Southern Africa Revealed

SOUTH AFRICA, NAMIBIA, BOTSWANA,
ZIMBABWE AND MOZAMBIQUE

ELAINE HURFORD

Southern Africa Revealed

SOUTH AFRICA, NAMIBIA, BOTSWANA, ZIMBABWE AND MOZAMBIQUE

First published in 1999
by Struik Publishers (Pty) Ltd
(a member of Struik New Holland Publishing (Pty) Ltd)
London • Cape Town • Sydney • Auckland

24 Nutford Place
London W1H 6DQ
United Kingdom

14 Aquatic Drive
Frenchs Forest
NSW 2086, Australia

80 McKenzie Street
Cape Town 8001
South Africa

218 Lake Road
Northcote, Auckland
New Zealand

2 4 6 8 10 9 7 5 3 1

Managing editor: Annlerie van Rooyen
Designer: Janice Evans
Editor: Lesley Hay-Whitton
Cartographer: Éloïse Moss
Picture researcher: Cara Cilliers
Proofreader: Mariëlle Renssen
Indexer: Gill Gordon

ISBN 1 86872 274 0

Reproduction by Hirt & Carter Cape (Pty) Ltd
Printed and bound by Tien Wah Press (Pte.) Ltd, Singapore

Page 1: *Sossusvlei in Namibia's Namib Desert.*
Pages 2 and 3: *Tourists experience Botswana's Okavango from a* mokoro.
This page: *Blue wildebeest in the Kalahari, South Africa.*

Contents

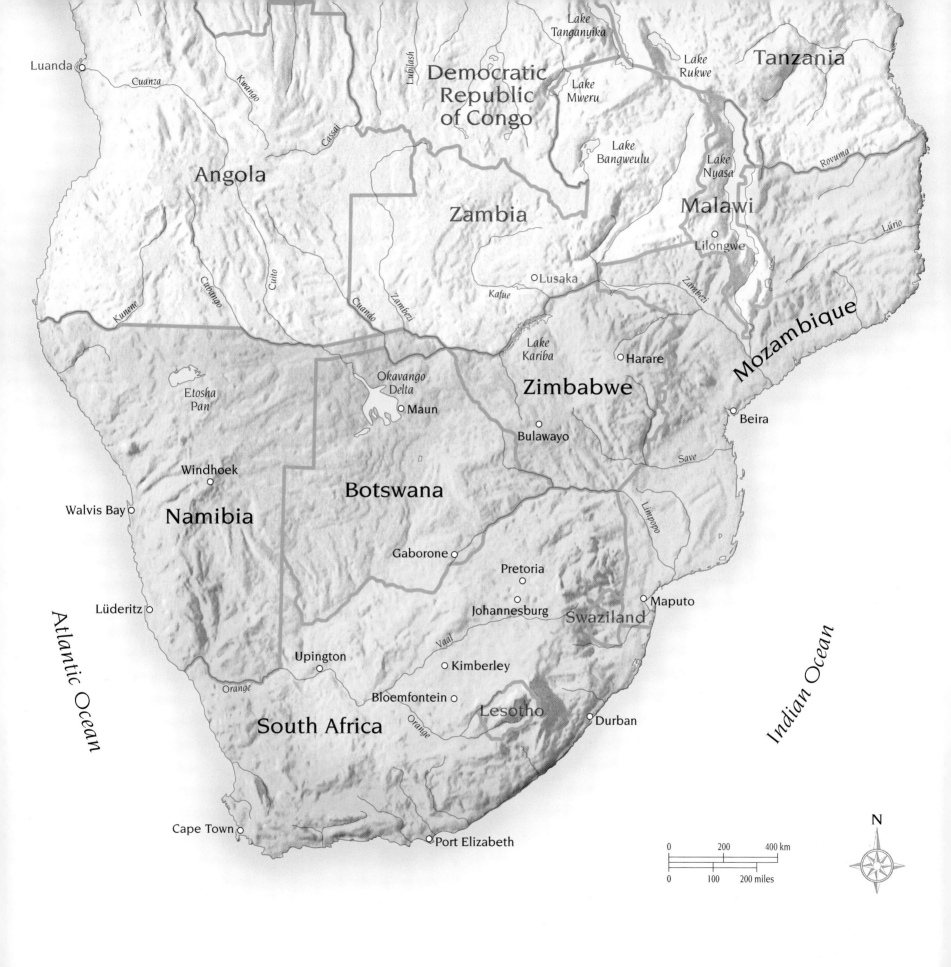

Introduction

The five major nations of Southern Africa – South Africa, Namibia, Botswana, Zimbabwe and Mozambique – lie between the Atlantic and Indian oceans, bisected by the Tropic of Capricorn. Together they occupy at most one-sixth of the continent but, in their scenic drama and natural diversity, they offer a compelling view of all that is best about Africa.

Their habitats embrace shorelands and marine environments, high mountains and subtropical swamps, wetlands and deserts and, in the interior, tracts of grassland – the savannah – which support herds of game protected from the encroachments of 'civilization' in sanctuaries that are among the world's finest.

The southern subcontinent does not lay claim to many cities of international stature, but those that do exist are every bit as sophisticated, albeit with a uniquely African flavour, as their counterparts on other continents. Their hotels, restaurants, museums and art galleries rank with the best in the world. Their airports, stations and, in some cases, harbours are the axes of major travel routes, with international carriers taking millions of travellers to destinations within Africa and beyond. Roads in South Africa are excellent. Elsewhere they are generally good, with the exception of Mozambique, Botswana and some parts of Namibia. Mozambique's major routes are being upgraded after decades of war, but most of Botswana's roads outside of Gaborone, Maun and Francistown are unlikely ever to be more than tracks in a wilderness of Kalahari sand. Many tourists use four-wheel-drive vehicles or single-engined air 'taxis' that transfer visitors, game rangers and staff from the lodges and camps to otherwise almost inaccessible areas.

Three of the five countries have extensive coastlines, sweeping from the tropical Indian Ocean waters of Mozambique, along the temperate shores of the southern Cape coastline where the Indian and Atlantic oceans meet at Cape Agulhas – the southernmost tip of the African continent – and on up the western seaboard of South Africa to Namibia's desert coastline on the Atlantic Ocean. The subcontinent boasts 7,500 kilometres of magnificent ocean frontage with beaches that by world standards are undeveloped, unpolluted and, in some cases, even unpopulated. Many are within reserves set aside to protect the coastal flora, its lakes and dunes, the birds and all the creatures of the seas.

A male lion. This majestic creature, king of the beasts, is one of the Big Five so prized by game-viewers, the other four being leopard, elephant, rhinoceros and buffalo.

Mozambique can lay claim to 2,500 idyllic kilometres of white, sandy beaches, coral isles and tropical reefs stretching up the east coast of Africa. These reefs are the home of the dugongs which gave rise to mermaid mythology.

South Africa's 3,500-kilometre coastline boasts numerous whale-watching sites of international significance, since southern rights and humpbacks breed here for six months of the year. The coastal terrace includes the famous Cape Peninsula, Table Mountain, many of South Africa's renowned winelands, and the Cape Floral Kingdom, the smallest but richest of the world's six plant kingdoms.

Namibia's 1,500 kilometres of sea frontage is composed of a remote and mysterious coastal desert which guards the welwitschia, the world's most bizarre plant, and great mineral riches.

On the other hand, the subcontinent's two landlocked countries – Botswana and Zimbabwe – have been richly compensated for the lack of a coastline. Each holds miracles and mysteries of such wonder and magnitude that their lack of beaches and harbours seems a paltry loss by comparison. Zimbabwe has ownership of the legendary Victoria Falls – twice the size of Niagara – and the majestic ruins at Great Zimbabwe ('houses of stone'). Great Zimbabwe, believed to have been the seat of the Shona kings from the 13th to the 15th centuries, is considered by many as the most important cultural site on the African continent.

Botswana is curator of the magnificent Okavango Delta which sprawls, fan-shaped, across 15,000 square kilometres of thirstland at its highest flood, creating a miraculous wilderness of wetlands and channels, floodplains and islands in an otherwise dry land.

The Southern African interior, high sunbaked plateauland, is mostly hot, dry and sparsely populated. Human settlements are often hundreds of kilometres apart. People visiting these areas will find the rewards

substantial: horizons are wider, the sky seems higher and, at night, the stars are brighter. In Namibia, only one percent of land is arable and the most precious resource is, surprisingly enough, not diamonds but water. Some regions are so remote they can be reached only on foot or by air, and one could easily get lost among the peach-coloured dunes with their shifting shapes and shadows or in the depths of the ancient Fish River Canyon. The oddly shaped Caprivi Strip is both a geographical and ecological anomaly which includes a small but pristine wetland ringed by desert.

South Africa is mostly dry beyond the great mountain chain that rings the eastern and southern regions and divides a narrow coastal terrace from the interior plateau. The mountain chain reaches from the folded mountains of the Western and southern Cape, and continues on through the breathtaking Drakensberg, culminating in the great Escarpment in the north-east. Here a dramatic change takes place, where the interior plateau ends at the rim of the Escarpment before plunging 1,000 metres to the subtropical plains of the game-rich Lowveld adjoining Mozambique. There are beautiful gateways through and over the many thousands of kilometres of the mountain chain, but none perhaps as majestic as the Swartberg Pass at the entrance to the interior plateau on the threshold of the Great Karoo in the south-western Cape. One-third of the country is composed of the semi-arid Karoo, which is an empty sun- and starlit space composed of big horizons and tiny towns, which transits into savannah and desert en route to Namibia, Botswana and Zimbabwe.

The savannah plains of the southern region of Mozambique rise towards a central and northern plateau, consisting of rugged highlands, which are incised by deep river valleys. The most distinguishing feature

ABOVE LEFT *Wilderness is one of the most popular resort towns of the scenic Garden Route, in South Africa.*

ABOVE CENTRE *Wildebeest in the South African Kalahari. Botswana and South Africa have removed the fences between their two Kalahari parks, to form one 80,000-square-kilometre reserve.*

ABOVE RIGHT *The Victoria and Alfred Waterfront is frequented by both locals and visitors to Cape Town. The Waterfront's attractions include an oceanarium, cinemas, restaurants to suit all pockets, and two craft markets.*

INTRODUCTION

of Mozambique is the Zambezi River, which creates a massive geographical and cultural divide between the north and the south.

Botswana, although officially falling almost entirely in the Kalahari Desert zone, is covered with light grass and savannah, as well as mopane woodland and a variety of other habitats which support a surprising diversity of fauna, including countless birds.

Zimbabwe too has its hot, dry lowveld plains but, where the country is bisected by a high diagonal ridge, the land is cool and fertile and many of the country's richest farms are established here. The Eastern Highlands provide an extraordinary contrast in a high mountain rampart running from north to south, a region of green and misty uplands more English than African.

Visitors may go to South Africa to drink wine, Zimbabwe to eat beef, Mozambique to feast on shellfish – but food is not the subcontinent's main drawcard. It is the Big Five (elephant, rhinoceros, lion, leopard and buffalo) that bring millions of visitors to the region each year. Most visitors now include South Africa's whale route, and the important whale-watching sites centred on Hermanus along the southern Cape coast, in their game-viewing itinerary. Whale-watching is at its best from May to November, when southern right and humpback whales come inshore to mate and calve each year.

No one region can claim superiority in terms of natural riches and diversity. Each is curator to at least one of Africa's big game parks and, if a new international movement gains ground, 'Peace Parks' will open boundaries between nations to allow the vast herds to move freely along their natural migration paths. One of these may well be on the South African–Mozambican border, which is also the eastern boundary of South Africa's Kruger National Park, one of the world's greatest national parks. This would also assist the rehabilitation of some of Mozambique's formerly great reserves, of which only three have reopened since the end of the war. These are the islands of the Bazaruto Archipelago, the Maputo Elephant Reserve and Gorongosa National Park in central Mozambique.

Botswana offers the visitor not only its fabulous Delta, but also the magnificent Chobe National Park north-east of the delta and the extra-ordinary Makgadikgadi Pans Game Reserve in the centre of the country. After rain, this reserve transforms from salt desert to shimmering lake and attracts millions of waterbirds, among them pelicans and flamingoes. Namibia's Fish River Canyon and Etosha National Park are but two of 14 national parks that compete for the visitor's attention, unforgettable in their stark, wild beauty.

South Africa's reserves embrace a range of contrasting systems, from the remote mountain wilderness of the Richtersveld in the arid north-west to the Greater St Lucia Wetland Park in the sub-tropical north-east. Game-rich KwaZulu-Natal's Hluhluwe-Umfolozi Park and world-renowned Kruger National Park (straddling Mpumalanga and Northern Province) are the country's oldest, both considered role models in park and conservation management. Zimbabwe boasts a staggering 40 national parks, ranging from the huge Hwange National Park (said to have more wildlife than anywhere else in the world) south of the Victoria Falls to the beautiful Matusadona National Park on the shores of Lake Kariba.

None of the Southern African nations is anything but acutely conscious of the value of its wildlife, but each must find an often-precarious balance between conservation, the needs of the people and the requirements of housing and industry. And, as is so often the case in Africa, conservation must frequently take a back seat to regular civil and political disruption.

Some, such as Botswana, have intentionally made tourism expensive to reduce impact and increase returns. Others have found a partial solution in 'wildlife management' or 'safari areas' where controlled hunting deposits tourism revenue in rural communities. Zimbabwe was among the African pioneers of this relatively new approach to combining the needs of the people with tourism requirements. The system works well, channelling much-needed funds from tourism – which includes controlled trophy hunting – into local communities.

ABOVE LEFT Xhosa homesteads in South Africa's Eastern Cape.

ABOVE CENTRE Buffalo in the Okavango, Botswana.

ABOVE RIGHT Dias Cross, a copy of the padrão *erected by 15th-century Portuguese explorer, Bartolomeu Dias, in Lüderitz, Namibia.*

INTRODUCTION

11

South Africa

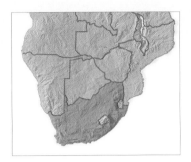

S outh Africa, freed at last of the stigma which haunted it through the unhappy decades of apartheid, has enjoyed a high international tourism profile since its entry into democracy in 1994. Overseas visitors are flocking to the country to enjoy its natural treasures, the hospitality of its people and, not least of all, its affordability. Tourism has quite simply boomed. Since the first democratic elections were held in April 1994, South Africa has risen fast in the list of the most popular international travel destinations. The world's airlines have laid on direct flights to Cape Town and Johannesburg international airports, and cruise liners are coming back into Cape Town's Table Bay and Durban's harbour. Accommodation in turn has mushroomed to meet the demand, in the shape of countless bed and breakfast establishments, comfortable guesthouses, country house hotels and guest farms, and, in the bigger cities, luxury world-class hotels.

Johannesburg and Cape Town are the prime launching pads for a South African holiday or business trip. Johannesburg, the financial hub of Southern Africa, is an axis for other business and leisure destinations on the subcontinent. Cape Town's beaches, mountains and winelands hold an irresistible lure for tourists, who as a result are clamouring for increasing volumes and styles of accommodation

OPPOSITE *Ten minutes' drive from the centre of Cape Town, Blouberg Beach provides the classic view of the flat-topped sandstone massif that is Table Mountain. To the left is Devil's Peak, and to the right Lion's Head and Signal Hill.*

RIGHT *The majestic King Protea, South Africa's national flower.*

The Quiver Tree of South Africa's semi-arid north-western regions was used by the San (Bushmen) for making arrows.

as they plan their trips to include this must-see city. Cape Town is also eclipsing Johannesburg as an important centre for international seminars and incentive awards which invariably target the world's most alluring destinations.

South Africa's challenged currency generates gloom on the home front, but there are one or two upsides. It keeps the locals at home to service an increasingly sophisticated and extensive tourist infrastructure. Visitors, on the other hand, can afford to stay longer, in better accommodation and, when they go home, there's the welcome jangle of change in their pockets.

In the meantime, untouched by the ephemeral storms buffeting international financial markets, South Africa's timeless treasures continue to make this one of the world's most blessed countries. It is a land of fabulous contrasts, incorporating deserts and tropics, plains and mountains, rivers and valleys. The topography moves through the haunting, almost lunar landscapes of the Northern Cape's remote Richtersveld, through all of nature's wide spectrum to end in the mangrove swamps of north-eastern KwaZulu-Natal. Accordingly, the climate can be both harsh and kind, wet or devastatingly dry, but is most often moderate with tolerable extremes at both ends of the thermometer. It is these contrasts that create specialized ecological niches for the astonishing varieties of birds, animals, marine life and plants that find habitats in South Africa.

This is also the land of the Rainbow Nation which has emerged as a resilient group of people, most of whom are determined to see their land safely through a passage of turbulence and change.

Throughout Southern Africa, the original occupants were almost always the San, simple, gentle hunter-gatherers who, when confronted with aggression, simply withdrew into ever-more remote and usually inhospitable regions until today they have almost disappeared. They remain, in their natural environment, only in small enclaves of Namibia. Their close relations, the Khoikhoi who, in the 15th century, encountered the Portuguese navigators exploring sea routes round the Cape, have effectively ceased to survive as a separate race. The eastern Cape was also, at that time, occupied by the Nguni people who spoke Xhosa, Zulu, Swazi and Ndebele. Traditionally they live in the south-eastern Cape (Xhosa), today's KwaZulu-Natal (Zulu), the sovereign independent country of Swaziland (Swazi) and in the northern provinces (Ndebele). Furthermore, Tsonga and Shangaan people live in the north-eastern region of Northern Province (former Gazankulu), as well as further north in Zimbabwe and in Mozambique. And the Venda people are settled along the Limpopo River bordering on Zimbabwe.

The Cape, with its rugged Peninsula, was the first part of South Africa to be settled by Europeans: the Dutch, British, and French colonists who have left an indelible stamp on life at the southern tip of this huge continent. As did the many thousands of slaves from other African lands and from the East, and the so-called 'indentured labourers' who were brought from Natal to work the young sugar plantations. The 'slaves' included many high-born exiles from the Dutch possessions in the East, such as Sheikh Yusuf who succeeded in founding Islam in South Africa.

After centuries of relative peace, South Africa became an open battlefield; British settlers brought to the eastern Cape in 1820 were intended to establish a buffer zone of farms between the colony west of the Great Fish River, and the cattle-farming Boers and Xhosa on the east. Instead, bloody conflict erupted and the border became a war zone. The Boers, dissatisfied with foreign control in the south, began to plan their Great Trek to new territories in the north, far from British intervention. And in the meantime, in what is now KwaZulu-Natal, an extraordinary leader was mobilizing Nguni-speakers into an expansionist force which would, through conquest and terror, create untold misery among the Southern African peoples. This was the Difaqane, which translated to 'forced migration' or 'the crushing' depending on whose side you were on.

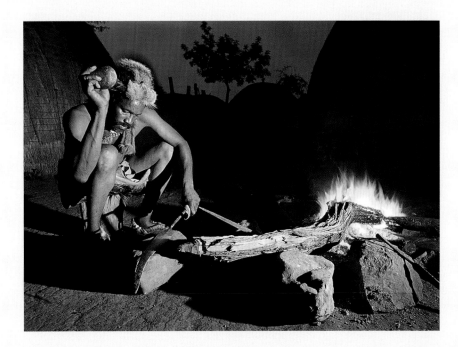

One of the few remaining Zulu spear-makers, Goboti crafts the stabbing spear (iklwa) that was introduced by Shaka, who revolutionized Zulu fighting techniques.

Waves of migrants fled before the force of the advancing conquered armies, amid widespread chaos, into the hands of Shaka, chief of a small Zulu group. As they fled, some as far north as Lake Tanganyika, so they conquered. It was into this scenario of disorder and conflict that the Boers arrived to settle their new territory and claim their freedom bringing 'civilization' to an untamed land. By 1828, Shaka was dead, killed by his half-brother Dingane, and the following few years saw the collapse of the Zulu

Around 8,000 elephants are resident in the Kruger National Park, South Africa's premier wildlife sanctuary. The park's 20,000 square kilometres provide a habitat for all of the Big Five – lion, elephant, leopard, rhino and buffalo.

'empire'. Displaced and poorly organized, what little Zulu resistance remained was easily overcome as the Boers cut a swathe to the north.

As history has shown, it took many more decades, many more wars, before democratic rule was able to be established in South Africa with the world's most famous political prisoner, Nelson Mandela, as its president. Unlike many of the other Southern African nations, South Africa's transition to democracy, after centuries of turbulence, has been triumphantly peaceful.

In terms of the physical faces of South Africa, its topography consists of three main parts – coastal plain, mountain chain and interior plateau. The lush, green coastal terrace lies between the mountains and the warm Indian Ocean on the southern and eastern seaboard. In the west, the cold Atlantic Ocean creates a stark coastal desert with rugged wilderness areas. A series of mountain ranges separates the interior from the coast, holding the greater part of the country in a rough semi-circle, beginning in the north-east with the majestic Drakensberg and ending in the folded mountains of the southern and Western Cape.

Beyond the mountain chain, a high, dry plateau comprises the remaining two-thirds of the country. The vast Karoo region beckons with its unending horizons, rich fossil and plant history and a treasury of small, often charming towns preserved by their isolation. The plateau rolls on beyond the Karoo for thousands of kilometres to meet the Kalahari Desert and boundaries of Namibia, Botswana and a tiny slice of Zimbabwe in the north; in the north-east, it continues through the grasslands of the Free State and Mpumalanga to the edge of the Escarpment. Here the land drops dramatically to the subtropical plains of the Lowveld. Adjoining the Mozambican border, this is the home of the world-renowned Kruger National Park and a host of private reserves which are sanctuary to the country's great game animals.

The Kruger and its neighbouring attractions vie with the beaches, mountains and winelands of the Cape Peninsula for first place as the country's premier holiday destinations. Not only is the Kruger Africa's oldest game park, but it is world-renowned for its model management, which uses tourism revenues to fund conservation.

Sprawling across two million hectares, the park contains a variety of ecosystems hospitable to the 'Big Five' – elephant, lion, leopard, rhino and buffalo – and a supporting cast of antelope, birds, reptiles, small mammals and insects. Its eastern boundary abuts Mozambique and, if plans for the proposed Peace Park materialize, animals will again be able to follow their natural migration routes between the two territories. Depending on their interests, visitors could easily spend an entire holiday in the north-eastern regions where the Kruger heads a host of very desirable destinations which include many other notable reserves.

The Highveld Escarpment is breathtakingly beautiful, a land of mysterious gorges, misty waterfalls, trout streams and evergreen forests. The Blyde River Canyon Nature Reserve contains more than 20,000 hectares of spectacular natural features, not least of which is God's Window, aptly always open to an unending near-mystical vista of river, mountain and forest.

The KwaZulu-Natal Drakensberg, central Escarpment and the Free State's Maluti Mountains are no less awesome. Three thousand metres above sea level, the lofty buttresses and spears of the Drakensberg are home to magnificent raptors, including the endangered Bearded Vulture, or Lammergeier, some antelope and mountain tortoises – hardy species able to endure the semi-alpine conditions at this altitude. The province of KwaZulu-Natal alone has about 100 game parks and nature reserves including two of the most significant in the world. The black and the white rhino, once on the brink of extinction, have now established a stable breeding population in the Hluhluwe-Umfolozi Park. And the Greater St Lucia Wetland Park, containing a string of parks and reserves along the northern coastline of Maputaland, including Sodwana Bay and Mkuze Game Reserve, is one of the world's most important wilderness areas.

Like the Kruger, all of the country's national parks have comfortable accommodation in numerous rest camps. These are fairly reasonably priced but should be reserved well in advance. More luxurious accommodation is available in exclusive private reserves which offer well-heeled foreign travellers a real 'Out-of-Africa' holiday experience.

The lush province of Mpumalanga is renowned for its numerous waterfalls which are without rival anywhere in the country. Near Graskop the Lisbon River cascades 95 metres into a deep pool below, forming the Lisbon Falls.

SOUTH
AFRICA
___

17

Robben Island, the former leper colony and prison where South Africa's first democratically elected president, Nelson Mandela, was incarcerated for two decades, lies 11 kilometres from Cape Town, separated from the mainland by the cold Atlantic Ocean. In January 1997 the Island was declared a Cultural Institution.

More and more visitors are using the Mother City, Cape Town, as a gateway to Africa. Although steeped in history, with fascinating architecture, galleries, museums and theatres, these are not the primary attractions for most tourists. The beaches, the winelands and the V&A Waterfront – the world's first leisure development in a working harbour – are rather what keep them coming back. Cape Town, at the foot of the world's most famous flat-topped mountain whose rugged massif culminates in the tip of a windy peninsula, is undeniably glamorous. While Johannesburg is where the big money changes hands, Capetonians lead a more laid-back lifestyle dominated by the pursuit of high-quality leisure.

The country's oldest vineyard, Groot Constantia, is in the suburbs of Cape Town, past the National Botanical Gardens at Kirstenbosch and en route to the fishing village and holiday resort of Hout Bay which, a mere 20 minutes from the city limits, has the air of a holiday resort with its picturesque harbour and leisurely pace . The famous vineyards of Stellenbosch, Paarl, Franschhoek and many others are accessible within an hour's drive or less, and make ideal venues for extended lunches as most estates have a small restaurant open on weekdays.

While the north lays claim to the Big Five, the south has put a feather in its regional cap with the 'Big Six' – which adds whales to the South African wildlife showcase. Hermanus, just an hour's drive from Cape Town, is one of the world's top 13 whale-spotting venues. The Eastern Cape not only boasts abundant game-viewing at the Addo Elephant National Park; it also shares the 900-kilometre Whale Route with the Western Cape. The route extends from the West Coast, around the Cape Peninsula and along the southern and Eastern Cape coast to the Garden Route resort of Plettenberg Bay. Other Western and Eastern Cape reserves are dedicated to flowers, including the region's wealth of fynbos ('fine-leaved bush', or scrub), elephant and mountain zebra. Even fossils may be found in the Karoo National Park at Beaufort West.

No matter what spectacular scenery a country may have to put on show, the welcome that visitors receive from the locals is what makes the experience unforgettable. South Africans of every stripe are renowned for their hospitality (and the food on their tables). Visitors have a fascinating array of culinary offerings from the various people of the 40 million-strong Rainbow Nation. Cultural villages and township tours have revealed lifestyles that were previously out of the public's reach. Overnight stays and meals within the simple confines of a Zulu, Xhosa or Ndebele dwelling can easily be arranged, or a table booked in a chic ethnic restaurant in downtown Johannesburg or sprawling Soweto.

Very broadly speaking, Port Elizabeth is the place for Chinese food and Durban for Indian, Cape Town is the centre of Cape Malay heritage and cuisine, while country areas dish up traditional Afrikaner-style

West Coast fishermen may take out the delicious local lobster only according to strict quota.

boerekos (hearty country food), with lamb being the signature dish of the Karoo. The West Coast deserves a special mention for its fabulous crayfish (rock lobster, or kreef) and other fresh seafood including snoek, best served out of doors straight off the barbecue. Big-city restaurants, on the other hand, are as sophisticated and diverse as any in the world, serving international-class cuisine from every region of the globe.

In a country with wonderful natural resources, fishing and agriculture are, naturally enough, among the high-ranking revenue earners which, in turn, create desperately needed jobs. It is estimated, too, that every tourist creates 10 opportunities in the workplace but, although tourism earnings have soared in the last few years, manufacturing is presently still the biggest contributor to the gross domestic product. Gold exports have fallen to second place, with financial services, mining, commerce and forestry bringing up the rear. The informal sector has become a considerable money-spinner, as well as making a small dent in the unemployment figures that are still one of the biggest headaches for South Africa's relatively new government.

ABOVE Cape Town reverberates with the festivities of the traditional Minstrel Carnival at New Year. The procession winds through the streets from the old Malay quarter of the Bo-Kaap, to the judging which takes place in the suburb of Observatory.

LEFT Hundreds of flower sellers make the old parade grounds in Darling Street, Cape Town, a colourful place. Bargains are to be had at the close of day or on quiet weekend afternoons.

OPPOSITE The V&A Waterfront, a huge and vibrant leisure venue, offers a vast choice of entertainment in its shops, restaurants, cinemas, museums and the superb oceanarium.

PAGES 22 AND 23, CLOCKWISE FROM LEFT The Cape Peninsula is blessed with beautiful sandy beaches on both sides. On the western side Camps Bay lies under the mountain range known as the Twelve Apostles; and on the eastern side are the coastal village of Fish Hoek, the Jackass Penguin colony at Boulders near Simon's Town, and St James with its colourful bathing huts.

ABOVE AND LEFT Chapman's Peak Drive leads from Hout Bay to Noordhoek along a ledge 160 metres high. Snoek may be bought fresh off the boats in Hout Bay.

OPPOSITE TOP AND BOTTOM Cape Point, the tip of the Peninsula, is set in the 7,750-hectare Cape of Good Hope Nature Reserve. A funicular leads to a viewpoint which commands staggering views.

ABOVE *Groot Constantia, South Africa's oldest wine estate, was the home of Cape Governor Simon van der Stel from 1699 to 1712. Today the estate is still producing wines of international distinction.*

RIGHT *The Kirstenbosch National Botanical Garden in Cape Town attracts half a million visitors a year. Covering 528 hectares of the eastern slopes of Table Mountain, the garden provides a showcase for the celebrated flora of the Cape Floral Kingdom.*

SOUTH
AFRICA

LEFT Visitors to the Boschendal wine estate (Franschhoek) can dine in- or outdoors in beautiful gardens, buy fine wines and view a splendid collection of Dutch East India Company treasures, including porcelain. The historic manor house is a superbly preserved example of Cape Dutch architecture.

ABOVE The leafy university town of Stellenbosch, South Africa's second oldest settlement after Cape Town, boasts magnificent Cape Dutch architecture and beautiful avenues of oaks. No visit to the town is complete without popping in at Oom Samie se Winkel in Dorp Street, to browse among its fascinating range of goods, which includes jams, wines, books and curios, or to eat a light al fresco meal.

OPPOSITE A carpet of vines covers the floor of the Hex River Valley between Worcester and Touws River, where most of South Africa's export table grapes are produced.

LEFT The Old Harbour in the town of Hermanus on the southern Cape coast is an open-air museum and aquaculture site for perlemoen, which is a protected seafood delicacy. Walker Bay, around which the town is centred, is one of the 13 top whale-viewing sites in the world. Each year from May to November southern right whales (RIGHT) come inshore to mate and calve.

ABOVE The lighthouse at Agulhas, the southernmost tip of Africa, has warned ships of the treacherous seas since 1849.

PAGES 32 AND 33 Wilderness is one of the top destinations on the southern Cape's lovely Garden Route.

THIS PAGE, CLOCKWISE FROM TOP LEFT The Heads, two massive sandstone bluffs, are the gateway to the Knysna Lagoon; Featherbed Nature Reserve is on the Western Head shown on the right. A charming 19th-century Norman-style church graces Belvidere estate near Knysna. The stone 'castles' at Noetzie east of Knysna are the holiday retreats of several Zimbabwean families. A centuries-old Outeniqua Yellowwood, at Storms River, towers 46 metres high.

OPPOSITE Holidaymakers revel in the fine sand and mild waters of the tourist resort, Plettenberg Bay. Its Central Beach, dominated by the Beacon Isle Hotel, is flanked by two other beautiful swimming beaches.

BELOW Many a Karoo farmer has made and lost fortunes through the trade in ostrich meat, feathers and leather. Oudtshoorn, the world's ostrich capital, was founded on the turn-of-the-century feather boom. Female ostriches are less showy than the males, being dun-coloured for daytime camouflage. The black males sit on the nests at night.

OPPOSITE The Cango Caves burrow deep into the heart of the Swartberg range which divides the Little and the Great Karoo. Considered among the finest dripstone caves in the world, their management and conservation is currently being reassessed – a result of rapid deterioration and damage in recent years.

OPPOSITE BOTTOM Port Elizabeth's King's Beach lies below the main beachfront boulevard which connects the city with Humewood and Summerstrand. The area's warm winters and long hot summers ensure that its beaches are populated almost all year round. The city's oceanarium (OPPOSITE TOP) is world-renowned for its dolphins, many of whom have been bred in captivity. The complex also houses a snake park and museum on the Humewood beachfront.

ABOVE The occupants of Addo Elephant National Park near Port Elizabeth eat a nourishing diet of the indigenous succulent, the 'spekboom'. Plans are under way to extend the park considerably, perhaps even to include a large portion of marine reserve. The park also hosts black rhino, hippo, antelope, birds (including ostriches), buffalo and bushpig. An equally famous resident is the small dung beetle – signs on the park's roads warn visitors to watch out for them.

SOUTH
AFRICA

39

OPPOSITE One of the best-known sights of the Eastern Cape's Wild Coast is Hole in the Wall, an archway in an island of rock gouged by the action of centuries of waves.

ABOVE Resorts such as Coffee Bay, with its safe beach, attract sunbathers and holidaymakers, while the region's wild seas are beloved by anglers. The environment is a composition of coastal forest and high vegetated cliffs against a canvas of sea and sky.

LEFT The Xhosa, who are centred in the Eastern Cape, wear elaborate attire when they marry.

SOUTH
AFRICA

41

BELOW *Victoria Embankment in Durban's busy harbour provides shelter for small craft.*

OPPOSITE, CLOCKWISE FROM TOP LEFT *Rickshaw drivers, with their spectacular adornment, attract custom for their tours of Durban's beachfront. Marine Parade, at the heart of the Golden Mile, is the starting point for all beachfront attractions — an open-air theatre, surfing and life-saving displays, snake park and aquarium. Clay vessels, crafted by Zulu women, can be bought at craft stalls on the Marine Parade. Visitors to Durban's Indian market may take home silk, baskets, brassware or a variety of spices.*

OPPOSITE *As a mark of respect (hlonipha), a Zulu woman's head should never be higher than a man's. Women traditionally serve food from a kneeling position, as demonstrated here at Shakaland in KwaZulu-Natal.*

ABOVE *Zulu men learn stick fighting from an early age, and demonstrate their skills at weddings and other important ceremonies. Here, the men dance before the stick fighting challenges begin.*

SOUTH
AFRICA

45

PAGES 46 AND 47 *Few camps can claim such a spectacular backdrop as Tendele Camp in KwaZulu-Natal's Drakensberg, encircled as it is by the Amphitheatre.*

LEFT *A number of well-regulated horseback and walking trails allow visitors to appreciate the beauties of the Drakensberg. One of South Africa's largest rivers, the Tugela, has its source at Mont-aux-Sources in the 'Berg (BELOW). From here it drops 2,000 metres into rapids that provide superb white-water rafting along the gorge below.*

OPPOSITE, CLOCKWISE FROM TOP *A viewpoint from Giant's Castle shows Monk's Cowl and Cathkin Peak covered in snow in mid-winter. A rich collection of San rock paintings may be found in the region. The rare Lammergeier, or Bearded Vulture, nests on ledges in the cliff face.*

ABOVE Renowned for the success of Operation Rhino, Hluhluwe-Umfolozi Park in KwaZulu-Natal is home to the endangered black rhino and the white rhino (pictured here), as well as many other game species, amongst them the giraffe (LEFT).

OPPOSITE, CLOCKWISE FROM TOP LEFT Greater St Lucia Wetland Park is a major marine and wetland environment, with the waters of Lake St Lucia – rich in fish, micro-organisms and crustaceans – attracting numerous waterbirds. A female Nile crocodile carries her hatchlings from the nest to the water at the St Lucia Crocodile Centre. Loggerhead turtles emerge from the sea at night to lay their eggs in the sand of the beaches of Maputaland. Fanie's Island is one of the idyllic camps on Lake St Lucia.

OPPOSITE, CLOCKWISE FROM TOP LEFT *One of South Africa's most scenic regions, Mpumalanga numbers among its attractions Bourke's Luck Potholes in the Blyde River Gorge, God's Window near Graskop, and the historic gold-mining town of Pilgrim's Rest, which dates back to 1873.*

ABOVE *The vast beauty of the Blyde River (River of Joy) Canyon is protected in a nature reserve. The quartzite-capped Three Rondavels, also known as the 'Chief's Wives', overlook the river and an immense dam 600 metres below on the floor of the 16-kilometre-long Blyde River Canyon.*

SOUTH
AFRICA

PAGES 54 AND 55 The vast Kruger National Park straddles Northern Province and Mpumalanga, and borders on Mozambique. One of its great drawcards is that it lays claim to the Big Five: buffalo, rhino and elephant (PAGE 54, TOP LEFT AND RIGHT, AND BOTTOM), leopard and lion (PAGE 55, BOTTOM LEFT AND RIGHT). Olifants Rest Camp (PAGE 55, TOP) boasts one of the finest views in the whole park, overlooking the Olifants River with the Lebombo Mountains in the east.

OPPOSITE Pretoria, the 'Jacaranda City', is South Africa's administrative capital. Its neoclassical Union Buildings (pictured here) were designed by Sir Herbert Baker.

ABOVE Ndebele women are famous for their brightly coloured geometric mural decorations. In traditional society, a married woman never takes off the metal neck rings (dzilla) which her husband gives her, but these days they are usually removable, as is the case with this woman

SOUTH
AFRICA

ABOVE Johannesburg, the financial hub of Southern Africa, lies 60 kilometres from Pretoria. The Hillbrow Tower dominates the Johannesburg evening skyline.

RIGHT A glittering oasis has risen from the bare African veld north of Johannesburg. Sun City – the biggest resort in Africa – has grown over 20 years to include four hotels, casinos, golf courses, an inland 'sea', man-made forests and lakes, an entertainment superbowl and (pictured here) the Palace of the Lost City.

SOUTH
AFRICA
—
58

ABOVE The Basotho people are the traditional inhabitants of the high mountain territories of the Free State and the little kingdom of Lesotho, west of the KwaZulu-Natal Drakensberg. Life here is challenging, revolving mainly around subsistence agriculture in the face of summer droughts and heavy snowfalls in winter.

RIGHT The uplands of the Free State end in the shadows of Lesotho's Maluti Mountains, the highest point of South Africa's great Escarpment. The beautiful Golden Gate Highlands National Park contains some of the most dramatic mountain landscapes in the country – strikingly coloured and sculpted peaks of sandstone coloured by iron oxide. Entrance to the park is east of the town of Clarens.

SOUTH
AFRICA
———
60

South Africa and Botswana have removed the fences between their Kalahari parks to create an 80,000-square-kilometre reserve. The animals of this thirstland survive on sweet grasses and desert succulents, aided by man-made dams and waterholes.

LEFT The cheetah, smaller and slimmer than the leopard, reaches speeds of up to 110 kilometres per hour when hunting.

RIGHT A male Kalahari lion feeds off the remains of a springbok.

BELOW The park is named for the gemsbok, whose rapier-like, near-vertical horns are a powerful defence against predators.

ABOVE *The Namaqua people called the Augrabies Falls in the Northern Cape 'the place of great noise'. The Orange River plunges 56 metres into an 18-kilometre-long ravine. There are several impressive cataracts, such as the 75-metre Bridal Veil Falls, in the Augrabies Falls National Park.*

OPPOSITE *The barren landscape of the Northern Cape is transformed into a flower carpet after spring rains. The short-lived miracle of the annual Namaqualand flowers is a spectacle witnessed by thousands of tourists every year, when a 'flower hotline' informs visitors of the best displays.*

ABOVE The Maltese Cross is one of the intriguing sandstone rock formations of the Cedarberg Wilderness Area, some 200 kilometres north of Cape Town.

LEFT Bird Island on the West Coast is a breeding colony for Cape Gannets.

OPPOSITE TOP AND BOTTOM Langebaan Lagoon is the focal point of the West Coast National Park. A few quaint West Coast fishing villages, such as Paternoster, still follow a traditional way of life.

Namibia

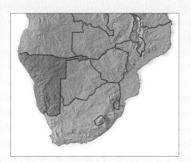

Everything about Namibia is larger than life – a little like Texas. In fact, Namibia is actually larger than Texas, and perhaps entitled to even more extravagant claims: home to the oldest desert, the strangest plant, the richest diamond deposits, possibly even the most beautiful landscapes on earth. It is also harsh, arid and inhospitable, many of its regions inaccessible except with rugged four-wheel-drive vehicles – in pairs – loaded with survival kits, making this a perfect habitat for the adventure traveller.

Despite its intractable nature, Namibia holds the visitor in its thrall, with surreal images of shifting multi-hued sand dunes, stark gravel plains, astonishing canyons, desolate mist-shrouded shores, ancient mountains and extraordinary plants and animals.

The country is bounded on the west, along 1,500 kilometres of desert shoreline, by the cold Atlantic Ocean. This is the Namib, the world's oldest desert. The coast is hostile, home to only the most adaptable flora and fauna, among them desert-dwelling elephants, Cape fur seals, sea- and shore-birds – including vast numbers of migrant waders – prolific fish species, rare reptiles and bizarre plants.

The desert also yields mineral riches – tungsten, uranium and a phenomenal quantity of gem-quality diamonds. And, in the south, the rewards are rich from karakul sheep, Namibia's 'black diamonds', whose valuable pelts are a major export product.

OPPOSITE *Sand dunes rise up to 500 metres around Sossusvlei in the huge Namib-Naukluft Park.*

RIGHT *The Himba maintain a nomadic lifestyle, moving as often as 10 times each year to find grazing for their goats and cattle.*

Although only one percent of Namibia's land is arable and the country must import some foodstuffs, more than half its people are subsistence farmers. Mining sustains the economy, accounting for almost 25 percent of the gross domestic product. Three of the country's 14 national parks are in the narrow strip of the Namib – the Skeleton Coast Park, National West Coast Tourist Recreation Area and the vast Namib-Naukluft Park. All are rugged and challenging, managed in an environmentally sensitive way, and in some areas accessible only on foot or in the company of strictly controlled fly-in safari operators.

Namibia is also home to one of the world's finest game parks, at Etosha ('place of mirages'), and the Fish River Canyon, which is exceeded in majesty only by the Grand Canyon. Etosha National Park occupies 23,000 square kilometres of wilderness in north-western Namibia. At its centre is a vast pan that, aeons ago, was a lake. When it dried, a salt desert remained, inhospitable to plants but supporting game in great numbers and diversity.

Desert elephant in the Kaokoveld, north-western Namibia, will range up to 70 kilometres a day to find food and water.

The pan occupies almost a quarter of the area of the park, which is served by 700 kilometres of dirt roads leading to major places of interest. Here, in Namibia's oldest and best-known park, all the animals associated with the southern savannah plains of Africa can be found. It is also the habitat of five rare species including black rhino, Hartmann's mountain zebra, the elegant black-faced impala and the tiny Damara dik-dik.

The Fish River Canyon in the extreme south, created by 1,800 million years of erosion, is 161 kilometres long, several kilometres wide and half a kilometre deep. One of Africa's true wilderness regions, the canyon is an awe-inspiring manifestation of the power of nature's forces. Backpacking is the way to get close to the beauty and profound stillness. An 85-kilometre trail leads from the northernmost viewpoint and terminates at Ai-Ais where 'firewater' awaits the tired traveller at a well-equipped resort with hot mineral springs. The trail is open only between May and August; for the rest of the year there is real danger of being swept away by floods, or suffering heatstroke.

Namibia is separated from Angola in the north by two of the country's four perennial rivers, the Kunene and the Okavango. In the north-east, the border is marked by a portion of the mighty Zambezi at the furthest tip of a narrow ribbon of land, the Caprivi Strip. In the east, the country is bordered by Botswana and South Africa and in the south by South Africa, separated by the broad Orange River.

Its more than 824,000-square-kilometre surface area is divided into three main geographical regions: a high central plateau from north to south, with the Namib Desert to the west and the Kalahari Desert to the east.

The plateau, although rising to 1,800 metres in places, lies at an average height of 1,100 metres. In this cool and elevated position in the very centre of the country, known as the Khomas Hochland, Namibia's largest city, the capital Windhoek is located. Although the city's main thoroughfare, Kaiserstrasse, has been renamed Independence Avenue, Windhoek retains a pleasant sense of *Gemütlichkeit* and a strong German colonial flavour.

The Quiver Tree has adapted to desert conditions by storing water in its small fleshy leaves. A forest of these unusual specimens has survived, and is now a national monument, near Keetmanshoop.

More precious than its fabled diamonds and other minerals (copper, uranium, gold, lead, tin, lithium, cadmium, zinc, salt, vanadium, natural gas, coal and iron ore), water is Namibia's scarcest, and most valuable, commodity. With the country's four major perennial rivers on its extremities, there is little natural water supply other than the irregular flow of six rivers which run only after good rains. This is supplemented with water pumped from man-made boreholes, or with ground water lying beneath the dry river beds, perennial springs and artesian wells. Other sources are pans or depressions such as Etosha.

Rain, such as it is, falls mainly in summer from November to February, varying from 50 millimetres a year in the harsh Namib to around 150 millimetres in the southern interior and 560 millimetres in the north. Occasionally the entire annual rainfall is dumped on a region all at once, causing great floods which close access roads and drown people and livestock. More often than not, rain comes in short-lived afternoon thunderstorms with crackling skies and flaming sunsets to follow.

Several Namibian towns retain some fine examples of German colonial architecture. Hohenzollern House in Swakopmund, 35 kilometres north of Walvis Bay, was originally built as a hotel in 1905.

The country falls in the Tropic of Capricorn in the continental tropical climatic zone but, although it is generally hot to sweltering, there are no jungles and few of the swamps associated with the tropics.

The Caprivi Strip, however, is lush in places by comparison with the rest of the country. The strip encompasses a variety of eco-systems and associated vegetation zones which include deciduous woodland and floodplains with reed and papyrus, riverine forest, and mopane woodlands. The Linyanti Swamp is a pristine wetland which, although much smaller, is as beautiful as Botswana's Okavango Delta.

Maximum summer daytime temperatures average 35°C, with nights dropping to 6°C in mid-winter. The coast is generally cooler than the interior but, with chilly seas and 117 foggy days a year, Namibia is not the average traveller's dream beach destination. The towns of Lüderitz, Walvis Bay and Swakopmund are the only major coastal holiday resorts.

Walvis Bay, the biggest port, is the headquarters of a massive fishing industry. Various powers have argued over its possession since 1784, when the bay was first used by American whalers. It was seized alternately by the Dutch and the British, who annexed it in 1878. For the next century, the 1,124-square-kilometre territory bounced between the British Cape Colony, the Union of South Africa, the Republic of South Africa, and South Africa's Cape Province. In 1992 it was placed under the joint administration of the Namibian and South African governments. Only after South Africa's own democratic elections in 1994 was it integrated as part of the young Namibian Republic.

Walvis Bay was, and still is, covetable territory. It is between two internationally significant nature reserves, the National West Coast Recreation Area to the north and the Namib-Naukluft Park to the south. The bay also borders the most important coastal wetland for birds in Southern Africa, the Walvis Bay wetland, which is home to enormous populations of plovers, flamingoes and sandpipers. The southern portion of the Walvis Bay lagoon includes the delta of the Kuiseb River. Among this region's offshore riches are vast hauls of fish, especially Whitefish and Pilchard, and a fabled, but as yet undiscovered, cargo of treasure spilled by a ship that was wrecked en route to England from India.

Inland from Walvis Bay are the Welwitschia Plains, home to one of the world's strangest plants. The giant *Welwitschia mirabilis* can live for over 1,000 years, producing only two leaves and one bloom in a lifetime.

Lüderitz Bay is sheltered by a peninsula which provides safe anchorage for fishing boats and a playground for dolphins. The town itself, backed up against the desert dunes, is a picturesque repository of quaint German colonial townhouses lined up along the steep, narrow streets of the old town. Just 90 years ago, Lüderitz rang with the shouts of men made wealthy overnight from the rich pickings of 'desert ice' – diamonds which lay scattered in the open sands.

Kolmanskop, once a diamond boom town, suffered a different fate: when supplies of water and diamonds dried up in 1950, the town closed its doors and turned out the lights. The empty mansions, theatre and German bakery with its sun-bleached Gothic lettering, the swimming pool, playgrounds and once-lavish gardens lie silent and half-buried beneath the ever-shifting sands while the wind plays games with the ghosts.

Namibia's 1.4 million people are sparsely distributed across the land; about one in four lives in the towns; the remaining inhabitants, an unusually diverse, multilingual range of cultural groups,

A specimen of one of the world's most bizarre plants, the Welwitschia mirabilis, *can be seen east of Swakopmund or Walvis Bay on the Welwitschia Plains. The oldest survivor of the species is believed to be 1,500 years old.*

occupy traditional areas and are engaged in subsistence agriculture. Afrikaans is commonly spoken, and, although English is the official language, it is used by only about seven percent of Namibians. Most indigenous people speak Oshivambo, Herero and Nama.

The Wambo people are the biggest group, making up easily half the population and traditionally occupying a large territory, Owambo, which stretches from north-west to north-east, just below the Angolan border. The Himba, a tiny sub-group of the Herero, is one of the smallest. The Himba

The Bogenfels Archway, the result of eons of erosion, rises 60 metres above the Atlantic waters, and is a landmark on the Namib Desert's southern shoreline.

cling fiercely to strict traditions and follow a nomadic pastoral lifestyle, moving constantly to find grazing for their goats and cattle in the hostile north-western area known as the Kaokoveld.

Although each population group is distinctive, the stately Herero women fascinate visitors with their elaborate costume – full-length dresses styled on those of 19th-century European missionary wives.

The San's forefathers have lived in this region for 2,000 years. Today only 34,000 San remain in three subgroups in northern Namibia. Visitors to the small Kaudom Game Park on the Botswana border are likely to encounter some of these light-skinned fine-boned people, but few of their traditional customs are still practised. The exception is the small Topnaar group of Khoisan – descendants of the hunter-gatherer San (Bushman) people and the Khoikhoi (Hottentots) who moved north from the Cape – in the Kuiseb area to the west of the Namib-Naukluft Park. For the rest, the nomadic lifestyle, with bow and arrow, and traditional dress of loincloth have largely given way to a more settled existence which sometimes included employment as farm workers. The greatest concentration of San rock art is to be found in the north-west, in the Damaraland wilderness.

At first the peace-loving San had the region to themselves. Their first competitors were the more aggressive Khoikhoi who dominated the region until around 1500. Then from the south came the Nama (descendants of the Khoikhoi), Oorlams and Basters of Dutch-Nama origin, and from the north the Wambo and Herero.

The Herero and the Namas fought each other over water, grazing and land rights – bloody and inconclusive clashes that continued until 1884 when Germany annexed the entire territory. From 1890, with the establishment of a German protectorate, a period of colonialization began and the Herero and Khoikhoi were now engaged in battles, not with each other, but against their German 'protectors'. This reached its tragic conclusion in a massive, four-year-long uprising of the Herero people, which cost them their lands, their social structures and 60,000 lives. By 1908 when the uprising had been quelled, a network of white farms was in place and the once-mighty Herero were reduced to just 15,000 impoverished survivors.

When, on being urged by Britain to do so, the South African military forces took control of the German colony in 1914, it was the start of a 60-year-long hold on the territory. History began to move forward again only in June 1971, when the International Court of Justice ruled that South Africa with her expanding apartheid policies was an illegal presence in South West Africa.

South Africa's refusal to relinquish the territory fanned the flames for the black African nationalist movement, SWAPO. Led by Sam Nujoma, they embarked on guerrilla warfare which continued until December 1988. By this time, major western powers were also exerting pressure on South Africa, who agreed to trade South West Africa's independence for the removal of Cuban troops from Angola. In 1990 Namibia gained independence with Sam Nujoma as the elected president.

ABOVE *Skeleton Coast gate at Ugab in the remote north-west of Namibia. Countless vessels have gone aground off this inhospitable shore since the first European navigators set sail to find a sea route to the East.*

BELOW *Namutoni Fort, one of Etosha National Park's three rest camps.*

Opposite The Fish River Canyon runs almost vertically for 161 kilometres down southern Namibia to Ai-Ais near the Orange River boundary with South Africa.

Above One of the empty mansions of the ghost town Kolmanskop, near Lüderitz.

Right Lüderitz's architecture is a pleasing mix of art nouveau and German colonial. The busy harbour and the bays of the peninsula encourage activities such as dolphin-spotting, boating, fishing and birding.

LEFT A hot air balloon is a leisurely way to view the
game in the reserves of the Namib Desert.

TOP Among the hardiest desert survivors is the gemsbok.
It is capable of surviving for months without drinking
water, obtaining moisture from the plants it eats.

ABOVE The entrance to the Namib-Naukluft Park is
at Sesriem, one of the few places in the desert where it
is possible to drive a sedan car.

NAMIBIA

OPPOSITE *Thousands of vessels have met their end on the Skeleton Coast of the Namib Desert.*

ABOVE *Greater Flamingoes feed in the shallows of the lagoon at Sandwich Harbour, south of Walvis Bay. The lagoon and its environs are protected and may only be visited with a permit.*

LEFT *A common resident is the large, Whitebreasted Cormorant, seen in abundant numbers along the Namibian coastline.*

NAMIBIA

ABOVE Leopard can be seen at close range from the discreet shelter of a hide at a private guest lodge near Otjiwarongo.

RIGHT Damaraland in north-west Namibia has a rich archive of rock engravings at Twyfelfontein.

OPPOSITE North-east of Swakopmund, Gros Spitzkopf and the two lesser peaks nearby are relics of ancient volcanic extrusions.

NAMIBIA

——————

82

PAGE 84 TOP *One of the most colourful reminders of the former German colonial presence in the capital city of Windhoek is the red-brick Lutheran Church, built in 1910.*

PAGE 84 BOTTOM AND PAGE 85 *Independence Avenue, Windhoek's main thoroughfare, is lined with markets and craft stalls displaying hand-painted curios, baskets and produce. Herero women sell their dolls from the pavements.*

OPPOSITE The Etosha National Park is one of the finest reserves in Africa. Most of the wildlife activity focuses on the vast Etosha Pan and the park's western regions, where game throngs during the wet season. The first camp to open to tourists was at Okaukuejo (TOP) situated on the south-western edge of the pan. The park supports huge numbers of elephant (BOTTOM) today, attracted by man-made waterholes.

ABOVE Almost all animals are at their most vulnerable when they are drinking at waterholes. In order to minimize the risk, some drink while others remain on the lookout for predators. This mixed group of giraffe, zebra and springbok slake their thirst in one of the perennial waterholes in Etosha next to the Chudob viewsite, which is an excellent spot for game-viewing.

NAMIBIA

ABOVE The Kunene River plunges into a series of roaring cataracts south of the remote village of Ruacana, on the Angolan border in northern Namibia. Upstream, the river banks are lined with Fan Palms, Himba trading posts and viewsites with vistas across neighbouring Angola.

OPPOSITE The north-eastern portion of Namibia's narrow Caprivi Strip is bordered by the majestic Zambezi River. At Katimo Mulilo visitors enjoy unrivalled views across the waters over sundowners at Zambezi Lodge's floating bar.

Botswana

Botswana is a land of subtle seduction, its beauty and mystery lingering in the memory and the senses, calling the traveller again and again to its majestic wild animals, great open spaces, blood-red sunsets and the miracle of a great delta, the legendary Okavango, at its heart.

Surrounded by a vast thirstland, the delta is a labyrinth of channels and islands, lagoons and floodplains – sustaining an extraordinary collection of birds, plants, insects and animals.

Botswana's 600,000 square kilometres are wedged between Namibia, Zambia, Zimbabwe and South Africa. The Zambian border – a mere 700 metres – is the world's shortest international boundary. Situated 600 kilometres from the nearest coast, and with few sources of water, Botswana is critically dry. Drought is a way of life in a country so parched that even its currency, the pula, translates wistfully to 'rain'. Botswana's two perennial rivers, the Okavango and the Chobe, are both in the extreme north. Streams in the east sometimes flow into bigger rivers such as the Limpopo, but these seldom hold their contents up until the dry winter. With more than two-thirds of the land falling into the Kalahari, towns are rare, the population thinly distributed. Most of Botswana's people live in the east or south-east where rainfall is higher and two rivers – the Limpopo and the Motloutse – run after the December to April summer rains.

OPPOSITE The Okavango Delta traces a network of islands and waterways across 15,000 square kilometres of Kalahari Desert.

RIGHT The African Fish Eagle is a conspicuous resident

Mokoros, *nowadays made of eco-conservative fibreglass rather than indigenous wood, are a traditional mode of transport.*

Although thinly inhabited by humans, Botswana is one of Africa's wealthiest wildlife regions. A high 17 percent of the land – 99,000 square kilometres – has been set aside for reserves and national parks and this already generous area is supplemented by large wildlife management regions. Although tourism and conservation go hand in hand and have been prioritized by the government, there is nevertheless pressure from the people for grazing land for livestock, which is a major capital and social asset.

The Kalahari, although termed a desert, is technically sandveld. While true deserts support no plant life and have no surface water, Botswana's 'desert' sustains grasses and savannah. The Kalahari is nevertheless the biggest sand mantle in the world, hundreds of metres deep in places, and in Botswana it makes life a challenging process. Roads through the desert are no more than sand tracks. Supplies and services are many kilometres away, making life in the bush a rugged affair.

For Botswana's many awestruck tourists it is exactly this isolation that makes their wilderness adventure a truly African experience. Sipping chilled drinks on the deck of a luxury camp, few travellers are aware that everything, down to the toothpicks and olives in their martinis, must be trekked from distant depots. Dry goods are transported overland in robust vehicles, sometimes only once a month, while people and perishables are ferried by air. Light aircraft are not just for the privileged few: guests coming in to the luxury camps in the single-engined charter planes that serve as air taxis will often exchange places with staff being flown out for leave or medical services. Not least of all it is these transport costs that make Botswana an expensive destination. The government, too, has a tourist policy of low volumes and high prices, which helps maintain the country's most vulnerable assets in a near-pristine state. Even the most luxurious safari lodges must be built so that they can be dismantled and Botswana's newest camps provide 'Out of Africa' style accommodation under canvas, using indigenous timbers and reeds.

The only sources of water are subterranean streams and the fugitive pools left in the pans after summer rains. The pans – some as big as a small European country – bring life to the parched wilderness, holding water, with luck, into the winter months. These shallow basins and dry lake beds vary in size from a few metres to several hundred metres or even kilometres wide. Makgadikgadi, a complex of two huge and several smaller pans in north-eastern Botswana, was once the biggest lake in Africa but it has been dry for 2,000 years. However, even the pans dry out eventually, with enormous demands by game, people and their livestock. In addition, with little or no cover in searing summer heats, huge volumes of moisture are lost through evaporation. One of Botswana's saddest sights is animals crowding round dwindling pans with faint hope of more water to come until the next rainy season several desperate months away.

Botswana, after rain, is swiftly and sweetly renewed. Makgadikgadi becomes a shimmering lake, a paradise for millions of flamingoes and fellow-waders who migrate here to breed each year. The pans create a temporary habitat for hordes of animals, especially browsing game species and the predators who follow them to the fresh new grasses on the surrounding floodplains. The Savuti area of Chobe National Park is spectacular after rain; vast herds of elephant, zebra, buffalo, wildebeest and antelope migrate there, with all the associated carnivores in their wake: leopard, lion, hyaena, cheetah and one of Africa's most threatened predators, the endangered wild dog.

Most of the country lies at 900 to 1,000 metres above sea level, an almost entirely flat tableland. Among the rare interruptions on the level landscape are the Tsodilo Hills, 400 kilometres via a tortuous route north of the central town of Maun. These four rocky outcrops, which the San named 'male, female, child and orphan', rise 300 metres above the desert floor like islands from a sea of sand, and provide awesome views of the Kalahari. The site, which holds a valuable outdoor gallery of ancient rock art and relics of Stone and Iron Age settlements, was described by Sir Laurens van der Post as 'the Louvres of the desert'. The San in Botswana, as in almost all of Southern Africa, were the earliest inhabitants, occupying the region between 25,000 and 40,000 years ago.

Entering Botswana's more modern history, however, the Ndebele were the catalysts for 150 years of change after many centuries of peace. These powerful people were a force to be reckoned with, aggressive invaders who displaced the peaceful locals and annexed their lands. When 20,000 Boer 'refugees' – escaping the British in the Cape Colony – entered Botswana in 1836, the Tswana enlisted their help in recovering their ancestral land from the Ndebele. With the aid of guns and ammunition – introduced to Botswana for the first time – the Ndebele were easily driven off but, in a swift about-turn, the Boers then claimed the lands for themselves. The dispossessed Tswana now

Intricately woven baskets emerge from natural raw materials such as Ilala Palm fronds and vegetable dyes.

appealed to the British for assistance, and, in response, Bechuanaland was declared a British protectorate in 1885. When the new Union of South Africa was formed in 1910, provisions were made to incorporate both Bechuanaland and then Rhodesia within its boundaries at some time in the future. This was not to be. When South Africa began to put pressure on the Tswana chiefs to join the Union, the offer was declined. South Africa retaliated with sanctions which almost brought the country to its knees. Struggling simultaneously with successive seasons of cruel drought, the country fell into swift economic disarray. Most of the male population was absent, working in South Africa and, as a result, the traditional fabric was fragmented, with far-reaching social consequences. Even today, traditional structures are fragile and 'urban drift' is an unfortunate social phenomenon.

Buffalo, close relatives of the domestic cow, congregate in huge herds in the dry season. The adults are preyed on by lion, the calves by spotted hyaena.

The Tswana people began, in the early 1950s, to think of independence, and, in just over a decade, the momentous transition had been swiftly and elegantly achieved. In 1966, Bechuanaland became the Republic of Botswana with Sir Seretse Khama as its first president. He remained, with his British wife Lady Ruth, a loved and respected leader until his death in 1980.

Today everyone who is a Botswana national is a Batswana, irrespective of origins. Although the majority of people are of Tswana heritage and culture, there are quite a number of other significant groups including the Bayei, Bakalanga, Hambukushu, Bakgalagadi, San, and relative newcomers such as the Herero community. Both Setswana and English are widely spoken and understood. Botswana's future is bright, given added sparkle by the discovery of diamonds which, since 1967, has accelerated economic growth into overdrive and built phenomenal foreign currency reserves. This wealth has made the pula the strongest currency in Africa, backed up with further mineral resources such as copper, nickel, coal, cobalt, manganese, soda ash, asbestos, and salt. And now tourism is a major money-spinner too. Getting to the bush is made easy with international scheduled flights via Johannesburg and Harare, and thence to the Botswana capital of Gaborone, Maun and a handful of other bigger centres. Maun, once little more than a dusty village, is now a rapidly developing base for safari operators, air charter, car hire and peripheral safari service providers.

Most of the luxury camps and lodges are concentrated in Moremi, the Delta and in the Savuti region of Chobe in the north-west. Kalahari accommodation on the other hand is limited to campsites with the most basic amenities, such as at Makgadikgadi and Nxai pans. Luxury in the bush is a relative term: while operators must charge high prices because of the set-up and maintenance costs, the most lavish camps would fall into the 'comfortable' category anywhere else. The average, well-heeled traveller will opt for a lodge, but many foreign visitors relish the romantic notion of a Hemingway-style mobile safari with a comfortable four-wheel-drive vehicle, private guide and well-trained camp staff to take care of them.

A familiar sight around the marshes and floodplains of the Delta are the richly coloured red lechwe. The antelopes' splayed hooves prevent them sinking in sedge.

Adventure travellers may also traverse the plains on horseback, perched on the back of an elephant, or by motorbike or on foot, under strict supervision. And, although motorized boats are permitted, the traditional *mokoro* dugout canoe is the most appropriate way to explore the myriad channels and lagoons of the Delta. Deftly manoeuvred by skilled Bayei polers, the *mokoros* quietly skim the waterways without leaving a ripple in their wake. Nor do they ruffle the flowering water lilies or disturb the birds or wake the crocodiles dozing on the reeded banks. Once made from the trunks of mature Strangler Figs and other large tree species, *mokoros* are now more often of fibreglass – a conscious move towards conservation of the country's limited timber reserves.

Few visitors will leave Botswana with regrets; perhaps it has to do with living, for a while, on the edge of a little danger? There's something to be said for eating in an outdoor *boma*, interrupted by a curious elephant, or having the gaze of a languid leopard settle on you from a branch just metres above your head, or hearing the rip and tear of newly dead flesh as lion settle in on a buffalo kill. And, never to be forgotten, the silence that allows you to hear a lion lap in the new dawn at the edge of a mirrored pan.

PAGE 96 *The Bayei are skilled polers who never lose their way, although the Delta map is constantly being redrawn by the ebb and flow of water and the seasons. Chief's Island, 1,000 square kilometres in extent, the biggest land mass in the Delta, contains a host of private camps. Gunn's Camp (*PAGE 97 TOP*) on the Moro River is accessible from Maun. An observation platform at Xaxaba Camp (*PAGE 97 BOTTOM*) offers an excellent view of the Delta's game.*

ABOVE *The Black Egret when hunting forms a shaded dome with its wings, which cuts surface glare on the water while luring small fish into its 'shelter'. Black egrets occupy both permanent swamp and the grasslands of the floodplains.*

BOTSWANA

98

RIGHT *The last, swiftly flowing stretch of the Okavango River is known as the Panhandle. From here the Delta fans out into three, then dozens and hundreds of smaller channels.*

LEFT Visitors to the Okavango are often surprised to find not only the anticipated game and a wealth of birds, but also plant life of extraordinary beauty and variety. The channels of the Delta support richly coloured reeds and grasses on their banks. The Day Waterlily (shown here) forms spreading carpets on undisturbed water.

OPPOSITE A typical sight at sunset on the Delta is the Bayei polers in their mokoros.

PAGE 102 Open game-viewing vehicles are as common a sight in the Delta as the Red Lechwe (TOP), the signature antelope of floodplains and marshlands; here they graze on the river bank in the Moremi Wildlife Reserve to the east of Chief's Island. Skilled guides know just when and where to find game. Invariably they know the animals by sight, keep a keen count on numbers and observe the movement of individuals or herds. Lion (BOTTOM) are always lazy after feeding, the male more so than the female, and are more active at night.

PAGE 103 Six-day elephant safaris are one of the most stately and gentle ways of experiencing the Okavango Delta and its environs. The project came to fruition through the vision of conservationist, author and elephant trainer, Randall Moore.

LEFT A hippo bull wallows in the waters of a lagoon in the Moremi Wildlife Reserve. These huge amphibian mammals rest in the water by day and forage on land by night.

BELOW The markings of the Yellowbilled Stork only become apparent in the mature bird, while the chick is a dull grey.

OPPOSITE TOP Reed and thatch are typical materials used to build safari camps in Botswana, where the rule is that all such structures must be able to be dismantled, such as Camp Okuti in Moremi (shown here).

OPPOSITE BOTTOM The Moremi Wildlife Reserve, in the north-eastern flange of the Okavango Delta, provides comfortable accommodation beneath a canopy of tall trees.

BOTSWANA

PAGES 106 AND 107 *The Chobe National Park, in the north-eastern corner of the country, is a showcase for breathtaking landscapes, huge populations of elephant* (PAGE 106), *lion and buffalo, and annual zebra migrations of up to 25,000. Like all camps in the area, Linyanti* (PAGE 107 TOP) *is tented. A tiny Carmine Bee-eater* (PAGE 107 BOTTOM), *one of the summer migrants in the region, hitches a ride on the back of a Kori Bustard.*

RIGHT *Mother and child in the wild. The African lion is territorial and lives in prides of up to a dozen individuals. The greater part of the day is spent in rest — the male is particularly indolent — but both male and female are powerful, aggressive and fast hunters. Although they have no natural foes, they are prey to parasitic diseases and death as a result of injury inflicted by their prey when they are hunting.*

BOTSWANA

108

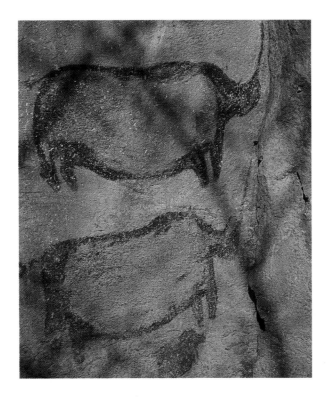

PAGE 110 *Africa's 'upside-down tree', the baobab. The ancient stand, the 'seven sisters', at Nxai Pan National Park, was immortalized by the artist and engineer Thomas Baines, who painted them in 1862.*

PAGE 111 *One of the few trees able to survive the saline soils of the Makgadikgadi Pans is the Ivory Palm.*

ABOVE AND RIGHT *West of the Panhandle an extraordinary outcrop of rocky inselbergs rises from the surrounding plains. The stories of the hills are inseparable from the legends of the San people who still live in traditional settlements at their base. The rock faces were canvases for the art of their ancestors, who painted animals, people and even fish. Today's San hunters are still armed with bow and arrow.*

BOTSWANA

Zimbabwe

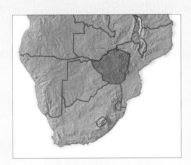

One of the youngest independent nations in Africa, Zimbabwe emerged from a decade of war and faced a future which, back in 1980, appeared radiant. Until recent upheavals, it was not only a safe and relatively well-organized country, but it had also set out to manage its many natural assets in an exemplary manner.

Among its priceless array of natural treasures, Zimbabwe is also the proud custodian of three World Heritage sites: the spectacular Victoria Falls and Mana Pools, both on the Zambezi River which is the country's northern boundary, and the mysterious ruins of Great Zimbabwe in the south-east, from which the country's name is taken.

Zimbabwe stands head and shoulders above some of its neighbours in many respects: its parks and their accommodation facilities are models of comfort and hospitality; wildlife management is shared between the government and the people; conservation has been made a national priority that encompasses not only animals but also the vegetation and winged occupants of its many habitats. Zimbabwe has a large number of mammal, reptile, fish, butterfly and indigenous tree species. Among its numerous bird species are Africa's biggest concentration of Black Eagles in the Matobo Hills.

OPPOSITE *The Victoria Falls, among the world's top tourist destinations, are 1.7 km wide and plunge 90 to 107 metres into the Zambezi Gorge.*

RIGHT *Makishi dancers in fantastic costumes perform ritual dances at the Victoria Falls Hotel.*

ZIMBABWE

115

In a land of many granite outcrops, none is quite so strange as Epworth's Balancing Rocks near Harare. The rocks are depicted on Zimbabwe's $10 note.

Zimbabwe has had its most notable successes with the management of its elephant and endangered black rhino populations. Although they are under constant threat from poachers, the country's black rhino are more numerous than anywhere else in the world – currently around 1,500.

The country's advanced conservation policies include 'safari areas', or controlled hunting, which brings immeasurable financial benefit to local people in wildlife management zones. The high price placed by game hunters on trophies has encouraged rural communities to value 'their' animals. Zimbabwe's conservation policies are based on the understanding that tourism revenue is fundamental to the country's well-being, manifesting returns to rural areas in the form of schools and hospitals. As a result of fortunes being ploughed back into education after independence, almost every Zimbabwean can speak English.

Among Zimbabwe's 40 national parks and reserves are several of international stature. These include Victoria Falls and Mana Pools on the Zambezi River, and the huge Hwange National Park south of the falls, said to have the highest diversity and density of wildlife in the world.

Zimbabwe is bounded in the north and south by two of Africa's great rivers, the Zambezi and the Limpopo. Its longest boundary is with Mozambique in the east, then Botswana in the west, Zambia in the north and South Africa in the south. A few metres of common frontier are shared with Namibia's Caprivi Strip in the north-west, where four countries (Zimbabwe, Namibia, Zambia and Botswana) meet within 100 metres of each other in a blur of heat and sand.

The country is diagonally sliced by a ridge, the Highveld, which occupies 25 percent of its space and contains most of its largest towns, including the capital Harare, at a cool and comfortable altitude of more than 1,000 metres above sea level. The ridge reaches its highest point at 1,500 metres in the tumbled granite hills of the Matobo National Park, where the grave of Cecil John Rhodes commands a spectacular panorama at World's View.

From this high plateau, the land descends in broad slopes to the hot, dry plains below, rolling on towards the river valleys of the Zambezi and the Limpopo to the north and south respectively, and to the Kalahari and Botswana in the west.

The eastern plains, Zimbabwe's Lowveld, are rich in game, and when irrigated are remarkably fertile, producing sugarcane and winter wheat. When not under irrigation, the natural dryland vegetation reverts to grasses, mopane woodland and baobab, able to survive searing temperatures and devastating dehydration. The southern Lowveld is home to Zimbabwe's second largest park, Gonarezhou – wild, rugged 'place of elephants' – which runs along the Mozambican border between the Save and Limpopo rivers.

Incredibly, the north-eastern extremities are lavishly green, quite unlike anything one might expect to find in central Southern Africa, the lush product of a 300-kilometre-long mountain belt running from north to south. A gentle tapestry of misted peaks, and downs, dells and dales more typical of the British Isles, these verdant uplands are the domain of trout lakes, exclusive golf courses and secluded holiday villages with English country churches. There are huge tobacco, coffee and tea plantations, groves of bananas and other tropical fruits, nuts, and vast forests of pine. It is the birthplace of rivers and limitless waterfalls, a paradise for birders and hikers, and, with its stunningly clear night skies, offers the celestial delights of stargazing.

Visitors have a bird's-eye view of the sunset from a hide at Deka, one of Hwange National Park's seven camps.

This area, the Eastern Highlands, holds some of Zimbabwe's finest scenery in the remote and beautiful Nyanga National Park, the Bvumba mountain promontory near the regional capital of Mutare, and the mountainous Chimanimani National Park in the south. Nyanga's Mount Inyangani is Zimbabwe's loftiest point, at 2,593 metres. Seventeen rivers flow from Inyangani, including the Pungwe (or Pungoe) which drops to a deep forested gorge in a series of impressive falls. Entry to the Highlands is via the pretty town of Mutare. Zimbabwe's fifth biggest town, Mutare lies back-to-back with the Mozambican province of Manica and is linked by road and rail to Beira and the Mozambican coast. Positioned in a compelling setting ringed by mountains, the town's several imperative attractions include the Bvumba Botanical Gardens, which are laid out on a mountain promontory where the sweeping views extend across the border to the plains of Mozambique some 1,000 metres below.

The Impala Lily, also known as the Sabie Star, carries its multiple blooms on a heavy fleshy trunk, usually growing below ground to conserve moisture.

While Zimbabwe's hinterland has plenty to keep the most adventurous traveller happily engaged, the country's most famous sights are concentrated in the northern and north-western extremities, which are home to the awesome Victoria Falls, Lake Kariba and huge Hwange National Park. Aside from these, this area boasts the remote mountain wilderness of Chizarira, the small, almost inaccessible Kazuma Pan and faraway Mana Pools on the edge of the Zambezi escarpment. Beautiful Matusadona on the southern shores of Lake Kariba, some travellers aver, is the loveliest of all Zimbabwe's national parks. This serene composition of water, islands, floodplains and mountain ridges is not only lovely to behold, but also creates habitats for a fabulous variety of birds, game and fish – including the Sabre-Toothed Tigerfish so loved by sporting fishermen. The name Matusadona, which translates as 'constant dropping of dung', says it all.

But it is 'Vic Falls' that is the primary destination for Zimbabwe's annual one million visitors. The Falls were patriotically named after Britain's reigning queen by Scottish missionary David Livingstone on 16 November 1855, although centuries-old indigenous descriptions of this mighty cataract were of 'water rising as smoke'. The falls thunder off a 1.7-kilometre-wide ledge 100 metres above the Zambezi Gorge, delivering up to five million cubic metres of water per minute when in full flood in April. The Victoria Falls, double the size of Niagara, have created

Getting away from it all is re-defined in the remote Mana Pools National Park. The park incorporates a series of pools on the alluvial floodplains of the Zambezi, where phenomenal numbers of game congregate in the dry season.

their own surrounding rainforest irrigated by the clouds of spray, visible 70 kilometres away, that are thrown high into the sky above the roaring cataract.

The Victoria Falls are the most spectacular natural feature of the Zambezi River, which rises in Zambia and flows for 2,700 kilometres before reaching the Indian Ocean in the Mozambique Channel. The Zambezi also supplies the vast lakes of Kariba and Cahora Bassa. These lakes generate enormous supplies of hydro-electric power, create extensive sources of food as well as jobs from fishing, a variety of habitats for animals and splendid recreational opportunities on the water and its shores.

While the majestic river, the Falls and the wildlife are Zimbabwe's natural attractions, the ruins of a once-mighty city provide the key to the country's social and cultural archives. The relict kingdom of Great Zimbabwe, second only to the Falls, and sprawled across more than 700 hectares of the Mutirikwe Valley in south-eastern Zimbabwe, is one of the most awe-inspiring sights of the southern continent.

The 'great houses of stone', which gave their name to modern Zimbabwe, were the seat of a powerful 13th- to 14th-century Shona-Karanga dynasty with some 40,000 subjects at the height of its influence. Trading in gold and ivory, and farming with cattle, sheep and goats, the people of this medieval African city state wove an affluent and stable society, expressing themselves in art and architecture.

Such was the mystery of its origins that the Great Zimbabwe complex was long thought to be the site of King Solomon's mines, perhaps Queen Sheba's court, or maybe the Valley of the Ancients. These myths have been exploded, and there is irrefutable proof that this was the royal court of the Shona kings until the 15th century. The site museum houses totemic soapstone birds, a wealth of archaeological treasures including gold, bronze, iron and copper relics, and trade objects of porcelain and glass. Modern Zimbabweans, particularly the Shona, are a nation of gifted craftspeople, creating covetable

ZIMBABWE

A 32-km-long sandstone massif, Chilojo, rises above the Runde River in Gonarezhou National Park, southern Zimbabwe.

wood and stone carvings and sculpture, clay pots, cloth, crochet work and items such as bags and rugs from Msasa tree bark. Venda baskets are a favourite tourist trophy, as are Ndebele hats woven of straw.

When the Shona-Karanga empire fell in the 15th century, lesser dynasties emerged – not without some territorial rivalry – which left the way open for Portuguese conquistadors hell-bent on claiming the gold, source of the fabled wealth of Zimbabwe's interior.

For the next three centuries the Mutapa and the Torwa held sway as the new, albeit lesser, Shona dynasties, establishing autonomous states and amassing great fortunes. The Mutapa controlled northern and eastern present-day Zimbabwe and most of Mozambique, imposing lucrative taxes on the trade routes to the coast. The Torwa of the south-eastern regions were more intent on farming and crafting granite-block structures than engaging in commerce or war with the neighbours (evidence of their skills as architects and sculptors is to be found in sites throughout Zimbabwe). Once almost invincible, the Mutapa, through the succession of lesser leaders, eventually lost their kingdom to the Changamire dynasty which swiftly went on to absorb the Torwa territory as well. The result was the establishment of a powerful new state, Rozwi, which maintained control of almost all of modern-day Zimbabwe for almost two hundred years.

In the south, Zulu chief Shaka's mission of ruthless expansionism had set many of the Nguni groups on a path of northward flight to escape his reign of terror. One of these, the Xumalo, was a subgroup of the aggressive, powerful Ndebele, 'the people who disappear behind long shields', led by 'great bull elephant' Mzilikazi. They assassinated the Rozwi leader and the state was dismantled by force. Mzilikazi set up his military state at Inyati, 60 kilometres from Bulawayo near the rugged hills of Matobo.

For the last half of the 19th century, the Shona and Ndebele remained enemies, until outrage over forced labour and land appropriation united them in an attack on Cecil John Rhodes' English settlers who had established farms and a luxurious lifestyle in the green and fertile uplands. Nevertheless, white rule continued for 85 years in British Rhodesia (as Zimbabwe was then called), with Salisbury (now Harare) as its capital. But, in the late 1950s, history stirred itself and rose up. White Rhodesians were urging Britain to give them independence while black Rhodesians, with the same goal, mobilized themselves into the Southern Rhodesian African National Congress headed by Joshua Nkomo. Ian Smith became Prime Minister in 1964 and, a year later, seized independence by means of a unilateral declaration (UDI).

In the meantime, the Rhodesian ANC had split into two opposed and antagonistic groups – the Zimbabwe African National Union (ZANU) and the Zimbabwe African People's Union (ZAPU). As a result, the nationalist movement was kept to no more than a slow simmer for the next seven years. The movement was brought to the boil by combining forces with Mozambique in full-scale guerrilla warfare, which wrought devastation for the next decade. Leaving 27,000 people dead, and 15,000 refugees in its wake, the war ended with an all-party conference in London in 1979. The first free elections were held early the next year, and Robert Mugabe became the prime minister of the new Zimbabwe.

Zimbabwe feeds its 13 million people from its immense farmlands, exporting tobacco, tea, coffee, sugar, flowers, maize, and timber, and earning huge revenues from tourism and gold,

Pools along the Mwenezi River in western Gonarezhou ensure excellent game-viewing. The Mwenezi area supports flourishing populations of sausage trees and, on the Mozambican border, a valley of ironwoods, the country's only stand of these trees.

in that order. Its other exports include nickel and asbestos. The economy is further sustained by a wide range of manufactured goods – a relatively new, but vibrant sector born of necessity during the lonely years of post UDI sanctions.

Today, although Zimbabwe shares Africa's problems of unemployment, soaring population figures, urban drift and Aids, it remains a popular destination with tourists because of all that it has to offer in terms of its glorious natural attractions.

ZIMBABWE

LEFT *The Main Falls are at their most impressive in full flood between February and May. The best views are via an approach through the adjacent rainforest, a jungle of orchids, vines and trees drenched in a perpetual fine mist.*

BELOW *River cruisers ferry thousands of awestruck tourists along the broad tranquil reaches of the Zambezi, which is at its widest point above the Falls.*

ZIMBABWE

123

ZIMBABWE

—————

124

ABOVE *Curios on sale at Victoria Falls and other tourist attractions around the country include hand-crafted items made from soapstone and woods such as teak and ebony.*

OPPOSITE *Shooting the rapids on the Zambezi is an exhilarating sport which attracts millions of television viewers worldwide during the annual Zambezi River Festival.*

Hwange, Zimbabwe's oldest and most easily accessible national park, is not far from the Victoria Falls.

OPPOSITE Elephant at Caterpillar Pan in the eastern zone close to Hwange's Main Camp.

LEFT Several private lodges augment the National Parks Board facilities, offering luxurious and sometimes novel accommodation, such as this tree house at Ivory Safari Lodge.

BELOW Five hundred kilometres of road lead to the park's biggest pans and other major game-viewing sites.

OPPOSITE Iron Age ruins with intricate geometric patterns in the style of Great Zimbabwe are to be found at many sites throughout Zimbabwe. Those at Nalatale, some 100 kilometres east of Bulawayo, are relics left by the dynasties of the Torwa, and their successors, the Rozwi.

ABOVE South of the city of Bulawayo, the Matobo Hills unfold in a rugged wilderness of tumbled granite boulders. Once owned by Cecil John Rhodes, who is buried on a spectacular hilltop site named World's View, the Matobos are the core of a spectacular national park.

ZIMBABWE

Left The Great Enclosure, the central
structure of the 13th- and 14th-century
ruins at Great Zimbabwe, lies in a wide
basin in the Mutirikwi Valley. It is seen here
from the Hill Complex, a cliff-face royal
castle made of hand-hewn granite boulders.
The oldest ruins have been dated back to
1270. These 'great houses of stone' give
Zimbabwe its name, and form the greatest
man-made structure south of the Pyramids.

Above The Great Zimbabwe site also
has a reconstructed Shona village, small
museum and curio shop, where curios such
as these soapstone birds can be bought.

ZIMBABWE

131

OPPOSITE Chimanimani National Park encloses part of Zimbabwe's cool, mountain regions, the Eastern Highlands. The Bridal Veil Falls are at the park's western edge.

RIGHT The Leopard Rock Hotel, built by Italian prisoners of war in WWII, is named for the natural granite monolith near the Bvumba Botanical Gardens at Mutare.

BELOW Pickers in Honde Valley plantations carry baskets to hold the freshly picked tea leaves. Coffee and tropical fruit are also grown here, at the foothills of Mount Inyangani.

ABOVE AND ABOVE RIGHT *Modern Zimbabwean stone sculpture has gained world acclaim in the last thirty years. Many fine examples of the work of leading artists – of whom at least seven are represented in galleries in Europe and America –* *are housed in the National Gallery in Harare. Other examples can be seen in the Chapungu Kraal Craft Village in the Msasa area of the capital city. The pieces shown here, which are of a massive scale, are displayed out of doors in the Sculpture Garden at Chapungu.*

OPPOSITE *Many attractive and elegant buildings grace the wide thoroughfares of Zimbabwe's capital city, Harare.*

ZIMBABWE

THIS PAGE, CLOCKWISE FROM TOP LEFT *Mana Pools National Park, a place of unspoilt beauty, boasts several specialized and endemic species as well as a rich variety of other African wildlife such as eland, zebra, wild dog and lion.*

LEFT While many of the activities of Lake Kariba are priced for the upper income brackets, the lake is a destination not to be missed on any Zimbabwean itinerary.

ABOVE The proliferation of wildlife in and around Kariba has been phenomenal since its construction in May 1960. Many of the best game-viewing areas, such as the Matusadona National Park on the lake's southern shore, are most easily accessible by boat.

ZIMBABWE

139

ABOVE A private safari boat sets out from Fothergill Island in the Matusadona National Park. Other game-viewing options are offered on foot or by air.

RIGHT Elephant walk the shoreline below the Bumi Hills. The pachyderms and other game sometimes swim from island to island in the park's lagoons, such as Sibilobilo.

ZIMBABWE

140

Mozambique

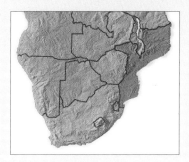

What has happened in Mozambique in the last few peaceful years has been nothing less than a renaissance. Emerging from the ashes of almost two decades of civil war, the country is preparing to resume its place as one of the most beautiful and romantic travel destinations in the world.

Foreign funding is helping to rehabilitate nature parks ravaged by war. Off-shore investors are focusing on property development. Roads are re-opening and communications have improved. Farmers are re-establishing plantations of copra, cashew nuts, citrus and tea, neglected by a nation at war. Red tape has unravelled and visitors may travel with every expectation of security and assistance all the way. Mozambique has defined its future in tourism and, when one considers the country's fabulous assets, this is as it should be.

Opposite The dhow, a legacy of centuries of Arab domination of the East African coastline, is still a common form of transportation.

Above right The Coral Rock Cod is among 1,200 species of fish in the oceans off Mozambique.

Mozambique's 2,500-kilometre tropical coastline is a paradise of palm-fringed beaches and aquamarine ocean, coral reefs and tiny, languid islands. Seven of the ten provinces have coastal frontage and it is here that most activity, however leisurely, is focused. Some of the islands have low-budget *pensões* and *pousadas* (luxurious lodges), and the major cities boast opulent hotels, but many visitors drift into beach huts or campsites, and the simple diversions of game fishing, scuba diving or simply finning through the crystalline waters, adrift over coral reefs in the company of tropical fish, turtles, dolphins, harmless whale sharks and dugongs.

The rare dugong (only about 15 of them are left today), which are believed to have given rise to the mermaid legend, breed in small areas off the south coast of the province of Inhambane, around the Bazaruto Archipelago, and off the northern province of Zambezia. Around 1,200 species of fish have been identified in the waters around Mozambique and several world records are held for deep-sea game fishing catches made here.

Most of the coastal communities make their living from subsistence fishing, settled in traditional villages in the shelter of high, forested sand dunes. Their daily haul will include giant prawns, clams and a wealth of other seafood for which Mozambique is renowned.

Mat weavers show off their craft at a traditional market near the coastal village of Palma, in Cabo Delgado province in the far northern reaches of Mozambique.

Fresh seafood is always high on the menu – peri-peri prawns may almost be regarded as a national dish – and Mozambican food as a whole is simple, but often spicy. Cashew nuts, also coated with peri-peri, are offered in even the humblest establishments, along with Portuguese beer.

The Mozambique Channel, lying between the mainland and the eastern Indian Ocean island of Madagascar, supports shoals of the pelagic sardine, anchovy and barracuda with game fish such as marlin and tuna found in deeper waters. These harvests from the sea not only underpin a significant commercial fishing industry, but also deliver desperately needed revenue from fishing tourism.

Mozambique's earliest peoples were hunter-gatherers, gradually integrated by the more dominant Bantu-speaking people who were moving southwards ahead of the shifting sands of the Sahara Desert. By 400 AD Arabs were trading with the indigenous peoples, in the process swiftly gaining a hold on all the ports of East Africa, and later dominating trade in gold, ivory and cloth, a monopoly that would endure until the middle of the 16th century.

The first Europeans arrived in the late 15th century, seafaring Portuguese explorers who, within 100 years, had wrested this monopoly from the Arabs. Formidable fortresses were built and, along with treasured cargoes of gold and ivory, hundreds of thousands of slaves were 'exported'. At first they were sent to work the sugar plantations in French Indian Ocean territories, and, later, to America. In 1828 alone 30,000 slaves left Mozambique.

After centuries of Portuguese rule, the first stirrings of the struggle for liberation began in 1962 with the formation of Frelimo (Mozambican Liberation Front). The first attack in the armed struggle was launched in 1964 and when the resistance movement Renamo was formed in 1977, civil war ensued and was to last for 17 years. From the time of his appointment as head of Frelimo in 1969 to his death in 1986, the liberation movement was headed by the late Samora Machel. Although Machel later shunned the Marxist policies adopted by Frelimo since independence in 1975, it was not until the collapse of communism in 1990 that Frelimo formally denounced these policies. A 1992 cease-fire finally brought an end to the hostilities and, two years later, Mozambique held its first independent, democratic multiparty elections under UN supervision.

There are countless reminders of centuries of both Arab and Portuguese cultures – and some remnants of the

Because of its isolation in the north-western corner of Mozambique, the Niassa Reserve was relatively unscathed by the war. Buffalo, elephant and antelope, lion and hunting dog are predominant.

communist era – throughout Mozambique today. Although Portuguese is the official language and is fairly widely spoken in the cities, most of the rural people speak one or another of the 17 ethnic languages. Many of the young are fluent in English, the legacy of early childhood years in refugee camps in neighbouring countries.

Mozambican architecture is an intriguing mix. Its rich and exotic history is preserved in centuries-old Catholic churches and mosques, fortresses and palaces, ornate Victorian mansions and some superbly

MOZAMBIQUE

Rice, which is harvested in winter, is an important crop of Mozambique's northern provinces.

preserved Art Deco buildings in Maputo. Tiny Mozambique Island, 1,500 kilometres north of Maputo and for 200 years the country's capital, is a living museum of Arab, Indian, African and Portuguese cultures, dominated by a 16th-century fortress and palace housing the national museum.

The country's art, which once reflected only the glory and grandeur of historical superpowers, has begun to show a more African face and there is much to covet or collect. The intricate and often bizarre wood carvings produced by the Makonde of the northernmost province of Cabo Delgado and the huge bold paintings by several highly-prized local artists have helped create a profile for indigenous art.

Only three of Mozambique's eight national reserves and nature parks have re-opened since the end of the war – the Bazaruto Archipelago, Maputo Elephant Reserve and Gorongosa – while others, such as Niassa near the Tanzanian border, may be visited with permits and are presently being redeveloped. Conservationists are looking ahead, too, at long-term plans to open the South African-Mozambican border in a Peace Park project that will allow animals to resume their ancient migratory routes.

While big game was the prime target for poachers and hungry soldiers, the country's coral reefs and birdlife remain untouched. The idyllic islands – most notably the five islands of the popular Bazaruto Archipelago – are once more drawing tourists to their romantic shores, and a fabulous array of avian fauna, with many rare species, keeps Mozambique on the list of priority destinations for serious birders and ornithologists from all over the world. Although most visitors gravitate to the coast, the mountains and rivers, flora and fauna of the interior plateau provide a fascinating contrast and welcome respite from the heat and humidity of the plains. Most visitors will find it more comfortable to travel in winter, April to September, and to avoid the hot, very humid, rainy months from October to March.

The southern and western interior are the driest parts of the whole country, with Pafuri in the Gaza province receiving a mere 300 millimetres over the whole year, by comparison with the wet northern provinces of inland Niassa and its neighbour Cabo Delgado situated on the coast, where up to 300 millimetres will fall in the course of just a few weeks during the rainy season.

A silversmith practises his skilled craft at Fort Alezi on Ibo Island, northern Mozambique, between Pemba and Mocímboa da Praia.

Eight major rivers flow through Mozambique, of which two have enormous impact on the political, social and economic status of the region. In the far north, the Rovuma River is a massive natural boundary between Mozambique and Tanzania. There are no bridges or ferries; the only passage is by dugout canoe. Further south, the mighty Zambezi River slices the country in two; this not only creates two distinct geographic regions but is also a traditional social, cultural and trade divide which, to this day, limits movement between north and south.

The river travels some 3,000 kilometres before entering Mozambique in the far north-west, where its force is contained in the mammoth Cahora Bassa hydro-electric project. From there it is released to flow south-east for another 600 kilometres before feathering out into a broad delta whose major tributaries once supported busy ports. The game in the delta escaped relatively unscathed by the war and it is possible to view the animals as well as the lovely channels and islands of the 1,500 square-kilometre delta by light aircraft.

MOZAMBIQUE

The length of the coast is threaded with estuaries. Some have never reached the sea, settling instead into inland lakes. These are bounded by forested dunes, among the highest in the world, formed along with a myriad sand spits and islands, by forces from the countercurrents of the powerful Mozambique Channel. This is the 'lagoon district' which begins near Ponta do Ouro (Golden Point) in the extreme south and stretches northwards for 500 kilometres through a string of 24 lakes in what explorer Vasco da Gama named 'Terra da Boa Gênte' (Land of Good People) 500 years ago.

Mozambique's largest city is its capital Maputo, followed by Beira, the capital of central Sofala province and an important ocean port on the Pungoe (or Pungwe) River. Maputo became the capital in 1897, succeeding Mozambique Island off the northern province of Nampula. Known as 'the meeting point of civilizations', the island had been occupied by the Portuguese since 1507.

Maputo is still nostalgically named L.M., or Lourenço Marques, by South Africans, who holidayed there in the pre-war years. Today its tropical lifestyle and pulsating nightlife give it the air of a little Rio, with echoes of elegant Lisbon in its planning and often grandiose colonial architecture. Maputo has several world-class hotels and restaurants and a substantial treasury of architecture, art, history and theatre. Among the city's landmarks are the 18th-century Catholic cathedral, several excellent museums, botanical gardens, a number of extraordinarily opulent cinemas, a fascinating craft market

The road north from Mocímboa da Praia to Palma in remote Cabo Delgado province is impassable after the heavy summer rains.

and the buzzing central market, Mercado Municipal. The nearby islands – Inhaca, Xefina Grande and Portuguese Island – the Maputo Elephant Reserve, and the lagoon coast stretching northwards for hundreds of kilometres are enough to keep holidaymakers happily distracted for weeks.

Beira gained prominence only in the late 19th century and again during the civil war years for its strategic position at the mid-point of Mozambique's long coastline. The former provincial capital of Sofala, which was for centuries an Arab trading post and gateway to the legendary gold deposits of the interior, is now partially buried by shifting

The Jesuit Mission of Boroma, a short distance from Tete town in north-western Mozambique, was built in 1890 on the banks of the Zambezi River.

dunes. Beira today is of more interest due to its historic squares and architecture, art galleries, Makonde sculpture workshop, and graveyard for wrecked and scuttled warships. It is now also possible to drive – with a 4x4 vehicle – all the way from Beira, across the Zambezi, to Tete in the north-west. The 500-metre-long suspension bridge near Tete is still the only reliable all-year-round Zambezi crossing, although there is one other road bridge and a ferry.

Historic Inhambane lies on the shores of a beautiful sheltered bay. It was established as a Portuguese trading post in 1534 and is one of the oldest surviving European settlements in Southern Africa. The town has a distinctly oriental air which is lent by hundreds of dhows – the traditional Middle-Eastern craft still widely used as a means of transport – plying the waters of the bay, and by the Indian stores and spice markets lining its streets.

Quelimane, the fourth-largest town in Mozambique, is the provincial capital of Zambezia, one of Africa's most important river ports and a major tea, rice and coconut-producing area.

MOZAMBIQUE

BELOW The Edwardian Polana Hotel reflects the glamour and sophistication that is Maputo, Mozambique's capital city, principal port and home to well over a million people.

OPPOSITE TOP Mozambicans are largely a nation of craftspeople – artists, potters, sculptors, jewellery-makers and weavers. Colourful handwoven cotton fabrics are displayed in an open-air bazaar (bairro).

OPPOSITE BOTTOM Silverio Sitoe is one of Mozambique's many fine artists who have gained prominence during the years since independence. He lives and works in Beira.

OPPOSITE *Mozambique's coral reefs are rated alongside those of Australia's Great Barrier Reef. These exquisite but fragile ecosystems sustain a host of marine creatures.*

ABOVE *The brilliantly-striped Emperor Angelfish is a common resident of the coral reefs of Maputaland. It is seen most often during the summer months.*

MOZAMBIQUE

RIGHT Five coral isles off Inhambane form the Bazaruto
Archipelago, one of the loveliest destinations in the country.
Accommodation, island style, is in thatched and reeded
huts (TOP) almost on the water. Supplies for the lodges are
delivered mainly by dhow (ABOVE).

MOZAMBIQUE

———————

154

LEFT The marimba (shown here) is a kind of xylophone similar to the timbila, which, with the addition of hollow gourds, produce an infinite range and depth of tone.

ABOVE Clay pots are still commonly made and used in the rural parts of central Mozambique.

RIGHT Maize is strained and sorted before it is ready for pounding.

Tiny Ilha de Moçambique, which is 2.5 kilometres long and less than 1 kilometre wide, lies at the narrowest point of the Mozambique Channel, between mainland Mozambique and the Indian Ocean island of Madagascar. This once hugely strategic island was known as 'the meeting point of civilizations' and today remains a living museum of all the varied and colourful influences – Eastern, African and European – that have helped create modern Mozambique. The Bairro Museum, sprawling across two-thirds of the island, has been declared a World Heritage Site. A mosque overlooks the fishing boat anchorage on the mainland side of the island.

MOZAMBIQUE

OPPOSITE A Portuguese church, one of the architectural relics on Ilha de Moçambique. Others are St Paul's Palace, a second World Heritage site, constructed in 1619 and now a museum, and the Fortress of San Sebastian, built in 1558.

BELOW Fishermen on Ilha de Moçambique pull up rich daily hauls from the Mozambique Channel. The vast majority of the country's coastal inhabitants earn a living from subsistence fishing.

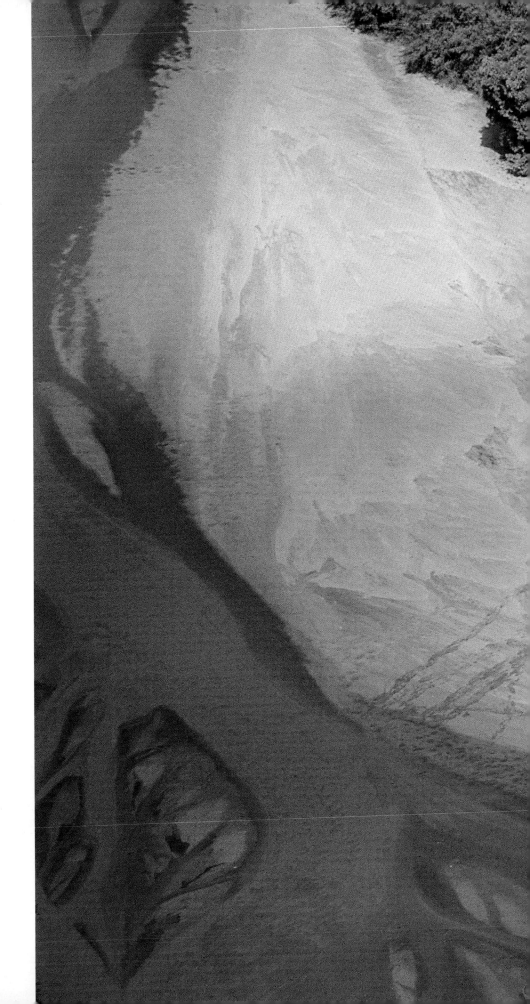

Niassa Reserve is situated in an isolated area in Niassa province, in the extreme north of Mozambique near the border with Tanzania. As a result, its game population largely escaped the devastation during the civil war that was the fate of animals in many other reserves. Today Niassa Reserve has the highest numbers of game in the country, which includes the elephant.

MOZAMBIQUE

Index

Page numbers given in **bold** indicate a main entry; those in *italics* indicate a photograph.

Photographic credits

ABPL = Anthony Bannister Photo Library; DB = Daryl Balfour; ET = Erhardt Thiel; GC = Gerald Cubitt; GD = Gerhard Dreyer;
HvH = Hein von Hörsten; IM = Ian Michler; IvdB = Ingrid van den Berg; JdP = Jean du Plessis; JK = J Kloppers; KB = Keith Begg;
LvH = Lanz von Hörsten; MH = Martin Harvey; MS = Mark Skinner; ND = Nigel Dennis; PA = Photo Access; PP = Peter Pickford;
PvdB = Philip van den Berg; RdlH = Roger de la Harpe; SA = Shaen Adey; SIL = Struik Image Library; WK = Walter Knirr

Front cover RdlH/SIL (top and bottom); **back cover** MH (top), IM (bottom left), JK (bottom right); **cover spine** MH; **back flap** Corrie Hansen;
endpapers KB/SIL, (left page, top), WK/SIL (left page, bottom), IM (right page, top), JdP (right page, bottom left), MH (right page, bottom right);
Pages **1** GC; **2–3** MH; **4–5** ND/SIL; **7** PP/SIL; **8** WK (left and centre), JdP (right); **9** WK/SIL (left), ND/SIL (centre), Lionel Soule (right); **10** HvH/SIL
(left), JK (centre), DB (right); **11** RdlH/SIL (left), MH (centre), JdP (right); **12** WK; **13** RdlH; **14** LvH/SIL; **15** RdlH/SIL; **16** DB; **17** WK; **18** MS;
19 ET/SIL; **20** WK (top), MS/PA (bottom); **21** GC; **22** WK; **23** WK/SIL (top), SA (centre and bottom); **24** WK (top and bottom); ET/SIL (top);
SA/SIL (bottom); **26–7** MS/PA; **28** SA/SIL (left), Anthony Johnson/SIL (right); **29** GC; **30** SA/SIL; **31** WK/SIL (top), Ken Findlay (bottom);
32–3 GD/SIL; **34** MS (top left and right, and bottom right), GD/SIL (bottom left); **35** WK; **36** MH; **37** MS; **38** MS (top), HvH/SIL (bottom);
39 HvH/SIL; **40** WK; **41** WK (top), RdlH/SIL (bottom); **42** RdlH/SIL; **43** RdlH/ABPL (top left), David Steele/PA (top right), WK (bottom left),
LvH/SIL (bottom right); **44** and **45** RdlH/SIL; **46–7** WK; **48** David Rogers/PA (top), SA/SIL (bottom); **49** RdlH/SIL (top), Terry Carew/PA (bottom
left), SA/SIL (bottom right); **50** ND/SIL (top), SA/SIL (bottom); **51** RdlH (top left), RdlH/SIL (top right), Pat de la Harpe (bottom); **52** and **53** WK
(all); **54** ND/SIL (top left), LvH/SIL (top right), SA (bottom); **55** LvH/SIL (top), Richard du Toit (bottom left), HPH Photography/IvdB (bottom right);
56 and **57** WK; **58** WK/SIL; **59** WK; **60** WK/SIL; **61** WK/PA; **62** ND/SIL; **63** Tony Camacho (top), ND/SIL (bottom); **64** CLB/SIL; **65** WK; **66** JK (top),
MH (bottom); **67** GD/SIL (top), WK/SIL (bottom); **68** JK; **69** PP/SIL; **70** HPH Photography/PvdB; **71** MS; **72** GC; **73** Carol Polich; **74** GC; **75** JdP (top),
GC (bottom); **76** GC; **77** JdP (top and bottom); **78** RdlH; **79** MH (top), JdP (bottom); **80** GC; **81** RdlH (top), HPH Photography/PvdB (bottom);
82 DB (top), HPH Photography/Heinrich van den Berg (bottom); **83–5** MS (all); **86** GC (top), DB (bottom); **87** HPH Photography/IvdB; **88** Mark
van Aardt; **89** GC; **90** MH; **91** RdlH; **92** and **93** MH; **94** IM; **95–6** MH; **97** MH (top), GC (bottom); **98** and **99** IM; **100–1** MH; **102** MH (top), IM
(bottom); **103** DB; **104** Richard du Toit (top and bottom); **105** and **106** MH (all); **107** IM (top), DB (bottom); **108–111** MH; **112** IM; **113** PP/SIL;
114 MS; **115** RdlH/SIL; **116** MH; **117** GC; **118–21** KB/SIL; **122** RdlH/SIL; **123** ND/SIL; **124** MS; **125** Patrick Wagner/PA; **126** GC; **127** GC (top),
RdlH/SIL; **128** and **129** MS; **130** KB/SIL; **131** and **132** RdlH/SIL; **133** RdlH/SIL (top and bottom); **134** and **135** MS (all); **136** KB/SIL (all); **137** JK;
138 RdlH/SIL; **139** DB; **140** RdlH/SIL; **141** GC; **142** IM; **143** **Danja Kohler;** 144–51 IM (all); **152** and **153** Geoff Spiby; **154–63** IM (all).

The following is from a Treasury Department Press Release giving an extract from testimony by Secretary Morgenthau before the Sub-committee of the House Appropriations Committee on December 18, in response to questioning by Chairman Ludlow: [32]

"Secretary Morgenthau:—so if it gets down to the question of—which it has—Great Britain needing financial assistance to pay for the orders that she wants to place with us, I think that is a matter for Congress to decide—as to how that financial assistance should be given to Great Britain, that is how I feel.

"Mr. Ludlow: But you feel that she has arrived at the point where she needs financial assistance?

"Secretary Morgenthau: I said so—they have so advised me as to further orders. They do need financial assistance for the orders they want to place with us for airplanes and boats and munitions."

HULL

[For text of radio address by President Roosevelt, December 29, 1940—the "arsenal of democracy" speech—see Department of State *Bulletin*, January 4, 1941, page 3.]

CONCERN OF THE UNITED STATES OVER THE FATE OF THE UNITED KINGDOM AND THE BRITISH FLEET AFTER THE COLLAPSE OF FRANCE

740.0011 European War 1939/2952 : Telegram

The Ambassador in the United Kingdom (Kennedy) to the Secretary of State

LONDON, May 15, 1940—2 a. m.
[Received May 14—10 : 15 p. m.]

1211. For the President and Secretary of State. I just left Churchill [33] at 1 : 00 o'clock. He is sending you a message tomorrow morning saying he considers with the entrance of Italy, the chances of the Allies winning is slight. He said the German push is showing great power and although the French are holding tonight they are definitely worried. They are asking for more British troops at once, but Churchill is unwilling to send more from England at this time because he is convinced within a month England will be vigorously attacked. The reason for the message to you is that he needs help badly. I asked him what the United States could do to help that would not leave the United States holding the bag for a war in which the Allies expected to be beaten. It seems to me that if we had to

---

[32] Louis Ludlow, Representative from Indiana.
[33] Winston Churchill, British Prime Minister.

fight to protect our lives we would do better fighting in our own backyard. I said you know our strength. What could we do if we wanted to help you all we can. You do not need money or credit now. The bulk of our Navy is in the Pacific and we have not enough airplanes for our own use and our Army is not up to requirements. So if this is going to be a quick war all over in a few months what could we do. He said it was his intention to ask for the loan of 30 or 40 of our old destroyers [34] and also whatever airplanes we could spare right now.

He said regardless of what Germany does to England and France, England will never give up as long as he remains a power in public life even if England is burnt to the ground. Why, said he, the Government will move to Canada and take the fleet and fight on. I think this is something I should follow up. If the Germans carry on there will be some conversation on what England will eventually do. Churchill called in the First Lord of the Admiralty Sinclair and Eden [35] and although they are tough and mean to fight they are very low tonight.

KENNEDY

740.0011 European War 1939/3435½

Memorandum of Conversation, by the Under Secretary of State (Welles)

[WASHINGTON,] May 21, 1940.

The British Ambassador [36] called to see me this morning. The Ambassador talked about the military situation in Europe. He seemed to believe that it was desperately serious, although he felt that there was still hope that a counter-offensive could be undertaken under the personal direction of General Weygand [37] which would prevent the Germans from achieving what now looked to be a crushing victory. The Ambassador said that he had heard that if Hitler succeeded in occupying Paris, Hitler and Mussolini would then jointly present Great Britain and France with peace terms in the form of an ultimatum with the proviso that if these terms were not promptly accepted, both countries would be completely destroyed. The Ambassador asked if I had any confirmation of this report.

I told him that I had no confirmation, but that it seemed to me entirely possible, although I nevertheless felt that what was more probable was that Great Britain would be subjected to bombing operations prior to the presentation of any peace terms.

---

[34] See pp. 49 ff.
[35] Anthony Eden, British Secretary of State for War.
[36] Marquess of Lothian.
[37] Gen. Maxime Weygand, Commander in Chief of the French Army.

The Ambassador spoke of his conversation with the President a few nights ago in which the question of the disposition of the British fleet in the event of British defeat had arisen. The Ambassador stated that in his judgment there was still hope for the world of the ultimate defeat of Germany so long as the British fleet remained out of German hands and so long as the British fleet could cooperate with the United States in controlling the Atlantic. The Ambassador felt that so long as the American fleet was in the Pacific and so long as the British fleet, and perhaps a portion of the American fleet, was in the Atlantic, Germany could not win a decisive victory. He said he felt, however, that in the event of a British defeat, the United States would have to become the focal point upon which the British fleet and the policy of the British Dominions could be based. He stated that only in such a manner could Germany, in the event of a victory, be prevented from strangling the South American Republics economically and forcing them thereafter to submit to German political control, and that also only in such manner would the British Dominions be enabled to continue in the struggle.

S[UMNER] W[ELLES]

740.0011 European War 1939/3005⁷⁄₁₀ : Telegram

The Ambassador in the United Kingdom (Kennedy) to the Secretary of State

LONDON, May 24, 1940—noon.
[Received May 24—11 a. m.]

1344. Personal for the Secretary. I saw Halifax [38] last night. The situation according to the people who know is very very grim. The mass of the people just never seem to realize that England can be beaten or that the worst can happen to them. I think the people in charge have in mind, realizing that the situation at the minute in France is precarious, that if necessary France will probably retreat to some line and hold on and England will get ready for attacks of all kinds. They feel that they will protect themselves well in the daytime and at night the efforts of the Germans cannot be anything but indiscriminate and they expect to return the attack on German locations, and in this way hold on for some time until help can arrive from the United States. Frankly I don't think that, if the French and British expeditionary force are licked in their present struggle, things will turn out quite as well as the English hope. I do not underestimate the courage or guts of these people but from the reports brought back by American newspapermen who were with the forces in Belgium and

---

[38] Lord Halifax, British Secretary of State for Foreign Affairs.

Northern France, it is going to take more than guts to hold off the systematic air attacks of the Germans coupled with air terrific superiority in numbers.

There is no question that everybody is mystified as to how the French were driven back so easily. They all seem to be looking for the answer but there is no doubt that there is terrific disappointment.

Halifax does not think that Mussolini has any influence at all with Hitler. He is definitely of the opinion that if anybody is able to save a debacle on the part of the Allies if it arrives at that point it is the President. Halifax still believes that that influence is one that the Germans still fear.

KENNEDY

740.0011 European War 1939/3487²⁄₁₀ : Telegram

The Ambassador in the United Kingdom (Kennedy) to the Secretary of State

LONDON, June 6, 1940—5 p. m.
[Received June 6—4 : 40 p. m.]

1524. Personal for the Secretary. Brief summary of the political and military situation as I see it here.

There is a terrific agitation going on, accelerated by the return of the powers who have very emphatic complaints against the Chamberlain [39] administration for lack of preparedness, to turn out the members of the old Government who are still in the present Government: Chamberlain, Halifax, Kingsley Wood,[40] Caldecote,[41] Butler.[42] I saw Chamberlain and he admits that the situation is very tense and that he is ready to go if Churchill so desires. I understand that Churchill will not force either Halifax or Kingsley Wood or Chamberlain out but that the force of public opinion may bring this about. Beyond that there is no political discussion at all. Everybody is with Churchill and his Government and it is unlikely that there will be much criticism aside from that directed against the old crowd while the military situation remains so tense.

From the military point of view most people feel that the French, if the pressure gets very heavy, will quit. The British are determined to fight on and Bracken [43] told me today that the fleet will not surrender in any event and that he considers that regardless of any deal the

---

[39] Neville Chamberlain, British Lord President of the Council of Ministers; formerly Prime Minister, May 28, 1937, to May 10, 1940.
[40] Kingsley Wood, British Chancellor of the Exchequer.
[41] Viscount Caldecote, British Secretary of State for the Dominions.
[42] Richard Austen Butler, British Parliamentary Under Secretary of State.
[43] Presumably Brendan Bracken, Parliamentary Private Secretary of the Prime Minister.

politicians may make regarding France, that the French naval crowd will join the British naval crowd. The French are crying for airplanes and there is now a plan going forward today to give them the use of a substantial number of British planes, to be flown by the French, the British say their flyers are too tired to go over there now. A plan is also being considered today to send the B. E. F.[44] now in England although not properly equipped to France and use French equipment and artillery.

There is also being discussed today here a very definite financial deal whereby England and France and their respective Empires pool their assets so that neither country will sell to the other what it needs but will hand over without charges. This is to keep the French reasonably happy.

There is constant agitation here in the newspapers, alleging that the Allies have asked for help from the United States; planes are mentioned most often and destroyers occasionally. I think it is important that some kind of statement should be made over there by some important person or over here after the policy has been decided explaining just why the United States is limited as to what she can give the Allies. I suggest this in order to save a great deal of ill-will that will arise towards the United States if nothing is done because refusal to give them destroyers or planes will unfortunately appear to the British public as American unwillingness to help them in their battle of death rather than because the United States has not the equipment that would be of service to them. If it is not deemed advisable to make such a statement in the United States, I could make an occasion for doing it here if you send me the material. I regard this as a major matter to be attended to because there is no point in having the Allies expect what there is no physical possibility of their getting, and it would be much better to explain why we could not meet their wishes than to hope the matter go by default. Particularly if at some later date we might want the British to take action on the Navy, that might be of service to us. We do not want a united hostile people in England.

KENNEDY

740.0011 European War 1939/3487²⁄₁₀ : Telegram

The Secretary of State to the Ambassador in the United Kingdom
(Kennedy)

WASHINGTON, June 7, 1940—noon.

1120. From the Under Secretary. Your 1524, June 6, 5 p. m. The Secretary and I feel that the suggestion contained in the last paragraph of your telegram is admirable. It seems to us, however, that

---

[44] British Expeditionary Force.

a statement of the character you suggest would carry more conviction if made by the British purchasing agent in the United States and given publicity through British governmental agencies in London.

I have brought up the question with Lord Lothian and he assures me that he will undertake to see that this is done immediately.

As you have probably been informed, War and Navy have now released to private manufacturers for immediate resale to the British and French Governments a very considerable amount of armaments and ammunition, together with a considerable number of airplanes. In all probability the number of airplanes to be made available can be still further increased.

If you feel any additional statement is desirable, please telegraph accordingly. [Welles.]

HULL

740.0011 European War 1939/3487⁴⁄₁₀ : Telegram

The Ambassador in the United Kingdom (Kennedy) to the Secretary of State

LONDON, June 10, 1940—1 p. m.
[Received June 10—10:17 a. m.]

1571. For the Secretary and Under Secretary. My 1524, June 6. Your 1120, June 7. I have carefully considered the plan outlined in your 1120 and it is impossible for me in London to judge what is the best action to take from the American point of view in America. My only knowledge of what is going on in the United States is taken from press clippings from America, mostly clipped from the *New York Times* and *Herald Tribune* and speeches of Senator Pepper; therefore you know what is best. Let me reiterate, however, that the feeling of the people of Great Britain towards the United States is going to be a matter of major importance, not only in this crisis but for many years to come. Regardless of what appears on the surface there is a very definite anti-American feeling in this country based primarily on the fact that the majority of the English people feel America should be in this fight with the Allies and in spite of the fact that the President's popularity is much greater than that of the United States itself, nevertheless many people in high places constantly say among themselves all they get from America is conversation. If things go badly for Great Britain everyone here is going to look around for somebody to blame. As it stands today they have the Baldwin and Chamberlain governments, but the attack on them is going to pale into insignificance when they have some one like the United States to blame. We can say we are sorry but it cannot be helped. I recognize that also, but nevertheless the fact remains that we are well on our way to becoming the "patsys" when Great Britain looks for somebody to blame. Over there it may not seem important as to whether the people in Great Britain will blame the United States either at the conclusion of this crisis or for years to come, but it appears to be a most serious matter. I can visualize their possible eventual acceptance of a German victory, but they will never forgive us for not having come to their aid. I therefore feel that this matter requires much more serious attention and thought than the mere statement by the British Purchasing Commission which I have seen issued this morning and does not at all answer the situation. Perhaps they are going to issue further statements. The position of the United States should be put right here; selling them "old material" is not solving the problem by any manner of means. The British are going to forget that they did not prepare and that the entry of the United States into the war would be only to hold the bag, but nonetheless the United States will receive severe criticism for years to come, and to me this is entirely unjustified. I hope for your further serious consideration of this matter.

KENNEDY

740.0011 European War 1939/3487⅗₀: Telegram

The Ambassador in the United Kingdom (Kennedy) to the Secretary of State

LONDON, June 10, 1940—9 p. m.
[Received June 10—7 p. m.]

1579. I have just seen the Prime Minister and words fail me in repeating what he thinks of Mussolini, but he looks forward to a degree of ferocity from him in the near future that is beyond anyone's imagination. He is quite hopeful that the French will not quit. He thinks the attack will now come against England and for that reason he is loath to give up any of his men, air force or equipment that will assist England in carrying on the war. He still is pleading for destroyers, and I should judge from his conversation that he believes that with the bombing of well known places in England the United States will come in. He assured me that as long as he lived the British Fleet will not be handed over to the Germans, but of course it is possible some other government, the Moseley [45] government for instance, might turn over anything that Hitler wanted in order to save England from destruction. England definitely wants a moral uplift and it looks to me that they feel the only way they could get it would be by a declaration of war by America even though nobody can point out just where America would fight the battle. The British public up to the declara-

---

[45] Sir Oswald Mosley, leader of the British Union of Fascists.

tion tonight [45a] are still ignorant of how terrible the situation is, in fact we had a hundred cancellations on the *Washington* today because people thought things were looking better. Needless to say the rush is on again tonight.

KENNEDY

841.30/176

Memorandum of Conversation, by the Secretary of State

[WASHINGTON,] June 11, 1940.

The British Ambassador called at his request and said that he had received from Mr. Churchill, the Prime Minister, a suggestion that there might be staff conferences between the naval people of our two Governments in regard to fleet movements both in the Atlantic and the Pacific. I made clear to him my views about all the public talk in regard to the disposition of the British fleet in the event of the defeat of Great Britain. I said, in brief, that any friend of Great Britain like myself would expect her to fight to the last dollar, to the last man and to the last ship, if necessary; that the people primarily interested in the Navy were the members of the British Empire; that, of course, Great Britain would not think of turning the fleet over to Germany if she expected to recover from a wholly unexpected temporary defeat due to sudden attack with new devices or weapons. The Ambassador said Churchill's position did not remotely contemplate Germany's getting the British fleet so far as his Government was concerned; that the only contingency in this respect would arise in connection with some successor government of the Mosley or Communist type. I then remarked that in the World War a new peace government took charge in Germany to negotiate peace, but that that peace government sank the German fleet [46] before peace terms were formulated. I then added that I doubted whether there would be any occasion for staff conferences, but that I would be glad to pass the suggestion on to the President.

The Ambassador stated that Argentina was slow to ban submarines from her ports and that the British were afraid that the Italians might send submarines to Argentine ports. I replied that we would give attention to this matter and that Argentina would probably come around to our position before long.

The Ambassador then inquired whether the British Military Attaché here might confer with the appropriate officials in the War

---

[45a] Declaration of war by Italy against France and the United Kingdom.

[46] On June 21, 1919, the German fleet interned in Scapa Flow, in the Orkney Islands, was scuttled by the German crews under orders of the German admiral in command. See *Foreign Relations*, The Paris Peace Conference, 1919, vol. VI, references listed in index, p. 1007.

Department in regard to the effect of British and French bombings inside Germany. I replied that I was sure our military people would be glad to give his Attaché any information at all feasible; that, of course, we could not be connected with any exchange of information of that nature.

740.0011 European War 1939/3487⅙₀ : Telegram

The Ambassador in the United Kingdom (Kennedy) to the Secretary of State

LONDON, June 12, 1940—2 p. m.
[Received June 12—11 : 07 a. m.]

1603. My view of the situation this morning. The condition of Britain's preparedness equals [*sic*] her ability to fight the kind of war Hitler wages still appears to be appallingly weak. I am of the opinion that outside of some air defence the real defence of England will be with courage and not with arms. No matter what action the United States takes towards this war it is only fair to say that short of a miracle this country after, and if and when, France stops fighting will hold on in the hope that the United States will come in. Churchill said quite definitely to me he expects the United States will be in right after the election; that when the people in the United States see the towns and cities of England, after which so many American cities and towns have been named, bombed and destroyed they will line up and want war. The people here are kept buoyed up by the inference in the papers and the publication of clippings from the *New York Times*, *Herald Tribune* and political speeches. This morning an American correspondent of an English paper mentions that all it needs is an "incident" to bring the United States in. If that were all that were needed desperate people will do desperate things. The point of all this is the fact that the preparedness for carrying on a war here is pitiful, this in spite of the fact that production and war effort are now for the first time going ahead in excellent fashion. We should know this in the light of any action we in America might see fit to take. A course of action that involves us in any respect that presupposes the Allies have much to fight with except courage is, as far as England goes, I think fallacious. The United States would have nothing to work with with these two countries in their present condition. Unless France and England are dealing or will deal Germany really crippling blows at her industrial production and seriously affect her strength in the air and in tanks as a result of these battles, the United States will have plenty to worry about in their own country. The cry should be prepare for anything right there, right now.

KENNEDY

740.00119 European War 1939/447 : Telegram

The Chargé in Germany (Heath) to the Secretary of State

BERLIN, June 26, 1940—9 p. m.
[Received June 27—6 : 30 a. m.]

2118. Yesterday the Italian Ambassador [47] sent word that he would be glad to have me call on him this afternoon. He discoursed at length on the allegedly critical situation of Great Britain. He stated that Britain had failed to prepare its defense in time and was now, he asserted, in no condition to prevent German attack and invasion which, he added, would be successful within a very short time. He remarked the King understood that Churchill thought that resistance could be prolonged over a period of months until greater assistance could be drawn from overseas but by virtue of his position as Ambassador of an Allied Power he had been given insight into German plans and preparations and that he was convinced no such possibility existed. Neither was there, he indicated, any possibility of relief through a diversion created by Russian advance in the Balkans.

He asserted that it was neither the desire nor the interest of either Germany or Italy to destroy England nor was it in the interest of the United States or the world at large that England and the British Empire be destroyed. There yet remained a few days but only a few in which the catastrophe might be averted. He was confident that peace terms which would be acceptable to England under the circumstances would be offered by the Axis Powers but that the request had to come from England. He had devoted thought to who might take such initiative in order to prevent the "catastrophe." The Pope was regrettably no longer in such a position. The King of England might act in an emergency but he indicated doubt that without prompting the King would take upon himself such responsibility, although a move of England for peace, he argued, would not constitute a national disgrace for England since it would be excused by the crushing and unexpected defeat of its ally France. He asserted that it was not even necessary that Churchill resign. It would suffice that there be some changes in the composition of the present British Cabinet.

He avoided making the direct suggestion that the United States intervene to persuade England to ask for terms beyond saying at the conclusion of the interview that the responsibility for the continuance of the war and the prevention of what he termed a catastrophe rested largely and primarily on the United States. He remarked possibly with intention that he had been several times at the Fuehrer's headquarters and that that afternoon he had had a long talk with State Secretary Weizsaecker.

HEATH

---

[47] Dino Alfieri.

740.00119 European War 1939/447 : Telegram

The Secretary of State to the Chargé in Germany (Heath)

WASHINGTON, June 28, 1940—3 p. m.

1792. Your 2118, June 26, 9 p. m. We desire you to call upon the Italian Ambassador and to say to him that you have informed your Government of the conversation of this afternoon. You should further state that for purposes of clarification you desire to know whether his remarks were made with the knowledge of the Italian and German Governments, and also whether he understands that the Italian Government desires the United States to take any action in the sense of his remarks.

HULL

740.0011 European War 1939/4264½ : Telegram

The Ambassador in Italy (Phillips) to the Secretary of State

ROME, June 29, 1940—7 p. m.
[Received 7 : 40 p. m.]

658. At his request King Alfonso of Spain came to see me this afternoon for the purpose, he said, of offering his services to the President if he could be of help in any move to initiate conversations between the Germans, Italians and the British before the supreme effort against England had begun. He reminded me that he had many intimate contacts among the British including Churchill, that he was in close touch with Italian court circles and he mentioned in passing that the German Ambassador was lunching with him tomorrow.

He offered no plan but felt that no effort should be spared to prevent the blow from falling upon England.

While he was careful to explain that he was speaking only on his own initiative and was without any information on the subject of peace proposals he thought he had accurate military information.

He was certain that the Italian movement on the Italo-French frontier had been seriously checked, that the Italian Army had been thrown back into Italian territory with 1,000 dead and many casualties and that this was the position when the Italo-French armistice [48] was signed. Furthermore the King said that a similar situation had developed in Cyrenaica and that British troops had already penetrated beyond the first line of Italian forts and to a depth of 30 kilometers.

In spite of the King's assertion I am not entirely convinced that his message to the President is made solely on his own initiative

---

[48] Signed June 24, 1940 ; for text, see *Documents on American Foreign Relations,* July 1939–June 1940, vol. II, p. 436.

and yet I have nothing to confirm this view. But the apparent urgency of his call and the fact that he has never before called on me leaves me open to suspicion. He asked me in conclusion to send his cordial greetings and regards to the President.

PHILLIPS

740.00119 European War 1939/448 : Telegram

The Chargé in Germany (Heath) to the Secretary of State

BERLIN, June 29, 1940—8 p. m.
[Received June 30—9 : 25 a. m.]

2217. The Department's telegram No. 1792 June 28, 3 p. m. was delivered at the Embassy at 3 : 20 p. m. today. I saw the Italian Ambassador at 6 and recalled in summary his views as reported in my No. 2118, June 26, 9 p. m. He said that it was a correct recital of his views and while he was not authorized to speak for his Government or that of the Reich in the matter he stated that they were also the views of the two Governments as he understood them. However, he had not consulted his or the German Government before the conversations with me which he desired to be considered personal nor was it his intention to make a report to his Government or to the German Government of that interview or of today's conversation.

He said that for him to do so would expose himself and the Axis Governments to the accusation of having initiated an overture for peace whereas in view of the present military situation it was very obvious that the initiative must come solely from the British side. For him to report or in any way take up the matter with his Government would have an effect opposite to that desired.

He remarked that the American Government without prompting had made two efforts for a peaceful understanding prior to the outbreak of war and was of course always within its rights to take any move in furthering its policy, but if it took any action in the present situation it must not be based on or refer to the interview and he again repeated that the initiative for peace must come solely from Great Britain. He asked that the conversation be held strictly confidential within the Department of State in order to protect his own position.

Alfieri was anxious to convince me that he had acted without specific instructions from his Government during our first conversation. I had the feeling, however, that Alfieri had represented his Government in recent conversations in Berlin on the subject of the desirability of propagating abroad the impression that it was necessary that Great Britain lose no time in initiating overtures for the cessation of hostilities and that by acting before the impending attack the British could obtain relatively favorable terms.

In view of Alfieri's request that this be held confidential within the Department, to which I felt it necessary to accede, I am not repeating this telegram to Rome.

HEATH

740.0011 European War 1939/4264¾ : Telegram

The Secretary of State to the Ambassador in Italy (*Phillips*)

WASHINGTON, June 30, 1940—1 p. m.

271. Your 658, June 29, 7 p. m. Please say to King Alfonso that your Government greatly appreciates his friendly and helpful message but that, in view of the situation and present policies of this Government, it would seem better for the purpose which the King has in mind for him to approach directly the Governments immediately concerned.

HULL

740.0011 European War 1939/4357 : Telegram

The Ambassador in Spain (*Weddell*) *to the Secretary of State*

MADRID, July 2, 1940—noon.
[Received 5 : 44 p. m.]

290. In a conversation last night with [member?] of the Embassy staff the Duke of Windsor declared that the most important thing now to be done was to end the war before thousands more were killed or maimed to save the faces of a few politicians.

With regard to the defeat of France he stated that stories that the French troops would not fight were not true. They had fought magnificently, but the organization behind them was totally inadequate. In the past 10 years Germany had totally reorganized the order of its society in preparation for this war. Countries which were unwilling to accept such a reorganization of society and its concomitant sacrifices should direct their policies accordingly and thereby avoid dangerous adventures. He stated that this applied not merely to Europe, but to the United States also. The Duchess put the same thing somewhat more directly be [by?] declaring that France had lost because it was internally diseased and that a country which was not in condition to fight a war should never have declared war.

These observations have their value if any as doubtless reflecting the views of an element in England, possibly a growing one who find in Windsor and his circle a group who are realists in world politics and who hope to come into their own in event of peace.

WEDDELL

740.0011 European War 1939/4578

Memorandum of Conversation, by the Secretary of State

[WASHINGTON,] July 5, 1940.

The British Ambassador called at his request and handed me an *aide-mémoire* dated July 3, 1940 (copy attached), which reviewed at length the altered situation of the British in view of the collapse of the French. This *aide-mémoire* pointed out certain considerations and situations which the British Government hoped would receive the careful attention of the United States Government.

I thanked the Ambassador and said the matters would receive due attention.

C[ORDELL] H[ULL]

[Annex]

The British Embassy to the Department of State

AIDE-MÉMOIRE

His Majesty's Government in the United Kingdom desire to invite the attention of the United States Government to the grave consequences to the Allies and to the cause of civilisation, of the collapse of French resistance to totalitarian aggression. They feel that they are entitled to place the results of their own review of the conditions thus created before the United States Government, because the United States Government have repeatedly stated that they are deeply concerned with the preservation wherever possible of free institutions, because successive United States Administrations have declined to recognise the validity of the forcible annexation of territory by an aggressor, and because within the limits imposed by their international obligations and the Neutrality Act [49] they have throughout rendered all the assistance they could to the Allies.

2. His Majesty's Government do not wish to discuss in this *Aide-Mémoire* the military consequences of the collapse of France further than to say that the economic and manufacturing resources of almost the whole of Europe are now at the disposal of the Nazi and Fascist Powers for the purposes of attack on Great Britain, now almost the last free country left in Europe. They would only repeat what they have said before, that the immediate sale of destroyers and power boats, aeroplanes and seaplanes, and guns, rifles and ammunition of all kinds is of the utmost importance if the impending attack on Great Britain is to be beaten off before winter sets in. His Majesty's Government gratefully acknowledge the great value of the war material

[49] Neutrality Act of 1939 ; 54 Stat. 4.

that the United States Government have already released to them, but feel constrained to emphasise once more that further releases, if promptly made, would be of immeasurable value.

3. His Majesty's Government desires in this *Aide-Mémoire* rather to call attention to the economic situation which follows from the French collapse. In this field they desire to impress upon the United States Government the conviction to which they have been driven, that if victory over Nazi aggression is to be achieved, they must seek from the United States equipment, supplies of aircraft and other munitions and essential raw materials on an altogether larger scale than hitherto. This is partly because the Nazi successes in Europe have deprived the Allies of many sources of supply to which they have hitherto had access and partly because incessant bombing is likely to reduce their own manufacturing capacity, while intensive submarine and air blockade is likely to reduce the quantity of food-stuffs and materials they can import from abroad.

4. In these altered circumstances, His Majesty's Government believe that the United States Government will not take it amiss if they express the conviction, founded upon their own experience, that the United States Government will find that if they are to complete their own rearmament programme in the shortest possible time and at the same time provide the increased supplies necessary to enable Great Britain and the Dominions and their allies to maintain the struggle, that far-reaching changes in the industrial organisation of this country are essential. His Majesty's Government have found that their own programmes have suffered severely from slowness in realising this necessity and they are anxious to place their own experience in this matter at the disposal of the United States Government.

5. The natural tendency of all democracies engaged in rearmament is to believe that it is possible to expand the production of guns and to enjoy a full supply of butter at the same time. His Majesty's Government have found by bitter experience that this is not true and that full production cannot be secured solely by expansion and development of munitions and auxiliary industries, other industries being left unaffected. The establishment of requisite priority for labour, materials, machine tools, etc., necessarily involves the early curtailment of production for domestic civil consumption. This reorganisation becomes all the more necessary if more than one country is engaged in expanding its production of armaments and if raw material supplies are limited. Where total available supplies are restricted (e. g. raw materials such as aluminium and steel or machine tools) His Majesty's Government hope that the Administration will agree to open immediate discussions with them on allocations as between themselves, Great Britain and Canada to secure the maximum possible

production with the utmost promptitude. As regards raw materials they hope also that it will be possible that those Central and South American States who are important producers should be included in the proposed arrangements.

6. So long as gold and other foreign assets at their disposal permit, His Majesty's Government will of course continue to pay cash for essential armaments, raw materials and food stuffs. They feel however that they should in all frankness inform the United States Government that it will be utterly impossible for them to continue to do this for any indefinite period in view of the scale on which they will need to obtain such resources from United States. Their immediate anxiety arises from the necessity of entering into long term contracts.

7. There is a considerable risk that, with the development of total war and the consequent great increase in the calls on the Royal Navy, the merchant marine serving the Allies may for a time at least suffer from a much higher rate of losses than hitherto. The temporary expansion of Allied shipping facilities due to the fact that certain Norwegian, Danish and other merchant vessels are now available would not offset the situation created by such losses. His Majesty's Government therefore feel compelled to ask whether the United States Government can take steps by whatever procedure seems most expeditious, to secure the withdrawal of the present prohibition on ships flying the United States flag entering the "combat areas" and belligerent ports to the extent necessary to permit such ships to bring imports to Great Britain. If they are prepared to do this His Majesty's Government would urge that the Administration jointly with themselves should immediately examine the possibilities of taking measures to secure the most effective joint use of the mercantile fleets of the United States, of the United Kingdom and their Allies and those of the Central and South American states.

8. His Majesty's Government regard it as a matter of the utmost urgency, from the point of view of wartime control as well as from that of post-war reconstruction, that the plans of the British nations and their Allies for dealing with their export surpluses should be concerted with those of the United States and of the other American Republics for dealing with theirs, and this is especially so as regards those products of which there is likely to be a world surplus, e. g. cotton, corn, wheat, edible oils. A fuller statement of the view of His Majesty's Government on this subject is given in the British Ambassador's separate memorandum "A" of July 3rd, 1940. [50]

There are a number of ways in which Germany and Italy might obtain resources from America, and His Majesty's Government accordingly desire to urge strongly that:—

[50] *Post*, p. 134.

(*a*) The United States Government should use any means in their power to cut off from Germany, Italy and the territories occupied by those states, including France, all direct and indirect exports from the United States of America; and to limit exports to other destinations from which they might subsequently reach German or Italian controlled territory. The more detailed views of His Majesty's Government on this vital subject are contained in the British Ambassador's separate memorandum "B" of July 3rd, 1940.[51]

(*b*) The United States Government should take measures to block financial balances belonging to Germany or Italy, as has been done in the case of occupied countries, and obtain any supplementary powers needed for this purpose. The previous exchange of views on this subject, ending with Mr. Sumner Welles' letter to His Majesty's Ambassador of 20th June, 1940,[52] has not been overlooked, but His Majesty's Government would once more emphasise the great importance which they attach to action of this kind, and would urge that the previous decision should be reconsidered.

(*c*) Steps should be taken to prevent the return from the United States to Europe of German and Italian technicians either for military service or for employment as skilled operatives in the war industries.

9. In the event of His Majesty's Government in the United Kingdom deciding to invite the Governments of the Central and South American States to adopt measures parallel with those referred to in paragraph 8 of this *Aide-Mémoire*, His Majesty's Government wish to express the earnest hope that the United States Government may see their way either to take the initiative in the matter or to use their good offices with those Governments in support of that approach. These governments have an equal interest with the United States in preventing the Nazi and Fascist powers from obtaining the resources which may enable them to adopt a policy of aggression in America.

As regards financial measures, His Majesty's Ambassador had a preliminary discussion on the 26th June with Mr. Sumner Welles,[53] who promised to look further into the matter. Certain action has been taken by the Governments of the Argentine Republic, Brazil, and Uruguay, but it does not appear to go far enough, while in Chile no action has been taken. A note giving more detail of the direction in which action is desired will shortly be submitted to the United States Government.

10. His Majesty's Government in the United Kingdom realise that in the above statement they are making wide and even difficult requests to the United States Government. It is only right therefore that they should conclude by stating in the gravest possible manner their considered opinion that the measures outlined are necessary if the civilisation which the United States and the nations of the British

---

[51] Vol. II, p. 52.
[52] Not printed.
[53] No record of this conversation found in Department files.

Empire share in common is to be successfully defended from attempts to overthrow it.

WASHINGTON, July 3, 1940.

740.0011 European War 1939/2855²⁷⁄₂₈ : Telegram

The Chargé in Italy (Reed) to the Secretary of State

ROME, August 1, 1940—11 a. m.
[Received August 1—10: 50 a. m.]

777. I am reliably informed that important officials of the German Embassy here have declared on several occasions that Roosevelt's defeat is of vital importance to Germany; that the German Government has authentic information of an undertaking by the President to bring the United States into the war after the elections and that Germany will therefore spare neither money nor effort to prevent his reelection.

REED

740.00119 European War 1939/476½ : Telegram

The Chargé in Germany (Kirk) to the Secretary of State

BERLIN, August 2, 1940—5 p. m.
[Received 11 : 10 p. m.]

3368. My 2960, July 15, 6 p. m.[54] Responsible Government officials continue to stress the view that England should sue for peace and that it is foolhardy for it to attempt to withstand the forces that are about to be directed against Great Britain. Furthermore private individuals of various neutral nationalities are professing that they are receiving projects for peace in conversations with the highest German authorities but exclusive of Hitler himself and that they are attempting to or have succeeded in conveying those projects directly to prominent persons in England. The aforementioned Government officials insist on the point that the United States is encouraging the British Government to resist and the private individuals in question are prone to link their peace efforts with references to the importance of American mediation or intercession in a peace settlement.

In all these efforts conspicuous emphasis placed on the opportunity for peace talks which the last Reichstag speech is alleged to offer and all seem to be entirely impervious to the argument that it is difficult to characterize as a peace offer a statement wherein Hitler makes clear that although he professes no wish to destroy the British Empire he will proceed to that destruction unless the British Government

---

[54] Not printed.

accepts a peace which in the Nazi mind is termed reasonable but which to others tokens the ruin of that Empire as the immediate champion of democracy in the world.

In the meanwhile reports of projects of imminent action against the British Isles accumulate and the rumored date is set from one week end to another.

KIRK

811.34544/12a

The Secretary of State to the British Ambassador (Lothian)

AIDE-MÉMOIRE

The Prime Minister of Great Britain is reported to have stated on June 4, 1940, to Parliament in effect that if during the course of the present war in which Great Britain and the British Commonwealth are engaged the waters surrounding the British Isles should become untenable for British ships of war, the British Fleet would in no event be surrendered or sunk but would be sent overseas for the defense of other parts of the Empire.

The Government of the United States would respectfully inquire whether the foregoing statement represents the settled policy of the British Government.

WASHINGTON, August 29, 1940.

811.34544/13

The British Ambassador (Lothian) to the Secretary of State

AIDE-MÉMOIRE

In his *Aide-Mémoire* of August 29th, 1940, the Secretary of State enquired whether the Prime Minister's statement in Parliament on June 4th, 1940, regarding the intention of His Majesty's Government in the United Kingdom never to surrender or sink the British Fleet in the event of the waters surrounding the British Isles becoming untenable for His Majesty's Ships "represents the settled policy of His Majesty's Government."

His Majesty's Ambassador is instructed by the Prime Minister to inform Mr. Secretary Hull that this statement certainly does represent the settled policy of His Majesty's Government. Mr. Churchill must however observe that these hypothetical contingencies seem more likely to concern the German fleet or what is left of it than the British Fleet.

WASHINGTON, September 2, 1940.

740.0011 European War 1939/5798½ : Telegram

The Ambassador in the United Kingdom (Kennedy) to the Secretary of State

LONDON, September 27, 1940—9 p. m.
[Received September 28—4 : 22 a. m.]

3247. For the President and the Secretary. I have seen Halifax and Kingsley Wood. The Dakar situation [55] is a bitter pill for the entire Cabinet and, from my observation, for the entire country. The newspapers have been most critical. It is the first real break in the Churchill popularity and there is a definite feeling that they have not a Prime Minister but a Generalissimo. The night raids are continuing to do, I think, substantial damage and the day raids of the last three days have dealt most serious blows to Bristol, Southampton and Liverpool. Production is definitely falling, regardless of what reports you may be getting, and with transportation being smashed up the way it is, the present production output will continue to fall.

The Government still publicly say they do not want America to come into the war because if she did they could not get supplies. I think this is only for public consumption because they have been advised by their American representatives that that is the course to proceed along. But they are hoping and praying every minute that something will happen that will bring the United States in.

First of all, Halifax in describing the Spanish, Egyptian and Turkish situation admitted these countries would practically be governed by the course of events in Great Britain. In other words, if things go well with Great Britain they will withstand Axis pressure; if things look as if they are going badly, they are liable to tumble over any day. Secondly, the British regard the need for financial aid as most serious and they realize they could get it easier and without any question or discussion if America were in the war.

My own feeling is that they are in a bad way. Bombers have got through in the day time on the last 3 days and on four occasions today substantial numbers of German planes have flown over London and have done some daylight bombing. Moreover, all their six naval units at Dakar received some damage, two or three of them substantial damage. Without being an expert, I cannot help feeling that the evidence in Norway, Dakar and Dunkirk and the fate of the destroyers traveling in the English Channel indicate that naval units are in a bad way when they are within a couple of hundred miles of the enemy's aerodromes.

I cannot impress upon you strongly enough my complete lack of confidence in the entire conduct of this war. I was delighted to see that

---

[55] Dakar, French West Africa, was unsuccessfully attacked by British and Free French forces, September 23–25, 1940.

the President said he was not going to enter the war, because to enter this war, imagining for a minute that the English have anything to offer in the line of leadership or productive capacity in industry that could be of the slightest value to us, would be a complete misapprehension. The morale of the British is as high as can be expected. They have concentrated all their attention on the victories in the air. They have sloughed over their losses at sea. They cannot cover up Dakar, however, and people are drawing their own conclusions. If there was not the hope of the United States in the offing, Japan's signing with Germany and Italy would be another nail in the coffin. If by any chance we should ever come to the point of getting into this war we can make up our minds that it will be the United States against Germany, Italy and Japan, aided by a badly shot to pieces country which in the last analysis can give little, if any, assistance to cause. It breaks my heart to draw these conclusions about a people that I sincerely hoped might be victorious but I cannot get myself to the point where I believe they can be of any assistance to the cause in which they are involved.

KENNEDY

NEGOTIATIONS FOR TRANSFER OF AMERICAN DESTROYERS TO THE BRITISH NAVY AND FOR ESTABLISHMENT OF AMERICAN NAVAL AND AIR BASES IN BRITISH POSSESSIONS IN THE WESTERN HEMISPHERE

811.34544/1½ : Telegram

The Secretary of State to the Ambassador in the United Kingdom (Kennedy)

WASHINGTON, May 16, 1940—1 p. m.

872. Your 1216, May 15, 6 p. m.[56] Please transmit the following message from the President to the former naval person:[57]

"I have just received your message and I am sure it is unnecessary for me to say that I am most happy to continue our private correspondence as we have in the past.

I am, of course, giving every possible consideration to the suggestions made in your message. I shall take up your specific proposals one by one.

First, with regard to the possible loan of 40 or 50 of our older destroyers. As you know a step of that kind could not be taken except with the specific authorization of the Congress and I am not certain that it would be wise for that suggestion to be made to the Congress

---

[56] Not printed; this telegram transmitted a message from British Prime Minister Churchill to President Roosevelt. For text of message, see Winston S. Churchill, *Their Finest Hour*, p. 24.
[57] Code name for Winston Churchill.

at this moment. Furthermore, it seems to me doubtful, from the standpoint of our own defense requirements, which must inevitably be linked with the defense requirements of this hemisphere and with our obligations in the Pacific, whether we could dispose even temporarily of these destroyers. Furthermore, even if we were able to take the step you suggest, it would be at least 6 or 7 weeks as a minimum, as I see it, before these vessels could undertake active service under the British flag.

Second. We are now doing everything within our power to make it possible for the Allied Governments to obtain the latest types of aircraft in the United States.

Third. If Mr. Purvis [59] may receive immediate instructions to discuss the question of anti-aircraft, equipment and ammunition with the appropriate authorities here in Washington, the most favorable consideration will be given to the request made in the light of our own defense needs and requirements.

Fourth. Mr. Purvis has already taken up with the appropriate authorities here the purchase of steel in the United States and I understand that satisfactory arrangements have been made.

Fifth. I shall give further consideration to your suggestion with regard to the visit of the United States Squadron to Irish ports.

Sixth. As you know, the American fleet is now concentrated at Hawaii where it will remain at least for the time being.

I shall communicate with you again as soon as I feel able to make a final decision with regard to some of the other matters dealt with in your message and I hope you will feel free to communicate with me in this way at any time.

The best of luck to you.

Franklin D. Roosevelt"
Hull

811.34544/1¾₁₂ : Telegram

The Ambassador in the United Kingdom (Kennedy) to the Secretary of State

London, May 18, 1940—6 p. m.
[Received May 18—1 : 14 p. m.]

1267. Your 872, May 16 and my 1243, May 17, noon.[60] Secret and personal for the President from Former Naval Person.

"Many thanks for your message for which I am grateful. I do not need to tell you about the gravity of what has happened. We are determined to persevere to the very end whatever the result of the great battle raging in France may be. We must expect in any case to be

---

[59] Arthur B. Purvis, Director-General, British Purchasing Commission.
[60] Latter not printed.

attacked here on the Dutch model before very long and we hope to give a good account of ourselves. But if American assistance is to play any part it must be available [soon]."

KENNEDY

811.34544/13½₂ : Telegram

The Ambassador in the United Kingdom (Kennedy) to the Secretary of State

LONDON, May 20, 1940—1 p. m.
[Received May 20—8 : 40 a. m.]

1271. Secret and personal for the President from Former Naval Person :

"Lothian [61] has reported his conversation with you. I understand your difficulties but I am very sorry about the destroyers. If they were here in 6 weeks they would play an invaluable part. The battle in France is full of danger to both sides. Though we have taken heavy toll of enemy in the air and are clawing down two or three to one of their planes, they have still a formidable numerical superiority. Our most vital need is therefore the delivery at the earliest possible date of the largest possible number of Curtiss P–40 fighters now in course of delivery to your Army.

With regard to the closing part of your talk with Lothian, our intention is whatever happens to fight on to the end in this Island and, provided we can get the help for which we ask, we hope to run them very close in the air battles in view of individual superiority. Members of the present administration would likely go down during this process should it result adversely, but in no conceivable circumstances will we consent to surrender. If members of the present administration were finished and others came in to parley amid the ruins, you must not be blind to the fact that the sole remaining bargaining counter with Germany would be the fleet, and if this country was left by the United States to its fate no one would have the right to blame those then responsible if they made the best terms they could for the surviving inhabitants. Excuse me, Mr. President, putting this nightmare bluntly. Evidently I could not answer for my successors who in utter despair and helplessness might well have to accommodate themselves to the German will. However there is happily no need at present to dwell upon such ideas. Once more thanking you for your good will."

KENNEDY

---

[61] Marquess of Lothian, British Ambassador in the United States.

740.0011 European War 1939/3938 : Telegram

The British Prime Minister (*Churchill*) *to President Roosevelt* [62]

WASHINGTON, June 11, 1940.

We all listened to you last night [63] and were fortified by the grand scope of your declaration. Your statement that material aid of the United States will be given to the Allies in their struggle is a strong encouragement in a dark but not unhopeful hour. Everything must be done to keep France in the fight and to prevent any idea of the fall of Paris, should it occur, becoming the occasion of any kind of parley. The hope with which you inspired them may give them strength to persevere. [They should] continue to defend every yard of their soil and use full fighting force of their army. Hitler thus baffled of quick results will turn upon us and we are preparing ourselves to resist his fury and defend our Island. Having saved British Expeditionary Force we do not lack troops at home and as soon as Divisions can be equipped on much higher scale needed for Continental service they will be despatched to France. Our intention is to have a strong army fighting in France for campaign of 1941. I have already cabled you about aeroplanes including flying boats which are so needful to us in the impending struggle for the life of Great Britain. But even more pressing is the need for destroyers. Italian outrage makes it necessary for us to cope with much larger number of submarines which may come out into the Atlantic and perhaps be based on Spanish ports. To this the only counter is destroyers. Nothing is so important as for us to have 30 or 40 old destroyers you have already had reconditioned. We can fit them very rapidly with our asdics and they will bridge over the gap of 6 months before our wartime new construction comes into play. We will return them or their equivalents to you without fail at 6 months notice if at any time you need them. The next 6 months are vital. If while we have to guard the East Coast against invasion new heavy German and Italian submarine attack is launched against our commerce the strain may be beyond our resources; and ocean traffic by which we live may be strangled. Not a day should be lost. I send you my heartfelt thanks and those of my colleagues for all you are doing and seeking to do for what we may now indeed call a common cause.

---

[62] This telegram was sent through the British Embassy, which transmitted it to the Department on June 11 for delivery to the President.

[63] For text of President Roosevelt's speech at Charlottesville, Virginia, see Department of State *Bulletin*, June 15, 1940, p. 635.

740.0011 European War 1939/3728½: Telegram

The Ambassador in the United Kingdom (Kennedy) to the Secretary of State

LONDON, June 15, 1940—9 p. m.
[Received June 15—6 : 37 p. m.]

1677. Secret and personal for the President from Former Naval Person:

"I am grateful to you for your telegram [64] and I have reported its operative passages to Reynaud [64a] to whom I had imparted a rather more sanguine view. He will, I am sure, be disappointed at nonpublication. I understand all your difficulties with American public opinion and Congress, but events are moving downward at a pace where they will pass beyond the control of American public opinion when at last it is ripened. Have you considered what offers Hitler may choose to make to France. He may say, 'Surrender the fleet intact and I will leave you Alsace-Lorraine', or alternatively 'If you do not give me your ships I will destroy your towns'. I am personally convinced that America will in the end go to all lengths but this moment is supremely critical for France. A declaration that the United States will, if necessary, enter the war might save France. Failing that in a few days French resistance may have crumbled and we shall be left alone.

Although the present Government and I personally would never fail to send the fleet across the Atlantic if resistance was beaten down here, a point may be reached in the struggle where the present Ministers no longer have control of affairs and when very easy terms could be obtained for the British islands by their becoming a vassal state of the Hitler empire. A pro-German government would certainly be called into being to make peace and might present to a shattered or a starving nation an almost irresistible case for entire submission to the Nazi will. The fate of the British Fleet as I have already mentioned to you would be decisive on the future of the United States because if it were joined to the fleets of Japan, France, and Italy and the great resources of German industry, overwhelming sea power would be in Hitler's hands. He might, of course, use it with a merciful moderation. On the other hand he might not. This revolution in sea power might happen very quickly and certainly long before the United States would be able to prepare against it. If we go [down] you may have a United States of Europe under the Nazi command far more numerous, far stronger, far better armed than the New [World].

[64] See telegram No. 1, June 13, 1 p. m., to the First Secretary of Embassy in France, vol. I, p. 247.
[64a] Paul Reynaud, French Premier, Minister for Foreign Affairs, and Minister for Defense.

I know well, Mr. President, that your eye will already have searched these depths but I feel I have the right to place on record the vital manner in which American interests are at state [*stake*] in our battle and that of France.

I am sending you through Ambassador Kennedy a paper on destroyer strength prepared by the naval staff for your information. If we have to keep as we shall, the bulk of our destroyers on the east coast to guard against invasion, how shall we be able to cope with a German-Italian attack on the food and trade by which we live? The sending of the 35 destroyers as I have already described will bridge the gap until our new construction comes in at the end of the year. Here is a definite practical and possible decisive step which can be taken at once and I urge most earnestly that you will weigh my words.

Since beginning of war Britain and France have lost 32 destroyers with displacement of 47,380 tons which were complete losses. Out of these 25, with displacement of 37,637 tons, were lost since 1st February.

There is always a large number of destroyers out of action for repairs to damages caused by enemy action and hard service. From outbreak of war up to Norwegian invasion approximately 30% of British destroyers in home waters were in this condition but since then the percentage has greatly increased and for instance, out of 133 destroyers in commission in home waters today, only 68 are fit for service, which is lowest level since war started. In 1918 some 433 destroyers were in service.

The critical situation which has arisen in land operations has unfortunately made less apparent the grave difficulties with which we are faced on the sea.

The seizure of the Channel ports by the enemy has provided him both with convenient bases and stepping off ground for descents on our coast. This means that our east coast and Channel ports will become much more open to attack and in consequence more shipping will have to be concentrated on west coast ports. This will enable the enemy to concentrate their submarine attacks on this more limited area, the shipping lanes of which will have to carry the heavy concentration of shipping.

This alone is a serious enough problem at a time when we know that the enemy intend to carry out the bitter and concentrated attack on our trade routes, but added to our difficulties is the fact that Italy's entry into the war has brought into the seas another 100 submarines many of which may be added to those already in the German U-boat fleet, which at a conservative estimate numbers 55.

The changed strategical situation brought about by the possession by the enemy of the whole coast of Europe from Norway to the Channel has faced us with a prospect of invasion which has more hopes of success than we had ever conceived possible. While we must concentrate our destroyers on protecting the vital trade, we must also dispose our naval forces to meet this threat.

If this invasion does take place, it will almost certainly be in the form of dispersed landings from a large number of small craft and the only effective counter to such a move is to maintain numerous and effective destroyer patrols.

To meet this double threat we have only the 68 destroyers mentioned above. Only 10 small type new construction destroyers are due to complete in next 4 months.

The position becomes still worse when we have to contemplate diverting further destroyer forces to the Mediterranean as we may be forced to do when the sea war there is intensified.

We are now faced with the imminent collapse of French resistance and if this occurs the successful defense of this island will be the only hope of averting the collapse of civilization as we define it.

We must ask therefore as a matter of life or death to be reinforced with these destroyers. We will carry out the struggle whatever the odds but it may well be beyond our resources unless we receive every reinforcement and particularly do we need this reinforcement on the sea."

KENNEDY

811.34544/1½₂ : Telegram

The Ambassador in the United Kingdom (Kennedy) to the Secretary of State

LONDON, July 5, 1940—9 p. m.
[Received July 5—7 : 22 p. m.]

2001. Personal for the Secretary of State. I have just seen Halifax [65] and he said that Sir Stafford Cripps [66] felt he was getting along very well in Russia; that he had seen Stalin and liked him; that Stalin had told him they had no further demands in the Balkans; that they are not helping Germany any more than is necessary; that they anticipate that Germany intends to take them on next spring, in the meantime, of course, having polished off the British. Halifax said that from all their information, although Cripps did not get this from Stalin, the Italians and Germans were unaware of the Russian move against Rumania. The Russians asked England to help keep the Turks calm. By that, Halifax thinks the Russians mean to try to get

[65] Viscount Halifax, British Secretary of State for Foreign Affairs.
[66] British Ambassador in the Soviet Union.

the British to persuade Turks to be reasonable in their attitude in the Dardanelles, but I judge from Halifax's side remarks that this would not get very serious consideration. The trade agreement negotiations, Cripps feels, are proceeding very well.

As to the French situation, Halifax said, of course they are terribly upset about the battle yesterday and he says it is not unlikely that France might even go so far as to declare war. At any rate he is quite sure that they will break off diplomatic relations although up to 6 o'clock tonight they have heard nothing on this. They are still waiting on word from Lothian as to what your attitude is on the Martinique situation which he was instructed to take up with you.[67] Regarding the French at Alexandria; that seems to be all settled, the agreement being that (a) fuel oil is to be discharged (b) ships to be made incapable of fighting (c) that the disposal of the ships' companies is to be a matter of further negotiations, but French advise them they will repatriate all the crews. Their fleets are watching the *Richelieu* and the *Jean Bart* which are on the west coast of Africa, but they are expecting to have a battle with them. That accounts for most of all of the ships except those at Toulon where the British are not likely to take them on because they understand the shore batteries are too strong. Out of this terrible mix-up with the French have arisen terrific problems of trade, currency, ships, et cetera.

Halifax showed me a message that Churchill was sending to Lothian to take up with President which again takes up the question of destroyers. I think that Churchill was making too much of a demand on the President and I pointed out that the President had all the information in regard to destroyers and that he would settle it in his own way in his own time and that to try to give him the "hurry up" or to point out again the dangers to America was not likely to influence him much. I think they may change it when you finally get it. His original memorandum to the President also said that the Irish situation was very bad and that he suspected that De Valera[68] and his crowd were going over to the Germans. Halifax admitted to me that this was too pessimistic and I said again I thought if Churchill were going to send a message he had better send the facts as they were and not make them better or worse than they were in order to try and influence the President. I said I had known the President for quite a while and had never found him subject to a "rush aggression".

Halifax said that Churchill had asked all departments which had got any information secret or otherwise from Germany to tabulate it and try and approximate the date of invasion. They have arrived

---

[67] See vol. II, pp. 505 ff.

[68] Eamon de Valera, Prime Minister and Minister for External Affairs, Ireland.

at either the 8th or 9th of July or the 15th. I realize that this is a day out of the sky, but I am passing it on to show you that the Prime Minister of England thought it worthwhile to have a study made of all available information.

KENNEDY

811.34544/1½₂ : Telegram

The Ambassador in the United Kingdom (Kennedy) to the Secretary of State

LONDON, July 31, 1940—6 p. m.
[Received 6 : 37 p. m.]

2490. Strictly secret and personal for the President from Former Naval Person:

"It is some time since I ventured to cable personally to you, and many things both good and bad have happened in between. It has now become most urgent for you to let us have the destroyers, motor boats and flying boats for which we have asked. The Germans have the whole French coastline from which to launch U–boats, dive-bomber attacks upon our trade and food, and in addition we must be constantly prepared to repel by sea action threatened invasion in the narrow waters, and also to deal with breakouts from Norway towards Ireland, Iceland, Shetlands and Faroes. Besides this we have to keep control of the exit from the Mediterranean, and if possible the command of that inland sea itself, and thus to prevent the war spreading seriously into Africa.

Point 2. We have a large construction of destroyers and anti-U–boat craft coming forward, but the next 3 or 4 months open the gap of which I have previously told you. Latterly, the air attack on our shores has become injurious. In the last 10 days we have had the following destroyers sunk: *Brazen, Codrington, Delight, Wren*; and the following damaged: *Beagle, Boreas, Brilliant, Griffin, Montrose, Walpole, Whitshed*, total 11. All this in the advent of any attempt which may be made at invasion. Destroyers are frightfully vulnerable to air bombing, and yet they must be held in the air bombing area to prevent seaborne invasion. We could not keep up the present rate of casualties for long, and if we cannot get a substantial reinforcement, the whole fate of the war may be decided by this minor and easily remediable factor.

This is a frank account of our present situation and I am confident, now that you know exactly how we stand, that you will leave nothing undone to ensure that 50 or 60 of your oldest destroyers are sent to me at once. I can fit them very quickly with asdics and use them against U–boats on the western approaches and so keep the more modern and better gunned craft for the narrow seas against invasion.

Mr. President, with great respect I must tell you that in the long history of the world, this is a thing to do now. Large construction is coming to me in 1941, but the crisis will be reached long before 1941. I know you will do all in your power but I feel entitled and bound to put the gravity and urgency of the position before you.

Point 3. If the destroyers were given, the motor boats and flying boats which would be invaluable, could surely come in behind them.

Point 4. I am beginning to feel very hopeful about this war if we can get 'round the next 3 or 4 months. The air is holding well. We are hitting that man hard, both in repelling attacks and in bombing Germany. But the loss of destroyers by air attacks may well be so serious as to break down our defense of the food and trade routes across the Atlantic.

Point 5. Tonight the latest convoys of rifles, cannon and ammunition are coming in. Special trains are waiting to take them to the troops and home guard, who will take a lot of killing before they give them up. I am sure that with your comprehension of the sea affair, you will not let this crux of the battle go wrong for the want of these destroyers. I cabled to Lothian some days ago, and now send this through Kennedy, who is a grand help to us and the common cause."

KENNEDY

Memorandum by President Roosevelt [69]

[WASHINGTON,] August 2, 1940.

At Cabinet meeting, in afternoon, long discussion in regard to devising ways and means to sell directly or indirectly fifty or sixty World War old destroyers to Great Britain. It was the general opinion, without any dissenting voice, that the survival of the British Isles under German attack might very possibly depend on their getting these destroyers.

It was agreed that legislation to accomplish this is necessary.

It was agreed that such legislation if asked for by me without any preliminaries would meet with defeat or interminable delay in reaching a vote.

It was agreed that the British be approached through Lord Lothian to find out if they would agree to give positive assurance that the British Navy, in the event of German success in Great Britain, would not under any conceivable circumstances fall into the hands of the Germans and that if such assurances could be received and made public, the opposition in the Congress would be greatly lessened. I sug-

---

[69] Photostatic copy obtained from the Franklin D. Roosevelt Library, Hyde Park, N. Y.

gested that we try to get further assurance from the British that the ships of their Navy would not be sunk, but would sail for North America or British Empire ports where they would remain afloat and available.

It was agreed that I would call up William Allen White,[70] who has recently talked with Willkie [71] on this subject; ask White to come to Washington at once to see Hull, Knox [72] and Stimson [73] and after that to see me; then returning to see Willkie and seek to get, with Willkie's approval, the support of Joe Martin [74] and Charlie McNary [75] for such a plan. It was agreed that if this procedure went through successfully that I would, at once, send a definite request to the Congress for the necessary legislation.

I stressed the point that in all probability the legislation would fail if it had substantially unanimous Republican opposition—and that the crux of the matter lay in the vote of the Republican minority in each house. I stressed the importance of having the issue acted on without regard to party politics in any way.

At 8:30 P. M., I talked with William Allen White, who was in Estes Park, Colorado; explained the above to him and asked him to come East.

He told me that he was sure that Willkie's attitude in the matter was the same as mine. I explained to him that that was wholly insufficient, and that the Republican policy in Congress was the one essential.

White told me he would get in touch with Willkie and let me know at the earliest possible moment.

F[RANKLIN] D. R[OOSEVELT]

Memorandum by the Legal Adviser (Hackworth) [76]

[WASHINGTON,] August 2, 1940.

THE SALE OF VESSELS OF WAR AND AUXILIARY VESSELS

Section 23, Title 18, of the United States Code makes it unlawful to fit out and arm, or attempt to fit out and arm, or to procure to be fitted out and armed, or knowingly to be concerned in "furnishing, fitting out, or arming of any vessel, with intent that such vessel shall be employed in the service of any foreign prince, or state" etc., to

---

[70] Editor, *Emporia Gazette*.
[71] Wendell Willkie, Republican Presidential candidate in 1940.
[72] Frank Knox, Secretary of the Navy.
[73] Henry L. Stimson, Secretary of War.
[74] Joseph W. Martin, Jr., Representative from Massachusetts; Minority Leader of the House.
[75] Charles L. McNary, Senator from Oregon; Minority Leader of the Senate.
[76] Photostatic copy obtained from the Franklin D. Roosevelt Library, Hyde Park, N. Y.

cruise or commit hostilities against the subjects, citizens, or property of any foreign prince, or state, etc., with which the United States is at peace.

Section 33 of the same Title of the Code provides that during a war in which the United States is neutral it shall be unlawful to send out of the jurisdiction of the United States any vessel built, armed, or equipped as a vessel of war, with any intent or under any agreement or contract, written or oral, that such vessel shall be delivered to a belligerent nation, or to an agent, officer, or citizen of such nation, or with reasonable cause to believe that the said vessel shall or will be employed in the service of any such belligerent nation after its departure from the jurisdiction of the United States.

Section 14 (*a*) of the act entitled "An Act to expedite national defense, and for other purposes" (Public—No. 671—76th Congress [77]), approved June 28, 1940, provides that "notwithstanding the provisions of any other law, no military or naval weapon, ship, boat, aircraft, munitions, supplies, or equipment, to which the United States has title, in whole or in part, or which have been contracted for, shall hereafter be transferred, exchanged, sold, or otherwise disposed of in any manner whatever unless the Chief of Naval Operations in the case of naval material, and the Chief of Staff of the Army in the case of military material, shall first certify that such material is not essential to the defense of the United States."

Section 33, *supra*, is perhaps the most difficult provision of statutory law to surmount in connection with any sale of vessels built and intended for belligerent operations. It would be possible to amend this section in broad general terms so as to cover the other provisions referred to without specifically mentioning them, thus making it possible to release such vessels as it might be deemed desirable to release. The amendment might read somewhat as follows:

Nothing contained in Section 33, Title 18, of the United States Code or in any other provision of law shall be so applied as to prevent the departure from the United States of any vessel which belonged to the Government of the United States and which the President, after consultation with the Secretary of War and the Secretary of the Navy, shall decide may be sold without detriment to the national defense of the United States: *Provided*, that prior to the departure of the vessel title thereto shall have passed to the foreign purchaser and compensation, which in the judgment of the President, the Secretary of War and the Secretary of the Navy shall be deemed adequate, shall have been paid to the United States.

An amendment of this kind would be applicable to the sale of any kind of vessel but it undoubtedly would be necessary to explain to the committees just what is in contemplation. If an amendment

---

[77] 54 Stat. 676, 681.

should be passed on the basis of the explanation, it might be found difficult later to extend the authority to other larger craft.

None of the foregoing would relieve us of the charge that the sale of war craft by this Government to a belligerent government would be unneutral.

GREEN H. HACKWORTH

Memorandum by the Secretary of State for President Roosevelt [78]

[WASHINGTON,] August 4, 1940.

I enclose a memorandum [79] by Mr. Hackworth, approved by Judge Townsend of the Department of Justice, relating to the sale of vessels of war and auxiliary vessels. You will find on page 3 of this memorandum a proposed draft [80] of a bill to be offered in Congress.

I had a long talk with William Allen White over the telephone yesterday afternoon, in which I got before him to a fairly satisfactory extent the important points relating to danger to this country and to this hemisphere. He said repeatedly that he appreciated the benefit of this; second, that Mr. Willkie agrees in principle on these and other methods of aiding Great Britain; third, that he would desire to see the proposed draft for Congress before approving it; and, fourth, Mr. White said that he had not conferred with Mr. Willkie about the attitude of McNary and Joe Martin towards the bill, but that he would take this up with him.

William Allen White telegraphs me today that he will be glad to get a copy of the bill right away. We in the office will wait tomorrow until you receive this proposed draft and telephone us your approval before sending it to White.

I enclose a copy of a statement [81] I am giving to the press today for publication in Tuesday afternoon papers. I hope you will see that it does not seep out in any way to the public.

C[ORDELL] H[ULL]

740.0011 European War 1939/5010½

The British Ambassador (Lothian) to President Roosevelt

WASHINGTON, August 5, 1940.

DEAR MR. PRESIDENT: I enclose, as I promised, a note summarising an appreciation of Hitler's probable future strategy sent to the Prime Minister by General Smuts.[82]

---

[78] Photostatic copy obtained from the Franklin D. Roosevelt Library, Hyde Park, N. Y.

[79] *Supra.*

[80] Paragraph beginning "Nothing contained in Section 33 . . .", p. 60.

[81] Department of State *Bulletin*, August 10, 1940, p. 103.

[82] Jan Christian Smuts, Prime Minister and Minister for External Affairs and Defense, Union of South Africa.

I also enclose a note of the proposals about landing grounds and naval facilities in British possessions off the East Coast of the United States which Mr. Churchill would agree to as one of the elements in the possible deal about destroyers. It is important that no public statement should be made about this as His Majesty's Government have to make the necessary arrangements with the various Colonial Governments concerned.

Believe me, Dear Mr. President,

Yours very sincerely,   LOTHIAN

[Enclosure 1]

The British Embassy to the Department of State

MEMORANDUM

General Smuts was sent a copy of the *Aide-Mémoire* presented to the State Department on July 12th [83] setting forth the anxiety of His Majesty's Government as to possible economic peace proposal to be launched by Hitler. The essence of this proposal was that the world would enter a new and unparalleled era of prosperity if it accepted the totalitarian management of Europe by Germany and that the only obstacle in the way of this era of prosperity was the resistance of Great Britain. To this General Smuts has replied saying that he thinks that it is probable that Hitler will start a peace offensive at an early date with either suggestions for a conference or of peace proposals launched before or after an attack on Britain. General Smuts has doubts about a blitzkrieg on Britain for the present because he thinks that British naval supremacy and the efficiency of the Royal Air Force are two formidable obstacles.

General Smuts thinks therefore that an alternative plan may be in contemplation, that would consist of further encirclement of Great Britain by attempts to seize the Faroe Islands and Iceland on the right flank and Spain, Portugal and Gibraltar on the left. Hitler would then have isolated Britain from Europe, especially if the surrender of Gibraltar entailed the withdrawal of the British fleet from the Mediterranean and the loss of the middle East. With practically the whole of Europe in his hands and with Russia and the Balkans in his pocket Hitler might think that the auspicious time to launch his peace offensive would be just before winter comes. He would then pose as the regenerator of an effete European system and would propose a United States of Europe composed of so-called free states, between whom tariff walls and economic barriers would have been abolished and some currency plan of Dr. Schacht's [84] devising would

---

[83] Not printed.
[84] Hjalmar Schacht, Reichsminister without Portfolio.

have been instituted. Being in fact master of Europe Hitler could afford to restore a semblance of freedom to his victims. America would then be plausibly reminded of the Monroe Doctrine and the Continent would well have become a closed German market from which Britain and America would be largely excluded.

A scheme of this kind could be dressed up in such a plausible appearance as to make a formidable appeal to world public opinion sickened by the horrible destruction of war and the spectre of threatened famine in Europe. If, in addition, Hitler were big enough to renounce annexations and indemnities the appeal might become irresistible and might induce Europe to accept a peace which would be a moral and political disaster of the first magnitude. General Smuts thinks consultation and agreement with the United States on a positive alternative plan will be essential. Meanwhile a warning note could be sounded in the press and in speeches in both countries to help prepare public opinion against Hitler's manoeuvres. Advance ridicule, Smuts thinks, might well take much of the strength out of it.

AUGUST 5, 1940.

[Enclosure 2]

The British Embassy to the Department of State

The facilities which His Majesty's Government in the United Kingdom are prepared to extend to the United States Government are as follows:—

(1) The continuation of the facilities already granted to the United States Government in June, 1939 allowing United States aircraft and ships to use the waters of Trinidad, St. Lucia and Bermuda and the United States naval authorities to lease premises, land stores and in general make use of the ports in these three islands. Leases embodying these facilities were drawn up and signed by the United States authorities and the appropriate British Colonial authorities in the second half of 1939.

(2) American military aircraft to be allowed to land at Jamaica, British Guiana and Trinidad.

(3) Pan-American Airways acting as agents of the United States Government to be allowed to lease a small area approximately 1500 feet by 500 feet adjacent to the Trinidad aerodrome where they could store supplies, erect a small radio station etc.

(4) Pan-American Airways acting as agents for the United States Government to be allowed to lease an area of approximately one square mile near Georgetown, British Guiana on which an aerodrome could be constructed.

(5) Pan-American Airways acting as agents for the United States Government to be allowed to construct an aerodrome near Kingston,

Jamaica on similar terms to the seaplane station which the Company already operates there.

(6) The United States Army aircraft to be authorised to make occasional training flights to Newfoundland and make use of the airport there.

811.34544/1⁹⁄₁₂

The British Ambassador (Lothian) to the Acting Secretary of State

WASHINGTON, August 8, 1940.

DEAR MR. WELLES: I have now heard from London regarding the proposed naval assurances.

The Prime Minister says that if Great Britain were over-run the present Government would certainly use the Fleet, or such of it as was intact, to defend the Empire overseas and would neither sink nor surrender it. At the same time he finds it difficult to make any further reference publicly to the subject at the present time because to do so would inevitably provoke discussion and would involve grave risk of creating both in the minds of the British people and of their enemies abroad the impression that the Government had in mind the collapse of Britain as a possible contingency.

In this connexion it is relevant to quote the following extract from the last declaration by Mr. Churchill as to the future of the British Fleet made on June 4th:—

"We shall defend our island whatever the cost may be; we shall fight on beaches, landing grounds, in fields, in streets and on the hills. We shall never surrender and even if, which I do not for the moment believe, this island or a large part of it were subjugated and starving, then our empire beyond the seas, armed and guarded by the British Fleet, will carry on the struggle until in God's good time the New World, with all its power and might, sets forth to the liberation and rescue of the Old."

As regards the naval and air facilities of the East Coast I have been authorised to confirm that the facilities which His Majesty's Government in the United Kingdom are prepared to extend to the United States Government are those which I enumerated in my letter to the President of August 5th, copy of which was sent to you on the same date. For convenience of reference a copy of the document enclosed in that letter is attached.[85]

I have however been instructed to make it clear in this connexion that His Majesty's Government feel obliged to stipulate that any British air transport undertaking designated by His Majesty's Government, engaged in the operation of air transport services between the West Indies and North and South America will have the uncon-

---

[85] Enclosure 2, *supra.*

ditional use of these facilities—i. e. aerodromes, wireless installations, etc.—established by American interests on British soil and that these facilities will be made available to such British undertakings at reasonable commercial charges.

[Complimentary closing illegible]

LOTHIAN

811.34544/16½ : Telegram

The Acting Secretary of State to the Ambassador in the United Kingdom (Kennedy)

WASHINGTON, August 13, 1940—6 p. m.

2316. Please deliver as soon as possible the following message from the President to the former naval person:

"I have been studying very carefully the message transmitted to me through the British Ambassador in Washington on August 8, and I have also been considering the possibility of furnishing the assistance in the way of releases and priorities contained in the memorandum attached to your message.

It is my belief that it may be possible to furnish to the British Government as immediate assistance at least 50 destroyers, the motor torpedo boats heretofore referred to, and, insofar as airplanes are concerned, five planes of each of the categories mentioned, the latter to be furnished for war testing purposes. Such assistance, as I am sure you will understand, would only be furnished if the American people and the Congress frankly recognized that in return therefor the national defense and security of the United States would be enhanced. For that reason it would be necessary, in the event that it proves possible to release the matériel above mentioned, that the British Government find itself able and willing to take the two following steps:

1. Assurance on the part of the Prime Minister that in the event that the waters of Great Britain become untenable for British ships of war, the latter would not be turned over to the Germans or sunk, but would be sent to other parts of the Empire for continued defense of the Empire.

2. An agreement on the part of Great Britain that the British Government would authorize the use of Newfoundland, Bermuda, the Bahamas, Jamaica, St. Lucia, Trinidad and British Guiana as naval and air bases by the United States in the event of an attack on the American hemisphere by any non-American nation; and in the meantime the United States to have the right to establish such bases and to use them for training and exercise purposes with the understanding that the land necessary for the above could be acquired by the United States through purchase or through a 99-year lease.

With regard to the agreement suggested in point 2 above, I feel confident that specific details need not be considered at this time and that such questions as the exact locations of the land which the United States might desire to purchase or lease could be readily determined upon subsequently through friendly negotiation between the two Governments.

With regard to your reference to publicity concerning the contingent destination of the British fleet, I should make it clear that I have not had in mind any public statement by you but merely an assurance to me along the lines indicated, as for example, reiteration to me of your statement to Parliament on June 4.

I should welcome a reply as soon as may be possible."

WELLES

811.34544/1⁷⁄₁₂ : Telegram

The Ambassador in the United Kingdom (Kennedy) to the Secretary of State

LONDON, August 14, 1940—noon.
[Received August 14—6 : 50 a. m.]

2711. Your 2316, August 13, 6 p. m. It would be helpful to me here if I could know the gist of Lothian's message of August 8.

KENNEDY

811.34544/1⁷⁄₁₂ : Telegram

The Acting Secretary of State to the Ambassador in the United Kingdom (Kennedy)

WASHINGTON, August 14, 1940—10 a. m.

2330. Your 2711, August 14, noon. The gist of the message was (1) reference to the statements regarding the British fleet made by the Prime Minister in the House of Commons on June 4; (2) certain restricted and entirely unsatisfactory suggestions with regard to the granting of limited facilities to Pan American Airways in certain of the British West Indies and with regard to the granting of rights for military or naval aviation of the United States to make occasional visits to Newfoundland; and (3) a very ample statement of British desiderata for naval vessels and airplanes far greater both in scope and in kind than it would be possible to consider.

WELLES

811.34544/1⁹⁄₁₂ : Telegram

The Ambassador in the United Kingdom (Kennedy) to the Secretary of State

LONDON, August 15, 1940—1 a. m.
[Received August 14—8 : 44 p. m.]

2730. Your 2316, August 13, 6 p. m. Secret and personal for the President from Former Naval Person.

"I need not tell you how cheered I am by your message or how grateful I feel for your untiring efforts to give us all possible help. You will, I am sure, send us everything you can, for you know well that the worth of every destroyer that you can spare to us is measured in rubies. But we also need the motor torpedo boats which you mentioned and as many flying boats and rifles as you can let us have. We have a million men waiting for rifles.

The moral value of this fresh aid from your Government and people at this critical time will be very great and widely felt.

We can meet both the points you consider necessary to help you with Congress and with others concerned, but I am sure that you will not misunderstand me if I say that our willingness to do so must be conditional on our being assured that there will be no delay in letting us have the ships and flying boats. As regards an assurance about the British fleet, I am of course, ready to reiterate to you what I told Parliament on June 4th. We intend to fight this out here to the end and none of us would ever buy peace by surrendering or scuttling the fleet. But in any use you may make of this repeated assurance you will please bear in mind the disastrous effect from our point of view and perhaps also from yours of allowing any impression to grow that we regard the conquest of the British Islands and its naval bases as any other than an impossible contingency. The spirit of our people is splendid. Never have they been so determined. Their confidence in the issue has been enormously and legitimately strengthened by the severe air fighting of the past week.

As regards naval and air bases, I readily agree to your proposals for 99-year leases which is easier for us than the method of purchase. I have no doubt that, once the principle is agreed between us, the details can be adjusted and we can discuss them at leisure. It will be necessary for us to consult the Governments of Newfoundland and Canada about the Newfoundland base in which Canada has an interest. We are at once proceeding to seek their consent.

Once again, Mr. President, let me thank you for your help and encouragement which means so much to us."

KENNEDY

811.34544/11⁹⁄₁₂ : Telegram

The Ambassador in the United Kingdom (Kennedy) to the Secretary of State

LONDON, August 15, 1940—noon.
[Received August 15—9 : 25 a. m.]

2734. Personal and strictly confidential for the Acting Secretary. After I left the Prime Minister last night I talked with a member of the War Cabinet who had discussed with the Prime Minister the President's telegram regarding destroyers. He said to me though not in an unfriendly way, "Isn't it rather a hard bargain for you to drive?" I said "Certainly not; we are only asking them to reiterate what the Prime Minister said in principle on June 4th".

But, having sat in with Churchill and other members of the Cabinet at the time of the French debacle at Bordeaux, I am reminded that they were bemoaning the fact that when Reynaud was Premier and Darlan was Admiral of the Fleet, they both agreed that if any situation ever arose where the French would have to give in, the fleet was the one thing that would never surrender and in part would be handed over to the British. Now, Churchill, in his agreement with us, promises a good deal less than that, but nevertheless to all intents and purposes agrees to make disposition of the fleet that will not be unacceptable to us. I think, for the protection of the President and State Department, it would be well to consider that if the occasion arose here where a surrender was imminent, it is not at all unlikely that the entire Churchill government would be thrown out and another government come in that would make peace and, in that event, is it too much to imagine that the new government might very well not consider itself bound by promises of Churchill and dispose of the fleet to its own best advantage? I therefore think it might be well to decide how we can protect ourselves in this event.

KENNEDY

811.34544/11½ : Telegram

The Ambassador in the United Kingdom (Kennedy)
to the Secretary of State

LONDON, August 22, 1940—5 p. m.
[Received August 22—12:52 p. m.]

2856. Secret and personal for the President from Former Naval Person.

"I am most grateful for all you are doing on our behalf. I had not contemplated anything in the nature of a contract, bargain or sale between us. It is the fact that we had decided in Cabinet to offer you naval and air facilities off the Atlantic coast quite independently of destroyers or any other aid. Our view is that we are two friends in danger helping each other as far as we can. We should therefore like to give you the facilities mentioned without stipulating for any return and even if tomorrow you found it too difficult to transfer the destroyers, et cetera, our offer still remains open because we think it is in the general good.

I see difficulties and even risks in the exchange of letters now suggested or in admitting in any way that the munitions which you send us are a payment for the facilities. Once this idea is accepted people will contrast on each side what is given and received. The money value of the armaments would be computed and set against the facilities and some would think one thing about it and some another.

Moreover Mr. President as you well know each island or location is a case by itself. If for instance there were only one harbor or site how is it to be divided and its advantages shared. In such a case we should like to make you an offer of what we think is best for both rather than to embark upon a close cut argument as to what ought to be delivered in return for value received.

What we want is that you shall feel safe on your Atlantic seaboard so far as any facilities in possessions of ours can make you safe and naturally if you put in money and make large developments you must have the effective security of a long lease. Therefore I would rather rest at this moment upon the general declaration made by me in the House of Commons yesterday, [86] both on this point and as regards the future of the fleet. Then if you will set out in greater detail what you want we will at once tell you what we can do and thereafter the necessary arrangements, technical and legal, can be worked out by our experts. Meanwhile we are quite content to trust entirely to your judgment and sentiments of the people of the United States about any aid in munitions, et cetera, you feel able to give us. But this would be entirely a separate spontaneous act on the part of the United States arising out of their view of world struggle and how their own interests stand in relation to it and the causes it involves.

Although the air attack has slackened in the last few days and our strength is growing in many ways I do not think that bad man has yet struck his full blow. We are having considerable losses in merchant ships on the northwestern approaches, now our only channel of regular communication with the oceans, and your 50 destroyers if they came along at once would be a precious help."

KENNEDY

---

[86] In his speech of August 20 to the House of Commons Mr. Churchill announced that suitable sites in British transatlantic possessions were to be leased to the United States to facilitate the defense of the Western Hemisphere and that the British and American democracies "will have to be somewhat mixed up together in some of their affairs for mutual and general advantage." He indicated that if Great Britain were seized by Germany the British Government would provide as far as possible for the naval security of Canada and the Dominions and make sure they had the means to carry on the struggle. For text of speech, see *Parliamentary Debates*, House of Commons, 5th ser., vol. 364, p. 1159.

811.34544/2⅔ : Telegram

The Ambassador in the United Kingdom (Kennedy) to the Secretary of State

LONDON, August 25, 1940—3 p. m.

[Received August 25—10 : 27 a. m.]

2892. From Former Naval Person to President, personal and secret. "I fully understand the legal and constitutional difficulties which make you wish for a formal contract embodied in letters but I venture to put before you the difficulties and even dangers which I foresee in this procedure. For the sake of the precise list of instrumentalities mentioned which in our sore need we greatly desire we are asked to pay undefined concessions in all the islands and places mentioned from Newfoundland to British Guiana "as may be required in the judgment of the United States". Suppose we could not agree to all your experts asked for should we not be exposed to a charge of breaking our contract for which we have already received value. Your commitment is definite, ours unlimited. Much though we need the destroyers we should not wish to have them at the risk of a misunderstanding with the United States or indeed any serious argument. If the matter is to be represented as a contract both sides must be defined with far more precision on our side than has hitherto been possible.

But this might easily take some time. As I have several times pointed out we need the destroyers chiefly to bridge the gap between now and the arrival of our new construction which I set on foot on the outbreak of war. This construction is very considerable. For instance we shall receive by the end of February new destroyers and new medium destroyers 20. Corvettes which are a handy type of submarine hunter adapted to ocean work 60. MTBs 37. MASBs 25. Fairmiles a wooden anti-submarine patrol boat 104. 72-foot motor launches 29. An even greater inflow will arrive in the following 6 months. It is just in the gap from September to February inclusive while this new crop is coming in and working up that your 50 destroyers would be invaluable. With them we could minimize shipping losses in the northwestern approaches and also take a stronger line against Mussolini in the Mediterranean. Therefore time is all important. We should not however be justified in the circumstances if we gave a blank cheque on the whole of our transatlantic possessions merely to bridge this gap through which anyhow we hope to make our way through with added risk and suffering.

This I am sure you will see sets forth our difficulties plainly.

Would not the following procedure be acceptable. I would offer at once certain fairly well defined facilities which will show you the kind of gift we have in mind and your experts could then discuss these or any variants of them with ours, we remaining the final judge of what we can give. All this we will do freely trusting entirely to the generosity and good will of the American people as to whether they on their part would like to do something for us. But anyhow it is the settled policy of H[is] M[ajesty's] G[overnment] to offer you and make available to you when desired solid and effective means of protecting your Atlantic seaboard. I have already asked the Admiralty and the Air Ministry to draw up in outline what we are prepared to offer leaving your experts to suggest alternatives.

I propose to send you this outline in 2 or 3 days and to publish in due course. In this way there can be no possible dispute and the American people will feel more warmly towards us because they will see we are playing the game by the world's cause and that their safety and interests are dear to us.

If your law or your Admiral [87] requires that any help you may choose to give us must be presented as a *quid pro quo* I do not see why the British Government have to come into that at all. Could you not say that you did not feel able to accept this fine offer which we make unless the United States matched it in some way and that therefore the Admiral would be able to link the one with the other.

I am so very grateful to you for all the trouble you have been taking and I am so sorry to add to your burdens knowing what a good friend you have been to us."

This telegram in four sections is the one referred to in my 2891.[88]

KENNEDY

811.34544/2⅔ : Telegram

The Ambassador in the United Kingdom (Kennedy) to the Secretary of State

LONDON, August 29, 1940—7 p. m.
[Received August 29—5 : 40 p. m.]

2948. My 2933, August 29.[89] The Cabinet is advising Lothian to tell the President that while they accept his proposition they want the right to announce that they offered these bases as part of reservations and that they are making the deal this way because of legal and constitutional difficulties in the United States.

Now, of course, as I told you, I know nothing about the background in the United States for all these negotiations but I am sure that

---

[87] Presumably Adm. Harold R. Stark, Chief of Naval Operations. On June 28, 1940, Congress approved a bill prohibiting transfer or sale of naval weapons, ships, etc., to which the United States had title, to anyone unless the Chief of Naval Operations should first certify it not essential to the defense of the United States (54 Stat. 676, 681).
[88] Telegram No. 2891, August 25, not printed.
[89] Not printed.

there is a complete misunderstanding on the part of the British Cabinet as to the situation in the United States. Halifax wants to do it any way the President wishes it done, believing that the idea of the England–United States tie-up on anything is of more value than either bases or destroyers.

Beaverbrook,[90] who has persuaded the Prime Minister says, "If we are going to make a gift, well and good, if we are going to make a bargain, I don't want to make a bad one and this is definitely a bad one." Another opinion has been advanced that the President will make great political capital out of getting these valuable bases for destroyers that are worth nothing to anybody except England for a few months and if that is the case then England should stand out for a better deal.

Don't misunderstand me, England never gets the impression they are licked and therefore they never can understand why they should not get the best of a trade. I have seen these undercurrents growing here and realize that delays have taken place but because I had no background I have not been able to do anything about it. I have told Halifax, however, that the provision he is sending to Lothian about making the announcement here was in my opinion a bad one. Besides we shall continue legal and constitutional difficulties, about which I am not informed, it strikes me that a very definite idea might arise that, although the British were willing to give all the bases for nothing, the President's insistence that they allocate some against the destroyers will persuade the United States that it was the President's method of getting the destroyers to the British. Therefore, I don't see how you can agree to their desire to make a public announcement that they were willing to give something for nothing, because it may give a completely wrong impression but again I may be completely out of tune because I am not familiar with the background.

KENNEDY

811.34544/2⅚ : Telegram

The Ambassador in the United Kingdom (Kennedy) to the Secretary of State

LONDON, August 29, 1940—11 p. m.
[Received August 29—7 : 35 p. m.]

2952. Have just seen Churchill and Halifax. Churchill has omitted the subject which I have discussed in my 2948, August 29, 7 p. m., and says he will leave the matter open. England will handle her politics in the manner which she thinks best and the United States will

---

[90] Lord Beaverbrook, British Minister for Aircraft Production.

of course handle hers in her own way. I think this is much the better way but I do believe that it is important that the President get his statement and sign first in order that the direction of Churchill's remarks will be more or less channeled.

I think that they are inordinately happy about the result and feel that the President has obtained something for his country that not even the remote possibility of a war between the two countries would have accomplished. As he says, it puts a ring of steel around the United States that it would be impossible for Germany to penetrate and what could the President of the United States accomplish for his country greater than this? And no matter what criticism may be leveled at the giving of a few destroyers, the President can very properly say: "At least I have conducted the affairs of this country in such a manner that it has been possible to obtain these important bases for 99 years with no real loss of anything worth while to America."

KENNEDY

Executive Agreement Series No. 181
811.34544/130

The British Ambassador (Lothian) to the Secretary of State

WASHINGTON, September 2, 1940.

SIR: I have the honour under instructions from His Majesty's Principal Secretary of State for Foreign Affairs to inform you that in view of the friendly and sympathetic interest of His Majesty's Government in the United Kingdom in the national security of the United States and their desire to strengthen the ability of the United States to cooperate effectively with the other nations of the Americas in the defence of the Western Hemisphere, His Majesty's Government will secure the grant to the Government of the United States, freely and without consideration, of the lease for immediate establishment and use of naval and air bases and facilities for entrance thereto and the operation and protection thereof, on the Avalon Peninsula and on the southern coast of Newfoundland, and on the east coast and on the Great Bay of Bermuda.

Furthermore, in view of the above and in view of the desire of the United States to acquire additional air and naval bases in the Caribbean and in British Guiana, and without endeavouring to place a monetary or commercial value upon the many tangible and intangible rights and properties involved, His Majesty's Government will make available to the United States for immediate establishment and use naval and air bases and facilities for entrance thereto and the operation and protection thereof, on the eastern side of the Bahamas, the southern coast of Jamaica, the western coast of St. Lucia, the west coast of Trinidad in the Gulf of Paria, in the island of Antigua and in British Guiana within fifty miles of Georgetown, in exchange for naval and military equipment and material which the United States Government will transfer to His Majesty's Government.

All the bases and facilities referred to in the preceding paragraphs will be leased to the United States for a period of ninety-nine years, free from all rent and charges other than such compensation to be mutually agreed on to be paid by the United States in order to compensate the owners of private property for loss by expropriation or damage arising out of the establishment of the bases and facilities in question.

His Majesty's Government, in the leases to be agreed upon, will grant to the United States for the period of the leases all the rights, power, and authority within the bases leased, and within the limits of the territorial waters and air spaces adjacent to or in the vicinity of such bases, necessary to provide access to and defence of such bases, and appropriate provisions for their control.

Without prejudice to the above-mentioned rights of the United States authorities and their jurisdiction within the leased areas, the adjustment and reconciliation between the jurisdiction of the authorities of the United States within these areas and the jurisdiction of the authorities of the territories in which these areas are situated shall be determined by common agreement.

The exact location and bounds of the aforesaid bases, the necessary seaward, coast and anti-aircraft defences, the location of sufficient military garrisons, stores and other necessary auxiliary facilities shall be determined by common agreement.

His Majesty's Government are prepared to designate immediately experts to meet with experts of the United States for these purposes. Should these experts be unable to agree in any particular situation, except in the case of Newfoundland and Bermuda, the matter shall be settled by the Secretary of State of the United States and His Majesty's Secretary of State for Foreign Affairs.

I have [etc.]   LOTHIAN

Executive Agreement Series No. 181
811.34544/130

The Secretary of State to the British Ambassador (Lothian)

WASHINGTON, September 2, 1940.

EXCELLENCY: I have received your note of September 2, 1940, of which the text is as follows:

[Here follows text of note printed *supra*.]

I am directed by the President to reply to your note as follows:

The Government of the United States appreciates the declarations and the generous action of His Majesty's Government as contained in your communication which are destined to enhance the national security of the United States and greatly to strengthen its ability to cooperate effectively with the other nations of the Americas in the defense of the Western Hemisphere. It therefore gladly accepts the proposals.

The Government of the United States will immediately designate experts to meet with experts designated by His Majesty's Government to determine upon the exact location of the naval and air bases mentioned in your communication under acknowledgment.

In consideration of the declarations above quoted, the Government of the United States will immediately transfer to His Majesty's Government fifty United States Navy destroyers generally referred to as the twelve hundred-ton type.

Accept [etc.] CORDELL HULL

811.34544/122

The British Ambassador (Lothian) to the Secretary of State

No. 459 WASHINGTON, September 26, 1940.

SIR: Following on our conversation on September 9th,[91] I have the honour under instructions from His Majesty's Principal Secretary of State for Foreign Affairs [92] to invite reference to the following passage occurring in State Department press release No. 403 of the 7th September [93] dealing with a notification by the United States Government to the Governments of all other American Republics touching the understanding reached with His Majesty's Government in the United Kingdom for the lease of naval and air bases in Newfoundland and in the islands of Bermuda, the Bahamas, Jamaica, St. Lucia, Trinidad, and Antigua, and in British Guiana.

"The resulting facilities at these bases will, of course, be made available alike to all American Republics on the fullest cooperative basis for the common defence of the hemisphere and in entire harmony with the spirit of the pronouncements made and the understandings reached at the conferences of Lima, Panama and Habana".

The question as to the access which His Majesty's forces are to have to the sea and air bases is a matter which will have to be settled by common agreement later. With respect to the passage quoted above I am instructed hereby formally to reserve the position of His Majesty's Government in the United Kingdom, and to state that it is assumed by them that the United States Government will ensure that

---

[91] No record of this conversation found in Department files.
[92] Anthony Eden.
[93] For text, see Department of State *Bulletin*, September 7, 1940, p. 196.

303207—58——6

His Majesty's ships and aircraft in the leased areas will enjoy the equivalent of any facilities and privileges which the United States Government may contemplate granting to the Governments of the other American Republics.

Further I am to invite attention to the last paragraph of my letter to Mr. Sumner Welles, dated August 8th, 1940, in which I informed him that His Majesty's Government felt obligated to stipulate in connection with the air facilities which they were offering for development by Pan American Airways on behalf of the War Department, that any British air transport undertaking designated by His Majesty's Government, engaged in the operation of air transport services between the West Indies and North and South America will have the unconditional use of these facilities—i. e. aerodromes, wireless installations, etc.—established by American interests on British soil and these facilities will be made available to such British undertakings at reasonable commercial charges. This question of commercial access is no doubt also a matter which will have to be considered when the details of the leases are under discussion.

I have [etc.]　　　　　　　　　　　　　　　　　　　　LOTHIAN

811.34544/122

The Secretary of State to the British Chargé (*Butler*)

WASHINGTON, December 30, 1940.

SIR: I refer to the Embassy's note no. 459 of September 26, 1940 in which it was stated in connection with the understanding reached between our two Governments concerning the use of certain naval and air bases, that the Government of the United Kingdom assumes that the United States Government will ensure that His Majesty's ships and aircraft in the leased areas will enjoy the equivalent of any facilities and advantages which the United States Government may contemplate granting, as indicated in the State Department's press release no. 403 of September 7, to the governments of the other American republics.

I have given careful and sympathetic consideration to this statement on the part of your Government and have the following observations to make in reply. This Government made available to the other American republics the facilities under reference on the fullest cooperative basis in view of important inter-American considerations. The twenty-one American republics have adopted in their character as neutrals a common attitude and have affirmed their joint determination to maintain and defend their sovereignty against any foreign activity that may threaten them. They have unanimously declared that any attempt against the integrity or inviolability of the territory, sovereignty, or independence of any American state should be considered an act of aggression against all the American republics. Having jointly declared in formal pronouncements their solidarity in behalf of their peace and vital interests, all the American republics have mutually associated themselves in understanding looking toward cooperation in maintaining the peace and vital interests of the Americas. In these circumstances my Government feels that it cannot appropriately extend the same offer of use of these facilities to the Government of the United Kingdom which is at present a belligerent and which, in any event, could hardly be expected to limit its use of the bases in question strictly to the defense of this hemisphere. Accordingly, and considering the long period of time that these bases will be under lease, my Government is of the opinion that it cannot guarantee to the Government of the United Kingdom any general right to the use of the bases but believes that specific questions of use should be decided when they arise and in the light of all the circumstances and conditions then existing.

I also take note of the reference to the last paragraph of the Embassy's letter of August 8, 1940 to Mr. Sumner Welles in which it was stipulated, in connection with air facilities offered for development by Pan American Airways on behalf of the War Department, that any British air transport undertaking, designated by the British Government, engaged in the operation of air transport services between the West Indies and North and South America will have unconditional use of these facilities established by American interests on British soil and that these facilities will be made available to such British undertakings at reasonable commercial charges.

In reply you are advised in view of the present projects to establish Army and Navy bases on areas to be leased from the British Government, that the original plans to have Pan American Airways construct certain facilities on British soil have been abandoned with the exception of seaplane facilities at Port of Spain, Trinidad. Pan American Airways plans to expand its seaplane facilities at Port of Spain, Trinidad, on behalf of the War Department, but such facilities will be commercial in character and not under the control of the United States Government. It is not contemplated that commercial aircraft will be authorized to operate from any of the Army and Navy bases to be constructed in the leased areas, except in case of emergencies or for strictly military purposes, under supervision of the War and Navy Departments. Should arrangements be made at some future time, however, to permit American commercial aircraft to operate from these bases, sympathetic consideration will then be given to the granting of similar facilities to British air transport undertakings at reasonable commercial charges.

Accept [etc.] CORDELL HULL

ARRANGEMENT FOR EXCHANGE OF SECRET TECHNICAL INFORMATION BETWEEN THE UNITED STATES AND THE UNITED KINGDOM

811.24Ei/1

The British Ambassador (Lothian) to President Roosevelt

AIDE-MÉMOIRE

The British Government have informed me that they would greatly appreciate an immediate and general interchange of secret technical information with the United States, particularly in the ultra short wave radio field.

It is not the wish of His Majesty's Government to make this proposal the subject of a bargain of any description. Rather do they wish, in order to show their readiness for the fullest cooperation, to be perfectly open with you and to give you full details of any equipment or devices in which you are interested without in any way pressing you beforehand to give specific undertakings on your side, although of course they would hope you would reciprocate by discussing certain secret information of a technical nature which they are anxious to have urgently.

I presume that, if you approve in principle of this interchange of information, you would wish to discuss it further with the War and Navy Departments before giving a decision, and, should you so wish, I would be glad to place my Air Attaché and the scientific assistant to the Air Attaché at the disposal of the staff of the C. G. S. (General Marshall) and the C. N. O. (Admiral Stark) with a view to their discussing what technical matters might be of interest to these Services.

As to subsequent procedure, should you approve the exchange of information, it has been suggested by my Government that, in order to avoid any risk of the information reaching our enemy, a small secret British mission consisting of two or three service officers and civilian scientists should be despatched immediately to this country to enter into discussions with Army and Navy experts. This mission should, I suggest, bring with them full details of all new technical developments, especially in the radio field, which have been successfully used or experimented with during the last nine months. These might include our method of detecting the approach of enemy aircraft at considerable distances, which has proved so successful; the use of short waves to enable our own aircraft to identify enemy aircraft, and the application of such short waves to anti-aircraft gunnery for firing at aircraft which are concealed by clouds or darkness. We for our part are probably more anxious to be permitted to employ the full resources of the radio industry in this country with a view to obtaining the greatest power possible for the emission of ultra short waves than anything else.

LOTHIAN

[WASHINGTON,] 8 July, 1940.

811.24Ei/1

The Acting Secretary of State to the British Ambassador (Lothian)

WASHINGTON, July 29, 1940.

EXCELLENCY: I have the honor to refer to your *Aide-Mémoire* dated July 8, 1940, proposing a general interchange of secret technical information between the United States and British Governments, particularly in the ultra short wave radio field.

I have brought your *Aide-Mémoire* to the attention of the Secretary of War and the Secretary of the Navy, who now state that they are prepared to undertake conversations with a small secret British Mission, consisting of two or three service officers and civilian scientists. The furnishing of any technical or scientific information to your Government will, of course, be based on the understanding that the procurement of related articles or devices from sources of supply in this country will be subject to approval by the War and Navy Departments, such approval being dependent upon non-interference with our own procurement program.

General Sherman Miles, Assistant Chief of Staff of the War Department, and Rear Admiral Walter S. Anderson, Director of Naval Intelligence, have been designated representatives of the War and Navy Departments, respectively, to coordinate the details for the interchange of information covered in your *Aide-Mémoire*. It is suggested that, in the first instance, your Air Attaché and the scientific assistant to the Air Attaché communicate with General Miles and Rear Admiral Anderson with a view to discussing the scope of the proposed conversations and also in order that the British Mission, before its departure for the United States, may be informed of the information in which the War and Navy Departments are interested.

Accept [etc.]   SUMNER WELLES

REPRESENTATIONS TO THE BRITISH GOVERNMENT WITH REGARD TO CENSORSHIP OF AMERICAN MAIL [94]

841.711/2895 : Telegram

The Chargé in the United Kingdom (Johnson) to the Secretary of State

LONDON, January 17, 1940—noon.
[Received January 17—8 : 40 a. m.]

146. Your 1664, December 22, 9 p. m.[95] Following note dated January 16 received today from Foreign Office:

"I have the honour to invite reference to your note No. 1730 of the 27th December in which you drew attention to certain specific instances

---

[94] Continued from *Foreign Relations*, 1939, vol. II, pp. 266–272.
[95] *Ibid.*, p. 270.

of the removal from British, United States and other neutral ships, and of the examination by the British censorship authorities, of United States mail addressed to neutral countries and of sealed letter mail despatched from the United States. You also stated that your Government admitted the right of His Majesty's Government to censor private mails originating in or destined for the United Kingdom or private mails which normally pass through the United Kingdom for transmission to their final destination, but that in view of The Hague Convention No. 11,[96] your Government could not admit the right of the British authorities to interfere with United States mail in United States or other neutral ships on the high seas or to censor mail in ships which have involuntarily entered British ports.

2. His Majesty's Government in the United Kingdom are happy to note that there is substantial agreement between them and the United States Government as regards the rights of censorship of terminal mails and that the only point of difference seems to lie in the interpretation of The Hague Convention in regard to correspondence in ships which are diverted into British ports.

3. The view of His Majesty's Government as regards the examination of mail in ships on the high seas or involuntarily entering British ports is that the immunity conferred by Article I of The Hague Convention No. 11, which in any case does not cover postal parcels, is enjoyed only by genuine postal correspondence, and that a belligerent is therefore at liberty to examine mail bags and, if necessary, their contents in order to assure himself that they constitute such correspondence and not articles of a noxious character such as contraband. This view must, in the opinion of His Majesty's Government, be regarded as established by the practice during the war of 1914–1918, when none of the belligerents accepted the view that Article I of this convention constituted an absolute prohibition of interference with mail bags, and the general right to search for contraband was regarded as covering a full examination of mails for this purpose. Reference to the correspondence between the United States Government and His Majesty's Government in 1916 shows that at that date the United States admitted in principle the right of the British authorities to examine mail bags with a view to ascertaining whether they contained contraband.[97]

4. It will be appreciated that the letter post as well as the parcel post can be used to convey contraband; and that even though letters may be addressed to a neutral country, their ultimate destination may be Germany. For instance the letter mails may be used to convey securi-

---

[96] Convention relative to right of capture in naval warfare, signed at the Second International Peace Conference held at The Hague, October 18, 1907, *Foreign Relations*, 1907, pt. 2, p. 1236.
[97] See *ibid.*, 1916, supp., pp. 591 ff.

ties, cheques or notes or again they may be used to send industrial diamonds and other light contraband. It must be remembered that the limit of size, weight and bulk of letters sent is sufficient to allow the passage of contraband of this nature which may be of the utmost value to the enemy. It was presumably for this reason that the United States Government in their note of the 24th May 1916 [98] stated that 'the Government of United States is inclined to the opinion that the class of mail matter which includes stocks, bonds, coupons and similar securities is to be regarded as of the same nature as merchandise or other articles of property and subject to the same exercise of belligerent rights. Money orders, cheques, drafts, notes and other negotiable instruments which may pass as the equivalent of money are, it is considered, also to be classed as merchandise.' It is clear that in the case of merchandise, His Majesty's Government are entitled to ascertain if it is contraband intended for the enemy or whether it possesses an innocent character, and it is impossible to decide whether a sealed letter does or does not contain such merchandise without opening it and ascertaining what the contents are. It would be difficult to prevent the use of the letter post for the transmission of contraband to Germany, a use which has been made on an extensive scale, without submitting such mail to that very examination to which the United States Government is taking objection.

5. The Allied Governments in their correspondence with the United States Government in 1916 also had occasion to demonstrate the extent to which the mails were being employed for the purpose of conveying contraband articles to Germany. The position in this respect is identical today, and, in this connexion, I have the honour to invite reference to an *aide-mémoire* dated the 23rd November, 1939,[99] which was communicated to a member of your staff and in which clear evidence was given of the existence of an organised traffic in contraband on a considerable scale between German sympathisers in the United States and Germany through the mail. An article in a newspaper [1] published in German in the United States, which was handed to him at the same time, showed that an organisation existed in United States territory for the purpose of facilitating this traffic.

6. Quite apart from transmission of contraband the possibility must be taken into account of the use of the letter post by Germans to transmit military intelligence, to promote sabotage and to carry on other hostile acts. It is in accordance with international law for belligerents to prevent intelligence reaching the enemy which might assist them in hostile operations.

[98] See note of the same date to the French Ambassador and footnote 1, *Foreign Relations,* 1916, supp., p. 604.
[99] Not printed.
[1] *New Yorker Staatszeitung und Herold,* October 4, 1939, not reprinted.

7. I may add that in another respect, namely the destruction of mails on board ships sunk by the illegal methods of warfare adopted by Germany, the situation today is identical with that which existed in the war of 1914–1918. Between the 3rd September, 1939 and the 9th January, 1940 the German naval authorities have destroyed without previous warning or visit, in defiance of the rules of war and of obligations freely entered into, the S. S. *Yorkshire*, the S. S. *Dunbar Castle*, the S. S. *Simon Bolivar* and the S. S. *Terukuni Maru*, all of which are known to have been carrying mails to or from neutral countries, with as little regard for the safety of the neutral correspondence on board as for the lives of the inoffensive passengers and crew. Yet His Majesty's Government are not aware that any protest regarding this destruction of postal correspondence has been made to the German Government.

8. In contrast to this reckless and indiscriminate destruction of neutral property the examination conducted by His Majesty's Government of the mails which are under discussion does not involve innocent mail being either confiscated or destroyed. In accordance with the terms of The Hague Convention mail found in ships which have been diverted to British ports is forwarded to its destination as soon as possible after its innocent nature is established. In no case is genuine correspondence from the United States seized or confiscated by His Majesty's Government.

9. For the above reasons His Majesty's Government find themselves unable to share the views of the United States Government that their action in examining neutral mail in British or neutral shipping is contrary to their obligations under international law. They are, however, desirous of conducting this examination with as little inconvenience as possible to foreign nations, and you may rest assured that every effort has been and will be made to reduce any delays which may be occasioned by its enforcement. If the United States Government have occasion to bring any specific complaints to the notice of His Majesty's Government concerning delays alleged to be due to the examination of these mails, His Majesty's Government will be happy to examine these complaints in as accommodating and friendly a spirit as possible. While the task of examination is rendered heavy as a result, it is believed that arrangements which have been made to deal with this correspondence will ensure that all genuine correspondence will reach its destination in safety and with reasonable despatch."

Foreign Office assumes that since our note of protest has been published we shall have no objection to eventual release here of the reply.

JOHNSON

841.711/3134

The Department of State to the British Embassy [2]

AIDE-MÉMOIRE

In view of the difficulties and inconveniences which are now being experienced by American firms due to delays in transmitting shipping documents to and from Europe, the American Government has been giving consideration to possible ways and means of obviating such delays. During the World War the British Government proposed that if the United States postal administration would consent to dispatch in special bags marked "shipping documents" bills of lading, invoices, et cetera, referring to cargo in the ship by which the documents in question were dispatched, arrangements would be made for the rapid examination of the contents of these bags by one or two officers of the censorship at the ports of call and for the forwarding of such documents by the same ship.[3] As a result of this proposal special pouches were used for forwarding shipping papers from the United States to Europe and from certain European countries to the United States. It is believed that this arrangement proved helpful in the delivery of shipping documents and certain American firms are now asking that a similar arrangement be introduced at the present time.

The American Government, without prejudice to the general position which it has already taken with respect to the interference with its mails by the British Government, would consent to the dispatch of shipping documents in special pouches on the understanding that the Government of Great Britain would provide for a rapid examination of the contents of these pouches by censorship officials and for forwarding of such documents without delay.

Many of the complaints received from American firms relate to delays in the receipt of shipping documents originating in the United Kingdom. It is obviously in the interest of both countries to eliminate all avoidable delays and it is hoped that the British Government may also give attention to this problem.

WASHINGTON, January 18, 1940.

---

[2] A similar *aide-mémoire* was presented to the French Embassy on the same day, but no reply has been found in Department files.

[3] See telegram No. 4162, April 15, 1916, from the Ambassador in Great Britain, *Foreign Relations*, 1916, supp., p. 603.

841.711/2961 : Telegram

The Chargé in the United Kingdom (Johnson) to the Secretary of State

LONDON, February 3, 1940—noon.
[Received February 3—7 : 42 a. m.]

306. Your 1448, November 17, 7 p. m.[4] Following note dated February 1 received from Foreign Office.

"I have the honor to inform you that the competent authorities have now completed their investigation of all the cases to which Mr. Kennedy was so good as to draw my attention in his note No. 1563 of the 20th November last [5] on the subject of the interference by the British censorship authorities with United States diplomatic and consular mail.

2. With regard to the instance numbered (1) in your note, I have the honor to state that according to the censorship regulations both diplomatic and consular correspondence, if addressed to a state department and if certified as emanating from a diplomatic mission or consulate (in order that its authenticity may be assured), is exempt from examination, though discretion has inevitably to be left to examiners as to whether a particular governmental institution is to be regarded as a state department for the purposes of examination. Enquiries are therefore being made in Madras into the case cited.

3. With regard to items (2) and (3), I have the honor to state that the correspondence of consular officers is not exempt from examination unless emanating from or addressed to a state department or diplomatic mission, except, as stated in Foreign Office circular Note No. W 13673/13452/50 of 26th September, 1939,[6] in the case of a consul who is the senior representative of his government in the absence of a diplomatic mission in the country concerned. Unless, therefore, the correspondence cited in your note was recognisable as emanating from a privileged address, it would appear that the censorship authorities acted correctly in examining it. The same considerations apply to the case of the censorship of the correspondence of the United States Consulate at Stuttgart, to which Mr. Schoenfeld [7] drew the attention of this department on 27th October last.

4. While in view of the above consideration I regret that instructions cannot be issued in the general sense desired by the United States Government, the censorship officials have been ordered to bear constantly in mind the high desirability of exercising the utmost consideration in dealing with consular mail, and I shall be happy to make enquiries into any cases to which you care to draw my attention where privileged correspondence appears to have been subjected to examination."

For Foreign Office circular note referred to in paragraph 3, above, see Embassy's telegram 1841, September 27.

[4] *Foreign Relations*, 1939, vol. II, p. 267.
[5] Copy of note No. 1563, November 20, 1939, was sent to Department as an enclosure to despatch No. 4548, February 3, 1940; neither printed.
[6] See telegram No. 1841, September 27, 1939, from the Ambassador in the United Kingdom, *Foreign Relations*, 1939, vol. II, p. 274.
[7] Rudolf E. Schoenfeld, First Secretary of Embassy in the United Kingdom.

Final sentence of paragraph 3 above relates to the opening by British censors of four letters addressed to the American Consulate at Stuttgart (two for the American Consul, one for Mr. Honaker [8] and one for an American employee) brought to attention of Foreign Office at instance of Embassy, Berlin.

JOHNSON

841.711/3135

The British Embassy to the Department of State

AIDE-MÉMOIRE

His Majesty's Embassy duly informed His Majesty's Government in the United Kingdom of the contents of the State Department's *aide-mémoire* of January 18th. In this *aide-mémoire* it was suggested that in order to facilitate the transmission of shipping documents from this country to Europe the United States Postal Administration should despach in special bags marked "shipping documents" bills of lading, invoices, etc., referring to cargo in the ship by which the documents in question were despatched, on the understanding that His Majesty's Government for their part would arrange for the rapid examination of the contents of these bags by the British authorities at the ports of call and for the onward transmission of the documents without delay. An arrangement on these lines was in fact in force during the war of 1914–1918.

His Majesty's Embassy is glad to be able to inform the State Department that a reply has now been received from the Foreign Office indicating that His Majesty's Government will be happy to comply with this suggestion. The necessary arrangements have in fact already been made to put the scheme into operation on the British side.

WASHINGTON, February 20, 1940.

841.711/3151

Memorandum of Conversation, by the Assistant Secretary of State (Berle)

[WASHINGTON,] March 26, 1940.

Lord Lothian [9] called today, at his request. He merely wished to inquire whether the conversations regarding the censorship of the mails were coming to a definite outcome. I pointed out that it was practically impossible to bring them to a definite conclusion until they had indicated to us what their own policy was to be. I had heard that they were planning to establish a control station at Sydney, Nova Scotia. Lord Lothian said that this was their intent, but they

---

[8] Samuel W. Honaker, Consul General at Stuttgart.
[9] British Ambassador in the United States.

were still hampered a little by the Canadians, who had been holding off any decision in the matter until after election. He hoped I would speak to the Canadian Minister about it.

I said that obviously we could hardly be in the position of suggesting any course of action in connection with control stations to the Canadian government, or any other belligerent. We had entered a general reservation against our ships or mails being taken into any control station. If there were to be a control station, presumably Sydney would be no worse than any other; but we obviously would not care to be in the position of suggesting it. I said I thought that Mr. Christie [10] understood this; in any event, there was no reason why he should not be given as frank a statement of our views as we had already given the British government.

A. A. BERLE, JR.

[Further correspondence on British mail censorship, not printed, deals with excessive delays and with details of censorship administration.]

DECLARATION BY THE UNITED STATES TO THE BRITISH GOVERNMENT THAT REMOVAL AT PORT SAID OF TWO GERMANS FROM PHILIPPINE SHIP WAS ILLEGAL

811B.85/17

The Secretary of State to the Chargé in the United Kingdom
(Johnson)

No. 1154   WASHINGTON, January 10, 1940.

SIR: In 1938 the Government of the Commonwealth of the Philippines through the National Development Company, a wholly owned instrumentality thereof, extended financial assistance to the De la Rama Steamship Company, a Philippine corporation, for the construction by the Fried Krupp Germaniawerft Aktiengesellschaft, Kiel, Germany, of a motorship, the *Don Isidro*. On June 16, 1939, for purposes of security in connection with this Government loan, the De la Rama Company was required to assign and transfer all its rights, interests and properties in the contract to the aforementioned National Development Company.

Pursuant to arrangements made with a British shipping firm, the *Don Isidro*, manned by an English crew under a British captain, together with four Filipino engineers and two German engineers, whose names are Repenning and Zuehl, sailed on August 24, 1939 from Kiel. The vessel was flying the American flag and operating under a pro-

---

[10] Loring C. Christie, Canadian Minister.

visional certificate of Philippine registry issued by the American Consul General at Hamburg under instructions of the Department, with Manila as the ultimate port of destination. According to the construction contract the two German engineers were to accompany the vessel to Manila and to remain there for a stipulated period in order "to guarantee construction and demonstrate proper manning of ship". When the *Don Isidro* put into Port Said preparatory to its passage through the Suez Canal, the two German engineers, without participation by the Egyptian authorities in whose territorial waters the vessel happened to be, were removed from the vessel and taken into custody by the British naval authorities under Vice Admiral Bedford, following a conference or conferences between the Vice Admiral and the British master of the *Don Isidro*. Thereupon, the vessel passed through the Canal on September 5 bound for Manila where it subsequently arrived safely, while the two German engineers were sent to Great Britain for internment.

On September 28, 1939 the American Legation at Cairo reported [11] that the British naval authorities justified their action in arresting the German engineers on the ground that war having been declared, the two German engineers were enemy subjects not too old for military service; that they possessed dangerous technical knowledge; and that the authorities suspected that definite title to the ship had not passed to the Philippine Government.

On the basis of information received from the United States High Commissioner to the Philippine Islands,[12] it has been concluded that the Philippine Government has not and will not suffer any monetary damages as a result of the arrest of the two German engineers.

Although the Department in this instance is not interested in determining the relationship between the United Kingdom and Egypt in the present hostilities in Europe or in determining the rights to which the Egyptian Government may be entitled with respect to such an incident occurring within its territorial waters, it is unwilling through silence to acquiesce in an act which, from information available, appears to be in violation of the neutral rights of the United States. The Department desires, therefore, that the Embassy request the British authorities to inform this Government of the legal basis upon which the action of Vice Admiral Bedford was predicated in exercising belligerent rights against a neutral vessel in the harbor of Port Said, the territorial waters of Egypt, en route to Manila via the Suez Canal.

For your information there are enclosed copies of messages received and transmitted by the Department with respect to this matter.[13] The

---

[11] Telegram No. 122, September 28. 1939, 10 a. m., from the Minister in Egypt, not printed.

[12] Francis B. Sayre.

[13] None printed.

confidential information contained in the last paragraph of Cairo's telegram no. 122, September 28, 10 a. m. should not be conveyed to the British authorities, as such action might be harmful to the British Commandant of the Suez Canal Police who gave that information in strict confidence to the Consul at Port Said.

Very truly yours,   For the Secretary of State:
                                                    SUMNER WELLES

811B.85/21

The Secretary of State to the Ambassador in the United Kingdom
(Kennedy)

No. 1361   WASHINGTON, April 29, 1940.

SIR: Reference is made to the Department's instruction No. 1154 of January 10, 1940 requesting that the Embassy ascertain from the British Government the legal basis for the removal by British naval authorities of two German engineers from the motorship, *Don Isidro*, while that vessel was at Port Said en route to Manila via the Suez Canal, and to the Embassy's despatch No. 4798 of March 6, 1940 [14] enclosing a copy of the British Foreign Office note No. W 3022/31/49 of March 2, 1940. In this note the British Foreign Office stated that, under the Anglo-Egyptian Treaty of Alliance of 1936,[15] "the Egyptian Government undertook in the event of war to come to the assistance of the British Government as an ally"; that the British Government is "authorized to station forces in Egyptian territory with a view to insuring, in cooperation with the Egyptian forces, the liberty and entire security of navigation of the Suez Canal"; and that, in the effectuation of these measures "the British Naval and other forces in the Canal Zone therefore act as agents of the Egyptian Government".

Because of these provisions, the note continues, "the British naval forces cooperating with the Egyptian authorities at that port (Port Said) were fully entitled to board the vessel for the purpose of satisfying themselves that neither the vessel, nor her crew, nor her cargo represented any threat to the security and free navigation of the Canal". As the presence on board the *Don Isidro* of two German engineers was regarded as constituting a menace to the safety and free navigation of the Canal, they were therefore removed. By way of addendum, paragraph numbered four of the note states that since these Germans were of military age and possessed "technical knowledge of considerable value to the German war effort", they were persons which the British Government was entitled to remove from neutral ships in the exercise of belligerent rights.

[14] Not printed.
[15] League of Nations Treaty Series, vol. CLXXIII, p. 401.

The Department is not aware that the Egyptian Government has declared itself to be a belligerent. That Government, therefore, could not legally exercise any belligerent rights nor authorize the British naval forces as its agent to do so. Accordingly, since it is clear that the removal and internment of the German citizens under reference would have been warranted only if Egypt were a belligerent, the action of the British authorities was clearly illegal and cannot be justified by any provisions of the Anglo-Egyptian Treaty of Alliance of 1936. The Department is, therefore, unable to regard the note of the British Foreign Office as a satisfactory answer to the question presented and still adheres to the position that the action of the British authorities was illegal and constituted a violation of the neutral rights of the United States. In as much as no pecuniary damage was suffered in this instance, however, the Department, on the assumption that similar instances will not be permitted to recur in the future, is willing to regard the matter as closed.

The Embassy is requested to inform the British authorities of the views of this Government as hereinabove set forth.

Very truly yours,   For the Secretary of State:

SUMNER WELLES

REPRESENTATIONS TO THE BRITISH GOVERNMENT ON EFFECTS OF IMPORT CONTROLS ON AMERICAN BUSINESS AND AGRICULTURE [16]

641.116/2578

Memorandum of Conversation, by the Secretary of State

[WASHINGTON,] January 22, 1940.

The British Ambassador [17] called at my request in order that I might, in the strongest possible terms, make representations to him and his Government regarding the recent announcement from London that the British would, to all practical intents and purposes, cease further purchases of tobacco in this country, and at the same time would undertake to make purchases from such countries as Turkey and Greece.

I brought up the general situation as it exists between our two Governments at this time and expressed my genuine concern at the increasing tension and feeling of resentment steadily rising in this country due to a multiplicity of what are considered here as excesses by the British Government in prescribing and carrying out war restrictions on trade and finance. I said there is a feeling that the British Government is ceasing to show any consideration to my Government and

---

[16] Continued from *Foreign Relations*, 1939, vol. II, pp. 213–234.
[17] Marquess of Lothian.

the people of this country as it makes more drastic a number of its war policies and methods, such as interference with mails,[18] forcing United States ships into the combat area, American loss due to British blockade of German exports, the navicert system, discrimination in favor of Italian ships against American ships at Gibraltar, et cetera, et cetera. I did not go into detail of what are considered by this Government and the American people as unnecessary, unreasonable and injurious restrictions to trade and other interests. I made it clear that this Government has in mind very fully every phase of the British situation as a belligerent engaged in a terrific war for its existence and the consequent need for many war regulations and restrictions of a temporary and abnormal nature. I then stated that there is a steadily increasing feeling in this country that American commercial and other interests are being severely injured by discriminations and unnecessary restrictions, the effect of which will extend into peacetime, perhaps permanently, to the detriment of American interests; there is a further growing feeling that in the pursuit of these policies the British Government will soon reach a stage where the advantages of these discriminations and restrictions will be decidedly less than the bad reactionary effects in this country. I elaborated on these lines and made it just as emphatic as I possibly could. I frequently appealed to the Ambassador from the standpoint of his own Government, if for no other reason, very urgently to request his Government to modify its reported attitude in making this recent tobacco announcement. I pointed out each time that his Government would know well how to put before the public a statement that would give reassurance to our tobacco growers who have built up this industry mainly on the strength of British purchases, especially during recent years. I made it clear that we could not defend this recent British action for a moment.

The Ambassador, of course, sought to defend the British side by pointing out the life and death struggle and the necessity for doing the things they were doing. I said that was not the question, but whether the British Government is not doing itself much more harm than good,—a fact in which I strongly believe. The Ambassador appeared to realize the strength of this view and said he would take it up at once with his Government and discuss it fully in the hope that something could be worked out along the lines of my representations.

C[ORDELL] H[ULL]

---

[18] See pp. 79 ff.

841.711/3027

Memorandum of Conversations, by the Chief of the Division of European Affairs (Moffat)

[WASHINGTON,] January 25, 1940.

The British Ambassador called on Judge Moore [19] and Mr. Moffat [20] this morning.

He began by saying that he had been puzzled, if not somewhat hurt, by the recent publicity in the American papers indicating considerable irritation against the British on a variety of subjects. When the war broke out, Secretary Hull and he had agreed to try and deal informally with cases as they arose and, whenever possible, to dispose of them without the writing (and particularly without the publication) of notes. The Ambassador had not been aware that so much irritation existed, and he wondered if he had not been in some way at fault. Whatever the causes, "the heat had been turned on," and he was trying to see whether ways and means could not be found of easing the situation.

Judge Moore replied that there were, in fact, many causes of irritation, some justified and some growing out of an inadequate knowledge of the facts. A reading of the recent Senate debates, as well as conversations he had had with Congressmen, editors, et cetera, had convinced him that this feeling was widespread. Judge Moore instanced the feeling on tobacco where the North Carolina population was as pro-English as in any State of the Union, but where it felt its entire economic future to be jeopardized. He spoke of the situation in the South with regard to the purchases of lumber, where he felt that there had been considerable worry, but which was now being relieved by the sale of ships (specially earmarked) for its transportation.

Mr. Moffat stated that perhaps the Ambassador was asking for more fundamental reasons for the feeling that has grown up, not connected with individual commodities or individual disputes, but based on certain fears which, although not concretely expressed, were perhaps widely felt. In the first place, there was a general feeling that the United States had been particularly friendly to Great Britain, had even gone out of its way to give special forms of help, but that Great Britain had taken this friendship so much for granted, that she was giving more favorable treatment to countries which had not shown as friendly an attitude. A second cause was a fear that while Great Britain was bending all its energies toward pursuing a military war, it was at the same time entering into a series of com-

---

[19] R. Walton Moore, Counselor of the Department of State.
[20] Jay Pierrepont Moffat, Chief of the Division of European Affairs.

mitments in its economic war which would have serious repercussions on American trade long after the war itself was over. Cases in point might be the agreements with Turkey, with the Argentine, et cetera. A third and more concrete fear was that in specific commodities there might be a change of taste on the part of the British consumer which would result in the permanent,—not merely the temporary,— loss of the British market.

The Ambassador said that this background was of real help to him. Of course, we knew the situation in which Great Britain found herself, struggling with all her resources against a powerful foe. The expenses of Britain's war efforts were rising by leaps and bounds. Everything that was not an immediate necessity to life or limb had to be subordinated to the purchase of direct war matériel. In fact, the greatest error which, in his opinion, the British and French were making was in not restricting much further the consumption on the part of their populations. For instance, he felt there should be severe rationing of food, clothing, and other forms of normal purchases. Total British purchases in the United States had risen sharply. Foreign exchange was limited, and every cent of it was being mobilized. Turkey, which was a necessary bastion in the east, had virtually blackmailed Great Britain. Most non-military supplies which could be purchased elsewhere must be sought in alternative markets in order to save Britain's vital dollar exchange.

With this background, the Ambassador hoped that we would be more understanding of the failure of the British to come into the American market for non-essentials. He was thinking about setting forth this picture as cold-bloodedly as possible, and perhaps inviting the suggestions of the American Government as to how the British could proceed within the limits of their available exchange so as to cause the least damage to American economy. Judge Moore and Mr. Moffat both said that the more information this Government had available the better, but that no American Government official could choose between American products and assume the responsibility of robbing Peter to pay Paul.

The Ambassador then came back to the question of publishing notes, which he felt created a bad press, particularly as the Neutrality Bill [21] had the paradoxical effect of removing counterbalancing causes of friction between the United States and Germany. Mr. Moffat said that in principle we agreed that publication was inadvisable, and it had only been when a number of problems were not settled that the different Divisions in the Department and the different Departments of the Government felt the time had come to make their stand public. At the same time, it was pointed out that while the British objected

---

[21] Act approved November 4, 1939; 54 Stat. 4.

to the publication of our notes, the official spokesmen in England had been commenting on the very points under discussion and not always in a way which had the happiest effect upon American psychology. A number of instances were mentioned. The Ambassador said that he was much impressed with the seriousness of the situation, and was already in telegraphic touch with his Government with a view to settling some of the points at issue.

Judge Moore said he thought that nothing would be more useful at the moment than for Britain to adopt a less rigid and more yielding attitude. On the matter of the censorship of Clipper mail at Bermuda, for instance, he wondered whether the advantages were worth the feeling that it had aroused. He feared that the British stand would even result in our having to route our Clippers by other routes, although it was very much to the interest of Britain to have speedy transatlantic mail service. The Ambassador agreed that the criterion should be: "Is a given course of action which is irritating to the United States absolutely necessary to win the war? If so, American public opinion cannot prevail; if it is merely a convenience and not a necessity, the British Government should definitely bear American reaction in mind."

The Ambassador was going to see Mr. Hull when he recovered next week. Meanwhile, he would endeavor to keep in close touch with the Department, and hoped that we would feel free to call on him whenever desired. He said that he wanted to be of help, and that he did possess real influence in London. It was also suggested that members of his staff might make a practice of dropping down from time to time to talk things over informally with members of the Department, rather than of waiting until a specific case had arisen. The Ambassador pointed out that it was most unfortunate that Mr. Kennedy was not at his post in London [22] as he was in a position to go to the Prime Minister,[23] Lord Halifax,[24] et cetera, and explain exactly how the American public would react in various contingencies. He himself had been hampered by the departure of Victor Mallet [25] and the temporary absence of Hoyer Millar.[26] He believed, however, that while there would always be questions arising between us, a better system of liaison would be able to keep these from developing into real friction.

3 p. m. Later in the afternoon Sir Owen Chalkley, Commercial Counselor of the British Embassy, called on Dr. Feis [27] and Mr.

---

[22] Ambassador Kennedy was on a visit to the United States from November 29, 1939, to March 7, 1940.
[23] Neville Chamberlain.
[24] British Secretary of State for Foreign Affairs.
[25] Counselor of the British Embassy in Washington, 1936–39.
[26] First Secretary of the British Embassy in Washington.
[27] Herbert Feis, Adviser on International Economic Affairs.

Moffat, more particularly to discuss the tobacco situation. He explained at some length the Turkish agreement which was limited to the purchase by Britain of about nine hundred thousand pounds of Turkish tobacco a year; it was, nonetheless, a twenty-year agreement. Dr. Feis said that perhaps of all American products tobacco was most dependent upon the British market; Senator Bailey [28] had told him that sixty percent of the North Carolina crop was sold to England and the Dominions. Sir Owen Chalkley said he had been giving a great deal of thought as to ways and means of finding the necessary exchange to increase British purchases of American tobacco, and was examining the suggestion made by Dr. Feis a few days ago that the excess of dollars obtained by virtue of the United States buying more rubber, tin, jute, et cetera than had been estimated might be allocated for this purpose.

Sir Owen Chalkley then talked at some length about British purchases of war materials, on which he supplied some interesting figures, and then about British purchases of agricultural products which are made in London and not in the United States. He was going to recommend that the British Government accredit an agricultural attaché to the Embassy at Washington who could keep in close touch with our Department of Agriculture, give the necessary facts and figures, and sense when any particular commodity situation became hazardous from the point of view of adverse public opinion.

He concluded by an earnest appeal that we endeavor to moderate the publicity about British "wrongdoing", in return for which they would do their best to remedy the situations of which we complained. They would like very much to be restored to the status of a "good boy", and hoped for some sort of public recognition to be given of their reform.

PIERREPONT MOFFAT

641.116/2579 : Telegram

The Chargé in the United Kingdom (Johnson) to the Secretary of State

LONDON, January 26, 1940—8 p. m.
[Received January 26—5 : 47 p. m.]

247. Your 158, January 25, 7 p. m.[29] Since presentation of my note of December 28 [30] I have more than once taken occasion to mention the matter informally at the Foreign Office and the Agricultural At-

[28] Josiah Bailey, Senator from North Carolina.
[29] Not printed; it instructed the Chargé to inquire from the Foreign Office when a reply to the Embassy's note of December 28, 1939, might be expected and gave information as to the importance of the British market to American tobacco producers (641.116/2568).
[30] See *Foreign Relations*, 1939, vol. II, p. 233, footnote 22.

taché [31] has also continued to manifest our interest in informal talks at the Board of Trade. While the matter is not one in which the Foreign Office is the determining factor, the official with whom the matter has been discussed is thoroughly conversant with the background and I have had the definite impression in talking with him that the authorities are under some embarrassment as to how to reply to our note. As I understand it one of the main reasons for the embarrassment is their reluctance to put on formal record the real reasons for curtailment of purchases of American tobacco which the official stated plainly were the problems of exchange. He remarked that the purchases from Turkey, although a valuable asset in Anglo-Turkish relations, formed but a very small proportion in value of what had been the annual purchases of American tobacco and that actually they would not mind very much if the tobacco purchased from Turkey had to be thrown into the sea. What they are faced with the official said is the impossibility of making purchases of American tobacco for a very long time to come, an impossibility which would be little if any affected were the agreement for the purchase of Turkish tobacco to be repudiated.

The Department will recall in this connection the Ambassador's conversations with Mr. Oliver Stanley [32] reported in his telegrams 1468, September 6, 1 p. m.,[33] 1620, September 13 and 1659, September 15, 3 p. m.[34] as well as a talk with Sir John Simon [35] reported in the Ambassador's telegram 2232, November 1.[36]

I venture to suggest that we might come somewhere nearer finding a solution of this problem if the United States could offer some practicable plan to the British which they could fit into their war economy and through the operation of which the market in this country for American tobacco might be protected.

There would seem to be two possible courses of procedure, one to endeavor to preclude increased use of Turkish tobacco in this market, the other to accept the temporary necessity of British use of a limited quantity of such tobacco. Assuming the first course we might either induce the British themselves to hold or otherwise dispose of the tobacco, or come to an understanding involving cooperation by the United States. If the second course were pursued we might urge upon the British a plan suited to protect our longer range interests. This would certainly involve withdrawal of any preferential treatment for Turkey after the war and, during the war, an understanding as to how Turkish (and Greek) tobaccos are utilized. The Board of Trade has

[31] Loyd V. Steere.
[32] President of the British Board of Trade.
[33] Not printed.
[34] *Foreign Relations*, 1939, vol. II, pp. 215 and 216, respectively.
[35] British Chancellor of the Exchequer.
[36] *Foreign Relations*, 1939, vol. II, p. 225.

suggested for example that a 15% general "adulteration" of present cigarette tobaccos with Turkish would not destroy their "Virginia" character and would enable a ready shift back after the war, whereas a scheme to encourage consumption of pure or distinctly Turkish type cigarettes might well involve permanent loss of a part of the market for the United States.

JOHNSON

641.116/2603

Memorandum of Conversation, by the Under Secretary of State
(Welles)

[WASHINGTON,] February 9, 1940.

The British Ambassador called this morning at his request and advised me confidentially that an announcement would be made next week by the British and French Governments that the two Governments were sending to the United States Mr. Ashton-Gwatkin, Economic Adviser to the British Foreign Office, and Mr. Charles Rist, the French financial expert, to discuss with the appropriate authorities in this country the manner in which some constructive solution might be given to the purchase by the Allies of American tobacco and other American agricultural commodities. The Ambassador said that he believed that the sending of these two experts would be a constructive step and that he believed results satisfactory to this Government would be derived therefrom.

I told the Ambassador that I could not emphasize too strongly the need for some satisfactory solution of this problem since the stoppage of purchases of American tobacco as well as other commodities would create a situation in this country which would be of real concern. The Ambassador said that he fully understood that, and that it was for this very reason that he had urged the sending of some competent authority to discuss the matter here.

S[UMNER] W[ELLES]

641.116/2621

The Department of State to the British Embassy

[WASHINGTON,] February 21, 1940.

MEMORANDUM

It is recognized that the British Ambassador's memorandum of February 14, as amended by the memorandum of February 16,[37] is

---

[37] Neither memorandum printed. In presenting the memorandum of February 14, the British Ambassador explained that it was not an official document and that his Government had not seen it. The memoranda gave information to show the necessity of the British Government to control agricultural purchases to conserve gold and dollar resources.

tentative in its various estimates. The following comments are likewise in part tentative and in any event would be subject to amendment to correspond to any further changes which might be made by Lord Lothian in his memorandum.

I

FOREIGN EXCHANGE RESOURCES OF THE UNITED KINGDOM

The great importance to the United Kingdom of its gold and foreign capital assets is fully understood. It may be inquired, however, why the estimate of "the total capital assets of Great Britain" which is given on page three of the Ambassador's memorandum should include only gold and negotiable dollar securities and should omit

(a) The British short-term balances in this country, estimated by the Federal Reserve Board to have been 595 million dollars at the end of August, 1939.

(b) The British "direct and other investments" in the United States cited in the same survey.

(c) British direct and security investment in third countries which if liquidated at all are likely to be sold to American investors.

(d) The central gold reserves of the rest of the sterling area (a half-billion dollars).

Further, although the memorandum justifiably does not include the gold, dollar balances and American investments of Canada and France, it may be noted that these amounted to over 4.5 billion dollars and constitute a fund which in some measure undoubtedly will be available, directly or indirectly, for the needs of the British Government in a protracted war.

These inquiries and comments are put forward in our endeavor to appraise whether the "total capital assets of Great Britain" may not lie somewhere above the 2,735 million dollars cited in the Ambassador's memorandum.

II

ESTIMATED BALANCE OF PAYMENTS BETWEEN THE "STERLING AREA" AND THE UNITED STATES

(1) It is the estimate of the memorandum that, omitting the sale of newly mined gold, the "sterling area" will have a negative balance of payments with the United States for the first year of the war (September 1939–August 1940) of 117 million pounds sterling or 470 million dollars. Considerations of caution would obviously indicate the wisdom of making such an estimate on a most conservative basis. However, it would appear that, even on a conservative basis, the net result presented by this estimate may overestimate the prospective net adverse British balance—perhaps by as much as 100 to 150 million dollars. Without entering into detailed discussion, it would seem pertinent to inquire:

(*a*) Whether it is justifiable to assume that American imports from the United Kingdom will be as low as in 1934 or the exceptional year of 1938, as is done in the British estimate.

(*b*) Whether the dollar value of American imports from the rest of the sterling area is not likely to be substantially in excess of the 1939 value, which is the value assumed in the British estimate.

(*c*) On what basis the British Treasury has reduced the "net balance of invisible exports" to the United States to 5 million pounds (20 million dollars) when, according to our estimates, the "service" items in the balance of payments between the two countries has varied between 66 and 134 million dollars annually in the past six years (always in favor of the United Kingdom).

(2) It would be useful to have more information on the state of the adverse balance of the sterling area (as defined) other than the United Kingdom for which the newly mined gold will be required.

Since most of this newly mined gold will undoubtedly be sold, directly or indirectly, to the United States Government, it is pertinent to inquire why the dollar exchange proceeds cannot be spent for American agricultural products instead of diverting the British purchases of the *same* products to other countries, paying therefor with the proceeds of American purchases of newly mined gold (assuming of course that American prices are competitive world prices).

III

THE SITUATION IN AGRICULTURAL PRODUCTS

The American Government is aware of the gravity of the British foreign exchange problem and fully understands that the British Government has strong reasons for reducing imports of non-essential products in order to conserve its resources for the procurement of commodities essential to Great Britain in time of war. With respect to any particular product, the cogency of the British position is such as to command the sympathetic understanding of the American Government. Unfortunately the cumulative effects of British measures for the control of trade bring direct loss and curtailment to American agriculture, which has a longstanding interest in the maintenance of foreign markets, while fostering an ephemeral trade in certain products directly related to the prosecution of the war, and for which the demand will largely cease with the end of the war. Hence, although fully understanding the position of the British Government, this Government cannot avoid concern over the loss of export outlets for its agricultural products in the United Kingdom. This loss would furthermore appear to be in considerable part the result not of reduced total British imports and consumption of such products, but of policies of diversion from American to other sources of supply. The United States is faced with the danger that its agricultural products may be shut out of their normal market in Great Britain because the United States is in a position to supply other products which are of the utmost importance to the British Government.

Approximately 35 percent of American agricultural exports (about 50 percent, excluding cotton) normally have gone to the United Kingdom, and a considerably higher percentage in the case of a number of individual products. For example, almost half of the total of American tobacco exports and about 85 percent of our ham exports are normally sent to the United Kingdom. It appears that various measures adopted by the British Government have completely closed the British market for American products which in recent years have accounted for almost half of our agricultural exports to the United Kingdom, that the trade in a number of other products has been severely curtailed, and that the outlook for the other agricultural products is far from reassuring.

The Department is currently giving attention to the various individual agricultural and forest products discussed in the Ambassador's memorandum. It would not appear to serve any useful purpose to enter into discussion of the details of the Embassy's comments, pending the more complete and, it is to be hoped, definitive talks which will be held upon the arrival of Mr. Ashton-Gwatkin. It may be remarked in general, however, on the basis of such incomplete information as the Department has been able to obtain from London and other sources, that the outlook for American agricultural exports to the United Kingdom (with the possible exception of cotton) is decidedly uncertain, particularly with respect to tobacco, fresh fruits and pork products.

Finally, note may be taken of the Ambassador's statements that ". . . cash purchases of non-essential American agricultural products and even of those now regarded as essential, must be reduced to a minimum" (page 16), that "imperative political considerations . . .[37a] may necessitate the diversion of purchases of some agricultural products from the United States to other countries" (page 17), and that diversion of trade from the United States to other countries "is imposed on us by war necessity and by the 'cash' and 'carry' requirements placed on Great Britain for the conduct of its wartime trade with the United States" (page 17).

It is true that loans to belligerent governments are prohibited. But it may be observed that it is unjustified to conclude that this imposes trade diversion upon Great Britain and the British Empire.

(a) The memorandum claims that the sterling area has large adverse balances elsewhere for which it has to reserve the equivalent of its new gold production. Since these balances are not settled by credits

---

[37a] Omissions indicated in the original memorandum.

or even by bilateral barter, there can be no economic reason (even of a wartime character) for diverting trade in agricultural products from the United States to these other countries. In either case the balance has to be met out of British resources.

(b) It is stated that Great Britain is making loans for "imperative political considerations" to third countries and diverting trade from us in order to be repaid.

(c) It is stated that Great Britain is buying in other countries to keep them out of the German orbit or to keep goods from getting to Germany.

Actions (b) and (c) may be understandable enough for a nation at war. However, it cannot be maintained that the *diversion* is due to American legislation. Even if American loans were legal and American investors were willing to extend such credits, it would appear that the British Government would still be motivated by the same political and strategic considerations and would still be trying to divert trade in important products away from the United States. And such diversion may or may not "come to an end when the war is over". The experience of countries which have embarked upon bilateral arrangements and trade diversion under the plea of emergency needs bears witness to the fact that such systems of trade tend to create their own justification for continuance and although the "emergency" may change in nature, it seldom passes.

641.116/2642 : Telegram

The Secretary of State to the Chargé in the United Kingdom
(Johnson)

WASHINGTON, February 28, 1940—7 p. m.

373. Your 480, February 27.[38] I am appreciative of the Embassy's efforts paralleling our own to induce the British Government to resume purchases of American agricultural products. While tobacco is the most important agricultural product which has been restricted, we are continually pressing at this end for a consideration of all of our normal agricultural exports to Great Britain. I pointed out to Lothian on February 23 [39] that 50 percent of our entire agricultural exports ordinarily go to Great Britain and that at one swoop the British Government has cut off most of our agricultural exports to that country (exclusive of cotton); that this action is easily capable of starting an uprising of the farm population and the resulting arousal of nation-wide sentiment of an unfavorable and unfriendly nature; and that since the British Government is expending huge sums of dollars annually it might find it extremely important to consider the

[38] Not printed.
[39] Memorandum of conversation not printed.

salutary effect of allotting what would be almost a nominal amount of this sum for the purchase of agricultural products in this country. The Ambassador said he would continue to work to that end.

I discussed this whole question with Ambassador Kennedy in some detail while he was here, and I am sure that he will be interested in this latest conversation here.

HULL

641.116/2612½

The British Ambassador (Lothian) to the Secretary of State

MEMORANDUM

The British Ambassador appreciates the understanding shown in Mr. Cordell Hull's memorandum of February 21st, 1940, of the grave conditions with which Great Britain is confronted in financing its maximum war effort and of the reasons which compel the United Kingdom Government to reduce imports of non-essential products in order to conserve its resources for the procurement of commodities essential to Great Britain in time of war. He also fully recognizes the concern of the United States Government over the loss of export outlets for its agricultural products in the United Kingdom, and about the dislocation which may consequently be caused to American agriculture.

With reference to sections I and II of that memorandum it should be stated that the object of the Embassy memorandum of February 14th [40] was not to give an exhaustive picture, accurate in every detail, of Britain's economic position, but to set forth the main features. Whether the amount of Britain's foreign capital assets, and the amount of her adverse balance of payments, are taken at the highest or at the lowest estimates, Britain has to face the possibility that her foreign capital assets may be wholly exhausted before the war is over.

The decision which has just been taken in principle to adopt a supplementary Anglo-French programme of aeroplane purchases in the United States, costing perhaps $1,000 million for that purpose alone, brings the exhaustion of our resources measurably nearer, and shows how the scale of war requirements is capable of rising.

The amount of the capital assets and of the current balance of payments alone do not give the whole picture. There is always the possibility of the loss of foreign currency through evasion of the British regulations, and—more important—it is not known to what extent United States citizens or others will take advantage of their freedom to withdraw their balances and investments from the United Kingdom.

---

[40] Not printed.

These considerations already answer in some measure the enquiries in sections I and II of the State Department memorandum of February 21st. But some further answer to the detailed questions may still further clarify the position.

I

FOREIGN EXCHANGE RESOURCES OF THE UNITED KINGDOM

(*a*) Short-term balances are always set off, in part at least, by short-term obligations. Britain's short-term obligations to the United States at the end of August, 1939, were estimated at $67 million. Further, banking relations generally require the maintenance of certain minimum balances, so that the short-term balances referred to could not be available in full for expenditure. The passage of the Neutrality Act has caused the withdrawal by the United States of an unknown but substantial amount of short-term credit formerly available to the United Kingdom. Lastly (a special feature) the London exchange market was over-sold on United States dollars when the war broke out to the extent of $107 million, and this had to be covered shortly after by the sale of gold.

(*b*) and (*c*). It may, as suggested, be necessary at a later stage to consider the realization of British "direct" investments in the United States, and of British assets in third countries; even perhaps of British assets within the Empire. But it is impossible to say at present how far such assets may be saleable at all in the United States at proper prices, or to make any estimate of their total realizable value.

The very fact that Britain may be forced to sell such assets as these, representing in the main the results of decades of saving and enterprise, should be sufficient to show how essential it is for Britain to conserve to the utmost her resources.

The more Britain is impoverished by the war, the less will she be able after the war to maintain the import surplus which has been the counterpart of the export surplus of other countries.

It should be noted that the United States statistics certainly include, as part of United Kingdom holdings of investments and short-term balances, substantial amounts which are in fact held for the account of third parties.

It should also be noted that, since there are substantial foreign investments in the United Kingdom (including some $500 million of American investments), the net foreign income of the United Kingdom will vanish before all her foreign investments are sold.

II

BALANCE OF PAYMENTS BETWEEN THE "STERLING AREA" AND THE UNITED STATES

While the British Government must be in the best position to estimate the effect of the war on the balance of payments, it is true that the figures of necessity be liable to large margins of error in either direction. There seem, however, to be good grounds for the variations assumed from the pre-war balance of payments, and there is no reason to suppose that the estimated adverse balance of $470 million could possibly be so much as $100 or $150 million too large. It should be noted that no allowance has been made for contingencies in the form of additional purchase requirements which are bound to arise. The adoption of the new aeroplane programme alone will probably make the present estimate too small, and will seriously affect the position in the second year of war.

1 (a) and (b). The approximate accuracy of the British estimates of the dollar value of United States imports from the United Kingdom and from the rest of the sterling area during the first year of war can only be known when the respective trade returns are available. It is greatly to be hoped that the possibility indicated in the memorandum of their being substantially in excess of the estimates may be realised. These returns are of such importance to an informed consideration of the whole problem under discussion that the British Embassy would be grateful if it could be supplied month by month, if that is possible, with the earliest advance figures of both classes of imports, and at the same time with the corresponding figures of United States exports by classes of merchandise.

1 (c). The net balance of invisible exports is bound to fall very substantially owing to the effect of the war and of the Neutrality Act on American travelling abroad, (including the prohibition of travelling on belligerent ships), and apparently on British freight earnings. Other service items will also be adversely affected, though economies may be possible in certain directions.

2. The British Ambassador is not in possession of full details of the adverse balance of the sterling area with countries other than the United States. But from the information at present in his possession it appears that the only case where gold or dollars are being used in any sense to purchase agricultural products which could alternatively be purchased in the United States, is that of Turkey, where imperative political necessities arise. Apart from political necessities, it is in such cases as the hire of neutral ships, where the United States is closed as a source of supply by the Neutrality Act, that the British Government have been unable in many cases to resist the demand for payment in dollars.

Where payments are thus made in gold or dollars, they increase of course the ability of the receiving country to purchase in the United States goods which they are unable, owing to war conditions, to obtain from their usual sources. This is part of a diversion of trade in favour of the United States which is inevitably brought about by the war.

III

THE SITUATION IN AGRICULTURAL PRODUCTS

It is noted that the State Department is currently giving attention to the individual agricultural and forest products discussed in the Ambassador's memorandum of February 14th and hopes that more complete and definitive talks will be held upon the arrival of Mr. Ashton-Gwatkin. Mr. Ashton-Gwatkin, however, will not be empowered to discuss increased British purchases of agricultural products, although Viscount Halifax has telegraphed that he welcomes the opportunity for Mr. Ashton-Gwatkin to hear and report to him personally the American point of view on current trade and economic problems generally. It will rather be the joint task of Messrs. Ashton-Gwatkin and Rist to explain the reasons for which the Allied Governments are constrained to abstain from purchases in the United States other than those required to cover their minimum needs.

With regard to agricultural products in general, Lord Lothian is unable to agree with the argument in the first paragraph of III of the State Department memorandum that the loss of United States export trade to the United Kingdom is caused in considerable part by British measures for the control of trade, by policies of diversion to other sources of supply, and by the fact that the United States is in a position to supply other products which are necessary to the British Government for the purposes of the war. In his opinion the reasons are those set out at length in the Embassy memorandum of February 14th, which are briefly that British consumption of and dollar expenditure on non-essential agricultural products must be increasingly restricted as an imperative condition of financing the war until it reaches a successful conclusion. There can be no ground for suggesting that if the United States had not been in a position to supply other products which are of the utmost importance to the British Government, the purchases of these non-essential agricultural products would not have been restricted and these losses would not have occurred.

Lord Lothian fully realises Mr. Cordell Hull's apprehension in regard to diversion of certain United Kingdom agricultural imports from the United States to other countries but such diversion is imposed by imperative political considerations and war necessity. The trade value of the reduction in United Kingdom imports from the United States of agricultural products due to diversion arising from these political considerations is small in comparison with the reduction due to the reasons given in the preceding paragraph.

The loss to American agriculture is likely to be heaviest in exports of the non-essential products referred to in the second and third paragraphs but these include tobacco and it would be premature to assume that the discussions and consultations referred to in the Embassy memorandum of February 14th will fail to produce any alleviation of this exceptional problem.

Against the loss of exports of these agricultural commodities should be considered the maintenance and even increase of others, also the indirect benefit of the stimulation of domestic consumption of all farm products brought about by heavily increased British purchases of industrial products and aircraft and other military supplies. This indirect benefit is bound to become an increasingly important factor as these purchases expand under the programmes which are contemplated. Public speakers of all shades of political opinion, including spokesmen for the trade agreements programme, have constantly emphasized the benefit to agriculture of increased industrial production.

The reference in the Embassy memorandum of February 14th to the "cash" and "carry" requirements of the Neutrality Act for the conduct of British wartime trade with the United States was intended to apply not only to the relatively small volume of imports diverted but also to the whole volume of imports from the United States of agricultural and other products which must necessarily be restricted for economic reasons flowing from the "cash" requirement. That necessity was recognized in the statement of the Secretary of Agriculture made to the House Committee on Agriculture on February 15th, 1940, that for farm products Great Britain and France must turn wherever possible to countries other than the United States where they can acquire these commodities "in exchange for their own goods or buy them with sterling or on credit."

The reference to the "carry" requirement is that United States ships are prohibited from carrying agricultural or any United States products purchased by the United Kingdom and that the United Kingdom is compelled to provide for their transport in British or other ships, under the limitation imposed on shipping by German submarine, mine, and aerial attack. The loss of exports to the United Kingdom of United States lumber and cotton which has been and may be increasingly occasioned by this shipping situation will no doubt be made apparent in the detailed examination of individual products which the State Department has undertaken. Moreover, although not relevant to this requirement, the disabilities placed on British ships as a result of Section 2, subsections (c), (g) and (l) of the Neutrality

Act, as regards the shipment of cargoes from the United States to belligerent territories in the "(g) areas", result in loss of earnings which would have contributed to British dollar resources for purchases in the United States, in the perhaps permanent loss of established British shipping connections, and to strong feeling in British shipping and other circles.

Lord Lothian fully realises the force of the last sentence of Mr. Cordell Hull's memorandum and can only draw his attention to the Prime Minister's speech of January 31st last,[41] expressing the hopes and intentions of His Majesty's Government in regard to multilateral trade after the war. But the probability of its being possible to return to multilateral trade will obviously depend upon the duration and the result of the war.

IV

The broad position would seem to Lord Lothian to be as follows:—

1) As a result of the war United Kingdom purchases in the United States will increase very largely. The pre-war average was $460 million a year. Present estimates are that purchases will amount to at least $720 million in the first year of the war, and well over $2,000 millions in the first two years of the war. These are only minimum figures; substantial new requirements are bound constantly to arise and are already arising. The increase in purchases will be represented in the main by aircraft, engineering products and munitions. There will be no equivalent increase in United States purchases of British goods.

2) There will be a reduction in the purchase of agricultural products and in particular products this reduction may be a considerable portion of the normal pre-war export. The total value of agricultural and lumber purchases by the United Kingdom in the first year of war, based on the estimates communicated to the State Department, seems likely to be more than 80 per cent of a five-year average of pre-war United States exports to the United Kingdom. If so, the reduction in agricultural purchases will be of the order of $55 million per annum as against the increased purchases of $250 million in the first year of the war and $1,500 million in the second, as above, for other commodities. There will be in addition a substantial indirect benefit to agriculture from the increase in domestic purchasing power in the United States as a result of the vast increase in British industrial purchases in the United States.

3) A reduction in the purchase of aircraft, engineering supplies and munitions would not have the effect of increasing British pur-

---

[41] For text of speech, see the London *Times*, February 1, 1940, p. 10.

chases of agricultural products for the reason that the reduction in such purchases is in the main the consequence of the need for rationing and the reduction of consumption in Great Britain, among other domestic measures regarded as necessary for winning the war and to the necessity for purchasing some of these products in other countries for imperative political reasons, e. g. Turkish and Greek tobacco. The only result of cutting down British engineering and munitions purchases would be to run the risk of prolonging the war or even possibly of losing it.

4) If the war goes on for much more than two years the United Kingdom will have transferred to the United States all of its easily negotiable dollar securities, most of its gold and (if the necessity arises which is suggested on page 2 of the State Department Memorandum) a part at least of its "direct" investments in the United States and of its assets in other countries outside the United Kingdom. A large part of British foreign investments and foreign income will thus be lost, and the consuming power of the British population, and thus their ability to purchase American agricultural products, will be correspondingly reduced.

WASHINGTON, March 1, 1940.

641.006/526 : Telegram

The Ambassador in the United Kingdom (Kennedy) to the Secretary of State

LONDON, March 9, 1940.
[Received March 9—11 : 50 a. m.]

606. The Board of Trade today informed the Embassy that consideration is being given to the introduction of some form of restriction upon imports, or at least purchase, of all products the importation of which is not yet restricted or controlled; and that, in the meantime, it has become necessary to take the action in regard to canned fruits indicated in the following *aide-mémoire:*

Tinned and bottled fruit is being imported and bought [*brought?*] forward in such large quantities that it has become necessary to take immediate measures to control the trade. An order will accordingly be made next week (probably on Thursday) with effect from 19th March adding tinned and bottled fruit to the list of goods which may not be imported except under license meanwhile, in order to check the flow of imports, which has recently become quite abnormal, the banks will, as from Monday 11th March, refuse to open any new credits and will refuse all transfers of currency outside the sterling area in respect of new purchases which are not yet on the water."

The Embassy pointed out that the proposed restriction would apparently differ from previous orders in permitting the importation without license only of goods actually afloat on the specified date, whereas hitherto goods actually rolling have been admitted without license. The Board of Trade official thought that it would be best to take up cases of goods shipped but not yet afloat if and when they arise; but, when recent difficulties of this nature with other commodities were pointed out, he did not exclude the possibility that the formal order when issued would be in the form hitherto followed.

He emphasized that the recent volume of purchases had been of very abnormal proportions, and that stocks on hand and supplies recently acquired were adequate to meet needs for a considerable period. This did not mean, however, that purchases were being suspended entirely; but that licenses would, in his opinion, probably be granted when the need again arose.

When questioned, he also held out the possibility that some special consideration might be given to goods packed specially for this market.

KENNEDY

641.006/543 : Telegram

The Ambassador in the United Kingdom (Kennedy) to the Secretary of State

LONDON, March 18, 1940—2 p. m.
[Received March 18—9 : 18 a. m.]

666. Embassy's 606, 9th (opening sentence of which refers to all *food* products not *all* products).

Board of Trade today advised that there would be announced tomorrow March 19 a general order prohibiting importation except under license of all foodstuffs not already subject to license except wines and spirits, fresh and cured fish and live animals. Open general licenses will be issued for time being in respect of certain foodstuffs which are not now subject to Ministry of Food control. The order will be published March 21 and will apply to goods despatched after March 20 and imported after March 27.

KENNEDY

641.116/2634a : Telegram

The Secretary of State to the Ambassador in the United Kingdom (Kennedy)

WASHINGTON, March 18, 1940—5 p. m.

511. Announcement of British restrictions on canned fruit resulted in widespread distorted press comment. For your information, the British Embassy and Ashton-Gwatkin are disturbed by the reaction

and telegraphed London on Saturday, strongly advising against the issuance of any other such dramatic announcement. The effects of such restrictions are extremely serious in themselves. Moreover, the manner in which they have been announced has given rise to misinterpretations and unnecessary misunderstandings which the British themselves, in their own interest, should seek to avoid.

HULL

641.006/543 : Telegram

The Secretary of State to the Ambassador in the United Kingdom (Kennedy)

WASHINGTON, March 18, 1940—6 p. m.

512. Your 666, March 18. Confirming Mr. Grady's [42] telephone conversation of today with the Ambassador,[43] please urge strongly a reconsideration of impending order to license imports of all foodstuffs and telegraph decision of British authorities.

HULL

641.006/576

The British Ambassador (Lothian) to the Secretary of State

WASHINGTON, March 19, 1940.

MY DEAR MR. SECRETARY: After the conversation which Mr. Grady had with Mr. Ashton-Gwatkin and Sir Owen Chalkley on Saturday last,[44] I sent a telegram to my Government pressing strongly for postponement of any action affecting imports from the United States.

I have received this morning a telegram from Viscount Halifax in which he much regrets that my telegram was not received until after an announcement had been made to the United Kingdom press for publication in to-day's papers of the issue of a General Order placing under licence the importation of all foodstuffs not already subject to licence.

Viscount Halifax asks me to send you a personal message of his deep regret at this mischance and to express his hope that it will not prejudice the renewal of the Trade Agreements Act.[45]

I am informed that a statement in explanation of the new General Order is being handed to American correspondents in London to the effect that it is more in the nature of a consolidation than an extension of existing restrictions and will not affect any items of outstanding importance to the United States. Some 90 percent of im-

---

[42] Henry F. Grady, Assistant Secretary of State.
[43] No record of this conversation has been found in Department files.
[44] March 16; no record of conversation has been found in Department files.
[45] Trade Agreements Act of June 12, 1934, extended by Joint Resolution of Congress, approved April 12, 1940; 48 Stat. 943 and 54 Stat. 107.

ports of foodstuffs from the United States are already subject to licence and the value of imports covered by the new Order is less than 10 percent. The statement concludes with a reference to relevant extracts from the speech made by the Prime Minister on January 31st when he referred to the necessity of concentrating our dollar resources upon essential requirements and to our intention to return to the most-favoured-nation principle on the conclusion of the war.

Believe me [etc.]   LOTHIAN

641.006/546 : Telegram

The Ambassador in the United Kingdom (Kennedy) to the Secretary of State

LONDON, March 19, 1940—1 p. m.
[Received March 19—7 : 50 a. m.]

683. Your 514, March 18, 7 p. m.[47] Following is text:

Steps are to be taken to unify the control of the trade in imported foodstuffs. The more important foodstuffs are already controlled by the Ministry of Food, and some, but not all of these, can only be imported under a Board of Trade import license; other foodstuffs require an import license but are not at present controlled by the Ministry; and there are certain foodstuffs which have not hitherto been subject to any control at all.

It has now been decided that the Ministry of Food shall take control over foodstuffs generally, and, in order to complete the scope of the control, a general order is being made by the Board of Trade and will be published on Thursday, March 21, prohibiting the imports of all foodstuffs, including feeding stuffs for animals, except under license. The only exceptions from the order are wines and spirits, fresh and cured fish, and live animals.

The order will apply to all foodstuffs, not already subject to license, which are despatched after March 20 and arrive in this country after March 27. Open general licenses will be issued permitting, until further notice, the importation of consignments of the following classes foodstuffs without separate licenses.

From all sources: cod liver oil; all cheese except cheddar, cheshire, gouda, and edam types; vegetables in salt or brine; dried vegetables; bananas; tomatoes; Barcelona nuts; hazel nuts; Brazil nuts, and chestnuts; vinegar; arrowroot; tapioca, cassava, mandioca; meat extracts and essences; malt extracts; isinglass and agar-agar; yeast.

From British countries: fresh fruit and nuts used as fruit, fruit juices, and crystallized fruit; fruit pectin; jams and marmalade; fresh vegetables; chutney; curry powder; honey; biscuits; peel, candied or drained; pepper; shell fish, fresh.

---

[47] Not printed; it requested that text of British press release on imposition of import licenses for foodstuffs be sent the Department (641.006/545).

All foodstuffs can be imported from Eire without separate licences except meat (including bacon and sausages), butter, condensed milk and milk powder, cream, margarine, lard and imitation lard.

The existing open general licences for the importation of goods from France, Algeria, and Tunis will remain in force. Importers are warned that impending shipments of all foodstuffs not covered by these open general licences should be cancelled immediately or postponed until an import licence has been obtained; applications for import licences should be addressed in future to the Ministry of Food in respect of all foodstuffs, except the following: coffee; chicory; biscuits; nuts used as fruit; caviare; cider and perry; fruit juices; table waters; spices, including pepper and liquorice. Applications in respect of these foodstuffs should be addressed to the Import Licensing Department, Board of Trade.

KENNEDY

641.006/547 : Telegram

The Ambassador in the United Kingdom (Kennedy) to the Secretary of State

LONDON, March 19, 1940—8 p. m.
[Received March 19—3 p. m.]

692. Department's 512, March 18 and Embassy's 682, March 18, 7 p. m.[48] Further energetic representations have been made in appropriate quarters today, and it is believed that they gained some appreciation of the unfavorable reception recent British import orders have had in the United States. Board of Trade advises tonight that supplementary statement has been prepared for release by Embassy in Washington which they expect to cable immediately.

KENNEDY

641.006/547 : Telegram

The Secretary of State to the Ambassador in the United Kingdom (Kennedy)

WASHINGTON, March 20, 1940—noon.

526. Your 692, March 19. Appreciate your continuance of vigorous representations. Please urge with utmost vigor that order licensing foodstuffs to be issued tomorrow follows the form of the press release issued Monday[49] and does not follow the form previously employed of lists in Schedules I and II. See the Prime Minister regarding this if necessary.

HULL

[48] Latter not printed.
[49] March 18.

641.006/548 : Telegram

The Ambassador in the United Kingdom (Kennedy) to the Secretary of State

LONDON, March 20, 1940—10 a. m. [*p. m.?*]
[Received 5 : 02 p. m.]

703. Your 526, March 20, noon. Went to work immediately on your instructions. I have just received word from Board of Trade that "there was only one form which the order could legally take so that I fear it is impossible for us to meet the suggestion of the Secretary of State". They have sent me copy of order in the form in which it is being made and also a copy of a notice to importers. This notice and order have already been made. I realize how important this is but it has been made clear to me that while they recognize the importance of doing what you suggest, that the law makes it impossible for them to do so. If you have any suggestion at all let me have it tonight and I will be on it the first thing in the morning. The only place I get cooperation in this particular thing is in conversation.

KENNEDY

641.116/2641

Memorandum of Conversation, by the Secretary of State

[WASHINGTON,] March 20, 1940.

The British Ambassador called at my request. Without preliminaries I proceeded to say that the manner in which his Government, whatever might be its intention, is dramatizing the restrictions it has placed and is placing on American exports of agricultural products is a matter of very great concern to this Government. I remarked that those who put out the publicity on this subject seemed to do so fairly frequently and to dramatize to an increasing extent the detailed commodities comprised in the restrictions. Furthermore, the definite impression created in the United States by this publicity is that an absolute embargo continuing indefinitely is being imposed by Great Britain on all or virtually all American agricultural exports to Great Britain, with each commodity listed separately and conspicuously. I then said that if the British officials would announce instead that they were imposing certain restrictions on some of the agricultural imports from the United States, with the view not of prohibiting all imports indefinitely, but with the idea of enabling the British Government to restrict the amount of imports of a given commodity or commodities to conform to the ability of Great Britain, by reason of war conditions, to make purchases of such agricultural products from the United States; and that the British Government expects from time to time in the future to be in the market for

American agricultural products to the extent and in the light of the foregoing. I elaborated to some extent regarding the danger and the injury which is threatening his own country by this sort of extremely hurtful publicity for which there is absolutely no excuse. The Ambassador agreed to everything I said in this connection and seemed very much interested and concerned.

The Ambassador wrote down the substance of my remarks and said that he would be glad to return at once to his Embassy and telephone to the appropriate official in London in an earnest effort to have the publicity situation dealt with in accordance with my suggestion. He said it would be necessary for him to leave at once to enable him to get in touch with the appropriate official in London before night and before it was too late to deal with tomorrow's publicity.

One or two hours later I received a message from the British Embassy to the effect that the Ambassador had contacted the proper official and hoped that he had accomplished his purpose in calling him.[50]

C[ORDELL] H[ULL]

641.116/2644

Memorandum of Conversation, by the Secretary of State

[WASHINGTON,] March 22, 1940.

The Ambassador agreed that the British Government should give out the statement accompanying his letter to me of yesterday's date [51] explaining the British license policy and the less injurious effects that such policy would have on our exports of agricultural products than an absolute embargo with the resulting harmful impression created in this country. I readily agreed with him that this statement to be most effective should be put out at London rather than by the British Embassy in Washington.

641.116/2671 : Telegram

The Ambassador in the United Kingdom (Kennedy) to the Secretary of State

LONDON, April 22, 1940.
[Received April 22—9 : 35 a. m.]

1019. Referring to Department's instruction 1276, March 14, 1940,[52] regarding American Tobacco Company, matter has been thoroughly discussed with Board of Trade which has communicated informally

[50] On the afternoon of March 20 the Marquess of Lothian informed the Secretary of State that he had just received a telegram from Lord Halifax stating that the British Government was issuing a statement to the press somewhat along the lines here suggested (641.116/2646).
[51] Letter dated March 20, received in the Department March 21, not printed.
[52] Not printed.

after due consideration its refusal to allow tobacco imports on credit, basing the decision on grounds which it is believed may be of immediate interest to the Department. Board states

"There are two main reasons for this refusal. The first is that the Treasury do not regard a loan from an associated company as justifying the issue of a license to import which would not otherwise have been granted. As you know, I think, the Import Licensing Department have had many similar proposals made to them on other products and all have been turned down. In the second place you will I am sure appreciate that it would be very difficult indeed for us to maintain a position in which this one American Company was able to get supplies of tobacco while all British companies were precluded from doing so."

Board still considering permit for one previous transaction. Despatch follows.[53] I personally discussed this whole matter with Sir William Brown[54] and he told me that before any decision would be made it would be taken up with Duncan, President Board of Trade. There are some angles of this situation that seem to me quite serious. When Simon originally told me they were cutting out tobacco purchases in order to conserve sterling he made it clear that it certainly was not done with the idea of hurting American tobacco growing. Now here is an opportunity to buy tobacco without losing sterling and I am not at all sure this refusal may not encourage the belief that the British want to do away with American tobacco buying. Of course there is also the danger that some people may believe that purchases on credit that might be made from American companies are being held off to increase the pressure on the broad question of credit for all purchases.

KENNEDY

641.116/2671 : Telegram

The Secretary of State to the Ambassador in the United Kingdom
(Kennedy)

WASHINGTON, April 25, 1940—2 p. m.

755. Your 1019 April 22 has been greatly appreciated. The Board of Trade has apparently misunderstood the Department's motive in supporting this single application for an import license. Our representations did not purport to secure for the American subsidiary an advantage over the British companies, but rather to remedy the disadvantage it suffers relative to British companies in the matter of supply position. That is all we ask in this particular case and we are indifferent as to whether the tobacco is imported on credit (the

---

[53] No. 5337, June 4, not printed.
[54] Member of British Board of Trade.

company's own suggestion) or on a license involving an exchange transaction. Department's Instruction 1344, April 18,[55] contains statement by the company indicating aggravation of its stock shortage. Please press the matter along the foregoing lines.

HULL

611.4131/2487a

The Department of State to the British Embassy

MEMORANDUM

Products on which the United Kingdom granted concessions in the trade agreement with the United States [56] and which are now subject to United Kingdom wartime import restrictions are set forth in the attached list.[55] These products account for approximately 90 percent of the value of the American export trade covered by Schedule I of the agreement. Trade-agreement commodities not as yet subject to United Kingdom restrictions represent a normal annual trade of only $30,000,000 and approximately one-third of this total is accounted for by raw fur skins.

The restrictions upon American agricultural products included in the trade agreement are particularly severe. There is official information that no licenses are being issued at present for a number of such products which normally account for about one-half of our agricultural export trade with the United Kingdom. American agricultural products thus prohibited were valued at $113,000,000 in 1936. As regards other agricultural-agreement products subject to licenses, no licenses are being issued for several other important products, according to unofficial information, and restrictions on most of the other items appear to be extremely severe.

To summarize, it appears accurate to state that all agricultural products included in the trade agreement, with the exception of cotton and a few relatively minor items, are either prohibited by British regulations or subjected to restrictive measures so severe as to amount, for practical purposes, to prohibitions. Furthermore, the outlook for cotton, which is subject to indirect United Kingdom import regulations through the operation of the Commodity Control, and the Ministry of Shipping, is not entirely reassuring.

The seriousness of the effect of these restrictions upon the trade agreement and upon American agriculture is even more apparent when it is recalled that approximately two-thirds of the American

---

[55] Not printed.
[56] See *Foreign Relations*, 1938, vol. II, pp. 1 ff. For text of agreement, signed November 17, 1938, see Department of State Executive Agreement Series No. 164, or 54 Stat. 1897.

trade covered by the agreement is accounted for by agricultural products and that approximately 95 percent of American agricultural exports to the United Kingdom, normally our overwhelmingly most important export market for agricultural products, are included in the trade agreement.

As regards American non-agricultural products included in the trade agreement, no British import licenses are being issued for certain of these commodities which accounted for trade valued at about $9,000,000 in 1936. Licenses are also required for other non-agricultural products included in the trade agreement which represented American export trade to the United Kingdom valued at about $49,000,000 in 1936, and it is understood that in most instances the operation of the licensing system is already causing severe curtailment of trade. In other words, almost 75 percent of the American non-agricultural trade—valued at approximately $58,000,000 in 1936—on which the United Kingdom made concessions in the agreement is subject to the British import-license system. It is noted that a number of highly important products, from the American export point of view, are subject to these prohibitions and restrictions, e. g. automobiles, lumber and lumber products, certain office machinery, and canned salmon.

Other wartime economic measures, in addition to the import prohibitions and restrictions, are adversely affecting American trade.

It is noted that the British arrangement to purchase Turkish tobacco, an arrangement covering a twenty-year period, is prejudicial to the interests of American tobacco producers and exporters and incompatible with the provisions of the trade agreement.

In addition to the restrictions on imports into the United Kingdom, there are also severe restrictions on imports from the United States into the other British territories included within the scope of the trade agreement.

In view of the sharp curtailment of American exports to the United Kingdom and the British colonies of products included in the trade agreement, and the depreciation of British currency, the maintenance of the trade agreement is becoming increasingly difficult.

WASHINGTON, May 4, 1940.

641.116/2728

The British Ambassador (Lothian) to the Secretary of State

The British Ambassador wishes to refer to his communication to the State Department of May 24, 1940, [58] on the subject of the importation of cotton into the United Kingdom.

---

[58] Not printed.

The British Government have now reviewed their programme of purchases from the United States during the second year of war in the light of their dollar resources. In the case of cotton they have had to reach the conclusion that, having regard to existing stocks in the United Kingdom and to the balance of the cotton, estimated at 77,000 tons, which remains to be shipped during the coming year under the cotton-rubber exchange agreement, their further commercial purchases of United States cotton during the 12 months ending August 31, 1941, will not exceed 7,000 tons (or say 30,000 bales) for which licences have already been issued for shipment in September and 3,000 tons (or say 15,000 bales) for which it is proposed to issue licences for shipment in October, with the addition of any forward contracts which it may prove impossible to cancel.

The United States Government will realise that the British Government must take any step open to them to conserve their dollar resources to pay for their essential war requirements and they regret that the existing exchange position does not permit them to see any possibility of exceeding these estimates.

With regard to purchases from other countries, it is contemplated that Brazilian cotton will be purchased at about the pre-war average (50,000 tons) and that certain purchases will be made of other growths of American-type cotton from the African colonies, especially from the Belgian Congo, which are necessary to support belligerent Allied countries and do not involve exchange difficulties.

WASHINGTON, September 18, 1940.

641.116/2736

The British Embassy to the Department of State

Reference is made to the British Ambassador's communication to the State Department of September 18th, 1940, on the subject of importation of cotton into the United Kingdom.

The British Government will make no announcement about their further purchase programme of United States cotton until after the end of October. Nevertheless importers in the United Kingdom will have to be informed in accordance with the usual practice how much cotton they will be allowed to import during October. It is proposed to announce that shipping space in October will be provided for 15,000 bales of American cotton and, later, that similar provision will be made in November. This would cover the 15,000 bales mentioned in paragraph 2 of the earlier communication referred to and 14,000 bales for which licences were issued for shipment in June, July and August but for which shipping space in practice could not be found.

The proposals to subject to licensing the use of all foreign cotton will have to be announced very shortly and importers may infer that further restrictions of imports from the United States may be contemplated, but as explained above no announcement to this effect will be made in the next few weeks.

WASHINGTON, September 27, 1940.

REPRESENTATIONS REGARDING BRITISH IMPORT AND EXCHANGE RESTRICTIONS IN KENYA COLONY AND THE MANDATED TERRITORY OF TANGANYIKA IN VIOLATION OF AMERICAN TREATY RIGHTS [59]

648T.006/12 : Telegram

The Secretary of State to the Chargé in the United Kingdom
(Johnson)

WASHINGTON, January 6, 1940—4 p. m.

38. Department's mail instruction 1134 December 26 [60] with regard to Kenya Colony regulations effective November 15, 1939, and American commercial rights in that colony.

The Japanese Embassy has made inquiry of us concerning this subject and we are informing the Japanese Embassy that you have been instructed to bring the matter appropriately to the attention of the British Government. When you make the approach to British officials contemplated in the final paragraph of the Department's instruction of December 26 the Department suggests that you inform those officials orally of the Japanese approach to us and of our reply.

HULL

648T.116/8

The Chargé in the United Kingdom (Johnson) to the Secretary of State

No. 4392   LONDON, January 17, 1940.
                                          [Received February 5.]

SIR: Referring to the Department's instruction No. 1134 of December 26, 1939 [60] (File No. 648T.006/12) directing this Mission to bring to the attention of the appropriate British authorities certain considerations respecting American commercial rights in Kenya and other East African areas and the effect thereon of recent British import licensing and exchange control measures, I have the honor

---

[59] Continued from *Foreign Relations*, 1939, vol. II, pp. 320–324.
[60] Not printed.

to report that the subject was yesterday discussed with Mr. Nigel B. Ronald, Chief of the General Department of the British Foreign Office. There was also left with him a copy of the enclosed *aide-mémoire*. At the same time he was informed of the inquiry made by the Japanese Embassy in Washington and of the Department's reply to that Mission.[61]

Mr. Ronald said that he was unable at the moment to indicate the precise position but that the general problem of the control of imports in the British colonies and mandates was being given active consideration at this time. The Japanese Government, he said, had approached the British Government on the subject, as he recalled, about the end of November. The Italian Government had also touched on the matter.

Speaking informally, Mr. Ronald said that the problem was one of the availability of exchange. The relative position of exports and imports and the resultant excess of exchange or the lack of it necessarily had an influence. With Great Britain engaged in a life and death struggle, it was necessarily obliged to use its exchange resources as effectively as it could. To his inquiry as to the American attitude the reply was made that in the past the United States Government had on a number of occasions strongly urged the view that measures rendering access to markets contingent on the relative position of bilateral trade balances were discriminatory.

Mr. Ronald indicated that as soon as the study now being made of the general question brought up in the Embassy's *aide-mémoire* had progressed to a conclusion, the Foreign Office would be glad to give the Embassy a considered answer.

Respectfully yours,   HERSCHEL V. JOHNSON

[Enclosure]

The American Embassy to the British Foreign Office

AIDE-MÉMOIRE

The attention of the United States Department of State in Washington has been called to the entry into effect on November 15, 1939 of a system of licensing and control of imports in the Colony of Kenya, British East Africa, under which licenses and foreign exchange permits are required, with certain exceptions, for all American products entering the colony. Essentially the same type of import and exchange control is understood to have been introduced in all the territories of British East Africa. It is reported, moreover, that applications to import American products are being disapproved in the

---

[61] For text of the inquiry from the Japanese Embassy, dated November 25, 1939, see *Foreign Relations*, 1939, vol. II, p. 320 ; no record of reply found in Department files.

majority of cases, while those applications which are approved encounter considerable delay.

The Governments of Great Britain and the United States, it will be recalled, are among the signatories to the Congo Basin Convention signed at St. Germain-en-Laye on September 10, 1919,[63] Article 2 of which provides that merchandise belonging to nationals of the Signatory Powers shall have free access to the interior of a specific region in Africa and that no differential treatment shall be imposed on such merchandise on importation or exportation. The import permit requirements and exchange control which have been established in the specified region, apparently without the consent of the Signatory Powers to the St. Germain-en-Laye Convention, not only seem to overlook the right of free access but to involve discriminatory treatment of American goods. These regulations are therefore, in the opinion of the Department, clearly inconsistent with the provisions of Article 2 mentioned above.

It is also the opinion of the Department of State that, in so far as the mandated territory of Tanganyika is concerned, the new regulations are inconsistent with the provisions of Article 7 of the Mandate, to the benefits of which the United States and its nationals are entitled under the terms of the American-British Convention signed at London on February 10, 1925.[64] The Department is now studying the effect of recent measures taken by the British authorities in other British territories, including those under British mandate, in Africa and in western Asia, and may wish to address a communication on that subject to the British Government at a later date.

Meanwhile the United States Government confidently expects that the British Government will recognize the right of American merchandise to enter British East Africa freely and without discriminatory treatment under the Congo Basin Convention, and, in view of the serious adverse effect which the regulations may be expected to have on American trade, that appropriate steps will be promptly taken to this end.

LONDON, January 16, 1940.

648T.006/17

The Secretary of State to the Consul at Nairobi (*Smith*)

WASHINGTON, March 13, 1940.

SIR: The receipt is acknowledged of your despatch no. 338 of December 20, 1939,[65] setting forth your conversation with the Acting

[63] *Foreign Relations*, 1928, vol. I, p. 437.
[64] *Ibid.*, 1925, vol. II, p. 203.
[65] *Ibid.*, 1939, vol. II, p. 323.

Governor in regard to the possible contravention of certain provisions of the Treaty of Saint-Germain of September 10, 1919 by the system of licensing and control of imports recently established in British East Africa. In this connection there is enclosed for your information a copy of an instruction addressed to the American Chargé d'Affaires at London on December 26, 1939.[66] It will be observed from that instruction that it is the opinion of this Government that the measures recently introduced into British East Africa constitute not only a violation of the pertinent provisions of the Treaty of Saint-Germain but also, in the case of the mandated territory of Tanganyika, a violation of certain provisions of the American-British Convention of February 10, 1925, concerning the rights of the United States and its nationals in East Africa.

In conclusion, the Department cannot agree with the remarks in the penultimate paragraph of your despatch under reference to the effect that "the question of the infraction of the Congo Basin treaties was of little importance". This Government has made clear in numerous statements published during the past few years that it attaches the highest importance to the sanctity of treaties and that violations of treaty rights wherever they occur tend to spread still further the forces of disorder.

Very truly yours,   For the Secretary of State:
                                          HENRY F. GRADY

648T.006/21 : Telegram

The Ambassador in the United Kingdom (Kennedy) to the Secretary of State

LONDON, April 9, 1940.
[Received April 9—11 : 47 a. m.]

883. Your 1638, December 19, 7 p. m.[67] and your mail instruction 1134, December 26 [66] regarding exchange control and import license system in Palestine, other British Mandates and British Territories within the Congo Basin. A lengthy note today received from Foreign Office [68] is being forwarded by pouch leaving April 11.

KENNEDY

---

[66] Not printed.
[67] *Foreign Relations*, 1939, vol. IV, p. 815.
[68] Note of April 8 (see especially par. 10), from the British Secretary of State for Foreign Affairs to the American Ambassador, p. 859.

REPRESENTATIONS REGARDING MONOPOLY FEATURES OF BRITISH COCOA CONTROL SCHEME FOR BRITISH WEST AFRICA

611.48N16/70 : Telegram

The Ambassador in the United Kingdom (Kennedy) to the Secretary of State

LONDON, November 16, 1939—7 p. m.
[Received November 16—1 : 20 p. m.]

2379. The Colonial Office has announced that the British Government is to purchase as a war measure the whole British West African cocoa crop for 1939/40. The prices to producers will be on a basis of 9 shillings per load for Gold Coast fermented and 16 pounds 10 shillings per ton for Nigerian f. a. q. cocoa ex scale port of shipment. The crop will be handled by shippers already established in the trade who will act as agents for the Government, purchases by each shipper to be allocated mainly on a quota system based on purchases in the last three seasons or in the case of smaller shippers in the last season only. Distribution and sales will be under the direction of the Ministry of Food with assistance of a Trade Advisory Committee and will be handled through existing trade channels. Am informed by Colonial Office that the Government purchasing scheme is not the result of any shortage of cocoa actual or prospective but on the contrary is intended to meet a condition of relative overproduction in relation to reduced demand arising from the war situation since the German market which absorbed 100,000 tons last season is now closed and the nearby neutral markets will have to be carefully rationed to prevent supplies going to Germany. Colonial Office states that while prices to consumers have not yet been definitely fixed it is expected that they will be maintained at approximately current levels and that there will be ample supplies available for the American market. The Colonial Office appears desirous of reassuring the American Government and American consumers that there is no intention of profiteering in this commodity or of restricting supplies. Regret was also expressed that it had not been found possible to proceed with the purchasing scheme proposed recently by Rockwood and Company as it had been found necessary to restrict distribution to organizations already established in the trade in line with general Government policy in the handling of essential commodities.

KENNEDY

611.48N16/70 : Telegram

The Acting Secretary of State to the Ambassador in the United Kingdom (Kennedy)

WASHINGTON, November 21, 1939.

1463. Your 2379, November 16, 7 p. m. Since the Department has been kept fully informed regarding the lengths to which the British cocoa trading firms have gone, including pressure on Government, in an effort to sabotage the legitimate cocoa buying scheme of Rockwood and Company, it is not surprising to learn that participation in the new Government program is limited to established shippers. It is appreciated that the Government would wish to bring its new plan into operation with the least possible maladjustment, and that it may therefore seem easier to use only the established concerns. The effect of the decision in the case of the cocoa scheme, however, will be to strengthen the monopoly control of the entrenched interests and to close the West African cocoa trade to American participation in spite of the very large amount of West African cocoa taken by American consumers.

In view of the progress made by British governmental agencies during the past year or so in the study of the cocoa marketing situation in the Gold Coast and Nigeria, and of the well-advanced plans for direct American purchasing in those areas, the Department desires you to press strongly at the Foreign Office for a reconsideration of this feature of the British Government scheme, unless in your opinion there is clear evidence that this feature of the scheme is essential as a war measure and that the decision has been reached on sound grounds and quite apart from considerations arising out of pressure exerted by the established British cocoa shipping organizations.

It is believed that the Government scheme would not be less effective if it should provide for the participation of American concerns in cases where such concerns are able to satisfy the British authorities that they would cooperate fully in the scheme and would efficiently carry out the functions to be assumed by them. If the British Government desires, as indicated in your telegram, to reassure this Government and American consumers that there is no intention of profiteering in cocoa or in restricting supplies, then it should welcome the direct participation of one or more responsible American concerns in the present scheme, thus indicating that Government policy respecting cocoa is not influenced unduly by the established British traders. It is recalled that before the British trading companies opened up their campaign of opposition to the Rockwood plan, the responsible British authorities, both in London and in Lagos and Accra, encouraged the representatives of interested American concerns to believe that the British Government would welcome American participation in this trade.

There is of course some element of choice in the market as between West African cocoa and cocoa from other sources, and no doubt American consumers will be more inclined to maintain or increase their purchases of West African if they have evidence that the virtual monopoly maintained by British trading houses up to the present is not to be strengthened and perpetuated by Government regulations.

Please report the results of your representations by telegraph.

WELLES

611.48N16/76 : Telegram

The Chargé in the United Kingdom (Johnson) to the Secretary of State

LONDON, December 12, 1939—10 p. m.
[Received December 13—12 : 14 a. m.]

2605. Department's 1587, December 11, 7 p. m. [70] Immediately upon receipt of the Department's 1463, November 21, an officer of the Embassy discussed the subject matter informally but fully with the appropriate official of the Colonial Office. The reasons assigned for the decision to limit the operation of the Government cocoa control scheme to established companies were essentially the following:

1. The full cooperation of the trade which was considered essential for the proper functioning of the control could be obtained only on condition that no new companies were permitted to participate.

2. The only practicable basis for allocation of the controlled trade was past performance which it was claimed automatically excluded Rockwood and Company for the duration of the control.

3. The policy of limiting participation in Government control schemes to existing trade channels was uniform in all controlled trades and to make an exception in the case of cocoa would probably lead to difficulties in other trades as well.

4. There were other claimants including certain native groups and London brokers who were also eliminated from participation in the controlled trade and who would be more difficult to deal with if an exception were to be made for Rockwood or other American concern.

Regret was again expressed on behalf of the Colonial Office at the apparent necessity for excluding Rockwood from direct participation, especially in view of the encouragement given earlier to Rockwood's proposals, and an impression was received that the principal reason for this exclusion was the Colonial Office view that the established companies would not cooperate in the proper functioning of the control scheme on any other basis.

It was intimated nevertheless that if the United States Government felt strongly in the matter it might be possible to give the situation

[70] Not printed.

further consideration. However as other Government departments including the Treasury and the Ministry of Food were now concerned it would not be practicable to deal with the question informally through the Colonial Office but that it would need to be taken up with the Foreign Office. This has accordingly been done and we are pressing for an early decision.

JOHNSON

611.48N16/70 : Telegram

The Secretary of State to the Chargé in the United Kingdom (Johnson)

WASHINGTON, December 13, 1939—5 p. m.

1596. Department's 1463, November 21. In view of the fact that buying season for West African cocoa will be over within a few weeks, it is hoped that an early reply to your representations will be made by the British authorities. The Department understands that the Government cocoa control went into full effect on December 5 but that prompt action would still enable American interests to participate in the market.

Please bring the seasonal element forcefully to the attention of the appropriate officials and endeavor to expedite a decision.

HULL

611.48N16/78 : Telegram

The Chargé in the United Kingdom (Johnson) to the Secretary of State

LONDON, December 14, 1939—3 p. m.
[Received December 14—2 : 20 p. m.]

2623. Department's 1596, December 13, 5 p. m. Importance of seasonal factor in cocoa buying has been emphasized to British authorities and is fully recognized by them. An early reply to our representations is promised, if possible within the next few days, but with an informal intimation that a favorable reply is doubtful.

An unconfirmed impression has been gained in the course of the discussions that the attitude of the British authorities toward the Rockwood proposals may possibly have been colored by the fact that earlier attempts on the part of American interests to enter the West African cocoa buying trade have not only failed for purely commercial reasons but have in some instances resulted in difficulties of various kinds. For example, the latest effort of this kind, that of . . . has ended with the deportation from the Gold Coast of their representative . . . who is now stranded in England. This is probably not a determining factor in the decision to be reached regarding Rockwood but at any rate doubt has been expressed by British officials as to whether Rockwood's efforts would have proved successful even if Government control had not intervened.

Full report follows by mail.

JOHNSON

611.48N16/81 : Telegram

The Chargé in the United Kingdom (Johnson) to the Secretary of State

LONDON, December 16, 1939—4 p. m.

[Received December 16—11 : 40 a. m.]

2653. My 2623, December 14, 3 p. m. Following are pertinent excerpts from a letter dated December 15 received today from the Foreign Office:

"Copies of the memorandum were at once communicated to the interested departments who have now asked the Foreign Office to convey to you the following reply:

In the first place it is to be explained that the Control Scheme does not in any way discriminate against United States interests. To enable the scheme to be introduced quickly and with as little dislocation of the trade as possible, it has been necessary to limit it to established shippers of cocoa from West Africa, among whom the exportable cocoa crop has been divided in proportion to their past business. This arrangement has excluded from participation in the scheme all firms, whether of British or other nationality, which had not operated during previous years. It is regretted that this arrangement unfortunately results in the exclusion from direct participation in the scheme of a United States concern which it is understood was proposing to establish itself as a buyer in British West Africa. At the same time it may be pointed out that this and all United States interests will be able to purchase British West African cocoa on exactly the same terms and conditions as other buyers and that they will be in no different position as regards buying than would have been the case if they had a direct purchasing arrangement in West Africa. If at any time United States interests should feel that the cocoa control is operating unfairly, the competent authorities will be happy to investigate the matter carefully and to endeavour to remedy any complaints. In this connexion the Minister of Food would be very glad to arrange for a member of his Department to explain the Cocoa Control Scheme and to discuss it fully with a representative of the United States Embassy. In Mr. Morrison's view, this would perhaps be the most satisfactory method of removing any misunderstanding which may exist and of clearing up any difficulties. You will, no doubt, let me know should the Embassy wish to avail themselves of Mr. Morrison's suggestion."

JOHNSON

611.48N16/78 : Telegram

The Secretary of State to the Chargé in the United Kingdom (Johnson)

WASHINGTON, December 22, 1939—6 p. m.

1661. Your 2623, December 14, 3 p. m. Before receipt of the British reply, please bring the following additional considerations urgently to the attention of the Foreign Office:

1. The Rockwood proposals were made as the result of direct encouragement from the Colonial Office. They not only entailed a substantial expenditure, but will place the company in an embarrassing position if the arrangements which were approved in principle are now turned down.

2. Rockwood and Company is obviously not the type of firm which unfortunately happened to be represented by . . . but is a long established and fully responsible American concern. It states that it has 20,000 pounds on deposit in West African banks for immediate cocoa purchases if a quota is granted.

3. The reasons assigned for limiting the operation of the Government control scheme to established companies are not regarded here as wholly convincing. In particular, it seems difficult to understand how the British Government can permit itself to be intimidated in war time by an apparent threat on the part of the established firms not to cooperate in the control, except on the understanding that none but they should be allowed to participate.

4. If the British authorities definitely feel that no new company can be admitted to share in the quotas allocated to the established firms, it is at least believed that the quota formerly set aside for German trading firms in British West Africa should be made available for American participation. This would relieve the British fear of overproduction in relation to demand and could impose no hardship on the established companies. As a minimum requirement for the present season, it might satisfy the American interests involved.

Please keep the Department informed by telegraph.

HULL

611.48N16/78 : Telegram

The Secretary of State to the Chargé in the United Kingdom (Johnson)

WASHINGTON, January 24, 1940—7 p. m.

150. Department's 1661 of December 22, 6 p. m. Please endeavor to obtain a definite statement as to the British attitude.

HULL

611.48N16/93 : Telegram

The Chargé in the United Kingdom (Johnson) to the Secretary of State

LONDON, January 26, 1940—10 p. m.
[Received January 26—5 : 51 p. m.]

248. Department's 150, January 24. Embassy has continued to press strongly with both Foreign Office and Colonial Office for reconsideration of position taken by British authorities regarding American participation and has repeatedly urged the considerations in the Embassy's telegrams 2379, November 16 and 2623, December 14.

Final reply not yet received but British Colonial Office hold out little hope of any relaxation of existing regulations to permit direct American participation at least during current season. This attitude continues to be based chiefly on the ground that restriction of quotas to established firms is considered essential to efficient functioning of control scheme and that Rockwood's plans have not matured sufficiently to entitle that company to participate on this basis.

In connection with the foregoing the Foreign Office official who is responsible for contact with the Colonial Office in matters of this kind told me this afternoon that his private opinion based upon various things that have been said at inter-departmental committee meetings is that the cocoa control scheme has grown out of bounds; the officials administering it are worried that it is not going to work, that it has been over-expanded and that they are going to have on their hands a much larger amount of cocoa than they can get rid of. The Foreign Office official said that if his judgment of the situation is correct anyone outside the control scheme may later have reason to be glad.

JOHNSON

611.48N16/100 : Telegram

The Ambassador in the United Kingdom (Kennedy) to the Secretary of State

LONDON, March 26, 1940—6 p. m.
[Received March 26—2 : 50 p. m.]

738. Your 1661, December 22, 6 p. m., and Embassy's 248, January 26, 10 p. m. Following letter dated March 24 received from the Foreign Office:

"I must apologize for the delay which has occurred in replying to your letter of the 27th December last on the subject of the exclusion of Messrs. Rockwood and Company from the British West African cocoa control scheme. Unfortunately I have not until now been in a position to deal with the points you raised. The considerations put forward in your letter were, as a matter of fact, immediately brought to the attention of the Department concerned and I understand that the difficulties in the way of making any alterations in the scheme have been fully explained to Mr. Homer Fox [70a] by Mr. Melville of the Colonial Office.

It is hardly correct, I am informed, to say that the proposals of Messrs. Rockwood and Company were made as the result of direct encouragement from the Colonial Office. Mr. Singer [71] who is, I think, what we would call managing director of the company, has from time to time sent the Colonial Office copies of his correspondence with West Africa in connection with his plan. No doubt in acknowledging these various letters interest has been expressed in what he was doing but nothing beyond that. It is true that, while Mr. Singer was in Lagos before the cocoa control scheme was proposed, the Governor of Nigeria gave him every facility for carrying out his investigations and laying his plans for direct buying. These plans were not however approved in principle either by the Nigerian Government or by the Colonial Office; indeed under peace time conditions when trade was free, it was not the business of the Government to approve plans made by a commercial organization.

It is regretted that the company incurred some expense in making investigations which, for the time being, must be regarded as fruitless.

No question of course has been raised as to the status or responsibility of Messrs. Rockwood and Company, who are recognized as one of the largest chocolate manufacturers in the United States, or as to their ability to finance cocoa purchases in West Africa.

I note that the reasons for limiting the operations of the export control scheme to established companies do not appear wholly convincing in Washington. The suggestion that limitation was decided on under pressure from the established firms is incorrect. Under the wide powers given to the Colonial Governments by the Defence Act it would have been possible for them to allocate quotas on any basis which they chose to adopt but clearly some equitable basis had to be found. The only satisfactory basis was that of a standstill arrangement, which would leave the various shippers, after control was removed, in relatively the same position as before the war. It follows that during the period of control, no new entrants could be admitted to the trade. The principle has been applied generally and Messrs. Rockwood and Company have not been the only prospective new entrants to be excluded. There have been many claims both from European and African organizations who have presented even stronger grounds than those presented on behalf of Messrs. Rockwood and Company. The same answer has been given to these applicants as has been given to the United States company.

The reference to a quota formerly set aside for German trading firms in British West Africa must I think be the outcome of a misapprehension. In the period before the war German trading firms in Nigeria purchased about 17% of the total crop. When the control scheme came into force naturally German firms were not included in quota purchasing arrangements. The whole crop was divided pro-

---

[70a] Assistant Commercial Attaché.
[71] A. Alexander Singer.

portionately amongst other established shippers both European and African on the basis of their purchases of previous crops.

The marketing of the main crop in Nigeria is now I understand practically completed and sales to United States manufacturers both from Nigeria and from the Gold Coast have proved relatively satisfactory. These manufacturers have been able to purchase British West African cocoa on the same terms and conditions as other buyers and in the absence of any complaint from Messrs. Rockwood and Company or from any of the other manufacturers it is assumed that the Government purchase scheme has not imposed upon them any serious difficulties in obtaining their requirements of West African cocoa."

KENNEDY

611.48N16/93 : Telegram

The Secretary of State to the Ambassador in the United Kingdom (Kennedy)

WASHINGTON, August 27, 1940—4 p. m.

2528. Your No. 248, January 26, 10 p. m. Unless you perceive objection please inquire informally of Foreign Office whether the British authorities will be willing to give consideration to participation by American interests in the West African cocoa quota for the period following expiration of the present regulations.

HULL

611.48N16/120 : Telegram

The Ambassador in the United Kingdom (Kennedy) to the Secretary of State

LONDON, September 10, 1940.
[Received September 10—2 : 12 p. m.]

3053. Your 2528, August 28 [*27*], 4 p. m. Informal inquiry of Foreign Office resulted in invitation to Agricultural and Commercial Attachés to attend informal discussion with representatives Colonial Office and Ministry Food which was held today. It was explained by British representatives that it was the intention to continue the cocoa control scheme for another year with only minor modifications and that after careful consideration the Departments concerned with administration of scheme had reluctantly concluded that it would be very impracticable to attempt to arrange participation of American interests in West African quota allocations. They were careful to avoid a categoric refusal but obviously hoped that we would not press the matter. Grounds for their conclusion essentially those advanced year ago when American participation originally refused. Ministry Food representatives suggested that as regards Rockwood arrangements were being made by Ministry to meet certain special requirements of Rockwood and that latter under war time conditions is probably in more advantageous position on the whole than if they were to participate as direct purchasers. It was also claimed that relations with Rockwood had been excellent during past year and cocoa control officials stated they were under impression that Rockwood had more or less abandoned idea of direct participation for duration war. Final arrangements next crop year expected to be completed this week.

KENNEDY

611.48N16/124

Memorandum of Conversation, by Mr. Henry S. Villard of the Division of Near Eastern Affairs

[WASHINGTON,] September 11, 1940.

I telephoned to Mr. Singer the substance of the attached telegram from London, no. 3053 of September 10,[72] in regard to the results of the Embassy's renewed representations in behalf of Rockwood and Company. I added that in my opinion the Department had now done about all that it could do to obtain a direct share in the West African cocoa quotas for American interests, and that pending the outcome of the war no useful purpose would be served by continuing to press the point with the British authorities.

Mr. Singer replied that he thoroughly agreed with this viewpoint and that he did not wish to badger the British any more than was necessary at this critical time. He wished to point out, however, that Rockwood and Company had not abandoned the idea of direct participation in the West African market. I said that it seemed to me the British authorities were under no misapprehension in this regard and that the record indicated that they would be prepared for a revival of Rockwood and Company's interest after the termination of the war.

Mr. Singer said that for the duration of hostilities, therefore, he would not ask us to renew our representations. He expressed great appreciation for the Department's efforts and said that the excellent relations now enjoyed by Rockwood with the British authorities is principally due to the attempts of the Department to obtain favorable treatment for the company.

---

[72] *Supra.*

ANGLO-AMERICAN DISCUSSIONS REGARDING POSTWAR RELIEF AND INTERNATIONAL CONTROL OF COMMODITIES

840.48/3994

King George VI to President Roosevelt [74]

BUCKINGHAM PALACE, 2 April, 1940.

MY DEAR PRESIDENT ROOSEVELT: In the midst of the preoccupations connected with the progress of the war, I have from time to time turned my mind to the question what is likely to be the condition of affairs in Europe and perhaps elsewhere when the war comes to an end. This is a matter which no doubt is in your mind too.

I think we must take it for granted that, at the moment when hostilities do cease, there will be in many parts of Europe and possibly elsewhere a serious dearth of the necessaries of life.

We cannot assume that, when that time comes, rapid initiative, followed by the requisite activity, will be forthcoming. On the contrary, I think it may be taken for granted that the responsible authorities will be very fully occupied. There is consequently a danger that, unless our preparations are made beforehand, there may be widespread distress and misery. I feel, therefore, that it would be wise to consider now whether some form of international organization should not be set up in the near future so that plans might be ready to be put into operation as soon as the right moment arrived. It seems to me that it is not too early even now to set on foot a preliminary study of potential stocks of the most vital articles of food and clothing, the sources of supply of these articles, and the possibilities of routing them to Europe and distributing them in the various countries which may stand most in need of them.

If you agree with me that a preliminary investigation of this kind would be of considerable value and importance, I should be very glad to have your views as to the best method of bringing it about.

Believe me

Yours very sincerely   GEORGE R. I.

840.48/3994

President Roosevelt to King George VI [74]

MAY 1, 1940.

MY DEAR KING GEORGE: The suggestions contained in your letter of April 2 have been very interesting to me indeed. I feel as you do that the constructive thought of those in authority in all parts

---

[74] Photostatic copy obtained from the Franklin D. Roosevelt Library, Hyde Park, N. Y.

of the world should be devoted to the manner in which the emergency conditions which will exist, after the present hostilities are ended, may best be alleviated.

I am appointing a governmental committee to make an immediate study of the stocks of food and clothing which are at present available in various parts of the world, as well as the manner through which production of those supplies which would be most vitally necessary may most effectively be increased as an added reserve.[75]

It occurs to me that if the British Government were to constitute a similar organization in England, there could, of course, be a useful and helpful interchange of information with regard to the findings of the two organizations through governmental channels.

I should be glad to know whether this suggestion seems practicable to you.

Believe me

Yours very sincerely, FRANKLIN D. ROOSEVELT

840.48/3994

King George VI to President Roosevelt [76]

BUCKINGHAM PALACE, 22 June, 1940.

MY DEAR PRESIDENT ROOSEVELT: Your letter of May 1st dealing with the emergency conditions which will exist at the end of the war, was very welcome to me. Every day which passes goes to show that these conditions will indeed be grave and the expert study which you suggest of available stocks of food and clothing, and of the possibility of increasing vitally necessary supplies should be of great value in making it possible to direct effort in the best way when the time comes.

It has been decided to undertake, through a Governmental Committee in this country, an enquiry on the lines indicated in your letter, and I am hopeful that the interchange of information through Governmental channels between the American and British Committees may prove to be of real assistance in preparing to meet this most serious problem.

I am very grateful for your ready cooperation in this work, which will mean so much to the peoples of Europe.

I am,

Yours very sincerely, GEORGE R. I.

---

[75] An interdepartmental group to consider postwar economic problems and policies was called together on May 27, 1940; see Department of State, *Postwar Foreign Policy Preparation, 1939–1945* (Washington, Government Printing Office, 1949), pp. 29–40 *passim*.

[76] Copy transmitted to the Secretary of State by the British Ambassador under covering letter dated July 9.

610.1131/442

The British Embassy to the Department of State

MEMORANDUM

His Majesty's Government in the United Kingdom are greatly interested in that part of the statement issued to the press by the President on June 21st relating to proposals which are being placed before other American Governments for cooperative economic action by the American Republics and possibly by other countries, to include an effective system of joint marketing of the important staple exports of the American Republics.[77]

His Majesty's Government have themselves been making a survey of the problem of dealing with surplus commodities produced in territories of the British Empire and in such parts of the French, Dutch and Belgian Colonies as can be controlled. This survey will include the investigation of the possibility of dealing with surpluses by regulated sales, storage, destruction where necessary, and restriction of excess production.

His Majesty's Government will give full information to the United States Government on the progress of their survey. They hope that the United States Government will do likewise and that any decisions taken on the United States proposals at the forthcoming Pan-American Conference at Havana [78] will not preclude cooperation with them.

The United Kingdom and the British Empire provide the principal foreign markets for a large-range of surplus commodities from North and South America. At the same time British Empire surpluses of commodities which the American Republics also produce might, if unregulated, impinge upon American interests. From the point of view of wartime control and also from that of post war reconstruction it appears to His Majesty's Government that American regulation and British Empire regulation should be brought into line, and it is their desire to find agreement with the United States as well as with other American countries on this question.

As regards those products of which there is likely to be a world surplus, (e. g. cotton, corn, wheat, edible oils) His Majesty's Government feel that it is of the utmost urgency that the plans of the British nations and their Allies for dealing with their export surpluses should be concerted with those of the United States and of other states in the Western Hemisphere.

His Majesty's Government realise that in origin the examination of the United States Government was directed to an economic and politi-

---

[77] See vol. v, section entitled "Program proposed by the United States for Inter-American economic cooperation." For text of the June 21 press statement, see Department of State *Bulletin*, June 22, 1940, p. 675.

[78] See vol. v, pp. 2 ff.

cal problem while theirs is at least to an equal extent an urgent problem of withholding supplies from Germany and countries under her control. On this aspect of the question His Majesty's Ambassador is addressing a separate memorandum to the Secretary of State.[79] WASHINGTON, July 3, 1940.

610.4115/42

The British Ambassador (Lothian) to the Secretary of State

MEMORANDUM

I

In memorandum "A" attached to his *Aide-Mémoire* of July 3rd, 1940,[80] the British Ambassador informed the Secretary of State that His Majesty's Government in the United Kingdom were greatly interested in the United States proposals to be made at the Habana Conference for dealing with the export surpluses of the Western Hemisphere, and that the United Kingdom Government were engaged on a survey of the problem of the surpluses of countries of the British Empire and Allied as well as British Colonial territories. It was suggested that the United Kingdom and United States Governments might exchange information as to their respective plans for dealing with the export surpluses of the two groups of countries, and give consideration to the possibilities of concerting them.

2. The Habana Conference referred the further study of the problem of surpluses as affecting American countries to the Inter-American Financial and Economic Advisory Committee in Washington [81] and Congress has since passed a bill to increase the lending authority of the Export–Import Bank by $500,000,000 for the purposes of "assisting in the development of the resources, the stabilisation of the economies, and the orderly marketing of products of the countries of the Western Hemisphere".[82]

3. The main new development on the United Kingdom side is the Prime Minister's announcement in the House of Commons on August 20th [83] that His Majesty's Government would do their best to encourage the building up of reserves of food and raw materials all over the world and arrange for their speedy entry into any part of

---

[79] Memorandum dated July 3, vol. II, p. 52.
[80] For text of the *aide-mémoire*, see p. 42 ;memorandum "A" is printed *supra*.
[81] See Department of State, *Second Meeting of the Ministers of Foreign Affairs of the American Republics, Habana, July 21–30, 1940, Report of the Secretary of State* (Washington, Government Printing Office, 1941), pp. 25 and 80.
[82] See 54 Stat. 961.
[83] See W. N. Medlicott, *The Economic Blockade*, vol. I (London, His Majesty's Stationery Office, 1952), pp. 551 and 666.

occupied Europe once it has genuinely regained its freedom. This proposal would at one and the same time contribute to a solution of the problems of surpluses and be a constructive basis for repairing the economic ravages of the war, both now and in the post-war period.

II

4. It appears to His Majesty's Government from the consideration which they have so far been able to give to the subject of world surpluses that the problems which the American and the non-American groups of countries have to face necessarily overlap and cannot be solved in isolation, not only as regards storage or marketing or control of production, but also as regards satisfaction of the import needs of the surplus producing countries. It would obviously be useless to store surpluses in one country if in other countries surpluses of similar or competing commodities continue to be produced and to be marketed at bankrupt prices, while producing countries want to be assured not only of a reasonable market for their product but also of the supply of their essential import requirements. The financial problems involved are equally vast and interlocking. Their solution is probably beyond the capacity of the United Kingdom and the individual countries in the non-American group and equally of the United States and the individual countries in the American group. Certainly the capacity of the United Kingdom to assist by purchases from the countries of the American group is limited to what can be financed by means of United Kingdom exports or credits or payments agreements.

5. The survey of the problem which the United Kingdom Government is preparing has not been completed but it appears to them that different remedies will have to be explored for various groups of commodities, which for this purpose would seem to fall in the following categories:—

(a) Some, e. g. wheat,[84] cotton,[85] maize, sugar,[86] were pre-war problems though the difficulties have been accentuated by war conditions. Their scope is vast and it may be considered that they must in the main be dealt with by means of storage schemes financed by producing countries and accompanied by efforts to regulate production.

(b) Others, such as copper [87] and perhaps meat and meat products [88]

---

[84] See bracketed note regarding preliminary negotiations for a conference to conclude an international wheat agreement, *Foreign Relations*, 1939, vol. II, p. 27.

[85] For previous correspondence regarding international regulation of production and marketing of cotton, see *ibid.*, pp. 20 ff.

[86] For correspondence regarding arrangements for the wartime operation of the international sugar agreement, see *ibid.*, vol. I, pp. 948 ff.

[87] For correspondence concerning copper, see vol. II, pp. 300 ff.

[88] For scheme for an international beef conference to regulate the supply of beef to the United Kingdom market, January 1, 1937, see International Labour Office, *Intergovernmental Commodity Control Agreements* (Montreal, 1943), p. 69.

might have to be dealt with by regulation agreements operated by industries or governments.

(c) A most acute problem is that of colonial products which cannot easily be stored or regulated or financed by the local governments and which have suffered most by loss of European markets. The United Kingdom Government are committed to supporting the economic situation in Allied as well as in British colonies and India. In these cases purchases seem to be the only method of helping or production must be discouraged by allowing prices to fall to a low level.

The United States and other American countries and the British Dominions are mainly concerned with (a) and (b) but the United Kingdom and its Allies are also deeply interested in (c).

6. Definite proposals on the wider objectives are still under examination by the United Kingdom Government but it appears to them that among the questions to which consideration will have to be given are:—

(a) What arrangements can best be made for the storage of existing surplus commodities both to ensure orderly marketing and to provide reserves for relief of Europe, when the time comes;

(b) How far storage can be financed locally by producing countries, and how far it would involve purchases or credits from other countries;

(c) What plans can be devised for dealing with the residue of existing surpluses;

(d) What steps can best be taken to alleviate the position (both as regards exports and imports) of producing countries, which find themselves owing to war conditions cut off from their normal markets;

(e) As regards the future, how far production of various surplus commodities in the various countries concerned can be planned or regulated so as to prevent as far as possible accumulation of fresh surpluses.

7. Where possible it would seem to His Majesty's Government that such questions should be dealt with on an international basis and that where international organisations exist they should be called into action. The advisability might be considered of asking the chairmen of such bodies, e. g. of the Wheat Advisory Committee and International Sugar Council, to summon informal meetings to consider the possibilities of appropriate action in the international field. The possibility might also be considered of creating new international organisations where they do not exist, e. g. for oil seeds or fats.

III

8. Pending the full consideration by the United States and United Kingdom Governments, either independently or in consultation, of the problems of export surpluses in general and their possible remedies and of these wider objectives, it seems probable, and possibly inevitable, that the United States Government may take *ad hoc* measures in regard to particular surplus commodities of particular American

countries as well as those of the United States itself, while the United Kingdom Government must take similar action to assist Empire and Allied countries, notably in respect of the commodities of category (c) of paragraph 5 of this memorandum. It would be unfortunate if the situation developed in such a way that ad hoc measures are devised on inconsistent lines by the United States for Western Hemisphere countries and by the United Kingdom Government for the British and Allied countries, as this would complicate not only the technical but the political problems involved.

9. It therefore appears to His Majesty's Government that in the first instance it would be most useful and mutually advantageous if an exchange of information with the United States Government could be instituted and maintained in regard to the ad hoc measures which they have taken or may contemplate taking for dealing with particular export surpluses, especially agricultural surpluses, of the producing countries within the respective groups. If this proposal is acceptable to the United States Government, His Majesty's Government for their part would be glad to arrange immediately for such an exchange, using either the American Embassy in London or the British Embassy in Washington as a channel of communication.

WASHINGTON, September 18, 1940.

840.48/4527½ : Telegram

The Director General, British Ministry of Economic Warfare (Leith-Ross),[89] to the Assistant Secretary of State (Grady)[90]

LONDON, November 30, 1940.

Personal. I have recently been asked by my Government here to take charge of the surplus problem and to formulate proposals for remedial action. I hope to rope in Cairns [91] as my chief assistant. It is a big subject and I have not yet been able to give much time to it. But I should like to outline to you the position as I see it and invite your interest in the whole problem and your views on practical steps that can be taken.

2. I assume that you have seen the memorandum about the question submitted to the State Department by Lord Lothian on September 18th, but I am not sure that the implications of this memorandum were made sufficiently clear. Superficially, both your country and ours are faced with various ad hoc surplus problems in our own territories and other countries throughout the world which demand some

---

[89] Chief Economic Adviser to the British Government since 1932.
[90] Transmitted by the British Ambassador under covering letter of December 3.
[91] Andrew Cairns, Canadian, Secretary of the International Wheat Advisory Committee.

immediate measures of relief. While some of these problems are due wholly to war conditions, others are largely repetitions of chronic maladjustments of supply and demand accentuated by the war. In either case, neither the United States nor the British Empire, acting alone, can hope to do more than supply expensive short lived palliatives, whereas in cooperation real solutions may be initiated which, combined with temporary war-time measures, should not only tide the world over the present emergencies but also lay foundations for a definite improvement in the economic organization of the post-war world. Thus it seems to me that the surpluses problem should be viewed as a great whole and as a collection of the problems of individual surpluses in particular countries. It is an opportunity to set on foot an international cooperative effort of great post-war as well as war-time significance.

3. Viewed from this angle the solution seems to lie in an international programme for storage of surplus supplies accompanied by appropriate regulation of production and marketing. A programme for storage of surplus supplies and regulation of production and marketing links up of course with the immense needs of Europe after the war. With the dangers of a sudden reversal in the supply situation unless stocks can accumulate beforehand, there may be a serious delay in food relief and in a restoration of economic activity in Europe, while outside Europe there will be great economic instability as result of a repetition of post-war credit and slumps of a future 1919–1920. The interests of the United States as well as those of the British Empire require that every possible effort should be made to avoid these dangers and restore normal conditions of international trade throughout the world as quickly and smoothly as is humanly possible.

4. As to methods, my personal and provisional views are as follows:

(a) I take it that neither your Government nor ours will be anxious to purchase surpluses not needed for consumption, and producing countries must not look to us as Fairy Godmothers who will take the existing surpluses off their hands and leave them free to start producing another next year. The producing countries should therefore be encouraged to formulate measures for carrying on their own surpluses and storing as much as possible of them on the basis of internal financing. Many of them will however need some financial support and this might be found on condition that schemes are reasonably economic and that there is adequate cooperation both as regards regulation of production or export and coordinated marketing.

(b) My idea is that the international committee should be revived and asked to get on to this as regards wheat as soon as possible. Similar international committees should conjointly be internationally created to deal thereafter with coffee [92] and cotton. Copper might be

---

[92] For correspondence regarding the Inter-American Coffee Agreement signed November 28, 1940, see vol. v.

dealt with through a cartel. Maize, linseed, wool and jute could be dealt with on similar lines by the producing countries concerned.

(c) There would still remain a number of colonial products especially vegetable oils, which are more difficult to store, and these would have to be dealt with by creating some storage corporation, which could buy up surpluses at appropriate prices and turn them over so as to have a supply available when the need arises. Finance would have to be provided for this corporation; but the problem would be greatly reduced in dimensions if more storable commodities could be dealt with on the basis of international schemes.

5. It seems to me that the United States and the British Empire should take the lead in formulating this programme and in securing the cooperation of the principal producing countries. Immediate *ad hoc* measures for dealing with particular problems or particular countries ought to be fitted into the framework of a programme on these lines. I should like to see a joint Anglo-American committee set up to agree to the general lines of policy and to initiate action and such a committee could later on be extended to include representatives of other countries and act as a coordinating body to which various committees on wheat and other commodities could refer.

6. If and when it seemed desirable, I would arrange to come to Washington for consultation. It will not be easy for me to get away from here but a good deal of prospecting work could usefully be done here before that stage comes, provided that the United States Administration would favour action on the above lines in principle. It would be the greatest help to me if you could let me know whether you think something can be developed on the above lines. I am not fully aware of what transpired at the Havana Conference and it may be that your experiences there were such as to make you hesitate to initiate any further efforts at international cooperation. The difficulties in the way of such action are of course considerable but the alternative of unregulated competition by overseas producers is so serious that I believe there is a better chance today of securing agreements than in the past.

F. LEITH-ROSS

840.50/4527⅜ : Telegram

The Chargé in the United Kingdom (Johnson) to the Secretary of State

LONDON, December 16, 1940—10 p. m.
[Received December 16—5:50 p. m.]

4093. The Department may be interested to know that Embassy has learned from reliable sources that British Embassy, Washington, has informed Leith-Ross by way of comment on his recent personal message to Grady that Department does not seem disposed toward a favorable response. Our attitude is described as strongly influenced by

Habana Conference and subsequent *ad hoc* commitments in Latin America. Leith-Ross is accordingly described as taking a somewhat pessimistic line about possibility of United States collaboration on surpluses and British program is said to be marking time. Embassy is informed, however, that Leith-Ross would welcome an opening to explore informally in Washington the possibilities of collaboration and would bring Cairns with him.

It is also understood that British Surplus Committee is interesting itself in next meeting of Sugar Council (Embassy's 4063, December 13 [93]) the proposed date for which is January 6. Secretary of the Council states informally that British are concerned about new expanding tendency of sugar production in certain Dominions and colonies.

JOHNSON

840.48/4527⅝ : Telegram

The Secretary of State to the Chargé in the United Kingdom (*Johnson*)

WASHINGTON, December 17, 1940—8 p. m.

3832. Your 4093, December 16, 10 p. m. The matter has been discussed with Sir Owen Chalkley.[94] Grady is in California. The Department has also discussed subject with him by telephone and there appears no basis for impression of unfavorable reception. Grady states the letter was received just prior to his departure for California and it was not understood that immediate reply was necessary. While general approach is sympathetic, further preliminary study, now going on, is necessary. The whole subject will be discussed again upon Grady's return next week.

HULL

840.48/4527⅞ : Telegram

The Chargé in the United Kingdom (*Johnson*) to the Secretary of State

LONDON, December 27, 1940—5 p. m.
[Received 6 : 35 p. m.]

4220. Department's 3832, December 17, 8 p. m. The substance of this telegram has been communicated to Leith-Ross (who expressed much appreciation) and incidentally was subsequently confirmed by cable from Chalkley.

For Department's information, Leith-Ross has instructed Cairns (who is shortly to become Leith-Ross' assistant) to be completely

---

[93] Telegram not printed.
[94] Commercial Counselor of the British Embassy in Washington.

frank with Steere [95] on the surplus question and to show him Ministry's surplus file which accordingly has been read. From this, certain things seem clear (1) that there has been mutual misunderstanding of the use being made of the term "*ad hoc*" and (2) that British Embassy officials in Washington have been under some misapprehensions about surplus questions and lack background on previous approaches to these problems. The British here understand *ad hoc* measures as special measures of a definitely restricted character i. e. pertaining to a local problem or problem of a particular country. They consider international schemes even for single commodities as outside the meaning of the term. They had therefore understood Department's references to *ad hoc* measures (which British Embassy did not clarify or explain and apparently understood in the British sense) to refer to some of the individual arrangements (credit, etc.) recently made between the United States and certain Latin American countries.

The Department appears to use the term *ad hoc* in a less restricted sense i. e. as extending to individual commodity schemes even of an international character such for example as a sugar or wheat agreement. If so the views of the two Governments regarding an approach to surplus problems are not so far apart.

From his perusal of the file above referred to which included a Cabinet document on the subject Steere has the definite impression that the British while naturally motivated by self interest in broaching the surplus problem are none the less taking a broad view of it, are aware of the necessity of British and Empire contributions if progress is achieved and are cognizant of the necessity of meeting the United States halfway; it also appears they feel the necessity lacking American collaboration of proceeding with certain *ad hoc* measures of their own but will have to confine them to Empire and Allied countries if a broader basis of cooperation cannot be worked out with the United States.

As regards wheat there is a bare possibility that British might press Canadians to take initiative or themselves take it if they thought it would start ball rolling. This is only a possibility not a probability.

JOHNSON

AGREEMENT BETWEEN THE UNITED STATES AND THE UNITED KINGDOM CONCERNING THE ESTABLISHMENT OF A STRATEGIC RESERVE OF AUSTRALIAN WOOL IN THE UNITED STATES, EFFECTED BY EXCHANGE OF NOTES SIGNED DECEMBER 9, 1940

[For texts of notes, see Department of State Executive Agreement Series No. 195, or 54 Stat. 2477.]

---

[95] Loyd V. Steere, Agricultural Attaché in the United Kingdom.

AUSTRALIA

TREATY BETWEEN THE UNITED STATES AND AUSTRALIA AMENDING IN THEIR APPLICATION CERTAIN PROVISIONS OF THE TREATY OF 1914 FOR THE ADVANCEMENT OF PEACE BETWEEN THE UNITED STATES AND GREAT BRITAIN, SIGNED SEPTEMBER 6, 1940

[For text of treaty, see Department of State Treaty Series No. 974, or 55 Stat. 1211.]

143

CANADA

ESTABLISHMENT OF THE PERMANENT JOINT BOARD ON DEFENSE, THE UNITED STATES AND CANADA

842.20 Defense/1½

The Minister in Canada (Moffat) to the Acting Secretary of State (Welles)[1]

OTTAWA, August 14, 1940.

DEAR SUMNER: Ever since I have been here, but more particularly in the last two or three weeks, there has been growing a public demand throughout Canada for the conclusion of some form of joint defence understanding with the United States. Even elements which in the past have been least well disposed toward us, such as the Toronto public and the English-speaking sections of Montreal, are now outspoken in its favor. The principal newspapers, such as the Montreal *Gazette*, the *Winnipeg Free Press*, the *Vancouver Sun* and such periodicals as *MacLeans* and *Saturday Night* are committed to the idea. Questions have been asked in Parliament and some of the political leaders are putting pressure on the Government behind the scenes. As a matter of practical politics the Prime Minister may ultimately be forced to recognize the existence of this popular demand; if Great Britain should suffer serious reverses the demand would immediately become very acute.

To Canadians such a joint defense understanding,—whether it took the form of a treaty or merely of publicly announced staff talks,—seems a reasonable reinsurance policy. The old fear that cooperation with the United States would tend to weaken Canada's ties with Great Britain has almost entirely disappeared. Instead, Canada believes that such cooperation would tend to bring Britain and the United States closer together, rather than to force Britain and Canada apart.

The press is increasingly pointing out that Canada has two lines of defense: the first in Great Britain, the second in a coordinated plan for the protection of North America. A few Canadians, but still rela-

---

[1] Photostatic copy obtained from the Franklin D. Roosevelt Library, Hyde Park, N. Y.

tively few, would add a coordinated plan for the protection of the Western Hemisphere.

That an understanding between Canada and the United States must necessarily be limited to the defense of North America is everywhere accepted here. Any suggestion that it would obligate the United States, even morally, to become involved overseas is recognized as outside the realm of practical possibilities. But conversely, the average Canadian fails to see why the United States, which unanimously supported the President's Kingston pledge,[2] should hesitate to work out ways and means of implementing the pledge. The argument that this would be difficult while Canada is a belligerent and the United States a neutral is generally brushed aside as a technical one, which ignores the basic fact that an understanding would only become operative in the event of a physical attack on Canada or the United States.

The recent advocacy by the *Chicago Tribune* and the *New York Herald Tribune* (which in political philosophies are as the poles apart) of a defensive alliance between Canada and the United States has made a deep impression on the average Canadian. He has jumped to the conclusion that the United States is ready for an understanding, and that it is the Canadian Government that is holding back.

Mr. Mackenzie King,[3] who knows us well, appreciates that any initiative on Canada's part toward a more formal understanding would cause embarrassment or at best controversy in the United States, which he wants at all costs to avoid. He believes that if an emergency should arise, the United States would act and act quickly, and that the recent secret talks between American and Canadian military and naval officers, although without commitment, have at least had the result that American aid would be effective.

On the other hand, dependent on future events, Mr. Mackenzie King may well be subjected to very heavy political pressure to make some approach to us either (*a*) to formalize the Kingston pledge or (*b*) to make a public admission that "staff talks" have in fact taken place. In a war situation where the picture changes overnight, I could not hope to prophesy when the pressure on Mr. Mackenzie King might be expected to reach its maximum intensity.

The purpose of this letter, Sumner, is merely to give you a feeling of the way Canadian opinion is growing, so that you in turn may be able to consider it in relation to the development of political opinion (pro or con) at home.

    With every good wish

        As ever yours   PIERREPONT MOFFAT

---

[2] Address delivered at Queens University, Kingston, Ontario, August 18, 1938, Department of State *Press Releases*, August 20, 1938, p. 123.
[3] Canadian Prime Minister.

842.20 Defense/14

Press Release Issued by the White House August 18, 1940

The following joint statement was issued by President Roosevelt and the Prime Minister of Canada, W. L. Mackenzie King:

"The Prime Minister and the President have discussed the mutual problems of defense in relation to the safety of Canada and the United States.

"It has been agreed that a Permanent Joint Board on Defense shall be set up at once by the two countries.

"This Permanent Joint Board on Defense shall commence immediate studies relating to sea, land, and air problems including personnel and matériel.

"It will consider in the broad sense the defense of the north half of the Western Hemisphere.

"The Permanent Joint Board on Defense will consist of four or five members from each country, most of them from the services. It will meet shortly." [4]

842.20 Defense/2 : Telegram

The Ambassador in Brazil (Caffery) to the Secretary of State

Rio de Janeiro, August 22, 1940—11 a. m.
[Received 1:45 p. m.]

417. For the Under Secretary. President Vargas and Aranha [5] are both harrying me with questions about our recent negotiations with Canada. Is there anything that you can let me have for them on this?

Caffery

842.20 Defense/2 : Telegram

The Acting Secretary of State to the Ambassador in Brazil (Caffery)

Washington, August 22, 1940—7 p. m.

262. Your 417, August 22, 11 a. m. I explained this matter fully to Ambassador Martins yesterday evening. The creation of a Joint Permanent Defense Board composed of Canadian and United States members is solely for the purpose of determining in advance the steps of a military and naval character which should be taken by both Governments in the event that Canada is attacked by a non-American power. In essence the objective of the arrangement is identical with the objective of the staff conversations held between Brazil and the

---

[4] On August 22 the White House announced the membership of the Board and that its first meeting would be held at Ottawa on August 26. See Department of State *Bulletin*, August 24, 1940, p. 154.
[5] Oswaldo Aranha, Brazilian Minister for Foreign Affairs.

United States. Please assure both the President and Aranha that this Government will keep the Brazilian Government fully informed of all matters of this kind.

WELLES

842.20 Defense/2a : Circular telegram

The Secretary of State to Diplomatic Missions in the American Republics Except Brazil

WASHINGTON, August 24, 1940—4 p. m.

In accordance with our policy of keeping the governments of the other American Republics fully informed as to action taken by this Government in matters of continental interest, you are requested to call informally on the Foreign Minister with regard to the recently created Joint Permanent Defense Board, composed of Canadian and United States members. You should state that this Board was created solely for the purpose of determining in advance the steps of a military and naval character which should be taken by both governments in the event that Canada is attacked by a non-American power.

HULL

842.20 Defense/43

Memorandum by the Secretary of the American Section of the Permanent Joint Board on Defense of the United States and Canada (Hickerson)

[WASHINGTON,] October 23, 1940.

I have learned informally from Mr. Moffat, our Minister to Canada, that a few days ago General Crerar, the Chief of Staff of the Canadian Army, in conversation with Norman Armour [6] concerning the Permanent Joint Board on Defense, remarked that as the Canadian Government had no secrets from the British Government he personally favored converting the Permanent Joint Board on Defense into a triple British-Canadian-American Board; or, if this were not possible, to invite British representatives to sit in at some of the meetings.

This is the first suggestion of this sort which I have heard, and I earnestly hope that the Canadian Government will not raise such a question; I do not believe there is much chance of their doing so. May I point out, against the possibility of someone raising this question with you, that such an addition would virtually destroy the premise on which we have thus far worked in the Joint Board. We have stated quite frankly to the Canadian Section that the job of the Joint

---

[6] Ambassador to Argentina; formerly Minister to Canada, 1935–38.

Board is to consider the *defense* of Canada and the United States from attack, and no other question. We have added that it is of course the policy of the American Government to give every possible assistance short of actual participation in the war to the British Government and to the Canadian Government in its overseas effort, but that such assistance will be given by agencies other than the Permanent Joint Board on Defense. It seems to me that this is a sound basis upon which to proceed.

I repeat, I seriously doubt whether the Canadian Government will raise with us General Crerar's suggestion; I certainly hope they do not. Mr. Moffat informs me he does not believe Crerar's point of view finds any favor with the civilian authorities in Canada.[7]

J[OHN] D. H[ICKERSON]

AGREEMENT BETWEEN THE UNITED STATES AND CANADA REGARDING THE APPLICATION OF THE RUSH–BAGOT AGREEMENT OF APRIL 28 AND 29, 1817, AS TO THE ARMAMENT OF NAVAL VESSELS CONSTRUCTED ON THE GREAT LAKES

[For text of agreement effected by exchange of notes signed October 30 and November 2, 1940, see Treaties and Other International Acts Series No. 1836.]

AGREEMENT BETWEEN THE UNITED STATES AND CANADA REGARDING THE GREAT LAKES–ST. LAWRENCE WATERWAY, EFFECTED BY EXCHANGE OF NOTES SIGNED OCTOBER 14 AND 31 AND NOVEMBER 7, 1940[8]

711.42157SA29/1640

The Secretary of State to the Canadian Minister (Christie)

WASHINGTON, January 3, 1940.

SIR: I have the honor to acknowledge the receipt of your note of December 26, 1939[9] relative to the proposed general treaty providing for the development of the Great Lakes–St. Lawrence Basin. I note especially that the Canadian Government considers it desirable that a number of questions be taken up by representatives of the United States and Canada, and that it suggests a meeting in Ottawa in the near future between members of the public services of the two countries and their technical advisers for the purpose of clarifying a number of the issues involved, such meeting to be informal and preparatory in character.

---

[7] The following notations appear on this memorandum: "I fully agree. S[umner] W[elles]"; and "OK. C[ordell] H[ull]."
[8] For previous correspondence, see *Foreign Relations*, 1939, vol. II, pp. 333 ff.
[9] *Ibid.*, p. 335.

I refer to the informal conversations which have taken place following the receipt of your note between officers of the Department and you concerning the earliest date on which the suggested conversations could take place in Ottawa, and I am happy to state that arrangements have been made to send a group to Ottawa at the end of this week.

The group will be composed of Messrs. Berle and Hickerson, of this Department, and Mr. Lelands Olds, Chairman of the Federal Power Commission. They will arrive in Ottawa on January 7th next to take part in the conversations proposed in your note.[10]

I avail myself [etc.]   CORDELL HULL

711.42157SA29/1652

Press Release Issued by the Department of State on January 24, 1940

The Canadian Delegation on the Great Lakes-St. Lawrence Basin Project arrived in Washington on January 21st. On Monday, January 22nd, conversations with the United States Delegation were resumed in the Department of State. These conversations continued through the afternoon of January 24th. Dr. O. D. Skelton, Under Secretary of State for External Affairs and head of the Canadian Delegation, and his associates left Washington to return to Ottawa this afternoon. Before their departure, the following joint statement on behalf of the two Delegations was agreed upon:

"During the discussions the whole field was covered, and definite progress was made. The discussions have now reached the point where it is necessary for the two Delegations to report to their respective Governments on various matters of policy requiring their consideration and decision.

"The engineering advisers of the two Governments have reached substantial agreement on the feasibility and desirability of a project in the International Rapids section of the St. Lawrence River which would involve a main dam in the vicinity of Barnhart Island, with a power house in each country, and control dam upstream. This project is based upon a plan which was discussed in some detail in the 1926 report of the Joint Board of Engineers.[11] The engineers of the two countries are in agreement that such a project is sound from an engineering standpoint, cheaper in cost than the project on which the 1932 Treaty[12] was based, and affords full protection for all the interests in the various sections of the St. Lawrence River.

"The negotiations will continue through diplomatic channels."

---

[10] The conversations in Ottawa began on January 8 and lasted through January 10. The delegations next met in Washington on January 22 to resume their conversations.

[11] Senate Document No. 183, 69th Cong., 2d sess.; and *Report of Joint Board of Engineers on St. Lawrence Waterway Project* (Ottawa, F. A. Acland, printer to the King's Most Excellent Majesty, 1927).

[12] Unperfected treaty between the United States of America and Canada relating to the Great Lakes–St. Lawrence Waterway, signed at Washington, July 18, 1932, *Foreign Relations*, 1932, vol. II, p. 69.

711.42157SA29/1739½

Memorandum of Conversation, by the Assistant Secretary of State (Berle)

[WASHINGTON,] September 11, 1940.

Participants: Franklin D. Roosevelt, the President of the U. S.;
Leland Olds, Federal Power Commission;
Adolf A. Berle, Jr., Department of State.

Mr. Leland Olds of the Federal Power Commission and I saw the President today at his request.

The President brought up the attached letter from Governor Lehman of New York, dated August 28, 1940,[13] accompanied by a memorandum describing the possible plans for developing the international rapids section of the St. Lawrence River. This letter in substance proposes a "special agreement" with Canada for the development of the power facilities of the international rapids section, without waiting for the signature and ratification of the St. Lawrence Waterway Treaty. He asked our comment.

I said that at dinner two or three days ago the Canadian Minister had indicated to me that he wished to come in to discuss St. Lawrence power and that he had an appointment this afternoon. I surmised that he would ask for a statement of our intentions as to developing the St. Lawrence; and that he would do so because the Ontario Hydro-Electric, on which fell the burden of supplying much of Canadian power for defense purposes, was already approaching capacity and had to plan further development. They would look for power either in the St. Lawrence, or if they were blocked there, then go to the Ottawa River. Likewise, certain private companies, notably Beauharnois, were asking for substantial diversions of water from the St. Lawrence, and his government would have to deal with that situation.

Mr. Olds observed that there were three courses to take: either do nothing; or do something along the lines of the Governor's proposal; or consummate the St. Lawrence Power Treaty and send it up.

The President said that we obviously were not ready for the St. Lawrence Power Treaty; that would have to wait until January.

Leland Olds presented figures showing that New York State would need additional power; by 1945 it would have exhausted not only the power that it has but would be using the St. Lawrence power, if developed, for defense purposes; should defense needs cease they would need that power anyway by 1948.

The President said that in principle he was opposed to taking the Great Lakes–St. Lawrence situation one bite at a time. His dream had always been a single, unified solution including the full use of the

---

[13] Not attached to file copy of this document.

Niagara power. His conception remained that of a unified development, and I gather that his planning was to send the St. Lawrence Waterways Treaty up for ratification as soon as the January Congress met.

After considerable discussion he requested us to draw four documents:

(1) An answer to Governor Lehman;
(2) An Executive Order appointing a Board to supervise the additional borings and detailed engineering plans, the Board to be composed of Leland Olds, myself, a member from the New York Power Authority, and a member designated by the Chief of Army Engineers, presumably General Robins.

This Board was to have among its duties the job of cooperating with any similar board or group designated by the Canadian Government.

(3) A letter to the Director of the Budget allocating one million dollars out of the President's contingent defense fund to the Army Engineers for the purpose of doing the necessary boring and engineering work;
(4) A message for the information of Congress setting forth this allocation, the reason for it, the need of power for defense, and indicating that as soon as this work reached the necessary point, legislation would be asked making available necessary funds for construction.

The President authorized me to tell this to the Canadian Minister; and to ask that we get assurance from Ontario Hydro that the million dollars will be included in the cost of operations, part of which are reimbursable by the Canadian Government as they use the power.

[Here follows a paragraph on unrelated subjects.]

A. A. BERLE, JR.

711.42157SA29/1739⅔

Memorandum of Conversation, by the Assistant Secretary of State (Berle)

[WASHINGTON,] September 11, 1940.

The Canadian Minister came in to see me today at his request. He had previously indicated that he wished to discuss St. Lawrence water power.

It appeared that the Ontario Hydro needs additional water now; and has been interested in knowing whether it could not have additional diversion rights at Niagara. He wanted to know whether he could have any assurance on this score.

I then told him the substance of the proposal which Governor Lehman had made to President Roosevelt, and the substance of the suggested solution which the President had made (see memorandum of September 11, 1940, conversation between the President, Mr. Leland

Olds, Chairman of the Federal Power Commission and myself). I said that the President had been opposed to piecemeal solution; but that I thought that it would be possible to consider a solution both at short and long range. Under this conception we ought to discuss together:

(1) A temporary immediate diversion of Niagara power to take care of the Ontario Hydro;
(2) The immediate initiation of the engineering work for development of power at the international rapids; and
(3) As and when convenient, the signature of the St. Lawrence waterway treaty.

Following the President's instruction I asked whether, were the engineering work on the international rapids commenced with American financing, this item would be considered as a part of the cost of the operation, and reimbursed in accordance with the agreed proportion by the Canadian Government as and when the power came to be used.

The Minister suggested that we put the suggestion in the form of a wholly informal memorandum for discussion, which he could report textually to Ottawa. I said that I would endeavor to get up such a memorandum and let him have it. I have accordingly requested Leland Olds to work out such a memorandum for discussion here.

A. A. BERLE, JR.

711.42157SA29/1714

Memorandum of Conversation, by the Assistant Secretary of State (Berle)

[WASHINGTON,] September 16, 1940.

The Canadian Minister called this morning, at my request. In our previous interview he had asked, and I had agreed to have drawn up, a memorandum covering the plan to get boring and survey work started for the St. Lawrence power development.

I handed him such a memorandum,[14] prepared by Mr. Leland Olds and by Mr. Hickerson. It will be found in the files of EU.[15]

Mr. Christie said that he had received a telegram from Ottawa, based on some newspaper reports that the President had decided to go ahead with the St. Lawrence power features, eliminating the seaway. This had caused some concern. From reading the memorandum, however, he gathered that this was not the case.

I said that it certainly was not the case. The growing needs of defense, the possible shipping situation now and later, and con-

[14] Not printed.
[15] Division of European Affairs.

ceivable changes in the Atlantic all heightened in our minds the need of inland navigation and possibly inland ship-building, as well. The President had expressed himself as not wishing to take the St. Lawrence–Great Lakes matters "in bites", but as a whole, which of course included navigation. All that we were trying to do here was to get matters started so as to make construction necessary for the most immediate requirements, namely, power, but with full intention of going forward with the whole project as rapidly as circumstances permitted.

The Minister said that he would send this to Ottawa.

A. A. B[ERLE], JR.

[For text of agreement between the United States and Canada regarding Great Lakes–St. Lawrence Waterway effected by exchanges of notes, signed October 14 and 31 and November 7, 1940, see Department of State Executive Agreement Series No. 187, or 54 Stat. 2426.]

ARRANGEMENT BETWEEN THE UNITED STATES AND CANADA FOR RECIPROCAL RECOGNITION OF LOAD LINE REGULATIONS FOR VESSELS ENGAGED IN INTERNATIONAL VOYAGES ON THE GREAT LAKES, EFFECTED BY EXCHANGE OF NOTES

[For texts of notes, signed April 29, August 24, October 22, 1938; September 2, October 18, 1939; and January 10 and March 4, 1940, see Department of State Executive Agreement Series No. 172, or 54 Stat. 2300.]

AGREEMENT BETWEEN THE UNITED STATES AND CANADA CONCERNING THE ESTABLISHMENT OF A BOARD OF INQUIRY FOR THE GREAT LAKES FISHERIES, SIGNED FEBRUARY 29, 1940

[For text of agreement, see Department of State Executive Agreement Series No. 182, or 54 Stat. 2409.]

AGREEMENT BETWEEN THE UNITED STATES AND CANADA CONCERNING EXEMPTIONS FROM EXCHANGE CONTROL MEASURES, EFFECTED BY EXCHANGE OF NOTES SIGNED JUNE 18, 1940

[For texts of notes, see Department of State Executive Agreement Series No. 174, or 54 Stat. 2317.]

TREATY BETWEEN THE UNITED STATES AND CANADA AMENDING IN THEIR APPLICATION TO CANADA CERTAIN PROVISIONS OF THE TREATY OF 1914 FOR THE ADVANCEMENT OF PEACE BETWEEN THE UNITED STATES AND GREAT BRITAIN, SIGNED SEPTEMBER 6, 1940

[For text of treaty, see Department of State Treaty Series No. 975, or 55 Stat. 1214.]

ARRANGEMENT BETWEEN THE UNITED STATES AND CANADA GIVING EFFECT TO ARTICLE III OF THE AIR TRANSPORT ARRANGEMENT SIGNED AUGUST 18, 1939, EFFECTED BY EXCHANGE OF NOTES SIGNED NOVEMBER 29 AND DECEMBER 2, 1940

[For texts of notes, see Department of State Executive Agreement Series No. 186, or 54 Stat. 2422.]

SUPPLEMENTARY TRADE AGREEMENT BETWEEN THE UNITED STATES AND CANADA WITH REGARD TO FOXES AND FOX FURS AND SKINS, SIGNED AT WASHINGTON AND NEW YORK DECEMBER 13, 1940

[For text of the supplementary agreement, see Department of State Executive Agreement Series No. 216, or 55 Stat. 1319.]

INDIA

REPRESENTATIONS BY THE UNITED STATES CONCERNING ARREST AND INTERNMENT OF NATURALIZED AMERICAN CITIZEN BY THE GOVERNMENT OF INDIA WITHOUT FURNISHING REASONS THEREFOR

345.1121 Benz, Heinrich/1 : Telegram

The Consul at Calcutta (Groth) to the Secretary of State

CALCUTTA, July 20, 1940—6 p. m.
[Received July 20—1 : 55 p. m.]

This Consulate General is informed by the Government of India that it considers that Heinrich Benz, a naturalized American citizen of German origin registered as an American citizen at the American Consulate at Bombay, has been engaged in anti-British activities and his arrest ordered.

The American Consul at Bombay [1] states that Benz arrested same day and that his business in Bombay is in hands of custodian of enemy firms. Two-thirds of firm in question owned by two German brothers of Benz who were interned outbreak of hostilities.

Donovan strongly of the opinion that suspicions of the Government of India are groundless and are due to the fact that Benz is a naturalized American citizen of German origin.

Could the Department cite precedents which might be conveyed to the Government of India with a view to effecting Benz' release and possible deportation.

GROTH

345.1121 Benz, Heinrich/2 : Telegram

The Consul at Calcutta (Groth) to the Secretary of State

CALCUTTA, July 24, 1940—11 a. m.
[Received July 24—9 : 10 a. m.]

Referring to my telegram of July 20, 6 p. m., the following telegram received from the Consul at Bombay.

"July 23, 1 p. m. Heinrich Benz interviewed last night at my instance prior to being sent to internment camp Ahmed Nagar, denied the vague charges against him and said that his detention solely due

---

[1] Howard Donovan.

155

to German birth and brothers' nationality. He reported that police told him they had notified this office of his arrest although first official notice was received yesterday. Benz said he frequently asked to see a consular officer but that these requests were not communicated to me.

Wishes the Department to notify wife at 73 Park Street, Binghamton, New York, of the situation and that her husband is well.

Custodian of enemy property is holding radio, camera and some other articles of Benz. Inquiries are being made.

Benz only desire is to return to the United States. Suggest recommendation to the Department that strong representations be made for his release."

GROTH

345.1121 Benz, Heinrich/4 : Telegram

The Acting Secretary of State to the Consul at Calcutta (Groth)

WASHINGTON, July 27, 1940—4 p. m.

Your July 20, 6 p. m. and July 24, 11 a. m. in regard to arrest of Heinrich Benz. If there is reasonable ground to warrant belief that Benz has engaged in anti-British activities, this Government could not properly question the propriety of his arrest and would not be warranted in making representations for his release based on Benz's assertion of innocence and Bombay's acceptance of his assertion.

However, this Government has a right to be informed of the grounds and supporting evidence on which the arrest was made and you are instructed to request the appropriate authorities to furnish that information, pointing out that while this Government has no desire to intervene in behalf of any American citizen who may have violated the laws of India, it has the duty of protecting American citizens who may, through no fault of their own, be unjustly suspected of engaging in improper activities. You may add that if Benz has engaged in subversive activities it is desirable that adequate information concerning those activities be in the possession of this Government.

Mrs. Benz notified in accordance with request in Bombay's telegram to you.

WELLES

345.1121 Benz, Heinrich/10

The Consul at Calcutta (Groth) to the Secretary of State

No. 1720   CALCUTTA, September 5, 1940.
                                            [Received September 30.]

SIR: I have the honor to refer to my telegrams of July 24, 11 a. m. and July 20, 6 p. m. and to the Department's reply thereto of July 27th regarding the arrest and internment of Heinrich Benz by the

Government of India, and in connection therewith to report that although this office has on several occasions since the receipt of the Department's instructions endeavored to ascertain the cause for his arrest, the Government of India has thus far failed to inform this office as to the offences committed by Mr. Benz—other than to state that he is understood to be pro-Nazi—under the Defence of India Act or any other law of this country, which fact seems to confirm the opinion originally held by the Consulate at Bombay, viz., that the suspicions held against him are groundless. Were this not so there would be no reason for the Government of India so long to withhold an explanation regarding Mr. Benz' arrest and internment.

As there seems to be no prospect of a reply being forthcoming from the Government of India, it is respectfully suggested that the matter be referred to London so that the necessary instructions may be given which will result in Benz' release and in this office receiving a reply from the Government of India.

The Department's attention is invited to my despatch No. 1719 of September 5, 1940,[2] regarding Hans Richard Schilling, who is being detained under similar circumstances by the Government of India.[3]

Respectfully yours,   EDWARD M. GROTH

345.1121 Benz, Heinrich/8 : Telegram

The Secretary of State to the Consul at Calcutta (Groth)

WASHINGTON, September 18, 1940—7 p. m.

Department's July 27, 4 p. m. Telegraph briefly reply of Indian Government in regard to the Benz case. If a reply has not yet been received you should request that it be expedited.

HULL

345.1121 Benz, Heinrich/11 : Telegram

The Consul at Calcutta (Groth) to the Secretary of State

CALCUTTA, September 30, 1940—5 p. m.
[Received 9 : 30 p. m.]

Referring to the Department's telegram of July 27, 4 p. m., the Government of India now states that it will give further consideration to the release for return to the United States of Benz and Schilling (the latter referred to in the Department's telegram of June 24

---

[2] Not printed.
[3] In a telegram of October 16, 1940, 9 p. m., the Department instructed the Consulate General at Calcutta that since Mr. Schilling was unable to overcome presumption of expatriation he was not entitled to the protection of the United States, but that if released he could be issued a passport for return to the United States. Mr. Schilling was retained in a concentration camp. (130 Schilling, Hans Richard)

to Bombay ⁴) upon the recommendation of this office and the giving by it of a guaranty that these men will not disembark in the Far East and engage in undesirable activities. Upon receipt of Department's instructions the Consulate General will recommend the release of the aforementioned individuals on condition that they be placed aboard a ship of the American President Line at Bombay for return to New York, consequently they will be unable to disembark at any Far Eastern port.

GROTH

345.1121 Benz, Heinrich/12 : Telegram

The Secretary of State to the Consul at Calcutta (*Groth*)

WASHINGTON, October 4, 1940—8 p. m.

Your despatches 1719 and 1720 of September 5 ⁵ and your September 30, 5 p. m. Please inform the Government of India that you are instructed to state that its failure to comply with this Government's request for a statement of the grounds on which Benz was arrested and interned, warrants the presumption that his arrest and internment did not result from any violation of the laws of India or anti-British activities on his part. In this situation it is hoped that the Indian Government will recognize the clear impropriety of requiring any recommendation or guarantee from a representative of the United States as a condition to permitting Benz to return to the United States.

You may point out, however, that his repatriation is feasible by a route which will not take him via the Far East. Also that the passports of American citizens are taken up upon arrival in this country and are subject to review if further foreign travel is contemplated.

If Benz is released, passport should be made valid only for the journey to the United States, and the passport when issued should be delivered to the purser of the ship upon which he sails for release only to the immigration authorities at American port of entry. The Indian Government authorities may be apprised informally of these instructions.

The Department should be notified by telegram of the date of sailing and the name of the vessel in order that the appropriate authorities in this country may be notified.

Referring to your despatch no. 1719, as Schilling's case presents material differences, you should refrain from further representations for his release except on specific instructions from the Department.

HULL

---

⁴ Not printed.
⁵ Despatch No. 1719 not printed.

345.1121 Benz, Heinrich/13 : Telegram

The Consul General at Calcutta (Wilson) to the Secretary of State

CALCUTTA, December 23, 1940—noon.
[Received December 24—8 a. m.]

Reference the Department's telegram of October 4, 8 p. m. The Government of India has announced that it will release Benz for repatriation. As Benz is understood to be practically destitute can the Department arrange with American Export Line through Maritime Commission for his transportation from Calcutta at nominal rate? Please refer to despatch No. 147 dated November 15, 1940, from American Consul at Bombay.[6]

WILSON

345.1121 Benz, Heinrich/18 : Telegram

The Consul at Calcutta (Groth) to the Secretary of State

CALCUTTA, February 10, 1941—9 a. m.
[Received 7 : 04 p. m.]

Reference Department's telegram of October 4, 8 p. m. Heinrich Benz departed Calcutta as member of crew of SS *Explorer* due at New York about March 12.

GROTH

---

[6] Not found in Department files.

IRELAND

DISCUSSIONS WITH THE IRISH GOVERNMENT RELATING TO THE PURCHASE OF ARMS BY IRELAND AND THE USE OF IRISH PORTS BY THE UNITED KINGDOM

841D.01/179 : Telegram

The Minister in Ireland (Gray) to the Secretary of State

DUBLIN, May 18, 1940—11 a. m.
[Received May 18—11 a. m.]

16. Premier [1] confidentially requests me to inquire whether possible for our Government to proclaim Irish *status quo* vital to American interests in view of strategic position commanding Atlantic air and sea traffic; considers it would greatly strengthen his leadership; if reply favorable he would consult his Legislature and make formal approval. Situation very complicated, army's ability to cope with parachute raid in conjunction with submarine arms landing and Fifth Column with aim of establishing temporary air bases as diversion very doubtful. Premier asked me not to request permission for our Military Attache [2] to inspect dispositions on ground Germans might ask same privilege. They doubtless know them. Premier admits privately he depends for protection on Great Britain but says he dare not authorize staff consultations for fear of bad effect on public opinion. Urgently trying to obtain 500 machine guns from Great Britain. He says but small minority disloyal to the Government but dares not arm volunteer force. Asked if he intends to prepare public mind for the realities replied yes but slowly. He lacks a positive formula for rallying support. Declines thus far to make material concessions that might bring about concerted action with North.

GRAY

841D.01/179 : Telegram

The Secretary of State to the Minister in Ireland (Gray)

WASHINGTON, May 22, 1940—4 p. m.

18. Your 16, May 18, 11 a. m. Please inform the Prime Minister that while we should be glad to be of assistance to Ireland, we regret

[1] Eamon de Valera.
[2] Brig. Gen. Sherman Miles.

160

that it is impossible for this Government to take the action which he suggests. Any such declaration would imply that we are departing from our traditional policies in regard to European affairs, and would inevitably lead to misunderstanding and confusion in the United States and abroad. The extent to which such a declaration would contribute to the safety of Ireland is, in our opinion, open to question.

In explaining the foregoing confidentially to the Prime Minister, please tell him that his country enjoys a very special position in the hearts of our people and that we hope and pray that Ireland will be spared from the conflagration now raging.

HULL

841D.24/14 : Telegram

The Minister in Ireland (Gray) to the Secretary of State

DUBLIN, June 4, 1940—6 p. m.
[Received June 4—3 : 35 p. m.]

31. De Valera instructing his Minister in Washington to attempt to purchase certain arms which British in crisis cannot supply. He requests me earnestly to ask President to help facilitate obtaining them. He says situation here more dangerous than he dare specify. Possible that inability to defend neutrality opens back door. Personally I believe he does not exaggerate. He must rely in the circumstances on rapid fire small arms. If his specified requirements cannot be obtained can military experts suggest alternate equipment that is available? Irish use Enfield rifle and should have uniform ammunition. Could they be rearmed with weapons using uniform ammunition made in America? No time for economy.

GRAY

841D.24/14 : Telegram

The Secretary of State to the Minister in Ireland (Gray)

WASHINGTON, June 7, 1940—7 p. m.

29. Your no. 31, June 4, 6 p. m. The Irish Minister has informed the Department of his instructions and of the list of arms which he is to endeavor to purchase. The Department has arranged a meeting between the Minister and the Interdepartmental Committee charged by the President to act as liaison with foreign purchasing missions. The Committee will give the Minister all necessary information and assistance. After his consultation with the Committee, the Minister will be in a position to reply direct to his Government to the question asked in your telegram under acknowledgement.

HULL

841D.24/14a : Telegram

The Secretary of State to the Ambassador in the United Kingdom (Kennedy)

WASHINGTON, June 12, 1940—1 p. m.

1159. The Irish Minister in Washington has been instructed by his Government to purchase with the least possible delay a large quantity of arms of various types including rifles, artillery, armored cars and aircraft. If these arms are purchased without special assistance from and special action by this Government it will be many months before they could be delivered. Delivery could be greatly expedited if this Government were to arrange for priority for the Irish purchases. Please ascertain and report to the Department the attitude of the British Government in regard to possible efforts on the part of this Government to facilitate and expedite the purchase and delivery of these arms.

HULL

841D.24/16 : Telegram

The Ambassador in the United Kingdom (Kennedy) to the Secretary of State

LONDON, June 17, 1940—7 p. m.
[Received June 17—5 p. m.]

1692. Your 1159, June 12, 1 p. m., was taken up immediately with Foreign Office which has informed me today that a full reply in the matter has been telegraphed to Lord Lothian[3] with instructions to communicate it to the Department. The gist of this reply to your inquiry is that the British Government desires Lord Lothian and Mr. Purvis[4] to assist the Irish Government as far as possible in obtaining the material desired provided it does not impede or postpone delivery of any similar material ordered by the British Government.

KENNEDY

841D.34/2

Memorandum of Conversation, by Mr. Edgar P. Allen of the Division of Controls

[WASHINGTON,] July 15, 1940.

Mr. Denis Devlin, Secretary of the Irish Legation, came in to see me this afternoon. Mr. Devlin indicated that the Legation has re-

---

[3] British Ambassador in the United States.
[4] Arthur B. Purvis, Director General of the British Purchasing Commission in the United States.

ceived a cable from its Government, requesting the Legation to make immediate inquiry in regard to the possibility of the Irish Government obtaining immediately a destroyer from the United States Government. Mr. Devlin indicated that the need is urgent and said that the Irish Government would like to obtain several additional destroyers at a later date. He said that he felt that, in view of the political situation, the Legation would receive a negative answer.

I informed Mr. Devlin that it is my understanding of the law on the subject that there is no existing legislation which would authorize the Government of the United States to sell destroyers to the Government of Ireland. I mentioned briefly also the present endeavors of this Government to build up its Navy and expressed the view that because of our own national defense requirements at this time, it seemed inconceivable to me that the Navy Department, even if legal authority existed, would be in a position to give favorable consideration to the Legation's request. I told Mr. Devlin that I would place the Legation's inquiry before officials of the Department and that if the Department had any comment to offer other than that which I had already given him, I would so inform him.

EDGAR P. ALLEN

841D.34/2 : Telegram

The Minister in Ireland (Gray) to the Secretary of State

DUBLIN, July 19, 1940—6 p. m.
[Received July 19—2 : 16 p. m.]

61. The Ministry for External Affairs informs me that a request made by the Irish Minister in Washington [5] for the purchase of one to four destroyers for this Government has apparently met with some difficulties. The Ministry here has therefore asked me to repeat this request for one to four destroyers and to ascertain whether there is any possibility of obtaining delivery. Would appreciate any information which I may transmit to the Ministry in this connection.

GRAY

841D.24/24 : Telegram

The Minister in Ireland (Gray) to the Secretary of State

DUBLIN, August 15, 1940—5 p. m.
[Received August 15—1 : 22 p. m.]

168 [*68*]. Reference Department's telegram No. 39, June 20, 4 p. m.,[6] Irish Premier today informs me that purchase of rifles appears stale-

---

[5] Robert Brennan.
[6] Not printed.

mated in Washington. Is there yet hope for delivery. Need for these arms unquestionably pressing.

GRAY

841D.24/24

Memorandum by Mr. Edgar P. Allen of the Division of Controls

[WASHINGTON,] August 16, 1940.

Upon the receipt of the attached telegram number 68 dated August 15, 1940,[7] from the American Legation at Dublin, I telephoned Colonel MacMorland of the Army and Navy Munitions Board for information in regard thereto. Colonel MacMorland said that the President had directed the sale of the final lot of eighty thousand surplus Lee-Enfield rifles to Canada, having had before him at the time both the Canadian and Irish requests. He said that it was his understanding that the British Purchasing Commission would supply the Irish needs from the quantity which was sold in Canada. In a later conversation with Colonel MacMorland, after my discussions with Mr. Buckley and Mr. Ballantine, related below, Colonel Mac-Morland said that he had not been present at the final meeting at which the disposal of these rifles was decided upon and that he is in agreement with the view that the question of supplying rifles to the Irish is one for determination between the British and Irish authorities.

I telephoned Mr. Buckley, who is acting, in Mr. Young's absence, for Mr. Philip Young, Chairman of the President's Liaison Committee charged with coordinating sales to foreign governments with the needs of our own services. Mr. Buckley read to me a letter which he addressed to the Irish Minister under date of August 15, 1940, in which he referred to the Minister's request of June 17 to purchase twenty thousand Lee-Enfield rifles and informed the Minister that there are no surplus Lee-Enfield rifles available for sale at this time. The Minister was given the pertinent facts in regard to the sale of the eighty thousand rifles to Canada.

Mr. Buckley said, as had Colonel MacMorland, that when the eighty thousand rifles were up for disposal, the President had before him both the Canadian and Irish requests and that the President endorsed the document "O. K. for Canada." Mr. Buckley said that it was his understanding that any rifles supplied to Ireland would have to be taken care of out of the quantity sold to Canada. He expressed the feeling that this was a question for discussion and determination between the British and Irish authorities.

---

[7] *Supra.*

Mr. Ballantine of the British Purchasing Commission was in Mr. Buckley's office at the time of my discussion with Mr. Buckley and I conferred briefly by telephone with Mr. Ballantine who informed me that the Canadians did not originally have in mind purchasing as many as eighty thousand rifles and that this larger quantity of rifles was made available to Canada for the sole reason of hemisphere defense. He indicated that he has discussed the question with the Secretary of the Irish Legation but was rather positive in indicating the feeling that there would be a breach of confidence if any of these rifles were to be turned over to Ireland. Neither Colonel MacMorland nor Mr. Buckley has any record of any such understanding and they are both strongly of the opinion that if the British wish the Irish to have these rifles, it is up to the British to provide them in one way or another.

EDGAR P. ALLEN

841D.24/24 : Telegram

The Secretary of State to the Minister in Ireland (Gray)

WASHINGTON, August 28, 1940—noon.

57. Your 168 [*68*], August 15, 5 p. m. As the Department informed you in its telegram of June 20 [8] and as the Irish Minister here was informed at the time, it was then believed that the Irish Government's needs could be met, at least in part. This now appears impossible and the Irish Minister has been informed that no rifles are available for sale at this time.

For your own confidential information the final 80,000 Lee-Enfield rifles were sold at the President's direction to Canada through the British Purchasing Commission. The Irish Minister has been informed of this sale and it has been suggested to him that the possibility of supplying Ireland's needs from the quantity sold to Canada be discussed with the British or Canadians. It is understood that there have recently been discussions between the Irish Minister and the British Purchasing Commission on this subject.

HULL

841D.24/27 : Telegram

The Minister in Ireland (Gray) to the Secretary of State

DUBLIN, September 12, 1940—10 p. m.
[Received September 12—10 : 50 a. m.]

81. Department's No. 57, August 28, noon. The Irish Premier has explained to me the urgent need of at least 20,000 rifles. There appears to be no immediate prospect of obtaining these from the allot-

---

[8] Telegram No. 39, not printed.

ment sold to Canada. He has been informed of the possibility of another lot being made available shortly from which Lothian and Purvis suggest to Brennan Irish requirements might be supplied. De Valera asks me to convey to the President his hope that delivery of at least 20,000 may be made possible without delay in view of critical possibilities of which the President is fully aware.

GRAY

841D.24/27 : Telegram

The Secretary of State to the Minister in Ireland (*Gray*) [9]

WASHINGTON, September 20, 1940—6 p. m.

64. Your no. 81, September 12, 10 p. m. There are no surplus rifles available for sale at this time. All rifles which were declared surplus have been already disposed of to foreign governments.

HULL

841D.24/27 : Telegram

The Secretary of State to the Minister in Ireland (*Gray*)

WASHINGTON, September 25, 1940—noon.

66. Department's No. 64, September 20, 6 p. m. An additional lot of rifles has been declared surplus and is being sold to the British. It is suggested that the Irish Government may wish to instruct Brennan to discuss this matter further with Lothian and Purvis.

HULL

740.0011 European War 1939/6918

Memorandum of Conversation, by the Under Secretary of State (*Welles*)

[WASHINGTON,] November 9, 1940.

The Irish Minister called to see me this morning. The Minister gave me a copy of the speech of Mr. de Valera of November 7 with regard to the utilization of Irish ports by the British Government.

The Minister likewise gave me a memorandum of the points which he made in our conversation. Both of these documents are attached herewith.[10]

In reply to the Minister I stated that the statement which he had made and the speech of Mr. de Valera made the position of the Irish Government very clear and that I could inform him categorically that

---

[9] This telegram was based on reply to inquiry made to Henry L. Stimson, Secretary of War.

[10] Speech not attached to file copy of this document.

no approach had been made to this Government by the British Government in regard to this subject.

I said that I did not, of course, intend to imply that I was questioning the wisdom of the policy of the Government of Eire, but that I wondered what the situation of the Irish people would be if Germany defeated the British, or were placed in a position of domination over the British Isles. I said, of course, the Minister had agreed with me that the utilization of southern Irish ports would be of great service to the British Navy under present conditions and that it would seem as if through its attitude on this question the Irish Government was jeopardizing its own security. The Minister said that there was no question about the value to the British of southern Irish ports, but that there was likewise no question but that if the Irish Government permitted this step, feeling in Ireland would turn bitterly against the British and it was highly probable that revolution would develop within the Irish Free State. Moreover, the Minister added, the Irish had absolutely no means of withstanding aerial attack and the Government was unable to obtain either planes or anti-aircraft artillery. Under such conditions, he said, the Irish Government could do nothing else than adhere to a policy of neutrality.

S[UMNER] W[ELLES]

[Annex]

The Irish Legation to the Department of State

At the outbreak of the war the Irish Government in accordance with previously stated policy declared Ireland's neutrality. This policy was supported by all parties in the Dail and by the entire press of the country.

Britain did not question Ireland's right to declare this policy and no attempt was made to interfere with it. The policy of neutrality has been scrupulously observed. The Government established a costly Coast Watching Service to see that none of the warring powers should take advantage of it. In order to defend Ireland's independence and safeguard its neutrality the Government raised the armed forces to 200,000 men, all volunteers. A similar force in the United States in proportion to population would be eight million men.

The friendly feeling between the British and Irish peoples which had arisen after the settlement of 1938 [11] was steadily increasing in spite of the fact that the last remaining grievance of the Irish people, that of Partition, had not been remedied.

---

[11] Agreements between the United Kingdom and Ireland signed April 25, 1938; see *British and Foreign State Papers*, vol. CXLII, pp. 10 ff.

On November 5th the British Prime Minister [12] in the course of a speech in the House of Commons said that Britain's deprivation of the use of Irish ports as naval and air bases was a serious handicap in fighting the war being waged on British shipping. This was followed by a chorus of demands in the British Parliament and in the British press for the return of these ports to England and this campaign found an echo in the American press. Press statements emanating from London asserted that the good offices of the President of the United States might be enlisted to induce the Irish Government to concede the use of the ports by Britain.

In the view of the Irish Government cession or lease of the ports would be a breach of neutrality which would bring Ireland into the war contrary to the declared policy of the Government and the wishes of 99% of the people.

Mr. de Valera asserted on the 7th November that Ireland would resist by force any attempt to occupy the ports or to impair Ireland's sovereignty by any of the belligerents. That is the determination of the Government and of the people. Under no circumstances will this policy be departed from.

The Government and people of Ireland are in hopes that America, the cradle and home of democracy, will realise the justice of Ireland's attitude in thus seeking to preserve its independence, its peace and its democratic institutions.

740.0011 European War 1939/6579 : Telegram

The Minister in Ireland (Gray) to the Secretary of State

DUBLIN, November 10, 1940—1 p. m.
[Received 6 p. m.]

99. Referring to my telegram No. 98,[13] had confidential and friendly talk with Walshe, External Affairs, who lunched November 7 before Prime Minister statement regarding Irish ports. This statement as foreshadowed in our telegram has received warm approval throughout country, memorandum of Walshe conversation being forwarded by pouch.[14]

Walshe stated that Irish Government would never give England the ports. Aside from question of neutrality his Government believed that they would never get them back. That also was his belief, unless there were American guarantee. I asked what would happen if United

---

[12] Winston Churchill.
[13] Dated November 8, 6 p. m., not printed.
[14] Transmitted by the Minister in Ireland as an enclosure to his despatch No. 96, November 13, not printed.

States were attacked and so brought into war and needed Irish air and sea bases. He said he thought that could be arranged without great difficulty. Discussed these same points the following day with Dillon, Opposition leader and member of Defense Council, who lunched here Friday. He said that if he proposed giving England the ports De Valera would beat him 14 to 1. That if he proposed giving the United States the ports and De Valera opposed it he would beat De Valera 3 to 1. He said that De Valera had told him he would lease the ports to no one.

One practical difficulty not discussed but important alike to De Valera's supporters and opponents is the defenselessness of Irish cities from air attack. Eire has no anti-aircraft guns or fighter planes. Adequate defense of cities would be prerequisite to taking over ports. Armament discussion with Great Britain continues in [a?] circle. Premier complains he is not trusted and cannot get arms. British feel they cannot supply essential kinds of armament to Government which withholds sympathy. Such arms might be used against them. Premier says they would not be so used unless Irish sovereignty were menaced. England says such a step if taken would only be for Irish protection. De Valera answers, "Give us arms and we will protect ourselves and you too," so on endlessly.

Referring back to conversation with Walshe I told him that I thought his Government must be prepared for support of Great Britain in the American press in case Churchill, moved by what he conceived to be a necessity, announced that he would occupy the ports by force after presenting publicly his brief which would probably include what is reported to be Chamberlain's undocumented understanding at the time he surrendered them,[15] that in case of need the harbors would be available.

Walshe suggested that if we should be brought in against our will the approach to bases should be along the lines of regrouping of democracies after victory, an enterprise in which his Government would be glad to participate. He said that his Chief was thinking in this direction. He suggested even permanent American air and sea bases in Ireland for the control of the North Atlantic. He would want us evidently as a buffer against England.

As we see it here any attempt by Churchill to negotiate for the ports will be hopeless. He has the choice between seizing them and paying the price in possible bloodshed and certain hostility and doing without. If he said that he could not any longer supply Ireland in British vessels it would probably bring home the situation to the Irish people and cause discontent with the Government but De Valera would probably capitalize it for his own political advantage. His whole

---

[15] By agreement of April 25, 1938. Neville Chamberlain was British Prime Minister at the time.

power is based on his genius for engendering and utilizing anti-British sentiment. His administration otherwise is generally unsuccessful. He is probably the most adroit politician in Europe and he honestly believes that all he does is for the good of the country. He has the qualities of martyr, fanatic and Machiavelli. No one can outwit him, frighten or blandish him. Remember that he is not pro-German nor personally anti-British but only pro-De Valera. My view is that he will do business on his own terms or must be overcome by force.

GRAY

740.0011 European War 1939/6589 : Telegram

The Minister in Ireland (Gray) to the Secretary of State

DUBLIN, November 11, 1940—11 a. m.
[Received November 11—8 : 59 a. m.]

100. My telegram number 98, November 8, 6 p. m.[16] Very confidentially informed that Churchill's reference to Irish ports was an expression of personal nature of which Cabinet had not been advised. British representative here coincides with views and conclusions set forth in my telegram under reference.

GRAY

740.0011 European War 1939/6749 : Telegram

The Minister in Ireland (Gray) to the Secretary of State

DUBLIN, November 18, 1940—1 p. m.
[Received 3 : 38 p. m.]

102. Reference my telegram No. 99, November 10, 1 p. m. and to the memorandum of conversation transmitted with my despatch No. 96, November 13.[17]

Contributing to conjecture as to the real but concealed attitude of the Ministry for External Affairs toward Great Britain, I am informed in strict confidence that 3 days ago the Permanent Secretary stated his belief that Germany would [win?] the war; that England at best could not alter "the new order" in Europe; that we would not become involved; that our aid to Great Britain would be unavailing; that the disabling of three Italian battleships,[18] if a fact,

---

[16] Not printed.
[17] Despatch and enclosure not printed.
[18] The British Fleet Air Arm inflicted heavy damage on Italian warships at Taranto during the night of November 11–12, 1940; three Italian battleships were among those damaged.

spelled the downfall of British sea power as Italian airplanes could sink British ships. Asked if he did not think Great Britain was fighting for something worthwhile he replied that no one outside of Great Britain believed that.

He apparently is very closely watching American opinion through Brennan for he stated that American press had given friendly reception to Irish Premier's speech about the ports, that Conboy's [19] speech had been well received and that Ireland's offer to receive refugees had changed United States opinion antagonistic to Ireland overnight. This probably is not far from De Valera's beliefs. For our guidance please telegraph your estimate of press opinion as to each of these three points. We have been trying to explain unofficially that while our Government understood Irish neutrality policy any anti-Irish interpretation of it by uncensored American newspapers was likely to excite hostile criticism and endanger our happy relations.

GRAY

740.0011 European War 1939/6749 : Telegram

The Acting Secretary of State to the Minister in Ireland (Gray)

WASHINGTON, November 19, 1940—6 p. m.

77. Your 102, November 18, 1 p. m. Please communicate to Mr. De Valera at the earliest opportunity the following views which represent the substance of my reply to the Irish Minister, when on November 9, he handed me a copy of Mr. De Valera's speech of November 7 with regard to the utilization of Irish ports by Great Britain:

I said that undoubtedly his Government had good reason for its policy but it seemed to us that through its attitude the Irish Government is jeopardizing its own security. What would be the situation of the Irish people if Germany should defeat Britain or should be in a position to dominate the British Isles? There would be no question in those circumstances of freedom or democracy for the Irish people.

The utilization of the Irish ports apparently was imperative to the success of the British Navy under present conditions. Although there had been no approach to this Government by the British Government with regard to this matter I was moved to express an opinion because my view coincides with that of virtually the entire American press and the vast preponderance of public opinion as well.

WELLES

---

[19] Martin Conboy, New York lawyer.

740.0011 European War 1939/6832 : Telegram

The Minister in Ireland (Gray) to the Secretary of State

DUBLIN, November 24, 1940—noon.
[Received 6 : 06 p. m.]

105. Reference your telegram No. 77, November 19, 6 p. m. Pursuant to your instructions I conveyed to De Valera on November 22 the views expressed in your telegram under reference. In a letter to him requesting an interview, I explained that your message was in response to my request for confirmation of my previously expressed interpretation of the trend of American opinion that Americans, as I had told Walshe, viewed Irish enjoyment of security and neutral rights under international law as being secured by and at the expense of Great Britain, as well as the unrationed standard of living here. I expressed that his unwillingness to explore the possibilities of cooperation might produce criticism that would have bad effect on our happy relations.

He received me cordially but said that any discussion of leasing an inch of this country's territory to anyone was out of the question. It was not a war of Ireland's choosing and that it was strange that the neutral United States should deny the right of neutrality to a small nation. I replied that we were not denying any right but that as all right ultimately depended on power he might be relying on the power of American public opinion to support him and that he might fail to receive this support. He said that there was a God in Heaven who would support him and they would all die if need be in defense of their sovereignty.

He then gave his views on the probable postwar set-up of the world suggesting a German-controlled Europe with England and Ireland aligned with the commonwealth of nations and the Americas. He told me that he had believed in Hitler up to the taking of Czechoslovakia. Now he condemns him. He again complained of not being able to get suitable arms from England though admitting that he intended to use them against Great Britain if trespassed upon.

Before this interview I was informed very confidentially that the Deputy Leader of the Opposition [20] had on November 20th warned De Valera that his policy appeared to be ranging him against Britain and the United States and on the side of Germany, that if it came to a question of declaring war on England the Deputy Leader would go to the country even if it brought on civil war here. In my view great care must be taken if any pressure is to be exerted that it give him no grounds for strengthening his political position. Churchill played

---

[20] James Dillon.

into his hands. His genius for capitalizing such tactical errors cannot be overestimated. Despatch with details will be forwarded by pouch.[21]

GRAY

740.0011 European War 1939/7148

Memorandum of Conversation, by the Under Secretary of State (Welles)

[WASHINGTON,] December 9, 1940.

The Irish Minister called to see me at his request. He stated that he had been advised by his Government of a recent conversation which Mr. Gray had had with Prime Minister de Valera by instruction of the Department. In this conversation Mr. Gray was alleged to have said to the Prime Minister that in the last conversation which the Minister and I had had, I had indicated to the Minister that the United States was going to get into the war in the near future and that in such event the naval bases in Eire which the British desire to use would have to be made available to the United States anyway and that, consequently, there was no reason why the Irish Government should not make these bases available at once to the British. The Minister said that to the best of his recollection no references of this character had been made in our conversation and he was consequently at a loss to know on what grounds Mr. Gray's conversation is based.

I replied that the Minister was entirely accurate in his recollection and that no such remarks had been made by me, directly or indirectly, nor, for that matter, did such remarks represent the policy of this Government. I stated that I felt sure there was some misunderstanding which could readily be clarified.

I stated that I could merely reiterate in general terms what I had said in my previous conversations, namely, that as the Irish Minister had admitted to me, naval and air bases in Eire would be of the greatest assistance and value to the British in their struggle for self defense and that, in as much as it was the announced policy of this Government to give all possible support and assistance to the British, this Government could not fail to view with sympathy any steps which the Government of Eire might take to assist the British in their struggle. At the present time, I stated, it was, of course, clear that the German submarines and raiders were concentrating on the North Atlantic approach to the British Isles and that so long as the British

[21] No. 101, November 25, not printed.

were deprived of the facilities which they could enjoy in Ireland, they were to that extent handicapped in their resistance against the attacks made upon their convoys. I told the Minister that the President had asked me to let him know that he desired to speak with him immediately after his return to Washington and I felt that this was a matter which the President would wish to discuss in some detail with the Minister. The Minister repeated to me the arguments he had advanced in all previous conversations, namely, that Eire was not prepared and that if she relaxed her neutrality in this regard she would be at once subjected to the kind of aerial bombardment from which Great Britain, herself, is now suffering. Furthermore, he said that any steps taken to relax Irish neutrality would result immediately in revolution in Ireland. To my comment that if Great Britain were defeated and invaded, Ireland would in any event suffer the same fate and be subjected to German domination, the Minister replied that he was in entire agreement that that would be the case but the alternatives that they were now up against were either inevitable destruction from the air and possible invasion from the sea by the Germans, or else potential domination by Germany in the event of the British defeat. He said that the complete neutrality policy of de Valera was becoming more and more firmly determined upon and that every message the Minister received from de Valera made this clearer.

The Minister then said that he was very much concerned by the activities of the William Allen White Committee.[22] He said that agents of the Committee were circularizing prominent Irishmen throughout the United States urging them to come out for the cession of bases in Ireland to the British and that these agents of the Committee had had so little tact in their representations as to select old time Fenians as the objects of their representations. This, the Minister said, was creating a violent disturbance upon the part of the Irish element in the United States and he feared that very soon there would be on foot Irish-American propaganda to the effect that the British were seeking these bases in Eire solely as a means of restoring British domination over Ireland. He stated this kind of reaction was already well under way in Massachusetts and that from a conversation which he had had in Philadelphia with Cardinal Daugherty two days ago he learned that it was already rife in Pennsylvania.

The Minister said that he had talked with Lord Lothian on this subject and that he stated steps would be taken to prevent the William Allen White Committee from continuing along these lines. He said it was particularly unfortunate that this should happen at a moment

[22] Committee to Defend America by Aiding the Allies.

when the Irish-American feeling in general had become sympathetic to the British cause. If this propaganda did not stop, he said, all the progress towards British-Irish understanding which had been made in recent years would be lost.

S[UMNER] W[ELLES]

NEW ZEALAND

ARRANGEMENT BETWEEN THE UNITED STATES AND NEW ZEALAND WITH REGARD TO THE IMPORTATION INTO NEW ZEALAND OF AIRCRAFT AND AIRCRAFT COMPONENTS MANUFACTURED IN THE UNITED STATES, SIGNED AT WELLINGTON JANUARY 30 AND FEBRUARY 28, 1940

[For text of the arrangement, see Department of State Executive Agreement Series No. 167, or 54 Stat. 2263.]

TREATY BETWEEN THE UNITED STATES AND NEW ZEALAND AMENDING IN THEIR APPLICATION CERTAIN PROVISIONS OF THE TREATY OF 1914 FOR THE ADVANCEMENT OF PEACE BETWEEN THE UNITED STATES AND GREAT BRITAIN, SIGNED SEPTEMBER 6, 1940

[For text of treaty, see Department of State Treaty Series No. 976, or 55 Stat. 1217.]

176

UNION OF SOUTH AFRICA

TREATY BETWEEN THE UNITED STATES AND THE UNION OF SOUTH AFRICA AMENDING IN THEIR APPLICATION CERTAIN PROVISIONS OF THE TREATY OF 1914 FOR THE ADVANCEMENT OF PEACE BETWEEN THE UNITED STATES AND GREAT BRITAIN, SIGNED APRIL 2, 1940

[For text of treaty, see Department of State Treaty Series No. 966, or 55 Stat. 1130.]

UNION OF SOVIET SOCIALIST REPUBLICS

REPORTS ON DEVELOPMENTS OF SIGNIFICANCE CONCERNING SOVIET RELATIONS WITH OTHER COUNTRIES, ESPECIALLY WITH THE UNITED STATES [1]

700.00116 M.E./10

Memorandum by the Chief of the Division of Controls (Green)

[WASHINGTON,] December 15, 1939.

After consultation with Mr. Moffat [2] and Mr. Henderson,[3] and after receiving instructions from the Secretary [4] that the policy of discouraging the sale of information in regard to the manufacture of high quality aviation gasoline was to be extended to the U. S. S. R.,[5] I called Mr. C. S. Reed, president of the Lummus Company, New York, and Mr. Carter, secretary of the Universal Oil Products Company, Chicago, by telephone this afternoon.

I told Mr. Reed that I understood that his company had two employees—Raymond Barton Owens and Viggo E. Hanson—now in the U. S. S. R. engaged in constructing a plant for the manufacture of gasoline products. I suggested that the company instruct these men to leave the U. S. S. R. without delay and to communicate with the American Ambassador in Moscow.[6] Mr. Reed asked no questions. He said that he would act immediately upon my suggestion.

I told Mr. Carter that I understood that his company had two employees—Hugh Rodman and Orion Newall Miller—now in the U. S. S. R. engaged in constructing a plant for the manufacture of gasoline products. Mr. Carter said that the company also had a third American employee—A. C. Rassmussen—in the U. S. S. R. I made the same suggestion to Mr. Carter that I had made to Mr. Reed. Mr. Carter asked whether he was correct in his understanding that Mr. Halle, president of the company, who had attended a conference at the Department yesterday, would understand the reasons for my mak-

---

[1] Continued from *Foreign Relations*, The Soviet Union, 1933–1939, pp. 731–809.
[2] Pierrepont Moffat, Chief of the Division of European Affairs.
[3] Loy W. Henderson, Assistant Chief of the Division of European Affairs.
[4] Cordell Hull, Secretary of State.
[5] For the institution of the moral embargo, see telegram No. 265, December 4, 1939, 6 p. m., to the Ambassador in the Soviet Union, and footnote 2g, *Foreign Relations*, The Soviet Union, 1933–1939, p. 801; also telegram No. 313, December 24, 1939, 4 p. m., to the Ambassador in the Soviet Union, *ibid.*, p. 806.
[6] Laurence A. Steinhardt.

ing this suggestion. I replied in the affirmative. Mr. Carter said that he would immediately communicate with Mr. Halle and would take appropriate action.

J[OSEPH] C. G[REEN]

700.00116 M.E./14

Memorandum by the Chief of the Division of Controls (Green)

[WASHINGTON,] December 26, 1939.

Mr. C. S. Reed, President of the Lummus Company, telephoned me from New York this morning. He said that he had received another telegram from the company's engineers at Ufa stating that the Soviet authorities had refused to permit them to leave that city. He said that the company's officials were in great anxiety in regard to the safety of its engineers and he asked what, if anything, the company should do in the circumstances.

I replied that the Department was fully aware of the situation, was in frequent communication with our Embassy in Moscow in regard to the matter, and was taking all necessary steps to insure the safety of the engineers and their immediate departure from the Soviet Union. I said that I did not believe that the company should attempt to take any further action at this time.

Mr. Reed said that Amtorg [7] had been making every effort to persuade the company to send four more engineers to the Soviet Union, that the company was refusing to do so, and was citing the desires of this Government as a reason for its refusal.

J[OSEPH] C. G[REEN]

700.00116 M.E./39 : Telegram

The Ambassador in the Soviet Union (Steinhardt) to the Secretary of State

Moscow, January 6, 1940—noon.
[Received January 6—10 : 19 a. m.]

26. My 9, January 3, 11 a. m.[8] Rassmussen, Rodmans, Hansons, Millers and Owens are now in Moscow. Permission for them to leave the Soviet Union has not yet been granted but the resistance to their departure appears to be weakening and I believe that after the Soviet authorities have exhausted all of the obstructive tactics they can think of exit visas will be forthcoming.

STEINHARDT

---

[7] Amtorg Trading Corporation, official purchasing and sales agency of the Soviet Union in the United States.
[8] Not printed.

700.00116 M.E./64 : Telegram

The Ambassador in the Soviet Union (*Steinhardt*) to the Secretary of State

Moscow, January 15, 1940—6 p. m.
[Received 7 : 10 p. m.]

59. After 10 days replete with evasions, obstructions, and delays exit visas were finally issued this afternoon to Rassmussen, the Hansons, Millers and Owens. As an example of the tactics employed, Rodman's exit visa is being withheld by the Soviet authorities pending an extension of his permit to reside in the Soviet Union which has expired since his arrival in Moscow. I hope to be able to obtain Rodman's exit visa within the next 2 or 3 days.

STEINHARDT

861.50/934

The Ambassador in the Soviet Union (*Steinhardt*) to the Secretary of State

No. 269   Moscow, January 24, 1940.
[Received March 5.]

SIR: I have the honor to refer to the Embassy's despatch No. 2312, of May 10, 1939,[9] transmitting a memorandum relating to the self-sufficiency and export capacity of the Soviet Union in respect of twenty-five essential raw materials, and to present below in summary form the gist of comment which has recently been published in the central and trade press concerning the utilization of Soviet resources of certain rare metals and of iron ore and coal.

Rare Metals.

Pravda of January 4, 1940, carries an article in which it is pointed out that the requirements of the domestic demand for such rare metals as tungsten, molybdenum, cobalt, tin and others have not been fully supplied by home production, but must be met to a greater or lesser degree by importation. The article raises the query as to whether it would be possible to expand domestic output so as to render possible the elimination of imports, and answers this question in the affirmative, claiming that Soviet resources are sufficient to enable the country to become self-supporting in these minerals. It is pointed out that the mining and smelting of rare metals is largely under the supervision and control of the Chief Administration of the Rare Metals Industry, which works ore deposits having a comparatively high content of the metals in question. Such deposits, on the other hand, it

---

[9] *Foreign Relations*, The Soviet Union, 1933–1939, p. 762.

is stated, constitute only a small fraction of the total known resources of rare metals within the confines of Soviet territory.

The article continues that the major portion of Soviet resources of rare metals are found in combination with other minerals, as secondary metal. Thus, for example, 70 percent of the total known reserves of molybdenum are encountered as secondary or accompanying metal in the copper ores of the Conrad, Pirdoudan and other mines. None of these mines, however, is engaged in the extraction of molybdenum. A similar condition prevails with respect to cobalt. Only 2 percent of the total resources of this metal are directly encountered, 80 percent being met with in combination with nickel and 18 percent in iron and manganese ores. The situation with regard to other rare metals such as tungsten and cadmium is stated to be the same. Such metals as indium and germanium, it is added, are only obtained as by-products from tailings of other metals, which they accompany.

The article urges that there is every reason to organize the intensive extraction of rare metals from ferrous and non-ferrous ores, to be undertaken, of course, in conjunction with increased mining of those ores in which rare metals appear as basic element. At present such extraction is conducted on a very small scale only and is disproportionate with the large possibilities it offers, according to the cited source. The main obstacle to the greater development of the extraction of secondary metals is stated to be the predominance of the so-called "mono-metallist" theory among Soviet engineers and scientific organizations. Many of them, the article alleges, have the vaguest idea of the properties and usefulness of rare metals, and concentrate their attention upon the production of the basic metal, making the increased output of this their main concern. In the last 10 years, the article concludes, millions of rubles have been invested in the enterprises of the Chief Administration of the Rare Metals Industry, but the returns on this investment are being realized very slowly, the volume of production being low and the cost high.

The comment may be made in connection with the article which has been summarized above that the problem of rare metal supply is one of the utmost importance in the Soviet Union, since, as has been suggested and as the Department is aware, the major portion of the country's requirements in many of these metals, which are essential to the war industries, has hitherto been met by importation. Deterioration of the already strained relations between the Soviet Union and Great Britain might lead to stoppage of the inflow of these metals and threaten to cause a dangerous shortage. On the other hand, the extraction and separation of rare metals from other ores is not a simple matter. It would in many instances require complex processing schemes, involving the employment of special equipment.

Iron Ore.

Pravda of January 5. 1940, contains an article discussing the problem of a better utilization of the iron ore resources of the Soviet Union. Emphasis is placed by this article on the need for an intensified working of low-grade iron ore deposits, mentioning in particular those found in the Krivoi Rog basins. It is averred that experimental data which have been assembled leave no doubt as to the possibilities for the practicable employment of such ores in the Soviet metallurgical industry.

Industriya of January 8, 1940, also carries a number of articles discussing the problems of iron ore shortage and of the highest possible utilization of low-grade iron ores. The content and general tone of these articles clearly disclose the anxiety which the Soviet authorities feel concerning the growing scarcity of iron ore, with its direct influence upon the country's steel industry.

The foregoing material is seen to confirm earlier information reported by the Embassy to the effect that the Soviet steel industry is seriously threatened with a shortage of iron ore and that the existing deposits of rich ores are being rapidly depleted. The problem of low-grade ore utilization, moreover, presents considerable difficulties, since this would entail the construction of a good many ore dressing plants, and since the Soviet blast furnaces and particularly their operators are poorly adapted for the execution of this task, the latter having neither sufficient experience nor the requisite training.

Coal.

Industriya of January 4, 1940, publishes a leading article dealing with the extremely low utilization of productive capacities in the Soviet coal industry and pointing to the very large sums invested annually in the construction of shafts and other coal mining equipment, without a commensurate increase in the output of coal. The article remarks that a majority of the shafts which have been put into operation in recent years are operating only to a portion of their normal capacity, which results in a noticeable disproportion between the productive capacity of the coal industry and the actual output of coal. Thus, large capital investments are immobilized and the national economy is deprived of adequate coal supplies.

Izvestiya of January 6, 1940, offers a leading article discussing developments in the coal industry during 1939. It states that the functioning of this industrial branch was unsatisfactory. Although the total production is stated to have exceeded the preceding year, the State plan was nevertheless not fulfilled. Poor technical management and a shortage of experienced and qualified workers are blamed for this condition.

Respectfully yours, LAURENCE A. STEINHARDT

861.00/11850 : Telegram

The Ambassador in the Soviet Union (Steinhardt) to the Secretary
of State

Moscow, February 17, 1940—6 p. m.
[Received 7 : 35 p. m.]

185. I returned to Moscow today following 6 days in transit through Riga, Tallinn, Narva and Leningrad. As a result of my observations and conversations with well-informed persons during the past week I have gained the following impressions:

(1) While there are persistent rumors in Latvia and Estonia to the effect that the Soviet Government contemplates further control over those states,[10] Wiley [11] and I were assured by the Foreign Ministers of both countries that no important demands have recently been made of them by the Soviet Government and that they do not anticipate such demands. It was apparent to me nonetheless that Soviet influence in Latvia and Estonia is already very great, is steadily increasing, and that the Latvians and Estonians in general feel that the Soviet military forces which are everywhere in evidence especially on the railways constitute virtually an army of occupation.

(2) It is evident that the Swedish Government is actively engaged in the Baltic States in an endeavor to bring about action leading to the cessation of the Finnish-Soviet conflict.[12] I believe that in these activities Sweden is at present acting independently of Germany and Estonia both of which countries are likewise engaged in similar activities.

(3) There has been a decided improvement recently in conditions in Leningrad which I found to be far better than previous reports would indicate. Food conditions at the present time in that city do not appear to be worse than usual, transportation appears to be normal. I could detect no signs of tension or discontent. The shops appeared to be better stocked than those in Moscow. I saw no wounded or other signs of the war in progress but a few miles distant aside from the blackout.

(4) On the journey from Tallinn to Leningrad and especially after passing Narva I observed large military concentrations which in-

---

[10] For correspondence concerning the interference by the Soviet Union in the Baltic States in 1939, see *Foreign Relations*, The Soviet Union, 1933–1939, pp. 934 ff. For correspondence on the forcible occupation and the absorption of the Baltic States into the Soviet Union in 1940, see *Foreign Relations*, 1940, vol. I, pp. 357 ff.

[11] John C. Wiley, Minister in Estonia and Latvia, with residence in Riga.

[12] For correspondence regarding the aggression by the Soviet Union against Finland and outbreak of the Winter War in 1939, see *Foreign Relations*, 1939, vol. I, pp. 952 ff. Concerning the developments in the war and in Finnish-Soviet relations in 1940, see *ibid.*, 1940, vol. I, pp. 269 ff.

cluded abundant light field artillery and light and medium tanks, field kitchens, and troops of all categories including substantial bodies of ski troops. At one airfield near which the train stopped for some time I observed abundant quantities of gasoline and approximately 30 large tri-motored bombers of modern design. I assume that these forces are being assembled in the neighborhood of Leningrad primarily as reserves for the offensive operations in progress on the Karelian Isthmus although it is possible that should the Gulf of Finland freeze to a degree that would make such an operation practicable they might be utilized in an attempt to outflank the Mannerheim positions.

(5) With respect to the policy of the Soviet Government toward the Finnish conflict all of the persons with whom I spoke confirmed my impression that the Soviet Government has thus far not been responsive to attempts to bring the conflict to an end through mediation or otherwise although it is generally felt that should the present offensive fail the Soviet Government might thereafter be willing to give consideration to a negotiated settlement provided virtually all of its terms could be met. I observed a general belief that in that event the Soviet Government might be inclined to accept mediation on the part of Germany, Estonia, Sweden or the United States, or at least avail itself of the good offices of one of these countries. I am convinced, however, that until the Soviet Government has satisfied itself that it cannot achieve a decisive military victory it will not entertain any proposals for mediation and that as a result of its lack of success thus far it is now devoting much more serious attention to the technical measures necessary for the prosecution of the war and is now attaining a greater degree of proficiency in organization and attack than heretofore.

(6) I was particularly impressed by the noticeably bad condition of the Soviet railway system especially by the deteriorated condition of the rolling stock which is in a far worse state than the roadbed. There appears to be a grave shortage of locomotives and in addition to this lack of hauling capacity a decidedly inefficient organization inasmuch as I observed thousands of freight cars lying idle on sidings. Judging by the chalked date markings on the sides and their appearance, most of these cars had been on such sidings for several weeks. The speed of the passenger trains on which I traveled was only a few miles an hour. The trip from Moscow to Riga required 42 hours. The second night the train was unlighted, without sleeping accommodations, and without food or even water throughout the whole trip.

STEINHARDT

861.002/189 : Telegram

*The Ambassador in the Soviet Union (Steinhardt) to the
Secretary of State*

Moscow, March 1, 1940—4 p. m.
[Received 6 : 40 p. m.]

228. The press today announces the transfer of Potemkin[13] from the post of Assistant People's Commissar for Foreign Affairs to that of Commissar for Education of the Russian Soviet Federated Socialist Republics. No explanation is given as to the reason for the transfer nor is there any indication as to who is to succeed Potemkin. The absence of Potemkin from the luncheon given in my honor by Molotov[14] had already given rise to the customary speculation as to the possibility of the imminence of his removal from the Commissariat for Foreign Affairs, but up to the present there has been no indication or even rumor as to the reason for his transfer. However, in view of the fact that Potemkin, although an experienced diplomat and long associated with the conduct of Soviet foreign relations has never been regarded as having any voice in the determination of policy, it is doubtful that his removal is of any great significance.[15]

STEINHARDT

861.002/190 : Telegram

*The Ambassador in the Soviet Union (Steinhardt) to the
Secretary of State*

Moscow, March 6, 1940—noon.
[Received March 6—10 : 30 a. m.]

246. My telegram No. 228, March 1, 4 p. m. The German Ambassador[16] told me last night in strict confidence that Potemkin's dismissal had its origin in part in the failure to prevent the Anglo-French-Turkish alliance[17] and that Stalin[18] and Molotov had held

---

[13] Vladimir Petrovich Potemkin, First Assistant People's Commissar for Foreign Affairs of the Soviet Union.
[14] Vyacheslav Mikhailovich Molotov, People's Commissar for Foreign Affairs of the Soviet Union.
[15] In an attached note, Loy W. Henderson, Assistant Chief of the Division of European Affairs, commented: "I would not be greatly surprised, in view of Soviet urgent need for better relations with this country if someone like Troyanovsky [Alexander Antonovich Troyanovsky, former Ambassador of the Soviet Union in the United States, 1934–39] would be appointed to succeed Potemkin."
[16] Friedrich Werner, Count von der Schulenburg.
[17] Treaty of Mutual Assistance signed at Ankara on October 19, 1939; for text, see League of Nations Treaty Series, vol. cc, p. 167.
[18] Iosif Vissarionovich Stalin, Secretary General of the Central Committee of the All-Union Communist Party (Bolsheviks) ; member of the Politburo and Orgburo of the Party, etc.

Potemkin responsible for the reorientation of Turkish policy away from the Soviet Union. He also said that in his opinion either Sobolev [19] who is at present Secretary General of the Foreign Office, or Lozovski [20] would probably succeed Potemkin.

Repeated to Ankara.

STEINHARDT

361.11 Employees/373

Memorandum of Conversation, by the Assistant Chief of the Division of European Affairs (Henderson)

[WASHINGTON,] March 15, 1940.

Mr. Max B. Miller, of the Max B. Miller Corporation of New York City, flew down from New York this morning in order to discuss certain problems connected with the lubricating oil plant which his firm is building for the Soviet Government in Batum, the chief Soviet Caucasian Black Sea port.

Mr. Miller said that he wished to ask my advice as to what steps he should take with respect to recalling his technicians from Batum. The plant had already been completed, but apparently the Soviet authorities could not get it started without the assistance of his men. He felt that the letter of his contract had already been carried out and that he would be fully justified in withdrawing his engineers at once without subjecting himself to suit for breach of contract. On the other hand, if he were to carry out the spirit of the contract, he would leave his men in Batum for at least a reasonable period of time, in order to help the Soviet authorities get the plant into full operation. He said that some time ago he had warned the Soviet authorities that on March 23 he would withdraw three of his engineers, and sixty days later the remaining three. He was under the impression that at the present time the withdrawal of any of his men would cause serious dislocation in the plant.

He wanted to know if in my opinion his employees would be in exceptional danger if they should remain several months longer in Batum. I replied that it was, of course, impossible to foresee the future; that in my opinion they would not be subjected to unusual danger; that our Embassy in Moscow was watching the situation closely, and that it would in all probability call the men out in case it should feel that the situation required such action.

Mr. Miller said that one of his difficulties lay in the fact that because of the inability of Soviet operating engineers the Soviet au-

---

[19] Arkady Alexandrovich Sobolev.
[20] Solomon Abramovich Lozovsky, an alternate member of the Executive Committee of the Third (Communist) International, elected at the VII Congress in 1935; appointed an Assistant People's Commissar for Foreign Affairs of the Soviet Union on June 9, 1939.

thorities would undoubtedly continue for an indefinite period to request extensions of the stay of his engineers.

I told him that in similar cases American manufacturers had set an absolute date upon which their men must be recalled and had given the Soviet Government reasonable notice in advance of their intention. It seemed to me that the Soviet Government could not accuse him of having failed to carry out the spirit of the contract if he should act in such a manner. He said that he believed that he would adopt this policy and would probably set the first of June or thereabouts as the deadline.

Mr. Miller said that he would draw the men out at once if I would authorize him to inform the Soviet Government that we had requested it. I told him that the Department of State was in no position to make such a request.

Mr. Miller stated that he had been under considerable pressure from some of his business friends in the Shell Oil Company to approach the State Department along with other lubricating oil people, with the request that the moral embargo against the Soviet Union be extended to cover the granting of technical assistance in the manufacture of lubricating oil and the sale of lubricating oil. He said that he had resisted such pressure thus far, but that it was rather strong, and he hoped that his company would not be labelled as disloyal or as disinclined to carry out the policy of this Government if it continued to keep its men in Batum. I told him that the loyalty of his company had never been subjected to doubt, and that if he desired to discuss the moral embargo I would arrange for him to see someone in the Division of Controls. He replied that he did not care to go further into the matter at this time.

Mr. Miller said that it was his understanding that the Russians had in this country a commission which was shopping around with the hope of making arrangements to spend several million dollars in obtaining American technical assistance to build gasoline and oil refineries. It was, therefore, possible that the question of whether American firms should accept contracts for the building of additional aviation lubricating oil plants might become active. I thanked Mr. Miller for this information.

760D.61/1346 : Telegram

The Ambassador in the Soviet Union (Steinhardt) to the Secretary of State

Moscow, March 20, 1940—1 p. m.
[Received 1 : 25 p. m.]

316. Following the termination of hostilities with Finland the subject of future Soviet policy is arousing considerable speculation in

diplomatic quarters here. The following observations on the general position of the Soviet Union and the probable lines of its policy in the immediate future may therefore be of interest to the Department.

1. The conclusion of peace with Finland testifies to the policy of realism and prudence which has on the whole been characteristic of Stalin's conduct of Soviet foreign relations. Diplomatic sources which were in close touch with the negotiations attributed to him personally the decision to conclude a negotiated peace with the present Finnish Government against the strong opposition of the Red army and certain members of the Politburo.[21] It is clear that the principal motive which impelled him to abandon the complete conquest of Finland, to which he was committed by the "treaty" with the Kuusinen Government,[22] was his realization that despite the penetration of the Mannerheim Line by the Red army further and perhaps extended military operations would be required to achieve his maximum aim and that such continuation would involve a serious risk of war with England and France. (I assume that the Soviet Government was not unaware of the decision of the British and French Governments to intervene in Finland and the preparations for active military support which have been disclosed by Daladier [23] and Chamberlain [24] in their recent declarations.)

2. Inasmuch as Soviet alarm at the prospect of war with England and France centers chiefly upon the possibility of an attack in the Black Sea and Caspian areas directed against Batum and Baku it is regarded here as certain that relieved of anxiety in regard to its northern frontiers the Soviet Union will now endeavor to safeguard its frontiers in the Black Sea and Caucasus and to this end concentrate its diplomatic activity towards the Balkans, Turkey and the Near East.[25]

3. Since it is assured that peace was concluded with Finland to avoid the possibility of war with England and France, I doubt that the Soviet Government, in endeavoring to strengthen its diplomatic position in the Balkan and Black Sea areas, will on its own initiative and under present conditions undertake any aggressive or openly provocative action which might provide England and France with the justification for an attack in either area. It is more likely that the Soviet Government will seek to improve its relations with Turkey (the possibility of an attempt by the Kremlin to renew the negotia-

---

[21] The Political Bureau of the Central Committee of the All-Union Communist Party (Bolsheviks).
[22] A pact of mutual assistance and friendship was signed on December 2, 1939, between the Soviet Union and its puppet Democratic Republic of Finland, whose government at Terijoki was led by Otto W. Kuusinen; for text of the treaty, see *New York Times*, December 3, 1939, p. 53.
[23] Edouard Daladier, President of the French Council of Ministers.
[24] Neville Chamberlain, British Prime Minister.
[25] For correspondence concerning the activities of the Soviet Union in these areas, see vol. I, pp. 444 ff.

tions with that country which broke down last October should by no means be excluded) and with the Balkan countries and Iran, in an endeavor to counteract French and British influence in these countries.

4. In view of the importance of Italy as a factor in the Balkan peninsula and Near East and the possibility of a community of interest between that country and the Soviet Union in preventing the war from spreading to those areas, development of Soviet-Italian relations is of special significance at the present time. It is generally regarded here that at least one of the purposes of Ribbentrop's visit [26] and a possible subject of discussion in the meeting between Hitler and Mussolini [27] was an attempt by Germany to bring about an improvement in the relations between Italy and the Soviet, and as indicated in my telegram No. 279, March 12, 7 p. m.,[28] it is of interest that the Soviet press has recently adopted a more friendly tone towards Italy.

5. In taking such diplomatic steps as may appear feasible to strengthen its position in the Balkans, Black Sea, and Caspian areas, and if possible to close these areas against a British and French attack, I anticipate that the Soviet Government, while in no sense departing from its policy of collaboration with Germany,[29] will endeavor to relieve the strain on its relations with England and France by seeking to convey the impression to those countries that its policy with respect to the European war is one of strict neutrality. Since the conclusion of peace with Finland, there has been a noticeable diminution of the violent press attacks on England and France which were characteristic of the preceding period. Any such appearance of a changed attitude towards France and England [30] should, however, in my opinion be regarded solely as a maneuver rather than an expression of a change in policy as there is not the slightest evidence that the Soviet Union intends in any way to alter its basic policy of collaboration with Germany. On the contrary there is evidence emanating from the German Embassy that a Soviet attempt to appease Britain and France has German acquiescence and approval.

The foregoing outline of the present Soviet attitude is based on the supposition that the political situation and the military situation in Europe remains static.

STEINHARDT

---

[26] Joachim von Ribbentrop, Reich Foreign Minister, visited Rome on March 10–11, 1940.
[27] Adolf Hitler and Benito Mussolini met at the Brenner Pass on March 18, 1940.
[28] Not printed.
[29] For correspondence on cooperation between Germany and the Soviet Union, see vol. I, pp. 539 ff.
[30] For correspondence regarding the relations between Great Britain, France, and the Soviet Union, see vol. I, pp. 589 ff.

861.00 Supreme Soviet/27 : Telegram

The Chargé in the Soviet Union (Thurston) to the Secretary of State

Moscow, March 29, 1940—10 a. m. [*p. m.?*]
[Received March 30—10:30 a. m.]

337. My 336, March 29, 4 p. m.[31] Molotov spoke for an hour on Soviet foreign policy this evening at a meeting of the Supreme Soviet and while an analysis of his remarks must await the publication of the full text his speech was generally regarded as moderate with emphasis on the "neutrality" of the Soviet Union in the present war. He spoke of Soviet-German friendship and the mutual advantages which will result from the development of trade following the conclusion of the economic agreement in February.[32] His remarks in regard to England and France, while critical were more in the nature of complaints of hostile treatment without just cause. Fully half of his speech was devoted to a review along previous lines of the Finnish-Soviet conflict and in citing the aid received by Finland stated that "even such a lover of peace as the United States sent military supplies." He said that when Finland proposed peace the People's Government was consulted which after expressing assent dissolved itself. He reiterated Soviet objections to the proposal for a defensive alliance between Sweden and Norway and Finland and stated that Finnish participation therein would not only be in contravention of Article III but of the entire peace treaty [33] and warned Finland and the Scandinavian countries against any policy of "revanche."

In regard to the Near East and Balkans he said that recently the foreign press had been manifesting suspicious interest in Soviet frontiers in the region of the Caucasus and with Rumania and stated that the anti-Soviet implications of the concentration of the Anglo-French army under General Weygand in the Near East had forced the Soviet Union to take counter measures for defense. In the only reference to Turkey he stated that Soviet-Turkish relations remain unchanged and mentioned that the Soviet Union has a nonaggression pact with both Turkey [34] and Iran.[35] In regard to Rumania he stated that no

---

[31] Not printed.
[32] The commercial agreement between Germany and the Soviet Union signed on February 11, 1940, is described in a German Foreign Office memorandum dated February 26; Department of State, *Nazi-Soviet Relations, 1939–1941* (Washington, Government Printing Office, 1948), p. 131.
[33] Treaty of Peace between Finland and the Soviet Union signed at Moscow on March 12, 1940; for text, see Department of State *Bulletin*, April 27, 1940, p. 453, or Finland, Ministry for Foreign Affairs, *The Finnish Blue Book* (Philadelphia, 1940), p. 115.
[34] Treaty of Neutrality and Mutual Nonaggression signed at Paris on December 17, 1925, League of Nations Treaty Series, vol. CLVII, p. 353; prolonged by protocols signed on December 17, 1929, *ibid.*, p. 360; on October 30, 1931, *ibid.*, p. 366; and finally on November 7, 1935, for 10 years, *ibid.*, vol. CLXXIX, p. 127.
[35] Treaty of Guarantee and Neutrality signed at Moscow on October 1, 1927, League of Nations Treaty Series, vol. CXII, p. 275.

such pact exists since the question of Bessarabia remains unsolved adding that while the Soviet Union had never recognized Rumania's possession of Bessarabia the question of its restitution by force had not been raised and there was therefore no obstacle to normal relations with Rumania. In a brief reference to Japan Molotov stated that great satisfaction cannot be expressed over present relations.

Molotov stated that relations with the United States [36] had not changed, leaving aside the moral embargo which is still in force despite the conclusion of peace with Finland. He added that Soviet imports from the United States were greater in 1939 than in the previous year and that the Soviet Union was prepared to buy even more if the American authorities would not place obstacles in the way.[37]

In conclusion he outlined Soviet policy as follows:

(1) Neutrality and non-participation in the European war;
(2) Opposition to the extension of the war; and
(3) Continued efforts to strengthen the defenses and safeguard the frontiers of the Soviet Union.

THURSTON

_____

861.00 Supreme Soviet/28 : Telegram

The Chargé in the Soviet Union (Thurston) to the Secretary of State

Moscow, March 30, 1940—7 p. m.
[Received March 30—5 : 17 p. m.]

338. Embassy's telegram 337, March 29, 10 p. m. The text of Molotov's speech as published in the press today follows without important departures the outline given in the Embassy's telegram under reference and as the full text has been sent abroad in English translation by Tass,[38] no further general summary will be telegraphed.

Molotov's speech in general followed the expected lines in emphasizing the intention and the desire of the Soviet Union to avoid participation in the present European war as well as a willingness on that basis to have improved relations with England and France, but he likewise made it clear that the Soviet Union has no intention of altering its present attitude toward Germany which makes Soviet "neutrality" a matter of definition. The most specific part of the speech dealt with relations with Rumania and may be regarded as an

_____

[36] For difficulties affecting relations between the United States and the Soviet Union, see pp. 244 ff.

[37] Regarding trade and the renewal of the commercial agreement with the Soviet Union by an exchange of notes signed on August 6, 1940, see pp. 441 ff.

[38] Telegraph agency of the Soviet Union, an official communications organization of the Soviet Government.

assurance to that country that the Soviet Union has no intention at present to attempt a forcible solution of the Bessarabian question but at the same time intimating that a genuine improvement in Soviet-Rumanian relations would require a settlement of that question. A reference to the "long delay in the appointment of a Minister to Rumania" due to the Butenko affair [39] is regarded by some as forecasting the appointment of a Soviet Minister in the near future, possibly with the intention of opening through diplomatic channels discussions in regard to Bessarabia. The slight note of dissatisfaction with the progress of relations with Japan is believed due in large part to the failure of Japan to respond to previous indications of a Soviet willingness to adjust its political relations with that country.[40]

As a whole the speech is regarded as moderate in tone and as indicating a disposition on the part of the Soviet Government to avoid any complications if possible in its relations with other countries while continuing the policy of collaboration with Germany.

THURSTON

861.00 Supreme Soviet/30 : Telegram

The Chargé in the Soviet Union (Thurston) to the Secretary of State

Moscow, April 1, 1940—noon.
[Received 1:40 p. m.]

341. My 337, March 19 [*29*], 11 a. m. [*10 p. m.*]. In its leading editorial yesterday devoted to Molotov's speech on foreign policy *Pravda* asserted that this address indicated that Soviet foreign policy continues to carry out the four tasks outlined by Stalin in his speech to the Eighteenth Party Congress.[41] The editorial selected for quotation Molotov's statement that "the new good Soviet-German relations have been put to the test in connection with the events in Poland and have sufficiently demonstrated their firmness" as well as his "warning to the English and French ruling classes that the Soviet Union had never violated [a treaty?] and never would be an instrument for

---

[39] Fedor Butenko, Soviet Chargé d'Affaires in Bucharest, who left Rumania in February 1938, and went to Rome, where an emissary of the Rumanian Government identified him on February 27. The Soviet Government professed not to believe in this flight, and attempted to put pressure on Rumania.

[40] For Japanese relations with the Axis Powers and the Soviet Union, see vol. I, pp. 633 ff.

[41] Held in Moscow, March 10–21, 1939; for an account of Stalin's speech on March 10, see telegram No. 99, March 11, 1939, 4 p. m., from the Chargé in the Soviet Union, *Foreign Relations*, The Soviet Union, 1933–1939, p. 739, and despatch No. 2213, March 30, 1939, from the Chargé, *ibid.*, p. 747.

the policy of others." After quoting Molotov's assertion that the conflict with Finland had not been with that country alone but with the united forces of a number of imperialist countries hostile to the Soviet Union including the reference to the help received from the "peace loving" United States, the editorial points out that Molotov indicated that those anti-Soviet plans had not been abandoned in imperialist circles and mentioned the projected defensive alliance in Scandinavia and the "suspicious hullabaloo" in regard to the Near East. In this connection it stated "Comrade Molotov warned those of our neighbors who might let themselves be drawn into this dangerous game of playing with fire and becoming instruments of an agressive policy against the Soviet Union."

Resolutions of approval of the foreign policy of the Soviet Union as outlined by Molotov which have been adopted at meetings throughout the country likewise emphasize "the miscalculations of the British and French imperialists" who hoped to use the Soviet Union as an "instrument for their criminal policy."

THURSTON

861.00 Supreme Soviet/31 : Telegram

The Chargé in the Soviet Union (Thurston) to the Secretary of State

Moscow, April 1, 1940—2 p. m.
[Received April 1—1 : 43 p. m.]

343. At the joint session of the Supreme Soviet yesterday the Commissar for Finance Zverev [42] introduced the consolidated state budget for 1940 the principal items of which are as follows in millions of rubles.

Revenue: (1) Turn over tax 108,349. (2) Deductions from profits 22,368. (3) Direct taxes and collections from population 9,704. (4) State loans 11,171. (5) Other revenues 30,994. Total revenues 182,586.

Expenditures: (1) Financing of national economy 57,118. (2) Social and cultural measures 42,875. (3) People's Commissariats for Defense and Navy 57,067. (4) Commissariat for Internal Affairs administrative judiciary organs 14,206. (5) Other expenditures 8446. Total expenditures 179,711.

Discussion of the budget will be continued by the two Houses sitting separately today.

THURSTON

---

[42] Arseny Grigoryevich Zverev.

861.00/11855 : Telegram

The Ambassador in the Soviet Union (Steinhardt) to the Secretary of State

Moscow, via BERLIN, April 13, 1940—6 p. m.
[Received April 14—3 : 08 p. m.]

380. My telegram No. 378, April 13, 10 a. m.[43] During my trip to the Caucasus Black Sea area, Crimea, and the Ukraine, I observed that a serious food shortage exists throughout the greater part of the districts visited attributable in my opinion to a considerable degree to inadequate distribution facilities and methods. At most of the towns where I stopped long lines of people were waiting to buy bread and other foodstuffs. At the important port of Odessa this condition was particularly noticeable, food lines being so continuous on the main street that thousands of people were visible from a single point. While in my judgment crop prospects for the coming season range from fair to medium, I have no reason to believe that even good crops this year would result in any material amelioration of the food situation.

My impression of the rail transport condition is that little is being done to augment existing distribution facilities either in respect of new railroad construction, the acquisition of rolling stock, or additional highway building. Maintenance of existing lines is negligible. I observed single track lines at many strategic points, particularly into and out of Grozny and a substantial part of the line from Baku to Batum. Roadbed was generally in poor condition and are unballasted in certain sections. Maintenance of way was non-existent for hundreds of miles and the condition of locomotives and rolling stock was mediocre with many in bad order on siding. With respect to the Grozny oil fields I noted that the refining plants are densely congested over a large area with some plants not in operation. Storage tanks in units of from 6 to 20 are extremely closely grouped, at some places only a few yards apart; the railway sidings are oil soaked. The entire area is extremely vulnerable to fire. The equipment in use appeared old but serviceable.

At Baku, I lunched with officials of the oil trust who furnished the following data, part of which I believe has not hitherto been given. 75% of the entire production of the Soviet Union originates from the Baku fields (this does not include Grozny). 20% of the production of the Baku fields is transported by a single 14-inch pipeline, for crude oil only to Batum, the daily run is about 15,000 tons or some-

---

[43] Not printed.

what over four and one-half million tons per annum, about 4,000 tons are shipped out of Baku daily by rail and the balance is transported by barges and some tankers to Caspian ports, principally Astrakhan, and thence up the Volga. The officials claimed an average annual production increase of approximately 8%, including 1940, but in view of their admission of salt water intrusion, sulphur content, and visible evidence of a large number of abandonments, I seriously doubt this claim.

The officials admitted Grozny output was not increasing; other sources indicate a considerable current decrease in that area. The total number of wells in the Baku fields was given as about 20,000 ranging in depth from 1,000 to 12,000 feet. From my observation most of these are under pump with few, if any, free flowing wells. Refining plants appeared less extensive than at Grozny. Gathering lines are above ground and in bad condition. Wells very close together in different fields and plants extremely closely grouped, with main line and feeder shut off valves above ground oil soaked and many leaking. Docking facilities primitive, antiquated, and limited. Baku, however, being less congested appeared less vulnerable than Grozny. I saw no evidence at either Grozny or Baku of military activities of any kind and noted no signs of defensive preparations.

Soviet shipping and port facilities in the Black Sea are conspicuously inadequate. From what I observed and was told I incline to the view that the Soviets have grossly exaggerated their naval strength in the Black Sea. Stopping at some 10 ports and spending several days at sea, I saw in all but 2 small coast guard cutters, 1 old destroyer in bad condition, and 1 mine layer. As far as I could see there was a complete absence throughout the areas visited of military or naval preparations. I was struck by the apparent failure to take the most elementary and obvious measures essential for the defense of such strategic points as Baku, Batum and Odessa. While at Batum I motored to and along the Turkish border, and saw no evidence of military preparations. The antiquated forts were normally manned, but I could observe no exceptional measures.

I conclude from the foregoing that the Soviets do not contemplate, at least for the present, engaging in any offensive military venture in the Black Sea area and that they are extremely vulnerable to naval and air attack in this region. The conditions I found in this region do not, of course, preclude the possibility of military preparations along the Bessarabian frontier.

With respect to potential Soviet economic aid to Germany I believe from what I saw in its industrial, agricultural and transport conditions in the important areas visited, that it is doubtful the Soviets will be able to render sustained economic assistance to Germany of a decisive character without subjecting Soviet internal economy to an excessive strain.

I saw no signs of political unrest. I am sending a more detailed report by pouch.[44]

STEINHARDT

361.11 Employees/377

Memorandum of Telephone Conversation, by Mr. Edward Page, Jr., of the Division of European Affairs

[WASHINGTON,] May 1, 1940.

Mr. A. O. Hartley, of the Max B. Miller and Company, Incorporated, New York, telephoned this morning and stated that the Soviet authorities had requested the seven engineers of his company to depart from the Soviet Union, and that four engineers had already left. Mr. Hartley requested the Department to telegraph Moscow at his expense and endeavor to confirm this information, and to ascertain the whereabouts and travel plans of the three engineers remaining and their families. He stated that he did not know the reasons for the decision of the Soviet authorities to request the engineers to leave, and was surprised at this move, in as much as the oil refinery under construction at Grozny by his company had not yet been put into operation. Mr. Hartley stated that Willis, Hackstaff and Midlam were the names of the engineers still in the Soviet Union.

E[DWARD] P[AGE]

461.11/867 : Telegram

The Chargé in the Soviet Union (Thurston) to the Secretary of State

Moscow, May 8, 1940—5 p. m.
[Received May 9—9 : 18 a. m.]

502. On April 26 the Commissariat for Foreign Affairs addressed a note to this Embassy transmitting a copy of an "instruction" issued by the Commissariat for Justice on February 28, 1940, "on the subject of claims connected with the nationalization of foreign properties in the territories of western Ukrainia and of western White Russia." The note remarked that this "instruction" has been approved by the Soviet of People's Commissars of the U. S. S. R.

---

[44] Despatch No. 418, April 15, not printed.

The "instruction" reads as follows in the English translation: [45]

"In connection with the presentation of claims, in reference to the nationalization of foreign properties in the territories of Western Ukraine and of Western White Russia, by individual foreigners to organs of justice of the U. S. S. R., the People's Commissariat for Justice of the U. S. S. R. instructs the local organs of justice to be guided by the following:

1. The measures nationalizing estate owners' land, banks and large industries in the territories of Western Ukraine and of Western White Russia were approved and proclaimed by decisions of October 28 and 30, 1939 of the National Assemblies of Western Ukraine and [of] Western White Russia.

The said measures were carried out in the territories of Western Ukraine and Western White Russia prior to the incorporation of Western Ukraine and Western White Russia into the U. S. S. R.,[46] and were carried out not by central or local organs of state authority or of the state administration of the U. S. S. R., but by authoritative organs established by the sovereign peoples of Western Ukraine and [of] Western White Russia.

Thus, there are no bases for the presentation of said claims to the Union of Soviet Socialist Republics or to its organs.

2. The fact, that the property for which said claims are presented is at present at the disposition of the organs of the U. S. S. R., also imposes no responsibility upon the U. S. S. R. in regard to the former owners who have lost all right to this property by virtue of its nationalization by the sovereign peoples of Western Ukraine and Western White Russia as represented by the authoritative organs established by them, from whom this property, as nationalized and [consequently] as state property has legally been transferred to the U. S. S. R."

The Embassy has not acknowledged the receipt of the note above referred to and will not do so unless so instructed by the Department.[47]

Since the seizure of Eastern Poland by the Soviet Union, the Embassy has addressed several notes to the Commissariat for Foreign Affairs requesting protection of property in that area in which American interests are involved or the return of American owned property believed to have been taken over by the Soviet authorities. With the exception of those concerning certain motion picture films which apparently are to be surrendered to the Embassy all such notes have been disregarded.

It was my intention to report the foregoing by despatch but have learned today that the United Press correspondent has been informed of the "instruction" above cited and is preparing to file a story regard-

---

[45] Telegraphed translation has been slightly revised in accordance with translation sent by the Chargé in his covering despatch No. 455, May 9, not printed.
[46] See telegram No. 826, October 28, 1939, 4 p. m., from the Ambassador in the Soviet Union, and footnote 83, *Foreign Relations*, The Soviet Union, 1933–1939, p. 785.
[47] See Department's telegram No. 276, May 16, 6 p. m., p. 201.

ing it. I have decided therefore to submit this cable so that the Department will be informed.

THURSTON

860C.01/546 : Telegram

The Chargé in the Soviet Union (Thurston) to the Secretary of State

Moscow, May 8, 1940—6 p. m.
[Received 6 : 11 p. m.]

503. The Commissariat for Foreign Affairs yesterday returned to the Embassy without an accompanying communication a note from the Embassy (on a routine matter) in which the phrase "Soviet-occupied Poland" was employed. This phrase was underscored by the Commissariat with a red pencil. I sent Mr. Ward [48] to the Commissariat at once to discuss the matter with the Chief of the American Section.[49] Mr. Valkov informed Mr. Ward that the note had been returned as the Commissariat cannot accept a note in which an integral part of the Soviet Union such as western Ukraine and western White Russia is referred to in the manner described. Mr. Ward left the note with Mr. Valkov who promptly returned it to the Embassy together with an earlier note which merely referred to the death of an American citizen which "apparently occurred some time during the occupation of Poland."

I requested an appointment with Assistant Commissar Lozovski and saw him this afternoon. I informed him that I assumed that the Commissariat had no intention to offend the Embassy and that the Embassy surely had had no such intention with respect to the Commissariat when employing the phrase to which exception was taken. I suggested therefore that a solution of the problem which confronted both offices would be for the Commissariat to accept the two notes which it had so rudely returned to the Embassy and for the Embassy to employ a more acceptable phrase in its future notes when referring to the territories in question. I also pointed out that the phrase "Soviet-occupied Poland" had been consistently employed by the Embassy for many months past and that it would have been a more proper procedure on the part of the Commissariat had it indicated either in writing or orally its objection to that phrase—the employment of which would have, of course, thereupon ceased. Mr. Lozovski replied that it was precisely because the Embassy had consistently used the offending term (he said he had a list of at least 100

---

[48] Angus I. Ward, Chief of Consular Section and Second Secretary of Embassy in the Soviet Union.
[49] Vasily Alexeyevich Valkov.

notes in which it appeared) that it had been decided to put a stop to it.

After considerable further discussion Mr. Lozovski proposed that the Embassy address one or two new notes to the Commissariat on the subjects concerning these areas, in which the term to which exception is taken should not be used. He said he would in the meantime "give consideration to the matter" and within a few days would summon me to the Commissariat to discuss the question again. He would not promise that if the Embassy followed this proposed procedure the Commissariat on its part would then accept the two notes now rejected.

I am disposed to accept this arrangement although it is by no means certain that the rejected notes will ever be accepted; but before doing so, I should appreciate your instructions.[50]

THURSTON

861.20/502 : Telegram

The Chargé in the Soviet Union (Thurston) to the Secretary of State

Moscow, May 9, 1940—5 p. m.
[Received May 9—4 : 30 p. m.]

508. Reference Embassy's 499, May 8, 11 a. m.[51] *Pravda* today announces the formation of a Government commission "to recommend candidates for the titles of General and Admiral". The president of the commission is Voroshilov.[52]

In a leading editorial devoted to the reintroduction of these military titles *Pravda* states that the measure is designed "to raise still further the authority of our commanding personnel". The customary references to military commissars [53] are omitted.

One editorial continues:

"The necessity for introducing the titles of Soviet General and Admiral has long been under consideration. Their introduction at the time (it has even been somewhat overdue) represents the completion in a link of the chain of measures for the organizational strengthening of the armed forces of the Soviet Union." [54]

---

[50] See Department's telegram No. 271, May 11, 3 p. m., p. 201.
[51] Not printed.
[52] Kliment Efremovich Voroshilov, Marshal, relieved as People's Commissar for Defense and appointed a vice president of the Council of People's Commissars of the Soviet Union on May 7, 1940.
[53] Political, or military commissars were reintroduced into the armed forces of the Soviet Union by resolution of May 11, 1937, and approved regulations of May 17, 1937. The statutes of the military commissars of the Red army were approved by the Central Executive Committee and the Council of People's Commissars of the Soviet Union on August 15, 1937. In part their duty was to control the military commander, and to supervise the greater political study and education in the training of the Red army.
[54] The Chargé in the Soviet Union reported in his telegram No. 680, June 15, 1 p. m., that in all 948 generals and 108 admirals of different ranks had been newly appointed to date (861.221/27).

Despite protestations that the titles cannot be compared to those of the old Tsarist army because of the new character of the Red forces, it is believed that their introduction is a further step toward the removal of some of the less practical revolutionary characteristics of the Red army. The Military Attaché [55] is inclined to the view that the move foreshadows the curtailment of the system of military commissars.[56] If so, the measure is of far reaching significance in restoring unity of command within the fighting forces.

THURSTON

860C.01/546 : Telegram

The Secretary of State to the Chargé in the Soviet Union (Thurston)

WASHINGTON, May 11, 1940—3 p. m.

271. Your 503, May 8, 6 p. m. Since the Soviet Government objects to the use of the term "Soviet occupied Poland," the Embassy in the future should draft its notes in such a way as to designate localities under discussion in this area without employing the expression to which offense is taken. It is believed that, as a rule, the names of towns or villages and of territorial subdivisions should be sufficient to designate given localities. If the Soviet Government insists, there is no objection to the use of the Russian names of towns and subdivisions. In case it becomes necessary to refer to the whole area the Embassy may employ expressions similar to the following: "the territory now referred to as the western Ukraine and western Belorussiya".

The Department does not consider that the use of Russian place names or of expressions similar to that suggested above indicates that this government recognizes Soviet claims to sovereignty over Soviet occupied Poland. The Embassy will of course take care not to describe localities in Soviet occupied Poland as being a part of the U. S. S. R. or of a Soviet republic.

HULL

461.11/867 : Telegram

The Secretary of State to the Chargé in the Soviet Union (Thurston)

WASHINGTON, May 16, 1940—6 p. m.

276. Your 502, May 8, 5 p. m. Please draft a reply to the Commissariat acknowledging receipt of its note of April 26 and informing it that you have been instructed by your Government to state that your Government looks to the Government of the Union of Soviet Socialist Republics for the compensation of any American nationals or firms

---

[55] Maj. Ivan D. Yeaton.
[56] See telegram No. 1011, August 13, 11 a. m., from the Chargé in the Soviet Union, p. 211.

who may have suffered losses as the result of the acts of nationalization of foreign property in the territories referred to in the instruction of the Commissariat for Justice of February 28 as Western Ukraine and Western Belorussiya.[57]

HULL

861.22/93

The Chargé in the Soviet Union (Thurston) to the Secretary of State

No. 568   Moscow, June 25, 1940.
                                            [Received August 14.]

SIR: I have the honor to inform the Department that an editorial published in *Krasnaya Zvezda* of June 23, 1940, reported that the People's Commissar for Defense [58] of the Union of Soviet Socialist Republics has issued an order in accordance with which all Soviet soldiers on or off duty must salute their superiors, and officers of equal rank must salute each other.

The editorial in question points out that the salute will be a sign of discipline and respect for a superior. Saluting will permit individual cases of violation of military procedure to be "uprooted decisively". Familiarity between officers and soldiers and "false democracy", which are stated to have impaired the army's capacity for fighting, must be ended forever, according to this editorial, and the desire of an officer to display his "democracy" is characterized as a crime against his service duties.

The recent restoration in the Soviet army and navy of the titles of general and admiral has been reported to the Department, and the present order represents a further step toward the elimination of "military communism" as well as of the duality of command which has been thought by most military observers in Moscow to have constituted a most serious handicap to the effectiveness of the Soviet army as a fighting unit.

Respectfully yours,   WALTER THURSTON

861.5041/61 : Telegram

The Chargé in the Soviet Union (Thurston) to the Secretary of State

                                        Moscow, June 27, 1940—3 p. m.
                                            [Received 5 : 38 p. m.]

760. A ukase [59] of the Presidium of the Supreme Soviet is published in today's newspapers giving effect to the recommendations of the labor unions reported in the Embassy's 755, June 26, 1 p. m.[60]

---

[57] The Chargé in the Soviet Union reported in his despatch No. 483, May 17, that a note in compliance with this instruction had been addressed to the People's Commissariat for Foreign Affairs (461.11/874).
[58] Marshal Semen Konstantinovich Timoshenko, since May 7, 1940.
[59] Dated June 26.
[60] Not printed.

The ukase which became operative today provides for the 8-hour day and 7-day week, Sunday to be the day of rest. Unnecessary change of employment is strictly forbidden and absence without leave penalized not by dismissal as heretofore but by corrective labor at the place of employment and by fines up to 25 percent of wages for 6 months.

A resolution of the Soviet of People's Commissars of the U. S. S. R. provides that present wages are maintained while production norms are raised and piecework rates lowered in proportion to the increased length of the working day.

The pronouncement of the labor unions yesterday stressed the need to strengthen the defenses of the country, especially the Red army and navy and air forces and stated that more metal, coal, oil, planes, tanks, guns, shells, locomotives, railway cars, machine tools and automobiles are required. An editorial in *Krasnaya Zvezda* yesterday stated that while the Soviet Union now enjoys the blessings of peace no predominance by the capitalistic countries should be permitted and added "the backward are being defeated but we do not want to be defeated." The same sentiment was expressed by the Secretary [61] of the All Union Central Soviet of Labor Unions in a speech delivered June 25th and published in today's *Pravda* in these words: "To be less prepared means to be backward and weak, and as is well known the backward and weak are being beaten."

Although more than 2 pages of *Pravda* and 1½ pages of *Izvestiya* yesterday and about 2 pages of *Pravda* today are devoted to resolutions adopted by meetings throughout the country of factory workers, railway men, office workers, miners, etc., approving the recommendations of the labor unions, a Russian-speaking informant has advised me that during a tour of numerous shops yesterday, which were as usual congested, he overheard much outspoken hostile criticism.

THURSTON

711.61/741 : Telegram

The Chargé in the Soviet Union (Thurston) to the Secretary of State

Moscow, July 6, 1940—10 a. m.
[Received 1 : 55 p. m.]

813. Embassy's 814, July 6, 11 a. m., which will follow.[62] An American journalist in Moscow told a member of the Embassy staff several days ago that a Secretary of the Japanese Embassy here had

---

[61] Nikolay Mikhailovich Shvernik. Speech before the IX Plenum of the All-Union Central Soviet (Council) of Labor Unions.

[62] Not printed ; this telegram reported a Tass communiqué which denied as "gutter gossip" a rumor published by the New York *Daily News* regarding a secret agreement between the United States and the Soviet Union against Japan in the Far East. (711.61/742)

inquired of him as to the reasons for which I had been seeing Molotov frequently in recent weeks and had intimated that the Japanese Embassy had reason to suppose that some basis of negotiations were in progress between the United States and Soviet Governments looking toward an agreement with respect to the treatment of Far Eastern questions, which, it was also intimated, would not be favorable to Japanese interests there.

Yesterday the same Japanese Secretary brought up this matter along similar lines in conversation with me and I pointed out that I had only seen Molotov once since I had been in charge of this Embassy and that I knew of no negotiations whatever which were in progress or under contemplation between the United States and the Soviet Union of any such character.

Please repeat to Tokyo.

THURSTON

711.61/743 : Telegram

The Chargé in the Soviet Union (Thurston) to the Secretary of State

Moscow, July 6, 1940—3 p. m.
[Received 4: 35 p. m.]

821. After having replied to the Japanese Secretary in the sense reported in the Embassy's 813, July 6, I remarked that it has been suggested that the Japanese Government had made representations to the Soviet Government regarding the furnishing of military supplies to China similar to those recently made to the British and French Governments. The Secretary answered that no such representations have been made and added that they would have been superfluous in any event since as a result of the Finnish war and the subsequent movements of the Red army the Soviet Union can spare no military equipment. He expressed the opinion that Soviet aid to China has in fact diminished considerably and asserted that most of the Soviet advisers have been recalled from China.

With respect to strictly Japanese-Soviet relations the same informant stated that conversations are in progress regarding Sakhalin Island and the fisheries problem and that a commission will be formed shortly to undertake the actual demarcation of the boundary of Mongolia–Manchuria.[63]

Repeated to Tokyo.

THURSTON

---

[63] For further details of Soviet-Japanese relations, see vol. I, pp. 633 ff.

861.60/337 : Telegram

The Chargé in the Soviet Union (Thurston) to the Secretary of State

Moscow, July 15, 1940—5 p. m.
[Received July 15—12 : 58 p. m.]

859. Today's newspapers publish a ukase [64] of the Presidium of the Supreme Soviet of the Union of Soviet Socialist Republics in which it is stated that the issuance of poor quality or defective industrial products or the issuance of goods below the obligatory standards constitutes anti-state crime equivalent to wrecking. Directors, chief engineers and chiefs of departments or others responsible for such conditions are subject to trial and imprisonment ranging from 5 to 8 years. Editorials in *Pravda* and *Izvestiya* praise the ukase and cite various examples of poor quality or defective production.

THURSTON

861.00B/697

The Chargé in the Soviet Union (Thurston) to the Secretary of State

No. 634   Moscow, July 23, 1940.
[Received August 17.]

SIR: Owing to a confusion in the notes upon which the Embassy's despatch No. 465, of May 10, 1940,[65] was based, certain errors in fact were incorporated in it. Additional data on the subject have now appeared, and it is possible not only to correct these errors, but to provide a more complete statement of membership of the Communist Party in the Soviet Union.

In Stalin's report on the work of the Central Committee to the Eighteenth Party Congress, in 1939,[66] he stated that there were 1,874,488 Party members represented at the Seventeenth Party Congress, held in 1934,[67] and that the number represented at the Eighteenth Congress was approximately 1,600,000. The reduction in numbers was attributed to the "purge of Party members and candidate members begun in 1933". On July 14, 1940, a *Pravda* editorial stated that 605,627 new members had been accepted during the period since the Eighteenth Party Congress, or from April 1, 1939, to June 1, 1940. Thus, by adding this figure to the previously cited figure of 1,600,000 given for the membership at the time of that Congress, it may safely be assumed that the present membership of the Party amounts to approximately 2,200,000.

[64] Dated July 10.
[65] Not printed.
[66] See footnote 41, p. 193.
[67] January 26–February 10, 1934.

The Embassy's despatch No. 465, of May 10, 1940, referred to a statement in a *Pravda* editorial of May 6, 1940, to the effect that the Party had doubled its membership in the past two years. Thus, if the figure 2,200,000 just cited be divided by two, it would appear that the membership in the spring of 1938, a year before the Eighteenth Congress, was only 1,100,000. This would mean that the Party lost some 774,000 members between early in 1934 and early in 1938, and gained some 500,000 between the spring of 1938 and March 1939. The 1938 figure doubtless represented the low point in membership because it coincided with the sharpest phase of the purge, but such violent fluctuations as are indicated by this calculation seem somewhat improbable. The possibility cannot be excluded that the *Pravda* statement of May 6 might have counted candidates for membership as within the ranks of the Party; the wording admits of this possibility. If this were the case, it would destroy the validity of the calculation just given.

The number of candidates for membership as of June 1, 1940, is 1,127,802, according to the *Pravda* editorial of July 14. Thus the total number of members and candidates is well over three million.

Pravda's editorial of July 14 praises the achievements of the Party in attracting to its ranks such a large number of new members, but goes on to stress the point that perhaps this growth has been too rapid. It refers to a recent resolution of the Party Central Committee, as yet unpublished, in which organizational deficiencies in the acceptance of new members were indicated. It appears that in many Party organizations there exists a tendency to seek a rapid quantitative growth, which is attained without sufficient attention to the proper procedure. It cites examples of *oblast* and constituent republic organizations which have increased by from 50 per cent to nearly 100 per cent in the past year their number of candidates for membership. Outstanding among these are Central Asiatic Party organizations.

The primary Party organizations and the *raion* committees are sharply criticized for the wholesale admission of new members without proper attention to the required process. Leaders of organizations which indulge in this practice are to be held responsible before the Party. If candidates realize that admission to the Party is being done in a perfunctory manner, then backward and undesirable elements will enter the Party ranks. *Raion* and city committees are guilty of not checking up on the work of lower organs in this respect. Even *oblast* and *krai* committees and the central committees of the Parties of constituent republics are blamed for their failure to do more in respect to the membership question than to review the numerical gains. Henceforth every Party organization must make a report at every plenum in which not only the statistics of growth are recorded, but in which a qualitative analysis is made. The previously simplified procedure of accepting new members must cease. The editorial also dwells on the need for increased activity in training new members properly, in imbuing them with the correct faith, and in testing their abilities and devotion. The period of candidacy has become an empty formality. Candidates should be thoroughly tested and should be given responsible work during their period of candidacy.

In conclusion it may be remarked that the shortcomings outlined above are by no means new in the Party, and that they are a favorite theme of the Soviet press. Nevertheless, this criticism is founded upon a resolution adopted by the Central Committee, and its appearance is coupled with figures on the growth of the Party. It would be logical to assume therefore that the Party may have been growing somewhat too rapidly to please its leaders.[68]

Respectfully yours, WALTER THURSTON

861.00 Supreme Soviet/37 : Telegram

The Chargé in the Soviet Union (Thurston) to the Secretary of State

Moscow, July 24, 1940—1 p. m.
[Received July 24—12 : 20 p. m]

896. A ukase is published in this morning's papers convoking the Seventh Session of the Supreme Soviet of the Union of Soviet Socialist Republics in Moscow on August 1st.

It is to be presumed that this meeting of the Supreme Soviet will deal with the incorporation of the Baltic States into the Soviet Union and the reorganization of the Moldavian Autonomous Republic along the lines mentioned in the Embassy's 837, July 19 [*10*], 2 p. m.,[69] and 844, July 11, noon.[70]

THURSTON

860C.01/559

The Polish Ambassador (Potocki) to the Secretary of State [71]

49/SZ–L–2 [WASHINGTON,] July 26, 1940.

SIR: Acting upon instructions of my Government I have the honor to communicate to you the following:

---

[68] In despatches No. 559, June 24, and No. 625, July 19, the Chargé had related that at the XI Plenum of the All-Union Leninist Communist Union of Youth (Komsomol) which had met in Moscow June 7–11, 1940, the membership of this body was announced as being 10,223,000. There was considerable criticism reported of the organization of the Komsomol and of the lackadaisical attitude of much of its membership. (861.00B/695, 696)

[69] Vol. I, p. 492.

[70] Not printed.

[71] Acting Secretary of State Welles acknowledged the receipt of this communication in his note of August 6, 1940.

The Government of the U. S. S. R. has recently annexed the territories of three Baltic States. This annexation also embraces the territory of Wilno which already in September, 1939, had been illegally occupied by the Soviet troops and in October, 1939, ceded to the Lithuanian Government, and at the present time reoccupied by the Soviet troops simultaneously with the rest of the Lithuanian territory.

The Polish Government file a solemn protest against this new violation of international law by the U. S. S. R., and formally reserve all their rights in relation to the territories of the Republic of Poland occupied by the Soviet troops in September, 1939, as well as at the present time. The act of violence performed by the U. S. S. R. does not entitle them to any rights to the territories thus occupied and the Polish Government reserve for themselves the right to claim at the opportune time reparations from the Soviet Government for all the damages already caused by the Soviet occupation and which may be perpetrated to the detriment of Poland and her citizens.

Accept [etc.]   POTOCKI

761.00/339 : Telegram

The Chargé in the Soviet Union (Thurston) to the Secretary of State

Moscow, August 1, 1940—midnight.
[Received August 2—5 : 16 p. m.]

945. At this evening's joint session of the Supreme Soviet Molotov read a report on Soviet foreign relations from which the following excerpts are presented in the order of delivery:

1. After reviewing developments in the European war, he stated that "of the two Allies that confronted Germany and Italy only England remains and she has decided to continue the war relying on the assistance of the United States". He attributed the collapse of France in part to the fact that "unlike Germany, ruling circles in France adopted too light minded an attitude toward the role and weight of the Soviet Union in European affairs". He added "We are now on the eve of a new stage of intensification of the war between Germany and Italy on one side and England, which the United States is assisting, on the other."

2. He reiterated Soviet policy with respect to the war in these words: "All these events have not changed the foreign policy of the Soviet Union. Due to its policy of peace and neutrality the Soviet Union is not taking part in the war".

3. With respect to Germany he asserted that relations are governed by the Nonaggression Pact of last year,[75] which has been strictly ob-

---

[75] Signed at Moscow on August 23, 1939; for text, see Department of State, *Nazi-Soviet Relations, 1939–1941* (Washington, Government Printing Office, 1948), p. 76, or *Documents on German Foreign Policy, 1918–1945*, Series D, vol. VII, p. 245.

served by the Soviet Government. "Developments in Europe not only have not weakened the strength of the Soviet–Germany Nonaggression Pact but have on the contrary emphasized the importance of its existence and further development". Referring to speculation regarding the possibility of disagreement between the Soviet Union and Germany and "attempts to intimidate us by the prospect of the growth of Germany's might" he repeated that the friendly relations between the two countries "are not based on fortuitous considerations of a transient nature but on fundamental state interests of both the Soviet Union and Germany".

4. Relations with Italy have improved. No essential change in relations with the British has occurred "although the appointment of Cripps [76] as Ambassador to the Soviet Union possibly reflected a desire on the part of Britain to improve relations with the Soviet Union".

5. A description of the restoration of Bessarabia and transfer of North Bukovina to the Soviet Union implies that the conflict between the Soviet Union and Rumania has been "peacefully settled".

6. An extensive discussion of recent events in the Baltic States contains nothing new.

7. After referring to postwar negotiations with Finland he stated "further development of Soviet-Finnish relations favorable to both countries depends mainly on Finland herself. It is understandable that if certain elements of the Finnish ruling circles do not cease their repressive acts against some of the Finnish public which are striving to improve good neighborly relations between the Soviet Union then harm may come to relations between the Soviet Union and Finland".

8. The statement that no important changes have taken place in the relations of the Soviet Union with Turkey was qualified by the assertion that the German White Papers [77] had cast "an unpleasant light on certain aspects of activity in Turkey". Reference was also made to the flight last April of a "certain foreign airplane from Turkish territory" to the area of Batumi. Relations with Iran were dealt with in the same manner and it was charged that in March two foreign airplanes coming from the direction of Iran were sighted in the Baku area. In consequence it was decided that the Soviet Government must intensify its vigilance on those southern frontiers.

[76] Sir Stafford Cripps, appointed British Ambassador to the Soviet Union on June 12, 1940.

[77] Reference is to the publication during 1940 of captured Polish documents (in March) and documents of the French General Staff (in July). The Soviet press depicted the latter especially as revealing alleged Anglo-French intentions for an attack upon the Soviet Union, particularly for the bombing of Baku and Batum, and implicating Turkey and Iran. The Chargé reported to the Department in telegram No. 820, July 6, 2 p. m., that it seemed likely that "the Soviet Government is in part at least distorting the evidence for domestic consumption and for its possible ulterior purposes." (740.0011 European War 1939/4449)

9. Relations with Japan have lately begun to assume a somewhat normal character and there are indications that Japan desires to improve relations with the Soviet Union. This is feasible "with mutual recognition of the interests of both parties and as soon as both parties will understand the necessity of removing obstacles on this path which have lost their significance. There is much however that is unclear in the program of the new Japanese Government concerning the establishment of the 'new political structure'.

10. The following references to the United States were delivered by Molotov in a sarcastic manner and, although they seem devoid of any humor, provoked general laughter and applause among the deputies:

"I shall not dwell on our relations with the United States if only for the reason that there is nothing good that can be said about them. We have learned that certain people in the United States are not pleased by the successes of Soviet foreign policy in the Baltic Countries. But we confess that we are little concerned over this circumstance inasmuch as we are coping with our tasks without the assistance of these displeased gentlemen. Nevertheless the fact that the authorities in the United States unlawfully detained gold which our State Bank recently purchased from the Banks of Lithuania, Latvia, and Estonia evokes a most energetic protest on our part.[78] In this case we can only remind both the Government of the United States and the Government of Great Britain, which adopted the same procedure, of their responsibility for these illegal acts."

11. Chinese relations were dealt with briefly "as regards our relations with Great National China fighting for her existence, they have retained their good neighborly and friendly character in line with the Soviet-Chinese nonaggression pact." [79]

12. In concluding his report Molotov indulged a final taunt at United States in the following statement:

"Imperialist appetites are growing not only in distant Japan but also in the United States where there are more than a few people who like to conceal their imperialist plans by well advertised 'concern' for the interests of the entire 'Western Hemisphere' which these gentlemen are prepared to turn into their property with all its numerous republics and with the colonial possessions of other countries on islands in the neighborhood of the American continent. All this harbors the danger of a further extension and kindling of war and its conversion into a world imperialist war."

13. The prospect just alluded to is then in conclusion cited as justification for measures strengthening the Soviet Union so that "no tricks of our foreign enemies could catch us unaware."

THURSTON

---

[78] This Soviet protest was transmitted to the Department in telegram No. 885, July 20, 9 p. m., vol. I, p. 395.
[79] Signed at Nanking on August 21, 1937, League of Nations Treaty Series, vol. CLXXXI, p. 101.

740.0011 European War 1939/5089 : Telegram

The Chargé in the Soviet Union (Thurston) to the Secretary of State

Moscow, August 13, 1940—11 a. m.
[Received 2 : 10 p. m.]

1011. Embassy's despatch No. 568, June 25, 1940. The press this morning publishes a ukase of the Presidium of the Supreme Soviet concerning the strengthening of the unity of command in the Red army and fleet which states that since the system of political commissars has in the main carried out its basic tasks and with a view to establishing full unity of command in the units of the army and fleet and to increasing the authority of the commander who is "the sole directing authority of the armed forces bearing full responsibility also for political work" the regulations concerning military commissars of August 15, 1937 are abolished and the post of assistant commander for the political sector in units of the Red army and fleet is created. Military Soviets are held responsible for "daily, active control of the political work in the armed forces".

THURSTON

861.50/940

The Chargé in the Soviet Union (Thurston) to the Secretary of State

[Extracts]

No. 705
Moscow, August 22, 1940.
[Received October 8.]

SIR: With reference to the Embassy's despatch number 451 of May 6, 1940,[80] and to previous similar despatches relating to economic conditions in the Soviet Union, I have the honor to submit on the following pages a brief review of the principal features upon which definitive information is currently available of the development of Soviet national economy during the quarter ending on June 30, 1940.

Introduction.

In the economic realm the second quarter of 1940 was particularly marked by the introduction of additional far-reaching and extraordinary measures designed to tighten labor discipline and to increase the productivity of Soviet industry. The policy of territorial expansion to which the Government is apparently committed was further manifested toward the close of the period by the occupation of Bessarabia, and northern Bukovina, and the intensification of defence preparations has gradually reached such a scale, both in respect of the number of men under arms and in the placing of industry on a

[80] Not printed.

war footing, that the entire economic structure of the country must, for practical purposes, be regarded as mobilized for war. The acceleration of this trend has imposed an added strain upon the material resources of the country and the authorities have been constrained to accentuate their already heavy demands upon the working masses in the drive to speed up military preparations. These increased demands, as suggested have taken the traditional form of drastic efforts to induce high productivity of labor, as well as to restrict consumption and to force economy in the use of materials and in monetary expenditures.

Mention was made in the Embassy's economic review covering the first quarter of the year (despatch number 451, May 6, 1940) of the increase in work norms and decrease of wage rates applied in many branches of Soviet industry, as well as of the increase in retail prices effected early in the year. These steps appear to have failed to improve the situation, since further price increases were resorted to during the quarter under survey. Moreover, the results of industry continued to be unsatisfactory, falling far short of the ambitious requirements felt to be imposed by the hazards of the international situation. On June 26, 1940, therefore, as has been separately reported,[81] a law was issued under which the return to the 8-hour day in industry and to the 7-day week was provided, and under which severe penalties for unnecessary change of employment or for absence from work without leave were imposed. Simultaneously an adjustment of work norms and wage rates was again made. The provisions of the law of June 26 were shortly made applicable in general to tractor and combine operators working in machine tractor stations and press comment which has subsequently appeared seems to indicate that it may soon be extended to collective farmers also.

With the view to precluding attempts at passive resistance on the part of the workers, usually manifested in an increase in the proportion of defective production, as well as to put an end to the so-called liberal attitude of managers and technical staffs toward such workers, a law was issued on July 10, 1940,[82] by which it is provided that the issuance of poor-quality or defective industrial products, or of goods below the obligatory standards, shall be considered as "wrecking." Under this law directors, engineers, chief of departments of technical control in industrial enterprises, and others responsible for defective, non-standard or incomplete production, are liable to imprisonment of from five to eight years.

---

[81] Telegram No. 760, June 27, 3 p. m., from the Chargé in the Soviet Union, p. 202.
[82] See telegram No. 859, July 15, 5 p. m., from the Chargé in the Soviet Union, p. 205.

The foregoing legislation, taken together with the new and drastic agricultural procurement regulations which have been separately reported by the Embassy, constitutes a formidable intensification of the pressure on industry and agriculture in the Soviet Union. The third issuance of the State Loan of the third five-year plan, approved on July 1, 1940, did nothing to ease the situation, as this in effect amounts to a forced loan. All these measures were presented to the people as made urgently necessary by the growing threat of the spread of the "capitalist war" to the confines of the Soviet Union. The labor laws have been very strictly enforced and it is reported that they have encountered a considerable amount of passive resistance.

Curtailments of administrative and office personnel, referred to in the Embassy's economic review for the first quarter of the year, have continued during the second quarter.

The developments described have accentuated the tendency toward reduction of the income of the civil population and the resultant decrease in purchasing power has contributed to producing a greater apparent availability of foodstuffs. A more real and immediate alleviation of the food situation has been afforded by the good vegetable crop this year.

Light Industry of June 10, 1940, *Machine Building* of June 9 and 18, and *Industriya* of June 10 have devoted editorials to continued over-expenditure of wage funds, increased production costs, and poor management. The new labor laws are, of course, also connected with these conditions. The press campaign urging economy of raw materials and reduction in monetary expenditures has, as indicated, continued unabated during the quarter under survey.

The principal economic problems with which the authorities are confronted as the third quarter proceeds remain substantially unchanged from the Embassy's previous economic review. The steps taken are intended to eliminate these difficulties and while their nature is such that rigid and unremitting application of them might induce some temporary improvement, past experience indicates rather that the dislocations which they are likely to cause may vitiate to a large degree their remedial value. It has been unofficially reported to the Embassy, for example, that in one shop of a local automobile factory where 400 men are employed 50 of these have already had their wages docked by one third for a period of six months for being late in arriving at work. Such pressure on the workers is regarded by them as out of all proportion to their fault, since transport facilities are so inadequate that it is practically impossible to avoid being a few minutes late from time to time. On the other hand, some observers suggest that the Government's desire for greater economy in wage expenditures has led it to resort deliberately to such methods in order to attain the desired end, while characterizing tardy workers as deliberate saboteurs. It is undoubted that the financial strain of the enormous defence expenditures is great and there seems every reason to believe that the funds required to meet this outlay will be disproportionate to any savings which may be achieved in the civil branches of the national economy. Efforts to control the latent inflationary tendency which the Embassy has repeatedly indicated in its despatches may thus be expected to become increasingly manifest.

Industry: general summary.

With the view of improving technical management in industrial enterprises the authorities have issued a number of decrees ordering mass transfers of qualified engineers and technicians from offices and designing bureaus to enterprises and workshops. A decree of May 28, 1940, also gives wider responsibility to foremen in the heavy machine-building industry, according them higher wages and a number of new prerogatives, such as the right of dismissing and employing workers, setting of wages, awarding of premiums and imposing of fines. The functions and power of a Soviet foreman are now believed to be very similar to those possessed by the foreman of a prerevolutionary plant.

According to the press, the majority of the machine-building plants are at present being switched over to two-shift operation, instead of a three-shift operation as before. The press contends that three-shift operation has been uneconomic and that the actual volume of production on the three-shift basis was in many cases below that turned out in two shifts. On the other hand, all mining enterprises have been ordered to operate in three shifts, current repairs and overhauling to be effected during and in the periods between the shifts.

As in the first quarter, no comprehensive statistics have been published showing the volume of industrial production. Information derived from press sources, however, tends to indicate that a certain improvement was recorded by a number of industries as compared with the preceding trimester. Nevertheless, the total volume of industrial production during the first half of 1940, with the probable exception of the defence industry and of some branches of the machine-building industry, apparently did not show any appreciable increase over that of the first half of 1939, and lagged behind the plan figure.

According to *Izvestiya* of June 8, 1940, a number of industries, among which were the steel, oil, and coal branches, were backward during the first five months of the year. *Industriya* of June 15, 1940, also points to considerable under-fulfillment by these industries. At the same time, the paper emphasizes marked improvement in the work of the gold industry.

Machine Building of June 12, 1940, mentions successes achieved by heavy machine building, locomotive, and press and forge equipment plants. On the other hand, the operation of machine-tool, railroad-car, and agricultural-machine plants is condemned.

During the period under survey, the textile industry is stated to have recorded improvement over the first quarter, but owing to the poor showing of the earlier months the plan of the first six months was not fulfilled.

The light and food industries also improved their working during the period under survey, it is stated.

It should be observed in this connection that because of the very low general level of production for the first quarter of 1940 that period scarcely provides a fair yardstick by which to measure the good functioning of Soviet industry.

Press comments reveal that the execution of the industrial capital construction program during the first six months of the year was far from satisfactory. This is apparently due in part to the fact that in 1940 far greater attention is being paid to the construction and equipping of military enterprises in the strict sense of the word than was the case heretofore.

. . . .

Defence industries.

The Soviet press pays close attention to problems concerning armaments and their manufacture, but carefully refrains from releasing any factual or comprehensive data pertaining thereto. Particular emphasis has been laid by the press upon the construction of naval vessels and military aircraft.

In this connection *Machine Building* of May 21, 1940, writes that over two hundred plants belonging to all branches of industry are now participating in the supply of material to the shipyards. The latter are now said to be operating on a "speed system" in the construction of warships, according to this source.

Machine Building of July 28, 1940, states that "the change in the international situation which took place during the year . . . [84] requires that we redouble our efforts in the work toward increasing the military power of our socialist fatherland." The paper further states that during the first six months of this year the volume of production turned out by the shipyards has greatly increased in comparison with the same period of 1939.

Machine Building of May 21, 1940, devoted a number of articles to the introduction of mass production methods in the construction of military aircraft. The paper urges the adoption of American methods of mass production. The same paper for June 5 and June 14 dis-

[84] Omission indicated in the original despatch.

cussed the quality of the new planes and their characteristics in action, emphasizing the necessity for the rapid development of new models. The industry is urged to accelerate immediately the designing, construction, and testing of new experimental models, and it is stated that very often delays render the new model practically useless, because of the rapid advances in technique.

.   .   .   .

Conclusion.

The fear of involvement in the European war, coupled with an urgent desire to acquire additional territory as rapidly and with as little serious military effort as possible, have caused the Soviet authorities to apply sharply increased pressure to both industry and agriculture in the months under review, with the avowed aim of erecting the most formidable defensive machinery which can be achieved and with the less publicized purpose of enabling them to take advantage of the European struggle to realize their territorial aspirations while their principal potential adversary is preoccupied elsewhere. As stated earlier in this despatch, Soviet economy has reached at the present date what can only be described as a war footing, with the result that needs of the people are entirely subordinated to the inherent demands of this condition, as well as that the fundamental weaknesses of the economic organization of the country are becoming more rather than less apparent.

Respectfully yours,   WALTER THURSTON

———————————

861.011/51

The Chargé in the Soviet Union (Thurston) to the Secretary of State

No. 726   Moscow, September 4, 1940.
[Received October 8.]

SIR: I have the honor to enclose herewith a translation made in the Embassy of a law adopted on August 7, 1940, by the Supreme Soviet of the U. S. S. R., which makes certain routine alterations in the Constitution of the U. S. S. R., in connection with the organization of the newly acquired territories of Bessarabia, Northern Bukovina, Lithuania, Latvia, and Estonia.

Respectfully yours,   WALTER THURSTON

[Enclosure—Translation]

LAW OF THE SUPREME SOVIET OF THE U. S. S. R. CONCERNING THE AMENDMENT AND SUPPLEMENTATION OF ARTICLES 13, 23 AND 48 OF THE CONSTITUTION (FUNDAMENTAL LAW) OF THE U. S. S. R.

In connection with the organization of the Constituent Moldavian Soviet Socialist Republic and the admission into the Union of Soviet

Socialist Republics of the Constituent Lithuanian Soviet Socialist Republic, the Constituent Latvian Soviet Socialist Republic, and the Constituent Estonian Soviet Socialist Republic, to introduce amendments and supplementations into Articles 13, 23, and 48 of the Constitution (Fundamental Law) of the U. S. S. R., stating these articles as follows:

"*Article 13.* The Union of Soviet Socialist Republics is a federal state, formed on the basis of the voluntary association of Soviet Socialist Republics having equal rights, namely:

> The Russian Soviet Federated Socialist Republic,
> The Ukrainian Soviet Socialist Republic,
> The White Russian Soviet Socialist Republic,
> The Azerbaidzhan Soviet Socialist Republic,
> The Georgian Soviet Socialist Republic,
> The Armenian Soviet Socialist Republic,
> The Turkmen Soviet Socialist Republic,
> The Uzbek Soviet Socialist Republic,
> The Tadzhik Soviet Socialist Republic,
> The Kazakh Soviet Socialist Republic,
> The Kirgiz Soviet Socialist Republic,
> The Karelo-Finnish Soviet Socialist Republic,
> The Moldavian Soviet Socialist Republic,
> The Lithuanian Soviet Socialist Republic,
> The Latvian Soviet Socialist Republic,
> The Estonian Soviet Socialist Republic".

"*Article 23.* The Ukrainian Soviet Socialist Republic consists of the *oblasts*: Akkerman, Vinnitsa, Volyn, Voroshilovgrad, Dnepropetrovsk, Drogobych, Zhitomir, Zaporozhe, Kamenets–Podolsk, Kiev, Kirovograd, Lvov, Nikolaev, Odessa, Poltava, Rovno, Stalino, Stanislav, Sumy, Tarnopol, Kharkov, Chernigov, and Chernovitsy".

"*Article 48.* The Supreme Soviet of the U. S. S. R. shall elect, at a joint session of both houses, the Presidium of the Supreme Soviet of the U. S. S. R. to be constituted as follows: The President of the Presidium of the Supreme Soviet of the U. S. S. R., sixteen assistants to him, the Secretary of the Presidium, and 24 members of the Presidium.

The Presidium of the Supreme Soviet of the U. S. S. R. is accountable to the Supreme Soviet of the U. S. S. R. for all its action."

M. KALININ
President of the Presidium of the
Supreme Soviet of the U. S. S. R.

A. GORKIN
Secretary of the Presidium of the
Supreme Soviet of the U. S. S. R.

Moscow, August 7, 1940.

861.02/25 : Telegram

The Chargé in the Soviet Union (Thurston) to the Secretary of State

Moscow, September 7, 1940—2 p. m.
[Received September 8—5 a. m.]

1130. *Pravda* today publishes a ukase [85] of the Presidium of the Supreme Soviet of the Union of Soviet Socialist Republics concerning the organization of the People's Commissariat for State Control of the Union of Soviet Socialist Republics. This ukase states that the Commissariat is organized with the objective of establishing a very firm control over the accounting for and expenditure of state funds and materials and of verifying the execution of the decisions of the Government "on the basis of the reorganization of the commissions of Soviet control and of chief military control". It grants to this Commissariat the right to issue instructions which shall be binding upon all People's Commissariats chief administrations committees attached to the Soviet of People's Commissars of the Union of Soviet Socialist Republics and their local organs and also upon all other state cooperative and other public enterprises, institutions and organizations concerning the presentations of their accounts and concerning explanations, information and other matters connected with questions which come within the complexities of state control. It gives the Commissariat the right to impose upon those guilty of non-fulfillment of the decisions of the Government and also of neglect in accounting and of wasteful expenditure of materials or money disciplinary measures including removal from office. In cases of malfeasance or other criminal activities the Commissariat is empowered to hold guilty persons answerable to a court in accordance with the procedure established by law. It may impose and collect monetary fines in cases of discovery of incorrect activities on the part of officials damaging to the state.

A separate ukase appoints L. Z. Mekhlis as People's Commissar for State Control and as an Assistant President of the Soviet of People's Commissars of the Union of Soviet Socialist Republics.

THURSTON

711.61/752 : Telegram

The Chargé in the Soviet Union (Thurston) to the Secretary of State

Moscow, September 13, 1940—4 p. m.
[Received September 14—12 : 49 p. m.]

1159. The Chinese Ambassador [86] called on me yesterday by appointment and stated that he had been specifically directed by his

---

[85] Dated September 6.
[86] Shao Li-tsu.

Government to inquire of me as to the present status of Soviet-American relations.[87] He then referred to a previous question along the same lines to me and added that as I already knew, it was his personal hope that the relations between the United States and the Soviet Union might be put on as firm and friendly a foundation as possible. I replied that I had no information concerning any new developments in Soviet-American relations nor any indication that any change was imminent. (I presume that the reports of the Soviet Ambassador's [88] recent visits to the State Department had given rise to the instruction to the Chinese Ambassador to make a special inquiry in the premises.)

During the course of the resulting conversation, I asked the Ambassador as to the present status of Soviet-Chinese relations, with particular reference to Soviet assistance to the Chungking Government. The Ambassador replied that there had been no marked change in the Soviet attitude toward his Government but that recently he had not been successful in obtaining a favorable reply to several specific requests for aid, which however, he attributed not to any change in the policy of the Soviet Government but to difficulties of transportation between China and the Soviet [Union] and Soviet military and domestic industrial requirements.

In reply to my inquiry regarding Soviet-Japanese relations, the Ambassador said that although information in the premises was difficult to obtain, he had no reason to suspect that any change had occurred or was likely to occur in Soviet policy toward Japan and that he had been assured specifically by Molotov that the recent Chita conversations are exactly what they appeared to be, namely, a local settlement of local boundary and related questions.

In respect of the Ambassador's statement that the failure to obtain certain types of material assistance from the Soviet Union was due to physical reasons primarily, it may be mentioned that there is no reason to believe that the transportation problems involved are any greater than in previous years when, according to the information received in the strictest confidence from the Chinese Embassy here (see Embassy's 592, September 22, 6 p. m.[89]) the material assistance from the Soviet Union to China was on a very large scale.

THURSTON

---

[87] For the discussions regarding the settlement of difficulties affecting relations between the United States and the Soviet Union, see pp. 244 ff.
[88] Konstantin Alexandrovich Umansky.
[89] *Foreign Relations*, 1939, vol. III, p. 261.

861.00/11867 : Telegram

The Ambassador in the Soviet Union (Steinhardt) to the Secretary of State

Moscow, September 19, 1940—7 p. m.
[Received 10 : 55 p. m.]

1194. The following observations made in the course of my trans-Siberian trip may be of interest to the Department:

1. Military preparations: On both sides of the Soviet-Manchurian frontier extreme measures were taken by both the Japanese and Soviet authorities to conceal fairly extensive military measures. While entering and departing from the frontier stations of Manchuli and Otpor the blinds were carefully drawn, the passengers supervised and the train was not permitted to depart until after dark. Through the entire 7 days from Otpor to Moscow large numbers of soldiers and officers were in evidence and in all of the stations stopped at one out of three men were in uniform. I noted a large number of airfields along the entire route spaced from three to four hundred miles apart. The airfields were large but the hangars and facilities appeared to be in a poor state of repair and the buildings very small in relation to the size of the fields. Such planes as were visible appeared to be antiquated, consisting largely of single or twin motored bombers and small pursuit craft. I observed no important troop movements either east or west and did not see a single troop train moving in either direction during the entire trip.

2. Trans-Siberian Railway line: In general the eastern and central Siberian roadbed showed evidence of heavy wear with little maintenance work in progress. There was a noticeable improvement in the condition of the roadbed the farther west the train proceeded. From Otpor, the eastern frontier station, to Omsk, the line was double tracked in part but not for the entire length. Some of the double tracking was obviously of recent date. From Omsk to approximately 200 miles west of Sverdlovsk, a total distance of some 800 miles, I can categorically state from personal observation that the line is single track with not the slightest evidence of double tracking in progress or laid out. Furthermore the three principal bridges across the Irtysh, Enesei and Ob Rivers are single span, too light to carry double track and in respect of the two last bridges they would have to be entirely reconstructed or duplicated in order to carry a second track. I am of the opinion, based on my observations of the roadbed and the great width of these rivers that it would require at least 2 years to double track the section of 800 miles referred to above. I saw no evidence that this work is in contemplation.

3. General conditions: From my observations at the stations at various points there appeared to be a shortage of food in Eastern Siberia. Conditions appeared somewhat better in Central Siberia improving progressively the farther west we went. In Eastern and Central Siberia little agricultural machinery or evidence of modern methods of farming was to be seen and I was struck by the small number of cattle which were to be seen in areas which appeared to be excellent grazing country. The condition of the cereal crop appeared to be poor in the east and fair in the west.

STEINHARDT

811.20 Defense (M)/441

Memorandum by the Acting Chief of the Division of European Affairs (Atherton)

[WASHINGTON,] September 25, 1940.

Under instructions from the Under Secretary, Mr. Henderson and I were present in Mr. Morgenthau's [90] office this afternoon at four o'clock to meet with Mr. Jesse Jones [91] and the Soviet Ambassador. Before the arrival of the latter Mr. Morgenthau stated that it was over a question of the possible purchase of manganese and other ores from the Soviet Government by the United States in return for which consideration would be given by the Soviet Government to increasing its export of arms and munitions to China. Mr. Morgenthau stated that subsequent to the conversation the other day on this subject the Soviet Ambassador had informed the Treasury that he had received instructions from his Government. When the Soviet Ambassador arrived he stated that the instructions of his Government empowered him to inform Mr. Morgenthau that the United States would be permitted to purchase from Soviet Russia manganese, platinum, chromium, asbestos and other raw materials mentioned with the exception of mica. He then outlined at some length a route via the Caspian Sea, the Iranian Railway and the Persian Gulf, by which these ores could be exported. But, continued Mr. Oumansky, I am further directed to say that this sale of ores to the United States can in no way relate to Soviet-Chinese trade. Mr. Morgenthau said that he was very pleased with this message and it would be something for the consideration of the United States authorities before the matter would be further pursued. Mr. Jones then asked in what quantities these ores were available. The Soviet Ambassador replied that he felt that the emphasis was misplaced in that, naturally the Soviet Government would want to know in what quantities the ores were required by the United States. He thereupon withdrew. After his departure Mr.

---

[90] Henry Morgenthau, Jr., Secretary of the Treasury.
[91] Secretary of Commerce.

Morgenthau said he hoped the representatives of the State Department would convey to Mr. Hull the substance of the Soviet Ambassador's remarks, which he felt were very encouraging and, after reference to Mr. Jones the latter said he shared this opinion. Mr. Morgenthau then inquired of the State Department officers their opinion and the reply was given that, in so far as these materials were desired by the United States there was no more advantage in buying in the Soviet market than anywhere else.

Mr. Morgenthau then asked the two officers whether they did not think that at a moment of tension between the United States and Japan when Mr. Hull was contemplating reprisals, that an announcement of an embargo on scrap iron, etc. to Japan coupled with a statement that with an increase of commercial trade between Soviet Russia and the United States had already taken place, would be in the nature of a diplomatic success for the United States. The State Department officers replied that the situation was not dissimilar to that which existed recently when an attempt was made to conclude a trade agreement between Great Britain and the Soviet Union. The Soviet Union, it was understood, had entered into these negotiations only after having previously consulted with Berlin because it was in need of foreign exchange or certain commodities controlled by Great Britain. In the present state of the world when undoubtedly both Tokyo and Berlin would have full knowledge of any conversations of the Soviet Ambassador in Washington, there was no basis for considering purchases from Soviet Russia in any light other than the advantage to be derived by the United States in securing such raw materials as it may need. At the end Mr. Morgenthau said, however, that he felt the conversation with the Soviet Ambassador had been very satisfactory and opened the way for Mr. Hull to carry on the negotiations if he felt it would be advantageous to do so.

In conclusion, Mr. Morgenthau said that he would like the State Department officers present to inquire of Mr. Hull what the next step would be and he felt the time element was important.

R[AY] A[THERTON]

711.61/753 : Telegram

The Ambassador in the Soviet Union (Steinhardt) to the Secretary of State

Moscow, September 25, 1940—5 p. m.
[Received September 26—1:09 a. m.]

1230. I have learned from a source which I regard as entirely reliable that instructions were recently issued to the Soviet press and radio authorities not to publish or broadcast statements hostile to the United States.

STEINHARDT

711.61/754 : Telegram

The Ambassador in the Soviet Union (Steinhardt) to the Secretary of State

Moscow, September 25, 1940—6 p. m.
[Received September 26—1 : 29 a. m.]

1231. With reference to the information contained in my 1217, September 24, 2 p. m.,[92] the Soviet press has continued through the medium of news despatches and summaries of the American press, as well as occasional articles, to display great interest in various aspects of American policy. The views set forth in the comments have followed along lines previously reported in that up to the present the mainsprings of American policy have been presented as purely imperialistic and based upon the desire of the United States to take advantage of the war in Europe to consolidate its hegemony over the Western Hemisphere and strengthen its position in the Far East. However, as previously reported, the prominence given to developments in American foreign policy, despite the criticism of the alleged motives thereof, would appear to indicate that the Soviet Government is not displeased with the recent negotiations with England nor to what is characterized as the "intensification" of American policy in the Far East in opposition to Japan.

STEINHARDT

893.24/887 : Telegram

The Ambassador in the Soviet Union (Steinhardt) to the Secretary of State

Moscow, September 25, 1940—11 p. m.
[Received September 26—1 : 17 a. m.]

1235. In the course of a conversation with the Chinese Ambassador this afternoon he stated that the Soviets were continuing to furnish munitions and supplies to China in amounts less than before the outbreak of the European war in September, 1939, but greater than during the spring of 1940. He added that he had recently been instructed by his Government to request new types of planes in view of the improvement in the Japanese planes and that the Soviet Government had taken his request under advisement stating that they had recently shut down some of their plane factories for the purpose of installing equipment for newer types, and that when the factories were reopened about the end of October his request would be given consideration.

---

[92] See vol. I, p. 346, footnote 62.

The Ambassador said that in the course of a recent conversation with "high Soviet officials" he had expressed to them the hope of closer relations between the Soviet Union and the United States to which the Soviet officials had replied that two barriers stood in the way, the first being the distance separating the two countries, and the second the interference by the United States in matters affecting the Soviet Union and other countries and which were of no direct concern to the United States.   The Ambassador added that in this connection the Finnish-Soviet controversy had been specifically mentioned.

STEINHARDT

711.61/782

Memorandum by Mr. Edward Page, Jr., of the Division of European Affairs

[WASHINGTON,] October 3, 1940.

CERTAIN ASPECTS OF SOVIET ETHICS IN ITS FOREIGN RELATIONS

I

SOVIET-AMERICAN RELATIONS

The resumption of diplomatic relations with the Soviet Union on November 16, 1933 [93] was contingent upon certain definite conditions set forth in a series of notes exchanged between the President of the United States and Mr. Litvinov.[94]   Two of the most important conditions dealt with (1) interference by persons or organizations on Soviet territory or under the control of the Soviet Government in the internal affairs of the United States, and (2) the legal protection of American citizens in the Soviet Union.   In addition, a joint statement was issued by the President and Mr. Litvinov in which the hope was expressed for a speedy and satisfactory solution of the question of indebtedness and claims.

In spite of the first mentioned pledge, organizations such as the Communist International, which maintain headquarters in the Soviet Union, and of which the highest officials of the Soviet Government are members, have, with the encouragement of the Soviet Government consistently interfered in the internal affairs of this country.   A protest against this practice was presented to the Soviet Government on August 25, 1935 and was rejected on the grounds that the Communist International was not covered by the pledge.[95]   This refusal of the

---

[93] For the establishment of diplomatic relations between the United States and the Soviet Union, see *Foreign Relations*, The Soviet Union, 1933–1939, pp. 1 ff.

[94] Maxim Maximovich Litvinov, People's Commissar for Foreign Affairs of the Soviet Union, 1930–39.

[95] For text of the protest, see press release issued by the Department of State, August 25, 1935, *Foreign Relations*, The Soviet Union, 1933–1939, p. 250; for correspondence, see *ibid.*, pp. 218 ff.

Soviet Government to fulfill its written obligation was not accepted by this Government since the control of that Government over the Communist International is beyond cavil. Thus, less than two years after the resumption of diplomatic relations, the Soviet Government revealed its disregard for its written commitments.

Although there is circumstantial evidence that the Communist International has continued to interfere in American internal affairs and although the American Government still refuses to accept the Soviet Government's disclaiming of responsibility for the actions of that organization, no further protest has been made to the Soviet Government, since it is believed that such a protest would only result in an insulting reply and would tend to embitter still further present relations between the two countries. The activities of the Comintern and its American section would in no way be curtailed.

It might be added that within recent weeks Communist agents in this country have endeavored to incite to mutiny the crew of an Estonian vessel in New York with an object of persuading it to murder their Captain and to sail the vessel back to a Soviet port, contrary to the Captain's orders.

At the time of the establishment of diplomatic relations assurances were given by the Soviet Government which caused the American Government to believe that its representatives in the Soviet Union would be able to render certain assistance to American citizens under detention in that country.[96] On the basis of most-favored-nation treatment, the Soviet Government undertook to inform the appropriate American consul of the arrest of an American citizen in the Soviet Union within from three to seven days after the arrest had been made. It furthermore agreed on the same basis to accede without delay to requests of American consular representatives that they be permitted to visit American nationals under arrest. Although a number of American citizens have been arrested in the Soviet Union since these assurances were given, *in not one instance* has the Soviet Government notified the American consular representatives of such an arrest until after repeated inquiries relating to such citizens have been made by the American Embassy in Moscow to the Soviet authorities. The confirmations by the Soviet authorities of reports received by the American Embassy at Moscow from other than Soviet Governmental sources of arrests of American citizens have never been received until many weeks or months after the arrests have been made.

Furthermore, the Soviet authorities have not acceded without delay to requests of American consular representatives to visit American nationals under detention by the Soviet Union. A member of the Embassy was not permitted to proceed to Murmansk at the time the

---

[96] Regarding the arrest and detention of American citizens by the Soviet Government, see *Foreign Relations*, The Soviet Union, 1933–1939, pp. 904 ff.

S. S. *City of Flint* was being detained at that port.[97]   American citizens detained in Soviet-occupied Poland have not been allowed to proceed to the Embassy at Moscow for the purpose of obtaining passport and citizenship services and protracted obstructions have been placed in the way of representatives of the Embassy who have been ordered to localities in which these Americans were encountering difficulties.[98]   The Soviet authorities have even endeavored to limit the assurances given in this respect by stating that they are not obligated to permit such visits before the termination of the investigation of the American national under arrest or while such national is serving sentence in conformity with a court decision.   Since the period between the termination of the investigation of the American citizen and the sentence may be extremely brief, such an interpretation of these assurances, if adhered to by the Soviet Government and accepted by the American Government, would render still more doubtful the ability of representatives of the American Government in the Soviet Union to protect and assist American citizens in that country and would constitute a further example of the reluctance, in fact refusal, of the Soviet Government to fulfill its written obligations.

At the time of establishment of relations it was definitely understood that the Soviet Union would be willing to make payments on the Russian debts to the United States and on American claims arising from property destruction and confiscation during and since the Revolution provided the United States Government would be willing to arrange for the granting of credits to the Soviet Government.[99]   A declaration was made to the effect that the exchange of views which had taken place with regard to methods of settling all outstanding questions of indebtedness and claims permitted the hope for a speedy and satisfactory solution of these questions.   Negotiations were instituted for the purpose of reaching a definite agreement in regard to this matter shortly following the resumption of relations.   It soon became evident that the Soviet officials were entirely indifferent to any settlement and that they had no intention of arriving at any agreement.   Since the termination of the negotiations there have been no developments which have given this Government ground to believe that the re-opening of negotiations would serve any constructive purpose.   In fact, the American Government feels that the Soviet Government acted in bad faith in being a party to the hope expressed in the joint statement of November 16, 1933,[1] "for a speedy and satis-

---

[97] For correspondence concerning the detention of the steamer *City of Flint* and its crew at Murmansk, see *Foreign Relations*, The Soviet Union, 1933–1939, pp. 984 ff.

[98] For correspondence regarding the trouble in connection with the repatriation of American citizens, see *Foreign Relations*, 1939, vol. I, pp. 574 ff.

[99] The failure of the negotiations in regard to claims, debts, and credits is presented in *Foreign Relations*, The Soviet Union, 1933–1939, pp. 166 ff.

[1] *Ibid.*, p. 37.

factory solution" of the question of indebtedness and claims when it later became obvious that such a hope was never seriously entertained by the Kremlin.

In addition to the above, there were various agreements of a lesser nature in which the Soviet Government has exhibited its lack of good faith. For example, prior to the establishment of a mission in Moscow, Mr. Litvinov gave Ambassador Bullitt definitely to understand that the Soviet Government was prepared to enter into an agreement whereby the American Embassy at Moscow would be able to obtain rubles from official sources at a reasonable rate of exchange and therefore would not be compelled, like other diplomatic missions in Moscow, to purchase Soviet currency from unauthorized sources. Following the establishment of the Embassy, the Soviet Government categorically refused to enter into any such arrangement.

In further regard to the question of American claims, it might also be pointed out that since the outbreak of the present war, property owned by American citizens has been nationalized or confiscated in certain territories of Eastern Poland, Finland and Rumania, and in Latvia, Estonia, and Lithuania while those areas were under control of Soviet armed forces. In the case of Soviet-occupied Poland, the Soviet Foreign Office has informed the American Embassy at Moscow that since measures nationalizing land, banks and large industries had been approved and proclaimed before the formal incorporation of Soviet-occupied Poland into the Soviet Union, there was no basis for presentation to the Soviet Union of claims arising from such measures even though the property with respect to which such claims represented may subsequently have passed into the possession of organs of the Soviet Government.[2] A similar pronouncement is expected with regard to the nationalization and confiscation of American property in Bessarabia and the Baltic States. The American Government has informed the Soviet Government that it holds and will hold the Soviet Government responsible for all losses to American citizens resulting from such acts of nationalization and confiscation and other acts injurious to property or interests of such nationals.[3]

II

SOVIET FOREIGN RELATIONS WITH OTHER COUNTRIES

In its relations with other nations of the world, the Soviet Government has shown a like disregard for its obligations, written or tacit. It need only be recalled that the Soviet Union was the first great

---

[2] See telegram No. 502, May 8, 5 p. m., from the Chargé in the Soviet Union, p. 197.

[3] See telegram No. 276, May 16, 6 p. m., to the Chargé in the Soviet Union, 201.

Power to ratify the Kellogg-Briand Pact [4] which was put into effect between the U. S. S. R., Finland, Latvia, Estonia, and Lithuania by the Litvinov Protocol of February 9, 1929.[5]   Moscow thereby bound itself "to renounce war as an instrument of national policy" and to seek "the solution of settlement of all disputes or conflicts only by pacific means".   The Soviet Union and Finland concluded an agreement on January 21, 1932, later extended to 1945, renouncing aggression,[6] in which it was stated that the High Contracting Parties "declare that they will always seek to solve in a spirit of justice all conflicts of whatever character or origin which may arise between them, and that in the regulation of these conflicts they will resort exclusively to pacific means".   Similar treaties of non-aggression were signed with the other states adjacent to the Soviet Union.

In 1933 the Soviet Union signed an agreement with all its neighbors,[7] including Finland, Latvia, Estonia, Lithuania, Poland, and Rumania, to the effect that the aggressor in an international conflict would be considered the state which would be the first to (1) declare war against another state; (2) invade by armed forces even without a declaration of war; and (3) give aid to armed bands formed on the territory of a state and invading the territory of another state, etc.   "No consideration of a political, military, economic or other nature can serve as an excuse of the justification of aggression."   In an appendix to this convention it was asserted that the internal position of any state, as, for example, its political, economic, or social structure; the alleged shortcomings of its administration; the international conduct of any state; a rupture of diplomatic or economic relations; border incidents, etc., may not be used to justify any act of aggression.

All of these obligations which the Soviet Union took the initiative of proposing were binding at the time of the invasion of Poland by the Red Army, of the Soviet-Finnish War and of the occupation by Soviet troops of Latvia, Estonia, and Lithuania, as well as the Bessarabian and Bucovina provinces of Rumania.   These obligations were wantonly swept aside in a manner legally and ethically indistinguishable from the aggressive acts committed by Germany, Italy, and Japan and the oft repeated pronouncements of the Soviet Government of its condemnation of war and its advocacy of peaceful relations with its neighbors have proved to be deceitful misrepresentations of its true

---

[4] Signed at Paris on August 27, 1928, *Foreign Relations*, 1928, vol. I, p. 153.

[5] Signed at Moscow, League of Nations Treaty Series, vol. LXXXIX, p. 369.

[6] Signed at Helsinki, League of Nations Treaty Series, vol. CLVII, p. 393; prolonged until December 31, 1945, by a protocol signed at Moscow on April 7, 1934, *ibid.*, vol. CLV, p. 325.

[7] The Soviet Union concluded a convention for the definition of aggression at London on July 3, 1933, with Estonia, Latvia, Poland, Rumania, Turkey, Iran, and Afghanistan; for text, see League of Nations Treaty Series, vol. CXLVII, p. 67. A similar convention with Lithuania was signed at London on July 5, 1933; for text, see *ibid*, vol. CXLVIII, p. 79.

policies. It now becomes clear that, in spite of repeated claims that the Soviet Union stands only for peace, the leaders of that country have never departed from the ultimate aim to enlarge their domain and to include under the Soviet system additional people and territories.

It should be borne in mind that the Communist state is based on the principle of revolution and class warfare; that the Kremlin is still irreconcilably hostile toward what it calls the "capitalist world"; and that its success in bringing under its rule most of the territories of the former Russias, as well as over a million square miles of China, has whetted its appetite for further territorial acquisitions.

It will be recalled that in the Spring and early Summer of 1939 the Soviet Union was negotiating with England and France over the possibility of rendering assistance, in case of aggression, to Poland and Rumania.[8] It was later revealed that the Kremlin was simultaneously carrying on double dealings with Germany.[9] The former Allies, it has subsequently been ascertained, refused to admit the right of the Soviet Union to interfere in the internal affairs of the Baltic States since it was realized that such a course would ultimately lead to the reduction of those States to Soviet satellites. Germany agreed to the Soviet domination of this area and the Soviet Union late in August suddenly and secretly joined the forces of Germany, thereby making war inevitable. The ensuing months witnessed the occupation by Soviet forces of parts of Poland, Finland and Rumania, as well as the Baltic States in their entirety in spite of the treaty obligations above mentioned.

FINAL OBSERVATIONS

Machiavelli defined the prudent ruler as one who "ought not to keep faith when by so doing it would be against his interests and when the reasons which made him bind himself no longer exist". This definition applies in full to Stalin and his advisers. The Soviet Government, because of the situation in the Far East and for reasons of prestige, desired to resume diplomatic relations with the United States. Once this end had been obtained it did not hesitate to break those pledges which were made a condition of recognition. In a like manner, the Soviet Union signed non-aggression pacts with all its neighbors in order to ward off an aggression feared at that time. When it became apparent, however, that the forces of destruction were turned against the Western Democracies, the Kremlin did not hesitate to violate its written pledges and to subjugate its weaker neighbors. In view of the developments described above, it becomes apparent

---

[8] See *Foreign Relations*, 1939, vol. I, pp. 232 ff.
[9] Regarding German-Soviet negotiations culminating in the treaty of non-aggression signed at Moscow on August 23, 1939, see *ibid.*, pp. 312 ff.

that no action or policy should be based upon the word of the Kremlin however solemnly pledged.

E. Page

861.504/352 : Telegram

The Ambassador in the Soviet Union (Steinhardt) to the Secretary of State

Moscow, October 3, 1940.
[Received October 4—12 : 35 a. m.]

1275. The press today publishes a ukase [10] of the Presidium of the Supreme Soviet providing for the creation of state labor reserves in the Union of Soviet Socialist Republics. The ukase states that in order to assure "a continuing reserve of labor for industry" it is essential to provide for the training annually for transfer to industry in trade schools, railroad schools and factory apprentice schools of a labor reserve of 800,000 to 1,000,000 youths. The trade schools will provide a 2-year course for the training of skilled workers for metallurgy, chemical, mining, oil and other industries and for water transport and communications. The railroad schools will provide the same period of training for all branches of railroad work. The factory apprentice schools will provide 6-month preparation of ordinary workers for certain industries. Students in the above mentioned schools will receive no pay but will be supported at the expense of the state. The state reserves of labor thus created will be at the disposition of the Soviet of People's Commissars alone and will not be available to commissariats and enterprises without permission of the Government. The trade and railroad schools will take youths from 14 to 15 years of age and the factory apprentice schools youths from 16 to 17 years. The decree further directs the presidents of collective farms to "mobilize" annually for every 100 members of the collective farms, 4 young men to be sent to these schools. The number of young men to be provided by the town soviets is to be determined each year by the Soviet of People's Commissars. The ukase further provides that when young men have completed their courses in the above mentioned schools they "shall be considered as mobilized and shall be obliged to work for 4 consecutive years thereafter in state enterprises by order of the Chief Administration of Labor Reserves"; that during the period of instruction and the subsequent 4-year period they shall not be liable to military service.

The press likewise publishes two decrees of the Soviet of People's Commissars implementing the foregoing ukase. One establishes a "Chief Administration of Labor Reserves" (with P. C. Moskatov [11]

---

[10] Dated October 2.
[11] Peter Grigoryevich Moskatov.

as head) attached to the Soviet of People's Commissars which is given entire control over the preparation and utilization of these labor reserves. The second decree sets forth the details of the organization and operation of the trade, railroad and factory apprentice schools and provides that in the period from November 10 to November 25, 1940, 350,000 young men shall be admitted either through mobilization or through voluntary enlistment to the trade and railroad schools and 250,000 to the factory apprentice schools.

A decree of the Soviet of People's Commissars also published today abolishes the system of free education in the secondary schools and higher educational institutions in the Soviet Union and provides that from September 1, 1940, students in the 8th, 9th and 10th grades of the secondary schools shall pay tuition fees of 150 or 200 rubles a year depending on the location of the school and university students fees of from 300 to 500 rubles. The decree further provides that from November 1, 1940, the system of stipends to students shall be abolished except for those students whose work has been outstanding.

STEINHARDT

861.504/353 : Telegram

The Ambassador in the Soviet Union (Steinhardt) to the Secretary of State

Moscow, October 3, 1940—8 p. m.
[Received 9 : 02 p. m.]

1277. Reference Embassy's *en clair* 1275, October 3. In addition to providing the Soviet Government with a system of labor conscription which will insure an annual increment in the labor forces of approximately 1,000,000 young men for Soviet industry the ukase of the Supreme Soviet published today is likewise apparently designed to remedy one of the outstanding deficiencies of Soviet industrial developments; namely, a shortage of skilled labor and foremen. The measures introduced for the compulsory training of skilled workmen are, it is believed, likewise intended to diminish the already disproportionate number of white collar workers and engineers. The decree abolishing free education in the secondary schools and higher institutions of learning is apparently directed towards the same end. The willingness of the Soviet Union to openly adopt a system of compulsory labor and the abolition of certain types of free education which are so completely at variance with the professed principles of the Soviet State constitutes eloquent testimony of the extent to which all other considerations are being subordinated by the Soviet Government to a hurried attempt to prepare the Soviet Union against the possibility of armed attack.

STEINHARDT

711.61/757 : Telegram

The Ambassador in the Soviet Union (Steinhardt) to the Secretary of State

Moscow, October 8, 1940—5 p. m.
[Received 10 : 30 p. m.]

1307. Department's 614, October 3, 2 p. m.[12] I endeavored yesterday to make an appointment with Molotov to discuss with him the questions authorized in the Department's telegram under reference. His secretary in reply to my request for an appointment stated that Molotov was so busy that he could not receive me at once and suggested that I see Lozovski, the Assistant Commissar for Foreign Affairs. His secretary was told that I would prefer to wait until Molotov could receive me as the questions which I had to discuss with him could best be discussed with him rather than Lozovski or any other official of the Commissariat for Foreign Affairs. I have as yet had no further word from Molotov. It is possible, especially in view of the British Ambassador's conversation with him reported in my telegram No. 1293, October 5, 7 [6] p. m.,[13] and particularly the rumors from London of American-Anglo-Soviet negotiations that the Soviet Government, being uncertain and apprehensive as to the future German policy resulting from the German-Japanese-Italian alliance,[14] desires to avoid even the appearance of any negotiations with England and the United States pending the clarification of German intentions. Such clarification may be anticipated following the return of the German Ambassador, who is expected at the end of this week.

STEINHARDT

861.504/354 : Telegram

The Ambassador in the Soviet Union (Steinhardt) to the Secretary of State

Moscow, October 21, 1940—2 p. m.
[Received 4 : 13 p. m.]

1377. *Pravda* yesterday published a ukase [15] of the Presidium of the Supreme Soviet concerning the obligatory transfer to other enterprises of economic personnel of the sixth category or higher which includes skilled workmen, employees, technicians, foremen, engineers, draftsmen, etc. The ukase states that in view of the necessity of

---

[12] *Post*, p. 388.
[13] Vol. I, p. 617.
[14] Signed at Berlin on September 27, 1940; for text, see League of Nations Treaty Series, vol. cciv, p. 387, or *Foreign Relations*, Japan, 1931–1941, vol. II, p. 165.
[15] Dated October 19.

assuring qualified personnel for new factories and other economic enterprises and also for enterprises which are transferring their production to new types of products, the existing situation whereby the various Commissariats do not have the right to transfer higher personnel from one factory to another constitutes an obstacle to development of national economy. The ukase accordingly grants to the Commissariats the right to effect the obligatory transfer of the categories of personnel referred to above from one enterprise to another irrespective of the logic of the enterprise. In the cases of such transfers the transportation expenses of persons transferred together with their families and effects, subsistence during the journey, and certain financial assistance in establishing themselves in their new places of work are to be paid for by the Commissariat effecting the transfer.

Persons transferred will retain their uninterrupted period of service and will be credited with 1 year of additional service. Refusal to obey a transfer order will place the individual so refusing within the same category as persons who have voluntarily separated themselves from their employment and will make them subject to criminal action under the terms of the ukase of June 26, 1940 reported in the Embassy's 761 [*760*], June 27, 3 p. m.

The ukase cancels, as of Oct. 20, 1940, the individual work contracts which have been concluded by Commissariats and enterprises with the personnel referred to and grants to the Commissariats and directors of [enterprises?] the right to continue the employment of such personnel without contract.

While the ukase of June 26, 1940 forbade voluntary change of employment, the new ukase referred to above takes the more positive step of placing in the hands of the authorities the legal right to compel trained personnel to accept transfers to any enterprise to which it may be desired to send them under penalty of criminal action should they refuse. In addition, the limited degree of protection afforded to personnel by their individual work contracts is withdrawn placing them still more at the mercy of their superiors. The ukase is in line with the steps already taken to tighten further labor discipline and direct state control of labor.

STEINHARDT

861.22711/3 : Telegram

The Ambassador in the Soviet Union (Steinhardt) to the Secretary of State

Moscow, October 24, 1940—7 p. m.
[Received 9 : 45 p. m.]

1409. In sharp contrast to the condition which has prevailed during the past 2 years the Military and Assistant Military Attachés of this Mission were taken yesterday by the liaison officer of the Commissariat for Defense on a tour of inspection of an aviation technical school in the vicinity of Moscow where they were shown every consideration and apparently afforded full facilities for observation. Furthermore, Major Yeaton and Captain Michela [17] have been invited by the Commissariat for Defense to visit Leningrad on October 30 as the guests of the Commissariat for the purpose of visiting and inspecting a military school and an infantry and artillery regiment now stationed there. Although I am informed that the Military Attachés of other nations will be taken on similar visits and in consequence the change of attitude towards the Military Attachés of this Embassy appears to be a general policy of the Soviet military authorities it is of some interest that these courtesies have first been extended to the Attachés of this Mission. I am of the opinion that the courtesies, limited though they may be, about to be extended to the American Military Attachés reflects the desire of the Soviet authorities to overcome the unfavorable impression heretofore created by the absolute denial to our Military Attachés of access of military establishments, and refusal of information concerning them, which has now extended over a period of 2 years, and to prepare the ground for courtesies about to be requested in Washington in connection with the American rearmament program.

STEINHARDT

861.20211/67 : Telegram

The Ambassador in the Soviet Union (Steinhardt) to the Secretary of State

Moscow, November 5, 1940—1 p. m.
[Received 6 : 12 p. m.]

1487. The Department may wish to take cognizance of the following statements recently made at the Embassy by one of the more intelligent visa applicants who has been experiencing difficulties in obtaining a Soviet exit visa.

The applicant stated that he was in considerable disfavor with the local authorities in the town of his residence in Soviet occupied Poland because he had refused to accept repeated offers from them to issue to him the desired exit visa and to facilitate his departure from the Soviet Union in every possible way and even to pay him substantial and regular compensation in the United States provided he would sign an agreement to undertake espionage work in the United States. He said the Soviet authorities had told him they were not granting permission to anyone to leave the Soviet Union unless the individual

---

[17] Joseph A. Michela, Assistant Military Attaché in the Soviet Union.

gave an undertaking to the foregoing effect and that he was foolish to refuse if he really wished or hoped to leave the Soviet Union. The authorities further stated that they already had many new agents working for them in the United States and that he should seize the opportunity extended to him as it was only a question of a short time before the Soviets would take over the Government of the United States.

The foregoing which reflects a common practice long known to the Department and recently applied in the Baltic States indicates that many visa applicants and doubtless many among the individuals who acquire American passports to return to the United States are being solicited to sign such agreements as a condition precedent to the issuance of exit visas. Nearly all of these individuals have relatives remaining in Soviet territory and are therefore subject to pressure in the United States if they fail to carry out their agreement. Furthermore the undertaking required of them might be availed of to bring about their deportation from the United States or to prevent them from ultimately acquiring American citizenship thus constituting a continuing form of blackmail during their stay in the United States.

I accordingly feel fortified in my previously expressed view that the best interests of the United States are not served by permitting aliens residing in territory under Soviet dominion to emigrate to the United States at the present time in any large numbers.

STEINHARDT

861.415/63 : Telegram

The Ambassador in the Soviet Union (Steinhardt) to the Secretary of State

Moscow, November 8, 1940—5 p. m.
[Received 9 : 25 p. m.]

1503. Contrary to his previous practice Molotov did not speak at the annual meeting on the eve of the November 7 holiday.[18] The address this year was made by Kalinin [19] who avoided any definite statements concerning Soviet foreign affairs or any reference to Soviet relations with other countries. He merely emphasized that the Soviet policy is one of peace and neutrality and in this connection asserted

[18] Following the policy adopted by the United States in 1939 (see telegram No. 228, November 4, 1939, to the Ambassador in the Soviet Union, and footnote 95, *Foreign Relations*, The Soviet Union, 1933–1939, p. 790), no message of felicitation was sent by President Roosevelt on this anniversary, but cards were left at the Embassy of the Soviet Union in Washington (861.458/14, 17).
[19] Mikhail Ivanovich Kalinin, President (Chairman) of the Presidium of the Supreme Council of the Soviet Union.

that "of the great states in actual fact the Soviet Union is the only one which remains outside of the war observing strict neutrality." He stated that the present international situation "does not give us the right to be indifferent observers and tranquil spectators of developing events" and characterized the chief task of the Soviet people as one of strengthening the economic and defensive power of the Soviet Union thereby carrying out their duty to the international proletariat.

In respect of international [*internal*] affairs he spoke of the recent improvement in industrial production which occurred during the summer months as a result of the new measures taken by the Government to improve labor discipline. He spoke of the past successful agricultural year and stated that the "gross production of grains this year was close to seven billion poods".[20] This would indicate that the 1940 grain crop, as indicated in the Embassy's No. 1432, October 28, 6 p. m.,[21] was almost equal to the 1937 record crop. However, it should be noted that the figure given by Kalinin refers to gross production and consequently does not reveal the actual barn production.

STEINHARDT

861.20211/67

The Under Secretary of State (Welles) to President Roosevelt

WASHINGTON, November 22, 1940.

MY DEAR MR. PRESIDENT: Since I know of your deep interest in the matter of the activities in this country of foreign agents, I am bringing particularly to your attention the attached telegram of November 5, 1940 from Mr. Steinhardt.[22] You will note from this telegram that Mr. Steinhardt is of the opinion that the Soviet Government is endeavoring to enlist as its agents in the United States persons immigrating to the United States from territory under Soviet control, and that it follows the practice of extracting promises to engage in espionage from such persons before granting them permits to depart. This is the first information which the Department has received that places under suspicion all persons emigrating from the Soviet Union to this country. Heretofore the Department has endeavored to prevent the issuance of visas to persons suspected of intending to come to this country to act as espionage agents, and if discovered after entry, to place them under investigation. In view of the instant communication from Mr. Steinhardt the Department will transmit to the appropriate agencies of this Government such information as it may succeed in obtaining which would cause any group of immigrants

[20] One pood equaled 36.113 pounds.
[21] Not printed.
[22] Telegram No. 1487, p. 234.

to fall under suspicion of coming to this country to act as Soviet agents.

Faithfully yours,   SUMNER WELLES

893.24/1014

Memorandum of Conversation, by the Under Secretary of State (Welles)

[WASHINGTON,] November 27, 1940.

The Soviet Ambassador called to see me this afternoon.

I said to the Ambassador that as he knew, this Government regarded with the utmost interest the situation of China and that it was prepared to give further material assistance to China. I stated that the maintenance of the independence and integrity of China was a primary objective in the foreign policy of the United States. The Ambassador stated that he was authorized likewise to say that the policy of the Soviet with regard to China was identical with that of the United States. He agreed that insofar as Russia and the United States were concerned, there was no conflict of interest between them in the Pacific, but that, on the contrary, their objectives were similar. I asked the Ambassador if it was true that his Government had ceased to give material assistance to China in recent months. He stated that so far as he was informed this was not correct and that in a recent conversation which he had had with Dr. T. V. Soong,[23] Dr. Soong had assured him that Russian military supplies were still being received by the Chinese Government from the Soviet. The Ambassador expressed great interest in Japanese movements in southern Asia.[24] He expressed the opinion that Japan was probably preparing through Indochina and Thailand some movement against Singapore from the rear. I said that this might well be the case although some attack against the Netherlands East Indies was, of course, likewise possible. I said that I had no very clear impression as yet that the Japanese Government had in fact determined what course it was going to pursue. I stated that it seemed to me undoubtedly true that Japanese activities in southern Asia would be far less in scope and extent if the Chinese Government had both the moral and material support of Russia.[25]

S[UMNER] W[ELLES]

---

[23] Chairman, Board of Directors, Bank of China; formerly Finance Minister.
[24] Details of the Japanese southward advance are given in vol. IV, pp. 1 ff.
[25] See also memorandum of November 27 by the Under Secretary of State, p. 413, and the memorandum of December 16 by the Assistant Chief of the Division of European Affairs, p. 420.

740.00111 European War 1939/565

Memorandum of Conversation, by the Assistant Chief of the Division of European Affairs (Henderson)

[WASHINGTON,] December 17, 1940.

Participants: Mr. C. A. Oumansky, Soviet Ambassador;
  Mr. Sumner Welles, Under Secretary of State;
  Mr. Ray Atherton, Acting Chief, Division of European Affairs;
  Mr. Loy W. Henderson, Ass't Chief, Division of European Affairs.

At the conclusion of discussions on various matters regarding Soviet-American relations which took place yesterday afternoon between the Under Secretary and the Soviet Ambassador,[26] the Soviet Ambassador stated that in his previous conversation [27] with Mr. Welles several questions had been raised with regard to the foreign policy of the Soviet Union. The Ambassador said that he was prepared to formulate his answers to those questions and expressed his certainty that these answers represented the point of view of his Government. The Ambassador's statement was as follows:

"The Soviet Government stands on its position of a policy of peace and remains out of war. At the same time the Soviet Government endeavors to maintain normal political and economic relations with all Powers, including the belligerents. The character of the Soviet Union's relations with China remains invariably good neighborly and is guided by the spirit of the Chinese-Soviet non-aggression pact of 1937.[28] The Near Eastern policy of the Soviet Union is determined by the principle of further improvement of economic and political relations with all Near-Eastern States."

Mr. Welles replied that it was his understanding that during the previous conversation Mr. Oumansky had agreed with him that the policy of the United States towards China is similar to that of the Soviet Union. It is the present intention of the United States, Mr. Welles continued, to increase assistance to China in such manner as might be further possible. He added that he assumed that the Soviet Government had similar intentions. The Soviet Ambassador replied that in his opinion there could be no doubt that the intention of the Soviet Government to continue aid to China could be read into the

---

[26] See the memorandum of December 16 by the Assistant Chief of the Division of European Affairs, p. 419.
[27] See the memoranda by the Under Secretary of State of November 27, *supra* and p. 413.
[28] Signed at Nanking on August 21, 1937, League of Nations Treaty Series, vol. CLXXXI, p. 101.

statement which he had just made, in view of the wording of the non-aggression pact of 1937 between China and the Soviet Union.

Mr. Welles stated that the statement which had just been made was of the utmost importance and was most gratifying to the Government of the United States.[29]

861.20211/72 : Telegram

The Ambassador in the Soviet Union (Steinhardt) to the Secretary of State

Moscow, December 26, 1940—3 p. m.
[Received December 27—3 a. m.]

1780. [The portion of the telegram here omitted gives detailed information received from an American citizen who had been residing in a Baltic State, but who had received an exit visa to return to the United States with his wife only on condition of acting there as a Communist agent.]

The foregoing information, which corroborates previous information received by the Embassy (see my 1487 of November 5, 1 p. m.) with regard to attempts of the Soviet authorities to recruit American citizens and emigrants leaving the Soviet Union and Soviet occupied areas for the United States, and which in this particular case is more detailed and circumstantial than usual, is in my opinion entitled to full credence. In this connection it is important to emphasize that a substantial proportion of the individuals who are permitted to depart, having relatives remaining in the Soviet Union or Soviet occupied areas, whether American citizens or emigrants, must rest under the presumption of having been approached by the Soviet authorities. Their failure to notify the Embassy or other American officials that they have been approached in no sense indicated that they have not been solicited or have not accepted the proposals that may have been made to them.

STEINHARDT

---

[29] Notations by both Mr. Atherton, Acting Chief of the Division of European Affairs, and Mr. Henderson, Assistant Chief of the Division, state that this text was edited by the Soviet Ambassador on December 18, 1940. The substance of this memorandum, and the complete statement made by Ambassador Umansky, were sent to the Ambassador in the Soviet Union in telegram No. 883, December 18, 6 p. m., not printed. For a summation by Ambassador Steinhardt of the apparent readiness of the Soviet Union to conclude a political agreement with Japan, although on its own terms, see his telegram No. 1788, December 27, 6 p. m., vol. I, p. 680.

861.50/946

*The Ambassador in the Soviet Union (Steinhardt) to the Secretary
of State*

[Extracts]

No. 1110   Moscow, February 1, 1941.
                                                 [Received March 12.]

SIR: With reference to the Embassy's despatch No. 868 of October 21, 1940,[30] and to previous similar despatches [31] relating to economic conditions in the Soviet Union, I have the honor to submit on the succeeding pages a brief review of the principal features upon which definitive information is at present available of the development of the economic situation in the Soviet Union during the quarter ending on December 31, 1940.

Introduction.

The far-reaching and extraordinary measures in the field of strict labor regulation which were introduced by the Soviet Government during preceding quarters of 1940 were followed at the outset of the fourth quarter by two further ukases of the Presidium of the Supreme Soviet of the U. S. S. R., the one relating to the obligatory transfer of engineers, technicians, foremen, office employees and skilled workers from one enterprise or institution to another, and the second concerning the organization of state labor reserves. According to the latter of these ukases, issued on October 19, 1940,[32] the People's Commissars of the U. S. S. R. are accorded the right of obligatory transfer of all skilled labor from one to another of the enterprises within their respective jurisdictions. The earlier ukase (October 2, 1940) [33] decreed the organization of state labor reserves by investing the Soviet of People's Commissars of the U. S. S. R. with the right to mobilize annually from 800,000 to 1,000,000 persons from among the city and village youth of the male sex aged from 14 to 17 for training in special trade schools. This mobilization and training of the country's youth was to be commenced at the end of November 1940. To supervise the training and handling of the new labor reserves a special Chief Administration of State Labor Reserves was set up. The texts and apparent implications of both of these ukases have been reported to the Department separately in detail.

---

[30] Not printed.

[31] See despatch No. 705, August 22, from the Chargé in the Soviet Union, p. 211.

[32] See telegram No. 1377, October 21, 2 p. m., from the Ambassador in the Soviet Union, p. 232.

[33] See telegram No. 1275, October 3, from the Ambassador in the Soviet Union, p. 230.

The importance attached by the authorities to the labor legislation put into application during 1940 is further emphasized by the following statements made by Shcherbakov,[34] Secretary of the Moscow Party Committee, in a speech delivered on January 21, 1941, on the occasion of the 17th anniversary of Lenin's death: "The Party and the Soviet Government must not disregard the quality of new admissions to the ranks of the working class. Loafers, shirkers and all kinds of ill-starred, good for nothing persons should not be permitted to enter the factories and shops".

Shcherbakov further stated that 600,000 youths have already been mobilized and have started their training. "From one year to another their numbers will increase. This means that in the near future our country will have new contingents of qualified and politically trained young workers burning with the desire to devote their energies to the good of the fatherland and to the strengthening of its power".

According to Shcherbakov the labor laws introduced during 1940 are directed against "those who have wrongly understood the right to work to mean the right to choose their own places of employment, in disregard of the interests and the needs of the state".

Shcherbakov further admits that the losses caused to industry by "shirking" and "loafing" during the period of the Second Five-Year Plan ran into billions of rubles.

These statements bring out the fact that the labor policy of the Soviet Government as inaugurated during 1940 has not been prompted solely by the progress of the European war and the changes in the international situation occasioned by it, but that it was also a direct result of internal difficulties arising out of the peculiar methods pursued in the development of the Soviet national economy. It is equally evident that the labor laws introduced in 1940 are not a series of extraordinary measures put into effect for a short period of emergency, but that they constitute an expression of a long-term policy.

The drive for drastic enforcement of the labor legislation continued unabated during the final quarter of the year and press reports ascribe to the wholesome influence of these laws the fact that the working of many branches of the national economy during that quarter showed "satisfactory" improvement.

Every precautionary measure has been taken by the authorities to check any increase in the wages paid to workers and employees. Thus, according to *Trud* of January 3, 1941, the establishment of progressive systems of payments for piecework as well as of premiums for overfulfillment of work norms should be effected with the greatest possible reserve and care, since many such systems of payment have in the past been based on wrong principles and have provided for

---

[34] Alexander Sergeyevich Shcherbakov.

excessively high rates of remuneration.   Moreover, *Trud* of December 27, 1940, hints at further upward changes in work norms to be effected in 1941.

The trend during the fourth quarter of 1940 was emphatically toward a reduction in wage funds and toward further drastic economy in public expenditures as well as in the utilization of raw materials in industrial enterprises.

.   .   .   .

The sweeping restrictive measures applied by the authorities in the course of 1940 with respect to labor, wages and work norms, taken together with the repeated price increases, have resulted in a marked decline in the purchasing power of the population, as mentioned in the Embassy's economic review for the third quarter of the year.[35] In the final quarter this decline became even more pronounced.   In this connection it will be noted, however, that the persons mostly affected have been those engaged in civil life, whereas expenditures in connection with the armed forces, policy, national defense and certain of the machine-building industries have been steadily rising.

The Government has obviously exerted great pressure in order to check inflationary tendencies, which have long been latent in the Soviet economy and which were particularly noticeable toward the end of 1939.   In order to avoid sharp currency inflation the Soviet authorities have resorted, among other things, to an inflation of prices—a step which they had hitherto been very reluctant to take. Having realized that the growing monetary inflation was accentuating the shortage of consumers' goods in the state stores and occasioning a rapid upward movement of prices on the so-called open or kolkhoz market, it was logically concluded by the authorities that price inflation would inevitably follow monetary inflation and that they had better introduce the latter themselves in order to check the first.   Price increases alone could not bring about a stabilization of Soviet finances; accordingly, the authorities began in addition to curtail severely the earnings of the population by the means described. During the quarter under review this policy was carried out with some success, but it is too soon as yet to characterize the present state of Soviet finances as stabilized.   The rumors current in Moscow several weeks ago concerning a possible revaluation of the ruble may have reflected a desire of the authorities to introduce some measure of this kind eventually, but the present time does not appear propitious for such a step.

.   .   .   .

---

[35] Despatch No. 868, October 21, not printed.

Industry: General Summary.

According to press reports the working of most branches of Soviet industry during the final quarter of 1940 was satisfactory. Particularly good results were achieved by the major branches of heavy industry, such as steel, iron ore, and coal. The petroleum industry also improved its operation during the quarter. The textile, light and food industries have likewise shown good results. On the other hand, most branches of the machine-building industry were characterized as backward.

In a statement made in a speech delivered on the occasion of the twenty-third anniversary of the establishment of the Soviet state and published in *Pravda* of November 7, 1940, Kalinin said [36] that the production of Soviet industry during 1940 was expected to exceed that of the preceding year by about 11 percent. This estimated percentage, however, represents the increase in industrial output in terms of gross production by value and is thus of very restricted usefulness. Kalinin also stressed the fact that during the first 6 months of the year industry had encountered numerous difficulties in executing its plan assignments, these difficulties being mostly due to international complications.

The marked improvement in operation which was achieved by Soviet industry during the latter portion of the year is attributed by the Soviet press to the strict enforcement of the new labor laws and a consequent increase in labor productivity. The influence of state-organized "social competition" campaigns upon the expansion of industrial output has also been favorably commented upon by the Soviet press.

Judging from official reports the poor operation of industry as a whole during the first six months of the year prevented the majority of its branches from accomplishing their annual plan assignments. Steel, coal, petroleum and other major branches of industry failed to fulfill their production programs for 1940 by a wide margin, although most of them augmented their output in comparison with the preceding year. The plan of the final quarter was likewise executed by few branches of industry only, notwithstanding that the percentage of execution was said to have come nearer to plan figures than during any of the preceding quarters.

Indirect evidence may be had from press sources to the effect that the production program for some industries has been reduced in the course of the operating year. This makes the estimating of actual production in kind in 1940, which is attempted in the following pages of this survey,[37] difficult and of doubtful reliability. On the whole,

---

[36] See the report on Kalinin's speech in telegram No. 1503, November 8, 5 p. m., from the Ambassador in the Soviet Union, p. 235.

[37] These estimates are not printed.

however, it may reasonably be assumed that the original provisions of the Third Five-Year Plan have been considerably modified and can no longer be considered as effective.

. . . .

Conclusion.

The main lines of Soviet economic policy remain essentially unchanged since the Embassy's last economic survey. Close collaboration with Germany has been reaffirmed by the economic agreements recently entered into, and there is every reason to presume that this will be continued under existing circumstances. The desires to avoid involvement in a major military adventure, to build up the country's defensive strength to the highest possible degree in the shortest possible time, and to profit to any extent which may be found practicable within the terms of these aims from the progress of international events remain basic, it is believed, in the minds of the Soviet leaders. The economic legislation applied during the latter months of 1940 seems thus far to have resulted in a speeding up of Soviet industry—with national defence emphasized as a major consideration behind the measures passed. There is no doubt that the pressure on the Soviet worker and peasant has been augmented during the year which has just drawn to a close, but the depth of their capacity to endure is, so far as can now be seen, as yet unplumbed.

Respectfully yours,   LAURENCE A. STEINHARDT

DIFFICULTIES AFFECTING RELATIONS BETWEEN THE UNITED STATES AND THE SOVIET UNION, AND DISCUSSIONS CONCERNING THEIR ALLEVIATION [38]

124.61/145 : Telegram

The Ambassador in the Soviet Union (Steinhardt) to the Secretary of State

Moscow, January 5, 1940—7 p. m.
[Received January 5—6:17 p. m.]

24. Evidence that the Soviet Government is endeavoring to isolate the Soviet Union from the outside world to a greater extent than ever before is accumulating. The Diplomatic Missions are no exception to this policy. Since the reestablishment of the press censorship (see my telegram No. 1153, December 29, 2 p. m.[39]) the following progressive steps have been taken by the Soviet authorities. Until about December 10 open mail addressed to members of the Embassy staff, while

---

[38] For previous correspondence regarding difficulties from Soviet authorities, see *Foreign Relations*, The Soviet Union, 1933–1939, pp. 837 ff.
[39] Not printed.

surreptitiously opened and read, was not withheld. During the past 3 weeks formal censorship has been in effect and open mail addressed to me and members of the Embassy staff in addition to being censored is now being held for approximately 2 weeks after its arrival in Moscow before being delivered. This morning, on endeavoring to telephone Riga, I was advised by the director of the telephone system that hereafter only local calls would be accepted from the Embassy and that long distance calls may only be made on personal appearance at the central telephone station.

STEINHARDT

700.00116 M.E./89

Memorandum by President Roosevelt for the Secretary of State

[WASHINGTON,] January 10, 1940.

I note in Steinhardt's cable No. 24, January 5, 1940, that long distance calls can no longer be made from the Embassy in Moscow except by personal appearance at the central telephone station.[40]

I am wondering whether we might apply the same rule to the Russian Embassy here—or at least tell Oumansky we are thinking of doing it. What is sauce for the goose might well be sauce for him too!

F[RANKLIN] D. R[OOSEVELT]

740.00116 European War 1939/171

Memorandum of Conversation, by the Chief of the Division of European Affairs (Moffat)

[WASHINGTON,] January 10, 1940.

The Soviet Ambassador [41] called this morning at his own request. He said that he had many observations to make about the course of American-Russian trade relations.[42] For years he had been working in the direction of building these up, and now for a series of reasons, partly political and partly economic, the direction had been reversed and his work was rapidly disintegrating. For the moment he wished to talk to me about one case which he said he regarded as somewhat in the nature of a test case. This was the Wright Aeronautical Company case.

In the last few days of August, 1939, the Soviet Government had signed with the Wright Aeronautical Company a five-year contract for

---

[40] The Ambassador in the Soviet Union reported in his telegram No. 68, January 20, 11 a. m., that the Embassy's long distance telephone service had been restored (124.61/146).

[41] Konstantin Alexandrovich Umansky.

[42] For correspondence regarding trade relations and renewal of the commercial agreement signed on August 6, 1940, see pp. 441 ff.

technical assistance, involving the construction of three types of airplane engines. The contract was signed after six years of relationship between the company and the Soviet authorities, and after the contract had been shown by the company to the authorities in Washington. Under this contract, which provided that several models of the engines should be shipped to Russia and manufactured there, fifteen Soviet engineers were to participate in receiving plans, drafts, and other facilities in the company's factory. All was going well when about December 27 or 28 Mr. Vaughn, the President of the company, informed Amtorg [43] that "by order from Washington" no Soviet engineers would any longer be admitted to the factory, and all passes were revoked. As a result, the execution of the contract has become impossible, and neither the company nor the Soviet authorities see any way in which work can be continued. Substantial sums are involved. The whole thing amounts to a unilateral breaching of contract, with the company referring to orders from Washington as justification for this unilateral breaching of contract. The Ambassador said that he did not know what officials had given this order.

In other factories the situation was not yet quite as bad, but little by little Soviet engineers were being refused permission to visit parts of the factories on the ground that orders were being filled therein for the United States Army and Navy. The Ambassador feared that there was widespread discrimination against Soviet engineers.

I told the Ambassador that I did not know anything specific about the Wright Aeronautical Company case and would try and find out for him. On the other hand, I showed him the two press releases that we had issued on December 15 and December 20 regarding the moral embargo.[44]

The Ambassador said that he had read these releases not once but many times. He pointed out that Soviet Russia was not mentioned therein. I replied that that was true but that it would be difficult to maintain that Russia had not been guilty of unprovoked bombing of civilians in Finland.[45] Furthermore, the Soviet Government had not answered the President's request for an assurance against the bombing or machine-gunning of civilians by Soviet Russia during the Finnish hostilities.[46] The Ambassador said that in the first place Mr. Molotoff [47] had in effect answered the President, though he seemed

---

[43] Amtorg Trading Corporation, official purchasing and sales agency of the Soviet Union in the United States.

[44] See footnote 5, p. 179.

[45] For reports by the American Minister in Finland of Soviet air raids on Helsinki during the first days of Soviet aggression, see Department of State *Bulletin,* December 2, 1939, p. 610.

[46] See telegram No. 255, November 30, 1939, 6 p. m., *Foreign Relations,* The Soviet Union, 1933–1939, p. 798.

[47] Vyacheslav Mikhailovich Molotov, People's Commissar for Foreign Affairs of the Soviet Union.

somewhat hazy as to the form in which it was done.[48]   However, he claimed that the facts spoke for themselves and that President Kallio of Finland had yesterday only claimed that 200 Finnish civilians had been killed by bombardment from the air despite what he alleged to be constant Soviet bombing of open cities.   Actually, the Ambassador said, Russia had limited herself entirely to military objectives and Finland's own figures were the best proof of the foregoing.

However, quite apart from the foregoing, he thought that paragraph 3 of the press release of December 15 [49] almost amounted to an invitation to the various companies to divest themselves of their contractual obligations with Soviet companies.   He felt that this was contrary to announced American policy, which had always upheld the sanctity of contracts and emphasized the necessity of equal treatment to all, without discrimination.

In conclusion, the Ambassador asked three things: first, that I endeavor to find out the facts in the Wright Aeronautical Company case; second, that we explore the possibilities of working out some effective means of continuing work under the contract,—some sort of *modus vivendi;* third, that we be prepared to discuss with him at a somewhat later date the whole subject of the general trade relations between the two countries, with particular reference to discriminations which he feels in fact are being practiced.

P[IERREPONT] M[OFFAT]

740.00116 European War 1939/172

Memorandum by the Assistant Chief of the Division of Controls
(Yost)

[WASHINGTON,] January 15, 1940.

After the receipt of Mr. Moffat's memorandum of January 10 of his conversation with the Soviet Ambassador in regard to what the Ambassador described as "a unilateral breaching of contract" in connection with the requested withdrawal of 15 Soviet engineers from the plant of the Wright Aeronautical Company and since it appeared that this withdrawal was a result of the control exercised by the War and Navy Departments over visits by foreigners to American armament plants rather than a result of the "moral embargo", I asked Mr. Moseley [50] to ascertain the pertinent facts from the War or the Navy Department.   Mr. Moseley spent the morning of January 13 at the Navy Department and obtained the following information.

---

[48] See *Foreign Relations*, The Soviet Union, 1933–1939, p. 799, footnote 2b.
[49] Department of State *Bulletin*, December 16, 1939, p. 685.
[50] Harold W. Moseley, of the Division of Controls.

On December 26, 1939, the Inspector of Naval Aircraft at the factory of the Wright Aeronautical Corporation, under instructions from the Navy Department, addressed a letter to the corporation requesting that "all authorizations extended heretofore for visits by Russian technicians and representatives be canceled, and that such representatives be no longer admitted to the company's factory in accordance with Article XV of the Agreement between the Wright Aeronautical Corporation and Stalin Plant of U. S. S. R." A copy of this letter is attached hereto.[53] It will be seen that the Navy Department objects to the presence of such a large number of foreign engineers in the Wright plant for the reason that "it operates to permit needless opportunity for observation of our production and development of military engines at a time when it is particularly to the best interest of the United States Government to exercise the utmost vigilance to prevent such observation". It may be added that the authority under which the Navy Department restricts visits of foreigners to armament plants is its constitutional authority to safeguard the interests of the national defense, as specifically implemented by the United States Naval Regulations of 1920, a copy of the pertinent section of which is attached hereto.[53]

It should also be noted that the Naval Inspector makes it clear in the third numbered paragraph of his letter that the intent is not to cut off altogether visits of foreigners to the Wright plant, but merely to reduce the number and duration and to limit them in general to visits made in connection with the actual purchase of American aircraft matériel.

In connection with Mr. Oumansky's reference to a "breaching of contract", attention is invited to the excerpts from the Wright–Soviet contract in question attached hereto.[53] It will be observed that the contract provides that Soviet technicians shall be stationed at the Wright factory only when the United States Government permits and shall be withdrawn whenever the United States Government shall refuse to grant such permission.   The action taken by the Navy Department on December 26 was therefore foreseen and provided for by the contract and could not be considered to be a violation of the contract.

Charles W. Yost

195.2/3649½

Memorandum of Conversation, by the Assistant Chief of the Division of European Affairs (Henderson)

[Washington,] January 19, 1940.

The Soviet Ambassador telephoned me today in order, as he said, to bring to my attention a new series of difficulties which the Soviet Gov-

---

[53] Not attached to file copy of this document.

ernment was encountering in connection with its endeavors to carry on commercial relations with the United States.

Soviet purchasing and shipping organizations in this country were encountering difficulties and obstacles in connection with their efforts to charter vessels for the purpose of transporting Soviet purchases made in this country to the Soviet Union. The Ambassador said that he wanted, particularly, to draw the attention of the Department of State to the case of the steamship *Ogon*, which had been chartered by the Amtorg Trading Corporation on December 30, with the hope that the Department may give some assistance in the matter. This vessel apparently was operated by the Intercoastal Packing Company and was scheduled to leave Seattle around January 25.

I asked the Ambassador what was the precise nature of the difficulties. He replied that he was sure that if the State Department took up the matter with the Maritime Commission it could obtain all the details of the case, since the Maritime Commission must be acquainted with them. He added that he hoped that steps would be taken so that it would be possible for the steamship to sail at a date not distant from that scheduled.[54]

811.22761/20 : Telegram

The Ambassador in the Soviet Union (Steinhardt) to the Secretary of State

Moscow, January 22, 1940—noon.
[Received January 22—8:45 a. m.]

89. During an interview at the Foreign Office yesterday Potemkin [55] brought to my attention two recent developments which appear to have been deeply resented by the Soviet Government. The first is the exclusion of Soviet representatives from the Wright Airplane factories, an act which Potemkin insisted was discriminatory. The second is a public address alleged to have been made recently by Assistant Secretary of War Johnson [56] in the course of which Potemkin asserted, Johnson had made remarks derogatory to the Soviet Union and to the honor of the Soviet Army. Potemkin was especially bitter and caustic on this subject. As I had no knowledge whatsoever of the address I contented myself with a reminder that freedom of speech prevails in the United States.

STEINHARDT

---

[54] During a telephone conversation with the Soviet Ambassador on February 2, Mr. Henderson told him that his inquiry had been taken up with the appropriate authorities, but that as yet there was no answer to make (195.2/3649 4/8). For the eventual reply, see the memorandum of March 14 by Mr. Henderson, p. 253.

[55] Vladimir Petrovich Potemkin, Assistant People's Commissar for Foreign Affairs of the Soviet Union until March 1, 1940.

[56] Speech by Louis Johnson before the New York State Bankers' Association at New York City on January 15; see *New York Times*, January 16, 1940, p. 13, and memorandum by the Secretary of State, February 1, p. 250.

811.22761/20 : Telegram

The Secretary of State to the Ambassador in the Soviet Union
(Steinhardt)

WASHINGTON, January 25, 1940—7 p. m.

54. Your 89, January 22, noon. As explained to the Soviet Ambassador on January 18: (1) The Army and Navy have the right to decide whether aliens will be permitted in plants manufacturing equipment for national defence; (2) The Wright plant is manufacturing such equipment and the Army and Navy requested that visits of foreigners to the plant be permitted only when necessary for the purchase of equipment; (3) The Soviet engineers excluded were not engaged in purchasing equipment; and (4) The Wright contract contained a provision to the effect that visits of Soviet technicians to the plant might be refused if disapproved by the United States Government.

A copy of memorandum of conversation will be transmitted by pouch.[57]

HULL

711.61/713

Memorandum of Conversation, by the Secretary of State

[WASHINGTON,] February 1, 1940.

The Soviet Ambassador came in at his own request. He said he had two points to bring up, one relating to a personal matter and the other to the interference of trade between our two countries.

The Ambassador drew out a manuscript of the recent speech of Assistant Secretary of War Louis Johnson on January fifteenth before the New York State Bankers Association in New York City, and proceeded very vigorously to condemn the criticism in the speech of totalitarian countries, and especially the comparison between Finnish soldiers and Soviet soldiers, greatly to the disadvantage of the latter. He made bitter complaint. I then proceeded to say that he must realize that statesmen and officials in his country, and particularly the government-controlled press, including *Pravda*, have been in the habit of applying almost every sort of epithet to the United States and to our officials and statesmen, but that this action has been passed unnoticed here. The Ambassador must understand, however, that this habit of applying epithets in his country has naturally created a general feeling here that, if persons in the United States should occasionally talk back in similar language, the Soviet Government, having set the example, ought not to think of making complaint. He sought to palliate and in effect to deny my statements about these

---

[57] Missing from Department files.

practices in his country. I adhered to my contention. Furthermore, I said that when the American Minister [58] and well-known and trusted American newspaper correspondents in Finland send unequivocal reports back to this Government to the effect that Russian bombers are killing numerous unarmed men, women and children in Finland, the Soviet Government must realize that people in a country like the United States or in most countries will insist on voicing the bitter feeling they entertain in regard to such assassinations and that no one can control them in this respect even if they should so desire. I added that this was another phase of the situation that might well be considered in connection with the utterance of Colonel Johnson, which, by the way, I stated I had not seen. The Ambassador sought to deny any bombing of civilians from the air, but I insisted that the evidence of our Government was beyond any contradiction from such a roundabout way as Moscow.

The Ambassador then took up the alleged breach of the gasoline contract between American citizens and Soviet agencies somewhat like the one pending with Japan. My replies and comments on this subject were similar to those I made to the Japanese Ambassador [59] on January thirty-first.[60] This included a reminder of how the Soviet Government had violated contracts and agreements with this Government. In particular, I mentioned the agreement entered into at the time of Russian recognition [61] by this Government and enumerated a number of very indefensible acts and practices toward this Government and its citizens by the Soviet Government or under its authority. The Ambassador sought to palliate these statements but without any serious attempt. He stated that this country was retaliating with respect to all trade relations between the two countries, even including a refusal to lease American ships to the Soviet Government for commercial transportation.

I again referred to the general state of lawlessness existing in so many parts of the world and unprovoked fighting going on for purposes of conquest, and said that, in the general state of turmoil and violation of all agreements and laws, anything may happen with the result that this country is more or less on a day-to-day basis with regard to many of its methods and practices, until such fighting slows down. At this point I was called in to the press conference and the Ambassador said that he was virtually through and would not remain.

C[ORDELL] H[ULL]

---

[58] H. F. Arthur Schoenfeld.
[59] Kensuke Horinouchi.
[60] *Foreign Relations*, Japan, 1931–1941, vol. II, p. 53.
[61] For correspondence concerning the recognition by the United States of the Soviet Union on November 16, 1933, see *Foreign Relations*, The Soviet Union, 1933–1939, pp. 1 ff.

138 Emergency Program/595 : Telegram

The Ambassador in the Soviet Union (Steinhardt) to the Secretary of State

Moscow, February 1, 1940—noon.
[Received 2 : 30 p. m.]

120. Department's telegram No. 69, January 31, 7 p. m.[62]   I am of the opinion that under present conditions it is advisable that passports good for travel in the Soviet Union should not be issued to any category of American citizens other than officers of the Foreign Service and accredited newspaper correspondents.   My reasons are : (1) the steadily increasing irritation of the Soviet authorities at the anti-Soviet manifestations in the United States; (2) the known sympathies of Americans with the Finnish cause [63] and the outspoken references in the American press to various kinds of assistance to Finland; (3) the possibility that the presence of additional Americans within the Soviet Union may be seized upon by the Soviet authorities to create incidents; (4) the difficulties of travel and living conditions; (5) the difficulties encountered by the Embassy in maintaining contact with American citizens within the Soviet Union; (6) the failure of the Soviet authorities to reply with reasonable promptness to communications and inquiries concerning the welfare or whereabouts of American citizens,[64] and the present extreme difficulty of obtaining exit visas and the possibility of a refusal to issue the same or of delay tantamount to refusal.

I do not recommend that any suggestion be made to those American citizens, particularly engineers, now in the Soviet Union that they depart prior to the expiration of their contractual obligations but I suggest that serious consideration be given to declining to grant further passports good for travel here, except for the most urgent and compelling reasons, among which I would not regard business or study as urgent or compelling.

I strongly recommend that whatever decision may be arrived at by the Department should not be made public and that such policy as the Department may decide upon should be kept strictly confidential if for no other reason than to avoid adding to the irritation which already exists among the Soviet authorities.

STEINHARDT

---

[62] Not printed.

[63] For correspondence concerning the Winter War carried on by the Soviet Union against Finland, see vol. I, pp. 269 ff.

[64] Regarding the arrest and detention of American citizens by the Soviet Government, see *Foreign Relations*, The Soviet Union, 1933–1939, pp. 904 ff.

700.00116 M.E./113a

The Secretary of State to the Amtorg Trading Corporation, New York, N. Y.

WASHINGTON, March 2, 1940.

SIRS: Your attention is invited to the enclosed documents [65] in regard to the policy of this Government in respect to the exportation of airplanes, aeronautical equipment, and materials essential to airplane manufacture to countries the armed forces of which are engaged in unprovoked bombing and machine-gunning of civilian populations from the air, and in regard to the exportation of certain listed commodities essential to the national defense.

In view of the fact that your company is an American corporation incorporated under the laws of New York, it is assumed and expected that you will wish to abide by the policies of this Government set forth in the enclosed documents. I should appreciate it if you would inform me that the Department is correct in this assumption and in this expectation.

Very truly yours,

For the Secretary of State:
JOSEPH C. GREEN

195.2/3688

Memorandum of Conversation, by the Assistant Chief of the Division of European Affairs (Henderson)

[WASHINGTON,] March 14, 1940.

In pursuance of my promise to reply to Mr. Oumansky's inquiry as to the reasons which caused the Maritime Commission to refuse a number of Amtorg applications to charter or acquire American ships, I read to him over the telephone today Mr. Berle's memorandum to Mr. Dunn of February 29.[66]

Mr. Oumansky said that he accepted with reserve some of the statements made in the memorandum since according to information in his possession the Maritime Commission, while rejecting Amtorg applications, almost simultaneously granted applications to other parties to charter American ships in similar circumstances.

---

[65] None attached to file copy of this document. The enclosures were statements issued by the Army and Navy Munitions Board dated October 11, 1939, and January 19, 1940, *Foreign Relations*, 1939, vol. I, p. 855, and *ibid.*, 1940, vol. II, p. 252, respectively; the President's statement of December 2, 1939, Department of State *Bulletin*, December 16, 1939, p. 686; and the Department of State's press release of December 15, 1939, *ibid.*, p. 685.
[66] The annex to this document.

He asked if he would not be justified in telegraphing his government that the Maritime Commission had definitely decided to refuse charters to Amtorg.

I replied that in my opinion such a telegram would be unjustifiable, in view of what I had just told him. Each application, according to my understanding, rested entirely on its own merits. There was no reason why Amtorg should not apply for the charter of an American ship whenever it desired to do so, and I had no reason to doubt that if in the opinion of the Maritime Commission American interests would be served by the granting of a charter, an application for such charter would not be refused. I said I was not prepared to enter into a discussion with him regarding his intimation that the Maritime Commission was discriminating against Amtorg. The information which we had received from the Maritime Commission, as I had already told him, was to the effect that decisions with respect to the questions of applications for charters rested solely on the domestic policy of the United States. I did not believe that any person who was not in possession of all the facts which entered into the various decisions made by the Maritime Commission was qualified to accuse that Commission of discrimination against any foreign country.

[Annex]

Memorandum by the Assistant Secretary of State (Berle) to the Adviser on Political Relations (Dunn)

[WASHINGTON,] February 29, 1940.

I have discussed with the Maritime Commission their policy with respect to the Amtorg applications to charter or acquire American ships.

Commissioner Woodward [68] informs me that the policies and action of the Maritime Commission in respect to applications for transfers of American ships are guided entirely by considerations of American domestic policy. They take into consideration the present employment of American shipping; the desirability of removing such shipping from the possibility of American use; the demands for tonnage in various parts of the world, and, as for example the relative transportation requirements in the Atlantic and Pacific; the possible need of certain kinds of vessels for naval reserve or national defense purposes, and the like.

In the case of each application, these and similar factors are considered by the Commission; and wherever an application for transfer

---

[68] Thomas M. Woodward, Vice Chairman of the United States Maritime Commission.

is denied the reason for such denial rests on these considerations, which rest solely on the domestic policy of the United States.

A. A. BERLE, JR.

700.00116 M.E./137

Memorandum by the Assistant Chief of the Division of Controls (Yost)

[WASHINGTON,] March 14, 1940.

Mr. Cook of the Aeronautical Chamber of Commerce telephoned this morning to inquire whether or not the moral embargo continues to apply to the export of aviation equipment to the Soviet Union since the cessation of hostilities.[69] I informed him that this question was still under consideration.

After the Secretary's announcement at his press conference this morning to the effect that there is no change in the application of the embargo,[70] I telephoned Mr. Cook and communicated this decision to him.

CHARLES W. YOST

700.00116 M.E./141

The Amtorg Trading Corporation, New York, N. Y., to the Chief of the Division of Controls (Green)

NEW YORK, March 14, 1940.

SIR: The Amtorg Trading Corporation wishes to acknowledge the receipt of your letter dated March second, 1940, with enclosures.

The Amtorg Trading Corporation as a company incorporated under the laws of the State of New York is acting under and respecting the laws of this country. This corporation is aware of the recommendations contained in the enclosures.

Yours very truly, AMTORG TRADING CORPORATION
K. I. LUKASHOV
Chairman of the Board
and President

---

[69] The Finnish–Soviet war was ended by the peace treaty signed at Moscow on March 12, 1940; for text, see Department of State Bulletin, April 27, 1940, p. 453, or Finland, Ministry for Foreign Affairs, The Finnish Blue Book (Philadelphia, 1940), p. 115.
[70] For text of the announcement, see New York Times, March 15, 1940, p. 10.

811.22761/30

Memorandum by the Assistant Chief of the Division of European Affairs (Henderson)

[WASHINGTON,] March 19, 1940.

Attached hereto you will note a memorandum prepared by EA [71] regarding the practice of the Soviet Government of sending engineers and technicians into American plants in order to observe and learn the technical processes.

The Amtorg Corporation has recently made inquiries regarding the possibility of arranging to place Soviet engineers in American rubber manufacturing plants. Mr. Viles, President of the Rubber Manufacturers Association, has inquired as to what our attitude would be with respect to the conclusion of such an arrangement.[72] Mr. Veatch of EA has discussed the matter with Colonel MacMorland of the Army and Navy Munitions Board. Colonel MacMorland, after a conversation with appropriate Army officers, has indicated that M. I. D.[73] would like to see an end put to the practice of admitting Soviet technicians into American plants. M. I. D. apparently is of the opinion that such representatives act as an espionage service, and suggests that in order to check or discourage the practice, the Department of State might inform the Soviet Government that this Government would not be prepared to approve the entry of Soviet technicians into American plants unless the Soviet Government is prepared to welcome American observers (either private or governmental) into Soviet plants. M. I. D. feels that we should, for instance, insist that our Military Attaché in Moscow [74] be allowed to inspect Soviet manufacturing establishments.

We do not believe that the procedure suggested by M. I. D. is desirable or practicable. In the first place, we do not want American engineers flocking just now to the Soviet Union to inspect Soviet plants. Ambassador Steinhardt has been urging for some time that we restrain American citizens from visiting the Soviet Union. Furthermore, if the Soviet Government should accept an arrangement of the character suggested (this is not, of course, likely), we should find ourselves in a position which would render it almost necessary for us to view with favor Soviet requests that Soviet technicians be admitted into American plants. Such an attitude on our part would

---

[71] Memorandum of March 12 by the Office of the Adviser on International Economic Affairs, not printed.

[72] In an attached memorandum of March 22 Mr. Veatch of the Office of the Adviser on International Economic Affairs noted that "Mr. Viles has now expressed the opinion that the rubber industry, entirely on its own responsibility, will wish to avoid any arrangement for Soviet engineers to visit or work in American rubber factories."

[73] Military Intelligence Division, War Department.

[74] Maj. Ivan D. Yeaton.

undoubtedly be resented by many American manufacturers, who, as a result of experience, do not desire visits from Soviet technicians.

In general, it may be said that any kind of arrangement for permitting Soviet technicians to enter American plants in consideration for the granting of permission for American engineers and Government officials to inspect Soviet plants would be sure to lead to endless disputes involving our manufacturers, the Soviet Government, and ourselves.

There appears to be no legal way for keeping Soviet engineers and technicians out of our plants. If the Army and Navy have strong feelings on this subject, however, it is possible that with the cooperation of other Departments of the Government and of various trade organizations they may exercise, at least during the period of the war, effective control over such visits.

It is possible, for instance, that the Army and Navy could arrange for such a control to be exercised, through some appropriate Governmental institution, such as the Army and Navy Munitions Board. This institution could prepare a list of the types of plants in which Soviet engineers would not be welcome and could notify the pertinent trade organizations, as well as particular plants, in certain instances, that for the protection of the public interests no foreign officials or technicians should be permitted to inspect American plants of the types contained in the list without permission in each individual case from the institution in question. This institution might also inform the Department of State of the situation and the Department could instruct the American Embassy in Moscow not to grant visas to Soviet engineers and technicians desiring to come to this country for the purpose of entering industrial plants of the character set forth in the list until after each individual visa application had been referred to the Department and until after the Department had had an opportunity to obtain the views of the institution in question as to the desirability of the proposed visit. Since each request for a visa or a visit would be decided upon its individual merits, it would be difficult for charges of discrimination against any one country to be substantiated.

A procedure of the type above outlined would be extremely cumbersome and certainly should not be adopted unless the Army and Navy feel that positive steps should be taken to exclude Soviet engineers and technicians from American plants.

It might be pointed out in this connection that recently representatives of a number of American plants have endeavored to persuade me to authorize them to inform Amtorg that the State Department did not look with favor upon the visits of Soviet engineers in their plants. They have stated that these visits result in little business; that the engineers when once admitted make all kinds of requests for information and privileges; and that in the end it is found necessary to refuse some of these requests, so that frequently the visits result in the creation of bad feelings rather than in increased good will. Officials of American firms frequently say that they dislike to refuse to admit Soviet engineers in their plants, since such a refusal might result in their being placed on the Amtorg "black list".[75]

700.00116 M.E./141

The Secretary of State to the Amtorg Trading Corporation, New York, N. Y.

WASHINGTON, March 20, 1940.

SIRS: The receipt is acknowledged of your letter of March 14, 1940, with further reference to certain policies of this Government in respect to the exportation of certain articles and commodities. It is noted that you are aware of the policies in question. It would be greatly appreciated if you would inform me at your earliest convenience whether the Department is correct in its assumption that, as you are aware of these policies, you will act in conformity thereto.

Very truly yours,　　　　　　For the Secretary of State:
JOSEPH C. GREEN
Chief, Division of Controls

311.6121½

Memorandum of Conversation, by Mr. Edward Page, Jr., of the Division of European Affairs

[WASHINGTON,] March 20, 1940.

Participants: Mr. Andrei Gromyko, Counselor of the Soviet Embassy;
Mr. Loy W. Henderson, Assistant Chief, Division of European Affairs;
Mr. Edward Page, Division of European Affairs.

Mr. Gromyko states that on March 1 three Soviet citizens by the names of Zhukov, Gapuzin and Davidyarov and an American translator, Kroll, were arrested on leaving the Melrose Hotel in Toledo. It appears that four bandits had crossed into Ohio from Michigan and that the above men had been picked up by the police. They were detained for two hours and were not permitted to get in touch with

---

[75] The Adviser on International Economic Affairs, Herbert Feis, wrote "I agree" at the end of this memorandum.

the Soviet Consulate General in New York. Mr. Gromyko stated that he wished the Department would investigate the matter and cause the Toledo police to be reprimanded.

Mr. Henderson stated that during recent years many American citizens had been detained in the Soviet Union for taking photographs and for other minor offenses, and that the Soviet police had not permitted them immediately to communicate with the Embassy. Mr. Henderson asked if he was to understand, in view of Mr. Gromyko's representations, that the Soviet authorities would permit American citizens detained by the Soviet police immediately to communicate with the Embassy.

Mr. Gromyko, somewhat embarrassed, stated that he was not making a protest, but merely wished to bring the matter to our attention. He obviously desired to let the matter drop once Mr. Henderson had injected his remarks regarding American citizens in the Soviet Union.

Mr. Henderson said that he would bring the matter to the attention of the proper authorities in the Department.

It is suggested that no action be taken in this matter.[76]

E[DWARD] P[AGE]

711.61/720 : Telegram

The Ambassador in the Soviet Union (Steinhardt) to the Secretary of State

Moscow, March 28, 1940—10 a. m.
[Received 3 : 58 p. m.]

332. Assistant Commissar for Foreign Affairs Lozovski requested me late last night to call at the Foreign Office. Upon my arrival he stated that he desired to call my attention somewhat informally to a series of unfriendly actions in the United States against the Soviet Union and he proceeded to cite what he described as "only some" of the particular incidents to which exception is taken. He stated that a memorandum listing several grievances was in course of preparation and would be delivered to me this morning. The memorandum has been received and is transcribed below in free translation.

The attention of the Embassy of the United States of America is hereby directed to the following occurrences which have recently taken place.

---

[76] A postscript was added by Mr. Henderson which stated: "I told Mr. Gromyko that judging from his story, I was convinced that the arrest and investigation were not prompted by the nationality or the occupation of the Amtorg employees. When a dragnet for criminals is out the police are likely to subject all persons who might meet the description of the fugitives to careful scrutiny. He insisted, however, that the police should be given a lecture for failing to allow them to telephone the Embassy."

1. Assistant Secretary of War Louis Johnson at a dinner of the Bankers Association on January 15, 1940 delivered a speech containing rude attacks against the Soviet Union and insults against the armed forces of the Soviet Union.

The Government of the United States of America took and is taking no action whatsoever in connection with unfounded charges and insults which have been directed against the Soviet Union and its representative in Washington, Mr. Oumansky, by the American press and in the Dies Committee.[79]

2. American authorities have "humiliated" Soviet citizens. For instance, Soviet engineers Kolesnikov, Davydov and Tsyganovski and his wife whose documents and American visas were in full order were upon their arrival in New York on December 6, 1939 on the steamer *Gripsholm*, prevented from landing and were taken to the "island of tears"[80] for examination as immigrants. Moreover, immigration officials subjected these Soviet citizens to an absurd investigation, asking them whether "they had come for purposes of espionage."

3. The American authorities have adopted the course of encouraging the disruption of commercial contracts between American firms and Soviet economic organizations, even to the extent of setting up a discriminatory regime against the Soviet Union.

The so called "moral embargo" on aviation equipment, airplanes, molybdenum, aluminum, technical assistance for the production of aviation fuel, et cetera, has been applied to the Soviet Union.

In connection with the "moral embargo" the American firms Lummus and Universal have recalled all their specialists from the Soviet Union.[81] The Lummus firm in a letter to Machinoimport[82] stated that it had recalled its specialists in accordance with instructions received from the Department. A telegraphic communication from the Lummus Company dated January 4, 1940 and subsequent communications from Amtorg in February and March indicate that the American firms Lummus and Universal, although they had not fulfilled their contractual obligations to send specialists to enterprises in the Soviet Union, cited the refusal of the Department of State to grant visas for the travel of American specialists to the Soviet Union.

5 [4]. Government authorities of the United States have recommended to industrialists that they apply the "moral embargo" to the Soviet Union and by so doing have encouraged firms having connections with economic organizations in the Soviet Union to violate their contracts and to render more difficult the placing of Soviet orders as is proved by the refusal to accept our orders on the part of several firms such as Pratt Whitney, Brown Lebland Hunday, Cincinnati, as well as by impeding the placing of our orders in respect of prices and dates of delivery as in the cases of the firms Glisson Fellow Leblabor [Lebland] Weeks.

---

[79] Martin Dies, member of the House of Representatives from Texas, Chairman of the Special Committee to Investigate Un-American Activities.

[80] Presumably intended as a reference to Ellis Island.

[81] For correspondence regarding the recall of experts from the Soviet Union, see memorandum of December 15, 1939, by the Chief of the Division of Controls, and later papers, pp. 179–197, *passim.*

[82] All-Union Combine for the import of equipment, electrical goods, and hauling machinery.

5. Visits by Soviet specialists to American plants are made difficult, even sometimes impossible. The firms concerned in this connection apply for decision on this point to the War, Navy and State Departments. Thus Soviet engineers in compliance with decisions by the War and Navy Departments were refused permission to visit the Wright plant.

6. On March 6, the Chase National Bank referring to instructions from the State Department notified Amtorg that the bank would settle accounts with firms only upon advice from Amtorg in each case that the purchases involved did not contravene governmental regulations applying to the non-export of deficit raw materials.

7. The American Merchant Marine Commission places difficulties in the way of the chartering of steamers designated to export goods to the Soviet Union.

8. Soviet citizens and institutions in the United States are persecuted and court proceedings are being instituted against organizations connected with the Soviet Union. When the Attorney General at Washington held a hearing of the Board of Directors of Bookniga, Nikolsky and Ilin, Directors of Bookniga, were accused of violating the law requiring the registration of foreign agencies operating in the United States despite the fact that Bookniga was registered with the State Department in May 1939.[83] Under the circumstances the institution of criminal proceedings against members of the Board of Directors of Bookniga and the imposition of a fine of $1000 upon Nikolsky, of $500 upon Ilin and $1000 against the Board of Directors is incomprehensible. Persecutions of such organizations as Bookniga and Amkino,[84] and the New York Intourist [85] Office have already resulted in the curtailment of their activities and doubtless is adversely affecting the cultural and economic relations between the two countries.

9. Unfriendly acts with respect to the Soviet Union on the part of American governmental officials such as those described above have taken place within recent days.

During the conversation last night, I remarked to Mr. Lozovski that with a few exceptions the complaints recited by him had already been the subject of discussions between Potemkin and myself quite some time ago [86] and that he would doubtless find a record of those discussions in his files. Specifically, I reminded him that, in so far as Mr. Johnson's comments are concerned, while I was not aware of the exact nature of the remarks attributed to him they must of course be viewed in the light of the fundamental American principle of the right of free speech; as to the attacks on Ambassador Oumanski, I stated that I was aware of no such attacks of recent date; as to the detention of the three

---

[83] Regarding difficulties with the Soviet Government over the requirement for the registration of agents of foreign principals, see *Foreign Relations*, The Soviet Union, 1933–1939, pp. 926 ff.

[84] Amkino Corporation, New York, N. Y., the Soviet motion picture film organization in the United States, distributors.

[85] All-Union Corporation for Foreign Tourism in the Soviet Union, official Soviet travel agency.

[86] See the Ambassador's telegram No. 89, January 22, noon, p. 249.

engineers at Ellis Island, I pointed out that the granting of a visa did not in itself guarantee admittance into the United States and remarked that taking into consideration the hundreds of Soviet citizens who have been entering the United States each year and who continue to enter in great numbers, any minor difficulties in connection with the admission of three would not seem to constitute adequate basis for a complaint.

I took the occasion to remind him of the persistent Soviet practice of refusing visas for Americans and of causing inordinate and inconvenient delays in the case of Americans desiring to enter the Soviet Union; with respect to the alleged breaches of contract by American firms, I pointed out that the American courts afford equal treatment to foreigners who may regard themselves as aggrieved; as to the moral embargo, I commented rather extensively on the abhorrence felt in the United States toward the bombardment and machine gunning of open towns, with the resultant loss of life among noncombatant civilians, women, and children and stated that it could hardly be expected that American citizens and their industrial enterprises should through cooperation with the Soviet war industries be parties to such attacks.

Mr. Lozovski denied that the bombardment of open towns had been deliberate and pointed out what he described as "the comparatively small number of civilian casualties as proof of Soviet restraint in this respect." I remarked that the recall of the Lummus and Universal engineers was attributed to the same sentiment in the United States; regarding the difficulties said to have been placed in the way of Soviet engineers who desired to visit American factories I expressed the opinion that the Soviet Government had come to expect unreasonable facilities in this respect and as he had particularly referred to the Pratt and Whitney and Curtiss factories I could see no reason why American factories engaged in providing for the American national defence and especially under present war conditions should be open for inspection by foreigners.

I requested him in this connection to cite a single instance where an American citizen had been allowed to inspect any Soviet aircraft factory; I stated that I have no knowledge of the incidents complained of in conjunction with the alleged action of The Chase National Bank and the Maritime Commission, but that as our banks are independent organizations and the Maritime Commission is an autonomous body they were of course at liberty to accept or [reject?] business in their own discretion; in so far as concerned the complaints regarding the difficulties encountered by Bookniga, Amkino, and Intourist, I pointed out that in the United States the entering of a plea of guilty was equivalent to an admission that the charge was well-founded and that under the circumstances it seemed to me that the sentences imposed had been extremely light particularly in the case of Bookniga which had admitted its failure to observe our laws.

The interview took place in an atmosphere of reasonableness and personal cordiality. Lozovski stated in conclusion that in the opinion of the Soviet Government the series of actions above listed could only be regarded as unfriendly and would affect the political as well as the economic relations between the two countries and increase tension. I remarked at the close of our interview that in all frankness as he was doubtless aware from reports received from the Soviet representatives in the United States of America the attack on Finland had aroused very deep feeling on the part of the American people and that it could hardly be expected that this feeling would not take some tangible form.

STEINHARDT

711.61/726

Memorandum by the Chief of the Division of European Affairs (Moffat) to the Secretary of State [87]

[WASHINGTON,] April 1, 1940.

MR. SECRETARY: The Soviet Ambassador, who is coming in to see you on Tuesday [88] at 11 a. m., wishes to discuss Soviet-American commercial matters. He will probably reiterate several of those "grievances" set forth in a memorandum which was presented to Mr. Steinhardt on March 28. You will note from the attached telegram from Moscow [89] concerning this memorandum that these "grievances" or "unfriendly actions" relative to Soviet-American commercial relations consist of (1) the application of the moral embargo; (2) the visits by Soviet specialists to American plants; (3) the application of this Government's policy with regard to the non-export of deficit raw materials; and (4) the policy of the Maritime Commission with regard to the charter of vessels to the Soviet Union.

THE APPLICATION OF THE MORAL EMBARGO

In regard to the charge that the American authorities in applying the moral embargo to the Soviet Union (section one, pages 2, 3, 4) are encouraging the breaching of contracts between American firms and Soviet industrial organizations and are setting up a discriminatory regime against the Soviet Union, it is probable that Mr. Oumansky will repeat Mr. Molotov's remarks made on March 29 in a speech

---

[87] Initialed by Mr. Moffat, but drafted by Edward Page, Jr., and Loy W. Henderson of the Division of European Affairs.
[88] April 2; see *infra*.
[89] *Supra*.

before the Supreme Soviet of the U. S. S. R.[90] to the effect that Russian-American relations have neither improved nor deteriorated "if we do not consider the moral embargo against the Soviet Union, which, now that peace with Finland has been concluded, is devoid of significance", and that "Soviet imports were increased and could be increased even more if the United States Government did not place obstacles in the way of trade". It can be adduced from the above remarks that the Soviet Government is inaugurating a campaign to have the moral embargo terminated so far as the Soviet Union is concerned.

It is, of course, untrue that this Government, as charged in the memorandum, has adopted a policy of encouraging the disruption of commercial contracts between American firms and Soviet economic organizations or has set up a discriminatory regime against the Soviet Union. It is true that the moral revulsion of the American people at the wanton invasion of Finland resulted in the refusal of a number of firms to sell products of a military character to the Soviet Union. It is also true that in response to popular feeling this Government has supported a policy of discouraging the sale of certain American products and technical knowledge to countries which follow the practice of bombing civilians from the air.

You are so thoroughly acquainted with our policies relative to the moral embargo that it appears unnecessary to go into that subject in this memorandum.

Your attention should be called, however, to the possibility that Mr. Oumansky will charge that the moral embargo is in violation of at least the spirit of our commercial agreement with the Soviet Union which provides in part that

"natural or manufactured products exported from the territory of the United States of America and consigned to the territory of the Union of Soviet Socialist Republics shall in no case be subject with respect to exportation and in regard to the above-mentioned matters, to any duties, taxes, or charges other or higher, or to any rules or formalities other or more burdensome, than those to which the like products when consigned to the territory of any third country are or may hereafter be subject".

It would be absurd to interpret our commercial arrangement with the Soviet Union in such a manner as to obligate us to cooperate in the bombing of civilians from the air by the furnishing of materials or certain types of technical information.

Our intentions at the time of our entering into our agreement with the Soviet Union are evidenced by a subsequent provision in the ex-

---

[90] See telegram No. 337, March 29, 10 a. m., from the Chargé in the Soviet Union, p. 191.

change of notes to the effect that "nothing in the agreement shall be construed to prevent the adoption . . . of such measures as the Government of the United States of America may see fit with respect to the control of the export or sale for export of arms, ammunition, or implements of war, and, in exceptional cases, all other military supplies".

THE VISITS OF SOVIET SPECIALISTS TO AMERICAN PLANTS

Mr. Oumansky may protest against the difficulty certain Soviet engineers are now encountering in regard to receiving permission to visit certain American factories. It is surprising that the Soviet Government should take the attitude that Soviet engineers have some kind of an inherent right to enter American factories. For many years Soviet engineers have been granted numerous courtesies in this respect by American industrialists, and according to the Department's information they are continuing in relatively large numbers to inspect and study American industrial plants at the present time. They have shown a tendency, however, to take offense in case some industrialist, for military or other reasons, refuses to allow them to enter his plant. There is no reason why American factories which are engaged in providing for American national defense should be opened for inspection by foreigners. As you are perhaps aware, American citizens have never been permitted to enter Soviet military factories or related industries, and it is rare that they are admitted into Soviet factories of any kind.

THE NON-EXPORTATION OF DEFICIT RAW MATERIALS

With regard to the alleged action of the Chase National Bank (section one, page 4) this action would appear to be quite reasonable in view of the policies of this Government regarding the exportation of strategic raw materials. There is no record, however, which would indicate that this Department has issued the alleged orders to the Bank.

RULING OF THE MARITIME COMMISSION

With respect to the failure of the Maritime Commission to approve the charter of vessels to Soviet commercial organizations in this country, Mr. Oumansky has already been informed that the charter of vessels by the Maritime Commission is guided entirely by considerations of domestic policy, such as the employment of shipping, possible naval reserve needs, and the necessity of not permitting vessels to proceed too far away from American ports and that each request for charter is judged on its own merits. There is no question of discrimination or moral embargo in this respect.

711.61/726

Memorandum of Converation, by the Secretary of State

[WASHINGTON,] April 2, 1940.

The Soviet Ambassador called at his own request. He cited, at the request of the Soviet Government, most of the grievances contained in telegram No. 332 of March twenty-eighth from our Ambassador at Moscow. His main inquiry concerned itself with the question of whether this Government, in the light of the various alleged acts of obstruction of commerce between the two countries, et cetera, intended to abandon or to continue commercial relations with Russia and I was particular not to comment thereon.

In addition to the replies made by Mr. Moffat and myself heretofore to the grievances mentioned in telegram No. 332, I emphasized further our view regarding several of them. I said that one or two minor phases would be looked into as to the full facts, although I was satisfied that I had ample facts on which to predicate answers. One of these related to the refusal of some American companies to permit a Russian engineer or purchaser within their plants while admitting all others. Another was the protracted detention on Ellis Island of Russian men and women of some prominence who come over on temporary visas. The Ambassador spent a great deal of time repeating these small complaints, referred to above, and I remarked that I had very little time to give to the things he had said, and I then proceeded to dispose in rather short order of his fifty minutes of talk in the manner herein set out.

The Ambassador referred to our circular letter requesting citizens of this country not to export eleven strategic materials [91] and brought forward the idea that this prohibition only applied to Russia. I made it clear to him that this applied to all nations alike. I went back to the agreements entered into between this Government and the Soviet Government on the occasion of Minister Litvinoff's [92] visit here, in which it was agreed that Russia would pay certain indebtedness [93] and would refrain from propaganda in this country directed from Moscow.[94] I said that my Government does not feel that it has been at fault about any disturbance of relations since we took the difficult step in this country of recognizing Russia in 1933 for reasons of peace and

---

[91] See the *aide-mémoire* of April 9 to the Soviet Embassy, p. 287.

[92] Maxim Maximovich Litvinov, People's Commissar for Foreign Affairs of the Soviet Union, 1930 to May 3, 1939.

[93] For correspondence on the failure of the negotiations to obtain a settlement of debts, claims, and credits with the Soviet Union, see *Foreign Relations*, The Soviet Union, 1933–1939, pp. 166 ff. See also *ibid.*, pp. 567–582, *passim*.

[94] For correspondence concerning the protest by the United States against interference in the internal affairs of the United States and the activities of the VII Congress of the Communist International, see *ibid.*, pp. 218 ff.

mutual progress. I added that, of course, we had been tremendously disappointed in the general accumulation of acts on Russia's part leading up to the present situation today. I then stated that Russia knew just what had happened, from the breach of the debt and the propaganda obligations down to recent occurrences, all of which have placed this country in an undesirable situation, so far as some phases of its relations with Russia are concerned; that his Government knows very well how to conduct itself so as to make possible normal relations on a thoroughly friendly and mutually satisfactory basis; that this Government does not know what new policy or step Russia may take at any time; that, for example, she plunged into fighting with Finland to the surprise of all of us; that she may take any similar step with no greater surprise than this; and that in these circumstances we are naturally conserving our shipping, our strategic and other materials for the reason that we never know when fighting in the world may call for some kind of self-defense on our part and that we do propose to be ready. I gave the Ambassador no definite answer as to when the moral embargo would terminate except to say, as stated, that we do not know when his country may embark upon another war. I then dismissed the matter because the South African Minister had been waiting for more than thirty minutes.

He denied bombing from the air by his Government, to which I replied that this Government has the most satisfactory evidence of Russian bombing of civilian populations and that I could not convince the Ambassador any more than the Ambassador could convince me to the contrary, in view of the tone of his discussion of the matter.

The Ambassador referred to the fact that his Government had not received any communication from this Government on economic reconstruction after the war, such as was sent to most all other countries.[95] I made no definite reply.

He referred to the latest address of Foreign Minister Molotov as setting forth Russian foreign policy. I asked him what kind of neutrality his Government stood for, adding that there are many shades of neutrality as practiced by some countries. His only reply was that it was a neutrality based on the idea of keeping out of war. I inquired whether this meant being drawn into war contrary to the desire or purpose of his Government or war rising out of aggressor action. He would not depart from his original reply to the effect that Russian neutrality was based on keeping the country out of war while disclaiming any aggressor role or purpose. I endeavored to convey a tone of doubt about each profession of the Soviet Government, as referred to by the Ambassador.

---

[95] See telegram No. 340, March 14, noon, from the Chargé in France, vol. I, p. 16; see also Department of State *Bulletin*, May 4, 1940, p. 461.

The Ambassador stated that his Government had no intention to interfere with Bessarabia and that it was slow to believe that Turkey would become a party to any interference with the Baku oil area by the Allies; and that Russia had no designs on any portion of the Near Eastern area.[96] He avoided the subject of Finland as he did Germany.

C[ordell] H[ull]

700.00116 M.E./202

Memorandum of Conversation, by the Assistant Chief of the Division of European Affairs (Henderson)

[WASHINGTON,] April 4, 1940.

Participants: Mr. Feis, Adviser on International Economic Affairs;
Mr. Pierrepont Moffat, Chief, Division of European Affairs;
Mr. Loy W. Henderson, Assistant Chief, Division of European Affairs;
Mr. Constantine A. Oumansky, Ambassador of the Soviet Union;
Mr. Andrei A. Gromyko, Counselor, Soviet Embassy.

Mr. Oumansky stated that he had sought the present conference at the suggestion of the Secretary. The conversation, as he understood it, was to be limited for the most part to a discussion of matters of an economic nature. He could not refrain, however, from repeating what he had already told the Secretary; i. e., that in the opinion of the Soviet Government there had been no basis for applying the moral embargo to the Soviet Union since the Soviet military forces had not been guilty of bombarding civilians from the air.

Mr. Oumansky said that the primary purpose of the conference from his point of view was to enable him to ascertain whether or not it would be possible for Soviet-American trade to continue. Soviet foreign trade was of a planned character. During recent years the Soviet authorities had assigned an important place to American manufacturers when planning Soviet purchases from abroad. In planning Soviet economic life the Soviet authorities had acted under the assumption that they would be able to obtain from the United States certain machinery and materials. Recent events have caused them to doubt whether in the future such an assumption would be justified.

According to Mr. Oumansky the moral embargo, while harmful, had not necessarily delivered a fatal blow to Soviet-American trade.

---

[96] For correspondence regarding the diplomatic activities of the Soviet Union in the Near East and the seizure of Bessarabia, see vol. I, pp. 444 ff.

That trade, even without the commodities listed under the moral embargo, was extremely important. The Soviet Government, however, was disturbed at the failure of the American Government to lift the moral embargo, now that the alleged reason for its application had certainly ceased to exist, and at the tendency of American authorities and industry to extend the discrimination against trade with the Soviet Union into other fields. Certain circles in the United States had taken advantage of the moral embargo in order to endeavor to undermine Soviet-American commercial relations from various directions. The questions therefore presented themselves as to whether the American Government intended to extend the moral embargo into other fields, and as to whether Soviet-American commercial relations were to continue. The Ambassador stated that having presented the two questions which were uppermost in his mind, he would now lay down a five-point agenda for the continuance of the discussion.

The five points which he intended to take up were:

(1) The extent to which the moral embargo has affected the status of contractual obligations between American manufacturers and Soviet trading agencies;

(2) Various pressures which have been brought to bear upon American manufacturing and commercial firms in order to prevail upon them to discriminate against Soviet business;

(3) The discrimination which is being shown in American plants against the visits of Soviet engineers and technicians;

(4) The discrimination against the Soviet Union in the matter of the chartering of American tonnage in order to ship Soviet purchases to the Soviet Union;

(5) The status of Amtorg and the place of Amtorg in American trade.

Mr. Oumansky stated that as a result of the moral embargo there had been a tendency of certain American manufacturers to treat lightly their contractual obligations towards the Soviet Union. Furthermore, numbers of American firms which in the past had been handling Soviet orders were now displaying an inclination either to refuse such orders or to delay the delivery of orders which had been previously taken. As a result, Soviet-American trade was in a chaotic condition and it was extremely difficult for Amtorg and other Soviet purchasing agencies to carry out the tasks assigned them.

Mr. Feis stated that he was not in a position to discuss the political aspects of the moral embargo and that it was his understanding, as Mr. Oumansky had already pointed out, that the conversations would be limited to matters of an economic nature. With respect to Mr. Oumansky's remarks regarding the indirect and almost invisible extension of the moral embargo into fields not contemplated in the original announcements, he would like to point out that undoubtedly the same surge of sentiment in this country which had prompted the decision to apply the moral embargo was also responsible for the reluctance of certain American trade groups and manufacturers to carry on business with the Soviet Union. It was his impression that the American public was in general so shocked with the events which have transpired in Finland that many American business men did not desire to furnish material and other assistance to the Soviet Union. Certain American commercial and industrial groups had gone so far as to request the Department that the embargo be extended into their fields.

Mr. Oumansky replied that the information which he possessed caused him to believe that the extension of the moral embargo into other fields was the result of pressure brought to bear upon business men and that American business men in general were reluctant to apply discriminatory measures against the Soviet Union. He said that of course he had not personally come into close contact with American business men, but that he had obtained the distinct impression through sources in which he had full confidence that the pressure for further discriminations against Soviet trade came from above rather than from below, that is, that American officials were attempting to persuade American business men to discriminate against the Soviet Union. This was particularly true with respect to the machine tool trade. If such a regime of discrimination were to continue in this country there was nothing left for the Soviet Union to do except to wind up its business with the United States. The moral embargo policy seemed to be like a snowball rolling down hill; its size and importance increased as time went on.

Mr. Feis stated that it was still his opinion, based on approaches which had been made to him by leaders of American business groups, that certain American business circles desired the moral embargo to be extended to them. Mr. Oumansky asked if he had been approached by American machine tool manufacturers. Mr. Feis replied that according to his recollection most of the American business men who had approached him were connected with the handling of raw materials. Mr. Feis continued that although he personally had little occasion for coming into contact with American machine tool manufacturers, it was his understanding that the American machine tool manufacturing business was in an over-rushed state; that the tool manufacturers were continually being forced to decide between competing orders that were beyond their capacity; and that they themselves were uncertain as to what their own policies should be.

Mr. Henderson stated that during recent months a number of American machine tool manufacturers had either called on him or telephoned him in order to inquire as to what the policy of the Department would be towards their accepting Amtorg orders. Some of them had merely asked if in the opinion of the Department it would be advisable to refuse such orders, whereas others had stated that they would like to refuse such orders and would appreciate it if the Department could authorize them to inform Amtorg that the American Government would prefer that they should not accept such orders. Mr. Henderson pointed out that certain American manufacturers had taken the attitude that in the past they had had satisfactory trade with the Soviet Union; that they did not wish to be placed on Amtorg's black list by refusing to accept orders at the present time; that in view of what was taking place in Eastern Europe they did not wish to accept orders; and that they would appreciate it if the American Government would extend the moral embargo so as to justify their rejection of Soviet orders. Mr. Henderson stated that so far as he knew the Department had always taken care to make it clear that the moral embargo was limited to the articles listed. He asked Mr. Oumansky if Mr. Oumansky had obtained the impression that officials of the State Department were endeavoring individually and unofficially to extend the moral embargo. Mr. Oumansky replied that he had never received any information which would indicate that officials of the State Department were engaging in such activities. Officials of other Departments, including the Treasury Department, were undoubtedly, however, endeavoring to persuade American manufacturers to discriminate against the Soviet Union. He knew of one instance, for example, in which American manufacturers had been urged to give British and French orders precedence over Soviet orders.

Mr. Moffat suggested that if Mr. Oumansky had any complaints to make regarding the activities of certain officials or Departments of the Government, he should present to the Department a well-documented memorandum on the subject. The Department would then be in a position to give the matter consideration. It would be difficult for the Department to take any action upon general statements of the kind which had thus far been made. Mr. Feis agreed that if Mr. Oumansky desired the Department to give weight to his charges that American officials were endeavoring to persuade American firms to discriminate against Amtorg, he should present his complaints in a documentary form.

Mr. Oumansky stated that he would endeavor to prepare a memorandum on the subject. He said that if it is true that the pressure for the extension of the moral embargo comes from below and that American business men desire to curtail trade with the Soviet Union, the answers to his general questions are apparent. There is little to be accomplished by conversation. The Soviet Union must make plans to trade elsewhere.

Mr. Oumansky added that he would like to kill the myth that the Soviet Union has been purchasing exceptionally large amounts of raw materials in this country. The fact is that it was buying less raw materials than formerly. In order to support this statement, he read certain trade statistics purporting to show that during recent months the Soviet Government had purchased practically no raw materials of a strategic character other than copper. The fact is, he said, that the United States is purchasing more raw materials of a strategic character from the Soviet Union than the Soviet Union is purchasing from the United States. After all, it should be borne in mind that commerce in strategic materials is of a reciprocal character.

Mr. Feis said that he was glad that Mr. Oumansky had made the remark regarding the reciprocal character of the trade in strategic materials, because it afforded him an opportunity to point out that the Soviet Government had often followed the policy of refusing to permit commodities to be exported abroad which were of strategic importance to the Soviet Union. Since the Soviet Government followed such a policy, it should be in a position to understand the desire of the American Government to restrict the export of strategic materials which were needed in the United States. Mr. Feis said that he would arrange to have prepared for Mr. Oumansky a memorandum relating to the American Government's policy with respect to the export of strategic materials. In this connection he would like to point out that Amtorg had created more difficulties in the enforcement of the embargo upon strategic materials than any other company in the United States. Mr. Oumansky suggested that if such a memorandum should be prepared it should show whether there had been any difficulties created by Amtorg during recent weeks.

Mr. Oumansky said that he wished at this point to state that so far as he was aware the Soviet Union had not engaged in the practice of discriminating against American trade and that it seemed to his Government that the present discrimination on the part of the American Government against the Soviet Union was not in harmony with general American foreign trade policies as enunciated by Mr. Hull.

Mr. Henderson said that the foreign trade policies and methods of the Soviet Union were so different from those of the United States that it would serve no purpose to endeavor to draw comparisons between them. Even the terminology which usually applies to foreign trade practices frequently has a different meaning when used in connection with Soviet foreign trade. It was impossible, for instance, to use the term "discriminate" in its usual foreign trade sense when discussing Soviet foreign trade policies. Through its foreign trade monopoly the Soviet Government was able to buy or sell as it chose without subjecting itself to charges that it was discriminating against one or another country. Nevertheless there could be actual discrimination. It should be recalled in this connection that during recent years the Soviet Government had suddenly decided to curtail its sales to the United States of such commodities as timber, fish and coal. As a result, American firms which had built up a trade in these Soviet products had suffered considerable losses. It was, of course, not possible, in view of the peculiarities of the Soviet foreign trade procedure, to substantiate charges that the Soviet Government had been discriminating against the United States in planning sales of raw materials.

Mr. Feis emphasized the fact that the embargo upon the sale of strategic materials applied to all countries with equal force, and that therefore it could not be said that the inability of the Soviet Government to purchase such materials in this country involved elements of discrimination.

Mr. Oumansky stated that he would like to take the occasion to discuss the status of Amtorg. He hoped that it would be possible to discuss this matter in a non-legalistic manner. Amtorg is a corporation organized under the laws of the State of New York. Its capital, however, is owned 100 percent by the Soviet Government. During its sixteen years of existence it has done more than two billion dollars worth of business, of which probably 80 percent consisted of Soviet purchases in the United States. While it is true that Amtorg is an American corporation, it is nevertheless much more than an American corporation. It is the chief purchasing agency in the United States of Soviet governmental organizations, and for many years it has been recognized as such by the American Government. As the chief Soviet purchasing agency in this country it should have a special position and it has enjoyed a special position. There has been a tendency of late, however, for the American Government to treat it in a narrow, legalistic manner, as being merely an American corporation.

Mr. Moffat stated that he was interested in Mr. Oumansky's remark, because he had gained the impression during recent years that Amtorg had at times endeavored to have its cake and eat it too. In other words, it apparently desired to obtain all the benefits which could be derived from its status as an American corporation and at the same time it showed a tendency to claim certain exemptions in view of the fact that it was a Soviet purchasing agency.

Mr. Oumansky said that he felt that Mr. Moffat had stated the facts in the reverse; that whenever it served its purposes the American Government treated Amtorg as an American corporation, and that on the other hand the American Government sometimes made demands on Amtorg which it would not make upon an American corporation. He pointed out that, for instance, the Department had just recently demanded that the Soviet Embassy furnish it regularly with lists of Soviet nationals who were employees of Amtorg. It seemed peculiar that the Soviet Embassy should be called upon to give information regarding the employees of an American corporation.

Mr. Henderson pointed out that he had already explained that situation in detail to Mr. Oumansky; that Mr. Oumansky must therefore be aware that the American Government regarded Soviet officials and employees who had been sent to this country to carry out orders issued by Soviet governmental organizations as Soviet governmental officials and employees, regardless of the fact that they may be attached to Amtorg; and that there was nothing peculiar about the request that the Soviet Embassy furnish the State Department with certain information regarding Soviet officials and employees in this country.

Mr. Oumansky said that this matter had already been settled and that therefore he could not go any further into it at the time. He would like, however, to read several letters which had been exchanged recently between the Department of State and Amtorg. He then read a letter addressed to Amtorg and signed by Mr. Green, Chief of the Division of Controls, which informed Amtorg of certain American governmental policies relating to the non-export of certain strategic materials, aeronautical equipment, and so forth. He also read the reply of Amtorg to the effect that it intended as an American corporation to comply with all American laws, and that it had taken note of the Government's policies outlined in the Department's letter. Mr. Oumansky then read the reply of the Department to Amtorg's letter, in which the Department stated that it assumed that since Amtorg had been made aware of the policies of this Government it would adhere to them, and invited Amtorg to confirm this Department's assumption.

Mr. Oumansky said that it could be seen from this exchange of letters that the Department of State was requesting Amtorg, the Soviet purchasing agency in this country, to state that it would adhere to the policy of the moral embargo against the Soviet Union; in other words, to promise to cooperate with the American Government in discriminating against the Soviet Union. Such a request seemed to him, to put it mildly, most unusual.

Mr. Moffat stated that he saw nothing unusual in the request. Amtorg was an American corporation, and as such should be expected to adhere to the policies of the American Government to the same extent as other American corporations. Mr. Feis said that he agreed with Mr. Moffat.

Mr. Oumansky argued that the fact should not be overlooked that although Amtorg is an American corporation, it is nevertheless a Soviet purchasing agency. Its primary object is to promote trade between the United States and the Soviet Union. How could it, therefore, subscribe to a policy the purpose of which is to strangle that trade? What kind of impression would it make upon an American firm which might approach Amtorg with an offer to sell certain articles listed under the moral embargo, if Amtorg should reply that in view of the policies of the American Government it could not make the purchase? Could Amtorg be placed in a position of cooperating to enforce discrimination against the Soviet Union?

Mr. Henderson stated that in his opinion such a reply on the part of Amtorg would enhance the prestige of Amtorg in the United States, and would cause it to be regarded with more respect even by such firms as might make proposals of the nature described. It was only proper that the State Department should desire to assure itself that Amtorg intended to limit its activities in the United States in such a manner that they would not conflict with policies of the American Government.

Mr. Oumansky asked if all American firms received letters similar to those which had been sent to Amtorg.

Mr. Henderson replied that it was his understanding that the Department had taken care to see that information regarding American governmental policies had reached all interested firms and that in case any particular firm should conduct itself in such a way as to cause the Department to doubt that it thoroughly understood the policies of this Government, special communications were sent to it. He said that it was his impression that the Department had received information which caused it to believe that Amtorg was either not aware of the policies of this Government or did not feel that it was expected to adhere to such policies. Therefore, it was only natural that the letters of the kind which Mr. Oumansky had read should be addressed to it.

Mr. Oumansky said that in his opinion Amtorg should not reply to the Department's last letter to it, and asked if it would not be better to let the matter drop without the exchange of further correspondence. Mr. Feis replied that he was not prepared to answer this question without discussing it with the Secretary, but that he was inclined to believe that what Amtorg might do was more important than what it might say. He wished to emphasize again the fact that in the past Amtorg, to a greater extent than any other firm or organization, had apparently endeavored to engage in transactions which were not in conformity with the policies of this Government so far as the export of strategic materials was concerned.

Mr. Oumansky said that he would like next to discuss the question of the discrimination which was being practiced in certain plants against the visits of Soviet engineers. The Army and Navy Departments apparently were permitting certain American plants to admit British and French technicians and at the same time were refusing to permit Soviet technicians to enter these plants. He had already discussed at some length with Mr. Moffat [97] the refusal of the Army and Navy to allow Soviet engineers to visit certain parts of the plant of the Wright Aeronautical Corporation. An explanation had been made to the effect that Soviet engineers were not being permitted to visit those parts of the plants in which French and British engineers were admitted because no Soviet orders were being executed at the time. Mr. Oumansky stated that this explanation in his opinion failed to conceal the fact that an injurious discrimination was being made against Soviet engineers in the Wright plant.

Mr. Feis said that certain urgent matters required his immediate attention, and asked if the discussion could not be continued at a later date. It was decided that another meeting would be held on Tuesday, April 9, at 2 : 30 p. m.* Mr. Oumansky said that at that meeting he would like to discuss the following subjects:

(1) The discrimination in American plants against the visits of Soviet employees;
(2) The recall from the Soviet Union of the experts of the Universal Oil Company and the Lummus Company, who had been lending technical assistance in the building of aviation gasoline plants;
(3) The non-granting of passports to new American experts to assist in the construction of these plants;
(4) Discrimination against the Soviet Union in the matter of the chartering of tonnage; and
(5) The status of Amtorg and the question as to whether it would be necessary for Amtorg to reply to the Department's last communication to it.

711.61/720 : Telegram

The Secretary of State to the Ambassador in the Soviet Union (Steinhardt)

WASHINGTON, April 4, 1940—6 p. m.

197. You are commended for the able manner in which you replied to Lozovski's complaints as set forth in your 332 of March 28.

The Soviet Ambassador made similar complaints to me yesterday [98] during the course of a long conversation in which we discussed the whole field of American-Soviet relations. He asked in particular whether this Government intended to break off commercial relations with the Soviet Union, and again raised the question of the moral embargo. I made it clear to him that this Government was not

---

[97] See memorandum of January 10 by the Chief of the Division of European Affairs, and the Department's telegram No. 54, January 25, 7 p. m., pp. 245 and 250, respectively.
* Later changed to 3 : 30 p. m. at Mr. Oumansky's request. [Footnote in the original. The continuation of this conversation is recorded in the memorandum of April 9 by Mr. Henderson, p. 277.]
[98] See memorandum of April 2 by the Secretary of State, p. 266.

responsible for such disturbances as may exist in Soviet-American relations. I gave the Ambassador no definite reply as to when the moral embargo would terminate, pointing out to him that we do not know whether the Soviet Union will embark upon another war and will engage again in the bombing of civilians.

HULL

711.61/732

Memorandum of Conversation, by the Assistant Chief of the Division of European Affairs (Henderson)

[WASHINGTON,] April 9, 1940.

Participants: Mr. Feis, Adviser on International Economic Affairs; Mr. Moffat, Chief, Division of European Affairs; Mr. Loy W. Henderson, Assistant Chief, Division of European Affairs; Mr. Constantine A. Oumansky, Ambassador of the Soviet Union; Mr. Andrei A. Gromyko, Counselor of the Soviet Embassy.

Mr. Oumansky referred to the conversation of April 4 of which the present conference was a continuance, and asked if any one desired to raise any questions before he proceeded with the presentation of the Soviet views. After having received a reply in the negative, he said that the next matter which he desired to discuss was the difficulty which Soviet agencies were encountering in chartering tonnage in United States Pacific ports for Vladivostok.

Mr. Oumansky pointed out that early in January he had brought to the attention of Mr. Henderson, of the Department, the refusal of the Maritime Commission to approve Amtorg's charter of the steamship *Ogon*. He had informed Mr. Henderson that the Soviet Government was of the opinion that the refusal of the Maritime Commission to approve the charter represented a discrimination against the Soviet Union, and he had expressed the hope that the State Department would take up the matter with the Maritime Commission. Mr. Henderson promised him that the matter would be referred to the appropriate authorities and would be discussed with Mr. Oumansky at a later date. Mr. Oumansky said that he had hoped that as a result of his conversation with Mr. Henderson the Soviet Embassy would receive assurances that no discrimination was being planned against Soviet cargoes by the Maritime Commission, as well as a satisfactory explanation of the reasons for the refusal of the charter of the *Ogon*.

Mr. Oumansky continued that almost a month had elapsed before Mr. Henderson had replied to his representations.[99]   Mr. Henderson's reply was that officials of the Department had discussed the matter with the Maritime Commission and had been informed by that Commission that it was not discriminating against the Soviet Union. The Maritime Commission, according to Mr. Henderson, had also informed the Department that the decision with respect to each application for the approval of a charter was based upon the merits of the individual case and that in passing upon applications the Maritime Commission was guided by considerations of domestic policy, such as the number of American vessels available, the advisability of permitting vessels to proceed to distant ports, possible naval reserve needs, and so forth.   Since the refusal of the Maritime Commission to approve the charter of the *Ogon* that Commission had also disapproved the chartering by Amtorg of two more vessels, the *California* and *Liberty Glow*.   In all three cases the charters had been disapproved after all arrangements had been made with the owners of the vessels to transport commodities, for the most part industrial equipment purchased in the United States, from United States Pacific ports to Vladivostok.   At almost the same time that the Maritime Commission disapproved the chartering by Amtorg of these vessels, it approved the chartering of vessels for the transport of freight from United States Pacific ports to Japanese ports.   For example, exporters in this country to Japan had been successful in chartering the steamships *Clifton* and the *City of Alma* (name doubtful).

Mr. Oumansky appreciated the reply which Mr. Henderson had been able to give to him, but the Soviet Government was not satisfied in view of the obvious discrimination against Soviet shipping.   The Soviet Government did not wish to exaggerate its need for American tonnage. It had needed that tonnage, however; it needed tonnage at the present time; and it was possible that it would need tonnage still more in the future.   The disapproval of the three charters by Amtorg had cost the Soviet purchasing agencies more than $450,000.   He hoped that the matter would be taken up again with the Maritime Commission with the purpose of bringing about a change in what appeared to be the fixed policy of the Maritime Commission to discriminate against cargoes destined for the Soviet Union.

Mr. Moffat stated that he did not agree that such was the fixed policy of the Maritime Commission; that it had already been pointed out to Mr. Oumansky that the Maritime Commission decided each case of an application for charter upon its own merits; and that he was unable to add to the explanation of the procedure and policies of the Maritime Commission which had already been furnished.   There were a whole

---

[99] See footnote 54, p. 249.

series of factors which entered into decisions relating to the approval of charters and it was unjustifiable to make charges of discrimination merely because circumstances caused the Maritime Commission to disapprove a number of charters.

Mr. Oumansky replied that he could not be satisfied with statements of the kind which Mr. Moffat had made. Although there was not perhaps *de jure* discrimination, there was certainly discrimination *de facto*, and he would appreciate it if the Department would make a more thorough investigation of the whole matter.

Mr. Moffat stated that the matter would again be brought to the attention of the Maritime Commission, but he was not sure that more information than that already given could be obtained. The Department of State had no authority to review the decisions of other Departments, particularly when such decisions related primarily to matters of domestic concern.

Mr. Oumansky said that in his opinion the Department should be interested in any matter which tended to prevent the flow of products from the United States to another country. The Department of State should be interested, for instance, in ascertaining why Japan received more favorable treatment than the Soviet Union in this respect.

Mr. Moffat insisted that the responsibility with respect to the approval of charters rested with the Maritime Commission, but that the Department was quite willing to pass on to that Commission the views expressed by Mr. Oumansky.

Mr. Oumansky said that the Soviet Government must be left a margin in which it could decide for itself, based on such information as is available to it, the question whether or not acts of discrimination were taking place. The Soviet purchasing agencies would like to discuss with the appropriate American shipping authorities the whole question of cargo needs on a purely commercial basis. They desired to make clear just what space they would need and to ascertain what space may be available to them. If it should become clear that discrimination was intended, the Soviet Government, of course, could then draw its own conclusions.

Mr. Oumansky stated that he wished again to take up the question of the refusal of American governmental authorities to permit Soviet engineers to enter the plant of the Wright Aeronautical Corporation. He referred to the conversation which he had had in January with Mr. Moffat on this subject and in which he had been informed that the restriction on the Soviet engineers was not connected with the moral embargo. In spite of the explanation which Mr. Moffat had given him, namely, that engineers of only those countries which were actually making purchases were being admitted into the plant, the Soviet Government took the view that the refusal of the American authorities to permit Soviet engineers into the plant while at the same time allowing British, French and Japanese engineers to enter, was a most serious act of discrimination against the Soviet Union.

Mr. Oumansky went on to explain that the engineers, according to a contract of long standing between Soviet purchasing agencies and the Wright Aeronautical Corporation, had the right to enter the Wright plant in order to keep in touch with the latest processes and inventions. This contract was along the lines of numerous agreements which the Soviet Union had entered into with various American firms in accordance with the well-established Soviet policy of linking up foreign technical assistance with foreign purchases. The obtaining of foreign technical assistance was one of the most important features of the Soviet foreign trade policy and any actions on the part of American Governmental officials which would tend to deprive Soviet industry of American technical assistance must be regarded as serious.

Mr. Moffat drew Mr. Oumansky's attention to the fact that according to the terms of the contract between the Wright Aeronautical Corporation and the Soviet purchasing agency the Corporation had a right to close its factory to inspection by Soviet engineers whenever it was requested so to do by the War and Navy Departments. Mr. Oumansky replied that most of the Soviet contracts calling for the giving of technical assistance contained clauses of this kind and that the fact that the War and Navy Departments should take advantage of these clauses so far as Soviet engineers were concerned while they were permitting engineers of other countries to visit the plant constituted discrimination. He again stated that the whole Soviet foreign trade system was based on the obtaining of technical assistance from abroad.

Mr. Moffat stressed the fact that the Soviet engineers who were refused admittance to the plant had desired to enter it in order to obtain technical assistance, whereas the other foreign engineers who were admitted entered the plant in order to make or inspect purchases. He failed to see, therefore, any justification for charges of discrimination on the basis of nationality.

At this point Mr. Moffat received a message that his presence in the Office of the Secretary was necessary, and he was compelled to leave the conference.

Mr. Oumansky stated that he regretted that he could not finish his conversation on the subject of the engineers with Mr. Moffat since the matter of the exclusion of Soviet engineers from the Wright plant was regarded with so much seriousness by his Government.

Mr. Henderson remarked that the Department had demonstrated its willingness to talk with Mr. Oumansky regarding the situation in the Wright plant; that in general the Department desired to take a reasonable attitude in discussing matters of this kind since it wished to remove any false impressions which Mr. Oumansky might have relative to discrimination against the Soviet Union; Mr. Oumansky should, nevertheless, understand that decisions as to who might or might not visit American industrial establishments fell primarily in the field of the internal affairs of the United States. The American Government, in cooperation with American industrialists, must have the right to restrict to such extent as may be compatible with American national interests, the visits of aliens at American industrial and commercial institutions. It should be understood that the decision of American authorities not to permit an alien or several aliens to inspect an American plant did not justify the Government of the country of which such alien might be a citizen to bring charges of discrimination. American governmental authorities who are charged with protecting national interests may take many factors into consideration when refusing to permit an alien engineer to visit an American plant, and they could not permit their decision to rest entirely upon the fact that a national of some other country had been or had not been admitted into the plant in question. The fact that the national of one country in a certain set of circumstances was permitted to visit a plant did not mean that the nationals of all countries should have the right to enter that plant. In other words, the American Government had no obligation to permit any alien to enter American plants and did not feel that it was necessary for it to explain to any other Government why an alien had been refused admittance to an American plant.

Mr. Henderson added that it was his understanding that at the present time more Soviet engineers than engineers of any other country were visiting American industrial plants and that he was certain that Mr. Oumansky could not substantiate charges of discrimination.

Mr. Oumansky said that Mr. Henderson's remarks shed an entirely different light upon the problem; that he was surprised to learn that the American Government did not consider that the right to enter American plants rested on a most-favored-nation basis. He said that furthermore he did not agree with Mr. Henderson's statement that at the present time Soviet engineers were being permitted freely to visit American plants. During previous years such might have been the case; unfortunately the situation had greatly changed.

Mr. Feis asked if Mr. Oumansky would like to place the right to visit industrial plants on a reciprocal basis, that is, would he desire to make the suggestion that an arrangement be entered into whereby Soviet engineers should be permitted freely to visit American plants provided American engineers should be permitted freely to visit Soviet plants.

Mr. Oumansky said that he did not know whether Mr. Feis was joking or not; that the situation in the Soviet Union was quite different from that in the United States; that it was his understanding that in the past more American technicians had been admitted into Soviet plants than the technicians of any other country; that the American Military Attaché in Moscow had on occasions been admitted to plants which no other Attaché had ever inspected; that unfortunately the situation in this respect had also changed recently, but that if the American Government desired the reestablishment of close commercial relations with the Soviet Union he saw no reason why the régime in which the Americans were the most favored visitors could not be reestablished. In fact, he thought that he might be willing to accept Mr. Feis' challenge, provided it should be understood that American engineers who visited Soviet factories would be doing so for the bona fide purpose of making purchases or the visits should be in connection with purchases that had already been made, as was the situation with respect to the visits of Soviet engineers in American plants.

Mr. Feis said that his remark had not been intended as a challenge, that he, of course, had no authorization to propose an agreement of the kind referred to; his statement had been intended merely as an aid in clarifying the discussion.

Mr. Henderson said that he quite agreed that during certain periods in past years American engineers had been admitted into Soviet plants probably in larger numbers than the engineers of other countries, but that many instances had come to his attention while he was in the Soviet Union in which American nationals were not permitted to visit Soviet plants to which technicians or engineers of other countries had been admitted. The American Embassy in Moscow, however, had not at the time made any representations on the subject since it had taken the attitude that the Soviet authorities had the right to decide who should be admitted into their plants. At no time, however, had the Soviet authorities been as generous in admitting Americans into Soviet plants as the American anthorities had been in allowing Soviet nationals to visit American plants. Since 1937 practically no Americans had been admitted in Soviet plants, whereas hundreds of Soviet engineers had been thronging through American plants.

Mr. Oumansky said that he wished to return to the subject of the Wright Aeronautical plant. He hoped that the State Department, which, after all, is the only organization to which he could appeal, would have sufficient interest in the development of Soviet-American commercial relations to discuss the situation in the Wright plant again with the appropriate American authorities and would endeavor to prevail upon them to remove the discriminatory regulations. Mr. Henderson asked Mr. Oumansky if he had in mind any other cases of alleged discrimination against the visits of Soviet engineers in American plants. Mr. Oumansky said that several instances of such discrimination had come to his attention, but that he was not prepared to advance them at the present time. In fact, he desired to focus the full attention of the American Government on the situation in the Wright plant, and he hoped that for the sake of Soviet-American relations the State Department would approach the War and Navy authorities again on the subject.

Mr. Henderson replied that a final decision must remain with the Army and Navy authorities since responsibility for safeguarding the public interests in this respect rested with them. Nevertheless the Department would undertake to convey the views which he had expressed to these authorities. Mr. Oumansky stated that he hoped that when this matter was discussed with the War and Navy officials the State Department would not fail to stress the international aspects of the matter.

Mr. Oumansky said that he was now prepared to discuss the question of the recall from the Soviet Union of the experts of the Universal Oil Products Company and of the Lummus Company who had been engaged in lending technical assistance to the Soviet Government in the construction of aviation gasoline plants in the Soviet Union. He had discussed this matter in January with Mr. Moffat. During the course of that discussion Mr. Moffat had informed him that the State Department had not requested the companies to recall the experts. The companies in question, however, had informed the Soviet Government that these experts had been recalled at the request of the State Department. Apparently the statement of Mr. Moffat conflicted with the statements of the oil companies. He regretted that Mr. Moffat was not present in order to assist in obtaining a clarification of the facts.

Mr. Henderson said that he had read Mr. Moffat's memorandum of the conversation, and he did not believe that Mr. Oumansky had accurately repeated the statements made by Mr. Moffat. Mr. Henderson suggested that before discussing the matter it might be advisable to examine Mr. Moffat's memorandum of that conversation. At Mr. Henderson's telephonic request, Mr. Page, of the European Division, brought in Mr. Moffat's memorandum of January 18,[1] and Mr. Henderson read the following extract from it:

"The Ambassador . . . came to the question of the article in the *Herald-Tribune*, according to which the United States Government had advised the representatives of oil firms in Russia to leave the country, and inquired whether this was true. I told him that it was not true as stated; that the engineers had been recalled by the companies; but that the companies' action had been taken in accordance with an announced expression of policy by the United States Govern-

---

[1] Missing from Department files; for a summary, see telegram No. 54, January 25, 7 p. m., to the Ambassador in the Soviet Union, p. 250.

ment. I agreed that the practical effect was not very different from that contained in the article, even though the development of facts contained in the article was inaccurate. The Ambassador then said that in effect we were asking firms unilaterally to breach their contracts with Soviet Russia. I replied that we had set forth our policy, and the firms in question without any pressure on our part were endeavoring to carry out this policy as they understood it."

Mr. Oumansky stated that the situation as he understood it was that the moral embargo had been extended by the American Government in such a manner as to prohibit the lending by American companies of technical assistance to the Soviet Union in the construction of aviation gasoline plants; that the American Government had informed the various interested companies that this extension of the moral embargo was to apply not only to future transactions but also to contracts already entered into. In other words, the American Government had informed the interested companies that in order to conform with American Governmental policies they should breach existing contracts with the Soviet Union. Such action on the American Government's part was a double discrimination against the Soviet Union in that it placed the Soviet Union in a worse position even than Japan, the other country to which the moral embargo applied. In enforcing the moral embargo against Japan, the American Government, according to his understanding, had not taken the position that it applied retroactively. The Soviet Union, therefore, in insisting that the moral embargo upon the lending of this type of technical assistance be not applied retroactively was merely requesting that it be given a position no worse than that of Japan. He would be interested in learning why the American Government apparently desired to place the Soviet Union in a worse position than Japan.

Mr. Henderson said that Mr. Oumansky was apparently laboring under a false impression; that the moral embargoes applied with equal force and in the same manner to both the Soviet Union and Japan. Mr. Oumansky replied that he had facts to back his statements; that he could show that for months after the application of the moral embargo upon Japan airplanes and airplane parts were being shipped to Japan. Mr. Henderson stated that it was his understanding that since the announcement of the extension of the moral embargo American firms had also been executing their contracts with the Soviet Union which called for the delivery of airplanes or airplane parts. Mr. Oumansky said that he begged to differ with Mr. Henderson; that he had with him a communication from the Bendix Company in which the Bendix Company stated its inability to carry out an agreement entered into some time ago to supply certain airplane parts on the ground that for it to do so would be a violation of the policies of the American Government. Mr. Henderson stated that since the announcement of the extension of the moral embargo cases had come to his attention in which American companies had been permitted to send airplane parts to the Soviet Union in conformity with contracts entered into before the bombing in Finland had taken place.

Mr. Oumansky said that he had been given to understand that the American Government had not only requested the American firms in question to withdraw their engineers but that it had refused to grant passports to other engineers to go to the Soviet Union to complete the construction of the plants. He would like to know precisely what the policy of the American Government was in this respect. Had the American Government taken the attitude that it desired American firms to break contracts with the Soviet Union?

Mr. Feis said that he personally was not prepared to enter into a detailed discussion of this matter. Mr. Henderson said that he also was not prepared to enter into a detailed discussion of the so-called moral embargo. Mr. Moffat perhaps would have been in a better position to continue conversations which he had already had with Mr. Oumansky on the subject. Mr. Oumansky suggested that this matter be postponed for further discussion.

Mr. Oumansky thereupon again raised the question relative to the status of Amtorg. He said that he hoped that it would not be necessary for Amtorg to reply to the communication of the Department in which the suggestion had been made that Amtorg inform the Department that it intended to adhere to the policy of the American Government with respect to the moral embargo. Mr. Feis said that he wished to take this occasion to hand Mr. Oumansky the *aide-mémoire* which he had promised him during the course of the last conversation relative to the policy of this Government with respect to the exportation of certain strategic materials and to the attitude of Amtorg with regard to that policy.

Mr. Oumansky said that before accepting this memorandum he would like to know if it was a circular addressed to all governments, or whether it was applicable particularly to the Soviet Union. He did not wish to give consideration to a document the delivery of which might be an additional act of discrimination against the Soviet Government.

Mr. Feis said that this memorandum had been drawn up particularly for Mr. Oumansky, but that the policies laid down in it applied equally to all governments, and that in case reason therefor should arise he would not hesitate to present a similar memorandum to the representative of any other government. A copy of this memorandum is attached hereto.[2]

---

[2] *Infra.*

Mr. Oumansky examined the memorandum and said that the figures in it tended to confirm his previous statements that Amtorg had not during the past few weeks been engaging in transactions which were not in harmony with the policies of the American Government.

Mr. Feis replied that it was true that the figures set forth in the memorandum showed that the Soviet Government had of late made few purchases of articles the export of which it was the policy of this Government to discourage. Nevertheless it was only fair to point out that the figures were low because Amtorg had been unsuccessful in making purchases of these articles and not because Amtorg had been endeavoring to adhere to the policies of this Government. During the last sixty days at least thirty dealers in tin and rubber had informed the Department that Amtorg had been attempting to purchase one or another of these commodities from them.

Mr. Oumansky stated that he was glad to have this information. It was quite new to him. He would give the memorandum his closest consideration.

In reply to Mr. Oumansky's question whether Amtorg should answer the Department's letter, Mr. Feis said that he had not had an opportunity to discuss the matter further in the Department and he was not prepared to give a definite reply. It was his personal belief, however, that it was much more important that Amtorg adhere to the policies of this Government than that it should state that it intended to do so. Mr. Oumansky replied that he was relieved to hear this since it would be extremely embarrassing for Amtorg to reply to the letter from the Department.

Mr. Oumansky said that he desired to revert to his general questions regarding the future of Soviet-American trade. He would like to know what the American Government's policy was in that respect. Did it desire to encourage trade with the Soviet Union or was it no longer interested in the development of that trade?

Mr. Feis replied that he thought the best answer to the question was the fact that trade between the two countries was proceeding; that commercial transactions were taking place between the two countries every day. Mr. Oumansky could be sure that if this Government were endeavoring to bring about a cessation of trade, the present volume of Soviet-American trade would not be as large as it was. Mr. Oumansky said that the Soviet-American trade could be much larger; that the spirit of Soviet foreign trade policy was non-discriminatory; and that the Soviet Union desired that the principle of equality remain the basis of foreign trade. The Soviet Union hoped to increase its trade with the United States, and that trade could be increased without difficulty. Soviet-American trade had grown steadily during the past nine years. He hoped that the American Government would not permit this flourishing business to be pushed into the shadows by war-purchase activities of other countries. It would be unfortunate if the demands of certain countries for munitions and machinery of war should be allowed to prevent the Soviet Government from satisfying its needs for industrial equipment. Commercial difficulties between the two countries could be removed. The Soviet Government was prepared to take all appropriate steps on its part to see that there should be no obstacles to Soviet-American trade. The Soviet Government could not remain quiescent, however, in the face of measures which gave the Soviet Union a position even less favorable than that of such a country as Japan.

Mr. Oumansky emphasized his hope that two specific problems could be solved favorably. One was the admission of Soviet specialists into the Wright plant. The other was connected with the aviation gasoline experts. He hoped that the American Government could see its way clear to permit American engineers to go to the Soviet Union in order to complete the unfinished aviation gasoline plants. He would not press for an early conference with respect to the moral embargo because he was more anxious that the outcome of such a conference should be favorable than he was that the conference should take place in the immediate future. If the American Government would consent to the return of the aviation gasoline experts to the Soviet Union, he was certain that the Soviet Government would not raise further questions with regard to past applications of the moral embargo or with regard to the breach of contracts. It would be content to drop the past if it could be assured of the future.

811.24 Raw Materials/829a

The Department of State to the Embassy of the Soviet Union [3]

AIDE-MÉMOIRE

Since September 26, 1939, it has been the announced policy of this Government to discourage, in the interest of the national defense, the exportation of certain strategic materials except shipments in normal quantities to customers in foreign countries who normally obtained their supplies of these materials from American exporters before the outbreak of the present war in Europe.

The strategic materials to which this policy applies are:

Antimony	Manila Fiber	Rubber
Chromium	Quartz Crystal	Silk
Manganese,	Quicksilver	Tin
ferrograde	Quinine	Tungsten

---

[3] Handed to the Soviet Ambassador by the Adviser on International Economic Affairs during the conversation on April 9; see *supra*.

Foreign trade statistics of the United States Department of Commerce indicate the following reexports from the United States to the Union of Soviet Socialist Republics of strategic materials covered by the policy mentioned above:

REEXPORTS OF FOREIGN MERCHANDISE

	Crude Rubber		Tin in bars, blocks, pigs, etc.	
1939	*pounds*	*dollars*	*pounds*	*dollars*
Oct.	11, 271, 538	2, 496, 366	—	—
Nov.	111, 487	24, 942	67, 192	34, 268
Dec.	—	—	1, 889, 458	977, 446
1940				
Jan.	—	—	2, 743, 574	1, 403, 428
Feb.	—	—	509, 205	186, 768
March *	50, 080	13, 738	—	—

This policy was adopted, in the interest of national defense, as a means of safeguarding United States supplies of the materials listed. In response to the Government's invitation, the vast majority of dealers, brokers and others concerned in the market are cooperating with this policy by refusing to export these materials, or to sell them for export, in any unusual channels irrespective of the country of destination. The policy is in no sense designed to deny supplies to foreign buyers on any other basis.

It has been inevitable that the unusual activity of the Amtorg Corporation in seeking to secure large quantities of some of these strategic materials in the American market has led to the impression in the market that the principal unusual export demand for such products is that created by Amtorg and that shipments, or inquiries regarding purchases for shipment, to some other export destinations may be connected with a transshipment trade from such destinations to the Soviet Union. It would seem desirable, from the standpoint of the Soviet Union as well as of this Government, to remove the impression that the activities of the Amtorg Corporation are in conflict with the policy of this Government in this matter. The most effective way of achieving this result would appear to be the cessation of all efforts by the Amtorg Corporation, either direct or indirect, to secure from this market the strategic materials covered by this Government's policy.

WASHINGTON, April 9, 1940.

---

*Incomplete. [Footnote in the original.]

702.6111/324

Memorandum of Conversation, by Mr. Loy W. Henderson and Mr. Edward Page, Jr., of the Division of European Affairs

[WASHINGTON,] April 16, 1940.

Participants: Mr. Andrei A. Gromyko, Counselor, Soviet Embassy;
Mr. Dmitri Chuvakhin, First Secretary, Soviet Embassy;
Mr. Loy W. Henderson, Assistant Chief, Division of European Affairs;
Mr. Edward Page, Division of European Affairs.

Mr. Gromyko and Mr. Chuvakhin of the Soviet Embassy called today to discuss the Departmental circular note of March 30, 1939 [4] sent to all foreign missions in Washington requesting reports on consular officers and employees and all other employees and officers of their governments.

Mr. Gromyko stated that the Embassy had classified Soviet nationals in this country into three categories, namely: (1) Government employees; (2) employees of independent commercial organizations, such as Machinoimport, Raznoimport, et cetera; and (3) employees of Amtorg. Mr. Gromyko stated that complete lists of the Government employees (category 1) would be furnished the State Department by May 3–4, and would contain all the information requested in the aforementioned note.

With regard to the second category, Mr. Gromyko first stated that the Embassy would furnish the Department with a list containing all the names of the Soviet nationals employed in this country by Soviet commercial organizations. Mr. Henderson replied that the furnishing of only the names of the employees would not be in compliance with the Department's regulations.[5] Mr. Chuvakhin advanced the usual arguments regarding the private, non-governmental character of these organizations, accused the Department, as usual, of discrimination, maintained that the Embassy had gone half way to meet the demands of the State Department, and pleaded that the State Department also go half way to meet the desires of the Embassy. After approximately an hour's bickering, during which the Soviet representatives did all in their power to press Mr. Henderson and Mr. Page to agree to the Soviet contention, the Soviet representatives with great reluctance tentatively agreed, subject to the approval of the Ambassa-

---

[4] *Foreign Relations*, The Soviet Union, 1933–1939, p. 926; see also the correspondence *ibid.*, pp. 928–933, illustrative of the difficulties with the Soviet Government over the requirements for the registration of agents in the United States of foreign principals, under the Foreign Agents Registration Act, approved June 8, 1938; 52 Stat. 631.
[5] Department of State, *Agents of Foreign Prinicpals, and of Foreign Governments* (Washington, Government Printing Office, 1939).

dor, to furnish the Department with lists of Soviet employees, such as engineers, translators, technicians, et cetera, in the employ of commercial organizations, such lists containing the names, business and home addresses, and capacities of the Soviet nationals in question. It was agreed that only the permanent address need be given, and that should an employee leave his permanent given address for a short period of time no change of address need be sent to the Department. However, should an employee change his address for an extended period, for example, to take up residence in another locality in order to study in an American factory, the change of address would be given. The Soviet representatives agreed to furnish in the near future a complete list of all the commercial organizations in the United States, of which there are four or five, which lists would contain the names, addresses, et cetera, of their employees.

Turning to the third category, another hour was passed going over the old arguments concerning the American character of Amtorg. Mr. Chuvakhin in all seriousness stated that the Embassy could not ask Amtorg for information regarding its employees since Amtorg was a private American corporation. Mr. Henderson remarked that Mr. Oumansky never hesitated in making representations for Amtorg whenever the interests of that company were involved. It was suggested that if the Embassy did not wish formally to apply to Amtorg for a list of its employees, it might without embarrassment request Mr. Lukashev, Chairman of Amtorg, to give such a list in his capacity of a Soviet citizen.

Again, with great reluctance the Soviet representatives agreed to furnish the Department in the near future with a list of the Soviet employees of Amtorg which would show their names, home addresses, and capacities. Mr. Henderson said that he saw no objection to the use in the Soviet lists of the terms "engineers" or "office workers" in setting forth the capacity of the various Soviet employees.

811.22761/37

Memorandum by Mr. Harold W. Moseley, of the Division of Controls

[WASHINGTON,] April 24, 1940.

At Mr. Green's [6] request I called at the Navy Department today where I discussed with Commander Phillips, Lieutenant Taylor, and Captain Nixon a matter relating to the withdrawal of Soviet engineers from the plant of the Wright Aeronautical Corporation.

---

[6] Joseph C. Green, Chief of the Division of Controls.

I explained to the naval officers that my mission was purely a fact-finding one and that I wished to ascertain if there had been any new developments in this case since my last discussion with them on January 15, 1940. I informed them that the Soviet Ambassador had recently called at the Department and had again complained that his country was being discriminated against by the request of the War and Navy Departments that the Soviet engineers be kept out of the Wright plant.

Commander Phillips and his colleagues quickly replied that there had definitely not been any discrimination against the Soviet engineers and that the Soviets were receiving the same treatment as the representatives of any other country. They pointed out that temporary visits to the plant are approved for the representatives of all foreign countries who are calling to inspect engines or other machinery which the foreign country had contracted for. They said that this type of visit will be permitted for the Soviets as well as any other nationality. For proof of this statement they gave me copies of grants (attached hereto) [7] of permission to visit the Wright plant which had recently been issued in behalf of Soviet engineers. These authorized visits of the Soviet technicians were for the purpose of inspecting 10 Cyclone engines which were being built for the Russians. Thus the Soviets were being granted the same treatment as the representatives of other countries, as the visits of the French, English, and other representatives were authorized for the purpose of a temporary visit to inspect equipment that had been contracted for.

Referring to the request of the Inspector of Naval Aircraft on December 26, 1939, that previous authorizations for visits to the plant by Russian technicians be cancelled, Commander Phillips pointed out that this request had reference only to the Soviet engineers being continually present in the plant, and that it had been stated at the time that temporary visits to inspect work contracted for would still be permitted. He stated that there was no discrimination involved in this request as it was the opinion of both the War and Navy Departments that the interest of the national defense suggested that the representatives of a foreign government should not be continually present in a plant which was doing confidential work for the armed forces of the United States. It was maintained that this was no slur upon the Russians and the same treatment would have been accorded any nationals of any other country. I may add, however, that the naval officers frankly stated that they thought that all Soviet engineers were spies. I inquired whether the activities of the Soviet engineers at the Wright plant had appeared to be sus-

[7] Not printed.

picious and the officers replied that their suspicions in this case were based on the fact that there was a rapid turn-over in the representatives at the plant and the number of engineers at the plant had been increased to 23 from the 15 who had been granted permission to be in attendance at the plant according to the original contract. The officers were of the opinion that there had been discrimination in the past in behalf of the Soviets rather than against them as their engineers had been in the Wright plant for several years which was a privilege few other countries had enjoyed.

The officers pointed out that the Soviets were still obtaining the technical assistance and information that they had originally contracted for as the Wright company was conducting its relations with them in a separate building apart from the main plant. It was pointed out that this was quite in accord with the original contract as for all intents and purposes the technicians were at the Wright plant, although they were not necessarily given access to all the buildings. To the claim that under the contract the Soviets were entitled to a knowledge of the latest processes and inventions, the officers pointed out that this information was still being released to them by the Wright officials at the special plant which had been set aside for them, subject only to the general restriction that they should obtain information on equipment which had been officially released.

Summing up this discussion it seems apparent that the Soviets are receiving the same treatment as anyone else as far as being granted permission to visit the Wright plant to inspect work that has been contracted for. Their right to have their technicians continually present in the main plant has been denied in accordance with the provisions in their contract. A privilege of this type has not been granted to any other nation and thus the claim of discrimination hardly seems justifiable. If the Soviets are dissatisfied with the present arrangements under which they receive technical information at a building apart from the main plant, this would seem to be a matter to be taken up with the Wright company.

I called Colonel Thornton of the War Department and asked him whether he had any facts regarding this case which were not known to the Navy. He replied in the negative stating that the War and Navy Departments had acted jointly in this matter and that the information of the War Department on this case was the same as that held by the Navy Department.

H. W. MOSELEY

701.6111/984

Memorandum by Mr. Edward Page, Jr., of the Division of European Affairs

[WASHINGTON,] April 26, 1940.

THE HOSTILE ATTITUDE OF THE SOVIET AMBASSADOR TO THE STATE DEPARTMENT

Last evening I dined at the Lithuanian Legation. Among those present were the Soviet Ambassador, the Latvian, Lithuanian, and Bulgarian Ministers, the Counselor and First Secretary of the Soviet Embassy, and Mr. Todd, Tass [8] representative in Washington.

During after-dinner coffee, Mr. Oumansky adopted a smug, complacent and domineering attitude over his colleagues (Ministers whose countries exist under the shadow of the Soviet Union).[9] The Ambassador also went out of his way to be hostile toward the State Department. He started the after-dinner conversation by suggesting that we all enter into a short discussion, and then adjoined with words somewhat as follows: "But perhaps this would not be fair, for I am sure we would all be grouped together against Mr. Page". He then went on to explain in a sarcastic tone that the American Government had instructed American flagships to refuse to carry mails to the Soviet Union and to the Baltic States, and added that this was not surprising. I asked the Ambassador where he had received this information, and was told that he had read it in the press. I stated that I felt sure that the press report was false, since I had been informed only that morning that mails, with the exception of parcel post, to the Soviet Union and the Baltic were being despatched via Italy and Germany. I observed that the parcel post question was under consideration, and that I doubted whether the temporary absence of this service would create much hardship, since I did not believe that, with the exception of small shipments through Intourist, the volume of parcel post amounted to much.* The Ambassador stated that he was glad to receive this news, and changed the subject.

---

[8] Telegraph agency of the Soviet Union, official communications organization of the Soviet Government.

[9] For correspondence concerning the activities of the Soviet Union in the Baltic States, see *Foreign Relations*, The Soviet Union, 1933–1939, pp. 934 ff., and *Foreign Relations*, 1940, vol. I, pp. 357 ff.

* Mr. Lammiel, Director of the Foreign Mails Section of the Post Office, confirmed this morning what I had told Mr. Oumansky, that is, that mails were going to the Soviet Union and the Baltic via Italy and Germany, and that there had been no refusals to carry mails to these countries on the part of American ships. Mr. Lammiel also informed me that the Post Office was endeavoring at this time to make arrangements with the Rumanian postal authorities for despatching parcel post to the Soviet Union via Rumania. [Footnote in the original.]

Mr. Oumansky then pointed out to all those present that because of the unfriendly attitude of the State Department, Intourist, as well as Bookniga and Amkino, had been forced to close down. I interposed that there was no reason why such firms should not carry on their legitimate business provided they registered with the State Department as agents of foreign principals. Mr. Oumansky remarked that it was unlikely that Intourist, Bookniga, et cetera, would open up again, in view of the attitude of the State Department. He commented at length on how Soviet citizens had been insulted and humiliated in this country by being photographed, handcuffed to police authorities, and by being commented upon in the American press in an insulting manner.

The Latvian, Lithuanian and Bulgarian Ministers maintained a discreet silence during this tirade. I was of the opinion that they considered the Ambassador to be acting in extremely bad taste in criticizing in fairly strong terms the Government to which he was accredited. I did not wish to enter into a heated discussion with Mr. Oumansky, and merely observed that the firms in question had not complied with our regulations regarding registration, and had been prosecuted according to law.

Later, in commenting on the difficulties which the Soviet Embassy was encountering in receiving radio broadcasts from Moscow, Mr. Oumansky, in a joking, yet extremely sarcastic manner, observed that it would not surprise him to learn that the State Department had deliberately arranged interference in order to hinder the Embassy's radio reception. This remark was typical of the critical and hostile manner in which Mr. Oumansky conducted himself throughout the entire joint conversation.

Mr. Oumansky later drew me aside and after commenting at length on the discriminatory attitude of the State Department in regard to the much-discussed question of the notification by the Embassy of the presence of Soviet officials in this country, stated that he had reluctantly approved of the procedure of notification agreed upon by Messrs. Gromyko, Chuvakhin, Henderson and Page early last week. He then brought up the usual complaints regarding the Maritime Commission, moral embargo, et cetera, and inferred that the State Department was principally to blame for the present strained situation in American-Soviet relations. I advanced some of the usual rejoinders, and stated that I saw no purpose in going into the matter again. Mr. Oumansky concluded by asking me to tell Mr. Henderson that he was still expecting a reply in regard to his representations over the refusal of the Maritime Commission to charter vessels to Amtorg. His favorite word throughout the evening appeared to be "discrimination".

I was strongly impressed during the entire evening by the out-spoken animosity and hostility toward the American Government, and especially towards the State Department, on the part of Mr. Oumansky, and the First Secretary, Chuvakhin. Mr. Gromyko, Counselor of the Soviet Embassy, on the other hand, appeared to be quite friendly, and conducted himself much more befitting a diplomat in a country to which he is accredited.[10]

E[DWARD] P[AGE]

195.2/3727

Memorandum by the Chief of the Division of International Communications (Burke) [11]

[WASHINGTON,] May 13, 1940.

With reference to various discussions held with Ambassador Oumansky by your Division and others on the subject of the reasons for the disapproval of charter of American vessels for Russian Government account by the United States Maritime Commission, the statements made to the Ambassador in regard to the Maritime Commission have been checked with the Commission as to whether they correctly represent the Maritime Commission's position and as to whether that position is in any way altered by current developments.

We are assured by the Commission that it follows a fixed policy in considering charter applications under Section 9 of the Merchant Marine Act, 1916, as amended.[12] This "fixed policy" is to consider on the merits each individual case as it comes before the Commission. The Commission gives consideration in each individual case and is largely guided by availability of and requirements for tonnage—

a. For the domestic market (coastwise and intercoastal)

b. For the hemisphere trades (in recent months South America, East and West Coasts)

c. The length of time required of a vessel to comply with the charter requirements

d. The various aspects of questions of national defense, and

e. The proposed charter rate and its possible effect on the foreign and domestic rate structure,

and any other matters which, in the judgment of the Commission, appear to be pertinent and bear on the sound development of our merchant marine policy.

---

[10] Andrey Andreyevich Gromyko had been in the United States only since the previous November; see the memorandum of November 17, 1939, by the Acting Secretary of State, *Foreign Relations*, The Soviet Union, 1933–1939, p. 794.

[11] Addressed to the Division of European Affairs.

[12] Approved September 7, 1916; 39 Stat. 728, 730.

The Commission denies any discrimination against Russian interests and asserts that in its approach to this problem the current domestic tonnage situation and the shortage of world tonnage generally, both largely affected by war conditions, are of great weight in the Commission's deliberations. The Commission asserts further, as evidence of its impartiality, that its failure to approve these charter applications in each instance has weighed heavily on the American owner of the vessels.

THOMAS BURKE

811.20 Defense (Requisitions)/1

Memorandum by the Assistant Chief of the Division of Controls (Yost)

[WASHINGTON,] May 16, 1940.

Commander Carney of the Office of the Secretary of the Navy called this morning to inform me that at a conference held at the White House the day before yesterday the President had instructed the Secretary of the Navy to requisition large quantities of machine tools now being manufactured by American firms for certain foreign governments and companies. In compliance with these instructions the Secretary of the Navy is sending out today letters to various American manufacturers requisitioning machine tools to a value of about $3,500,000. It is proposed to extend these requisitions in the near future to apply to tools valued at a total of between $21,000,000 and $22,000,000. The tools involved in the initial requisitions are chiefly large lathes for the production of heavy ordnance. Later requisitions may also involve machine tools for the aircraft industry.

The two countries chiefly affected by the initial requisitions are Japan and the Soviet Union. It is proposed in the future to extend these requisitions to orders placed by Norway, Sweden, Holland and Belgium. It is hoped that these latter requisitions may be made with the consent of the governments involved since it is believed that, with the possible exception of Sweden, deliveries could not be effected in any case. It is also believed that future requisitions may affect orders placed by Italy, and there is even some question of requisitioning a large Italian order which is already on the docks in New York ready for shipment. Commander Carney assured me that no steps would be taken in regard to this particular requisition until we had been consulted.

As I understand it these requisitions are not to be made under the authority of any law but simply on the basis of contractual relationships between the Navy Department and the companies concerned and on the basis of the general interests of the national defense. Some of the pertinent contracts between American manufacturers and foreign buyers provide that the goods shall not be delivered if the United States Government should express a desire to procure them. Other contracts, however, do not contain this provision and will have to be broken by the companies concerned. The Navy Department proposes to furnish to these companies not only funds to reimburse the foreign purchasers for partial payments which have already been made but also funds to pay any damages which they may incur for violation of contracts.

Though the War Department is not yet doing so, it is believed that it will in the near future participate in this program.

Commander Carney has promised to supply us with complete data in regard to all orders which will be requisitioned now and in the future.

CHARLES W. YOST

811.20 Defense (Requisitions)/5

Memorandum of Conversation, by the Assistant Chief of the Division of European Affairs (Henderson)

[WASHINGTON,] May 22, 1940.

Mr. Oumansky, the Soviet Ambassador, called me by telephone this afternoon and in an extremely agitated tone of voice told me substantially the following:

An event which I fear will be of tremendous importance to American-Soviet relations has just taken place. I feel it my duty at once to bring this to your attention, and hope that I may have some explanation regarding it in the near future, in order that I may explain the situation to my Government.

On September 6, 1939 Stankoimport,[13] a Soviet purchasing organization, ordered a machine tool (a planer) from the Consolidated Machine Tool Company, of Rochester, New York. The purchase price was $95,269. On May 13 the machine tool company notified the purchaser that the tool was ready for delivery. The machine was inspected by the purchaser and accepted. On May 20 the machine tool company announced that it was released for export. On May 22, that is, today, the machine tool company notified the purchaser that upon the request of the Assistant Secretary of the Navy it would not be able to effect delivery of the tool.

I feel that the act of American officials in preventing the delivery of this tool goes far beyond the moral embargo or acts directed against the Soviet Union to which I have called the attention of the Department during my several conversations with the Secretary and with representatives of the Department in Mr. Feis' office. Would you

---

[13] All-Union Combine for the import of machine tools and instruments.

please make the appropriate investigations and let me know the reasons for this intervention on the part of the American Government.

I told Mr. Oumansky that I would look into the matter immediately; that the information which he had just conveyed to me was the first intimation I had had regarding the action of the Assistant Secretary of the Navy; that although I was not yet in a position to state the reasons for the action, I was quite sure that there was no act of discrimination involved; that if I were to hazard a guess I would say that it had possibly been decided that the machine tool in question was needed in connection with our program to enlarge our defense industry; and that I would make inquiries and convey to him such information as I could obtain as soon as possible.

Mr. Oumansky replied that he was shocked at the information which had been given him; that he had communicated with me on the subject within five minutes after having received the news; and that he hoped that he could have a reply either today or tomorrow. He said that if the machine tool was to be taken over for the use of the American Government or for American defense industry, it was extremely important that he be informed whether or not machine tools being manufactured in this country for all foreign governments were being taken over, or whether those of only certain governments were being requisitioned. It was imperative that he make clear to his government whether or not a new policy of discrimination against Soviet trade was being inaugurated.

Mr. Oumansky also referred again to the conversations which he had had with Mr. Feis, Mr. Moffat, and myself several weeks ago, and said that he was still waiting for an answer to several questions which he had posed during that conversation. He pointed out that seven weeks had elapsed since his talk with the Secretary, and that he had not as yet received a definite answer whether these conversations would yield any positive results.

I told Mr. Oumansky that I understood that we were now prepared to discuss the matters to which he referred and hoped that within the next few days it would be possible for him to have a conversation with Mr. Moffat or some other official of the Department on the subject. I pointed out that extremely urgent matters arising from recent developments in Western Europe had subjected this Department and other Departments to such abnormal pressure that we were not able to move as fast as we would like.

Mr. Oumansky said that he hoped to be able to complete our discussions this week, since he would probably have to leave town over the week end for several days.

611.6131/613

Memorandum of Conversation, by the Assistant Chief of the Division of European Affairs (Henderson)

[WASHINGTON,] May 23, 1940.

Participants: Mr. Constantine A. Oumansky, Ambassador of the Soviet Union;

Mr. Pierrepont Moffat, Chief, Division of European Affairs;

Mr. Loy W. Henderson, Assistant Chief, Division of European Affairs.

It will be recalled that a number of weeks ago during conversations with members of the Department in the office of Mr. Feis, Mr. Oumansky expressed dissatisfaction with the reasons given for the refusal of the Maritime Commission to approve charters of American vessels for trips to Vladivostok, and he also stated that he was not satisfied with the reasons advanced for the refusal of the Navy Department to permit Soviet engineers stationed in the Wright Aeronautical plant to enter certain sections of the plant. He stressed the seriousness of the effect which the attitude of the Maritime Commission and the Navy Department would be sure to have on Soviet-American relations, especially commercial relations, and requested that the Department again approach these two agencies of the American Government on the subject and inform him regarding the outcome of the conversations.

Yesterday afternoon Mr. Oumansky called Mr. Henderson by telephone, and with considerable agitation said that he had just been informed that a large machine tool ordered from an American firm a number of months ago by a Soviet purchasing agency and now ready for delivery had been requisitioned by the Navy Department. He asked for an immediate explanation of the action of the Navy Department and for assurances that the requisitioning of the tool was not the beginning of a new series of discriminations against the Soviet Union. He also informed Mr. Henderson that he would appreciate receiving as soon as possible a report of the conversations of the Department with the Maritime Commission and the Navy Department.

In pursuance of Mr. Oumansky's request it was arranged for him to see Mr. Moffat today at noon. Mr. Henderson was present during the conversation.

Mr. Moffat opened the conversation by referring to Mr. Oumansky's request that the Department take up again with the Navy Department the refusal to permit Soviet engineers freely to visit various parts of the Wright Aeronautical plant. Mr. Moffat said that this matter had again been discussed with the Navy Department and that he desired to read a memorandum, a copy of which is attached hereto,[14] setting forth the views of that Department.   Mr. Moffat thereupon read the memorandum, which had been prepared by the Division of Controls, while Mr. Oumansky made notes.

Following the reading of the memorandum, Mr. Oumansky stated that he found that the detailed reply did not correspond fully to facts.   For instance, the Navy Department maintained that temporary visits to the plant were still being approved for representatives of the Soviet Union for the purpose of inspecting engines and other machinery.   It was true that since his last conversation with the Department on the subject as an exception and for only a short time several Soviet inspectors had been admitted into the Wright plant, but the general practice was still to exclude them.   He wished to point out that the Navy has rendered it impossible for the technical assistance contract in existence between the Wright Aeronautical Corporation and the Soviet Union to be carried out.   On the other hand, the engineers of other countries were being allowed the freedom of the plant.   China, for instance, has a technical assistance contract with the Wright Aeronautical Corporation, and Chinese engineers stationed at the plant, in accordance with that contract, were being accorded privileges to visit sections of the plant to which the Soviet engineers were being denied access.

Mr. Moffat stated that he could not discuss individual cases.   He desired again to point out that the Navy Department had stated that there has been no discrimination.   The Ambassador said that he regretted that the situation had shown no improvement since his last conversation on the subject with the Department.   There was no change and no improvement.   Mr. Moffat added, "and also no discrimination".

Mr. Moffat then referred to Mr. Oumansky's request that this Department again take up with the Maritime Commission the matter of the refusal of the Commission on several occasions to approve the charter of American vessels for Vladivostok.   Mr. Moffat read to Mr. Oumansky the attached memorandum of the Division of International Communications, dated May 13,[15] setting forth the factors which the Maritime Commission considers in passing upon applications for charters.   Mr. Oumansky made copious notes while Mr. Moffat was reading.

When Mr. Moffat had finished reading the memorandum Mr. Oumansky stated that he appreciated the detailed answer, that he had no criticism to make of the form of the reply, but he regretted

---

[14] Not attached to file copy of this document, but see memorandum of April 24, p. 290.
[15] *Ante*, p. 295.

to learn that in spite of his representations in the matter there was no change and no improvement. He was sure that Mr. Moffat would again add "and no discrimination". He could not, however, agree with Mr. Moffat in this connection. Japan and Vladivostok were in approximately the same geographical area. There were only about 36 hours' difference in sailing time between them. At least six or seven times since January Japanese importers had been able to obtain charters of American vessels, whereas no charters had been obtainable for Soviet vessels. He had failed to find among the factors listed by the Maritime Commission as those which guided it in its decision, any factor which might account for a failure to approve charters for Vladivostok, at a time when charters for Japanese ports were being approved. He had noticed that in addition to the factors specifically listed the Maritime Commission had referred to "any other matters, which, in the judgment of the Commission, appeared to be pertinent and bear on the sound development of our merchant marine policy". Perhaps some of these unspecified matters might have influenced the decision of the Commission.

Mr. Oumansky then produced an article clipped from the *New York Herald-Tribune* of April 24 regarding the refusal of the Maritime Commission to approve charters for Vladivostok. He said that in his opinion this article which frankly admitted discrimination against the Soviet Union stated the truth. He referred in particular to a statement contained in the article to the effect that in addition to refusing to approve charters the Maritime Commission was "cracking down" on other tonnage for the Soviet Union. He charged that the Maritime Commission was making it impossible for Amtorg not only to charter vessels but even to obtain space for cargo destined for Vladivostok in vessels bound for the Far East. As a result of the pressure brought upon American ship owners, Soviet purchasing and shipping agencies had been unable of late to find space for a single ton of merchandise destined for the Soviet Union. Millions of dollars worth of machinery and other merchandise purchased by the Soviet Government in the United States were occupying warehouses in this country at enormous expense to the Soviet Government. He added:

"I wish to thank you again for your detailed answer, but find in it no explanation. I can't be emphatic enough in stressing the damage to American-Soviet trade which is being caused by the attitude of the Maritime Commission. The situation is worse than it was when I talked with you in Mr. Feis' office, because we are now unable to obtain not only charters but also cargo space. I must, therefore, reserve my position on this point."

Mr. Moffat then referred to Mr. Oumansky's complaint of the previous day that the Navy Department had requisitioned a machine tool ordered by a Soviet purchasing agency from the Consolidated Machine Tool Company of Rochester. To assist the Ambassador in understanding the situation, Mr. Moffat read excerpts from the attached memorandum of May 22 prepared by the Division of Controls.[16] Mr. Moffat said that in order to carry out certain extensive defense measures of this Government the Navy Department had found itself obliged to requisition from a number of machine tool manufacturers tools which had been ordered by several foreign governments or foreign concerns. He emphasized the fact that the sole reason for the requisitioning of these tools was that they were indispensable to the production of armaments which were essential to the expanding needs of the national defense of the United States. He assured Mr. Oumansky that the policy of requisitioning would not involve discrimination against any of the foreign purchasers.

When Mr. Moffat had finished his explanation of the situation, Mr. Oumansky remarked sarcastically that this must be terrible news for the British and French. No reply was made to this statement. He therefore repeated it, adding that he assumed that the measures which were being applied to machinery ordered by the Soviet Union in this country would also be applied in an equal measure to the British and French. Mr. Moffat said that the only criterion was our own need for the individual machine tools.

Mr. Oumansky said that he wondered if the American Government understood the full implication of the steps which it was taking. The most important activity of Soviet purchasing agents in this country was the buying of machine tools. A threat to cut off the supplying by the United States to the Soviet Union of American machine tools would be a serious step in the direction of disruption of Soviet-American trade. It should become apparent in the near future whether requisitioning of machinery ordered in this country by the Soviet Union would be on a large scale. It would also become clear in a short time whether similar measures were being applied to machinery and equipment under order by certain belligerent countries. Scores of millions of dollars were involved. The inauguration of such a policy of requisitioning produced an absolute uncertainty about orders placed. Soviet planning organizations had devoted much time and spent large sums of money in preparing to make purchases in this country; commissions had been sent to the United States at considerable expense to make purchases; inspectors had been maintained here in order to examine the machinery which had been ordered; Soviet plans had been built around the contemplated arrival of the machinery in the Soviet Union. The financial losses to the Soviet Union would therefore be much greater than the mere

---

[16] Not printed.

value of the machinery. His remarks were, of course, of a merely preliminary nature since the official answer to the measures which had just been taken by the American Government must come from the Soviet Government. He would like to point out, however, that Lozovsky, the Assistant Commissar for Foreign Affairs, was apparently right when recently he stressed the fact in a conversation with Mr. Steinhardt [17] that the measures (discriminating against Soviet-American trade) which were being taken by the American Government must affect that trade in the future as well as in the present.

Mr. Moffat stated that it was his understanding that the Soviet Government would be reimbursed for certain losses resulting from the requisitioning of equipment ordered by it.

Mr. Oumansky said that before telegraphing to his Government he would appreciate learning the extent to which the policy of requisitioning would be carried out—would this policy be carried so far as to render it impossible for the Soviet Government to purchase machinery in this country?

Mr. Moffat replied that so far as he knew the policy was being applied only to those machine tools which were most urgently needed. He was not in a position to state whether or not the policy would be extended to other fields. Mr. Oumansky said that in his own personal opinion it was tragic that in view of the lengthening chain of measures of a discriminatory character against Soviet trade in the United States the relationship between the two greatest neutrals was progressing in the direction of deterioration and ruin. The subject which had been under discussion was no mere routine matter. It merited the most careful consideration of the American Government. He would probably receive instructions in the near future to discuss it personally with the Secretary of State.

811.20 Defense (Requisitions)/6 : Telegram

The Secretary of State to the Chargé in the Soviet Union (Thurston)

WASHINGTON, May 27, 1940—7 p. m.

291. This Government is requisitioning from American manufacturers against compensation to the original purchasers various machine tools which have been ordered for delivery abroad. This requisitioning is being carried out solely because the tools being taken over are indispensable to the production of armaments essential to the expanding needs of our national defense.

---

[17] Doubtless in reference to the conversation reported by the Ambassador in the Soviet Union in his telegram No. 332, March 28, 10 a. m., p. 259.

The Soviet Ambassador complained to the Department on May 23 because of the requisitioning by the Navy Department of a machine tool which had been ordered by Stankoimport. Our policy was fully explained to him and he was informed that machine tools ordered and manufactured for other Governments are also being requisitioned and that the requisitioning was not an act of discrimination against the Soviet Government, the criterion being our own need for the machine tools in question.

He stated that he was reporting the matter to his Government, and would probably make formal representations within the next few days.[18] In case you are approached on the subject by the Soviet authorities you are authorized to explain the situation and to insist that the policy of requisitioning machine tools is not directed against the Soviet Government or any other particular government and is being carried out in a non-discriminatory manner.

HULL

740.0011 European War 1939/3423 : Telegram

The Chargé in the Soviet Union (Thurston) to the Secretary of State

Moscow, May 31, 1940—midnight.
[Received May 31—10 : 35 p. m.]

604. Molotov received me tonight at 10 p. m. I informed him almost verbatim of the reason for my visit as set forth in your telegraphic instruction No. 292, May 29.[19] Molotov stated that the Soviet Government is taking no unusual military measures; that such measures as it is taking are of a much less extensive nature than military measures being taken by Rumania; and especially less extensive than those being taken by the United States as to which the Soviet Government is unable to determine whether they are designed for peace or war.

Mr. Molotov (who had interrupted me before I had finished stating my errand to inquire if that was all I had come to see him about) then launched upon an extended and violent complaint against the treatment being accorded the Soviet Government by the Government of the United States which he described as unfriendly and intolerable. As he referred to the cancellation of orders placed with American firms by the Soviet Union I interjected that I had been informed by my Government of the [conversation] to which I assumed he was referring and that as Mr. Umanski had been informed already, orders placed for other governments were being requisitioned by us and

---

[18] See note of June 12 from the Soviet Ambassador, p. 319.
[19] Vol. i, p. 469.

that such a requisitioning did not constitute any act of discrimination against the Soviet Government.

Molotov replied that he was familiar with our attempts to explain our actions and to present them as being nondiscriminatory but that he did not regard our explanations as being substantiated by proofs. I inquired whether he therefore rejected the explanation I had offered and he stated that he did. He then resumed his criticism of our attitude toward the Soviet Union making such statements, for example, as that the United States had no mandate to revise the normal methods of intercourse between states and describing our action as unlawful and intolerable, and one for which we must assume full responsibility and which could bring no good to the United States. The foregoing subject was pursued by him at great length. But in general his remarks were a repetition in various forms of what I have just set down. He requested me to inform my Government of the views of the Soviet Government in this respect and I assured him that I would immediately do so.

At the conclusion of our interview I stated to Molotov that he had spoken to me with extreme frankness on a subject which interested him but that I did not feel that I had obtained the information I had requested from him with respect to Rumania. Mr. Molotov somewhat curtly replied that he had said all on that subject that he had to say.

THURSTON

811.20 Defense (Requisitions)/19

Memorandum of Telephone Conversation, by the Assistant Chief of the Division of European Affairs (Henderson)

[WASHINGTON,] June 1, 1940.

The Soviet Ambassador called me by telephone this morning. He said that he had a new problem which he desired to present to me. The Soviet steamship *Rodina* has been endeavoring to load in New York a cargo of machinery purchased by Soviet agencies in this country. The *Rodina*, according to the Ambassador, had noted a lack of cooperation on the part of various American officials in connection with its attempts to take on cargo and get under way. The Ambassador had just received a message from New York to the effect that a United States customs agent had, without advance notice, required additional data with regard to the cargo of the vessel, which data, so far as could be ascertained, had never previously been required with respect to American machinery bound for the Soviet Union, and apparently was not required by published regulations. The customs agent, for instance, was requesting additional information with regard

to the names of the manufacturers of the machinery, he was requesting full description of the machinery, and he was asking for serial
numbers, and so forth. As a result of the demands of the customs
agent, it had become necessary for the vessel to cease loading. In response to questions put to him, the customs agent had said that he had
been instructed to obtain the additional information for the use of
the Department of State.

The Ambassador said that he hoped that what appeared to be a
studied endeavor to interfere with the loading of the Soviet vessel
would not turn out to be another instance of American discrimination
against Soviet trade. He would appreciate it if I would take up
the matter with the appropriate authorities and endeavor to find out
who was responsible for the holding up of the loading of the vessel
and whether new regulations requiring additional data regarding
machinery leaving the United States had been put into effect. He was
particularly interested in learning whether similar measures were
being applied with respect to shipments destined for countries other
than the Soviet Union.

I informed Mr. Oumansky that although I knew nothing whatever about this matter, I was confident that the customs agent was
in error in stating that the information desired was for the use of
the Department of State. I felt quite sure that such information
as serial numbers, description of machines, and so forth, must be for
the use of the Treasury authorities rather than for members of the
State Department. I told him that I would gladly look into this
matter and would inform him of the results of my investigation.

After discussing the matter with Mr. Berle [20] and Mr. Dunn,[21] and
having learned from them the circumstances responsible for the delay in the loading of the *Rodina*, I called the Ambassador by telephone and told him that I was in a position to give him a preliminary reply to the questions which he had put to me earlier in the
day. I referred to the conversation which he had had several days
ago with Mr. Moffat and myself, during which he had been informed
that the American Government was being compelled to requisition
against compensation certain machinery manufactured in this country
for export abroad which was considered as essential in the carrying
out of our defense program. As a result of the adoption by the
American Government of the policy of requisitioning, the duty rested
upon American authorities not to permit machine tools, and perhaps other machinery, which might be essential to the American
defense program, to leave the United States. These authorities, therefore, were endeavoring to obtain data much more comprehensive than

---

[20] Adolf A. Berle, Jr., Assistant Secretary of State.
[21] James C. Dunn, Adviser on Political Relations.

previously requested regarding machinery consigned abroad, in order to enable themselves to judge whether or not such machinery was needed in the United States. I said that apparently the additional information requested with respect to the machinery which was scheduled for loading on the *Rodina* was requested in order to help our authorities to determine whether such machinery might be exported or should be requisitioned.

Mr. Oumansky said that my explanation had left him speechless; that he did not know just how to reply to a statement of the kind which I had made. He asked if I understood that the policy of requisitioning on the part of the American Government was making trade between the Soviet Union and the United States impossible. He said that trade could not be carried on in such circumstances.

I told Mr. Oumansky that the American Government realized and regretted that the policy of requisitioning must result in a certain amount of temporary confusion in certain branches of our export trade. It was hoped, however, that in a short time the situation would be sufficiently clarified to enable our foreign trade to be carried on normally within the framework of new regulations which undoubtedly would be issued. I said that I felt that he was taking an unnecessarily alarming view of the situation; that my understanding was that only that machinery which was deemed essential for our defense program would be requisitioned; and that there was no reason why machinery which was not considered as essential should not be sent to its destination. I emphasized the fact that this measure was in no sense directed against the Soviet Union or against Soviet interests, and that it certainly was not discriminatory. The United States Government was faced with what might be considered as an emergency situation, and in order to meet that situation, it was compelled to take all necessary measures for the national safety. It was regrettable that certain of these measures adversely affected Soviet interests; it should be remembered that they also similarly affected the interests of other countries.

Mr. Oumansky said that he feared that it would be difficult to persuade his Government that the action of the American Government in requisitioning machinery in the United States manufactured for the Soviet Union was not a policy of discrimination. I said that I hoped that in reporting this matter to his Government he would emphasize my statement to him that the policy of requisitioning was not directed against the Soviet Government or against Soviet interests, that it had been adopted solely as a measure for securing the safety of the United States, and that the American authorities would deeply regret it if the execution of this policy should result in inconvenience to the Soviet Union.

Mr. Oumansky said that he would faithfully report to his Government my statements, but, at the same time, he would be compelled to add that he had thus far not been assured that the policy of requisitioning was also to be applied to machinery ordered in the United States by Great Britain and France. I told Mr. Oumansky that obviously I was not in a position to state the extent to which individual countries would be affected, since the policy of requisitioning would be executed on the basis of investigations and reports of technicians. I could say with confidence, however, that if it should be decided that the requisitioning by this Government of certain machinery manufactured in this country was essential to our national security and to the execution of our national defense program, such machinery would be requisitioned regardless of the country for which it had been manufactured.

Mr. Oumansky asked if the Department had as yet received from Mr. Thurston the report of his conversation with Mr. Molotov on the preceding day.[22] I replied in the affirmative, and said that I had noted that Mr. Molotov apparently felt very deeply about the matter. Mr. Oumansky said that he did not know what would be the reaction in Moscow, since the delay of the loading of the *Rodina* must be considered as an answer to Mr. Molotov's statement to Mr. Thurston. I replied that it hardly seemed necessary, after what I had already said, for me to say that the difficulties encountered in connection with the loading of the *Rodina* were in no way related to Mr. Molotov's conversation with Mr. Thurston. The request made by the customs authorities for additional information with respect to the *Rodina* cargo was prompted only by their desire to carry out certain policies of the American Government adopted solely for the advancement of our defense program.

The Ambassador said that he would like to add in confidence that it was unfortunate that just at a time when trade relations between the Soviet Union and Great Britain were showing marked signs of improvement,[23] the American Government should be taking steps which were certain to result in consequences unfavorable to trade between the Soviet Union and the United States. I said that I was of the opinion that if the Soviet Government could be made to understand that the steps which we were taking with respect to requisitioning were not directed against trade between the two countries, the results of these steps would not be so catastrophic as he seemed to believe.

---

[22] *Supra.*

[23] For correspondence concerning relations between Great Britain, France, and the Soviet Union, see vol. I, pp. 589 ff.

811.20 Defense (Requisitions)/43

*Memorandum of Telephone Conversation, by the Assistant Chief of
the Division of European Affairs (Henderson)*

[WASHINGTON,] June 6, 1940.

Mr. Oumansky talked to me this morning by telephone from New
York. He said that the situation with regard to the loading of the
Soviet steamship *Rodina* is much more serious than he had realized
during his previous conversation with me on the subject. For five
days the *Rodina* has not been able to continue loading as a result of
the obstructionist tactics of the customs officials. These officials are
asking numberless questions, many of which do not appear to have
any direct relation to the question whether or not it is legal to export
the machinery destined for the *Rodina*. They are asking questions
relating not only to the machinery but also to the activities of Amtorg.
When certain questions are answered, new ones are raised. The officials, furthermore, continue to maintain that they are acting under
orders of the Department of State and not under the Departments of
Treasury or Navy in pursuing their queries. In the meantime, the
financial loss to Amtorg and to the Soviet Government is terrific.
Queries made by officials of Amtorg of the customs officials as to the
law or regulations upon which they are basing their actions have not
been answered. It appears, therefore, that Amtorg is suffering losses
as a result of actions of the customs authorities which are not authorized by law.

Mr. Lukashev, the President of Amtorg, has asked Mr. Oumansky
the following question:

"I have received instructions from my clients in the Soviet Union
to place millions of dollars worth of orders for machine tools and
other machinery. I have no certitude that even if these orders are
accepted they will be executed. I have no guarantee that even if the
orders are executed the machinery will not be requisitioned. What
shall I do? Shall I inform my clients in the Soviet Union that I
have suspended the placing of orders or shall I seek to place orders,
only to learn later that the machinery will not be delivered?".

The Ambassador stated that he was unable to answer Mr. Lukashev's
question, and he asked me what kind of a reply I would suggest.

I told the Ambassador that I was not in a position to give any
advice on the matter. I said that in our previous conversation I had
told him that the situation should be somewhat clarified in a short
time. It might be easier then for Amtorg to decide for itself the
policy which it should pursue. The Ambassador said he wished that
the Department would present Mr. Lukashev's question to the Navy
Department or to those officials who were responsible for the present

situation. He added that he could not stress too strongly the fact that conditions at present were such that it was physically impossible for the Soviet Union to engage in commercial transactions with the United States. The outcome of this matter was certain to have a profound effect upon Soviet-American trade, not only in the present but in the future.

I told Mr. Oumansky that I would convey the statements which he had made to me to the appropriate American authorities.

700.00116 M.E./305

Memorandum by Mr. Harold W. Moseley of the Division of Controls

[WASHINGTON,] June 6, 1940.

At Mr. Yost's request I attended a meeting today at the office of Mr. Herbert Gaston, Assistant Secretary of the Treasury, in regard to the proposed embargo on machine tools. Mr. Huntington Cairns of the Treasury legal division, Mr. Basil Harris, Commissioner of Customs, and Captain Almy, of the Navy Department, were present.

The principal problem discussed was the requisitioning of machine tools which had been purchased by the Japanese and the Soviets and which were either on the docks or in vessels ready to leave. There were two Japanese vessels and one Soviet ship which were being detained in New York pending the requisitioning of machine tools by the Navy Department. On the West Coast the Soviets have a considerable quantity of machine tools ready for export although they have not yet succeeded in arranging for their transportation. Mr. Gaston stated that it was most desirable to expedite the departure of these vessels as the Japanese and the Soviets were not only complaining of discrimination but it was costing them $25,000 a day to hold the vessels there. Captain Almy said that he already had naval officers going over the cargo and that they would remove as quickly as possible those machine tools which the Navy had decided to requisition. This apparently solved the immediate problem of permitting the early departure of these ships. With regard to the Soviet shipments Mr. Gaston stated that Amtorg was apparently fairly cooperative [24] and was anxious that the Navy speedily decide which machines it wanted and permit the early departure of those that were remaining. It was further decided that the procedure for the requisitioning of machines and machine tools on which title has already passed to a foreign purchaser should be that the customs officials in all ports of exit would inform the Navy Department

---

[24] A marginal notation by Mr. Loy W. Henderson reads: "Navy says Amtorg has not been cooperative."

when shipments of this type were ready for export. The Navy Department in turn would send one of its men to the port to requisition the material which it felt was needed.

I raised the question of discrimination and inquired whether it was planned to requisition machine tools which were going to France and England. The gentlemen present agreed that at least a gesture should be made to prevent the charge of discrimination and that a few non-consequential items such as grindstones might be requisitioned from shipments destined to the Allies. I stated that the Department had been besieged with inquiries from machine tool makers during the past two days who wished to learn if the newspaper accounts of an embargo on machine tools were true. I asked Mr. Gaston if he had any suggestions to make as to how we should reply to these inquiries. He said that it was quite proper to inform the machine tool makers, as we have been doing, that there was no embargo on the export of machine tools at the present time, but he thought that in all fairness they should be informed of the pending legislation which would give the President power to proclaim an embargo. Mr. Gaston stated that the proposed legislation in question was being taken up by the Senate today and that there was a very good possibility of it becoming law within the next few days.[25]

H. W. MOSELEY

811.20 Defense (Requisitions)/43½

Memorandum of Telephone Conversations, by the Assistant Chief of the Division of European Affairs (Henderson)

[WASHINGTON,] June 7, 1940.

I had two telephone conversations with Mr. Oumansky today regarding the difficulties encountered by the Soviet steamship *Rodina* in taking on cargo and the policy of the American Government with respect to the requisitioning of Soviet machine tools.

Shortly before noon Mr. Oumansky telephoned me to ask if I had any answer as yet to give him to the requests and inquiries made by him during his conversation with me of yesterday. He wanted to know specifically if the authorities in Washington were taking any steps to make it possible for the *Rodina* to load and depart.

I told Mr. Oumansky that the Department had been informed by the interested governmental authorities that the main reason for the delay in the loading of the *Rodina* was the failure of Amtorg to cooper-

[25] The Export Control Act, approved July 2, 1940; 54 Stat. 712. Proclamation No. 2413 setting up the necessary controls under this act was issued by the President on July 2; for text, see Department of State *Bulletin*, July 6, 1940, p. 12.

ate in furnishing the customs officials promptly with sufficient information regarding the character of the cargo to enable them to decide whether or not the various items were needed in the United States in connection with our defense program. Mr. Oumansky asked if that was all that I had to tell him. I replied that it seemed to me that what I had said was rather important if it was desired that the *Rodina* sail without further delay. I added that according to my understanding, exporters to a number of countries other than the Soviet Union had displayed full cooperation in giving to the customs authorities the information desired regarding machinery destined for export. The authorities therefore had been able to set aside such machinery as was needed by the American Government, and to permit the other machinery to depart. I said I was convinced from the information I had received that if Amtorg had at once given all the information requested the *Rodina* would probably not have been held up.

Mr. Oumansky said that he was surprised that in reply to his complaints regarding what seemed to be the illegal methods employed in delaying the sailing of the *Rodina* we were making complaints to him regarding the failure of Amtorg to furnish promptly certain information requested by the customs authorities. I told Mr. Oumansky that we were not complaining, we were merely trying to explain the basis of some of the difficulties of the *Rodina*. Mr. Oumansky said that it was his understanding that Amtorg had now replied to all of the questions asked it; nevertheless, the loading of cargo was not being permitted. He then went on at great length again to emphasize the fact that the United States Government was discriminating against the Soviet Union in that it was permitting machinery to go forward to Great Britain and France at a time that it was holding up shipments to the Soviet Union. He said that he had no doubt that shipments to other countries were also being held up. Nevertheless, as long as shipments were allowed to go forward freely to Great Britain and France, he must insist in the name of his Government that similar treatment be granted to machinery destined for the Soviet Union.

He asked me if I had any advice to give him which might aid him in replying to the question raised by Mr. Lukashev, the President of Amtorg, on the preceding day. It will be recalled that Mr. Lukashev had asked Mr. Oumansky whether, in view of uncertain conditions in American industry, he should inform his clients in the Soviet Union that he must suspend placing orders in American plants. I told Mr. Oumansky that I had nothing to add to what I had said on the previous day. I said that I was sure that in a short time the situation would be sufficiently clarified to make it possible for Mr. Lukashev to make his decision without advice from us.

Mr. Oumansky asked me if I had any answer to make to his inquiry as to the laws and regulations upon which the various actions of the customs authorities which resulted in the holding up of the ship were based. I told him that I was not prepared to discuss the various laws and regulations involved, some of which appeared to be rather complicated; that if Amtorg desired to raise the question of the legality of what the customs authorities were doing, it could refer the matter to its own legal counsel; and that the only answer that I could make was that during the present national emergency in this country our authorities were being compelled, in order to protect the important interests of the United States, to make use of certain powers which they usually do not employ. I said that although I was convinced that the actions of the customs and other authorities involved were legal, the question as to their legality could be decided only in our courts.

I told Mr. Oumansky that as long as we were on the subject of Amtorg I might tell him that I was very much surprised to hear yesterday that apparently Amtorg had sold for export to Italy 300 tons of rubber which it had imported into this country, despite the fact that it had been informed of our policies with respect to the export of rubber. I said that I hoped that the information which I had received with respect to this, and which apparently had not been fully verified, was inaccurate. It would be exceedingly unfortunate if it should be ascertained that Amtorg had become involved in a transaction which it must know was not in harmony with American governmental policies.

Mr. Oumansky said that he was sure that Amtorg had not engaged in any transaction contrary to American governmental policies. If the records of Amtorg's purchases during the last two months should be examined, "it would be found that Amtorg had been meticulously carrying out the policies of the American Government, the purposes of which were to curtail Soviet-American trade". I told Mr. Oumansky that I chose to consider his last remark as a touch of sarcasm to which he did not intend any reply to be made. I did not propose to make any since I had already on numerous occasions endeavored to impress upon him the fact that our policies of curtailing the exports of certain commodities were based primarily upon the necessity for protecting our own interests, and were not aimed at the interests of any other country.

Mr. Oumansky reviewed at length the various ways in which the American Government was discriminating against Soviet trade, and said that he could not emphasize sufficiently strongly the seriousness with which our attitude was being considered in Moscow. It would be impossible for his Government not to take cognizance of what we were doing.

I told Mr. Oumansky that I realized that it was difficult for a person in my position to talk to him in a personal rather than in an official manner. I would, nevertheless, like to make a remark to him which I had no authority to make, provided he would be willing to regard it as a personal comment from myself. He replied that he would be glad to hear what I had to say and would consider it as personal rather than official. I then said, "For a number of months you have been talking to me about discrimination against the Soviet Union, and I have been endeavoring to reply to you. I feel it is terribly unfortunate, in the light of the present world situation, that your Government cannot be made to understand or to take an attitude which will allow us to know that it understands that what we are trying to do may eventually be of benefit not only to the American Government and the American people, but also to the Soviet Government and to the people of the Soviet Union."

Mr. Oumansky said that my remark was the first indication he had ever received to the effect that what our Government was doing might eventually operate to the benefit also of the Soviet Government. He said that he would be glad at any time to discuss this matter in full with me either personally or officially. This was a subject which certainly deserved exploring. Nevertheless, he must continue his protests and he must make such protests emphatically, so long as the only concrete facts before him were acts of discrimination on the part of the American Government against Soviet trade.

Late in the day Mr. Oumansky again told me by telephone that he had just received word from New York that the customs authorities had ordered the *Rodina* to unload 60-odd cases of machine tools from among the 80-odd cases which had been taken aboard. He said that this order was a great disappointment to him since he had hoped that in case the American Government decided to requisition some of the tools on board the *Rodina* the requisitioning could have been limited to a small number. He said he wished, however, to point out that so far as the matter of principle was concerned, it was just as unpermissible from the Soviet point of view for the American Government to seize one tool as for it to seize 50 or 60. He must therefore again make the request that the *Rodina* be allowed to load all the cargo, including the machine tools destined for the Soviet Union, which it had planned to carry and be permitted to depart at once. I told him that I would convey this information to the appropriate American authorities.

Mr. Oumansky said that perhaps on Monday, June 10, he would request an opportunity to discuss the matter of the *Rodina* with the Secretary or some other ranking official of the Department.[26]

---

[26] See memorandum of June 12 by the Secretary of State, p. 315.

811.20 (D) Regulations/5745

Memorandum of Telephone Conversation, by the Assistant Chief of the Division of European Affairs (Henderson)

[WASHINGTON,] June 10, 1940.

Mr. Oumansky called me late in the afternoon by telephone. He said that he wished to inform the Department that he had just been advised by Amtorg that of the 2700 tons of machine tools which had been loaded on the Soviet steamship *Rodina* in New York harbor, 1286 tons had been unloaded at the request of the United States customs officials. Most of the unloaded cargo seemed to be machine tools of the ordinary type—that is, they had not been made under special order for particular types of work. Furthermore, he had been informed that four very important machine tools which had been partly paid for by Soviet purchasing agencies had been requisitioned by the American authorities at a machine tool factory in Niles, Ohio. Soviet inspectors, moreover, were now being refused permission to enter the machine tool factory where these four tools were being made.

Mr. Oumansky said that he wished again to repeat his request that (1) all machine tools ordered by the Soviet Government which had been requisitioned should be at once returned to the Soviet Government, and (2) that the steamship *Rodina* should be permitted to sail at once with its cargo. He also wished to reserve the right to press claims for any damages suffered by the Soviet Government as a result of the requisitioning of the machine tools and the holding up of the sailing of the *Rodina*.

Mr. Oumansky asked if the Secretary had been made personally acquainted with his various representations with regard to discrimination which was being carried on in this country against Soviet-American trade. I replied in the affirmative. He said that he was anxious that the Secretary should have full knowledge of this important matter.

711.61/738

Memorandum of Conversation, by the Secretary of State

[WASHINGTON,] June 12, 1940.

The Ambassador of the Union of Soviet Socialist Republics called, at his request. I was familiar with his numerous conferences with other officials in the Department and of the topics discussed, as well as the rather vituperative tone and demeanor of the Ambassador. I therefore proceeded to do most of the talking.

First I reviewed and discussed at some length the extremely dislocated and lawless state of the world as a result of the policies of those who are carrying out plans of conquest by force and applying force in carrying out almost all of their governmental activities. I again reviewed the course of our relations with Soviet Russia, especially since 1933, and referred to our wishes to comply with the urgent desire of Russia for recognition on account of dangerous relations between her and Japan in particular. I pointed out how I and some of my associates had incurred bitter criticism during all the past seven years because of our earnest efforts to cooperate with Russia. We had hoped that this cooperation would be not only for our mutual benefit but that it would be a stabilizing factor in the international situation, and that it would result in discouraging heavy armaments and in preventing possible war in the future. I pointed out how we had been hopelessly disappointed in many important respects in these efforts. I then passed in review the world situation relative to peace and the developments of danger to peace during the past seven years, notwithstanding the constant preachments and strenuous efforts of this Government to work with every other country at all disposed to go in the direction of peace. This especially included Russia. I then said that it was with unspeakable disappointment and regret that all of the efforts of this country in pursuing the foregoing objectives had come to naught; that the world was being rapidly subjected to a reign of force and destruction of most of the worthwhile things; that in these circumstances this Government had proceeded on a new policy of arming and arming and arming in order to defend itself against anybody wherever defense might legitimately be called for; that to this end this Government has no hesitation in taking necessary materials and otherwise conserving all of the commodities needed for this day-and-night program of military armament; that if anything unlawful is done this Government is responsible; that I am not intimating anything on that question; that I need not do so for the purpose of what I am saying; that my Government has no notion of making further sacrifices or engaging in further delays that would in the slightest retard or handicap its program of armament; that here it stands, and the Government of the Ambassador ought to be able to understand and realize that this is exactly our position.

I then said that it was a matter of great disappointment that we could not have the cooperation of Russia to a much fuller and broader extent than we have had during the past seven years, especially in view of the far-reaching extent to which we have gone to encourage and induce such broader cooperation for peace and mutual welfare. The Ambassador then began to speak of the trade discriminations which he says this Government is practicing. I said that I was surprised, in the existing far-reaching exigencies, to see his Government engaging in such small topics of controversy. I said that his Government is discriminating in favor of other countries in its trade methods and that we are saying nothing; that this includes immense war supplies to Germany.[27] The Ambassador said this was normal trade. I replied in any event that it comprised immense supplies urgently needed for war, which fact made it vastly different from normal trade. I added that Russia had a perfect right to pursue this trade so far as this Government is concerned, but that we followed a very different policy toward Italy with our trade during the Italian-Ethiopian war,[28] holding it down to the pre-war level by a moral embargo. I rested my contention, however, paramountly and primarily on our present policy of conserving supplies and materials for increasing our armaments, and that these references to Soviet policies were only casual.

I said then that in our extreme desire to see Russia pursue a course that would give her a great influence for peace, the President generously offered his good offices to Russia before she invaded Finland.[29] The Ambassador rather sarcastically said, yes, but his Government did not very well respond or react to the President's speech on a certain occasion at that time. I replied that when a giant country has a little microscopic helpless country by the throat and is choking it to death, I must agree that the Government of the large country is not in a position to respond or to react; that naturally the deepest possible silence is about the only recourse in such circumstances. The Ambassador looked uncomfortable but said not a word in reply.

I then said that I was not sure that Mr. Litvinov and Mr. Molotov are really friendly toward this country in view of the disposition to haggle and engage in vituperative language about a number of matters so infinitely small in the light of the present terrific problems that are being grappled with; (and having in mind the bitter and patronizing talk of Molotov to Thurston at Moscow a few days ago, and the loud and vituperative talk of the Ambassador himself here in Washington on all possible occasions) I proceeded to say that Mr. Molotov seems to have gotten on a "high horse" and that I have been hearing of the vituperative talks about Washington by his representative. I then said that this is, in part, my compensation for having undergone biting criticism for seven years in my efforts to

---

[27] For correspondence on wartime cooperation between the Soviet Union and Germany, see vol. I, pp. 539 ff.

[28] For correspondence concerning United States neutrality in the Ethiopian-Italian conflict, see *Foreign Relations*, 1936, vol. III, pp. 188 ff.

[29] See telegraphic instruction No. 252, November 29, 1939, 3 : 13 p. m., to the Chargé in the Soviet Union, *ibid.*, 1939, vol. I, p. 1003.

keep up anything like desirable relations with Soviet Russia and the reward for my hope of their improvement.

The Ambassador then handed me the accompanying note from Molotov,[30] which is self-explanatory. I said that I had already anticipated the contents of this paper, because I had heard nothing harped on except these comparatively small items, and that I must again call his attention to our policy of conserving materials for emergency armament purposes and that nothing would stand in the way of it. There were some brief references to these questions in virtually the same language that they have been discussed between the Ambassador and my associates in the Department and, to some extent, between him and myself some weeks ago. I said that other governments are not raving like his about similar conditions existing between us and those other governments, and that soon even his Government will be obliged to see more clearly that in view of our determination to conserve strategic and other needed materials for armament purposes the operation of the policy is general. The Ambassador repeatedly returned to the matters of difference set out in the written statement handed to me from Molotov. I said it was useless to protract this sort of discussion since I had made clear the broad policy of conservation on which our action primarily rested.

The Ambassador again denied that his Government was aiding Germany any more than normal relations would aid her. I again replied that the Soviet Union had the privilege of taking any of the various courses to which I had referred that she might see fit; that I was not raising any question for discussion on its merits but merely to point out that in effect Russia discriminates as between different countries.

When the Ambassador again returned to some of his complaints I replied that my Government could list a whole ream of earnest complaints against Russia, but that I would not undertake to do so in this connection except to the extent I had gone. He invited me to list any that I might have in mind. I thereupon read off to him the first page of the statement in the files recently dictated by Ambassador Steinhardt,[31] and added that I could read several additional pages but would not do so.

Finally, I referred again to the long and earnest efforts I and others had made to get along amicably with Russia and on a broad basis of cooperation for all purposes, as heretofore stated, and added that this Government would be glad whenever Russia should see fit to return to a set of policies that would make possible the fuller development of the relations of peace and mutually profitable cooperation in every practicable way. I pointed out that while the amount of Russian

---

[30] See note by the Soviet Ambassador, June 12, *infra*.
[31] Not found in Department files.

trade with this country is relatively small, and that it would be a mistake to exaggerate any special importance that we might attach to it, we would be glad to see it retained and developed, provided it is possible for such development to take place under mutually acceptable relations between the two countries.

811.20 Defense (Requisitions)/33

The Ambassador of the Soviet Union (Umansky) to the Secretary of State [32]

WASHINGTON, June 12, 1940.

SIR: On behalf of the Government of the Union of Soviet Socialist Republics I have the honor to bring to your attention the continuing irregular and discriminatory measures adopted by the Government of the United States of America and directed against the Union of Soviet Socialist Republics. These measures undertaken and directed against the Union of Soviet Socialist Republics are regarded by the Government of the Union as incompatible not only with the principle of "unconditional and unrestricted most-favored nation treatment" embodied in the letter and spirit of the agreement of August 4, 1937,[33] which continues to regulate the commercial relations between the two countries, but also with the spirit of normal intercourse between nations.

Discriminatory measures tendentiously directed against the Union of Soviet Socialist Republics not only continue to be applied but are being exercised in the United States of America against my country on an ever-increasing scale. Besides the facts of discriminatory practices which on various previous occasions in recent months I had the honor to bring to the attention of the Government of the United States, the Government of the Union is now faced with new and grave instances of discriminatory measures undertaken by the authorities of the United States against the Union of Soviet Socialist Republics.

Thus, on May 22nd, 1940, the Consolidated Machine Tool Corporation of Rochester, New York, received an order from the Assistant Secretary of the Navy not to deliver a machine tool (a planer of standard type) manufactured by the above-mentioned company on order placed in 1939 by the Soviet commercial organization, Stankoimport, and which had been inspected and accepted on behalf of Stankoimport by the Amtorg Trading Corporation, New York City.

---

[32] Handed to the Secretary of State during the conversation on June 12; see memorandum *supra.*

[33] Effected by exchange of notes, Department of State Executive Agreement Series No. 105, or 50 Stat. 1619; for correspondence concerning negotiations, see *Foreign Relations, The Soviet Union, 1933–1939,* pp. 405 ff.

On June 1st, 1940, United States customs authorities ordered suspension of the loading of the S. S. *Rodina* of Soviet register which had arrived in Hoboken, N. J. from the Union of Soviet Socialist Republics on May 22 and which had commenced loading in Claremont Terminal, N. J. on May 30th. Notwithstanding my repeated representations to the Department of State, the customs authorities not only continued to prevent the loading of the S. S. *Rodina* but shipments already loaded on the steamer were ordered by the customs authorities to be unloaded. On June 8th the shipper, the Amtorg Trading Corporation, was informed that of 2,736 tons which were declared for export on the above-mentioned steamer, 1,286 tons consisting of 426 items were being detained by the customs authorities for further examination with the intention of partial requisition of those items by the Navy Department of the United States. The items in question consist of machinery, especially machine tools, ordered in 1939 by Stankoimport, Machinoimport and other Soviet commercial organizations.

In connection with the inspection of the cargo of the S. S. *Rodina* the United States customs authorities requested from the agents of Soviet commercial organizations the presentation of a series of supplementary data over and above those contained in the usual declaration of export and going far beyond the customs formalities in ordinary usage in the United States and in contradiction to the Soviet-American agreement of August 4, 1937, which stipulates that ". . .[34] natural or manufactured products exported from the territory of the United States of America and consigned to the territory of the Union of Soviet Socialist Republics shall in no case be subject with respect to exportation . . .[34] to any rules or formalities other or more burdensome than those to which the like products when consigned to the territory of any third country are or may hereafter be subject."

I have been informed that similar discriminatory procedures are being instituted in regard to the loading and clearing of cargos owned by Soviet commercial organizations and assigned for shipment on the S. S. *Valiente* of Panama register in New York and on the S. S. *Ecuador* of Swedish register in Tacoma, Washington.

I understand further that the delivery of four heavy duty engine lathes by the General Machinery Corporation, Niles Tool Works Division, Hamilton, Ohio, to the purchaser, Stankoimport, which ordered these lathes in 1939, has been halted in similar manner by order of United States authorities.

In response to previous representations referring to several of the above-mentioned discriminatory measures, I was informed by the Department of State that the official orders for nondelivery or sus-

[34] Omission indicated in the original note.

pension of loading of manufactured goods purchased by Soviet Commercial organizations, is connected with the policy of the Government of the United States to requisition machine tools essential for national defense of the United States.

The Government of the Union finds itself compelled to record the fact that the Government of the United States of America which orders or permits the requisition of equipment belonging to Soviet economic organizations and which in this connection refers to the needs of the national defense of the United States, at the same time permits and in every way furthers the delivery on a large scale to certain belligerent countries of machine tools and other equipment as well as various materials for military use.

The Government of the Union considers that the Government of the United States can not fail to realize that the above-mentioned measures, being acts of direct and indisputable discrimination against the Union of Soviet Socialist Republics, disrupt the trade between the two countries and are prejudicial to Soviet-American relations.

On behalf of the Government of the Union of Soviet Socialist Republics I hereby present to you its emphatic protest against these irregular and, moreover, discriminatory measures of the Government of the United States of America toward the Union of Soviet Socialist Republics and inform you hereby that the Government of the Union reserves its right to present to the Government of the United States of America claims for compensation for all losses caused by the above-cited measures.

At the same time the Government of the Union feels confident that the Government of the United States of America after having considered the full significance of the facts described in this note as well as the facts referred to in previous representations, will take immediate steps to discontinue the measures directed against the rights and the interests of the Union of Soviet Socialist Republics and to restore normal conditions of trade between the two countries.

Accept [etc.] C. Oumansky

711.61/739

Memorandum of Conversation, by the Under Secretary of State (Welles)

[Washington,] June 18, 1940.

The British Ambassador [35] called to see me today.

The Ambassador first referred to the conversation which he had had at the White House with the President and myself on the evening of Sunday, June 16, and in the course of which the Ambassador had

---

[35] The Marquess of Lothian.

referred to a message he had received from the newly appointed British Ambassador to Moscow, Sir Stafford Cripps.

Lord Lothian said that he now had received instructions from his Government supporting the point of view taken by Sir Stafford Cripps, namely, that while there was no indication that the Soviet Union was as yet prepared to break away from her agreements with Germany, there was a very clear indication that increasing apprehension existed on the part of Mr. Molotov and of the Soviet Government with regard to the unexpected German victories and the strengthening of Germany's position vis-à-vis Russia as a result thereof. The British Government desired Lord Lothian to suggest that, inasmuch as Russia was believed to be very anxious to improve her relations with the United States, it would be most helpful if the United States would indicate to Russia its desire that the equilibrium in Europe be maintained and that closer relations between Great Britain and the Soviet would do much to accomplish such an end.

I said to Lord Lothian that I imagined that certain practical steps would have to be taken by this Government if the Soviet were to believe that we were sincerely desirous of improving relations with Russia, and I mentioned as being necessarily included among such steps the undoubted insistence of the Soviet that we make it possible for Russia to obtain all of the products within the United States that she desired without restriction, including machine tools, et cetera, which undoubtedly would be regarded as required by our own national defense program. I said that among other complaints recently made by the Soviet Ambassador was our advice to the oil companies not to furnish aviation gasoline and materials required in aviation construction to the Soviet,[36] as well as our unwillingness to permit Soviet agents to have free and untrammelled access to our factories and manufacturing plants. I said Lord Lothian would undoubtedly understand that it would not be the policy of this Government to satisfy Soviet desires in this regard under present conditions. Lord Lothian said he quite understood, and remarked that it was in the interest of Great Britain that we should not do so. I said that nevertheless I would discuss the matter with the Secretary of State and see if there was any way in which we could be helpful with regard to the British request.

S[UMNER] W[ELLES]

---

[36] In a series of letters sent on March 26, 1940 (700.00116 M. E./148a), many firms were reminded that there had been "no change in the application of the policy" of the moral embargo in these matters, as the Secretary of State had announced on March 14; see memorandum of March 14 by the Assistant Chief of the Division of Controls, p. 255.

811.20 Defense (Requisitions)/33

The Secretary of State to the Ambassador of the Soviet Union
(Umansky)

WASHINGTON, July 1, 1940.

EXCELLENCY: I have the honor to acknowledge your note of June 12, 1940 in which you state that the Government of the United States of America has adopted certain measures which are discriminatory against the Union of Soviet Socialist Republics and incompatible with the principle of unconditional and unrestricted most-favored-nation treatment embodied in the agreement of August 4, 1937, between the two countries, as extended.

After examining the contents of your note and after giving full consideration to oral statements recently made by you to various members of the Department, as well as to the statements made during your call upon me on June 12, I have to inform you that my Government is of the opinion that it has taken no measures and has pursued no policies incompatible with any of its agreements with the Union of Soviet Socialist Republics. In this connection, attention is called to the fact that the seventh paragraph of section one of the agreement of August 4, 1937 permits the Government of the United States to take "such measures as the Government of the United States of America may see fit with respect to the control of the export or sale for export of arms, ammunition, or implements of war, and, in exceptional cases, all other military supplies".

In view of the present world situation, for which this Government is in no way responsible, my Government has been compelled to take certain measures for the purpose of ensuring the national defense of the United States. In connection with these measures, my Government has found it necessary to adopt a policy which calls for acquiring certain machinery manufactured in this country under order of foreign firms and governmental commercial organizations. This policy, as has been explained to you on a number of occasions, is not directed against the Soviet Union or any other country and is being applied without any intention of discrimination against the Soviet Union. It is being carried out solely for the purpose of providing essential materials and equipment necessary for our national security. I can assure you that my Government is endeavoring to administer this policy in such a manner as to minimize, so far as the interests of our national defense will permit, inconveniences to Soviet commercial and industrial organizations. My Government sincerely regrets the inconveniences which have already been experienced and hopes that the effects upon those organizations of this policy, following the perfection of the procedure for executing it, will be less severely felt. It is prepared to cooperate with the Soviet Government in an endeavor to maintain between the United States and the Soviet Union commercial relations of as normal a nature as is possible in the present international situation.

With regard to your statement relative to compensation for losses resulting from the policies of this Government, it is suggested that you inform your Government that arrangements are being made for compensating the owners of the property being requisitioned.

Accept [etc.]   CORDELL HULL

811.20 (D) Regulations/148

Memorandum by the Assistant Chief of the Division of European Affairs (Henderson)

[WASHINGTON,] July 19, 1940.

Mr. Oumansky, the Soviet Ambassador, telephoned this afternoon and told me substantially the following:

He has just been informed by the Amtorg Trading Corporation that the Maritime Commission has refused permission for the chartering of an oil tanker of the Standard Oil Company of California from a Pacific port to Vladivostok. The name of the tanker is believed to be the *Miller*. It is hoped that the decision of the Maritime Commission may be reconsidered since adherence to it will be a distinct blow to Soviet-American trade. The Soviet Union for a number of years has purchased gasoline of low octane content for use in the Soviet Far East. It fails to understand why at this time the American Government should place obstacles in the way of the continuance of this trade.

The problem might be approached from two angles: (1) That of discrimination. In other words, are charters being approved which would enable American gasoline to be delivered to other countries? (2) That of Soviet-American trade. The second approach is preferable. Is it, after all, to the interests of the United States or the Soviet Union that trade of this kind should be strangled?

I told the Ambassador that I would be glad to see that his views are conveyed to the Maritime Commission.

711.61/776

Memorandum by the Assistant Chief of the Division of European Affairs (Henderson) to the Adviser on Political Relations (Dunn)

[WASHINGTON,] July 26, 1940.

The situation with respect to our trade with the Soviet Union has become so critical that I feel that I should call it to your attention. The facts are as follows:

1. During the months of May and June the Navy began to inform certain American manufacturers, who were producing machine tools for Soviet purchasing organizations, that these machine tools were required by the Navy and should not be delivered. They even went so far as to order machine tools removed from Soviet vessels in our harbors. The number of machine tools thus detained is not ascertainable. It appears, however, that almost a thousand were involved. (Apparently approximately another 2000 which had been examined were released for shipment.) These figures I wish to emphasize are subject to considerable correction.

2. The Soviet Embassy in Washington and the Minister for Foreign Affairs in Moscow complained vigorously at this action. The Soviet Ambassador, after instructions from his government, wrote a strong note on the subject.

[3?] The appropriate officials of the Navy Department informed us that the machinery in question was being requisitioned by the Navy since it was needed for the carrying out of our national defense program. They further stated that naturally the purchasers of the machinery would be compensated for what had been taken. This information was conveyed to the Soviet Government both in Washington and in Moscow orally, and similar statements were incorporated in a note on the subject to the Soviet Ambassador.[37]

4. The Naval authorities gave us to understand that there was no doubt about the Government's right to requisition this machinery. Officials of the Navy furthermore informed us that legislation which would take care of the whole matter was being enacted.

5. A short time ago we were told by Captain Almy of the Navy, who is now working with Colonel Maxwell,[38] that the Navy has no authority to requisition the machine tools until the President first issues a proclamation stating that we are on the verge of war. Captain Almy also has pointed out that the new legislation which has been enacted gives the Government the right to refuse to permit certain machinery to be exported; it does not, however, authorize the Government to purchase machinery thus detained.

6. There are, therefore, in this country several hundred machine tools which have been bought by Amtorg for Soviet purchasing organizations. Title to them has already passed to the Soviet organizations. Navy has asked Amtorg to sell these machine tools to various American manufacturers who need them in the carrying out of the defense program. Amtorg has replied that the title to the machinery rests not with it, since it acts merely as an intermediary, but with the Soviet purchasing organizations, and that these Soviet organizations

[37] Dated July 1, p. 323.
[38] Lt. Col. Russell L. Maxwell, Administrator, Office of Administrator of Export Control.

have no authority to sell machinery which they have purchased in this country.

7. In addition to machinery ordered for the Soviet Government which our Government wishes to keep here permanently, there are several hundred machines which Navy detained only long enough to examine and which it returned to Amtorg for export. However, the new law demanding licenses for the export of machine tools came into effect before shipping space for these tools could be found. Therefore, these tools are also being held up pending the issuance by the Government of the appropriate export licenses in spite of the fact that we do not need them.

8. Navy has taken the position that it will not now approve the granting of licenses permitting the release of any machine tools whatsoever for the Soviet Union until such time as the Soviet export agencies are willing to sell the machine tools which are needed here. Navy has also suggested that the Department approach the Soviet Ambassador on the subject and inform him that if he or his government can prevail upon the appropriate Soviet purchasing agencies to sell to various American firms the machine tools which they want, other machine tools in this country destined for the Soviet Union will be released.

9. In view of the repeated statements which we have already made to the Soviet Government that our Government was requisitioning the machine tools which it was holding up, and in view of the present state of relations between the two governments, we have grave doubts that an approach along the lines suggested to the Soviet Ambassador would be wise or successful.

10. After discussing the matter with Mr. Grady [39] I suggested to Mr. Green that the recommendation be made to Colonel Maxwell that an amendment be made at once to the recent export license act which would give the Government the right in certain circumstances to purchase such commodities and materials, the export of which it has forbidden.[40] Mr. Grady thought that perhaps such an amendment might go through without any great loss of time. Mr. Green apparently acted on our suggestion and such a memorandum went over to Colonel Maxwell two days ago.

11. In the meantime, the export trade of machine tools of all kinds to the Soviet Union is at a standstill; Soviet irritation with us is growing; we are in a position of having informed the Soviet Government that we were requisitioning tools, whereas now we are asking Soviet export agencies to sell them to American private companies;

---

[39] Henry F. Grady, Assistant Secretary of State.
[40] An act for the requisition of certain articles and materials for the use of the United States, with provision for payment for property taken, was approved on October 10, 1940; 54 Stat. 1090.

Colonel Maxwell's organization is telling American firms that none of the machine tools which they have manufactured for the Soviet Union can be released until the Soviet organizations sell us machines which we want. Moreover, dozens of American firms are losing money and are being handicapped in producing machine tools to be used in connection with our preparedness programs because the floors, stockrooms, and shipping rooms of their factories are chocked with tools made for the Soviet Government.

12. I feel that every effort should be made by the highest officials of the Department to insure the swift passage of an amendment to the present law which will give the Government the right to requisition and to sell materials and machinery which have been produced in this country but which the Government will not permit to be exported.

711.61/749

Memorandum of Conversation, by the Acting Secretary of State

[WASHINGTON,] July 27, 1940.

The Soviet Ambassador called to see me this morning at my request. I handed the Ambassador a copy of the President's proclamation of regulations covering the export of petroleum products, tetraethyl lead and its derivatives, and iron and steel scrap,[41] and stated to the Ambassador that these regulations had been issued solely because of our national defense requirements and that they were general in character and applied equally to all nations without any discrimination against any particular nation or nations.

The Ambassador was evidently fully informed of the contents of these documents before he came to see me, since he merely stated that the Soviet Government was not interested in the products mentioned and that the effects of the proclamation would have no prejudicial effect upon Soviet interests.

The Ambassador then commenced the same type of statement which he has recently made to the Secretary of State and to other officials of the Department regarding the policies pursued by this Government towards the Soviet. He said that as a result of the proclamation and regulations issued by the President on July 2,[42] the Amtorg Corporation had made application for over a thousand export licenses and that as yet not a single one of these licenses had been granted.

---

[41] Proclamation No. 2417, issued by the President on July 26, 1940, Department of State *Bulletin*, July 27, 1940, p. 49. For further limitations on additional material subject to export license, see the following proclamations issued by the President: No. 2423 of September 12, *ibid.*, September 14, 1940, p. 213; No. 2428 of September 30, *ibid.*, October 5, 1940, p. 279; No. 2449 of December 10, *ibid.*, December 14, 1940, p. 529; No. 2451 of December 20, *ibid.*, December 21, 1940, p. 559.
[42] See footnote 25, p. 311.

He stated that the most urgent requirement of Russia was machine tools and that machine tools which had been manufactured for the Soviet within the United States could not possibly be utilized in the American rearmament program since they were entirely different from machine tools utilized in the United States and even the measurements were metrical and, consequently, not usable in American factories. The Ambassador stated furthermore that while the United States was refusing to issue licenses for exports to Soviet Russia, it was granting licenses for the export of exactly the same products to other belligerent countries.

I stated to the Ambassador that the question of what was or was not required in our own national defense interests was a matter to be determined solely by the competent authorities of this government and not by the representative of a foreign government. I stated that the Ambassador was fully familiar with the policy of the United States, namely, that it intended to afford every possible assistance to the British Government short of war and that if the Ambassador was complaining of the fact that export licenses had been granted by American authorities to the British authorities, that was clearly a matter to be determined upon by the government of the United States and was not open to question. I added, however, that within the limits of the policy of the United States, one feature of which I had already mentioned and another feature of which was an unwillingness to approve exports of materials which could assist governments indulging in the practice of bombing civilian populations from the air, I had been informed by the officials of the Department who were in close contact with these questions that there had been no discrimination whatever against the Soviet Government and that whatever action might have been taken or might in the future be taken in the way of refusing licenses for exports to Russia, I could assure the Ambassador that such determinations would be controlled solely by what was regarded here as our own national defense requirements.

I stated that I was likewise informed, however, that there were innumerable incidents of discrimination against American nationals by the Soviet government and that I was under the belief that these incidents had been brought to the attention of the Ambassador. The Ambassador said that certain attempts had been made to show discrimination against American nationals but that he had never yet learned of any proven case.

I said that since that was the situation according to the Ambassador, it seemed to me that it might serve a useful purpose for the Ambassador and myself to sit down in the near future and to take up the complaints which he desired to make and the incidents regarding which we believed we had a valid ground for complaint, in order that we might thresh the whole question out. I stated that it seemed to me regrettable in the present moment of the world's history for two great powers like the United States and Russia to have their relations constantly deteriorating. I said it seemed to me it would be far more constructive and in the better interests of the peoples of the two countries for an effort to be made by both sides, including the Ambassador himself, not to spend their time complaining and finding causes of contention, but rather in a friendly spirit to try and solve the alleged grievances which both sides might possess in order that the efforts of the two countries might be directed towards a rehabilitation of world order and legitimate trade at a time when anarchy seemed about to engulf the entire civilized world.

The Ambassador said that he was very much relieved to hear the statement that I had made and that he himself believed that such an objective would be in the highest interests of the two countries.

The Ambassador then said that he would like to divest himself of his official role for a few minutes and speak to me personally. I said I would be very glad to have him do so. He then stated that the official statement which I had issued three days before regarding the action taken by the Soviet against the three Baltic republics [43] had heightened ill-feeling against the United States in Soviet Russia and had been regarded as most offensive by his Government, and had not given an accurate statement of the facts. The Ambassador went on to say that the action taken by the Soviet should have been applauded by the United States since it had obliterated the growth of "fascism" in the three Baltic republics and had made it possible for the suffering peoples of those three nations to come under the sheltering protection of the Soviet Government as a result of which they would obtain the blessings of liberal and social government.

I stated that the statement which I had issued represented the official view of the government of the United States and that it was impossible for me to discuss the matter with the Ambassador. I said that the policy of this government was known throughout the world, that it opposed the use of force and the domination of free and independent peoples, and that so long as this Administration continued, it would not fail to raise its voice in protest against acts of aggression of this character.

The Ambassador interjected to say that it seemed to him that I was placing the freely expressed will of the Baltic peoples to come under Russian domination on a par with the military invasion and occupation by Germany of the small Western European nations.

---

[43] Statement of July 23 regarding the independence and territorial integrity of the Baltic Republics; for text, see vol. I, p. 401, or Department of State *Bulletin*, July 27, 1940, p. 48.

I said that I had made it clear in the statement to which the Ambassador referred that we saw no difference in principle between the two cases. I further said that there was no useful purpose to be served by continuing a discussion of this matter and that it would be well for the Ambassador and myself to regard the question as one upon which we agreed to disagree.

I then said that it had been a matter of great regret to this government that after a period of 20 years, during which the Soviet Government had time and again reiterated its desire to maintain the cause of world peace, to uphold the principle of the right of free and independent peoples to have their independence and territorial integrity held inviolate, to see that the Soviet government during the past year had apparently departed completely from its former policy. I said that I need not detail the events of the past year since the Ambassador was as fully familiar with this page of history as I was. I stated that it seemed to me, however, that in the months and the years to come there undoubtedly would arise many dangers which would affect the Soviet Union and that I believe this situation was obvious. I remarked that it seemed to me that the Soviet Union would appear logically to desire to obtain more friendly relations with a government like the United States from which it never had and never would have anything to fear, rather than to pursue a policy which necessarily must result in a deterioration of the relations between the United States and Russia.

The Ambassador replied that he was completely in accord. He wished, however, to advance two considerations in this connection:

He said, first, that trade between the United States and Russia today had fallen to the zero point and that he believed that in order to accomplish what he himself greatly desired, namely, the objective I had just mentioned, a practical basis must be laid down so that a reasonable volume of trade between the two countries might exist.

Second, he said, conversations between the two governments looking towards an improvement in relations, to be fruitful, must take place independently of the policy of either of the two governments with regard to third powers.

I replied immediately that I was entirely in accord with what the Ambassador said and that I would be very glad to engage in further conversations with him on the basis which he had proposed, although I interpreted his remarks to mean, when he said that such discussions as might take place must be independent of the relations of each of the two governments with third powers, that the discussions would be such as not to conflict with the established policy of this government with regard to its moral and material support of Great Britain. The Ambassador assented to this interpretation.

I said before concluding the conversation that I should remind the Ambassador once more of all of the efforts which the present government of the United States had made over a period of seven years, from the time when Mr. Litvinov visited Washington, to establish friendly relations with the Soviet government. I said I need hardly remind the Ambassador that from our point of view the assurances contained in the Litvinov agreement had not been carried out by the Russian government and that I feared that no satisfactory result would be obtained from the discussions which we had in mind unless both parties to these discussions were assured that confidence could be obtained on both sides as to the good faith and the good will of the other party to the conversations.

I said to the Ambassador that I would ask him to come to see me again the latter part of next week and at that time I would be glad to review with him some of the precise questions which he desired to bring up and which we ourselves desired to raise.

S[UMNER] W[ELLES]

711.61/777

Memorandum by the Assistant Chief of the Division of European Affairs (Henderson)

[WASHINGTON, undated.[44]]

CERTAIN FACTORS AFFECTING SOVIET-AMERICAN RELATIONS

I. DIFFICULTIES ENCOUNTERED BY SOVIET ORGANIZATIONS RELATIVE TO THE PURCHASE AND DELIVERY OF MACHINE TOOLS

The Soviet Union during the last ten years has perhaps been our best customer for machine tools. Soviet industry to an extent has been built up with the aid of American machine tools and is still dependent upon them. The ability to obtain American machine tools is therefore much more important to the Soviet Government than it is willing to admit.

The machine tool trade with the Soviet Union at the present time is in a state of chaos. The situation is set forth rather fully in a memorandum attached hereto which was prepared by Mr. Henderson on July 26.[45] In view of the complicated nature of this matter it has been deemed inadvisable to make a summary of the memorandum.

---

[44] This memorandum was undoubtedly prepared between July 27 and August 1, 1940.
[45] *Ante*, p. 324.

II. THE "FREEZING" OF LATVIAN, LITHUANIAN AND ESTONIAN CREDITS IN
THIS COUNTRY

The Assistant Commissar for Foreign Affairs presented to our Chargé d'Affaires in Moscow on July 20 a strong note of protest [46] against the withholding from the Soviet State Bank by American banks of gold which it claims already to have acquired from Estonian, Latvian, and Lithuanian banks. The Soviet note stated that the gold in question was acquired by the Soviet State Bank on the basis of a sale purchase agreement and was subject to transfer to the deposit of the State Bank by virtue of telegraphic orders dated July 13, 1940; that instead of immediately executing the transfer, the Federal Reserve Bank informed the State Bank on July 16 that it was soliciting the permission of the Federal Treasury for the transfer; that the Federal Reserve Bank at the same time referred to Executive Order No. 8484 of July 15, 1940 [47] which prohibits such transfers; and that no further communications have been received concerning the matter since that date.

The Soviet Government, continued the note, maintained that the Federal Reserve Bank had no legal right for suspending the operation since transfer instructions had already been received prior to the issue of Order No. 8484; that, furthermore, "neither this nor any other Order can limit the rights of the U. S. S. R. to the receipt of property which it has purchased or to the disposal of this property as property of a sovereign state". In conclusion the note stated that "the Soviet Government expects an immediate transfer to the gold which it has purchased" from the Baltic Banks and "charges the government of the United States with all responsibility for the losses inflicted upon the U. S. S. R. by the actions of the American institution".

The Department is awaiting the comments of the Treasury Department before replying to this note.[48]

III. THE DIFFICULTIES ENCOUNTERED BY SOVIET COMMERCIAL ORGANIZATIONS IN CHARTERING AMERICAN TONNAGE

The Soviet Ambassador has protested informally on a number of occasions during the last few months regarding the inability of Soviet commercial organizations in this country to charter American vessels from the Maritime Commission. He maintains that outright discrimination exists since charters are granted to Japanese firms for vessels destined to Japanese ports but are refused to Soviet firms for shipments to Vladivostok. The State Department always contends that in passing upon applications for charter, the Maritime Commis-

---

[46] See telegram No. 885, July 20, 9 p. m., from the Chargé in the Soviet Union, vol. I, p. 395.
[47] 5 *Federal Register* 2586.
[48] See the Department's telegraphic reply No. 423, August 9, 6 p. m., vol. I, p. 410.

sion is guided entirely by considerations of domestic policy, that each charter is decided upon its own merits and that there is no discrimination against any country.

Since an American tanker, the *Miller*, was granted a charter last week to carry gasoline to Vladivostok, and since charters had previously been refused for two Japanese shipments, it is likely that this situation has eased somewhat. The Ambassador may continue to press, however, for a promise on our part to permit American tankers and freighters to ply freely between Vladivostok and our Pacific ports. It is possible that the State Department may consider it expedient to request the Maritime Commission to take under consideration the advisability of granting charters from time to time to Soviet commercial organizations in the future unless important considerations of domestic policy prevent such action.

IV. THE EXPORT OF GASOLINE TO THE SOVIET UNION

On July 26 the President issued a proclamation and regulations adding aviation motor fuel, lubricating oil, and gasoline blending agents to the list of articles which, under the Act of July 2, 1940, may not be exported from the United States except when licensed by the Secretary of State.

During recent years the Soviet Union has purchased such commodities in this country in small quantities and only for experimental purposes. It has, however, purchased large quantities of ordinary gasoline for shipment to Vladivostok. Exports amounted to 1,544,000 barrels in 1937; 1,120,000 barrels in 1938; and 844,000 barrels in 1939. Exports in 1940 have been negligible because of lack of shipping.

It has been reported from the Embassy at Moscow that in the course of the Soviet-Swedish trade negotiations, the Soviet authorities have agreed to deliver substantial quantities of petroleum products to Sweden provided such exports are more than offset by oil shipments to the Far East from the United States.

At the present time we can see no objection to the sale of limited quantities of low grade gasoline to the Soviet Far East provided tankers can be obtained by Soviet commercial organizations to bear the traffic, and provided we have no reason to believe that the delivery of this gasoline results in Soviet gasoline being released to Germany.

V. THE APPLICATION OF THE "MORAL" EMBARGO OF DECEMBER 20, 1939 CONCERNING THE DELIVERY OF PLANS, PLANTS, MANUFACTURING RIGHTS, OR TECHNICAL INFORMATION REQUIRED FOR THE PRODUCTION OF HIGH TEST AVIATION GASOLINE

The advisability of including such plans, plants, etc., under the Act of July 2, 1940 is at present under discussion. It is likely that Soviet commercial organizations in this country will bring suit for breach of contract against certain American firms which complied with the "moral" embargo policy of this Government and which recalled from the Soviet Union engineers who were engaged there in the erection of aviation gasoline plants.

There would appear to be no reason why American companies engaged in the construction of ordinary gasoline plants in the Soviet Union (The Lummus Corporation) or ordinary lubricating oils (The Max Miller Company) should not continue construction, or if they so desire, undertake new construction provided they would not send American personnel to the Soviet Union.

VI. DIFFICULTIES ENCOUNTERED BY SOVIET ENGINEERS DESIRING TO ENTER AMERICAN INDUSTRIAL PLANTS

The Soviet Ambassador has alleged on numerous occasions that American governmental officials and firms have discriminated against Soviet engineers and technicians by refusing to permit them to enter certain American plants. In answering such allegations the Department has emphasized that the American Government considers that decisions as to who may or may not visit American industrial establishments fall entirely in the field of the internal affairs of this country; that the American Government has the right to cooperate with American industrialists in taking steps to restrict to such an extent as may be compatible with American national interests the visits of aliens in all kinds of American industrial and commercial institutions. Should the Soviet Ambassador again refer to this subject, it is suggested that he be informed that such restrictions as may be laid down may not appropriately be the subject of diplomatic representations.

It should not be difficult for the Soviet Government to understand the position of this Government in the matter since that Government has for many years followed the policy of admitting aliens into Soviet industrial establishments only when it is convinced that the visits of such aliens would be to the advantage of the national interests of the Soviet Union. On numerous occasions American citizens have been refused permission to enter Soviet plants at a time when citizens of other countries were permitted to visit them.

In this connection it should be pointed out that according to such information as is in this Department's possession, Soviet engineers and technicians are at the present time being admitted almost daily into American industrial plants and establishments on the same basis as nationals of other countries.

VII. THE ROUTING OF MAIL TO THE SOVIET UNION

Early in June the United States postal authorities took the initiative in requesting the cooperation of the Soviet postal authorities in the routing of United States mails destined for Eastern Europe and the Mediterranean countries via the Pacific and Siberia. The Soviet authorities signified their willingness to cooperate. On July 2 the American postal authorities informed the Department that it had abandoned the project in view of the establishment of a regular steamship line between New York and Lisbon and that all mail for the Soviet Union would be routed in that manner.

The Soviet Ambassador informed the Department on July 11 [49] that he was of the opinion that mail destined for the Soviet Union, and especially Soviet diplomatic pouches, should not be entrusted to this route. He subsequently stated that, in accordance with instructions from his Government, the Soviet Government would prefer that mail for the Soviet Union should not cross Western Europe but should be despatched via the Pacific and Siberia.

It is possible that the mail route across Siberia is more certain and perhaps even faster than that across Western Europe. The Post Office might therefore be requested to re-examine the situation with regard to American-Soviet mail only (not including mail to Eastern Europe and the Mediterranean countries) and, if possible, to take steps to re-route this mail via the Pacific and Siberia. Even if the Post Office should not see its way clear to change its policy, it would seem likely that some arrangement could be made to despatch Soviet diplomatic pouches over the route desired by the Soviet Embassy.

VIII. ALLEGED MISTREATMENT OF TWO SOVIET ENGINEERS BY THE PITTSBURGH POLICE

On July 6 the Soviet Ambassador made strong representations to the Department regarding the alleged mistreatment of two Soviet engineers by the Pittsburgh police. The Ambassador's story is that the engineers in question were attacked by a group of unknown persons who accused them of being communistic; members of the police arrived and knocked one of the engineers unconscious and beat up the other; they were then taken to the police station where they were further mistreated; subsequently, they were taken to the Pittsburgh office of the F. B. I.[50] where they were examined concerning their political beliefs, their connections with the Communist Party and the Soviet Government; they were released, on the day following their arrest, after having been fined.

---

[49] Memorandum of conversation not printed. By letter of August 9, the Acting Postmaster General advised the Secretary of State that "instructions were issued on the 5th instant pursuant to a cable request from the Postal Administration of the Soviet Union to employ the route via Vladivostok for all mails destined for the Soviet Union, Estonia, Latvia and Lithuania." (811.71261/7)

[50] Federal Bureau of Investigation, Department of Justice.

A representative of the Special Agent of the State Department examined the matter and reported [51] that the engineers had been fighting in the street; that one was found by the police lying on the ground dead drunk; and that the other was bleeding at the face and waving a bloody handkerchief and shouting, "This is my flag". The men were arrested, according to the agent's report, for drunkenness and disorderly conduct. Officials at the Police Station disclaimed the allegations of mistreatment and maintained that the injuries were caused by the engineers themselves. The Soviet Ambassador has not been informed regarding the findings of the Chief Special Agent since we prefer waiting for a report requested from the Governor of the State of Pennsylvania [52] before discussing the matter further with him.[53]

The Ambassador took special offense at the reply which Mr. Berle made to him when he informed Mr. Berle by long distance telephone from New York of the arrest. According to the Ambassador's story, which has been confirmed to an extent by Mr. Berle, Mr. Berle informed the Ambassador in reply to his complaints, that although naturally the American Government deplored acts of violence, nevertheless, so long as Moscow-directed communists in this country continue to intervene in our internal affairs and to attempt to undermine the American Government and to attack American governmental policies, it would be difficult to prevent spontaneous expressions of resentment, some of which might take the form of physical violence, against Soviet citizens in this country.

IX. AMERICAN INTERESTS IN SOVIET-OCCUPIED TERRITORIES

The occupation of the Polish Ukraine, White Russia, Bessarabia, a part of Finland, Latvia, Lithuania, and Estonia by Soviet armed forces and the incorporation of these territories into the Soviet Union has presented this Government with numerous problems relative to the protection of American citizens and interests therein.[54] Not only is the question of the evacuation of American citizens from these areas still to be solved but also the question of American property. The Soviet Commissariat for Foreign Affairs informed our Embassy at Moscow on April 26, 1940 [55] to the effect that since the measures nationalizing property in the Western Ukraine and Western White

---

[51] Report dated July 15 of examinations made on July 10–11, not printed.
[52] Report dated August 15 transmitted by Gov. Arthur H. James under covering letter of September 23, not printed.
[53] See memorandum by the Assistant Chief of the Division of European Affairs, August 20, p. 382.
[54] For correspondence concerning the protection of American citizens in Europe and their repatriation, see vol. II, pp. 68 ff.
[55] See telegram No. 502, May 8, 5 p. m., from the Chargé in the Soviet Union, p. 197. For Department's reply, see telegram No. 276, May 16, 6 p. m., p. 201.

Russia were approved and proclaimed by decisions of October 28 and 30, 1939 [56] of the National Assemblies of the Western Ukraine and Western White Russia prior to the incorporation of these areas into the U. S. S. R., and were carried out by authoritative organs established by the people of the Western Ukraine and Western White Russia, "there is no basis for the presentation of claims to the U. S. S. R. or to its organs." The Soviet Foreign Office continued that the U. S. S. R. had no responsibility in regard to the former owners who had lost all property rights by virtue of the nationalization decrees of the sovereign people of Western Ukraine and Western White Russia. This property, according to the Commissariat, as nationalized and as State property, had legally been transferred to the U. S. S. R.

A similar statement will probably be issued following the incorporation of the Baltic States into the Soviet Union since nationalization and confiscation legislation has already been enacted in those countries.[57]

The American Government cannot accept such an interpretation and holds the Soviet Government responsible for all American property which has been confiscated, nationalized or expropriated by organs under the jurisdiction of the Soviet Government. This Government firmly believes that Soviet officials exercised full control over the governments and organs of the nations and areas which were later incorporated into the Soviet Union, and that any legislation concerning nationalization or confiscation were, in fact, legislation of the Soviet Government. This Government, therefore, cannot accept the interpretation as cited above and holds the Soviet Government responsible for compensation for any American property in the areas in question.

It may be stated that the Soviet Union has never informed the American Government regarding the status of American property in these areas.

With respect to Bessarabia it may be pointed out that all of the property of the Rumanian Telephone and Telegraph Company, which is almost entirely American owned, was seized by the Soviet authorities. Efforts on the part of the American Embassy in Moscow to ascertain the status of this property thus far have brought forth no response.

---

[56] See telegram No. 826, October 28, 1939, 4 p. m., from the Ambassador in the Soviet Union, and footnote 83, *Foreign Relations*, The Soviet Union, 1933–1939, p. 785.

[57] For correspondence regarding the forcible occupation of the Baltic States and their incorporation into the Soviet Union, see vol. I, pp. 357 ff.

X. THE TREATMENT ACCORDED TO AMERICAN CITIZENS IN SOVIET-OCCUPIED
POLAND

The Embassy in Moscow informed the Department on July 26 [58] that the Soviet authorities have consistently refused to permit American citizens in Soviet-occupied Poland to proceed to Moscow for the purpose of applying for passport services. Thus American citizens with expired passports or without passports are deprived of any opportunity to appear at the Embassy in order to apply for new passports and only those American citizens bearing valid passports can be evacuated from that area. (It is believed that there are over 200 persons in the area claiming American citizenship.) The Embassy is of the opinion that the Soviet authorities are now forcing those American citizens trapped in Soviet-occupied Poland without valid passports to accept Soviet passports and Soviet citizenship. Evidence of this policy has come to the attention of the Embassy.

It is suggested that emphatic representations be made to the Soviet Ambassador with regard to this situation and that he be informed that any restrictions of the freedom of movement of American citizens in the Soviet Union and any efforts to force American citizens to accept Soviet passports and citizenship, such as have been reported by the American Embassy in Moscow, are matters of grave concern to this Government. It is also suggested that the Ambassador be informed that until this situation is corrected to the satisfaction of the American Government no real improvement in Soviet-American relations can be effected.

XI. OPENING OF A CONSULATE AT VLADIVOSTOK

At the time of establishment of diplomatic relations between the American and Soviet Governments it was planned to open a consulate at Vladivostok. This plan did not materialize because the Soviet Government showed by its attitude that it did not desire that such a consular office be opened and the State Department realized that little could be accomplished by any consular officer in Vladivostok whose presence there was not agreeable to the Soviet authorities.

Since the Soviet Government has adopted a policy of reciprocity in regard to consular offices—that is, it takes the position that no country should maintain in the Soviet Union more consular offices than the Soviet Union maintains in the second country—we might well demand that the Soviet Government permit us to open a consular office in Vladivostok. We could even go so far as to insist that unless permission is given to us to establish such an office, the Soviet Government must close its consular offices in San Francisco and Los Angeles.

---

[58] Telegram No. 914, July 26, 3 p. m., vol. II, p. 146.

It is not believed, however, that any useful purpose would be served at this time by adopting such an attitude. The Department has decided that it is preferable to request from the Soviet Government a frank statement regarding its views on the matter, since the full cooperation of the Soviet Government and Soviet officials would appear to be essential to the successful functioning of an American consular office in the Far East. It may be pointed out that arrangements have just been concluded for the opening of a German consular office in Vladivostok.

The American Embassy at Moscow was requested about two weeks ago to take the matter up along these lines with the Soviet Foreign office.[59] No reply has as yet been received from the Embassy regarding its representations. It is not believed that the question of a consulate at Vladivostok should be made a bargaining point.

XII. THE TREATMENT ACCORDED TO THE AMERICAN EMBASSY IN MOSCOW

The difficulties and irritating experiences which our representatives continue to encounter in the Soviet Union strongly operate to injure the relations between the two countries. It is firmly believed that it will be almost impossible to have what might be truly called cordial relations so long as the Soviet authorities continue to employ methods which seriously hamper the proper functioning of the Embassy and alienate the American personnel.

The unprecedented regime of customs inspection to which official supplies and personal effects of American diplomatic officers must be continuously submitted, the delay which is usually encountered in the obtaining of Soviet visas, the obstructionist, and in fact discourteous treatment frequently shown to our officials, such as for instance the rudeness and lack of cooperation shown to Mr. Ward [60] on his recent trips to Lvov, the bureaucratic manner in which the Soviet authorities take advantage of their monopoly on property and services in order to cause difficulties in connection with leases for and upkeep of property used by the Embassy are but a few examples of the annoying "pin pricks" which cause constant irritation. Mention has been made of the refusal to permit American citizens in Soviet-occupied Poland to come to Moscow for passport services. It should also be recalled that persons, American citizens and foreigners, are often detained and sometimes arrested upon entering or leaving the Embassy; that the Soviet Foreign Office has refused, even as a matter of courtesy, to furnish the Embassy with information concerning the welfare and whereabouts of persons of dual (American-Soviet) nationality and

---

[59] See telegram No. 377, July 18, 6 p. m., to the Chargé in the Soviet Union, p. 460.
[60] Angus Ivan Ward, Consul, First Secretary, and Chief of Consular Section of the American Embassy in the Soviet Union.

has sometimes shown reluctance to cooperate with the Embassy in respect to the welfare and whereabouts of American citizens in the Soviet Union. It still refuses to permit certain Soviet wives of American citizens to depart from the Soviet Union, although for a period last year it did show more than usual liberality in this respect.[61]

It cannot be too strongly emphasized that the above-mentioned irritations and annoying incidents, which show no signs of decreasing, not only prevent our Embassy from functioning in a normal manner but also make it appear that the attitude of officials responsible for them is not friendly to the United States.

711.61/743½

Memorandum of Conversation, by the Assistant Chief of the Division of European Affairs (Henderson)

[WASHINGTON,] August 1, 1940.

Participants: Mr. Constantine A. Oumansky, Soviet Ambassador;
                Mr. Sumner Welles, Acting Secretary of State;
                Mr. James C. Dunn, Political Adviser;
                Mr. Loy W. Henderson, Assistant Chief, Division of European Affairs.

In pursuance of the understanding reached between Mr. Welles and the Soviet Ambassador during the course of their conversation on July 27, the Soviet Ambassador called upon Mr. Welles this afternoon for the purpose of discussing certain problems affecting relations between the United States and the Soviet Union. At the request of Mr. Welles, Mr. Dunn and Mr. Henderson were also present.

The Ambassador announced upon his arrival that he had come at the invitation of Mr. Welles to discuss various phases of Soviet-American relations in the hope that the conversations may aid in the settlement of certain problems outstanding between the two governments.

Mr. Welles stated that it was his understanding that one of the chief problems in the Soviet-American relations at the present time arose from the situation with respect to machine tools which the Soviet Government had ordered in this country, and suggested that this be the first problem discussed.

The Soviet Ambassador replied that the difficulties which the Soviet purchasing agents were encountering in this country in obtain-

---

[61] For earlier difficulties in connection with this matter, see memorandum by the Ambassador in the Soviet Union of a conversation with the People's Commissar for Foreign Affairs on March 14, 1938, and footnote 34, *Foreign Relations, The Soviet Union, 1933–1939*, pp. 533 and 534; and despatch No. 19, August 16, 1939, from the Ambassador in the Soviet Union, *ibid.*, p. 844.

ing the right to export machine tools which they had purchased was one of the outstanding problems in the relations between the two countries. He dwelt in some detail upon the great amount of inconvenience and the heavy losses which his government had incurred as a result of the refusal of the American authorities to permit machine tools ordered for the Soviet Union to leave the country. He pointed out that the machine tools under detention fell into several categories. In the first category were those which representatives of the Navy had, before July 2, the date of the passage of the Export License Act, set aside as needed in this country. A second category were those which prior to July 2 the Navy had released to Amtorg for export but which, for various reasons, including the lack of shipping facilities, Amtorg had not been able to get out of the country before the passage of the Act. A third category were those ready for shipment which Navy had apparently not examined before July 2, some of them apparently having been completed only after that date. Another category were those which had been ordered but which had not yet been manufactured or were still in certain stages of manufacture.

Applications for licenses had been made for the first three categories and applications had also been filed for the export of certain of the machine tools falling in the fourth category. Since the entry into force of the export license system, the American authorities, however, had not issued any licenses for the export of machine tools to the Soviet Union. Some 218 applications pertaining to some 327 tools were still pending. About 4,400 tons of machine tools valued at more than $4,000,000 were lying in docks and warehouses waiting export license permits. It was the understanding of the Ambassador that export license permits were being issued daily covering machine tools destined for countries other than the Soviet Union. It seemed, therefore, that the export license law was being used as a weapon against Soviet-American trade.

At Mr. Welles' request, Mr. Henderson stated that during the latter part of May it became apparent to this Government that in order effectively to carry out its preparedness program it must take over for the use of American defense industry machine tools available in the country of which that industry might be in urgent need. In order to ascertain what tools might be needed, most tools ready for export were detained until technicians could be given an opportunity to examine them and to determine their utility. For a brief period following the decision to examine these tools, there was a certain amount of confusion arising from the fact that it took some time to prepare the facilities for such examination and to train the personnel for the rather exacting work. Unfortunately, foreign purchasers of American machine tools suffered considerable inconvenience during the period of examination since it was impossible to state, until the examination had been completed, which machines would be permitted to leave the country and which would be detained.

Mr. Henderson pointed out that it was the desire of the American authorities that no machine tools be held up unless they were essential for the national defense. In order to make sure that the Governmental authorities would not make the error of taking over machine tools which were not needed, it was eventually decided that each machine detained would be assigned to a specific American firm engaged in carrying out various phases of the defense program. The Government, instead of taking title to these machines, followed the practice of requesting the purchasers to sell them to the American firms to which they had been assigned. This procedure was in general working out satisfactorily. Difficulties had, however, arisen with respect to the machine tools destined for export to the Soviet Union. It appeared that title to most of these machines had already passed to various Soviet importing organizations and that these organizations were unwilling to conform to the suggestions of the American authorities that they sell their machines to the American firms designated. In view of the failure of the principals of Amtorg to cooperate with them, the authorities responsible for the distribution of machine tools among American industry and for the issuance of export licenses had taken the position that they could not facilitate action upon the various applications for licenses which had been made by Amtorg in pursuance with the provisions of the law of July 2. The present situation, therefore, was that practically no licenses were being issued to Amtorg and that the export of machine tools and other equipment which could be shipped only under license to the Soviet Union was at a standstill. Mr. Henderson was of the opinion that the best way to break this jam and to permit the resumption of the natural flow of trade was for the Soviet Government to issue instructions to its importing agents to sell such machine tools as were needed in the United States to American firms as suggested by the appropriate American authorities. If this should be done, it seemed certain that the jam would be broken and that almost automatically hundreds of licenses which had been held up would be released and the export trade to the Soviet Union would become as nearly normal as could be expected in the present world situation. Mr. Henderson stressed the fact that the sale to American firms by the Soviet importing agencies of the machine tools for the export of which licenses were being refused would do much to eliminate the present unhappy situation.

The Soviet Ambassador replied that instructions which he had received from his government were to the effect that he should request an undertaking from the American Government that all machine tools which had been ordered in the United States on behalf of Soviet importing organizations be granted export licenses at once, and that irrevocable licenses be issued in the future before the negotiations for purchases would be concluded. He had no authority to accept, even as a basis for discussion, a proposal for any arrangement which would be less favorable than that requested by his government. He would, of course, convey any suggestion to his government which the American Government might desire to make. Before conveying the suggestion which had just been made, however, he would like to have a more definite idea regarding the number and type of machine tools which this Government would agree to release, and the same information with respect to those which it proposed that the Soviet importing agencies should sell.

Mr. Welles suggested that perhaps the Department might have two lists prepared—one setting forth the machine tools which this Government might be willing to release, and the other a list of those which it could not permit to leave the country. These lists might be submitted to the Ambassador at the next meeting, and after examining them the Ambassador might be in a better position to discuss them with his Government.

The Ambassador agreed to this proposal provided it should be understood that he was not receding in the slightest degree from the request which his government had instructed him to make.

Mr. Welles stated that he would give instructions at once to have the two lists prepared. The Ambassador again made the plea that the State Department impress upon the authorities charged with the issuance of licenses the fact that since most of the machine tools manufactured for Soviet use were equipped with instruments of the kind suitable to a country which employed the metric system and a 50 cycle electric current, they must be considerably altered and in some cases entirely rebuilt if they were to be adapted to American industry. He said that he wished again to emphasize the point that he did not know whether his government would be willing to permit Soviet importing organizations to sell any machine tools to American firms. He felt certain, however, that if the list of machine tools which the American Government wanted the Soviet organizations to sell was not exceedingly small, his government would not listen to the suggestions which had been made.

Mr. Welles replied that the Ambassador could be sure that the list would be as short as the needs for national defense would permit. The Ambassador should understand, however, that the American Government at the present time must give first consideration to its preparedness program and that it could not, of course, take any action which might seriously affect that program.

Mr. Welles said that he understood that the Ambassador on several occasions had complained to the Department with respect to difficulties encountered by Amtorg in chartering American vessels for the purpose of transporting merchandise from the United States to the Soviet Union.

The Soviet Ambassador replied that the question of obtaining tonnage had been indeed a very serious one. Since the Maritime Commission had recently permitted Amtorg to charter an oil tanker in order to carry gasoline from an American Pacific port to Vladivostok, he had some ground to hope that these difficulties were not [now?] at an end. Nevertheless, he wished to emphasize the fact that during the last six months the Maritime Commission had clearly been discriminating against the Soviet Union by refusing to approve Amtorg applications for charters of American vessels to Vladivostok, while at the same time it had been freely approving charters for American vessels to transport merchandise to Japanese ports. As a result of this discrimination the Soviet Government had suffered losses amounting to hundreds of thousands of dollars, in addition to inconveniences arising from the failure of needed machinery to arrive on scheduled time at plants in the Soviet Union.

The Ambassador mentioned in particular the incident of the steamer *Wildwood*. This American vessel, he said, was loaded with machinery and other merchandise bound for Vladivostok. In the middle Pacific the vessel suddenly turned around and went back to an American Pacific port. The operators of the vessel claimed that they had received orders from the Maritime Commission to return to the United States. He was not sure whether such orders had actually been given. In any event, the losses arising from loading and unloading and storage of the cargo amounted to more than $260,000. Amtorg was suing the owners of the *Wildwood* for damages and was confident that it would win the suit.[62]

The Ambassador added that he hoped that such incidents would not occur in the future and that the American authorities would find it possible to permit freighters and tankers to proceed from American Pacific ports to Vladivostok under charters from Amtorg. He said that according to information which he possessed there was plenty of tonnage available and certainly American steamers were safer on this route than on the Atlantic Ocean.

---

[62] The Amtorg Trading Corporation brought a libel for breach of contract against the American steamship *Wildwood* for $350,000 in District Court, Western District, State of Washington, Northern Division. The decision of this Court of November 13, 1941 (41 F. Supp. 956), was appealed by the owners of the *Wildwood* to the Circuit Court of Appeals, 9th Circuit, which reversed the decision of the lower Court on February 23, 1943 (133 F. 2d 765). The case was closed when the United States Supreme Court denied a writ of certiorari on June 14, 1943 (319 U. S. 771).

Mr. Welles stated that he would undertake discussions on the subject with the Maritime Commission. He wished to point out, however, that the Maritime Commission, in passing upon applications for charters usually considered the circumstances surrounding each individual case.[63] It would therefore be difficult for it to give any undertakings of a general nature for the future. He would probably be prepared to discuss this matter in more detail at the next meeting since by that time he hoped to have had an opportunity to go into it with the Maritime Commission.

Mr. Welles referred to the request which the Soviet Government had made through the Soviet Embassy in Washington to the effect that mails from the United States to the Soviet Union be routed across the Pacific Ocean and Siberia rather than across the Atlantic Ocean and through Western Europe. Mr. Welles said that after giving the matter careful consideration he had come to the conclusion that the request of the Soviet Government was reasonable and that he would be glad to ask the appropriate postal authorities to accede to it. He pointed out that he would take the matter up with the postal authorities regardless of the fact that it would probably cost the American Government much more to send mail by the Pacific-Siberian route than by the Atlantic-Western European route. Mr. Oumansky said he was happy to hear this and added that if proper arrangements could be made, he thought that his government would not be adverse to sharing the additional cost involved. Mr. Welles informed the Ambassador that he would notify him of the outcome of his conversation with the postal authorities at the next conference.

Mr. Welles said that it was his understanding that the Soviet Embassy had made some complaints with regard to the difficulties which the Soviet Union has encountered in obtaining gasoline from the United States. He did not believe, in view of recent events,[64] that it would be worthwhile to discuss this subject at the present time. Mr. Oumansky stated that he agreed with Mr. Welles as far as gasoline was concerned but that he felt that he must at this point stress the losses which the Soviet Government had suffered and was still suffering in consequence of the so-called moral embargo which the American Government had placed upon the lending of technical assistance and upon the export of materials to the Soviet Union which would enable the Soviet Government to enlarge its aviation gasoline industry. As a result of the manner in which this embargo was enforced, American engineers who under contract had been assisting

[63] See memorandum of March 14 by the Assistant Chief of the Division of European Affairs, p. 253; and memorandum of May 13 by the Chief of the Division of International Communications, p. 295.

[64] See Proclamation No. 2417 by President Roosevelt and the regulations of July 26, 1940, Department of State *Bulletin*, July 27, 1940, p. 49.

in constructing aviation gasoline plants in the Soviet Union had been called home, and the American firms which had entered into the contracts with Soviet organizations had been forced to break their agreements. Thus far, the firms in question had refused to send American engineers back to the Soviet Union to finish the construction of the plants on the ground that the State Department would not grant the requisite passports. He said that he hoped that arrangements could be effected which would make it possible for the American engineers to return to the Soviet Union in order to complete their work and for the firms to go on with the contracts which had been breached.

Mr. Welles said that it seemed to him that two questions were involved here. One question related to the moral embargo and the other to the refusal of the State Department to issue passports to American engineers which would enable them to go to the Soviet Union. Mr. Oumansky agreed, adding that these two questions, however, were interlocked; that the contracts for technical assistance would have no value if the American Government did not permit American engineers to go to the Soviet Union to assist in the erection of plants, and that on the other hand it would be useless for American engineers to go to the Soviet Union unless their employers were allowed to extend technical assistance.

Mr. Welles said that Mr. Oumansky, in raising the questions of the visits of American engineers to the Soviet Union, forced him to refer to the treatment which the Soviet Government had been giving to American citizens in the Soviet Union and in Eastern Poland. The Under Secretary stressed the fact that so long as American citizens in the Soviet Union were not given freedom of movement and were not allowed at will to appear at the American Embassy at Moscow, this Government did not feel that it could afford to facilitate the visits of American citizens to the Soviet Union by the issuance to them of passports. According to his understanding the Soviet Government was making it impossible for American citizens in Soviet-occupied Eastern Poland to report to the Embassy at Moscow in order to register or to have their citizenship papers put in order. Furthermore, he had been informed that in some instances the Soviet authorities were endeavoring to prevail upon the American citizens in Eastern Poland who did not have access to the American Embassy to accept Soviet citizenship. Other instances had also come to his attention in which American citizens in the Soviet Union proper who desired to report to the American Embassy at Moscow had been prevented from doing so by local authorities. Mr. Oumansky said that the difficulties encountered by American citizens in that part of the Soviet Union which formerly had belonged to Poland in reporting to the American Embassy at Moscow had not previously been brought to his attention. He would be glad, however, to report the matter to his government and to inquire with respect to it. He said that he wondered if the persons who were being detained were really American citizens in possession of documents evidencing their citizenship. Mr. Henderson stated that it was his understanding that the refusal of the Soviet authorities to permit American citizens in Soviet-occupied Poland to go to the American Embassy at Moscow was not based upon any doubts regarding the American citizenship of the persons in question. He believed that the Soviet Government had given the Embassy to understand that American citizens in Eastern Poland could not go to Moscow in any circumstances.

Mr. Oumansky said that he would take up the matter at once with his government. It would be of assistance to him, however, to have the names and addresses of the various American citizens who had been prevented from appearing at the American Embassy at Moscow.

Mr. Welles suggested that the conversation end for the time being and be resumed during the early part of the following week. Mr. Oumansky replied that before the conference terminated he wished to raise one point which was first in order of importance, namely, the freezing of the gold in American banks which the Baltic States had sold to the Soviet Union.[65] The Soviet Government regarded with extreme seriousness this act on the part of the American Government. It was his understanding that the People's Commissariat for Foreign Affairs had handed Mr. Thurston a note on the subject.[66] He had nothing to add to the note other than to say that it deserved the full consideration of the American Government.

Mr. Welles replied that this matter was being given consideration and that a reply would probably be ready for the Ambassador at the next conference.[67]

Mr. Oumansky said that he had been working on a memorandum which would set forth 15 points of issue between his government and the American Government. He hoped to be able to present this memorandum at the next conference. It was his suggestion that it be studied and replied to either in the form of a memorandum or orally. Mr. Welles stated that it had been his experience that the exchange of memoranda was not the best method for composing differences. It seemed to him that informal discussions such as the conversation which had just taken place were more likely to be fruitful of results. Mr. Oumansky said that he would be glad to have

---

[65] For text of Executive Order No. 8484 issued July 15, 1940, see 5 *Federal Register* 2586; for correspondence on this subject in connection with the forcible occupation of the Baltic States by the Soviet Government, see vol. I, pp. 357 ff.

[66] See telegram No. 885, July 20, 9 p. m., from the Chargé in the Soviet Union, vol. I, p. 395.

[67] See telegram No. 423, August 9, 6 p. m., to the Chargé in the Soviet Union, vol. I, p. 410.

the conversations conducted in such a manner as would be agreeable to Mr. Welles.

It was decided tentatively that the next conference would take place on Tuesday morning, August 6.[68]

711.61/827½

Memorandum of Conversation, by the Assistant Chief of the Division of European Affairs (Henderson)

[WASHINGTON,] August 7, 1940.

Participants: Mr. Constantine A. Oumansky, Soviet Ambassador;
               Mr. Sumner Welles, Acting Secretary of State;
               Mr. Ray Atherton, [Acting] Chief, Division of European Affairs;
               Mr. Loy W. Henderson, Assistant Chief, Division of European Affairs.

The second of the series of conversations between Mr. Welles and the Soviet Ambassador with regard to problems affecting relations between the United States and the Soviet Union took place this afternoon. At the request of Mr. Welles, Mr. Atherton and Mr. Henderson were present.

After greeting the Ambassador Mr. Welles stated that he thought there was cause for gratification at the progress which had been made at the last meeting and expressed the hope that these conversations would continue to yield favorable results. Mr. Oumansky replied that in spite of the narrow basis on which the conference had taken place he also was pleased at the results achieved.

ROUTING OF MAIL TO THE SOVIET UNION

Mr. Welles suggested that the first point to be taken up was that of the routing of mail to the Soviet Union. He said that he was glad to state that instructions had already been issued by the appropriate United States authorities for the routing through Vladivostok of mail to the Soviet Union and to the three Baltic countries of Latvia, Lithuania, and Estonia. Mr. Oumansky expressed his appreciation of this step. He added that he had been surprised at the recent smoothness of the transmission of mails from Moscow to Washington. Whereas during the past Winter and Spring it frequently happened that it took three or four months for mails to travel from Moscow to Washington, the Embassy was now receiving mail within four weeks from the date of its despatch from Moscow. He said he would appreciate it if inquiries would be made of the American postal authorities as

---

[68] The next conference was held on August 7; see *infra*.

to the routing of these mails. It might be that if these mails are coming across Europe and if there can be some assurance that they will continue to come with such satisfactory speed, the Soviet Government would be satisfied with the European routing and would not desire to put the American postal authorities to the inconvenience of routing mail through Vladivostok. Mr. Welles informed Mr. Oumansky that appropriate inquiries would be made and the Embassy would be informed regarding the route over which recent mails had come.

CHARTERING OF AMERICAN VESSELS BY AMTORG OR OTHER SOVIET AGENCIES

Mr. Welles referred to the complaints which Mr. Oumansky had made at the previous conference regarding difficulties encountered by Soviet agencies in chartering American vessels for the transport of merchandise to or from the Soviet Union. Mr. Welles stated that he was glad to say that Soviet agencies would probably not encounter any more difficulties with respect to tankers since for the present, at least, tankers seemed to be available for the run between American and Soviet Pacific ports. The situation with respect to dry cargo vessels was somewhat more difficult. It was frequently impossible to meet the demand for such vessels with the present supply of tonnage. He felt quite certain that any difficulties which might be encountered in chartering such vessels would be only of a temporary nature, and that in general dry cargo vessels would be available for trips to the Soviet Union.

The Soviet Ambassador replied that he was glad to receive this statement. He felt that he should point out, however, that the situation at present remains unsatisfactory, although for reasons other than those which existed a few months ago. Prior to last June there were large consignments of merchandise destined for the Soviet Union piled up on the wharfs and in the warehouses awaiting ships, the chartering of which the Maritime Commission would not approve. Now there were plenty of ships available but unfortunately the American authorities would not permit the release of merchandise destined for the Soviet Union which was ready for shipment. The abundance of ships arose from the fact that Soviet boats were commencing to operate between Murmansk and American ports. The third Soviet vessel from Murmansk had recently arrived in the United States. There was also considerable Swedish tonnage available for the Soviet trade at the present time and, now that some American tonnage could be used, the question of obtaining bottoms for the transfer of merchandise was no longer serious. Cargo rather than tonnage seemed to be the outstanding problem at the present time

The Question of the Detention in the United States of Machine
Tools Purchased by Soviet Governmental Agencies

Mr. Welles referred to the promise which had been made at the last
conference that he would furnish the Soviet Ambassador two lists of
machine tools—one list itemizing the machines which the American
Government desired the Soviet owners to sell to American manufacturers, and the other enumerating tools which could be released in case
the sale of the machine tools in the first list should be agreed to. Mr.
Welles handed the two lists [70] to the Ambassador pointing out that the
goods which were to remain in the United States aggregated only
about $800,000 in value, whereas the value of those which might be
permitted to leave the country would amount to more than $2,800,000.
Mr. Welles also emphasized the fact that although the lists had been
compiled with considerable care and undoubtedly represented the
situation correctly, there was, nevertheless, a possibility that a few
machines might subsequently be transferred from one list to another.

The Ambassador, after glancing at the lists, said, "Bad news, Mr.
Secretary, very bad news. I had hoped to have a very different kind
of a reply from you."

Mr. Welles suggested that the Ambassador take the lists with him
and have them subjected to careful study by his technical assistants.
He said that in case the Ambassador should feel that there were cogent
reasons why certain machines should be transferred from one list to
the other, he would be pleased to have the Ambassador present them
to him.

The Ambassador again expressed his disappointment at finding in
the first list so many articles of great importance to Soviet economy.
He said that it was his understanding that the purpose of the present
conversations was to eliminate tension in the relations between the
two countries. The policies of the American Government, even though
they might not be aimed directly against the Soviet Union, were resulting in the placing of obstacles in the way of Soviet-American
trade. For years the Soviet Union had occupied first place as foreign
purchaser of American machine tools. It had now fallen down to
fourth place. It was the belief of the Soviet Government that a much
broader approach to this question could have been possible. It seemed
to it that this problem could best be solved in the way suggested
by Mikoyan,[71] namely, that the President's proclamation of July 2
be not given retroactive force. The Ambassador then proceeded to
point out at length the unfairness of the attitude of the American
Government. He emphasized the fact that in placing orders in this

---

[70] Neither attached to file copy of this document.
[71] The proposals of Anastas Ivanovich Mikoyan, People's Commissar for Foreign Trade of the Soviet Union, were reported by the Chargé in his telegrams
No. 936, July 30, 6 p. m., and No. 937, July 31, 9 a. m., pp. 446 and 449, respectively.

country under the present system, the Soviet Government had no guarantee that machines which might be ordered in the United States would ever be delivered. In general, his complaint was upon two grounds—1) that of insecurity and 2) that of discrimination—in view of the fact that the Soviet Government was not being granted most-favored-nation treatment.

Mr. Welles replied that our Government fully understood the inconveniences which the Soviet Government was bound to suffer and regretted them. It was precisely because of this understanding that he had suggested that the Ambassador feel free to advance reasons why any particular machines which our Government desired to retain in the country should be released.

Mr. Welles pointed out that in times like the present questions of international defense must rise above everything. When the American experts tell the President that certain machine tools which are in this country are necessary for the execution of the national defense program, there is only one thing to be done—that is, to take steps to retain them. Mr. Welles also expressed the opinion that when the situation with respect to the needs of American industry had become more clear, it would be found that there would be a relative security in the trade between the two countries. Soviet purchasing agencies would probably be able to count with reasonable assurance on obtaining goods for which export licenses had been granted.

Mr. Oumansky said that another thought had occurred to him. He would advance this thought as a personal suggestion since he had no instruction from his Government with respect to it. If, for instance, machine X which the American Government felt should be retained in this country because of present urgent needs could be duplicated, say within four months, could the American Government issue licenses which would permit the Soviet Government to have a copy of the machine within that period? Mr. Welles replied that this seemed to be a fair question and would be given consideration. The Ambassador again stated that he had no authority to raise the question. Mr. Welles stated that the suggestion would be considered as having come from himself.

Mr. Oumansky said that after casually examining the lists he found them more unsatisfactory than a first glance would indicate. He found that the most valuable machines were among those to be detained. The element of quality made the lists still more unfavorable than that of quantity. He did not know what kind of a shock absorber he could devise in transmitting these lists to his Government. He hoped that the matter would not be considered as entirely closed. If it should be so considered, the outlook would be very gloomy.

Mr. Welles stated that in his opinion it would be wise, during the course of these discussions, not to consider anything as a closed book.

THE MORAL EMBARGO

Mr. Oumansky referred to the exchange of remarks which had taken place at the last conference relating to the so-called moral embargo upon the granting of technical assistance to the Soviet Government in the matter of the building of aviation gasoline plants. In that conference the general question of the moral embargo and its effects had not been dwelt upon. The Soviet Government had never purchased large quantities of the commodities which had been covered by the moral embargo. Soviet industry, however, had suffered considerable injury as the result of its inability to receive American technical assistance in the construction of aviation gasoline plants, at the cessation of the supplies of molybdenum, and at its failure to receive the newest models of American airplanes for which it had been contracting over a period of many years. The worst result of the moral embargo, however, was the effect which it had upon the attitude of American business towards Soviet trade. The public, to an extent, followed the line laid down by the Government. By announcing that the moral embargo was applicable to the Soviet Union, the American Government raised in the minds of wide business circles doubts as to the morality of having any dealings with the Soviet Government, or at least caused these circles to feel that they might be criticized if it should be known that they were having such dealings. If there was to be a different atmosphere in the relations between the two governments it was important that something be done to cause the American public to feel that no stigma should be attached to Soviet trade. He did not wish to suggest the form of action which should be taken to eliminate the unwholesome effects of the moral embargo.

Mr. Welles replied that the situation as outlined by the Ambassador would be given serious consideration and would be discussed later.

IMPORTS OF SOVIET GOLD INTO THE UNITED STATES

The Ambassador stated that several years ago he had had a "paradoxical talk" with Mr. Morgenthau regarding shipments of Soviet gold into this country. Mr. Morgenthau had told him during this conversation that it would be unfortunate if the United States should at any time be flooded with Russian gold. At the present time the trade balance between the United States and the Soviet Union was distinctly unfavorable to the Soviet Union. The Soviet Union must of necessity, therefore, sell gold in the United States in order to be able to continue its purchases of American goods. In view of numerous difficulties which the Soviet Government has encountered during the last year it desired to make sure that no unpleasant surprises might await it with respect to gold. It was hoped, therefore, that the American Government could agree that during the coming year it would take no steps which might interfere with the sale of Soviet gold in the country.

Mr. Welles asked Mr. Henderson if he would clarify the situation somewhat with respect to gold. Mr. Henderson replied that according to his understanding the American Government for many years had followed the policy of declining to make any undertakings which would bind its hands in the matter of restricting the importation or exportation of gold. He was certain that the American authorities could not, therefore, give an undertaking of the kind which Mr. Oumansky suggested. So far as he had been able to ascertain, no restrictions on the import or sale of Soviet gold were being considered at the present time. Nevertheless, he doubted that any commitments could be made.

The Ambassador said that he felt confident that if the American Government was unable to give any formal undertaking not to restrict the sale of Soviet gold in the United States during the coming year an informal letter to the effect that no such restrictions were being contemplated at the present would be sufficient. In his personal opinion there was no great danger of such restrictions being placed upon the imports of Soviet gold. He did not, therefore, attribute as much importance to the matter apparently as did his Government. Mr. Welles asked Mr. Henderson to have prepared a memorandum for him on the subject of our policies with respect to gold.

DIFFICULTIES ENCOUNTERED BY SOVIET ENGINEERS WITH THE WRIGHT AERONAUTICAL PLANT IN PATERSON, NEW JERSEY

The Soviet Ambassador said that he now desired to pass on to a matter which had been the subject of several conversations between members of the Department, including Mr. Moffat, Mr. Feis, Mr. Henderson and himself. He referred to the exclusion of Soviet engineers from certain sections of the Wright Aeronautical Plant in Paterson, New Jersey.

The Ambassador went on to explain that an agreement for technical assistance had existed for a number of years between the Wright Aeronautical Plant and an agency of the Soviet Government; that under this agreement the Wright plant was obligated to furnish the Soviet engineers plans of improvements and new devices and to permit them to enter the plant in order to observe the manufacturing processes called for in the production of new types of equipment; that this contract had worked out satisfactorily until seven or eight months ago; and that subsequently Soviet engineers allegedly under orders of American Governmental authorities had been restricted to certain parts of the plant and were thus not able to obtain the information called for in the contract. In consequence of these restrictions Soviet engineers have been placed in a humiliating position. In the first place they have themselves been wasting their time. In the second place they have been given to feel that they were considered as less worthy of trust than engineers of other countries who were being allowed to enter sections of the plant from which they were being excluded.

The Ambassador said that in reply to previous protests which he had made to the Department relating to this subject he had been informed that no discrimination against Soviet engineers existed. He had been given to understand that the engineers only of those countries for which airplanes were being manufactured in mass production were being given privileges denied to the Soviet engineers. He had learned, however, that such was not the case. Although airplanes were not being made in large numbers for China, for instance, nevertheless Chinese engineers were being admitted in parts of the plant from which Soviet engineers were being excluded. This contract of technical assistance was extremely important to the Soviet Union. It would lose its meaning unless some arrangements could be made which would permit the Soviet engineers to go into all parts of the plants except naturally those parts where work was actually being done on secret devices for the American Government. He firmly believed that some kind of a *modus vivendi* could be found whereby Soviet engineers could be admitted at least to those parts of the plant, admittance to which was necessary for the proper functioning of the agreement.

Mr. Welles replied that he considered that the suggestion of the Ambassador was reasonable and that he would look into the matter at once and discuss it later with the Ambassador. The Ambassador said that he could give personal assurances that the Soviet engineers would show full respect for all secrets of American national defense and would not take advantage of such privileges as might be granted them in accordance with their contracts.

INCORRECT DECISIONS OF COURTS IN THE UNITED STATES WITH RESPECT TO CONDITIONS IN THE SOVIET UNION

The Ambassador stated that the next question which he desired to discuss related to actions taken by the Judicial Branch of the Government. He realized the independence of both branches and the reluctance of the Executive Branch to take any action which might be considered as an infringement upon the independence of the Judicial Branch. He hoped, however, that the Executive Branch of the Government could give certain explanations to the Judicial Branch with regard to conditions in the Soviet Union with respect to which the Judicial Branch apparently was without knowledge.

He wished in particular to refer to a question which had arisen during the last year relating to the transfer of the residue of estates from the United States to the Soviet Union. The amounts affected were modest but the principle was important. In November 1939, the Surrogate Court of King's County, New York, in deciding not to approve the transfer of certain property to heirs in the Soviet Union stated that private property in the Soviet Union had been abolished. This decision served as a signal to the courts in various other counties in New York and in other states. A series of decisions of a similar character have followed. It must be quite well known to the Department of State that the statement made by the Surrogate Court of King's County was not in accordance with fact; the constitution of the U. S. S. R. itself takes cognizance of private property rights in the Soviet Union.

Mr. Welles stated that this matter had not previously been brought to his attention and he suggested that the Ambassador send a description to Mr. Henderson of the various cases in which the decision in question and similar decisions had been made, together with the appropriate citations. He assured the Ambassador that upon receipt of this information, the Department would be glad to investigate the matter.

ANNOYANCES SUFFERED BY SOVIET CITIZENS IN THE UNITED STATES AS THE RESULT OF PERSECUTIONS BY FEDERAL AND STATE AUTHORITIES

The Ambassador stated that during the past year there had been an endless number of incidents involving mistreatment of Soviet citizens in the United States by State and Federal officials. Unfortunately the number of these cases was increasing. It would appear that Federal agents, as well as agents of the State, did not have instructions from the American Government regarding the manner in which Soviet citizens should be treated. Many of the 160 Amtorg officials who had recently departed from the United States had left because of the humiliations which they had suffered while in the country. Numbers of them had told him frankly that they could not tolerate the type of treatment which had been meted out to them and would not live in a country in which they were compelled to suffer such indignities.

The Ambassador described in some detail a number of cases in which Soviet engineers and other Soviet citizens had been detained or arrested on suspicion by Federal or local authorities, had been subjected to examination, and had been given inconsiderate, if not insulting, treatment while being examined. He mentioned the case of the arrest of the two engineers in Pittsburgh and referred to a recent incident in Baltimore in which Federal police had seized and examined the baggage of Soviet engineers and had compelled one of them to parade through the corridors of the hotel in his underwear.

The Ambassador said that a number of incidents involving mistreatment of Soviet officials had already been reported to Mr. Henderson. Mr. Henderson stated that several cases had been brought to his attention; none of them, however, except that of the arrest of the engineers in Pittsburgh,[72] had involved Federal officials. Mr. Henderson said that furthermore he did not feel that any of the cases, except the Pittsburgh case, which had been reported to him were of a serious nature. They seemed to him to represent mere instances of temporary detention by perhaps overzealous local authorities of Soviet engineers traveling through the country. No evidence had been submitted which would show that these detentions were other than a part of the efforts of the local authorities to make sure that the aliens in the area for the order of which they were responsible were not engaged in activities contrary to the laws of the United States.

Mr. Welles suggested that the Ambassador cause to be prepared a memorandum describing in some detail instances of mistreatment of Soviet citizens, and that the memorandum be given to Mr. Henderson.

The Ambassador said that he wished to refer to difficulties which Soviet officials and members of Amtorg had been encountering with respect to admittance into the United States and to the extension of visas. These Soviet citizens had often been compelled to wait for months for the receipt of replies to petitions for the extension of permits to reside in the United States. There were also cases in which Soviet engineers or members of their families had been detained in Ellis Island upon their arrival in the United States, despite the fact that they had been in possession of valid visas issued by the American Embassy at Moscow. He had been told in the Department that the possession of a valid American visa did not necessarily guarantee that the immigration authorities would admit any alien into the United States.

---

[72] On July 6, Ambassador Umansky had made representations to Mr. Henderson in regard to the alleged mistreatment of two Soviet engineers, Viktor Chichkov and Viktor Korsoun, by the police of Pittsburgh, Pennsylvania. After a series of investigations, in a conversation on October 2, Mr. Atherton read to the Ambassador the report on the incident received from the Governor of Pennsylvania, which denied any mistreatment of the engineers and described how they had been arrested for intoxication, disorderly conduct, and for involvement in a street brawl. As the Ambassador was not disposed to accept this explanation of the affair, Mr. Atherton proposed that the Soviet Embassy and the Department of State should each make their own records and that the matter be considered closed. Apparently no further representations were made.

Mr. Henderson stated that such was in fact the case. The immigration authorities had the right to investigate and to reject aliens entering the United States even though the travel documents of such aliens might be in order. Mr. Henderson asked if there had been any recent cases of detention in Ellis Island and the Ambassador referred to the detention several weeks ago of a Soviet official who had departed on the *President Washington* and had been compelled to return with that vessel when it had changed its course upon instructions from the American Government, and instead of going to Genoa, had proceeded only as far as Lisbon.

The Ambassador said he desired to dwell upon one case which had been particularly irritating to the Soviet Government. That was the case of Bookkniga. It would be recalled that Bookkniga had been prosecuted for having failed properly to register as the agent of a foreign Power.[73] The fact was that Bookkniga had registered and had been given to understand that its registration was in order. Nevertheless, upon the flimsiest of technicalities a case had been built up against it. The officials of the corporation, which had been engaged in importing and exporting printed matter between the United States and the Soviet Union, had been coerced into confessions of guilt and had been fined. In pursuance of an agreement with the authorities they had pleaded guilty and had been released upon the payment of a fine. As a final insult, however, the Federal authorities during the 20 minutes which elapsed between the filing of the plea of guilty and the payment of the fine handcuffed them and permitted the press to photograph them. Some of the most learned professors in American law schools after a careful examination of this case had stated that the defendants had been indicted unlawfully and that charges against them were of an extremely technical nature.

As a result of the treatment given to Bookkniga, the corporation had ceased conducting business. It has since been almost impossible for American universities and learned institutions to obtain Soviet scientific and economic publications for their libraries.

PRONOUNCEMENTS OF OFFICIALS OF THE UNITED STATES GOVERNMENT HOSTILE TO THE SOVIET UNION

The Ambassador said that he desired now to discuss certain incidents in the political field which had given rise to much resentment in the Soviet Union. He referred in particular to pronouncements against the Soviet Union which had been made during recent months by responsible officials of the Government of the United States. Numerous statements of this nature had been made. He would limit his remarks, however, to three of them.

---

[73] See *Foreign Relations*, The Soviet Union, 1933–1939, pp. 926 ff.

In the first place he wished to refer to the recent pronouncement made by Mr. Welles relating to developments in the Baltic States. Statements of this kind made the task of improving relations between the two governments extremely difficult. He failed to understand why so violent exceptions should have been taken to the advancement of democracy in Eastern Europe. The American Government should realize that if the Soviet Government had not interfered to the extent of introducing Soviet democracy into certain areas in Eastern Europe, those areas would have fallen easy prey to an expanding movement which was the antithesis of democracy. An important section of public opinion in the United States viewed what had happened in the Baltic area in an open minded manner. They were pleased to see such doctrines as those which the present administration of the United States advocates, namely, social equality and reform and racial equality introduced into new areas in Eastern Europe. The Baltic people historically had lived together with the Russian people for a period longer than that during which the United States had been independent. It could not be understood why the resumption of normal relations between the Baltic people and the Russian people should have produced an expression from the American Government which was not the type of statement usually made by one government regarding another government maintaining friendly relations with it. The Ambassador said that in making this protest he wished it to be understood that he had no desire to place the conversation on a personal basis.

Mr. Welles replied that he understood the position of the Ambassador and that the Ambassador, of course, must realize that the statements to which the Ambassador referred were not an expression of personal views of Mr. Welles but that of the views of the American Government. The Ambassador replied that, if the views expressed were those of the American Government, the pronouncement was indeed serious.

The Ambassador said that the second statement to which he wished to take exception was the speech which had been made some time ago by Assistant Secretary of War Johnson before a group of American bankers in New York City.[74] He had already referred to this statement in conversations with Mr. Hull. During the course of this speech Mr. Johnson had made remarks which were insulting to the armed forces of the Soviet Union. He called them forces of bigotry and oppression. Other remarks contained in Mr. Johnson's speech were equally offensive to the Soviet Union. No replies had as yet been made to his protests with regard to this speech to the Secretary.

---

[74] See footnote 56, p. 249.

The Ambassador said that the third instance was the statement made on May 1, 1940, by General Marshall before a Congressional subcommittee to the effect that the Soviet Government was fortifying Big Diomede Island which lies only a few miles from American-owned islands adjacent to the Alaskan coast. He could not understand why such a statement had been made. Historically there never had been any contradictions between Russia and the United States. It seemed unfortunate that just at this time statements which might have the result of artificially creating such contradictions should be made. The impression created by these statements was that it was necessary for the United States to arm because of the menace of the Soviet Union. The Ambassador said that he could not understand why the head of the American Army should be taking such an attitude with respect to the Soviet Union.

Mr. Welles replied that he was not acquainted with the nature of the statements nor with the situation which had given rise to them. He could only infer from what the Ambassador had told him that General Marshall must have had cause to believe that the island in question was being fortified, and that that fact would be of interest to members of the Congressional committee. He said that he would be glad to look into this matter.

There were further complaints, the Ambassador continued, which he could register with respect to unfriendly statements which had been made by American governmental officials. Some of these statements had been made by persons in much higher positions than those whose names he had already mentioned. He considered, however, that it might be in bad taste and probably would serve no purpose to register protests against statements emanating from such high sources.

Mr. Welles called the attention of the Ambassador to the fact that during their first conversation regarding Soviet-American relations, the Ambassador had mentioned the statement made by Mr. Welles with regard to Soviet actions in the Baltic States. At that time it was agreed that with respect to this point the two governments would agree to disagree but that they would endeavor, so far as possible, to eliminate other points of disagreement between them. The Ambassador, however, had raised this question again. In the same friendly spirit in which the Ambassador had made his protests Mr. Welles would therefore endeavor to reply to them.

For almost 20 years, Mr. Welles continued, the American Government has looked with sympathy upon certain aspects of the foreign policy of the Soviet Union, namely, the apparent desire of the Soviet Government for peace. It was unfortunately the view of the United States that the policy of the Soviet Union had undergone a change during the last year. The invasion of Finland last winter [75] was regarded in the United States as an unprovoked attack by a great Power upon a small neighboring country. The ties of friendship between the United States and Finland were close. There were many persons in this country who were of Finnish origin or who had relatives in Finland. People in the United States admired the genius of the Finnish people and Finnish institutions. Somewhat similar sentiments existed with respect to the three Baltic countries which recently had been invaded by Soviet forces. In view of the well established policy of the American Government, it was impossible to let these things pass unnoticed and undeplored at a time when the forces standing for international law and order must hold firmly against tendencies towards agression and the use of force.

Mr. Welles said that in this connection he felt impelled to refer to a matter which he would not have mentioned if the Ambassador had not just made his complaints. He wished to point out that unfriendly remarks with regard to the United States had been made by Soviet officials. Not long ago, for instance, Mr. Molotov had declared that the United States Government was imperialistic and was keeping Cuba under its domination. [76]

With respect to the speech made by Mr. Johnson, Mr. Welles continued, the American Government did not consider that address as an official pronouncement. So far as contradictions between the United States and the Soviet Union were concerned, he agreed that there was no occasion whatsoever for any conflict of interest between the two countries. The remarks which had already been made belonged to the past. He hoped that in the future there would be no occasion for the making of further statements by the American Government or American officials critical of the foreign policy of the Soviet Union.

The Ambassador stated that he regretted that the impression should have been created in the United States that the policy of peace of the Soviet Union belonged to the past. Soviet policy had not changed. The situation had altered. It was not the fault of the Soviet Government that the system of collective security had collapsed. The Ambassador himself had been in Moscow during the period of the negotiations which had resulted in the signing of the non-aggression pact between the Soviet Union and Germany. [77] He therefore could per-

---

[75] See *Foreign Relations*, 1939, vol. I, pp. 952 ff.
[76] See telegram No. 847, November 1, 1939, from the Ambassador in the Soviet Union, *Foreign Relations*, The Soviet Union, 1933–1939, p. 786.
[77] Signed at Moscow on August 23, 1939; for text, see Department of State, *Nazi-Soviet Relations, 1939–1941* (Washington, Government Printing Office, 1948), p. 76; or *Documents on German Foreign Policy, 1918–1945*, series D, vol. VII, p. 245.

sonally vouch for the truth of the statements which he had made above.

The Ambassador said that he had returned to the United States with a message from Stalin suggesting that peace might possibly be brought about by the common efforts of the United States and the Soviet Union. No answer to this suggestion had ever been made. It was unfortunate that Soviet relations with countries the foreign and internal policies of which were in sharp contradiction with those of the Soviet Union, seemed to develop more satisfactorily than relations with countries with which the Soviet Union had much in common. The desire for security had forced the Soviet Union to improve its international position. The steps which the Soviet Government had taken during the last year were not in contradiction to its previous record.

Mr. Welles replied that there could be no question that the government and people of the United States had assumed that the policies of the Soviet Government had undergone a change. He was therefore extremely interested in the statements made by the Ambassador to the effect that no such change had taken place. The Ambassador had pointed out that a change had occurred in the international situation. This statement was, of course, true, and that is precisely one of the reasons why the two governments should endeavor to work out some practical method for closer cooperation. The forces represented by the Soviet Union and the United States should work together more closely during these troublesome periods.

The Ambassador said that Mr. Welles was making statements of real importance and was looking ahead.

The Ambassador stated that he had no more complaints to register at the present time. When the conversations started it had been his intention to protest on fifteen different points. However, in view of the spirit in which they were being conducted he had decided that it would be better to limit his protests to matters of real importance; therefore he had reduced the number to nine. In summarizing the result of the day's conversations, he understood that:

(1) The freezing of the Baltic funds would, if possible, be discussed at the next conference.

(2) The question of the issuance of licenses for Soviet machine tools would be studied by the Embassy and would be discussed further at the next conference.

(3) The American Government would take into consideration his comments with respect to effects of the moral embargo upon Soviet-American trade.

(4) The matter of Bookkniga and similar instances of persecution would be considered as a thing of the past.

(5) The matter of the sale of Soviet gold in the United States would also be discussed at the next meeting.

(6) The Soviet Embassy would prepare and give to Mr. Henderson a memorandum setting forth some of the cases in which Soviet engineers in this country had been mistreated by Federal and local authorities.

(7) The Soviet Embassy would furnish Mr. Henderson a memorandum regarding the decisions of the American courts to which the Soviet Government took exception.

The Ambassador said that he was especially pleased at the spirit in which outstanding differences had been discussed. Mr. Welles stated that he hoped that the conferences could continue on the same plane and suggested that questions relating to political matters be regarded as closed.

Monday, August 12, at 3 p. m. was tentatively set as the date for the next meeting.[78]

711.61/746½

Memorandum of Conversation, by the Assistant Chief of the Division of European Affairs (Henderson)

[WASHINGTON,] August 12, 1940.

Participants: Mr. Constantine A. Oumansky, Soviet Ambassador;
Mr. Sumner Welles, Acting Secretary of State;
Mr. Ray Atherton, Acting Chief, Division of European Affairs;
Mr. Loy W. Henderson, Assistant Chief, Division of European Affairs.

Mr. Welles and Mr. Oumansky engaged in a further conversation this afternoon regarding various problems of American-Soviet relations. At the request of Mr. Welles, Mr. Atherton and Mr. Henderson were also present.

The Soviet Ambassador stated that he understood that there were four problems to be discussed in this conference—namely, 1) the retention in the United States of Baltic gold; 2) the attitude of the American Government with respect to the issuing of export licenses covering merchandise destined for the Soviet Union; 3) the so-called moral embargo; 4) the difficulties encountered by Soviet engineers in the Wright Aeronautical Plant at Paterson, New Jersey. The Ambassador suggested that these problems be taken up in the order indicated.

---

[78] See *infra*.

TRANSFERS OF ASSETS OF BALTIC COUNTRIES IN THE UNITED STATES

Mr. Welles agreed to the Ambassador's suggestion. He thereupon handed the Ambassador 1) a copy of the memorandum [79] which Mr. Thurston had been instructed to give to the Assistant People's Commissar for Foreign Affairs in reply to the Soviet memorandum [80] protesting at the retention of Baltic gold in this country, and 2) a copy of the first-person note [79] which the American Chargé d'Affaires in Moscow has been instructed to address to the People's Commissar for Foreign Affairs informing the Commissar that the American Government was holding the Soviet Government responsible for certain losses inflicted upon American citizens in territories under Soviet control. When giving these documents to the Soviet Ambassador, Mr. Welles suggested that the Ambassador might desire to read them at his leisure; that if the Ambassador cared to discuss them, he could do so at another conference. The Ambassador agreed.

ROUTING OF MAILS FROM THE SOVIET UNION TO THE UNITED STATES

Mr. Welles suggested that before passing to the second point on the agenda he would like to reply to an inquiry which the Ambassador had made at the preceding conference. During the course of that conference the Ambassador had stated that recent mails from Moscow had come to him with unusual speed and he would like to know the route over which they had come. Inquiries to the Post Office Department had elicited the information that these mails had passed through Vladivostok and crossed the Pacific Ocean. Mr. Welles said that it would appear that mails were coming with greater speed along this route because there had been better timing of their arrival at various ports with the departure of westward bound vessels.

EXPORT LICENSES FOR MACHINE TOOLS

With respect to some of the problems that had been raised involving licenses, Mr. Welles said that he was very glad to inform the Ambassador that in view of the desire of the American Government to demonstrate the friendly spirit in which the present conversations were taking place, arrangements had been made for the immediate issuance of export licenses covering all merchandise ordered by Soviet agencies which was not needed in the United States. In other words, licenses were being granted at once which would make it possible to export without delay various machine tools contained in the list numbered (2) which had been handed to the Ambassador at the last conference.

---

[79] The text, which was presented in Moscow on August 12, 1940, was sent to the Chargé in the Soviet Union in the Department's telegram No. 423, August 9, 6 p. m., vol. I, p. 410.

[80] Text quoted in telegram No. 885, July 20, 9 p. m., from the Chargé in the Soviet Union, vol. I, p. 395.

303207—58——24

The Ambassador stated that he appreciated this information very much. The action of the American Government in releasing these machine tools would advance Soviet-American trade.

Mr. Welles stated that in order to expedite the elimination of problems relating to machine tools, he would appreciate having as early as possible such information as the Ambassador might desire to give him relative to the various machine tools contained in list numbered (1) which, in the Ambassador's opinion, should be released. He also hoped that information would be furnished at once which might be useful in deciding whether orders could be placed for the purpose of substituting new machine tools for those which must be detained.

The Ambassador said that he was afraid that he must disappoint Mr. Welles. He had made a careful study of the list of tools which the American Government proposed to retain. He and his technical advisers had worked very hard on this matter. They found, however, that the picture was such that the ceding of any articles contained in this list would cause heavy losses to certain branches of Soviet industry. These machines had been ordered with much care and at great expense. Each machine was for a definite purpose and the failure of any machine to take the place for which it was destined would be sure to result in considerable disorganization. The fact must not be overlooked that some of this machinery, as a result of certain policies of the American Government, had already been detained in the United States for a period of five or six months. The damage which had already been done to Soviet industry in consequence of the delays encountered in the export of machinery from this country, delays which had not been the fault of the Soviet Government or Soviet organizations, was tremendous.

Mr. Oumansky stated that Mr. Molotov, himself, had suggested that the conversations, with respect to the solution of problems at hand, should be placed on an entirely different basis—that is, that they should follow the lines laid down by Mr. Mikoyan in his conversation of July 30 with Mr. Thurston. It would be recalled that Mr. Mikoyan had made the following proposals: (1) that assurances be given that the United States Government would consider in a favorable spirit applications of firms for licenses for export to the Soviet Union of merchandise ordered after July 2, 1940; (2) that an assurance would be given that manufactured goods ordered by Soviet purchasing agencies prior to the President's Proclamation of July 2 would be released and that all export licenses issued for goods purchased or ordered after July 2, 1940 would be considered as irrevocable; (3) that assurance would be given that impediments to Soviet-American trade such, for instance, as those obstacles created by the so-called moral embargo, would be removed; (4) that a general assurance would be given that trade with the Soviet Union would not be discriminated against, and, in particular, that the Soviet Government would not be subjected to discrimination with respect to the purchase of gold by the Government of the United States.

The Ambassador recalled the fact that Mr. Mikoyan had asked that exchanges of letters on the subjects mentioned above take place in connection with the signing of the trade agreement. Mr. Thurston had suggested to the Commissar, however, that those subjects be discussed in conversations independent of any trade agreement negotiations. Exchanges of letters were very desirable since they were needed for purposes of precision and in order to restore the confidence of the Soviet authorities in the stability of trade with the United States.

Mr. Welles informed Mr. Oumansky that in principle the American Government would have no objection to exchanges of letters with respect to various points on which they might be able to come to agreement. He felt certain that it would not be possible for the United States Government to give all of the undertakings which had been requested by Mr. Molotov and Mr. Mikoyan. With regard to the first point raised by Mr. Oumansky there could be no difference of minds. The American Government would consider in a friendly spirit applications by Soviet agencies for licenses to enable them to export various machine tools to the Soviet Union.

Mr. Welles said that it was his understanding with regard to point no. 2 that the Soviet Government was asking the Government of the United States, notwithstanding the needs of the United States for certain machine tools, to issue licenses permitting such machine tools to be exported to the Soviet Union. His government could not agree to such a proposal. In his opinion the suggestion which he had advanced in previous conversations was a reasonable one—that is, that Mr. Oumansky and he go with care over the machine tools enumerated in list no. 1 in order to ascertain if any of these tools might be released without severe damage to American interests.

Mr. Oumansky pointed out that the value of machine tools contained in lists no. 1 and no. 2 aggregated roughly $4,000,000. The value of machine tools ordered by Soviet agencies in this country before July 2 which had not yet been delivered, totaled about $10,000,000. (Mr. Oumansky later telephoned that he had under-estimated the value and should have said $15,000,000.) Licenses for all of these machine tools had not been applied for at the time lists no. 1 and 2 had been compiled. Since August 3, applications for licenses had been submitted by Soviet agencies to the Department covering machine tools of a much greater value than the value of machine tools contained in the lists no. 1 and 2 combined. The Ambassador proceeded to analyze the various categories of machine tools for which licenses had been applied. Roughly, there were approximately 925 different items involved. He said that the Soviet Government recognized and respected the needs of the national defense of the United States. It realized that such needs were bound to affect the character and volume of Soviet purchases in that country. Nevertheless, in spite of this fact it seemed certain that if a basis could be found for eliminating present difficulties, Soviet purchases in the United States would increase enormously without in any way interfering with the American defense program. He had gone carefully through each item contained in list no. 1. He must repeat that the loss to the Soviet Union of any one item would create disorganization and loss of production. Furthermore, he was confident that practically all of the items listed could be spared without perceptively affecting the interests of American defense. Soviet needs in comparison with American production were infinitesimal. He had found, for instance, that Soviet orders covering one type of lathes comprised less than $\frac{7}{10}$ of 1% of American production. The release of all the machines on list No. 1 would, after all, only partly compensate to the Soviet Government for the millions of dollars which it had lost as a result of delays in shipment.

Mr. Welles stated that he would suspend answer with respect to point No. 2 until the next conference and that during the interim he would give the matter further reconsideration. He said that he must admit that the problem was somewhat confused since the applications for licenses covering all Soviet purchases in this country had not as yet been received. Mr. Welles then requested Mr. Henderson to take steps to have drawn up at once, if possible for consideration at the next conference, two new lists enumerating all the machine tools for which Soviet agencies had applied for export licenses, and which had not been included in the two lists already compiled. The first of the new lists should embrace those machines which could not be released and the second list those which could be exported. He said that it was only fair, however, that the Ambassador should understand that national needs must have first consideration. He still adhered to the conviction that the only proper procedure would be to go over the lists item by item. Mr. Oumansky asked if he could be accompanied at the next meeting by Mr. Lukashev, the President of Amtorg, who could discuss various technical problems. Mr. Welles replied that there would be no objection to the presence of Mr. Lukashev at the conference.

Mr. Oumansky said that in connection with the granting of export licenses covering machine tools, he wished again to emphasize the suggestion made by Mr. Mikoyan that the American Government agree that export licenses issued to Soviet agencies at the time of purchasing of machine tools be considered as irrevocable. The issuance of irrevocable licenses would do much to dispel some of the elements of uncertainty and lack of confidence which at present existed.

Mr. Welles replied that for the American Government to give such an understanding might well be considered as an act of discrimination unless similar assurances would be given to other governments. No sovereign government under present world conditions could promise that regardless of what might transpire in the future, certain machinery which might be of great value to its national defense would be permitted to leave the country. The American Government could not, on August 12, in view of the rapidly shifting world situation, state irrevocably that it would not, say on September 1, be in sore need of certain machine tools.

Mr. Oumansky replied that in view of the exceptional losses which the Soviet Government had suffered as a result of American policies during the last six months, the American Government might find some means of giving exceptional treatment to Soviet orders placed in the United States during the coming year. Mr. Welles said that inescapable facts must be taken into consideration as a basis for any negotiations. One of the facts that must not be overlooked was that the United States must place first the interests of national defense.

Mr. Oumansky pointed out that the American Government seemed to be overlooking the tremendous damages which it had caused the Soviet Union during the past months. It was true that the American Government had assured the Soviet Government that it would reimburse it for any machinery which might be requisitioned. It should bear in mind, however, that the losses to the Soviet Government were much greater than the mere purchase price of the machines.

THE MORAL EMBARGO

The Soviet Ambassador said that it was his understanding that the next point to be discussed was that of the moral embargo. Mr. Welles agreed. He stated that the so-called moral embargo had been instituted for the purpose of preventing private industry from implementing by the sale of supplies and technical knowledge certain policies of various foreign governments. Naturally, when the situation which had given rise to the moral embargo no longer existed, the embargo also should cease. In case the two governments should find it possible to solve the various problems in their relations, and if the situation which had given rise to the moral embargo no longer existed, the moral embargo would naturally be lifted. It should be understood, however, that in case the situation continued to exist, the moral embargo must stay in force.

Mr. Oumansky inquired if it was to be understood from the remarks of Mr. Welles that the matter of the moral embargo was to be considered as an organic part of the present conversations. Mr. Welles replied in the negative. He said that the moral embargo resulted from a certain situation which could have no connection with the present conversations and therefore it could not be considered as a part of the present negotiations. Suppose, he continued, that a certain country, which might be referred to as Tasmania, pursued certain policies which caused the American Government to declare that the so-called moral embargo be applied to it. If, at a later date, it should become clear that Tasmania no longer pursued such policies, the moral embargo would be lifted. If, however, after the moral embargo had been lifted, Tasmania should again resort to the policies which resulted in the application of this embargo, naturally the embargo would again be applied.

Mr. Oumansky said that he understood from the remarks of Mr. Welles that the American Government considered that acts of enforcing the moral embargo were of a unilateral, not a bilateral, nature. Mr. Welles replied in the affirmative.

Mr. Oumansky said that the attitude of the American Government with regard to the moral embargo raised important questions which must be referred to his government. In the meantime he wished again to express the hope that the American Government would without delay lift the embargo or take some act to mitigate its effect on Soviet-American trade. Such an act should be of a retroactive nature. He felt that he must also make one reservation—that is, it was the firm conviction of his government, supported by the evidence of American citizens who had been in Finland, that there had been no situation justifying the application of the embargo to the Soviet Union.

ASSURANCES OF NON-DISCRIMINATION AGAINST SOVIET TRADE

The Ambassador said that point No. 4 raised by Mr. Mikoyan related to the general subject of discrimination in the United States against trade with the Soviet Union. The Soviet Government felt, in view of what had transpired during the past 12 months, that such assurances were necessary for the stabilization of Soviet-American trade.

Mr. Henderson remarked that in the commercial agreement which had just been signed,[81] there were the usual assurances of non-discrimination. Mr. Oumansky replied that such assurances had been included in the commercial agreement which expired on August 5;[82] nevertheless, discrimination had taken place. Soviet merchandise,

---

[81] For correspondence concerning the renewal of the commercial agreement by an exchange of notes signed on August 6, see pp. 441 ff.

[82] For correspondence on the negotiation of the commercial agreement effected by an exchange of notes signed on August 2, 1939, see *Foreign Relations, The Soviet Union, 1933–1939*, pp. 809 ff.

for instance, had been retained by Customs authorities in the United States in accordance with procedures which had not been applied to merchandise destined for other countries. New assurances which were of a more precise and emphatic nature were necessary. Special undertakings were required with respect to the ability of the Soviet Government to charter American vessels and to sell gold in the United States.

Mr. Welles said that he had already informed Mr. Oumansky that it was not the present intention of the American Government to discriminate against any government with respect to the purchase of gold. This matter had been taken up with the Treasury and he suggested that discussion of the subject be postponed until the next morning.

Mr. Welles said it had been his understanding that the question with respect to charters had already been answered. Mr. Oumansky replied that his government felt that more formal undertakings with respect to these matters were desirable. Mr. Welles suggested that these questions be taken up again in subsequent conversations.

The Alleged Discrimination Against Soviet Engineers at the Wright Aeronautical Plant at Paterson, New Jersey

The Soviet Ambassador said that he wished again to refer to the discriminatory manner in which Soviet engineers at the Wright Aeronautical Plant at Paterson, New Jersey, were being treated. Mr. Welles stated that this matter had already been given attention and was to be discussed with the appropriate governmental authorities later on in the afternoon. He therefore would ask that it also be carried over to the next meeting.

The Desirability of an American Consulate in Vladivostok

Mr. Welles stated that during the recent conversations Mr. Oumansky had on several occasions referred to the mutual benefits which could be derived from satisfactory trade relations between the two countries. He said that some time ago the American Chargé d'Affaires at Moscow had asked the People's Commissar for Foreign Affairs what the Soviet attitude would be with regard to the opening of an American consular office in Vladivostok.[83] The American Government was inclined to believe that such an office might be useful in the advancement of American-Soviet trade relations, particularly in case the present conversations should develop satisfactorily. He added that he would appreciate it if Mr. Oumansky would inquire of his government regarding the status of this matter. Mr. Oumansky said he would be glad to do so.

---

[83] See telegram No. 995, August 9, 10 a. m., from the Chargé in the Soviet Union, p. 460.

861.20111/2

Memorandum of Conversation, by the Assistant Chief of the Division of European Affairs (Henderson)

[WASHINGTON,] August 15, 1940.

Captain Sherman and Lieutenant Commander Oliver, who represents the Navy in the Wright Aeronautical Plant at Paterson, New Jersey, came in to see me this afternoon.

They said that they were considering the advisability of cutting down the privileges granted to the Chinese engineers in the plant so that the Russians could not claim discrimination. I told them that what the Russians wanted was not curtailment of privileges to the Chinese but more privileges for themselves. I asked if, in view of our desire at the present time to come to a better understanding with the Russians, it might not be possible for them to make some kind of a friendly gesture by giving the Russians a little more leeway in the plant without endangering in any degree the public interests of the United States.

Lieutenant Commander Oliver said that one of the difficulties with the Russians arose from the fact that there were about 20 of them in the plant; that they apparently wanted to roam almost at will through those portions of the plant which were not regarded as strictly secret. Employees of the Wright plant had resented the manner in which the Russians had been allowed to see almost everything despite the fact that signs were posted by the Company enjoining secrecy on the part of the employees. The rule had been formerly that the Russians would go around in groups—that is, three Russians accompanied by an official of the Wright plant. These groups were very inquisitive and their presence had not contributed to the work of production. Furthermore, there was a fear on the part of both ONI [84] and MID [85] that the Soviet engineers, after obtaining a thorough knowledge of the layout of the plant, might communicate what they had learned to certain subversive elements in the United States.

Captain Sherman and Commander Oliver stated that, in view of our hope that some sort of a gesture to the Russians could be made, they would hold a conference with the representatives of the Army in the plant and try to devise some means to let the Russians see more of what was going on without interfering with production or endangering public interests. They said that there was one suggestion they would like to have made to Mr. Oumansky—namely, that the number of Russian engineers in the plant be reduced. It was absurd for 20 Soviet engineers to be stationed in a plant of this kind since it

[84] Office of Naval Intelligence, Department of the Navy.
[85] Military Intelligence Division, War Department.

was obviously impossible to be showing to all of them simultaneously the various processes of production. If the number could be reduced to three or four it would be much easier to give these few men a thorough knowledge of the manufacturing methods employed. They further suggested that pending the outcome of the conversations, Mr. Oumansky might be informed that a thorough examination of the situation was being made and that within a few days it would be possible to determine what, if any, changes could be made which would give the Soviet engineers a better opportunity to observe the manufacturing processes.

I said that it was my feeling that it would not be appropriate for the details of any scheme which might be worked out, such as the number of men to be kept at the plant, to be discussed during the conversations between Mr. Welles and Mr. Oumansky. Such details should preferably be worked out at the plant. I promised, however, to pass the views expressed by them on to the Acting Secretary.

711.61/743½

Memorandum of Conversation, by the Assistant Chief of the Division of European Affairs (Henderson)

[WASHINGTON,] August 15, 1940.

Participants: Mr. Sumner Welles, Acting Secretary of State;
Mr. Constantine A. Oumansky, Soviet Ambassador;
Mr. Ray Atherton, Acting Chief, Division of European Affairs;
Mr. Loy W. Henderson, Assistant Chief, Division of European Affairs.

Late this afternoon another conversation took place between Mr. Welles and the Soviet Ambassador regarding certain problems of American-Soviet relations. At the request of Mr. Welles, Mr. Atherton and Mr. Henderson were present. Mr. Lukashev, the President of the Amtorg Trading Corporation, accompanied Mr. Oumansky.

Mr. Welles requested Mr. Oumansky to give suggestions as to the order of subjects to be discussed. Mr. Oumansky stated that it would perhaps be advisable first to discuss the lists of applications for export licenses which he understood Mr. Welles had caused to be prepared; then to take up one by one the questions of future policy with respect to export licenses, to the moral embargo, to assurances of non-discriminatory treatment, and to privileges to be allowed to Soviet engineers in the Wright Aeronautical Plant. After these matters had been examined, there were some additional subjects for discussion, during the course of which the presence of Mr. Lukashev would not be required. Mr. Welles agreed to this procedure.

Export Licenses Covering Merchandise Ordered or Purchased by Soviet Agencies in the United States Before July 2, 1940

Mr. Welles handed Mr. Oumansky four documents,[86] namely:

1. An amended copy of the list which has been referred to in previous conversations as List No. 1. (This list enumerates the machine tools ordered by the Soviet Union for which licenses have been applied prior to August 3, and which the American Government has decided should be retained in the United States.)

1a. A list supplementing List No. 1. (This list enumerates machine tools covering which, for the most part, applications for export licenses have been filed subsequent to August 3, and which the American Government has decided should be retained in the United States.)

2. An amended copy of List No. 2. (This list enumerates machine tools for which licenses have been applied for prior to August 3 and which the American Government has decided could be exported.)

2a. A list supplementing List No. 2. (This list enumerates machine tools applications for export licenses covering which have been filed for the most part subsequent to August 3. The machine tools on this list may be exported.)

Mr. Welles explained briefly the nature of the lists and pointed out that the American Government had found it necessary to transfer five machine tools from the original List No. 2 to List No. 1 since it had been decided that they were urgently needed in the United States. He said that he understood that these lists contained practically all of the machine tools ordered by Soviet agencies for which export licenses had been applied.

Mr. Oumansky thanked Mr. Welles for having had the lists prepared. He said that Mr. Welles already knew the point of view of his government. This point of view had been expressed in certain instructions which he had outlined during the course of the previous conversations, and with respect to which there had been no change. It would therefore serve no purpose for Mr. Lukashev and himself to endeavor to analyze the lists which had just been given him. He must continue to adhere to the position that without exception all machine tools which had been ordered in the United States prior to July 2 should be released at once.

Mr. Welles replied that certain principles were here involved which he had attempted to make clear during previous conversations. The interests of the national defense must be superior to all other interests. He had devoted much time and energy in endeavors to assist the Soviet Government in obtaining without delay those machine tools which were not necessary for the national defense of the United States. To attain this end he had carried on discussions with ranking officials of the Army and Navy. The lists which he had just given to the Ambassador were the result of careful study by the highest

---

[86] None attached to file copy of this document.

military authorities of the American Government. When these authorities stated that the machine tools set forth in Lists No. 1 and 1*a* were necessary for the carrying out of the Government defense program, he could not ignore their statements. He was willing to go even further. He was prepared to enter into a careful and friendly study with the Soviet Ambassador and his assistants of the various items contained in Lists 1 and 1*a* in order to make sure that no machine tools set forth in them could possibly be spared.

Mr. Oumansky replied that he also had tried to make his point of view clear. He suggested that Mr. Lukashev might make a statement on the subject.

Mr. Lukashev said that he, of course, understood that the demands of national defense could not be ignored. He hoped, however, that the State Department could still prevail upon the appropriate American authorities to release all machines ordered by Soviet agencies before July 2. The State Department might explain that each of these machines fitted into a carefully worked out scheme of Soviet industry. The orders for some of them dated back to 1938 and 1939. Many American manufacturers in conversations with him had expressed amazement at the action of the American authorities in withholding machines manufactured for the Soviet Union when duplicates of them could be made almost immediately for the use of the American Government.

Mr. Welles stated that he had already made it clear that he was prepared to receive suggestions with respect to any machine tools enumerated in Lists 1 and 1*a* which Amtorg had reason to believe could not be used to advantage by the American Government or which could be duplicated for the American Government in a short time. Any information of a specific nature along these lines which could be furnished him would be received in a friendly manner.

Mr. Oumansky replied that it would be impossible for Mr. Lukashev to enter into a factual discussion of the lists which had been submitted to him since his Soviet clients had forbidden him to do so. His clients had taken the stand that there should be no retroactive action, so far as tools destined for the Soviet Union were concerned, in the enforcement of the Act of July 2, 1940. Furthermore, while private American manufacturers might be willing to talk privately with Mr. Lukashev, they would probably be unwilling to permit themselves to be quoted in, or to enter into, official conversations. He must adhere, therefore, strictly to the instructions of his government and request a quite different approach to the export license problem. He again referred to Mr. Mikoyan's proposals and said that he desired to call attention to the fact that Mr. Thurston had assured Mr. Mikoyan that the American Government would be willing to give friendly consideration to such proposals in conversations not related to the trade agreement. The Soviet Government and Soviet industry as a whole were involved in the discussions. Production schedules had been upset. It was imperative that the element of stability be re-introduced into Soviet-American trade.

Mr. Welles replied that he feared that the Soviet Ambassador and he were going rapidly into the direction of an impasse and that was precisely what he wished to avoid. If the Ambassador continued to insist that the conversations relating to machine tools must follow the lines just indicated, he was afraid the discussions on this subject must cease. He could only repeat to the Ambassador that it was the desire of the American Government to facilitate the granting of every possible license to the Soviet Government. If it should be found that any machine tools, the export of which had been denied, could be duplicated for the use of the American Government within a reasonable time, that information would be helpful. There would be no occasion for embarrassment to the manufacturers. It would not be necessary to quote them or to bring them into the conversations. Statements from the Ambassador or Mr. Lukashev to the effect that certain machines were not suitable for the use of the American Government or that certain machines could be speedily duplicated for the use of American industry would be sufficient to warrant a re-examination of the decisions covering the machines in question. It seemed to him that such a procedure was the correct approach. They could make no progress exchanging statements of principles with each other.

Mr. Oumansky said that he had the displeasure to agree with Mr. Welles that they were rapidly getting into an impasse. His point of view was not merely a matter of principle although it represented the platform of Mr. Mikoyan. It was also a matter of compensation for heavy losses incurred by the Soviet Government as a result of the protracted detention of machine tools which Soviet agencies had ordered in the United States months ago. He suggested that for the time being it be considered that the two governments had reached an impasse in their efforts to solve the problem of the detention of machine tools ordered prior to July 2. In the meantime he would convey to his government the new information which had just been given to him by Mr. Welles and ask for new instructions. He hoped that the American Government would consider again and yet again the proposals which he had made, so that discussion with respect to them could be resumed at a later meeting. It should be borne in mind, however, that hundreds of Mr. Lukashev's clients were pressing him for the machines which they had ordered through Amtorg.

Mr. Welles stated that he was prepared to postpone discussions of this problem until the next meeting. He felt that he must candidly state, however, that in his opinion the Government of the United States could not recede from the position which he had outlined. He was sure that if the Soviet Union would be faced with a similar situation its position would be no different from that of the American Government.

THE QUESTION OF THE ISSUANCE OF IRREVOCABLE EXPORT LICENSES FOR MACHINE TOOLS ORDERED BY THE SOVIET GOVERNMENT AFTER JULY 2

Mr. Oumansky stated that he wished at this time again to ask that the American Government would agree to issue irrevocable export licenses covering machine tools ordered by the Soviet agencies in the United States. His government took the view that unless such licenses could be issued at the time of the placing of orders, it could have no assurance that the goods purchased would ever be delivered. He therefore hoped that Mr. Welles could offer some kind of a constructive suggestion with regard to a formula which would meet the desires of the Soviet Government and at the same time be satisfactory to the American Government. If in the future irrevocable licenses would be issued whenever a Soviet order was placed, there would be little cause for new difficulties with regard to the detention of merchandise. The Soviet Government could then have the feeling of security which was necessary in the carrying on of normal trade between two countries.

Mr. Welles said that in the present insecure world situation it was difficult to give assurances which could afford absolute security. It would not [now?] be difficult to state that in the absence of a change in the world situation, licenses would rarely be revoked. In his opinion, a reasonable element of security could be achieved by constant and friendly cooperation between Amtorg and the American Governmental authorities charged with the consideration of export license applications. He could promise the Ambassador that the appropriate American authorities would deal in a sympathetic and cooperative manner with Amtorg. It would be impossible for them, however, to issue irrevocable licenses in view of the uncertainties of the international situation.

Mr. Oumansky said that he appreciated the first part of the statement made by Mr. Welles but regretted that the second part showed that the American position with respect to the issuance of irrevocable licenses had not changed. He hoped that perhaps it might be possible in spite of the difference in the views of the two governments to work out some formula that would be satisfactory to both. Mr. Welles stated that he would discuss this matter with the appropriate governmental authorities. It might be possible to devise a formula to the effect that it would be the policy of the American Government, in administering the export license law and regulations, to cause a minimum amount of inconvenience to Soviet purchasing agencies.

THE SO-CALLED MORAL EMBARGO

Mr. Oumansky raised the question as to the manner in which an exchange of statements relating to the so-called moral embargo might be formulated.

Mr. Welles said that he thought that he had made it clear to Mr. Oumansky during the last conversation that any statement which the Government of the United States might make with respect to the moral embargo must be of a unilateral nature. Mr. Oumansky inquired to whom and in what form such a statement might be made. Mr. Welles replied that in his opinion a declaration relating to the moral embargo should be made in a form similar to that of the announcement that such an embargo was in effect, namely, by a public statement. Mr. Welles said that he could summarize the position of the American Government by stating that: (1) any announcement relating to the moral embargo must be of a unilateral nature; (2) it could be made simultaneously with the successful conclusion of the present negotiations; and (3) it could be made only if the conditions which were responsible for the decision to declare such an embargo should no longer obtain.

Mr. Oumansky said that the position of the American Government in this respect was now clear to him.

ASSURANCES OF NON-DISCRIMINATION IN THE PURCHASE OF GOLD BY THE GOVERNMENT OF THE UNITED STATES

Mr. Oumansky said that in his opinion there should be no great difficulty with regard to the Soviet desire for assurances that the American Government would not discriminate against the Soviet Union in buying gold.

Mr. Welles replied that the Department had prepared a statement relating to its policy with respect to gold purchases. To this statement was attached the text of a speech which had been made recently by the Secretary of the Treasury.[87] He believed that the contents of the statement and of the speech should assure the Soviet Government that it was not the intention of the Government of the United States to discriminate against any country in purchasing gold. Mr. Welles thereupon read to Mr. Oumansky the statement, as well as certain paragraphs from the speech in which opposition was expressed to discriminating against any country in connection with the pur-

---

[87] Not attached to file copy of this document. For the address by Secretary of the Treasury Henry Morgenthau, Jr., on the gold holdings of the United States, given before the National Institute of Government at Washington on May 3, 1940, see S. Shepard Jones and Denys P. Myers (eds.), *Documents on American Foreign Relations, July 1939–June 1940* (Boston, World Peace Foundation, 1940), vol. II, p. 512.

chase of gold. Mr. Oumansky said that the statement and the text of the speech were helpful. He would like to give the matter consideration. It was his suggestion that the points in the statement and speech of importance to the Soviet Government be boiled down and incorporated in an exchange of letters between the two countries.

Mr. Welles said there would be no objection to incorporating what he had just read in a letter to the Soviet Government if the Soviet Government preferred a letter to a statement. A copy of the statement and letter are attached hereto.[88]

ALLEGED DISCRIMINATION AGAINST SOVIET ENGINEERS IN THE WRIGHT AERONAUTICAL PLANT AT PATERSON, NEW JERSEY

Mr. Oumansky asked if anything had been done as yet to relieve the situation of the Soviet engineers in the Wright Aeronautical Plant who were unable, because of the attitude of the American authorities, to visit portions of the plant in which processing of airplane motors and equipment was taking place.

Mr. Welles stated that he had personally talked the matter over with the Chief of Naval Operations [89] and that only this afternoon Mr. Henderson had had a conference with the Naval Inspector of the Wright Aeronautical Plant on the same subject. Both the Chief of Naval Operations and the Inspector had shown an interest in this matter, and it was hoped that within a week arrangements could be made which would remove grounds for complaint.

Mr. Oumansky thanked Mr. Lukashev for his assistance and told him he was no longer needed. Mr. Lukashev thereupon left the conference.

THE ATTITUDE OF THE UNITED STATES WITH RESPECT TO THE DIPLOMATIC MISSIONS AND CONSULAR OFFICES OF LITHUANIA, LATVIA, AND ESTONIA IN THE UNITED STATES

The Ambassador stated that there was another very urgent matter which must be discussed at this conference, a matter which he had already mentioned in a tentative manner to Mr. Atherton and Mr. Henderson. Following the incorporation of the countries of Lithuania, Latvia, and Estonia into the Soviet Union, diplomatic relations between those countries and other countries had ceased.[90] He had been ordered by his government to take possession of the property and archives of the diplomatic missions and consulates of these three Baltic States in the United States. He was, of course, acquainted with the statement which Mr. Welles had made with respect to the Baltic States on July 23, and which he had already discussed with

---

[88] Neither attached to file copy of this document.
[89] Adm. Harold R. Stark.
[90] For correspondence regarding the occupation of the Baltic States and their incorporation into the Soviet Union, see vol. I, pp. 357 ff.

Mr. Welles. This statement had not indicated, however, whether the American Government intended to continue to recognize the Legations and consulates of the countries in question in the United States. He had been unable to find any statement on this subject. In response to inquiries made by himself, Mr. Atherton and Mr. Henderson had replied that so far as they knew, no formal statement on the subject had been made public. He had before him the task of protecting the interests and property of the nationals of Lithuania, Latvia, and Estonia, and of taking possession of the archives and consulates of these States. He asked that the American Government assist him in the performance of this task. In making this request he would like to point out that the situation in the Baltic States could in no way be compared with the situation in certain countries which had lost their independence in an entirely different manner. He would like to suggest Austria as a possible precedent.

Mr. Welles replied that he was sure that the position of the American Government in this matter was clear. The public statement which he had made, as well as his remarks during the course of previous conversations with the Ambassador on the subject of the Baltic States, should leave no doubt that the United States could not recognize the absorption of these States by the Soviet Union. The Government of the United States, furthermore, continued to recognize the Legations and consulates of the Baltic States in this country. He did not consider that the situation of the Baltic States was analogous to that of Austria. He could cite a much more similar situation. He wished to remind the Ambassador that the Soviet Government had continued to recognize the Czechoslovak Legation in Moscow for a long period after Czechoslovakia had been occupied by the forces of another Power.

The Ambassador replied that the taking over of Czechoslovakia could not be compared to the entry of the Baltic States into the Soviet Union. He regretted that the American Government apparently did not appreciate the situation in the Baltic States. There was a difference between the re-inclusion into a great country of smaller countries which were historically a part thereof. The three Baltic States in question had always belonged to his country. In this connection it should be pointed out that the statement of July 28, 1922 [91] of the Government of the United States announcing the decision to recognize the three Baltic countries in question contained certain reservations opposing the alienation of Russian territory.

Mr. Henderson remarked that Mr. Oumansky had not given an entirely correct impression regarding the nature of the announcement.

---

[91] For text, see telegram No. 98, July 25, 1922, to the Commissioner at Riga, *Foreign Relations*, 1922, vol. II, p. 873.

Although the announcement did contain a statement of the opposition of the American Government to the alienation of Russian territory, it also stressed the fact that the recognition of the Baltic States was no departure from the American Government's policy in this respect since the governments of Lithuania, Latvia, and Estonia had been set up by an indigenous population and had maintained stability over a long period.

Mr. Oumansky said that he feared that the attitude of the American Government with regard to the Baltic States would make it difficult to achieve the purpose for which he understood the present conversations were being held—namely, to effect an improvement in the relations between the United States and the Soviet Union. So long as the United States Government addressed communications to the Soviet Government of such a nature as that stick of dynamite on the subject of the frozen Baltic funds which had been given to him at the last conference, an improvement in the relations between the two countries would not be easy to achieve. Those communications in form and content were not the type of communications which friendly governments customarily addressed to each other. He noticed in one of these communications such offensive expressions as "duress", "force", etc.

Mr. Welles stated that the communications in question were entirely of a factual nature, and if one considered the charges against the American Government to which they were a reply they could not be regarded as offensive. He pointed out that the Soviet memorandum to the American Government on the subject of the Baltic funds could certainly not be described as a communication of a friendly nature. The American Government was not accustomed to being accused of engaging in illegal acts or of violating principles of international law. Mr. Welles suggested, however, that no constructive purpose would be served by devoting time to matters of this kind.

It would appear that there were some problems between the two countries which it might not be possible to solve for the present. There were other difficulties which it might be possible to eliminate. The purpose of these conversations was to remove, so far as possible, all obstacles to good relations.

Mr. Oumansky stated that he was agreeable to keeping the conversations on the economic level. He could not refrain from adding, however, that differences between the two governments at higher levels might well sag down into the economic level and add to the difficulties of improving even economic relations between the two countries.

It was suggested by Mr. Welles that further conversations be postponed until Monday afternoon, August 19, at 4 o'clock.[92]

---

[92] No record of a conference on this date has been found in Department files.

191.1/499

The Chargé in the Soviet Union (Thurston) to the Secretary of State

No. 699   Moscow, August 19, 1940.
[Received September 17.]

Sir: I have the honor to inform the Department that Mr. V. A. Valkov, Chief of the Division of American Countries of the People's Commissariat for Foreign Affairs, today called to his office Mr. Ward of the Embassy staff and stated that it is the desire of the Soviet Government that the Embassy observe the practice followed by the other foreign displomatic missions in Moscow with regard to the payment of foreign consular fees, i. e., that Soviet currency be accepted in payment of such fees.

Mr. Ward explained to Mr. Valkov that fees collected by the Foreign Service are prescribed in the Tariff of United States Foreign Service Fees and are payable in United States currency or its equivalent in local currency. He also informed Mr. Valkov that since there is no means, other than under authority from the People's Commissariat for Finance in each instance, whereby rubles may be converted into United States currency, there is no free equivalent in Soviet currency for United States currency, and that notwithstanding the current rate of exchange observed by Soviet banks is Rubles 5.30 to $1.00 this rate of exchange is a free equivalent only in exchanging United States currency into Soviet currency, and that even Soviet currency received in consequence of such an exchange may not be re-exchanged into United States currency without special permission from the People's Commissariat for Finance. Mr. Valkov was informed that should arrangements be made whereby Soviet currency accepted by the Embassy in payment of fees may be converted into United States currency and/or bills of exchange on New York upon demand by the Embassy at the Bank for Foreign Trade of the Union of Soviet Socialist Republics, or any other bank in Moscow, it would seem that these arrangements would create what could be considered a free equivalent in Soviet currency for United States currency and that the Embassy would then be able to accept Soviet currency in payment of fees. Mr. Valkov stated that such an arrangement would hold no interest for the Soviet Government, which desires that the Embassy accept Soviet currency in payment of fees without any obligation on the part of his Government or any of its organs to redeem such currency in foreign currency—he added that the Soviet currency thus received could be applied to local expenses, upon which he was informed that funds received in payment of fees are remitted to the Treasurer of the United States, and that funds required for local expenses are obtained against bills of exchange drawn on the Treasurer of the United States or the

Secretary of State, a system precluding the adoption of the system suggested by him.

Mr. Valkov requested that the Embassy submit to the Department for consideration by the United States Government the request of the Soviet Government that special arrangements be made whereby Soviet currency may be accepted in payment of Foreign Service fees at the official rate of exchange without regard as to whether or not the Soviet currency thus accepted may be converted into United States currency. It was suggested that since the realization of the request set forth by him would probably require a change in existing statutes this request be stated in writing to which he replied that the request is clearly understood by the Embassy and he failed to perceive any need for it being formulated in writing.

In the ensuing conversation Mr. Valkov requested that the Embassy should inform its Government that should it not be able to accept Soviet currency at "the bank rate of exchange" (i. e., Rubles 5.30 to $1.00) the Soviet Government will be obliged to take "reciprocal action" in the matter of fees from American citizens. When questioned regarding the "fees" to which he had reference he made specific mention of Soviet residence permits (present fee Rubles 5.50) and copies of public records (present fee Rubles 11.00), upon which he was informed that all Soviet currency remitted by the Embassy in payment for copies of public records is purchased from the Bank for Foreign Trade unless the American citizen desiring the record is resident in the Soviet Union. It was further pointed out to Mr. Valkov that such action on the part of the Soviet Government would not be "reciprocal" but would constitute a discrimination against American citizens since the nationals of no other country are required to pay in foreign currency the fee for a Soviet residence permit, whereas "reciprocal action" would be the collection of fees in Soviet currency by the Soviet Embassy and the Soviet consular offices in the United States. Mr. Valkov stated that Soviet currency is not available in the United States since its exportation from the Soviet Union is prohibited by law, upon which he was reminded that by this statement he himself had explained why Soviet currency may not today be accepted in payment of American fees—Soviet currency thus accepted may not be remitted to the Treasurer of the United States. Mr. Valkov withdrew his request that the Embassy inform its Government of the previously mentioned "reciprocal action", and stated that the action which may be taken upon the receipt by the Soviet Government of a reply to its request that Soviet currency be accepted in payment of Foreign Service fees will be discussed subsequent to the receipt of such reply.

It was pointed out to Mr. Valkov that in accepting only United States currency in payment of fees the Embassy is not discriminating against Soviet citizens since American citizens and all non-American citizens alike are required to pay these fees in United States currency. He was reminded that in actual practice Soviet individuals and organizations enjoy a privilege under the Embassy's "exchange order" system not even enjoyed by American citizens (this system is explained in an accompanying memorandum [94]).

While the Soviet Government's request, as set forth orally by Mr. Valkov, is hereby submitted to the Department for its consideration, it is the Embassy's opinion that the desired special arrangements should not be made since the inability of the Embassy to accept Soviet currency as a local currency equivalent of United States currency issues not from any restriction set up by the United States Government but is the consequence of currency restrictions set up and enforced by the Soviet Government. Were the Soviet statutes and regulations restricting the buying and selling of Soviet currency removed, thereby permitting the ruble to become a free currency, the Embassy would be able to exchange rubles into dollars freely and could therefore accept Soviet currency in payment of Foreign Service fees.

Respectfully yours,   WALTER THURSTON

311.6121 Chichkov, Viktor

Memorandum of Conversation, by the Assistant Chief of the Division of European Affairs (Henderson)

[WASHINGTON,] August 20, 1940.

Mr. Gromyko, Counselor of the Soviet Embassy, came in to see Mr. Henderson this afternoon in order to present to him the attached memorandum.[94] This memorandum set forth instances in which Soviet citizens, particularly engineers, had been allegedly mistreated by American police or other officials.

In handing Mr. Henderson the memorandum Mr. Gromyko said that the instances described therein must be considered as merely illustrative since many more could be cited. These instances, he said, fell into three categories:

1. Cases in which Soviet citizens in this country on official business for the Soviet Government had been detained or treated discourteously by American police officers, local, or Federal.

---

[94] Not printed.

2. Cases in which Soviet engineers and other Soviet citizens entering the United States on official business for the Soviet Government had been detained or inconvenienced by United States immigration authorities, although in possession of valid visas.

3. Cases in which United States customs officials had examined the baggage of Soviet consular officers entering the country.

Mr. Gromyko discussed the first category of cases in some detail. He said that the Soviet Government was convinced that these cases of mistreatment of Soviet engineers and other Soviet citizens in this country were linked together and were systematic. It was felt that American Federal officials were responsible for the unfriendly attitude shown by the local police authorities to Soviet citizens. It was the request of the Soviet Government that the police officials responsible for the mistreatment described in the memorandum be instructed that there was no justifiable cause for the detentions which had taken place and that in the future every consideration was to be shown to Soviet citizens. It was also the desire of the Soviet Government that the appropriate Federal and State officials of the United States be informed by circular or other means, (*a*) that Soviet engineers, Amtorg officials, etc. in the United States were in the country legally and should be treated with consideration; (*b*) that if there was any doubt whatsoever regarding the status of any person claiming himself to be a Soviet citizen, such person should be permitted at his request to communicate by telephone with the appropriate Soviet consular office or with the Embassy in Washington in order to prove his identity. The Soviet Government desired assurances from the American Government that incidents of the kind described in the first part of the list should cease.

Mr. Henderson told Mr. Gromyko that he was convinced after glancing at the list of instances, that there could be no link between them. There was no systematic persecution of Soviet officials or citizens of the Soviet Union. In view of the present international situation, police officials throughout the United States were in general on the alert for so-called Fifth Columnists or persons engaging in activities injurious to public interests. It was not surprising, therefore, that strange aliens in many instances should be detained and examined. He was confident that the cases of detention and examination of Soviet citizens in the United States were rare in comparison with the detention and examination of citizens of a number of other countries.

Mr. Henderson also remarked that in view of the peculiar dual system of the American Governmental apparatus, it was difficult for the Federal Government to supervise rigidly the work of the local police authorities. It would therefore not be possible to give assurances that no instances similar to those which had taken place in the past would occur in the future. Mr. Henderson said that nevertheless he was sure that the proper steps would be taken in order to reduce the number of such cases to a minimum.

Mr. Gromyko said that the duty of the Soviet Embassy was to protect Soviet citizens in the United States. The Soviet Embassy was not interested in what happened to citizens of other countries. It must, however, under instructions from its government, insist that steps be taken which would terminate at once instances of the nature set forth in the memorandum. Mr. Henderson informed Mr. Gromyko that the statements which he just made would be brought to the attention of the appropriate officials of the American Government. Mr. Henderson said he could not refrain, however, from pointing out that it is the duty of American police officials in their efforts to protect the interests of the United States to investigate from time to time the activities of persons who, for some reason or other, might fall under suspicion. Among these persons there might conceivably be some Soviet citizens. In the Soviet Union similar problems existed. Dozens of cases of temporary detention of American citizens had been brought to the Embassy during the period that Mr. Henderson was in Moscow.[95] Most of these cases had not even been reported to the Foreign Office since it had been clear that the police, in detaining such American citizens, had been doing so merely for the purpose of ascertaining their identity and acquainting themselves with the nature of their activities. In Mr. Henderson's opinion it would be impossible for the American Government to issue instructions which might prevent the police from engaging in their usual activities of protecting American public interests.

Mr. Gromyko referred to the alleged mistreatment of Soviet citizens by immigration officials of the United States. He said that since August 1939 there apparently had been an almost systematic mistreatment of Soviet citizens entering the United States or already in the United States by immigration officials. He hoped that steps could be taken to make sure that Soviet citizens legally in this country would not be molested or inconvenienced by the action of American immigration officials.

Mr. Henderson told Mr. Gromyko that his statements would be given careful consideration. Mr. Gromyko should understand, however, that since the outbreak of the war immigration laws were being enforced with strictness and no relaxation in this respect could be expected in the immediate future. He was certain that if Soviet officials had been detained or inconvenienced, there were legal grounds therefor. In any event he was confident that there was no systematic

---

[95] For correspondence on the arrest and detention of American citizens by Soviet authorities, see *Foreign Relations*, The Soviet Union, 1933–1939, pp. 904 ff.

mistreatment of Soviet citizens. The cases which had been cited would be looked into and the matter could be discussed again at a later date.

Mr. Gromyko said that it was the feeling of the Soviet Government that if Soviet citizens upon entering the United States were in possession of valid Soviet visas, they should not be detained by the immigration authorities. In particular, the immigration authorities should not subject them to examination with respect to the persons for whom they had voted in the last Soviet elections, and so forth.

Mr. Henderson replied that it had already been pointed out, in a number of conversations with the Soviet Embassy on the subject, that the United States Immigration officials had the right to question and examine aliens entering the country regardless of whether or not such aliens were in possession of valid visas. The immigration authorities bore the final responsibility for preventing the entry into the United States of inadmissable aliens, and neither the State Department nor any other Department of the Government was in a position to interfere with their work of carrying out the laws and immigration regulations.

Mr. Gromyko stated that the examination by United States customs officials of the baggage of Soviet consular officers entering the United States was discrimination against the Soviet Union. The Soviet Government had noted in particular that these examinations were taking place at the specific request of the Department of State. A customs officer in New York had informed one of the Soviet consular officers who was protesting at such an examination that he had received a letter from the State Department requesting that the examination be made.[96]

Mr. Henderson replied that according to American customs laws and regulations, consular officers of foreign countries must be given the same customs treatment as that extended to American consular officers in entering the countries which such consular officers represented. The treatment given to foreign consular officers entering the United States was based on the principle of reciprocity.

Mr. Gromyko said that the Soviet Government could not accept discrimination. According to Soviet law, the baggage of consular officers of all foreign countries entering the Soviet Union must be examined by the customs officials. The consular officers of the United States in this respect were given treatment just as favorable as that of the consular officers of any other country. There was no discrimination against the consular officers of the United States. The So-

<hr/>

[96] For correspondence regarding the examination by United States Customs authorities of the baggage of Dmitry Ivanovich Zaikin (Zaikine), Soviet Vice Consul at New York, the case here under reference, see *Foreign Relations*, The Soviet Union, 1933–1939, pp. 857–868, *passim*.

viet Government therefore requested that no discrimination be shown Soviet consular officers entering the United States.

Mr. Henderson replied that the policy of the American Government of applying the principle of reciprocity in deciding the customs treatment to be given any foreign consular officer entering the country had been established long before there was a Soviet Union. This policy was applied universally. There were many countries the customs officers of which insisted on examining the baggage of American consular officers. The United States customs officials were accustomed to giving like treatment to the consular officers of those countries. For the United States to order the United States customs officials not to examine the baggage of Soviet consular officers would mean discrimination against other countries which did not grant customs courtesies to American consular officers. In the opinion of Mr. Henderson no purpose could be served in discussing the possibility of the United States departing from its long-established policy of applying the principle of reciprocity in the customs treatment to be given to foreign consular officers.

711.61/756 : Telegram

The Ambassador in the Soviet Union (Steinhardt) to the Secretary of State

Moscow, September 27, 1940—1 p. m.
[Received September 28—5 : 30 a. m.]

1238. I had a long, and unusually frank discussion with Molotov yesterday regarding the various problems which have vexed the Embassy during the past 4 or 5 months. Molotov was extremely cordial. I told him that in line with our desire to improve relations between the two countries steps had been taken in Washington to remove some of the causes of Ambassador Umansky's complaints and that I now expected that like good will would be exhibited on the part of the Soviet Government. I pointed out to him that a favorite accusation of the Soviet Government against the United States in connection with the most trivial incidents was that the Soviets were being discriminated against and that I had brought with me a list of acts of discrimination by the Soviet Government against the United States. I invited his attention to a number of obstacles encountered by the Embassy during recent months and asked him specifically to remove these as a first evidence of good will.

I then enumerated certain of the difficulties and the cases of lack of cooperation on the part of Soviet authorities which the Embassy had encountered such as the question of the opening of a Consulate at Vladivostok; [97] in the liquidation of our Baltic Missions and the refusal of Soviet authorities to permit the departure of the alien clerks of those Missions; difficulties placed in the way of the departure of American citizens from Soviet occupied Poland; and the continued failure to grant exit visas to the Soviet wives of American citizens. In connection with the foregoing I mentioned that other nations maintain Consulates at Vladivostok and that the Missions of other countries in the Baltic had not encountered the same difficulties as ourselves in effecting the departure of their alien clerks and certain other matters which appeared to reflect less favorable treatment of the United States. I also discussed with him the question of additional space for our increased staff, the demand of Burobin [98] that official obligations of the Embassy be paid in rubles obtained at the official rate through the State Bank and other matters of a minor nature.

Molotov replied that he would give these matters his personal attention and would endeavor to see to it that we obtain relief from vexations of this character. Insofar as concerned a Consulate at Vladivostok, while he made no commitment, he indicated quite clearly that he was favorably disposed. I then inquired as to his disposition concerning a Consulate at Riga to which he replied that the Soviet Government had recently decided in principle that there would be no Consulates at Riga. When I asked whether this included Japan and Germany he replied in the affirmative. He remarked that the subjects which had been mentioned were of secondary importance and expressed his disappointment at the action by our Government in taking over the machine tools purchased by the Soviet Government in the United States.

I thereupon explained to him the necessities of our national defense program, seizing the opportunity to impress upon him the magnitude thereof and the fact that the American Navy and Air Force would be the most powerful in the world within 2 years, pointing out that it was my understanding that a substantial percentage of the machine tools in question had been or were about to be released for export to the Soviet Union. He then brought up the subject of the gold of the Baltic States sequestered by our Government and afforded me an opportunity of referring to the indebtedness of the Baltic States to the United States Government and the sizeable amount of American capital invested there in respect of which no compensation has as yet been tendered or offered by his Government and in passing I referred to the substantial amount of American capital that had been nation-

---

[97] For correspondence regarding the establishment of an American Consulate General at Vladivostok, see pp. 460 ff.
[98] Central Bureau for Services to Foreigners.

alized in Soviet occupied Poland and Bessarabia. After some further discussion on the same lines Molotov reverted to the question of the retention of machine tools ordered by the Soviet Union. When I spoke of the need in the United States for these tools Molotov replied that the Soviet Government needed them just as badly and that as the United States was a highly industrialized country he could not understand why what he described as an unimportant number of [tools?] should have been taken over. To this I replied that the Soviet Government already had considerable armament whereas the United States, as is well known, was only beginning to arm and that as events moved rather rapidly these days it seemed more desirable that the United States should have some armament quickly than that the Soviet Government should increase its armaments further.

Molotov did not seem disposed to contradict this observation and I gained the general impression that the American armament program is not at all displeasing to the Soviet Union. He gave every indication of a desire to see an improvement in our relations and indicated clearly that if the American Government should show a desire to improve relations his Government would be glad to cooperate.

Neither of us touched upon general political subjects and I thought it preferable to reserve any attempt to draw him out with respect to Soviet intentions in the immediate future for a subsequent meeting as I will be able to judge his disposition to discuss the Soviet position vis-à-vis countries other than the United States by the action taken by him in respect of the matters I brought to his attention. Should these be promptly dealt with and the general attitude of the Foreign Office undergo any marked change as a result of my talk with him yesterday afternoon I shall endeavor to see him again in the near future for the purpose of drawing him out on Soviet policy in Europe and the Far East.

STEINHARDT

711.61/756a : Telegram

The Secretary of State to the Ambassador in the Soviet Union (Steinhardt)

WASHINGTON, October 3, 1940—2 p. m.

614. Section I. During the month of August a series of conversations were carried on between the Soviet Ambassador and Mr. Welles with a view to settling certain outstanding problems, principally of a commercial nature, in American-Soviet relations. Although constructive results were obtained in several instances, other problems still remain unsettled. A summary of the most important issues dis-

cussed and of the present situation with respect to them follows herewith:

1. *The exclusion of Soviet engineers from the Wright Aeronautical Plant.* In compliance with the request of the Ambassador, arrangements have been made whereby such engineers, under certain restrictions, may now have access to various sections of the plant for the purpose of studying manufacturing processes.

It is believed that this problem is now settled in a manner satisfactory to the Soviet Ambassador.

2. *The obtaining of American tonnage.* The Ambassador has been informed that Soviet agencies in this country would probably not encounter any difficulties in obtaining American tankers for Pacific shipments; that although there was a shortage of dry cargo boats in the Pacific, any difficulties in obtaining charter thereof would be of a temporary nature and that in general such vessels would be available.

This question also appears to have been settled to the satisfaction of the Ambassador.

3. *The routing of mails to the Soviet Union.* Upon the request of the Ambassador appropriate instructions were issued to the Post Office authorities to route mail destined for the Soviet Union across the Pacific.

4. *The purchase of Soviet gold.* Reference is made to the note contained in your 937, July 31, 9 a. m.,[99] Section D. The Ambassador was orally informed that this Government did not intend to discriminate against any country in the purchase of gold and that it was willing to express its views on this subject in a note to the Soviet Ambassador. This note, which has not yet been presented, reiterates the established gold purchasing policy of this Government. It also declares that this Government cannot enter into any undertaking which might tend to limit its freedom of action in the purchase of gold.

There is no reason to believe this should not be satisfactory to the Soviet Government.

5. *Assurances of non-discrimination against Soviet trade.* The Ambassador has requested written assurances of non-discrimination in conformity with the letter requested by Mikoyan in your 937, July 31, 9 a. m., Section B. The Department has under consideration the presentation of a memorandum to the Soviet Embassy stating in effect that it is the intention of this Government (*a*) to consider in a friendly spirit applications for export licenses, and (*b*) not to apply to orders or purchases of goods destined for the use of the Union of Soviet Socialist Republics any measures of a discriminatory character except in accordance with the policy of my Government as set forth below. It is then pointed out that the application of the policy of my Government as expressed above is subject to the limitation that it must obtain for itself full freedom to adopt any export prohibitions which it may consider to be in the interests of national defense, and to take any measures which it may deem to be necessary for insuring the security of the United States, its territories, or possessions.

Since no written undertakings are entered into as requested by Mikoyan regarding the question of irrevocable export licenses, the

---

[99] *Post*, p. 449.

releasing of goods purchased prior to July 2, the charter of vessels, or the moral embargo, it is doubtful whether this note, if presented, will be acceptable to the Soviet Government.

6. *Moral Embargo.* The Ambassador has been informed that the moral embargo should not be considered an organic part of the conversations since it resulted from a situation which could have no connection with them; that because of the unilateral policy of this Government of refusing to facilitate the carrying on of certain types of warfare which it condemns, it could not enter into any bilateral agreement which might prevent it from continuing that policy; however, upon the successful termination of the present conversation, the American Government might be prepared to issue a statement raising the embargo provided the conditions which were responsible for the decision to declare it should no longer obtain.

The Ambassador stated that he would advise his Government with respect to these views.

7. *The granting of passports to American engineers for travel to the Soviet Union.* The Ambassador was informed that so long as the freedom of movement of United States citizens in the Soviet Union was restricted, this Government did not feel it could afford to facilitate the visits to that country of American citizens. The difficulties regarding our citizens in Soviet-occupied Poland were emphasized.

The Ambassador stated that he would take this matter up with his Government.

8. *The despatch of American transport planes to China via Siberia.* In reply to inquiries regarding the position of the Soviet Government on this matter, the Ambassador stated that in view of the present state of relations between the American and Soviet Governments, and the tension produced as a result of charges in the American press to the effect that the Soviet Government was fortifying the Diomede Islands, the Soviet Government could not agree to the transfer of planes from Alaska to China via Siberia. Asked specifically on August 24 whether the Soviet Government did not wish to assist China in this instance and to cooperate with the United States in the Pacific, the Ambassador stated that in view of the aforementioned question, he would request new instructions from his Government.

The Ambassador has not subsequently mentioned the receipt of any new instructions.

9. *The situation regarding the export of machine tools.* In view of the extremely complicated nature of this question, it is believed inadvisable to endeavor to explain the developments which have taken place here. This Government must give first consideration to its national defense program and it cannot take any action, such as the granting of irrevocable export licenses, which might seriously affect it. In the application of the Export License Act this Government is retaining as few machines ordered or purchased by Soviet import agencies as national defense requirements permit.

10. *The questions regarding the withholding of Baltic assets in this country and the disposition of Latvian and Estonian vessels in American waters* were touched on in the conversations but did not form an integral part since at the time the agenda was agreed on this question did not arise. The position of the United States in regard to its refusal to recognize the absorption into the Soviet Union of the Baltic

States and to its continued recognition of the Baltic Legations and Consulates in this country was reiterated. The Ambassador was further informed that the problems in American-Soviet relations arising out of recent developments in the Baltic were insoluble for the time being and that it would be better to concentrate on difficulties which could be eliminated.

Section II. The Department now has under consideration the advisability of resuming the conversations under discussion. It would appear from your 1238, September 27, 1 p. m., that Molotov desires to see an improvement in Soviet-American relations and the Department believes that under ordinary circumstances the logical way to effect this end is through the continuation of discussions here. However, in view of the cordiality between you and Molotov, and the non-cooperative aggressiveness, in spite of the concrete results attained, which Oumansky continues to display here, the Department feels that more positive results might be accomplished through the transfer for discussion and negotiation in Moscow of many of the existing problems. The Department is of the opinion that Oumansky, in an endeavor to strengthen his personal prestige by playing a lone hand, may well be working at cross purposes with his Government. There is reason to doubt that he has reported accurately to his Government on all that has transpired here, especially on the concessions already made and on how this Government has sincerely endeavored to cooperate in these recent conversations. It is, of course, difficult for the Department to judge how extensive the instructions received by Oumansky have been, and also whether he interprets them in the way intended by his Government.

It is suggested that you see Molotov in the near future, inform him of the progress of the conversations as related in Section I (omitting any reference to the contents of the notes contained in paragraphs 4 and 5), and endeavor to ascertain what impression he has obtained not only of the results achieved thus far but also of Oumansky's reports on the present outstanding problems.

After your conversation with Molotov, the Department would appreciate your views on the advisability of transferring to Moscow certain of the points now under discussion in Washington. In view of Oumansky's attitude it is felt, for example, that since the notes regarding the purchase of Soviet gold and non-discrimination originally formed a part of the commercial negotiations, they may well be taken up in Moscow; that the problem regarding the granting of passports may be used by you as a bargaining point in your representations regarding the protection of American citizens in Soviet-occupied Poland; that Moscow is perhaps the more logical place to discuss the questions regarding the transfer of planes to China, the Vladivostok consulate, the additional quarters for the Embassy, and the other points raised in your 1238, September 27, 1 p. m.   On the other hand, it is believed that the problems relating to the export of machine tools, the Baltic ships, and the moral embargo should form the agenda of future conversations here.

HULL

191.1/499

The Secretary of State to the Ambassador in the Soviet Union (Steinhardt)

No. 318   WASHINGTON, October 7, 1940.

SIR: The receipt is acknowledged of your despatch No. 699, August 19, 1940, regarding a request of the Soviet Government that the Embassy accept Soviet currency in payment of consular fees.

Whenever the Soviet Government is prepared to permit the exchange of its currency, received by the Embassy in payment of consular fees, for United States currency or dollar drafts at a rate of exchange approximately equivalent to that at which it will permit the exchange of dollars for rubles, the Embassy may accept rubles in payment of fees.   Until then, the Department will have no interest in rubles tendered in payment of fees which Foreign Service Officers are by law required to collect "in the coin of the United States or at its representative value in exchange" (22 U. S. C. 128).

Very truly yours,   For the Secretary of State:
                                        BRECKINRIDGE LONG

711.61/757a : Telegram

The Secretary of State to the Ambassador in the Soviet Union (Steinhardt)

WASHINGTON, October 9, 1940—11 a. m.

630. Department's 614, October 3, 2 p. m.

1. The Soviet Ambassador called yesterday [1] at his request on Mr. Welles to inform him of the following instructions received from Molotov:

(a) The Ambassador is authorized to recede from his adamant position in refusing to agree to the retention in the interests of national defense of equipment ordered by Soviet purchasing agencies prior to July 2.   He is instructed, however, to obtain assurances that irrevocable export licenses will be issued in the future.

---

[1] October 7 is the date intended; no record of conversation found in Department files.

(*b*) The Soviet Government has taken note of Mr. Welles' statement regarding the gold purchasing policy of this Government and desires that a formula be worked out in accordance with this statement for inclusion in an exchange of notes between the two governments.

(*c*) The Soviet Government has noted with satisfaction the results obtained in regard to the availability of American tonnage to Soviet commercial organizations.

2. The Department has been informed by the Financial Adviser to the Chinese Government[2] that it has been decided to ship to Hongkong by sea the airplanes mentioned in the Department's 614, October 3, 2 p. m., and that it would no longer be necessary for the Government of the United States to approach the Soviet Government on this question. If you have not yet done so, it is suggested that you do not raise this issue with Molotov at the present time but that the question be left open since it is possible that endeavors [may?] be made next year to fly additional planes to China via Siberia.

HULL

861.56/192 : Telegram

The Ambassador in the Soviet Union (Steinhardt) to the Secretary of State

Moscow, October 10, 1940—7 p. m.
[Received October 10—6 : 40 p. m.]

1329. The Embassy has been endeavoring to obtain permission for eight Soviet spouses of American citizens to depart from the Soviet Union. In discussing these cases today Valkov,[3] of the People's Commissariat for Foreign Affairs, stated that the Soviet authorities are examining their petitions for permission to renounce Soviet citizenship and intimated that the petitions of the following spouses will probably be approved in the near future: Mariya Scott, Neonila Magidoff and Louis Salant. John Scott and Robert Magidoff, the American husbands of Mesdames Scott and Magidoff, are now in Moscow and Julia Salant, the American wife of Louis Salant, is at 1086 President Street, Brooklyn, New York.

In discussing the 360 persons of known or alleged American citizenship in Soviet occupied Poland on whose behalf the Embassy has been striving for months to obtain permission for their travel to Moscow, Valkov indicated that their cases are being examined by the Soviet authorities and that those who are not vested with Soviet citizenship will probably be permitted to visit the Embassy. The Embassy is unaware of the number of dual nationals among these persons.

STEINHARDT

[2] Arthur N. Young.
[3] Vasily Alexeyevich Valkov, Chief of the American Section in the People's Commissariat for Foreign Affairs.

811.20 (D) Regulations/5434

Memorandum of Conversation, by Mr. Edward Page, Jr., of the Division of European Affairs

[WASHINGTON,] October 15, 1940.

Participants: Mr. Constantine A. Oumansky, Soviet Ambassador;
Mr. Atherton, [Acting] Chief of [the Division of] European Affairs;
Mr. Page.

Mr. Atherton opened the conversations by remarking that he had requested the Ambassador to come in for the purpose of informing him of the results of the preliminary studies of the Ambassador's memorandum; [4] that he wished the conversation to be of an informatory and not controversial character and that there could be no question of negotiations since neither Mr. Atherton nor Mr. Page were empowered to negotiate the questions at issue. Mr. Oumansky agreed to keep the conversation on this basis.

Mr. Atherton then explained that the Department was prepared to furnish the Ambassador with the following three lists of applications for export licenses for machine tools:

(1) Applications rejected during the period July 1–October 1;
(2) Applications previously approved and contained on the lists of approved licenses handed to the Ambassador on October 14 which had subsequently been revoked;
(3) Applications which have previously been rejected but which may now be resubmitted for consideration. Mr. Atherton added that in addition to the above there existed a further list of thirteen applications to the value of approximately $250,000 which the Defense Commission intended to revoke. This list was still under consideration and could not be given to the Ambassador.

The Ambassador was then informed that in the preliminary conversation with Colonel Maxwell and other interested officers the Soviet position, as stated in the Ambassador's memorandum, had been fully explained; that the Department had been advised that one of the basic policies of the Defense Commission was to keep machine tool plant capacities free for future Government orders and for this reason it was quite impossible to make any definite commitments for future deliveries of Soviet orders; that it was strongly recommended that Soviet purchasing agencies in this country resubmit their orders for machine tools for which export licenses had been rejected to the President's Liaison Committee and that these agencies inform the Committee which tools were most urgently needed. Mr. Atherton added that should the Ambassador agree to this course

---

[4] Dated October 7, not printed.

it was likely that Mr. Welles would recommend to the Committee that special consideration be given to Soviet replacement orders.

The Soviet Ambassador received the above remarks with considerable displeasure. After brief references to the illegality of the retroactive effect of the President's Proclamation of July 2,[4a] the Ambassador stated that it was evident that the American authorities were not prepared to authorize the automatic renewal of existing contracts as provided for in point 4(a) of the Ambassador's memorandum; that since these authorities were demanding that new applications should be made, the possibility existed of new rejections and postponements. He stated that he would willingly discuss all new orders with the Liaison Committee but that his present instructions were limited to the liquidation of the past which did not include the course suggested by the Department of considering renewal orders as new orders. He continually maintained that the Soviet Government was entitled to be permitted to renew automatically contracts for machine tools not released for export. Mr. Atherton remarked that the present conversations were of an informatory and not controversial character and suggested that Mr. Oumansky's attention be directed to the lists prepared by the Soviet Embassy and by the Department. The Ambassador stated that according to his figures applications for licenses for machine tools and other equipment to the value of $7,592,558 had been denied or had not been acted upon. He itemized the figures as follows: Applications denied for machine tools already in United States ports—$845,466. Applications denied for machine tools in American factories—$3,335,176. Applications, the disposition of which is unknown, $2,503,466. Machine tools contracted for which have been taken over ("requisitioned") by American manufacturers $907,450, and total $7,592,558.

The Ambassador added that Soviet purchasing agencies had accepted all the tools in American ports, tools to the value of $849,133 of the "unknown disposition" category and tools to the value of $264,718 orders in "requisition" by American manufacturers or a total of $1,959,317. He stated that he assumed that the second part of point 3 of the Soviet memorandum had been accepted by the American Government. He was informed that just the contrary was true since the President's Proclamation referred to exports and not to the acceptance of equipment by Soviet purchasing agencies. The Ambassador again commented on the retroactive effect of the Proclamation and stated that as far as he could see the conversations had not advanced during the course of the last seven weeks.

Mr. Atherton suggested that the Ambassador study the new lists and then inform the Department which machine tools the Soviet

---

[4a] Department of State *Bulletin*, July 6, 1940, p. 12.

Government desired to replace. The Ambassador stated that he believed that his Government would probably wish to replace practically the entire list.

Summing up the conversation, the Ambassador stated that it would appear that the American and Soviet Governments were still as far apart in the matter of the principle of the application of the President's Proclamation as they were at the last conversation and especially so with regard to point 3 and 4(a) of the memorandum; that insofar as the practice was concerned the situation had greatly deteriorated since now rejections amounted to about 50%, whereas on August 1 such rejections amounted to 30% and on August 15 to about 35%.

It was explained to the Ambassador that our defense program had changed drastically in the last 2 to 4 weeks; that early in August we believed that this program would not seriously interfere with our export business in machine tools, but that in the development of the program it became clear that we had been prematurely optimistic, and that there was now a tendency to manufacture tools only for United States defense industries.

Mr. Atherton then informed the Ambassador that he had been called to the Secretary's office. Before leaving he again strongly advocated that the Soviet purchasing agencies in this country approach the President's Liaison Committee with regard to their problems.

Mr. Oumansky, Mr. Page and Mr. Schnee [5] discussed several minor details concerning the disposition of applications not yet acted upon and it was suggested to the Ambassador that after study of the new lists he advise the Department concerning those applications still not heard from. He requested the investigation of an application for the export of a catalyst cracking unit to the value of $74,000. Mr. Schnee promised to look this matter up.

861.24/434½

Memorandum by Mr. Edward Page, Jr., of the Division of European Affairs to the Under Secretary of State (Welles)

[WASHINGTON,] October 17, 1940.

MR. WELLES: Before a definite answer is given to Mr. Oumansky concerning the release for export of the machine tools to the amount of approximately $2,000,000 which have been accepted by Soviet purchasing agencies, I believe that it would be advisable carefully to examine the list of such tools which the Ambassador has been asked to furnish the Department. We know that this list will show certain machines

---

[5] Alexander Schnee, of the Division of Controls.

which have already been diverted to and are in use by American manufacturers under national defense contracts. It may also show other tools which are of such vital importance to our defense program that their release may seriously disrupt a key industry. I do not believe that any improvement in American-Soviet relations which might result from the release of these machines would be sufficient compensation for the possible serious disruption which might follow in our defense industries. Furthermore, I believe that unfavorable public reaction might result should it be learned that certain vital equipment had been released for export to the Soviet Government.

On the other hand, it may be possible to undertake the immediate replacement of certain of these machines without disrupting to a too great extent our defense program. It is also quite possible that many of the "accepted" tools lying in American ports whose applications have been rejected may be released immediately. It is probable that certain of the other machines mentioned by the Ambassador may be released or replaced in the near future without serious injury to our national defense. I believe that the value of these machines may well amount to more than one million dollars.

In view of the above, I do not see how we can give the Ambassador any blanket assurance that *all* the machines accepted by Soviet purchasing agencies will be released.

I feel reasonably sure, however, that after examination by Colonel Maxwell and other interested officers of the list promised by the Ambassador, we will be able to release a considerable proportion of the "accepted" machines without serious damage to our defense program.

711.61/762 : Telegram

The Ambassador in the Soviet Union (Steinhardt)
to the Secretary of State

Moscow, October 20, 1940—7 p. m.
[Received October 20—6 : 50 p. m.]

1373. Reference my 1307, October 8, 5 p. m.[6] My request for an interview with Molotov remains unanswered and an inquiry yesterday of his secretary elicited the response that the matter would again be brought to Molotov's attention. Since the instructions contained in the Department's telegram 614, October 3, 2 p. m. were not urgent and in view of the circumstances set forth in the last paragraph of my telegram under reference which I am more convinced than ever constitute the reason for the secretary's unusual delay in obtaining an appointment with Molotov I have refrained from pressing my request with vigor.

---

[6] *Ante*, p. 232.

However, as it is now 12 days since my original request I believe that I should either insist upon seeing Molotov immediately or cancel the request and made an appointment with Lozovski or Vishinsky in order to take up the questions outlined in the Department's instructions. In view of the publicity which has apparently been given to reports of British-American-Soviet negotiations (in this connection see Berlin's 4379, October 18 [7]) I would appreciate the Department's views as to the advisability at the present time of insisting upon an interview with Molotov.

I might add that despite the assurances given me by Molotov on September 26 (see my 1238, September 27, 1 p. m.) of the disposition of the Soviet Government to settle satisfactorily certain problems of a secondary nature as he termed them, there has up to the present been little evidence that the Soviet Government intends to take favorable action in these matters. For example the question of the departure of American citizens from Soviet occupied Poland is still unsettled; no reply has been received to a further note concerning the Vladivostok Consulate, commerce [*Embassy?*] is still without additional housing.

STEINHARDT

611.6131/615½

Memorandum by the Under Secretary of State (Welles) to the Acting Chief of the Division of European Affairs (Atherton)

[WASHINGTON,] October 23, 1940.

MR. ATHERTON: I had a personal conference yesterday with the Secretary of the Treasury. Mr. Morgenthau tells me that should I consider it desirable, he will approve an exchange of letters between the Soviet Ambassador and myself containing the affirmative assurance of the attitude of this Government regarding gold and silver as contained in the phraseology set forth in the memorandum I attach.[8] This, of course, covers completely what Oumansky desired.

I suggest that the necessary correspondence be prepared and that should we make progress in the next few meetings, and always provided that the political status of Russia does not change in the meantime, we can inform Oumansky that this exchange of letters is agreeable to this Government.

---

[7] Not printed.
[8] Not printed. The phraseology contained in unsigned memorandum of October 17, 1940, gave as the essential wording of the proposed letter "The assurances that no prohibitive or restrictive measures would be applied to export or import of Soviet gold or silver which would not be applied to all other countries."

In a letter of July 16, 1941, to Secretary of the Treasury Henry Morgenthau, Jr., Acting Secretary of State Welles recalled: "In view of certain considerations of an international character the contemplated exchange did not take place." (611.6131/634a)

711.61/762 : Telegram

The Secretary of State to the Ambassador in the Soviet Union
(Steinhardt)

WASHINGTON, October 24, 1940—1 p. m.

685. Your 1373, October 20, 7 p. m. Department believes that it would be inadvisable for you to insist at this time upon an interview with Molotov for the purpose of discussing the questions set forth in the Department's 614. Oumansky has recently received fairly comprehensive instructions from his Government permitting our negotiations here to be resumed.

Since the Department intends in the near future again to bring to the Ambassador's attention the problems set forth in the last sentence of your telegram, it believes that it might be better for you not to press your appointment with Molotov until Oumansky has had occasion to bring to the attention of his Government the Department's interests in these matters. On the other hand, the Department perceives no objection to your maintaining normal relations with Lozovski or Vishinski.

HULL

711.61/762a : Telegram

The Secretary of State to the Ambassador in the Soviet Union
(Steinhardt)

WASHINGTON, October 26, 1940—3 p. m.

699. Section 1. In view of recent developments in Washington, the Department desires that you disregard general instructions contained in part II of telegram 614, October 3, 2 p. m. On the other hand, if you can obtain the opportunity of being received by Molotov, at an early date, or otherwise with some other appropriate official, please develop orally the following views as under instructions from your Government:

As is known to Mr. Molotov there have been recent exchanges of views between the two Governments in the hope that certain difficulties of an administrative or commercial nature which have arisen between them might be eliminated. The fact that these conversations have taken place demonstrates that there is a sincere desire on the part of the American Government to see a spirit of greater cooperativeness. You may add that your Government is particularly gratified at the successes which have thus far been achieved and hopes that by a continued exchange of views in the same spirit the two Governments may be able to extend these successes to broader and more important fields.

The Tripartite Pact[9] which has been recently announced uniting the aggressor nations emphasizes the common danger from the policies pursued by these nations which faces peace-loving and peace-abiding countries. The United States Government is hopeful that peace-loving nations will continue to resist pressure for commitments incompatible with their own national integrity. You may add that doubtless your Government has suggested this approach at the present moment because of the announcement of this Pact which has the positive feature of clarifying for the benefit of the whole world a situation which has existed for some time; the fact that the aggressor bloc has been forcing nation after nation to succumb to its dominance clearly indicates that the bounds of its aggressiveness are without limit.

Such considerations cannot be ignored by even those great Powers which for the moment find themselves beyond the scope of the immediate activities of these aggressor forces. These great Powers, furthermore, must not be unmindful of the fact that any undertakings limiting freedom of action given by them to the signatories of this Tripartite Pact not only tend to isolate these powers from other free nations but also amount in reality to the granting of a mortgage on their future in favor of those powers which seem bent on world domination through conquest. The Government of the United States welcomes at this time the opportunity afforded by the conversations already initiated of removing the causes for friction and misunderstanding which have arisen between our two Governments, and of thus preparing the way for a closer and more friendly association which it believes will be a valuable factor in preventing a further spread of warfare.

Section 2. Should you have any reason to doubt the advisability of the aforementioned action, or should you desire to make any suggestions in this connection, the Department desires you to telegraph your views.

HULL

711.61/771 : Telegram

The Ambassador in the Soviet Union (Steinhardt) to the Secretary of State

Moscow, October 30, 1940—8 p. m.
[Received October 31—4 : 55 a. m.]

1454. Department's 699, October 26, 3 p. m. I was received yesterday by Vyshinski who granted the interview immediately upon request.

---

[9] Signed at Berlin on September 27, 1940, by Germany, Italy, and Japan. For text, see League of Nations Treaty Series, vol. cciv, p. 387, or *Foreign Relations, Japan, 1931–1941*, vol. ii, p. 165.

I began our conversation by referring to the sincere desire of my Government to work for greater cooperation with the Soviet Government as evidenced by the discussions which have been taking place in Washington with respect to certain administrative and commercial difficulties and cited in this connection the successful settlement of certain specific questions which had been the subject of complaint on the part of the Soviet Government. I remarked that the efforts of my Government in this respect unfortunately had not thus far been reciprocated and cited several pending matters which I had hoped the Soviet authorities might have found it possible to dispose of. At this point Vyshinski stated that while he was informed that such discussions were in progress in Washington nothing had come of them in so far as he was aware and he inquired what matters had been settled. I outlined to him the understandings already reached with Oumanski, referring particularly to the granting of permission for Soviet engineers to visit the Wright Aeronautical Plant, the assurance of the release of machine tools, not required for our national defense and the favorable decision with respect to the Soviet request for American tankers. Vyshinski then stated that irrespective of any concessions made in Washington, of which he appeared to be uninformed, the Soviet Government had in principle decided to agree to the establishment of a Consulate in Vladivostok and that by November 15 the Embassy would receive additional housing facilities. With respect to the American citizens in Soviet-occupied Poland he was noncommittal and said that he would look into the matter.

Having enlightened Vyshinski as to some of the steps which the Department has already taken in an endeavor to develop a spirit of greater cooperation and to eliminate friction between the two Governments and having received his assurances that the Soviet Government also desires to see an improvement in [relations?], I outlined to him the views contained in the Department's telegram under reference. Vyshinski listened carefully and then made the following observations which he stated I could accept as the view of his Government:

(1) The Soviet Government has always taken cognizance of aggression, the definition of which has been publicly expressed by Molotov, and it likewise recognizes that aggression is "sometimes without limit".

(2) The foreign policy of the Soviet Union is a consistent policy directed towards the furtherance of the foreseeable peace. The Soviet Union bases its relations with other countries on this principle and all treaties concluded by it are directed towards this goal since the Soviet Government regards the maintenance of peace as fundamental to its future. In its foreign affairs the Soviet Government is guided by a desire to maintain friendly relations with all countries, a principle which it also regards as of fundamental importance to its future

development. Past events have demonstrated that the pursuance of the foregoing policy has not resulted in limiting the freedom of action of the Soviet Union or in isolating it from other countries thus demonstrating the correctness of a Soviet policy.

(3) The Soviet Union is able to protect itself against any aggression.

As you will observe Vyshinski's remarks which he delivered without hesitation are little more than an exposition of the stereotyped declarations which have been publicly made by Soviet leaders concerning Soviet foreign policy for a long time past and consequently reveal little as to the real intentions of the Soviet Government at the present time.

In the general conversation which ensued I had occasion to ask Vyshinski whether the Soviet Union contemplated an agreement with Japan in the near future to which he replied that he was not in a position to give me any information on this subject. He then referred to the view which I had expressed to him in accordance with the Department's instruction that any undertakings limiting its freedom of action given by a great power to the signatories of the above tripartite pact would tend to isolate that power from other free nations and observed in this connection that in his opinion any such development would depend on the nature of the undertakings given and added that the existing agreements between the Soviet Union and Germany [10] had not isolated the Soviet Union from other countries nor, as our conversation proved, had it stood in the way of an exchange of views.

Although Vyshinski's reply provided little information of a concrete nature as to the intentions of the Soviet Union at the present time in view of his subsequent observation I received the impression that the Soviet Government contemplates an agreement with Japan the extent and exact nature of which cannot be accurately forecast [11] and that Vyshinski was endeavoring indirectly to persuade me that should such an agreement be effected it should not result in an impairment of Soviet relations with other countries particularly the United States.

My conversation with Molotov on September 26th reported in my 1238, September 27th, 1 p. m., and my talk with Vyshinski, tend to confirm the Department's suspicion that Oumanski has not kept his Government fully informed of the progress made in Washington or the spirit in which the concessions were made. This suspicion is further strengthened by a statement recently made to Ward by Valkov, Chief of the American Section of the Foreign Office, that, due to the

[10] For correspondence concerning wartime cooperation and agreements made between Germany and the Soviet Union, see *Foreign Relations*, 1939, vol. I, pp. 477 ff.; *ibid.*, 1940, vol. I, pp. 539 ff.

[11] The Soviet Union did conclude a neutrality pact with Japan valid for 5 years, signed in Moscow on April 13, 1941. For text, see Department of State *Bulletin*, April 29, 1945, p. 812.

attitude of our Government, Soviet-American relations instead of improving have been deteriorating. I venture to suggest therefore that until the Soviet Government indicates that it is entirely aware of the extent of the concessions made to it and the spirit in which the same have been made no further concessions be granted.

I regard Vyshinski's immediate and glib exposition of the official and public interpretation of Moscow foreign policy in response to the message I conveyed to him as indicative of a desire to avoid any form of political discussion with the United States at the present time and I am more than ever of the opinion that any concessions made to the Soviet Union in administrative and commercial fields should be affected on the basis of strict reciprocity and with no expectation that they will in the slightest degree affect the political policy of the Soviet Government.

STEINHARDT

860N.85/1

Memorandum of Conversation, by the Under Secretary of State (Welles)

[WASHINGTON,] October 31, 1940.

The Soviet Ambassador called to see me.

The Ambassador again undertook a discourse upon the subject of Baltic ships within United States jurisdiction.

I stated that I would investigate the matter further and would discuss the problem with him once more in an early conversation.

S[UMNER] W[ELLES]

861.24/441

Memorandum of Conversation, by the Under Secretary of State (Welles)

[WASHINGTON,] October 31, 1940.

The Soviet Ambassador called to see me in accordance with the agreement we had reached at the last general conference I had had with the Ambassador and his advisers.

The Ambassador appeared to be in a far more satisfied and conciliatory mood than I had ever seen him. He expressed the greatest appreciation of the "cooperation and courtesy" shown him by Colonel Maxwell and his associates, and by Mr. Philip Young [12] and the latter's associates, and expressed the opinion that while the amount of detailed work involved in the study of the machine tool license question was

---

[12] Special Assistant to the Secretary of the Treasury.

enormous and would necessarily take some time, he himself was entirely satisfied that every effort was being made to reach an equitable and expeditious solution.

Surprisingly, he referred only once, and that only casually, to what he had in previous conversations claimed was the small percentage of concessions made by this Government covering the export licenses for machine tools to the Soviet.

The Ambassador and I agreed in principle that the time had now come when a certain amount of drafting could be undertaken to cover agreements in principle already reached, but that of course, until an agreement had been reached on both sides with respect to all of the questions in which the two Governments were interested, there would be no formalizing of any specific agreements in principle already reached.

I took occasion to say to the Ambassador that I had been very glad to see from a telegram received this afternoon from Ambassador Steinhardt [13] that the Soviet Government had agreed in principle to the establishment of an American consulate in Vladivostok after November 15. The Ambassador had not yet received this message.

I stated, however, that I regretted to see from the same telegram that Mr. Valkov, Chief of the American Section of the Soviet Foreign Office, had recently expressed the opinion to an official of the United States Embassy that there had been no improvement in Soviet-American relations in as much as the United States Government was doing nothing to improve such relations. I expressed the opinion that a remark of this kind was in the first place inaccurate, and in the second place, hardly calculated to improve the atmosphere between the two Governments.

The Ambassador turned a bright red and immediately said that the remark was completely unjustified and in no sense represented his own views, nor the views of Mr. Molotov nor of other high officials of the Soviet Foreign Office. He stated that both Mr. Molotov and himself were exceedingly appreciative of the friendly attitude which had recently been shown by this Government and were likewise under the impression that a far more friendly feeling between the two Governments had come about.

I asked the Ambassador whether he had informed his Government fully of all of the conversations which I had with him and he told me that they had been reported by him and that he had received specific approval from his Government of every agreement in principle which had been reached.

S[UMNER] W[ELLES]

---

[13] Telegram No. 1454, October 30, 8 p. m., p. 400.

711.61/773 : Telegram

The Ambassador in the Soviet Union (Steinhardt) to the Secretary of State

Moscow, November 19, 1940—9 p. m.
[Received November 20—9 : 44 a. m.]

1579. For the Under Secretary. During the course of an interview with Lozovski this afternoon I took up with him the following matters : failure to grant permission for the Soviet wives of American citizens to leave the Soviet Union; failure to grant the Embassy free access to an imprisoned individual claiming American citizenship; failure to grant permission for the greater part of the Americans in the Lemberg [14] area to depart for the United States; failure to provide on November 15 additional housing for the Embassy personnel as promised; failure to grant exit permits to three non-American employees of our Legation in Kaunas; failure to reply to my written request for permission to export a limited quantity of gasoline to our Legation in Stockholm; the conduct of the Moscow Customs authorities in having damaged a substantial part of a recent shipment of foodstuffs for the Embassy by tearing open containers and thrusting iron rods through each bag; refusal to afford most American citizens in transit through Moscow the necessary time within which to obtain requisite visas including Soviet exit visas; arrest without notice of a Soviet employee of the Embassy leaving his wife and 6 months old child to be fed and provided for by me personally; quadrupling the freight charge on our food shipments from Vladivostok so that the rate now exceeds 2,000 rubles per ton; refusal to grant a permit for the installation of a gasoline container within the Embassy premises although similar containers have been installed by the Soviet authorities in like premises; confiscation by Soviet frontier authorities of the $5.00 generally furnished by the Embassy to American citizens in process of repatriation and refusal to return the same to the Embassy insisting that application of refund be made by the individual concerned.

I asked Lozovski how he could reconcile the foregoing course of conduct with the concessions made to the Soviet Government in Washington. He replied that very few concessions had been thus far granted in Washington and then read to me the following list of matters in respect of which he said no action has as yet been taken : the sequestered gold and ships of the Baltic States, the continued recognition by the Department of the representatives of the Baltic States, the moral embargo and licenses for the export of machine tools. He stated that Colonel Maxwell had recently told Umansky that it

[14] Lvov, Lwow.

would not be possible to grant export licenses in conjunction with machine tools and concluded with the observation that out of 297 machine tools for which $3,085,000 had long since been paid by the Soviet Government only one costing $7,090 has been released.

When Lozovsky concluded his recital of the concessions which the Soviet Government is still seeking in Washington I told him bluntly that I would oppose any further concessions in Washington until the Soviet Government had given tangible evidence of its appreciation of those already granted by removing the grievances I had cited. Lozovsky thereupon adopted a more reasonable attitude and assured me that permission would be granted forthwith for the export of a reasonable quantity of gasoline to our Legation at Stockholm, that he would give immediate instructions that I be permitted to interview the arrested individual claiming American citizenship, that he would also give instructions that American citizens in transit through Moscow be granted a reasonable period of time within which to perfect their papers, that he would issue instructions that all individuals in the Lemberg area in possession of American passports either now valid or which have expired within the past 3 years be granted exit visas and allowed to proceed to Moscow, that he would "look into" the matters of the Soviet wives of American citizens and the employees of our Legation in Kaunas, that he would "look into" the freight rates and also the matter of the arrested Embassy employee. He also said that he had informed himself with respect to the additional housing promised for the Embassy personnel on November 15 and that one apartment would be made available by the end of the current month and a second apartment "sometime in January".

STEINHARDT

711.61/798

Memorandum by the Acting Chief of the Division of European Affairs (Atherton) to the Under Secretary of State (Welles)

[WASHINGTON,] November 26, 1940.

MR. WELLES: I am sure that you will be interested in the extracts set forth below taken from a confidential letter which Mr. Steinhardt has written to Mr. Henderson under date of October 20, 1940 relating to various problems facing the Embassy in Moscow. Since the portions of the letter devoted to Soviet-American relations might be of interest to you and might be even of help in connection with your conversations with Mr. Oumansky, we are submitting them to you despite the personal character of the letter.

"Disposing briefly of the political side, we have been uncertain of the Department's policy and purposes arising out of the series of conferences with Oumansky, which of course have been given extraordinary publicity in the European press. Taken at its face value, the telegram [15] advising us of the matters of secondary importance discussed between Oumansky and Mr. Welles would indicate that the conferences had no purpose other than to iron out routine difficulties. However, I have not been so certain but that there was a deeper purpose, and as long as I have not been certain that there *was* a deeper purpose, it has been difficult to orient our course here. Whether or not there was a deeper purpose, it has been made abundantly clear to me that the British have read a very profound objective into this series of conferences. You have my report [16] that Cripps [17] seized upon the opportunity to threaten Molotov with the United States; that may not be very diplomatic language, but in effect that was his object and I am certain that Molotov received his remarks as being more than those of 'a third party'. Of course, it may well have been that this is exactly what the Department wanted, but we here have been uncertain. There is not the slightest doubt in my mind but that the publicity going the rounds that an Anglo-American-Soviet alliance was 'in the making' has had a very bad effect in the Kremlin. I do not need to labor the point with you that this is the wrong approach to these people. They are realists, if ever there are any realists in this world. Their fear of the German army—no longer held by the French army—is, of course, even greater than before France collapsed. The idea that they would change their policy and run the risk of a German invasion because the British *wish* them to do so, is childish beyond belief. In my opinion, there will be no change of basic or fundamental Soviet policy in respect of a shift of weight away from the Axis Powers unless and until the German army is no longer regarded in the Kremlin as the principal threat to the Soviet Union. If I am correct in this interpretation, approaches by Britain or the United States must be interpreted here as signs of weakness and the best policy to pursue is one of aloofness, indicating strength, rather than an approach which can have no prospect of success as long as the German military force remains intact and there is no sign of a weakening of German moral. In the Far East, it seems to me that the Soviet objective must be war between the United States and Japan. Nothing would be more to their liking and they have apparently decided that this purpose would be best accomplished by a Soviet-Japanese non-aggression pact which, in their opinion, would bring about such a conflict. Once the conflict has begun, and barring extraordinary pressure from Germany, I should expect the Soviet position to shift so as to withhold any assistance to Japan, particularly insofar as concerns oil, in the hope that Japanese naval power will be destroyed and that the fruits of any such war would fall into the Soviet lap without any effort. It is difficult to envisage a Japanese-American naval war, the ultimate outcome of which will not be of material value to the Soviet Union, for should Japanese naval power be destroyed, it would inevitably result in a Japanese collapse which would allow the Soviet Union to re-occupy sufficient territory to assure the safety of Vladivostok.

---

[15] Telegram No. 614, October 3, 2 p. m., p. 388.
[16] See telegram No. 1293, October 5, 6 p. m., from the Ambassador in the Soviet Union, vol. I, p. 617.
[17] Sir Stafford Cripps, British Ambassador in the Soviet Union.

"The British attempts to use the United States as a trial balloon for a continuance of their appeasement policy. This point needs no elaboration, as you are familiar from the telegrams with the publicity given by the British to their unsuccessful attempts to wean the Soviet Union away from Germany—with the United States cast in the role of 'wet nurse'."

"To make matters worse, the Soviet authorities have been more recalcitrant, uncooperative, and stubborn than usual during the past three or four weeks. This is easy to explain. As long as the attitude in Washington was unfriendly, we were getting results here. As soon as the Oumansky–Welles conferences began to take shape in Washington, Oumansky undoubtedly reported the same as a great personal victory and I have little doubt reported the United States as seeking the good graces of the Soviet Union in anticipation of war with Japan. As you know, from your own experience, the moment these people here get it into their heads that we are 'appeasing them, making up to them, or need them', they immediately stop being cooperative. With Oumansky's vindictive nature, I can just imagine what some of his reports to Molotov must look like. I am sure that he has been gloating and the impression has been created here that the Embassy can be ignored because of the 'jitters' in Washington. It would, of course, have been far better to have specifically conditioned the concessions to be made by our Government on the complete removal of our grievances here and to have layed down as a condition precedent to any concessions that the Vladivostok Consulate be granted and some two hundred Americans released from the Lwow area, not to speak of our own difficulties in connection with living conditions, space, etc., but I assume that the 'higher ups'—regarded international 'policies' as more important than profitable results and are still fooling themselves into believing that the Soviet Government responds to kindness or evidences of good will. My experience has been that they respond only to force and if force cannot be applied, then to straight oriental bartering or trading methods and that they would have valued the concessions made in Washington much more had they been on a bargaining basis, such as the charter of a tanker in exchange for a Consulate in Vladivostok or five hundred tons of marine tankers for each American now over a year in the clutches of the local authorities at Lwow. That, in my opinion, is the only language they understand and the only language productive of results. It also has the advantage of gaining their respect. In my opinion, our prestige here has not been at all enhanced by the concessions made to Oumansky, without asking for a semblance of a *quid pro quo*. I can imagine just what you are up against in trying to get this point of view across. It must be all the more difficult with the British and American press endeavoring to formulate our foreign policy."

R[AY] A[THERTON]

861.24/436½

Memorandum Prepared in the Division of European Affairs

[WASHINGTON,] November 26, 1940.

For purposes of convenience there is attached an outline [18] showing the present status of the conversations with the Soviet Ambassador. This outline divides the subjects which have been discussed or may properly be discussed into three major headings:

A. Soviet complaints or requests.
B. Extraneous matters which the Soviet Ambassador continuously endeavors to inject into the conversations.
C. American complaints or requests.

Soviet complaints or requests are divided into two groups:

1. Those on which no further action is called for;
2. Those still pending.

On the list of those still pending are six headings—namely, the machine tool problem, the moral embargo, the import of Soviet gold into the United States, a pledge of non-discrimination against Soviet trade in general, the alleged persecution suffered by Soviet citizens and officials in the United States, and the refusal of the Department to grant passports good for travel in the Soviet Union to American engineers.

The machine tool problem. It is understood that Mr. Oumansky is irritated at his lack of success thus far in obtaining more machine tools. The Administration of Export Control tells us that when Colonel Maxwell informed the Ambassador that the Administration could let him have only one machine tool valued at approximately $7000 out of some 103 tools valued at approximately $3,000,000, Mr. Oumansky replied that apparently the negotiations had returned to the point from which they had started, and that the matter must again be taken up through diplomatic channels. The situation seems to be as follows in regard to the negotiations between Colonel Maxwell and Mr. Oumansky:

Two lists of machine tools apparently were submitted by the Ambassador with the request that the decision to deny them export licenses be reconsidered. The first list, which was presented through the Department and which was discussed in the Department, was composed of some 61 machine tools which had already been manufactured and were awaiting shipment. The Administration permitted the export of 29 of the less complicated of these tools, retaining 32. The second list of 103 tools was composed of tools applications for export licenses covering which had already been rejected. Of this number, only about 80 could be identified during the course of a conversation early

---

[18] Not printed.

in November.   On November 12, Colonel Maxwell, as has been pointed out, informed the Ambassador that only one of these machines could be released.   It is understood that the remaining 20 have finally been identified and will be discussed by the Administration of Export Control on the afternoon of November 26.   In any event, the Soviet Ambassador is disappointed at the results of his negotiations with Colonel Maxwell and will undoubtedly try to re-introduce the subject of machine tools into the current conversations.

It will be recalled that it has already been agreed in principle that notes will be exchanged with respect to the non-discrimination in connection with the purchase of Soviet gold by the United States Treasury, and with respect to Soviet trade in general.   It is believed that for the present it would be advisable to postpone further detailed discussions on these points pending developments in other phases of our conversations and a clarification of Soviet international policy.

The Ambassador is almost sure to raise during the next conversation the question of the moral embargo since he has on previous occasions displayed some impatience at our delay in lifting it.   In this connection he will probably again request that we give assurances that we will permit the Kellogg Company to sell the Soviet Government gasoline cracking equipment in the value of approximately $12,500,000.

With regard to alleged persecutions suffered by Soviet officials and citizens of the United States, there does not seem that much more can be said on either side.   We might, perhaps, as a gesture, inform the Ambassador that we have gone carefully into the charges of persecution and discrimination and have convinced ourselves that there has been no organized or systematic effort to cause unpleasantness to Soviet officials and citizens in this country or to handicap them in their work.   If we care to go so far, it might be added that we are preparing to inform the Department of Justice that the Soviet engineers employed by Amtorg are considered by the Department of State as Soviet officials and that it is to be hoped that the appropriate American law enforcing authorities will treat them with the courtesy due officials of foreign governments who possess no diplomatic immunities or rights.   At the same time, it might be desirable to impress the Ambassador with the fact that Soviet officials in the United States not connected with the Embassy or with Soviet consular offices should realize that they are subject to American laws and should endeavor to conduct themselves in such a way that they will not be likely to come into conflict with the law enforcing authorities.

It is possible that the Ambassador may again raise the question of our refusal thus far to issue passports to American engineers good for travel in the Soviet Union.   If he does, it might be best for us to continue to follow the line that until we see a change in the treatment accorded to American citizens in the Soviet Union on the part of the Soviet Government, we feel that in the interest of good relations between the two governments, it would be wise to reduce to a minimum the number of American citizens in the Soviet Union. It is not believed that it would be advisable to endeavor to solve this problem by an exchange of notes for two reasons:

1. In view of the uncertainty of the future we cannot afford to promise definitely that we will allow American citizens to go to the Soviet Union in cases where it is useful for the Soviet Government to have them;

2. Any promise on the part of the Soviet Government to give us most-favored-nation treatment with regard to the freedom of travel of American citizens in the Soviet Union would be of little value since the travel of all foreigners, including even that of Germans, is so restricted that we would not be able to use such a Soviet promise in endeavoring to improve the position of our own nationals in that country.

It seems, therefore, that this problem can be solved only by a change in the attitude of the Soviet authorities with regard to American citizens already in the Soviet Union.

Under extraneous matters which the Soviet Ambassador continues to inject into the conversations fall various problems connected with the Baltic States. Although the Ambassador thus far has limited his demands of recognition of Soviet conquests to the Baltic, there seems to be little doubt, in view of the development of conversations between Great Britain and the Soviet Union, that if he should receive any encouragement with respect to this area, his demands will be enlarged to include Eastern Poland, Bessarabia, etc. His demands with respect to the ships and frozen funds, of course, merely represent Soviet endeavors to drive a wedge into our whole policy of refusing to recognize Soviet conquests in Europe and perhaps later in Asia.

It will be observed that under the heading of American complaints or requests we have thus far gained nothing, unless the Soviet agreement to establish an American Consulate General in Vladivostok may be considered as a concession arising from these conversations.[19] If the opportunity presents itself, it is suggested that it be made clear to Mr. Oumansky that the establishment of a consular office in Vladivostok has no direct connection with the outcome of the conversations. Our request for such an office was made prior to the opening of the conversations and we feel that since there are two Soviet consular offices at present on the Pacific coast,[20] our consular office should

---

[19] For correspondence concerning the negotiations for the establishment of an American Consulate General in Vladivostok, see pp. 460 ff.

[20] The Soviet Union maintained a Consulate General in San Francisco, California, and a Consulate in Los Angeles, California.

be opened in Vladivostok without further delay and regardless of the outcome of the present conversations. You may care to point out that we are appointing Mr. Ward, now First Secretary in Moscow, as Consul in Vladivostok and are ordering him to proceed as soon as possible to that city for the purpose of arranging for offices, living quarters, etc., and for the opening of the Consulate General. You may care to add that we appreciate the decision taken by the Soviet authorities to permit the opening of the consular office and that we are depending upon their sympathetic cooperation for the successful conduct of the office.

The difficulties encountered by our Embassy in Moscow have *not* been appreciably lightened as a result of the conversations. It might be well to impress this fact upon Mr. Oumansky. It will be noted from Mr. Steinhardt's telegram that he brought the following matters to the attention of Lozovsky, the Assistant Commissar for Foreign Affairs, on the afternoon of November 19:

1. The continued difficulties of the Embassy in protecting and assisting American citizens in the Soviet Union arising from the lack of cooperation on the part of the Soviet authorities.

(*a*) The reluctance of the Soviet authorities to grant the Embassy access to persons in prison claiming American citizenship. (It will be noted that since this conversation the Soviet authorities have permitted the Embassy to see another American citizen in jail.)

(*b*) The failure of the Soviet authorities to permit American citizens in certain areas under Soviet control to depart to the United States, or even to appear at the Embassy in order to arrange for travel documents.

(*c*) The refusal of the Soviet authorities to grant permission for the Soviet wives of American citizens to leave the Soviet Union in company with, or to join their husbands.

(*d*) The refusal of the Soviet authorities to give American citizens in transit through Moscow the necessary time with which to obtain requisite visas, including Soviet exit visas.

2. The continued lack of consideration shown by the Soviet authorities with regard to the Embassy and members of the Embassy staff, as for example:

(*a*) The unfriendly treatment still shown by the Soviet Customs authorities which was recently illustrated by their act of damaging certain foodstuffs destined for the Embassy by thrusting iron rods through the containers.

(*b*) The quadrupling of freight charges on food shipments from Vladivostok to Moscow so that at the present time the rate exceeds 2000 rubles a ton.

(*c*) Arresting without notice another Soviet employee of the Embassy, leaving his wife and 6-months-old child without any means of support. (This is the fifth employee to be arrested.)

(*d*) Refusal to permit installation of a gasoline container within the Embassy premises, although similar containers have been installed by the Soviet authorities in like premises. (This refusal means much loss of time and inconvenience.)

(*e*) The failure of the Soviet authorities thus far to grant additional quarters to the Embassy which is desperately in need of them since its work has been greatly increased as a result of the taking over by the Soviet Government of the Baltic States and Eastern Poland and the refusal of the Soviet authorities to permit the maintenance of a consular office in Riga.

711.61/799

Memorandum of Conversation, by the Under Secretary of State (Welles)

[WASHINGTON,] November 27, 1940.

The Soviet Ambassador called to see me this afternoon. I went over with him point by point all of the problems set forth in the memorandum attached herewith,[21] prepared by the European Division, which had to do with the machine tool controversy and with our own complaints against the Soviet Government.

Rather to my surprise, the Ambassador's attitude was most conciliatory and friendly, and, while he complained vehemently, as was to be expected, with regard to the decisions reached by the Administrator of Export Control, he stated that his reception both by Colonel Maxwell and by the committee headed by Mr. Philip Young had been exceedingly courteous and friendly and that every consideration had been given to the arguments which he had set forth. He again insisted, however, that the Soviet Government be permitted to obtain the thirty-four machine tools now in ports of the United States and that the Administrator of Export Control be requested to reconsider the decisions reached with regard to List C. I stated to the Ambassador that as he well knew, the Department of State had to be guided in matters of this kind by the decisions reached by the experts in charge of national defense problems and that I was sure he would realize that public opinion in the United States would never sanction in times like these the overruling by officials of the Department of State of the competent authorities in charge of the national defense program. I said, however, that I would be glad to discuss the matter once more with Colonel Maxwell and that I would then let the Ambassador know the result of such conversation.

The Ambassador adopted a sympathetic and responsive attitude when I read to him a list of the American complaints against the

---

[21] *Supra.*

Soviet Government but classified them as of minor importance compared with the grievances of the Soviet Government against the United States. I said that it seemed to me impossible to weigh in the balance the importance of the complaints of one side or of the other and that as he and I had agreed, our conversation should be directed towards the removal of legitimate causes for complaint in the interest of paving the way to a more profitable relationship between the two Governments. The Ambassador said that he would take up all of the complaints I had read to him once more with his Government. He mentioned one or two of these complaints on the ground that he felt the cause therefor had already been removed. I insisted, however, that the principle of permitting individuals claiming American citizenship to go to the American Embassy in Moscow and there be afforded the opportunity of proving their citizenship to our own authorities was one of the greatest importance and one upon which we must insist. He appeared to be responsive in this regard.

The Ambassador brought up again the question of the Baltic ships. I said that it seemed to me that he and I must recognize that we were up against a question of principle here upon which this Government was not prepared to yield and upon which I assumed, from what he told me, the Soviet Government was not prepared to yield. I said if there were any practical way of solving the question of the Baltic ships without bringing up the question of principle, I would be very glad to consider it. I asked him what the attitude of his Government had been with regard to the requisition of Baltic ships in British ports by the British Government. The Ambassador said the Soviet Government had objected vigorously. He then remarked that he thought a practical solution which would not raise the question of principle would be for the authorities of the United States to issue clearance papers to the Baltic vessels which desired to proceed to Baltic or Russian ports. I said that I would give the entire question further consideration.

The Ambassador complained that the arrangement which had been agreed upon with regard to the visits of Soviet engineers to the Wright Aeronautical Corporation in Paterson was not being carried out. I told him that I would be happy to have this matter looked into immediately.

Upon the conclusion of the discussion of these matters, which took a very considerable period, I asked the Ambassador whether he had any information with regard to recent political developments affecting his Government which he felt disposed to communicate to me. The Ambassador said that the reports regarding Molotov's visit to Berlin [22] had been greatly distorted and were completely fantastic. He said that he was authorized to state to me that the foreign policy of the Soviet Union remained completely independent after Molotov's visit to Berlin and that the policy of the Soviet Union would continue to be a policy of complete neutrality and of avoidance of participation in war. He stated that the Soviet was anxious to enlarge its commercial relations with Germany and that his Government believed that as a result of the visit, progress in this regard would be made.

I said to the Ambassador that as he knew, this Government regarded with the utmost interest the situation of China and that it was prepared to give further material assistance to China. I stated that the maintenance of the independence and integrity of China was a primary objective in the foreign policy of the United States. The Ambassador stated that he was authorized likewise to say that the policy of the Soviet with regard to China was identical with that of the United States.[23] He agreed that insofar as Russia and the United States were concerned, there was no conflict of interest between them in the Pacific, but that, on the contrary, their objectives were similar. I asked the Ambassador if it was true that his Government had ceased to give material assistance to China in recent months. He stated that so far as he was informed this was not correct and that in a recent conversation which he had had with Dr. T. V. Soong,[24] Dr. Soong had assured him that Russian military supplies were still being received by the Chinese Government from the Soviet. The Ambassador expressed great interest in Japanese movements in southern Asia. He expressed the opinion that Japan was probably preparing through Indochina and Thailand some movement against Singapore from the rear. I said that this might well be the case although some attack against the Netherlands East Indies was, of course, likewise possible. I said that I had no very clear impression as yet that the Japanese Government had in fact determined what course it was going to pursue. I stated that it seemed to me undoubtedly true that Japanese activities in southern Asia would be far less in scope and extent if the Chinese Government had both the moral and material support of Russia.

S[UMNER] W[ELLES]

[22] Molotov visited Berlin November 12–14, 1940. German accounts of the conversations held are published in Departmet of State, *Nazi-Soviet Relations, 1939–1941* (Washington, Government Printing Office, 1948), pp. 217–255.
[23] Concerning the attitude toward China, see memorandum of November 27 by the Under Secretary of State, p. 237.
[24] Chairman, Board of Directors, Bank of China; former Finance Minister of China.

711.61/775 : Telegram

The Ambassador in the Soviet Union (Steinhardt) to the Secretary of State

Moscow, November 29, 1940—7 p. m.
[Received 10 : 25 p. m.]

1645. For the Under Secretary. Since my interview with Lozovski on November 19 (reported in my No. 1579, November 19, 9 p. m.), the following matters which I discussed with him have been dealt with : I have been permitted to visit the imprisoned individual whose American citizenship was established in the course of the interview and whose release I now anticipate; 38 Americans in the Lwow area have been permitted to depart for the United States; permission has been granted to export a limited quantity of gasoline to our Legation at Stockholm; corrective measures have been promised with respect to the handling of Embassy shipments by the Customs authorities; assurances have been given that in the future American citizens in transit through Moscow will be permitted to remain here for the time necessary to effect their documentation; the matter of the arrested Soviet employee of the Embassy is being satisfactorily disposed of; an investigation has been promised of the excessive freight charges levied on our food shipments from Vladivostok; assurances have been given Soviet frontier authorities will be instructed to discontinue the confiscation of small amounts of American currency from American citizens departing from the Soviet Union.

No action has as yet been taken by the Soviet authorities in respect of the other matters referred to in my telegram under reference but I am now hopeful that they may also be disposed of.

STEINHARDT

———————

711.61/773 : Telegram

The Secretary of State to the Ambassador in the Soviet Union (Steinhardt)

WASHINGTON, December 3, 1940—4 p. m.

828. Your 1579, November 19, 7 [9] p. m. The Department approves the steps you have taken and the policy you have adopted in your conversations with Lozovski and is especially glad that you have brought this matter to its attention at this time. You may be sure that you will have its full support in your efforts to solve the problems confronting the Embassy.

On November 27 Mr. Welles personally discussed with the Soviet Ambassador the various matters referred to in your telegram under reference. In response to the Ambassador's contention that these problems were of minor importance compared with the grievances of the Soviet Government against the United States, Mr. Welles pointed out that it appeared impossible to weigh in the balance the importance of the complaints of one side or of the other, and referred to the understanding between the Ambassador and Mr. Welles that their conversations should be directed towards the removal of legitimate causes for complaint with the purpose of paving the way to a more profitable relationship between the two governments. The Ambassador adopted a sympathetic and responsive attitude and promised to transmit Mr. Welles' remarks to his Government.

The Department is pleased to note the favorable results attained so far, as reported in your 1645, November 29, 9 [7] p. m. It would appear from Oumansky's present conciliatory and friendly manner that the Soviet Government, for the present at least, is assuming a more reasonable attitude in regard to the solution of outstanding problems in Soviet-American relations. In your discretion you may inform the appropriate Soviet authorities that your Government is appreciative of the tendency of Soviet officials to adopt a more cooperative attitude towards the Embassy and its problems.

Please continue to keep the Department informed of further developments.

HULL

---

138 U.S.S.R./605a : Telegram

The Secretary of State to the Ambassador in the Soviet Union
(Steinhardt)

WASHINGTON, December 13, 1940—4 p. m.

869. Since the receipt of your 120 of February 1, noon, the Department has been issuing no passports valid for travel to the Soviet Union except to American government officials, in certain instances to accredited newspaper correspondents, and to fur buyers who have built up a business based on Russian purchases. We are now considering the advisability of resuming the issuance of passports to American engineers proceeding under contract to various parts of the Soviet Union since we understand from your 1645 of November 29, 7 p. m., that the treatment of American citizens in the Soviet Union has improved considerably. The Department would like to have your views before a final decision is taken.

The Soviet Ambassador is calling on Mr. Welles on Monday afternoon, December 16. If there are any matters which you wish Mr. Welles to discuss with the Ambassador please include them with your recommendations relative to passports.

HULL

811.20 (D) Regulations/3652

Memorandum by Mr. Edward Page, Jr., of the Division of European Affairs to Mr. Alexander Schnee of the Division of Controls

[WASHINGTON,] December 14, 1940.

MR. SCHNEE: Many thanks for bringing this matter to my attention. There would appear to be no objection to the issuance of the attached license [25] since the Soviet Union has been in past years a fairly large purchaser of non-aviation gasoline for shipment to Vladivostok. Shipments so far this year (not including that contemplated in the attached license) have amounted to:

January–September	559, 571 barrels
October	246, 310 "
November 1–25	---
Total	805, 881 barrels.

If the present purchase amounting to about 521,000 barrels is included in the 1940 exports, a total of approximately 1,325,000 barrels will have been exported to the Soviet Union. This is below former annual exports amounting in the past to an average of 1,500,000 barrels.

---

138 U.S.S.R./606 : Telegram

The Ambassador in the Soviet Union (Steinhardt) to the Secretary of State

Moscow, December 15, 1940—7 p. m.
[Received 8 : 02 p. m.]

1733.   Department's 869, December 13, 4 p. m.   At the present time I see no objection in principle to the resumption of the issuance of passports to American engineers desiring to proceed under contract to various parts of the Soviet Union.   However, in view of the difficult living conditions, inadequate communication facilities and the fact that travel within the Soviet Union and particularly exit therefrom are made difficult by the Soviet authorities and entail excessive delays it would seem preferable to limit the issuance of such passports to special cases.

It would be extremely helpful if, when advising Umanski of the decision in principle with respect to the resumption of the issuance of passports to American engineers to enter the Soviet Union, Mr. Welles would say that he expects the Soviet Government to grant exit visas to the six Soviet wives of American citizens, to provide the prom-

---

[25] Not attached to file copy of this document.

ised additional housing for the Embassy personnel and to desist from discriminating against American newspaper correspondents in the application of the censorship.

With respect to the foregoing the following background may be useful to Mr. Welles: Three of the wives in question are married to American correspondents. Although I have been able during the past 16 months to extract a not inconsiderable number of exit visas for the Soviet wives of other American citizens, the three in question have been studiously passed by each time by the Soviet authorities. As all three of the husbands have over a period of years shown pronounced Leftist tendencies in their writing I presume that the Soviet Government may not desire their departure in view of the probability that they would be replaced by correspondents whose despatches might be more objective. The failure to obtain exit visas for their wives in at least two of the cases has, to my knowledge, operated conveniently to enable the husbands for several years to avoid transfer from Moscow.

Insofar as concerns the matter of housing the apartment definitely promised us by November 15 has not materialized, and there seems little prospect that without Mr. Welles' assistance any housing will be forthcoming for an indefinite period of time. I am particularly concerned on this subject as several of the new clerks are due here within the course of the next few days and as our existing apartments are still badly overcrowed they will be compelled to reside in a hotel.

Insofar as concerns the discrimination against the representatives of the Associated Press and United Press they have for over a year now been denied telephone facilities which are regularly granted to the German and Italian correspondents and their despatches have been subjected to a much more severe censorship as evidenced by a comparison of identic despatches.

STEINHARDT

861.24/434½

Memorandum by the Assistant Chief of the Division of European Affairs (Henderson)

[WASHINGTON,] December 16, 1940.

Lieutenant Stout, assistant to Colonel Maxwell, gave me the following information today with regard to the various lists which have been under discussion between the Soviet Ambassador and Mr. Oumansky [*Welles*].

It appears that Mr. Oumansky submitted early in November or late in October through the Department to Colonel Maxwell a list of 62 items which he desired to have exported. It seems that all of these items represent machines which had already been manufactured and were ready for export. Colonel Maxwell's office broke this list into two: list A was composed of 32 items which it was decided should not be exported; list B was composed of 29 items, the export of which was agreed to. Apparently an additional item was not considered as a machine tool and so was not included in either list.

Of the 32 items on list A it was subsequently found that 4 items were aeronautical equipment rather than machine tools. One of these 4 items has been released for export and the other 3 are under discussion. The list of 21 machine tools, which Colonel Maxwell on December 12 informed us it had been decided to release, has been made as list F. List F is composed of machine tools taken from the 32 items on list A which we had originally decided not to release. Five other items on list A have been requisitioned by the Government and 2 have been turned over to American firms; therefore, of the 32 items originally on list A, 7 have been retained in the United States, 22 are to be released, and 3 aeronautical items are being discussed.

Sometime early in November, Mr. Oumansky submitted a list of 103 items, for which export licenses had been refused, to the Ministry of Export with the request that the refusal be reconsidered. This list was known as list C. Subsequently, list C was amended by an additional 15 items. The additional list is known as list D. Thus, lists C and D together comprise 118 items. From list C only 1 item was released. From list D 2 items have subsequently been released and it is learned that 2 had already been released. Lists C and D are made up of heterogeneous items which the Soviet Government wished particularly to have.

On December 11 a list of 6 items was sent to the Department by the Administrator of Export Control with the statement that it had been decided that these items should be released. None of these items have appeared on any lists, with the exception of 2 which apparently have been carried on list D referred to above.

711.61/780½

Memorandum of Conversation, by the Assistant Chief of the Division of European Affairs (Henderson)

[WASHINGTON,] December 16, 1940.

Participants: Mr. C. A. Oumansky, Soviet Ambassador;
Mr. Sumner Welles, Under Secretary;
Mr. Ray Atherton, Acting Chief, Division of European Affairs;
Mr. Loy W. Henderson, Assistant Chief, Division of European Affairs.

At Mr. Welles' suggestion, the Soviet Ambassador called upon him at 4 o'clock this afternoon in order to continue the discussions which had been in progress regarding various phases of Soviet-American relations. Mr. Atherton and Mr. Henderson of the Division of European Affairs were also present.

MACHINE TOOLS

Mr. Welles informed the Ambassador that as a result of efforts made by the highest officials of the American Government—efforts in which the head of the United States Government himself had shown an interest—it has become possible to arrange for the release to the Soviet Union of an additional 21 machines out of the list of 61 which the Ambassador had submitted to the Department a number of weeks ago. Mr. Welles reminded the Ambassador that these 61 machines formed a group which had already been manufactured and delivered and were lying in warehouses awaiting export. He pointed out that 29 of these machines had already been released; that with the release of the additional 21 plus one machine which was an aeronautical device rather than a machine tool, the situation with respect to the 61 items on the list was now as follows:

```
Released to the Soviet Union . . . . . . . . . . . . 51
Requisitioned by the American Government . . . 5
Turned over to American firms with the
    consent of Stankoimport . . . . . . . . . . . . 2
Airplane parts still held in the United States . . 3
                                                    —
    Total . . . . . . . . . . . . . . . . . . . . . 61
```

Mr. Oumansky expressed his appreciation of the interest which Mr. Welles and other officials of the American Government had displayed in the matter. He said that the release of these machine tools must be regarded as an indication of a friendly spirit on the part of the American Government towards the Soviet Government. He nevertheless felt that it was his duty to point out that his Government was disappointed that the American Government had not been able to adopt his suggestion that all the machines lying in port ready for shipment be released; that the American Government had decided to divide them into two groups, one group to be detained in this country and the other to be exported to the Soviet Union. He said that although the release of 51 of the 61 machines was now being permitted, it was necessary to point out that the American Government during recent weeks had requisitioned machine tools from its list of 61 in the value of $851,354. He pointed out that the five machines which had been requisitioned were apparently worth over $800,000, whereas the 51 which had been released were valued at less than $1,200,000. The concessions which the American Government had made were not as great as it would seem when one considered the value of the machines which had been detained.

The Ambassador asked Mr. Welles if he had any additional information to impart regarding the lists of machine tools known as "List C" which he had given to Colonel Maxwell. This list, the Ambassador stated, as amended, was made up of 118 machines at a value of approximately $4,300,000. The machines in this list had already been ordered and some were in the various stages of manufacture but no export licenses covering them had as yet been obtained. After a number of conversations on this subject with Colonel Maxwell, Colonel Maxwell had informed the Ambassador that one machine valued at $7000 could be exported. Subsequently, it had been agreed that licenses could be issued for machines in the C list to the value of an additional $72,000. The picture was most disappointing. The Soviet Government had in good faith placed orders in the United States for machine tools amounting to over $4,000,000 and it had been informed that from these machine tools it could have items valued at less than $100,000. Another most disturbing matter had come to the attention of the Ambassador. Mr. Seldyakov of Stankoimport had engaged in some discussions with Mr. Mason Britton, Chief of the Machine Tool Division of the Advisory Committee to the Council of National Defense, with regard to the question of priorities for Soviet machine tools. Mr. Britton had frankly informed Mr. Seldyakov that the American machine tool industry was at present so choked with orders for machines necessary for national defense that the delivery of machines to the Soviet Union for which licenses had already been granted would probably have to be postponed until the end of 1941 or until 1942. The Ambassador said that therefore there were two urgent problems which still remained for discussion: (1) the granting of licenses for the export of those tools set forth in List C which had already been ordered; (2) the question as to how soon it would be possible for American machine tool shops to turn out machine tools for which export licenses had already been granted. The Ambassador added that he felt that thus far the American officials in the Administration for Export Control and in the Defense Commission had failed to take into consideration Soviet needs. He had been treated with great courtesy by these officials but had obtained the impression that they were thinking only of the interests of American national defense and were ignoring entirely the problems of Soviet industry. A full satisfaction of Soviet needs would require only two percent of present American machine tool shop production. It seemed to him, therefore, that without any great sacrifice of American interests, more consideration for the Soviet position should be shown.

The Ambassador added that he was particularly disappointed that Mr. Welles had not informed him that more of the machine tools contained in List C could be released. He had spoken with Colonel Maxwell on the subject recently and Colonel Maxwell had given him to understand that the Administration for Export Control had not been asked by the Department of State to reconsider the decision which it had made with respect to the machines on List C.

Mr. Welles told Mr. Oumansky that it had been the feeling of the American officials with whom he talked that the machine tools on the docks belonged to a special category and that, therefore, they had made every possible effort to obtain the release of such of them as could possibly be spared. As a result of their efforts, the American Government had retained only 10 items out of the 61. The 51 which had been released were also needed by the American Government and their release represented considerable sacrifice. With regard to machine tools belonging to other categories which had not already arrived at the dock ready for shipment, he must frankly state that it would be possible to release them only when the national defense program of the United States permitted. Soviet needs would be given consideration, however, when decisions were made with respect to the delivery of such machine tools. There must be some misunderstanding regarding List C since Mr. Welles knew personally that the Colonel had been making a study of the list in the hope that it might be found possible to release to the Soviet Union certain tools set forth in it. Mr. Welles thereupon handed to the Soviet Ambassador a second list containing six additional items which it had been found possible to release. Mr. Oumansky asked whether these items had been set forth in List C. Mr. Welles replied that in his opinion some of them had been contained in that list. In any event, the decision to release them, Mr. Welles said, showed that Colonel Maxwell was continuing his efforts to release as many machine tools as could be spared for Soviet use.

Mr. Oumansky said that he would appreciate it if:

(1) Mr. Welles would find it possible to advise Colonel Maxwell to do what he could to expedite decisions with regard to the issuance of export licenses, since the first of the year was approaching and the Soviet Government should know without further delay what it might expect to be able to purchase in the United States. The Soviet economy was planned and therefore the Soviet Government must have some idea in advance regarding markets in which it could buy;

(2) Steps could be taken to clarify as far as possible the possibilities of the manufacturing of goods for which licenses had been issued or would be issued. Mr. Britton had stated that it was possible that in some instances licenses might expire several times before it would be possible for American industry to produce the machine tools covered by such licenses. As he had already pointed out, Soviet orders would

require only two percent of the production capacity of American machine tool plants. His Government believed, therefore, that it would be possible without injury to the American defense program to give a reasonable degree of priority to Soviet orders. The Soviet Government must realize that in the priority order, place No. 1 must be given to tools needed for American consumption. What place would Soviet orders have? Some kind of stability seemed to be necessary in order to make it possible for the Soviet purchasers to continue their activities in the United States.

Mr. Welles said that he was sure that Colonel Maxwell was doing all that he could to expedite decisions with regard to the issuance of licenses covering orders already placed. He added that he felt that the Soviet Government was fully entitled to such clarity as could be obtained with respect to the possibility of obtaining merchandise already ordered and for which licenses had already been issued. He would take steps to inquire into this matter.

Mr. Oumansky stated that there was still a third point to be discussed:

(3) It was important that the Soviet Government should know what the attitude of the American Government might be with regard to orders which had as yet been unplaced and which the Soviet Government desired to place as soon as it had received authorization so to do. About ten days ago applications for permission to place orders aggregating approximately $1,200,000 had already been submitted to Mr. Buckley of the President's Liaison Committee. It was hoped that these and future applications would be given favorable consideration so that the Soviet Government could continue to obtain a fair share of its needs for machine tools in the United States.

Mr. Oumansky said that to sum up, he would like to discuss the manner in which the compromise suggestions which he had advanced on October 7 had been carried out. In his memorandum of that date,[26] he had suggested, (1) that the American Government release all machine tools on the docks; (2) that in considering applications for export permits the American Government would take Soviet needs into consideration; (3) that a system of compensation be adopted which would be similar to that used by the American Government during the last World War. Unfortunately, none of these three suggestions had thus far been followed by the American Government. With regard to suggestion No. 1, apparently about 40 percent of the machine tools on the docks in terms of value had been retained in the United States. With respect to No. 2, results make it evident that Soviet needs have not been taken into consideration. With regard to the means of compensation, the Soviet Government has as yet had no answer. So far as compensation is concerned, the question of principle is really more important than that of the amounts involved.

---

[26] Not printed.

Mr. Welles replied that the Soviet Government must recognize the fact that the American Government had gone very far in endeavoring to meet the Soviet desires. The American Government had made a real sacrifice in releasing so many of the machine tools lying on the docks. Furthermore, the American authorities were examining still further the possibility of releasing certain tools contained in List C. The question of compensation was also receiving the attention of the American Government. The procedure for the items which had been requisitioned would probably be the procedure which would be followed in case of additional requisitioning. As soon as the two Governments had reached an agreement with regard to the machine tools contained in List A—that was, just as soon as the Soviet Government agreed that the matter of List A was closed—the American Government was willing to begin negotiations with respect to the matter of compensation.

The Question of the Moral Embargo

The Soviet Ambassador pointed out that negotiations had been going on for a period of five months. He said that he was personally willing to continue them indefinitely. The question involved was not, however, that of his personal pleasure but that of promoting the interests of his Government and increasing economic intercourse between the Soviet Union and the United States. In spite of numerous conversations which had taken place, the moral embargo was still in force. The Ambassador was aware of Mr. Welles' suggestion that the question of the lifting of the embargo be discussed when the machine tool problem was definitely settled. So far as he could see, however, the machine tool problem would probably continue for some time to come. It seemed that the question of machine tools would be active for almost an indefinite period.

Mr. Welles replied that it was his hope that at the very next conference the general questions and policies with respect to machine tools would be definitely settled so that the machine tool problem would be considered to be out of the way. Of course, there would be certain details to be worked out, but the main outline could be agreed upon. The Ambassador replied that the possibility of an agreement would be greatly facilitated when a clarification of the three points which he had already raised could be made.

Financial Transactions Between the Soviet and Rumanian Governments

The Ambassador said that according to a financial agreement which had been reached in July 1940 between the Rumanian and Soviet Governments, the Rumanian Government was to pay to the Soviet Government the sum of approximately 110,000,000 lei in final payment of salaries due railway employees in the Province of Bessarabia. The Rumanian Government on December 11 had therefore applied to the Treasury Department for a license to pay that amount, which represented $501,907.25, to the Soviet Government from the account of the National Bank of Rumania in the Chase National Bank of the City of New York.[27]

The Ambassador said that the Rumanian Legation in Washington had already requested that a license for the release of this shipment be issued.

Mr. Welles suggested that the Soviet Embassy prepare a memorandum or a note on the subject and said that upon the receipt of such memorandum or note the matter would have the attention of the appropriate Government authorities.

DIFFICULTIES ENCOUNTERED BY SOVIET ENGINEERS IN THE WRIGHT AERONAUTICAL PLANT

The Ambassador asked Mr. Welles if he had as yet succeeded in obtaining information regarding the difficulties encountered by the Soviet engineers in the Wright Aeronautical Plant at Paterson, New Jersey. He reminded Mr. Welles that in a previous conversation he had pointed out that the system governing the movements of these engineers, which had been worked out by the Navy, was not satisfactory since it failed to take into consideration the fact that the engineers were in the plant in accordance with a technical assistance contract. Mr. Welles said that he had taken the matter up but had as yet received no answer. He asked Mr. Henderson to make inquiries, with regard to the subject, of Mr. Orme Wilson of U–L.[28]

"SECONDARY MATTERS" RELATING TO THE WORK OF THE AMERICAN EMBASSY IN MOSCOW

The Ambassador said that in the previous conversation with Mr. Welles, Mr. Welles had brought to his attention certain "secondary matters" and "everyday questions" relating to the work of the American Embassy at Moscow. He had referred the matter to his Government and he had been able to obtain the following information on the subject:

The Soviet Government had been leaning over backwards in its endeavors to make sure that persons in the Western Ukraine and Western White Russia who stated that they were American citizens and who might possibly be American citizens be given the opportunity to go to the American Embassy at Moscow to verify their American

---

[27] Rumanian assets in the United States had been frozen by Executive Order No. 8565 of October 10, 1940. For text, see 5 *Federal Register* 4062. For the regulations issued by the Treasury Department on October 10, 1940, see 5 *Federal Register* 4063.

[28] Liaison Officer, Liaison Office of the Under Secretary of State.

citizenship and obtain passports. It had therefore permitted numbers of such persons who did not possess valid documents showing themselves to be American citizens, to appear at the American Embassy. It would appear that 60 American citizens have been permitted to leave. Mr. Steinhardt had said that there were 140 American citizens still in that portion of the Soviet Union, and the American Embassy in a later note had said that there were 350 American citizens. The Soviet authorities, after careful examination of these cases, had ascertained that the bulk of them were really former Polish citizens and, therefore, had become Soviet citizens. For instance, the American Embassy at Moscow had written to the Soviet Government about a certain Rozkowsky.[29] The Embassy had maintained that Rozkowsky was an American citizen in jail. The Soviet Government, after investigating the matter, had learned that the person in question was not an American citizen, and he had never been in the United States. It seemed, however, that on January 8, 1939 he had applied for his first papers. The case of Rozkowsky is a typical case. The Under Secretary said that there must be a mistake since no one could take out first papers without being in the United States. Mr. Henderson stated that he felt sure that certain circumstances not mentioned by the Ambassador must be involved since the American Embassy would not claim that Mr. Rozkowsky was an American citizen unless it was in possession of some information which caused it to believe that he had a claim to American citizenship. Mr. Oumansky said that if there were any special circumstances, he knew nothing with respect to them.

Mr. Oumansky then took up the question of American citizens in prison in the Soviet Union. He said that of the six persons in jail in the Soviet Union whom the American Government considered to be American citizens, only two had turned out to be American citizens. Of this number, one had already departed for the United States and the other, who had been visited in prison by the Ambassador and a member of his staff, could leave the Soviet Union whenever funds for that purpose were received from the United States.

With respect to the Soviet wives of American citizens who could not leave the Soviet Union, the Ambassador said that only six cases, so far as he knew, were pending. Since the definite departure of these persons meant loss of Soviet citizenship, their applications to leave

---

[29] Mieczyslav Ignatyevich Roszkowski, born at Fall River, Massachusetts, on October 29, 1920, had been seized in Soviet-occupied Poland on June 29, 1940, for alleged illegal possession of firearms and had eventually been sentenced to 3 years imprisonment. This term had been reduced to 1 year. After intercession by the American Embassy in Moscow, Roszkowski was finally deported to the United States in 1941. Correspondence on this case will be found in *Foreign Relations*, 1941, vol. I, pp. 926–954, *passim*.

the country must necessarily be considered by the highest Soviet authorities. The procedure was rather elaborate and much time must necessarily be consumed before final decisions could be made.

With respect to the issuance of visas permitting American citizens coming out of the Western Ukraine and Western White Russia to remain in Moscow long enough to obtain American passports, he said he had been advised that orders had now been issued which would permit them to remain in Moscow for five days.

The Ambassador then said that one of the complaints of the Embassy apparently was the lack of sufficient living and office space. He had been instructed by his Government to state that two apartments would be furnished the Embassy in December and five more in January. He said that anyone who had lived in Moscow must realize, in view of the shortage of housing in that city, that the furnishing of these apartments represented a real sacrifice on the part of the Soviet Government.

He then referred to a complaint of the American Embassy that the Soviet Government would not permit a gasoline container to be sunk in the court of the Embassy. He said that the permit could not be issued since it was contrary to the Soviet fire regulations to permit a large supply of gasoline to be stored so close to a residence. The Soviet Government was, furthermore, surprised that the Embassy should make such a request since no limitation had been placed upon the amount of gasoline which the Embassy might use. He said that the Soviet Government had no intention to limit the Embassy's supply of gasoline and that new regulations which had been issued curtailing the use of gasoline in the Soviet Union would not be applied to the American Embassy.

The Ambassador said that he felt that the Customs difficulties which the Embassy had encountered with respect to the shipment of food supplies were for the most part due to misunderstandings. The Embassy had stated recently that a large shipment which had arrived in Vladivostok was composed entirely of canned foods. Later, however, it had been learned that bottled beverages were also in the shipment. Since there was a great difference between the cost of the freight of canned goods and that of bottled beverages, much delay had been encountered in separating the contents of the shipment and cataloguing them for the purpose of calculating freight rates.

With regard to the request that four former employees of the American Legation at Kaunas be permitted to leave Lithuania, the Soviet Government regretted that it could not permit them to leave the country. These persons, he said, were former Lithuanian citizens and were now Soviet citizens and therefore subject to Soviet laws and regulations.

The Ambassador said that Lozovsky had instructed him to state that the Soviet Government could not accept from the American Government such minor complaints as those about which he had just discussed as set-offs to Soviet representations of real importance. The Soviet Government felt that the matters which the Soviet Ambassador had been instructed to discuss with the Under Secretary pertained to the basic economic relations between the two countries, and should not be confused with minor irritations. The Ambassador said that on the Soviet side there were numerous matters relating to difficulties encountered by Soviet officials in this country which he could take up during these conversations. He did not feel, however, that it would be appropriate to deal with them in this manner. His secretaries were taking them up from time to time with Mr. Page and Mr. Henderson. The Ambassador said that, for instance, questions arising from laws relating to fingerprinting and to registration for the draft had already given rise to an unpleasant incident and probably would occasion more difficulties in the future. For some reason the American Government was refusing to issue any documents to Soviet officials in the United States which would show that they had been registered with the Department as Government officials and, therefore, were not required to have their fingerprints taken or to register for the draft. A week or so ago a Soviet official while in the hospital was disturbed by the American authorities who insisted that while he lay ill he should register as an alien and have his fingerprints taken. They refused to listen to his explanation that he had been registered in the State Department as a Soviet official and therefore was not required to register as an alien. The Ambassador said that it seemed to him that it should be to the interest of the American Government as well as the Soviet Government to take steps to prevent incidents of this kind from occurring.

The Under Secretary said that he thought it was a reasonable request that foreign officials in the United States be furnished with some kind of document in order to show that they were Government officials and were therefore not required to register for the draft or as aliens.

Mr. Henderson informed the Under Secretary that he understood that the matter had been discussed in the Department of State and with the Department of Justice and it had been decided that since no documents were issued to aliens who had registered, it had been decided that there was no necessity for issuing documents to those aliens who were not required to register. Mr. Henderson said that although the American Government was not issuing such documents, he could see no reason why the Soviet Embassy could not furnish Soviet officials in the United States with documents showing that they had been registered with the State Department as Government officials and therefore should not be required to register either for the draft or as aliens.

Mr. Oumansky said that he had suggested such a procedure some time ago and had obtained the impression that it would not have the approval of the American Government.

Mr. Welles said that he felt strongly that some steps should be taken in order to prevent incidents such as that which had taken place in the hospital from occurring and requested Mr. Henderson to give him more information regarding the matter so that he could give it his personal attention.

Mr. Welles stated that he did not wish the remarks of the Ambassador to the effect that the American Government was endeavoring to introduce minor irritations in the discussions to pass unanswered. He wished it to be understood that it was not his intention to oppose complaints by the Soviet Government with statements regarding the various difficulties encountered by the American Embassy at Moscow. He had referred to these difficulties only because it had been his understanding that the purpose of these conversations was not only to solve certain problems in Soviet-American relations but also to eliminate as far as possible various sources of irritation between them. He was glad to learn from Mr. Oumansky's explanations that steps had been taken by the Soviet Government for the purpose of removing some of the obstacles to the functioning of the American Embassy at Moscow.

Statement of the Foreign Policy of the Soviet Union

The Soviet Ambassador stated that in his previous conversation with Mr. Welles several questions had been raised with regard to the foreign policy of the Soviet Union. The Ambassador said that he was prepared to formulate his answers to those questions and expressed his certainty that these answers represented the point of view of his Government. The Ambassador's statement was as follows:

"The Soviet Government stands on its position of a policy of peace and remains out of war. At the same time the Soviet Government endeavors to maintain normal political and economic relations with all Powers, including the belligerents. The character of the Soviet Union's relations with China remains invariably good neighborly and is guided by the spirit of the Chinese-Soviet non-aggression pact of 1937.[30] The Near Eastern policy of the Soviet Union is determined by the principle of further improvement of economic and political relations with all Near-Eastern States."

Mr. Welles replied that it was his understanding that during the previous conversation Mr. Oumansky had agreed with him that the

---

[30] Signed at Nanking August 21, 1937; for text, see League of Nations Treaty Series, vol. CLXXXI, p. 101.

policy of the United States towards China was similar to that of the Soviet Union. It is the present intention of the United States, Mr. Welles continued, to increase assistance to China in such manner as might be further possible. He added that he assumed that the Soviet Government had similar intentions. The Soviet Ambassador replied that in his opinion there could be no doubt that the intention of the Soviet Government to continue aid to China could be read into the statement which he had just made,[31] in view of the wording of the non-aggression pact of 1937 between China and the Soviet Union.

Mr. Welles stated that the statement which had just been made was of the utmost importance and was most gratifying to the Government of the United States.

Mr. Welles said that he had no further official business to discuss but he would like to mention a matter informally which was very much on his mind. That pertained to the desire of the many friends in the United States that Rabbi Schorr, one of the outstanding Jewish scholars, who at the present time is in or near Lwow, be given an exit visa so that he may come to the United States. Mr. Welles said that he thought that probably Mr. Oumansky was familiar with the case and that therefore it would not be necessary to go into it in detail. He pointed out that not only a great section of the Jewish community in the United States was interested in the matter but also some of the most important officials of the American Government.

The Ambassador said that he would look into the matter and take it up with his Government.

SUPPLEMENTARY STATEMENT OF THE SOVIET AMBASSADOR

The Soviet Ambassador subsequently informed Mr. Henderson that during the conversation with Mr. Welles on December 16 he had failed to stress properly the desire of his Government that in case export licenses should be revoked or refused covering machine tools produced in the United States under order of the Soviet Union, steps be immediately taken which would make possible the replacement of such tools. The Ambassador said that one of the conditions under which the Soviet Government had expressed a willingness to permit the American Government to retain some of the machine tools manufactured for the Soviet Union was that licenses be issued at once permitting the manufacture of identical tools for export to the Soviet Union.

The Soviet Ambassador also stated that careful checking of the lists which had been given to him thus far showed that with respect to value, only 57 percent of the machine tools which had been de-

---

[31] See memorandum of December 17 by the Assistant Chief of the Division of European Affairs, p. 238.

livered at the docks to Soviet foreign trade agencies had been released. The Ambassador said that he hoped that during the conversation with Mr. Welles he had made it clear that his Government continued to adhere to the conditions set forth in his memorandum of October 7, 1940. In presenting that memorandum, his Government had made certain sweeping concessions in order to contribute to the breaking of the deadlock in negotiations. These concessions had been made on certain conditions. Although the American Government had taken notice of the concessions it apparently had not given due attention to the fact that they were conditional. The situation at present, therefore, was that the Soviet Government had made contributions to the breaking of the deadlock and the American Government had not met it half way. The Soviet Government had asked that 100 percent of the machines already at the docks be released for use in the Soviet Union. Only 57 percent of them had been released. The Soviet Government had asked that Soviet needs be taken into consideration when decisions were being made with respect to the release of machine tools for which orders had already been placed. So far, with respect to values, less than one-eighth of a percent of the machine tools ordered, not yet manufactured,—that is, those contained in List C—were being released.

---

138 U.S.S.R./606

Memorandum of Conversation, by the Assistant Chief of the Division of European Affairs (Henderson)

[Washington,] December 17, 1940.

During the course of the conversation yesterday between Mr. Welles and Mr. Oumansky, Mr. Welles informed Mr. Oumansky that the Department had been giving serious consideration to the matter of issuing passports to American engineers proceeding to the Soviet Union in accordance with contracts calling for the rendering of technical assistance between themselves and the Soviet Government.

Mr. Welles said that it had been decided by the Department to give sympathetic consideration to the passport applications of American engineers desiring to proceed to the Soviet Union in case the Department should be convinced that their visits to the Soviet Union would be advantageous to the United States or helpful to the promotion of Soviet-American economic relations. This decision was based on the understanding that American citizens in the Soviet Union would be free to visit the American Embassy at any time or to leave the Soviet Union when they desired so to do.

Mr. Welles added that if at any time the Soviet Government was especially anxious to have the services of any particular American engineer or technician, it would be appropriate for Mr. Oumansky to bring the matter to the attention of the Department so the Department might give special consideration to the passport application.

861.24/438½

Memorandum of Conversation, by the Assistant Chief of the Division of European Affairs (Henderson)

[WASHINGTON,] December 20, 1940.

The Soviet Ambassador telephoned me late this afternoon. He said he had just returned from a talk with Colonel Maxwell; that as a result of the conversation, the machine tool situation had been somewhat clarified but, unfortunately, clarified in a negative manner.

The Ambassador stated that Colonel Maxwell had informed him that a number of the machine tools contained in the list of 21, which on December 16 the Under Secretary of State had informed could be released for export, had already been handed over to American manufacturers, were being used in American factories, and could not possibly be dismounted and sent to the Soviet Union. As a result, instead of the $670,000 worth of machine tools which Mr. Welles had promised him, the Soviet Government would receive tools only in the value of $270,000.

The Ambassador said that Colonel Maxwell stated that the error was entirely the Colonel's own fault. This confession of error on the part of Colonel Maxwell, however, did not relieve the situation so far as the Soviet Union was concerned. It would seem that the machine tools in question had been seized by the Navy without legal authority prior to July 2 and, without any requisitioning or any authority, had been diverted to use in American plants.

The Ambassador said that he has asked Colonel Maxwell regarding the machine tools in List C; that the Colonel had told him that the tools on List C were being given a constant study with the hope that it might be further possible to release more of them to the Soviet Union. The Colonel, however, was unable to give any assurances that any more of them would be released.

The Ambassador also referred to the list of six items which the Under Secretary had given him on December 16 with the statement that they were not needed for national defense and may be released. The Ambassador said that Colonel Maxwell had told him that he could make no definite promise that these machines would be released for export. Colonel Maxwell had said that they "may be released". Colonel Maxwell could give no absolute assurance that these or any other machines, regardless of whether or not export licenses had been obtained for them, could really be exported.

The Ambassador said that he regretted to say that he felt there had been little improvement in the whole situation with respect to machine tools. The many discussions had yielded few concrete results. He appreciated the fact that the Under Secretary had endeavored to be of assistance and regretted that the joint efforts of the Under Secretary and himself should have been almost in vain. Apparently the American Government had no intention to accept the conditions laid down in the Ambassador's memorandum of October 7.[32]

711.61/775 : Telegram

The Secretary of State to the Ambassador in the Soviet Union (Steinhardt)

WASHINGTON, December 21, 1940—2 p. m.

896. Your 1579, November 19, 9 p. m., and 1645, November 28 [*29*], 7 p. m.

Section 1. The Soviet Ambassador stated to Mr. Welles on December 16 that he had brought to the attention of his Government "certain secondary matters" relating to the work of the Embassy and had been informed as follows:

a. The Soviet Government had been leaning over backwards in its endeavors to make sure that persons in Soviet-occupied Poland who have any claim to American citizenship be permitted to proceed to the Embassy to verify their citizenship and to obtain passports. A number of persons who did not possess valid documents had been permitted to appear. The majority of those persons alleged to be American citizens by the Embassy had proved after careful examination by the Soviet authorities to be former Polish citizens and consequently Soviet citizens.

b. Of the six persons in jail whom the Embassy had considered to be American citizens, only two had proved to be such. One of these had been permitted to depart from the Soviet Union and the other could leave upon receipt of travel funds.

c. Considerable time must necessarily elapse before a decision could be reached with regard to the six Soviet wives who wished to depart since an elaborate procedure of renouncing Soviet citizenship was involved.

d. Orders had been issued which would permit American citizens proceeding from Soviet occupied Poland to remain in Moscow 5 days in order to obtain passports.

e. Two apartments would be furnished the Embassy in December and five more in January.

f. The sinking of a gasoline container in the Embassy court was contrary to Soviet fire regulations and would not be permitted. No limitation had been placed upon the amount of gasoline which the Embassy might use and the Soviet Government had no intention to

---

[32] Not printed.

limit the Embassy's supply. The new gasoline regulations did not apply to the Embassy.

g. The Customs difficulties regarding the food shipment had been due to misunderstandings over the contents of shipment.

h. The four former employees of the Kaunas Legation would not be permitted to depart since they were now Soviet citizens subject to Soviet law.

Section 2. The Ambassador added that his Government had instructed him to state that it objected to endeavors to oppose Soviet representations of real importance with "such minor complaints".

HULL

811.20 (D) Regulations/5437

Memorandum of Telephone Conversation, by the Assistant Chief of the Division of European Affairs (Henderson)

[WASHINGTON,] December 23, 1940.

Mr. Oumansky called me by telephone this afternoon and said that he was sorry to inform me that more machine tools sold to the Soviet Union were being requisitioned. He said that the Soviet purchasing agencies had bought ten machine tools from the Gear Grinding Machine Company of Detroit, Michigan. Export licenses had been issued covering all of them. Of these ten machines, six had been inspected, accepted, and shipped to the docks in New York. They had arrived at the docks on December 16. According to the Customs authorities, a telephone call from Mr. Schnee of the State Department stopped the loading of these machines. Mr. Schnee had informed the authorities that the export licenses which had been granted would be revoked. Out of the six machines at the docks, four have already been requisitioned and diverted to American use. The value of the ten machines was $64,349.

The Ambassador said that another machine had been purchased by Soviet authorities from the Federal Machine and Welding Company of Warren, Ohio. This machine was an electrical welding machine. The licenses which had been issued for the export of this machine had also been revoked. The Ambassador said that he had discussed this machine with Mr. Welles in October, and Mr. Welles had promised to look into the matter. The value of the welding machine was $200,000.

The Ambassador expressed the hope that the Department could take some steps in order that new export licenses would be issued permitting the forwarding of these machines to the Soviet Union where they were badly needed.

711.61/779 : Telegram

The Ambassador in the Soviet Union (Steinhardt) to the Secretary of State

Moscow, December 23, 1940—11 p. m.
[Received December 24—10 : 29 a. m.]

1776. Department's 896, December 21, 2 p. m. In the event that the Under Secretary should desire to reply to Umanski's statements on December 16, I submit the following comments.

(*a*) Of the approximate 600 persons in Soviet-occupied Poland whose claims to American citizenship have seemed sufficiently well-founded to warrant investigation by the Embassy, permission for only approximately 100 to depart from the Soviet Union or to come to Moscow for the purpose of obtaining American passports has been obtained by the Embassy during the past 15 months. Repeated representations have been made by the Embassy to the Commissariat for Foreign Affairs with respect to the other approximately 500 cases but without avail. Thus the extent to which the Soviet Government has "been leaning over backwards" in this matter is not likely to cause it to lose its balance.

(*b*) While the Embassy does not know which "six persons" Umanski referred to the four most recent cases which have come to the Embassy's attention were of individuals either bearing American passports or for whom the issuance thereof has been authorized.

(*c*) Of the six Soviet wives, three of them have been endeavoring to renounce Soviet citizenship for 3 years and I have been actively pressing for the entire six since my first arrival in Moscow. As evidence that the elaborate procedure cited by Umanski does not always necessitate the lapse of considerable time, I may point to the fact that when a British citizen endeavored to circumvent the procedure by abducting his wife in an airplane, the Soviet authorities enabled her to relinquish her Soviet citizenship within 2 or 3 days; and that in the case of one of the employees of the Embassy some years ago similar promptness was forthcoming.

(*d*) The orders to which Umanski referred have apparently been effective as the Embassy has had no further complaints on this score.

(*e*) I hope that Umanski's assurances as to the dates on which the apartments will be available will prove to be more reliable than the assurances received from the Soviet authorities in Moscow that these apartments would be furnished some months ago and the more recent assurances that at least some additional housing would be available not later than November 15.

(*f*) Apparently those administering the Soviet fire regulations consider the fire hazard greater in the ample garden of the American Embassy than from containers installed immediately adjacent to buildings in the center of Moscow. It is quite correct that no limitation has been placed upon the amount of gasoline which the Embassy may use nor is it the general practice of the Soviet Government to ration or limit purchases. A far more simple method is in vogue of limiting the total supply available to the city of Moscow with the result that for days and sometimes weeks at a time gasoline cannot be bought.

The mishandling of our food shipment took place despite the presence of an Embassy representative who exhibited detailed packing lists so that there could not have been any "misunderstanding" over the contents of the shipment. The misunderstanding to which Umanski refers arose subsequently out of a demand for quadruple the freight rate on another shipment and was in no sense related to the destruction of our food.

I am indebted to Umanski for information as to the position of the Soviet authorities with respect to the four former employees of our Legation in Kaunas as repeated representations to the Commissariat for Foreign Affairs have failed to elicit a definite response.

With respect to Umanski's final observations, the Under Secretary may wish to suggest to him that as a result of his years of residence in the United States, he may no longer attach as much importance to freedom of movement, housing, transportation, and a modest food supply as those of us who reside in his native city.

STEINHARDT

861.24/434½

Memorandum of Telephone Conversation, by the Assistant Chief of the Division of European Affairs (Henderson)

[WASHINGTON,] December 26, 1940.

The Soviet Ambassador called me this afternoon in order to make further representations regarding the requisitioning by the American Government of machine tools which had been ordered by Soviet purchasing agencies from the Gear Grinding Machine Company of Detroit, Michigan. The Ambassador said that he had discussed the matter with Colonel Maxwell and regretted to report that eight of the ten machines were to be requisitioned. He said that although the total value of these machines amounted to only $64,349, nevertheless, they were very important to Soviet economy. They were needed by the Soviet automobile plant in Gorki. Soviet engineers had spent much time in designing and inspecting these machines and the loss to the Soviet Government was much greater than their value.[33]

The Ambassador said he hoped that steps would be taken to revoke the requisition orders which had already been issued for them. He added that the Customs office in New York had informed him that Mr. Schnee had instructed them by telephone to detain the machines if they had not already been placed on board the ship, and said that if they were already loaded, they were to be permitted to proceed. The Ambassador also referred again to the welding machine, the license for which had been revoked, and said that he hoped that steps would be taken to permit it to go forward.

The Ambassador stated that he had had another conversation with Colonel Maxwell which was not at all satisfactory. Colonel Maxwell could not guarantee that any machines would go forward, including those on the lists given to Mr. Oumansky by Mr. Welles. The Colonel had stated that the presentation of lists of this kind to the Embassy merely signified that the appropriate officials of the American Government were willing to reconsider the question of the export of the machines on the list.

Colonel Maxwell also had as yet no good news for the Ambassador with respect to List C. Thus far, the Colonel maintained the position that it had been found impossible to grant export licenses for additional machines on this List.

711.61/781 : Telegram

The Ambassador in the Soviet Union (Steinhardt) to the Secretary of State

Moscow, December 26, 1940—8 p. m.
[Received 11 : 35 p. m.]

1781. Molotov asked me to call to see him this afternoon. He was in especially good humor and extremely cordial. He opened the conversation by asking me whether I could tell him the "present status" of the Baltic gold, ships and Legations in Washington and what was the "present attitude" of the United States towards the entry of the Baltic States into the Soviet Union. I replied that I was not conversant with the day to day status of the discussions between Mr. Welles and Umanski and was unaware of the extent to which these questions had been under discussion recently in Washington but that

---

[33] Mr. Henderson wrote at the beginning of this memorandum: "Note. The Soviet Ambassador called Mr. Henderson by telephone on December 30 in order to state that he had been advised by his Government that the gear grinding machines were urgently needed in the Soviet Union and to press for their release. L. W. H."

I assumed he was receiving regular reports from Umanski. Molotov then stated that he had been informed that the names and flags of the Baltic States [*ships*] were being changed and that some had already actually been sent to South America where they would be out of reach of the Soviet Union as it has no diplomatic representation in that area. He was quick to add that he understood that this action has been taken by the diplomatic representatives of the Baltic States in Washington but "with the full knowledge and consent of the American Government." He then inquired whether this procedure would continue. At this point I inquired whether he had not instructed Umanski to discuss the subject with Mr. Welles. He then asked me, "Do you think this matter can be separately dealt with—apart from the general conversations that are being carried on in Washington?" and concluded his inquiry with the statement that the Soviet Government must protest at these acts of the Baltic representatives with the consent of the United States. I replied that the question whether this subject could be separately dealt with was for the State Department to determine but that I would be glad to report his inquiry. There then ensued a general discussion as to the course of the conversations in Washington and I seized the opportunity to impress again upon Molotov the concessions that have already been made by the Department. Molotov replied by reciting what he described as the discriminatory acts of the United States, including what he referred to as unfriendly speeches by public officials in the United States. At this point and without conceding the accuracy of his statements I invited him to specify a single act since August which he regarded as discrimination. He conceded that there had been none, pointing out that at no time had there been any discrimination or unfriendly utterances emanating from Soviet sources. I then asked him whether he would like me to cite a few instances of discrimination against the United States and American interests which I added, did not cease in August but have continued up to the present time and referred to the negotiations with Sweden and Germany to compensate their respective nationals for property located in the Baltic States and to recent acts of discrimination against American newspaper correspondents. Molotov made the lame excuse that special conditions affected the German negotiations, such as transfer of population. When I inquired whether these special conditions also applied to Sweden he merely smiled. At one point in the course of our general discussion he intimated that since he understood that the talks in Washington did not include all questions between the two Governments there was no reason why the subject of the Baltic gold, ships and Legations could not be separately disposed of. He said that he regarded this question as the most important issue between the two

Governments. [?][34] of the American Government. When I asked him whether he did not think that the American Government during the past 3 or 4 months had already given ample evidence of its good will and desire to establish friendly relations, he replied "In a very small way." I then pointed out to him that the Soviet Government had not yet responded "even in a small way" by referring to the unsolved difficulties previously reported which the Embassy was still encountering. There followed a discussion in the course of which Molotov defended the failure of the Soviet authorities to take appropriate action in those matters which have not yet been adjusted on the grounds that they involved rules, regulations, and provisions of law, culminating with a promise to give personal consideration to these questions.

Towards the close of our talk Molotov remarked that while he still hoped that the discussions in Washington would eventually lead to some results he felt that they were progressing extremely slowly and in this connection referred to the failure of the Soviet Government to receive any substantial amount of machine tools. I asked him specifically whether the Soviet Government genuinely desired to restore what I described as the "cordial relations" which have always existed between the two countries and he responded in the affirmative with some degree of enthusiasm. In this connection I gained a stronger impression this afternoon than ever before that Umanski's reports to Molotov have not only failed to give the substance but to reflect the spirit in which these negotiations have been carried on.

STEINHARDT

861.24/434⅝

Memorandum by the Assistant Chief of the Division of European Affairs (Henderson) to the Under Secretary of State (Welles)[35]

[WASHINGTON,] December 30, 1940.

MR. WELLES: You will observe from the two attached memoranda of conversations between the Soviet Ambassador and Mr. Henderson of December 23 and December 26, respectively,[36] that the Ambassador is asking:

1. that steps be taken to revoke requisitions which have been issued for a number of machine tools which the Soviet Government has purchased from the Gear Grinding Company of Detroit, Michigan;

2. that a new export license be issued to replace a revoked license covering the export of a welding machine valued at $200,000 manufactured for the Soviet Government by the Federal Machine and Welding Company of Warren, Ohio.

[34] Cipher group missing.
[35] Mr. Welles wrote on this memorandum: "I agree. S. W."
[36] *Ante*, pp. 435 and 437, respectively.

The matter of the machines mentioned above has been taken up informally with Colonel Maxwell who insists that these machines are necessary for the national defense. In view of Colonel Maxwell's statement, it is suggested, subject to your approval, that we inform the Soviet Ambassador that unfortunately in view of the demands of national defense it has been found impossible to release these machines for Soviet use.

You will note also attached hereto a telegram [37] to the Amtorg Trading Corporation notifying Amtorg of the revocation of licenses authorizing the export of a grinding machine and two lathing machines. This telegram has been held up until the matter could be discussed with Colonel Maxwell who advises us that the machines in question have not yet been manufactured and that the manufacture of them for the Soviet Government just now would not be in the interests of national defense. This telegram has, therefore, been initialed by Eu.[38]

None of these machines have appeared on any lists thus far presented by the Ambassador to Colonel Maxwell.[39]

711.61/781 : Telegram

The Secretary of State to the Ambassador in the Soviet Union
(Steinhardt)

WASHINGTON, January 2, 1941—9 p. m.

4. We have read your telegram No. 1781 of December 26, 8 p. m. with interest and fully approve the attitude taken by you during the conversation. The matter of the Baltic gold, ships, Legations and so forth will be made the subject of a subsequent telegram to you.

HULL

TRADE RELATIONS BETWEEN THE UNITED STATES AND THE SOVIET UNION: RENEWAL OF COMMERCIAL AGREEMENT BY EXCHANGE OF NOTES, SIGNED AUGUST 6, 1940 [40]

611.6131/582½

Memorandum by Mr. Leander B. Lovell of the Division of Trade Agreements

[WASHINGTON,] June 14, 1940.

The time is approaching for the annual consideration of commercial agreement negotiations with the Soviet Union. This year the subject

---

[37] Not attached to file copy of this document.
[38] Division of European Affairs.
[39] A final note by Ray Atherton, Acting Chief of the Division of European Affairs, reads: "31st. The Soviet Ambassador is pressing for a reply today. R. A."
[40] For previous correspondence, see *Foreign Relations, The Soviet Union, 1933–1939*, pp. 809 ff. For text of the exchange of notes signed August 2, 1939, see Department of State Executive Agreement Series No. 151, or 53 Stat. 2404.

is complicated by many non-commercial factors which have arisen since the negotiations last year.[41]

The present commercial agreement with the Soviet Union, which expires on August 5, 1940, provides for full most-favored-nation treatment by the United States of imports from and exports to the Soviet Union. Exceptions are provided, among other things, with respect to the "export or sale for export of arms", et cetera, and the operation of the Neutrality Act of 1937.[42] A reservation, accompanied by a termination provision, (giving the U. S. S. R. the right to terminate the agreement on thirty days' notice), is made on the subject of imports of coal from the Soviet Union.

On its part the Soviet Union agrees to "increase substantially the amount of its purchases" from the United States of "articles the growth, produce or manufacture of the United States of America," such purchases to amount to no less than $40,000,000 in the agreement year.

While figures of Soviet purchases from the United States in recent months have not been made available by the Soviet Government (nor have import figures been published for several months), United States exports of domestic products to the Soviet Union have already amounted to over $60,000,000 in the first nine months of the current agreement year. United States imports from the Soviet Union amounted to about $18,000,000 in the same period. The limitations on trade between the two countries have arisen mainly from developments entirely beyond the scope of the commercial agreement.

With respect to imports into the United States from the Soviet Union, while this Government's commitment to give Soviet products most-favored-nation treatment when imported into this country is of material benefit to the Soviet Union, the principal limitation on that country's exports to the United States are not so much American tariff barriers as Russian internal needs. A possible decline in Soviet exports to this country was indicated early last year and no doubt was partly responsible for the lack of a desire on the part of the Soviet authorities for an agreement containing tariff reductions by the United States on products of which the other country is an important supplier. Imports of Soviet manganese and certain types of furs into the United States have been maintained in the first nine months of the current agreement year while many other imports from the Soviet Union have declined.

United States exports to the Soviet Union undoubtedly would have been larger if they had not encountered various difficulties in this

---

[41] For attempts to resolve difficulties arising in relations between the United States and the Soviet Union, see pp. 244 ff.
[42] Approved May 1, 1937; 50 Stat. 121.

country. A moral embargo was applied in December 1939 to the export to the Soviet Union of American "airplanes, aeronautical equipment, and materials essential to airplane manufacture" (including by interpretation molybdenum and aluminum) and of "plans, plants, manufacturing rights or technical information required for the production of high quality aviation gasoline." (Direct quotation from Department of State releases of December 15 and 20, 1939.)[43] All countries, the Soviet Union included, have been subject to the moral restriction against the export of certain strategic materials such as rubber and tin for the supplies of which the United States depends on imports. Moreover, American manufactures of machine tools have raised difficulties to the placing of new orders for such machinery in the United States by the Soviet Union.

In addition to the aforegoing restrictions, there has been the shipping difficulty, and the Soviet Government has been unable to ameliorate this condition by obtaining the use of available American ships since the United States Maritime Commission has disapproved applications of private companies to charter such ships to the Soviet Government.

There is pending in Congress a bill (S. 4025) which would give the Executive the power to embargo the export of practically anything that might be considered to be useful for war purposes. This bill may be expected to become law in the very near future.[44] As an indication of its applicability to our exports to the Soviet Union, there is attached a table [45] giving the commodity nature of this trade in the first four months of 1940.

611.6131/585 : Telegram

The Chargé in the Soviet Union (Thurston) to the Secretary of State

Moscow, July 6, 1940—5 p. m.
[Received July 6—4 : 15 p. m.]

823. After Stepanov [46] handed to me the communication reported in the Embassy's 824, July 6 (to follow this message) [47] I endeavored to engage him in conversation by inquiry as to the working of the present commercial agreement. He replied that the Soviet Government was encountering many difficulties in its trade with the United States and that if such difficulties could be removed trade would increase. I

[43] For texts, see Department of State *Bulletin*, December 16, 1939, p. 686, and *ibid.*, December 23, 1939, p. 714. See also *Foreign Relations*, The Soviet Union, 1933–1939, p. 801, footnote 2g.
[44] This became the Export Control Act of 1940, to expedite the strengthening of the national defense, approved July 2, 1940 ; 54 Stat. 712.
[45] Not printed.
[46] Mikhail Stepanovich Stepanov, Assistant People's Commissar for Foreign Trade of the Soviet Union.
[47] *Infra.*

replied that as he of course was aware some of the difficulties to which he alluded and about which Molotov [48] had spoken to me were produced by special circumstance of the moment.[49] I then inquired whether in the event negotiations are undertaken for the extension of the commercial agreement his Government intends to bring up these "difficulties" for discussion. Stepanov replied that it does.[50]

THURSTON

611.6131/584 : Telegram

The Chargé in the Soviet Union (Thurston) to the Secretary of State

Moscow, July 6, 1940—6 p. m.
[Received July 6—5 : 26 p. m.]

824. I was requested to call at the Commissariat for Foreign Trade this afternoon. Upon arriving there I was received by Mikhail Stepanovich Stepanov, Assistant People's Commissar for Foreign Trade, who read and then handed to me the following communication :

"Moscow, July 1940. Article 3 of the trade agreement of 1937 between the U. S. S. R. and the United States of America, which was renewed on August 6, 1939, provides that the parties must begin negotiations concerning prolongation of the agreement not later than 30 days before the expiration of the period of validity of this agreement.
The receipt by the People's Commissariat for Foreign Trade of the U. S. S. R. of a communication from the Embassy of the United States of America about whether the Government of the United States intends to enter into the above-mentioned negotiations and, in case it does intend to do so, where, when and through what plenipotentiary persons, would be timely."

I informed the Assistant Commissar that I would bring the matter to the attention of my Government, and that I would advise him promptly of any reply I might be instructed to make to his communication.

THURSTON

611.6131/586a : Telegram

The Secretary of State to the Chargé in the Soviet Union (Thurston)

WASHINGTON, July 10, 1940—6 p. m.

360. The question of a possible renewal of the Commercial Agreement of 1937, as extended to expire August 6 of this year, is receiving consideration in the Department at the present time. In order to

---

[48] Vyacheslav Mikhailovich Molotov, People's Commissar for Foreign Affairs of the Soviet Union.
[49] See telegram No. 604, May 31, midnight, from the Chargé in the Soviet Union, p. 304.
[50] A note by Loy W. Henderson, Assistant Chief of the Division of European Affairs, attached to telegram No. 824, July 6, 6 p. m. (*infra*), reads : "This tends to confirm our belief that the inauguration of negotiations for the renewal of the agreement will open the door to renewed Soviet protests."

facilitate the Department's consideration of this matter, you are instructed at the earliest opportunity to obtain an expression of the views of the Soviet Government concerning the renewal of the Agreement in its present form. In your discussions with the officials you may indicate that while a further extension of the Agreement would be entirely agreeable to this Government, it is nevertheless recognized that the adoption of certain measures by this Government for the purpose of insuring the national defense, and in particular the Act of Congress signed July 2, 1940 authorizing the President in the interests of national defense to prohibit or curtail the export of certain material or equipment, may have an adverse effect on the availability for export of certain types of commodities and equipment which have heretofore entered into Soviet purchases in this country. The Department realizes, therefore, that in the circumstances the Soviet Government may desire to make certain suggestions with respect to the commitments which it may care to make for the coming year. You are accordingly instructed to inform the appropriate officials that this Government is prepared to give careful consideration to any suggestions which they may care to offer.

For your information. The Soviet Government, particularly through the Ambassador here,[51] has on various occasions charged discrimination on the part of the United States against Soviet trade. In a formal note dated June 12, 1940 [52] the Soviet Ambassador referred to a number of cases of alleged discrimination against Soviet trade and alleged that the measures adopted by the United States Government were incompatible with the principle of unconditional and unrestricted most-favored-nation treatment embodied in the commercial agreement. In my reply of July 1, 1940 [53] the Soviet Ambassador was informed that this Government was of the opinion that it had taken no measures and pursued no policies incompatible with any of its agreements with the Soviet Union, and in this connection cited the seventh paragraph of Section 1 of the agreement of August 4, 1937 [53a] which permits this Government to take such measures as it may see fit with respect to the control of the export or sale for export of arms, ammunition, et cetera.

For your guidance in the event that the subject of discrimination and alleged violation of the most-favored-nation principle is raised by the Soviet officials, the following portion of my note of July 1 is quoted.

[Here follows quotation of the third and fourth paragraphs of the note of July 1, printed on page 323.]

HULL

---

[51] Konstantin Alexandrovich Umansky.
[52] Ante, p. 319.
[53] Ante, p. 323.
[53a] Department of State Executive Agreement Series No. 105, or 50 Stat. (pt. 2) 1619.

611.6131/587 : Telegram

The Chargé in the Soviet Union (Thurston) to the Secretary of State

Moscow, July 12, 1940—11 a. m.
[Received 5 : 50 p. m.]

849. Your telegram 360, July 10, 6 p. m.   I called on Mr. Stepanov this morning and informed him that I had been instructed to say, in response to his communication of July 6, that the Department of State has been giving attention to the question of a possible renewal of the 1937 commercial agreement as extended to the 6th of August 1940 and that in this connection I should be glad to receive an early expression of the views of his Government with respect to the renewal of the agreement in its present form.   Mr. Stepanov stated that he would communicate my statement to his superiors and inform me of their reply as quickly as possible.

I then stated that I had been authorized to say that while a further extension of the agreement would be entirely agreeable to my Government, it is recognized that the adoption of certain measures designed to insure our national defense may adversely affect the availability for export of certain types of equipment and commodities heretofore purchased in the United States by the Soviet Government and that under these circumstances it is realized that the Soviet Government may desire to advance certain suggestions.   I stated that if so, my Government is prepared to give careful consideration for use in such suggestions.   Mr. Stepanov again stated that he would convey this information also to his superiors.

As it was quite apparent that Mr. Stepanov was not empowered to enter into any conversations with me at this time, I did not take up the question of alleged discrimination or of your note of July 1 to Oumansky.[54]   These questions will of course, come up in later conversations and I will then discuss them along the lines of your instruction.

THURSTON

611.6131/589 : Telegram

The Chargé in the Soviet Union (Thurston) to the Secretary of State

Moscow, July 30, 1940—6 p. m.
[Received July 31—5 : 25 a. m.]

936. Department's 392, July 27, 6 p. m.[55]   I was received this afternoon by Stepanov who took me to the office of Mikoyan,[56] the Com-

---

[54] *Ante*, p. 323.
[55] Not printed.
[56] Anastas Ivanovich Mikoyan.

missar for Foreign Trade. Although I had explained when requesting the interview that it was for the purpose of ascertaining whether the Soviet authorities were as yet prepared to present proposals with respect to the renewal of the commercial agreement Mikoyan waited for initiative in the conversation.

When I had restated my [purpose?] and Mikoyan replied that after my talks with Stepanov he had proceeded to draft a statement of the views of his Government with respect to the agreement but that just as he was doing so the United States Government had seized the gold which the Soviet Government had acquired in the United States from the three Baltic States.[57] This action of the United States Government he said had been construed by the Soviet Government as a clear indication that the United States Government was not interested in maintaining good relations with the Soviet Government or in facilitating trade between the two countries. He had accordingly decided not to present the Soviet proposals.

In this connection he stated that the Soviet Government is a great power; that it is not confronted by the necessity of trading with the United States; and that if the United States continued its present practices that trade could very easily be diverted to other countries or the requirements of the Soviet Union be met by its own industries.

He continued by referring to our seizure of machinery and other articles purchased in the United States by the Soviet Government, to the Executive Order forbidding the exportation of certain commodities and articles except under license,[58] which he said was in itself acceptable insofar as exports subsequent to its promulgation were concerned but was not acceptable if applied retroactively.

At this point, following a procedure which I had determined to adopt in all future interviews with Soviet officials after my experience with Molotov some weeks ago, I stated to Mikoyan that I must observe that the United States also is a great and powerful nation which could easily dispense with the volume of trade resulting from its commercial relations with the Soviet Union. I felt, however, that two great States such as we represented should find it possible to come to a prompt agreement which would surely be of mutual advantage despite incidental difficulties and that I would be glad to contribute toward such an outcome if he were so disposed. Mr. Mikoyan thereupon relaxed and became amiable, and stated that he had not finished his remarks. He had, he continued, caused Oumansky

---

[57] The President signed Executive Order No. 8484 on July 15, 1940, regarding property of Estonia, Latvia, and Lithuania in the United States. For text, see 5 *Federal Register* 2586. For text of regulations by the Treasury Department issued on July 15, 1940, see 5 *Federal Register* 2593.

[58] For text of the President's proclamation of July 2, setting up the controls considered necessary under the Export Control Act of July 2, 1940, see Department of State *Bulletin*, July 6, 1940, p. 12.

to take up with the State Department the question of the difficulties to which he had just referred and Oumansky had now reported that he had had an interview with Mr. Sumner Welles in which the latter had stated that the Government of the United States desires to improve relations with the Soviet Union.[59] He had, in consequence, decided to present to me the draft of the Soviet proposals with respect to the commercial agreement.

He wished however, he said, to comment still further on obstacles to American-Soviet trade such as, for example, the failure of the American authorities for the past 20 days to grant export licenses to Amtorg.[60] Over 200 applications by Amtorg for export licenses, on articles which in the opinion of the Soviet Union are not affected by our current laws and regulations, have been filed and disregarded. He stated that while the Soviet draft agreement would, as in previous years, signify the intention of the Soviet Government to purchase at least 40,000,000 dollars worth of American goods during the 12 months to be covered by the agreement, this undertaking could not, of course, be observed by the Soviet Government if the United States Government persists in hampering Soviet purchases.

When Mikoyan had concluded I stated that the subject of the Baltic gold in the United States had been taken up with me by Lozovski[61] recently and that I had referred his protest[62] to the Department. Pending the receipt of any instructions from the Department in answer thereto I was unable to discuss the matter.[63] With respect to the necessity which my Government had encountered of acquiring certain machinery or other articles purchased in the United States by foreign governments including that of the Soviet Union I referred Mikoyan to the report undoubtedly made by Umansky following the receipt of the Department's note to him dated July 1, 1940,[64] excerpts from which as quoted in the Department's 360, July 10, 6 p. m., I read to him. With respect to the delay in granting export licenses to Amtorg I stated that I would make special mention of this point in my report of our conversation to the Department.

At the conclusion of our interview, Mikoyan handed to me the documents comprising the Soviet draft proposal. He stated that

---

[59] See memorandum by the Acting Secretary of State, July 27, p. 327.
[60] Amtorg Trading Corporation, official purchasing and sales agency of the Soviet Union in the United States.
[61] Solomon Abramovich Lozovsky, Assistant People's Commissar for Foreign Affairs of the Soviet Union.
[62] See telegram No. 885, July 20, 9 p. m., from the Chargé in the Soviet Union, vol. I, p. 395.
[63] For the Department's reply, see telegram No. 423, August 9, 6 p. m., vol. I, p. 410.
[64] *Ante*, p. 323.

the Russian text would be the official one, with the English text merely for convenience. Although I am aware that this constitutes a reversal of the practice followed last year, I did not consider it to be advisable at the time to attempt to reestablish the principle that the English text must govern, with the Russian text occupying the subsidiary position. This point, if the Department so desires, probably can be gained during later conversations.

The draft proposal consists of four documents which are being transmitted in a separate telegram following this.[65] It incorporates provisions designed from the Soviet point of view to overcome the difficulties which the Soviet Government has encountered in conducting its trade with the United States, most of which, with the exception of that regarding the chartering of American vessels and the "moral embargo", have been discussed with me either by Lozovski or Mikoyan. It omits, probably by oversight, reference to Soviet coal imports into the United States.

THURSTON

611.6131/590 : Telegram

The Chargé in the Soviet Union (Thurston) to the Secretary of State

Moscow, July 31, 1940—9 a. m.
[Received 1 : 40 p. m.]

937. Embassy's telegram No. 936, July 30. The documents comprising the Soviet draft proposal for the 1940–41 commercial agreement follow:

(*a*) A letter to be addressed to me by Mikoyan in the following terms:

"Mr. Chargé d'Affaires, in accordance with the conversations which have taken place I have the honor to confirm on behalf of my Government the agreement which has been reached between the Governments of our respective countries that the agreement regarding commercial relations between the Union of Soviet Socialist Republics and the United States of America recorded in the exchange of notes of August 4, 1937, between the People's Commissar for Foreign Affairs of the Union of Soviet Socialist Republics and the Ambassador of the United States of America, which came into force on August 6, 1937, on the date of approval thereof by the Council of People's Commissars of the Union of Soviet Socialist Republics and proclamation thereof by the President of the United States of America and which was renewed on August 5, 1938,[66] and August 2, 1939,[67] shall continue in force until August 6, 1941.

---

[65] *Infra.*
[66] Executive Agreement Series No. 132, or 53 Stat. (pt. 3) 1947.
[67] Executive Agreement Series No. 151, or 53 Stat. (pt. 3) 2404.

The present agreement should be approved by the Council of People's Commissars of the Union of Soviet Socialist Republics and proclaimed by the President of the United States of America."

(*b*) A letter to be addressed by me to Mikoyan in the following terms:

"Mr. People's Commissar, during the conversations which have lately taken place with respect to prolonging until August 6, 1941 the operation of the Commercial Agreement of August 4, 1937 between the United States and the Union of Soviet Socialist Republics, there was a discussion of difficulties in Soviet-American trade which have arisen in connection with the entrance into force of the law of July 2, 1940 concerning the control of exports of materials necessary for national defense.

Referring to these conversations, I have the honor on behalf of the Government of the United States of America to inform you as follows:

(1) For the facilitation of trade between the United States of America and the Union of Soviet Socialist Republics the Government of the United States of America shall consider favorably applications of firms for licenses for export to the Union of Soviet Socialist Republics of the goods subject to the provisions of the law of July 2, 1940. Furthermore, the Government of the United States of America undertakes to grant to such firms in each individual case irrevocable export licenses before the transaction is concluded and not to impede in any way the export of goods manufactured or sold by the firms to the Union of Soviet Socialist Republics under the above-mentioned licenses.

(2) The goods purchased or ordered in the United States of America by the Amtorg Trading Corporation or by Soviet economic organization[s] prior to the entrance into force of the law of July 2, 1940, concerning the control of exports of materials necessary for national defense shall not require any licenses whatsoever for their export to the Union of Soviet Socialist Republics and the Government of the United States of America shall not in any way impede the export of the said goods to the Union of Soviet Socialist Republics.

(3) The Government of the United States of America shall take the necessary measures to the end that the appropriate organs facilitate the chartering of American vessels by Soviet or American economic organizations for the transportation of exports from the USSR, and of imports into the USSR and to the end that in each case these organs without hindrance permit the chartering of American vessels for shipments from the USSR into the United States of America and from the United States of America into the USSR, if the existing procedure in the United States of America shall require that such permission be granted.

(4) The Government of the United States of America shall not apply to orders or purchases of goods for the USSR, as well as to the export of such goods from the United States of America, any measures which have a discriminatory character with respect to the USSR, in particular the so-called 'moral embargo'."

(*c*) A letter to be addressed to me by Mikoyan as follows:

"Mr. Chargé d'Affaires, in reply to your inquiry regarding the intended purchases by the Union of Soviet Socialist Republics in the United States of America in the course of the next 12 months, I have the honor to inform you that the economic organizations of the Union of Soviet Socialist Republics intend to buy in the United States of America in the course of the next 12 months American goods to the value of $40,000,000 or more.

Nevertheless, the Soviet Party, having in view the existing restrictions in the United States of America affecting the export of goods from the United States of America, cannot guarantee the above-mentioned value of its purchases in the United States of America. The value of the purchases of the USSR in the United States of America can reach $40,000,000 or more only under conditions in the United States of America which are entirely favorable for imports of the USSR from the United States of America as well as for exports of the USSR to the United States of America."

And (d), a letter from me to Mikoyan stating:

"Mr. People's Commissar, with reference to paragraph 7, sentence 1 of the Commercial Agreement of August 4, 1937, the Government of the United States of America explains that it will not take with respect to the Union of Soviet Socialist Republics any measures prohibiting or curtailing exports or imports of gold or silver which shall not be applied with respect to all other countries.

In any case, in view of the adverse balance of the USSR in Soviet-American trade, Soviet economic organizations will be permitted, directly or through the State Bank of the USSR without hindrance to import gold into the United States to the amount necessary for all their payments in the United States.

The Treasury of the United States will purchase the above-mentioned amount of gold from the Soviet economic organizations or from the State Bank of the USSR."

THURSTON

611.6131/590 : Telegram

The Secretary of State to the Chargé in the Soviet Union (Thurston)

WASHINGTON, August 1, 1940—5 p. m.

405. Your 936, July 30, 6 p. m., and 937, July 31, 9 a. m. In support of your statement to Mikoyan to the effect that the United States and the U. S. S. R. should find it possible promptly to reach an agreement on commercial matters you may inform the Soviet authorities that this Government is entirely agreeable to renewing the agreement on the basis suggested by them as outlined in the documents referred to in parts (a) and (c) of your 937. In view of the possible unavailability here of certain commodities of interest to the Soviet Union this Government has no objection to including a suitable qualification to the Soviet agreement to purchase "American goods to the value of $40,000,000 or more" along the general lines indicated in your part

(*c*). It is suggested, however, that the second paragraph of the document given in part (*c*) of your telegram be deleted and the following paragraph added in its place:

"If, however, restrictions imposed on exports by the Government of the United States should render it difficult for Soviet economic organizations to satisfy their needs in the United States, it may be impossible for these organizations to carry out their intentions. The Government of the Union of Soviet Socialist Republics is therefore not in a position at the present time to guarantee the above-mentioned value of its purchases in the United States."

This Government does not consider that the points mentioned in the documents referred to in parts (*b*) and (*d*) are appropriate subjects of commercial negotiations. In recognition of this position these matters have in one form or another been excluded or specifically excepted from the operation of all commercial or trade agreements concluded by the United States. This Government, however, is prepared in a friendly spirit to enter into discussions not connected with the negotiation of this agreement of various problems affecting relations between the United States and the Soviet Union.

HULL

611.6131/591 : Telegram

The Chargé in the Soviet Union (Thurston) to the Secretary of State

Moscow, August 2, 1940—7 p. m.
[Received 9 : 05 p. m.]

954. Dickerson [69] and I were received by Mikoyan this evening and I presented to him a paraphrase of the confidential portions of the Department's 405, August 1, 5 p. m.

As to the substitution of the second paragraph of draft (*c*), Mikoyan stated that as he understood it from its oral translation, it is apparently acceptable. With respect to drafts (*b*) and (*d*), however, he stated that what is wanted is a practical solution not merely a general discussion and he queried how we could trade if these problems were not solved. He also asked where and when the suggested discussions might take place. To his second question I replied that although the Department had given no indication of its plans in this respect I assumed that the discussions could take place according to his wishes either in Moscow or Washington and at once.

Mikoyan then stated that he was naturally not satisfied with the answer of the American Government which he construed to mean that what it desired was merely the maintenance of the *status quo* and that it did not wish to take the trouble to endeavor to solve the problems

---

[69] Charles E. Dickerson, Jr., Consul and First Secretary of Embassy.

posed by the Soviet draft proposals. He added hastily, however, that he would think the matter over, consult his Government and let me know its decision.

I said that I was glad he was not making a final decision now as I was compelled to disagree with him thinking him mistaken in the view he had expressed. I said that I had good reason to believe that the United States Government sincerely wished to negotiate a new agreement pointing out that some days ago the Department had telegraphed inquiring as to the present status of the negotiations, observing that if agreement were not reached Soviet coal imports [70] would immediately be subject to tax. In this connection and following a remark of mine as to the desirability of speed particularly in view of the effect upon Soviet coal imports of a lapse of the current agreement Mikoyan said that it was not through any oversight that he had failed to mention coal imports in his draft proposals but that he had done so in recognition of the opposition to that arrangement on the part of American producers and that he had intended the omission to be a friendly gesture to which we had not made the hoped for response.

Mikoyan then stated that he had not intended to imply that either Government was disinterested in concluding a new agreement but that the United States Government was not taking steps which would facilitate the Soviet Government from a practical point of view in conducting its trade with us. He insisted that if the American Government were really interested in this trade it would not have rejected his drafts (b) and (d).

I replied that I must be permitted to disagree once more; that it was not the substance of (b) and (d) to which we necessarily objected but their inclusion in these particular commercial negotiations as we are quite willing to enter into friendly discussion of the problems concerned but only as a separate negotiation. In answer to this Mikoyan repeated he would consider the matter definitely with me later.

THURSTON

611.6131/591 : Telegram

The Secretary of State to the Chargé in the Soviet Union (Thurston)

WASHINGTON, August 3, 1940—2 p. m.

413. Your 954, August 2, 7 p. m. For your information consideration is still being given to the desirability of including the coal notes in the renewal of the agreement.

HULL

---

[70] In a press release of August 7, 1940, the Department of State indicated that there had not been any imports of Soviet coal since October 1939 (Department of State *Bulletin*, August 10, 1940, p. 105).

611.6131/592 : Telegram

The Chargé in the Soviet Union (Thurston) to the Secretary of State

Moscow, August 5, 1940—11 a. m.
[Received August 5—10 a. m.]

961. Embassy's telegram 954, August 2, 7 p. m. Dickerson was informed this morning by the Trade Agreements Section of the Commissariat for Foreign Trade that "the People's Commissar although displeased had decided having in view the shortness of time to extend the agreement on the basis offered." He was handed at the same time final draft notes consisting of the following documents: (1) a note from me to Mikoyan identical *mutatis mutandis* with that transcribed as draft (*a*) in the Embassy's 937, July 31, 9 a. m.; (2) second note from me to Mikoyan inquiring in terms identical with those of the same inquiry made in 1939 as to the value of Soviet purchases to be made during the next 12 months; and (3) a letter from Mikoyan to me identical with that submitted to the Department in the Embassy's 937, July 31, 9 a. m., as (*c*) as amended in its second paragraph to conform with the substitute paragraph transmitted in the Department's 405, August 1, 5 p. m.

All the foregoing documents are dated August 5 and it was indicated to Dickerson that it was desired that signature take place at 2 o'clock this afternoon. The documents are to be signed in Russian and English duplicate sets. I assume in the absence of comment from you that you are agreeable to the Russian text being the official one with the English subsidiary.

The complementary letter from the Commissar to me which corresponds to (1) above was shown to Dickerson but not delivered to him. He read it, however, and it appeared to be identical *mutatis mutandis* with the note from me to him.

I have informed the Commissar that I cannot sign these documents in the absence of specific instructions but that I expect to have them from you before midnight tonight. He has replied that signature up to midnight tonight or even later will be agreeable to him.

Please send your instructions triple priority.

THURSTON

611.6131/594 : Telegram

The Chargé in the Soviet Union (Thurston) to the Secretary of State

Moscow, August 5, 1940—noon.
[Received August 5—9 : 35 a. m.]

962. In the course of the conversation described in the Embassy's 961, August 5, the officials of the Commissariat for Foreign Trade

told Dickerson that they hoped negotiations with respect to the matters excluded from the conversations with respect to commercial agreement and which were contained in documents (*b*) and of the Embassy's 948 [*937*], July 31, might begin "in a friendly spirit" and at an early date.

THURSTON

611.6131/596a : Telegram

The Acting Secretary of State to the Chargé in the Soviet Union (Thurston)

WASHINGTON, August 5, 1940—6 p. m.

415. Department's 413, August 3, 2 p. m., and Embassy's 961, August 5, 11 a. m. Renewal of the principal exchange of notes alone for another year almost certainly would be sufficient to insure that imports of coal from the Soviet Union would be free of the import tax. Therefore, even if the Soviet authorities are for the present not interested in the question of coal exports to this country, the Department desires, because of the domestic situation in this country, to have the note referring to the 400,000 ton limitation renewed again.

Hence in expressing to Mikoyan appreciation for the motives which led to his failure to mention coal imports you should inform him that your Government feels that it is necessary to have the coal notes repeated in connection with the renewal of the agreement for the reasons given above.

You are authorized to sign the pertinent documents referred to in your telegram under reference and in this telegram. The Department prefers that the English and Russian texts should be considered equally authentic.

Please inform the Department promptly upon signing the agreement so that the appropriate release may be given here. You may inform the press in Moscow upon signing, using, if you wish, the preliminary figure of $67,779,000 as the value of U. S. exports to the Soviet Union in the first 11 months of the 1939–40 agreement year. In the entire 1937–38 and 1938–39 agreement years the figures were $64,224,000 and $50,255,000, respectively.

WELLES

611.6131/595 : Telegram

The Chargé in the Soviet Union (Thurston) to the Secretary of State

Moscow, August 6, 1940—9 p. m.
[Received August 6—3 p. m.]

976. Exchange of notes extending commercial agreement to August 6, 1941, including notes on Soviet coal, took place at 8 o'clock Moscow time tonight. Details follow in a separate telegram.[71]

THURSTON

[For text of the agreement effected by exchange of notes signed August 6, 1940, and effective August 6, 1940, see Department of State Executive Agreement Series No. 179, or 54 Stat. (pt. 2) 2366. For text of press release issued by the Department August 7, see Department of State *Bulletin*, August 10, 1940, page 105.]

611.6131/597 : Telegram

The Chargé in the Soviet Union (Thurston) to the Secretary of State

Moscow, August 6, 1940—10 p. m.
[Received August 7—5 : 11 a. m.]

978. Your 415, August 5, 6 p. m., was not received until 9 : 45 o'clock this morning. In view of your desire to include in the exchange the customary notes regarding Soviet coal it was necessary to reach agreement with the Commissariat for Foreign Trade on this point before signature could take place. For this reason it was not possible to sign the notes until this evening as reported in the Embassy's 976, August 6, 9 p. m.

The exchange of notes consists of the following:

1. The letter referred to in the Embassy's 937, July 31, 9 p. m. [*a. m.*] as document (*a*) which concludes Accept Mr. Chargé d'Affaires the assurances of my highest consideration. In this letter as signed the words "of August 4, 1937" follow "Ambassador of the United States of America" and not "exchange of notes" as given in the Embassy's 937.

2. An identical note *mutatis mutandis* from me to Mikoyan, addressed Mr. People's Commissar and concluding Accept Mr. People's Commissar the assurances my highest consideration.

[3.] A note from me to Mikoyan inquiring as to the value of intended Soviet purchases in the United States during the ensuing 12 months and identical to that addressed to him by Grummon[72] last year. This note, however, begins Mr. People's Commissar and [ends

---

[71] Telegram No. 982, August 7, 11 a. m., from the Chargé in the Soviet Union, p. 458.

[72] Stuart E. Grummon, First Secretary of Embassy in the Soviet Union and Chargé d'Affaires.

Accept] Mr. People's Commissar the renewed assurances of my highest consideration.

4. A reply from Mikoyan to the foregoing identical to document (c) in the Embassy's 937 introduces open door principle pursuant to the Department's 405, August 1, 5 p. m. This note concludes Accept Mr. Chargé d'Affaires the renewed assurance of my highest consideration. In this note the words Union of Soviet Socialist Republics are written in full in all cases and not abbreviated.

5. A note from me to Mikoyan beginning Mr. People's Commissar identical to Grummon's note to him last year regarding the admission of Soviet coal which concludes Accept Mr. People's Commissar the renewed assurances of my highest consideration.

6. A note in answer thereto from Mikoyan to me identical to his reply to Grummon last year. All documents are dated August 6. All documents from Mikoyan to me are signed A. Mikoyan and addressed Mr. Walter Thurston, Chargé d'Affaires of the United States of America, Moscow, and all notes from me to Mikoyan are signed Walter Thurston and addressed Mr. A. I. Mikoyan, People's Commissar for Foreign Trade of the Union of Soviet Socialist Republics, Moscow.

Mikoyan stated that the approval of the extension of the commercial agreement by the Council of People's Commissars will be given tomorrow and he expressed the desire that the President issue his proclamation thereof tomorrow so that both may be announced simultaneously.

I have informed the American journalists in Moscow that the exchange of notes took place tonight and that it is identical to the exchange of last year with the exception of an addition thereto made necessary by present world conditions. I have not given them the texts. Owing to the garbled state in which the last paragraph of your 415, August 5, 6 p.m., was received and to serious discrepancies between the figures cited therein and those released last year regarding trade statistics I did not give them any prepared statement on this subject.

THURSTON

611.6131/598 : Telegram

The Chargé in the Soviet Union (Thurston) to the Secretary of State

Moscow, August 6, 1940—11 p. m.
[Received August 7—9 : 01 a. m.]

979. Embassy's telegram No. 978, August 6, 10 p. m. An understanding was reached with Mikoyan to the effect that the English and Russian texts shall be considered equally authentic. I left with him a note on the subject reading as follows:

"Mr. People's Commissar, it is my understanding, which I shall be glad to have you confirm to me that the English and Russian texts of the exchange of notes we have just effected extending the commercial agreement shall be considered equally authentic.

Accept Mr. People's Commissar the renewed assurances of my highest consideration."

Mikoyan stated that he will address a note to me tomorrow confirming my understanding in this matter.[73]

THURSTON

611.6131/599 : Telegram

The Chargé in the Soviet Union (Thurston) to the Secretary of State

Moscow, August 7, 1940—11 a. m.
[Received August 7—10 : 08 a. m.]

982. The signature of the exchange of notes extending the commercial agreement took place last night in an atmosphere of definite cordiality. Mikoyan was accompanied by six or seven of his associates and I by Dickerson and Armstrong,[74] both of whom have been of great assistance. At the conclusion of the ceremony of signature Mikoyan served champagne and we conversed in an informal and friendly manner for some time and all this presumably was preliminary to the broaching again of the subject of the initiation of discussions regarding problems affecting the relations between the United States and the Soviet Union, as at the conclusion of the meeting Mikoyan emphasized that he hopes that these discussions will begin at an early date. I believe that he feels that having [yielded?] in the light of the Department's wishes regarding the exclusion of this subject from the negotiations for the extension of the commercial agreement, in view of our statement that we are prepared to discuss it separately, something in the nature of a commitment has been made, and that it would be helpful if the Department would give an early indication of its intentions in this respect.

THURSTON

611.6131/597 : Telegram

The Acting Secretary of State to the Chargé in the Soviet Union (Thurston)

WASHINGTON, August 9, 1940—7 p. m.

424. Your 977, August 6, 9 p. m.,[75] and 978, August 6, 10 p. m.

1. A press release similar to last year's[76] was issued here in the afternoon of August 6 and was reported in the morning newspapers of

---

[73] The Chargé reported the receipt of this confirmation on August 7.
[74] Willis C. Armstrong, translator in the American Embassy at Moscow.
[75] Not printed.
[76] For text of press release issued by the Department of State on August 5, 1939, see Department of State *Bulletin*, August 5, 1939, p. 96.

August 7. The release gave trade figures by agreement years, referred to the proviso to the Soviet purchase commitment, and reported the fact that there have been no imports of Russian coal since October 1939.

2. In my press conference of August 7, I read the following statement:

"It may be noted that notes were exchanged yesterday between this Government and the Soviet Government extending until August 6, 1941 the commercial agreement which in its present form was first concluded between the two countries on August 4, 1937. The present agreement is similar to those in effect during the previous 3 years, in all respects except that there has been added a proviso to the note referring to the minimum amount of purchases ($40,000,000) to be made in the United States by the Soviet Economic organizations. This proviso takes into account the possibility that various export restrictions imposed by the United States in the course of its national defense program may make it impossible for these organizations to carry out their intentions.

"It is a source of deep gratification that we are able by means of this agreement to continue our commercial relations with the U. S. S. R. on the present basis and it is to be hoped that during the coming year they will develop in a manner advantageous to both parties."

3. What appeared to be a discrepancy between the trade figures given you in the Department's 415, August 5, 6 p. m., and those in last year's press release may be explained by the fact that the former were American export figures as indicated in the Department's telegram and the latter were Soviet import figures.

You should at the next opportunity point out to the Soviet authorities that while the agreement refers to the value of Soviet purchases in the United States in the given period, the Soviet Government has been unwilling, despite repeated requests, to furnish this Government with figures indicating the amount of such purchases in the United States. Moreover, for a year no figures giving Soviet imports from the United States have been released. Hence for comparative purposes it was necessary to use American domestic export figures for all agreement years in our press release (mentioned in paragraph numbered 1 above). These figures, beginning with the 1935–36 agreement year, are in thousands of dollars as follows: 33,286; 31,018; 64,224; 50,255; and in the first 11 months of the 1939–40 agreement year 67,779 (preliminary).

In last year's press release figures were given for the value of United States imports for consumption from the Soviet Union through the 1937–38 agreement year. For the 1938–39 agreement year and the first 11 months of the 1939–40 agreement year, the figures are 24,761 and 23,916 (preliminary) respectively.

WELLES

ESTABLISHMENT OF AN AMERICAN CONSULATE GENERAL AT VLADIVOSTOK [77]

125.977/26 : Telegram

The Secretary of State to the Chargé in the Soviet Union (Thurston)

WASHINGTON, July 18, 1940—6 p. m.

377. Unless you perceive some objection thereto, you are instructed to call upon the appropriate officials of the Commissariat for Foreign Affairs and to make a statement along the following lines:

"My Government for some time has been giving consideration to the advisability of opening a consular office in Vladivostok. Under existing conditions it is inclined to the view that certain advantages might be derived from the establishment of such an office in the immediate future. Before making any final decision in the matter it would like to have a frank statement from the Soviet Government regarding its views since the full cooperation of the Soviet Government and Soviet officials would appear to be essential to the successful functioning of a consular office of the United States in the Soviet Far East."

It is also suggested, unless you perceive some objection thereto, that following your conversation you leave an *aide-mémoire* with the Commissariat containing the substance of the above statement.

In case Soviet officials should endeavor to discuss the matter with you in more detail, you may point out that the advantages to both Governments of the establishing of such an office should be obvious; that, for instance, it seems likely that for some time to come communications across Europe between the Soviet Union and the United States will be difficult. During the course of your conversation, however, it should be made clear that we have no desire to persuade the Soviet Government against its will to permit the establishment of such a consular office, or to seek permission for the opening of such an office as a special favor.

HULL

125.977/27 : Telegram

The Chargé in the Soviet Union (Thurston) to the Secretary of State

MOSCOW, August 9, 1940—10 a. m.
[Received 12 : 24 p. m.]

995. Department's 377, July 18, 1 [6] p. m. On July 19 I called on Assistant Commissar Lozovski [78] and made a statement to him

---

[77] For correspondence on the closing of the former American Consulate at Vladivostok, see *Foreign Relations*, 1923, vol. II, pp. 792 ff.

[78] Solomon Abramovich Lozovsky, Assistant People's Commissar for Foreign Affairs of the Soviet Union.

along the lines indicated in the instruction under acknowledgement. I left with him an *aide-mémoire* paraphrasing the quoted section of your telegram.

On August 5 Dickerson [79] inquired of Valkov,[80] chief of the American Section, whether he had any observations to convey concerning the attitude of the Soviet Government with respect to the opening of an American consular office at Vladivostok. Valkov replied that he would inquire of Lozovski and endeavor to answer Dickerson's inquiry in the course of the day. As no word has been received from the Commissariat I took the occasion of my visit to Valkov this morning to inquire again whether Soviet Government had reached any decision in the matter. Valkov replied that the matter was under consideration but that decision had been postponed in view of the activities connected with the current sessions of the Supreme Soviet [81] but that a statement on the subject might be expected in the near future.

THURSTON

125.977/31 : Telegram

The Ambassador in the Soviet Union (*Steinhardt*) *to the Secretary of State*

Moscow, November 5, 1940—5 p. m.
[Received 11 : 33 p. m.]

1495. Vyshinski,[82] who had asked me to call on him yesterday evening, told me he wanted to clear up a misunderstanding which apparently had arisen concerning the opening of a Consulate at Vladivostok. He said that according to a report received from Oumanski [83] the Under Secretary [84] on November 1 had expressed satisfaction that the Soviet Government had agreed to the opening of an American Consulate in Vladivostok on or after November 15.[85] Vyshinski said that as he had not assured me that we might open the Consulate on or after November 15 he felt there must have been a misunderstanding. I told Vyshinski that he had made it quite clear to

[79] Charles E. Dickerson, Jr., Consul and First Secretary of Embassy in the Soviet Union.

[80] Vasily Alexeyevich Valkov, Chief of the American Section of the People's Commissariat for Foreign Affairs of the Soviet Union.

[81] The VII Session of the Supreme Council of the Soviet Union was held in Moscow August 1–7, 1940.

[82] Andrey Yanuaryevich Vyshinsky, Assistant People's Commissar for Foreign Affairs of the Soviet Union.

[83] Konstantin Alexandrovich Umansky, Soviet Ambassador in the United States.

[84] Sumner Welles, Under Secretary of State.

[85] See memorandum by the Under Secretary of State, October 31, p. 403.

me at our conference on October 29th [86] that the date of November 15 referred to the date on which additional housing facilities in Moscow would be made available to the Embassy and not to the matter of the Consulate in Vladivostok and that I had so reported to the Department and that in consequence the misunderstanding must have arisen as a result of a garble in telegraphic transmission. To this he readily agreed. He then said that the Soviet Government was prepared definitely to agree to the opening of an American Consulate General in Vladivostok after November 20, 1940, and handed me a memorandum which, after drawing my attention to the misunderstandings above referred to, concluded:

"Insofar as the substance of the question concerning the opening of the Consulate General of the United States at Vladivostok is concerned, if on October 29 I did not yet have the instructions from my Government on this question, at the present time I can inform Mr. Steinhardt that the Soviet Government has agreed to the opening of the Consulate General after November 20, 1940 as soon as housing facilities have been prepared and certain technical questions connected with the matter have been decided."

In view of Vyshinski's observations concerning a misunderstanding I have checked and verified the wording of my telegram as well as the coding thereof which "the Soviet Government had in principle decided to agree to the establishment of a Consulate in Vladivostok and that by November 15 would receive additional housing facilities." It would seem therefore that this sentence must have been garbled in transmission as the Department will observe from Vyshinski's memorandum the Soviet Government agrees to the establishment of a "Consulate General" in Vladivostok although in accordance with the Department's instruction in its original and subsequent notes on the subject the Embassy referred to "Consulate." In agreeing to the establishment of a Consulate General the Soviet Government has probably been motivated by the fact that the only two consular establishments permitted in Vladivostok, namely, the Japanese and the German, are both Consulates General.

Having disposed of the subject of the Consulate Vyshinski reaffirmed his previous statement that additional housing would be available after the 15th and also added that immediately after the Soviet holidays [87] he would make every effort to dispose of the question of the American citizens still remaining in Soviet-occupied Poland and to accelerate the issuance of exit visas to the Soviet wives of American citizens.

STEINHARDT

---

[86] See telegram No. 1454, October 30, 8 p. m., from the Ambassador in the Soviet Union, p. 400.
[87] Anniversary of the Bolshevik Revolution of October 25/November 7, 1917.

125.9777/9 : Telegram

The Ambassador in the Soviet Union (Steinhardt) to the Secretary of State

Moscow, December 30, 1940—2 p. m.
[Received 4 p. m.]

1800. Reference ultimate paragraph Department's 780, November 19, 7 p. m.[88] The Embassy's repeated inquiries of the Commissariat for Foreign Affairs regarding the extent of the Vladivostok consular district elicited no reply until today when Valkov stated orally that the district will be limited to the city of Vladivostok.[89] The German and Japanese Embassies state that this is the extent of their consular districts at Vladivostok.

STEINHARDT

[Mr. Angus I. Ward, Consul and First Secretary of Embassy at Moscow, was assigned as Consul in charge of the Consulate General at Vladivostok on November 28, 1940. He reported on January 15, 1941, the opening of provisional offices at Vladivostok. The Consulate General was opened to the public on February 13, 1941. Mr. Ward became Consul General at Vladivostok on October 31, 1941. Further correspondence regarding the administrative details of establishing the Consulate General, the difficulties in obtaining suitable accommodations, etc., is not printed.]

---

[88] Not printed.
[89] In an unnumbered instruction dated February 18, 1941, the Department advised Consul Ward at Vladivostok that it had been decided "formally to delimit your consular district as the City of Vladivostok only".

THE NEAR EAST AND AFRICA

EGYPT

IMPACT OF THE EUROPEAN WAR ON EGYPT AS A NEUTRAL STATE HAVING SPECIAL POLITICAL RELATIONS WITH THE UNITED KINGDOM [1]

740.0011 European War 1939/2136 : Telegram

The Chargé in Egypt (Hare) to the Secretary of State

CAIRO, April 12, 1940—noon.
[Received 12 : 38 p. m.]

53. I have been advised authoritatively but in strictest confidence that the Prime Minister [2] yesterday ordered the Minister of War and the Commander of the Territorial Waters to prepare for submission to him within 48 hours a program for general mobilization.

I am informed that this action was taken owing to apprehension of hostile action by Italy in the Mediterranean should Great Britain be unable to repel the Germans in Norway promptly and decisively. Under the circumstances and acting entirely on his own initiative the Prime Minister desired to be ready for immediate action in case of emergency.

The impression is given in this connection that reasonably adequate defense has been prepared against a land attack from Libya but that defense against aerial attack is less adequate particularly since a considerable quantity of anti-aircraft guns intended for shipment here several months ago are said to have been diverted to Finland.

Other military developments here involve (1) continued study of an attack on the Caucasus in which connection Turkish hesitancy to cooperate appears to be the most important deterrent factor, and (2) anticipated increase of British forces in Egypt, including impending arrival of 2 divisions of New Zealand troops, to about 100,000 and in Palestine to about 50,000 by the end of May whereas the plan several months ago is understood to have called for concentration of 100,000 in Palestine.

HARE

---

[1] Only a few reports on military operations are printed here to show setting of the political situation with respect to military events. The Legation in Egypt sent to the Department of State numerous reports regarding military developments.

[2] Aly Maher Pasha.

465

740.0011 European War 1939/2226 : Telegram

The Chargé in Egypt (Hare) to the Secretary of State

CAIRO, April 15, 1940—4 p. m.
[Received April 15—1 : 55 p. m.]

54. The Legation's 53, April 12. The Legation is authoritatively informed that the British Ambassador [3] received a telegram from the Foreign Office in London on April 12 indicating apprehension regarding possible action by Italy and requesting that the Egyptian Government be informed to that effect and asked to take appropriate preparatory measures.

The Legation is further authoritatively informed that the Prime Minister has received reports of Italian Fleet concentration at Bari and Taranto which he fears may be preparatory to an attack on Yugoslavia or on Greece via Albania. In the latter event Great Britain would automatically come to Greece's aid and the Prime Minister feels that Egypt could not escape being drawn into the war.

Although many qualified observers discount the probability of imminent Italian [attack?] and the local Italian colony appears calm, there is no doubt that the Egyptian Government is seriously concerned.

HARE

740.0011 European War 1939/2607 : Telegram

The Chargé in Egypt (Hare) to the Secretary of State

CAIRO, May 2, 1940—3 p. m.
[Received May 2—12 : 16 p. m.]

59. Legation's telegram No. 54, April 15. Reports of British reverses in Norway, Italian troop concentrations on Yugoslav frontier, belligerent statements by Italian officials and press and particularly the closing of the Mediterranean to British shipping have caused renewed tension here and the Egyptian Government is known to regard the situation as extremely grave. However, aside from the placing of special guards over essential utilities the situation remains one of watchful but apprehensive waiting.

HARE

---

[3] Sir Miles Lampson.

740.0011 European War 1939/2949 : Telegram

The Chargé in Egypt (Hare) to the Secretary of State

CAIRO, May 14, 1940—5 p. m.
[Received May 14—3 : 41 p. m.]

68. The Legation learns from a high British military source that Italian entry into war within next few days [4] is feared in which event no immediate land offensive against Egypt is expected but aerial attacks on Alexandria and Port Said and possibly Cairo would be anticipated. Impression given that British military here is less confident of ability to maintain adequate defense than was the case heretofore.

HARE

740.0011 European War 1939/3442 : Telegram

The Chargé in Egypt (Hare) to the Secretary of State

CAIRO, June 2, 1940—11 a. m.
[Received 2 : 45 p. m.]

87. I am informed by Levy, *New York Times* correspondent, that he has just learned from a high Government source that the British Government yesterday asked the Egyptian Government what position it would assume in the event of an attack by Italy on France and a consequent declaration of war on Italy by Great Britain.

Despite strong pressure by the Embassy and British military authorities here the Prime Minister invited attention to the fact that the Anglo-Egyptian treaty [5] did not call for a declaration of war by Egypt under the conditions outlined and that, although Egypt intended fully to carry out its specified treaty obligations, it could not without the consent of Parliament as provided by the constitution join Great Britain in declaring war on Italy unless the latter took the offensive against Egypt. The Prime Minister added that he would be prepared to present that matter to Parliament but he doubted if it could agree to the British proposal in view of general fear of war in the country.

Whether by taking such a position Egypt could actually avoid involvement in hostilities for any considerable length of time seems highly problematical due to the country's being a British naval military and air base and thus an obvious object of Italian attack.

---

[4] Italy entered the war on June 10.
[5] Anglo-Egyptian Treaty of Alliance, signed at London, August 26, 1936; for text, see League of Nations Treaty Series, vol. CLXXIII, p. 401.

Should the Department perceive no objection Levy would appreciate foregoing being brought to the attention of Krock [5a] for the information of the *New York Times* but not for publication.

HARE

740.0011 European War 1939/3689 : Telegram

The Chargé in Egypt (Hare) to the Secretary of State

CAIRO, June 11, 1940—noon.
[Received 3 : 22 p. m.]

98. Following Mussolini's speech, conversations with the British Ambassador and Italian Minister [6] and a meeting of the Cabinet, the Prime Minister late last night issued a noncommittal statement giving assurance that the Egyptian Government was following the situation closely with a view to safeguarding Egyptian interests and advising the population to remain calm.

The Egyptian Government is obviously on the horns of a dilemma. On the one hand, in keeping with the prevailing spirit of defeatism in official circles, they would like to put credence in Mussolini's declaration that Italy does not intend involving other countries, including Egypt, in the struggle and consequently they are hesitant to take any action which would give offense to Italy. On the other hand an objective appraisal of the situation including due consideration of Egypt's treaty obligations to Great Britain leaves little room for hope that Egypt can remain out of hostilities for long.

Diplomatic relations not yet severed.

HARE

701.8365/8 : Telegram

The Chargé in Egypt (Hare) to the Secretary of State

CAIRO, June 13, 1940—noon.
[Received June 13—11 : 40 a. m.]

103. Department's 42, May 25th.[7] The Under Secretary of State of the Egyptian Foreign Office informed me this morning that since the severance of relations with Italy yesterday the Foreign Office has been unable to communicate with the Egyptian Minister at Rome. The Under Secretary requested that the American Ambassador at Rome inform the Egyptian Minister there of the severance of relations and the termination of his mission and endeavor to arrange for the immediate departure, under appropriate guarantees, of the Minister

---

[5a] Arthur Krock, Chief of the Washington bureau of the *New York Times*.
[6] Serafino Mazzolini.
[7] Not printed.

and his staff overland via Yugoslavia, Turkey and Palestine. Upon arrival at the Yugoslav frontier the Egyptian Government should immediately be notified by telegraph in order that the Italian Minister and his staff here may be permitted to leave Egypt at the same time. It is requested that the foregoing be transmitted in the Department's discretion to the Ambassador at Rome and that he be requested to advise me immediately of the results of such action as he may take. There has not been a declaration of war by Egypt on Italy.

HARE

701.8365/8 : Telegram

The Secretary of State to the Chargé in Egypt (Hare)

WASHINGTON, June 14, 1940.

53. Your 103, 13th, noon, has been repeated to Embassy Rome for such action as may be possible in the circumstances.

HULL

740.0011 European War 1939/3804 : Telegram

The Chargé in Egypt (Hare) to the Secretary of State

CAIRO, June 14, 1940—4 p. m.
[Received 7 : 05 p. m.]

105. In a note received today the Egyptian Foreign Office communicated to the Legation the text of the declaration made by the Prime Minister in the secret session of Parliament on June 12 in respect of the attitude of Egypt regarding the entrance of Italy into the war. The following is a summary of the declaration:

(1) Fidelity of Egypt to its alliance with Great Britain and pledge to render all assistance demanded by its ally within the territorial limits of the country.

(2) Egypt will enter the war only if attacked by Italy in one of following three ways: (*a*) if Italian soldiers take the initiative in an incursion on Egyptian territory; (*b*) if Italy bombs Egyptian towns; (*c*) if Italy directs air raids against Egyptian military objectives.

(3) On the request of Parliament the Government agreed to submit this matter again to it should the circumstances warrant.

An obvious deduction from this declaration is that an air attack on British military or naval establishments in Egypt would not necessarily be considered an act of aggression against Egypt. This equivocal attitude serves to illustrate the observation made in the Legation's telegram No. 98, June 11, noon, regarding the tendency in Government circles to attempt to avoid or at least postpone hostilities with Italy while at the same time observing Egypt's treaty obligations to Great Britain.

Relations between the Prime Minister and the British Embassy have been increasingly difficult of late the principal contentious points being the declaration of war issue on which the Prime Minister refuses to give in and the Cairo open city plan which the British refuse to approve. This situation gave rise to reports several days ago of a possible change in the Government possibly the return of Wafd press [*party*] in view of the strong vote of confidence given the Prime Minister day before yesterday his position seems momentarily stronger, but the situation remains uncertain.

It is thought in certain quarters that one of the purposes of recent British attacks in Libya and Italian East Africa was to provoke reprisals and thus bring Egypt into the war and the failure of such reprisals to materialize is regarded as only a temporary respite dictated by political motives.

HARE

740.0011 European War 1939/3923 : Telegram

The Chargé in Egypt (Hare) to the Secretary of State

CAIRO, June 18, 1940—1 p. m.
[Received June 18—9 : 50 a. m.]

110. Although Italian bombing attacks during the last few days on Sollum and Mersa Matruh resulted in several Egyptian military casualties Prime Minister last night announced that such would be considered incidents capable of being settled by diplomatic means. Richard Mowrer, *Chicago Daily News* correspondent, suffered superficial injury from flying masonry during bombing at Mersa Matruh. He is now in Alexandria coming to Cairo tomorrow.

HARE

740.0011 European War 1939/4094 : Telegram

The Chargé in Egypt (Hare) to the Secretary of State

CAIRO, June 22, 1940—6 p. m.
[Received June 23—5 : 58 p. m.]

117. My telegram No. 115, June 22, 8 a. m.[8] An official communiqué issued this afternoon states this morning's air raid warning in Cairo was a false alarm and that the planes fired upon were Royal Air Force units. Several civilian casualties from anti-aircraft fire reported.

---

[8] Not printed.

Another communiqué states that 2 persons were killed and 23 wounded during last night's bombing in Alexandria. Consul there reports no American casualties.

HARE

883.00/1125 : Telegram

The Chargé in Egypt (Hare) to the Secretary of State

CAIRO, June 24, 1940—8 a. m.
[Received 11 a. m.]

118. Legation's telegram No. 111, June 18, 6 p. m.[9] Announcement was made yesterday of the acceptance of Aly Maher's resignation as Prime Minister but his successor has not yet been chosen. Dr. Ahmed Maher, the Prime Minister's brother, regarded as most likely candidate.

King Farouk was reluctant up to the last to yield to British pressure exerted to bring about removal and went so far several days ago as to make a personal appeal to King George but the latter courteously but firmly declined to intervene.

Before deciding to accept the Prime Minister's resignation the King on Saturday called a meeting of leaders of all parties at the Palace with a view to the formation of a National Government but Nahas Pasha [10] is reported to have refused to lead or cooperate with such a government [unless?] new elections were held. The formation of the new Cabinet was thereupon left to King.

It is regarded as significant that the political leaders at the meeting were unanimous in endorsing Aly Maher's foreign policy of living up to the treaty with Great Britain loyally but endeavoring to keep Egypt out of war despite fact that it was largely on this issue that the present crisis was precipitated. There is no doubt that public opinion here is still strongly against the entry of Egypt into the war.

HARE

883.00/1128 : Telegram

The Chargé in Egypt (Hare) to the Secretary of State

CAIRO, July 4, 1940—10 a. m.
[Received 11 : 35 a. m.]

130. The Legation's telegram No. 124, June 29, 10 a. m.[9] In a declaration before Parliament last night the new Prime Minister [11] said it would be his policy to safeguard the independence and safety of Egypt while fulfilling treaty obligations with Great Britain in both

---

[9] Not printed.
[10] Former Prime Minister, leader of Wafd Party.
[11] Hassan Sabri Pasha.

spirit and letter and in accordance with the motion approved by Parliament on June 12 (see Legation's telegram No. 105, June 14, 4 p. m.). The declaration was essentially identical with statements of the previous Prime Minister, Aly Maher, and is regarded as a full vindication of his policy.

In debate following the declaration a number of deputies strongly criticized British interference which had brought about the fall of Aly Maher at a time when he enjoyed the confidence of the people, Parliament and King.

A vote of confidence based on the Prime Minister's declaration was carried by a large majority in the Chamber of Deputies.

HARE

740.0011 European War 1939/4502 : Telegram

The Chargé in Egypt (Hare) to the Secretary of State

CAIRO, July 8, 1940—11 a. m.
[Received 2 : 05 p. m.]

138. The Legation is reliably informed that the British authorities have proposed to the Egyptian Government that since Egypt is apparently not disposed to enter the war certain Egyptian military material particularly artillery and mechanized equipment should be turned over to the British Army in Egypt which is short of such materials. The proposal is understood to make provision for compensation.

The reactions of the Egyptian Government to the proposal is not yet known but it would seem from first indications that it may develop into a highly contentious issue since aside from British need for such material it is believed that a motivating factor was probably distrust by the British of the Egyptian Army.

HARE

740.0011 European War 1939/5007 : Telegram

The Chargé in Egypt (Hare) to the Secretary of State

CAIRO, August 7, 1940—9 a. m.
[Received 4 : 47 p. m.]

168. In a communiqué issued by British General Headquarters, Middle East, last night it was stated that the first phase of operations in the western desert might be said to be finishing. During this period a small British mobile force had been most successful in operating along the eastern Libyan frontier and heavy toll has been taken of the Italians in both material and men. Now, however, hostilities were entering a second phase with the concentration of Italian troops

in the Monastia–Bardia [*sic*] area and the taking over of command by Marshal Graziani. Experience at Kassala and Moyale had shown that the Italians required a superiority of 10 to 1 before attacking but "in this coastal area they now have an even greater superiority and an attack must be expected". Plans have been made to meet this contingency and exaggerated claims which may be expected to emanate from Bari and Berlin should be discounted.

As background of foregoing it may be said that there has been increasing evidence recently of stronger Italian opposition in western desert area and qualified observers have predicted that under the circumstances a strategic British withdrawal was probably imminent in view of heavy strain on men and the difficulty of maintaining campaign so far from bases. Further reason for such a withdrawal has been seen in pressure recently brought to bear by Italian artillery on Sollum with result that its abandonment has seemed a foregone conclusion. Once this position were lost a further retirement would be expected owing to the strategic location of the escarpment immediately west of Sollum which dominates coastal plain to the east.

Reports on last night's American radio of mass Italian attack on Egypt are contradicted by a semi-official statement issued here this morning to the effect that there are no Italian troops at present on Egyptian soil. However an Italian attack in force which had formerly not been anticipated before the end of summer now seems in prospect and the question is whether the British will be able to sustain such an attack along their main line of defense in the Mersa Matruh area. The British still profess confidence but objective observers seriously question whether acknowledged British fighting qualities will be sufficient to make up for the great disparity between the two forces in men and equipment.

It is regarded as significant that since August 1 visits of war correspondents to the western desert have been prohibited. Incidentally the Legation learns on good authority that despite alleged British supremacy in the Mediterranean the Italians have maintained adequate communications with Libya by a successful convoy system.

HARE

883.032/49 : Telegram

The Minister in Egypt (Fish) to the Secretary of State

CAIRO, August 23, 1940—1 p. m.
[Received August 24—7 a. m.]

182. The Chamber of Deputies adjourned on August 21 until November 5 subject to call in case of need. Senate also recessed recently without fixing date for reconvening.

One of the acts of the Chamber was to adopt on the proposal of Dr. Ahmed Maher Pasha, President of the Chamber, a declaration confirming its previous declaration of June 12 (see the Legation's telegram No. 105, June 14, 5 [4] p. m.) regarding the entry of Italy into war and interpreting that declaration as meaning that "Egypt while not harboring enmity or hatred of any other nation cannot but defend herself by all means at her command if her territory or forces are attacked".

FISH

883.00/1129 : Telegram

The Minister in Egypt (Fish) to the Secretary of State

CAIRO, August 23, 1940—4 p. m.
[Received August 24—8 : 40 a. m.]

181. Following is comment on the Legation's telegram No. 182, August 23, 5 [1] p. m.   The approval of the declaration was preceded by a stormy debate, partly in open and partly in secret session, during which Ahmed Maher Pasha and other advocates of closer cooperation with the British and of a stronger stand on the defense issue sought to prevail upon the Prime Minister to refute the prevailing impression that the Egyptian Government would seek to avoid becoming involved in hostilities with Italy at any cost.   The Prime Minister refused to go further than reiterate adherence to the declaration of July [June] 12 but finally consented, after allegedly being at one time on the point of resigning, to accept the declaration proposed by Ahmed Maher Pasha.

The new declaration is regarded as significant because it apparently commits Egypt to defend itself if its territory or forces are attacked but makes no mention of declaration of war.   In other words the British are now apparently getting in substance what they formerly failed to obtain in insisting on a declaration of war (the British Ambassador recently told me he was no longer pressing this latter point).   However, it is believed that the predominant feeling in Egypt is still against involvement in hostilities and it remains to be seen whether, should the occasion arise, Egypt will actually take up arms against Italy.

FISH

883.00/1131 : Telegram

The Minister in Egypt (Fish) to the Secretary of State

CAIRO, August 28, 1940—11 a. m.
[Received August 29—4:45 p. m.]

186. Following a Cabinet meeting yesterday the Prime Minister made a statement to the press denying the report published in the morning papers regarding the resignation of the Cabinet, adding that the situation remained unchanged and that the Cabinet was remaining in office. However, the Legation is reliably informed that the Cabinet did in fact submit its resignation in writing to the King day before yesterday in a move designed to obtain Wafd support by removing Nokrashy Pasha from the Ministry of the Interior and by possibly even going so far as to eliminate all Saadists from the Cabinet but the British Embassy, which has recently been working in close cooperation with Dr. Ahmed Maher, President of the Saadist Party, is said to have intervened at the last moment and prevailed upon the Prime Minister to remain in office. Situation is still regarded as unsettled and either the reshuffling of the present Cabinet or the formation of a new Cabinet seems likely.

FISH

740.0011 European War 1939/5395a : Telegram

The Secretary of State to the Minister in Egypt (Fish)

WASHINGTON, August 31, 1940—3 p. m.

96. Please telegraph the Department any information that you may be able to obtain discreetly concerning the general military situation in Egypt and the Sudan, including the approximate number of British forces in Egypt and the Sudan and the estimated number of opposing Italian forces. In that connection the Department would be pleased to receive the opinions of the British military and civil authorities concerning the military situation so far as they may feel free to make such opinions known to you.

The Department would also be interested in receiving an estimate of the naval situation in the eastern Mediterranean and in the Red Sea, including whether the Red Sea is continuing to be used by the British for commercial shipping.

The Department assumes that you are maintaining close contact with the Consulates at Alexandria and Port Said with a view to forwarding by telegraph information of important developments in those districts. Such information should of course include any discreetly obtainable concerning damage of any significance by Italian air raids.

HULL

740.0011 European War 1939/5455 : Telegram

The Minister in Egypt (Fish) to the Secretary of State

CAIRO, September 10, 1940—11 a. m.
[Received September 12—9 a. m.]

198. Department's telegram 96, August 31. The following is the general military situation in Egypt and the Sudan and the naval situation in the eastern Mediterranean and the Red Sea.

1. Egypt: Italian forces in Libya are estimated about 220,000 metropolitan troops and about 80,000 native troops. Only a partial concentration has been effected on the border due to water supply problem. Bulk of concentration believed to be in Jebel-El Akhdar area and between Derna and Tobruk.

British forces in Egypt have been considerably increased of late [apparent omission] transfer of troops particularly Australians from Palestine and recent arrival of reenforcement of about 14,000 men from various parts of the Empire (see the Legation's telegram 180, August 23 [12]) and a few more convoys are expected in the near future. Furthermore early transfer of about 6,000 Polish troops from Palestine is expected and about 1,000 French volunteers are in training at Ismailia.

Total British troops in Egypt and the Sudan at present estimated at from 85,000 to 95,000 not including Egyptian troops. Although latter number over 30,000 only about 5,000 are trained and equipped for modern warfare. Given present forces available and expected reenforcements the British problem is not so much lack of manpower as inadequacy of equipment including anti-aircraft guns, artillery, tanks and above all airplanes. Most of the planes used are Blenheim bombers and Gladiator and Lysander fighters and there is great need of faster planes. Furthermore, airdromes and such important strategic points as Suez are deficient in anti-aircraft protection. Supplies including some Hurricanes are beginning to come in but it is understood problem remains acute. In this connection an informed source has it that some British bombers are now being flown from England to Egypt and are being used for bombing Italian objectives en route. According to the same source 30 German bombers with German crews recently reached Libya. Operations on the western desert since Italy entered the war have been summarized and analyzed in the Legation's telegrams No. 154 of July 19 [12] and No. 168 of August 7.

Despite their inferiority in men and material the British took the initiative at the outset of the war, British mechanized units penetrating over 50 miles into Libya but making no attempt to hold enemy

---

[12] Not printed.

territory and British airplanes raiding Italian bases along the Libyan coast, such raids being supplemented recently by bombardment by British naval units based on Alexandria. However, although air activity has been maintained land operations have been at a virtual standstill for the past month during which time both sides have been strengthening their forces in apparent anticipation of operations on a larger scale. That the offensive in such operations will be taken by the Italians is taken for granted but opinion is divided as to when the attack will come and whether the British defense will be sufficiently strong to withstand it.

About a month ago (see Legation's telegram 168, August 7) Italian troop concentrations on the Libyan border gave rise to fear of an imminent Italian attack and that possibility is still not to be excluded. However, in the absence of important developments of an unexpected nature the approach of the cool season in October and November is now mentioned as the most likely time for launching an attack possibly in conjunction with a move against the Sudan from Italian East Africa.

As regards the probable outcome of such an offensive the Italians although having great superiority in men and equipment must maintain a long line of communications in order to assure an adequate water supply and also meet the natural obstacles of trans-desert transportation. However, certain observers point out that the Italians have had years to develop means for meeting these obstacles and that wishful thinking in this respect is dangerous.

Many other responsible British military and civil authorities view the situation with obvious seriousness but at the same time with apparent confidence particularly since the arrival of additional troops and supplies.

2. The Sudan: The total Italian forces in East Africa are estimated at about 200,000 men including white and native troops but it is difficult to estimate how many of these could be released to attack the Sudan. Against this the British have a relatively small force of British and Sudanese troops but reenforcements are now being sent and the native population is said to be remaining loyal. Not long after hostilities began the Italians moved to a short distance over the border and seized certain Sudan border towns such as Kassda [Kassala] and Kurmuk but the rainy season halted further operations. However, it is expected attack will be renewed after wet season with Port Sudan as most likely objective and possibly Khartum. In the meantime the British are attempting to promote native uprisings in Abyssinia and for that reason brought Haile Selassie from England.

The basic fact regarding Italian East Africa is its complete isolation and lack of means of obtaining supplies except by occasional airplanes. Under the circumstances it is obvious that the Italians cannot afford to delay for long if they contemplate launching a serious offensive from East Africa.

3. The naval situation: The British Eastern Mediterranean Fleet is based on Alexandria and its composition is as follows: 5 battleships, 8 cruisers, 2 airplane carriers, 22 destroyers, 2 tenders and 32 submarines. Of these 1 battleship, 3 cruisers, 1 aircraft carrier and 6 destroyers were sent from England as reenforcements only last week and 2 more cruisers and possibly more destroyers are on the way with a convoy around the Cape. Generally speaking the new units are better fitted for anti-aircraft defense than those originally here. It is also expected that about one-third of the destroyers being acquired from the United States will be used in the Eastern Mediterranean or Red Sea area.

As matters now stand the British naval command in this area is said to feel sufficiently strong to defeat any Italian force sent against it in the open sea but not sufficiently strong to attack the Italian Fleet at their bases nor to stop Italian convoys from Italy to Libya which are said to be crossing without great difficulty. For a serious attack on the fleet and bases greater air strength would be needed and to stop convoys more destroyers would be required. Under the circumstances continuation of its raids against Italian bases such as those recently conducted is to be anticipated but no decisive action. Italian submarine losses in the Mediterranean are said to have been heavy.

As regards shipments to Egypt there is practically nothing coming by way of the Mediterranean but the convoy system in the Red Sea appears to be working efficiently although incoming cargo thus far has been almost exclusively military. However knowledge of resumption of commercial shipping in the Red Sea including direct sailings between Suez and New York by foreign registry ships is expected in the near future.

The Consulates at Alexandria and Port Said are under standing instructions to report any events of military interest in their districts not covered in official communiqués but thus far they have had little to report. Alexandria has been the objective of repeated air raids but attacks have been light and no important objectives have been hit and heavy damage done. Port Said and Suez were attacked for the first time last week but no damage was done although bombs dropped at latter which barely missed oil tanks.

FISH

740.0011 European War 1939/5607 : Telegram

The Minister in Egypt (Fish) to the Secretary of State

CAIRO, September 20, 1940—4 p. m.
[Received September 21—5 : 41 p. m.]

209. Legation's telegram No. 207, September 18, 4 p. m.[13] Official sources report that the Italians have made no effort to advance further since their occupation of Sidi Barrani on Monday but are confining their activity to consolidation their position and establishing communications with the rear. British reconnaissance is reported to reveal no extensive troop movements in the rear and it is still an open question whether the Italians intend pressing their attack on Egypt to a decisive issue at this time. In the meantime British action by armored units and by air is being continued and supplemented by harrying operations by the British Fleet from Sidi Barrani to Bengazi.

The attitude of the Egyptian Government in respect of this situation still remains obscure. The Cabinet met yesterday for the first time since the Italian advance started on Sept. 13 but the views of the Ministers are understood to have been divergent and no decision was reached. Dr. Ahmed Maher Pasha made two speeches at Mansura yesterday strongly urging that Egypt take steps to defend itself and the Saadist Party is supporting him but the Prime Minister is understood to oppose Egypt's becoming involved in hostilities at this time and most of the Cabinet are said to share his views. Since discussion of the matter seems to be taking a partisan turn it would not be surprising if a Cabinet crisis resulted. As far as can be ascertained the British are not attempting to force the issue.

Generally speaking public opinion in Egypt is opposed to becoming involved in war but at the same time there is no doubt that the vast majority of the population dislike the Italians intensely and hope for a British victory. Under the circumstances it seems probable that as matters progress the Egyptians, while hesitant to take up arms, may be disposed to lend certain assistance to the British such as turning over much needed military equipment.

FISH

883.00/1137 : Telegram

The Minister in Egypt (Fish) to the Secretary of State

CAIRO, September 23, 1940—3 p. m.
[Received September 24—9 : 43 a. m.]

211. Legation's telegram No. 209, September 20, 4 p. m. Following a meeting of the Egyptian Cabinet on September 21 to discuss the

---

[13] Not printed.

situation arising out of the occupation of Egyptian territory by Italy the four Saadist members of the Cabinet (see this Legation's despatch No. 2158, July 27 and telegram No. 192, September 3 [14]) resigned when the Cabinet refused to accept their proposal that Egypt should declare a state of war against Italy.   In the course of the discussion the Prime Minister is reported to have maintained that he perceived no reason for a precipitate change of policy at this time and to have stated that the British Ambassador had assured him that Great Britain was satisfied with the way Egypt was living up to its treaty obligations.   However, the Cabinet decided to increase the Egyptian Army by 5,000 men and 500 commissioned officers.   (A part of the Egyptian Army is now stationed in the western desert to the east of Mersa Matruh but it is not clear what disposition would be made of this force in case of a further Italian advance.   According to recent reports certain Egyptian motorized units being moved further to the rear.)   The posts of the resigning Ministers are being filled entirely by reshuffling the present Cabinet.   Suliman Pasha, formerly without Portfolio, takes Finance; Sirry Pasha takes Communications in addition to Public Works; Samy Bey, leaves Supplies and takes Commerce and Industry; Ibrahim Bey, formerly without Portfolio, takes Supplies.

In deciding against a change of policy with regard to the involvement of Egypt in hostilities the Cabinet was undoubtedly influenced by the following factors: (1) general opposition of the people to war, (2) the remoteness and relative unimportance of the area affected by the Italian occupation, (3) unpreparedness of Egypt for war, (4) disapproval of participation in the war by most Egyptian Army officers, (5) fear of Italian retaliation, particularly in the form of bombing of Egyptian cities, and (6) feeling that in the event of an Italian victory Egypt would be dealt with more generously if it had not taken up arms against Italy.   A point which many Egyptians of all parties stress in this connection is that they would be much more disposed to enter the conflict if Great Britain would now guarantee to withdraw completely from Egypt after the war, i. e., if the reward offered was complete independence rather than the continuance of the less objectionable of two foreign dominations.

FISH

740.0011 European War 1939/5607 : Telegram

The Secretary of State to the Minister in Egypt (Fish)

WASHINGTON, September 23, 1940—6 p. m.

102. Your 209, September 20, 4 p. m.   The Department would welcome a fuller analysis by you of the attitude of Egypt toward the

---

[14] Neither printed.

Italian invasion of Egyptian territory in the light of the declaration made by the Chamber of Deputies on August 21, as reported in your telegrams 182 and 183 [*181*] of August 23. Such an analysis should include an appraisal of the influence of the King, his cabinet, and that of Egypt's ally, Great Britain, as well as of any other factors which may be making themselves felt in the determination of Egypt's attitude toward this invasion.

It is assumed that you are maintaining contact with the Egyptian Prime Minister and Minister of Foreign Affairs, as well as with your British colleague, in order to inform yourself so far as may be possible concerning the course the Egyptian Government may take in the present conflict. Any information you are able to develop discreetly and informally through such contacts should be, of course, included in your telegraphic report.

HULL

740.0011 European War 1939/5730 : Telegram

The Minister in Egypt (Fish) to the Secretary of State

CAIRO, September 25, 1940—11 a. m.
[Received September 26—6 : 55 a. m.]

213. Department's 102, September 23, 6 p. m. The Legation's No. 211, September 23, 3 p. m. which apparently crossed the Department's telegram under reference is believed to have covered most of the points on which the Department desired to be informed. In recapitulation it may be said :

1. That the King is definitely anti-British and opposed to Egypt's entry into the war at the side of Great Britain.

2. That the Prime Minister and the Cabinet, while maintaining that the Egyptian Government will by its declaration to defend the country, are in fact opposed to Egypt's taking up arms except in case of absolute necessity and are disposed to seize upon any likely excuse to avoid so doing, the pretext now advanced being that it is not clear that the Italian advance into Egyptian territory should be regarded as a planned invasion.

3. That, except for followers of Ahmed Maher and a few other persons, the people do not feel that this is Egypt's war, are fearful of the consequences of entry into the war and are strongly opposed to such action.

4. That the British after having pressed for months for a declaration of war and while they would still welcome such action by Egypt, are apparently resigned to the fact that, given the strong popular opposition to such action, the best policy is not to attempt for the time being to force the issue.

In the event of an advance or prospective advance by the Italians into the Nile Valley itself it is possible that the Egyptian Government and people might take a less apathetic attitude particularly if effective

British pressure were applied. By that time, however, given Egypt's military unpreparedness, it might well be a matter of indifference to the British whether Egypt elected to remain a cooperative nonbelligerent or to become an active ally.

FISH

882.00/1142 : Telegram

The Minister in Egypt (Fish) to the Secretary of State

CAIRO, October 11, 1940—noon.
[Received 8 : 55 a. m.]

237. Legation's telegram No. 213, September 25, 11 a. m. As a result of continued agitation on the part of Dr. Ahmed Maher Pasha for the re-convening of Parliament in order to discuss the declaration of war issue the Cabinet met on October 9th and decided against calling Parliament into session at this time. The Prime Minister thereupon notified Dr. Ahmed Maher Pasha of the Cabinet's decision noting that Parliament would not necessarily have to be convened before November 16th and that under the circumstances a special session seemed unnecessary. In a written reply Maher Pasha agreed not to press the matter further.

FISH

740.0011 European War 1939/6081 : Telegram

The Minister in Egypt (Fish) to the Secretary of State

CAIRO, October 15, 1940—6 p. m.
[Received October 15—4 : 58 p. m.]

246. I attended a luncheon at the British Embassy today given in honor of Anthony Eden [15] who told me he left London Saturday and arrived yesterday. I gathered that the main reason Eden's visit was to conduct a personal inspection of the defenses of Egypt and the Sudan, but it seems likely that he may also take the occasion to seek to effect an improvement in Anglo-Egyptian relations particularly as regards the attitude of the King by whom Eden said he was being received.

The Ambassador told me that no reference to Eden's visit was being permitted in the press.

FISH

[15] British Secretary of State for Foreign Affairs.

740.0011 European War 1939/6139 : Telegram

The Minister in Egypt (Fish) to the Secretary of State

CAIRO, October 17, 1940—5 p. m.
[Received October 18—4 : 30 a. m.]

252. The Legation's telegram No. 246, October 15, 6 p. m. I am confidentially informed that in an audience with the King on October 15 Eden outlined British policy in respect of Egypt and particularly stressed that further obstructionist tactics on the part of the Palace could not be tolerated at a time when such vital issues were at stake.

The King is said to have received Eden's admonition in good part. In this connection please see the Legation's telegrams 178, August 17 [*18*] and 225, October 5.[16]

The ban on mention by the press of Eden's presence here was removed yesterday.

FISH

740.0011 European War 1939/6256 : Telegram

The Minister in Egypt (Fish) to the Secretary of State

CAIRO, October 26, 1940—3 p. m.
[Received 10 : 55 p. m.]

267. The Legation's telegram No. 252, October 17, 5 p. m. I am now informed by a usually reliable but unofficial source that on the occasion of his audience with the King, Eden delivered to him a letter from King George expressing the hope that Egypt would cooperate with Great Britain in the conduct of the war. I may add that in my several recent conversations with the Ambassador and Eden no mention of such a letter was made.

My informant also states that in talking with the King, Eden referred to a conversation with the Prime Minister in which the latter had given assurance that if Siwa were attacked Egypt would fight. The King replied that Egypt of course had a responsible Parliamentary Government and that such matters were for the decision of the Government. However, after the interview, the King is said to have summoned the Prime Minister and expressed his displeasure regarding the assurance given Eden.

Speaking generally, I am given to understand that although the King is not entirely satisfied with the close cooperation between the Prime Minister and the Embassy he is inclined to let matters drift up to the point of becoming involved in the war which he continues to oppose strongly. As a matter of fact the Prime Minister, despite

---

[16] Neither printed.

his assurance regarding Siwa, appears to be in essential agreement with the King in this respect and it is expected that in the new Parliament convening November 14th he will rely for support largely on the anti-war group.

FISH

883.00/1152 : Telegram

The Minister in Egypt (Fish) to the Secretary of State

CAIRO, November 16, 1940—9 a. m.
[Received November 17—5 : 16 p. m.]

304. Referring to the Legation's telegram 303, November 15, 7 p. m.,[17] announcement was made last night of the formation of a new Cabinet by Hussein Sirrey Pasha who, in addition to the Premiership, takes Foreign Affairs and Interior. Other Ministers remain the same as in the last Cabinet with the following exceptions: Abdel Kawi Ahmad Bey takes Public Works which Portfolio he held under Achen Maher; Hassan Sadek Bey, formerly Under Secretary of State for Finance, takes Finance; Youne Saleh Pasha, a former Royal Counselor, takes National Defense; Mohammed Abdel Galil Samra Bey takes Social Affairs; and Abdel Meguid Ibrahim Saleh takes Communications in addition to Supplies.

All of the new appointees are Independents except Samra Bey who is a Liberal Constitutionalist.

The Legation understands that the name of the new Prime Minister was submitted to the British for approval before final decision was made.

It is expected that Sirrey Pasha will follow in general the policy of his predecessor.

FISH

740.0011 European War 1939/6726 : Telegram

The Minister in Egypt (Fish) to the Secretary of State

CAIRO, November 16, 1940—3 p. m.
[Received November 17—4 : 20 p. m.]

305. The Legation's telegram 225, October 5.[17] The Legation has been informed by a strictly confidential but reliable source that the British military authorities here acting direct rather than through the Embassy have informally approached the Egyptian Government with a proposal for the solution of the problem of the Egyptian Army in respect of current hostilities on Egyptian territory. The proposed

---

[17] Not printed.

Egyptian troops in danger areas would be withdrawn to the rear for guarding communications and public utilities as well as other similar protective services and in addition the Egyptian Government would release to the British a certain quantity of war material including particularly tanks which the British are said especially to need.

As a first step in the withdrawal program Egyptian officers in the Sudan frontier and now stationed at Siwa would be replaced by British officers and the force integrated into the British Army.

According to my informant the British military do not now feel that the Egyptian Army is in a position to render substantial assistance under existing circumstances and they have decided therefore that the best services that Egyptian troops can render for the time being would be to insure against sabotage and destruction behind the lines.

My informant gives me to understand that this proposal met with initial favor on the part of the Egyptians and that an eventual agreement on that general basis is probable.

FISH

883.00/1153 : Telegram

The Minister in Egypt (Fish) to the Secretary of State

CAIRO, November 26, 1940—3 p. m.
[Received November 27—9 : 16 a. m.]

312. In a statement of policy before Parliament yesterday afternoon the new Prime Minister said that the preceding Cabinet had been able to meet the difficult situation confronting it by adopting the policy outlined in the speech from the Throne and that it was his intention to follow the same program.

It would appear under the circumstances that the Prime Minister will rely as did Hassan Sabry Pasha before him on anti-war sentiment for support in Parliament. It is interesting to note in this connection that on November 18 the Chamber of Deputies elected Dr. Ahmed Maher Pasha leader of the pro-war group as its President but it is not yet clear to what extent his election was due to personal popularity and to what extent to approval of his policies. Presumably this situation will be clarified in discussing the speech from the Throne which will come up for debate at a later date.

I understand that Sir Sabry Pasha's appointment by the King was made with the approval of Aly Maher Pasha who although out of office continues to enjoy the confidence of the King and to play an important role in Egyptian politics.

FISH

740.0011 European War 1939/6955 : Telegram

The Minister in Egypt (Fish) to the Secretary of State

CAIRO, November 29, 1940—3 p. m.
[Received December 1—10 : 55 a. m.]

320.   Referring to the announcement of the appointment of General
Catroux as Delegate General of General de Gaulle [18] for the Balkans,
the Near East and the Red Sea with headquarters at Cairo, the Legation learns from a British Embassy source that this decision was
originally reached at a conference of Catroux and De Gaulle at Fort
Lamy some 5 or 6 weeks ago.

According to the Embassy, General Catroux is regarded as particularly qualified in this position because of his experience in colonial
administration and his specialized knowledge of the Near East and
North Africa.   Concerning the choice of Cairo for the General's headquarters the following reasons were cited : (1) position with reference
to French population centers in the Near East such as Istanbul and
Athens; (2) as a listening post for Syria; (3) ready contact with
French Equatorial Africa; (4) presence of French Legion in Egypt.

The Embassy estimates the total number of white French in Egypt
at about 8,000 and says that beginning with about 20 members the
Free French now number about 1,400 men who with their families
would account for approximately half of the total French population
here.

The Embassy added that General Catroux puts the French
Minister [19] here in a difficult position but that the Ambassador had
approached the Prime Minister in the matter and the latter had agreed
to look the other way.   I may add that in talking yesterday with the
French Minister I was struck by the fact that whereas he had usually
preferred to be pro-British in his sentiments, on this occasion he was
strongly critical of the British who he said were driving the French
into the arms of the Germans.

In an interview with an American newspaper correspondent yesterday General Catroux stated that he had no hope for change of policy
by the Vichy Government but that he believed recent British and Greek
successes were having a favorable effect in North Africa and Syria
although he did not expect any immediate developments of importance
in those areas.   Regarding Syria he said he thought it best to leave
the situation undisturbed for the time being because the French Army
there would resist any attempt to take over the country by either the

[18] Leader of the Free French movement.
[19] Jean Pozzi.

British or the Italians. Questioned regarding Weygand [20] he said that it was difficult to say exactly [where ?] Weygand stood but that it was still possible that he might break with Pétain.[21] This statement was confirmed by the Embassy which [indicated ?] that it was known that Weygand had recently been requested to return to Vichy but had refused to do so.

FISH

740.00116 European War 1939/359 : Telegram

The Minister in Egypt (Fish) to the Secretary of State

CAIRO, December 3, 1940—5 p. m.
[Received December 4—9 : 45 a. m.]

325. In reply to a question raised in Parliament last night the Prime Minister is reported by the press to have stated that the Egyptian Government had protested against the bombing of the civilian population in Egypt. However upon inquiring at the Foreign Office this morning the Legation was informed that no actual protest had been lodged. What had been done was to call the attention of the Italian Government to damage resulting from Italian air attacks and to state that it was intended to draw against Italian property under sequestration to provide provisional relief for air raid victims and repair of their houses. The matter has been handled through the Swiss Government since it had particularly to do with property under sequestration and the Swiss were in charge of Italian interests here. Had it been desired to lodge a formal protest the Foreign Office said the message would have been communicated through the medium of American diplomatic channels.

In his statement before Parliament the Prime Minister gave total civilian casualties from air raids in Egypt from June 22 to date as 155 civilians killed and 425 wounded. It may be noted that half of these casualties resulted from a raid over Alexandria during the night of November 18–19 which according to a recently released report resulted in 76 persons killed and 204 wounded, most casualties occurring in the poor quarter of Babsidra. Aside from this raid loss of life and property, damage has been relatively light. Only five deaths outside Alexandria are on record, one at Maadi and four in the Port Said area.

FISH

---

[20] Gen. Maxime Weygand, in command of French Forces in Syria.
[21] Marshal Henri Philippe Pétain, French Chief of State.

740.0011 European War 1939/7121 : Telegram

The Minister in Egypt (Fish) to the Secretary of State

CAIRO, December 11, 1940—8 p. m.
[Received December 11—3 : 15 p. m.]

344. The British Ambassador told me this evening that General Wavell [22] had just advised him that the British had captured Sidi Barrani.

The number of prisoners was at the time unknown but included three generals.

General Wavell had further informed the Ambassador that the Italians were fleeing and the British were in pursuit.

FISH

740.0011 European War 1939/7128 : Telegram

The Minister in Egypt (Fish) to the Secretary of State

CAIRO, December 13, 1940—8 p. m.
[Received December 13—7 : 50 a. m.]

349. For Miles, War Department, from Fellers: [23]

"1805 : British General Headquarters confidentially discloses that the Italian western desert air force is practically grounded. First and Second Libyan and First and Fourth Blackshirt Divisions have been annihilated. 62nd and Catanzaro Divisions are now in Bardia area. Retreating 63rd Division has been attacked by R.A.F. with British mechanized force in pursuit. Prisoners estimated at 30,000, British losses light. Heavy sandstorm intensifies battle confusion."

FISH

740.0011 European War 1939/7253 : Telegram

The Minister in Egypt (Fish) to the Secretary of State

CAIRO, December 23, 1940—6 a. m.
[Received December 24—10 : 50 a. m.]

368. Following for Miles, War Department, from Fellers:

"1806. Elements of British armored [apparent omission] in contact with Italians in Bardia. Support group of armored division confronts Bardia–Tobruk roads. British plan immediate coordinated attack on Bardia by land, sea and air forces. At least 1830-infantry tanks, Australian division, armored division, 7 regiments of artillery, 16th brigade will attack western desert, Italian forces lost equipment, mate-

---

[22] Gen. Sir Archibald P. Wavell, Commanding General of British Forces in the Middle East.
[23] Maj. Bonner Frank Fellers, Military Attaché in Egypt.

rial, supplies, and transport of 5 divisions.   Parts of 3 divisions now occupy fortified Bardia.   British estimate 20,000 enemy in Tobruk. Supply situation alleviated by naval transport to Sollum and captured trucks.   Fourth Indian Division will go to Sudan.   New armored division and heavy equipment of motor transport and supplies arriving."

FISH

740.0011 European War 1939/7274 : Telegram

The Minister in Egypt (Fish) to the Secretary of State

[Extract]

CAIRO, December 26, 1940—10 a. m.
[Received December 27—9 : 40 a. m.]

370. For War Department.   Colonel Brower [24] returned to Egypt 19th from Greece.   Going to desert today.   He supplements Major Feller's report No. 1806 as follows.

Recent operation originally planned for January as flank attack on anticipated Italian advance.   Italians failed to advance, plan converted to limited attack on Sidi Barrani.   Surprise complete due extreme secrecy.   Weak resistance and captured supplies permitted British advance beyond all expectation.   Air force western desert had been reenforced from Sudan and England by direct route . . .

FISH

883.00/1156 : Telegram

The Minister in Egypt (Fish) to the Secretary of State

CAIRO, December 26, 1940—6 p. m.
[Received December 27—10 : 07 a. m.]

373. After a 3-day debate mostly in secret session the Chamber of Deputies last night gave the Government a vote of confidence of 122 to 68 on the question of the approval of the Government's foreign and military policy as set forth in the speech from the Throne.   The opposition consisted almost exclusively of Saadists.   The Wafd broke precedent by voting with the Government.

In the course of the debate in secret session the Prime Minister is reported to have stated that he had protested to the British Government regarding the passage in Churchill's speech to Italy [25] in which reference was made to Egypt as being under British protection and that he had demanded an immediate explanation.   This action is taken as illustrative of apprehension in Egyptian political circles that

[24] Col. Gerald E. Brower, observer and Assistant Military Attaché in Egypt.
[25] Speech appealing to Italian people, December 23.

Egypt's nonparticipation in the war may prejudice its position vis-à-vis the British after the war.

FISH

740.0011 European War 1939/7304a : Telegram

The Secretary of State to the Minister in Egypt (Fish)

WASHINGTON, December 26, 1940—9 p. m.

162. Please report whether or not combat operations of any kind have recently taken place on or over the Red Sea, the Gulf of Aden, and the Straits of Bab el Mandeb.

HULL

740.0011 European War 1939/7305 : Telegram

The Minister in Egypt (Fish) to the Secretary of State

CAIRO, December 28, 1940—10 a. m.
[Received December 29—8 : 15 a. m.]

375. Department's 162, December 26, 9 p. m. British naval and air headquarters advise confidentially that the Italians now have 1 submarine, 6 destroyers, 5 motor torpedo boats and 9 bombers in area specified. However, action during October and November was confined to air and averaged only 6 attacks per month by 1 or 2 planes. No attacks of any kind have been reported for December. Since the beginning of the war only 1 ship has been sunk and 1 damaged both from the air. All British merchant shipping is convoyed by destroyers and an air patrol of 2 or 3 planes. Total ships thus convoyed amounted to 156 in October and 274 in November.

FISH

883.00/1157 : Telegram

The Minister in Egypt (Fish) to the Secretary of State

CAIRO, December 30, 1940—5 p. m.
[Received December 31—10 : 51 a. m.]

379. The Legation's telegram No. 373, December 26, 6 p. m. An official communiqué has been issued by the Egyptian Government stating that as a result of the Egyptian Prime Minister's protest regarding the reference to Egypt in the Churchill speech, a reply has been received from Eden stating that the phrase in question implied nothing more than the obligation incumbent on Great Britain under its treaty with Egypt in respect of the defense of Egypt.

FISH

740.0011 European War 1939/7356 : Telegram

The Minister in Egypt (Fish) to the Secretary of State

CAIRO, December 31, 1940—3 p. m.
[Received 7:45 p. m.]

377. Following for Miles, War Department, and information of the Navy from the Military Attaché.

"No. 1807. Italian attacks by motor torpedo boats, submarines, bomber and attack planes against sea transport to Sollum delayed attack on Bardia. Ammunition is going forward overland. All other supplies are being sent to Sollum by sea. Bardia port is desired as a base for future operations. British plan to attack when supplies adequate.

Churchill is pressing commanders to clear Libya.

Reliable source claims monthly flow to Egypt of 40 American bombers and 45 fighters will begin in January. At the same time British Blenheims, Hurricanes and Fulmers will raise total monthly flow to 240 planes. Planes are being assembled and also tested at Takaradi and then flown to Egypt via Khartoum.

Quantities of supplies, motor transport and mechanized vehicles reliably reported as being assembled in South Africa.

There are several other indications that the British plan to organize, train and equip vast land army in Egypt.

Do you want a cable summarizing land operations against the Italians?

If practicable send code book and all regulations including finance for Military Attachés. Leaving for Libya."

FISH

ATTITUDE OF THE UNITED STATES TOWARD PROPOSED EGYPTIAN LEGISLATION REGARDING RELIGIOUS PROPAGANDA TENDING TO RESTRICT ACTIVITIES OF AMERICAN EDUCATIONAL INSTITUTIONS IN EGYPT

383.0063/3

The Minister in Egypt (Fish) to the Secretary of State

No. 1680   BULKELEY, ALEXANDRIA, June 12, 1939.
[Received July 5.]

SIR: I have the honor to report that both American and British missionary interests have in the past few weeks felt some concern at the attention given in the Egyptian Senate to a draft bill first proposed on June 22, 1938, by Senator Sheikh Abdel Khaliq Salim.

The bill, the first draft of which is appended as Enclosure No. 1,[26] would forbid, under certain penalties, propaganda among young people for the purpose of changing their religious convictions. Enclosure No. 2 [26] is an explanatory note submitted by Senator Salim

---

[26] Not printed.

outlining the disasters the bill is intended to circumvent. When first laid before the Senate in June 1938 the bill was shelved, then revived in February 1939, and referred to the Senate's Committee on Internal Affairs, which modified the draft by raising from 16 to 18 the age under which religious instruction other than that of parents or guardians should be forbidden. In March 1939 Dr. McClenahan of the American University and Dr. Adams of the American Mission in Cairo called at the Legation to express their alarm. They stated that they felt that a movement was afoot to give this bill the force of law. As long ago as 1933 they were conscious of the fact that the Egyptian Government desired to restrict missionary endeavor, and thereupon had issued a statement, adhered to by numerous missions of various nationalities, designed to set forth the general policy of the missionary societies and to allay the fears of supporters of measures directed against them. This statement of policy, said Dr. McClenahan and Dr. Adams, was distributed in quarters where they thought it would do the most good.

They then referred to the guarantee of religious liberty contained in the Egyptian Constitution, and expressed their belief that the Salim bill had not finally passed in its initial form as it could easily be interpreted as applying to Moslem institutions as well as Christian, and thus would not have served the desired end of discriminating against the latter. On a subsequent occasion they mentioned a recently issued fetwah [27] deciding that boys aged seven and upwards might be allowed to choose their religion, provided the choice operates from non-Moslem to Moslem; the fetwah would forbid boys in the same age group, already Moslem, to opt for another religion.

The above-named representatives of American missionary interests are collaborating with an inter-mission committee, a British member of which has placed the committee's views before the British Embassy. The secretary of the Legation recently interviewed Mr. E. F. W. Besly, Legal Adviser of the British Embassy, on this subject, and learned that that Embassy had referred the matter to the Foreign Office, with a request for instructions as to how far the Embassy should intervene if the course of Egyptian legislation renders this necessary. Mr. Besly stated that he hoped some cooperation would be forthcoming from this Legation especially as the American missionary interests in Egypt surpass the British. The object of the law, he says, is not so much its apparent substance, as a means adopted by the Opposition to annoy the Government. He has mentioned the matter on a few occasions to an Under-Secretary of the Ministry of the Interior, who informed him that the bill would be shelved if possible. The interested missionaries however fear that it may be passed notwithstanding.

---

[27] A formal interpretation of Mohammedan Canon law.

Mr. Besly does not believe that the proposed bill reflects any strong Moslem prejudice against Christian missionary work as such at the present time, but that it is principally designed to irk the Government.

Delay in voting the bill in the Senate is also due in part to the fact that the Ministry of the Interior itself is working on a similar bill. In the Senate's session of April 17, 1939, the report of the Committee of the Ministry of the Interior was read, and communication made of the following declaration of the Minister of the Interior to the Committee:

"The Government, while approving the principle of the bill, believes that the question has multiple aspects which have not been considered by the author of the bill. The Government's own bill is more complete. As soon as it has been studied it will be submitted to Parliament. And as it is not fitting that concerning such a serious question there should be two bills at the same time, or that one of them should modify the other, the Government is asking that the study of the law be adjourned pending introduction of the Government's own bill."

Dr. Salim hereupon objected, saying that the bill should not remain too long in abeyance. The Minister of the Interior responded that the Government's bill would be introduced during the present session.

As mentioned above, Mr. Besly has reason to believe that the Ministry of the Interior has no real desire to force the Salim bill through. It has probably adopted the policy of offering to draft its own bill to replace Dr. Salim's for purposes of delay and eventually to shelve it again if possible.

In view of the above situation, and the possibility feared by the American missionary interests involved that the bill, in one form or the other (its author's or the Ministry's) may have some chance of slipping through, the Legation would appreciate an indication from the Department as to how far it might cooperate with the British Embassy in any representations in this matter. The Legation will remain in contact with the Embassy on the subject, and will be informed of the instructions the latter expects to receive from the Foreign Office. If the bill does not pass in the present session of Parliament, the whole matter will rest in abeyance until the reopening of Parliament in the autumn.

Respectfully yours, BERT FISH

383.0063/3

The Secretary of State to the Minister in Egypt (Fish)

No. 413 WASHINGTON, August 25, 1939.

SIR: The Department has received your despatch no. 1680 of June 12, 1939 regarding the concern manifested by American missionary interests in Egypt with respect to a draft law under consideration by the Egyptian Parliament forbidding propaganda among the youth for the purpose of changing their religious convictions.

In that connection there are enclosed copies of correspondence [28] recently exchanged between Mr. A. L. Warnshuis, Secretary of the International Missionary Council, 156 Fifth Avenue, New York, and the Chief of the Division of Near Eastern Affairs [29] on this subject.

The Department desires that you continue to maintain close contact with your British colleague in the matter of the proposed legislation and that you keep the Department informed as to all developments which may occur in connection with consideration of and action on that legislation.

In view of the information contained on pages 6 and 7 of your despatch no. 1719 of July 8, 1939,[28] it would not appear that imminent action on the legislation is anticipated. However, if the proposed legislation, or legislation in substantially similar form, should be enacted it would seem difficult to avoid the conclusion that, for the reasons stated in the memorandum [30] accompanying the letter of Dr. Warnshuis, the law would render practically impossible the continued maintenance of American schools as now organized and conducted and would therefore constitute a violation of the obligation assumed by the Egyptian Government at Montreux with respect to American educational institutions.[31]

In the event that the proposed legislation should seem likely to be enacted, you are authorized to communicate the foregoing views informally to the Foreign Office and to express the confidence of this Government that the Government of Egypt will not permit the enactment of any legislation which would destroy or impair the rights of American institutions which have been expressly recognized and confirmed by the Egyptian Government.

Very truly yours,   For the Secretary of State:
R. Walton Moore

---

[28] Not printed.

[29] Wallace Murray.

[30] Not printed; it stated that the provisions of the proposed law were so strict that it would be impossible for a Christian school to risk the presence of non-Christian pupils at worship or at any kind of instruction which might deal with Christianity or Islam, and any objective dealing with Islam, even in a historical lesson, would be regarded as an infraction of the law (383.0063/4).

[31] See exchange of notes between the United States and Egypt dated May 8, 1937, Department of State Treaty Series No. 939, or 53 Stat. 1705.

383.0063/9

The Chargé in Egypt (Hare) to the Secretary of State

No. 2077   CAIRO, April 24, 1940.

[Received May 16.]

SIR: I have the honor to enclose a translation of a Bill prohibiting religious propaganda, together with an accompanying explanatory note,[32] which is reported to have been signed by King Farouk and to have been referred to Parliament for approval during the present session.

Article 1 of the Bill imposes a general prohibition on the carrying on of religious propaganda outside places of worship or the places designated for that purpose.

Article 2 provides in respect of schools that pupils shall be neither forced nor allowed to attend classes in which instruction is given regarding a faith other than the pupil's own; that pupils shall be neither forced nor allowed to join in prayers or attend religious services other than those of their own religion; and that pamphlets shall not be distributed to students setting forth religious principles contrary to their own faith. It is specified that these prohibitions apply to hospitals and charitable institutions as well as to schools.

Articles 3 and 4 provide for inspection of institutions by the police in connection with the enforcement of this law and, in addition to such punishment as may be prescribed in the Penal Code, specifies that offenses contravening the provisions of this law shall be punishable by one month's imprisonment or a fine of L.E. 10 or both.

Article 5 specifies a fine of L.E. 100 or imprisonment of one year in the case of persons found attempting to give religious instruction to young persons under eighteen years of age, even with their consent. Similar penalties are prescribed for proselitization by means of giving gifts, intimidation, or by the use of narcotics or hypnotism.

Article 6 provides for the enforcement of law by officials of the Ministries of Public Education and Public Health in agreement with the Ministry of the Interior.

The Bill is accompanied by an explanatory note in which it is stated that the Egyptian Constitution proclaims freedom of faith and accords adequate protection for worship within the bounds of public order and public morals, these principles being in conformity with the spirit of tolerance which marks the Moslem faith. In this connection the authorities have facilitated the granting of land for the erection of places of worship for all faiths and have granted facilities to religious organizations for the establishment of schools and hospitals. However, certain organizations have indulged in religious propaganda

---

[32] Neither printed.

in a manner which has been offensive to Moslems. Such religious propaganda when practised outside designated places of worship may lead to public disorder, and it is for that reason that the present law was drafted.

A full report on this subject is now under preparation. It was thought advisable, however, to transmit the text of the Bill to the Department in the pouch leaving today in as much as it may be necessary to request telegraphic instructions in the event that the question of possible intervention by the Legation should arise. It may be observed in this connection that Dr. Wendell Cleland, Dean of the Division of Extension of the American University; Rev. John S. Badeau, Dean of the College of Arts and Sciences of the American University, and Dr. E. E. Elder of the American Mission, called at the Legation yesterday to express their apprehension of the possible consequences of the passage of this Bill which they feared might be used as a lever to make the lot of American missionary institutions in Egypt so difficult that some or all of them might have to cease operation entirely. They said that similar fears were entertained by British missionary organizations and that the Anglican Bishop in Cairo had taken the matter up with the British Embassy and requested the Ambassador's intervention with a view to forestalling the passage of the Bill, at least in its present form. The Legation understands, however, that the Embassy has not yet decided what action, if any, it will take in the matter. Needless to say, the Legation will not take this case up with the Egyptian Government except under the Department's instructions.

Respectfully yours,   RAYMOND A. HARE

383.0063/11

The Chargé in Egypt (Hare) to the Secretary of State

No. 2092   CAIRO, May 7, 1940.
                                                              [Received June 1.]

SIR: I have the honor to refer to the Legation's despatch no. 2007 [*2077*] of April 24, 1940, enclosing a translation of a bill providing for the prohibition of religious propaganda which had been signed by the King and referred to Parliament for action.

The Legation has just been advised by Dr. Adams, Dean of the School of Oriental Studies of the American University of Cairo, that he has been informed by a source which he regards as reliable that action on the bill in question has been postponed until the next session of Parliament in December. However, the writer had in the meantime sought occasion to discuss this question informally with the French Minister and the Legal Counselor of the British Embassy with a view to ascertaining their views on the subject, which are set forth below as being of possible interest for background purposes.

The French Minister said that he was cognizant that a bill for the prohibition of religious propaganda had been prepared and submitted for legislative action but that he did not contemplate doing anything in the matter. He said that it had been his invariable rule to advise against all proselytizing activity in French institutions and that under the circumstances he would not want to become involved in any discussion on the subject with the Egyptian Government.

The Legal Counselor of the British Embassy said that the Embassy had been approached by various interested British organizations in connection with the proposed bill and that for a time the Ambassador was more or less inclined to intervene in the matter, basing his intervention on the assumption that the bill was intended to be strictly non-discriminatory and that it would therefore be equally applicable to proselytizing by Moslems as by Christians. Knowing that there was no small amount of Moslem proselytizing in Egypt, particularly in respect of Copts in the schools, it was the thought of the Ambassador that insistence on strict non-discrimination might serve to kill the bill or at least to effect its modification. However, the Oriental Secretariat of the Embassy had opposed such an approach for political reasons and it had therefore practically been decided not to pursue the matter further. In this connection the Legal Counselor said quite frankly that it is a fixed policy of the British Government to refrain from supporting Christian missionary activity in Moslem countries in view of the large number of Moslems in territories under British rule whose sensibilities the British Government would not want to offend.

There is enclosed as being of possible interest to the Department a copy of a letter written by the Anglican Bishop in Cairo,[34] signing himself as "Lover of Egypt", and sent to the *Egyptian Gazette* for publication, a copy of which was furnished the Legation in confidence by a member of the *Gazette* staff. However, the censors refused to pass the letter and it was not published.

Respectfully yours,   RAYMOND A. HARE

_____

383.0063/13

The Chargé in Egypt (Hare) to the Secretary of State

No. 2101   CAIRO, May 20, 1940.
                                        [Received June 17.]

SIR: I have the honor to refer to the Legation's despatches No. 2077 of April 24, 1940, and No. 2092 of May 7, 1940, regarding a bill sub-

_____

[34] Not printed.

mitted to Parliament providing for the prohibition of religious propaganda, and to report recent developments in that connection.

It will be recalled that in the Legation's despatch No. 2092 it was stated that Dr. Adams, Dean of the School of Oriental Studies of the American University of Cairo, had advised the Legation that he had been informed by reliable sources that action on the bill had been postponed until the next session of Parliament. . . . the missionary interests concerned suffered a rude awakening when, assuming that the matter had been dropped, they suddenly learned that the bill had been approved by the Senate Committee and was due to come up for vote before the Senate on May 16th. As a matter of fact, the Senate postponed action on the bill for one week, but the missionary interests concerned are not inclined to regard this short respite as particularly reassuring.

On May 18th Dr. Wendell Cleland called at the Legation to discuss this matter with a view to possible intervention by the Legation to prevent the passage of the bill. Dr. Cleland, whose apprehensions regarding the possible consequences of the passage of the bill were mentioned in the Legation's despatch no. 2077 of April 24, 1940, said that he felt that a basis for such representations was contained in the second paragraph of Article 2 of the Montreux Convention,[35] providing for non-discriminatory treatment of foreigners. He added that he felt certain that there would be no question of applying the proposed bill equally to propaganda activities conducted by Christians and Moslems and he seemed to feel that a suggestion to that effect to the Egyptian authorities and reference to Article 2 of the Montreux Convention might serve as a deterrent to the passage of the bill.

I observed to Dr. Cleland that I was doubtful whether the proposal which he suggested would be either justifiable or tactful; not justifiable, because it seemed doubtful if Article 2 of the Montreux Convention was intended to cover a case of this kind; not tactful, because it would amount to accusing the Egyptian authorities of discrimination in advance of any action on their part, an accusation to which they could, and undoubtedly would, take exception. However, I told Dr. Cleland that I would study the matter with a view to ascertaining whether there might seem to be any justifiable ground upon which objection to the bill could be lodged. I added that any approach to the Egyptian authorities by the Legation would, of course, be contingent upon obtaining advance approval from the Department.

---

[35] Convention for the abolition of capitulations in Egypt signed at Montreux May 8, 1937; for text, see Department of State Treaty Series No. 939, or 53 Stat. 1645.

The same day that I talked to Dr. Cleland I also received a telephone call from Mr. E. F. W. Besly, Legal Counselor of the British Embassy, who said that orders had been received from the Foreign Office in London authorizing the Embassy to take the matter up informally with the Egyptian Government, pointing out that a bill of such a sweeping nature as that under consideration was hardly compatible with the principles of modern legislation, and to express the hope that action on the bill would not be pressed. The Foreign Office had specifically enjoined the Embassy, however, against basing opposition to the bill on any provision of the Montreux Convention. Acting under these instructions Mr. W. A. Smart, Oriental Secretary of the British Embassy, called upon Aly Maher Pasha, the Prime Minister, and expressed the hope that action on the bill would not be pressed. According to Mr. Besly, Mr. Smart received the impression that his remarks had fallen on unreceptive ears, but it seemed a possibly encouraging sign that action on the bill had been postponed if only for a week when it had come up before the Senate. Mr. Besly said that the Embassy had been instructed by the Foreign Office to advise the Legation of the attitude of the British Government in this matter.

In conclusion, it may be said that after due consideration of this matter the Legation is inclined to the belief that its intervention with the Egyptian authorities in this connection would be inopportune since no sufficient legal ground is perceived upon the basis of which representations could be made and in so far as the possibility of an informal approach is concerned such action has already been taken by the British Embassy which, in view of its special relations with the Egyptian Government, is in a position to make such an informal approach more efficaciously than could be done by the Legation. It might, of course, be argued that informal representations by the Legation in support of the Embassy's intervention might be helpful but I am inclined to the belief that the contrary might in fact be the case since the Egyptian authorities might thereby gain the impression that they were being subjected to pressure tactics. Under the circumstances and unless otherwise instructed by the Department, the Legation does not propose taking up this question with the Egyptian Government at this time. However, should other facts emerge which would seem to justify revision of this decision, such facts will be reported to the Department and its instructions requested.

Respectfully yours,

RAYMOND A. HARE

383.0063/9 : Telegram

The Secretary of State to the Chargé in Egypt (Hare)

WASHINGTON, May 22, 1940—6 p. m.

38. Your despatch no. 2077 of April 24, 1940. Pending the receipt and study by the Department of your complete report, you should be guided in the meanwhile by the Department's instruction no. 413 of August 25, 1939.

HULL

383.0063/15

The Chargé in Egypt (Hare) to the Secretary of State

No. 2123   CAIRO, June 3, 1940.
                                                     [Received June 28.]

SIR: I have the honor to refer to the Legation's despatch no. 2101 of May 20, 1940, and previous reports, regarding a bill submitted to the Egyptian Parliament providing for the prohibition of religious propaganda and to the Department's telegram no. 38 of May 22, 6 p. m., 1940, advising that the Legation should be guided pending further developments in the matter by the Department's instruction no. 413 of August 25, 1939. Reference is also made to my letter of May 22, 1940 [36] to the Chief of the Division of Near Eastern Affairs outlining a conversation with Dr. Cleland of the American University at Cairo on this subject.

In accord with the Legation's policy of keeping in touch with the British Embassy regarding this matter, I called on Mr. E. F. W. Besly, Legal Counselor of the British Embassy, on May 25 with whom this question had been discussed on several occasions in the past. I observed that I had been advised by several American missionaries that they had been given to understand that opposition to the bill had developed on the part of Moslem interests which felt that such a law would prevent certain Moslem religious observances and activities conducted outside mosques and that revision of the bill to eliminate such restriction of Moslem activity was being urged. Mr. Besly said that he had also heard reports from British missionaries to that effect, which, if true, were most interesting since one of the reasons why it had been difficult to criticize the bill was its apparent nondiscriminatory nature.

In my discussion with Mr. Besly I mentioned the fact that the Department had given thought to this general question last year at a time when a similar bill was up for discussion in the Egyptian Parlia-

---

[36] Not printed.

ment and that it had been the opinion of the Department at that time that the enactment of such a law would so adversely affect American schools in Egypt as to constitute a violation of the obligation assumed by the Egyptian Government at Montreux with regard to American educational institutions. Mr. Besly said that the Embassy had in the past also attempted to advance a similar argument but with little success due to the fact that the Egyptian Government had always maintained that such legislature [*legislation*] was in conformity with the stipulation in the letter [37] of Nahas Pasha [38] that such institutions should be subject "to all measures necessary for the preservation of the public order". In fact it was for that reason that the Embassy had been instructed recently (see p. 4 of the Legation's despatch under reference) not to cite the Montreux Convention in opposing the religious propaganda bill but to confine its representations to the point that the proposed law was inconsistent with the principles of modern legislation (which incidentally is a provision of Article 2 of the Montreux Convention, although the Embassy did not apparently cite this fact in taking the matter up with the Prime Minister).

I also discussed with Mr. Besly the two points raised by Dr. Cleland of the American University and mentioned in my letter of May 22, 1940 to the Chief of the Division of Near Eastern Affairs regarding (1) the place of religious instruction and propagation of religious doctrine in the charters and curricula of American educational, medical and charitable institutions in Egypt and (2) the guarantee of liberty of worship in the Nahas Pasha letter. As regarded the first of these points Mr. Besly said he had no doubt that the Egyptian authorities would cite the "preservation of the public order" provision as a counter argument. As regarded the second point he said he could not see how a guarantee of freedom of worship could be construed to be applicable to religious instruction.

On May 27 the proposed bill finally came up for discussion in the Senate and a lively debate ensued centering around whether the bill was intended to prohibit Moslem as well as non-Moslem religious propaganda. Abdel Razzek el Kadi Bey, Rapporteur of the Committee introducing the bill, stated quite definitely that the bill was supposed to apply to all proselytizing whether Moslem or non-Moslem, whereas Mohamed El Chafei el Labbane, Director of the Criminal Section of the Ministry of the Interior who had been specially delegated to represent the said Ministry in the discussion of the matter, took the view that the purpose of the bill was to regulate religious activity of non-Moslems not sharing the faith of the majority of the

---

[37] Annexed to the convention for the abolition of the capitulations in Egypt, Department of State Treaty Series No. 939, p. 69.
[38] President of the Egyptian delegation to the Montreux Conference, 1937, and President of the Council of Ministers at that time.

inhabitants of the country and that it was by no means intended that the bill should apply to proselytizing by Moslems. In view of these conflicting opinions of the Rapporteur of the Committee and the Delegate of the Ministry of the Interior it was decided to send the bill back to committee for further study.

I understand in this connection that when this question was put up to the Prime Minister by the British Ambassador recently the former stated that the object was to put an end to all proselytizing because he felt that the changing of religion had unfortunate social consequences regardless of whether the person concerned was a Moslem, Christian or adherent of another faith.

Missionary representatives with whom this question has been discussed since the debate in Parliament are inclined to think that the bill will hardly come up for active consideration during the present session of Parliament which is expected to end as soon as action on the budget has been completed.

Respectfully yours,   RAYMOND A. HARE

383.0063/15

The Acting Secretary of State to the Chargé in Egypt (Hare)

No. 478   WASHINGTON, July 23, 1940.

SIR: The Department has received your despatch no. 2123 of June 3, 1940, with further reference to the draft law under consideration by the Egyptian Parliament on religious propaganda.

The Department has carefully considered the facts reported in this and in previous despatches, including particularly the views expressed by the Legal Counselor of the British Embassy in Cairo. While it is of course admitted that the activities of any person or group of persons which endanger the peace and good order of the community in which they reside cannot be permitted, the Department cannot recognize as valid the suggestion that the preservation of public order in Egypt may necessitate restrictions upon the lawful activities of American educational institutions in Egypt, which have been conducted for many years with definite and admitted benefit to that country. It is the Department's view that any attempt to justify interference with the lawful activities of those organizations on the ground of the preservation of public order would rest on extremely tenuous legalistic grounds.

The fact is indisputable that activities which would be forbidden by the proposed law have been lawfully performed for many years by the American institutions concerned with the full knowledge and approval of the Egyptian Government and the primary purpose of the assurance obtained from the Egyptian Government in the Montreux

Convention was to insure continued recognition of their right, at least during the transition period provided for in that Convention, to "continue freely to carry on their activities in Egypt."

The purpose of the Egyptian Government's assurance is confirmed by the express terms of the letter dated May 8, 1937, now forming part of the Montreux Convention, delivered to the American Delegate by the head of the Egyptian Delegation, particularly the paragraph which reads as follows:

"They (educational, medical and charitable institutions) shall retain their legal status and shall, as regards their organization and operation, be governed by their charters or other instruments under which they were created and also in the case of educational institutions, by their own curricula."

The Department, therefore, is still of the opinion that if the proposed bill should be enacted and applied to American educational institutions in Egypt, its practical effect would be the repudiation by the Egyptian Government of its commitment respecting the institutions mentioned.

While the provisions of Article 2 of the Montreux Convention stipulating that legislation to which foreigners will be subject "will not be inconsistent with the principles generally adopted in modern legislation" might be invoked against the enactment of the proposed bill, the Department believes that the difficulty of interpreting the term "modern legislation" renders that provision of the convention less definitely applicable to the proposed legislation than the assurance of the Egyptian Government that educational, medical and charitable institutions would be permitted to continue freely to carry on their activities.

While it seems not improbable from your despatch under acknowledgment that the proposed bill may not be enacted, at least in the near future, you are authorized in your discretion informally to bring the Department's views to the attention of the Foreign Office in the event the bill in substantially its present form seems likely to be enacted into law. The Department recognizes that the existing situation may render inexpedient any strong protest against the enactment of the pending legislation, particularly if it does in fact apply to all educational institutions irrespective of their racial or religious status and, accordingly, the manner and form of your representations in the circumstances indicated are left to your discretion.

You will, of course, continue to maintain close contact with your British colleague on the subject of the proposed legislation and it is expected that you will continue to keep the Department informed of all pertinent developments concerning it.

Very truly yours,   For the Acting Secretary of State:
                                                    R. WALTON MOORE

REPRESENTATIONS BY THE UNITED STATES REGARDING EGYPTIAN INTERPRETATION OF THE PROVISIONS OF THE MONTREUX CONVENTION PERTAINING TO THE EXPULSION OF FOREIGNERS FROM EGYPT

383.1124/4

The Minister in Egypt (Fish) to the Secretary of State

No. 1837   BULKELEY, ALEXANDRIA, September 23, 1939.
[Received October 19.]

SIR: I have the honor to refer to the Department's Instruction of January 17, 1939, [39] to the American Consul at Alexandria, Egypt, (File no. 383.1124, Jesenof, Boris), concerning Paragraph 4 of the Declaration of the Royal Egyptian Government of May 8, 1937, at Montreux, annexed to the Montreux Convention of that date.[40]

A circular Note has now been received from the Egyptian Foreign Office, of which the original French version and an English translation are enclosed.

The Legation has at this time merely acknowledged the receipt with no comment other than that it is reporting the statement to its Government. I have the honor to inquire whether the Department desires me to reply more fully to the Foreign Office on this subject, and if so, in what terms.

Respectfully yours,   BERT FISH

[Enclosure—Translation]

The Egyptian Ministry for Foreign Affairs to the American Legation

No. 83.122/121 (47C)

CIRCULAR NOTE

The Royal Ministry of Foreign Affairs presents its compliments to the Legation of the United States of America and has the honor to inform it that certain foreign nationals in Egypt to whom the terms of the Montreux Convention do not apply erroneously invoke the provisions of this Convention when they are called upon by the competent Royal Authorities to leave the country or when orders of expulsion are issued against them by the said authorities.

In order to put an end to this state of affairs and furthermore to forestall any possible misunderstanding in the interpretation of the above-mentioned Convention, as regards the expulsion of foreigners from Egypt, the Royal Ministry has the honor to make the following observations for all useful purposes:—

---

[39] Not printed.
[40] See Department of State Treaty Series No. 939, p. 69, or 53 Stat. 1645.

The Montreux Convention does not apply:

(1) To foreigners who entered Egypt after its effective date, nor to those who came less than five years before its effective date.

(2) To foreigners who had resided in Egypt before the treaty was concluded, for periods which have been successively renewed, even if these periods exceed a total of five years.

(3) To foreigners who had entered Egypt on a visa for a limited sojourn and had neglected to obtain an extension of stay, even in instances were they had remained, without authorization, for more than five years.

The Convention makes exceptions for foreigners in the following cases:

(a) If the foreigner has been convicted in respect of a crime or misdemeanor punishable by more than three months' imprisonment.

(b) If the foreigner has been guilty of activities of a subversive nature or to the prejudice of public order or public tranquillity, morality or health.

(c) If he is indigent and a burden upon the State.

Therefore, as the Convention is applicable only to foreigners subject to mixed jurisdiction, the right of the Ministry of the Interior to expel from Egypt, if it judges necessary, a foreigner belonging to one of the above-mentioned categories may not lie open to discussion.

The Royal Ministry of Foreign Affairs seizes this occasion to renew to the Legation the assurances of its high consideration.

CAIRO, September 20, 1939.

383.1124/4

The Secretary of State to the Minister in Egypt (Fish)

No. 425   WASHINGTON, November 1, 1939.

SIR: The Department has received your despatch no. 1837 of September 27, 1939, enclosing a copy of a circular note addressed to you by the Egyptian Minister for Foreign Affairs containing the latter's interpretation of the provisions relating to deportation contained in the international convention regarding the abolition of the capitulations in Egypt.

While the Department is unable to admit the validity of the interpretation of the Egyptian Government's Declaration regarding the expulsion of foreigners from Egypt, which is contained in the Circular Note, particularly paragraphs 1 and 2 thereof, the Department desires to obtain further information for its consideration in formulating instructions to the Legation on the subject. You are accordingly requested to ascertain and report the views of your interested colleagues respecting the Circular Note and whether they have taken, or have instructions to take, any action in regard to it. The Department also desires to be acquainted with your opinion concerning the validity of the interpretation set forth in the Circular Note under reference.

Very truly yours, For the Secretary of State:
R. WALTON MOORE

383.1124/5

The Chargé in Egypt (Hare) to the Secretary of State

No. 1993 CAIRO, February 9, 1940.
[Received March 8.]

SIR: I have the honor to refer to the Department's despatch No. 425 of November 1, 1939 in reply to the Legation's despatch No. 1837 of September 27, 1939, enclosing a copy of a circular Note addressed to the Legation by the Egyptian Minister of Foreign Affairs, setting forth the latter's interpretation of the provisions relating to deportation contained in the Declaration of the Egyptian Government of May 8, 1937 annexed to the Montreux Convention of that date. The Department stated that it was unable to admit the validity of the interpretation of the Egyptian Government's Declaration regarding the expulsion of foreigners contained in the circular Note in question, particularly Paragraphs 1 and 2 thereof, and the Legation was requested to obtain further information for the consideration of the Department in formulating instructions to the Legation on the subject. The Legation was further requested to ascertain and report the views of interested colleagues in respect of the Note and whether they had taken or had instructions to take any action in regard to it.

This matter has been discussed at length with Mr. E. F. W. Besly, Legal Counselor of the British Embassy, who handled the subject on behalf of the Embassy. Mr. Besly stated that after careful study of this matter he had reached the conclusion that the validity of the Egyptian Government's interpretation of the Declaration regarding the expulsion of foreigners from Egypt was inadmissible; that his views had been incorporated in a despatch dated October 13, 1939, to his Government, which had concurred in his findings; and that, acting upon instructions from London, the British Embassy had on December 5, 1939 addressed a Note to the Egyptian Ministry of Foreign Affairs stating that it was unable to accept as correct the interpretation placed by the Egyptian Government on the Declaration in question.

In support of this point of view the Embassy had maintained that the restrictions which the Egyptian Government undertook to accept during the transition period on the exercise of the right of deportation were expressed in clear and unequivocal language and that the

Declaration had further provided that any disputes on the subject of the length of residence in Egypt of a person whose deportation was under consideration should be examined by an administrative advisory committee especially created for the purpose. A copy of the Embassy's Note of December 5, 1939 is enclosed herewith.[41]

As regards the arguments adduced by the Embassy in this connection the following is a summary of that portion of the Embassy's despatch of October 13, 1939 to the British Foreign Office which the writer was permitted to read.

(1) With regard to the first class of persons to which the Egyptian Note of September 20, 1939 had maintained that the Montreux Convention did not apply—to foreigners who had entered Egypt after the effective date of the Convention, or who entered Egypt less than five years before its effective date—the Embassy had maintained that the date by which the five years residence must be completed should be the date on which the question of the exercise by the Egyptian Government of its right of deportation of a particular foreigner might come up for decision; that the use of the future tense "shall have" in the Declaration made at Montreux makes it virtually impossible to interpret the undertaking as referring only to foreigners who had resided in Egypt for five years before October 15, 1937; and that under the circumstances there seemed no ground upon which to distinguish between persons arriving in Egypt after October 1937 and those in the country before that date.

(2) With regard to the second class of persons covered in the circular Note of September 20, 1939,—foreigners who had resided in Egypt for broken periods even though those periods exceeded a total of five years—the Embassy had maintained that if it had been the purpose of the framers of the Convention to specify that the five year period in question should be unbroken it would have been perfectly easy so to state and that in the absence of such specification there seemed no ground upon which to justify such an interpretation. Furthermore, in practice it would be difficult to apply such a stipulation in Egypt where so many foreigners spend a considerable part of the year abroad, and, even if annual leave might be held not to involve a break in residence, there would still always remain the question of deciding at what point leave from Egypt should end and absence from the country begin.

(3) With regard to the third class of foreigners mentioned in the circular Note of September 20, 1939,—foreigners who entered Egypt on a visa for a limited sojourn but neglected to obtain an extension of stay although they might have remained without such authorization for more than five years—the Embassy took the point of view that the exclusion of this category of persons would seem to have a certain superficial justification on the principle that an abuse cannot create a right. But the answer to this contention would seem to be that, since the Egyptian Government has the right to expel foreigners who outstay the length of their temporary visas, their failure to expel such foreigners must be taken as acquiescence in their continued residence. The fact that there are many instances where such persons

---

[41] Not printed.

303207—58——33

have paid taxes and otherwise been treated by the Egyptian Government as lawful inhabitants of the country would bear out this argument.

In further discussion of the matter, Mr. Besly said that he had found it difficult to understand how the Egyptian Ministry of Foreign Affairs had felt justified in reaching the conclusions expressed in its Note of September 20, 1939, since this subject had been discussed fully in conversations between the British and Egyptian authorities before the Montreux Conference and it should have been well known to whoever drafted the Note that the contentions contained therein were not only contrary to the Montreux Declaration itself but were also opposed to the informal understandings which had been reached prior to the Conference. Mr. Besly stated that the Embassy had as a matter of fact said as much in a separate and informal communication to the Ministry of Foreign Affairs which was sent to accompany the Embassy's formal Note of December 5, 1939.

As regards the attitude of other interested colleagues in this matter, it is understood that the French and Greek Legations either have or have the intention of replying to the Ministry of Foreign Affairs in a similar sense to the British Embassy.

As regards the views of the Legation in this matter, it is respectfully submitted that a basic consideration would appear to be the provision made in the last paragraph of Article 4 of the Declaration on this subject by the Egyptian Government at Montreux for the setting up of an administrative advisory committee for the specific purpose of acting upon questions of this kind. Given this fact it is difficult to understand upon what valid ground the Egyptian Government could decide to treat the subject by a unilateral declaration. Under the circumstances it is the opinion of the Legation that a reply to the Ministry of Foreign Affairs refusing to admit the validity of the position taken in the circular Note of September 20, 1939 would be in order.

Respectfully yours,   RAYMOND A. HARE

383.1124/5

The Secretary of State to the Minister in Egypt (Fish)

No. 453   WASHINGTON, March 18, 1940.

SIR: The Department has received Mr. Hare's despatch no. 1993 of February 9, 1940 concerning the interpretation given by the Egyptian Government, in a circular note of September 20, 1939, to the provisions relating to deportation contained in a declaration made by the Egyptian Government included in the international convention of May 8, 1937, to which this Government is a party.

You should inform the Egyptian Ministry of Foreign Affairs that this Government is unable to admit the validity of the interpretation given by the Egyptian Government to its declaration in question, in as much as that interpretation is not in accordance with this Government's understanding of the unequivocal language of that declaration.

In the event the Egyptian Government should seek to apply to an American citizen the interpretation which it has given its declaration of May 8, 1937 in the circular note under reference, you should notify the Department promptly by telegraph. You should of course continue to keep the Department informed of all pertinent developments concerning this subject.

Very truly yours,   For the Secretary of State:
                                      R. WALTON MOORE

383.1124/6

The Chargé in Egypt (Hare) to the Secretary of State

No. 2080   CAIRO, April 26, 1940.
                                      [Received June 1.]

SIR: I have the honor to refer to the Department's instruction no. 453 of March 18, 1940, concerning the interpretation given by the Egyptian Government to its declaration in respect to deportation included in the Montreux Convention of May 8, 1937, and to enclose a copy of the Legation's note of April 26, 1940 to the Egyptian Foreign Office advising the Egyptian Government, under instructions from the Department, that the American Government is unable to admit the validity of the interpretation given by the Egyptian Government to its declaration.

In its despatch no. 1993 of February 9, 1940 on this subject, the Legation reported that the British Embassy had advised the Egyptian Ministry of Foreign Affairs that it was unable to accept the Egyptian Government's interpretation of its declaration and that it was understood that replies in similar sense were being made by the French and Greek Legations. In the meantime, the Legation has been advised by Count W. F. L. de Bylandt, the Netherland Chargé d'Affaires, that he also was instructed by his Government to oppose the action of the Egyptian Government in this respect. He said that in its initial instructions to him his Government had undertaken to refute one by one the points raised in the Egyptian Foreign Office's note of September 20, 1939. However, when the Chargé had pointed out to his Government that by so doing grounds might be afforded for endless discussion of the matter, his Government had agreed that a simple statement of refutation was sufficient. As a consequence it is understood that the reply made by the Netherland Legation was essentially similar to that made by this Legation except that it also invited attention to the provisions in Article 4 of the declaration for the setting up of an administrative advisory committee for the purpose of acting upon questions of this kind.

Respectfully yours,

RAYMOND A. HARE

[Enclosure]

The American Legation to the Egyptian Ministry for Foreign Affairs

No. 768

The Legation of the United States of America presents its compliments to the Royal Egyptian Ministry of Foreign Affairs and has the honor to refer to the latter's note no. 47C of September 20, 1939 interpreting the provisions relating to deportation contained in a declaration made by the Egyptian Government included in the international convention of Montreux of May 8, 1937, and to the Legation's reply no. 699 of September 23, 1939,[42] stating that this matter was being brought to the attention of the competent authorities of the Department of State at Washington.

The Legation is now in receipt of an instruction from the Department of State at Washington stating that the American Government is unable to admit the validity of the interpretation given by the Royal Egyptian Government to its declaration in question, in as much as that interpretation is not in accordance with the American Government's understanding of the unequivocal language of that declaration. The Legation was instructed to inform the Royal Ministry of the American Government's views in this respect.

The Legation of the United States of America avails itself of this opportunity to renew to the Royal Egyptian Ministry of Foreign Affairs the assurance of its highest consideration.

CAIRO, April 26, 1940.

PROPOSED CONSULAR CONVENTION BETWEEN THE UNITED STATES AND EGYPT; CONTINUATION OF CUSTOMS EXEMPTIONS TO CONSULAR OFFICERS ON BASIS OF RECIPROCITY[43]

711.8321/17

The Chargé in Egypt (Hare) to the Secretary of State

No. 2066

CAIRO, April 17, 1940.
[Received May 16.]

SIR: I have the honor to refer to the Department's instruction no. 416 of September 13, 1939 [44] enclosing a draft Consular Convention to

---

[42] Not found in Department files; see last paragraph of despatch No. 1837, September 23, 1939, from the Minister in Egypt, p. 504.

[43] For previous correspondence regarding a proposed consular convention, see *Foreign Relations*, 1939, vol. IV, pp. 477 ff.

[44] *Ibid.*, p. 477.

be presented to the Egyptian authorities, and to the Legation's despatch no. 1903 of November 6, 1939 [45] reporting that the draft had been submitted to the Foreign Office and duly acknowledged.

In this connection the Legation has recently been giving consideration to that part of Article 11 of the Montreux Convention [46] which provided that consuls should continue to enjoy the immunities possessed at the time of the signature of the Convention pending the conclusion of Consular Conventions "and in any case during a period of three years as from the date of the signature of the present Convention". The Convention having been signed on May 8, 1937, the three year period prescribed in Article 11 therefore terminates on May 7, 1940. The question thus arose whether in the absence of the signature of a Consular Convention within the specified three year period consular officers in Egypt would continue to enjoy the immunities to which they were previously entitled. Since the American Government had some months ago submitted a draft Consular Convention for the consideration of the Egyptian Government and since responsibility for delay in such negotiations therefore lay with the Egyptian Government for having failed to pursue the matter further, it seemed to the Legation that a strong case could be made for arguing that American consular officers would be entitled to the continuance of their immunities regardless of such action as the Egyptian Government might contemplate taking in other cases. However, it was thought advisable to look into the matter with a view to avoiding possibly unforeseen complications.

The matter was first discussed informally with Mr. E. F. W. Besly, Legal Counselor of the British Embassy, who said that the British Government had in fact prepared a draft Consular Convention for submission to the Egyptian Government but that it had been decided not to submit it until after the war. He said that it was his opinion that under the terms of Article 11 of the Convention the specification of a three year period was not intended to indicate the period within which a Consular Convention should be concluded but rather the period during which consuls would be entitled to previous immunities regardless of whether or not a Consular Convention was concluded. However, when it was observed to Mr. Besly that such an interpretation would, if correct, make it possible, by merely adopting obstructionist tactics, indefinitely to delay the conclusion of a Consular Convention and thus ensure by such tactics the maintenance of consular immunities, he admitted that he might perhaps have been somewhat precipitate in reaching the decision that the conclusion of

---

[45] Not printed.
[46] Signed at Montreux May 8, 1937; Department of State Treaty Series No. 939, or 53 Stat. 1645.

Consular Conventions could be postponed beyond the three year period without running the danger of loss by consuls of their immunities. In this connection he thereupon consulted a published work on the Montreux Convention by Messrs. Aghion and Feldman and found that it was categorically stated in the commentary on Article 11 that in the absence of the signature of a Consular Convention within the three year period specified in the Article consuls would cease to enjoy their customary immunities. Mr. Besly said he was glad this matter had been brought to his attention because he thought the Embassy might wish to reconsider the matter and possibly to submit its draft Convention in the early future.

This question was also raised informally on April 6 with Mohamed Said Bey, Acting Director of the Administrative Section of the Foreign Office, who appeared to be thoroughly conversant with the subject and said that although the Foreign Office was aware that the three year period specified in Article 11 of the Montreux Convention was approaching its termination no immediate action in respect of the abolition of the immunities of consuls was anticipated. The matter was, however, under study by the appropriate authorities and it was his understanding that the final decision reached would probably be to propose that the privileges of consuls should be placed on a reciprocal basis. In any event, he reiterated, he could give assurance that no precipitate action was in prospect.

Under the circumstances the Legation is of the opinion that there is adequate assurance that the immunities of American consular officers in Egypt are adequately safeguarded for the time being. It is also reassuring to learn that the Egyptian Government contemplates adopting the principle of reciprocity as a basis for according such immunities in the future in view of the liberal treatment specified in Article IV of the draft Consular Convention referred to above which the American Government is prepared to accord Egyptian consular officers.

Respectfully yours, RAYMOND A. HARE

711.8321/19

The Chargé in Egypt (Hare) to the Secretary of State

No. 2091 CAIRO, May 7, 1940.
[Received June 1.]

SIR: I have the honor to refer to the Department's instruction no. 416 of September 13, 1939,[47] transmitting a draft consular convention for presentation to the Egyptian Foreign Office and to enclose a copy of a note dated May (?), 1940, received yesterday from the Foreign

---

[47] *Foreign Relations,* 1939, vol. IV, p. 477.

Office transmitting a printed model consular convention just completed by the Foreign Office. A translation of the note has been made and is enclosed but in as much as the note was received only yesterday and the pouch closes tomorrow morning there has not been sufficient time to prepare a translation of the model convention. Such a translation will be made, however, and forwarded to the Department at a later date,[48] together with such comments thereon as may seem appropriate.

In the short time intervening between the receipt of the note from the Foreign Office and the writing of this despatch the only point in respect thereof which the Legation has been able to look into with any degree of thoroughness is that of the liability of consular officers to payment of customs duties, a point which, as brought out in the Legation's despatch no. 2066 of April 17, 1940, is of particular interest at this time in view of the fact that the three year period prescribed in Article 11 of the Montreux Convention expires today. In this connection I may say that after my discussion of this matter with the Acting Chief of the Administrative Section of the Foreign Office on April 6, as reported in the Legation's despatch no. 2066, certain less reassuring reports reached the Legation to the effect that drastic action curtailing consular customs exemptions would be taken, effective May 8, and I accordingly again took the matter up with the Acting Chief of the Administrative Section and with the Chief of Protocol who both professed to believe that there was no cause for apprehension but said that they would look into the matter and advise me of its status. I may say that in my discussions with both of these officials I was given the impression that in matters of this kind one branch of the Egyptian Government very often does not know what another branch may be doing. This is particularly true of legal matters in which Badawi Pasha, Chief of the Legal Department, usually has the final word and often reaches his decisions with little if any consultation with the Foreign Office, and it was gathered that the customs exemption question might be a case of this kind.

Upon the receipt of the communication from the Foreign Office yesterday, the Legation was somewhat reassured to note that it was stated that the Egyptian Government was in essential agreement with the draft submitted by the American Government, particularly as regarded the third paragraph of Article 11 of the Montreux Convention pertaining to the immunities of consular officers. However, the language of the Foreign Office note was so involved in its more specific discussion of this question that it was thought advisable to take the matter up with the Foreign Office with a view to ascertaining

---

[48] Not printed; it was transmitted to the Department by the Minister in Egypt in his despatch No. 2229, October 16, p. 520.

its specific intentions in respect of American consular officers after May 8 and pending the conclusion of the negotiation of a convention.

This point was accordingly taken up yesterday with Sharara Pasha, Under Secretary of State for Foreign Affairs, who had signed the Foreign Office note in behalf of the Foreign Minister. Sharara Pasha said that the situation was very simple, that is to say, during the period after May 8 and pending the conclusion of a consular convention with the American Government American consular officers in Egypt would receive exactly the same treatment as was accorded Egyptian consular officers in the United States. I told Sharara Pasha that it was my understanding that Egyptian consular officers in the United States (see Department's instruction no. 75 of March 12, 1935 [50]) enjoyed the privilege of importing articles for their personal use free of duty during their official residence without limitation as to the number of officers to whom the free importation privilege was granted. Sharara Pasha said that in that case the Egyptians would be prepared to extend similar privileges in respect of American consular officers and suggested that the Legation address a letter to the Foreign Office confirming my observations regarding the treatment accorded Egyptian consular officers in the United States. It is believed that on the basis of the instruction cited above such a letter might have been written without requesting further authorization from the Department but to avoid any possible misunderstanding such authorization is being requested today by telegraph.[51]

It may be noted in this connection that when the matter of extending customs exemption to all American consular officers in Egypt rather than to two officers at each post has been taken up in the past the invariable reply was that the Foreign Office was powerless to grant such a privilege on the basis of reciprocity so long as Article 9 of the Egyptian Customs Regulations was in force. That this aspect of the matter may have slipped Sharara Pasha's mind when he said that Egypt would be prepared to grant complete reciprocity in this respect seems possible. However, the indicated course of action appeared to be to take him at his word and trust that we may be more successful in this instance than we have been in the past.

In conclusion the attention of the Department is invited to Article 31 of the Egyptian draft providing that the provisions of the convention would be applicable to diplomatic agents invested with consular functions, a point which the Department may wish to consider in connection with the anticipated giving of dual commissions to officers at this post.

Respectfully yours,   RAYMOND A. HARE

---

[50] Not printed.
[51] See telegram No. 63, May 8, 4 p. m., *infra*.

[Enclosure—Translation]

The Egyptian Minister for Foreign Affairs (*Aly Maher Pasha*) *to the American Chargé* (*Hare*)

No. 28/76/7 (16 Cir.)   CAIRO, May 1940.

MR. CHARGÉ D'AFFAIRES: The object of Article 11 of the Montreux Convention was to put an end to the special status which consuls of the Capitulatory Powers enjoyed up to that time in Egypt, the prerogatives and privileges of such consuls, henceforth having to be in conformity with international law and usage on condition of reciprocity.

However, with regard to immunities in respect of consular premises and with regard to taxes, customs duties and other public dues, the system then in force was provisionally maintained pending the conclusion of consular conventions, it being understood that this special regime should not continue in effect beyond a period of three years from the date of the signature of the Convention. Upon the termination of that period, the said regime was to end completely and be replaced by common law.

I have, therefore, the honor to bring to your attention that as from May 8, 1940, the immunities which consuls enjoy in Egypt with regard to consular premises and taxes, customs duties and other public dues, will be those recognized by international law and usage on condition of reciprocity.

In your letter no. 708 dated October 21, 1939,[52] you communicated to me in the name of the American Government a draft consular convention which has been given attentive study by the Egyptian Government. After a study of this draft and of others presented by other countries, the Egyptian Government, being anxious to define by means of conventions its consular relations, not only with the United States of America but also with other countries, has drawn up a draft of a consular convention which you will find attached and which has also been communicated this day to the other signatories of the Montreux Convention.

This draft indicates how the Egyptian Government envisages, in consular matters, the rules usually sanctioned by international law and what it understands by international usage.

In fact, pending the conclusion of consular conventions, the Egyptian Government has the intention, in applying Article 11, to be guided, on the condition of reciprocity, by these rules and customs which moreover arise from existing conventions and international practice.

Moreover, comparison of the draft transmitted by your government with the Egyptian draft shows that both are inspired by the same

---

[52] See despatch No. 1899, October 21, 1939, from the Minister in Egypt, *Foreign Relations*, 1939, vol. IV, p. 486.

principles and that there exists between them no fundamental difference, particularly with regard to the matters dealt with in paragraph three of Article 11 of the Montreux Convention.

I would appreciate your kindly transmitting to your government the draft of the convention which will meet, I hope, with its approval and will permit the conclusion of a consular convention between our two countries in the near future.

I take this occasion [etc.]   For The Minister of Foreign Affairs

M. CHARARA

611.83241/80 : Telegram

The Chargé in Egypt (Hare) to the Secretary of State

CAIRO, May 8, 1940—4 p. m.
[Received May 8—1: 38 p. m.]

63. In a circular note to all signatories of the Montreux Convention delivered to this Legation on May 6 [54] the Foreign Office transmitted a draft consular convention and gave notice of the termination on May 8 of the special regime specified in the third paragraph of Article Number 11 of the Montreux Convention. Beginning today and pending the conclusion of a consular convention such immunities would be extended in accordance with international law and usage on the basis of reciprocity. In this connection the Foreign Office has requested a statement with reference to the treatment of Egyptian consular officers in the United States. Am I authorized to reply in the sense of the Department's instruction Number 75 of March 12, 1935 [55] pointing out that the American Government does not limit the number of Egyptian consular officers entitled to customs exemption? Copy of the note and draft convention sent in today's pouch.

HARE

611.83241/80 : Telegram

The Secretary of State to the Chargé in Egypt (Hare)

WASHINGTON, May 17, 1940—7 p. m.

34. Your 63, May 8, 4 p. m. You are authorized to reply to the Egyptian Government in the sense of the Department's instruction no. 75 of March 12, 1935.[55] You should state that in as much as this Government does not limit the number of Egyptian diplomatic and consular officers to whom immunities are granted in this country, it is assumed that the immunities which the Egyptian Government pro-

---

[54] *Supra.*
[55] Not printed.

poses to extend to American Foreign Service Officers in accordance with international law and usage on the basis of reciprocity will likewise be without any numerical limitation. Your reply should also, in making reference to the draft consular convention which was transmitted to the Egyptian Government for negotiation on October 21, 1939,[56] inquire as to the views of the Egyptian Government concerning that draft.

HULL

683.11241/35

The Chargé in Egypt (Hare) to the Secretary of State

No. 2119

CAIRO, June 3, 1940.
[Received June 28.]

SIR: I have the honor to refer to the Legation's telegram no. 63 of May 8, 4 p. m., 1940, and the Department's telegraphic reply no. 34 of May 17, 7 p. m., regarding exemption from payment of customs duty by American consular officers in Egypt following the termination of the three-year period specified in the third paragraph of Article 11 of the Montreux Convention, and to enclose a copy of a note on this subject addressed to the Egyptian Minister of Foreign Affairs on May 29, 1940.

Following the delivery of the Legation's note I have had several conversations with the Chief of Protocol of the Egyptian Foreign Office regarding this matter and he has assured me that appropriate orders will be issued without delay restoring customs franchise to American consular officers to whom such exemption was accorded before May 8, 1940. Thus far, however, the Legation has not been furnished a definite reply in respect of the number limitation on consular officers entitled to such exemption. However, this question is somewhat academic for the moment in as much as at neither Alexandria nor Port Said, the only American consular establishments in Egypt outside the combined office at Cairo, does the personnel exceed the limitation hitherto imposed.

As regards the case of Cairo, reference is made to the Legation's despatch no. 2118 of this date entitled "Dual Commissions for Foreign Service Officers in Cairo" [57] in which the matter of the exemption from payment of customs duty by officers at this post was discussed.

Respectfully yours,

RAYMOND A. HARE

---

[56] See despatch No. 1899, October 21, 1939, from the Minister in Egypt, *Foreign Relations,* 1939, vol. IV, p. 486.
[57] Not printed.

[Enclosure]

The American Chargé (Hare) to the Egyptian Minister for Foreign Affairs (Aly Maher Pasha)

No. 774   CAIRO, May 29, 1940.

EXCELLENCY: I have the honor to refer to Your Excellency's note No. 28/76/7 (16 Cir.) received by the Legation on May 6, 1940,[58] in which you referred to the draft consular convention submitted by the American Government to the Egyptian Government under cover of the Legation's note of October 21, 1939 [59] and transmitted for the consideration of the American Government a printed draft consular convention prepared by the Royal Ministry of Foreign Affairs.

In confirmation of my conversation on May 6 with His Excellency Mohamed Sharara Pasha, Under Secretary of State for Foreign Affairs, I may say that a copy of the draft convention prepared by the Royal Ministry together with a copy of its note under reference was promptly transmitted to the Department of State at Washington. The Legation was gratified to note that it was the opinion of the Royal Ministry that the draft conventions prepared by our respective governments were inspired by the same principles and that there was no fundamental conflict between them, particularly as concerned Paragraph 3 of Article 11 of the Montreux Convention.

In this latter connection, i. e. the matter of consular immunities as prescribed in Paragraph 3 of Article 11 of the Montreux Convention, it is recalled that this question was discussed on May 6 with the Under Secretary of State for Foreign Affairs with particular reference to the matter of customs exemption, and that the Under Secretary stated that pending the conclusion of a consular convention between our two countries the Egyptian Government would be pleased to extend to American consular officers in Egypt the same customs privileges as were accorded Egyptian consular officers in the United States. Sharara Pasha suggested that a written communication be addressed to the Royal Ministry of Foreign Affairs setting forth the customs privileges accorded Egyptian consular officers in the United States to the end that similar privileges might be extended American consular officers in Egypt.

This matter was referred to the State Department at Washington, which has now authorized the Legation to state that Egyptian consular officers of Egyptian nationality in the United States are currently extended the privilege of free entry of duty on articles for their personal and household use during official residence, with the under-

---

[58] *Ante*, p. 515.
[59] See despatch No. 1899, October 21, 1939, from the Minister in Egypt, *Foreign Relations*, 1939, vol. IV, p. 486.

standing that no article the importation of which is prohibited by the laws of the United States shall be imported by the persons in question. The State Department further instructed the Legation to state that in as much as the American Government does not limit the number of Egyptian diplomatic and consular officers to whom immunities are granted in the United States, it is assumed that the immunities which the Egyptian Government proposes to extend to American Foreign Service Officers in accordance with international law and usage on the basis of reciprocity will likewise be without number limitation.

Accept [etc.]   RAYMOND A. HARE

683.11241/37

The Chargé in Egypt (Hare) to the Secretary of State

No. 2136   CAIRO, June 17, 1940.
                                              [Received July 12.]

SIR: I have the honor to refer to the Legation's despatch no. 2119 of June 3, 1940, enclosing a copy of a note addressed to the Egyptian Minister of Foreign Affairs on May 29, 1940, regarding the matter of customs franchise for American consular officers in Egypt, and to enclose a copy and translation of a note dated June 11, 1940 from the Foreign Office, stating that pending the conclusion of a consular convention between the United States and Egypt, the Egyptian Government is prepared to extend customs exemption to American consular officers in Egypt on the basis of reciprocity.

It will be noted that although the Legation in its note of May 29, 1940 particularly stressed that customs franchise was extended to Egyptian consular officers in the United States without limitation as to number, the Foreign Office's reply makes no reference to this point. Under ordinary circumstances this matter would have been taken up with the Foreign Office before reporting further on the subject to the Department, but it so happens that the Legation has just been advised that the boat which is to carry the pouch in which this despatch is to be sent is sailing this afternoon, several days in advance of its scheduled departure. A further report on this subject will, therefore, be submitted in due course.

I may add that so far as the Legation is aware, American consular officers in Egypt are the only such officers to whom customs franchise has been restored following the expiration on May 8 of the three-year period specified in the third paragraph of Article 11 of the Montreux Convention.

Respectfully yours,   RAYMOND A. HARE

[Enclosure—Translation]

The Egyptian Under Secretary of State for Foreign Affairs
(Charara) to the American Chargé (Hare)

No. 28.76/7 (203)   CAIRO, June 11, 1940.

MR. CHARGÉ D'AFFAIRES: I have the honor to acknowledge the receipt of your letter No. 774 of May 29, 1940, by which you were good enough to inform me, in reference to the draft consular convention to be concluded between our two Governments, that your Government grants to consular agents of Egyptian nationality who are performing their duties in the United States of America, the customs franchise on personal effects and household articles which they may import during their official stay. In this letter you requested to be informed whether, while awaiting the conclusion of a consular convention between the two countries, the Egyptian Government would be disposed to extend the same treatment to American consular agents performing their duties in Egypt.

In reply, I hasten to inform you that the Royal Egyptian Government sees no objection to extending the same treatment to American consular agents who are carrying on their duties in Egypt, on the condition of reciprocity and while awaiting the conclusion of a consular convention between the two countries.

I seize this occasion [etc.]   M. CHARARA

711.8321/22

The Minister in Egypt (Fish) to the Secretary of State

No. 2229   CAIRO, October 16, 1940.
                                                [Received December 11.]

SIR: I have the honor to refer to the Legation's despatches No. 2091 of May 7, 1940, and No. 2135 of June 17, 1940,[60] relative to the model consular convention drawn up by the Egyptian Foreign Office, and to transmit herewith a translation of this model convention together with certain comments prepared by the Legation.[61]

It may be pointed out that the comments which form enclosure No. 2 to this despatch are intended to be read in conjuction with the comments on the Egyptian draft convention compiled by Vice Consul Daniel Gaudin, Jr. at Alexandria and transmitted to the Department as an enclosure to the Legation's despatch No. 2135 dated June 17, 1940.

---

[60] Despatch No. 2135 and its enclosures not printed.
[61] Neither printed.

To summarize briefly the Legation's views regarding the Egyptian draft convention, there would appear to be no essential differences between this draft and the American draft transmitted to the Legation by the Department's instruction No. 416 of September 13, 1939.[62] The Egyptian model convention, however, is more detailed and in many respects more cumbersome than the American one and it is believed that the extra details serve to render it more difficult of interpretation and to lessen its practical applicability. It is consequently the opinion of the Legation that, providing the consent of the Egyptian Government were obtained to such a procedure, it would be preferable to use the simpler American draft as a basis for negotiation and to make such additions and emendations to that draft as might prove necessary in order to bring it into line with the desires of the Egyptian Government.

Respectfully yours,   BERT FISH

[In telegram No. 215, June 13, 1941, 7 p. m., to the Minister in Egypt, the Department stated that it would be preferable to use the American draft as a basis for negotiations and continued:

"This Government will gladly consider alterations in its draft which the Egyptian Government may deem desirable. Department is continuing to examine the American draft in comparison with the Egyptian counterdraft and in the light of further developments, and will communicate with the Legation concerning revisions to be made in American draft. Meanwhile endeavor to ascertain attitude of Egyptian Government regarding use of American draft as a basis." (711.8321/24)

No record of further negotiations on this subject has been found in Department files for the war period.]

---

[62] *Foreign Relations*, 1939, vol. IV, p. 477.

ETHIOPIA

INABILITY OF THE UNITED STATES TO PROVIDE ARMAMENTS FOR USE BY INSURGENTS IN ETHIOPIA AGAINST ITALIAN RULE

865D.24/1

The Counselor of Embassy in the United Kingdom (Johnson) to the Adviser on Political Relations (Dunn)

LONDON, July 3, 1940.
[Received July 15.]

DEAR JIMMY: I pass on to you the following matter, for whatever action, if any, it may be considered desirable to take.

Mr. W. Martin, the ex-Minister in London of Ethiopia, called to see me a day or two ago and asked if it would be possible for Abyssinian insurgents against Italian rule to be furnished armaments from the United States. The Minister said that until the loan was paid back his country could—provided it was successful in throwing off Italian rule—be placed under American protection; that facilities also would be granted for trade, for mineral and oil exploitation and Tsana Dam concessions.

I gave the Minister no encouragement, nor did I attempt to enter into any discussion with him as to the merits of his proposition or what the United States could or could not do. I merely told him that I would pass on the information to the Ambassador and that, if the Ambassador had no objection, I would forward an account of his conversation to appropriate officials in Washington.

Mr. Martin, who said that he was speaking with the full knowledge and authority of the Emperor Haile Selassie who is now in Great Britain, seemed to be quite confident that if Abyssinian tribesmen could be furnished with sufficient arms they would soon put an end to the Italian occupation. He also made the point that such action could only be beneficial to the Allied cause in that part of the Near East. He explained that the reason for coming to the Embassy about the matter instead of having it presented in Washington was that the Emperor had no representative, personal or otherwise, in the United States.

Yours sincerely,

HERSCHEL JOHNSON

522

865D.24/1

The Adviser on Political Relations (Dunn) to the Counselor of Embassy in the United Kingdom (Johnson)

[WASHINGTON,] August 16, 1940.

DEAR HERSCHEL: I wish to refer to your letter of July 3, 1940 in which you presented, without comment, a proposal made by Mr. W. Martin, the ex-Minister in London of Ethiopia, which was presented with the full knowledge and authority of the Emperor Haile Selassie, to enable the Abyssinian insurgents to be furnished armaments from the United States.

There is no need to go into the political aspects of this matter because, for all practical purposes, no arms could be supplied. The only armaments that would be available for sale by this Government to foreign Governments would be those which have been declared surplus and it is understood that the War Department supply of surplus arms is practically exhausted and that the British, Irish and Canadian Governments are now negotiating for what little is left. With respect to possible purchases of arms from private companies in this country, Emperor Haile Selassie would have to appoint a duly authorized representative to carry on negotiations direct with the companies, but this channel does not hold much promise as such companies are already booked to capacity and undoubtedly would not care to take on additional commitments.

With this picture in mind, I think you will agree that it is not necessary to take up the other aspects of the matter and it is noted that the entire business would be conditioned upon a loan from this Government, the collateral for which would be quite nebulous.

Sincerely yours, JAMES CLEMENT DUNN

GREECE

THE GRAECO-ITALIAN WAR

I. Italian Pressure Upon Greece

740.0011 European War 1939/2362 : Telegram

The Minister in Greece (MacVeagh) to the Secretary of State

ATHENS, April 20, 1940—5 p. m.
[Received April 20—3:40 p. m.]

70. The Under Secretary for Foreign Affairs [1] said to me this morning that his Government is increasingly confident of Italy's desire to have no war with England, and consequently with Greece, at this time. He said this confidence is based on both the logic of Italy's position after the recent British naval successes and on the incompleteness of her actual preparations. He explained Italy's present hostile press campaign and the rumors apparently started by herself regarding her bellicose intentions as owing to her need to keep the Allies impressed with her importance. In regard to Yugoslavia he thought it doubtful whether any attack on her could be made without Allied and even Balkan intervention.

MACVEAGH

740.0011 European War 1939/2611

Memorandum of Conversation, by the Chief of the Division of European Affairs (Moffat)

[WASHINGTON,] April 24, 1940.

The Greek Minister [2] called this morning.

After talking over various phases of the war, he said that from the Greek point of view the matter of greatest interest was Italian intentions. He recognized that the tension in Italy had somewhat subsided and he believed that Mussolini would, in no event, make a move until the Scandinavian campaign had been decided one way or the other.

If Italy moved, however, he thought it would not be against Yugoslavia. He said that the Serbs were magnificent fighters, and even the Croats had no sympathy for the Italians. If Italy moved, he believed it would be on Salonika, probably a march which would avoid violat-

---

[1] Nicholas Mavroudis.
[2] Cimon P. Diamantopoulos.

524

ing Yugoslav neutrality. Of course, the Greek Army would resist, and probably the Turkish Army would come to her assistance. If so, he foresaw that the Turks would move through western Thrace and not try to cross Bulgarian territory. If the Italians were fighting alone, the Minister thought that the Bulgarians would remain neutral. If Germany should also enter the Balkans, he felt that Bulgaria would adopt toward the Germans very much the same attitude as had the Danes. He had lived many years in Sofia and professed to know the Bulgars well. They would not want to fight, partly because their experiences in the last war had been unfortunate, and partly because they were very much afraid of the Turks. They were not in favor of a German victory, neither were they in favor of an allied victory. They were playing all their cards on the chance of a negotiated peace. The peace conference, they felt, would give them more than a military campaign.

P[IERREPONT] M[OFFAT]

740.0011 European War 1939/2640 : Telegram

The Minister in Greece (MacVeagh) to the Secretary of State

ATHENS, May 3, 1940—6 p. m.
[Received May 3—4: 06 p. m.]

76. The Director General of the Foreign Office [3] this morning expressed belief in Italy's intention to maintain a non-belligerent attitude, basing this belief on the logic of her situation and the assurances of the Italian Minister just returned from a "holiday" in Rome. Nevertheless, the Greek Government yesterday called up 10 classes of reserve officers of all arms, including medical services, about one-third to report May 15 and the others in July and August. The controlled press has denied that this move bears any relation to the international situation and the Director General described it as a routine measure, but the large numbers involved betray its essentially precautionary character and I am reliably informed that an additional decree is ready for signature which would call up seven classes of privates and noncommissioned officers. The dates given are, of course, subject to change, but as they stand would seem to indicate a present estimate of the situation similar to that of the Turkish Military Attaché reported in the Legation's telegram No. 75, April 25, 6 p. m.[4]

Unconfirmed reports from Albania state that the Italian laborers recently shipped to that country have started work on a railway to link the coast with the Greek frontier.

MACVEAGH

---

[3] Andre Delmouzos.
[4] Not printed.

740.0011 European War 1939/2664 : Telegram

The Minister in Greece (MacVeagh) to the Secretary of State

ATHENS, May 4, 1940—2 p. m.
[Received May 4—12:16 p. m.]

81. The Under Secretary for Foreign Affairs again expressed the opinion to me this morning that Italy will not enter the war unless and until Germany invades the Balkans or obtains what appears a decisive advantage elsewhere. In this connection he quoted the assurances given to the Greek Government by the Italian Minister on his return from Rome early this week as follows:

"Italy will not enter the war for the present and in any case has no intention of disturbing the peace of the Balkans."

Neither the Greek Government nor the British and Turkish representatives in Athens have any information concerning reported Italian concentrations in the Dodecanese. According to the Turkish Military Attaché, the Italian naval strength in those islands has recently amounted only to 6 submarines and 2 destroyers, 7 torpedo boats and 8 torpedo launches. Both he and the British Naval Attaché admit that there may have been some reinforcements in the last few days but both regard extensive reinforcements as unlikely and the former points out that concentrating in the Dodecanese would be dangerous for the Italians so long as they do not control Crete.

MACVEAGH

740.0011 European War 1939/2704 : Telegram

The Minister in Greece (MacVeagh) to the Secretary of State

ATHENS, May 7, 1940—8 p. m.
[Received May 7—4:15 p. m.]

83. During the past few days the German radio has made a number of startling but unfounded statements regarding Allied activity in this country. Actually there has been no influx of Allied aviators into Greece as alleged and there are no signs whatever of imminent Allied use of Greek territory for war purposes. In addition talks which I had yesterday with the King and the Crown Prince, the Under Secretary for War, the Under Secretary of Marine and the Chiefs of Staff of both the army and the navy all indicate that the Greek Government has no intention of abandoning the present non-belligerent attitude while the British and French Ministers both continue to affirm that they have no interest in persuading it to do so.

I am reliably informed that the Greek Military and Naval Staffs are closely cooperating with the Allies in the formulation of war plans but these are for defense and the German allegations can only constitute an uncomfortable reminder of pretexts used in other cases to "justify" aggression.

MACVEAGH

740.0011 European War 1939/3142 : Telegram

The Minister in Greece (MacVeagh) to the Secretary of State

ATHENS, May 18, 1940—7 p. m.
[Received May 18—2 : 35 p. m.]

97. Regarding the assurances of the Italian Minister reported in my telegram No. 81, May 4, 2 p. m., the King confirmed to me today that if Italy enters the war without attacking in the Balkans, Greece hopes it may be posssible to remain non-belligerent at least for a time though to maintain such a policy would be "like balancing on a knife edge" if Italy and the Allies should take to fighting over the use of Greek harbors and islands. Under direct attack from Italy he said his fears for Athens would be chiefly in connection with air bombardment and added that he has hopes of assistance from British air forces in such an eventuality.

The Swedish Chargé d'Affaires asked the Director General of the Foreign Office this morning how Greece could justify remaining nonbelligerent if Turkey fulfilled her obligations to the Allies and the latter replied that Greece's obligations to Turkey arise only in case that country is attacked and not if she attacks others in fulfillment of her own engagements.

One class reservists of all arms was called today for a month's "training" to begin May 25.

MACVEAGH

740.0011 European War 1939/3270 : Telegram

The Chargé in Germany (Kirk) to the Secretary of State

BERLIN, May 23, 1940—6 p. m.
[Received 8 : 25 p. m.]

1487. My 1027, April 17, 7 p. m.,⁵ last paragraph. Within the past 24 hours there has been an intensification of the anxiety in Greek circles here as to the possibility of imminent action on the part of Italy with regard to Greece, and I understand that this feeling is largely due to an intimation received from German sources to the effect that unless the Greek Government gives immediately some manifestation of a disassociation from its previous pro-Ally attitude, Italy will move to establish a protectorate over Greece.

⁵ Not printed.

According to this information, it is not clear whether military action is intended forthwith or whether demands in the form of an ultimatum may be presented to Greece as a preliminary step. In Greek circles this intimation is being connected with the rumors of an Italian move through Switzerland (see my 1465, May 22, 4 p. m.[6]) and the impression prevails in the same circles that such a move also may be preceded by a presentation to France by Italy of demands in the form of an ultimatum.

Repeated to Rome.

KIRK

740.0011 European War 1939/3289 : Telegram

The Minister in Greece (MacVeagh) to the Secretary of State

ATHENS, May 24, 1940—6 p. m.
[Received May 24—4 p. m.]

104. After telling me today that his Government still has no idea as to what Italy's intentions may be, the Premier [6a] reiterated the hope that she will at least not attack in the Balkans. As a foundation for the hope he stated his belief that zones of influence in this region have not been agreed upon and cannot be agreed upon between Germany and Italy and Russia. In addition he restated his stand that Greece will resist if attacked, and when asked how effective such resistance might prove, replied simply, "It will be war".

MACVEAGH

740.0011 European War 1939/3352 : Telegram

The Minister in Greece (MacVeagh) to the Secretary of State

ATHENS, May 28, 1940—6 p. m.
[Received 6 : 25 p. m.]

108. The Greek public has received the news of Belgium's surrender with consternation and an Italian attack on France is almost universally regarded as imminent. The Director of the Foreign Office however in telling me this morning that the Greek Government still has no information of any threatening Italian movements in this area suggested that Mussolini's next move might be a peace offensive rather than a military one, since "It is not to Italy's interest to have Germany too strong and if peace can be made now Italy will still count for something in the Axis". He indicated that Greece's official policy of defending herself if attacked remains unchanged.

---

[6] Not printed.
[6a] Joannes Metaxas.

The German Military Attaché told Johnson [7] this morning that Italy is sure to enter the war very soon but that she is unlikely to attack in the Balkans and especially in Greece because the strategic advantages to be gained are "secondary" and because "Germany does not wish it". In this connection it may be significant that the already large German Legation here has recently been reinforced and its increasing propaganda takes no account whatever of Italian pretensions.

MACVEAGH

740.0011 European War 1939/3687 : Telegram

The Minister in Greece (MacVeagh) to the Secretary of State

ATHENS, June 11, 1940—5 p. m.
[Received 10 : 39 p. m.]

124. The Director General of the Foreign Office told me this morning that Greece's policy remains unchanged for the moment. He confirmed rumors from Salonika that some fresh Italian troops have recently arrived in Albania, but neither he nor the Chief of Staff whom Johnson interviewed regard the concentrations there as sufficient for an offensive or see any reason at present to doubt Mussolini's assurances. Regarding Greece's course should Turkey enter the war against Italy, the Director General repeated his remark reported in my telegram No. 108 of May 28 to the effect that this would not necessarily affect Greece, but thought it worth mentioning that should Bulgaria attack Turkey the Balkan Pact [8] would come into play.

The British Minister [9] called to offer congratulations on the President's speech.[10] He informed me that he and the French Minister saw the Premier last evening after Mussolini had made his declaration [11] and that Mr. Metaxas reaffirmed his sympathy with the cause of the Allies and his belief in their ultimate victory by terms that "if he were not speaking the truth he is a greater liar than Mussolini or Hitler." He also said that Mr. Metaxas reasserted Greece's determination to resist whenever and wherever attacked and that in view of previous conversations he understands this blanket statement to include Crete as well as all other Greek territory. In this connection Sir Michael added that Great Britain will not make the first move to occupy any

[7] Capt. Max S. Johnson, formerly Assistant Military Attaché in France, on temporary duty in Greece pending arrival of permanent Military Attaché.
[8] Signed at Athens, February 9, 1934, by Greece, Rumania, Turkey, and Yugoslavia. For text, see League of Nations Treaty Series, vol. CLIII, p. 153.
[9] Sir Charles Michael Palairet.
[10] Address by President Roosevelt at Charlottesville, Virginia, June 10, 1940, Department of State *Bulletin*, June 15, 1940, p. 635.
[11] On June 10, 1940, Italy declared war on France and the United Kingdom.

point in Greece and that unless her policy has changed without his being notified, it will suit British plans to have Greece remain non-belligerent if Turkey enters the war. Finally he gave me a précis of a note which he said he felt unnecessary, but which he was instructed to communicate to Mr. Metaxas today expressing "the hopes of his Government that no country will be tempted to attach the least importance to the assurance offered by Mussolini in his speech of yesterday".

The President's speech has made a deep impression here, and summaries and quotations are published today in the entire controlled press despite an obviously inspired attempt to give no unusual space or emphasis to Italy's alarming decision. Only two papers, however, leading ex-liberal *Vima* and *Acropolis*, venture to quote the President's statement about the dagger in the neighbor's back.

MacVeagh

740.0011 European War 1939/3731 : Telegram

The Minister in Greece (MacVeagh) to the Secretary of State

ATHENS, June 12, 1940—6 p. m.
[Received 6 : 20 p. m.]

126. In addition to saying that there are no present indications of Italy to attack Greece, General Papagos, Greek Chief of Staff, told Captain Johnson yesterday:

(1) That Greece will seek to maintain her neutrality by impartially refusing all foreign demands for use of her facilities specifically mentioning the Corinth Canal.

(2) That he believes Turkey will try to remain neutral in the present circumstances.

(3) That his intelligence estimates show 100,000 Italians plus 12,000 in Albania, only 1 Bulgarian division on the Greek frontier and 3 on Turkish and 43 Russian infantry and 12 cavalry divisions plus 5 mechanized brigades opposite Rumania.

(4) That Greek assistance to Turkey or other Balkan States is obligatory only against Bulgarian aggression and finally

(5) That no additional measures are being taken towards Greek mobilization which is now only one-third completed.

Regarding Greece's obligations the General's statement would appear to be strictly military and to ignore the naval implications of the Greco-Turkish Pact of 1938 [12] (see my despatch No. 2240 of April 28, 1938 [13]). Furthermore, as regards mobilization, there are indications that quiet progress is actually being made with preliminaries

---

[12] Signed at Athens, April 27, 1938, League of Nations Treaty Series, vol. CXCIII, p. 175.
[13] Not printed.

to permit completion in perhaps 3 days. The discharge of the 1935 class on June 29 after 1 month refresher training was announced yesterday together with a call for the 1934 class for similar duty beginning June 25. Additional reserve officers also called for June 15. The Yugoslav Military Attaché states categorically that one Italian corps sailed from Trieste a week ago for an unknown destination and that another from the same area has been preparing departure. He confirms the Greek Staff's information that of the Italians in Albania only one division now faces Greece directly.

MACVEAGH

740.0011 European War 1939/4105 : Telegram

The Chargé in Germany (Heath) to the Secretary of State

BERLIN, June 22, 1940—8 p. m.
[Received 9 : 52 p. m.]

2034. Greek circles in Berlin profess optimism that they will not be involved in the present war nor suffer territorial losses in connection with the peace arrangement. On the contrary, they maintain that intimations have been received that if Greece pressed a claim to Cyprus that it would receive German support. From this intimation they argue that while Germany has conceded the Mediterranean as falling within Italy's sphere of influence, nevertheless, the Reich dislikes the idea of too marked Italian domination supplanting the previous balance of British, French and Italian territories and interests in the area.

HEATH

740.0011 European War 1939/4563 : Telegram

The Minister in Greece (MacVeagh) to the Secretary of State

ATHENS, July 10, 1940—8 p. m.
[Received July 10—5 : 42 p. m.]

165. The British Naval Attaché told Captain Johnson this morning that the Italian war plane reported last night to have landed damaged in Crete was one of a formation of three waves of such planes which attacked British surface craft south of Gavdos Island late Monday. Possibly these planes were attempting to intercept the British sweep toward Malta which resulted in yesterday's clash.

The Attaché also said that a British oiler engaged in refueling destroyers has recently three times violated Greek territorial waters the first occasion being in the Gulf of Argolis the second near the southern capes and the third off the northwest coast of Crete. At the instance of the Greek Government the Attaché has each time requested the

Commander-in-Chief of the Mediterranean Fleet to discontinue such action but has received non-cooperative replies.

The positions given for the refueling would seem to indicate the existence of constant British patrolling across the direct route from Italy to the Dodecanese and the tenor of the Commander-in-Chief's replies is reminiscent of the practical disregard of Greece's neutrality which was shown by the British in the last war.

The Union of Soviet Socialist Republics has now created resident service representation at this post by the appointment of a Naval Attaché who has just arrived.

MacVeagh

765.68/262 : Telegram

The Chargé in Italy (Reed) to the Secretary of State

Rome, August 14, 1940—3 p. m.
[Received August 14—12 : 10 p. m.]

816. I have learned from a confidential source in which I place considerable credence that the Italian Government will shortly demand that Greece cede Corfu and neighboring islands and possibly that portion of Greek territory inhabited by Albanians; also that the Italian Government will demand that Yugoslavia cede to it the Dalmatian coast.

Repeated to Athens and Belgrade.

[Reed]

740.0011 European War 1939/5115 : Telegram

The Minister in Greece (MacVeagh) to the Secretary of State

Athens, August 14, 1940—6 p. m.
[Received August 14—4 : 40 p. m.]

196. My telegram No. 195, August 13, 6 p. m.[14] Competent opinion in both official and unofficial circles here remains considerably mystified as to what lies behind the continuing Italian press and radio campaign against Greece, but in view of the general European situation it is believed that clarification may be expected soon. Meanwhile, the Italians do not appear to have reinforced their troops in Albania and the relative unimportance Corfu and the Albanian frontier at this juncture suggests that Italy's real desire at present may be to force concessions from Greece in a more immediately vital area. In this connection my Yugoslav colleague suggests the Aegean, and his Military Attaché after listening to a Rome broadcast last night accusing

---

[14] Not printed.

Greece of allowing the use of Cretan harbors to British warships has reversed his opinion of yesterday and now looks for an ultimatum demanding at least the use of Crete for the Italian forces during the war.

MACVEAGH

765.68/274

Memorandum of Conversation, by the Chief of the Division of Near Eastern Affairs (Murray)

[WASHINGTON,] August 15, 1940.

The Counselor of the Greek Legation called this morning by appointment and read to me the full text of the attached telegraphic communication, dated August 14, 1940, from the Prime Minister of Greece, stoutly denying the accusations made by the Stefani Agency in Tirana, Albania, regarding the purported killing of an alleged Albanian patriot by Greek emissaries.

Although Mr. Depasta was apparently not instructed to leave any copy of this communication with the Department and hesitated to do so, he nevertheless followed my suggestion and left with me the attached copy for our information.[15]

It will be noted that in the Greek Prime Minister's telegram to the Legation in Washington he refers to a conversation which took place yesterday between the Greek Under Secretary and the Italian Minister in Athens, who was called to the Foreign Office to be acquainted with the views of the Greek Government in this matter. It will be noted in particular that Mr. Metaxas states that the Under Secretary "left it to be understood clearly that in the event of an Italian assault (upon Greece) the decision of the Government to oppose any such assault remains firm".

Mr. Depasta seemed deeply perturbed over the situation in which his country now finds itself and apparently expects that the worst is yet to come.

765.68/267 : Telegram

The Minister in Greece (MacVeagh) to the Secretary of State

ATHENS, August 15, 1940—4 p. m.
[Received 8 : 50 p. m.]

197. Every year on this date the Greeks celebrate the Dormition of the Virgin with special rites at the town of Tinos in the Cyclades. Many devotees gather there in view particularly of the miraculous

---

[15] Not printed; the telegram stated that the Greek authorities had nothing to do with the murder and that the victim was a criminal at large with convictions for murder, robbery, kidnapping, etc.

cures said to be performed. This morning the Greek cruiser *Helli*, anchored off the quay, after having brought several officials to the ceremony and while bedecked with gala flags was torpedoed without warning by an unidentified submarine and sunk almost immediately with the loss of 1 officer and about 30 men. I am also informed that the submarine damaged the quay with one or two torpedoes which missed the cruiser and that civilian casualties occurred. The Premier has issued a request by radio to the people of Tinos to remain calm and has guaranteed the safe return of all excursionists. He has also consulted with the chiefs of the military and naval forces but no result of this conference has been divulged.

The cynical brutality of this attack is reminiscent of the Corfu incident of 1924 [*1923*],[16] as well as of the violation of Albania on Good Friday of last year [17] and the Greeks are in no doubt as to its author especially in view of the Italian anti-Greek press and radio campaign with its trumped up charges which was reported in my telegram No. 194, Aug. 13, 3 p. m.,[18] and which still continues. The demands which normally follow intimidation in this type of diplomacy are expected soon.

MacVeagh

765.68/269 : Telegram

The Minister in Greece (*MacVeagh*) to the Secretary of State

Athens, August 16, 1940—8 p. m.
[Received August 17—5 : 15 a. m.]

198. The Under Secretary for Foreign Affairs told me this morning that there has still been no official communication from the Italian Government and that the Greek Government is completely in the dark as to what demands may be made and when. He indicated that Greece might be willing to make minor concessions in the interest of maintaining the peace but would never give up her friendship with Great Britain or renounce the British guarantee [19] given her last year. He granted that an immediate objective of the Italians would seem to be the ousting of the present Government but feels that their current press and radio attack against Mr. Metaxas will strengthen rather than weaken his position locally. He dismissed an Italophile movement

---

[16] Occupation by Italy of the Island of Corfu. See League of Nations, *Official Journal*, November 1923, pp. 1276–1316, *passim*.
[17] For correspondence on this subject, see *Foreign Relations*, 1939, vol. ii, pp. 365 ff.
[18] Not printed ; the charges referred to related to the affair reported in the memorandum of August 15 by the Chief of the Division of Near Eastern Affairs, *supra*.
[19] Made by former Prime Minister Neville Chamberlain in a statement to the House of Commons, April 13, 1939. See *Parliamentary Debates*, House of Commons, 5th ser., vol. 346, p. 13.

within the country as impossible because of the deep seated and universal anti-Italian feelings of the people.

The press publishes full details of yesterday's outrage, which it characterizes as "a foul crime" but is careful to make no charges as to the identity of the attacking submarine. The unsuccessful bombing of the Greek passenger vessel *Frinton* off Crete yesterday is officially confirmed. Unofficial reports state in addition that the destroyers sent to convoy the returning excursionists from Tinos were also unsuccessfully attacked by planes.

The late afternoon papers announce the calling up of the 15 D class of reserves (said to number about 100,000) for "autumn maneuvers" beginning September 1.

MacVeagh

765.68/277 : Telegram

The Minister in Greece (MacVeagh) to the Secretary of State

ATHENS, August 21, 1940—6 p. m.
[Received August 22—6 : 27 a. m.]

206. The Director General of the Ministry of Foreign Affairs whom I saw early this afternoon told me that the German Foreign Office professes to regard the Greco-Italian situation as definitely less threatening and that the same view has been expressed to the Turkish authorities by Von Papen.[20] He pointed out however that this view seems hardly substantiated by recently reported movements of Italian troops in Albania from the Yugoslav to the Greek border and the continuance of Italian press and radio attacks against this country.

He indicated unmistakably that the Greek Government is still very apprehensive and regards the situation as one in which anything may happen or be made to happen at any time.

Some more special troops from among "auxiliary reservists" of the 1934 class were called today for a period of instruction beginning September 4 but according to the Director General Greece is still avoiding any military measures which might with any show of reason be seized upon by the Italians as provocative.

MacVeagh

765.68/278 : Telegram

The Minister in Greece (MacVeagh) to the Secretary of State

ATHENS, August 22, 1940—4 p. m.
[Received August 23—8 : 50 a. m.]

208. The Italian Minister visited the Foreign Office yesterday and, according to the political [apparent omission] whom I saw this

---

[20] Franz von Papen, German Ambassador in Turkey.

morning, only registered some new complaints regarding the handling of the Italian point of view in the Greek press. The Italian press and radio continues to attack Greece, the latest charges being that Greek authorities have been preparing armed bands for several months with a view to acting against the Albanians in Western Epirus and the Greek Government has issued a statement through the Athens press agency denying this categorically at some length.

The Director General mentioned concentration of Italian forces on the Greek frontier as continuing and this was confirmed to me by the British Military Attaché last night who estimated, however, that the total Italian strength in Albania still remains somewhere in the neighborhood of 140,000 including laborers.

The Turkish Military Attaché here is returning to duty with troops and being replaced by the former Military Attaché in Paris. During his final call on me today he gave me his personal views of the situation to the effect that the Italians intend to take action without much further delay and that the Greeks will resist. As to possible Turkish assistance to the country in such event, his tone was much more positive than when I last saw him (see my telegram No. 195, August 13, 6 p. m.[21]).

MacVeagh

765.68/280 : Telegram

The Chargé in Germany (Kirk) to the Secretary of State

BERLIN, August 23, 1940—4 p. m.
[Received August 24—1 : 59 a. m.]

3713. There has been scant reference in the German press to Italo-Greek relations since the transmission of my 3581, August 17, 4 p. m.[21] and the inference is being drawn that not only is the German Government refraining from published expression on this subject but may also be counseling moderation in Rome.

Following the accentuated press campaign in Italy against Greece, certain interested diplomats took occasion last week to inquire at the Foreign Office here in regard to the German view as to the gravity of the situation and gained the impression then that action on the part of Italy was not felt to be imminent. During the first days of the present week the Greek Government, alarmed by the reports of Italian troop concentrations on the Albanian border, caused an inquiry to be made in Berlin as to whether the German Government believed that Italy meant war and it is assumed that this information was sought by the Greek Government in order to determine the question

[21] Not printed.

of ordering general mobilization which it was feared might furnish a pretext to Italy to attack.

Up to the present it is understood no reply to the foregoing has been forthcoming. In certain well-informed but unofficial German circles it is stated that Italy has decided to take Corfu, Northern Epirus, certain of the islands and Salonika, and it is also advocated that Greece denounce the pact with England although such an act might precipitate the seizure of Greek ports by England. Although it is asserted that Germany would prefer that Greece remain unmolested it is acknowledged that at the present time Italy could not be successfully opposed by Germany even if it wished to and that the German Government would find it necessary to accept as an accomplished fact whatever action Italy might take against Greece.

KIRK

765.68/282 : Telegram

The Minister in Greece (MacVeagh) to the Secretary of State

ATHENS, August 23, 1940—5 p. m.
[Received August 24—8 : 45 a. m.]

210. The Director General of the Foreign Office has assured me that rumors retailed to me by American correspondents last night and this morning and which may have reached the United States to the effect that formal demands have been made on the Greek Government, that Corfu has been occupied, and that the British have seized Crete are false. He stated that the troop movements in Albania and the charges against Greece in the Italian press which are again denied today through the Athens news agency continue to be alarming but on the basis of information from the Greek Minister in Berlin "and other capitals" he spoke more confidently than heretofore of the exertion of German influence to insure the preservation of peace. In this connection he spoke with satisfaction of a Berlin "Transocean" despatch featured in all the Greek papers today which recites with evident approval the determination of the Greek Government to maintain its neutrality so long as the integrity and independence of the country are not threatened.

The Director General added interesting comment that intimations have come from the German Government that it would be [apparent omission] for Greece not to take any such military measures as might be construed in Rome as provocative. He admitted that this advice has its ambiguous side and may be intended to facilitate Italian plans but he said that it was necessarily being followed so far as appears safe. The Greek Government has announced no troop movements whatever but reliable observers have recently reported the departure from here of some small units by sea in the direction of Preveza and today four more special categories of recruits have been called up for a month's special training.

The view that Germany will restrain Italy from attacking Greece is not supported by the attitude of the German Legation here which remains officially noncommittal but privately seems to contemplate letting things take their course. A number of German correspondents arrived in Athens yesterday apparently to cover expected developments.

MACVEAGH

765.68/283 : Telegram

The Minister in Greece (MacVeagh) to the Secretary of State

ATHENS, August 24, 1940—3 p. m.
[Received August 25—4 : 20 p. m.]

211. The Under Secretary for Foreign Affairs told me this morning that he had received news from Rome to the effect that the Italian Government regards the present anti-Greek campaign as primarily an affair of the press (see telegram No. 839, August 23, noon from Rome [24]) and as reflecting a question of settlement between Greece and Albania. In consequence, he felt the situation today to be less tense but referred to the continuing concentrations on the frontier as definitely disturbing despite Italian assurances. Regarding the possibility that Germany may have advised Italy against extending the war, he said he thinks the two powers have been in agreement on this policy for some time but that Italy now wants a victory of some sort and will not be restrained from the use of arms if she can shift the responsibility. Hence, he emphasized the impossibility of this country's taking adequate defense measures (see my telegram No. 210, August 23, 5 p. m.) and described the present situation of the Greek Government as a positive "martyrdom". The Under Secretary confirmed that following further allegations in the press concerning Greek atrocities Italian forces have now reoccupied the frontier zone voluntarily evacuated last autumn (see my telegram 178, September 19, 1939 [24]). In this connection Salonika reports a gradual shift of Greek troops from eastern to western Macedonia but still there have been no general mobilization orders nor large scale military movements of any kind. A fire destroyed 10 million drachmas worth of military equipment in Piraeus last night during a high wind. Its origin seems to be as mysterious as the sinking of the *Helli* and as little likely to be clarified. Incidentally, the *Helli* now appears to

[24] Not printed.

have been recently converted into the Greek Navy's principal mine layer and to have been sunk with a considerable cargo of mines aboard.

MacVeagh

765.68/284 : Telegram

The Chargé in Germany (Kirk) to the Secretary of State

Berlin, August 26, 1940—2 p. m.
[Received 4:50 p. m.]

3744. My 3713, August 23, 4 p. m. The Greek Minister here was summoned yesterday to Salzburg to confer with Ribbentrop[25] and is expected to return to Berlin tomorrow. Although the Minister was apparently not informed of the purpose of this interview it is inferred that it is to acquaint him with the German position in regard to the relations between Greece and Italy.

Kirk

765.68/287 : Telegram

The Minister in Greece (MacVeagh) to the Secretary of State

Athens, August 26, 1940—9 p. m.
[Received August 28—3:35 p. m.]

214. The Political Director of the Foreign Office read me a telegram this morning from the Greek Minister to Italy stating that the German Ambassador in Rome had interceded with the Foreign Minister in the interests of the preservation of peace in this region. Coincidentally, I am privately informed on the best authority that the Greek Minister in Berlin was instructed last week to request intercession. If this is true it would seem that the Greek Government has incurred obligations toward the German Government which it may find difficult to ignore later on.

The Berlin broadcast in the Greek language denied last night "at the request of the Stefani Agence" (1) that Italy has presented an ultimatum to Greece; (2) that there are any concentrations of Italian troops on the Greco-Albanian frontier; (3) that Italy intends to take military action or occupy Corfu or Crete; and (4) that Italy has assumed in general a hostile attitude toward Greece.

Tension appears to be somewhat lessened here both in official and unofficial circles. Nevertheless, the Greek Government is remaining vigilant. In regard to No. 3 above, the Political Director again confirmed to me this morning that Italian troop concentrations on the border exist, he said they are even increasing and added that

---

[25] Joachim von Ribbentrop, German Minister for Foreign Affairs.

within the last few days, 6,000 more Italian troops have landed in Albania, most of whom have been sent to the southern section.

The Yugoslav Military Attaché who still puts the strength of the Italians in Albania at 150,000 men said today that without overt mobilization the Greeks now have between 300,000 and 320,000 men under arms in all services. Full mobilization consisting of 12 classes has been accomplished in Crete, the Ionian Islands and Epirus while in Macedonia 5 classes have been called up. There are 3 divisions in Epirus facing Albania 1 of them motorized and 6 in Macedonia. Completely mobilized services include the navy, the coast defense, the heavy artillery, the engineering corps, the anti-aircraft defense, aviation, and liaison.

MacVeagh

765.68/289 : Telegram

The Chargé in Germany (Kirk) to the Secretary of State

BERLIN, August 29, 1940—2 p. m.
[Received 5 p. m.]

3780. My 3744, August 26, 2 p. m. Following the interview between the Minister for Foreign Affairs and the Greek Minister the impression prevails in Greek circles here that the danger of Italian action against Greece is not immediate. On the basis of that impression it is not believed in those circles that the Greek Government need take any emergency military measures at the moment.

KIRK

765.68/290 : Telegram

The Minister in Greece (MacVeagh) to the Secretary of State

ATHENS, August 29, 1940—3 p. m.
[Received August 30—10 : 55 a. m.]

218. The Premier confirmed to me today that Italy has made no formal demands on Greece and that there is a lessening of tension between the two countries. He refused to be drawn into any predictions as to future developments in this matter saying merely that Greece is no longer placing any faith in Italian assurances and remains ready to defend herself to "the last man, the last woman, the last child". In regard to what has already happened he said he thought Italy had begun her campaign in mistaken contempt of Greece's morale and capacities but that the Germans have understood these better adding that "the Germans say they have exerted their influence for the preservation of peace". He avoided a possible question as to Greece's reported request for intercession in Berlin, see my telegram No. 214,

August 26, 9 p. m., by saying regarding his relations with the German Minister here that "Greece is no beggar". When I suggested that he might soon be invited to Vienna to settle Albanian claims he said that counterclaims would naturally come up at such a conference and asked if I thought the Italians would wish to discuss the very large number of Greeks in Albania and the question of the Dodecanese.

MACVEAGH

765.68/294 : Telegram

The Minister in Greece (MacVeagh) to the Secretary of State

ATHENS, September 6, 1940—4 p. m.
[Received September 7—2 : 45 p. m.]

227. The Under Secretary for Foreign Affairs told me today that the Italians are maintaining their concentrations on the Greek-Albanian frontier and confirmed that Greece is reinforcing her own troops in that region though he attempted to minimize the movement and emphasized that nothing like a general mobilization has occurred. He also said that the Italians are continuing to keep alive their anti-Greek campaign for possible future developments with what he described as "pin pricks ["] citing yesterday's accusations, in the Albanian press, that the Archbishop of Janina is organizing armed bands on the border and unreasonable protests lodged at the Foreign Office against Greek visa regulations for foreigners. Regarding Lord Halifax's reaffirmation of British guarantee yesterday [26] he obviously felt this rather inopportune in Greece's present delicate situation and said, "Thank God (and I cannot think how it got into his head) he at least included the statement that we are neutral".

In a talk with me yesterday Mr. Maximos, ex-Minister for Foreign Affairs, voiced the pessimism widespread in informed circles here. He said he believed the real Axis aim in regard to Greece is to bring her eventually under complete control and this could only result in war. In this connection the German Minister recently informed a friend of mine that immediately after Rumania had renounced British guarantee [27] the Axis intimated to Greece that it would be well for her to do the same but met with no encouragement. I asked the Under Secretary about this today and he admitted that suggestions had been thrown out remarking in addition that when the next serious pressure is applied against Greece he expects it to be by both Italy and Germany combined.

MACVEAGH

---

[26] In the House of Lords, September 5, 1940. See *Parliamentary Debates, House of Lords*, 5th ser., vol. 117, p. 368.
[27] On July 1, 1940.

740.0011 European War 1939/5731 : Telegram

The Minister in Greece (MacVeagh) to the Secretary of State

ATHENS, September 25, 1940—6 p. m.
[Received September 26—8 : 20 a. m.]

245. According to the Director General of the Foreign Office the Italian Minister for Foreign Affairs recently informed several diplomats in Rome, though not the Greek Minister, that despite serious and important complaints against Greece, Italy will take no action at present but await a general postwar settlement of this region's problems. The official attitude here, however, is still to take nothing for granted in regard to Italy and military preparations continue quietly.

Festivities in connection with the visit of the Yugoslav Minister of Commerce who attended the opening of the Salonika Fair last Sunday have been made the occasion for emphasizing solidarity between Greece and Yugoslavia but there is no indication here that Greece will cooperate with that country in a military sense unless she is herself attacked.

With regard to telegram No. 897, September 20, 4 p. m., from Rome,[28] paragraph 2, it may be said that Greek resistance being predicated on the maintenance of British power in the Mediterranean, this country would probably pass into the Italian orbit without a struggle should that power collapse.

MACVEAGH

II. The Italian Invasion of Greece

740.0011 European War 1939/6176 : Telegram

The Chargé in Italy (Reed) to the Secretary of State

ROME, October 21, 1940—9 p. m.
[Received 9 : 40 p. m.]

1001. Following information from excellent source believed correct:

"Invasion of Greece is planned for early morning October 25. Duce has given the order. Badoglio[29] strongly opposed this move on ground that British Fleet will seize bases in Greece from which to bomb oil fields in Rumania. Troops are being embarked at Bari and Brindisi."

It is reported that four large passenger steamers left Trieste October 18 for Bari and Brindisi and it was inferred by Buffum[30] that attack on Greece would begin in near future.

---

[28] Not printed.
[29] Marshal Pietro Badoglio, Chief of Staff of the Italian Armed Forces.
[30] David H. Buffum, Consul at Trieste.

Inform Navy Department that source of quoted information is Signor "X".

[REED]

740.0011 European War 1939/6181 : Telegram

The Chargé in Italy (Reed) to the Secretary of State

ROME, October 22, 1940—10 a. m.
[Received October 22—8 : 35 a. m.]

1004. My 1001, October 21, 9 p. m. Substantially identical information has been given one of our correspondents by a high German Embassy official who intimated that Italian attack this week would be on a relatively small scale for purpose of testing Greek temper and resistance.

REED

740.0011 European War 1939/6188 : Telegram

The Chargé in Italy (Reed) to the Secretary of the State

ROME, October 22, 1940—11 a. m.
[Received October 22—9 : 09 a. m.]

1005. My 1001, October 21, 9 p. m. Following from same source:

"Italian Fleet now assembling at Taranto will sail from that port the night of October 24 to attack Corfu early on morning October 25. Large numbers of parachutists are being assembled with ships and supplies at Taranto and Bari. Plans are all set and may be put into operation on a moment's notice. Present plan for attack on 25th might be delayed until 28th for technical reasons. Russia has been promised complete control of the Dardanelles for entry into the Axis."

Inform War and Navy.

REED

740.0011 European War 1939/6207 : Telegram

The Minister in Greece (MacVeagh) to the Secretary of State

ATHENS, October 22, 1940—5 p. m.
[Received 11 : 40 p. m.]

260. The Under Secretary for Foreign Affairs told me this morning that the Greek Government is completely at a loss to understand recent British agency and radio reports of Axis demands on this country in view of the fact that no such demands have been made. Furthermore he said that while the concentrations of Italian troops in Albania must still be considered as a potential menace, official

relations between Greece and the Axis powers are easier at the moment than for some time past. He personally suggested as a possibility that the British maneuver may be part of a campaign to alarm Russia over Axis intentions in the Balkans linking it up with recent false rumors from British sources in Rumania. Regarding the Albanian concentrations he said that they may have been effected in anticipation of the collapse of Great Britain this summer, when the moment would have been opportune for a Balkan snatch, and quoted a remark of the Italian Minister here to the effect that if Italy really wished to invade Greece she would have done so in August and not waited until now.

The British and Yugoslav Military Attachés both are informed that the condition of the Italian troops on the Albanian border, many of whom are under canvas, is rapidly becoming untenable, and believe that they must soon either advance or retire. In this connection the Under Secretary believes that retirement is the more likely not only because of the immediate difficulties in the way of advance, but because the latter would "certainly involve widespread consequences". He still thinks any war in the Balkans unlikely at least before next spring and in view of the difficulties to be surmounted by the Axis in attacking vital British centers in Asia or Africa without command of the sea, considers the final German decision may have to be to stake all on putting England out by direct attack.

MacVeagh

740.0011 European War 1939/6240 : Telegram

The Minister in Yugoslavia (Lane) to the Secretary of State

[Extract]

Belgrade, October 24, 1940—9 p. m.
[Received October 25—8 : 18 a. m.]

471. The following is the gist of conversations which I had today with two high Yugoslav authorities.

1. Relations between Soviet Union and Turkey are improving. Information which we transmitted regarding German offer to Russia of Iran, Iraq, Istanbul and the Straits is correct only in so far as Iran and Iraq is concerned. The German aim is to give Russia access to the Persian Gulf and thus keep her out of the Mediterranean.

2. The Italian Minister informed the Minister of Foreign Affairs yesterday that Yugoslavia need not be alarmed regarding the increase of troops in Albania as they are there primarily for use against Greece. When the Foreign Minister expressed his surprise that Italy had aims against Greece, Mameli said that the Greeks are continually provok-

ing Italy and are adopting a very unfriendly attitude. The situation greatly disturbs the Yugoslav Government especially as it is confirmed by information received directly from Athens.

.   .   .   .

LANE

740.0011 European War 1939/6247 : Telegram

The Chargé in Italy (Reed) to the Secretary of State

ROME, October 26, 1940—11 a. m.
[Received October 26—8 : 56 a. m.]

1019. My 1005, October 22, 11 a. m., and previous. Following from same source:

"As late as Thursday night [31] argument continued between Duce and followers on one side and Badoglio and General Staff on the other side regarding the attack on Greece. Badoglio insists that if attack is made it should coincide with advance in Egypt. Graziani [32] refuses to renew attack in Egypt until certain equipment and reinforcements have been received. It is probable attack on Greece will take place this week-end over Badoglio's protest.

On Thursday 24 Italian submarines left Sardinia and Sicily for Bordeaux."

Information received this morning that airplane service Rome to Athens discontinued for the present.

Inform War and Navy.

REED

740.0011 European War 1939/6253 : Telegram

The Minister in Greece (MacVeagh) to the Secretary of State

ATHENS, October 28, 1940—5 a. m.
[Received October 28—3 : 50 a. m.]

262. Following some more absurd Italian news agency charges of Greek armed action in Albania, fully denied by the Greek Government yesterday, the Italian Minister handed the Premier an ultimatum at 3 o'clock this morning to [expire?] at 6, demanding permission to occupy certain strategic points. When the Premier asked what points, the Minister said he did not know. This last I have from the British Minister who was at once called in consultation. Indications are that Greece will not comply. Athens is already blacked out.

MACVEAGH

---

[31] October 24.
[32] Rodolfo Graziani, Commander of Italian Forces in North Africa and Governor General of Libya.

740.0011 European War 1939/6274 : Telegram

The Minister in Greece (MacVeagh) to the Secretary of State

ATHENS, October 28, 1940—noon.
[Received 2 : 15 p. m.]

263. The Chief of Staff told Major Baker [33] this morning that no word has yet been received by the Greek Government of possible assistance either from Turkey or England. He said the Albanian frontier has not yet been crossed but that the opposing forces there have been in contact and the artillery firing since the ultimatum expired. The Tatoi Airfield and the Corinth Canal have already been bombed, the latter without effect according to the same source. General mobilization has been declared and we have had recurrent alerts in Athens since 7 o'clock, anti-aircraft guns being repeatedly in action. There have been some excited anti-Italian demonstrations in the streets but no bombs have so far exploded in the capital and all Americans are believed to be safe.

MACVEAGH

740.0011 European War 1939/6266 : Telegram

The Chargé in Germany (Morris) to the Secretary of State

BERLIN, October 28, 1940—1 p. m.
[Received October 28—9 : 50 a. m.]

4485. So far the Greek Minister has not received from his own or from the German Government any indication of the effect of the Italian aggression upon German and Greek official relations. When Hitler and Mussolini meet today at Florence it is believed that this matter will be determined and Hitler will also insist that Italian military operations must not endanger Greek historical treasures. Italy's immediate military objective is reported to be the establishment of air bases at Salonika and in the Peloponnesus probably at Kalamata to protect merchant vessels carrying Black Sea petroleum to Italy. The Italian fleet has been unable to attempt this task because it lacks sufficient fuel.

MORRIS

740.0011 European War 1939/6267 : Telegram

The Chargé in Italy (Reed) to the Secretary of State

ROME, October 28, 1940—1 p. m.
[Received October 28—9 : 48 a. m.]

1027. I have just seen the Greek Minister who said he was entirely without news of any kind from his Government. The Turkish Am-

[33] Maj. Joseph K. Baker, Military Attaché in Greece.

bassador, however, had told him that he had been called to the Foreign Office this morning and informed that as a result of the unsatisfactory response of the Greek Government to Italy's protests regarding Greek assistance to Great Britain the Italian Government had deemed it necessary to address a note to the Greek Government demanding the use of certain places in Greek territory as naval bases.

Today's newspapers just *published* Greek acts of provocation against Albania but do not mention any ultimatum or military action.

REED

740.0011 European War 1939/6289 : Telegram

The Chargé in Yugoslavia (Bonbright) to the Secretary of State

BELGRADE, October 28, 1940—4 p. m.
[Received October 29—4: 45 a. m.]

478. After unsuccessful efforts to see the Foreign Minister [34] who has received no one this morning, I saw the Assistant Minister for Foreign Affairs at 1 o'clock. Smiljanic stated that the Yugoslav Legation at Rome was formally advised by the Italian Government this morning of the action against Greece. The notification included further assurances that no action against Yugoslavia was contemplated.

My informant was obviously anxious concerning what Bulgaria would do and this anxiety was reflected from other sources. He professed to believe that Bulgaria would not move at least during the next few days. In this connection the Bulgarian Military Attaché informed Colonel Fortier [34a] that Bulgarian divisions are mobilized on the Greek frontier but that no attack would be launched unless Hitler gave the word.

In reply to my question Smiljanic stated that there would be no general mobilization here since the number and disposition of Italian troops on the Italian and Albanian borders of Yugoslavia did not constitute a direct threat to this country. He added that if the situation changed Yugoslavia would take the necessary measures.

He kept repeating that the attack on Greece is a development of the war between Italy and Great Britain in the Mediterranean; that this is not "a Balkan war"; that Great Britain and not Yugoslavia had promised to come to the aid of Greece; that "we should wait and see"; and that it is still in Germany's interest to maintain peace in the Balkans.

The Prime Minister returned by air from Cetinje this morning and a meeting of the Cabinet is expected to take place this afternoon.

The atmosphere in official circles in Belgrade this morning was one of confusion, indecision and fatalism. Unless there is a sudden

---

[34] Aleksander Cincar-Markovitch.
[34a] Louis J. Fortier, Military Attaché in Yugoslavia.

change following the meeting of the Cabinet it is our impression from the sources which we have consulted that Yugoslavia will continue her policy of watchful waiting in the hope that she will be spared actual hostilities even though the attack on Greece threatens her complete encirclement.

The British Military Attaché saw the Chief of Staff this morning and asked him pointblank if Yugoslavia would fight. The former told Fortier that the Chief of Staff's reply was "It all depends on the Government".

Repeated to Ankara and Sofia.

BONBRIGHT

740.0011 European War 1939/6288 : Telegram

The Chargé in Germany (Morris) to the Secretary of State

BERLIN, October 28, 1940—5 p. m.
[Received 9:20 p. m.]

4496. Except for short reports dated from Rome of border incidents on the Greek-Albanian border reported as having involved Greek and Albanian border guards, the German press contains no reports of developments between Italy and Greece.

MORRIS

740.0011 European War 1939/6280 : Telegram

The Ambassador in Turkey (MacMurray) to the Secretary of State

ANKARA, October 28, 1940—5 p. m.
[Received October 29—12:20 a. m.]

179. 1. At an early hour this morning, the Turkish Ministry for Foreign Affairs was notified by the Greek Ambassador of the Italian ultimatum and its rejection by the Greek Government. It is understood that a meeting of the Cabinet is being held this afternoon.

2. In conversation this afternoon, my Greek colleague recalled that Turkey is under no direct obligation to give military support to Greece except in the event of an attack by Bulgaria. Her obligations to Great Britain (under articles II and III of the treaty of October 19, 1939) [35] would apply upon Great Britain's acting in fulfillment of the guarantee to which Greece has already appealed; but the nature of the assistance to be given would be determined upon consultation in the light of the existing situation. He intimated, as his personal opinion, that it might be more advantageous, at any rate for the time being, if Turkey were to remain neutral and on guard against possible Bulgarian attack in Thrace.

---

[35] League of Nations Treaty Series, vol. cc, p. 167.

3. The first impression of popular reaction here seems to be a rather fatalistic acceptance of the belief that Turkey must soon fight for her existence.

MacMurray

740.0011 European War 1939/6298 : Telegram

The Chargé in Yugoslavia (Bonbright) to the Secretary of State

BELGRADE, October 28, 1940—6 p. m.
[Received October 29—7:45 a. m.]

479. My 478, of today. The Cabinet is now in session. We have been informed from a reliable source that an announcement is expected afterwards to the effect that Yugoslavia will maintain its neutrality but will defend its territory if attacked.

BONBRIGHT

740.0011 European War 1939/6325 : Telegram

The Chargé in Yugoslavia (Bonbright) to the Secretary of State

BELGRADE, October 29, 1940—11 a. m.
[Received October 30—8:30 a. m.]

480. The Chief of the Political Section of the Foreign Office [36] told me last night in strict confidence that there had been pressure during the day from the Italians for the issuance of a declaration of neutrality by the Yugoslav Government but that the latter had not complied.

He added that the Greeks had asked the Yugoslav Government not to permit any Italian troops to cross Yugoslav territory and that his Government had given assurances that any such request from the Italians would be refused. This has been confirmed this morning from an unimpeachable source.

Repeated to Rome, Athens and Ankara.

BONBRIGHT

740.0011 European War 1939/6309 : Telegram

The Chargé in Germany (Morris) to the Secretary of State

BERLIN, October 29, 1940—noon.
[Received October 29—11:40 a. m.]

4499. In Yugoslavian circles the opinion is expressed that the Greek Government, despite its announced resistance, may come to some com-

[36] R. Petrovic.

promise with Italy but the impression is gained that such predictions are offered by way of excuse for Yugoslavia's apparent intention not to support its neighbor against aggression and they are accompanied by the assertion that the Balkan Entente does not require Yugoslavia to take up arms for Greece against Italy. These circles take the line that Turkish action in support of Greece depends upon Russia's attitude which seems inscrutable. They maintain that no intimations have been received from the German Government that it will request the right of passage over Yugoslavia for German troops proceeding to the Mediterranean but admit that such a request can come as suddenly and unexpectedly as Italian demands on Greece.

These circles are puzzled by the timing of the Italian action since they share the opinion of certain other diplomatic observers—an opinion which is also occasionally heard in German circles—that the movement to obtain Spanish collaboration and French cooperation or acquiescence has been laid with a view to presenting before the American elections a picture of a Europe in submissive agreement with Axis plans for the exclusion of British influence from the Continent.

MORRIS

740.0011 European War 1939/6302 : Telegram

The Chargé in Italy (Reed) to the Secretary of State

ROME, October 29, 1940—noon.
[Received October 29—7 : 40 a. m.]

1033. The outbreak of hostilities with Greece has not yet been announced to the Italian people either in the press or on the radio. This morning's press however carries the text of the Italian ultimatum and editorials declare that any resistance on the part of Greece will be overcome by the Italian Armed Forces.

Text of the note will be forwarded by mail.

REED

740.0011 European War 1939/6327 : Telegram

The Chargé in France (Matthews) to the Secretary of State

VICHY, October 29, 1940—5 p. m.
[Received 9 : 20 p. m.]

852. I called this afternoon on the Greek Minister to express indignation at the act of aggression to which his country has been subjected.

He had no news of the day's developments nor of the attitude which either Turkey or Bulgaria may assume. The Foreign Office likewise has no news.

MATTHEWS

740.0011 European War 1939/6333 : Telegram

The Ambassador in Japan (Grew) to the Secretary of State

Tokyo, October 29, 1940—6 p. m.
[Received October 30—2 : 20 p. m.]

1079. Today's *Asahi, Hochi, Yomiuri* discussing question article 3 tripartite alliance [37] vis-à-vis war Italy–Greece state Japanese Government to withhold decision its attitude pending study detailed official reports today's Cabinet meeting. *Yomiuri, Hochi* assert Japan obviously fully prepared render every assistance Italy if requested. All newspapers declare Greco-Italian war result British intrigue instigation Greece. Evening newspapers report today's Cabinet meeting decision reached withhold final formation Japanese attitude pending further close study detailed cables. Domei reports observers believe interpretation tripartite pact should be agreed upon following tripartite consultations—pact designed prevent extension conflict therefore interpretation should be considered from "practical standpoint" not "literal".

Sent to Department via Shanghai.

GREW

740.0011 European War 1939/6326 : Telegram

The Minister in Rumania (Gunther) to the Secretary of State

Bucharest, October 29, 1940—9 p. m.
[Received October 30—8 : 30 a. m.]

682. A high official of the Greek Embassy told Huston [38] this afternoon that it was the Embassy's definite conviction that Berlin was taken by surprise by the Italian attack on Greece, that the attack was certainly not sponsored by Germany and even did not fit in with German plans.

The Military Attaché of this Legation gained a similar impression from his conversations today with service attachés of the German Legation.

Repeated to Athens.

GUNTHER

[37] Signed September 27, 1940, by Germany, Italy, and Japan; for text, see *Foreign Relations, Japan, 1931–1941*, vol. II, p. 165.
[38] Cloyce K. Huston, Second Secretary of Legation in Rumania.

740.0011 European War 1939/6329 : Telegram

The Chargé in Italy (Reed) to the Secretary of State

ROME, October 30, 1940—6 p. m.
[Received October 30—2 : 20 p. m.]

1044. In contrast with the exuberance displayed in connection with earlier military exploits the press has thus far restrained its enthusiasm regarding the invasion of Greece. Today's army communiqué states merely that the advance is continuing, the Greek rear guard forces having been overcome, and news columns give little additional information on the progress of the campaign. Considerable space is, however, devoted to explanations of the attack which assert that Britain itself had plans under way for a move into Greece and had once again been forestalled. Greece too comes in for a certain amount of opprobrium for alleged British use of Greek harbors and waters.

REED

740.0011 European War 1939/6373 : Telegram

The Minister in Yugoslavia (Lane) to the Secretary of State

BELGRADE, October 31, 1940—noon.
[Received November 1—8 : 30 a. m.]

483. The Greek Minister told Bonbright last evening that during the day the Yugoslav Government had received assurances from Bulgaria that the latter would not move against Greece. Rosetti assumed that this decision was in line with Germany's wishes.

Rosetti was still in a highly nervous state and expressed some dissatisfaction with the slowness of British aid. He said that he had seen the British Minister earlier in the day and had urged upon him the importance of immediately sending tangible aid, preferably in the form of planes to bolster up Greek morale and show that in this case the British guarantee really meant something. Otherwise he felt that there might be a collapse inside of a week followed by a change of government in Greece.

Later in the evening a high official of the Foreign Office confirmed the fact that assurances of Bulgarian neutrality had been received. He added that the British made two démarches yesterday, one to Sofia warning the Bulgarians to remain quiet, and the second here asking that Yugoslavia help the Greeks in every way possible. Most Yugoslav diplomatic missions abroad were reporting the opinion, he said, that the conflict between Greece and Italy would be localized, but news from Moscow attributed "sinister motives" to Germany, the thought being that when the Italians drive through to Salonika they will join up with the Bulgarians supported by the Germans.

The situation remains quiet here.

Repeated to Rome, Sofia, Athens, Ankara.

LANE

740.0011 European War 1939/6346 : Telegram

The Ambassador in Turkey (MacMurray) to the Secretary of State

ANKARA, October 31, 1940—1 p. m.

[Received 7 : 09 p. m.]

183. My telegram No. 180, October 28, 7 p. m.[39]

1. The Secretary General of the Foreign Office informed me today that in the conversations in progress with the British, his Government has outlined its position (which has also been made clear to the Greeks and is fully understood by them) that Turkey will participate in the war only in the event of either (first) a direct threat to Turkey or (second) an intervention by Bulgaria—in either of which contingencies she should "go the limit". As to the first, I inquired whether this Government contemplated the possibility of an offensive defense beyond its own borders: and he replied that if, for example, the Italians were to advance on Salonika the Turks would consider their own safety directly menaced and would act accordingly. With regard to the second possibility, he expressed the opinion that Bulgaria would not act unless provoked by Turkey or unless constrained to do so by Germany.

2. In amplification of the Turkish viewpoint he expressed his conviction that Italy had counted upon it that Greece would yield to the ultimatum but now found herself compelled to undertake action against almost insuperable natural obstacles: if free to concentrate their forces along that line of defense, the Greeks had every prospect of successful resistance. He believed the Bulgarians had no intention of attacking Greece on her exposed Thracian flank so long as the Turks maintained an armed neutrality on their common frontier. If, on the other hand, Turkey were to undertake the military support of Greece on the relatively small scale that is geographically possible, he felt sure that Bulgaria would enter the melee and thus compel a distraction of the Greek forces besides spreading the conflict and creating new problems and causing a further dispersion of Allied effort.

3. He recognized, however, that these provisions might be upset if it should prove that Germany (now overwhelmingly the controlling element of the Axis group) has other intentions not as yet evident. But although remarking that on first impression it would seem that

---

[39] Not printed.

Italy had acted without previous understanding with Germany he deprecated the assumption that the two powers would fail to coordinate their activities: it was of course to be assumed that Italy's action would be if it had not already been fitted into some larger plan. In view of the tremendous difficulties (the certainty of Turkish resistance, the enormous distances involved, and the great difficulty of the terrain particularly for a winter campaign) he did not think it probable that an Axis push along the eastern coast of the Mediterranean was to be expected at any rate for the time being.

4. With regard to Soviet Russia as a possible factor on the immediate situation he said that his Government had had no contacts whatsoever with Moscow in reference to the invasion of Greece and surmised that the Russians might be expected to hold aloof from the question.

5. As regards the relations of this country with Russia he was considerably more optimistic than the Minister had been a fortnight ago (my telegram No. 171, October 18, 6 p. m.[40]) stating that they might at last be said to have been brought back to the degree of cordiality that existed formerly (that is before the Molotov–Ribbentrop agreement of August 1939[41]).

Repeated to Athens.

MacMurray

740.0011 European War 1939/6347 : Telegram

The Minister in Bulgaria (Earle) to the Secretary of State

Sofia, October 31, 1940—7 p. m.
[Received October 31—3 : 40 p. m.]

150. The Foreign Minister has just informed me there is no change in Bulgaria's foreign policy of non-aggression against her neighbors. However, his voice lacked the positive snap of a few months ago in making this assertion.

He feels that even if according to rumor Germany is not in full accord with Italy in the attack on Greece there is certainly not enough friction in this action to cause a rift between the Axis powers.

In answer to my inquiry whether there was a possibility of the passage of German troops through Bulgaria to the Turkish frontier and what would be Bulgaria's action in such a contingency, he replied these were questions he dared not even ask himself. However, he saw no indication at present of such German action.

---

[40] Not printed.
[41] Signed at Moscow, August 23, 1939; Department of State, *Nazi–Soviet Relations, 1939–1941*, p. 76.

In answer to my inquiry regarding the proposed Jewish restrictions he said that often people were forced to do things they did not wholly approve but that he really thought "these measures and the way they would be enforced" would protect the Jews in that they would allay any violent anti-Semitism.

EARLE

740.0011 European War 1939/6353 : Telegram

The Chargé in Germany (Morris) to the Secretary of State

BERLIN, October 31, 1940—8 p. m.
[Received October 31—6 : 02 p. m.]

4549. Rumors that Germany will mediate between Greece and Italy are without foundation according to the Greek Minister who believes that Greek-German diplomatic relations will be broken shortly and that action to that end will await the return of Ribbentrop whose arrival is expected today.

MORRIS

740.0011 European War 1939/6384 : Telegram

The Chargé in Italy (Reed) to the Secretary of State

ROME, November 1, 1940—3 p. m.
[Received November 1—1 : 16 p. m.]

1050. The Greek Minister has asked for his passports and is expected to leave Rome with his staff on Sunday. It is understood that the Swiss Legation will take over Greek interests.

A restrained tone still characterizes press treatment of the Greek venture but reports are carried of enthusiastic demonstrations in Albania. In Italy, however, the reaction has been one of disapproval and disappointment and one frequently hears expressions of pity for Greece.

REED

740.0011 European War 1939/6407 : Telegram

The Minister in Yugoslavia (Lane) to the Secretary of State

BELGRADE, November 1, 1940—7 p. m.
[Received November 2—9 : 25 a. m.]

488. The Yugoslav Government has just given to the press a statement, the high points of which are as follows:

Even before the war the efforts of this country were directed towards establishing friendly relations with all her neighbors, particularly Germany and Italy. When war came Yugoslavia declared her neutrality which was based on the sole condition of respect for her independence and the security of her frontiers. In doing so she best served the vital interests of her people and at the same time fulfilled her obligations of a correct neighbor, as has been categorically and openly admitted by Berlin and Rome. Having relations of sincere friendship with Italy and Greece this country profoundly regrets the conflict between them. Yugoslavia must follow the new situation attentively while continuing to devote all her strength to the maintenance of peace. Taking into account the attitude which she has maintained up to now "Yugoslavia hopes that she will not see her interests threatened from any side by the future development of events".

LANE

740.0011 European War 1939/6412 : Telegram

The Minister in Yugoslavia (Lane) to the Secretary of State

BELGRADE, November 2, 1940—7 p. m.
[Received November 2—4:47 p. m.]

491. A high Foreign Office official said to me this morning that Bulgaria will not attack Greece or Yugoslavia as it would not be in Germany's interest. Bulgaria will follow the bidding of "the masters". The information received by the Foreign Office is that the invasion of Greece is not popular with Hitler but was necessary to recoup Mussolini's local prestige which had suffered serious setback because of his failure to bring Spain into the war and to defeat the British Fleet in the Mediterranean. My informant confirmed the impression which we have obtained from numerous sources that the Italian public is apathetic towards the war.

LANE

740.0011 European War 1939/6510 : Telegram

The Minister in Greece (MacVeagh) to the Secretary of State

ATHENS, November 4, 1940—5 p. m.
[Received November 7—5:55 a. m.]

279. The British Military Attaché told Major Baker confidentially last evening that Greek strategic movements and concentrations should be completed in another week. He confirmed the Greek communiqués as to the present situation on the front saying that at no place have the Italians made more than preliminary contact with the main defensive positions though in the Pindus sector difficulties of communication caused some early confusion and doubts as to the exact situation.

The Italian Minister and staff are leaving Athens by rail this afternoon. They have just driven off from the Legation watched by a quiet and orderly crowd. Many German businessmen and commercial travelers are also departing but there appears to be no general exodus yet of the German community. In this connection the Director General of the Foreign Office expressed the opinion this morning to me that Germany must eventually join Italy against this country and the Hungarian Minister who is taking over Italian interests here expects such action soon. He told my Brazilian colleague that Germany will not move through Bulgaria for this purpose, as she desires not to disturb Turkey, but through Yugoslavia. Incidentally the Turkish decision not to enter the war at present has been surprisingly well received by the Greek public which either understands the great service rendered by Turks in watching Bulgaria or is blinded to its own peril by initial frontier successes.

Johnson [42] reported this morning two more air raid warnings but no bombardment in the immediate vicinity; all Americans in the district are believed safe. The Governor General spoke to Gullion [43] personally yesterday about the urgent need for more Red Cross supplies and an appeal in this connection has also been made to the British authorities.

Johnson has today burned the Consulate's A–1 code and all cipher tables on hand. He would be grateful if the Department would inform his family that their cable has been received.

MacVeagh

740.0011 European War 1939/6472 : Telegram

The Chargé in France (Matthews) to the Secretary of State

Vichy, November 4, 1940—8 p. m.
[Received November 5—9 : 02 a. m.]

890. The prevailing impression in France now is that Mussolini launched his attack on Greece without consulting his senior partner. The French like to feel that the vision of a possible Franco-German *rapprochement* was so distasteful to the Duce that he timed his Greek adventure to upset the Hitler–Laval plans. Rochat [44] however is an exception; he finds it difficult to believe that Mussolini would dare to act except in complete accord with the Nazi leader. He does not agree with other views prevailing here that the tenacity and relative success of Greek resistance has proved surprising both to Italy and to the rest

---

[42] John D. Johnson, Consul at Salonika.
[43] Edmund A. Gullion, Vice Consul at Salonika.
[44] Charles Antoine Rochat, official of the French Ministry for Foreign Affairs.

of the world. He has, he says, no idea of the ultimate objective of the Axis Powers though Salonika must seem important.

Toward France, he said, Italy's attitude continues to be extremely unfriendly particularly that of the Italian press. He denies that any formal territorial demands have been received but knows that the Italians have large appetites.

It is certainly a fact in France today that while much is heard in Government circles of France's powerlessness to resist German demands, there is no tendency to yield an inch to Italy and no voice is raised to urge reconciliation with France's Mediterranean rival.

MATTHEWS

740.0011 European War 1939/6455 : Telegram

The Chargé in Germany (Morris) to the Secretary of State

BERLIN, November 4, 1940—8 p. m.
[Received 9 : 48 p. m.]

4590. Reference my 4551, November 1, noon.[45] The Greek Minister this afternoon gave me the following picture of the Greek-Italian conflict. Italy was disgruntled because it was not consulted or previously informed of the German intrusion into Rumania. He was very positive on this point. It felt justified in balancing the Axis scales by a thrust against Greece which it expected to succeed as easily as the Rumanian one. Italy therefore acted without previous notification to Germany just before Hitler and Mussolini had arranged to meet in Florence. Resentful of the Italian coup, Berlin officialdom is delighted at Greek resistance. From his first fears of a rupture the Minister has veered to strong hope of a German mediation on the basis of Greek surrender of some strategic points to Italy possibly with German participation in their control. It was evident to me he hoped for this solution to end hostilities. He expressed the feeling that German official circles regarded the Greek situation so far as an isolated one but Greece's acceptance of English military assistance will soon cause Greece to be looked upon as an ally of England in the war. The Minister spoke of a German ultimatum to Greece the preparation of which a few days ago was abandoned in favor of a more moderate policy tending to justify Greece's resistance but to wheedle her into "honorable concessions". The Minister had seen two high officials before he received me.

MORRIS

---

[45] Not printed.

740.0011 European War 1939/6493 : Telegram

The Minister in Rumania (Gunther) to the Secretary of State

BUCHAREST, November 5, 1940—noon.
[Received 12:14 p. m.]

705. My 695, November 1, 10 a. m. and paragraph 1 my 698, November 1, 5 p. m.[46] Since the Italian attack on Greece I have been impressed with the importance which persons in this country, one in particular, well versed in Balkan problems, attach to the following view. I believe the view which I interpret herewith worth considering and even expounding in the proper British quarters.

1. Even two divisions of British troops on the Greco-Italian front might turn the tide for the Greeks and result in a major disaster for the Italians far from their base and surrounded by a population which could easily turn exceedingly hostile at the first sign of real weakness. Simultaneous bombing of Durazzo and other Albanian ports would probably also be helpful.

2. Or a major disaster in Albania might have the most serious repercussions politically and socially in Italy.

On the other hand should the British be inclined to establish themselves in Salonika with its forlorn memories of the last war this might: (*a*) result in a general Balkan conflagration which would seem to be what the British want notwithstanding the great advantages enjoyed by Germany in such an event as the Germans would have to attack and it is doubtful whether British forces in sufficient number could be sent and maintained; (*b*) should the British be unable to hold or make ground all the Balkans would swing inevitably to the Axis and even Greece and Yugoslavia would probably go.

Whereas if the Italians were defeated first: (1) the Axis would be weakened and might even be dissolved by a separate peace; (2) Balkan resistance to German penetration would receive a new impulse; (3) the magnificent Greek resistance to date is buoyed up by hopes of real assistance from England. Should this fail Greece would probably go the way of other small countries. The parallel is already being made here of Norway with Yugoslavia in the role of Sweden.

GUNTHER

740.0011 European War 1939/6621a : Telegram

The Secretary of State to the Minister in Greece (MacVeagh) [47]

WASHINGTON, November 7, 1940—6 p. m.

248. You are instructed to inquire of the Greek Government whether it considers a state of war exists between Greece and Italy.

HULL

---

[46] Neither printed.
[47] The same, *mutatis mutandis*, as telegram No. 536, November 7, 7 p. m., to the Chargé in Italy.

740.0011 European War 1939/6591 : Telegram

The Minister in Sweden (Sterling) to the Secretary of State

STOCKHOLM, November 11, 1940—2 p. m.
[Received 3 : 55 p. m.]

1032. Regarding invasion of Greece : In opinion of Foreign Office, based on its reports from Continent, it came to ears of Mussolini some weeks ago that Hitler was offering French Morocco to Franco and at same time assuring Laval that no further territorial concessions would be demanded of France. This so angered Mussolini that since he had continuously received reports from his Minister at Athens that Greeks would offer absolutely no resistance, he decided on immediate invasion, expecting to face Hitler at their meeting in Florence with a *fait accompli*. Unlooked for stand of Greek Army and people has for moment set Axis collaboration awry and much annoyed Hitler who desired a *status quo* in Balkans.

STERLING

740.0011 European War 1939/6661 : Telegram

The Minister in Greece (MacVeagh) to the Secretary of State

ATHENS, November 12, 1940—5 p. m.
[Received November 14—9 : 32 a. m.]

299. Department's telegram No. 248, November 7, 6 p. m.   In reply to my formal inquiry the Under Secretary of State for Foreign Affairs informs me by his note No. 33953 dated November 11, 1940, that "a state of war exists in Greece since October 28th of this year at 5 : 30 a. m. at which time Italy launched an unexpected attack against Greece".

MACVEAGH

740.0011 European War 1939/6682 : Telegram

The Chargé in Germany (Morris) to the Secretary of State

BERLIN, November 14, 1940—5 p. m.
[Received November 14—5 : 15 a. m.]

4710. With the Greek-Italian war in its third week and no break in Greek-German relations Greek circles in Berlin still express belief that Hitler is seeking a basis for mediation of the conflict or if no basis is found will as a lesson to Mussolini let the Italians carry on unaided for a time.   They are however skeptical that any mediatory basis can be found which from the point of view of Italian prestige will be acceptable to Mussolini.

The belief of these circles that Germany is actually considering a mediatory action are based on intimations which are admittedly rather obscure and which do not proceed from the highest officials in the Foreign Office realm, such remarks as the expression of hope that Greek operations will not be conducted so fiercely as to inflict any great defeat on the Italians which would irrevocably commit the latter for prestige sake to continue the war. Greek circles continue to receive official intimations that Italy's action against their country was taken without prior consultation with Germany. The impression created in Greek circles by these intimations is reinforced by the still friendly reception accorded them by German officials and by their recollections of previous statements and incidents interpreted as evidence that Hitler has a mystic objection to the use of violence against historic Greece plus doubts as to the political and military advisability of such action. They assert that it was Hitler's personal opposition which prevented the Italian attack on Greece last August and go so far as to express their opinion that the invasion of their country marks the beginning of a definite rift in the Axis.

The belief in German mediation and refusal to lend assistance to Italian military operations in Greece is not shared by certain other observers in Berlin although the rumor is prevalent that as an object lesson Hitler will withhold military support for a time.

MORRIS

740.0011 European War 1939/6707 : Telegram

The Minister in Greece (MacVeagh) to the Secretary of State

ATHENS, November 16, 1940—7 p. m.
[Received November 17—5 : 50 p. m.]

311. A British squadron of 5 warships debarked troops apparently from Palestine and Egypt at Piraeus this afternoon. According to the British Consul there, the troops number "several thousand" and more are expected. Hundreds have already been brought to Athens for temporary billets, receiving an ecstatic reception from the people.

Department's telegrams 255 and 256 [48] received yesterday. Nos. 257 to 261 [49] inclusive received today.

MACVEAGH

740.0011 European War 1939/6661 : Telegram

The Acting Secretary of State to the Minister in Greece (MacVeagh)

WASHINGTON, November 16, 1940—9 p. m.

263. Your 299, November 12, 5 p. m. In view of the Greek Government's statement, a proclamation declaring the neutrality of the

---

[48] Neither printed.
[49] None printed.

United States in the war between Greece and Italy [50] is being issued today. If you consider it desirable you may inform the Greek Government that this action has followed the official confirmation by Greece of the state of war, and that similar action has been taken in respect to the other belligerents as they have become involved. You may state that the proclamation is to be construed in no way as being an indication of any lessening of the sympathy of this Government for Greece in its present conflict with Italy.

WELLES

740.0011 European War 1939/6785 : Telegram

The Chargé in France (Matthews) to the Secretary of State

VICHY, November 18, 1940—10 p. m.
[Received November 19—1:05 p. m.]

973. A member of the Italian Embassy in Paris has made the following explanatory statements to an official of the French Foreign Office which I pass on for what they may be worth:

The war in Greece was a "preventive war which had started too late"; the Italians were convinced that the British were making such headway in Greece that by next spring the country would have been a British stronghold; that the Italians now realized that the war will not be over this autumn, hence their need to move quickly, in spite of adverse advice of their military chiefs. The Germans would have preferred to wait and settle Greece in the fashion of Rumania; hence the sudden move at 6 o'clock on the morning that the Fuehrer was to meet Mussolini at Florence and without previous notification. As a result the Florence meeting had been unproductive.

MATTHEWS

740.0011 European War 1939/6781 : Telegram

The Minister in Yugoslavia (Lane) to the Secretary of State

BELGRADE, November 19, 1940—7 p. m.
[Received November 19—3:40 p. m.]

534. A responsible official of the Yugoslav Foreign Ministry informed us this morning in strict confidence that the Yugoslav Government has made new *démarches* to the Italian, British, and Greek Governments, presumably to warn them against further violations of Yugoslav territory by foreign aircraft. In this connection, the

---

[50] Department of State *Bulletin*, November 16, 1940, p. 426.

Prime Minister told me yesterday that violations of Yugoslav territory by Italian planes are taking place almost daily.

LANE

740.0011 European War 1939/6837 : Telegram

The Minister in Greece (MacVeagh) to the Secretary of State

ATHENS, November 22, 1940—8 p. m.
[Received November 23—4 : 15 p. m.]

326. Early this afternoon the Premier announced the fall of Koritza to a large crowd in Constitution Square. Details not yet available but the King's aide has confirmed to me that the booty is considerable and the British Military Attaché described the affair as a major victory. He believes that the Italians have thrown nearly the whole of their Albanian Army into the effort to hold the line, now broken at its most important point, and that withdrawal will be difficult. In this connection, he spoke of the opportunity now presented to deal Italy a serious blow before Germany comes on the scene and urged that while the British command in Egypt is already sending all the planes it can, not a moment should be lost in shipping others from America if such can be obtained. The retiring Rumanian Ambassador, who represents himself as in the confidence of the German Minister told me this morning that the German Legation here is uninformed of any plans to help the Italians, but that he believes personally German assistance of some sort cannot be long delayed.

Department's telegrams 270 to 274 inclusive and circular of November 20, 6 p. m.[51] received today.

MACVEAGH

740.0011 European War 1939/6819 : Telegram

The Chargé in Italy (Reed) to the Secretary of State

ROME, November 23, 1940—9 a. m.
[Received November 23—8 a. m.]

1115. Department's No. 536, November 7, 7 p. m.[52] By note dated November 20 just received the Foreign Office states that Greece is considered an enemy state since October 28.

REED

[51] None printed.
[52] See footnote 47, p. 559.

740.0011 European War 1939/6836 : Telegram

The Chargé in Germany (Morris) to the Secretary of State

BERLIN, November 23, 1940—4 p. m.
[Received November 23—3 : 40 p. m.]

4815. The German press after having in the recent past given a good deal of space to comment on the difficulty of terrain, communication and weather encountered by the Italians in northern Greece, now confines its reporting of the Greco-Italian war to the publication of the text of Italian war communiqués. Reports of the actual extent of Italian reverses are not published in such a way as to make them clearly discernible to the German public.

MORRIS

740.0011 European War 1939/6835 : Telegram

The Minister in Yugoslavia (Lane) to the Secretary of State

BELGRADE, November 23, 1940—4 p. m.
[Received 6 : 06 p. m.]

542. I asked the Minister for Foreign Affairs this morning what Yugoslavia's attitude would be in the event that Bulgaria attacks Greece and whether he considered the provisions of the Balkan Pact still in force in view of the collapse of Rumania. The Minister replied that today there is no such thing as pacts, that only the question of one's own interests is involved. He said that today one must regard facts and not obligations. (The British Minister whom I met subsequently at the Foreign Office informed me that the Minister for Foreign Affairs recently spoke to him in an identical manner.)

In reply to my inquiry regarding information as to Bulgaria's attitude, he said that this morning assurances had been received from the Bulgarian Minister for Foreign Affairs that Bulgaria had no intention to attack Greece or Yugoslavia and that Bulgaria had been informed by Germany that Germany did not intend any move in the Balkans. The Minister said, however, that in the event that Germany should request passage of troops through Bulgaria, Bulgaria would surely accede.

He said that the Yugoslav Government still is in doubt as to whether Germany intends to come to the aid of Italy against Greece. He said that the Yugoslav Government has received no information regarding the increase of German troops in Rumania. (This information was also given to Colonel Fortier this morning by the Yugoslav General Staff, although contradicting that transmitted in my 541, November 22, 7 p. m.[53])

LANE

---

[53] Not printed.

740.0011 European War 1939/6838 : Telegram

The Minister in Yugoslavia (Lane) to the Secretary of State

BELGRADE, November 23, 1940—5 p. m.
[Received November 23—3 : 42 p. m.]

543. We were informed by a member of the Turkish Embassy this morning that his Government has notified the Yugoslav Government that if Bulgaria moves against Greece, Turkey is definitely decided to come into the war. He added that although they had no precise information, they estimated the number of German troops in Rumania at 180,000 (see my telegram No. 542 of today).

Repeated to Ankara.

LANE

740.0011 European War 1939/6870 : Telegram

The Minister in Yugoslavia (Lane) to the Secretary of State

BELGRADE, November 25, 1940—6 p. m.
[Received 10 : 27 p. m.]

546. Discussed this morning with the Prime Minister the possibility of German military cooperation with Italy against Greece and against Yugoslavia. He said that he was certain Germany would take no part in hostilities in the Balkans. I emphasized the following points in the hope of obtaining more comprehensive and detailed information:

1. Even though Italy might be reluctant for reasons of pride to request German assistance against Greece, can Germany permit the loss of prestige to the Axis which Italy's apparent military reverses at the hands of a small power would entail?
2. Is it logical that Germany with hundreds of idle divisions will permit its ally to suffer defeat?

His comments were generalized but were to the following effect: Italy's hate for Great Britain and France dates from their help to Italy after the defeat at Caporetto in 1917. Germany realizes this. The granting of aid to Italy against Greece might therefore eventually seriously jeopardize the solidarity of the Axis. On the other hand he admitted that Italy is making the Axis appear "ridiculous".

I hope to be able to telegraph the Department more analytically within the next few days.

LANE

740.0011 European War 1939/6876 : Telegram

The Minister in Yugoslavia (Lane) to the Secretary of State

BELGRADE, November 26, 1940—noon.
[Received November 26—11:29 a. m.]

548. The Minister of the Court informed me last evening that in the opinion of the Yugoslav General Staff, Mussolini had chosen for his present military adventure the most difficult terrain in Europe and at a most impropitious moment because of snow and rain. In reply to my question as to whether Germany would come to the aid of Italy he said with emphasis "No, Hitler is too wise". He added that Hitler cannot afford a defeat and that his General Staff is fully aware of the difficulties of a campaign in Greece. He said that the difference between Hitler and Mussolini is that the former is more of a realist.

I asked him in view of his seeming confidence that Germany would not advance in the Balkans how he could explain the adhesion of Hungary and Rumania to the Tripartite Pact and the visit of King Boris to Germany. He showed astonishment at my question saying that of course these moves were for the purpose of intimidating the United States.

As to Bulgaria Antic said that the agitation at the present time for territorial revindication at the expense of Yugoslavia might be understood if Italy were now victorious in Greece; under present conditions such a move is ridiculous.

LANE

740.0011 European War 1939/6881 : Telegram

The Ambassador in Turkey (MacMurray) to the Secretary of State

ANKARA, November 26, 1940—5 p. m.
[Received 9:35 p. m.]

211. Referring to Belgrade's telegram to the Department, No. 543, November 23, 5 p. m., Turkish Foreign Office estimates number of German troops in Rumania at 25 to 30,000. Reliable Rumanian and Yugoslav sources here give a similar figure.

The Embassy understands that the Turkish Government, which is watching carefully for any evidence of German preparations for military operations in the Balkans, has no information indicating that such preparations are in progress.

Turkish official circles incline to the opinion that Germany (which they consider to be pleased at the demonstration of the political and military incapacity of its ally) does not contemplate going to the aid of Italy in the near future.

Repeated to Belgrade.

MacMURRAY

740.0011 European War 1939/6935 : Telegram

The Minister in Greece (MacVeagh) to the Secretary of State

ATHENS, November 27, 1940—7 p. m.
[Received November 29—10:33 a. m.]

336. The Director of the Foreign Office told me this morning the Greek Government feels definitely encouraged regarding the general Balkan situation and believes that a number of influences may be working together to localize the Greco-Italian conflict at least for some time to come. Among these influences he specified Germany's interest in not extending the war to regions economically important to herself and ostensibly a Secretary of the German Legation who is credited with being the chief Nazi agent in Greece as saying that Germany will not attack this country so long as the British do not compel her to do so presumably by bringing over sufficiently important forces to threaten the constitution of an eastern front. In addition he spoke of the stiffening attitude of Yugoslavia and the recent Turkish military precautions both of which together with possible confidential expressions of Russian interest he thinks may be having an effect on Bulgarian policy.

As regards the military situation which is very briefly dealt with in staff communiqués he said that the Greek Army cannot keep pace with the newspaper reports but that it is nevertheless advancing satisfactorily. He said the Italian Army has been badly demoralized by the recent fighting, declared that the port of Durazzo has been practically destroyed from the air and was very optimistic as to the future if international complications can be avoided.

MACVEAGH

740.0011 European War 1939/6942 : Telegram

The Chargé in France (Matthews) to the Secretary of State

VICHY, November 29, 1940—6 p. m.
[Received 10:35 p. m.]

1059. Unoccupied France is indulging in many chuckles at a sign which has been posted on the Franco-Italian frontier at Mentone reading as follows: "Notice to the Greeks: This is the French frontier". I understand that the Italians find no humor in the sign and have officially "protested" to the French Government. Our correspondents have not been permitted to cable the story.

MATTHEWS

740.0011 European War 1939/6983 : Telegram

The Chargé in Italy (Reed) to the Secretary of State

ROME, December 3, 1940—noon.
[Received 1:10 p. m.]

1144. From an informed source I learn that the original plan for the invasion of Greece called for landings in force on Corfu and Cephalonia to support operations through the passes from Albania and was expected to overcome all Greek resistance in 8 days. The plan of operations had the approval of Badoglio who, however, was opposed to the campaign.

Storms along the Greek coast are said to have prevented the landing operations and thus led to the major reverses suffered by the Italian forces. Italian losses are described as very heavy and although reinforcements are reaching Albania satisfactorily, in large part by air, it is not believed that a strong counteroffensive can be begun for another 3 or 4 weeks. The High Command now considers that 4 or 5 months will be required for the successful conclusion of the campaign.

REED

740.0011 European War 1939/7160½

King George II of Greece to President Roosevelt [54]

TO THE PRESIDENT OF THE UNITED STATES:

In this hour in which my country is engaged in a hard and unequal struggle, forced upon it by an enemy whose actions are motivated by cruelty and violence, I am deeply moved by the warm sympathy and the keen interest manifested by the great Nation whose destinies you guide.

The noble American people have often in the past rendered assistance to my country in all critical moments of its history, and the recent organization of the Greek War Relief Association is further proof that philhellenism continues to inspire Americans of today in their lofty aims.

Guardians across the seas of the ideals for which throughout the centuries Greeks have lived and died, Americans today are aware that the Greek nation is again fighting for the principles of justice, truth and liberty, without which life for us is inconceivable.

I wish to assure you that with the help of the Almighty, we will march forward until our sacred struggle is crowned with success. All moral and material assistance will strengthen the heroic Greek army and bring it nearer to victory.

GEORGE II

---

[54] Transmitted to the President on December 3, 1940, by the Greek Minister.

740.0011 European War 1939/7160½ : Telegram

The Secretary of State to the Minister in Greece (MacVeagh)

WASHINGTON, December 6, 1940—3 p. m.

293. On December 3 the President received the following message from the King of Greece transmitted through the Greek Minister in Washington:

[Here follows text of message printed *supra*.]

The President has authorized the following message to be sent to the King as a reply.

"I thank Your Majesty for your friendly message which comes at a time when all free peoples are deeply impressed by the courage and steadfastness of the Greek nation.

The American Red Cross has already sent substantial amounts of funds and supplies for the relief of suffering in your country and I am sure that my countrymen will give generously to the new organizations which are being established for the same purpose.

As Your Majesty knows, it is the settled policy of the United States Government to extend aid to those governments and peoples who defend themselves against aggression. I assure Your Majesty that steps are being taken to extend such aid to Greece which is defending itself so valiantly."

Please see that the President's reply is delivered to the King as soon as possible.

Arrangements are being made with the Greek Minister here for release of the texts to the press December 7 at 10 : 30 a. m.[55]

HULL

740.0011 European War 1939/7063 : Telegram

The Minister in Greece (MacVeagh) to the Secretary of State

ATHENS, December 6, 1940—8 p. m.
[Received December 8—9 : 55 a. m.]

348. The Director General of the Foreign Office and the Turkish Ambassador both expressed to me yesterday their growing satisfaction with the present diplomatic situation in the Balkans and their belief that Germany intends to take no military measures here this winter. According to the former, routine relations between the Foreign Office and the German Legation continue smoothly.

On the Albanian front the Italians appear to be resorting to the rather desperate maneuver of throwing in reinforcements piecemeal. According to the British Military Attaché units of one and the same division have recently been captured at widely separated points along the front. He also said that the British are assisting the Greeks by

---

[55] See Department of State *Bulletin*, December 7, 1940, p. 503.

furnishing supplies and that the most pressing problem at present aside from obtaining planes is connected with the furnishing of ammunition most of the Greek cannon being of a different caliber from the British.

I have been confidentially informed from reliable sources that active Greek aviation has now been reduced from 105 to slightly over 30 planes owing not only to heavy outright losses but to the lack of repair facilities. There are 4 British squadrons now in Greece namely 1 pursuit squadron of gladiators, 2 of Blenheim bombers and 1 mixed. All are of reduced strength averaging 8 planes apiece although it is hoped that they may be filled up to 16 later on. In addition a fifth squadron is expected to arrive shortly but it is believed that no more than 5 can now be operated in Greece successfully on account of the present limited airfield capacity. With the exception of a military mission engaged in exploring the question of further assistance and despite radio and press propaganda to the contrary there are no British troops in this country today beyond those connected with the Royal Air Force as reported in my telegram 313 of November 18, 11 a. m.[56] These number abount 4,000.

MacVeagh

740.0011 European War 1939/7158 : Telegram

The Ambassador in Turkey (MacMurray) to the Secretary of State

ANKARA, December 14, 1940—noon.
[Received 6 : 32 p. m.]

219. In view of the repeated radio announcements from Germany that the Turkish Minister for Foreign Affairs has gone or is going to Athens to assist in arranging a compromise between Greece and Italy, it is perhaps not superfluous to report that the Minister has never entertained any such intention and is inclined to regard the reports as inspired by the Italians.

MacMurray

740.0011 European War 1939/7213 : Telegram

The Minister in Yugoslavia (Lane) to the Secretary of State

BELGRADE, December 19, 1940—1 p. m.
[Received 1 : 12 p. m.]

598. Yesterday afternoon a responsible Foreign Office official informed us confidentially as follows.

They have reports of dissatisfaction in Albania at the failure of Great Britain or Greece to announce specifically that their intention

[56] Not printed.

is to restore Albanian independence. The Albanians would welcome the immediate setting up of a provisional government at Koritza in order to set at rest their suspicions that Greece has designs on some of their territory. Such a move would also stir Albanians to greater behind-the-lines activity against the Italians.

Giving it as his personal opinion our informant added that it would be far [better] for Greece as well as for all the Balkan States if she had a satisfied Albania as a neighbor than if she tried to settle old claims by taking and keeping "a few Albanian towns". In the latter case Albania would again become a center of intrigue by any European power which desired to meddle in Balkan affairs.

Repeated to Athens.

LANE

740.0011 European War 1939/7244 : Telegram

The Minister in Greece (MacVeagh) to the Secretary of State

ATHENS, December 21, 1940—9 a. m.
[Received December 22—4:15 a. m.]

374. With reference to telegram No. 598, December 19, 1 p. m. from Belgrade, Albanian suspicions of Greek intentions would appear unjustified in view of a statement made by Mr. Metaxas over the radio after the fall of Koritza on November 23, "We are fighting not only for our existence but for the other Balkan peoples too, and for the liberation of Albania". The Director General of the Foreign Office with whom I have had several conversations, as also with the Under Secretary for Foreign Affairs and other officials on this subject, expressed the opinion to me this morning that Italian propaganda may be at work in this connection. Greek aims, he said, are clear so far as they go. On the other hand he professed to regard Albanian aid to either side in the present conflict as relatively unimportant.

What will be done if and when Albania is liberated is another question which the Greeks appear to feel had better be taken up when the time arrives. In addition they are quite aware that its solution will not depend upon them alone. They undoubtedly hope to regain southern Albania where the Greek population predominates but are indifferent as to the fate of the rest of the country. Meanwhile, according to the Director General, to set up a provisional Albanian government in the rear of the Greek Army is impractical on account of the necessities of the military situation and because of the existence of factional dissensions among the Albanians themselves.

MACVEAGH

740.0011 European War 1939/7240 : Telegram

The Chargé in Germany (Morris) to the Secretary of State

BERLIN, December 22, 1940—2 p. m.
[Received 5 p. m.]

5136. The Greek Minister here was recently approached by an unofficial but authorized German in regard to the Italo-Greek conflict. It was pointed out to the Minister that the defeat of England was a certainty within the next few months, Greece would then have to accept any terms imposed by Italy. At present a German mediation asked for by Greece could result in an honorable and even advantageous peace for Greece. Germany would not fail to weigh favorably to Greece its fine military accomplishments. As to procedure it was suggested that the Minister recommend that his Government request one of its neighbors, either Yugoslavia or Turkey, to lay before the German Government a Greek request for German mediation. The Minister rejected this proposal observing that a victorious nation does not ask for mediation and stating his belief that the successful resistance of Greece to the Italian attack had served the interest of Germany itself by eliminating Italian pretentions to a political overlordship in the Balkans which would eventually embarrass Germany's plans in this part of Europe. In the event of England's defeat the Minister felt confident that the Führer would take into consideration this fact together with his admiration of Greek spirit and culture to forbid Italy to impose any harsh terms. The Minister indeed felt that Greece would be allowed to retain the Greek inhabited portions of South Albania to which she has an ethnological ground and which her armies are conquering no matter which side wins.

Above message would have been repeated to Athens if records showed that they had this code.

MORRIS

740.0011 European War 1939/7329 : Telegram

The Ambassador in the Soviet Union (Steinhardt) to the Secretary of State

MOSCOW, December 30, 1940—4 p. m.
[Received 8 : 05 p. m.]

1802. The Greek Minister informed a member of my staff last night in confidence that it was the understanding of his Government based on intimations from the German Government that Germany would not intervene directly in the Italian-Greek war unless (1) the British attempted to establish a second general front in the Balkans through the dispatch of troops to Macedonia or (2) the British endeavored to use air bases in Greece for the purpose of bombarding the Rumanian oil wells. The Minister added that insofar as he was aware this remained the general policy of Germany in regard to the Italian-Greek war and he referred in this connection to the "entirely correct" behavior of the German Legation in Athens towards the Greek Government.

STEINHARDT

740.0011 European War 1939/7374 : Telegram

The Minister in Greece (MacVeagh) to the Secretary of State

ATHENS, December 31, 1940—6 p. m.
[Received January 1, 1941—1: 35 p. m.]

381. Department's telegram No. 316, December 28, 5 p. m.[57] When I queried him in general terms this morning the Under Secretary for Foreign Affairs would not say that there have been any German attempts at mediation in the Greco-Italian war though he admitted in this connection what he called "rumors in Berlin". On the same subject, the Director of the Foreign Office yesterday made a similar evasion but went on to say that mediation is out of the question in any case since Greece could accept only a victorious settlement at present including such things as territorial readjustment and the payment of a large indemnity as well as recognition of the fact that Greece cannot compel the British to leave the positions here which they have already occupied. Regarding "territorial readjustment" he said that he could make no official definition of Greek war aims but pointed to the fact which is becoming daily more evident in the press that national aspirations are being aroused as a result of Greek victories for the return of northern Epirus and the Dodecanese.

Since a rumor has reached here from Sofia alleging secret Greco-Bulgarian conversations in that city, I sounded out both the Under Secretary and the Director General on this subject. The Under Secretary said that he thought Bulgaria is now well content to remain neutral between the conflicting pressures of the colossi Germany and Russia. To a question as to whether under these conditions a move to attract her into a new entente for the preservation of Balkan integrity and independence might not be in order he replied, "This is not the time". In this connection he particularly cited Turkish suspicions of Bulgaria which he said would dictate the retention of Turkish military forces in eastern Thrace and thus practically nullify

[57] Not printed; it merely repeated the information contained in telegram No. 5136, December 22, 2 p. m., from the Chargé in Germany, p. 572.

any peace pact which might be made between the two. When I asked the Director General a question along the same lines but specifically citing the possibility of an Aegean exit I received only the old answers that Bulgaria has no right to such an exit and could not be trusted to be content with it if obtained.

The Under Secretary appeared more interested in what is going on in the West particularly in France at present than in purely Balkan developments, feeling that the former will decide the direction to be taken by the latter. Both he and the Director General indicated that despite local successes the military situation in Albania remains essentially as reported in my telegram 368, December 14, 7 p. m. section 2.[58]

Salonika was bombed again yesterday and some damage was done to property near the Consulate but there were few casualties and Consul Johnson has reported all Americans safe.

Department's telegrams 311, 312 received December 22; 313, 314 December 25; 315 December 28.[59]

MacVeagh

III. Requests by the Greek Government for Aid in Supplies and Credits From the United States

868.24/88 : Telegram

The Minister in Greece (MacVeagh) to the Secretary of State

ATHENS, June 21, 1940—6 p. m.
[Received 6:37 p. m.]

147. The Greek Chief of Staff today urgently requested Captain Johnson [60] to ascertain by telegraph whether the American Army or American industries can supply Greece promptly with 150 French 75-millimeter guns, 150 37- to 47-millimeter anti-tank guns, 30 light tanks and 5 or 6 anti-aircraft batteries with appurtenances.

In view of the existing impediments to delivery, the General's request would appear to merit comment. He maintained that transportation can be found which may of course be possible though it appears to me highly unlikely. But the possibility cannot be wholly excluded that he may be lending himself to some German maneuver to sew up remaining American material in advance of further Allied orders, since German influence here is increasing by leaps and bounds.

MacVeagh

---

[58] Not printed.
[59] None printed.
[60] Capt. Max S. Johnson, formerly Assistant Military Attaché in France, on temporary duty in Greece pending arrival of permanent Military Attaché.

868.24/88 : Telegram

The Secretary of State to the Minister in Greece (MacVeagh)

WASHINGTON, June 24, 1940—6 p. m.

149. Your No. 147, June 21, 6 p. m. The President has established an Interdepartmental Liaison Committee [61] to deal with foreign purchasing missions. That Committee is in a position to furnish all necessary information and advice to representatives of foreign governments referred to it by the Department. It cannot, however, undertake to deal with these matters by any other procedure. Therefore, if the Greek Government desires to purchase arms in this country, it should send appropriate instructions to its Legation here or to some other authorized representative acting on its behalf and not as a broker on commission. Should the Greek Minister or any other authorized representative of the Greek Government approach the Department in regard to this matter, the statements in paragraph 2 of your telegram under acknowledgment will be borne in mind when the matter is brought to the attention of the Liaison Committee.

HULL

711.00111 Armament Control—Military Secrets/3533

The Greek Minister (Diamantopoulos) to the Secretary of State

No. 1456

The Minister of Greece presents his compliments to His Excellency the Secretary of State and has the honor to request that the President's Liaison Committee be communicated with in order that a permit be granted to the Namstrad Inc., 405 Lexington Avenue, New York City, for the sale of fifty (50) to seventy-five (75) Vultee Pursuit Planes, to the Royal Greek Government.

In view of the urgency of the above request, the Minister of Greece should greatly appreciate receiving an early reply on this matter.

WASHINGTON, September 17, 1940.

711.00111 Armament Control—Military Secrets/3570

The Greek Minister (Diamantopoulos) to the Secretary of State

No. 1594

The Minister of Greece presents his compliments to His Excellency the Secretary of State and has the honor to enclose herewith two applications [62] for license to export arms, ammunition, or implements

[61] See *United States Government Manual*, Fall 1940, p. 59b.
[62] Not attached to file copy.

of war, for Mr. M. Cavalliotis, agent of the Aegean Trading Company, 154 Nassau Street, New York City, acting for the Greek Government for the supply of war materials, with the request that same be transmitted to the appropriate authorities.

The Minister of Greece wishes to express his thanks to His Excellency the Secretary of State for his good offices in this matter.

WASHINGTON, October 11, 1940.

711.00111 Armament Control—Military Secrets/3574

Memorandum by the Greek Legation [63]

WASHINGTON, October 16, 1940.

1. On September 17, 1940, letter No. 1456, was sent to the Department of State asking for 50–75 Vultee Pursuit Planes.

2. On October 14th, we asked for 50 Single Seat Fighters, produced by the Canadian Car and Foundry Company, but built by the Columbia Aircraft at Port Washington, New York. (Letter No. 1596— President's Liaison Committee).[64]

3. Also an application was made for the export of 60 Seversky Single Seaters, ordered by the Swedish Government, transmitted to the State Department by our letter No. 1594 of October 11th, 1940.

711.00111 Armament Control—Military Secrets/3574

Memorandum by the Under Secretary of State (Welles) [65]

[WASHINGTON,] October 17, 1940.

This urgent memorandum [66] was left with me by the Greek Minister yesterday. Under instructions from his Government, the Minister made an impassioned plea that Greece be given the opportunity to increase her defenses by obtaining the aviation matériel desired. I gave to the Minister as sympathetic a response as I could, but I made it clear that I was not informed as to the facts involved and that I feared that our own national defense requirements and our existing commitments would make it impossible for any immediate practical assistance to be afforded. Please look into the matter again and let me know what final reply I should make to the Minister.

---

[63] Handed to the Under Secretary of State by the Greek Minister, October 16, 1940.

[64] Not found in Department files.

[65] Addressed to the Chief of the Division of Near Eastern Affairs (Murray), the Acting Chief of the Division of European Affairs (Atherton), and the Chief of the Division of Controls (Green).

[66] *Supra.*

711.00111 Armament Control—Military Secrets/3574

Memorandum by the Chief of the Division of Near Eastern Affairs (Murray) to the Under Secretary of State (Welles)

[WASHINGTON,] October 23, 1940.

MR. WELLES: This Division has given consideration to the question of the export of airplanes to Greece in connection with each of the three groups of planes (Vultee, Columbia, and Seversky) mentioned by the Minister in his memorandum of October 16. I am of the opinion that it would be unwise to hamper our own defense needs by insisting upon the exportation of these military planes to Greece.

I am led to this conclusion from the following considerations, based on our best information regarding the situation in Greece: (1) Mr. MacVeagh, our Minister in Athens, has reported that although there is increasing Greek public opinion in favor of resisting aggression and that the Metaxas Government has repeatedly declared that Greece will fight "to the last man", Mr. MacVeagh still sees the possibility, if not the probability, that Greece still might submit, without fighting, to determined Axis demands. In view of our principal desire to avoid allowing planes to fall into Axis hands, the risk involved in sending valuable planes to Greece at this time is a major consideration. (2) Granted that Greece might resist, the Greek Army is neither well-trained nor well-equipped, and would probably offer little difficulty for a well-mechanized attacking force. Greece is particularly lacking in trained aviators and mechanics such as would be required to operate modern American-made planes. Therefore, even if American planes sent to Greece should avoid capture by Italy, they would probably not accomplish any important military result when manned by Greek pilots. (3) Since Great Britain has guaranteed Greek independence and is primarily responsible for the defense of that country, the planes which we are able to spare for export would be put to a much better use if supplied to Britain rather than to Greece.

Some considerations which might be listed in favor of selling a few planes to Greece are as follows: (1) Greece is faced with the question whether to resist aggression. There is strong public sentiment in favor of such resistance, and an indication from the United States, however small, of a desire to assist Greece might furnish the necessary encouragement to keep Greece in this frame of mind, while a refusal to permit Greece to obtain any of the three groups of airplanes so urgently requested by the Minister might cause his Government to feel that resistance is useless if the United States has no desire to lend any assistance. (2) Although some risk would undoubtedly be involved in supplying planes to Greece, a small number might be a sufficiently important token of our desire to assist Greece to hold the country in line, and the results which might be accomplished may be important enough to outweigh the risk, it being frequently impossible to avoid all risk in matters of this kind.   (3) Unlike some of the other countries which Britain has agreed to help, Greece is within the reach of the British Mediterranean fleet.   It is reported that the British would occupy Crete and some other Greek islands if Greece were attacked.   The Greek Government would doubtless find Greek soil on which to maintain resistance for a considerable time.   Aid to Greece would therefore not involve as much risk as would aid to a country not so favorably situated as regards assistance from the British fleet.   (4) Italy, which is already launched, apparently irrevocably, on its Egyptian compaign,[67] may hesitate to attack Greece if there is indication that any considerable fighting would result.   A little assistance to Greece on our part might be sufficient to enable that country to save itself from attack by a show of some resisting power, at least as long as the Egyptian campaign is in progress.

While the above considerations have merit, I am inclined to think the arguments *against* selling planes to Greece the stronger, and am accordingly not prepared to recommend that the refusals already made in the present cases be changed.

WALLACE MURRAY

711.00111 Armament Control—Military Secrets/3574

Memorandum by the Under Secretary of State (Welles) to the Chief of the Division of Near Eastern Affairs (Murray)

[WASHINGTON,] October 24, 1940.

MR. MURRAY: I agree completely with the opinion expressed in the last paragraph of your memorandum.[68]   Please see the Greek Minister for me and take care to explain to him that our present situation makes it impossible, after full consideration, for us to do anything in the way of assistance to Greece through supplying airplanes for some time to come.

711.00111 Armament Control—Military Secrets/3574

Memorandum by the Chief of the Division of Near Eastern Affairs (Murray) to the Under Secretary of State (Welles)

[WASHINGTON,] October 26, 1940.

Mr. WELLES: In accordance with the instructions contained in your attached memorandum of October 24 last,[68] I requested the Greek

---

[67] For correspondence on this subject, see pp. 465 ff.
[68] *Supra.*

Minister to come to see me today in order that I might discuss with him the desire of his Government, which the Minister conveyed to you on October 16 last, to obtain urgently certain aviation matériel set forth in a memorandum which the Minister left with you.

I explained to the Minister that he was doubtless aware of the dual effort which was being undertaken at the present moment both to accord every possible assistance to Great Britain in her hour of need as well as to meet the enormous requirements of this Government in its rearmament program. I said I felt sure that the Minister's Government shared our views as to the desirability and necessity of rendering Great Britain every possible aid short of war.

I furthermore referred to the recent instances of airplane orders from both Sweden and Siam and pointed out that in these cases the orders had actually been paid for and, in the case of Siam, shipped and under way to that country and that despite this fact this Government had felt it necessary to exercise its authority to take over the planes in both cases. Such being the case the Minister would of course understand that our attitude in the case of the present request for assistance to Greece was based upon considerations that were applicable in other equally urgent instances.

I added that the Greek Government undoubtedly appreciated the fact that aid without stint to Great Britain was indirectly aid to Greece in view of Great Britain's commitments to that country, and in this the Minister heartily concurred.

Mr. Diamantopoulos then went on to say that this whole incident had in fact served a very useful purpose as far as he was concerned, namely that it would afford him an opportunity to impress upon his Government the desirability of concentrating authority in matters of this kind entirely in his hands. He said he had been considerably embarrassed by the fact that in the case of these very planes now under discussion the matter had dragged along for several months in the hands of agents unfortunately authorized by the Greek Government to handle the matter, and that only after the agents had proved themselves incapable of getting results he had been requested to bring the matter urgently to your attention. I assured the Minister that we, too, could only welcome this simplification of procedure and reminded him that others of his colleagues, notably the Turk and the Egyptian, had, through personal experience, been able to persuade their governments to eliminate all intermediaries in the matter of arms orders and to concentrate authority solely in their hands.

Mr. Diamantopoulos thanked me profusely for the interest which the Department had shown in this matter and said he fully understood our position, which he would not fail to convey to his Government.

WALLACE MURRAY

868.24/89 : Telegram

The Minister in Greece (MacVeagh) to the Secretary of State

ATHENS, November 2, 1940—2 a. m.
[Received 1 : 50 p. m.]

275. Baker [70] has been informed by the British Military Attaché who has already taken up quarters with the Greek General Staff [71] that the Greek Army is short of anti-aircraft ammunition and desires 50,000 rounds of type Krupp 88 millimeters fuse type UZS–30 weight 385 kilograms. The Attaché has wired London to know whether this can be obtained anywhere in the Western Hemisphere either complete ammunition or a fuse suitable of being adapted. He is confident that his Government will soon communicate with Washington and suggests that a preliminary investigation of opportunities might be useful.

I transmit this for the Department's information and for such use as it may wish to make of it.

MACVEAGH

740.0011 European War 1939/6491 : Telegram

The Chargé in the United Kingdom (Johnson) to the Secretary of State

LONDON, November 5, 1940—7 p. m.
[Received 8 : 05 p. m.]

3639. The British Government has received both through the Greek Minister in London and the British Minister at Athens a long list of military requirements which the Greek Government desires urgently, covering the greatest variety of ammunition and different kinds of armament. According to a responsible Foreign Office official, although this request is now being given careful study by the departments concerned it will not be possible to meet all of the Greek desires, some of which were characterized as being beyond any reasonable requirement. It is quite evident that America is being looked to as the eventual source of supply for at least some of this material, and I understand that the British have under consideration working the matter through Purvis [72] with instructions for him to give all the assistance that he can, compatible with the good will of the American authorities and with British requirements, in support of Greek en-

---

[70] Maj. Joseph K. Baker, Military Attaché in Greece.
[71] Following outbreak of war between Italy and Greece, October 28, 1940. For correspondence on this subject, see pp. 524 ff.
[72] Arthur Blaikie Purvis, Director-General of the British Purchasing Commission, and Chairman of the Anglo-French Purchasing Board.

deavors to fill their needs in the United States. The Foreign Office informed me that the Greek Minister had stated a copy of the list of requirements he gave to the Foreign Office was likewise being given to me but I have not yet received it.

Responsible and well-informed officials with whom I have had various conversations on the subject of the new situation in the Mediterranean show, perhaps involuntarily, their satisfaction that the British forces in the Mediterranean will now have more advantageous bases for holding the eastern part of the sea and for offensive action against Italy. They speak of Great Britain's determination to give Greece all aid possible. Almost in the same breath however they manifest doubt as to the amount of material assistance which Great Britain will be able to give. Having advantageous bases in Crete and [apparent omission] is only of relative value, if defense against enemy bombers is inadequate and I have found little sign of certainty that sufficient help can be brought in time to save Greece itself from being overrun. Expressions of confidence go rather to a long view and to the improved position in the Mediterranean which occupation of Greek island and other bases should afford the British Fleet and Air Force.

JOHNSON

740.0011 European War 1939/6500 : Telegram

The Chargé in the United Kingdom (Johnson) to the Secretary of State

LONDON, November 6, 1940—7 p. m.
[Received November 6—3 p. m.]

3653. My 3639, November 5, 7 p. m. The Greek Minister informed me last night that he had been intrusted by his Government to make an appeal to the United States Government through this Embassy for its approval and support of the Greek requests for war requirements. M. Simopoulos [73] said that the request would be made of course directly to the Department by the Greek Minister in Washington, but that he had been specially instructed to parallel the request here. I also understand from the Minister that his Government does not contemplate sending a special purchasing or procurement mission to the United States, but that they hope to make arrangements whereby Purvis, the British purchasing agent, will likewise act on behalf of the Greeks.

JOHNSON

---

[73] Charalambos Simopoulos, Greek Minister in the United Kingdom.

868.24/108

Memorandum of Conversation, by Mr. George V. Allen of the Division of Near Eastern Affairs

[WASHINGTON,] November 6, 1940.

Participants: Mr. George S. Depasta, Counselor of the Greek Legation

Mr. Murray

Mr. Allen

Mr. Depasta said that his Legation had just received a long and urgent telegram from its Government listing numerous military supplies which it desired to purchase in the United States. Mr. Depasta said that a finished text of the telegram was not yet ready, but that he desired to leave a memorandum listing the principal types of material desired [74] and would transmit to the Department a complete text of the telegram as soon as possible.

Mr. Depasta said that his Government had also requested its Legation in London to approach the British Government in an endeavor to obtain the assistance of that Government in persuading the United States to permit Greece to purchase the desired supplies here. He said that he had telephoned to the British Embassy in Washington and had learned that the Embassy had not yet received any information from London on this subject.

Mr. Depasta said that in view of the fact that his country was engaged in armed resistance to an unprovoked attack, he hoped very much that his request would receive the most sympathetic consideration by the American Government. He referred to the friendly attitude the United States has maintained towards Greece and the well-known desire of the United States to assist small nations which are attacked by powerful neighbors.

Mr. Murray asked Mr. Depasta to supply detailed information regarding the material desired. He said that meanwhile due note would be taken of his memorandum.

868.248/74

Memorandum by the Chief of the Division of Near Eastern Affairs (Murray) to the Chief of the Division of Controls (Green)

[WASHINGTON,] November 7, 1940.

With reference to the request of the Greek Government to purchase military supplies in the United States, as embodied in a memorandum handed to me yesterday by the Counselor of the Greek Legation, I

---

[74] Not found in Department files.

may refer to my memorandum of October 23, 1940, addressed to Mr. Welles on the subject of the desire of the Greek Government to purchase airplanes in the United States. The conclusion was drawn that we should not recommend any reconsideration of the application for certain planes mentioned by the Greek Minister, which had already been refused.

Although the above-mentioned memorandum concerned only airplanes, the general considerations involved in the question of aid to Greece were discussed. Some of these considerations have been affected by developments since that time. On October 23 it was not certain whether Greece would actively resist with its armed forces an attack by Italy. It seems evident at present that the Greek Government is making a determined resistance, and with some measure of success. Greece is therefore in the category of a small nation, object of unprovoked aggression, which has resisted with the military force at its command. As such, its request for permission to purchase arms and material in this country would appear to be entitled to as sympathetic consideration as we may accord, depending of course on our own defense needs. A refusal to permit Greek purchases in the United States at this time could be based only on our own requirements of the materials desired. Certainly we would not be justified in withholding from Greece at present any material for which we have a surplus production capacity.

Decision regarding the Greek Government's present request for military supplies therefore seems to rest with the appropriate authorities of this Government familiar with our own defense needs. I recommend as sympathetic consideration as may be consonant with those needs.

WALLACE MURRAY

868.24/90 : Telegram

The Minister in Greece (MacVeagh) to the Secretary of State

ATHENS, November 8, 1940—7 p. m.
[Received November 9—4 : 50 p. m.]

290. For the President: Premier Metaxas has asked me to convey to you his personal felicitations on your re-election and the joy which he feels in its happy augury for the world. In addition both he and the King have asked me to bring to your attention efforts recently made by the Greek authorities to buy 60 pursuit planes in the United States, efforts which they say came to nothing because of British priority. They state that they have now requested the British, in view of the new situation and Greece's desperate need under indiscriminate bombing, to waive this priority and that all details together

with specifications covering other desired matériel are either in the hands of the Greek Legation in Washington or being forwarded by cable today.

The Premier has given me the following message for you.

"Because she wished to maintain her neutrality, Greece has been subjected to brutal aggression but has risen as one man to defend her liberty, her independence and her honor.   I appeal in this grave hour to Your Excellency's high sense of justice for an extension of aid to Greece in a struggle which however unequal must be victorious in a sacred cause.   Such aid could best consist in the prompt delivery of munitions and raw materials.   I have supplied a list of these to the Greek Legation in Washington and permit myself to call it to Your Excellency's personal attention through the kind offices of the American Legation in Athens."

Both the King and the Premier wish to make it clear that only the present critical situation and not a desire to escape from normal channels which they are using to the best of their abilities in any case prompts their addressing you personally in such a matter.

MacVeagh

868.24/97

Memorandum by the Chief of the Division of Controls (Green) to the Chief of the Division of Near Eastern Affairs (Murray)

[Washington,] November 9, 1940.

In the course of a telephone conversation late yesterday afternoon with Mr. Philip Young, Assistant to the Secretary of the Treasury and Chairman of the President's Liaison Committee, Mr. Young referred to our conversation on November 6 in regard to the desire of the Greek Government to purchase arms in this country.

I told Mr. Young that I had not seen the Greek Minister as yet, but that, as soon as the Minister called, I would send Mr. Young full information in regard to my conversation and in regard to the desires of the Greek Government.

Mr. Young told me that Mr. Purvis, Chief of the British Purchasing Commission, had called on him during the day and had informed him that he had just received a telegram from London in regard to this matter.   Mr. Purvis said that the military authorities in London were canvassing the situation with a view to furnishing the Greeks with such arms as they could spare.   Mr. Purvis said that his Government hoped that this Government would not make any commitments to furnish arms to the Greeks until the British Government had had an opportunity to ascertain what deliveries it could make to the Greeks from supplies now in its hands.   If, after the

British had delivered arms to the Greeks, the Greek Government still desired to obtain arms in this country, the British Government hoped that arrangements could be made whereby the British Purchasing Commission would be charged with making purchases on behalf of the Greeks.

I told Mr. Young that, when I saw the Greek Minister, I would suggest to the Minister that he call on him, and that, when the Minister called, he would have an opportunity to make the necessary suggestions to the Minister.

Mr. Young said that it was his understanding that the Greek Minister had already had some conversations with the British Purchasing Commission, had been informed of what the British were doing and were proposing to do for his Government, and had entered into some sort of tentative arrangement with the Commission.

JOSEPH C. GREEN

868.24/99

Memorandum of Conversation, by the Chief of the Division of Controls (Green)

[WASHINGTON,] November 12, 1940.

The Greek Minister called at my Office this afternoon. He handed me the attached list of arms [75] which his Government desires to purchase and told me that he had been charged with the duty of acting as agent for his Government in connection with purchases of arms in this country.

I told the Minister that I was very glad to hear that his Government had charged him with this duty. I said that this Government had found it highly undesirable to deal with intermediaries, brokers, commission merchants, etc., and that purchasing governments had also found that the results of using such intermediaries were unsatisfactory. I suggested that, as he was now in charge of this matter of purchasing arms, he should, as soon as possible, confer with Mr. Philip Young, Assistant to the Secretary of the Treasury and Chairman of the President's Liaison Committee charged with assisting foreign purchasing missions and coordinating their purchases with those of this Government.

The Minister thanked me for the suggestion and asked me to make an appointment for him with Mr. Young.

I told the Minister that I should be glad to do so. I said that I had already discussed the matter of purchases by the Greek Government, and that Mr. Young had informed me that he had already discussed it with Mr. Purvis, Chief of the British Purchasing Commission. I said

---

[75] Not printed.

that it was my understanding that the British Government was canvassing the situation in Britain with a view to determining the extent to which the Greek needs could be met from supplies of arms in that country; that, after this had been determined, the British Government would instruct its purchasing mission to canvas the possibility of making available to the Greeks some of the arms which it was purchasing in this country; and that only after that was it contemplated that the Greek Government would place its own orders here.

The Minister said that that was also his understanding, and that he had discussed the matter with Mr. Purvis.

The Minister then raised the question of credits, expressing the hope that this Government would make arrangements whereby long-term credits could be extended to facilitate Greek purchases in this country.

I told the Minister that that was a question which he would have to take up with Mr. Young.

November 13, 1940.

I called Mr. Young by telephone this morning and made an appointment for the Greek Minister to see him this afternoon. I told him of my conversation with the Minister and added that the Department hoped that some means would be found to furnish the Greeks with some of the arms which they desire to obtain.

JOSEPH C. GREEN

868.48/975 : Telegram

The Minister in Greece (MacVeagh) to the Secretary of State

ATHENS, November 13, 1940—3 p. m.
[Received November 15—1 : 55 a. m.]

302. To centralize and expedite the purchase and transportation to Greece of essential foreign products for civilian needs especially foodstuffs both for civilian and fighting forces but not military supplies the Government has created the Greek Supply Office with subsidiary agencies at New York (headed by Greek Consul General), Alexandria and Bombay. Purchases will be made on commercial basis without adjudication against payment in United States or British funds. Available Greek tonnage will be requisitioned by the Government to transport United States purchases as quickly as possible via South Africa. For some weeks at least authorities here anticipate such requisitioned vessels will be required exclusively for Government cargo but hope rapidly to elaborate the shipping facilities between Greece and the United States in expectation of increasing dependence on our sources of supply as German and other nearby sources decrease or disappear. The Minister of National Economy states the normal Greek import quota system is necessarily suspended and all private

imports will be subject to special permit on each shipment, issuance depending primarily on availability of shipping and essentiality of product.

MacVeagh

868.24/98

Memorandum of Conversation, by the Chief of the Division of Near Eastern Affairs (Murray)

[Washington,] November 13, 1940.

The Greek Minister called on me by appointment on November 12 and left with me the attached memorandum [76] setting forth in some detail the various items of military material which the Minister states is urgently needed by his Government and the furnishing of which his Government hopes will be facilitated by every possible means by this Government. The Minister added that this matter had been taken up with the British Government with a request that if necessary the British purchasing authorities in this country assist the Greek Government in obtaining these supplies.

Mr. Diamantopoulos added that his Government earnestly hoped in this connection that credits for the purchase of the present supplies could be furnished not only by the American Government but also by private concerns with which the orders would be placed.

The Minister also remarked that the present communication could be taken by us as an indication that the Greek Government desires it to handle orders of this kind exclusively through its Legation in Washington and that the endeavors of agents hitherto acting for the Greek Government in connection with such orders could in the future be ignored.

I told the Minister that I would bring his communication and remarks to the immediate attention of the appropriate authorities.

868.51/1614 : Telegram

The Minister in Greece (MacVeagh) to the Secretary of State

Athens, November 14, 1940—noon.
[Received November 15—9 : 40 a. m.]

305. The Minister of Finance called on me last Saturday in connection with the possible extension of dollar credits to Greece. I advised him that such a matter might better be taken up directly with the Department through the Greek Minister at Washington and this I understand is being done. He has also, however, addressed me a

[76] Not printed.
303207—58——38

5-page appeal which he requests that I forward together with a favorable report of my own.

Briefly summarized his appeal states: While the British have already extended an initial credit of 5,000,000 pounds it may be used only for purchases within the British Empire or for internal needs through the issue of drachma notes against cover in pounds. Consequently British credits will take care of only a fraction of Greece's urgent needs since such items as wheat, sugar, wool, iron, tires, sanitary materials, motor vehicles, etc., must be purchased from the United States or from other countries which demand payment in dollars. Since Greece's supply of dollar exchange is no longer being replenished her reserves will thus be quickly exhausted. American assistance is, therefore, implored in supplying the necessary credits or money or the goods themselves. If that extension of credit for the sale of military goods is impossible under American laws then the supply of non-military items or the granting of open credits available for purchases of the latter either in the United States or, in cases of emergency, in other countries, becomes a question of imperious necessity. The Minister mentions the recent transfer of $100,000 against interest due this month on the American section of the refugee loan as the latest evidence of Greece's determination to honor her obligations; and, citing the example of the United States' assistance to Finland, he appeals to American generosity and philhellenism in extending similar financial aid to Greece. He adds that the Greek Minister at Washington will approach the Department with regard to specific needs.

I am aware that the direct extension of credit to Greece is impossible under the terms of the Johnson Act.[78] Furthermore, I have suggested to the Minister of Finance as well as the King and the Prime Minister, in previous conversation that they might do well to handle the question of supplies from the United States through the medium of their British ally. However, Greece's need appears to be as urgent as her cause is just, and I hope that every possibility of the extension of indirect assistance will be explored with generous consideration.

MacVeagh

868.24/89 : Telegram

The Acting Secretary of State to the Minister in Greece (MacVeagh)

WASHINGTON, November 15, 1940—8 p. m.

262. Your No. 275, November 2, 2 a. m. The Department and other interested agencies of the Government have been annoyed by the

---

[78] 48 Stat. 574.

activities of private firms claiming to be authorized agents of the Greek Government for the purchase of arms. The Department has informed the Greek Minister here that his Government's requests could be dealt with more effectively if he or some responsible Greek official were appointed the Greek Government's official purchasing agent, and that endeavors to purchase through private agents, either American or Greek, be terminated. The Turkish Ambassador in Washington has acted successfully as agent for the large purchases of his Government in the United States, thus eliminating private dealings and commissions. The new arrangement by which it appears that Greek purchases are to be handled by the Greek Minister cooperating with the British Purchasing Commission is entirely satisfactory. The Minister and the Chief of the Commission are now in consultation in regard to this matter with the Liaison Committee charged by the President with assisting foreign purchasing missions and coordinating their purchases with those of this Government.

You are requested to inform the Greek Government of the foregoing.

WELLES

868.24/90 : Telegram

The Acting Secretary of State to the Minister in Greece (MacVeagh)

WASHINGTON, November 16, 1940—3 p. m.

266. Your No. 290, November 8, 7 p. m. The contents of your message have been conveyed to the President, who has expressed his sincere thanks for the Prime Minister's cordial remarks regarding the recent elections in this country, and his appreciation of the considerations which have led to the Minister's personal appeal for assistance to Greece.

As regards the latter, the President has instructed the appropriate authorities of this Government to pursue actively the negotiations which they have undertaken with the Greek Minister in Washington and the British Purchasing Commission in connection with the desire of Greece to obtain material in the United States.

In view of the extent to which the industry of the United States has already obligated itself to fill orders accepted from Great Britain, the Department believes that Greek purchases may most advantageously be handled through the British Commission and recommends the continuation of this procedure.

WELLES

868.24/99

Memorandum by the Under Secretary of State (Welles) to the Chief of the Division of Controls (Green)

[WASHINGTON,] November 18, 1940.

MR. GREEN: The Greek Minister called to see me to take up the matter mentioned in your memorandum.[79] I told him I would try to give him a definite reply by Wednesday afternoon. In other words, I see no reason for letting the Greek Government continue to have the hope of our doing something if it cannot be done. The question is one of vital importance to them as I understand it. I shall talk with General Marshall and the Secretary of War personally about this and let you know.

868.24/91 : Telegram

The Minister in Greece (MacVeagh) to the Secretary of State

ATHENS, November 18, 1940—7 p. m.
[Received November 19—7: 55 p. m.]

316. I saw the Prime Minister this morning and gave him the President's message as contained in the Department's 266, November 16. At the same time I informed him of the Department's views as expressed in that telegram and in the Department's 262, November 15, 8 p. m. In addition, I told him of the issuance of the President's proclamation of neutrality as suggested in the Department's 263, November 15 [16], 9 p. m.[80] And finally, I gave him a draft for $10,000 payable to the Greek Red Cross, together with a letter to that organization and an *aide-mémoire*, both stating explicitly the purpose for which this donation is made and adding the information regarding the purchase of milk in Yugoslavia, all as instructed in the Department's telegram No. 261, November 15.[81]

The Prime Minister expressed his appreciation but appeared very worried. He told me that though the Greeks have so far been able to advance satisfactorily, they were subjected yesterday to attack from no less than 500 bombers and dive-bombers and that today the Italians have brought up even more of these planes. The small Greek aviation, he added, is practically exhausted, and under such conditions the Greek troops not only cannot continue advancing but are hard put to it to hold their ground. He asked that I telegraph this information as confirming the urgent necessity reported in the Legation's telegram No. 290, November 8, 7 p. m.

---

[79] Memorandum dated November 12, p. 585.
[80] *Ante*, p. 561.
[81] Not printed.

I reminded him that to get planes from America, even if it were possible, must take a long time and in this connection he assured me that at the present critical moment, he is making every effort to obtain British airplanes from Egypt, estimating that 150 fighters and bombers would make all the difference between success and failure. He said that he had even telegraphed to Mr. Churchill, himself, in this regard and added that as nothing serious has as yet developed in Egypt, the planes so necessary on this front might conceivably be spared from there for return later. The Premier said that Germany has so far remained at least ostensibly neutral and has given no aid to the Italians either in troops or in planes but reiterated that should Italian bombing of Monastir and other Serbian towns provoke Yugoslavia to open hostilities, Germany might be forced to come in, in which case "we would be lost".

The Prime Minister's plain speaking is not paralleled by the General Staff which gave the Military Attachés this morning no information beyond that contained in the official communiqué.

Department's telegram No. 266 received today.

MacVeagh

868.248/59

Memorandum by the Chief of the Division of Near Eastern Affairs (Murray) to the Assistant Secretary of State (Berle)

[Washington,] November 18, 1940.

Mr. Berle: With reference to our telephone conversation this morning, regarding 100 fighter airplanes which might be available for export, we have considered the question from the point of view of the needs of countries in the Near East and I recommend that Greece be given first consideration with regard to the purchase of these planes.

When the question of aid to Greece was first being considered during October, it was not clear whether Greece would resist attack, and I recommended at that time that Greece be not permitted to purchase planes in this country on the grounds that planes shipped to Greece might result in a presentation of the planes to Italy. Since that time, however, events have taken place which have changed the picture fundamentally. Greece has shown that it intends to resist with its available forces and is doing so with some measure of success. On November 7 I recommended to the Division of Controls (memorandum attached [82]) that since Greece had entered the category of a small nation resisting attack by an aggressor, as sympathetic consideration should be given to Greece's requests for military supplies as might be consonant with our own defense needs.

[82] *Ante,* p. 582.

Since the 100 planes you mentioned could be spared apparently without seriously affecting our defense needs, I believe Greece should be allowed the first opportunity to acquire them, or a major portion thereof.

The Greek Minister has been after us almost every day since the Italian attack, begging for airplanes. Prime Minister Metaxas made a direct appeal to the President for help, and the Department has replied that the President appreciates the considerations pointed out by Metaxas and has instructed the appropriate authorities of the Government to pursue actively the negotiations taking place with the Greek Minister. Greek morale would doubtless be bolstered considerably, therefore, by the opportunity to acquire these planes at this time.

As regards other countries of the Near East, the Turkish Ambassador informs me that he has obtained all of the airplanes his Government has actually instructed him to purchase. He has been asked to undertake some preliminary investigation of the possibility of obtaining 50 additional planes from Curtiss–Wright, but he is not yet in a position to place an order for them.

As regards Iran, the Iranian Legation informed us this morning that in principle 30 additional pursuit planes and 50 bombers were desired, and it is very likely that the Iranians would be pleased at an opportunity to consider purchasing some of the 100 fighters you mentioned.   (We have not, of course, given any intimation to either the Turks, Iranians or Greeks of the availability of these planes.)   The Iranians frequently make difficulties over purchasing any planes except the latest models, and might not be so ready to act immediately in the present matter as the Greeks undoubtedly would. However, an offer of some of the planes, say 10 or 15, would be appreciated by them, might be taken at once, and would be a helpful gesture in my opinion. As you know, the Iranians have been after us for planes even longer than the Greeks.   I should like to encourage the Iranians by offering them a small number of these planes, provided this action would not deprive the British, Greeks or Turks of their requirements. I should like to make it clear, however, that in my opinion the Iranian claims should be considered as distinctly secondary to those of Greece and Turkey.[83]

WALLACE MURRAY

---

[83] For further correspondence regarding Iranian requests for planes, see pp. 638 ff.

868.24/92 : Telegram

The Minister in Greece (MacVeagh) to the Secretary of State

ATHENS, November 20, 1940—noon.
[Received November 21—12 : 10 p. m.]

320. Department's telegram No. 262, November 15, 8 p. m., Department's 266, November 16, 3 p. m., and my 316, November 18, 7 p. m. In a written communication dated November 19 the Prime Minister expresses his great appreciation of the President's prompt response to his appeal for the material aid so necessary to Greece in its hard and unequal struggle against an unprovoked aggression.

He confirms the full agreement of the Greek Government with the Department's point of view regarding Greek purchases in the United States stating that orders will be placed by the Greek Minister at Washington through the British Purchasing Commission liaison with which will be assured by the Greek Consul General at New York. He adds that lists of materials required have been drawn up in agreement with the British authorities and transmitted to the Greek Minister and that the necessary instructions have been issued by both the Greek and British Governments.

MACVEAGH

868.248/61

Memorandum by Mr. Charles W. Yost of the Division of Controls to the Chief of the Division (Green)

[WASHINGTON,] November 22, 1940.

MR. GREEN : Late Wednesday afternoon Mr. Welles informed me, in the presence of the Greek Minister, that 30 Curtiss P–40 pursuit planes would be made available to the Greek Government if it desires to purchase them. He asked me to make an appointment for the Minister to confer with Mr. Philip Young of the President's Liaison Committee in order to settle such details as the price and the date of delivery of the planes. In Mr. Young's absence, I made an appointment for the Minister to see Mr. Buckley of the Liaison Committee at 11 o'clock this morning. Later today Mr. Buckley informed me that he had seen the Minister and that the conversation had proceeded satisfactorily.

CHARLES W. YOST

868.248/55¼

The Greek Minister (Diamantopoulos) to the Under Secretary of State (Welles)

WASHINGTON, December 5, 1940.

MY DEAR MR. SECRETARY: I beg to inform you that the British Air Mission advises me that according to instructions from London they can not release to the Greek Government the 30 planes from the ones which are manufactured here for the British Air Force. I understand that they are going to suggest to the American Government to release an equal number from the planes destined for the American Air Force.

Owing to the vital importance of this question, which Your Excellency fully realizes as I know, I entreat you to do what you think fit to settle this matter according to the earnest wishes of my Government.

With highest consideration,

Sincerely yours,

C. DIAMANTOPOULOS

———————

868.248/55¼

Memorandum by the Under Secretary of State (Welles) to the Chief of the Division of Near Eastern Affairs (Murray)

[WASHINGTON,] December 6, 1940.

MR. MURRAY: I wish you would talk with Dr. Berle and Mr. Philip Young regarding the matter dealt with in the attached letter [84] from the Greek Minister. It is the President's most positive desire that these thirty planes be released to the Greek Government. Surely some satisfactory way can be found of doing it.

———————

868.51/1618 : Telegram

The Minister in Greece (MacVeagh) to the Secretary of State

ATHENS, December 7, 1940—2 p. m.
[Received December 8—11: 23 a. m.]

352. The Prime Minister called me to the Foreign Office this morning and gave me a written memorandum referring to the appeal of the Minister of Finance summarized in my telegram 305, November 14 and amplifying it to cover the extension of dollar credits in some form or other for desperately needed war material purchases by this country. In addition he asked that President Roosevelt be personally advised if possible of his views on the urgency of this matter as summarized below.

———————

[84] Supra.

General Metaxas said that operations are proceeding satisfactorily against the Italians but that it is absolutely necessary to bring the war in Albania to a close this winter because, without any doubt, Germany will attack in this region next spring. This explains why the Greek Army is not at present consolidating but pushing forward with all its strength despite the weather and difficult terrain. If Greece can drive the Italians out of Albania in the next few months as she now has the opportunity of doing the whole setup in the Peninsula will be changed and Yugoslav, Turkish and even, perhaps, Bulgarian resistance to Germany secured. Thus he regards the Greek war at present as a turning point in the battle for the freedom of all this region and perhaps in the whole war. But he emphasized and re-emphasized that Greece's munitions and what the British can spare for her use this winter are not sufficient for unremitting operations on the present scale over a period of months. He understands the limitations imposed by the Johnson Act but he urged that it is in the interests of all that America stands for as well as in those of this heroic little nation that some means be devised as soon as possible to insure an adequate flow of war munitions to insure the continuance and success of Greece's present effort.

The following is the text of the memorandum:

"On November 13th the Minister of Finance addressed to the United States Minister to Greece a long letter describing the insurmountable difficulties we are facing through lack of sufficient credit in dollars for our vital needs in supplies, and voicing a plea for American economic support so that the urgent requirements of the moment may effectively be met. With the evolution of the war situation our economic needs grow more pressing and facing them becomes an overwhelming problem. Although Great Britain has opened credits in our favor the problem still remains critical as the latter are limited to the sterling area, and a great number of goods of essential importance may only be procured in America and in countries requiring payment in dollars. Due to the decrease in exports to America, procuring dollars becomes extremely difficult, and our stock of dollars is running low at the very moment when we must apply to the American market for supplies of war material which Great Britain is unable to ensure. As the difficulties are becoming overwhelming, even endangering the successful outcome of the war, we deem it timely to appeal to the United States Government for financial aid.

"Consequently we request you to take the necessary steps in the name of the Greek Government and we trust that the United States Government will not deny Greece their aid so that she may effectively wage her struggle for liberty and the common ideals of our two nations."

MACVEAGH

868.51/1619 : Telegram

The Minister in Greece (MacVeagh) to the Secretary of State

ATHENS, December 9, 1940—noon.
[Received December 10—8 : 50 a. m.]

353. My telegram No. 352, December 7, 2 p. m. As a sequel to our conversation of yesterday I received last night a personal letter from the Premier in connection with Greece's urgent need for planes and credits. Regarding credits he refers once more to the inability of sterling to take care of all the crushing necessities imposed upon this country by the war and to the decrease in Greece's dollar holdings caused by the stoppage of her export trade. He then goes on "The amount of dollars at our disposal at the outbreak of the war totalling 23½ million inclusive of the Bank of Greece's gold deposits in the United States is already completely pledged for payments due on foodstuffs and raw materials as well as for war material in the United States. It covers the cost of munitions about to be purchased and of the 60 planes which we hope to obtain and which will be entirely paid for from these funds. The Greek Government is decided to use all the dollars at its disposition for purchases in the United States. Nevertheless being at the end of its resources and forced by present need to purchase munitions which Great Britain is not able to provide, it is constrained to address itself to the Government of the United States for assistance." The note closes with "the hope that in this time of crisis for Greece, which may become even more critical in the future, the Government of the United States will not allow the magnificent moral effort of the entire Greek nation to be compromised for lack of material to sustain it."

Regarding planes the Prime Minister enclosed in his letter the following distressing exposé, and furthermore spoke to me about the matter personally, and finally sent his secretary to see me to emphasize once more that Greece can and will pay for the planes concerned if only the gordian knot of their procurement can be cut:

"On account of the imperious necessity of obtaining pursuit planes as promptly as possible to meet the repeated attacks of Italian aviation directed chiefly against unfortified and defenseless towns, the Greek Government addressed to the American Government early in November an urgent plea for assistance in according it 60 combat planes.

"In reply the Government in Washington informed the Greek Minister on November 20th that upon the personal intervention of President Roosevelt it was prepared to cede to Greece a first lot of 30 planes of the most recent type destined for the American Army and that it reserved for future consideration the question of ceding 30 more.

"Later on the 27th of the same month the Under Secretary of State advised the Greek Minister at Washington that following an examination of the question by the competent American authorities the 30 planes promised should be furnished from those manufactured for England. Nevertheless the British Government, when consulted on the matter refused its consent to this solution, maintaining that the planes in question should come from those reserved for the United States.

"As a result the question remains at present in suspense awaiting a solution of this difference of opinion. But the resulting delay deprives Greece, engaged in an arduous struggle against an enemy better equipped, of means of opposing effectively the latter's aerial attacks.

"In view of the vital importance of prompt reenforcement for Greek aviation, not only to meet the present contingency but other contingencies now unforeseen which may arise in the near future, the Greek Government urgently prays that it may receive as soon as possible the assistance which it confidently expects from the Government of the United States and which only America can give."

MACVEAGH

868.51/1620 : Telegram

The Minister in Greece (MacVeagh) to the Secretary of State

ATHENS, December 9, 1940—3 p. m.
[Received December 10—10 : 20 a. m.]

355. With background reference to my telegram number 353, December 9, noon, I have the honor to transmit at the request of the Prime Minister the following personal message addressed by him to the President (translated from the original French) :

"Mr. President : At this time when Greece, the victim of unjustified aggression on the part of a great power has been fighting for 40 days with all her resources in defense of her independence and of the high principles which from the beginning have been the foundation of her national existence, she is confronted by problems whose solution depends on her obtaining adequate assistance. The question of necessary supplies of war material and that of the foreign exchange required to procure them constitute two of the most acute problems, against the stern realities of which this nation's spirit of sacrifice and its unflinching courage risk being broken.

Thus while the Greek Air Force engages the enemy at the front with the small resources at its disposal, the civil population, women and children are exposed to perfidious attack from the enemy's aviation, which prefers to attack towns whose lack of defenses lays them open to its assaults.

Moreover the Government is encountering extremely serious difficulties in its attempts to procure necessary supplies for the army and to ensure the provisioning of the civil population with foodstuffs, because of the shortage of foreign exchange resulting from its increased needs and the restriction of its resources by the war.

In every critical juncture throughout her national existence Greece has invariably found in your country the sympathy and the help she required. It is only natural therefore that at such times as the present she should turn with confidence in that direction.

Making myself the spokesman of this confidence I am once more, Mr. President, addressing you in person as the authorized head of the great American nation as well as the heir of its noblest traditions to beg you to exert your high prestige to assure to my country the assistance of which she stands in need.

Only yesterday you magnanimously intervened to assure the transfer to the Greek Air Force of 30 of the 60 pursuit planes we had asked for which were about to be delivered to the American Army. Encouraged by this gesture and awaiting the removal of the obstacles in the way of its fulfillment which have arisen, I beg you to be good enough to intercede for the satisfaction in the United States of the pressing needs of the Greek Air Force.

Many other supplies as well are essential to our army to enable it to accomplish the task before it. Unfortunately the country's available resources in foreign exchange are far from sufficient to meet the drain upon them. Therefore I hope that the possibility will be considered of according Greece such terms of payment as will allow her to place in the United States urgent orders for matériel which she cannot procure in England in spite of the generous help furnished her by that country.

The assistance which your great country could give to us at this time might be decisive in the struggle which has been forced on Greece and which she is now carrying on at the side of the British nation to ensure liberty and justice for all men. Knowing of your devotion to this ideal and to that of the supremacy of spiritual and moral forces over those of violence and oppression, the ideal which has always been the common heritage of our two peoples, I dare to hope that this further appeal which I am venturing to address to you will meet with a sympathetic reception.

In this hope I beg, Mr. President, that you will accept the assurance of my profound devotion. Signed J. Metaxas."

MacVeagh

868.24/106

*Memorandum by the Chief of the Division of Controls (Green)
to the Secretary of State*

[Washington,] December 16, 1940.

The Secretary: I called Mr. Philip Young, Assistant to the Secretary of the Treasury and Chairman of the President's Liaison Committee, by telephone this afternoon and asked him what progress the Committee was making in its efforts to make arms available to the Greek Government.

Mr. Young said that this Government, the Greek Government, and the British Government were endeavoring to work out a triangular arrangement to supply the Greeks with the thirty planes which they wished to obtain immediately. Under this arrangement, the British would furnish the Greeks immediately with thirty British Defiant planes—the type which the Greeks are already using; the British would be recompensed later by receiving thirty Curtiss–Wright P–40's now on order by this Government. Mr. Young said that this arrangement would be satisfactory both to this Government and to the Greek Government, and that it was hoped that the British would inform us of their agreement within the next day or two.

Mr. Young explained that, as far as the other arms and munitions desired by the Greek Government were concerned (see the list attached to my memorandum of a conversation with the Greek Minister on November 2 [12]), the agreement between this Government, the Greek Government, and the British Government was that the British would first determine which of the articles listed could be supplied to the Greeks from British stocks in Europe and Africa; that the British Purchasing Commission would then determine which of the remaining items could be supplied from orders already placed by the British in this country; and that the Liaison Committee would then endeavor to ascertain which of the items which still remain unaccounted for could be made available to the Greeks in this country without interference with our own defense program. Mr. Young said that there had been some delay in carrying out this agreement due to the fact that the Greek list mentioned above was full of errors so that the Greek Minister had been obliged to telegraph to Athens several times for clarification and correction of the list. The program would be carried out, however, as rapidly as possible.

JOSEPH C. GREEN

868.248/104

Memorandum of Conversation, by the Under Secretary of State (Welles)

[WASHINGTON,] December 16, 1940.

The British Chargé d'Affaires called this evening.

Mr. Butler stated that he had just received a telegram from his Government informing him that General Metaxas, the Greek Prime Minister, had advised the British Government that he would be quite satisfied to receive 30 planes from the British aviation forces in Egypt in substitution for the 30 P–40 planes offered by the United States Government, and that consequently the planes in the United States could be utilized by the British without any diversion.

I said to Mr. Butler that I was very glad that this arrangement had been made and that there would be no further difficulty in connection therewith.

S[UMNER] W[ELLES]

868.248/75

The Greek Legation to the Department of State

The Greek Government is very much concerned with the question of the reinforcement of its air forces and it feels the necessity of taking proper measures to face not only the present necessities but also other unforeseen developments which might arise in the near future from the situation in the Near East.

After a careful examination of the offer made in regard to the "Defiance" [*Defiant*] planes, the Greek Government came to the conclusion that these planes are not suitable and that Curtiss P–40 are the adequate ones. Their shipment should be hastened in order that they could reach Greece in time.

Therefore, the Greek Government want to renew their urgent appeal to the United States Government hoping that the latter will fully realize Greece's situation and bring the question to a satisfactory conclusion.

WASHINGTON, December 17, 1940.

868.51/1620 : Telegram

The Secretary of State to the Minister in Greece (MacVeagh)

WASHINGTON, December 18, 1940—9 p. m.

308. Your 355, December 9, 3 p. m. Please inform the Prime Minister that his appeal for financial assistance has been laid before the President, who has given it his most sympathetic consideration. The President now asks that you inform General Metaxas that in view of the clear intent of Congress, as expressed in existing legislation, it is impracticable to act favorably on the Prime Minister's appeal at this time.

However, financial assistance to Greece is being extended in substantial amounts through the American Red Cross and other organizations and this aid will doubtless continue and increase. Moreover, the Prime Minister may be assured that special consideration will continue to be given to facilitating the acquirement by Greece of military supplies in this country.

HULL

868.24/112

Memorandum by Mr. George V. Allen of the Division of Near Eastern Affairs

[WASHINGTON,] December 18, 1940.

The Greek Minister left with Mr. Murray the two attached lists of military supplies which Greece has expressed a desire to purchase in this country. According to the Minister the longer list, containing 27 items,[85] may now be disregarded, in as much as the Greek Government, after canvassing the availability of dollar exchange for purchases in this country, has decided that it must limit very strictly the expenditure of the exchange available. The shorter list,[86] containing six items, is said to be "rock-bottom" and to contain only material urgently needed. Only shells and cartridge cases are included in this list.

Mr. Condouriotis of the Greek Legation has informed the Near Eastern Division that he has learned that the American Government (Army or Navy) has on hand shells of the type listed in Items 3 and 6, and no others. Mr. Condouriotis said that Item 1 (Rondelle washers) could be obtained from the Bridgeport Brass Company and that this item had therefore been taken care of. He said that the Legation was most hopeful that the American Government would allow Greece to purchase from our own ordnance stores shells of the type listed in Items 3 and 6.

Mr. Condouriotis said that copies of the attached lists have been furnished by the Greek Minister to Mr. Philip Young, Chairman of the Interdepartmental Liaison Committee, Treasury Department.

868.248/55a : Telegram

The Secretary of State to the Minister in Greece (MacVeagh)

WASHINGTON, December 19, 1940—8 p. m.

309. Two or three weeks ago the Greek Minister in Washington was informed that Greece would be allowed to purchase 30 pursuit planes in this country. After reference to his Government, the Minister stated that his Government desired to purchase 30 Curtiss-Wright P–40 pursuit planes. In as much as all of the P–40 planes now being produced are earmarked for Great Britain, the British Government suggested to General Metaxas, through British officials in Athens, that Britain would immediately furnish Greece with 30 Defiant planes, in exchange for Greece's agreement to forego the 30 Curtiss-Wright planes we had promised. On December 16 the British Chargé d'Affaires in Washington informed the Department that he had received a telegram from his Government stating that General Metaxas had advised the British Government that Greece would be quite satisfied to receive 30 planes from the British aviation forces in Egypt in substitution for the 30 P–40 planes offered by the United States Government. On December 17, however, the Greek Minister

---

[85] Not printed.
[86] Not attached to file copy.

submitted a written communication to the Department, stating that "after a careful examination of the offer made in regard to the Defiant planes, the Greek Government came to the conclusion that these planes are not suitable and that Curtiss P–40's are the adequate ones. . ."[87] Therefore the Greek Government want to renew their urgent appeal to the U. S. Government. . ." On December 18 the Counselor of the Greek Legation in Washington agreed to telegraph his Government urging the acceptance of the Defiant planes.

It is possible that the misunderstanding in this matter will be clarified by the British and Greek authorities. For your information, however, it should be pointed out that while the American Government has no intention of withdrawing the offer made to Greece, the informed authorities of this Government consider that Greece would be well-advised to accept the British offer for several reasons: (1) the time of delivery and shipment to Greece of the P–40's is uncertain; (2) the P–40 plane is said to be particularly difficult to handle, and partly for this reason our Army is not accepting any further planes of this type; (3) with no spare parts or mechanics in Greece familiar with this plane, the P–40 might soon be more of a liability to Greece than an asset.

If the somewhat delicate situation with regard to these planes has not already been settled, the Department desires that unless you perceive some objection you take such measures as may be feasible and appropriate in an effort to persuade the Greek authorities that its advantage lies in accepting the Defiant offer. We desire to avoid any implication that the American Government is attempting to withdraw its offer to Greece. We are convinced, however, that the British offer is decidedly advantageous to Greece.

HULL

868.248/58 : Telegram

The Minister in Greece (MacVeagh) to the Secretary of State

ATHENS, December 27, 1940—6 p. m.
[Received December 28—12 : 45 p. m.]

379. My telegram No. 375, December 21, 3 [4] p. m.[88] My inquiries having disclosed no apparent agreement I laid before the Premier personally on December 23 the views expressed in the Department's telegram 309, December 19, 8 p. m., and have now received from him a communication dated yesterday setting forth his reasons for not agreeing with those views, and making a further urgent appeal for the fulfillment of the United States Government's offer to Greece.

---

[87] Omissions indicated in the original telegram.
[88] Not printed.

The Premier's appeal is contained in a first person note and an attached memorandum. Pertinent portions of the note read as follows: (in translation from the French)

"Two months have already passed since Greece became a victim of the unjustified aggression of a Great Power, 2 months during which this country, insufficiently equipped, has been obliged to sustain a hard struggle for her independence and for the principles of liberty trampled under the feet of the aggressor. Tomorrow unforeseeable developments may bring us to grips with still greater forces and oblige us to face considerably more formidable technical means. If under such circumstances we should not be assisted in our efforts to procure the material necessary to support the spirit of the nation, our sacrifices may have been made in vain and the consequences which would follow may be grave.

"I consider it necessary to insist very strongly on this point, Mr. Minister, and to appeal once again for the assistance which is necessary, nay indispensable, to enable us efficaciously to confront the imperious exigencies of the hour. I like to hope that your great country will not ignore Greece's confident appeal and that it will realize with all the sympathy which we feel we can expect, the necessity of coming to her assistance without delaying further."

The memorandum reads as follows:

"With reference to the communication of the United States Minister, according to which the Greek Government should accept the offer of the British Government of 30 Defiant planes instead of the 30 Curtiss-Wright P–40 which the United States finds difficult to deliver, owing to their having been reserved for the needs of Great Britain, it seems necessary to make the following observations.

"In answer to the Greek Government's appeal for the urgent supply of 60 fighters made to the United States Government, the American Under Secretary of State notified the Greek Minister to Washington, the 20th of November last, that, owing to President Roosevelt's personal intervention, the United States Government were conceding '30 planes of the latest type, of those under construction for the United States Army' reserving themselves to consider subsequently the ceding of the remaining 30.

"Shortly afterwards, on November 27th, the Under-Secretary of State informed the Greek Minister at Washington that, after consideration of the matter by the competent American authorities, the 30 promised planes would have to be ceded out of those under construction for Great Britain. However, the British Government, having been consulted in the matter, refused to consent to this solution insisting that they could not give up the planes being constructed on their account.

"On December 13th, the Department of State notified the Greek Minister to Washington that the competent Ministers, Messrs. Hull and Morgenthau, had attended to the question of the planes, but that the British Purchasing Commission had declared that they were unable to cede the P–40 planes, instead of which ought to be delivered to Greece an equivalent number of those under construction for the

United States. In any case, the Greek Minister was advised that the United States' promise concerning the delivery to Greece of 30 planes continues to hold good.

"Following this it was proposed that the Greek Government accept in lieu of the above the delivery of 30 Defiant planes which, it was asserted, without [*would*] suffice to meet the Greek needs.

"At this point a cable was sent to the Greek Minister in Washington, Mr. Diamantopoulos, making clear the reasons why the Defiants, proposed as a substitute for the promised planes, could not fill the needs which they would be called upon to meet. These reasons are that Greece, having to face a great power with a strong air force today and very probably having to confront one of the most modern and most powerful air fleets in the near future, must, in order to effectively meet the needs arising from the above, ensure the supply of the latest and most powerful aircraft. The Defiant plane, therefore, does not seem to possess the required qualifications. What is needed is a light pursuit plane of the latest type, while the Defiant is a rather heavy two-seater fighter plane, comparatively slow on the ascent. For these reasons it is no longer in use in Great Britain for the pursuit of the attacking German aircraft.

"It is unnecessary to point out how important it is for the effective carrying out of the war and to the end of repelling enemy aircraft attacks against the country, that the Greek Air Force be supplied with the most appropriate means, and not with material of substitution. Already it appears that Greek airplanes may shortly have to meet German airplanes on the front in Albania. In consideration of this possibility, and in view of the hard fight which the former is carrying on, in spite of insufficient means, the Greek Government are willing to accept any sacrifice in order to obtain the proper material. In fact, the latter, despite the limited means of payment in dollars, have decided to give over out of the meager stock of which they dispose the entire sum required for the payment in full of the 60 planes that were expected to be supplied from the United States. It is hoped, therefore, that the United States Government will not wish to deprive Greece of her precious aid at this critical hour, when she is engaged in an unequal struggle for her liberty and for the principles of freedom which the great American Nation has always defended.

"In this hope the Greek Government believes that they may without fear of misunderstanding insist upon their request for the supply of 'planes of the latest model out of the lot now being constructed for the United States Army' and which were the subject of the original promise of the United States Government. If this description did not refer to type P–40—of which mention was made later on, in the statement informing the Greek Minister of the refusal of the British Government to give up the planes of this type being constructed on their account—it certainly did not concern the 'Defiants' which are not being produced in the United States and which are already no longer being produced in England. What was meant, as was moreover clearly stated, was the latest type of fighter planes which is now being supplied to the United States Air Force and whose characteristics were not defined in the original communication to the Greek Minister.

"The Greek Government gratefully hastened to avail themselves of this offer, conscious of the fact that the planes at present being constructed in the United States—irrespective of type—rank among the finest in the world. They were willing, therefore, knowing that the country was in urgent need of such planes successfully to face the dangers threatening it, to undergo any sacrifice in order to obtain them.

"The reasons mentioned in the notice of the United States Minister, and concerning the difficulties which the use of such latest model aircraft would present to the Greek Air Force, do not seem to justify any anxiety. The fact that the mechanism of this type of plane is extremely complicated is not reason enough to prevent the supply of such planes to the Greek Air Force which is at present using several complicated planes of recent model, with which they are already familiar. It would, therefore, merely be a question of additional training for its pilots. As regards modern aerodromes, such are now in process of construction with the assistance of British engineers. Lastly, concerning the matter of spare parts, the aircraft being produced at present are always delivered with their spare parts. At any rate all the above are problems for which an appropriate solution may be found.

"It is sincerely hoped, therefore, that the United States Government, in their undoubted interest in the struggle of a small nation resolved to stake all its vital forces in the fight against brute force, will be willing to support this endeavor by supplying the Greek Government with the necessary technical means of which the United States dispose."

MacVeagh

868.248/106

Memorandum by the Under Secretary of State (Welles) to the Chief of the Division of Near Eastern Affairs (Murray)

[Washington,] December 27, 1940.

Mr. Murray: The British Chargé d'Affaires called to see me this morning. He conveyed a message from the British Government to this effect. The British Government is willing to provide the Greek Army immediately with thirty Mohawk planes which are either actually in Egypt or already en route from England to Egypt. This would be done by the British authorities on the understanding that the United States Government would arrange subsequently at the earliest possible date to replace these Mohawk planes with thirty Tomahawk planes now completed under British orders in the United States and that the United States would further agree to ship these thirty Tomahawk planes on an American ship to Basra. I told Mr. Butler that I would submit this suggestion to the appropriate authorities here for their consideration. It is my understanding that Mr. Arthur Purvis will make this same suggestion to Secretary of the Treasury Morgenthau this afternoon. I think that the Secretary of State should be informed of this suggestion at once so that the various phases of the question can be considered by him at the same time that the matter is under consideration by the Treasury and National Defense experts.

868.24/114

Memorandum of Conversation, by Mr. George V. Allen of the Division of Near Eastern Affairs

[WASHINGTON,] December 28, 1940.

Participants: Greek Minister
                Mr. Murray
                Mr. Allen

Referring to the memorandum which the Greek Minister left with Mr. Murray on December 23, 1940,[89] inquiring "if in the Navy and Army warehouses are kept available shells for 75 mm. and 155 mm. guns", Mr. Murray informed the Greek Minister that the Department had received word from an official of the Army and Navy Munitions Board that no shells of either type were available for sale by the American Army and Navy.

The Greek Minister said that he must of course accept this statement as an official reply to his inquiry and report it, with regret, to his Government. In an endeavor to clarify the situation, however, he said that two questions were involved: first, whether the American Government has in its possession shells of the type specified, and, second, if so, whether Greece would be able to purchase any of these shells. He said that his purpose in leaving the memorandum of December 23 was to find out first whether such shells existed, and that he had intended, after ascertaining that they did exist, to make an official request to purchase them.

Mr. Murray said that the statement he was now transmitting to the Greek Minister appeared to take care of both phases of the subject, since, regardless of whether the American Government has on hand shells of the type desired, the military authorities have stated that no such shells are available for sale by the Government.

---

[89] Dated December 23 but left with Mr. Murray on December 27; not printed.

868.51/1628

Memorandum by the Chief of the Division of Near Eastern Affairs (Murray) [90]

[WASHINGTON,] December 28, 1940.

The Greek Minister has just asked me to let him know some time today whether you would see any objection to General Metaxas, the Prime Minister of Greece, addressing a message to the Greek-American citizens of this country thanking them, so I understand, for the sympathy which they have shown to Greece in her present struggle and for the generous aid and assistance which has been forthcoming, from American citizens of Hellenic origin.

The plan would be, if it meets with your approval, for the Greek Prime Minister's message to be delivered through the Greek Minister in Washington over the radio in Greek and to the Greek Language Press in this country.

Will you kindly let me know as soon as possible what reply you wish me to give to the Greek Minister in response to his inquiry.

I personally am rather dubious about this.

WALLACE MURRAY

868.51/1617

Memorandum by the Chief of the Division of Near Eastern Affairs (Murray) [90]

[WASHINGTON,] December 30, 1940.

After discussing with you the request of the Greek Minister, as set forth in the attached memorandum,[91] I called Mr. Diamantopoulos by telephone on Saturday afternoon last and spoke to him as follows.

I stated that while this Government had, of course, every sympathy for Greece in her present struggle and were lending her substantial aid, I felt sure the Minister would understand that a suggestion of this kind might place us in an embarrassing situation. While we entertained the most cordial feelings toward General Metaxas, if we acceded to the present request that he be permitted to address a message direct to American citizens of Hellenic origin and to the Greek Language Press in this country, we might thereby be establishing a precedent which would make it difficult to deny similar requests from other Chiefs of State in Europe with whose policies this Government is by no means in agreement.

---

[90] Addressed to the Secretary of State and the Under Secretary of State.
[91] *Supra.*

The Minister said he understood fully our point of view and thought it entirely logical. He then informed me and *only then* that this suggestion had *not* come from his Government but had been his own and that there would, therefore, be no necessity to take the matter up with his Government.

WALLACE MURRAY

868.24/105

The Greek Minister (Diamantopoulos) to the Secretary of State

No. 2252   WASHINGTON, December 30, 1940.

MISTER SECRETARY: I am requested by my Government to bring to your Excellency's attention that the Greek General Staff is in urgent need of some assistance in order to secure war materials in the United States.

I have made every effort to ascertain whether it would be possible to purchase some in open market; but, unfortunately, they have been sold long ago. Hence, I have left copies of the list with Mr. Wallace Murray and Mr. Philip Young, requesting them to be good enough to let me know whether these materials could be obtained from the War or Navy Departments. Up to the present time, as I am informed, the only available ones are 10,000 shells of 57 calibre ammunition.

The Greek Government fully realizes that due to the American and British Defense needs, it would be difficult to secure immediately from the United States all the necessary military supplies. For this reason, my Government has requested me to appeal to Your Excellency so that, from the aforesaid numerous war materials, the most urgently needed be furnished for the defense of the country, namely:

40,000—75 m/m shells for Schneider Mountain Gun Type, 1919
10,000—105 m/m shells of Schneider Gun Type, 1925
10,000—155 m/m shells of Schneider Gun Type, 1917

Besides, my Government is expecting a favorable decision on their planes request of which Your Excellency is fully aware.

I am in the belief that you will find this appeal in accordance with the general policies of the United States Government as they have been authoritatively set forth.

Accept, Sir, the assurances of my highest consideration.

C. DIAMANTOPOULOS

868.248/111

Memorandum of Conversation, by the Chief of the Division of Near Eastern Affairs (Murray)

[WASHINGTON,] December 31, 1940.

Participants: The Greek Minister
Mr. Welles
Mr. Murray

The Greek Minister called by appointment with the Under Secretary this afternoon with further regard to the question of airplanes and military supplies needed by the Greek Army.

Mr. Welles informed the Minister of the substance of the message conveyed to him from the British Government by the British Chargé d'Affaires on December 27 last. This message was, in brief, that the British Government is willing to provide the Greek Army immediately with thirty Mohawk planes which are either actually in Egypt or already en route from England to Egypt. This would be done by the British authorities on the understanding that the United States Government would arrange subsequently at the earliest possible date to replace these thirty Mohawk planes with thirty Tomahawk planes now completed under British orders in the United States.

Mr. Welles explained in reply to an inquiry from the Minister that both the Mohawk and Tomahawk planes were of American manufacture and of the latest type. This information seemed to be very welcome to the Minister who apparently had in mind his Government's unwillingness to accept a previous offer of British Defiant planes.

The Under Secretary suggested to the Greek Minister that he might care to get in touch at an early moment with Mr. Arthur Purvis of the British Purchasing Commission in order to discuss the further details of the British proposal. Mr. Welles suggested, at the same time, that the Minister and myself might arrange to discuss the matter at an early moment with Mr. Philip Young in the Treasury. I am making the necessary arrangements to that end. The Minister then raised the question of munitions and stated that after a thorough investigation of the situation and after consultation with the British purchasing authorities he was now convinced that it would be absolutely impossible for him to obtain in this country some urgently needed supplies of shells, unless arrangements could be made by us to release certain quantities of such shells now held in the Army and Navy arsenals. The Minister laid great stress on this request of his Government and said he earnestly hoped that we might find it possible to let Greece have a certain quantity of these shells for her immediate need and that we in turn could place our orders for future delivery.

During the Minister's visit with Mr. Welles he referred to the very cordial manner in which the President had received him today and to the President's assurances that every effort would be made to render Greece such assistance as is needed at this time, while bearing in mind the paramount needs of Great Britain. The Minister added that while he did not, of course, go into detail in discussing with the President all phases of Greek military and aviation needs, the President was most emphatic in his assurances that we should do everything possible to assist Greece in her present need.

POSTPONEMENT BY GREECE OF TRADE AGREEMENT DISCUSSIONS WITH THE UNITED STATES[93]

611.6831/241 : Telegram

The Minister in Greece (MacVeagh) to the Secretary of State

ATHENS, January 20, 1940—1 p. m.
[Received January 20—10 : 10 a. m.]

11. Complying with instruction No. 622 of September 28, 1939,[94] I laid before the Under Secretary for Foreign Affairs and the Ministry of National Economy this morning the Department's views and proposals regarding the negotiation of a possible trade agreement. Further talks which may be necessary to facilitate the Greek Government reaching a decision regarding its readiness to negotiate can be carried on directly with the Minister of National Economy. While of necessity noncommittal at this stage, both Ministers appeared receptive to our advances and the latter, especially, expressed a hopeful attitude.

MACVEAGH

611.6831/243 : Telegram

The Minister in Greece (MacVeagh) to the Secretary of State

ATHENS, July 11, 1940—2 p. m.
[Received 2 : 48 p. m.]

166. Department's instruction No. 622, September 28, 1939 and my telegram No. 11, January 20, 1 p. m. After repeated attempts to secure a reply in this matter I have received a note from the Foreign Office today stating that our proposal is receiving profound study, in a friendly spirit with a view to the initiation of negotiations as soon as the normal situation shall be re-established and the difficulties affecting

---

[93] For previous correspondence, see Foreign Relations, 1939, vol. II, pp. 603 ff.
[94] Ibid., p. 603.

particularly communication with the United States as a result of the extension of the war to the Mediterranean shall have been removed.

MacVeagh

611.6831/245

The Minister in Greece (MacVeagh) to the Secretary of State

No. 4301   ATHENS, July 25, 1940.
                                            [Received September 9.]

SIR: Confirming my telegram No. 166 of July 11, 2 p. m., I have the honor to report that the Greek Government has at last replied to my *Aide-Mémoire* of January 20, 1940, conveying the Department's proposals for a definitive Trade Agreement to replace the existing *Modus Vivendi* [95] in commercial matters between the United States and Greece.

According to the *Note Verbale* of the Royal Hellenic Foreign Office, No. 19954 of July 10, 1940, copies of which I enclose in the original French and in English translation,[96] the contents of my *Aide-Mémoire* have been examined with interest by the competent Greek authorities, who have furthermore undertaken a profound study of the problems involved with a view to the initiation of negotiations when the present difficulties due to the extension of the war to the Mediterranean shall have been removed and the normal situation re-established.

There would seem to be little comment to make on this reply, which will perhaps cause no surprise to the Department. That it has taken me many special urgings to extract it from the Foreign Office may be explained partly by a natural reluctance to return such an answer to proposals actually at one time encouraged by the Greek authorities (see my despatch No. 3542 of November 7, 1939 [96]) and partly by continual preoccupation with the immediate problems arising from the rapid sequence of events in Europe during the past six months. I see no reason to doubt the sincerity of the Minister of National Economy's hopeful expressions of last fall, but since then the situation has grown worse for Greece rather than better. Difficulties connected with the British control of exports and imports, and with the absorption by Germany of country after country having commercial agreements with Greece, have been followed by the entrance of Italy into the conflict and the practical cessation of Mediterranean trade.

---

[95] Provisional Commercial Agreement signed at Athens, November 15, 1938. For text, see Department of State Executive Agreement Series No. 137, or 53 Stat. (pt. 3) 2046.
[96] Not printed.

Whether she likes it or not, it would seem that Greece must now submit more than ever to the dictates of the German clearing if she is to continue to live. It is her hope that this situation may be only temporary, but while it lasts, it is perhaps inevitable that she should regard discussion of mutual tariff concessions calculated to increase trade with us as somewhat utopian. As to the principles involved, these are already embodied in our Provisional Commercial Agreement, or *Modus Vivendi*, of 1938, and this backed by the vigilance and energy of the Commercial Section of the Legation should continue to afford useful and, in general, adequate protection to our commercial interests under prevailing conditions.

Respectfully yours,   LINCOLN MACVEAGH

REPRESENTATIONS BY THE UNITED STATES REGARDING DISCRIMINATORY TREATMENT AND NON-PAYMENT OF INTEREST BY THE GREEK GOVERNMENT ON THE AMERICAN LOAN OF MAY 10, 1929 [98]

868.51/1598

The Minister in Greece (MacVeagh) to the Secretary of State

No. 4062   ATHENS, April 26, 1940.
                                              [Received May 16.]

SIR: In reference to the parts of my despatches No. 3759 of January 27, 1940 and No. 3969 of March 29, 1940 [99] relating to a secret Anglo-Greek commercial accord I have the honor to enclose herewith a copy of an exchange of notes between Mr. Apostolides, the Greek Finance Minister, and Lord Bessborough, representing the League Loans Committee and the Council of Foreign Bondholders, dated respectively January 25th and 26th, 1940.[1] This exchange of notes, obtained from the International Financial Commission in Athens, confirms the report that Greece agreed to raise the percentage now being paid on her foreign debt from 40% to 43%.

In his note submitting the Greek proposition, Mr. Apostolides refers to the negotiations with the British Government "on various matters" and to the "strongest hope" expressed by the British Government that "the cordial relations between our two countries should be strengthened by an arrangement for the service of the External Debt". He then submits

"a definitive offer for the service of the debt, of which the most important point is that Greece is willing to pay 43% of the contractual

---

[98] For previous correspondence on the Greek debt, see *Foreign Relations*, 1936, vol. II, pp. 308 ff.
[99] Neither printed.
[1] For texts, see the *Sixty-Seventh Annual Report of the Council of the Corporation of Foreign Bondholders for the Year Ending 31st December 1940* (London), pp. 38–42.

interest, commencing 1st April 1940. The Greek Government, moreover, undertake to pay the same percentage throughout the duration of the war."

He requests the Committee to accept his assurance that

"this increase represents the utmost that Greece can pay in the present circumstance, and the undertaking to maintain this percentage throughout the war is, I hope, sufficient proof of the sincerity of our effort to reach an agreement."

The British reply paraphrases the Greek offer in detail and informs Mr. Apostolides that

"in view of the present exceptional circumstances and in view of the fact that your Government unconditionally undertake to maintain payments at 43% of the interest for the duration of hostilities, the Council and the Committee are prepared to recommend your Government's present offer to the acceptance of the bondholders. The Council and the Committee are further ready to recommend to His Majesty's Government that the Governments represented on the International Financial Commission in Athens should instruct the Commission to release to the Greek Treasury such balances in drachmas out of the assigned revenues as would become free under this arrangement."

The British note closes with the suggestion that the offer be made public as soon as possible, and that this be done, as in November, 1933, by the publication of the correspondence. Publication, however, has not been made in Greece.

The Department will observe that attached to the exchange of notes there is a list of the loans under the control of the International Financial Commission, and that this includes the United States Government's 4% loan of 1929. In addition the term "for the duration of the war" used in the body of the exchange suggests that the Greek offer was intended to give preferential treatment to loans floated in countries now engaged in hostilities. Under these circumstances, I took the occasion yesterday to inquire of the Under Minister for Foreign Affairs whether Greece regards the agreement reached with the bondholders in London as general or restricted in the manner indicated.

Mr. Mavroudis replied that the agreement between Mr. Apostolides and Lord Bessborough covers only British loans, but can be extended to French loans also if the French Government gives Greece similar concessions to those Great Britain has granted her. He said loans from other countries would, he supposed, continue to be serviced with the 40% hitherto offered. Great Britain merited a special concession, he said, by extending a loan of 2,000,000 pounds Sterling to Greece for the purchase of war materials, and by other helpful actions.

In view of the conflicting attitudes of the Greek and American Governments regarding the 1929 loan, and in advance of instructions from the Department, I made no comment to the Under Minister on his reply. The Legation's records fail to show, however, that any interest on the 1929 loan was paid to the United States in 1939, though 40% was paid in 1938. I did mention this to Mr. Mavroudis, and he laughed and remarked, "Well, that's a precedent".

Respectfully yours,   LINCOLN MACVEAGH

868.51/1598 : Telegram

The Secretary of State to the Minister in Greece (MacVeagh)

WASHINGTON, June 19, 1940—5 p. m.

141. Your despatch No. 4062, April 26. You are requested to inform the Greek Government immediately and in an emphatic manner that the Government of the United States expects that the Greek Government will accord to the American Government's loan of 1929 treatment no less favorable than that accorded the Stabilization and Refugee Loan of 1928 [2] and that, consequently, 43 percent of the interest which accrued to this Government on May 10, 1940, is due and payable, in accordance with Section 2 of Part II of the Debt Agreement of May 10, 1929.[3]

Furthermore, you should inform the Greek Government that since this Government understands that throughout the past 2 years the Greek Government has paid 40 percent of the interest due on the Stabilization and Refugee Loan of 1928, the same percentage of the interest which fell due on November 10, 1938, May 10, 1939, and November 10, 1939, on the American loan of 1929, is due and payable, no part of such interest having been received.

You should remind the Greek Government that this Government supplied Greece with $12,167,000 in 1929 on the specific condition that this new loan would be accorded treatment no less favorable than that accorded the Stabilization and Refugee Loan of 1928, and that the condition was accepted by Greece in order to obtain the loan. The American Government regrets that during the past 8 years it has been necessary to remind the Greek Government on more than one occasion of its clear and unmistakable obligations in this respect.

It should be made clear to the Greek Government that a most unfortunate impression would be created in this country should the Greek Government, despite the categorical terms of Section 2

---

[2] For terms of this loan agreement, signed at London, January 30, 1928, see League of Nations, *Official Journal*, April 1928, p. 494.

[3] Text printed in *Annual Report of the Secretary of the Treasury for the Fiscal Year Ended June 30, 1929* (Washington, Government Printing Office, 1930), p. 308.

of Part II of the Debt Agreement of 1929, accord to the American loan of 1929 treatment less favorable than that which has been or is to be accorded the Stabilization and Refugee Loan of 1928.

As regards the question of availability of exchange, you may remind the Greek authorities orally of the amount of free foreign exchange received by Greece as a result of such items as immigrants' remittances and veterans' payments, as well as the export balance of trade which in 1939 was in favor of Greece by a ratio of approximately 4 to 1.

Please keep the Department promptly informed by telegraph.

HULL

868.51/1602 : Telegram

The Minister in Greece (MacVeagh) to the Secretary of State

ATHENS, July 12, 1940—6 p. m.
[Received July 12—5 : 40 p. m.]

170. The Department's telegram No. 141, June 20 [*19*], 1940. I have now received reply in the form of a first person note signed by the Under Secretary for Foreign Affairs stating in substance as follows:

1. The Greek Government desires to assure the Government of the United States that it has "never dreamed" of treating the American Government loan of 1929 less favorably than the 6% 1928 stabilization loan.

2. It desires also to assure the Government of United States that the suspension of payments which has occurred since November 1938, and which has been due only to Greece's economic difficulties, is provisional and will disappear as soon as circumstances permit. At that time the service of the loan in question will be resumed in the same proportion as that of the stabilization loan and an attempt will be made at the same time to pay the interest in arrears.

The rest of the note is devoted to a defense of Greece's good faith and an exposition of her difficulties, which may be real enough at present but hardly explains the failure to make the payments now overdue.

MACVEAGH

868.51/1602 : Telegram

The Secretary of State to the Minister in Greece (MacVeagh)

WASHINGTON, July 17, 1940—5 p. m.

165. Your 170, July 12, 6 p. m. Please inform the Foreign Minister, in a formal communication, that the United States Government has noted with satisfaction the Greek Government's assurance that it has no intention of treating the American Government loan of 1929 less

favorably than the Stabilization and Refugee Loan of 1928. You should add that this Government cannot, however, regard as admissible the Greek Government's claim that "economic difficulties" constitute an adequate reason for the failure of the Greek Government to accord in fact the equal treatment in this matter to which it admits the United States is entitled. Therefore, if the present assurance is to be taken seriously the Greek Government should give effect to it without further delay by making the payments past due and payable to this Government as set forth in the first two paragraphs of the Department's 141, June 19, 5 p. m., and it should in the future so apportion its available financial resources for foreign debt service as to afford this Government the equal treatment to which it is warranted.

Please include in your written communication the statements you were authorized to make orally to the Greek Government in the penultimate paragraph of the Department's 141. Greek exports to the United States during 1939 were valued at $22,359,000, while imports into Greece from the United States were valued at only $6,391,000 according to the reports of the United States Department of Commerce. Veterans' payments to beneficiaries in Greece during the fiscal year ending June 30, 1939, amounted to $404,818. Figures for immigrant remittances and tourists' expenditures are not available but were of course substantial.

You should point out that the American Government is at present studying its position with regard to the free flow of dollar exchange abroad and naturally considers all relevant circumstances in that connection.

Please press this matter vigorously and keep the Department currently informed by telegraph of developments.

HULL

868.51 War Credits/770 : Telegram

The Minister in Greece (MacVeagh) to the Secretary of State

ATHENS, July 31, 1940—6 p. m.
[Received July 31—2 : 55 p. m.]

182. The Department's 165, July 17, 5 p. m. In my talks at the Foreign Office regarding that matter following presentation the Department's views as instructed I have met with some [opposition?] over our pressing Greece at a moment allegedly very difficult for her, but this morning the Permanent Under Secretary of Foreign Affairs definitely assured me that my note is being given the most careful consideration "with a view to seeing what can be done" and promised that I should have a reply in 3 or 4 days.

MACVEAGH

868.51 War Credits/772 : Telegram

The Minister in Greece (MacVeagh) to the Secretary of State

ATHENS, August 7, 1940—5 p. m.
[Received August 7—4 : 35 p. m.]

190. My number 182, July 31. Not having received a reply as promised, I again saw the Under Secretary for Foreign Affairs this morning, at which time he excused his delay on grounds of personal illness and the difficulty of evolving as satisfactory a reply as possible under the conditions now affecting the Greek treasury. He said he would need several more days as well as further conference with the Minister of Finance, which he arranged in my presence, adding that the contents and tenor of the Greek Government's message are of more importance than its date.

MACVEAGH

868.51 War Credits/773 : Telegram

The Minister in Greece (MacVeagh) to the Secretary of State

ATHENS, August 12, 1940—5 p. m.
[Received August 12—4 : 40 p. m.]

193. My telegram No. 190 of August 7, 5 p. m. Following further conversation with the Permanent Under Secretary for Foreign Affairs I am now in receipt of the Greek Government's reply in the form of another note signed by him as before and dated August 11th.

This note admits the Legation's argumentation regarding the foreign exchange normally received from the United States, but cites circumstances having to do with the recent course of the war as rendering "particularly critical the state of Greek economy from the point of view of foreign exchange." After some less important paragraphs of a deprecatory nature it then goes on as follows :

"However that may be, the Greek Government in spite of these very serious difficulties is not suspending the service on the American loan and declares on the contrary that within a short time and at the latest by the end of December 1940 it will meet its obligations. At the same time it renews the assurance that it has no intention of treating this loan in a manner less favorable than the stabilization loan of 1928." Finally the note concludes with the "hope that the Government of the United States will fully understand the realities involved in this problem and will allow the payment facilities we request."

The full text with translation ⁴ is being forwarded by air mail.

MACVEAGH

---

⁴ Not printed.

868.51 War Credits/773 : Telegram

The Acting Secretary of State to the Minister in Greece (MacVeagh)

WASHINGTON, August 15, 1940—6 p. m.

188. Your no. 193, August 12, 5 p. m. The Department has taken note of the Greek Government's renewed assurance that it has no intention of treating the American loan of 1929 in a manner less favorable than that accorded the stabilization loan of 1928, and of the Greek Government's undertaking to meet its obligations under the American loan within a short time and at the latest by the end of 1940.

As regards the assurances of an intention to accord equitable treatment, the Greek Government leaves unexplained and unmentioned the actual facts, which appear to point clearly to a contrary intention. During the period November 10, 1938, through November 10, 1939, when three payments on the American loan fell due, the Greek Government made no payment to the American Government although offering 40 percent of the interest due to holders of the 1928 loan, and when a further payment on the American loan fell due on May 10, 1940, the Greek Government made no payment to us although it had offered to holders of the 1928 loan 43 percent of the interest falling due during the Greek fiscal year beginning April 1, 1940. These obvious facts make it difficult to understand the Greek Government's repeated assurances of no intention to accord less favorable treatment to the American loan, particularly when these assurances are unaccompanied by any actual payment.

While appreciative of the fact that conditions in Europe are not normal, the American Government feels constrained to point out that the Greek Government was aware of its resources for foreign debt service when it made the above-mentioned offers to the holders of the 1928 loan, and that there has been no indication that the Greek Government intended to make any payment to the American Government until the matter was brought to the Greek Government's attention.

As regards the Greek Government's undertaking to meet its obligations under the American loan at the latest by the end of December 1940, this undertaking would naturally carry more assurance if accompanied by a substantial immediate payment on account of the arrears past due, as tangible evidence of the Greek Government's avowed determination to accord equitable treatment. This suggestion is made with the present European situation particularly in mind.

If you perceive objection to the submission of any of the foregoing to the Greek Government at this time, the Department will be glad to give consideration to your views. Any payment which the Greek Government may make should be made to the Federal Reserve Bank of New York for the credit of the Treasury of the United States as heretofore.

WELLES

868.51 War Credits/774 : Telegram

The Minister in Greece (MacVeagh) to the Secretary of State

ATHENS, August 20, 1940—5 p. m.
[Received 10 : 24 p. m.]

202. Department's telegram No. 188, August 15, 6 p. m. After embodying the Department's observations in a first person note addressed to the Premier, I took this today to the Under Secretary for Foreign Affairs to whom I made known its contents. He immediately remarked in some excitement that Greece's situation has become even worse since our last conversation on the subject but after I had expressed my personal sympathy in regard to Greece's present difficulties with Italy [5] and had stressed that my note dealt with a very different matter and one long under discussion between us he accepted it gracefully enough for the earliest possible attention.

In view of existing circumstances I am not sanguine as to prospects of any immediate payment as a result of this note but feel it should have a salutary influence on the future attitude of the Greek Government toward all financial questions involving us.

MACVEAGH

868.51 War Credits/776 : Telegram

The Minister in Greece (MacVeagh) to the Secretary of State

ATHENS, September 4, 1940—1 p. m.
[Received September 5—7 : 28 a. m.]

221. My telegram No. 202, August 20, 5 p. m. Following a further conversation with the Premier in which I personally urged the excellent impression which any payment on the Greek debt might be expected to make in America at this particular juncture in Balkan affairs I have received note from the Under Secretary for Foreign Affairs informing me that the sum of $87,168 has been telegraphed to New York to the order of the Secretary of the Treasury. This sum according to the Under Secretary for Foreign Affairs corresponds to the interest payable November 1, 1938 and its payment is intended as an earnest of the Greek Government's sincerity of intention regarding the fulfillment of its obligations. The rest of the letter contains a reaffirmation of the difficulties facing the Greek Treasury and a

---

[5] For correspondence on this subject, see pp. 524 ff.

statement that budgetary previsions have been entirely upset by the demands of national security in the present emergency.

MACVEAGH

868.51 War Credits/776 : Telegram

The Secretary of State to the Minister in Greece (MacVeagh)

WASHINGTON, September 5, 1940—7 p. m.

202. Your 221, September 4, 1 p. m. Confirmation has been received from the Treasury of the payment of $87,168 on the Greek debt. The Department is highly gratified at the outcome of your conversations with the Premier and commends you for the successful manner in which you have handled this matter.

HULL

868.51 War Credits/777

The Secretary of State to the Greek Minister (Diamantopoulos)

The Secretary of State presents his compliments to the Honorable the Minister of Greece and, at the request of the Treasury Department, has the honor to enclose a copy of the certificate of deposit issued by the Federal Reserve Bank of New York on September 3, 1940, evidencing the deposit in that bank of the amount of $87,168.00, representing payment by the Greek Government to the Government of the United States of forty percent of the semi-annual interest amounting to $217,920.00, due on November 10, 1938, on the four percent loan of 1929 made to the Greek Government by the United States under the agreement of May 10, 1929.

The Treasury Department has requested that the attention of the Greek Government be directed to the position previously taken by the United States with respect to payments of this character made by the Greek Government and that the latter be informed that the present payment has been received without prejudice to the contractual rights of the United States which are set forth in part II of the debt agreement of May 10, 1929, and in accordance with the position of the United States Government as stated in the note addressed to the former Minister of Greece on February 8, 1936.[6]

WASHINGTON, September 12, 1940.

[6] *Foreign Relations*, 1936, vol. II, p. 310.

IRAN

IMPACT OF THE EUROPEAN WAR ON IRAN; SOVIET PRESSURE ON IRAN

761.6211/232 : Telegram

The Chargé in Iran (Engert) to the Secretary of State

TEHRAN, October 3, 1939—2 p. m.
[Received 4 : 30 p. m.]

112. Legation's 103, September 18, 10 a. m. and despatch No. 1694, September 28,[1] in the last pouch.

(1) The Iranian Government views the Russo-German[2] and Russo-Estonian[3] treaties with the greatest alarm. For over a month German and Soviet diplomacy has been bending every effort to undermine Iran's morale and weaken her will to resist blandishments and threats from Berlin and Moscow. The partition of Poland[4] and the virtual loss of independence of the Baltic States[4a] have created fear that the Soviets will next turn their attention to the Black Sea and Caspian and that crucial days are ahead for Iran. But while hitherto the Iranian Government believed that the situation merely called for considerable diplomatic skill, there is now serious recognition of the fact that as one sensational event becomes the precursor of another it may have to adapt itself to a role which will be forced upon it by influences far beyond her control.

(2) I am reliably informed that Iran has already capitulated on practically all points in connection with the new commercial agreement with Russia which is also to give Germany transit rights for her exports to Iran. It has not yet been signed but only because the new Soviet Ambassador[4b] at the eleventh hour formulated a demand that exclusively Russian oil be used in the northern provinces and that all Communists imprisoned in Iran be released. He also protested against the concentration of Iranian troops in the north.

(3) There is a rumor for which I cannot vouch that the Ambassador likewise demanded recognition of Russia's "special rights" in Azer-

---

[1] Neither printed.
[2] Treaty of Nonaggression, signed at Moscow, August 23, 1939, Department of State, *Nazi–Soviet Relations, 1939–1941*, p. 76.
[3] Pact of Mutual Assistance, signed at Moscow, September 28, 1939, Department of State *Bulletin*, November 11, 1939, p. 543.
[4] See *Foreign Relations*, 1939, vol. I, pp. 477 ff.
[4a] See vol. I, pp. 357 ff.
[4b] Matvei Y. Filimonov.

baijan and Ghilan and if necessary the passage of troops to protect such rights.

(4) Nobody knows what precisely the Shah's [4c] state of mind is but he is reported to be showing increasing irritation at the hollowness and hypocrisy of both German and Russian propaganda. He has always taken a strong line against communism and is now more than ever afraid of the doctrine of world [domination?]. Ordinarily he would of course want to defend Iran's neutrality, territorial integrity, and independence by force of arms but there is a strong pro-German element in the army which has great respect for German ability and efficiency and which believes the German entente with Russia spells the doom of the democracies. The Government therefore may not feel strong enough to reject Soviet overtures or to indulge in heroic gestures.

(5) Japanese Military Attaché [4d] who is now in Khorassan reports to his Legation that Russia seems to be concentrating troops in Turkestan. This and similar rumors are causing considerable nervousness among better informed political circles who fear danger of recrudescence of events of 1918 to 1921 when the Soviets threatened Tehran. Consequently although there is of course no cause for immediate panic many wealthy merchants are already sending their families south.

ENGERT

761.91/195 : Telegram

The Chargé in Iran (Engert) to the Secretary of State

TEHRAN, October 17, 1939—9 a. m.
[Received 9 p. m.]

120. Since the Legation's 112, October 3, 2 p. m., I have had several informal talks with the Minister for Foreign Affairs [4e] and the Soviet Ambassador.

(1) Both assure me that no trade agreement has as yet been signed because neither side is willing to surrender what it considers vital interests. Without of course referring to the specific rumors mentioned in my No. 112 they admit that their economic problems are closely interwoven with political problems. But the Foreign Minister said frankly that Iran must preserve economic freedom as much as possible for without it she could probably not long maintain her political independence. He also intimated that normal negotiations were extremely difficult in "the present atmosphere" and that Iran was carefully watching her frontiers.

(2) The Foreign Minister appeared much impressed by the firmness shown by Finland and referred to President Roosevelt's telegram to

---

[4c] Reza Shah Pahlavi.
[4d] H. Fukuti.
[4e] Mouzaffar Aalam.

Moscow⁵ as a "noble gesture". He added that according to his information the Soviets were at present particularly bitter against Great Britain and the United States because they realized that a fundamentally successful democracy was the most dangerous enemy bolshevism could have. Moscow was now hoping that even victorious democracies would be too exhausted to stop Russian denomination [*domination*] in Eastern Europe and Near East and the furthering of Communist aims. And by that time the Soviets might be ready for open war against the capitalist world. He thought it was useless to put down Hitler only to let a much worse enemy of society take his place but it would require statesmanship of a very high order on the part of all democracies to prevent it. He himself did not believe the Soviets would ever become "good neighbors".

(3) Iran's foreign policy appears to be in a fluid state because the Government must tread carefully if it is to remain on equally good terms with Russia and Great Britain. The Shah undoubtedly wants to go his own way and has on the surface adopted an attitude of detachment toward the European war. He is above all intent on avoiding if possible the recurrence of the unfortunate experiences during the last war. He will probably do nothing reckless nor deliberately provoke displeasure in Moscow but many factors are already conspiring to make his task a very awkward one.

ENGERT

741.6711/25 : Telegram

The Chargé in Iran (Engert) to the Secretary of State

TEHRAN, October 23, 1939—10 p. m.
[Received October 24—6:15 p. m.]

128. My 59, May 23, 9 a. m., paragraph 3, 76, July 26, 11 a. m., paragraph 2⁶ and 120, October 17, 9 a. m. Also despatch No. 1701, October 10th.⁷

(1) News of failure of Turkish negotiations in Moscow and mutual assistance pact between Turkey, Britain and France⁸ was received in Iran with mixed feelings. Although there is strictly speaking no public mind there are a number of shrewd and competent political observers whose sparse and guarded comments occasionally reflect reactions of both the Government and the middle classes. The first impression is that there appears to have been a certain relaxation of

---

⁵ See telegram No. 194, October 11, 1939, 5 p. m., to the Ambassador in the Soviet Union, *Foreign Relations*, 1939, vol. I, p. 967.
⁶ Neither printed.
⁷ Not printed.
⁸ Signed at Ankara, October 19, 1939, League of Nations Treaty Series, vol. CC, p. 167.

the tension which had been created by the establishment of a virtual Russian protectorate over the Baltic States. It had been feared that Turkey would be induced to sign something which might sacrifice Rumania whereupon Iran's turn would follow soon. This danger seems now much less imminent.

(2) Iran as a signatory of the Saadabad pact [9] is obviously interested in the Anglo-French system of alliances and guarantees which Turkey has now definitely joined. German failure to localize the war and the determination of the democracies to fight to a finish have put Iran in a singularly delicate position and she realizes that it may ultimately lead to a complete reshaping of her foreign policy. Opinions are divided whether the Saadabad pact is destined to assume an ever increasing importance or whether recent events have not practically destroyed it. It must be frankly admitted that the moral issues involved in the war have so far made little appeal to either Iranian public or Government with the notable exception of the Foreign Minister whose sympathies have always been on the side of the democracies. Self interest being the determining factor in the Shah's policy he dreads the thought of being obliged to sign any defensive pacts with either Great Britain or Russia.

(3) This feeling is all the stronger because the treaty signed by Turkey is regarded as of little use against Soviet aggression which is precisely the danger that is looming increasingly large. Unlike Bulgaria or Yugoslavia Iran was never on friendly terms with Russia even before the last war, and the threat from the north is an ever present factor in her political and social life. Iran resents of course that Germany should have strengthened Moscow's hands in the Middle East but she does not fear Nazi aggression. Unless therefore Turkey shows willingness to fight Russia if necessary Iran will remain skeptical as to the practical value of cooperation with Turkey and the democracies.

(4) New Turkish Ambassador [9a] who has just been transferred here from Paris tells me that Turkey was not prepared to subordinate her own vital interests to the wishes of either Russia or Great Britain or anybody else but that it so happened that these interests coincided at the present time with the aims of the democracies. He intimated that Ankara's pride had been wounded by the Soviet's neglect to inform it of the negotiations with Hitler and of the decision to invade Poland.

(5) German propaganda in Tehran had until the last hoped for the defection of Turkey but is now spreading the report that Turkey had simply been "bought" by England and is trying to sow discord

---

[9] Treaty of Nonaggression signed at Saadabad Palace, Tehran, July 8, 1937, by Turkey, Iraq, Iran, and Afghanistan; League of Nations Treaty Series, vol. cxc, p. 21.

[9a] Suad Dava.

between Iran and Turkey by making it appear that the latter was intent on compelling Iran to abandon her policy of neutrality.

ENGERT

761.91/200 : Telegram

The Chargé in Iran (Engert) to the Secretary of State

TEHRAN, December 1, 1939—10 a. m.
[Received December 2—7:16 a. m.]

152. Minister of Finance [9b] who dined with me last night said the news from Finland was again causing the Government to take an extremely grave view of the immediate outlook (see also my telegrams 120 and 128). Breakdown of international law and the complete upheaval in Eastern Europe had brought distinctly increased dangers to Iran which no mere desire for detachment from the quarrels of others or a noncommittal policy in foreign affairs could avoid. Almost every hour seemed to develop new situations and the whole Near and Middle East was now dominated by the threat of force.

The Minister, whose wife is Russian, then said that although Iran had furnished no pretext whatever for a change in her relations with Moscow, all Iranian economic overtures toward a commercial agreement had recently been coldly rejected. He feared secret understanding with Reich under which Soviet Union could seek to revive her dominant position in the northern provinces. With an eye on Kirkuk and the Iranian oil fields Moscow would doubtless like to accuse Iran of resisting legitimate Soviet demands because encouraged by the British to do so presumably in order to become a base for the invasion of Russia! He thought that not unlike Japan in the Far East, the Soviets were now planning a "new order" for the Middle East by adroit opportunism and a cynical defiance of reason and justice. Unless therefore the end of this war saw the destruction of bolshevism, as well as nazism, the menace of freedom and civilization would not have been removed.

ENGERT

761.91/202 : Telegram

The Chargé in Iran (Engert) to the Secretary of State

TEHRAN, January 3, 1940—5 p. m.
[Received January 4—11:54 a. m.]

2. (1) The Iranian Government has ordered all German and Soviet nationals to leave the province of Kuzistan where the Anglo-Iranian oil fields are situated. This includes the officers and crews of

---

[9b] Rezaqoli Khosrovi.

the German vessels referred to in my despatch No. 1712, October 26.[10] They are now being repatriated via Russia.

(2) German propaganda whose principal object has been to create discord between Britain and Iran and between Britain and the Soviet Union has seized upon this measure to start a whispering campaign in the bazaars that England will now soon order Iran to decree a general mobilization and that the Soviets will have just cause to accuse Iran of playing the game of her "British masters". Although the Iranians—as do the Afghans—feel instinctively that the Germans look upon them as inferior peoples and really unfit to enjoy full independence the close economic bonds with Germany have offered merchants opportunities of easy profit and other advantages. The bazaar is therefore in a sense pro-German and lends itself to the dissemination of false reports.

(3) An exceptionally reliable source not connected with paragraph 5 of my 112, October 3, states that three new Russian divisions have recently arrived in Turkestan. Iran is quietly speeding up defensive measures but the Government officially denies that it is concentrating large forces in the north. However, foreigners are at present not allowed to travel in Mazanderan because it is rumored small fortifications and field defenses are being constructed as there are no modern fortified lines properly speaking. Otherwise there is as yet little evidence of special military precautions.

(4) There is a certain amount of cautious Bolshevist propaganda directed chiefly by Russian trained refugees and Armenians who are attempting to spread subversive doctrines among the peasants for whom the present regime has done very little and who are being promised distribution of lands. The Iranian authorities have recently arrested several Soviet agents including some officers in civilian clothes near the Turko-Iranian frontier.   ENGERT

761.91/209 : Telegram

The Chargé in Iran (Engert) to the Secretary of State

TEHRAN, March 7, 1940—9 p. m.
[Received March 8—8 : 13 p. m.]

40. The following information has been received from a very trustworthy source.

(1) Newly arrived German Minister [10a] has assured the Iranian Minister of Foreign Affairs on behalf of Hitler that Russia will not invade Iran. No such assurance has been received from the Soviet Ambassador.

---

[10] Not printed.
[10a] Erwin C. Ettel.

(2) Trade agreement between Iran and the Soviet Government is about to be initialed in Moscow. Discussions have since my 152, December 1, been proceeding both here and in Moscow in an atmosphere of great mystery and there have been exchanges of views without committing either Government. Official negotiations had been in abeyance since May 1939 as Iran feared they would almost certainly be stretched so as to include raw materials (see also my 112, October 3).

(3) Relative lack of Soviet success in the Finnish campaign [11] has appreciably stiffened Iranian attitude toward Moscow. The Shah is said to be deeply impressed by Finland's resistance against overwhelming odds and he will now probably stand firm in the face of unreasonable Soviet demands because he does not believe Russia can at present afford to put any additional strain on her army. Feeling is gaining ground that developments in Finland and in the Balkans are bound also to affect Soviet plans in the direction of the Black Sea and the Caspian.

ENGERT

761.91/210 : Telegram

The Chargé in Iran (Engert) to the Secretary of State

TEHRAN, March 16, 1940—7 p. m.
[Received March 17—11 : 45 a. m.]

46. By an odd coincidence for the third time in 3 years the Shah's birthday has been celebrated when attention was focused on the triumph of aggression. See, e. g., my telegram 22, March 16, 1939.[12] It was natural therefore that at the Crown Prince's dinner party last night the news from Finland should form the chief topic of conversation.

(1) The first reaction among highly placed Iranians was one of dismay. They did not conceal their great concern over the new international situation created by Finland's surrender. They feel frontiers everywhere are threatened if all such modifications of the map are permitted to go unchallenged. As stated in paragraph 3 of the Legation's 40, March 7, 9 p. m. the Iranian Government had been watching the Finnish war with intense interest and had hoped until the last that Finland might yet prevent extension of Soviet ambitions. But now they fear the Soviets may reach out after fresh objectives and as the world seems to be completely in the dark as to Moscow's real motives and intentions the implications of the events in the Baltic have not been lost on Iran.

---

[11] See vol. I, pp. 269 ff.
[12] Not printed.

(2) While Iranian official circles profess great satisfaction that the commercial agreement [13] referred to in my 44 of March 14, 9 a. m.[14] should have been concluded just at this juncture and cite it as proof of the improved atmosphere which now obtains between Iran and Russia, they are always prepared for disagreeable surprises from Moscow. Although Iran has displayed a genuine desire to reduce the tension and can justly claim the chief credit for such improvement in their relations as may exist, the unscrupulous system and methods for which Stalin stands may force her to adapt herself to a new relationship with Soviet Russia. In fact, the Russian Ambassador is reliably reported to have intimated to the Foreign Office here that his country desired settlements "on broad lines" which is interpreted as an intention to tighten Russia's grip on all border states.

(3) Iran's and Afghanistan's geographic position is such that close commercial relations with Russia are natural and both show anxiety lest the trade relationships be exploited by the Soviets to revive policy of aggression in Central Asia. Without taking the many recent rumors regarding Russian projects in the Middle East too literally, Iran has undoubtedly been marked out for greater commercial and diplomatic activity which may well translate itself into a demand for nonaggression or mutual assistance pact. Iran does not want such a pact with Moscow and she does not want to suffer the fate of Poland and Finland.

(4) As pointed out in earlier reports, e. g., my telegrams 112, 120, 128, and 151 [152] of 1939 and despatch No. 1755, January 10, 1940,[15] the Iranian Government is firmly convinced that the Soviets have reverted to and adopted most of the imperialism of the old Czarist Russia and are using the expansion of Bolshevist doctrines as an instrument of the new revolutionary imperialism. Influential Iranian circles are therefore longing for a sign that the democracies are prepared to call Stalin's bluff and the fact that Turkey, Egypt and Iraq are now all linked with the democratic nations would probably make the Government receptive to proposals to consolidate Iran's position in the Middle East. In any event, informed opinion here is now under no misapprehension as to what a German-Soviet victory would mean for the future of Iran.

ENGERT

---

[13] Treaty of Commerce and Navigation between the Soviet Union and Iran, signed at Tehran, March 25, 1940; for English translation, see *British and Foreign State Papers*, vol. CXLIV, p. 419.
[14] Not printed.
[15] Despatch not printed.

661.9131/183 : Telegram

The Chargé in Iran (Engert) to the Secretary of State

TEHRAN, April 17, 1940—9 a. m.
[Received 5:40 p. m.]

77. Legation's 63, April 5, 9 p. m.[16] It seemed best to await completion of English and French translations before commenting.

(1) Immediate result of the signing of the treaty was a distinct *détente* in Irano-Soviet relations. Feeling of optimism has taken the place of fear of grave developments which were freely predicted only a few months ago. Although the exact nature of the difficulties which have for nearly 2 years been found insurmountable has never been divulged, enough has leaked out to show that Moscow originally wanted an agreement of much wider scope than a simple treaty of commerce. Ever since the Soviets established military domination over the Baltic States, the Iranian Government has been expecting similar treatment. Moscow had already hinted that political relations with Iran could be "improved" by means of a so-called nonaggression or mutual assistance pact or even a military alliance. The present treaty has therefore been hailed as a pleasant surprise and as a welcome sign of a definite easing of the tension. Please see also my despatch No. 1694, September 28[16] and telegrams 120, October 17 and 152, December 1.

(2) Informed diplomatic circles express the view that had Finland yielded like the Baltic States, Iran's turn would probably have come next but the Finnish war—as stated in the Legation's telegram No. 40, March 7, 9 p. m.—had a direct influence on the negotiations. Iran adopted a somewhat firmer tone and avoided being drawn into political discussions. It seems also certain that Great Britain and Turkey lent their moral support and expressed great interest in the maintenance of the *status quo* in Iran. On the other hand, they are said to have advised the Iranian Government to make every possible concession consistent with her independence and neutrality in the hope that the Soviets might postpone pressing any political claims. The mere fact that the treaty was signed in Tehran instead of Moscow is considered by Iranians as a great diplomatic victory.

(3) Although the Foreign Minister denies that there are any secret clauses, it is generally believed that certain promises have been made by the Iranian Government such as, for example, the release of Communist prisoners reported in the Legation's 60, April 2[16] and facilities in case Russia should find it necessary to invoke articles V and VI

---

[16] Not printed.

of the treaty of 1921 [19] (see my despatch 820, February 2, 1922 [20]) it has been tacitly assumed by Iran that article VI had become a dead letter but it is clear from two specific references to the 1921 treaty that the Soviet Union wished to stress the fact that it considered the old treaty in full force.

(4) The clauses in the new treaty which worry Iranians most are those giving the Union of Soviet Socialist Republics the right to maintain trade representatives with diplomatic immunity and to establish filling stations. Distrust inspired by recent tendencies in official Soviet policy is so great that it is firmly believed these rights will be abused and exploited for propaganda purposes. So long as Russia's plans and ambitions remain obscure and subject to sudden change Iran feels she will have to keep the closest watch on her every move.

Comments regarding technical questions will be made by mail.

ENGERT

761.91/217 : Telegram

The Chargé in Iran (Engert) to the Secretary of State

TEHRAN, May 6, 1940—9 a. m.
[Received May 6—8 : 45 a. m.]

101. My 91, April 30, 4 p. m.[20] It now seems practically certain that the Iranian Government has been obliged to put several flying fields at the disposal of the Soviets. A number of Iranian refugees who were expelled from Russia—see my despatch No. 1294, May 13, 1938 [20]—have just been engaged by the Iranian Air Force presumably to serve as interpreters.

ENGERT

761.91/217 : Telegram

The Secretary of State to the Chargé in Iran (Engert)

WASHINGTON, May 8, 1940—5 p. m.

53. Your 101, May 6, 9 a. m. As soon as you are in a position to do so, please telegraph without delay further information and your views regarding the basis and significance of the Soviet demands for airfield facilities, including an explanation of the phrase "at the disposal of the Soviets".

HULL

---

[19] Treaty of Friendship, February 26, 1921, League of Nations Treaty Series, vol. IX, p. 383.
[20] Not printed.

761.91/219.: Telegram

The Chargé in Iran (Engert) to the Secretary of State

TEHRAN, May 10, 1940—9 a. m.
[Received 11 : 10 p. m.]

106. Department's 53, May 8, 5 p. m.

(1) According to an extremely reliable source Russia has demanded and has been granted the right to use if and when required 7 Iranian landing fields including 1 at Ahwaz near the oil fields and 1 at Khwash near the Afghanistan frontier. Four of them are being rapidly enlarged and at least 2 new ones are being constructed in compliance with Soviet wishes.

(2) The basis for the demand must of course be sought in article 6 of the treaty of 1921 referred to in paragraph 3 of the Legation's telegram No. 77, April 17, 9 a. m. But the ostensible reason for invoking it at the present time is probably contained in the last sentence of my 87, April 27, 9 p. m.[21] Ever since the concentration of Allied troops in the Middle East and foreign newspaper talk of bombing Baku I understand the Soviet Ambassador has been feigning apprehension lest Iran become a "tool of Britain" and force Moscow to take measures for the protection of the Baku oil fields against possible attacks from the south.

(3) Extreme secrecy has marked all recent Soviet moves in Iran and the precise details of the demands alluded to in my telegram 112, October 3, 1939, have never become available. However, the technique of their presentation seems to resemble closely that employed against the Baltic States except that the Soviets have evidently decided not to repeat the mistake made in the case of Finland of making public demands and threats without being sure that Iran will not fight.

(4) Soviet Embassy and German Legation are apparently working in close collaboration in Iran. Both seem determined, although each from different motives, to exploit fully all advantages the Russo-German understanding gives them. Germany has undoubtedly been inciting the Soviets to adopt greater aggressive policy toward Iran and Afghanistan in the hope of weakening and perhaps eliminating British influence. Moscow seems to be tempted by the chance for easy spoils and easy diplomatic or military victories and—as so often pointed out in these telegrams—to secure the larger Soviet objectives of overthrowing capitalism by causing a general social and economic breakdown in as many countries as possible. It is significant that in Iranian official circles the belief is frankly expressed that if the Soviet

---

[21] *Post,* p. 641.

Union should intervene actively in the European war its intervention would be decisive.

ENGERT

740.0011 European War 1939/3444 : Telegram

The Chargé in Iran (Engert) to the Secretary of State

TEHRAN, June 1, 1940—9 a. m.
[Received 1 p. m.]

117. 1. As the theater of war widens the nervous tension here is [increasing?]. Although political circles are more reserved and non-committal than ever, it is clear that the crisis on the western front is having a profoundly disturbing effect on the Iranian Government. Iran's attitude toward every question of foreign policy is of course decided by the Shah which means that irrevocable decisions may be taken overnight without previous discussion. No one knows what is happening behind the scenes but the swiftly moving political and military events are gradually altering the outlook. The Iranian masses are practically neutral or indifferent in thought and feeling. The principles the Allies are fighting for mean little to a people who can hardly be expected to understand democratic ideals, while among the governing classes and army there is a distinct tendency to favor the totalitarian regimes as best calculated to preserve internal order. See also paragraph 2 my telegram No. 2, January 3, and my telegram No. 113, May 24.[24]

2. Iran is of course much less exposed to German than to Russian aggression but usually well informed quarters believe that the effects of German military successes will soon be felt here. In fact it is rumored that the Reich has already offered Iran a joint Russian-German guarantee against "British aggression" and the German Legation here is combining boasts with veiled threats in talking to Iranians. A clever argument they use is that it was Hitler who prevailed on Stalin to leave Finland, an independent and non-Bolshevist Government, and they promise to do as much for Iran! In Germanophile circles one also hears the obviously inspired statement whispered that as soon as Germany has won the war she will not continue her present temporary understanding with the Soviets and could therefore assure Iran that Russia would not be permitted to expand southward. Incidentally, German propaganda promises a victorious Germany would see that Bahrein was returned to Iran.

---

[24] Latter not printed.

3. As Germany cloaks most of her political activities in Iran under commercial guises her principal aim is stated to be to increase the area where trade is closely regulated and organized on a bilateral basis at the expense of course of countries adhering to multilateral trade principles. The creation of such an immense Nazi and Soviet economic bloc would also give them overwhelming political influence in the Near East and Middle East to the exclusion and extinction of all democratic influences.

4. In the meantime I learn that some 300 alleged German commercial travelers have recently arrived in Iran via Russia making a total of approximately 2000 male German nationals of whom about 1500 are said to be in Tehran and the remainder in the provinces. In view of fifth column activities elsewhere a similar danger is not excluded here. There is evidence that Germans and Russians have suborned several high officials and many minor ones and although their methods are often obvious and crude the technique of subversion as a weapon of conquest has been well thought out. Lack of Iranian watchfulness is illustrated by the fact that the British have just discovered that 2 of the 5 German merchant vessels at Bander Shahpur (see the Legation's despatch No. 1712, October 26, 1939 [25]) were using radio transmitter sets which had been sealed by the Iranian authorities. The latter expressed surprise and merely resealed them instead of removing them from all five ships. British and French Ministers are now insisting that any suspicious activities of Germans and Russians must be promptly checked and that persons whose bona fide occupation cannot be established must be expelled.

ENGERT

740.0011 European War 1939/4471 : Telegram

The Chargé in Iran (Engert) to the Secretary of State

TEHRAN, July 8, 1940—8 a. m.
[Received July 8—4 : 48 a. m.]

153. Recent statements attributed to members of the Soviet Embassy are to the effect that in view of the German discoveries in Paris of documents proving Allied designs on Baku and Batum the Soviet Government will probably find it necessary to demand certain guarantees which will render the execution of such plans impossible.

This is interpreted here as foreshadowing Russian territorial claims in northern Iran. See also my telegram No. 106, May 10, paragraph 2.

ENGERT

---

[25] Not printed.

740.0011 European War 1939/4498 : Telegram

The Chargé in Iran (Engert) to the Secretary of State

TEHRAN, July 8, 1940—noon.
[Received July 8—11 : 40 a. m.]

157. My telegram number 153 of today. Editorial this morning expresses surprise that Russian broadcast should use alleged revelations in German White Book [26] to accuse Iran of being involved in Allied plans to bomb Baku. There is no evidence whatever that Iran knew anything at all about such plans. On the contrary from the documents published it appears clearly that Iran was not a party to them. Iran would defend her neutrality against anybody attacking it. She suspects Soviets are looking for a pretext.

ENGERT

740.0011 European War 1939/4739 : Telegram

The Chargé in Iran (Engert) to the Secretary of State

TEHRAN, July 18, 1940—11 a. m.
[Received 9 : 42 p. m.]

170. My telegram 153, July 7 [8], 8 a. m. It now seems reasonably certain that the Soviet Government has formulated definite demands of which the following are the most important.

1. The cession or at least occupation by Soviet troops of northern Azerbaijan including Tabriz. Portion of Ghilan and of Gorgan to the Gorgan River including port of Bandarshah on the Caspian Sea.

2. Control of the trans-Persian railway to the Persian Gulf.

3. Use of all Iranian landing fields, see also my telegram No. 106, May 10, 9 a. m., and especially third paragraph.

ENGERT

740.0011 European War 1939/5035 : Telegram

The Chargé in Iran (Engert) to the Secretary of State

TEHRAN, August 9, 1940—9 a. m.
[Received August 10—8 : 35 a. m.]

187. Legation's 186, August 7, noon [27] and 170, July 18, 11 a. m. Molotov's [28] reference to Iran [29] has revived many contradictory re-

---

[26] See footnote 77, p. 209.
[27] Not printed.
[28] Vyacheslav M. Molotov, Soviet Minister for Foreign Affairs.
[29] Presumably a reference to Molotov's speech on Soviet foreign relations to the Supreme Soviet, August 1, 1940. See telegram No. 945, August 1, midnight, from the Chargé in the Soviet Union, p. 208.

ports regarding Soviet aims in this part of the world but it is less than ever possible to be certain of the correctness of one's information. My contacts with the new Prime Minister [29a] are not yet what they were with his predecessor and even the Minister for Foreign Affairs has, since he signed the commercial treaty with Moscow become extremely reticent.

Inquiries among persons with unusually wide contacts indicate that Iranian anxiety had been momentarily allayed by the belief that the Soviets were not prepared to embark upon fresh ventures so soon after the Finnish campaign. However, the annexation of Bessarabia [30] and the Baltic States [31] has again given rise to pessimism and to a feeling that Iran's very existence may soon be threatened.

The Shah resents the role of a helpless pawn upon the slippery chess board of power politics and is pathetically anxious to give the impression that he is following his own policy and not that of some great power; nor does he want Iran to become a protectorate either in form or in fact. And as he can be very stubborn when aroused he is credited with a recent instruction to his Foreign Minister that there must be no undue compliance with Soviet demands for he had the firm intention of holding the northern provinces at all costs.

On the other hand his principal advisers are obviously carefully avoiding any action which might be considered provocative by the Soviets and are ready to give in regarding minor adjustments whenever prudence seems to recommend such a course. They recognize that traditionally northern Iran has always been a sphere of Russian influence and that Soviet Russia, having secured herself against the Axis in the west may now take similar measures in the Near and Middle East against Great Britain to link up with a bolshevikized Sinkiang and Mongolia erected against Japan. In any event Russia is at present Iran's most powerful neighbor for under present circumstances England can do little for Iran. Therefore, although there has never been much public sentiment here in favor of the Allies and the triumph of right and justice would mean little to the people, real anxiety is felt by the Iranian Government as to the outcome of the struggle between Britain and the Axis. The ultimate safety of Iran oddly enough is now considered closely linked with the British cause.

Effect of Jap [*Nazi?*]-Soviet cooperation is becoming daily more pronounced. Principal danger of the combination is believed to lie in the fact that the Reich is no longer afraid of the Soviets and may thus become the dominant partner in a discreditable scramble to secure strategic and political positions favorable to their ambitions. Backed by threats and bribes beyond this cynical disregard even of appear-

---

[29a] Ali Mansur.
[30] See vol. I, pp. 444 ff.
[31] See *ibid.*, pp. 357 ff.

ances, their joint diplomacy is trying to shake the nerve of the Iranian Government and to bluff or browbeat it into political and economic subordination.

Molotov's crude remarks about Soviet relations with the United States have been referred to by various persons in high positions as proof that Moscow like Berlin is holding the United States in contempt and that unless the democratic world combines against the common danger the last of the world's bulwarks against bolshevism will fall one by one. Iran considers herself as part of this remaining barrier and being still devoted to the ideal of collective security looks to the democracies to take common action against Soviet-Nazi policies which are [designed to?] frustrate everything the West has ever stood for.

ENGERT

761.62/803 : Telegram

The Chargé in Iran (Engert) to the Secretary of State

TEHRAN, November 14, 1940—3 p. m.
[Received November 16—6 : 30 a. m.]

248. In conversation with the Under Secretary of Foreign Affairs [31a] this morning he referred to Molotov's visit to Berlin [32] as fresh proof that Soviet policy was devoid of all moral foundations. Whenever Germany and Russia wished to impress an intended victim they got together and were apparently ready to use any means to attain their goal. This time he feared the Soviets might be tempted with the possibility of adding Turkish Armenia to their dominions in which case Iran might also become involved. He expressed great uneasiness over Iran's future relations with both Moscow and Berlin.

ENGERT

740.0011 European War 1939/6789 : Telegram

The Chargé in Iran (Engert) to the Secretary of State

[Extract]

TEHRAN, November 19, 1940—3 p. m.
[Received November 20—3 a. m.]

253. My 230, October 24, noon.[33] Similar source [34] now states:
(1) Soviets have promised Berlin not to interfere with German and Italian projects in the Balkans in return for Turkish Armenia and,

---

[31a] Djevad Amery.
[32] November 12–13, 1940. For the German account of this visit, see Department of State, *Nazi-Soviet Relations, 1939–1941*, pp. 217 ff.
[33] Not printed.
[34] Not identified.

if the Soviets should consider it vital, portions of northern Iran. See also Legation's 248, November 14, 3 p. m.

. . . .

ENGERT

740.0011 European War 1939/6956 : Telegram

The Chargé in Iran (Engert) to the Secretary of State

TEHRAN, November 29, 1940—10 a. m.
[Received November 30—9 a. m.]

260. Legation's 248, November 14, 3 p. m., and 253, November 19, 3 p. m. Acting Minister for Foreign Affairs [34a] states he believes ceaseless activity of German diplomacy bodes ill for Near and Middle East if Russia acquiesces. When I asked if he had any news from Moscow as to Soviet intentions he laughed and said he doubted whether Molotov himself knew! He feared the Russo-German understanding whatever it might consist of would be the source of many further dangerous complications for the world as it had become perfectly clear that no reliance whatever could be placed on Hitler's or Stalin's promises or guarantees. At the present moment the Soviets had an interest in prolonging the war as much as possible but they were afraid of Germany and their policy was influenced by the daily fluctuations in the fortunes of war. To my question how Iran's relations with Moscow were shaping he replied that the recent action now showed distinct signs of easing.

The impression is that Iranian fear of the Soviets is a German diplomatic asset which is being utilized for all it is worth. Germany knows that Iran's fundamental orientation is towards the West rather than Russia, and as Great Britain is at present not considered powerful enough to render effective assistance Germany is posing as Iran's next friend. The Shah's fear of communism leads him to hope that Hitler may yet protect Iran against a Bolshevist invasion. See also paragraph 2 of my telegram 117, June 1, 1940. But intelligent Iranians realize that Germany would not protect Iran any more than she protected Rumania and that both Moscow and Berlin are merely plotting to take advantage of Iran's weakness. In the meantime the Iranian Government is disposed to go as far as possible along the swap of collaboration with the Soviet Union but would probably not submit tamely to military aggression. Moscow's shadow is lengthening and although there is as yet no clear indication how extensive Soviet ambitions are it must be remembered that in Iran mistrust of Russia is likely to remain more deep and widespread than fear of the Axis.

ENGERT

[34a] Presumably the Under Secretary for Foreign Affairs.

IRANIAN REQUESTS FOR CREDITS, AIRPLANES AND EQUIPMENT, AND TECHNICAL ADVISERS FROM THE UNITED STATES [35]

891.51/529

Memorandum of Conversation, by the Chief of the Division of Near Eastern Affairs (Murray)

[WASHINGTON,] March 1, 1940.

The Iranian Minister came to see me yesterday by appointment and said that he desired again to touch upon the question of the extension of credit to the Iranian Government by the Export-Import Bank.

Mr. Schayesteh referred to his conversation with Mr. Pierson, President of the Bank, some little time ago, and to Mr. Pierson's statement that if and when the lending authority of the Bank was extended by congressional action it might be feasible to give further consideration to the requests of the Iranian Government. Mr. Schayesteh had in mind the recent extension of the lending authority of the Bank to $100,000,000, and he is obviously hopeful that in view of this development favorable action may be taken upon the Iranian Government's request for the extension of credit in connection with the very considerable purchases ($75,000,000 has been mentioned) which that Government proposes to make in this country. The Minister quoted Mr. Pierson as having had a favorable impression of Iran's credit position, and he mentioned in this connection the accomplishment of the Iranian Government in financing the Trans-Iranian Railway, costing nearly $150,000,000, out of current revenue. He added that the firms employed to do this construction had not had the slightest difficulty in collecting from the Iranian Government.

I told the Minister that it was my understanding that the Export-Import Bank extended credit to American exporters upon the presentation of a concrete proposal to the Bank and that it would therefore seem that the Bank might expect to have before it such proposals before serious consideration in this matter could be given. The Minister emphasized, however, that what he had in mind was the establishment of a given credit which could be drawn upon by American exporters or by American firms when they would have come to an agreement with the Iranian Government regarding specific purchases.

The Minister expressed the earnest hope that the Department would interest itself in this matter not only because it considered the Iranian Government's request to be a good "business proposal", but also because of the larger political aspects of the situation affecting Iran. He stated in this connection that since the Bank had financed certain

---

[35] For previous correspondence on the subject of Iranian request for a loan, see *Foreign Relations, 1939*, vol. IV, pp. 538 ff.

exports to Sweden he saw no reason why the same assistance should not be rendered in the case of Iran.

I promised the Minister that I would not fail to bring his views to the attention of Mr. Pierson and suggested at the same time that he discuss the matter further with him in person.

891.20/120

Memorandum of Conversation, by the Chief of the Division of Controls (Green)

[WASHINGTON,] March 29, 1940.

The Iranian Minister called at my office this morning. He told me that he had two problems which he wished to discuss.

He said that the Iranian purchasing mission now in this country had been negotiating with three aircraft companies but had delayed placing orders because of the necessity of settling beforehand such questions as whether the aviation gas obtainable in Iran was of sufficiently high quality for use in American aircraft engines, whether machine guns already in the possession of the Iranian Government could be installed on the airplanes which the mission was considering purchasing, etc., etc. The mission was now prepared to place orders but had been distressed to learn that the prices of the planes which it wished to purchase had increased somewhat since the beginning of its negotiations and that the large number of foreign orders recently accepted by the manufacturers would make it impossible for them to deliver planes to the Iranian Government as soon as the mission had hoped. The mission was therefore confronted by unexpected difficulties. The Minister asked me whether I could give him any advice as to how the mission should proceed.

I told the Minister that the President had recently established an Interdepartmental Liaison Committee under the Chairmanship of Captain Harry E. Collins, Chief of the Procurement Division of the Treasury,[36] charged with the duty of assisting foreign purchasing missions and coordinating their purchases with those of this Government. I told him that I thought it would be very much to the advantage of the mission to explain their difficulties fully to Captain Collins who would, I was sure, do everything possible to assist the mission. I said that I would be glad to arrange an appointment with Captain Collins if the Minister so desired.

The Minister said that he would discuss this matter with the mission and would call me by telephone within a few days to request a definite

---

[36] The President authorized this committee in a letter to the Secretary of the Treasury, dated December 6, 1939. See *United States Government Manual*, Fall 1940, p. 59b.

appointment with Captain Collins. He said that he would probably ask for an appointment for himself and for officers of the mission.

The second question which the Minister wished to discuss was in connection with the desire of the Iranian arms purchasing mission in Europe to buy in the United States contact mines for coast defense. He said that an officer of the purchasing mission had reported that he had endeavored to obtain the assistance of the American Minister in Bern but had been informed that the matter should be taken up direct in Washington. The Minister asked how he should proceed.

I told the Minister that this was also a matter in which Captain Collins could be of great assistance to his Government. I suggested that, when he called on Captain Collins, he should take this matter up with him in order that Captain Collins might give him information as to the companies with which his Government might wish to communicate.

JOSEPH C. GREEN

891.20/121

Memorandum of Conversation, by the Chief of the Division of Controls (Green)

[WASHINGTON,] April 2, 1940.

The Iranian Minister called me by telephone this morning. He told me that he and officers of the Iranian purchasing mission had had a very satisfactory conference with Captain Collins, Chief of the Procurement Division of the Treasury, and that Captain Collins had asked him to furnish detailed descriptions of the planes and contact mines which his Government desires to purchase and had offered to obtain, for the Minister, as soon as possible, a statement of the prices at which these arms could be purchased and of the dates on which they could be delivered. He thanked me profusely for having arranged the conference and said that he felt that the difficulties which the purchasing mission had encountered were now in the way of solution.

JOSEPH C. GREEN

691.1115/8

Memorandum of Conversation, by the Chief of the Division of Near Eastern Affairs (Murray)

[WASHINGTON,] April 8, 1940.

The Iranian Minister called on me this morning to advise me of the latest developments in connection with his efforts to obtain credits from the Export-Import Bank with a view to stimulating trade between the United States and Iran.

Mr. Schayesteh told me that he had recently had conversations on this subject with Mr. Grady [37] and Mr. Feis,[38] also with Mr. Jesse Jones, Administrator of the Federal Loan Agency, and Mr. Warren Pierson, President of the Export-Import Bank. From the Minister's account of his conversations I gathered that he was reasonably encouraged.

Mr. Schayesteh expressed the hope that officials of this Department would take a sympathetic interest in the matter of credits to Iran and in particular that any credits that might eventually be granted should not be too restricted to serve the purpose which his Government had in mind. In this connection I gathered that Mr. Feis and Mr. Jones as well as Mr. Pierson may have pointed out to the Minister that any such sum as the Iranian Government had had in mind would be out of the question but that study might be given to the possibility of credits in a far more modest amount.

891.248/77 : Telegram

The Chargé in Iran (Engert) to the Secretary of State

TEHRAN, April 27, 1940—9 p. m.
[Received April 28—5 : 45 p. m.]

87. Yesterday morning I was again sent for by the Prime Minister [38a] who seemed more agitated and worried than I had ever seen him and said that he had something important to tell me: the Iranian Government had decided to dismiss all British air craftsmen and technical advisers now employed in the Iranian airplane factory and to engage Americans in their stead. He therefore requested me to assist him. Does the Department believe that some 12 such skilled workmen and supervisors could be found?

Although he gave as a reason that the Government was buying planes in America and therefore wanted to adopt American systems and methods his embarrassment was so obvious that I fear this is but another instance of Soviet pressure. (See also Legation's telegrams 60, April 2,[39] second paragraph of 71, April 14 [40] and paragraph 4 of 77, April 17.[41])

Iran is of course prepared to go to the utmost limit in reorganizing her relations with the Soviets for the length of their common frontier gives Moscow power to bully Iran into "cooperation". Hence her [submission?] to Russia in relatively minor matters but there is grow-

---

[37] Henry F. Grady, Assistant Secretary of State.
[38] Herbert Feis, Adviser on International Economic Affairs.
[38a] Dr. Matine-Daftary.
[39] Not printed.
[40] *Post,* p. 694.
[41] *Ante,* p. 629.

ing preoccupation with the extent of Moscow's appetite. Since the developments in Scandinavia [42] the Soviet Ambassador in Tehran is said to have expressed solitude [*solicitude?*] for Iran's neutrality in order to prevent her from becoming "a basis for aggression against Russia."

ENGERT

891.248/78 : Telegram

The Chargé in Iran (Engert) to the Secretary of State

TEHRAN, April 28, 1940—11 a. m.
[Received 5 : 25 p. m.]

88. At the interview with the Prime Minister reported in my No. 87 of yesterday, he also said His Majesty had urged him to request me to bring the following to your attention :

1. The Iranian Minister in Washington was now negotiating for credits of 5 million dollars. But that was not nearly enough. The Shah desired credits of at least 10 million dollars to be used exclusively for the purchase of military aircraft in the United States. This, apart from and in addition to the airplanes which are being bought for the Aero Club.

2. The Iranian Government would like to have an American company undertake the erection and equipment of an airplane factory in Iran with the least possible delay.

ENGERT

891.248/78 : Telegram

The Acting Secretary of State to the Chargé in Iran (Engert)

WASHINGTON, May 2, 1940—7 p. m.

50. Your 87, April 27, 9 a. m. [*p. m.*] and 88, April 28, 11 a. m.

1. The question of engaging American airplane production experts can doubtless be handled best by the Iranian Aviation Mission now in this country. If desired the Department will of course be glad to put the Mission in touch with the proper people.

2. It is our understanding that one of the original objects of the aviation mission was to make arrangements for the construction and equipment of an airplane factory in Iran. The Department is not informed of the progress that has been made along this line. The Iranian Minister is also without precise information as the Mission apparently operates independently of him.

[42] The German occupation of Denmark and invasion of Norway; see vol. I, pp. 136 ff.

3. The Minister is negotiating with the Export-Import Bank for a credit but he understands that the Bank, owing to legal restrictions, is unable to grant any credit whatever for military purposes. We understand that the Minister is also negotiating with a private New York bank for a loan the proceeds of which could be used for any purpose. The Minister has been told as clearly as possible, and it is desired that you emphasize the point to the Iranian authorities, that it is utterly impossible for the Department to bring influence or pressure to bear regarding such matters.

4. The Minister has been informed of the substance of your No. 88.

WELLES

891.248/80 : Telegram

The Chargé in Iran (Engert) to the Secretary of State

TEHRAN, May 6, 1940—5 p. m.
[Received 7 p. m.]

103. I have just seen the Prime Minister and communicated to him the substance of your 50, May 2, 7 p. m. He was visibly disappointed and asked me whether I thought the Department understood how urgent it all was. I assured him that I felt the Department had from the beginning given most serious and sympathetic thought to all angles of his proposals and requests. After a few moments hesitation and looking very grave he requested me to transmit the following verbal message from him to the Secretary of State:

"I, the Prime Minister of Iran, on behalf of the Imperial Government request the Government of the United States to make it possible for Iran to purchase in the United States a comparatively large number of military airplanes of various types for delivery at the earliest possible date. In order to enable Iran to purchase these planes, I hope a credit can be arranged for $10,000,000 to be devoted exclusively to this purpose. Iran has, of course, no aggressive designs against any of her neighbors but merely wishes to be fully prepared to maintain the strictest neutrality and if necessary to defend her independence and territorial integrity."

The above is obviously intended to convey the impression that Iran is gradually feeling the impact of pressure from the Soviets. While neither the Prime Minister nor the Foreign Minister has mentioned to me the reports referred to in the last paragraph of my 87, April 27, and in my 100, May 5,[43] and 101 May 6,[44] statements from excellent sources though unconfirmed officially are beginning to lift the curtain behind which some unpleasant scenes must have been enacted. See

---

[43] *Post,* p. 661.
[44] *Ante,* p. 630.

also my 46, March 16.[45] The seriousness of the international situation has further been brought home to Iran by the turn events have taken in Norway and the uncertainties in the Mediterranean. It is felt that the new phase of the war which has just begun may greatly alter Iran's role in the Middle East. For the present this country is still clinging precariously to neutrality and shares the common desire of all neutrals to keep the war from spreading. Although the Shah keeps his feelings and intentions a secret he is said to have declared that he wishes to follow an essentially Iranian policy and to retain complete freedom of judgment of action. But he is every day faced with new and vital decisions and being conscious of Iran's military weakness he realizes that her very existence may hang in the balance. Iran is in a state of great perplexity and the message from the Prime Minister to Secretary Hull is perhaps meant to suggest that the world must do something to help neutrals warn off intending aggressors if all small nations are not to disappear.

ENGERT

891.248/80 : Telegram

The Secretary of State to the Chargé in Iran (Engert)

WASHINGTON, May 11, 1940—3 p. m.

56. Your 103, May 6, 5 p. m. Please again assure the Prime Minister that this Government has given and will continue to give full and sympathetic consideration to his various proposals. However, so far as concerns loans to foreign governments, their agencies and nationals, the only United States Government organization through which loans are made is the Export-Import Bank, which is prevented by the Act of March 2, 1940 [45a] from making "any loans for the purchase of any articles, except aircraft exclusively for commercial purposes, listed as arms, ammunition, or implements of war by the President of the United States in accordance with the Neutrality Act of 1939".[45b]

The Iranian Government is free to make purchases here of military and civil aircraft on the same basis as any other country. The Iranian Aviation Mission has already been placed in touch with manufacturers through the Inter-Departmental Committee and the Department stands ready to arrange further contacts upon request.

HULL

---

[45] *Ante*, p. 627.
[45a] 54 Stat. 38.
[45b] 54 Stat. 4.

891.248/84 : Telegram

The Chargé in Iran (Engert) to the Secretary of State

TEHRAN, July 29, 1940—noon.
[Received 4 : 56 p. m.]

178. The Foreign Minister sent for me this morning. In his office I found the Acting Minister of War [45c] who stated he had been instructed by His Majesty to request me to do my utmost to obtain from the United States about 50 heavy bombers and 30 pursuit planes. His Majesty had also reiterated his desire to engage the services of American aircraft experts and to erect an airplane factory as already reported in my 87, April 27, and 88, April 28.

As the Foreign Minister has been particularly helpful in bringing about a settlement of the school question [46] I should like, if possible, to assure him that the Department is continuing its efforts to assist. Could perhaps a smaller number of planes than indicated above be definitely promised? See also last paragraph of my 103, May 6.

ENGERT

891.248/85

Memorandum of Conversation, by the Assistant Chief of the Division of Near Eastern Affairs (Alling)

[WASHINGTON,] August 3, 1940.

I telephoned today to the Iranian Minister to tell him that we were continuing to look into the question of the airplanes which his Government had desired. I told him that, as he probably knew, several other Government departments had to be consulted in this matter and I was sorry to say that we still had nothing definite we could tell him. I added that it was hoped that we would have something definite next week and that Mr. Murray would probably get in touch with him at that time to arrange a conference between officers of the Department and the Minister and Major Chaltchi.[47]

The Minister said he sincerely hoped that something could be done to meet the wishes of his Government in its present circumstances. He went on to say that he thought it was most important to point out that at the time he had presented his letters of credence to the President the latter had emphasized his belief that Iran must continue to exist and must defend itself against possible aggressors. According to the Minister, the President had added that this Government would help in any way it could to assist Iran in defending itself. The Minister

---

[45c] Gen. Ahmed Nakhtchevan.
[46] See pp. 693 ff.
[47] Head of the Iranian Aviation Mission in the United States.

said he hoped that the President's views were known to the military authorities and that those authorities would bear those views in mind when arriving at a decision in regard to airplanes for his country.

I told the Minister that in my discussions with interested people here in the Department I had found every disposition to assist the Iranian Government as much as we could. At the same time I pointed out that, as he must realize, we had our own defense problem and other considerations which must be borne in mind. The Minister stated that he fully realized this, but he felt that we could spare at least a part of the planes which the Iranian Government desired since that small number could not possibly affect our own defense problem. I again assured the Minister that we were all working with the utmost good will to help, and although the situation was difficult we had hopes that something could be done to assist.

891.248/89

Memorandum of Conversation, by Mr. William S. Farrell of the Division of Near Eastern Affairs

[WASHINGTON,] August 6, 1940.

Major Chaltchi called this morning in response to my telephone message inviting him to do so. He stated that it is only in the past week that he has received orders from the Iranian Ministry of War authorizing him to make contact with government authorities in this country. Up to then he was limited to broaching his business affairs with private companies only. He mentioned the well-known axiom that Iranian military officers must in general have nothing to do with foreign government officials. He presumed that the contact established by the Iranian Ministry of Foreign Affairs between Engert and the Acting Minister of War (as reported in Engert's telegram of July 29) reflected the Shah's personal interest in the question of obtaining airplanes, and would explain the recent change in his orders giving him greater latitude for making official contacts in this country.

The Major's name, by the way, is officially spelled with French phonetics "Chaltchi", and he informs me that it is so written in his Iranian passport.

He first referred to a purchase of airplanes from the Curtiss company, effected several months ago, for 10 machines on "service order", construction to commence in December next, for completion in February or March 1941; payment terms, 50 percent down and the remainder guaranteed. This trial order, he says, has nothing to do with his present concern for 50 bombers and 30 pursuit planes. It is his government's hope that the 10 machines already contracted for can be used as models for further construction in the already existing plant in Iran.

His immediate concern is to obtain as soon as possible 50 Douglas bombers (DB320) and 30 pursuit planes (either "Curtiss P 46" or "North American 73"). He has received the letter from Philip Young [48] of last Saturday, which tells him that this Government has no objection to the release of the planes provided the factories can furnish them after fulfilling current orders for our own national defense.

The Iranian desiderata and arguments at this point are the following:

1. In view of the American friendship for Iran, cannot the Department prevail upon the War Department, National Defense Commission and any others interested to allow a very small proportion, up to the 50 desired units of bombers and the 30 of pursuit planes, to be earmarked for Iranian needs, for delivery as soon as manufactured? With the factories running full blast to produce for American needs, it would be a simple matter for them to turn out the equivalent number to make up the U. S. defense demand immediately after turning over the allowable quantity, up to the numbers above stated, to Iran. In other words, from a hypothetical U. S. order of 1000 bombers from a given company, could not the first 970 represent those immediately needed and to be turned over to U. S. Army and/or Navy, the following 30 for Iran, and the factory at that point to continue its mass production, by that time functioning at maximum speed, to produce the remaining 30 for U. S. needs.

2. The Shah desires that the existing Iranian aircraft manufacturing facilities be improved to produce a more up-to-date model of plane. It is hoped that the 10 "service order" Curtiss planes already booked, as well as any number no matter how small, of the bombers and pursuit planes now desired, can be used as models for manufacture in Iran. Hence the urgency for obtaining them before U. S. needs are completely fulfilled as outlined in Young's letter. In view of American friendship for Iran, cannot the Department prevail upon the Curtiss company to make available one of its experts to fly to Iran, examine the present manufacturing equipment there, recommend what is needed to modernize the Iranian factory, and fly back to the United States? This should not take more than three months at the most. Chaltchi states that he realizes that the airplane manufacturers in this country can not easily spare an expert under the present circumstances, but is hopeful that this Government can induce them to send one, out of friendship for Iran.

3. While half payment has already been effected, and remainder guaranteed, for the order of Curtiss planes already placed, the Iranians would like longer credit terms for subsequent orders for planes, and are hopeful that the Department will induce the American manufacturers to grant them.

---

[48] Member of the Interdepartmental Liaison Committee. See *United States Government Manual*, Fall 1940, p. 59b.

The Major states that his trip to Buffalo has no connection with the present endeavor to order new planes, but is concerned with the previous order for 10 Curtiss planes. He must translate the specifications from English into Persian for transmission to his War Ministry.

The Iranian Minister in suggesting a conference had in mind being put in contact by this Division with the appropriate officials of War and Navy Departments and National Defense Commission, to induce them to make available from current U. S. orders the small numbers of planes desired by Iran.

891.248/95

Memorandum of Conversation, by Mr. Gordon P. Merriam of the Division of Near Eastern Affairs

[WASHINGTON,] August 16, 1940.

Participants: The Iranian Minister, Mr. Schayesteh
　　　　　　　Mr. Murray
　　　　　　　Mr. Villard
　　　　　　　Mr. Merriam

The Iranian Minister came in this afternoon at Mr. Murray's invitation to discuss the desire of his Government to purchase 50 heavy bombers and 30 pursuit planes from American manufacturers. The Minister was informed that as the result of inquiries which had been made of the competent officials, there appeared to be no possibility of making available to the Iranian Government machines being constructed or to be constructed for the United States Government. It was pointed out to him, on the other hand, that military airplanes were being built for and delivered currently to foreign governments. Those governments had, however, placed their orders some time ago. If the Iranian Government wanted airplanes, it would seem desirable that orders be placed as soon as possible, since priority of delivery as between foreign buyers seemed to hinge essentially upon date of orders. However, we had no information that the Iranian Government had placed orders for the machines above mentioned or that it intended to do so in the immediate future.

Mr. Schayesteh was manifestly disappointed at receiving this information. He observed that in view of the immense size of the American armament program, surely a few airplanes could be spared for the Iranian Government without interfering with that program in any important way.

Mr. Murray reminded the Minister that the American program is at present almost entirely on paper, that recent international events had placed heavy responsibilities on our armed services, which felt themselves unable to permit the slightest interference with the plans for the manufacture and delivery of machines for our use. The Minister was informed of the view of the Under Secretary of State that the Department could not in any way bring pressure to bear on the competent officials to subordinate any part of our program to Iranian needs. The Minister was asked whether in fact the Iranian Government had placed any order for airplanes in this country apart from a few training machines.

Mr. Schayesteh replied in the negative, and stated that the interviews which Major Chaltchi, present head of the Iranian Aviation Mission here, had had with representatives of the manufacturers, were most unsatisfactory. Major Chaltchi, he said, had been informed by those representatives that Iran could not be supplied until the American program should be achieved, and that neither delivery dates nor prices could be quoted at this time.

As the result of considerable questioning it appeared, although it proved to be impossible to secure a categorical statement from the Iranian Minister on the point, that Major Chaltchi had not yet made any use of the letter which Mr. Philip Young, the Coordinator from the Procurement Division of the Treasury, had addressed to him on August 3 stating no objection is perceived, subject to the needs of the American armed forces, to permitting the supply of airplanes to Iran, and offering to place him in touch with American airplane manufacturers.

The Minister was told that the logical next step was for Major Chaltchi to avail himself of Mr. Young's offer and then to return to the manufacturers with Mr. Young's letter in hand.

It was arranged that Major Chaltchi should come to see Mr. Murray on Monday and that an endeavor would be made to make an appointment for Major Chaltchi with Mr. Young, whereupon the Iranian Minister departed evidently pleased that some way might yet be found of meeting the desires of his Government.

After clearing with Mr. Yost in Co,[49] Mr. Murray talked with Mr. James Buckley, assistant to Mr. Young (the latter being out of town), and arranged for Major Chaltchi to call on Mr. Young, Monday at 11:30. Mr. Buckley was informed that for political reasons it was desirable to do everything possible to meet the wishes of the Iranian Government in the matter, although, of course, we did not wish to urge any action which the Coordinator should consider unwise or impracticable. Mr. Buckley promised to take Major Chaltchi in hand and do what was possible. He felt, however, that little could be done until after the Major should have presented Mr. Young's letter to the manufacturers.

---

[49] Division of Controls.

891.248/96

Memorandum of Conversation, by Mr. Gordon P. Merriam of the Division of Near Eastern Affairs

[WASHINGTON,] August 20, 1940.

Participants: The Iranian Minister, Mr. Schayesteh
               Major Chaltchi
               Mr. Murray
               Mr. Villard
               Mr. Merriam

The Iranian Minister and Major Chaltchi, head of the Iranian Aviation Mission, came in prior to keeping an appointment at the Treasury with Mr. Philip Young of the President's Liaison Committee.

As the result of discussion and questioning, it developed from Major Chaltchi's remarks that on receiving instructions from his Government, he had approached Mr. Young on July 18 relative to the possibility of purchasing bombers and fighters of types approved by the United States Army. Mr. Young thereupon made inquiries, the results of which were embodied in his letter of August 3 to Major Chaltchi, a copy of which the Major handed to Mr. Murray, and is attached hereto.[50]

Major Chaltchi said that he had not availed himself of Mr. Young's offer to put him in touch with the Washington representatives of the manufacturers because he already knew them. He therefore approached them direct, but was informed that since delivery to the American armed forces must take precedence, no delivery dates on Iranian orders could be set; moreover, delivery of the Iranian requirements would occur after such a long lapse of time that the manufacturers could not quote prices. He reported to Tehran to this effect, with the result that the Iranian Government took up the matter with our Legation at Tehran.

Mr. Murray observed that Major Chaltchi's problem was by no means unique. It was faced by every foreign Government which wanted to buy airplanes here. He asked whether Major Chaltchi had inquired from the air attachés of other foreign countries represented in Washington, under what conditions they were obtaining airplanes. It would be interesting to know, for example, how the Turks were making out.

Major Chaltchi replied that the Turks were accepting planes of types not being supplied to the United States Army. The Iranian Government, however, would not purchase machines not approved by the American armed forces.

---

[50] Not printed.

Mr. Murray then said that the Iranian Government seemed to be seeking the solution for an insoluble problem. They could not expect this Government, under existing conditions, to give way to Iranian needs. Moreover, this country was deeply concerned with the outcome of the present attacks on Great Britain. It was obviously in the interest of this country to make every airplane which could be manufactured, and which was not required here, available for the British. However, Mr. Murray did not doubt that the Liaison Committee would do everything possible for the Iranian Government. At the same time, he pointed out that neither the Department of State nor even the Liaison Committee, in the last analysis, exercised control over the manufacturers, which were free enterprises at liberty to accept or reject any orders.

This morning Major Chaltchi telephoned to Mr. Merriam to say that, in company with his Minister, he had had an interview yesterday with Mr. Young, Colonel Morland, and Commander Young. He said that the American officials had manifested every willingness to do everything possible to meet the wishes of the Iranian Government, and would explore the situation further regarding the possibility of licensing the manufacture of pursuit planes in Iran, and of securing firm price and delivery quotations from the manufacturers.

Major Chaltchi said that he had received two more urgent telegrams from his Government on the subject, and that he hoped a reply from the Committee would be forthcoming in the next two or three days. He asked whether the Department could not urge the Committee to expedite the matter.

The Major was informed that there was every reason to believe the Committee would exert itself to the utmost. He was told quite frankly that it would be inadvisable for the Department to inject itself further into the matter at this time and that to do so would probably have the effect of a boomerang. If the Major should not receive a reply in a reasonable time, we would then consider what further steps might be taken.

891.248/97

Memorandum by the Under Secretary of State (Welles) to the Chief of the Division of Near Eastern Affairs (Murray)

[WASHINGTON,] August 23, 1940.

MR. MURRAY: The Minister of Iran called to see me this morning with regard to the aviation question.

The Minister stated that by instruction of his Government he was calling to ask me personally to interest myself in the problem of the airplanes desired by the Persian Government, since he and his Gov-

ernment both believe that in view of the very large production of airplanes for our own national defense, which would soon be under
way, the manufacture of the small number of planes desired by Iran
could in no sense be a detriment to our own defense requirements.

I explained to the Minister that it was, of course, my desire to do
everything possible to be of assistance and service to the Iranian Government but that I was sure the Minister understood that our own
national defense requirements had to rise superior at this time to
other considerations. I stated to the Minister, however, that as soon
as it was possible for me to do so I would be glad to ascertain if there
was any possibility of complying with the request made.

You have covered the situation personally with the Minister so many
times that I think there is really no need for me to do anything myself
in the matter but if you think it would be helpful, you may say to
the Minister that as soon as I return from my brief vacation I shall
be glad to take the matter up with the National Defense Advisory
Council.

S[UMNER] W[ELLES]

891.248/87 : Telegram

The Chargé in Iran (Engert) to the Secretary of State

TEHRAN, August 26, 1940—9 a. m.
[Received 3 : 05 p. m.]

193. Minister of Foreign Affairs inquires whether he may expect
a reply to my 178, July 29, noon.

ENGERT

891.248/98

*Memorandum of Telephone Conversations, by Mr. Gordon P. Merriam
of the Division of Near Eastern Affairs*

[WASHINGTON,] August 28 & 30, 1940.

On August 28 I telephoned to Mr. Buckley and informed him that
the Iranian Government, through our Legation at Tehran, was pressing us for a reply on the question of obtaining American military aircraft. Mr. Buckley replied that the Iranian request had been placed
before the War and Navy Departments and the National Defense
Council. He doubted whether any decision had been reached, but said
that he would be glad to ascertain the present status of the matter and
to let me know. He promised to get in touch with me the next
morning.

Not having heard from Mr. Buckley, I telephoned to him again on August 30. Mr. Buckley apologized for not having called me the day before, and said that it had not yet been possible for him to run down the present status of the question. However, he was positive that he would get hold of the facts before the end of the afternoon. He asked what the *quid pro quo* was and stated that if it was merely a matter of the payment of half a million dollars to some missionaries, that did not amount to much. I replied that the actual sum involved was in the neighborhood of a million and a quarter spread over three or four years. The first payment would be due in September, and while no understanding had been reached with the Iranians that the two questions were interdependent, it was a matter of some interest to keep the Iranians well-disposed.

Mr. Buckley then asked how far we wished to push the Iranian request, observing that the matter was primarily bound up with the question of priority in deliveries. I said that we most certainly did not desire to urge that Iranian needs be placed ahead of our own; that we had informed the Iranian Minister here of the deep interest of this country in the outcome of the "battle of Britain" and had given him to understand, without saying so directly, that the Iranians could not expect to be given priority over the British.

Mr. Buckley said that he was glad to know this, and asked how, from the viewpoint of our interests, we felt about Iran on the priority question with reference to the East Indies.

I said that this appeared to be a question for the authorities directly concerned, but that in considering it they would doubtless wish to bear in mind that the supply of airplanes to Iran was linked to the security of important American petroleum interests in the Persian Gulf, notably at Bahrein and in Eastern Arabia. Moreover, if there was a disposition to help the British war effort, sight should not be lost of the huge British petroleum production and refining installations in southern Iran.

Mr. Buckley replied that he was glad to be reminded of these points, and telephoned later to say that he had completed his survey. The most difficult part of the Iranian request to deal with related to pursuit planes. The Iranians wanted the very latest type, a machine designed to take the Allison engine. The production of fuselages is not much of a problem, but the production of the engine is the worst bottleneck in the industry. There have been several hitches in production already, another exists now, and more may occur in the future. No sooner do the manufacturers get started on production than something is found wrong and has to be ironed out. The Iranians have been given priority on delivery of these planes after ourselves and the British. However, it is not possible to give them a delivery date.

It may not be possible to deliver such machines to the Iranians for eighteen months. Next week it may be possible to make a guess. On the other hand, there are several fighters approved by our armed forces which are still being currently produced for their use. Here the production situation is much better. Thus far, however, the Iranians have insisted on the latest type.

As to bombers, the Iranians have not yet decided what type they want. In order to make up their minds, they need specifications which the Committee is in process of acquiring from the manufacturers. Only when the Iranians decide what they want will it be possible to go into the question of delivery and priority.

Regarding the Iranian desire to secure a license to manufacture in Iran pursuit planes of the type 75–A, it is to be noted that they will have to purchase engines and other parts here. However, the engine situation is generally difficult. It would be desirable for Major Chaltchi to ascertain from the manufacturers what they can promise on delivery of engines and parts for this type and then check with the Committee, which might well have plans for the manufacturers of which the latter would have no knowledge when talking with Chaltchi. After all this had been done, a decision would be taken whether or not to license manufacture in Iran.

Asked if there would be any objection to telegraphing the gist of his remarks to the Legation for delivery to the Iranian authorities, Mr. Buckley said there would be [no?] objection, provided we did not make any unjustifiable promises on behalf of the Committee. He added that he knew the Department well enough to know that we would not do that.

891.248/84 : Telegram

The Secretary of State to the Chargé in Iran (Engert)

WASHINGTON, September 3, 1940—8 p. m.

87. Your July 29, noon, and August 26, 9 a. m. Please deliver to the Minister of Foreign Affairs the substance of the following. The Department has been in repeated contact with the proper authorities of this Government in regard to the desire of the Iranian Government to purchase pursuit and bombing planes. The authorities here are doing their best, in the most friendly spirit, to arrange to meet Iranian requirements, but they are bound to place the defense needs of this country above all other considerations.

Specifically, it appears that Iran desires the latest type of pursuit plane designed for a certain engine. Iran has been given the first priority in delivery thereof consistent with our national interests. No delivery date can now be set, but it is hoped that it will soon be possible to set an approximate date which, however, would be subject to later developments.

There are several types of pursuit planes accepted by our armed forces and being currently produced for them in regard to which the delivery question is less difficult. In view of the situation described above, the Iranian authorities would apparently be well advised to consider them.

The Iranian authorities require further specifications on bombers before deciding on the type desired. The American authorities are in process of obtaining them. Until Iran decides on the type the delivery question cannot be given consideration.

Iran desires to secure a license to manufacture a certain type of pursuit ship, but would purchase engines and various parts here. It will be necessary for the Aviation Mission to ascertain from the manufacturers and from the American authorities the delivery prospects, particularly for the engines, whereupon the question of licensing will be decided.

HULL

891.248/99

The Iranian Minister (Schayesteh) to the Under Secretary of State (Welles)

No. 1164 [WASHINGTON,] September 6, 1940.

MY DEAR MR. UNDER SECRETARY: At the time of my call on August 21 [*23*], I had the honor of informing you that my Government desires a recommendation on behalf of the American Government granting permission for the purchase here in the United States of a certain number of airplanes. I at that time tendered you certain details regarding our desire, and as well, advised you that this question was taken up with the Near Eastern Division of the State Department as well as with the President's Liaison Committee of the Treasury Department.

I have assumed that you are already familiar with this question because your Chargé d'Affaires in Tehran has also been informed of this desire on the part of the Government of Iran.

You were so kind as to affirm to me that you will take this matter in hand and advise me of the result. As my Government is eager to know the decision of the United States Authorities in this regard, I shall be particularly grateful to you if you will kindly inform me of the action which has been taken in this respect.

With the assurance [etc.] M. SCHAYESTEH

891.248/99

The Under Secretary of State (Welles) to the Iranian Minister
(Schayesteh)

WASHINGTON, September 19, 1940.

MY DEAR MR. MINISTER: I acknowledge the receipt of your note, no. 1164, of September 6, 1940, in regard to the purchase of aircraft in this country.

I have inquired of the interested officers of the Department and of the President's liaison committee of the Treasury Department in regard to this matter and find that every effort is being made to meet the desires of your Government so far as is possible under existing circumstances. I understand that the President's liaison committee is in frequent consultation with Major Chaltchi and that it is expected that definite information can be conveyed to him within a few days in regard to the planes that can be obtained in this country and possible dates of delivery.

You may be assured that I shall keep this matter in mind.

I am [etc.]   SUMNER WELLES

891.248/114

Memorandum by the Chief of the Division of Near Eastern Affairs
(Murray) to the Assistant Secretary of State (Berle)

[WASHINGTON,] October 5, 1940.

MR. BERLE: With reference to my conversation with you yesterday on the above subject, this Division is of the opinion that, given the present outlook, the delivery of military airplanes to the Iranian Government would be undesirable.

Present indications are to the effect that Germany and Italy have told the Soviets to keep clear of the Turkish Straits but that the latter may be permitted, in order to satisfy their ever-present desire for warm water, to move in the direction of the Persian Gulf and India, taking the Anglo-Iranian oilfields in their stride. In such an eventuality, any American airplanes acquired by Iran would be used in self-defense against Russia. However, the military forces at the command of the Soviets are so overwhelmingly superior that the addition of fifty-odd machines to the small Iranian air force would have no effect on the outcome.

Under the Irano-Russian Treaty of 1921,[51] Russia has the right to send troops into Iran if a third country attempts to turn Iranian

---

[51] For text, see League of Nations Treaty Series, vol. IX, p. 383.

territory into a base for military activity against the U. S. S. R. In view of recent Russian performances, this provision constitutes a pretext ready-to-hand.

The Russians have already demanded airfield facilities in Iran and requested the Iranians to enlarge existing fields and to create new ones. There is evidence that these demands are being met. In consequence, delivery of American airplanes to Iran would be tantamount to delivery thereof to the Soviets. The Iranians are not last-ditch fighters.

It is open to serious doubt whether the Iranian pilots could handle or maintain the latest-type pursuit and bombing planes which they insist upon having. Americans who have traveled on Iranian commercial airlines have been impressed by the lack of mechanical and flying skill displayed. The Iranian Government turned down an opportunity two years ago to secure the services of an American Army Air Corps Reserve officer, Colonel Larner, who we understand was at that time one of the few reserve officers who maintained a constant ability to fly the latest machines. It is not believed that the Iranians have had anyone of Colonel Larner's caliber to train their air corps.

The Iranian Minister might be told that we have considered his country's desires in a thoroughly friendly spirit, and that, as Mr. Young has already informed Major Chaltchi, head of the Iranian Aviation Mission here, there is no objection of principle to supplying the Iranian Government with the types of machines it desires. However, in view of the present international situation and the production bottleneck, we cannot, in the national interest, press the requirements of his Government any further than has been done.

WALLACE MURRAY

891.248/105

Memorandum of Conversation, by Mr. Gordon P. Merriam of the Division of Near Eastern Affairs

[WASHINGTON,] November 18, 1940.

I asked Major Chaltchi to inform me of the present status of the airplane purchasing program of his Government in the United States.

Major Chaltchi stated that twenty-five Rearwin machines had been purchased for the Aero Club of Iran. Of these eight have been shipped, eight are ready for shipment, and nine are not yet completed.

Ten Hawk–75 pursuit planes have been ordered. These will be ready for Major Chaltchi's inspection from December 15, and are expected to be completed in January or February.

Major Chaltchi said that he had never been instructed by his Government to acquire specific quantities of additional machines, although from a telegram received by the Department from the Legation at Tehran he understood the additional number wanted was thirty pursuit planes and fifty bombers. He had merely been instructed to look into the question of purchasing additional planes but had been unable to get a promise of delivery prior to 1942, which would be too late for the purposes of his Government.

Major Chaltchi brought up the question of acquiring aluminum parts for British airplanes which were now in Iran. He said that in the past such parts naturally had been secured from Great Britain but were now unobtainable from that source. The application for this aluminum had been turned down, but he sincerely hoped this decision was not irrevocable, as it made things very difficult for his country's air force. He had heard that the application had been denied from fear that the parts would reach Germany. If this were the case, he did not think the decision was well taken. In the first place, the quantity involved was small. In the second place the sheets, etc., would be fabricated for the British machines in question in accordance with plans and specifications. The Major said he very much hoped the decision could be given reconsideration, and asked for such assistance as the Department could give.[52]

I thanked him for his information and said that his remarks regarding aluminum parts would be given careful consideration.

891.248/110 : Telegram

The Minister in Iran (Dreyfus) to the Secretary of State

TEHRAN, December 24, 1940—4 p. m.
[Received December 25—1 : 14 a. m.]

276. Acting Minister for Foreign Affairs [52a] informs me that Iranian Military Mission in the United States has arranged with Curtiss Company for a technical expert now in Australia to come to Iran to study the possibilities of manufacturing pursuit planes in this country with American equipment.

He stated that the plan now lacks only the authorization of the Department and requested the good offices of the Legation to obtain it. The foregoing is transmitted for the Department's information and any comment it may wish to make.

DREYFUS

---

[52] It is stated in a marginal note that the Division of Near Eastern Affairs did not recommend consideration of this proposal.
[52a] Presumably the Under Secretary for Foreign Affairs, Djevad Amery.

891.248/110 : Telegram

The Secretary of State to the Minister in Iran (Dreyfus)

WASHINGTON, December 30, 1940—9 p. m.

125. Your 276, December 24, 4 p. m. If the technical expert in question is an American citizen he should apply to the nearest American consulate for endorsement of his passport valid for travel to Iran.

While from the standpoint of foreign policy, the Department sees no objection to the establishment of an aircraft factory in Iran using American equipment, it is doubtful whether such equipment could be released for export in view of the needs of the national defense program.

HULL

OPPOSITION BY THE SOVIET UNION TO THE GRANTING OF AN OIL CONCESSION BY IRAN TO AN AMERICAN OIL COMPANY

891.6363 Standard Oil Co./422 : Telegram

The Chargé in Iran (Engert) to the Secretary of State

TEHRAN, December 21, 1939—7 p. m.
[Received December 21—2:05 p. m.]

170. Representative of Standard Oil Company of New Jersey, Lawrence Anderson, arrived today to seek an important oil concession. He believes his company advised the Department of the purpose of his coming.

ENGERT

891.6363 Standard Oil Co./423 : Telegram

The Secretary of State to the Chargé in Iran (Engert)

WASHINGTON, December 27, 1939—4 p. m.

71. The Department was not apprised of the intention of the Standard Oil Company of New Jersey to send a representative to Iran prior to the receipt of your 170, December 21, 7 p. m. However, the Washington representative of the company now states that Anderson is fully authorized to discuss petroleum trade and exploration possibilities in Iran.

HULL

891.6363 Standard Oil/424 : Telegram

The Chargé in Iran (Engert) to the Secretary of State

TEHRAN, January 8, 1940—9 a. m.
[Received 9 : 48 a. m.]

5. Department's 71, December 27, 4 p. m. Prime Minister [52b] tells me that under no circumstances would the Iranian Government consider granting the Standard Oil Company of New Jersey a concession which included an area in northern Iran but would be willing to negotiate regarding areas in the south.

I learn from a semi-official source that this decision is due entirely to Soviet insistence that Russia alone shall have the right to acquire oil concessions in the north, a rumor which was also current when I sent 112, October 3, 2 p. m.[53]

ENGERT

891.6363 Standard Oil/425 : Telegram

The Chargé in Iran (Engert) to the Secretary of State

TEHRAN, January 11, 1940—3 p. m.
[Received 8 : 45 p. m.]

6. Legation's 5, January 8, 9 a. m. Prime Minister told Lawrence this morning that the Iranian Government had decided not to grant any oil concessions to any company "in view of the uncertainties of the international situation while the war lasts". Lawrence states he gained the impression that the Soviets had increased their demands but I am inclined to believe that the Iranian Government wishes to avoid appearance of submitting to Soviet pressure by granting a concession outside northern areas.

Prime Minister was very apologetic and added that his Government would ordinarily welcome Standard Oil Company of New Jersey and would in any event consider its present application as giving it priority if and when the Government should decide to grant a concession.

ENGERT

891.6363 Standard Oil/427 : Telegram

The Chargé in Iran (Engert) to the Secretary of State

TEHRAN, January 17, 1940—11 a. m.
[Received 1 : 10 p. m.]

11. My 6, January 11, 3 p. m. I called on the Prime Minister this morning at his request and he told me that for "political reasons" he

[52b] Dr. Matine-Daftary.
[53] Not printed.

had been obliged to give a negative reply to Standard Oil application. However, he had given the matter much thought since then and felt the Government should reconsider its decision. He then referred to our conversation reported in my 9, January 16,[54] and said that if a concession could be granted in connection with a loan and closer general economic ties with the United States [55] there would be no danger of its being interpreted by third parties (presumably the Soviets) as a political move.

He suggested Anderson who left January 14 be recalled but I told him I hesitated to do so unless a more definite proposal could be submitted to him. Instead I promised to suggest to the Department that his general idea be conveyed to the Standard Oil Company of New Jersey.

I gained the impression that the Shah was personally much interested and that if the company could arrange for a loan a concession could probably be obtained on favorable terms.

ENGERT

891.6363 Standard Oil/428 : Telegram

The Secretary of State to the Chargé in Iran (Engert)

WASHINGTON, January 20, 1940—11 a. m.

8. The substance of your 11, January 17, 11 a. m., has been transmitted to the Standard Oil Company of New Jersey.

HULL

891.6363 Standard Oil Co./430 : Telegram

The Chargé in Iran (Engert) to the Secretary of State

TEHRAN, May 5, 1940—9 a. m.
[Received 10:18 p. m.]

100. Legation's 5, January 8. Minister of Finance [55a] told me yesterday that the Soviet Government has warned the Iranian Government that it would not permit the granting of an oil concession to an American company. When I asked whether he meant in the northern provinces he said "No, anywhere in Iran".

ENGERT

---

[54] *Post*, p. 663.
[55] For correspondence on this subject, see pp. **638 ff.**
[55a] Rezaqoli Khosrovi.

891.6363 Standard Oil/431 : Telegram

The Secretary of State to the Chargé in Iran (Engert)

WASHINGTON, May 8, 1940—4 p. m.

52. Your 100, May 5, 9 a. m. The Department has no information indicating that the Standard of New Jersey or any other American company is now actively interested in obtaining an oil concession anywhere in Iran. The question therefore arises why the Soviets should have considered it necessary to state their attitude on the subject at this time. We should appreciate any information you may be able discreetly to obtain which would throw light on this matter.

HULL

891.6363 Standard Oil/431 : Telegram

The Chargé in Iran (Engert) to the Secretary of State

TEHRAN, May 13, 1940—9 a. m.
[Received 1 : 35 p. m.]

108. Your 52, May 8, 4 p. m. Yesterday I had an opportunity to ask the Minister of Finance whether the subject had come up recently and I gathered from his reply that the Prime Minister—as stated in the third paragraph of my 68, April 4 [14], 1 p. m.[56]—continued to be interested even though there had been no negotiations with an American company since the Legation's 11, January 17, 11 a. m. It seems likely that either the Prime Minister or the Minister of Finance mentioned the matter to the Soviet Ambassador and received the answer reported in my 100, May 5, 9 a. m. The most significant thing about it is of course that while last January (see Legation's 5, January 8, 9 a. m.) the Soviets objected only to American concessions in the north, they now would object to them in other parts of Iran as well.

Incidentally, the Minister of Finance in referring to the latest victims of German aggression said textually, "and European neutrals are not the only neutrals that are in danger. We ourselves have evidence of it every day. Our northern neighbor is now deliberately seeking excuses for intervention". The Department will recall a similar conversation I had with the Minister as long ago as last November (see my 152, December 1 [57]).

ENGERT

[56] *Post*, p. 671.
[57] Not printed.

891.6363 Standard Oil/432 : Telegram

The Chargé in Iran (Engert) to the Secretary of State

TEHRAN, December 4, 1940—11 a. m.
[Received 9 : 44 p. m.]

264. Department's 8, January 20, 1940, and previous telegrams. Anderson returned yesterday and will propose to the Iranian Government that the Standard Oil Company be authorized to engage in geological explorations for not to exceed 3 years. This to create no obligation either on the part of the Government to deal with his company or opportunities for the company to apply for a concession. Main object would be to have the necessary data ready in case a concession should later be obtained and thus to save much time.

ENGERT

891.6363 Standard Oil/433 : Telegram

The Minister in Iran (Dreyfus) to the Secretary of State

TEHRAN, December 12, 1940—3 p. m.
[Received December 12—2 : 20 p. m.]

269. Legation's 264, December 4. Anderson left Tehran today. Acting Foreign Minister told Engert that the Iranian Government feared acceptance of his proposal might create apprehension in Soviet and Axis circles and draw attention to the oil question which Iran wished to avoid.

DREYFUS

RESUMPTION OF PRELIMINARY DISCUSSIONS FOR A TRADE AGREEMENT BETWEEN THE UNITED STATES AND IRAN [58]

166.934/197 : Telegram

The Chargé in Iran (Engert) to the Secretary of State

TEHRAN, January 16, 1940—9 a. m.
[Received 10 : 05 a. m.]

9. The Prime Minister [58a] again sent for me last night and said the Iranian Government would appreciate it so much if the Department could continue to take a friendly interest in its attempts to place large orders in the United States and if possible to obtain a loan.[59]

I told him of the Department's telegram 2, January 5, 6 p. m.,[60] which I had already communicated to the Minister of Finance [60a] and

---

[58] Continued from *Foreign Relations*, 1938, vol. II, pp. 757–762.
[58a] Dr. Matine-Daftary.
[59] For correspondence on the subject of credits, see pp. 638 ff.
[60] Not printed.
[60a] Rezaqoli Khosrovi.

pointed out the necessity of being as precise as possible in order to enable American firms to make offers.

From further remarks he made I saw that he had no clear idea as to what the various Ministries really wanted from America nor how they should go about it to obtain what they needed. I therefore advised him to inform his Legation at Washington of all their requirements and said that I felt sure the Department would be glad to assist in any way it properly could. From the fact that he seemed clearly disappointed when I made this suggestion and from the nature of his helpless questions I can only conclude that heretofore the German Legation must have relieved them of all necessity to think for themselves.

The Department may wish to refer to this conversation when the new Iranian Minister calls.

ENGERT

611.9131/106 : Telegram

The Chargé in Iran (Engert) to the Secretary of State

TEHRAN, January 19, 1940—8 p. m.
[Received January 20—8 : 50 a. m.]

14. Legation's 9, January 16, 9 a. m. Prime Minister and Minister of Industry [60b] have asked me whether commerce with the United States could not perhaps be put on some sort of private barter or compensation basis which would be mutually advantageous. I said I did not know but believed that an arrangement of this nature had recently been attempted by Turkey and that information on the subject could doubtless be obtained at Ankara.

The Prime Minister then requested me to submit his suggestion to the Department for comment or advice.

ENGERT

611.9131/107 : Telegram

The Chargé in Iran (Engert) to the Secretary of State

TEHRAN, February 3, 1940—8 p. m.
[Received February 5—7 a. m.]

25. My 14, January 19, 8 p. m. The Prime Minister handed me a memorandum this afternoon of which the following is the substance, including some explanations he added verbally.

1. Iran intends to spend about 70,000,000 dollars in the United States over a period of 3 years for the purchase of equipment required for factories, railways, ports and mines. In order to balance

---

[60b] Ali Mansur.

these purchases as much as possible Iranian exports to the United States are to be increased, and American advice would be sought as to the best means of intensifying the production of articles now being exported to America, or of developing new resources for which there may be a market in America.

2. In the absence of a clearing agreement it is suggested that the American Government recommend a financial institution which could act as purchasing agent, and help create and develop markets for Iranian products.

3. The Iranian Government proposes the immediate negotiation of a commercial agreement.

4. Should the American Government think well of this plan in principle the Iranian Government could designate experts to discuss details.

Although the Prime Minister did not refer to a possible oil concession it was obvious that he had this kind of arrangement in mind when he made the statement reported in my 11, January 17, 11 a. m.[61]

ENGERT

611.9131/108 : Telegram

The Chargé in Iran (Engert) to the Secretary of State

TEHRAN, February 3, 1940—9 p. m.
[Received February 5—4 : 45 a. m.]

26. Personal for Murray.[62] My 25 of today. Whatever the ultimate reaction of our competent authorities might be to the scheme outlined may I suggest that a courteous reply be sent at once indicating that it would be given serious consideration? Such a reply, coming at a psychological moment when we are trying to break a deadlock in connection with the evaluation of school properties,[63] might help.

ENGERT

611.9131/107 : Telegram

The Secretary of State to the Chargé in Iran (Engert)

WASHINGTON, February 8, 1940—3 p. m.

17. Your 14, January 19, 8 p. m. and 25, February 3, 8 p. m. You may inform the Iranian officials that this Government fully reciprocates the desire of the Iranian Government to widen and increase the scope of the economic relations between the two countries. The Iranian officials, therefore, may be assured that the officials of this Government take a thorough-going interest in the present proposals and will lend

---

[61] *Ante*, p. 660.
[62] Wallace Murray, Chief of the Division of Near Eastern Affairs.
[63] Missionary school properties expropriated by the Iranian Government. For correspondence, see pp. 693 ff.

their full cooperation in every way in which it is possible for this Government to act.

You should state that the Iranian plans and intentions apparently contemplate several arrangements, one of them being a commercial agreement. This Government would not, of course, be disposed to consider any arrangement for placing Iranian-American trade on a private barter or compensation basis since such arrangement would be contrary to the well-defined policy of this Government of conducting its foreign trade relations on a multilateral basis in accordance with the principle of unconditional most-favored-nation treatment. You should add, however, that this Government would be willing to give sympathetic consideration to a proposal for the resumption of conversations with a view to undertaking the negotiation of a trade agreement along the lines indicated in the Department's No. 50, October 5, 1937, 4 p. m.,[64] and No. 8, February 10, 1939 [*1938*], 6 p. m.[65]

It would not be possible to undertake active negotiations for a trade agreement with Iran, including public announcement thereof, until the Trade Agreements Act is renewed. However, this would not preclude the resumption of preliminary conversations.

With reference to your understanding that a barter or compensation arrangement had been attempted by Turkey,[66] the Department presumes that you have reference to recent unilateral action by the Turkish Government involving a system of exchange premiums covering exports to and imports from the United States. The system does not require export and import transactions to offset each other and is intended to lower the relatively high prices of Turkish products which have developed under the clearing and compensation system applied in Turkish foreign trade since 1933 and which, in the view of the Turkish Government, have seriously handicapped Turkish exports to the United States. Turkish-American trade does not rest, of course, on a barter or compensation basis, but upon a reciprocal trade agreement concluded on the same principles as the 18 other similar agreements negotiated by this Government and now in effect.

Before definite comment can be made on the other suggestions of the Iranian authorities, which do not appear to involve direct action by this Government, it will be necessary to explore the ground. The Department anticipates so doing in close association with the new Iranian Minister who has just arrived.

HULL

[64] *Foreign Relations*, 1938, vol. II, p. 757.
[65] *Ibid.*, p. 759.
[66] See pp. 964 ff.

611.9131/111

Memorandum of Conversation, by Mr. Gordon P. Merriam of the Division of Near Eastern Affairs

[WASHINGTON,] February 12, 1940.

Participants: The Iranian Minister (Mr. Schayesteh)
The Iranian Trade Representative (Mr. Amerie)
Mr. Murray
Mr. Alling [67]
Mr. Deimel [68]
Mr. Stinebower [69]
Mr. Merriam

Mr. Murray gave a brief account of the previous attempts which had been made to enter into active negotiations for the conclusion of a reciprocal trade agreement between Iran and the United States, and said that, although neither an announcement of an intention to negotiate nor formal negotiations could be commenced prior to the extension by Congress of the Trade Agreements Act, preliminary conversations would not be precluded. The general nature of reciprocal trade agreements and the procedure involved were explained. Mr. Murray added that Iran might find it possible to open up a market for carpet wool in the United States at this time, because of the fact that certain usual sources of supply, such as India, had been rendered uncertain. However, as carpet wool is on the free list, this particular matter seemed to resolve itself largely into the formation of trading contacts.

Mr. Amerie said that he had received some inquiries from American wool importers and he hoped, with the information which he had supplied, that some trade would follow.

The possibility of marketing Iranian caviar in the United States was discussed, in a general way.

The Iranian Minister said that what his Government had in view was not a temporary strengthening of the economic ties between the two countries for the period of the war, but a long-range program which would continue to operate after the conclusion of the war. The best means for bringing this about, he thought, would be some organization which could advise the Iranian Government on purchases in this country and sell Iranian products. The Iranian Government, he added, would facilitate the operations in Iran of such an organization.

A discussion ensued as to the best sources from which to obtain advice on using some existing organization for what the Iranian Government has in mind, or forming a new one. It was agreed that the

---

[67] Paul H. Alling, Assistant Chief of the Division of Near Eastern Affairs.
[68] Henry L. Deimel, Jr., Assistant Chief of the Division of Commercial Treaties and Agreements.
[69] Leroy D. Stinebower, Assistant Adviser on International Economic Affairs.

303207—58——43

Department would explore this question informally, and the hope was expressed that it might be possible to gather some information which would be of interest to the Iranian Minister in a week's time.

After the conference broke up, the Iranian Minister spoke to Mr. Murray of the hope of his Government that it might be possible to raise a loan in the United States.

611.9131/109 : Telegram

The Chargé in Iran (Engert) to the Secretary of State

TEHRAN, March 2, 1940—8 p. m.
[Received March 2—1 p. m.]

37. Department's 17, February 8, 3 p. m. In a conversation with the Foreign Minister yesterday he told me that so far reports from his Minister in Washington had not been very encouraging. He had therefore telegraphed him that the Iranian Government was disappointed. I drew his attention to the fact that the Department had for many months been cooperating wholeheartedly with the Iranian Legation in Washington and with this Legation in an endeavor to assist the Iranian Government, but that unlike totalitarian states we were obviously unable to bring pressure to bear on our commercial and financial institutions to engage in operations which were purely a matter of private enterprise. He said he realized that but he thought there were many informal ways in which a Government could encourage or discourage such activities in the foreign field.

ENGERT

691.1115/5

Memorandum of Conversation, by Mr. Gordon P. Merriam of the Division of Near Eastern Affairs

[WASHINGTON,] March 5, 1940.

Participants: Mr. Schayesteh, the Iranian Minister
Mr. Domeratzky, Chief of the Division of Regional Information, Bureau of Foreign and Domestic Commerce
Mr. Alling
Mr. Lary, Finance Division, Bureau of Foreign and Domestic Commerce
Mr. Merriam

The Iranian Minister referred to the memoranda [70] recently prepared by the Division of Regional Information and the Finance Division, Bureau of Foreign and Domestic Commerce, regarding the

---

[70] Dated February 16 and February 20; neither printed.

possibility of increasing Iranian exports to the United States and the choice of a general trading company in this country which could handle the trade in both directions. He briefly described the ideas of his Government along these lines. He said that the normal sources of supply to Iran of industrial equipment were not available owing to the war in Europe and to conditions arising therefrom, adding, however, that his Government desired to establish closer trade relations with the United States which would continue in effect after the war should terminate.

Mr. Domeratzky observed that the Iranian Government would have no particular trouble in obtaining materials and articles in this country, but that if Iran intended to pay for them with exports to the United States it would probably have difficulty in doing so in view of the size of the contemplated purchasing program on the one hand and the fact that it might prove difficult, if not impossible, for Iran to increase the sale of its products here to a comparable extent.

The Minister said he realized this but that money would be available to pay American suppliers even if the trade should not be balanced, since Iran had a favorable balance of trade with certain other countries.

Mr. Domeratzky said it had recently come to his attention that there was a market in this country for medium quality carpets owing to the fact that the Chinese supply had been cut off, and he inquired whether Iran was in a position to furnish rugs of this type or whether all Persian rugs were in the luxury class. Mr. Alling pointed out, in this connection, that perhaps the best way for Iran to increase the sale of carpets here would be to concentrate on the production of medium quality carpets, since there was bound to be a far larger market for them than for fine rugs which only a limited number of persons could afford to buy.

The Iranian Minister said he thought the point merited careful consideration, but that since Iranian rugs now had a reputation for high quality it might be questionable whether it would be advisable for Iran to make and export a type of rug which could bring about a loss of prestige for Iranian rugs in general.

Mr. Domeratzky said that he presumed Iran desired to make a choice of some American general trading company, and that the Department of Commerce was prepared to look into the matter and to make available to the Minister the names of several companies, without responsibility and without recommendation, one of which could be selected by the Iranian Government. Such a company would presumably work on a commission basis, and the commission charged would doubtless vary with the work accomplished. For example, a very small commission might be charged on making purchases of locomotives since that would be a relatively simple matter, whereas, if the company should, through its efforts, build up Iranian raw wool exports to this country from three to ten million dollars a year, a more substantial reward for its services would be in order.

Mr. Lary asked whether the plan was to have all Iranian trade in both directions handled by the company to be chosen, or whether commodity trade which was already well developed, would be left in the present channels. He said, in particular, that American wool buyers had expressed themselves as preferring not to work through such an organization but to make their trading contacts and arrangements themselves with the sellers in Iran.

The Minister replied that while nothing had definitely been decided it was his own view that it would be preferable to have all trade between the two countries centralized in the company, as the business would thereby be greatly simplified. In the case of wool, he thought that it also would be handled in this way, and that it would be a considerable advantage to have samples available with the company on the basis of which American buyers could make their purchases.

It was agreed that the Department of Commerce, through the New York office, would place the requirements of the Iranian Government before certain trading concerns, in a general way, and that the names of those companies which should manifest an interest therein would be communicated to the Minister, who said he fully realized that this Government was not in a position to concern itself more directly in this phase of the economic relations of the two countries.

611.9131/109 : Telegram

The Secretary of State to the Chargé in Iran (Engert)

WASHINGTON, March 9, 1940—5 p. m.

24. Your 9, January 16, 9 a. m., and the Department's 17, February 8, 3 p. m., last paragraph. You may inform the Iranian authorities that as a result of conferences between the Iranian Minister and officers of this Department and of the Department of Commerce, memoranda have been prepared and delivered to the Minister analyzing and discussing the export trade of Iran to this country and making several suggestions for its increase. Certain verbal suggestions have also been made. It is understood that the Minister is communicating this material to his Government.

Within a few days Commerce expects to make available to the Minister the names of several trading companies of good general reputation who have expressed an interest in handling trade between the two countries. These names will be communicated without recommendation or responsibility on the part of this Government and it will then be necessary for the Iranian Government to make its choice and to arrange details.

The Export-Import Bank has been informed of the plans of the Iranian Government to establish closer economic relations with this country, for consideration in reaching a decision on the question of making credits available for exports to Iran. The decision, when taken, will necessarily be rendered in the light of the Bank's statutes and policies which are not subject to the Department's control or influence. The Minister has been advised to approach the president of the bank direct.

With reference to your 37, March 2, 8 p. m., it seems unnecessary to add that the Department is doing its utmost to further the plans of the Iranian Government in every possible and appropriate manner.

HULL

611.9131/114 : Telegram

The Chargé in Iran (Engert) to the Secretary of State

[Extracts]

TEHRAN, April 14, 1940—1 p. m.
[Received April 15—8 : 35 a. m.]

68. The Prime Minister sent for me this morning to tell me that he hoped the Department and this Legation would not look upon the conclusion of the commercial treaty with Soviet Russia [71]—see my 63, April 4 [5] [72]—as in any way indicating a lessening of interest in trade relations with the United States. On the contrary the Iranian Government and he personally continued to believe that close and ever increasing commercial ties with the United States were most desirable and he would make every effort to bring them about.

.   .   .   .

The Prime Minister then said he still believed his memorandum transmitted with Legation's desptach 1723 [*1767*], February 5,[73] could form the basis for a satisfactory economic arrangement and asked me why so little progress had been made in the direction of its consummation. Incidentally, he again referred to the subject of the Legation's 11, January 17, 11 a. m.[74] I replied in the sense of my 37, March 1 [*2*], 8 p. m., and also reiterated to him certain statements in the Department's 17, February 8, 3 p. m. and 24, March 9, 5 p. m. and Murray's letter to me January 30, 1940.[75] . . .

---

[71] Signed at Tehran, March 25, 1940; for English translation of text, see *British and Foreign State Papers*, vol. CXLIV, p. 419.
[72] Not printed.
[73] Not printed, but see telegram No. 25, February 3, 8 p. m., from the Chargé in Iran, p. 664.
[74] *Ante*, p. 660.
[75] Letter not printed.

As the Prime Minister will expect some kind of reply could the Department telegraph briefly a few concrete instances of cooperation between the Department and the Iranian Minister which the latter does not seem to report sufficiently to his Government?

Last pouch received here left Washington about February 20.

ENGERT

611.9131/114 : Telegram

The Secretary of State to the Chargé in Iran (Engert)

WASHINGTON, April 20, 1940—2 p. m.

46. Your 68, April 14, 1 p. m. Please deliver the substance of the following message orally to the Prime Minister:

This Government welcomes the Prime Minister's statement that there has been no diminution in the interest of the Iranian Government in trade relations with the United States. Although this Government stated in February that it would give sympathetic consideration to an Iranian proposal to resume conversations looking to the negotiation of a reciprocal trade agreement, no specific observations in this regard have been received from the Iranian Government. It may be noted in this connection that the Trade Agreements Act has now been extended by Congress as from June 12, 1940 for 3 years.[76]

The other plans of the Iranian Government for promoting economic relations with the United States, as previously explained, involve arrangements by the Iranian representatives in this country with independent private and governmental organizations. The Department of Commerce, taking the Prime Minister's views as a point of departure, has supplied the Iranian representatives here with specific suggestions and with the specific results of its inquiries and studies concerning the prospects for increasing Irano-American trade and the means for bringing this about. We shall of course continue to give all appropriate counsel and assistance. The arrangements on which the Iranian representatives are working require careful thought and planning if they are to be of real value and effectiveness and cannot be completed overnight. We understand that these matters are being actively pursued under the guidance of the Iranian Minister with whom we are in frequent and cordial communication.

If the Iranian Government desires to follow up the question of granting an oil concession to the Standard of New Jersey, the Legation here would appear to be the appropriate channel of communication.

HULL

---

[76] Joint Resolution approved April 12, 1940; 54 Stat. 107.

611.9131/115 : Telegram

The Chargé in Iran (Engert) to the Secretary of State

TEHRAN, April 24, 1940—5 p. m.
[Received April 24—3 : 28 p. m.]

85. I called on the Prime Minister this afternoon and communicated to him the gist of your 46, April 20. He is very grateful for the interest the Department is taking and hopes that the efforts now being made will soon bear fruit and prove of mutual advantage to both countries.

With respect to the proposed trade agreement he assures me that he instructed both the Ministry for Foreign Affairs and the Ministry of Commerce last February and once or twice since then to start preliminary discussions immediately and he cannot understand why it has not been done. I informed him that all I had heard was that the Under Secretary for Foreign Affairs had been designated to interest himself in the matter and I suggested that it might perhaps be useful if an official of the Ministry of Commerce could be associated with him. The Prime Minister agreed and said he would see what could be done.

ENGERT

611.9131/116 : Telegram

The Chargé in Iran (Engert) to the Secretary of State

TEHRAN, May 1, 1940—10 a. m.
[Received 2 : 44 p. m.]

93. Referring to the second paragraph of my 85, April 24, I have since been informed by the Under Secretary for Foreign Affairs that he has been instructed by the Prime Minister to accelerate discussions. He explained delay by the fact that the draft which I submitted to the Foreign Office in March 1938 had been mislaid by the Ministry of Commerce. Iranian translation has been made but was so bad that he now requested the Legation to make one.

We have had several talks at which a director in the Ministry of Commerce was present. Both Iranian officials felt that in its present form the proposed treaty offered almost insuperable obstacles in view of the clearing agreement with Germany [77] and the commercial treaty with Russia. However, the Iranian Government would welcome suggestions as to a possible compromise formula which would enable them to sign a trade agreement with the United States.

Incidentally and to give the Department an idea of the difficulties confronting us both officials asked me very naively why I had not attached schedules I and II mentioned in the first articles!

ENGERT

[77] Signed at Tehran, January 4, 1939 ; German text printed in *Reichsgesetzblatt*, February 22, 1939, p. 120.

611.9131/116 : Telegram

The Secretary of State to the Chargé in Iran (Engert)

WASHINGTON, May 10, 1940—11 a. m.

55. Your 93, May 1, 10 a. m. It is assumed that the obstacles referred to in your second paragraph have to do with the standard general provisions which the Department transmitted to you for the information of the Iranian Government. In view of the fact that these provisions are merely an elaboration of the basic principles underlying this country's trade relations with other countries, it would be desirable to have an explanation by the Iranian Government as to the nature of the difficulties which the provisions appear to them to present.

Such an explanation should also indicate wherein the clearing agreement with Germany and the commercial treaty with Russia are deemed inconsistent with a trade agreement with the United States based on the principle of most-favored-nation treatment.

HULL

611.9131/122

The Chargé in Iran (Engert) to the Secretary of State

[Extract]

No. 1862   TEHRAN, June 25, 1940.
                                            [Received September 9.]

SIR: I have the honor to transmit herewith a copy, in English, of a proposed Trade Agreement between the United States and Iran which the Iranian Government desires me to submit to the Department for examination and comment.

The Persian text, without any translation, was only handed to me by the Under Secretary of Foreign Affairs, Mr. Djevad Amery, on Saturday, June 22, 1940, and the Interpreter of the Legation has ever since then been busy translating it. I have therefore not yet had a chance to study it closely or to compare it with the draft which the Department asked me to submit to the Iranian Government in 1938.

.   .   .   .

I have since then had a number of conferences with the Under Secretary of Foreign Affairs—who had been especially delegated by the Prime Minister to negotiate this agreement—and with the Minister of Commerce, Mr. Sadeq Vassighi, and the Chief of Economic Studies of the Ministry of Commerce, Mr. Ali Mohamed Oveicy. At first they were inclined to depart very widely from the draft treaty, but when I told them that it would be useless to submit a practically new treaty to the Department, and when I recommended that they study carefully the Trade Agreement between the United States and Turkey [78]—which the Department had sent me with its instruction No. 428 of April 7, 1939 [79]—they produced the draft which is forwarded herewith.

A cursory examination of the text would seem to indicate that the Iranian authorities tried to follow the agreement with Turkey as much as possible. But even so a number of apparently unnecessary changes have been introduced, and article 14 is entirely new.

Respectfully yours,   C. Van H. Engert

[Enclosure—Translation]

Iranian Draft of Proposed Trade Agreement Between Iran and the United States

His Imperial Majesty the Shahinshah of Iran and His Excellency the President of the United States of America, being desirous of maintaining the principle of reciprocity as the basis of commercial relations in order to strengthen the traditional bonds of friendship between the two countries, and of promoting the trade between the two countries by granting reciprocal concessions and facilities, have decided to conclude a Trade Agreement, and for this purpose have appointed their Plenipotentiaries as follows:

His Imperial Majesty the Shahinshah of Iran:

His Excellency the President of the United States of America:

Who, after communicating to each other their respective full powers, have agreed upon the following Articles:

ARTICLE 1

Natural or manufactured products of Iran as described in Schedule I annexed to this Agreement, and natural or manufactured products of the United States of America as described in Schedule II annexed to this Agreement shall not, on their importation into either country, pay customs duties in excess of those set forth in the said two Schedules.

Also no other duties, fees, taxes or exactions imposed on or in connection with imports, shall be collected on said articles in excess of those in force on the day of the signature of this Agreement.

The two Schedules I and II are considered as part of this Agreement, and all the contents thereof shall have the same force and effect as those in the text of this Agreement.

---

[78] Signed at Ankara, April 1, 1939, Department of State Executive Agreement Series No. 163, or 54 Stat. (pt. 2) 1870.

[79] Not printed.

ARTICLE 2

The provisions of Article 1 of this Agreement shall not prevent the Government of either party from imposing at any time on the importation of any product of the other party a charge equivalent to an internal tax imposed in respect of a like domestic product, and/or an internal tax on a commodity from which the imported product has been manufactured or produced in whole or in part.

Also either Government is free to increase the duties, charges or other impositions mentioned in Article 1 at any time that it may deem advisable.   But in this case such increase shall not be applied to the imports of the other party until two months after the date of approval, and the other party may act in accordance with Article 13.

ARTICLE 3

Natural or manufactured products of the Empire of Iran or the United States of America shall not, after importation into the other contracting country, pay any internal taxes, fees or charges other or higher than those payable on like products of national or foreign origin.

ARTICLE 4

No prohibitions, import or customs quotas, import licenses, or any other form of quantitative regulation, whether or not operated by means of any agency of centralized control, shall be imposed by Iran on the importation or sale of any natural or manufactured products of the United States as described in Schedule II, and/or by the United States of America on the importation or sale of any natural or manufactured products of Iran as described in Schedule I, other than what is in force and customary in accordance with current laws and regulations on the day of the signature of this Agreement.

The foregoing provision shall not apply to quantitative restrictions in whatever form imposed by the United States of America or Iran on the importation or sale of any natural or manufactured products of the other country, with a view to supporting governmental measures operating to ensure the following purposes:

1. Regulating or controlling production.
2. Adjusting prices of like domestic articles, and/or regulating market supply.
3. Increasing the labor costs of production of such articles in the interior of the country.

Whenever the Government of either country decides to establish or change any restriction authorized by this paragraph, it shall give notice thereof in writing to the other Government thirty days before such decision is put into effect, and the other Government may within this period state in writing its views in the matter or act in accordance with Article 13.

ARTICLE 5

With due regard to the provisions of Article 5 of this Agreement, either of the two Governments may impose prohibitions or quantitative restrictions upon the importation of natural or manufactured products of the other country, as well as upon the exportation of natural or manufactured products destined for the other country, provided this prohibition or restriction is general and applies also to imports of like products of other foreign countries, or exports of like products of that country to the territory of other countries.

If the Government of either country applies quantitative restrictions to the importation of any product in which the other country has an interest and allocates the share of each importing country of the quantity of imports, there shall be allocated to the other contracting country a share of the total quantity of importations of the said article proportionate with that country's share of the total imports of such article prior to the establishment of restrictions during a definite period.

ARTICLE 6

In the event that either Government shall establish or maintain, either directly or indirectly, any form of control of the means of international payment, it must, with respect to the transfer of all payments in connection with articles imported from the other country and also in the case of the rate of foreign exchange, the charges and dues on exchange transactions, and the rules and regulations relating to said transactions, unconditionally accord a treatment no less favorable than that accorded in the case of the imports of articles from other countries (except the countries with which they have compensation agreements).

ARTICLE 7

With respect to customs duties or charges of any kind imposed on or in connection with imports or exports and also with respect to the method of levying such duties or charges, (with respect to) all rules, laws and regulations in connection with importation or exportation, the sale or taxation or method of using imported goods, and also with respect to the application of administrative laws and regulations and administrative or judicial decisions pertaining to the classification of articles for customs purposes or to the determination of rates of duty, and also with respect to advancing the rates of duties or charges collected in the other country, under an established and uniform practise, from imports of either country, or regulations imposing new requirements with respect to such imports, and any other customs formalities, both Governments agree to accord to the imports of each other unconditional most-favored-nation treatment.

ARTICLE 8

1. Except as (otherwise) provided in the second paragraph of this Article, the provisions of this Agreement relating to the treatment to be accorded by the Iranian Government and the United States, respectively, to the commerce of the other country, shall not apply to the Virgin Islands, American Samoa, the Island of Guam, or to the Panama Canal Zone.

2. Taking into consideration the reservations specified in the second and third paragraphs of this Article, the provisions of this Agreement regarding most-favored-nation treatment shall apply to products of all territories under the sovereignty or authority of Iran or the United States of America, imported from or exported by either country to any territory under the sovereignty or authority of the other country.

It is understood, however, that the provisions of this paragraph do not apply to the Panama Canal Zone.

3. The advantages accorded or which may hereafter be accorded by Iran or the United States of America to adjacent countries in order to facilitate frontier traffic, and advantages resulting from a customs union to which either Iran or the United States of America may be a party so long as the right to enjoy such advantages is not extended to any other country, shall be excepted from the operation of this Agreement.

4. The advantages now accorded or which may hereafter be accorded by the United States of America, its territories or possessions, or the Panama Canal Zone to one another or to the Republic of Cuba are excepted from the operation of this Agreement.   The provisions of this paragraph shall continue in the future to apply in respect of advantages now or hereafter accorded by the United States of America, its territories or possessions or the Panama Canal Zone to one another, irrespective of any change that may take place in the political organization (*sic*) of any of the territories and possessions of the United States of America.

ARTICLE 9

Taking into consideration the point that under no circumstances shall there be any discrimination under any title, by either country against the country in favor of any third country, the provisions of this Agreement shall not extend to the following prohibitions or restrictions:

1. Prohibitions or restrictions imposed on moral or humanitarian grounds;
2. Prohibitions or restrictions relating to prison-made goods;

3. Prohibitions or restrictions relating to the protection of human, animal or plant life or health;
4. Prohibitions or restrictions relating to the enforcement of police affairs or fiscal laws;
5. Prohibitions or restrictions relating to public security.

None of the provisions of this Agreement shall prevent the adoption of measures prohibiting or restricting the exportation of gold and silver, or prevent such measures as either Government may, with a view to protecting its interests, take with respect to the control of the export or sale of arms, ammunition, or implements of war, and in exceptional circumstances, all military supplies, and it is agreed, further, that none of the provisions of this Agreement shall be construed to prevent the adoption of measures to ensure and enforce neutrality.

ARTICLE 10

On condition of observing the provisions of Article 13 of this Agreement, the Government of Iran and (the Government of) the United States of America reserve the right to cancel or modify the concession granted on any article under this Agreement, or to limit the quantity of imports of such article if, as a result of the extension of such concession to a third country, they find that such third country obtains the major benefit of such concession and in consequence thereof an unduly large increase in importations of the needed article takes place.

ARTICLE 11

Whenever the rate of exchange between the currencies of Iran and the United States of America varies unduly from the rate obtaining on the day of the signature of this Agreement, the Government of either country, if it considers the change in rate so important as to prejudice the industry or commerce of the country, shall be free to propose negotiations for the modification of this Agreement or to terminate this Agreement on thirty days' written notice.

ARTICLE 12

In the event that Iran or the United States adopts any measure which, even though it does not conflict with the terms of this Agreement, is considered by the Government of the other country to nullify or impair the effectiveness of this Agreement, the Government which has adopted such measures shall consider such proposals and protests as the other Government may make in this matter in such a manner as to effect a mutually satisfactory adjustment.

ARTICLE 13

Whenever the Government of either country has protests or proposals to make concerning any measures taken by the Government of the other country as a result of Articles 2, 4 (paragraph 4), 5, 7, 9, 10 and 12 of this Agreement, it will state its views in writing to the other party, and the other party shall receive them in a friendly spirit and give most careful consideration and special attention to the matter. If within thirty days after the receipt of such representations, an agreement is not reached between the two Governments, the protesting Government shall be free, within fifteen days after the expiration of the aforesaid period of thirty days, to terminate this Agreement on giving thirty days' notice.

ARTICLE 14

Inasmuch as the main object of concluding this Agreement is the extension of commerce between the two countries with a view to attaining a balance of trade, both Governments fully agree that each shall, within the limits of the laws and regulations in force in their respective countries, afford facilities to the imports of the other contracting country with all the means and powers in its hands, in such a manner that consequently the volume of trade between the two countries may steadily increase.

ARTICLE 15

The present Agreement shall come into full force on the thirtieth day following the issuance of a Decree by His Imperial Majesty the Shahinshah of Iran and His Excellency the President of the United States of America for its enforcement, and should these two proclamations be issued on two different days, on the thirtieth day following the date of the later proclamation, and shall remain in force for a term of three years thereafter.

The Government of each country must notify the Government of the other country of the date of its proclamation. Unless at least six months before the expiration of the above-mentioned term of three years either Government shall have given to the other Government notice of its intention to terminate this Agreement upon the expiration of the aforesaid term, this Agreement shall remain in force for six months after any date on which either Government shall have given notice to the other Government.

In witness whereof the Plenipotentiaries of both Governments have signed and sealed this Agreement.

Done at the city of . . . . on . . . . in duplicate in the Persian and English languages, both equal and authentic.

For His Imperial Majesty the Shahinshah of Iran:

For His Excellency the President of the United States of America:

611.9131/118 : Telegram

The Chargé in Iran (Engert) to the Secretary of State

TEHRAN, August 2, 1940—11 a. m.
[Received 2 : 52 p. m.]

182. Department's 55, May 10, 11 p. m. [*a. m.*]. Under date of May 30, I addressed a note to the Minister for Foreign Affairs reminding him of my note of March 28, 1938, which embodied the substance of the Department's telegram No. 8, February 10, 1938,[80] but to which I had never received a reply. By a note dated July 27, 1940, the Foreign Minister now informs me that the Iranian Government accepts the two points mentioned in the first paragraph of the Department's No. 8, but he refers to the conversations reported in the second paragraph of my telegram 93, May 1, 1940, and adds "Inasmuch as my Government has compensation agreements with certain foreign countries the principles and conditions of which are naturally different from general commercial conventions it cannot accept the same conditions and principles with respect to other countries or agree that other countries should benefit from the advantages of the said agreements without concluding with Iran agreements embodying the same conditions and principles."

As soon as the Department receives my despatch 1862, July [*June*] 25, 1940, a brief telegraphic reply would be appreciated by the Iranian Government whether the draft submitted therewith could form the basis of negotiation.

ENGERT

611.9131/124

Memorandum of Conversation, by Mr. Leander B. Lovell of the Division of Commercial Treaties and Agreements

[WASHINGTON,] August 24, 1940.

Participants: The Iranian Minister, Mr. Schayesteh
Mr. Deimel
Mr. Merriam
Mr. Lovell

The Iranian Minister said that he had received instructions from his Government concerning the possibility of trade agreement negotiations between the two countries; but owing to the fact that an earlier communication from his Government on the same subject had not as yet reached him, he was not altogether clear as to the status of the conversations.

---

[80] *Foreign Relations*, 1938, vol. II, p. 759.

Mr. Deimel indicated that there had been intermittent discussions over the past several years concerning the possibility of negotiating a trade agreement between the United States and Iran and that when these conversations were resumed in the latter part of 1937 and early in 1938, the Department had transmitted to the American Legation in Tehran an outline of our understanding of the nature of the proposed negotiations. Mr. Deimel read pertinent parts of the telegrams, to which he had reference, and said that this Government's position had been given in a note from the Legation in Tehran to the Iranian foreign office on March 28, 1938. He understood from a recent telegram (dated August 2, 1940) from the Legation that the Iranian Foreign Minister had replied accepting the position that any such negotiations should be based on the principle of reciprocal most-favored-nation treatment in respect of all forms of trade control but adding a qualification referring to the contents of certain compensation agreements to which Iran is a party.

The Minister said that these agreements were of a very special nature, providing for the purchases of certain commodities by each country and establishing prices and the means of payment for such purchases. He had thought before he came in that he would ask for a memorandum giving the American proposals but he now felt that this was unnecessary since he understood them well enough. There were some other things in which he was interested, however. The instructions from his Government had referred to the trade agreement between the United States and Turkey and he wished to have copies of that as well as of the provisional commercial agreement of May 11 [14], 1928 between his country and the United States.[81] He wished also to be told about the general provisions which we employed in trade-agreement negotiations.

Mr. Deimel replied that he would be glad to furnish the Minister with sets of the general provisions and also copies of the agreements mentioned. He pointed out that the standard general provisions, of which two copies were provided the Minister, were what this Government started with in trade agreement negotiations and that in each case the provisions were modified somewhat to suit the particular situation as the Minister could see from looking over some of the trade agreements concluded. Mr. Deimel briefly outlined the procedure followed here in trade agreement negotiations, referring to the public announcement of intention to negotiate and the all-inclusive list published with it and the period of at least five or six weeks after the announcement before the formal negotiations could begin. It was pointed out that in the nature of the procedure this Government was

---

[81] See exchange of notes, May 14, 1928, *Foreign Relations*, 1928, vol. III, pp. 724–729.

not in a position to make a commitment on any trade concession to the other country until after the hearings which are referred to in the public announcement. In this connection Mr. Deimel indicated the Minister might wish to give some thought to the products on which his country might like to have concessions, bearing in mind the fact that the United States follows in general the principle of limiting concessions to the other country to products of which that country is a major supplier.

The Minister was grateful for the discussion of the procedure and requested copies of the public announcement made in the case of Turkey [82] as well as copies of some publication which would contain a comparison of the rates of duty finally included in the Turkish agreement with those in effect prior to the agreement. In response to his request the Minister was furnished copies of the analysis of the trade agreement with Turkey as well as of the announcement. The Minister indicated he would send to the Department the pertinent parts of the most recent instruction from his Government.

611.9131/120 : Telegram

The Chargé in Iran (Engert) to the Secretary of State

TEHRAN, August 26, 1940—10 a. m.
[Received 2 : 15 p. m.]

194. The Prime Minister requests me to ascertain whether the quoted passage in the Legation's telegram No. 182, August 2 is considered an obstacle to the negotiation of a trade agreement. He hopes the Department will reply by telegraph even before receiving my despatch No. 1862, June 25.

ENGERT

611.9131/121 : Telegram

The Chargé in Iran (Engert) to the Secretary of State

TEHRAN, August 28, 1940—noon.
[Received 1 : 54 p. m.]

197. My telegram No. 194, August 26, 10 a. m. Consul Moose and I feel the following factors should be taken into consideration in connection with Irano-American trade relations.

1. Local dealers now claim definite discrimination against American automotive products through the operation of the clearing or barter agreements with Germany and Russia.

---

[82] Department of State, *Press Releases*, January 15, 1938, p. 108.

2. During the past year consular invoices certified for the shipment of Iranian products to the United States have doubled and local merchants report a marked increase in such exports. The United States is now the only important market supplying free exchange to Iranian exporters, but part payment of Iranian purchases from Russia and Germany is being made in dollars.

3. It is said that administration of exchange control is manipulated so as to favor purchase of German automobiles. It is represented that 413 trucks have just been ordered from Ferrostahl, Germany, which normally would have been ordered from America.

4. Reliable non-Iranian importer of American products states he has seen a strictly confidential circular issued by the Ministry of Finance requiring that all bids even the lowest on supplies for the Iranian Government are to be rejected if payment is demanded in dollars unless the articles are absolutely unobtainable elsewhere.

5. Referring to my despatch No. 1677, September 11, 1939,[33] it does not appear that a single payment has been facilitated to American creditors. The Consulate therefore suggests that consideration be given to the possibility of attaching Iranian Government funds on deposit for example with Irving Trust Company and Chase National Bank, New York, for the protection of the American firms.

ENGERT

891.5151/200

The Secretary of State to the Chargé in Iran (Engert)

No. 527   WASHINGTON, October 1, 1940.

SIR: Reference is made to the Legation's telegram No. 197 of August 28, noon, 1940, paragraph 5, and to previous correspondence concerning the problem of securing effective payment for American exporters who made shipments to Iran shortly before the enactment of the Iranian Foreign Exchange Law of March 1, 1936.

You are instructed, in your discretion, to continue your efforts to have dollar payments effected. It would appear appropriate to remind the Iranian authorities of the communication from the Ministry of Foreign Affairs dated September 4, 1939,[34] outlining the procedure whereby the American creditors concerned could be effectively paid, to indicate the cases which have come to your attention where payment has not yet been received, and to request an investigation with a view to the early removal of the difficulty.

In this connection there are enclosed a copy of a letter of August 28, 1940 from the Tuthill Spring Company, Chicago, Illinois, and

[33] *Foreign Relations*, 1939, vol. IV, p. 543.
[34] *Ibid.*, p. 544.

a copy of the Department's reply,[85] which are believed to be self-explanatory.

In regard to the suggestion made at the conclusion of the Legation's telegram above mentioned, it is not the Department's practice to be instrumental, in the supposed interest of American concerns, in attaching funds located in this country belonging to a foreign government. Such concerns are of course free to adopt any course which is open to them and which they may consider expedient.

Very truly yours,   For the Secretary of State:
                                                HENRY F. GRADY

611.9131/123 : Telegram

The Chargé in Iran (Engert) to the Secretary of State

TEHRAN, October 9, 1940—noon.
[Received 12:05 p. m.]

221. I should like if possible to communicate to the Prime Minister some sort of reply with regard to the matter referred to in my 194, August 26, 10 a. m.

ENGERT

611.9131/121 : Telegram

The Secretary of State to the Chargé in Iran (Engert)

WASHINGTON, October 10, 1940—2 p. m.

101. The Department presumes that reports are en route from the Legation or the Consulate enlarging upon paragraphs 1 to 4 inclusive of the Legation's no. 197 of August 28, noon. If not, such material should be prepared and forwarded as soon as possible. The Department's mail instruction of October 1 deals with the situation mentioned in paragraph 5.

The Department is continuing its study of the Iranian trade agreement proposal and anticipates reaching conclusions in the near future on the general factors involved.

HULL

611.9131/125 : Telegram

The Consul at Tehran (Moose) to the Secretary of State

TEHRAN, October 14, 1940—3 p. m.
[Received October 14—1:58 p. m.]

Reference is made to the Legation's telegram No. 197, August 28, noon, fourth paragraph.

---

[85] Neither printed.

The Consulate has been informed by reliable local importers that in the cases of various contracts awarded by the Iranian Government for the purchase of American products, the Iranian authorities have (1) attempted to change the currency of payment from dollars to Reichsmarks or pounds (sterling) or (2) failed to open dollar credits as agreed on or (3) revoked the remainders of letters of credit opened by the National Bank of Iran and [apparent omission] partially filled contracts.

It is not known whether this situation results from the current shortage of Iranian dollar reserves or from official policy. In any event, American manufacturers should exercise caution in submitting bids and in specifying terms of payment.

Moose

611.9131/135

The Consul at Tehran (Moose) to the Secretary of State

No. 264   Tehran, August [*October*] 19, 1940.
[Received January 8, 1941.]

Sir: I have the honor to amplify the Consulate's telegram of October 14, 1940, 3:00 p. m. with a description of the following specific cases which illustrate the difficulties encountered in the sale of American products to the Iranian Government when those products can be obtained, or when the Iranian authorities believe that they can be obtained, elsewhere.

On May 26, 1940, the Automotive Division of the Iranian Ministry of Finance approved a contract with the Firestone Tire & Rubber Co., Akron, Ohio, for the purchase of tires valued at about $200,000. According to the agreement, a credit was to be opened by the National Bank of Iran early enough to permit shipment of the tires from the United States before September 26, 1940. The credit has not yet been opened, and informal inquiries have been made of the local Firestone representative by Iranian officials to learn whether or not pounds sterling would be acceptable to the American firm instead of dollars.

Some months ago, the Iranian Department of Agriculture invited bids for supplying cyanide gas to be used in fumigating agricultural products. The invitation contained the usual stipulation that bids stipulating payment in rials would receive preference. When the bids were opened, a local businessman offering the products of the American Cyanamid Company, New York, was the lowest bidder. He was declared by the Department of Agriculture to be the recipient of the award, and was invited to refer to the Ministry of Finance to sign the formal contract. Despite the fact that his bid had specified payment in dollars, the Ministry of Finance refused to agree to pay any currency other than rials or reichsmarks, and the signature of the contract has been indefinitely postponed.

The two cases described above are typical of many others.

The Consulate has learned of a single case where a credit affecting the purchase of American goods has been revoked. On a date believed to have been June 23, 1940, the Iranian Railways Administration opened a credit for $93,766 in the name of Mr. Michel Saab, a commission merchant, in payment of articles to be purchased from various American manufacturers. Mr. Saab has informed this office that on August 26, 1940 (within the period of validity of the credit), the remainder of $27,000 was withdrawn by the National Bank of Iran acting on instructions from the Iranian Treasury General. The revocation of the credit prevented the placing of orders with the Track Specialties Company, 1775 Broadway, New York City, and with the Warren Tool Corporation, Warren, Ohio. The Consulate has now been informed that on October 16, 1940, the day on which the telegram cited above was sent, the credit was renewed and the order reinstated.

Mr. Saab states that the renewal of the credit was not an act of good faith on the part of the Iranian authorities, but was due to their belief that unless the $93,766 credit were made available in its entirety, the manufacturers would not ship the goods (about $67,000 worth) for which payment had already been made.

It has not yet been possible to learn whether cases such as those described above are due to official Iranian commercial or financial policy, or to current shortage of dollar exchange.

Unconfirmed reports are now current in Tehran that because the Iranian Government has succeeded in converting a part of its sterling reserves into dollars, there will henceforth be less difficulty in arranging for the opening of dollar credits.

It is further rumored that within the last week the operation of the Iranian-German clearing agreement has virtually ceased through failure of the Iranian authorities to grant import licenses for German goods. The Consulate has been able to learn from reliable sources that merchants have difficulty in obtaining import licenses for German products other than iron and steel products, chemicals and pharmaceuticals.

The significance of this situation, if any, is not yet apparent.

Respectfully yours, JAMES S. MOOSE, Jr.

611.9131/129

Memorandum of Conversation, by the Assistant Chief of the Division of Commercial Treaties and Agreements (Deimel)

[WASHINGTON,] November 15, 1940.

Participants: The Iranian Minister
Mr. Paul H. Alling, Mr. Gordon P. Merriam, NE
Mr. Deimel, TA

The Minister called by appointment for an informal discussion of various points raised in the Iranian draft proposal for trade agreement general provisions submitted some weeks ago by the Minister [86] as well as received (with some minor differences in translation) from the American Legation in Teheran.[87]

It was understood that the present discussions were of a tentative informal nature with a view to clarifying the situation for more definite action. Our procedure in the negotiation of trade agreements, particularly in regard to the necessity of obtaining the approval of the Trade Agreements Committee prior to the requisite public announcement of intention to negotiate, were reviewed for the Minister.

The Minister was told that we appreciated and shared the evident desire of his Government, as indicated by the care with which their proposal had been drafted, to seek the conclusion of a useful trade agreement; and that there were several points in the Iranian proposal which it was felt might be discussed in an informal manner before bringing the proposal before the Trade Agreements Committee. These points were then discussed in the following order:

(1) It was explained that the wording of article 14 which would set the equalization of trade between the two countries as an objective of the agreement would on general grounds not be acceptable; the Minister indicated that he would not expect any difficulty to the elimination of this provision with a view to emphasizing the increased interchange of goods as the essential objective.

(2) It was pointed out that the proposed agreement lacked any very definite commitment for the stabilization of such tariff concessions as might be agreed upon; that while of course certain provisions for exceptions would be necessary, the general structure of the Iranian proposal seemed to allow too much flexibility: it was believed that the trade agreements committee would probably insist upon some more definite degree of stability which of course would apply reciprocally. The Minister indicated that he did not anticipate any great difficulty with his Government on this score.

(3) The Minister's attention was called to the monopoly article in our standard draft general provisions with which he was familiar,

---

[86] This draft not found in Department files.
[87] *Ante*, p. 675.

and it was pointed out that the Iranian draft failed to contain any such provision. The Minister expressed the hope that this point could be left out since it was felt by his Government that any restrictions as to action by the Government in its own operations would be an unjustified limitation of its sovereignty. It was explained to him that the general purpose of the monopoly article was merely to assure fair and equal treatment of our trade in the general operation of government monopolies and that because government monopolies were of some importance in the Iranian economy it appeared unlikely that the Trade Agreements Committee would be willing to forego some sort of assurance in this regard. The Minister mentioned our own Government's position in regard to the export of war materials, et cetera, and indicated that he thought it would be difficult for us to live up to the provisions of the standard article; he stressed the opinion that his Government would be unwilling to tie itself up with regard to the operation of its monopolies and intimated that the difficulty probably lay in the dependent position of Iran in its relations with Soviet Russia.

(4) With reference to the proposed exchange control commitments in article 6 of the Iranian draft, it was pointed out that the blanket exception with respect to countries having compensation or clearing agreements with Iran was too far reaching; it was recognized that this question afforded a problem of some difficulty but that any exception which might be made would have to be developed in much more definitely restricted fashion, and would probably have to be formulated upon an actual detailed study of the compelling circumstances. The Minister gave an explanation of the Iranian position, referring primarily to Germany and Soviet Russia, the gist of which was that the problem lay in the specification of exchange rates in the clearing agreement with Germany and in the fact that the Soviet Government had no free currency.

It was agreed at the conclusion of the discussion that it would be desirable, in the light of this explanation, for the Iranian proposal now to be submitted definitely to the Trade Agreements Committee for its consideration with a view to developing more clearly this Government's viewpoint.

The Minister was told that we would endeavor to obtain the views of the trade agreements committee on the matter as promptly as possible.

891.02/25 : Telegram

The Acting Secretary of State to the Chargé in Iran (Engert)

WASHINGTON, November 19, 1940—5 p. m.

119. In connection with the proposed trade agreement, the Department is endeavoring to formulate a mutually acceptable provision ensuring fair treatment for American products in Iranian Govern-

ment purchases and for American suppliers and purchasers in their transactions with Iranian Government monopolies or other business organizations under Government control in law or in fact. Reference is made to the Legation's despatch No. 1825 of May 2, 1940,[88] from which it appears that a foundation was laid for the reorganization of business enterprise controlled by or connected with the Government. However, we lack a picture of the present situation.

Please prepare immediately in cooperation with the Consulate and forward by airmail a report describing the types and activities of the above-mentioned organizations, legal background, importance in the Iranian economy and to American trade as compared with purely private enterprise, and discrimination against American trade.

WELLES

611.9131/131 : Telegram

The Chargé in Iran (Engert) to the Secretary of State

TEHRAN, November 25, 1940—2 p. m.
[Received November 26—7 a. m.]

257. Report desired in the Department's 119, November 19, is being prepared. On November 23d I received a note from the Acting Minister of Foreign Affairs stating that according to information from the Iranian Legation in Washington officials of the State Department "appeared to have no knowledge of the existence of the proposed American draft. They stated that it had only been agreed negotiations should be continued between the two Governments on the basis of most-favored-nation treatment". He requests me to explain to you that the Iranian Government's project is the result of the consideration which was given to the Department's draft which I had communicated to the Iranian Government on March 28, 1938.

ENGERT

611.9131/136 : Telegram

The Chargé in Iran (Engert) to the Secretary of State

TEHRAN, December 5, 1940—2 p. m.
[Received December 6—1 : 05 a. m.]

265. The Prime Minister asked me this morning whether I had any reply to my telegram 257, November 25, 2 p. m.

ENGERT

---

[88] Not printed.

611.9131/134

Memorandum of Conversation, by the Assistant Chief of the Division of Commercial Treaties and Agreements (Deimel)

[WASHINGTON,] December 17, 1940.

Participants: The Iranian Minister
Mr. Merriam, NE
Mr. Deimel, TA

Mr. Merriam referred to a remaining balance of funds due American creditors which has been blocked in Iran since the imposition of exchange control in 1936. He said it was understood that the total amount involved was in the neighborhood of $50,000, that the Iranian debtors had not, apparently, questioned the validity of the debts and in some cases had made rial deposits in Iranian banks to cover them. The Legation at Tehran had taken the matter up repeatedly with the Foreign Office, with the result that the Iranian Government had agreed in principle to provide for the necessary dollar transfers, but for some reason this had never been done. The American creditors concerned were continually communicating with the Departments of State and Commerce and with our representatives in Iran in regard to the question and we should be glad to have it cleared up. The Iranian Minister said that he would make inquiries of his Government.

Mr. Deimel then referred to the preceding conversation with the Minister relative to a possible basis for trade agreement negotiations. He said that in accordance with the understanding reached at the meeting on November 15,[89] the subject had been discussed in the Trade Agreements Committee, which had, he felt, obtained a sympathetic understanding of the Iranian position with respect to the two problems involving particular difficulty, namely: the questions of Iranian exchange control and government monopolies. The necessity of our obtaining appropriate guarantees against real discrimination was pointed out to the Minister, who was told, however, that we wished to avoid raising difficulties of an imaginary nature; that we were therefore looking further into the subject, pending the arrival from our Legation at Tehran of a report which had been requested on the Iranian Government monopolies and their application to American trade, in the hope of discovering some effective solution; and that at the same time the commodity trade between the two countries was being reexamined.

The Iranian Minister was reminded that the standard provisions, copies of which had been supplied to him and to his Government, did

---

[89] See memorandum by the Assistant Chief of the Division of Commercial Treaties and Agreements, November 15, p. 688.

not constitute a definite proposal on our part but merely a basis for discussion. The Minister said that he quite understood this.

There followed a renewed discussion of the various points involved and also an explanation of our trade agreement procedure, including reference to the regular announcement of intention to negotiate, and the list of commodities customarily published therewith. The Minister said that since our last conversation he had discussed the matter with the Iranian trade representative in New York, Mr. Amerie, who assured the Minister that the difficulties with respect to exchange control and government monopoly commitments were not real difficulties at all, but the Minister said of course he had to follow the views of his own Government. However, it was suggested that Mr. Amerie might be of some assistance in this connection with respect to possible commodities to be covered in negotiations, and the Minister offered to ask Mr. Amerie to come down to Washington at any time this might prove desirable.

It was also agreed that we would call the Minister in again as soon as there was anything further to discuss with him.

611.9131/131 : Telegram

The Secretary of State to the Minister in Iran (Dreyfus)

WASHINGTON, December 20, 1940—9 p. m.

123. Your 257, November 25, 2 p. m. As the Iranian Minister was informed on August 24, the Department regards the standard general provisions, which reflect the basic principles this Government follows in its commercial treaties and agreements, as a basis for discussion, rather than a draft or proposal prepared with particular reference to Iran. We are exploring further in search of some formula which would cover our essential requirements and the special Iranian situation, and the Iranian Minister was so informed on December 16 [17].[90] Detailed explanation was sent December 13 by airmail.[91]

HULL

611.9131/133 : Telegram

The Minister in Iran (Dreyfus) to the Secretary of State

TEHRAN, December 21, 1940—11 a. m.
[Received 4 : 19 p. m.]

275. Referring to the Legation's telegram No. 265, December 5, 2 p. m., the Prime Minister and the Acting Minister for Foreign Affairs on the occasion of my official calls and the Shah himself when

---

[90] See memorandum, *supra.*
[91] Instruction No. 538, not printed.

I presented my letter of credence all pointedly expressed interest in the early conclusion of the trade agreement.

Report [92] called for in Department's 119, November 19, 5 p. m. will be forwarded in the next pouch, December 28, for transmission via trans-Atlantic airmail. DREYFUS

AGREEMENT BY IRAN TO MAKE PAYMENT FOR THE EXPROPRIATED PROPERTIES OF AMERICAN SCHOOLS IN IRAN [93]

391.1164/127 : Telegram

The Chargé in Iran (Engert) to the Secretary of State

TEHRAN, March 28, 1940—11 a. m.
[Received 12:44 p. m.]

54. I have on several occasions told the Prime Minister and Foreign Minister [93a] that the representatives of the Mission Board who have already spent 4½ months here are very much disappointed that their negotiations have not made much headway. I told them the principal difficulty seemed to be that the Iranian authorities maintained the original cost of the properties should form the basis of settlement while the Board naturally insisted that present market values should be the starting point. I said I feared that unless an equitable agreement were reached in the near future the negotiations were in great danger of breaking down altogether, leaving the entire problem in a most unsatisfactory state.

I believe the time has come when the Legation should address a formal note to the Foreign Office embodying the substance of the above remarks together with any statements the Department may wish to add with special reference to the valuation of the properties.

ENGERT

391.1164/127 : Telegram

The Secretary of State to the Chargé in Iran (Engert)

WASHINGTON, April 3, 1940—8 p. m.

35. Your 54, March 28, 11 a. m. Please place the following considerations before the representatives of the Board:

1. As the Mission is not a profit-making organization, the minimum terms of a fair settlement might include cost including, of course, any improvements, plus damages or expenses resulting from the transfer of the properties, together with satisfactory provisions for prompt and effective payment.

---

[92] Submitted as an enclosure to despatch No. 8, December 23, 1940, from the Minister in Iran; not printed.
[93] For previous correspondence, see *Foreign Relations*, 1939, vol. IV, pp. 525 ff.
[93a] Dr. Matine-Daftary and Mouzaffar Aalam, respectively.

2. The initial request of the Mission for compensation at market value would appear to have been amply justified as a starting point. However, the delay granted by the Iranian authorities for negotiations is rapidly running out, and since the passage of time tends to strengthen the tactical position of the Iranians, it appears unlikely that they will be the first to suggest a compromise solution.

3. In the last resort a claim founded in international law might be presented on the basis of market value after local legal remedies are exhausted and provided a denial of justice has occurred. But it might be difficult in practice to establish the inadequacy of any offered price owing to the circumstance that the market for such buildings is virtually restricted to the Iranian Government.

The foregoing is of course for communication to the Board representatives only. In any note which you may address to the Foreign Office at this time you should confine your remarks to an expression of the interest with which this Government has been following the course of the negotiations, of its regret that thus far no substantial progress has been made, and of its earnest hope that an equitable settlement will be reached in the near future.

HULL

391.1164/128 : Telegram

The Chargé in Iran (Engert) to the Secretary of State

TEHRAN, April 14, 1940—2 p. m.
[Received April 14—5:43 p. m.]

71. Department's No. 35, April 3, 7 [8] p. m. Soon after sending my 54, March 28, I happened to see the Foreign Minister and asked him if instead of dealing with the Ministry of Education the American negotiators could not establish direct contact with an official of the Ministry for Foreign Affairs. He promised to think the matter over and a few days later informed me that he had designated Under Secretary for Foreign Affairs Amery to handle the entire case for the Government. The American Committee has already had several meetings with him and has found him friendly and anxious to arrive at a fair settlement. I shall therefore not send a note to the Foreign Office for the present.

In a conversation with the Prime Minister this morning, I referred to the school problem. He said if it were only a question of the American schools the Government would gladly reconsider its decision, but as other nations were also involved he feared it was impossible. From his tone and manner I gathered he wished me to infer that there was something in the rumor reported in the Legation's telegram No. 114, October 9, 1939.[94]

ENGERT

---

[94] *Foreign Relations*, 1939, vol. IV, p. 533.

391.1164/128 : Telegram

The Secretary of State to the Chargé in Iran (Engert)

WASHINGTON, April 15, 1940—5 p. m.

42. Your 71, April 14, 2 p. m. It is observed that you consider it unnecessary to address a note to the Foreign Office at the present time. However, in as much as it is only through such a communication that the matter can be brought to the personal attention of the Shah, who in the last analysis must make the final decision, it is desired that you stand ready without further reference to the Department to send a note embodying the suggestions in the final paragraph of the Department's 35, April 3, 8 p. m. whenever the negotiations appear to be lagging.

In this connection and bearing in mind that the delay granted by the Iranians for negotiations will soon expire, the Department again calls your attention to the provisos in its 41, April 12, 5 p. m.[95] concerning your proposed visit to Meshed.

HULL

391.1164/133

Memorandum of Conversation, by Mr. Gordon P. Merriam of the Division of Near Eastern Affairs

[WASHINGTON,] April 29, 1940.

Participants: The Iranian Minister, Mr. Schayesteh
Mr. Murray [96]
Mr. Alling [97]
Mr. Merriam

Following a discussion with the Iranian Minister this morning bearing on the desire of his Government to obtain credits, locomotives, and assistance and supplies for the creation and operation of an airplane factory in Iran,[98] Mr. Murray observed that approximately five months had now gone by since the representatives of the Presbyterian Board had arrived in Tehran for the purpose of arranging the terms of payment for the Mission's educational properties.

For the information of Mr. Schayesteh, who had not been directly concerned with the matter thus far, Mr. Murray briefly reviewed the facts of the case, stating that it had been the original astonishing intention of the Iranian Government to take over the educational properties of the Mission, which had been working in Iran for a hundred years, on two weeks' notice, terms of payment to be discussed

---

[95] Not printed.
[96] Wallace Murray, Chief of the Division of Near Eastern Affairs.
[97] Paul H. Alling, Assistant Chief of the Division of Near Eastern Affairs.
[98] For correspondence on this subject, see pp. 638 ff.

subsequently. Following the intervention of this Government, the Mission was permitted to operate as before until the end of the school year, which would terminate in the latter part of May, thus affording an opportunity for a discussion of terms before the properties should be taken over.

Mr. Murray declared that five months had now passed without any progress having been made, and that the Iranian Government had shown no sign of making adequate, prompt and effective payment for properties worth more than two million dollars. The Iranian Government could not expect to assume control until the schools had been paid for; moreover, since the termination of the Mission's educational work would result in a drastic curtailment of its activities in Iran, the Mission would have no use for rials but would require payment in dollars.

The Iranian Minister observed that the Presbyterian Mission schools were very highly regarded in his country and that there was no objection to them. Everyone regretted that they would have to go. The fact of the matter was that his Government desired to get rid of the Russian schools, but, of course, it had been necessary to proceed on a non-discriminatory basis, with the result that the American schools were affected also.

Mr. Murray told the Iranian Minister that, if his Government should take over the schools without proper compensation, Iran would undoubtedly have a very bad press in this country, and that the relations of the two countries would doubtless be subjected to a certain strain. . . .

. . . .

Mr Murray terminated the interview by stating that the Department took a very deep interest indeed in the question of a proper settlement for the Mission properties. He expressed the earnest hope that the Minister would impress upon his Government the fact that we were following the matter very closely and anxiously.

391.1164/134 : Telegram

The Chargé in Iran (Engert) to the Secretary of State

TEHRAN, May 17, 1940—8 p. m.
[Received May 17—noon.]

110. A note in the sense suggested the last paragraph of the Department's 35, April 3, 8 p. m., was addressed to the Foreign Office on May 9. No reply has been received but the American negotiators were yesterday informed by the Under Secretary for Foreign Affairs that the Cabinet had decided not to purchase the school properties after closing the schools but to let the Mission dispose of them as they pleased. If they wished to sell to the Iranian Government the latter

would have the properties appraised and pay the price in rials in one payment. Or they could sell to private Iranian or foreign nationals. The reason he gave was that the Iranian Government had no foreign exchange with which to buy the school.

As the Government could of course easily influence any prospective private buyer either not to bid at all or to offer less than the Government, this decision would seem to be tantamount [to] a forced sale to the Government at its own figure. I shall await your instructions before discussing the above with Government officials.

Please inform Mission Board.

ENGERT

391.1164/134 : Telegram

The Secretary of State to the Chargé in Iran (Engert)

WASHINGTON, May 24, 1940—7 p. m.

61. The substance of your 110, May 17, 8 p. m. has been communicated to the Board and discussed with Boyce.[99] It would not appear advisable at this juncture to seek interpretations of the Cabinet decision from the Iranian authorities. It is desired that you consult the Board representatives and telegraph opinion whether the decision precludes the sale of part of the school properties to the government and part to individuals; also whether the lack of foreign exchange for the purchase means dollars only or foreign exchange of any kind. The Board could utilize sterling in several countries having sterling-linked currencies.

It is assumed that the representatives are reporting fully to the Board but it would be helpful to receive brief observations and recommendations by telegraph.

It does not appear from the face of the decision that forced sales would be involved since there is no time limit and no requirement to sell at all in the absence of offers satisfactory to the Board.

HULL

391.1164/136 : Telegram

The Chargé in Iran (Engert) to the Secretary of State

TEHRAN, May 29, 1940—4 p. m.
[Received 9 : 30 p. m.]

116. Department's 61, May 24. Following from representatives to the Board :

"Government's decision thoroughly disliked and quite contrary to Minister of Education's letter last August and subsequent conversations. Government is closing schools but has so far evaded all ques-

[99] Arthur C. Boyce of the Presbyterian Board of Foreign Missions.

tions as to price at which it would be willing to purchase, time limit and possibility of obtaining any foreign exchange whether properties sold to the Government or private individuals. Government unwilling to buy some properties and not others and in any event properties offer would presumably be totally inadequate and probably ineffective because in rials. Intervention of our Government essential to enable us to secure bids from Iranian Government with permission that mission retain without time limit for use or private sale such properties or portions as desired. Strongly urge Board now take initiative by requesting State Department to intervene in that sense and also to endorse reservation of right to following possible claims against Iranian Government:

1. Loss on land sales if time limit forces quick sale or if fair sale prevented by Government attitude or refusal to guarantee unhindered possession to purchaser;
2. Loss on building sales because of forced sale in market lacking adequate offers because unsuitable for ordinary use;
3. Loss because of failure of Government to provide adequate exchange facilities;
4. Travel of regular American teachers to new fields of work with salary compensation for reasonable interim;
5. Travel home or to new location of American contract teachers with adequate compensation for broken contracts;
6. Retiring allowances for Iranian teachers serving 10 years or more;
7. Expenses of negotiating commission and any subsequent litigation expense;
8. Interest on any delayed payments by Government."

ENGERT

391.1164/136 : Telegram

The Secretary of State to the Chargé in Iran (Engert)

WASHINGTON, June 13, 1940—6 p. m.

63. Your 110, May 17, 8 p. m. and 116, May 29, 4 p. m. If no objection is perceived, you are requested to communicate the following message orally to the Foreign Minister, leaving an *aide-mémoire* of your remarks. You are also authorized in your discretion to discuss the matter with the Prime Minister, leaving a copy of your *aide-mémoire* with him. The message, which has been approved by the Presbyterian Board, should also be communicated to its negotiators at Tehran.

The American Government understands that the representatives in Iran of the Presbyterian Board have been officially informed that the Iranian Government has decided not to purchase the Board's educational properties and that the Board may dispose of them at such time and in such manner as it may desire. It is the American Government's understanding, however, that by way of exception to the foregoing, the Iranian authorities will purchase the properties at an agreed price in one payment in case the Board desires to dispose of them to the Iranian Government and to accept compensation therefor in rials. Alternatively, the Board may dispose of the properties to private Iranian or foreign nationals. The reason for this announcement is understood to be the lack of dollar exchange available to the Iranian Government.

By its note dated May 14, 1928,[1] the Iranian Government authorized American educational work under certain stated conditions with which the Presbyterian Board and its representatives in Iran have carefully anl loyally complied. Notwithstanding its authorization, the Iranian Government adopted the policy of assuming the cost of all educational work for the purpose of unifying the educational system of the country. It has been apparent to the American Government for some time that the task of reaching an equitable and practicable settlement under this policy, which was announced before the outbreak of war, presents considerable difficulty under existing conditions.

If the Iranian Government cannot supply dollar exchange, the Board could utilize certain other foreign exchange in payment for the properties such as sterling or certain sterling-linked currencies. In the absence of such exchange, the Board would of course have but restricted use for such a large sum in rials as would result from payment by the Government in that medium for all of the educational properties in the near future. Under these circumstances, the American Government understands that the Board intends to use some of the properties in question for non-educational purposes or to dispose of them gradually over such period of time as it may require for the orderly and equitable liquidation thereof. Large units such as the school and dormitory buildings could be rented to the Government should the Government so desire and sold when and as the Board requires rials to support its non-educational activities in Iran. The Board may, in addition, wish to divide and to subdivide the properties in any manner that appears to it most suitable for sale or rental to the Government and to private interests.

For the information of the Board's representatives it is of course understood that they will be free to decline any inequitable offers.

HULL

[1] *Foreign Relations*, 1928, vol. III, p. 732.

391.1164/143 : Telegram

The Chargé in Iran (Engert) to the Secretary of State

TEHRAN, July 16, 1940—9 a. m.
[Received July 17—3:25 p. m.]

164. Just prior to receipt of the Department's telegram No. 63, June 13, I had prevailed upon the then Prime Minister to reconsider tentatively the Government's decision reported in my 110, May 17 and to resume negotiations on the basis of outright purchase by the Government. Conversations between the representatives of the Board and the Foreign Office were in progress when the Department's 603 [*63*] arrived. After several consultations with the American representatives and their local committee it was considered advisable to postpone further representations by the Legation pending the outcome of the conversations. These were unfortunately interrupted by the fall of the Cabinet June 25. As soon as practicable I called on the new Prime Minister [1a] and acquainted him briefly with all that had gone before. He said he was entirely unfamiliar with the case, but promised to study it. I then told him that the American representatives had already wasted much valuable time in fruitless negotiations in the course of which the authorities had not made any constructive suggestions and I felt it was decidedly up to them to contribute something toward a solution.

Speaking personally and informally I thought two alternatives presented themselves to the Government, one was to prolong the delay for another scholastic year and the other to offer immediate and adequate compensation. Prime Minister feared that to postpone the closing of the schools was out of the question. I then urged him to give careful thought to the following considerations before declining the second alternative.

1. I considered it nothing short of a miracle that the closing of the schools has not been referred to in the American press, but I felt quite sure that once the representatives had returned emptyhanded and the American personnel was scattered that the news would get into the papers and it was impossible to predict what they might say.

2. To leave the properties in the hands of the Board to be disposed of as best they could was hardly an equitable solution because the building laboratories and playgrounds, et cetera, had all been created for educational institutions and could only with difficulty and probably at a loss be sold for other purposes.

3. Even if properties could be sold to private purchasers the question of time limit and exchange restrictions would continue to plague us and would prevent a speedy termination of the cases.

4. It would be very difficult to convince the American public that a government which apparently had means of obtaining either dollar or sterling exchange for armaments, airplanes, and other expensive

---

[1a] Ali Mansur.

equipment from abroad could not afford a relatively small sum to acquire admittedly very desirable school buildings.

5. It would be equally difficult to convince the American people that the Iranian Government was genuinely desirous of interesting American commercial and financial institutions in a large-scale exchange of products and was anxious to sign a trade agreement with the United States [2] when at the same time it was not only snuffing out practically (the only information American stake?) [*sic*] in Iran but was seemingly unwilling to make an equitable settlement. I then referred further to the note of May 14, 1928,[3] in which Amercian educational work had been specifically authorized.

In view of all these circumstances and the fact that the representatives could not possibly prolong their stay, I urged that he authorize the Secretary for Foreign Affairs to offer the maximum sum which the Iranian Government would be prepared to pay in dollar exchange for the properties and I promised to use my good offices in discussing with the negotiators any proposal which seemed fair and just.

The Prime Minister thanked me for the frankness with which I had spoken and assured me that he would do his best to bring about a mutually satisfactory settlement.

I am now glad to be able to report that on July 14 the Under Secretary for Foreign Affairs stated that he had been empowered to offer $1,200,000 and that the negotiators have accepted in principle. But as the Government proposes to spread payment over 6 years and to pay the first installment only in May 1941, I have with the consent of the representatives suggested to the Prime Minister this morning that payment be completed in 3 years and the first installment be paid this year. He promised to see what he could do.

Please inform the Board of the substance of the above.

ENGERT

391.1164/144 : Telegram

The Chargé in Iran (Engert) to the Secretary of State

TEHRAN, July 19, 1940—11 a. m.
[Received 12 : 10 p. m.]

171. Legation's 164, July 16. Under Secretary of Foreign Affairs has informed the representatives that subject to the approval of the Council of Ministers he accepted that payments be spread over 3 years and suggested that a first payment of $100,000 be made in September 1940 and 200,000 by next March. Thereafter 300,000 1941, 1942 and 1943. Interest at 8 percent on all installments not paid on date due. Representatives have agreed in principle.

ENGERT

---

[2] See pp. 663 ff.
[3] *Foreign Relations*, 1928, vol. III, p. 732.

391.1164/144 : Telegram

The Acting Secretary of State to the Chargé in Iran (Engert)

WASHINGTON, July 27, 1940—1 p. m.

75. Your 164, July 16, 9 a. m. and 171, July 19, 11 a. m. The Department commends your efforts on behalf of Presbyterian Board and congratulates you on the successful outcome of your negotiations to obtain settlement from the Iranian Government.

Boyce cabled negotiators July 22 "Answering cable 19th, Board accepts terms outlined".

WELLES

391.1164/147 : Telegram

The Chargé in Iran (Engert) to the Secretary of State

TEHRAN, August 15, 1940—noon.
[Received 12 : 40 p. m.]

189. Department's 75, July 27, 1 p. m. was very much appreciated. Representatives of the Board deserve highest praise for tact, patience and intelligent cooperation with the Legation.

Contract was only signed today because of last minute disagreement as to precisely which properties were included in Tehran and in Tabriz.

ENGERT

391.1164/167 : Telegram

Dr. J. L. Dodds of the Presbyterian Board of Foreign Missions to the Chief of the Division of Near Eastern Affairs (Murray)

NEW YORK, December 19, 1940—12 : 40 p. m.
[Received 3 : 22 p. m.]

First payment 100,000 received this morning from Iran.

J. L. DODDS

[For statement on this subject released to the press January 9, 1941, see Department of State *Bulletin*, January 11, 1941, page 61.]

IRAQ

REPRESENTATIONS BY THE UNITED STATES TO THE IRAQI GOVERNMENT URGING A COOPERATIVE ATTITUDE IN ITS RELATIONS WITH THE UNITED KINGDOM

740.0011 European War 1939/4269

The Minister Resident in Iraq (Knabenshue) to the Secretary of State

No. 1572

BAGHDAD, May 29, 1940.
[Received June 28.]

SIR: I have the honor to report that until recently I had not visualized much difficulty in connection with the protection of American citizens and their evacuation in the event of the European war spreading to this area. My recent visit to the mountainous frontier points in northern and northeastern Iraq reassured me in respect to the difficulties which any invading army might experience in attacking this country through that area. Recently, however, two factors brought out by the war operations in Europe have changed the complexion of the situation, namely, preliminary attacks by air and parachutists, and secondly, fifth column activities.

From what has been observed in the war activities in Europe it would now seem evident that any attack on Iraq would most likely be made by air, which, together with fifth column efforts, would facilitate a rapid follow-up by mechanized land forces. The desert lends itself to airplane landings at most of the pumping stations along the Iraq petroleum pipeline from Kirkuk to Tripoli and Haifa on the Mediterranean. These pumping stations would seem to possess no anti-aircraft guns and their only form of protection is a few native armed guards and subsidized tribesmen. In any event, these stations would be very vulnerable to air bombardment. The lightning rapidity with which military campaigns in Europe have been moving does not leave much assurance that Iraq could resist for long a serious invasion by the Germans from the northwest or by the Russians from the northeast.

In my telegram no. 34 of May 18, 6 p. m.,[1] I reported the essence of a potential fifth column in Iraq. Heretofore, there was not a great deal of attention paid to this factor. It was well known that the former German Minister here, Dr. Grobba, was very active in spreading German propaganda, including anti-British propaganda, and that he

---

[1] Not printed.

subsidized not only many individual Iraqis but also some of the Iraqi newspapers. But it was not until the prominence given to fifth column activity, particularly as from the invasion of Norway that much attention was paid to this factor in Iraq. It is now widely acknowledged that most of the junior officers in the Iraqi Army are both pro-German and anti-British. It is also a fact that practically all of the young Iraqi students who have been educated in Germany during the past few years are distinctly pro-German and anti-British. It is also generally believed that there are large numbers of other Iraqis who are pro-German and anti-British in consequence of Dr. Grobba's activities which have been continued since the beginning of the war through local German agents. In addition to all this, the residence here of the Mufti of Jerusalem [2] and some four or five hundred of his Palestinian and Syrian followers, all of whom are at least anti-British and who are believed by some to be in German pay, constitute a potential section of a fifth column. As reported in my telegram no. 34, an alleged plot was recently discovered implicating the Mufti and his followers in a plan to attack British residents in Baghdad. The rumor in this regard was considered of sufficient importance to cause a Cabinet meeting. The Mufti was questioned, but he denied the existence of any such plot in respect to himself and his following. In spite of this, however, police precautions were taken and nothing occurred.

During the past few weeks tension has been increasing in Baghdad. The bazaars have been full of alarming rumors, excitement increased and there was a general fear that disturbances were imminent. It was believed that such disturbances would first manifest themselves by attacks upon Jews and that if this were not immediately suppressed it would spread to native Christians, British subjects and foreigners generally. I discussed the matter with the British Ambassador. He told me that he had taken it up with the Prime Minister and tried to impress upon him the necessity for some action to control the situation, allay public fears and maintain order. However, he said that he regretted that he did not seem to be able to impress the Prime Minister with the gravity of the situation and he suggested that I might succeed with the latter where he had failed. On the following day I saw General Nuri as-Said, the Foreign Minister, with whom I discussed this situation, pointing out of course, that my primary interest in the matter was the protection of American citizens. I said that I considered the matter sufficiently grave to warrant my seeing the Prime Minister about it and that I would be glad if he would accompany me. Nuri then became very frank and agreed with me that something ought to be done. He said that he himself had also spoken to the Prime Minister,

---

[2] Haj Mohammid Amin Effendi el Husseini.

but without avail, and he therefore suggested that I see him alone. Accordingly, he thereupon arranged by telephone an appointment for me with the Prime Minister for the following morning. I am enclosing for the Department's information a copy of a memorandum of my conversation with the Prime Minister, which brings out the highlights of that interview.

It will be noticed that I was very frank in my statements to him, for I felt that the situation demanded it. It will also be noted that I stressed the necessity for him to take some action to allay public apprehension and thus relieve the tension which might develop to serious proportions dangerous in the last analysis to American citizens, and in leaving him I stated specifically that I considered the safety of American citizens here to be his personal responsibility.

I am glad to be able to report that immediately after my conversation with him, he sent for the editors of all the local newspapers and instructed them to publish articles warning the public against the spread of false rumors and against the activities of German agents. I enclose copies of some of the editorials published in this respect.[3] I am also glad to report that the publication of these articles together with information reaching Iraq through the press and radio of the dangerous consequences of fifth column activity have had a sobering effect upon the populace, and that the tension has very materially eased. I also know that the Minister of Defense has called meetings of various grades of Army officers to warn them, first, that an allied defeat in northern France at this time does not mean ultimate defeat, and secondly, warning all Army officers against pro-German, anti-British sentiments. I am also informed that the secret police have been materially increased in number, in order to secure better and more information regarding the activities of German agents.

In the circumstances, I feel that my conversation with the Prime Minister had some material effect.

During the past few days when the plight of the isolated allied army in northern France became increasingly critical, and particularly since the capitulation of King Leopold, the Iraqi public seems to have become stunned and certainly distinctly sobered, particularly those who are anti-British and who have been using the Palestine situation as a whip with which to lash the British. Aside from the relatively few Iraqis who are distinctly pro-German, the other Iraqis are not basically pro-German and are only anti-British because of the latter's alleged treatment of the Arabs in Palestine. Many of them have felt that while in the last war the Arabs gained partial independence they could, as a result of the present war, gain complete

---

[3] Not reprinted.

independence if they would take advantage of the situation to black-mail the British by threatening attitudes. Until recently the Arabs no doubt entertained a confidence that the Anglo-French allies were invincible and would ultimately win the war, but the German military victories in Europe and the present plight of the Anglo-French isolated army in northern France has now shaken that confidence and it has caused them to speculate as to the consequences of final German victory in this general Arab area. Major Edmonds, the British Adviser to the Ministry of Interior, tells me that during the past few days he has been receiving an increasing number of visits from Iraqi politicians and other notables who show that they have been shaken and sobered by the present critical situation in northern France and who now do not hide their fears of a German invasion and occupation of these Arab countries. I believe that there is no question but that the Arabs not only would prefer British influence here, but that they would fear German influence. A British intelligence officer expresses the opinion that this fear is now even extending to the Mufti and his following who are commencing to visualize a German policy, in the event of victory, of using Palestine and the nearby Arab countries as a dumping ground for all Jews who come within their domination.

In view of the above factors, it is impossible to predict what might happen in the near future in Iraq, particularly in the event of further allied reverses and the entry of Italy in the war on the side of Germany, but at best it would seem that there will be an increasingly uneasy situation here.

Respectfully yours, P. KNABENSHUE

[Enclosure]

Memorandum of Conversation, by the Minister Resident in Iraq (Knabenshue)

BAGHDAD, May 21, 1940.

I informed His Excellency [4] that I had become very much concerned about what appeared to be a dangerous situation in Baghdad and that I felt it necessary in the interest of American nationals to discuss the matter with him. I told him that my many and various sources of information convinced me that there was intense apprehension among the public of impending disorders. I said that it would appear that the Jewish population of the city were fearful of being attacked and that these fears are spreading even to the native Christians. It would

---

[4] Rashid Ali al-Gailani, Prime Minister of Iraq.

also appear that the rapidly increasing anti-British feeling engendered by militant Palestinian refugees and German agents as well as by the Arabic broadcasts from Berlin was causing apprehension among British subjects who were fearful of being attacked as were the British in Egypt immediately after the last war. I also informed him that American citizens here were apprehensive lest such attacks spread to other foreigners, including Americans.

I told His Excellency that this situation which seemed to be a potentially dangerous one for American citizens made it incumbent upon me to bring the matter to his attention in the hope that he would find it possible to take some action with a view to allaying public apprehension and thus relieve the tension as well as other concrete action calculated to control the situation, and thereby, as far as I was concerned, afford protection to American citizens. I informed him that obviously I had been obliged to report my estimate of the situation and my fears to my Government. I also informed him that the Legation possessed armament for defensive purposes and that arrangements have been made for American citizens in Baghdad to take refuge at the Legation in the event of disturbances. I told him frankly that if the Legation should be attacked by rioters we would defend ourselves. He assured me that this would not be necessary, for the Government would be fully capable of rendering all protection necessary.

His Excellency thanked me for having spoken so frankly about the matter, but assured me that the situation was not as grave as I had been led to believe and he asked me to tell him more specifically the reasons for my apprehension. I thereupon told him that there was much evidence to indicate that there was a potential fifth column in Iraq made up of pro-German, anti-British junior officers of the Iraq army and Iraqi students who had been educated in Germany. I also mentioned the Palestinian refugees in Iraq and other Iraqis who are influenced by German propaganda and probably even in the pay of German agents. I said that it was the general belief that through such sources rumors were being circulated with a view to stirring up and exciting public opinion and with a view also to bringing about disturbances.

His Excellency replied that these facts were known to the Government and the precautions taken by the police would prevent occurrences of the sort I feared. I replied that while I felt sure that precautionary measures had been planned and ordered by his Government, nevertheless it would seem that this is unknown to the public, among whom the question is being asked, "What is the Government doing about it?" Consequently, I suggested that in order to allay public anxiety it would seem advisable or even necessary for him to take some action which the public could understand and appreciate and which would assure them of the Government's willingness and ability to protect them from disturbances which they, at the present time, actually believe to be imminent. He then told me that measures were recently taken in connection with the younger officers of the Army, that more restrictions were being put upon the local press and that the police authorities were keeping a closer watch upon the actions of suspected German agents and that as fast as evidence could be secured against such agents they would be appropriately dealt with. He said that he hoped that very soon the measures taken and to be taken by the Government would calm public fears.

His Excellency agreed with me in respect to the potential fifth column here and in that connection informed me that they had received reports from their Legation in Tehran and their consulates in Iran which indicated a very formidable fifth column in that country made up chiefly by the very large number of Germans residing there together with Russians and Iranians who had been won over by them. He said that this influence has now become so great that he believed the Shah would feel himself unable to oppose it. I thereupon remarked that this being so it should convince him all the more of the necessity of taking strong action in Iraq before a similar movement here would be developed to dangerous proportions.

In taking my leave of His Excellency, I informed him that my visit and my frank discussion with him were purely for the purpose of seeking action for the protection of American citizens. I said that two years ago one of our citizens was murdered at Dohuk and that up to date the perpetrators of the crime had not been captured or punished and that only a few days ago an American citizen had been attacked in his place of business by two young Iraqi army officers. Consequently, I said, I view with increasing anxiety the dangerous situation which had been developing here, and I repeated my hope that the measures which he said he had taken and which he said would be taken would soon dispel my fears. I said that I appreciated his grave responsibility as Prime Minister of this country in the present international situation and the possibilities of the extension of hostilities even to this area, but I added that my responsibility to my nationals had made it necessary for me to discuss the matter as I had with him, as their safety also became one of his responsibilities. In parting he again assured me that appropriate measures were being taken and would be taken to meet the situation.

P[AUL] K[NABENSHUE]

740.0011 European War 1939/4255 : Telegram

The Minister Resident in Iraq (Knabenshue) to the Secretary of State

BAGHDAD, June 28, 1940—1 p. m.
[Received 5 p. m.]

59. I am reliably informed that the Iraqi Prime Minister, following the oriental custom of using a third party intermediary, informally communicated to the British Ambassador that if Great Britain wants Iraq to state her position more clearly and to act in accordance with British ideas, the Iraqi Government is prepared to do so on the following conditions:

1. Syria to have complete independence.
2. The immediate implementation of the White Paper on Palestine,[5] calling for an Arab state with a fixed Jewish minority.
3. Great Britain should furnish Iraq at once with the arms which Iraq's new position would make necessary, in sufficient quantities and not "in driblets".

KNABENSHUE

890G.00/513 : Telegram

The Minister Resident in Iraq (Knabenshue) to the Secretary of State

BAGHDAD, August 29, 1940—noon.
[Received August 30—1 : 55 a. m.]

81. 1. In general there has been nothing of particular interest to report during the past few weeks, not even the usual local political intrigues. The populace is keenly but calmly following through radio and press the progress of the Battle of Britain as well as developments in the Balkans and North Africa and they are inclined to give more credence to British reports than formerly. The populace is impressed by American defense measures.

2. I received the following information from the Counselor of the British Embassy last night.

Recently extreme Iraqi pan-Arab protagonists have renewed pressure on the British Embassy demanding that the British Government take some concrete action at this juncture favorable to Arab cause in Palestine and Syria. They seem particularly interested in Syria and were even disposed to foment a rebellion there against the French hoping thereby to involve the British and thus bring about temporary British occupation of Syria. They were told that the British Government would stand by its declaration in respect to Syria [6] issued upon

---

[5] British Cmd. 6019: *Palestine, Statement of Policy*, May 1939.
[6] See telegram No. 1971, July 4, 1940, from the Ambassador in the United Kingdom, p. 896.

the collapse of France and would strongly discountenance any action by the Arabs calculated to disturb the situation there.

Nuri, the Minister for Foreign Affairs, has just returned from a visit to Egypt, Palestine and Syria where he tried to feel out the situation but he seems to have received no real encouragement. The Mufti is intriguing and trying to spread false propaganda with regard to British action in Palestine.

3. A Cabinet change might occur in the not distant future with either Nuri or Jamil Midfai as Prime Minister. In spite of the former's pro-British attitude the British would probably prefer the latter at this juncture as being more stable and more interested in Iraq than in pan-Arab policies.

KNABENSHUE

890G.00/514 : Telegram

The Minister Resident in Iraq (Knabenshue) to the Secretary of State

BAGHDAD, November 12, 1940—10 a. m.
[Received November 13—8 : 50 a. m.]

100. From an international point of view anti-British feeling in Iraq has recently been the outstanding feature of the political situation here. While there are various alleged reasons therefor the basic cause is the Palestine problem.

German propaganda through the German Minister before the war and since by secret agents and the Italian and German Arabic broadcasts nourished and inflamed this growing anti-British feeling and political Palestine Arab refugees headed by the Mufti have through increasing influence here seriously aggravated the situation, particularly during the past few months until this anti-British feeling whipped up by politicians is now widespread, including Army circles. Iraqi politicians, egged on by the Mufti and his followers, hoping to gain personal political kudos as the liberators of Palestine, have endeavored to take advantage of Britain's embarrassment in the stress of war to force an immediate British declaration regarding Palestine favorable to the Arabs, which Nuri explains to be should be implementation of the White Paper at once but with executive authority remaining for the present in the hands of British advisers and the High Commissioner similarly as in the case of Iraq from 1920 until 1932.

The British have resisted the pressure and Churchill [7] has emphatically refused to do anything about Palestine until after war. The Iraqis are now discouraged and resentful, including pro-British Nuri,

---

[7] Winston Churchill, British Prime Minister.

and I am reliably informed that the Iraqi Cabinet in drafting the Regent's address to Parliament November 5 contemplated the elimination of any mention of the British alliance in the address. The statement of the President of Turkey November 1, however, influenced their decision and finally persuaded them to make the briefest mention possible, namely "while our friendly relations with our ally, Great Britain, and with other friendly states continue to develop on a basis of friendship and mutual cooperation". The speech was also otherwise brief and colorless. The debates in Parliament now commencing may throw some further light on this subject.

It is believed even by the British that Iraqi anti-British [feeling?] will not be translated into any action which would materially impede the British in their prosecution of war measures.

Mail report follows.

Copies by pouch to Ankara, Beirut, Jerusalem, Cairo.

KNABENSHUE

890G.00/521

The Minister Resident in Iraq (Knabenshue) to the Secretary of State

No. 1661   BAGHDAD, November 14, 1940.
                                          [Received January 8, 1941.]

SIR: I have the honor to refer to my telegram no. 100 of November 12, 1940, reporting the salient features of the anti-British feeling which has become the most important factor of the political situation in Iraq.

Anti-British feeling here has existed since the tribal revolt against the British in 1920. From that time onward it was whipped up and kept alive by Iraqi politicians for the purpose of gaining their complete independence. Even after Iraq was admitted as a member of the League of Nations in 1932 local politicians remained unsatisfied with the relationship provided for by the Anglo-Iraqi Treaty of Alliance [8] and continued to utilize anti-British sentiment in their efforts to eliminate entirely all British influence and control, but it was not until the Palestine problem became acute in 1936 that Iraqi politicians commenced to use it seriously in their campaign against the British. Since that time the Palestine problem has been linked to their utopian ideal of Arab unity which they hold cannot be attained until the British solve that problem in favor of the Arabs.

With the outbreak of the present war the Arab revolt in Palestine was suspended, and the situation remained quiet for a time. However,

---

[8] Signed at Baghdad, June 30, 1930, League of Nations Treaty Series, vol. CXXXII, p. 363.

soon thereafter Palestinian refugees commenced to arrive in Baghdad, followed on October 16, 1939, by the Mufti himself, and it was not long before their influence became felt in local political circles.

In the meantime, the propaganda activities of the German Minister before the war were particularly successful in stimulating anti-British feeling and in promoting a pro-German sentiment. The activities of German agents and German broadcasts in Arabic since the war have also been effective in this regard. Iraqi students who had been sent to Germany returned violently pro-German. Pro-German officials of the Ministry of Education have been promoting, in recent years, a Youth Movement which has been developed on Nazi lines and which has engendered pro-German, anti-British sentiment. In the army practically all of the younger officers in particular are pro-German.

While there have been occasional displays of anti-British feeling on the part of the local population, and while the press has constantly shown anti-British bias, on the whole it has not been generally noticeable. In the circumstances, I was somewhat surprised during my recent leave, which I spent in Syria and Palestine, to be met on every hand by the question of why the Iraqis were so anti-British and pro-German. It was there also that I learned much of the reported growing influence of the Mufti in Iraqi political circles. After my return from leave I made an investigation of the situation and have come to the following conclusions:

First. The Anglo-Iraqi Treaty of Alliance provides scope for engendering a certain degree of anti-British feeling.

Second. The Palestine problem provides the most effective opportunity for generating anti-British feeling among the populace.

Third. German propaganda has taken advantage of these opportunities to inflame public opinion.

Fourth. Iraqi politicians have capitalized these opportunities to gain political prestige and power for themselves by whipping up a frenzy which otherwise would not be aroused to any serious extent. The Palestine problem and Arab unity are not, in fact, matters which are of vital direct interest to Iraq. I am satisfied that normally they would only receive the passing unemotional attention of the people here. But they do provide excellent material for politicians seeking a pretext for political agitation to gain their ends.

In further explanation of the fourth conclusion, I may add that the Iraqi politicians have been endeavoring to take advantage of Britain's present embarrassment to force the issue of the Palestine question, but the determination of the British Government to do nothing about the matter until after the war, seems to have discouraged them and made them feel resentful.

This resentment was made manifest in the Regent's address at the opening of Parliament on November 5, 1940. The Turkish Minister told me (and he has special opportunities for keeping well informed) that the Cabinet had deliberated the question whether to eliminate from the address all mention of the British and the British alliance, but that the speech of the Turkish President on November 1, 1940, affirming Turkey's determination to respect her alliance with Britain had decided the Cabinet to make but the briefest mention of the British alliance in the Regent's address.

With regard to the Mufti, my investigations convince me that he is the most highly respected and influential individual in Iraq today, both in religious and political circles. It appears that he is exercising his usual craftiness and astuteness and is exerting his influence only in matters affecting Palestine and the Arab cause generally, but as can be appreciated this gives him very great scope. He had gained a large following in Palestine and Syria and he is now developing a similar influence in Iraq. He is thus becoming a power to be reckoned with in the Arab world.

Finally I may express the opinion that this anti-British feeling in Iraq will not materially impede the British in their war effort unless a successful German thrust through Turkey should force the British to evacuate Iraq. In this connection I may mention that it has been reported to me that young Iraqi army officers have boasted that in such an event no Britisher will be permitted to leave the country alive. However, it is my opinion that basically, at least, Iraqi politicians and senior army officers are not so anti-British and pro-German as to permit any outrages to be perpetrated against them and would make every effort to protect them, but the probable activities of extremists and fifth columnists would undoubtedly make the occasion a serious one.

For the Department's further information I enclose a copy of a memorandum of my conversation with the Minister for Foreign Affairs on November 9, 1940.

I am also enclosing a copy of a memorandum of my conversation with the Turkish Minister, some of whose remarks will doubtless prove of interest to the Department.[8a]

Respectfully yours,

P. KNABENSHUE

740.0011 European War 1939/6829 : Telegram

The Chargé in Iran (Engert) to the Secretary of State

TEHRAN, November 21, 1940—9 p. m.
[Received November 23—2 : 25 a. m.]

254. I learn from two absolutely reliable sources that several German emissaries have recently arrived in Tehran and are trying to

---

[8a] Enclosures not printed.

get in touch with Iraqi officials with a view to reestablishing diplomatic relations between Iraq and the Reich. They are reported to be army officers who, before their departure from Germany received instructions from the former German Minister in Baghdad as to the methods to be adopted and the persons to be approached.

The feeling in Iranian official circles is now that at the Hitler–Molotov conversations [9] Iraq was definitely included in Germany's sphere and the whole of Iran including the southern oil fields in Russia's sphere.

Baghdad informed.

ENGERT

741.90G 11/27 : Telegram

The Minister Resident in Iraq (Knabenshue) to the Secretary of State

BAGHDAD, November 27, 1940—noon.
[Received 9 : 07 p. m.]

107. The British Ambassador told me last night that he has just had several talks with the Regent regarding the failure of the Iraqi Government to fulfill more completely and in a more friendly spirit its obligation under their treaty of alliance and that more particularly he protested against acts and maneuvers by the Iraqi Government (and especially the Prime Minister) favorable to Britain's enemies such as the recent re-establishment of telegraph communication between Iraq, Germany and Italy. He said that Germany's declaration of friendship for the Arab countries in October was made at the instigation of the Iraqi Prime Minister. He has demanded a change of attitude of the Iraqi Government vis-à-vis the British which, in his opinion, can only be realized through a change of government which I gathered he had insisted upon. He told me that he therefore hoped for and expected the fall of the present Cabinet very shortly.

KNABENSHUE

741.90G 11/28 : Telegram

The Minister Resident in Iraq (Knabenshue) to the Secretary of State

BAGHDAD, November 30, 1940—midnight.
[Received December 1—10 : 50 a. m.]

110. Referring to my No. 107 of November 27 and Engert's No. 254 of November 21, a critical situation has arisen in respect to British-Iraqi relations which will result probably within a matter of hours in the fall of the present Cabinet or Iraqi defiance of British and

---

[9] For the German account of these conversations held at Berlin, November 12–13, 1940, see Department of State, *Nazi-Soviet Relations, 1939–1941*, pp. 217 ff.

resumption of diplomatic relations with Germany. Nuri resigned yesterday in protest but resignation not yet accepted or generally known. Iraqi troops are being maneuvered into strategic positions around Baghdad. Further details tomorrow.

KNABENSHUE

741.90G 11/29 : Telegram

The Minister Resident in Iraq (Knabenshue) to the Secretary of State

BAGHDAD, December 1, 1940—11 p. m.
[Received December 2—6 a. m.]

111. The British Ambassador told me this evening during a long conversation that while in his conversation with the Regent and afterwards with the Prime Minister he had informed them that his Government was entirely dissatisfied with Iraq's failure to have cooperated with the British in accordance with the terms and spirit of the Treaty of Alliance, in many respects which he enumerated, he had officially protested only in respect to one matter, namely a resumption of diplomatic relations with Germany which his Government had reason to believe was about to be proposed by Germany to Iraq. However, he had made it clear to the Regent and to the Prime Minister that his Government had lost confidence in the good faith of the latter to fulfill his assurances of friendship and cooperation with the British, and implied strongly that the resignation of the Prime Minister would therefore be expected.

The Prime Minister telegraphed the Iraqi Legation in London to seek confirmation of the Ambassador's representations from Lord Halifax.[10] The Ambassador said that he understood the reply was received today and that he expects to receive further instructions from London tomorrow. He believes it probable but not certain that the matter will be settled without any untoward incidents. (To be continued).

KNABENSHUE

741.90G 11/30 : Telegram

The Minister Resident in Iraq (Knabenshue) to the Secretary of State

BAGHDAD, December 2, 1940—5 p. m.
[Received December 3—4 a. m.]

112. During the course of the conversation [11] the Ambassador outlined some of the causes of British complaints against the Iraqi Government as follows:

[10] British Secretary of State for Foreign Affairs.
[11] See *supra*.

(1) Resumption of telegraphic communication with Germany and Italy.
(2) Failure to rupture diplomatic relations with Italy.
(3) Failure to suppress pro-German anti-British propaganda in local press.
(4) Failure to deny rumor of imminent resumption of diplomatic relations with Germany.
(5) Suppression of criticism in the press of German declaration of October 1940.
(6) Attempt of Government to follow a policy of neutrality instead of a pro-British attitude such as would normally be expected from an ally and failure to make public pronouncements calculated to lead public opinion in this direction and show advantages to be gained by supporting their ally.

The Ambassador said that he had sound reasons for believing that Naji Shawkat, the Minister of Justice, returned from Turkey October 28 bringing from Von Papen [12] three German desiderata for consideration of the Iraqi Government as follows:

(1) Resumption of telegraphic communication with Germany.
(2) Enactment of anti-Jewish legislation.
(3) Resumption of diplomatic relations with Germany.

Britain's power to exert economic pressure on Iraq and to close the port of Basra and Turkey's need of transit through Iraq are factors which in the end should force Iraq to accept Britain's demands supported as they undoubtedly would be by Turkey.

It is rumored today that the present Cabinet is prepared to resign as soon as someone can be found willing to form a new government.

KNABENSHUE

741.90G 11/28 : Telegram

The Secretary of State to the Minister Resident in Iraq (Knabenshue)

WASHINGTON, December 3, 1940—5 p. m.

56. Your 110, November 30, midnight. Please seek immediately an interview with the Prime Minister, or, in your discretion, with the Foreign Minister, or with both, and set forth orally but vigorously the following considerations:

The United States Government has adopted as a firm and fundamental policy the rendering to Great Britain in the present struggle of all possible aid short of war. That aid is increasing daily and will continue to increase. State that in view of the determined policy of this Government, as set forth above, any decision or action of the

---

[12] Franz von Papen, German Ambassador in Turkey.

Iraqi Government which might result in a less cooperative attitude in its relations with Great Britain could not fail to create a most painful impression in the United States. Add that in the event of a lessening in that cooperative attitude, public opinion here could not avoid drawing a most unfavorable comparison between Iraq and its nearby neighbor, Turkey, which has remained steadfast in its contractual obligations with Great Britain. According to our information, defeat of the British would endanger the independent existence of Iraq as well as all other States of the Near and Middle East.

In your discretion please discuss this matter with your Turkish colleague with a view to seeing whether he would not be willing to take parallel action, if necessary after seeking instructions from his Government.

Please inform your British colleague of your instructions and telegraph an account of your interview.

Repeat paraphrase of your telegram under reference . . . and this instruction to Tehran for Engert's information and discreet use.

HULL

741.90G/125

Memorandum of Conversation, by Mr. George V. Allen of the Division of Near Eastern Affairs

[WASHINGTON,] December 3, 1940.

Mr. Murray informed the Turkish Ambassador [13] of the contents of Mr. Knabenshue's recent telegrams regarding the difficulties between the British authorities in Iraq and the Iraqi Government, and told him that the Department was instructing Mr. Knabenshue to express the interest of the United States in the situation and our hope that Iraq would not adopt any less cooperative attitude towards Great Britain. Mr. Murray said that the Department was of course aware of Turkey's great interest in Iraq and of the importance of that country's location astride the principal communication route to Turkey. Mr. Murray said that he thought the Turkish Government would be interested in learning the action the American Government was taking and that the Turkish authorities might possibly desire to take parallel action.

The Turkish Ambassador said that personally he agreed entirely with the position taken by the United States Government and that he felt confident his Government would desire to take parallel action.

---

[13] Mehmet Münir Ertegün.

741.90G 11/31 : Telegram

The Minister Resident in Iraq (Knabenshue) to the Secretary of State

BAGHDAD, December 5, 1940—2 a. m.
[Received 9 : 15 a. m.]

113. I have just received the Department's telegram 56, December 3, and will carry out the instructions at the earliest moment. In the meantime, I may report that it was generally reported throughout the city last night the Cabinet had, after consulting political and army leaders and tribal chiefs, definitely determined to defy the British by refusing to resign. If the British were to retaliate by economic pressure or more forceful means, public opinion might be whipped up and inflamed to a dangerous fanatical pitch and lead to serious consequences.

However, I am hopeful of local regency intervention and will report immediately.

KNABENSHUE

741.90G 11/32 : Telegram

The Minister Resident in Iraq (Knabenshue) to the Secretary of State

BAGHDAD, December 5, 1940—5 p. m.
[Received December 6—5 : 31 a. m.]

115. I saw the Prime Minister and Nuri at the Foreign Office at 10:45 this morning and fulfilled the Department's instruction No. 56 of December 3, 5 p. m. In view of the fact that in the Iraqi Government's telegram to their Chargé d'Affaires in London they embodied what they termed the British Ambassador's interference in internal affairs of Iraq, I deemed it advisable to assure the Prime Minister that it was not the desire of the United States Government to interfere in the internal affairs of any country but that with a world situation such as existed today some situations had become of international importance involving matters in which the United States was vitally interested.

The Prime Minister informed me that it has been and still is the policy of the Iraqi Government to fulfill in letter and spirit their treaty of alliance with Great Britain and that all rumors which I might have heard to the contrary are unfounded. Inasmuch as the effect of the Department's *démarche* might have been lessened had I unreservedly accepted his reply, I remarked that unfortunately the rumors in question which had not been publicly denied by the Government had created an atmosphere which had convinced the public and all observers that the Iraqi Government was anti-British and following a policy of non-cooperation with the British, but I was glad to receive his assurance that this was not true and that it is the intention of his Government to fulfill in both letter and spirit their treaty of alliance with Great Britain and that I would report accordingly to my Government.

Immediately after my meeting with the Prime Minister, I called on the Turkish Minister and discussed the situation with him. He is well aware of the true situation and of its potential dangers and we both agreed that it could be developed into a conflict between the Iraqis and the British which might interrupt Turkey's only means of contact with the world through Basra. Being convinced that it is to Turkey's interest that the Iraqi Government should respect its treaty of alliance with the British and cooperate fully with them he is telegraphing to his Government today requesting authority to take parallel action with us.

Before seeing the Prime Minister I called upon the British Ambassador and informed him of the Department's instruction which pleased him very much. I agreed to his informing the Regent whom he is seeing today, for it will strengthen Regent's hand in his efforts to bring about Iraq's cooperation with the British. He read to me his recent telegram to London and the replies—the last from Lord Halifax, informing him that he had told the Iraqi Chargé d'Affaires that the Ambassador at Baghdad had been acting on his instructions and that he had repeated to the Chargé d'Affaires that His Majesty's Government had lost confidence in the friendly good faith of the Iraqi Prime Minister but would leave it to the Iraqis themselves to decide what should be done in the matter. The Ambassador is determined that the only satisfactory solution is the resignation of the present Prime Minister and formation of a government willing to carry out its treaty obligations with Great Britain. . . .

While the [situation?] is still fraught with dangerous possibilities, particularly because the army is an uncertain factor, I am hopeful that after a brief delay a peaceful solution will be found.

KNABENSHUE

741.90G 11/33 : Telegram

The Minister Resident in Iraq (Knabenshue) to the Secretary of State

BAGHDAD, December 10, 1940—3 p. m.
[Received 11 : 30 p. m.]

117. Referring to the Legation's No. 115, December 5, 5 p. m., the Turkish Minister called to inform me today that a representative of his Government informed him that the Turkish Government had already been approached in the matter by the United States Government through the [Embassy?] in Washington; that in a conversation

with the Turkish Foreign Minister the Iraqi Minister at Ankara (a brother of the Iraqi Prime Minister) denied that any situation existed to rise [14] represented but would telegraph to his Government for advice; that until such reply is received the Turkish Government would postpone action.

The British Ambassador called immediately afterwards to thank me for our cooperation in the matter. He stated that he and his Government still insist on resignation of the Prime Minister and that Iraq politicians are trying to find a way of accomplishing it while at the same time saving the face of the Prime Minister and the prestige of Iraq.

He has now veered around to the advocacy, if necessary, of economic pressure de [or?] force, believing that any resultant disturbances would only damage the Iraqis themselves.

Anti-British newspapers did not appear yesterday and today their tone was milder than heretofore.

KNABENSHUE

890G.00/520

Memorandum of Conversation, by the Chief of the Division of Near Eastern Affairs (Murray)

[WASHINGTON,] December 11, 1940.

The Turkish Ambassador called yesterday to inform me that he had not failed to communicate to his Government the information which I had conveyed to him some days ago regarding the serious political situation in Iraq due to the apparently disloyal attitude of the Iraqi Government and the threat of the latter to reestablish relations with Germany. I had informed the Ambassador, at the same time, of the representations which this Government had instructed our Minister in Baghdad to make, and I had suggested to the Ambassador that he might care to communicate with his Government with a view to similar action being taken in Baghdad by the Turkish Minister there.

The Ambassador stated that he was now in receipt of a telegraphic reply from his Government to the effect that the Turkish Foreign Minister had immediately called in the Iraqi Minister to inquire regarding the situation in Iraq and that the latter, while denying all knowledge of any difficulty between the Iraqi Government and British officials in Baghdad, had promised to inquire at once of his Government and to let the Turkish Foreign Minister know. It appears that in the telegram received by Mr. Ertegün here the Turkish Foreign

---

[14] Sentence apparently garbled at this point.

Minister had furthermore stated that his reports from Iraq did not indicate any serious trouble. Nevertheless, it is the intention of the Turkish Government, when it will have received accurate information and if the situation is as serious as has been reported, to take steps along the lines already taken by our Minister.

762.90G/13 : Telegram

The Ambassador in Turkey (MacMurray) to the Secretary of State

ANKARA, December 14, 1940—1 p. m.
[Received 6 : 25 p. m.]

220. The Minister for Foreign Affairs last night took occasion to ask me whether I was familiar with my Government's proposal to the Turkish Ambassador in Washington of a joint Turkish-American *démarche* to the Government of Iraq as to its reported intention to take steps toward a *rapprochement* with Germany. Upon my acknowledging myself uninformed he told me that he had at once instructed Münir Bey to suggest that action on the proposal be withheld until he should have had opportunity to ascertain (as he felt he was in an especially advantageous position to do) whether or not there was actual reason to apprehend the development supposed. He feared that this instruction might not have arrived in time to forestall action by the American Government. But he said he wanted me to know (and presumably to report to you) that he had promptly taken up the question with the Iraqi Minister (brother of the Prime Minister) who had immediately assured him that he knew of no basis for the attribution to his Government of any such intention and who had just now confirmed to him on its behalf that it entertained no such purpose. The Minister added that if the Turkish Government had believed there was any substance in the reports in question it would have been more concerned than anybody else because of the fact that this country is now dependent upon the route through Iraq for its importations of necessary war materials.

Repeated to Baghdad.

MACMURRAY

741.90G 11/34 : Telegram

The Secretary of State to the Minister Resident in Iraq (Knabenshue)

WASHINGTON, December 14, 1940—5 p. m.

60. Your 117, December 10, 3 p. m. With reference to the second and third paragraphs of your telegram, the Department is confident that you appreciate the fact that our interest does not extend to

interference in the internal affairs of Iraq or an effort to bring about the overthrow of cabinets or the application of economic pressure. Our sole purpose is to stress to the Iraqi authorities our conviction that it is to their own interest to cooperate with the British in their efforts to resist totalitarian aggression.

HULL

711.67/104 : Telegram

The Minister Resident in Iraq (Knabenshue) to the Secretary of State

BAGHDAD, December 17, 1940—7 p. m.
[Received December 18—3 : 30 a. m.]

120. Referring to MacMurray's telegram to the Department, 220, December 14. The Turkish Minister read to me yesterday his entire dossier on the subject. It was evident that his Government had been inclined to give too much credence to the assurances of the Iraqi Minister. In his report of 2 days ago he made it clear to his Government that it had been misinformed by the Iraqi Minister at Ankara as to the true situation in Baghdad in respect to strained Anglo-Iraqi relations, pointing out that the instruction sent to Ankara by the Iraqi Minister for Foreign Affairs (which the Turkish Minister had seen) did not conform to what had been communicated by the Iraqi Minister to the Turkish Minister for Foreign Affairs and which was for the most part untrue or misleading. For instance the Iraqi Minister told the Turkish Minister for Foreign Affairs that in consequence of the Iraqi Government's vigorous representations direct to Lord Halifax the British Ambassador at Baghdad apologized to the Iraqi Prime Minister. That was not true for I saw Lord Halifax's telegram sent to the British Ambassador as reported in my telegram 115, December 5, and I know that the Ambassador has not apologized. The Turkish Minister suspects that the Iraqi Minister must have received private instructions from his brother the Iraqi Prime Minister and he intimated as much to his Government. In a telegram received December 16 by the Turkish Minister it appeared that the Turkish Government now appreciates this peculiar state of affairs and being convinced that in consequence of all that had transpired there is now no likelihood of this Government resuming relations with Germany and therefore considers it unnecessary to do anything further in the matter.

Repeated to Ankara.

KNABENSHUE

890G.5151/7 : Telegram

The Minister Resident in Iraq (Knabenshue) to the Secretary of State

BAGHDAD, December 18, 1940—3 p. m.
[Received December 19—1 : 55 a. m.]

121. The following is a confidential comment on my telegram No. 122, December 18, 4 p. m.[15] which will follow. While the British decision may be for financial reasons it is generally believed that it is also the beginning of a political and economic pressure to be increased in other directions until Iraq's attitude toward Britain becomes more cooperative.

KNABENSHUE

890G.5151/6 : Telegram

The Minister Resident in Iraq (Knabenshue) to the Secretary of State

BAGHDAD, December 18, 1940—4 p. m.
[Received 8 : 40 p. m.]

122. British banks in Iraq have received instructions from their head offices in London to refuse all applications for dollar exchange. The British maintain that Iraqi dollar credits resulting from their exports to the United States are more than sufficient to meet their normal purchases in the United States, but that the Iraqis have permitted their dollar exchange to be utilized for their purchase from Japan. In these circumstances Britain will not permit its meager dollar credits to be utilized by Iraq. It is estimated that Iraqi dollar credits lack by 30% enough to meet their normal American requirements plus the equipment for their army now on order in the United States. The Legation's banker informed me today that the local British banks endeavored to persuade Iraqi Government to institute exchange control in order to safeguard their foreign credits for legitimate needs such as American credits for American goods but no action was taken.

The effect of this situation will be a throttling of Iraqi purchases in America until steps are taken to control dollar credits for American purchases.

KNABENSHUE

---

[15] *Infra.*

890G.00/518 : Telegram

The Minister Resident in Iraq (Knabenshue) to the Secretary of State

BAGHDAD, December 18, 1940—7 p. m.
[Received 11 : 40 p. m.]

123. I was informed today by the chief British intelligence officer that the Regent called the members of the Cabinet to him yesterday and declared to them that the best interests of the state required their immediate resignations. The Prime Minister replied that he would consider the matter.

It is expected that a decision will be made within a few days. The attitude of the army is still an important factor, perhaps the most important.

KNABENSHUE

890G.00/519 : Telegram

The Minister Resident in Iraq (Knabenshue) to the Secretary of State

BAGHDAD, December 21, 1940—11 a. m.
[Received 5 : 35 p. m.]

122 bis. The Prime Minister has refused the Regent's invitation to resign. He can be forced to resign only by a vote of lack of confidence in Parliament. There are a sufficient number of influential political personalities who are willing and able to dislodge him on local issues in Parliament but personal feuds and enmities, engendered by previous *coups d'état* and vindictive persecutions, are making it difficult to form a group strong enough to take over the responsibilities of the Government at this critical period. However, influences are at work in an effort to bring this about.

KNABENSHUE

741.90G/121

*Memorandum of Conversation, by the Under Secretary
of State (Welles)*

[WASHINGTON,] December 21, 1940.

The British Chargé d'Affaires called to see me this morning. Mr. Butler stated first that his Government was deeply appreciative of the steps taken by the United States Government through its Minister in Baghdad to express the interest of the United States in the maintenance of close and friendly relations between Great Britain and Iraq.

S[UMNER] W[ELLES]

762.90G/14 : Telegram

The Ambassador in Turkey (MacMurray) to the Secretary of State

ANKARA, December 27, 1940—4 p. m.
[Received 5 : 58 p. m.]

227. Although it would appear from the Baghdad Legation's telegram to the Department No. 120, December 17 that the Turkish Government does not contemplate further action vis-à-vis the Government of Iraq, I should appreciate instructions for my guidance in the event that the Minister for Foreign Affairs should wish to discuss with me any aspect of the Department's suggestion of a joint *démarche* in this matter (my telegram No. 220, December 14).

MACMURRAY

741.90G 11/37 : Telegram

The Minister Resident in Iraq (Knabenshue) to the Secretary of State

BAGHDAD, December 29, 1940—8 p. m.
[Received January 12, 1941—10 a. m.]

127. In consequence of a long discussion I had with Nuri, the Minister for Foreign Affairs, when he paid me a visit December 26, he brought to me today a copy of his 2,300 word letter to the Prime Minister dated December 15 (approximately), copy of which I shall forward by airmail transpacific with a covering despatch.[16]

In this letter Nuri emphasized the importance of harmony and frankness as factors essential for the success of a Cabinet, especially at this particular time and he outlined some of the obstacles confronting them, particularly in their relations with Great Britain. In this connection he stated that the Palestine problem is the main cause of the disturbance and weakening of the once normally happy relations between Iraq and Britain. After reviewing Iraq's past efforts in behalf of the Arabs' cause and the Palestine situation in particular, he reminded the Prime Minister of the semi-official proposal of the Iraqi Government to the British Colonial Secretary whereby they offered that Iraq should enter the war by Great Britain's side in return for the British Government's solving the Palestine question (he means immediate establishment of a national government) and meeting the wishes of the Arabs of Palestine in a manner not opposed to their policy as set forth in the White Paper.

Referring further to the earlier reverses of the British he states that now it is evident that the British are able alone to stand against the two Axis powers and implies that Iraq's safety depends upon a British victory.

[16] Despatch No. 1687, January 7, 1941, and enclosure not printed.

He stated that for the first time in the history of Iraq they had received an official communication from the Government of the United States in which that Government expressed an earnest desire for the welfare of Iraq and for the preservation of its independence. He then reviewed what I had communicated to him and the Prime Minister in accordance with Department's telegram No. 56, December 3. Stating that the interest thus shown by America in regard to Iraqi affords them a fresh opportunity to serve the Arabian causes in a new field, he suggests the despatch to the United States of a deputation of Iraqis-Palestinians and Syrians to set out the problems arisen from the Syrian and Palestinian questions. He also recommended that this Government appoint a Minister Plenipotentiary to Washington instead of a Chargé d'Affaires.

I respectfully suggest that the Department reserve comment, if any, until the receipt of the full text of Nuri's communication and my despatch.

He expressed the opinion during his visit that the Prime Minister would resign within about 2 weeks and that a government of more or less neutral personalities would be set up to be succeeded after a few months by a stronger group.

KNABENSHUE

762.90G/14 : Telegram

The Secretary of State to the Ambassador in Turkey (MacMurray)

WASHINGTON, December 30, 1940—8 p. m.

104. Your 227, December 27, 4 p. m. The Department instructed Mr. Knabenshue on December 3 to inform the Iraqi Government that any action or decision of the Government of Iraq which might result in a less cooperative attitude in its relations with Great Britain could not fail to create a most painful impression in the United States. At the same time, the Department discussed the Iraqi situation with the Turkish Ambassador in Washington, with the idea that his Government might possibly desire to take parallel action. The Department has not had in mind a joint *démarche*. Our action was taken independently, in keeping with the American Government's traditional policy in such matters, and it was contemplated that any action Turkey might desire to take would also be taken independently.

According to Mr. Knabenshue's latest report, dated December 24,[16a] the difficulties between Great Britain and Iraq had not been settled . . . The Department naturally is not concerned with Iraq's conduct of its government and does not contemplate instructing the Legation

---

[16a] Not printed.

to make any further representations to Iraq in the matter at the present time. It will keep you informed of any further developments.

HULL

INFORMAL ASSURANCES BY THE IRAQI GOVERNMENT REGARDING APPLICATION OF NEW EDUCATION LAW TO AMERICAN SCHOOLS IN IRAQ [17]

890G.42/44

The Minister Resident in Iraq (Knabenshue) to the Secretary of State

No. 1459

BAGHDAD, January 3, 1940.
[Received February 16.]

SIR: I have the honor to refer to the Department's instruction No. 404 of November 21, 1939,[18] with which was enclosed for the Legation's information, a copy of a memorandum of conversation between Father Edmund J. Walsh, Vice President of Georgetown University and representatives of the Division of Near Eastern Affairs regarding the proposed educational law in Iraq.

Subsequent to the date of the Department's instruction under acknowledgment, the Department will have received my despatch No. 1427 of November 2, 1939,[19] with which I enclosed a copy of my note to the Ministry for Foreign Affairs, drafted in accordance with the suggestions contained in the Department's instruction No. 389 of September 14, 1939.[20] In this despatch, I informed the Department of the cooperation which I had secured from the British Ambassador. The Ambassador stated that, having referred my suggestions to his Government, he had been authorized to give full support to this Legation's representations in the matter. After our conversation, I received from the Ambassador a note, a copy of which is enclosed, outlining to me his conversation with the Minister for Foreign Affairs.

I feel confident that, in view of the tenor of my note to the Ministry of October 16, 1939,[21] and of the British Ambassador's conversation with the Minister for Foreign Affairs, the proposed educational law will undoubtedly be shelved for the moment, and that if and when later presented to Parliament, it will be so amended as to eliminate its more objectionable features. However, I will keep in touch with the situation, and should a new law be proposed I will hope to be given an opportunity of discussing it again with the Minister for

---

[17] For previous correspondence, see *Foreign Relations*, 1939, vol. IV, pp. 545 ff.
[18] Not printed.
[19] *Foreign Relations*, 1939, vol. IV, p. 551.
[20] *Ibid.*, p. 550.
[21] *Ibid.*, p. 552.

Foreign Affairs and report the matter to the Department before the law is presented to Parliament.

Respectfully yours,   P. KNABENSHUE

[Enclosure]

The British Ambassador in Iraq (Newton) to the American Minister Resident in Iraq (Knabenshue)

BAGHDAD, 14 November, 1939.

MY DEAR MINISTER: I spoke to Ali Jaudat [22] on November 9th about the draft educational law. He explained that they appreciated the good work done by the American schools and did not wish to harm them. But the Persians had closed several Iraqi schools in Persia and they wanted to retaliate on Persian schools in Iraq.

I pointed out that it would be a mistake to enact a foolish law merely because the Persians had set a bad example and the upshot of our talk was that Ali Jaudat made a note to talk the matter over with the Minister of Education with a view to finding some means to hit back at the Persians without damaging other foreign educational institutions.

With a two months' adjournment before them they should have time to think things over before Parliament meets again.

Yours very sincerely,   BASIL NEWTON

890G.42/47

The Minister Resident in Iraq (Knabenshue) to the Secretary of State

No. 1537   BAGHDAD, April 8, 1940.
                                              [Received May 16.]

SIR: I have the honor to refer to the Legation's despatches during the course of 1939 regarding the new education law which the Iraqi Government was proposing to enact. After lying dormant for some time, the proposal was revived a few days ago. It was brought to my attention that a committee of the Chamber of Deputies which had the proposal under consideration had finally prepared its report for presentation to the Chamber and that this report recommended the law as previously drafted with certain amendments which made it even more unacceptable so far as foreign schools were concerned and which did not eliminate any of its former undesirable features. I enclose a copy [23] of what is believed to be the text of the previous law with the committee's recommendations in parallel columns.

---

[22] Iraqi Minister for Foreign Affairs.
[23] Not printed.

Immediately the matter came to my attention I consulted with my French and British colleagues and I afterwards addressed a first-person note to the Acting Minister for Foreign Affairs, a copy of which I enclose. The French Minister is making strong representations in the matter, and the British Ambassador, although there are no British schools in Iraq, intends to support the representations of the French Minister and myself.

I will keep the Department informed of developments.

Respectfully yours,   P. KNABENSHUE

[Enclosure]

The American Minister Resident (Knabenshue) to the Iraqi Acting Minister for Foreign Affairs

No. 765   BAGHDAD, April 6, 1940.

EXCELLENCY: I desire to draw Your Excellency's attention to an exchange of notes which took place during the past year between this Legation and the Ministry for Foreign Affairs regarding a proposed new education law for Iraq which was being considered by the Iraqi Parliament.

In its note No. 668 of August 4th,[24] the Legation drew the attention of the Ministry to the fact that Baghdad newspapers had published what was alleged to be a proposed new public education law, which, it was said, would be submitted to Parliament for approval during its session at that time. The Legation called attention to the fact that several provisions of the proposed law, as published in the newspapers, appeared to be prejudicial to American educational institutions in Iraq and contrary in particular to the Declaration of the Kingdom of Iraq to the League of Nations on May 30, 1932.[25]

In its note No. 12/1117/11875/gh of August 12, 1939,[26] the Ministry was good enough to inform the Legation that what had appeared in the local press was nothing more than a draft law submitted to Parliament for examination and that the decision thereon had been postponed until the next session.

In its note No. 696 of October 16, 1939,[27] the Legation expressed its pleasure at learning from the Ministry that the bill under discussion had been drafted for the purpose of organizing cultural and educational affairs and that it was not intended to prejudice any foreign cultural institutions in Iraq, the aim of which, the Ministry recognized

---

[24] *Foreign Relations*, 1939, vol. IV, p. 548.
[25] League of Nations Document No. A.17.1932. VII: *Request of the Kingdom of Iraq for Admission to the League of Nations*, p. 3.
[26] *Foreign Relations*, 1939, vol. IV, p. 550.
[27] *Ibid.*, p. 552.

as "undoubtedly sincere service to the sons of the country within the existing law."

While gratified at the Ministry's assurance in this respect, the Legation remarked in its note of October 16th, that whether or not there be any technical discriminations in the proposed law itself, or other provisions which might be liable to prejudice American educational interests in Iraq, the ambiguity of some of the provisions of the proposed law that may depend for their interpretations and application upon administrative action, holds the possibility of prejudice and discrimination in practice. Furthermore, it was pointed out, the draft of the proposed law as published by the press appeared to contain provisions contrary to both the letter and spirit of Iraq's Declaration of May 30, 1932, to the League of Nations. In these circumstances, the Legation felt sure that the Ministry would agree that the Declaration established a standard of treatment applicable to all nations, from which Iraq would not desire to depart by *unilateral* action. The Legation therefore expressed the hope that any new legislation on this subject would be in harmony with the spirit of Iraq's Declaration to the League, and that there would be no abridgement of the long-established prerogatives of American educational institutions in Iraq.

I now desire to bring to Your Excellency's attention the fact that rumors are circulating to the effect that a committee of the Chamber of Deputies is on the point of recommending to the Iraqi Parliament the former proposed education law with certain suggested amendments and without eliminating the features of the proposed law which had been considered to be prejudicial to American educational institutions in Iraq.

While it is hoped that the present rumors relative to this matter are unfounded, in the circumstances, however, I hasten to review the situation to Your Excellency and to reiterate that my Government's point of view in this matter is as outlined in the fourth and fifth paragraphs of the Legation's note No. 696 of October 16, 1939.

I avail myself [etc.]   P. KNABENSHUE

890G.42/48

The Minister Resident in Iraq (Knabenshue) to the Secretary of State

No. 1542   BAGHDAD, April 12, 1940.
                           [Received June 1.]

SIR: I have the honor to refer to my despatch no. 1537 of April 8, 1940, regarding the proposed new Iraqi Education Law and to inform the Department that in consequence of the action taken by this and the French Legation and the British Embassy the proposed law was withdrawn from the Iraqi Parliament by the Ministry of Education for, it was announced in the press, the Ministry desired to make certain basic changes. Subsequently I received an acknowledgement from the Minister for Foreign Affairs of my note of April 6th,[28] with the statement that "I assure Your Excellency that the appropriate Iraqi authorities are attending to this matter in all its aspects and shall communicate the result thereof to you in the near future."

While the present Iraqi Government seems disposed apparently to meet our recent representations in a favorable manner, it is not impossible that we may be obliged to cope with a similar situation in the future. The Department will of course be kept informed of developments.

Respectfully yours, P. KNABENSHUE

890G.42/49

The Minister Resident in Iraq (Knabenshue) to the Secretary of State

No. 1567 BAGHDAD, May 16, 1940.
[Received June 17.]

SIR: I have the honor to refer to previous despatches regarding the proposed new Iraqi Education Law and particularly to my despatch No. 1542 of April 12, 1940, reporting that the draft law had been withdrawn for the moment from the Iraqi Parliament for further consideration by the Ministry of Education, and that in a note from the Foreign Office I was assured that the appropriate Iraqi authorities were studying the matter and that the result thereof would be communicated to me in the near future.

While I remarked that the Iraqi Government now seemed disposed to meet our recent representations in a favorable way, I added that it was not impossible that we may be obliged to cope with further difficulties in the future. My fears in this respect have now been realized.

On Sunday, April 14, I called to see the Minister for Foreign Affairs before proceeding the next day on a tour of northern Iraq. He told me that the new Education Law had been passed by the Chamber of Deputies, but that it would not be sent to the Senate during the present session, but would be held over until the next session in the autumn and that in the meantime discussions could take place with a view to arriving at a solution of the problem which would satisfy the foreign

---

[28] *Supra.*

school interests concerned. I pointed out to the Foreign Minister that the law as drafted was still considered to contain provisions which limited the freedom of action of foreign schools contrary to the terms of Iraq's Declaration to the League of Nations. I repeated my former statements to the effect that the passage of this law as drafted would seem to constitute unilateral action on the part of the Iraqi Government in respect to its international obligation, to which my Government is opposed. The Foreign Minister assured me that it was not the desire of the Iraqi Government to do anything which would constitute a nonfulfillment of its international obligation, and that he felt sure that during the interim period between now and the next session of Parliament a satisfactory solution could be found.

In view of the above circumstances, I was greatly surprised to receive an urgent request for me to visit him on May 6th and to learn from him that the Senate had actually passed the Education Law on the eve of its adjournment. He was full of profuse apologies and explained that he was not present at the session of the Senate when this took place and that had he been there he would have caused this law to have been held over until the next session. I thereupon made the suggestion that, in view of the circumstances, he might consider it desirable to cause the signature of the Regent to the law to be postponed pending further discussions. With this object in view, he at once telephoned to the Prime Minister. The Prime Minister informed him that if the Regent had not already signed the law he would ask him to postpone signature and that, if he had signed it, he (the Prime Minister) would postpone its publication in the official journal. According to Iraqi Law, even if a bill is passed by Parliament and signed by the Regent, it does not become a law until published in the Government Gazette.

I again pointed out to the Foreign Minister that the proposed law would seem to be a contravention of their Declaration to the League of Nations and as such constitute unilateral action on the part of the Iraqi Government in respect to their international obligation. He replied that he had been assured by his advisers that the law as drafted was not in fact inconsistent with their declaration to the League, and he felt sure that an agreement could be reached whereby the law could be administered in such a way as to give satisfaction to the foreign school interests. I pointed out that while it was possible that the present Government might be disposed to administer the law in a lenient and favorable manner in respect to foreign schools, there could be no assurance that succeeding governments would do likewise.

As a result of our further discussion of the matter, it was arranged that the Foreign Minister would furnish me with a copy of the proposed law as now passed by the Iraqi Parliament; that I would furnish copies of this law to the American school interests; that I would invite the heads of these schools to meet and formulate their objections to the law; and that this committee would then meet at the Foreign Office in order to discuss the matter with officials of the Ministry of Education with a view to bringing about reconciliation of the various points at issue. However, in agreeing to this procedure, I informed the Foreign Minister that I am not authorized to offer specific suggestions or to accept specific proposals, and that I could only urge that the Iraqi Government avoid taking unilateral action in respect to its international obligation, which would be prejudicial to American interests. I also informed him that even if the heads of American schools in Iraq should be disposed after consultation with officials of the Government to accept any proposed arrangement under the new law as enacted, it would still be necessary for me to submit the entire matter to my Government for its consideration, for individual American citizens are not entitled to waive their own rights or the rights of other American citizens guaranteed to them by treaties or other international instruments.

I will keep the Department informed of further developments, and, for its information, I am enclosing copies of the law [29] as translated from an Arabic text given me by the Minister for Foreign Affairs.

Respectfully yours,   P. KNABENSHUE

890G.42/51

The Minister Resident in Iraq (Knabenshue) to the Secretary of State

No. 1591   BAGHDAD, July 16, 1940.
                                                   [Received August 17.]

SIR: I have the honor to refer to my despatch No. 1567 of May 16, 1940, regarding the proposed new Iraqi education law, wherein I reported circumstances which led up to an arrangement whereby the heads of the American schools in Iraq would meet with representatives of the Iraq Government at the Ministry for Foreign Affairs in order to discuss the proposed law and its effect upon American school interests here. Subsequently, the meeting took place on July 10, 1940, and I have the honor to report as follows in connection therewith:

On July 9th the heads of the American schools met at the Legation in order that they might discuss together and formulate their position with regard to the proposed law before meeting the representatives of the Iraqi Government at the Ministry for Foreign Affairs. I received these American gentlemen and outlined the gen-

[29] Not printed.

eral situation to them. I pointed out to them that my reason for agreeing to their meeting with representatives of the Ministry of Education was that it would give them an opportunity as technical experts in the matter to demonstrate to the Iraqi officials in what specific respects the new law would interfere with the administration of their schools in contravention of the Iraqi Government's declaration to the League of Nations. I cautioned them that in their discussions with the Iraqi officials they should bear in mind that they were not authorized to waive their own rights or the rights of other American citizens guaranteed to them by treaties or other international instruments. I also informed them that as I myself was not authorized to offer any specific suggestions in respect to the amendment of the proposed law, I would refrain from joining their deliberations. They were then given a room at the Legation for the purpose of discussing the matter together and formulating their position. On the following day they met with representatives of the Iraqi Government at the Ministry for Foreign Affairs. I enclose herewith a copy of a translation of the minutes of this meeting signed by the persons who were present. I also enclose copies of two letters from Mr. John Van Ess dated July 12 and July 14 respectively,[30] reporting to me further details in connection with the matter.

On the day following the meeting, I deemed it desirable to send a note to the Minister for Foreign Affairs reminding him of our conversation on May 6th particularly in respect to the fact that individual American citizens are not entitled to waive their own rights or the rights of other American citizens guaranteed them by treaties or other international instruments and of the fact that he had given me assurance that the publication of the proposed law would be withheld pending further negotiations between us in the matter and I consequently repeated in my note my request that in the circumstances he be good enough to cause continued postponement of the publication of the law until I could communicate to him my Government's further point of view in the matter. I enclose a copy of this note.

The Department will observe from the enclosures that the representatives of the American schools in Iraq only questioned four articles of the proposed new law, namely, articles 27, 30, 35 and 36. The Department will also note that in view of the assurances given by the Iraqi representatives which they said would be officially confirmed by the Government, the American representatives were disposed to accept these assurances as the basis for the continuation of the schools under the proposed law under what they termed a gentlemen's agreement pending further negotiations between the Iraqi and United States Governments.

---

[30] Neither printed.

In these circumstances the matter is submitted to the Department for its decision as to whether it will recognize the proposed new law. In this event, it is assumed that the Department would desire the assurances given to the American school representatives to be officially confirmed in an exchange of diplomatic notes or in some other manner acceptable to the Department. The only alternative would be to refuse to accept the law and to insist upon its amendment by the Iraqi Parliament in order that this law might be made more precisely to conform to the undertaking of the Iraqi Government under article 15 of its declaration to the League of Nations in 1932.

It might be mentioned that the Iraqi Government maintains that the proposed new law is not in conflict with its declaration to the League of Nations. While it is no doubt true that in many respects the new law restricts to a certain extent "the free exercise of the . . . educational . . . activities of religious missions . . . ",[30a] the most important prohibition of such free exercise is that contained in article 36 which forbids Iraqi students attending foreign primary schools. In this connection the Iraqis seem disposed to permit American missions to offer primary education to Iraqi students through the intermediary of schools nominally registered in the names of Iraqis but which will be administered by Americans.

The Iraqis maintain, more or less confidentially, that the proposed law is directed primarily against certain other foreign schools in this country, particularly those of the Iranians which are largely subsidized by the Iranian Government.

I am also enclosing a copy of a note addressed to the Minister for Foreign Affairs by the British Ambassador,[31] in which it will be noted he in effect supports under instructions from his Government my representations to the Iraqi Government in this matter. The British Ambassador was kind enough to allow me to read the instruction which he received from his Foreign Office in this regard, a copy of which was also sent to the British Embassy in Washington where it is assumed the Department also will be permitted to see it.

There can be no doubt that Iraq is bound by an international obligation in this matter. It therefore remains for the Department and its legal advisers to decide to what extent in their opinion the proposed new Iraqi education law contravenes Iraq's obligation and to what extent the Department may be willing to make concessions, if any, to the Iraqi Government in the interpretation and administration of the law as it stands or whether the Department will insist upon refusing to accept the law as drafted and as already passed by the Iraqi Parliament, but not yet promulgated.

[30a] Omissions indicated in the original despatch.
[31] Not printed.

It will be noted that article 42 of the new law provides for the cancellation of Public Education Law No. 28 of 1929, which is the law under which education is at present administered. I am enclosing a copy of this law [32] in order that it might serve for comparison purposes when the Department is giving consideration to the proposed new law. I am also enclosing for ready reference a copy of article 15 of Iraq's declaration to the League of Nations of May 30, 1932.

As I fear that I may not be able to influence the postponement of the publication of the law very much longer, inasmuch as the Iraqi Government would like to make it effective before the next school year, I would be glad if the Department could telegraph me its decision in the matter briefly, with more detailed instructions, if necessary, to follow by airmail via the Pacific to the Consulate General at Calcutta for transmission from there by air to this office. (Through airmail service via the Pacific is not established.)

Respectfully yours,   P. KNABENSHUE

[Enclosure 1—Translation]

Minutes of Meeting Between the Iraqi Director General of Public Instruction and Representatives of the American Schools in Iraq

In accordance with the wishes of His Excellency the Minister for Foreign Affairs, Dr. Fadhel al Jamali, Director General of Public Instruction and Education, representing the Ministry of Education, met Mr. Van Ess, Dr. Staudt, Father Sarjeant, and Mr. Hakken, representing the American schools in Iraq, on July 10, 1940 in the office of Sayid Yusuf al Gailani, Director of Western Affairs of the Ministry for Foreign Affairs, and in the presence of Sayid Sadiq Shanshal, Legal Adviser to the Ministry for Foreign Affairs. Discussions proceeded on the subject of the new Educational Law as follows:

Mr. Van Ess starting the talk said that they did not come as advocates demanding a right but they have come to investigate certain points. Dr. al Jamali in reply remarked that his request was that none of them should feel that the object of the new law was to bring pressure against American schools or was directed against any one of them as its aim was to protect national public instruction and the Ministry of Education was prepared to co-operate with the American institutions which have proved their good intentions toward the Kingdom in general and education in particular.

Mr. Van Ess then asked about the object of including two articles, one providing for the appointment of directors and teachers of private and foreign schools with the approval of the Ministry of Education,

---

[32] Not printed.

and the other stipulating that the Ministry of Education will itself appoint the teachers of history, geography and the Arabic language. Dr. Fadhel al Jamali stated that the Ministry of Education, in addition to its desire to ensure the integrity of all teaching institutions, wishes to select itself those on whom it depends for civic studies.

Mr. Van Ess objected and said that he had good Iraqi teachers for these lessons, who have given long and praiseworthy services. Dr. Fadhel al Jamali replied that the Ministry of Education will take such good teachers into consideration and will not hesitate to nominate them to the school in which they were serving.

Father Sarjeant then inquired whether it would be possible for the American fathers to study the Arabic language and then teach these civic studies. Dr. al Jamali replied that his understanding of the spirit of the law was that the sons of the language itself will undertake the teaching of the branches of civic studies and the Arabic language.

A discussion then took place concerning the subject of the liability of the teachers who may be appointed by the Ministry of Education to the regulations of the schools to which they will be appointed. Dr. al Jamali stated that they will be treated like the other teachers attached to the school administration. They will account for their behaviour and the execution of their duties as if they were teachers in the Government schools and the Ministry of Education does not by the appointment of teachers for these lessons intend to weaken the discipline in these schools.

A discussion then ensued concerning the salaries to be paid to those teachers which may be less than those paid by the Ministry of Education. Dr. al Jamali replied that the Ministry of Education will treat this matter. It may appoint teachers who may not need high salaries or it may grant some of those teachers subsidies from its own budget, if it considers that necessary. Father Sarjeant then expressed his fears of the possibility of the appointment of teachers below the required educational standard but Dr. al Jamali assured him that their standard will not be lower than that of the teachers of the Ministry of Education in general.

Then Father Sarjeant brought up the question of differentiation in shortcomings between the school and between the administrative and teaching staffs, stating that the Ministry may punish the offending members of the staff and may not punish the school. Sayid Sadiq Shanshal replied that the school had a moral, legal character and Dr. Fadhel al Jamali added that assuming that a certain school adopts policies and aims contradictory to the Iraqi public interest and takes a harmful course, in spite of the changes in the members of its staff, the Ministry will undoubtedly punish the school by closing it.

Then Mr. Van Ess enquired about the periods of school holidays and whether it was intended to close American schools on the same days during which Government schools will be closed. Dr. al Jamali answered that the days during which the schools will be closed will be the official holidays during which Government departments will be closed and will not include Fridays.

Mr. Van Ess then brought up the problem which might arise as a result of prohibiting Iraqis from sending their children to foreign schools and reproached the Iraqi Government for taking such measures despite the fact that he has rendered loyal services to this country for a period exceeding thirty years. Dr. al Jamali replied that this measure was inevitable for the protection of the national culture and was not at all directed against him. After further discussions, it was agreed that the American primary schools be entrusted to Iraqis who will apply for permits to open these schools in their names as private schools provided that the Ministry of Education will assist them in accepting grants-in-aid which they may receive from America through the American schools. Dr. al Jamali then promised that he will personally intervene to offer all facilities for the execution of this transaction within one week from the date of the submission of the application and there would not be the least difficulty or obstacle.

The meeting ended with the provision that the talk was to be considered as a "word of honor" or a "gentleman's agreement."

(Signed) FADHEL AL JAMALI
Nazir al-Awwal
*Director General of Public Instruction
and Education*

(Signed) John Van Ess
" Bernard D. Hakken
" Calvin K. Staudt
" Francis B. Sarjeant, S.J.

[Enclosure 2]

*The American Minister Resident (Knabenshue) to the Iraqi Minister
for Foreign Affairs (Nuri as-Said)*

No. 790 BAGHDAD, July 11, 1940.

EXCELLENCY: During our conversation on May 6th when we discussed the proposed new education law, you informed me, with regret, that, contrary to your previous assurances to me that the law would not be submitted to the Senate until its next session in the autumn, the Senate had, however, just passed the law on the eve of its adjournment. Upon my request that the signature of His Highness the Regent be withheld until further discussions could take place and until I could refer the matter to my Government for further consideration, you were good enough to telephone to the Prime Minister and then to inform me that His Excellency had agreed to withhold publication of the law until the matter could be further discussed. It was then arranged between us that I should call a meeting of the heads of the American educational institutions in Iraq in order that they might formulate their position in respect to the proposed law and afterwards meet with representatives of the Iraqi Government at the Ministry for Foreign Affairs with a view, if possible, of bringing about a reconciliation of the various points at issue.

As Your Excellency is aware, the meeting in question took place at the Ministry for Foreign Affairs yesterday. It is my understanding that an arrangement was suggested whereby the American educational institutions in Iraq would tentatively accept certain conditions which would enable them to continue their schools under the proposed education law.

As I had informed Your Excellency on May 6th, individual American citizens are not entitled to waive their own rights or the rights of other American citizens guaranteed to them by treaties or other international instruments and that, consequently, I would be obliged to refer the proposed law to my Government, together with the recommendations of the American interests involved for its consideration. Having already forwarded a copy of the proposed law to my Government, I am now communicating to it the results of the meeting which took place at the Ministry yesterday. In the circumstances, I desire to ask that you be good enough to cause continued postponement of publication of the law until I can communicate to you my Government's further point of view in the matter.

I avail myself [etc.]   P. KNABENSHUE

890G.42/52

The Minister Resident in Iraq (Knabenshue) to the Secretary of State

No. 1592   BAGHDAD, July 17, 1940.
         [Received August 17.]

SIR: I have the honor to refer to my despatch no. 1591 of July 16, regarding the proposed Iraqi education law and to report that immediately after the preparation of that despatch I received a note from the Minister for Foreign Affairs, a copy of which is enclosed, in reply to my note to him of July 11, 1940, a copy of which forms an enclosure to my previous despatch. In view of the concluding statement of the Minister for Foreign Affairs that, in consequence of the alleged agreement come to between the heads of the American schools and officials of the Iraqi Government, no further negotiations between us would be required, I hastened to reply immediately by my note no. 791 of July 16, a copy of which is also enclosed, in which I informed His Excellency that I could not accept his thesis that no further negotiations were necessary.

In view of this new phase of the situation which has arisen, I would call the Department's attention to the minutes of the meeting which took place between the heads of the American schools and the officials of the Iraqi Government,[33] from which it will be noted that for the most part it consisted of a statement of the Americans' point of view and in assurances given by the Iraqis to meet these points of view. In only one instance was there mention of an agreement and that was in connection with that article of the proposed law which prohibited Iraqis from attending foreign primary schools. The memorandum concluded with the statement:

"The meeting ended with the provision that the talk was to be considered as a 'word of honor' or a 'gentlemen's agreement.' "

In this connection I would also call the Department's attention to Mr. Van Ess' letter to me of July 14 [34] in which he stated in connection with the opening of the meeting:

"We distinctly declared that we understood that the conference at the Foreign Office was exploratory only and that we had met only as conferees and that our signatures to the memorandum would in no sense prejudice our rights, to which Dr. Jamali and Yusuf Beg agreed."

In his letter to me of July 12th,[34] Mr. Van Ess stated:

"At the end of the conference, it was mutually emphasized that our deliberations and conclusions constitute a gentlemen's agreement, which, without quibble and in the spirit of honorable intention on both sides, shall result in a working arrangement, pending the official negotiations between the Iraq Government and the Government of the United States of America."

It is unfortunate that the Minister for Foreign Affairs should have assumed, as he did, that no further negotiations were necessary and especially so after my warnings to him both verbally on May 6th before the meeting of the American school heads and the Iraqi Government representatives, and on the day after the meeting in my note of July 11th.

I will keep the Department informed of developments and in the meantime will hope to receive as soon as possible the Department's instructions as suggested in the last paragraph of my despatch No. 1591 of July 16, 1940.

Respectfully yours,

P. KNABENSHUE

---

[33] *Ante*, p. 736.
[34] Not printed.

[Enclosure 1—Translation]

The Iraqi Minister for Foreign Affairs (Nuri as-Said) to the American Minister Resident (Knabenshue)

No. 12/2881/2881/gh   BAGHDAD, July 15, 1940.

MY DEAR MINISTER: Reference Your Excellency's note No. 790 of July 11, 1940, concerning the draft Public Education Law, I have the honor to state that the conference of which you made mention in your above quoted letter has taken place in the Ministry for Foreign Affairs and has resulted in an agreement of the viewpoints between the representatives of the Ministry of Education and this Ministry and the representatives of the American schools in Iraq and the consent of the latter to take certain administrative measures which would ensure the continuance of the accomplishment of their educational duties in Iraq without any difficulty. A minute for this understanding has been prepared which will be the basis for action in the future.

I consider it my duty to make mention of the thanks of the Ministry of Education and its appreciation to those who are responsible for the administration of the American schools for the good services they have rendered which the Iraqi Government is so anxious to see maintained within simple administrative measures which are required by the new law. Therefore, after obtaining this satisfactory result, there remains nothing which might call for entering anew into negotiations concerning the subject.

I avail myself [etc.]   NURI AS-SAID

[Enclosure 2]

The American Minister Resident (Knabenshue) to the Iraqi Minister for Foreign Affairs (Nuri as-Said)

No. 791   BAGHDAD, July 16, 1940.

EXCELLENCY: I have just received Your Excellency's note No. 12/2881/2881/gh of July 15, 1940, in reference to my note No. 790 of July 11, 1940, concerning the draft Public Education Law and the conference which took place at your Ministry between the heads of American schools in Iraq and representatives of the Iraqi Government which, you state, resulted in an agreement of the viewpoints between the representatives of the Ministry of Education and the representatives of the American schools and consent of the latter to take certain administrative measures which would insure the continuance of the accomplishment of the American educational institutions in Iraq without difficulty and that a minute for this understanding had been prepared which will be the basis for action in the future.

Your Excellency was also good enough to mention the thanks of the Ministry of Education and its appreciation to those who are responsible for the administration of American schools and the good services they have rendered, which the Iraqi Government is anxious to see maintained within simple administrative measures which are required by the new law. Your Excellency then concludes that there remains nothing which might call for continuing negotiations in connection with this subject.

As it would seem that Your Excellency has failed to understand the full purport of my note no. 790 of July 11, 1940, I hasten to call your attention to its third paragraph on page two, wherein I reminded Your Excellency that in our conversation on May 6th I had informed you (in connection with the proposed meeting between the American school representatives and representatives of the Ministry of Education) that individual American citizens are not entitled to waive their own rights or the rights of other American citizens guaranteed to them by treaties or other international instruments and that, consequently, I would be obliged to refer the proposed law to my Government together with the recommendations of the American interests involved for my Government's consideration. The understanding come to between the American school representatives and the representatives of the Ministry of Education was merely for a temporary arrangement which would permit the American schools to continue operating pending the conclusion of negotiations between the Iraqi and United States Governments on this subject, and as a result, there was no final or definite acceptance of the provisions of the proposed new education law either by the American schools or by the United States Government.

In this connection it may be relevant to quote to Your Excellency from letters I received from Mr. Van Ess in connection with the meeting in question:

"We distinctly declared that we understood that the conference at the Foreign Office was exploratory only and that we had met only as conferees and that our signatures to the memorandum would in no sense prejudice our rights, to which Dr. Jamali and Yusuf Beg agreed."

and also:

"At the end of the conference, it was mutually emphasized that our deliberations and conclusions constitute a gentlemen's agreement, which, without quibble and in the spirit of honorable intention on both sides, shall result in a working arrangement, pending the official negotiations between the Iraq Government and the Government of the United States of America."

In the circumstances, I am not able to accept Your Excellency's thesis that there remains no need for further negotiation in the matter.

In the circumstances, I must refer the matter to my Government, and I must ask Your Excellency to be good enough to continue postponement of the publication of the proposed law until I can communicate to you my Government's further point of view in the matter.

I avail myself [etc.]   P. KNABENSHUE

890G.42/53

The Minister Resident in Iraq (Knabenshue) to the Secretary of State

No. 1601   BAGHDAD, July 23, 1940.
                                        [Received August 27.]

SIR: I have the honor to refer to my despatches nos. 1591 and 1592 of July 16 and 17, respectively, and to report that after the receipt of my note no. 791 of July 16, 1940, the Minister for Foreign Affairs asked me to call at the Ministry for a further discussion of the proposed new education law with officials of the Ministry. Consequently, on July 22nd I complied with his request. The officials delegated to discuss the matter with me were Sayid Mousa Shabandar, Personal Assistant to the Minister for Foreign Affairs, Sayid Yusuf Gailani, Chief of the Bureau of Western Affairs, and Sayid Siddiq Shamshal, Acting Legal Adviser to the Ministry.

At the outset, I made it clear to these gentlemen that I was not authorized to make any specific suggestions in respect to the proposed new education law, but only to point out that the United States Government could not accept what would constitute unilateral action on the part of Iraq in the abrogation of rights which accrue to us by virtue of Iraq's declaration to the League of Nations of May, 1932. I also pointed out again that as individual American citizens or groups of American citizens are not legally empowered to waive their own rights or the rights of other Americans guaranteed by international treaties or other instruments, the recent meeting between the heads of American schools in Iraq and officials of the Iraqi Government and the memorandum of their conversations which was signed by those taking part in it could only be considered as advisory. I stated that I had forwarded a copy of the memorandum in question to my Government for its consideration, and that pending the receipt of my Government's further observations on the subject, I would expect the Iraqi Government to postpone promulgation of the proposed new education law in accordance with the assurances given to me in this respect by the Minister for Foreign Affairs and the Prime Minister.

The officials with whom I was holding this discussion desired to express to me for the Department's further information that in the opinion of the Iraqi Government the new law does not infringe upon

Iraq's declaration to the League. Taking up the two principal points of the new law which it is alleged provide for an interference with the free exercise of the educational activities of American schools operated by religious missions, they pointed out in respect to the first, namely, the appointment by the Ministry of Education of teachers for certain subjects in private schools as provided for in Article 27 was an essential safeguard to which the Iraqi Government felt itself entitled on moral and cultural grounds. In accordance with the assurances which had been given to the heads of American schools, the Iraqi Government would be willing to allow the American schools to nominate teachers for the studies in question from the list of which nominations the Government would make the choice.

In respect to the second feature of the law (Article 36) which prohibited Iraqi students from entering foreign primary schools, it was explained that this provision was necessary for two reasons: first, they deemed it essential for moral and cultural reasons that Iraqi children of tender ages during the early formative period of their lives should receive their primary education in Iraqi schools in accordance with Iraqi moral and cultural standards and ideals. The second reason was that because there are so many foreign primary schools (Persian and Jewish schools being meant) it was necessary to adopt a uniform law so that discrimination could not be claimed. However, as the Iraqi Government did not entertain any particular objection to American primary schools conducted in Iraq they had suggested to the heads of the American schools here that their primary schools be registered in the names of Iraqis and they agreed to permit these schools to be administered and operated as heretofore by the American personnel. It was explained that this would permit the Iraqi Government to issue permits for the transfer of such American primary schools to nominal Iraqi registration but to refuse permits for the transfer of other foreign schools in their discretion.

While the provisions of Article 27 and Article 36 of the proposed new law would seem to constitute the most flagrant interference with American schools contrary to Iraq's declaration to the League, there are other provisions of the law which, in a lesser degree, also would seem to be inconsistent with the declaration. However, it was pointed out by the Iraqi officials with whom I was holding the discussion that obviously it was not intended by Iraq's declaration to the League that foreign schools would be permitted to operate in Iraq without some form of control on the part of the Ministry of Education in order to protect the interest of their Iraqi students. In support of this contention, reference was made to Article 4 of the tripartite convention between Iraq, Great Britain and the United States of January 9, 1930,[36] which reads as follows:

---

[36] *Foreign Relations*, 1930, vol. III, p. 302.

"Subject to the provisions of any local laws for the maintenance of public order and public morals, and to any general educational requirements prescribed by law in Iraq, the nationals of the United States will be permitted freely to establish and maintain educational, philanthropic and religious institutions in Iraq, to receive voluntary applicants and to teach in the English language."

Thus it was pointed out that in spite of the provision which permitted nationals of the United States freely to establish and maintain educational institutions it was made obligatory that such schools comply with the general educational requirements prescribed by law in Iraq. While this latter provision was not included in Iraq's declaration to the League, it was maintained by the Iraqi officials that the principle involved must obviously be accepted.

Although I had frequently pointed out to the Minister for Foreign Affairs and other interested Iraqi officials the impropriety of unilateral action on the part of the Iraqi Government in this matter, they have constantly maintained and still maintain that the law as drafted does not, in their opinion, conflict with their declaration to the League and they consider that on moral grounds they are entitled to protect the interests of their young nationals along the lines covered by the draft law. Their firm stand in this respect will also be noted in the enclosed copy of a note from the Minister for Foreign Affairs to the British Ambassador dated July 15, 1940.[37]

In view of this attitude of the Iraqi Government and the fact that the British Ambassador now informs me that he fears he can do nothing further in the matter, and especially so as the British have no schools in Iraq, and in view of the fact that the French Minister, having been given a free hand by his Government is now not inclined to press further in the matter inasmuch as the heads of French schools here seem willing to accept the law and fear that their opposition might cause further difficulties for them, it would seem that there is no practical alternative to an acceptance of the Iraqi point of view, but perhaps with certain assurances to be given by them in an exchange of diplomatic notes. I am very reluctant to recommend this action, but I fear that if we continue to oppose the promulgation and enforcement of the new law it may result inevitably in certain retaliatory measures which we could not oppose, but which would have the effect of making the continued operation of American schools impracticable. For instance, the Iraqis maintain that the law does not prohibit foreign primary schools which would be permitted to accept foreign students, but the Iraqis maintain that they have the right to prohibit Iraqi students from attending such schools. Also, at the present time Iraqi students attending foreign secondary schools which

---

[37] Not printed.

follow the curriculum of the Ministry of Education are permitted to take Government examinations and secure Government certificates which qualify them for appointment to Government positions. It would seem to be within the rights of the Iraqi Government, if they so saw fit, to refuse to permit students attending foreign schools to take the Government examinations and secure Government certificates. Obviously, such forms of retaliation would be effective in causing the closing of foreign schools.

It is obvious to me that the real motive behind the new law is a nationalistic one, in order to bring foreign schools more and more under Iraqi control with a view eventually to their total or at least partial eradication, following, in this respect, what has been done and is being done both in Iran and Turkey.

May I ask that the Department be good enough to telegraph me its decision in the matter.

Respectfully yours,   P. KNABENSHUE

890G.42/50 : Telegram

The Minister Resident in Iraq (Knabenshue) to the Secretary of State

BAGHDAD, August 7, 1940—7 a. m.
[Received August 8—7 : 30 a. m.]

77. Reference is made to my despatch No. 1567, May 16, 1591, July 16, 1592, July 17, and 1601, July 23, regarding the new education law. In spite of the assurances given me by the Minister for Foreign Affairs and the Prime Minister, the new law has been signed by the Regent and promulgated without awaiting the Department's further consideration of it. I am reliably informed that the Regent opposed the law up to the last moment of the constitutional time limit and only signed it finally under pressure of the Cabinet's threat to resign. I respectfully request that the Department postpone further action pending consideration of my despatches cited above and in particular the last sent by airmail via the Pacific.

KNABENSHUE

890G.42/53 : Telegram

The Secretary of State to the Minister Resident in Iraq (Knabenshue)

WASHINGTON, September 7, 1940—2 p. m.

41. Your despatch no. 1601 of July 23. The Department considers that it might be desirable, in view of all the circumstances set forth by you in this and in previous despatches on the subject, to take no further action at this time in respect of the new Public Education Law.

The Department has in mind in this connection that any assurances which the Iraqi Government might give this Government in respect of the administration of the Public Education Law would not differ from the informal assurances already given representatives of American schools in Iraq by the Director General of Public Instruction and Education and would not necessarily offer any greater promise of fulfillment than those informal assurances.

HULL

PROPOSED CONSULAR CONVENTION BETWEEN THE UNITED STATES AND IRAQ

711.90G21/3 : Telegram

The Minister Resident in Iraq (Knabenshue) to the Secretary of State

BAGHDAD, January 29, 1940—10 a. m.
[Received January 29—9:40 a. m.]

8. With reference to my telegram No. 1, January 2, 10 a. m.,[38] I am now in receipt of an official communication from the Foreign Office expressing willingness of the Iraqi Government to conclude consular convention with the United States and desire to receive draft proposals.

KNABENSHUE

711.90G21/4

The Secretary of State to the Minister Resident in Iraq (Knabenshue)

No. 409

WASHINGTON, February 2, 1940.

SIR: The receipt is acknowledged of your telegram No. 1 of January 2, 10 a. m.,[38] stating that the Iraqi Government has agreed to commence negotiations of a series of treaties suggested by the Chief of the Division of Near Eastern Affairs in a letter to you dated November 9, 1939.[38]

There is enclosed herewith a draft of a consular convention between the United States and Iraq [38] which you are authorized to present to the Iraqi Government at such time as you may deem appropriate.

Nearly all of the provisions embodied in the enclosed draft have counterparts in provisions in treaties of friendship, commerce and consular rights or in consular conventions now in force between the United States and other countries. The texts of these treaties and conventions have, however, been reconsidered carefully and many improvements in language have been made in the enclosed draft.

As of possible interest there are enclosed three copies of the Treaty of Friendship, Commerce and Consular Rights between the United

[38] Not printed.

States and Norway signed June 5, 1928,[39] Articles XVI to XXVII of which relate to consular rights and privileges.

It is understood, of course, that the enclosed draft is tentative, and that if accepted by the Iraqi Government as a basis of negotiation, either Government may propose changes at any time during the course of the negotiations.

Very truly yours,

For the Secretary of State:
R. WALTON MOORE

711.90G21/6

The Minister Resident in Iraq (Knabenshue) to the Secretary of State

No. 1523

BAGHDAD, March 15, 1940.
[Received April 9.]

SIR: I have the honor to acknowledge receipt of the Department's instruction no. 409 of February 2, 1940, enclosing a draft consular convention and to report that on March 11, 1940, I personally presented the draft to His Excellency General Nuri as-Said, Prime Minister and Acting Minister for Foreign Affairs, together with my note to him dated March 8, 1940, a copy of which is enclosed herewith.[40] In presenting the draft convention to His Excellency, I pointed out that there was nothing exceptional in the phraseology or provisions of the convention which would give cause for delay in its consideration, and I expressed the hope that his Government would give the matter early attention in order that the convention, which is mutually desirable might be brought into effect as soon as possible.

Respectfully yours,

P. KNABENSHUE

[No record has been found in the Department files that the Iraqi Government took any further action on this proposed consular convention.]

---

[39] *Foreign Relations*, 1928, vol. III, p. 646.
[40] Not printed.

KENYA

[For correspondence on representations regarding British import and exchange restrictions in Kenya Colony and the mandated territory of Tanganyika in violation of American treaty rights, see pages 118 ff.]

LIBERIA

INTEREST OF THE UNITED STATES IN THE INTERNAL STABILITY OF LIBERIA

882.001 Barclay, Edwin/28 : Telegram

The Chargé in Liberia (Wharton) to the Secretary of State

MONROVIA, September 8, 1940—11 p. m.
[Received September 9—11 : 50 a. m.]

54. As a result of an alleged conspiracy to assassinate him President Barclay has arrested and is holding in Camp Johnson five young Liberians since September 4th. It is rumored that further arrests will likely follow and there is considerable tension here. While there is as yet no cause for alarm, opposition to President Barclay appears to be growing because of arrests. Any further developments will be telegraphed.

WHARTON

882.001 Barclay, Edwin/30 : Telegram

The Chargé in Liberia (Wharton) to the Secretary of State

MONROVIA, September 23, 1940—9 p. m.
[Received September 24—10 : 25 a. m.]

56. Referring to my telegram No. 54, September 8, 11 a. m. [*p. m.*]. On the afternoon of September 8, sixth young Liberian similarly imprisoned. It is said that the following day prisoners wrote scathing letter to President Barclay protesting against "kidnaping" by frontier force soldiers without charges first being preferred, and imprisonment in violation of constitutional guarantee of due process of law. Habeas corpus denied on the 13th and as yet no date fixed for the trial.

Referring to despatch No. 412, last February 21,[1] Bulletin 4 dated September 4 has been published accusing Secretary of State Simpson of plotting against Barclay and yesterday I received by mail Bulletin 5 against Simpson and Attorney General Brownell.

James S. Wiles, former Consul General at Hamburg and cousin of the Speaker of the House, today was arrested and imprisoned in

---

[1] Not printed. Bulletins referred to were being published anonymously attacking the Barclay administration.

Monrovia prison for alleged sedition. I am informed that writs for his arrest and commitment were issued simultaneously and that bail approved by Justice of the Peace was denied by Brownell.

I am of the opinion that Barclay's present course of action is unwise and ill-advised. Today's arrest has further increased tension, it is quite evident opposition to him steadily increasing and present situation causing some concern.

Department will be kept informed.

WHARTON

811.3340/1043 : Telegram

The Secretary of State to the Chargé in Liberia (Wharton)

WASHINGTON, October 1, 1940—5 p. m.

37. Please request permission for the U.S.S. *Omaha*, Flagship of Rear Admiral David M. LeBreton, commanded by Captain L. A. Davidson, to visit Monrovia informally from October 9 to 11, inclusive.

Telegraph reply.

HULL

882.001 Barclay, Edwin/31 : Telegram

The Chargé in Liberia (Wharton) to the Secretary of State

MONROVIA, October 3, 1940—9 p. m.
[Received October 3—12:05 p. m.]

58. Referring to my telegram 56, September 23, 9 a. m. [*p. m.*], I am informed that at preliminary hearing held since Monday evidence of Government witnesses has thus far failed to substantiate charges against prisoners.

Last Friday received anonymous letter addressed to me, British Chargé d'Affaires, Consuls and foreigners by "true hearted" Liberians airing grievances and threatening unless Barclay and Cabinet resign immediately drastic measures will be taken and foreigners will be insecure. I find that letter itself of little significance and it has caused no fear.

Referring to the Department's 37, October 1, visit will have salutary effect internationally and while it may have stabilizing effect on internal affairs I believe Department should be informed that it may also be misconstrued as prompted by letter referred to and might consequently tend to further strengthen opposition. Await further instructions before acting on 37.

WHARTON

882.00/1134 : Telegram

The Secretary of State to the Chargé in Liberia (Wharton)

WASHINGTON, October 4, 1940—7 p. m.

39. Your 58, October 3, 9 p. m.   Unless you have reason to believe, following receipt of this telegram, that the internal situation would be unfortunately affected by the arrival of the U. S. S. *Omaha*, you should at once request permission for a 24-hour visit beginning October 9 instead of the period stated in the Department's 37, October 1, 5 p. m. Vessel left Lisbon October 3 en route to the United States and will call at Pernambuco, Brazil, after making this courtesy visit to Liberia. Arrangements were made to include Monrovia in the itinerary because this Government was mindful of the cordial reception accorded to the *Boise* 2 years ago [2] and because it was believed that the Government of Liberia would appreciate the opportunity to receive another courtesy call by a United States war vessel in the face of present international developments.   If you consider the visit inadvisable, you should inform the Department immediately.

We had intended, in any case, to send you our views in regard to the disquieting reports received from various sources as to the political situation in Liberia.   The alleged attempts against the life of President Barclay and Secretary of State Simpson are a cause for perturbation at a moment which may be critical in the existence of Liberia as an independent nation.   As you are probably aware, intensified activity in Africa by the Axis Powers is foreshadowed with the approach of winter and the apparent postponement of action against the British Isles, and there is no way of predicting how the forthcoming events may affect Liberia.   At this juncture in world affairs, and in African affairs in particular, it would appear vitally important for the Government and people of Liberia to present a united front, to avoid scrupulously any appearance of internal dissension, and to refrain from any action which might be construed abroad as weakness.

We have long realized the great burden which President Barclay is carrying in loyally and patriotically endeavoring to discharge the duties of his office, and we have been concerned lest his health should suffer as a result of the tremendous strain he is constantly undergoing. One means of relieving the load which occurs to us would be the prompt filling of cabinet vacancies for administrative purposes, even if few candidates of outstanding calibre can be found at the moment.   If such posts remain long unfilled, the impression is inevitably created, as in certain European countries, that the head of the government desires to retain them for himself.   While we are aware that such suspicions would be grossly unfair in the case of President Barclay, we

[2] See *Foreign Relations*, 1938, vol. II, pp. 817 ff.

cannot avoid pointing out the danger of permitting them to develop in the minds of misguided or unintelligent persons.

You should bring the foregoing consideration to the attention of the President in whatever manner you deem most appropriate, but we shall leave to your discretion the advisability of acting now or waiting until after the departure of the *Omaha*. In view of the delicate internal situation, it would probably be undesirable to link the remarks directly with the projected visit of the warship, but to let the latter speak for itself. You could, however, make the utmost of the salutary international effect which the visit would have at this time, especially when the question of international and inter-continental air routes is a subject of attention and discussion. In this connection, you could take Rear Admiral LeBreton into your confidence and enlist his personal and informal assistance in mentioning to officials of the Liberian Government the need for national unity in democratic countries during these dangerous times.

In view of the shortness of time before the arrival of the *Omaha*, you should suggest to the Liberian Government that any entertainment provided should be of the most informal variety and that expenses in this connection might well be kept to a minimum.

HULL

811.3340/1045 : Telegram

The Chargé in Liberia (Wharton) to the Secretary of State

MONROVIA, October 6, 1940—1 p. m.
[Received October 7—8 : 10 a. m.]

59. In reply to my request for visit Simpson states his Government will be pleased to receive *Omaha*.

WHARTON

811.3340/1049

The Chargé in Liberia (Wharton) to the Secretary of State

No. 528   MONROVIA, October 12, 1940.
[Received November 8.]

SIR: I have the honor to report upon the visit to Monrovia of the U. S. S. *Omaha*, Flagship of Rear Admiral David M. LeBreton, commanded by Captain P. Powell, for a period of twenty-four hours beginning October 9, 1940, which was the subject of my telegram of October 10, 7 p. m.,[3] and earlier telegrams exchanged with the Department.

---

[3] Not printed.

Upon receipt of the Department's telegram no. 37 of October 1, 5 p. m., instructing me to request facilities for the *Omaha* to visit Monrovia informally from October 9 to 11, inclusive, I felt that owing to the tense internal political situation the Department should be informed of the facts set forth in my telegram no. 58 of October 3, 9 a. m. [*p. m.*]. Shortly thereafter, there was a slight lessening of the tension and when the Department's telegram no. 39 of October 4, 7 p. m. was received, I believed that the visit of the vessel would have no unfortunate effect on the internal situation and at once requested permission for the twenty-four hour visit. Permission for the visit was accorded by the Liberian Government.

The *Omaha* arrived in Monrovia harbor on October 9th at 5 : 15 p. m. Admiral LeBreton, accompanied by Flag Lieutenant Sylvester, called on me at the Legation that same evening. This call was apparently due to a misunderstanding caused by the Liberian boarding officer who met the ship telling the Admiral that he thought that he was expected ashore that evening.

I had a most enjoyable talk with the Admiral. When the tentative program for the next day had been arranged, I took the Admiral into my confidence as suggested by the Department's telegram no. 39 of October 4, 7 p. m. and he at once understood the Department's suggestions.

On the morning of October 10th, I paid my official call on Admiral LeBreton which was followed by the Admiral's visit to President Barclay. The visit to President Barclay was a most pleasant one. Honorable C. L. Simpson, Liberian Secretary of State, on behalf of the President, later made a return call on Admiral LeBreton.

At 1 p. m. President Barclay gave a luncheon to the Admiral, nine of the *Omaha's* officers, the cabinet, aide-de-camp, private secretary and myself at the Executive Mansion. The President in welcoming the Admiral and his guests said that he was happy that the United States Government had not forgotten this little sister Republic on the West Coast of Africa at this time and that he was always glad to have American naval vessels call at Monrovia just as often as possible.

Admiral LeBreton in responding said that in these times of turmoil and strife democratic countries were being tested and that to be strong and withstand the test, they must stand together. He further said that it was a great pleasure for him to visit Monrovia for the first time.

It is of interest to report that during the luncheon conversation Admiral LeBreton took the opportunity to inform the President that in these dangerous times there is great need for national unity in democratic countries, and I not only feel that the President got the significance of this remark, but also will be helped thereby.

After the luncheon President Barclay in conversing with the Admiral showed interest in the question of air communication between South America and West Africa. He sent for an atlas to point out that in his opinion the shortest distance across the South Atlantic and West Africa is between Brazil and Liberia. This conversation will most likely be reported to the Department by the Admiral.

On leaving the Executive Mansion I took the Admiral and his staff to the new Legation building at Mamba Point. These officers expressed delight at the building and splendid site selected for our new home.

From 4 to 5 p. m. I had the pleasure of receiving the Admiral, twenty of his officers, leading Liberian Officials, American colony, diplomatic and consular corps at the Legation. I estimate that about one hundred and eight people were present. Admiral LeBreton stated that he was indeed surprised at the size of the fine American colony here.

There are enclosed herewith my remarks [4] made on this occasion in welcoming the Admiral to Monrovia. The Admiral replied that he regretted very much that his orders would not permit him to remain longer than twenty-four hours in Liberia. He thanked the American colony, the Legation staff and myself for the cordial reception he and his men had received here. Immediately after the reception, the Admiral and officers left for the *Omaha* which cleared about 6 p. m.

There is no doubt whatever that the visit of the *Omaha* at this time has had a most salutary effect; in fact, the visit was timed to perfection, coming when nerves were jittery because of the uncertainty of Liberia's position internationally. Further, I feel that the visit had a healthy effect on present internal difficulties. While it may not be of any significance, it is interesting to report that the preliminary hearings of the men imprisoned for sedition was terminated the day before the arrival of the *Omaha*, the presiding Justice of Peace ruling that there was not sufficient evidence to hold the accused over for the grand jury.

Quite naturally there were a few rumors conjecturing on the reasons for the visit of the *Omaha*. I am glad to report that during the stay of the vessel, there were no unpleasant incidents and I consider the visit highly successful.

Respectfully yours,

CLIFTON R. WHARTON

---

[4] Not printed.

882.00/1135 : Telegram

The Chargé in Liberia (Wharton) to the Secretary of State

MONROVIA, October 17, 1940—10 a. m.
[Received October 18—8 : 55 a. m.]

63. Day before yesterday I informed President Barclay orally of the views contained in Department's telegram No. 39, October 4, 7 p. m.

He said that he accepted them in good part, expressed thanks, and stated that: (1) Department's observations on his country's present international position is what he has held all along; (2) present internal trouble only flare-up by few disgruntled office seekers and entire opposition not over 100 men in area limited to Monrovia; (3) feels people are with him as will be shown and as evidenced by many letters expressing disgust at anonymous bulletins and letters and increasing number of delegations to Executive Mansion expressing confidence in him; (4) arrests at first caused stir but as people learned truth tension lessened; (5) because of evidence presented at preliminary hearings which ended October 8, men charged with sedition which is not bailable are being held for grand jury and entire matter proceeding regular course under complete jurisdiction of Department of Justice; (6) appreciates considerations on Cabinet vacancies and plans to send nominations to Senate.

Tension has lessened to some extent but dissatisfaction naturally continues despite letters and expressions of confidence some of which may be inspired.

WHARTON

CONCERN OF THE UNITED STATES REGARDING SPANISH PROPOSALS FOR AN AIR NAVIGATION AGREEMENT WITH LIBERIA; DISCUSSIONS BETWEEN PAN-AMERICAN AIRWAYS AND THE LIBERIAN GOVERNMENT REGARDING ESTABLISHMENT OF AIR TRANSPORT SERVICES

752.822/1

The Chargé in Liberia (Wharton) to the Secretary of State

No. 474   MONROVIA, June 11, 1940.
[Received July 17.]

SIR: I have the honor to report that Honorable C. L. Simpson, Liberian Secretary of State, informs me that negotiations have been started in Paris by Baron O. de Bogaerde, Liberian Minister, and the Spanish Ambassador there for a treaty of friendship, commerce and navigation between Spain and Liberia.

Upon a suggestion made a few months ago by Baron de Bogaerde, Secretary Simpson authorized him to approach the Spanish Ambassador in Paris with a view towards recognizing General Franco's [5] government and beginning negotiations for a treaty of friendship, commerce and navigation along the lines of the recent treaty concluded between Liberia and France.

Baron de Bogaerde in an informal letter to Secretary Simpson written the latter part of April pointed out that, if he is appointed Liberian Chargé d'Affaires to Spain, he would be in a position to carry on in San Sebastian and Madrid Liberia's representation to both France and Spain in the event that the Liberian Legation has to evacuate Paris; and that the establishment of a small office in Spain by him would be without additional expense to the Liberian Government.

In an airmail letter received a few days ago by Secretary Simpson, Baron de Bogaerde suggests that the treaty be concluded as early as possible and that he be appointed Liberian Chargé d'Affaires to Spain. Following this letter, Bogaerde has telegraphed Secretary Simpson urgently requesting his appointment to Spain.

Secretary Simpson is at a loss to understand the urgency of concluding the treaty and appointing a representative to Spain. He says that, while President Barclay has given him authority to appoint Baron de Bogaerde to the position, he favors waiting for an explanation from Bogaerde as to the necessity of rushing the matter, especially since he has been told that General Franco has not indicated an early appointment of a representative to Liberia. According to Secretary Simpson, two Spaniards are supposed to have left Spain sometime in April for Monrovia as unofficial agents of the Spanish State to visit Liberia on a commercial mission and with an idea of again making Monrovia a port of call of *Trasatlantica* vessels sailing between the Spanish Peninsula, the Canaries and Fernando Po. These two men have thus far failed to reach Monrovia.

In ordinary circumstances, I would see no reason why Liberia should not conclude a treaty with Spain, particularly since a treaty quite likely may lead to beneficial commercial relations with that country. However, I believe that Secretary Simpson's position is well taken to wait for some explanation from Baron de Bogaerde despite any commercial advantages that might accrue to Liberia as a result of the treaty.

Apparently Secretary Simpson is not unmindful of the avowed friendship of General Franco for Germany and Italy and the latter's entrance into the war against the allies. He does not care to hasten into a treaty and exchange representatives with Spain at present.

Respectfully yours,   CLIFTON R. WHARTON

---

[5] Francisco Franco, Spanish Chief of State.

752.822/2

The Chargé in Liberia (Wharton) to the Secretary of State

No. 490   MONROVIA, July 18, 1940.
                                           [Received August 10.]

SIR: I have the honor to refer to my despatch no. 474 of June 11, 1940, concerning the Spanish-Liberian treaty negotiations, and now to report that on July 16, 1940, two Spaniards arrived in Monrovia from Fernando Po aboard the S. S. *Minero.*

Honorable C. L. Simpson, Liberian Secretary of State, states that these two Spaniards are Sr. Don Joaquin Fernandez Munoz who was commissioned Spanish consular agent at Monrovia by General Franco on May 8, 1940, and a Spanish physician who has offered his services to the Liberian Government. These two men were received by Secretary Simpson yesterday at the Department of State.

According to Secretary Simpson the conversation yesterday at the Department of State was of a general character only, but that the two Spaniards showed interest in obtaining authority from Liberia to use Monrovia as a port of call for Spanish planes on a West African run. Secretary Simpson said that he understands that the men will probably remain in Monrovia until November. Neither of the men can speak English and the conversation had to be carried on through an interpreter.

I called Secretary Simpson's attention to the fact that he had informed me earlier that two Spaniards were to come here as unofficial agents of the Spanish State on a commercial mission. He replied that he was as much surprised as I that an agent of the Spanish Government had been sent and that he was cabling de Bogaerde for an explanation of the actual status of these men.

I gather that de Bogaerde fled France upon the fall of Paris and hurried to San Sebastian, and that upon his insistence was later appointed Liberian Chargé d'Affaires there by Secretary Simpson. The two Spaniards now in Monrovia are the same men referred to in my previous despatch.

In view of the fact that Spain has no relations, commercial or other, with Liberia, the arrival of the two Spaniards is causing some comment here. The French Chargé des Affaires at once conjectured that the men are interested in obtaining the right for a Spanish airline to use Monrovia, which it will be seen is correct.

According to Secretary Simpson, the Liberian Government does not need the services of the Spanish physician and that in any negotiations with these men the Liberian Government will go slowly. He added that he planned to see them again within a few days and find out more definitely the real object of their mission here.

Respectfully yours,   CLIFTON R. WHARTON

752.822/2 : Telegram

The Acting Secretary of State to the Chargé in Liberia (Wharton)

WASHINGTON, August 14, 1940—7 p. m.

28. Your despatch No. 490, July 18. If it should develop that the Spanish representatives are in fact endeavoring to obtain a concession for an airline, the Liberian Government will undoubtedly recall the provisions of the confidential supplementary agreement [6] to the Air Navigation Agreement between the United States and Liberia signed June 14, 1939.[7]

The Department would be glad to be informed by telegraph as to the actual status and activities of the Spaniards now in Monrovia and the recognition accorded to them by the Liberian Government. We have no doubt that Secretary Simpson will desire to proceed most cautiously in establishing relations with the present government in Spain.

WELLES

752.822/3 : Telegram

The Chargé in Liberia (Wharton) to the Secretary of State

MONROVIA, August 18, 1940—9 p. m.
[Received August 19—6 p. m.]

47. Department's telegram 28, August 14. Inviting attention to agreement referred to, Liberian Secretary of State on August 12th addressed communication to Legation to the effect that Spanish Government approached Liberian Government recently looking towards negotiating and signing an aviation agreement and submitted proposal setting forth their desire to ascertain if Liberia approve and permit aviation camp here, construction of which has to be determined and decided by two Governments, for land planes for passengers and mail flying between Bata and Seville calling at Monrovia weekly both ways.

[The Liberian Secretary of State?] requests that the proposal be submitted to my Government with assurance that he will welcome any suggestion or advice you may be good enough to offer.

Delay in reporting to the Department was [explained?] by my telegram No. 46, August 14th.[8] No decision yet reached on the proposal and I respectfully request a reply as early as possible.

According to Secretary Simpson in addition to aviation proposal

---

[6] Exchange of notes between the Liberian Secretary of State and the American Minister, June 14, 1939, *Foreign Relations*, 1939, vol. IV, pp. 618–619.
[7] Department of State Executive Agreement Series No. 166, or 54 Stat. (pt. 2) 2018.
[8] Not printed.

Spanish proposals include: (1) exchange of representatives; (2) treaty as reported; and (3) Liberian labor for colonies.

Simpson repeats his Government does not desire services of physician and informs me that the other Spaniard not accorded recognition because of misunderstanding as to his status having presented commission as consular agent but claiming quasi-diplomatic rank and rank of Consul; further no word from Spanish Government or Bogaerde as to status and latter not yet recognized by Spanish Government.

Simpson further states that he is personally opposed to air agreement as well as labor. He adds President Barclay emphatically against labor proposal and told him his policy has been and will be to proceed most cautiously in establishing relations with Spain.

Activities of Spaniards thus far appear to be limited to proposals herein. They have been unsuccessful in trying to rent furnished house. I am informed that consular agent plans leaving by next steamer Spanish northward due at Monrovia in about 1 week to confer with his Government and clarify his status.

WHARTON

752.822/3 : Telegram

The Acting Secretary of State to the Chargé in Liberia (Wharton)

WASHINGTON, August 21, 1940—6 p. m.

32. Your 47, August 18, 9 p. m. We earnestly hope that the Liberian Government will take no action on the Spanish proposals pending our further study of the matter, the results of which will be communicated to you shortly.

WELLES

752.822/4 : Telegram

The Chargé in Liberia (Wharton) to the Secretary of State

MONROVIA, August 24, 1940—2 p. m.
[Received August 25—1:20 a. m.]

50. In answer to your telegram 32, August 21, 6 p. m., Simpson states that no action will be taken.

WHARTON

752.822/3 : Telegram

The Secretary of State to the Chargé in Liberia (Wharton)

WASHINGTON, August 26, 1940—8 p. m.

34. Your 47, August 18, 9 p. m. The Department fully understands President Barclay's reluctance to enter into relations with Spain at

this time, and it shares Secretary Simpson's misgivings with regard to the specific proposals of the Spanish representatives. President Barclay is, of course, well aware of the active colonial aspirations of certain European powers, and of the necessity of giving the most careful scrutiny to the background of proposals such as the present ones. Moreover, the President is probably not unmindful of the assistance rendered to General Franco by Germany and Italy during the Spanish Civil War and of the close relations maintained between the two Governments. In view of the lack of common interests between Liberia and Spain, and in the absence of any substantial trade or commercial prospects worth mentioning, no useful purpose would appear to be served by concluding a treaty between the two countries or exchanging diplomatic or consular representatives at this time.

With respect to the proposed Air Agreement, we are definitely concerned lest the right to construct an aviation "camp" in Liberia, which would undoubtedly serve as an important intermediate base for the flights between Seville and Bata, might involve commitments which would eventually enable Spain or possibly some other foreign Power with ulterior motives to secure a foothold in the country. However, since no nation enjoys exclusive air rights in Liberia, it would obviously be difficult to reject the Spanish request in its entirety. As an alternative, the Department would perceive no serious objection to granting to Spain for a reasonable period the right of air transit through Liberia, with the privilege of landing such as provided by the agreement between France and Liberia [9] approved by the Liberian Legislature on December 11, 1936. If any such transit right should be accorded, however, it should be distinctly understood that it would not include the right (a) subsequently to extend the Spanish services across the Atlantic from Liberian territory, (b) to designate the place of landing in Liberia, (c) nor to operate wholly between points in Liberia such as taking on passengers and cargo at one place in the country and discharging them at another place therein.

In this connection the Liberian Government may be interested to know that an American air transport company has made application to the Civil Aeronautics Board for permission to operate a transatlantic route from the United States to Africa via Puerto Rico and Brazil. In view of the uncertainty of finding proper terminal facilities in West Africa today, the Government of Liberia might desire to invite any American air transport enterprises that may be interested to consider the possibility of using Liberian territory as a transatlantic terminal point. Without any assurances on the part of this

---

[9] Signed at Paris, May 29, 1936. For text, see *Journal Officiel de la République Française: Lois et Décrets*, November 11, 1937, p. 12427, or International Commission for Air Navigation, *Bulletin of Information*, September 22, 1938, p. 14.

Government that a Liberian terminal would be deemed either expedient or practicable by the American company, we should be glad to transmit any suggestion on the part of the Liberian Government to the appropriate quarters.

Please keep the Department fully informed by telegraph as to the status of the Spanish negotiations, particularly with respect to the activities of Bogaerde as Liberian Chargé d'Affaires in Spain.

HULL

752.822/6 : Telegram

The Chargé in Liberia (Wharton) to the Secretary of State

MONROVIA, September 6, 1940—10 a. m.
[Received 12 : 12 p. m.]

53. Upon his request I have given to Secretary of State Simpson in strict confidence a paraphrase of pertinent sections of the Department's telegram 34, August 26, 8 p. m. President Barclay and Simpson state that the Department's telegram has correctly expressed Liberia's views and policy and that no immediate action on proposals is contemplated. Simpson believes that in time entire matter "may die a natural death". He hopes to advise me shortly with respect to possible invitation to American company and President Barclay appears favorably disposed to the suggestion.

Briefly, status is that negotiations on Spanish proposals have terminated for the present and as previously reported Spaniard is still awaiting steamer. According to Simpson there has been no word from, or information concerning, Bogaerde for some weeks.

WHARTON

811.79682/3 : Telegram

The Chargé in Liberia (Wharton) to the Secretary of State

MONROVIA, September 19, 1940—9 a. m.
[Received 9 : 10 a. m.]

55. Referring my telegram No. 53, September 6, 10 a. m. Secretary of State Simpson in a personal note informs me that the Liberian Government would appreciate if the American Government found it possible to intimate to a reliable air transport company of the United States the desire of his Government to negotiate or discuss with such company the practicability of undertaking civil aviation services between Liberia and our country.

Spaniards left here for Spain last Saturday.

It is reported that Bogaerde has been in Lisbon but now is in Vichy.

WHARTON

811.79682/14

Memorandum of Conversation, by Mr. Henry S. Villard of the Division of Near Eastern Affairs

[WASHINGTON,] September 30, 1940.

Mr. Firestone [9a] brought in a copy of an article which appeared in the *New York Daily Mirror* of September 21, 1940, pointing out the strategic importance to the United States of the Republic of Liberia on the west coast of Africa. Some of the statements made in this article were based on facts supplied by the Firestone organization, and Mr. Firestone desired to indicate that he was in entire accord with the description of Liberia as a point on which the defense of the Western Hemisphere might find support.

Mr. Firestone also brought in aerial photographs of the port of Marshall in Liberia, which he described as being suitable for seaplane landing operations. He had also obtained a report from an aviator who a few years ago made a photographic survey of Liberia for the Firestone Company and who expressed the opinion that Marshall, or possibly Monrovia, might be used for a seaplane base. Mr. Firestone inquired whether there was any possibility of an American airline running a service to Africa and stated that in his opinion such a service, using Liberia as first point of contact on the African continent, would be of very great value from the point of view of national defense and general strategy.

I then gave Mr. Firestone for his confidential information an outline of recent developments in connection with the desire of Pan-American Airways and American Export Lines to establish an air service from the United States to Africa. For background purposes I also outlined in confidence to Mr. Firestone the desire of the Spanish Government to inaugurate an airline from Seville to Rio Muni via Monrovia. I said that the Liberian Government had approached us for advice on this matter and had requested us to invite any American airlines that might be interested to use Liberia as an African terminal.

Mr. Firestone said that he was greatly interested to learn of these developments. He said that it would be of very considerable advantage to the Firestone Company if an American airline would offer a service to Liberia. The Firestone Company would send all its mail and express matter via plane in that case, and would assure the airline of a large percentage of its passenger list both coming and going. Mr. Firestone said that the present steamship services to West Africa were far from adequate for the Company's purposes and that to speed up communication and transportation between the offices in this country and the Liberian Plantations it would be of the greatest assistance to have an air transport service.

[9a] Harvey S. Firestone, Jr., president of the Firestone Tire and Rubber Co.

I suggested to Mr. Firestone the possibility of using Fisherman's Lake in Liberia as a landing place. He replied that according to the report of his aviator, this body of water was deceptively shallow and filled with tree stumps which were not visible at high water. Although the size and situation of the Lake were practically ideal, it might not be possible to use it for landing purposes. It was agreed, however, that if an air service were seriously contemplated it would be necessary to conduct a careful survey of all possible landing sites in Liberia.

Mr. Firestone said he would be glad to talk to Mr. Juan Trippe, President of Pan-American Air Lines, with regard to the use of Liberia as a terminal. He said he would also be in a position to supply us with information as to the business which the Firestone Company could give to any American air line operating between the United States and Liberia. Finally, said Mr. Firestone, even if a trip were made only once a month he believed it would be worthwhile for this Government to subsidize such operations for the sake of having a foothold in Africa to offset the development of air lines across the South Atlantic by totalitarian powers. It was obvious that Liberia offered the only place in Africa where there would be some justification for the United States to interest itself.

811.79682/15

Memorandum of Conversation, by Mr. Stephen Latchford of the Division of International Communications

[WASHINGTON,] October 9, 1940.

A conference was held in the office of Mr. Thomas Burke, Chief of the Division of International Communications, on October 3, 1940, for the purpose of discussing the question whether American air transport interests should be encouraged to seek operating rights to Liberia. Those present were as follows:

Department of State:

Division of International Communications:
Mr. Burke
Mr. Stephen Latchford
Division of Near Eastern Affairs:
Mr. Henry S. Villard
Division of European Affairs:
Mr. Lewis Clark
Division of the American Republics:
Mr. Walter N. Walmsley, Jr.
Mr. Livingston Satterthwaite

War Department:

Lieutenant Colonel A. Franklin Kibler

Navy Department:
  Commander Malcolm S. Schoeffel

Civil Aeronautics Board:
  Mr. Samuel E. Gates
  Major Melvin Hall
  Mr. Harry A. Real

In opening the meeting Mr. Burke made reference to certain negotiations between this Government and the Government of Liberia leading up to an invitation recently received from the Liberian Government through the American Legation at Monrovia for American air transport interests to apply for operating rights to Liberia. The following is a summary of Mr. Burke's remarks:

The United States entered into an aviation agreement with Liberia in June, 1939, which accords the right for aircraft of either country not engaged in scheduled operations to make flights in the other country. At the time this agreement was entered into, there was an exchange of notes between the American Legation at Monrovia and the Liberian Government, not given publicity, in which that Government undertook to notify the Government of the United States in the event that any foreign interests should seek to establish air transport services in Liberia. Subsequently, certain Spanish emissaries approached the Liberian Government with a view to acquiring aviation rights in Liberia. The American Chargé d'Affaires at Monrovia was instructed to point out to the Liberian Government the political implications which might be involved in granting to Spanish interests rights to conduct services wholly within Liberia or a transatlantic operation with Liberia as a base. The American Chargé d'Affaires was instructed to say that while no definite assurance could be given that a service by an American carrier would be considered economically feasible, we would be glad to give consideration to the appropriate disposition of any invitation which the Liberian Government might extend to American air transport interests to operate to Liberia. It appears from reports received from Monrovia that the Liberian authorities have not been disposed to grant operating rights to Spanish interests, and the Department is now in receipt of a telegram from the Chargé d'Affaires conveying an invitation from the Liberian authorities for American air transport interests to make application for operating rights in Liberia.

Mr. Burke said that while the representatives of the Civil Aeronautics Board would of course have views to express on the question of economic feasibility, he thought it would be well at that stage to invite the comment of the Army and Navy representatives on the national defense angle.

Commander Schoeffel said that it was his belief that the Navy Department would not have any direct interest from the standpoint of national defense in the establishment of an air base in Liberia, although he felt that it was highly important that everything possible be done to discourage the establishment of air bases in Liberia by the Axis powers or by any interests that might be affiliated with them. With respect to the technical aspects of the question, he stated that it would appear from his information that there are no suitable areas along the coast of Liberia which could accommodate naval planes. It is doubtful whether the Navy Department would favor the establishment of any base which it would not be in a position to defend and should any elaborate installations be made by American companies there would be the danger that they might later be taken over by the Axis powers. Commander Schoeffel said that he was in sympathy with any action which could properly be taken to discourage any approach by foreign powers to obtain a foothold with respect to aviation in Liberia, and suggested the possibility that an American commercial air transport company might be able to provide facilities at a reasonable cost which perhaps could be destroyed in an emergency. He also offered for discussion the suggestion that if some way could be found to conduct surveys in Liberia with the ostensible purpose of establishing aviation facilities, this might have the result of discouraging any approach on the part of foreign interests to establish themselves in Liberia, even though no definite steps should be taken by the American interests toward the actual establishment of air services.

Mr. Gates said he thought that as a rough estimate, the cost of operating an air transport service to Liberia might be as much as from five hundred thousand to three quarters of a million dollars a year, and that he did not believe that the Civil Aeronautics Board would be disposed to approve such a project unless it had a very definite national defense angle, and was desirable from the standpoint of international policy. In response to a question by Mr. Gates, Commander Schoeffel said that he personally did not believe that the Navy Department would be disposed to advocate an appropriation of such an amount on the theory that it was desirable from the standpoint of national defense.

Colonel Kibler stated that in general he believed that the Army would agree with the viewpoint of the Navy, that is, while the Army would not look with favor upon aviation facilities being established in Liberia by the Axis powers, the facts would not warrant any extended outlay from the standpoint of national defense for an air base which could not be defended by the armed forces of the United States.

Mr. Burke raised the question whether it would be desirable to acquire certain rights in Liberia which would pave the way for commercial operations, possibly by establishing a link in an air transport service which would extend into Liberia. Mr. Gates thought that this might present the same problem as would arise in connection with the establishment of an elaborate commercial base for transatlantic operations.

Mr. Villard presented for the general information of the conferees certain information which had been received from Mr. Harvey Firestone, Jr., who is interested in rubber plantations in Liberia. Mr. Villard stated that Mr. Firestone had presented a copy of an article appearing in the *New York Daily Mirror* of September 21, 1940, pointing out the strategic importance to the United States of the Republic of Liberia. Mr. Firestone indicated that he was in entire accord with the description of Liberia as a point upon which the defense of the Western Hemisphere might find support. He also presented aerial photographs of the port of Marshall in Liberia which he described as being suitable for seaplane landing operations, and said that it would be of very considerable advantage to the Firestone Company if an American airline would offer a service to Liberia. The Firestone Company would send all of its mail and express matter via plane in that case, and would assure the airline of a large percentage of its passenger business. He concluded by saying that Liberia offered the only place in Africa where there would be some justification for the United States to interest itself.

Mr. Gates asked in connection with any surveys made by Mr. Firestone whether it had developed that there were areas large enough for seaplanes to take off. It was stated by Mr. Gates in this connection that a run of at least five miles would seem to be necessary. Mr. Villard stated that he had in his conversation with Mr. Firestone referred to the possibility of using Fisherman's Lake about forty miles northwest of Monrovia, as a landing place, but that Mr. Firestone had replied that according to the report of his aviators, this body of water, which is six miles long, is deceptively shallow and is filled with tree stumps which are not visible at high water. Although the size and situation of the lake were practically ideal, it might not be possible to use it for landing purposes, and it was thought that if an air service were seriously contemplated it would be necessary to conduct a careful survey of all possible landing sites in Liberia. In answer to a question, Mr. Villard stated that the Firestone interests employ about 110 white persons. This led to some discussion as to what amount of potential traffic might be available to an American air carrier. Mr. Gates again stated that regardless of this factor, the actual cost of operation of a transatlantic service would be quite heavy as he had previously indicated. He said, however, that the problem of Liberia was not altogether academic, since there is actually pending an application before the Civil Aeronautics Board by Pan American Airways to operate a service from the United States to Capetown, via Puerto Rico, Natal (Brazil) and Bolama (Portuguese Guinea), and there might be involved the question whether the carrier should be authorized to use Liberia instead of Bolama as an alternate stop on the route to Capetown. Mr. Villard remarked that American Export Airlines had also expressed some interest in the possible extension of a service into Liberia.

Mr. Burke remarked that we had heard the comments of the representatives of the Army, Navy and Civil Aeronautics Board who had expressed their views without, of course, undertaking to commit their superiors, and that he thought it would be in order to have some discussion of the pending problem from the standpoint of foreign policy.

Mr. Clark of the European Division stated that he could not see that in view of the limited national defense interests, the payment of a large subsidy in order to establish an American service would be warranted from the standpoint of foreign policy so far as the European Division is concerned.

However, Mr. Satterthwaite and Mr. Walmsley of the Division of the American Republics thought that the matter was of considerable interest and importance in connection with the aviation situation in Brazil, from which it is likely that any South Atlantic air service would operate on a route to Liberia. Mr. Satterthwaite thought that in connection with any desire of this Government to discourage South transatlantic operations by French, German or Italian interests, the Brazilians would be more impressed if there was the possibility of a service by a United States carrier from Brazil to Liberia. Mr. Walmsley expressed the view that our prestige in Brazil would be enhanced by a transatlantic service between Brazil and Liberia.

Mr. Latchford made reference to the statements of Commander Schoeffel and Colonel Kibler to the effect that their Departments would not look with favor upon the establishment of air transport facilities in Liberia by the Axis powers, and suggested that perhaps an important point was to consider whether if American transport interests did not go into Liberia the Liberian Government would have difficulty in discouraging approaches by foreign interests looking to the establishment of aviation bases in Liberia. It was suggested in this connection that possibly consideration might be given to the negotiation of a brief air transport agreement giving United States air transport interests an option to establish air transport services. It was thought that if such an agreement should be given publicity it might lend moral support to the Liberian Government in holding off alien interests even though we do not take advantage of the option. There was some discussion of this point, and Mr. Burke expressed some doubt as to whether anything would be gained by establishing rights for American carriers which would not be availed of. Possibly even in this case the Liberian Government would have some difficulty in withstanding the pressure of foreign interests.

However, the Department's representatives indicated that they were expressing only their personal viewpoint and that any definite ruling in the matter would depend upon the decision of the policy officers of the Department.

811.79682/3 : Telegram

The Secretary of State to the Chargé in Liberia (Wharton)

WASHINGTON, October 18, 1940—6 p. m.

42. Your 55, September 19, 9 a. m. Department has informed the President of Pan American Airways and the President of American Export Airlines of the desire of the Liberian Government to discuss the practicability of undertaking air transport services between the United States and Liberia.

In making this statement for the information of these companies, the Department has pointed out that it cannot undertake to indicate what the attitude of the Civil Aeronautics Board would be in the event that either company should apply to the Board for a certificate authorizing an air transport service to Liberia.

HULL

8531.79682/6

Memorandum of Conversation, by Mr. Henry S. Villard of the Division of Near Eastern Affairs

[WASHINGTON,] November 22, 1940.

Participants: Mr. Harvey Firestone
Mr. Murray
Mr. Villard

Mr. Firestone stated that he had discussed with Pan-American Airways officials the possibility of offering a service to Monrovia in conjunction with the new winter route of the company, which uses Bolama, Portuguese Guinea, as a base in Africa. Pan-American Airways had agreed to run a shuttle service from Bolama to Monrovia once a week and a contract for this purpose had been offered to President Barclay of Liberia.

Mr. Firestone said that this service by Pan-American Airways would bring Monrovia within three days of New York and would be of inestimable aid to the Firestone Rubber Plantations in its operations in Liberia. The shuttle service between Bolama and Monrovia would connect with the trans-Atlantic Clipper planes flying between Lisbon and New York. The fare between New York and Monrovia would be about five hundred dollars, and the cost of the shuttle service to Pan-American Airways would be approximately ten thousand dollars a month. Seaplanes about the size of the Sikorsky would be used on this run.

Pan-American Airways had appointed Mr. George Seybold, general manager of the Firestone interests in Liberia, to represent the air transportation company in negotiations with the Liberian Government. The contract submitted to President Barclay was modelled on one recently concluded between the company and the Dominican Republic, but was designed to exclude any other American company from operating rights in Liberia. The contract provided for subsequent extension of Pan-American operations both within Liberia and across the South Atlantic, as the Pan-American apparently had in mind the eventual extension of its operations down the West Coast of Africa to Capetown. The present contract would give the company an entering wedge in Liberia to build up experience and background.

Mr. Firestone did not know whether it would be necessary to obtain the approval of the Civil Aeronautics Board for the shuttle service between Monrovia and Bolama, or whether the Pan-American Airways company intended to ask for a United States Government subsidy in this connection.

853i.79682/1 : Telegram

The Minister in Liberia (Walton) to the Secretary of State

MONROVIA, December 24, 1940—noon.
[Received December 24—11 : 20 a. m.]

91. President Barclay approved today contract between Liberian Government and Pan-American Airways to start operation of air mail services within a year from Liberia to Portuguese Guinea connecting with other air mail services to Europe, United States and other countries. Company has been granted limited monopoly as against other American companies for a term of 10 years.

WALTON

8531.79682/2 : Telegram

The Secretary of State to the Minister in Liberia (Walton)

WASHINGTON, December 27, 1940—4 p. m.

60. Your 91, December 24, noon. Department notes President Barclay has approved contract with Pan American Airways which grants monopolistic privilege as against other American companies. This Government does not look with favor upon contracts being entered into by American air carriers which contain such provisions excluding other American carriers.

Therefore, telegraph briefly conditions under which contract was signed with particular reference to monopolistic feature, and confirm by mail report.

HULL

8531.79682/3 : Telegram

The Minister in Liberia (Walton) to the Secretary of State

MONROVIA, December 30, 1940—11 a. m.
[Received 11 : 58 a. m.]

93. Referring to the Department's No. 60, December 27. Pan American Airways had acceded to Liberian Government's original demand that monopolistic clause be excluded. In the final draft of contract President Barclay incorporated monopolistic clause and stipulated that company furnish services within 1 year. Because concessionaires failed in the past to exercise rights President Barclay reasons that a specific time limit would mean nothing to Pan American Airways unless granted a monopoly.[10]

WALTON

---

[10] Contract as amended finally was signed at Monrovia, July 14, 1941

MOROCCO

RESERVATION OF AMERICAN TREATY RIGHTS AS AFFECTED BY EMERGENCY WAR MEASURES IN THE FRENCH ZONE OF MOROCCO AND THE TANGIER ZONE[1]

681.006/72

The Diplomatic Agent and Consul General at Tangier (Blake) to the Secretary of State

No. 1521

TANGIER, January 9, 1940.
[Received February 9.]

SIR: I have the honor to enclose herewith copy of a Note, dated January 9, 1940, which I have addressed to the Resident General of France at Rabat, as Foreign Minister of His Shereefian Majesty, in pursuance of Instruction No. 1054 of December 4, 1939[2] (File No. 681.006/67), reserving American treaty rights in relation to legislation introduced by the French Protectorate Government, incident to the present exceptional circumstances in French Morocco.

The general reservation formulated in my Note, follows as closely as possible the phraseology of the above mentioned Instruction, and will, I trust, be found by the Department, to meet the situation satisfactorily.

Respectfully yours,

MAXWELL BLAKE

[Enclosure]

The American Diplomatic Agent and Consul General at Tangier (Blake) to the Frence Resident General in Morocco (Naguès)

TANGIER, January 9, 1940.

MR. RESIDENT GENERAL: I had the honor to address to Your Excellency, under date of September 18, 1939,[3] a Note which, on behalf of my Government, made formal reservation of American treaty rights in Morocco, in relation to decrees establishing Foreign Exchange Control, the prohibition and reglementation of exports and imports, and similar emergency war time measures, which were published in the Official Bulletin of the Protectorate Government, No. 1402-bis of

---

[1] For previous correspondence on this subject, see *Foreign Relations*, 1939, vol. IV, pp. 684 ff.
[2] *Ibid.*, p. 692.
[3] *Ibid.*

September 15, 1939. My Note further protested against the pretention to afford preferential treatment to French and Algerian merchandise implied in certain of the decrees concerning the control of importations.

While confirming the tenor of the Note above mentioned, I am now instructed to extend the same reservations, to all war time measures promulgated subsequently to the decrees particularly referred to above, and to those which may be introduced in the future, incident to the present exceptional circumstances in French Morocco, insofar as they may be at variance with the treaty principles upon which American rights are based in Morocco.

I am instructed to remind Your Excellency that my Government cannot give its approval to the application to American nationals in French Morocco of legislation which might be regarded as direct governmental assistance to one belligerent against the interests of the opposing belligerent, because, as the Protectorate Government has been informed, such a result would not be in accord with the neutrality of the United States, which has been proclaimed by the President.

However, I am prepared to examine with the Protectorate Authorities, and to report to the Department of State at Washington, suggestions designed to avoid special difficulties prejudicial to the interests of the Moroccan community, which might result from the failure of my Government to give its approval to legislation enacted as a result of the present exceptional circumstances in Morocco. Such suggestions would have to be limited, of course, to those measures of co-operation which did not prejudice the neutrality of the United States, the maintenance of American treaty rights in French Morocco, or the legitimate activities and interests of American nationals there.

Please accept [etc.] MAXWELL BLAKE

681.006/73

The Diplomatic Agent and Consul General at Tangier (Blake) to the Secretary of State

No. 1522 TANGIER, January 12, 1940.
[Received February 9.]

SIR: I have the honor to enclose herewith English translations of laws which now regulate war-time trade in the Tangier Zone. Copies of the Official Bulletin of the Zone containing the French text of the laws are also enclosed.[4]

It will be recalled, as indicated in my despatch No. 1496 of October 9, 1939,[5] and in Mr. Doolittle's report: "Tangier and the War" of

---

[4] None printed.
[5] *Foreign Relations*, 1939, vol. IV, p. 688.

October 24, 1939,[6] that the French Protectorate Authorities were seeking to extend their control over the trade of the Tangier Zone, and attempted to make shipments of provisions and supplies for Tangier, from French Morocco, conditional upon the prohibition to export from Tangier to any destination, all merchandise, even goods in transit, of whatever origin. The Committee of Control were opposed to this contention as derogatory of the principles of the Moroccan treaties. The laws herewith enclosed purport to embody the compromise arrangements which have finally been agreed upon.

The main law is dated November 2, 1939; its principal provisions are:

(1) Prohibition to export from Tangier merchandise (figuring upon a practically all comprehensive list of goods) proceeding from France, French colonies, and particularly from the French Zone of Morocco, regardless of their national origin.

(2) The exportation of goods proceeding from places other than France or the French Zone, is subjected to the constitution of local security stocks.

(3) Goods in transit may be exported, but in case of necessity approved by the Committee of Control, they may be requisitioned for local consumption.

(4) The operation of the law is subjected to the supervision of a Special Commission, composed of a member of the Committee of Control, as President, one of the Vice-Presidents (in turn British, French, Spanish and Italian) of the Legislative Assembly, and the Administrator of the Zone. Advisory members are: A delegate of the Sultan's representative, the Assistant Director of Finance, the Chief of the Customs Service, and the Presidents of Chambers of Commerce of various nationalities.

(5) The provisions of the law shall have a duration of three months from the date of their official publication, but may be extended by periods of three months, through decision of the Legislative Assembly, subject to the approval of the Committee of Control, so long as the present circumstances shall prevail.

International supervision over the operation of these Tangier trade regulations is therefore preserved. The provisioning of the Zone appears now to be proceeding satisfactorily, under these arrangements.

Nevertheless, from a point of view of treaty principles, the restrictions imposed upon trade are obviously illegal, as the Committee of Control does not fail to note in a "Decision" published, as a preamble to the regulations, in the Official Bulletin of the Tangier Zone. (See Enclosure No. 1). In this decision the Committee of Control maintains that the law places limitations on economic liberty, as guaranteed "by the Statute and by the Treaties," and therefore decides to approve the regulations only as exceptional measures, occasioned by the vital necessities of the community, and on condition that the law

---

[6] Not printed.

shall be repealed when the normal provisioning of the Zone again becomes possible.

By this "Decision" the Committee of Control (i. e., the representatives of the foreign powers in Tangier) seeks to safeguard the treaty principle of "economic liberty."

However, since Article 2 of the Law did, in fact, admit a French derogation from the regime of "economic liberty," the Legislative Assembly has passed a complementary "Decision" dated November 22, 1939, (Enclosure No. 4) which, in the name of "equality among the nations" grants to any other country a similar right to violate that treaty regime.

To secure this right a Government has merely to request that, in respect of goods shipped by its country to Tangier, there should be established the principle of the interdiction to re-export, as provided in the case of France, by Article 2 of the Law of November 2, 1939.

This implication of the subversive effect of one treaty principle ("equality among the nations") upon another treaty principle ("economic liberty"), seems to be open to objection, but as this curious construction of treaty terms arises from the temporary difficulties and perplexities of an unusual situation, it may perhaps be overlooked as lacking significance.

The Resident General of France, as Minister for Foreign Affairs of the Sultan of Morocco, has requested that the Tangier Laws above referred to, regulating trade in the Tangier Zone, be made applicable to American *ressortissants* in that Zone.

I am of the opinion, however, that in view of the derogation, implied in the legislation, of treaty principles which we are anxious to maintain, we should decline to give any formal assent to the regulations, notwithstanding their presumably temporary character. I suggest that we should adopt towards the war-time regulations of the Tangier Zone, the same position as that which we have assumed towards similar legislation in the French Zone, and limit ourselves to assurances of co-operation designed to overcome particular difficulties arising from the present circumstances, as indicated in the Department's Instruction No. 1054 of December 4, 1939 [7] (File No. 681.006/67).

This policy is virtually being pursued in the Tangier Zone at the present time. Moreover, there are extremely few American concerns in this Zone which are affected by the trade regulations in question.

The only case which has hitherto been brought to the notice of this Legation is that of the Singer Sewing Machine Company. The Company's central depot of machines and spare parts is located in

---

[7] *Foreign Relations*, 1939, vol. IV, p. 692.

French Morocco, but the head office in Tangier deals with the distribution of these stocks to its clients throughout the entire country, including the Tangier and Spanish Zones.

Stocks sent up to Tangier, from the Central Depot in Casablanca, for transmission to the Company's branch offices in the Spanish Zone, may not be forwarded to Spanish Morocco under the provisions of Article 2 of the Tangier Law of November 2, 1939.

On his own initiative the Director of the Singer Sewing Machine Company is in contact with the Protectorate Authorities, and with those of the Tangier Zone, in an endeavor to reach a practical solution of this difficulty. The intervention of the Legation will be required only if the conversations above referred to fail to result in a satisfactory arrangement.

Respectfully yours,   MAXWELL BLAKE

_____

681.006/74

The Diplomatic Agent and Consul General at Tangier (Blake) to the Secretary of State

No. 1523   TANGIER, January 13, 1940.
                            [Received February 9.]

SIR: Under cover of my No. 1521 of January 9, 1940, I had the honor to transmit to the Department, copy of my Note of the same date addressed to the French Resident General at Rabat, in pursuance of Instruction No. 1054 of December 4, 1939 [8] (File No. 681.006/67), reiterating and amplifying the reservations formulated in a former Note, dated September 18, 1939,[9] (Enclosure No. 15 to my No. 1496 of October 9, 1939 [10]) in respect of wartime legislation of the French Protectorate at variance with the treaty principles governing the economic regime of Morocco.

I now have the honor to transmit herewith, in the French text and English translation, copy of a communication from the French Residency General at Rabat, commenting upon my first Note of September 18, 1939. By coincidence, this communication from the Resident General and my second confirmatory Note, are both dated January 9, 1940, and crossed in the post.

I submit that the Residency's communication is not unsatisfactory. While, as might be expected, it affirms in somewhat nebulous generalities assurances of the Protectorate Government's good intentions, it certainly does seem to contain what we may claim to construe as a commitment, on the part of the French and Protectorate Governments,

[8] *Foreign Relations*, 1939, vol. IV, p. 692.
[9] *Ibid.*
[10] *Ibid.*, p. 688.

to repeal the unorthodox legislation, upon the termination of the war conditions, which are alleged to have occasioned it.

This would seem to be no unimportant factor in support of the reservations which we have formulated for the safeguard of our position, in relation to the possible renewal of treaty negotiations concerning Morocco, after the termination of the war.

There has of course been insufficient time for the Residency to reply to my amplified Note of January 9, 1940, from which, the French Authorities should appreciate the spirit of understanding in which we regard their special difficulties, and the offer of practical co-operation in an endeavor to overcome them.

Respectfully yours, MAXWELL BLAKE

[Enclosure—Translation]

The Secretary General of the French Residency General in Morocco (Morize) to the American Diplomatic Agent and Consul General at Tangier (Blake)

RABAT, January 9, 1940.

MR. DIPLOMATIC AGENT: I did not fail to examine, with all the care which they deserve, the arguments and considerations which you have been good enough to develop in your letter of September 18, 1939.

It will certainly not have escaped the attention of the American Government that the various measures recently taken in commercial and financial matters, tend to protect the Moroccan economy, which the war threatened to throw out of balance. Moreover this support, of which France bears the entire burden, is profitable without distinction to all powers which entertain commercial relations with Morocco.

Neither is it the intention of the Government of the Republic to give longer duration to this regime than may be justified by the circumstances. The regime arises from these circumstances and will disappear with them. There is nothing to justify attribution to the Administration of the Protectorate, of the intention to take advantage, to the detriment of third parties, of necessities the inevitable character of which is self-evident.

The measures in question are therefore not destined to survive the conditions which have rendered their application indispensable. Finally, France and Morocco, far from desiring to seek weapons to be used for their own advantage, are firmly resolved, in practice, not to depart from the liberal spirit which, in this regard, has never ceased to animate them.

Please accept [etc.] MORIZE

681.116/60

The Consul General at Casablanca (Goold) to the Secretary of State

No. 281   CASABLANCA, January 22, 1940.
[Received February 23.]

SIR: With reference to Mr. Stanton's despatch No. 263 of December 5th, last [11] (files nos. 600/610.21/610.22), regarding the Protectorate's foreign trade control, in which mention was made of the fact that applications for the importation of automotive vehicles must be approved both by the Army and by the Public Works Department, I have the honor to report that, according to several local representatives of American automotive exporters, the following temporary quotas have been established for American trucks or truck chassis (for mounting locally-built truck and bus bodies) for the year ending September 30th next:

Quarter	Number of truck chassis
October to December 1939	282
January to March 1940	302
April to June 1940	202
July to September 1940	202
Total	988

The quota practically equals the average annual registration of imported trucks, including busses, during the three calendar years preceding the War, which is shown in the following table:

1936	885
1937	1,148
1938	950
Average	994

The allotment includes both gasoline and gasogene vehicles, since Public Works is endeavoring to promote the use of the second type to utilize fuel produced in this country. It is not necessarily confined to American vehicles, as arrangements have been made that imports of French, British or other non-American units during any quarter will be deducted from the "American" total for the ensuing quarter, but it is expected that it will be filled almost entirely, if not entirely, by exports from the United States for the reasons that American trucks are still preferred in this area, that present French military demands apparently preclude the prospect of obtaining truck chassis from France, and that the opportunity for importing British chassis does not appear to be much better, even though purchases from the Franc-Sterling Union are favored by the Foreign Exchange Control over

[11] Not printed.

orders placed in countries outside of that monetary combination. At present there is an actual shortage of trucks, the Army having requisitioned some 3,000, plus about 1,000 passenger cars, at the outbreak of hostilities, as indicated in the report entitled "French Moroccan Automotive Vehicle Registration Estimates for January 1, 1940", dated December 29th [12] (File No. 866.16). The real limitations are the shortage of dollar exchange and the interruptions to shipping service from the United States.

The allotment has been divided among local importers on the basis of their average receipts during the past several years, but the recent acquisition by a single company of the representation of a substantial number of leading American makes has given one Casablanca importer (Société France-Auto) more than half the total.

Patently, the establishment of the quota system and the theoretical priority accorded to French and British automotive interests are not consistent with the principle of the Moroccan Open Door—the policy of freedom of economic opportunity without any inequality. Even though local distributors do not anticipate much difficulty in keeping the market for American trucks during the prospectively near future, these violations of the principle are worth reporting—especially as they constitute modifications far more important commercially than the "free" sale of Moroccan gasoline discussed in my despatch No. 276 of January 11th, last [13] (File No. 869.6).

Respectfully yours, HERBERT S. GOOLD

681.006/76

The Chargé in Morocco (Doolittle) to the Secretary of State

No. 1530 TANGIER, February 14, 1940.
[Received March 5.]

SIR: In further reference to despatch No. 1523, which transmitted a copy of the French Residency General's reply dated January 9, 1940, to Mr. Blake's Note of September 18, 1939, formulating reservations in respect of wartime legislation in French Morocco, I now have the honor to enclose herewith copies of the French text, and English translation, of the French Residency General's acknowledgment, dated February 8, 1940, of Mr. Blake's further Note of January 9, 1940, drawn up in pursuance of the Department's Instruction No. 1054 of December 4, 1939, (File No. 681.006/67) on the same subject.

Respectfully yours, H. A. DOOLITTLE

---

[12] Not found in Department files.
[13] Not printed.

[Enclosure—Translation]

The Secretary General of the French Residency General in Morocco (Morize) to the American Diplomatic Agent and Consul General at Tangier (Blake)

RABAT, February 8, 1940.

MR. DIPLOMATIC AGENT: By letter of 9th January last, you have been good enough to give me certain complementary information concerning the reservations which you had formulated, under date of September 18, 1939, with regard to the application in the French Zone of Morocco of the various commercial and financial measures taken, since the commencement of hostilities.

In this connection I can only confirm the terms of my letter of January 9, in which I had the honor to define the character of these measures and the spirit in which the Shereefian Government contemplates applying them.

I add that the Residency General has taken note of the new considerations which you have been good enough to set forth in the second part of your aforementioned letter.

Please accept [etc.]   J. MORIZE

681.006/73

The Secretary of State to the Chargé in Morocco (Doolittle)

No. 1063   WASHINGTON, March 4, 1940.

SIR: The Department has received Mr. Blake's despatch no. 1522 of January 12, 1940 enclosing the text of legislation promulgated in the Tangier Zone on November 5 and November 30, 1939, regulating wartime trade in that Zone. In Mr. Blake's despatch it is stated that the legislation has been referred to him by the French Resident General with a view to obtaining the assent of this Government to its application to American nationals and American protected persons in the Tangier Zone.

You should inform the French Resident General that the Department cannot give its approval to the application in the Tangier Zone to American nationals and American-protected persons of legislation in derogation of American treaty rights in that Zone.

However, it may be stated in your communication that you would be prepared to examine with the French Resident General and to report to the Department suggestions designed to avoid special difficulties prejudicial to the interests of the Tangier community which might result from the failure of this Government to give its approval to legislation enacted as the result of the present exceptional circumstances in the Tangier Zone. It should be added that the suggestions would have to be limited, of course, to those measures of cooperation which did not prejudice the neutrality of the United States, the maintenance of American treaty rights in the Tangier Zone or the legitimate activities and interests of American nationals there.

Very truly yours, For the Secretary of State:

R. WALTON MOORE

681.116/60

The Secretary of State to the Diplomatic Agent and Consul General at Tangier (Blake)

No. 1066 WASHINGTON, March 20, 1940.

SIR: The Department has received Mr. Goold's despatch no. 281 of January 22, 1940, reporting the temporary establishment in the French Zone of the Shereefian Empire of import quotas on trucks. It appears that a copy of Mr. Goold's despatch has been furnished to you.

It is not apparent from the despatch whether the quotas have been introduced as a result of specific legislation or whether they have been imposed by administrative action. If the quotas in question have been authorized by legislation formally promulgated in the French Zone, the reservations which you were authorized to enter with the French Protectorate Authorities in pursuance of the Department's instruction no. 1054 of December 4, 1939,[14] concerning legislation introduced by the Protectorate Authorities incident to the present exceptional circumstances in French Morocco, would adequately protect our rights. On the other hand, if the imposition of the quotas is the result of administrative action it is considered that specific notice should be taken of this violation of our treaty rights.

Accordingly you should endeavor to ascertain the basis for the introduction of the quotas on trucks. Should your investigation disclose that the imposition of these quotas is not based on specific legislative authority you should address a note of protest to the French Protectorate authorities, reserving at the same time all American treaty rights as affected by this administrative action as well as by any action of the French Protectorate authorities incident to the present exceptional circumstances in French Morocco.

Very truly yours, For the Secretary of State:

R. WALTON MOORE

---

[14] *Foreign Relations*, 1939, vol. IV, p. 692.

681.116/65

The Diplomatic Agent and Consul General at Tangier (White) to the Secretary of State

No. 7   TANGIER, August 12, 1940.
[Received September 4.]

SIR: I have the honor to transmit herewith copy of a Note of protest dated August 12, 1940, which in pursuance of the Department's Instruction No. 1066 of March 20, 1940 to my predecessor, I have addressed to the Resident General of France in Morocco, as Minister for Foreign Affairs of His Shereefian Majesty, concerning quotas and other restrictions imposed by administrative action of Protectorate Departments, without specific legislative authority, upon the importation of automotive vehicles, parts and equipment into the French Zone of Morocco. The Note reserves, at the same time, all American treaty rights as affected by such action as well as by any action of the French Protectorate Authorities incident to the present exceptional circumstances in French Morocco.

Respectfully yours,   J. C. WHITE

[Enclosure]

The American Diplomatic Agent and Consul General at Tangier (White) to the French Resident General in Morocco (Noguès)

TANGIER, August 12, 1940.

MR. RESIDENT GENERAL: I have the honor to inform Your Excellency that, according to reports received by the Department of State from the American Consul General at Casablanca, quotas and other restrictive measures have been imposed upon the importation of automotive vehicles, spare parts and general automotive equipment, through the action of administrative departments of the Protectorate, unsupported by any specific legislative authority.

As instances of such administrative action reference is made to a reported convention between the Department of Public Works, the Foreign Exchange Control Office, and the principal local distributors of American truck chassis for the limitation of imports of chassis to a quota of 988 units over a period of twelve months from September 1939 to September 1940, and also to the rules laid down by the Director General of Public Works, at his conference, on February 5, 1940, with representatives of the "Groupement des Importateurs du Commerce de l'Automobile," rules which required importers, whenever possible, to limit the placement of their orders to France and Great Britain, purchases to be allowed exceptionally in other countries, listed in their order of preference, the United States coming last. It may be incidentally remarked that one of the avowed purposes of the rules was to replace the importation of products of the United States by that of similar products which might be obtained from other sources.

The fact is of course not overlooked that these administrative measures are intended solely to meet war time difficulties. I would recall however that the position of my Government in regard to legislation enacted in French Morocco in a similar intention, was stated in a Note dated January 9, 1940, addressed to Your Excellency by my predecessor, Mr. Maxwell Blake.[15]

I am further instructed by my Government to address to Your Excellency a protest against the administrative quotas and restrictions above referred to, and at the same time, to reserve all American treaty rights as affected by this administraive action as well as by any action of the French Protectorate Authorities incident to the present exceptional circumstances in French Morocco.

Please accept [etc.] J. C. WHITE

SPANISH OCCUPATION AND CONTROL OF THE TANGIER ZONE; ASSURANCES GIVEN BY SPAIN REGARDING HER INTENTIONS; RESERVATION OF RIGHTS BY THE UNITED STATES

740.0011 European War 1939/3801 : Telegram

The Ambassador in Spain (Weddell) to the Secretary of State

MADRID, June 14, 1940—1 p. m.
[Received 2 : 30 p. m.]

192. My 190, June 14, 11 a. m.[16] I have received a communication from the Minister of Foreign Affairs in which he transmits copy of a note which had been sent to the British Embassy as well as to the "other powers". Translation of the note follows : [16a]

"Excellency : The Minister of France in Tangier sent Captain Luiset, Military Attaché, to visit the Spanish Minister in Tangier informing him that he had addressed the French Government advising him of the suitability of preparing a mixed Franco-Spanish detachment with a view to reinforcing the services of vigilance and security in the international zone in anticipation of possible incidents which might disturb the neutrality of Tangier.

The Spanish Government addressed the French Government through its Ambassador in Paris, explaining its rights [*reservations*] [16b] and at the same time its opinion that such police operation

---

[15] *Ante*, p. 772.
[16] Not printed.
[16a] Translation revised on basis of Spanish text in Madrid Embassy files.
[16b] *reservas.*

should be left to Spanish forces, since Spain's attitude of non-intervention is the maximum guarantee of neutrality and of the statute.

Having obtained the agreement of France, as the Ambassador informed the undersigned Minister yesterday during his visit at 7 : 30 p. m., the High Commissioner of Tetuan was authorized to order Moorish [*Khalifan*] [16c] troops, in the name of the Sultan, to occupy Tangier with that view. Said forces have orders to enter the Tangier Zone this morning.

In accordance with the discussion with the French Ambassador, the occupation is of a provisional nature in conformity with and respecting the statute,[17] and guaranteeing the neutrality of its jurisdictional waters and the normal functioning of all public services.

I avail myself of this opportunity, Mr. Ambassador, to reiterate the assurances of my high consideration."

WEDDELL

740.0011 European War 1939/3793 : Telegram

The Diplomatic Agent and Consul General at Tangier (*Blake*) *to the Secretary of State*

TANGIER, June 14, 1940—3 p. m.
[Received June 14—11 : 30 a. m.]

20. At 7 a. m., this morning High Commissioner of Spain telephoned Acting Resident General of France in Morocco that Spanish military forces would occupy Tangier within 10 minutes. It is believed that Rabat responded expressing its accord and stated that note had been taken thereof. At 7 : 30 military forces entered International Zone and simultaneously Soviet [*Spanish*] naval vessel arrived in the port. French Residency's response is supposed to indicate occupation took place with consent of French Government although my colleagues, French and English, are without information as yet. I have reason to believe that Spanish representative here has addressed written communication to the British and French representatives, that Spain's intervention is provisional, designed to protect the neutrality of the zone, that the rights of the powers will be respected and that existing services will not be interfered with. Situation tranquil.

Copy of this telegram sent to Embassy Madrid.

BLAKE

[16c] *jalifianas.*

[17] Convention regarding organization of the Statute of the Tangier Zone, signed at Paris, December 18, 1923. For text, see League of Nations Treaty Series, vol. xxviii, p. 541. The United States did not adhere to this convention and made reservation of the rights of the American Government and its nationals. See note to the French Ambassador, June 18, 1925, *Foreign Relations*, 1925, vol. ii, p. 599.

740.0011 European War 1939/3815 : Telegram

The Diplomatic Agent and Consul General at Tangier (Blake) to the Secretary of State

TANGIER, June 15, 1940—11 a. m.
[Received June 15—10 : 08 a. m.]

21. I have received a note dated June 14, 1940, from the Spanish Minister in Tangier, identical in terms with notes addressed by him to all my colleagues reading in translation as follows : [17a]

"The military occupation of Tangier and of its hinterland having been effected by forces of the Shereefian Army [*Khalifan Mehalla*],[17b] in the name of the Sultan of Morocco and with the exclusive object of assuring the absolute neutrality of Tangier and its zone in the present circumstances, I have the honor[, in the name of my Government,] [17c] to inform you that this occupation is provisional in character and that the rights of the interested powers, and all the established services will be respected."

My reply has been limited to acknowledging receipt of the communication taking note of the assurances contained therein that the rights and interests of the treaty powers in Tangier would be respected and adding that the contents of the note was being brought to the attention of my Government.

Copy sent to Embassy at Madrid.

BLAKE

740.0011 European War 1939/3860 : Telegram

The Diplomatic Agent and Consul General at Tangier (Blake) to the Secretary of State

TANGIER, June 17, 1940—4 p. m.
[Received June 17—11 : 53 a. m.]

23. During a visit which they paid me this morning my Spanish colleague and the commander of the troops of occupation gave their solemn assurances that in no circumstances would there be any internment of civilian population of Allied Powers in Tangier Zone. Similar assurances have been given to my British colleague and in consequence the situation here is easier.

BLAKE

[17a] Translation revised on basis of Spanish text in Tangier Diplomatic Agency files.
[17b] *Mehal-la Jalifiana.*
[17c] *en nombre de mi Gobierno.*

881.00/1770 : Telegram

The Diplomatic Agent and Consul General at Tangier (White) to the Secretary of State

TANGIER, November 4, 1940—11 a. m.
[Received November 4—8 : 25 a. m.]

50. Referring to my telegram No. 48, November 2, 10 a. m.,[18] contents of which in the French text have been communicated to me by the Spanish Legation, the following has appeared, in this morning's paper:

["]I, Don Antonio Yuste Segura, Colonel of Infantry, Chief of the Column of Occupation of the Zone of Tangier, order:
That publication of this order, and in accordance with the present circumstances, the Committee of Control, the Legislative Assembly and the Mixed Bureau of Information (mixed Franco-Spanish Secret Service) shall cease to function. As a result I assume charge of the Tangier Zone as Governor General and as delegate of the High Commissariat of Spain in Morocco.
Tangier, November 3, 1940. (signed) Antonio Yuste."

Comment will follow.

WHITE

881.00/1771 : Telegram

The Diplomatic Agent and Consul General at Tangier (White) to the Secretary of State

TANGIER, November 4, 1940—11 p. m.
[Received November 4—5 : 03 p. m.]

52. Reference is made to Legation's No. 50, November 4, 11 a. m.
November 2. The Dutch and Belgian Consuls General, following a summons of High Commissioner, proceeded to Tetuan where they were invited to vacate their positions in both the Spanish and International Zones, High Commissioner offering to lodge them in his house. They replied that Spain had not broken off relations with their Government, and in the Tangier area their exequaturs emanated from the Sultan. After a telephone conversation with Madrid it was agreed that their consular capacity should not be disturbed provided that they agreed to abdicate from the Committee of Control. My colleagues signed agreement to this effect and were allowed to return home.

The same evening the Spanish Minister returned from Madrid and invited the British, French and Portuguese representatives to meet him, the Italian was advised separately. He explained that as some of the members were incapacitated from further activity on the com-

---

[18] Not printed.

mittee or words to that effect, it would be necessary to discontinue the three services mentioned in my telegram referred to above. He refused to state who was the authority for this decision (obviously reached in Madrid, Berlin or Rome) throwing the responsibility upon the military commander.

It is believed to be the intention of the Spaniards to retain the personnel of the existing administration for the present though it is rumored that Amieva, the administrator, is in trouble in his own country. Pending receipt of their instructions, my French colleague has stated in writing to the Consul General of Spain his views concerning irregularity of the above-mentioned supersession of international agreements and my British colleague asked me if in certain eventualities I would be [willing?] to take charge of British interests.

Another submarine made this harbor this afternoon under similar circumstances to those of yesterday.

WHITE

881.00/1772 : Telegram

The Ambassador in Spain (*Weddell*) *to the Secretary of State*

MADRID, November 5, 1940—5 p m.
[Received 10 : 32 p. m.]

613. I today called on the Foreign Minister at his request. He said he wished to tell me of Spain's attitude and the motive inspiring its recent action in the matter of Tangier whose former political status was in his opinion a "legal fiction and a monstrosity"; he remarked that in the first place the world existing at the time of its creation and the world of today were entirely different parts of speech, that Spain's relation to Tangier and nearby territory was allied to a natural right and that Spain's recent action although an isolated act as regards the general international situation had, however, a close relation thereto in its timing.

The Minister pointed out that the defeat of France had effaced that country from the picture as regards Tangier and declared that this was equally the case with certain other signatories of the instruments creating the international zone for example with Holland; that France had occupied in the administration an importance to which it had no real rights; that with France eliminated Spain's real rival was Italy and that very frankly Spain had profited by Italy's preoccupation in various directions to take the step of which the world was informed. Spain's action he desired to re-emphasize was the assertion of the natural right which Spain had to this territory.

With regard to the three major powers having interests under the instruments creating the administration and status of the zone the

Minister said that Great Britain had not exactly "protested" Spain's action; France had formally done so but that, very confidentially, the stiffest protest had come from Italy.

I told the Minister that we would naturally wish to conserve our rights and privileges in Tangier and that I was reporting his comment to my Government for such instructions as it might consider appropriate.

Repeated to Tangier.

WEDDELL

881.00/1774 : Telegram

The Chargé in the United Kingdom (Johnson) to the Secretary of State

LONDON, November 5, 1940—6 p. m.
[Received 8 : 05 p. m.]

3638. I was informed at the Foreign Office this morning that Sir Samuel Hoare [19] on his own had made a vigorous protest at Madrid against the Spanish action in taking over Tangier. This action of the British Ambassador appears to have cut across other action which the Government was contemplating, based on a plan for joint representations by the signatories and adherents of the Tangier Convention. They realize that under present conditions this would practically amount to a British protest as Sweden is the only other country a party to the convention which is not either in the enemy camp or under enemy occupation. They had felt that this approach would keep the protest strictly within the limit of treaty rights as the Spanish action is considered here to be a very high-handed move. Sir Samuel Hoare having already acted, they are now considering what the next step may be.

JOHNSON

881.00/1775 : Telegram

The Chargé in the United Kingdom (Johnson) to the Secretary of State

LONDON, November 6, 1940—8 p. m.
[Received November 6—3 : 20 p. m.]

3654. My 3638, November 5, 6 p. m. The Foreign Office has telegraphed instructions to the British Ambassador at Madrid to make a vigorous official protest against Spanish action at Tangier, protest being based upon Spain's violation of treaty rights. The British are

---

[19] British Ambassador in Spain.

also consulting the other parties to the Tangier Convention although they do not expect any effective action from them. Sweden has no representative at Madrid, Belgium and Holland will protest, but are under German occupation and they are doubtful that Portugal will do anything.

JOHNSON

881.00/1777 : Telegram

The Chargé in the United Kingdom (Johnson) to the Secretary of State

LONDON, November 7, 1940—9 p. m.
[Received November 7—3 : 20 p. m.]

3672. My 3654, November 6, 8 p. m. An official of the Foreign Office informed me today that according to secret and reliable information the Spanish were impelled to take the action they did at Tangier to forestall Italian occupation.

While Sir Samuel Hoare has been instructed to put an official protest on record with full reservation of all British rights under the international agreements governing Tangier, I gather that the Foreign Office does not view the Spanish action with any undue apprehension as far as the fact of occupation is concerned. They dislike the high-handed way the Spaniards acted without consulting this country as required by treaty commitments and as the Spaniards had specifically promised to do last June when the British consented to Spanish troops moving into the International Zone.

JOHNSON

740.0011 European War 1939/3801 : Telegram

The Secretary of State to the Ambassador in Spain (Weddell)

WASHINGTON, November 9, 1940—6 p. m.

297. Your 192, June 14, 1 p. m., and 613, November 5, 5 p. m. Please present the following note to the Spanish Minister of Foreign Affairs:

"I did not fail to communicate to my Government the note (here insert date) from your predecessor in explanation of the Spanish action in occupying the Tangier Zone on June 14, 1940, as well as the oral communication which Your Excellency was good enough to make to me on November 5, 1940, concerning the political status of Tangier.

My Government has also received from the American Diplomatic Agent and Consul General at Tangier the text of the following order dated November 3, 1940 issued by Colonel Antonio Yuste, who is described in the order as 'Chief of the Column of Occupation of the Zone of Tangier':

'That (upon) publication of this order, and in accordance with the present circumstances, the Committee of Control, the Legislative Assembly and the Mixed Bureau of Information (mixed Franco-Spanish secret service) shall cease to function. As a result I assume charge of the Tangier Zone as Governor General and as delegate of the High Commissariat of Spain in Morocco.'

While my Government has not adhered to the convention of December 18, 1923, revised on July 25, 1928 [20] regarding the organization of the Statute of the Tangier Zone, it possesses certain treaty rights in Morocco with which, of course, the Spanish Government is acquainted. It was undoubtedly with those treaty rights in mind that Your Excellency and Your Excellency's predecessor were good enough to acquaint me with the action taken by the Spanish Government in Tangier in June and again in November of this year.

My Government has taken note of the declaration made by Your Excellency's predecessor that the Spanish occupation of Tangier on June 14, 1940 was undertaken with a view to guaranteeing the neutrality of its jurisdictional waters and the normal functioning of its public services. It is the understanding of my Government that the oral explanations given me by Your Excellency on November 5 and the declarations in the public press of Tangier do not represent in any way a departure from the policy of the Spanish Government with respect to the Tangier Zone as formally communicated in the note of Your Excellency's predecessor under reference. My Government is confident that no such departure is intended by the Spanish Government.

It is of course to be understood that nothing in this note involves a recognition by the Government of the United States of America of any unilateral act of the Spanish Government affecting the Tangier Zone."

Please repeat foregoing to Tangier with the request that a copy of the note be made available to the French Resident General in his capacity as Minister of Foreign Affairs of the Sultan.

HULL

881.00/1796

Memorandum of Conversation, by the Chief of the Division of Near Eastern Affairs (Murray)

[WASHINGTON,] November 12, 1940.

Mr. Butler, British Chargé d'Affaires, called on me by appointment on November 12, when I informed him that this Government, in a telegraphic communication sent on November 9, had instructed the American Ambassador in Madrid to make written representations to the Spanish Foreign Minister as a result of Spanish activities in the

---

[20] For text of Agreement Revising the Convention of December 18, 1923, relating to the Organization of the Statute of the Tangier Zone, see League of Nations Treaty Series, vol. LXXXVII, p. 211. For prior reservation of American rights with respect to this revision, see telegram No. 76, March 15, 1928, to the Ambassador in France, *Foreign Relations*, 1928, vol. III, p. 371.

International Zone of Tangier subsequent to the Spanish occupation of that Zone on June 14, 1940.

I referred in particular to the order issued on November 3, 1940 by the "Chief of the Column of Occupation of the Zone of Tangier" abolishing the Committee of Control, the Legislative Assembly and the Mixed Bureau of Information in the International Zone as of that date.

I told Mr. Butler that in as much as his Government had been good enough to inform our Chargé d'Affaires in London that representations had been made at Madrid by the British Ambassador there as a result of recent Spanish actions in Tangier, I thought he might wish to inform his Government of the present representations of this Government.

I reminded Mr. Butler at the same time that the basis of our representations in Madrid were not the same as those of Great Britain by reason of the fact that this Government was not a party, nor has it adhered to, the Convention of December 18, 1923, revised on July 25, 1928, regarding the organization of the Statute of the Tangier Zone; that this Government, however, possesses certain treaty rights in Morocco which have been called to the attention of the Spanish Government and which we intend to maintain. Our treaty rights in Morocco flow from our treaty of 1836,[21] from the Madrid Convention of 1880 [22] and the Algeciras Act of 1906.[23] The 1836 treaty granted us capitulatory rights in the whole of Morocco, which we alone among all the great Powers still possess.

As for the present Spanish action in Tangier, presumably designed to abolish the International Zone and absorb it into the Spanish Zone, I pointed out to Mr. Butler that this action was wholly inconsistent with the written assurances which we had received last June from the Spanish Government as well as the oral assurances which we had received from the Spanish Foreign Minister on November 5, 1940 concerning the political status of Tangier. Under the circumstances, therefore, although we were not in a position to protest any action of the Spanish authorities in violation of the Tangier Statute, we nevertheless felt justified in recalling the above-mentioned assurances of competent Spanish officials in Madrid and in expressing the understanding of this Government that the present Spanish actions in Tangier do not represent in any way a departure from the policy of the Spanish Government with respect to the Tangier Zone as formally communicated to our Ambassador in Madrid by the Spanish Foreign Minister on June 14, last.

[21] Signed at Meccanez, September 16, 1836; Hunter Miller (ed.), *Treaties and Other International Acts of the United States of America*, vol. 4, p. 33.
[22] Signed at Madrid, July 3, 1880, *Foreign Relations*, 1880. p. 917.
[23] Signed at Algeciras, April 7, 1906, *ibid.*, 1906, pt. 2, p. 1495.

740.0011 European War 1939/6623 : Telegram

The Ambassador in Spain (Weddell) to the Secretary of State

MADRID, November 12, 1940—1 p. m.
[Received 10 : 40 p. m.]

635. Department's 297, November 9, 6 p. m.   I yesterday delivered to the Foreign Office a note concerning Tangier following the Department's text.   The Minister accepted the note without comment.

In the course of the ensuing conversation I referred to statements made in the former Minister's note of June 14 [24] concerning the neutrality of jurisdictional waters remarking that I understand that there were two Italian submarines at Tangier and that these statements would receive a practical illustration by the manner in which the Spanish authorities treated these naval units.

The Minister replied affirmatively and stated that as a matter of fact instructions had been issued that these submarines depart within a period of 20 days from their entry into port.

When I saw the Minister he had just concluded a long interview with the Military Governor of Spanish Morocco.

Repeated to Tangier.

WEDDELL

740.0011 European War 1939/6651 : Telegram

The Ambassador in Spain (Weddell) to the Secretary of State

MADRID, November 13, 1940—11 a. m.
[Received 11 : 38 a. m.]

639. My 635, November 12, 1 p. m.   The following decree of the Chief of State dated November 9 is published in today's *Boletín Oficial.*

"The organizations of the statute having been suppressed in the Zone of Tangier, the Governor Delegate of the High Commission of Spain in Morocco has provisionally assumed the functions of government and administration thereof until further notice extended thereto the general regime established for the Spanish Protectorate; and this juridical situation being incompatible with the character previously held by the former diplomatic representation of Spain in the said zone I decree on the proposal of the Minister of Foreign Affairs:

Article I : that from the time of publication of the present decree and as a consequence of the incorporation of Tangier in the zone of the Spanish Protectorate the Consulate General of Spain established there shall have the characteristics and functions of the other Consulates of our Protectorate."

WEDDELL

---

[24] See telegram No. 192, June 14, 1 p. m., from the Ambassador in Spain, p. 783.

881.01/83 : Telegram

The Ambassador in Spain (Weddell) to the Secretary of State

MADRID, November 26, 1940—noon.
[Received 3 : 30 p. m.]

676. The Council of Ministers is reported to have approved on November 23 a project of law establishing a new juridical regime for the Zone of Tangier "in view of its incorporation into the Spanish Protectorate in Morocco" but the text of this law is not yet available. As soon as it is obtained the Department and Tangier Legation will be informed of its content.

Repeated to Tangier.

WEDDELL

881.00/1788 : Telegram

The Diplomatic Agent and Consul General at Tangier (White) to the Secretary of State

TANGIER, November 28, 1940—noon.
[Received November 28—8 : 43 a. m.]

69. From recent remarks of leading Spanish officials here it seems to me probable that a distinct economic, and especially foreign exchange, regime will be maintained for this city and that Tangier rural districts will be incorporated in the Spanish Zone.

WHITE

881.00/1719a : Telegram

The Secretary of State to the Chargé in France (Matthews)

WASHINGTON, November 30, 1940—2 p. m.

777. Your 1044, November 27, 5 p. m.,[25] sections 2 and 3. Please comment on a report which has been received by the Department that the French Government has relinquished its rights in the Tangier zone and has accepted Spanish control over that zone.

HULL

881.01/84 : Telegram

The Ambassador in Spain (Weddell) to the Secretary of State

MADRID, December 2, 1940—11 a. m.
[Received 4 : 45 p. m.]

692. My 676, November 26, noon. There follows in translation the text of a decree law of the Chief of State "establishing the Juridical

---

[25] Not printed.

Regime of the Zone of Tangier" dated November 23, 1940, and published in the *Boletín Oficial* of December 1, 1940. The legislative organs of the Zone of Tangier having been suppressed and incorporated in that of the Protectorate of Spain in Morocco it is necessary to establish a juridical regime for that territory in order to avoid litigation and misinterpretation. In consequence thereof:

Article I. From the date of publication of the present law in the official Bulletin of State, the legislation which may be issued with application to the Spanish Protectorate in Morocco shall also have effect in the Zone of Tangier.

Article II. From the first of January 1941 all Spanish and "Hispano-Jalifiono" law antedating the publication of the present law in effect in the Protectorate shall be applied to the Zone of Tangier. The Minister for Foreign Affairs may place in effect even before that date that part of the said law which he deems suitable.

Article III. Without prejudice to the general principles established in article I of this law and with regard to the special circumstances of the Zone of Tangier there will be issued to the extent that this may be indispensable the corresponding special legislation with temporary or indefinite application to this Zone of the Spanish Protectorate.

Article IV. The Minister for Foreign Affairs may issue the necessary measures for the execution of the preceding and especially such temporary norms of law as may be necessary.

WEDDELL

881.00/1791 : Telegram

The Diplomatic Agent and Consul General at Tangier (White) to the Secretary of State

TANGIER, December 2, 1940—3 p. m.
[Received December 2—1 : 24 p. m.]

75. Embassy at Madrid undertook to cable the decree published this morning's *España*.

The four articles constituting the same and dated November 23 are clear as to intent to apply the laws of the Spanish Zone to Tangier. For the legal implications for American interests reference is made to the Legation's despatch 995, November 30, 1934 [26] concerning Spanish Zone taxation and references therein.

As regards nationals who will not have capitulatory rights the Assistant Administrator, for legal affairs, tells me that the juridical change will not be fundamental since the codes in Tangier are based on French and Spanish laws though they afford a more expeditious procedure than in Spain. He agreed that the decree presages the liquidation of the Mixed Court and of non-Spanish judicial personnel,

---

[26] Not printed.

himself included. He also said that it was impossible to give a juridical interpretation of a document that is essentially political.

Pending the interpretation which future developments may give, it appears to me that the meagerness of the information contained in the decree illustrates the difficulty now experienced by the Spanish Government in reaching a decision in regard to the administrative and legal implementation of its *fait accompli*.

WHITE

881.00/1792 : Telegram

The Chargé in France (Matthews) to the Secretary of State

VICHY, December 2, 1940—5 p. m.
[Received December 3—7 : 40 a. m.]

1074. Department's 777, November 30, 2 p. m. The Foreign Office states that the report received by the Department is "inexact". The Spanish took over the control of the Tangier International Zone for the duration of hostilities with the consent of the French and British Governments. However, when granting its permission the French Government "reserved all its rights" under existent treaties and has never signed any agreement relinquishing them.

A certain amount of curiosity was evinced as to the reasons for the "strong protest" which, according to the French representative at Tangier, was recently made by our Diplomatic Agent.

I replied that I had no details of this action but considered that as a signatory of the Algeciras Convention we were naturally interested in any change in the status of the International Zone.

The Foreign Office confirmed that conversations have been carried on "in Vichy and Madrid" in regard to territorial cessions to Spain in Morocco (my telegrams 1044, November 27, 5 p. m., and 1052, November 28, 7 p. m.[27])

While agreeing "in principle" to certain modifications of the existent frontier between Spanish and French North African possessions the French are opposed to any extensive cession of territory to the north of the Rabat–Meknes–Fez–Taza line because of its "strategic importance" to the defense of those cities.

Although the Spanish would like to have Agadir and the rich agricultural region surrounding it the Foreign Office considers it improbable that any territory will be ceded in that part of Morocco. Minor concessions may be made in the Rio de Oro sector.

MATTHEWS

---

[27] Neither printed.

881.00/1793a : Telegram

The Secretary of State to the Chargé in the United Kingdom
(Johnson)

WASHINGTON, December 10, 1940—3 p. m.

3736. Please forward Department by telegraph text of statement made in House of Commons by Butler on December 4 regarding Tangier and send copy to Tangier by mail.

HULL

881.00/1794 : Telegram

The Chargé in the United Kingdom (Johnson) to the Secretary
of State

LONDON, December 11, 1940—3 p. m.
[Received December 11—9 : 45 a. m.]

4035. Your 3736, December 10, 3 p. m. Hansard text only available this morning. Mr. Butler's statement about Tangier was in reply to a question as to the present position at Tangier; whether the area is now a Spanish protectorate; and whether the Italian submarines are still in the harbor and Italian sailors free to move about. Mr. Butler said: "On 1st December a law was published in Madrid establishing a new juridical regime for the Tangier Zone under which the laws which apply to the Spanish Protectorate of Morocco will also have force in the Tangier Zone. One of the articles of this law provides that in consideration of the special circumstances obtaining in the zone, such measures as may be considered indispensable together with special and suitable regulations will be framed with temporary or indefinite application to this zone. The precise effect of the document is not yet clear. His Majesty's Ambassador in Madrid has been informed by the Spanish Minister for Foreign Affairs that Spain will guarantee peace and will secure the economic rights of all foreigners in the Tangier Zone. In accordance with the instructions he had already received, His Majesty's Ambassador left the Spanish Government in no doubt regarding the attitude of His Majesty's Government to further unilateral Spanish action in the zone, and fully reserved His Majesty's Government's position.

The two damaged Italian submarines are still in Tangier. On 29th November His Majesty's Ambassador renewed his inquiries of the Spanish Government as to the length of time they would be allowed for repairs. His Majesty's Government have been promised an immediate reply. The answer to the last part of the question is in the affirmative."

In reply to a supplementary question as to whether in view of the guarantee of peace he could say anything about the attack on the British Legation reported by the B. B. C. December 7, Mr. Butler replied: "I think that report is a great exaggeration. I regret to say that a party of Italians did attack the British Post Office, for the purpose of taking down certain publicity notices, but I can inform the House that His Majesty's Consul-General has already protested to the Governor of the zone who has promised to take every precaution against any recurrence of such an incident. These British premises are now being guarded by the administration authorities and the publicity notices in question have been replaced."

A further supplementary question asked what precisely Mr. Butler meant by further unilateral action against which the British Government would protest and whether steps were being taken to insist that no permanent fortifications should be erected. Mr. Butler replied: "The answer to the first part of that question is that we regard the law of 1st December as a further example of unilateral action. With regard to the latter part of the question, I have already informed the Honorable Member that since the original Spanish occupation of the zone there has been a reinforcement of the Spanish forces and to that extent the position is not satisfactory. I cannot go further."

To additional supplementary question as to whether British authorities in Tangier have endeavored to make independent inquiries to ascertain to what extent submarines were damaged and how long they ought to be allowed to stay Mr. Butler replied: "We have done our best to procure the information which I know the House would desire to have. I am satisfied that the Spanish Minister of Foreign Affairs is fully aware of the importance which we attach to this matter and I hope that he will shortly give us a favourable reply about these two submarines."

JOHNSON

881.00/1798 : Telegram

The Diplomatic Agent and Consul General at Tangier (*White*)
to the Secretary of State

TANGIER, December 13, 1940—9 a. m.
[Received December 13—7 : 20 a. m.]

83. The British Ambassador at Madrid has been instructed to press for the maintenance of the existing rights of British subjects in Tangier, legal—with special reference to right of trial by the Mixed Court, property and commercial—including present rates of import duties; also retention of the Moroccan franc as legal tender, continuance of British officials now serving in international administration and of

the British Post Office.   He has also been directed to continue urging that the Straits be not fortified and to demand satisfaction for the British Post Office incident—in this connection I hear that the most conspicuous offender, though not under arrest, is to be brought into court.

In regard to the continued refuge given to the two hostile submarines the tone of the instructions is sharper.   If satisfaction is not forthcoming the British Government reserves freedom of action not only as to the promised supplies to Spain of wheat but also for its fleet.

Even in the absence of more positive action I presume that the English protests are an important factor in retarding a complete *Anschluss*.   The Franco-Spanish negotiations recently reported from Vichy doubtless have the same effect.   I am disposed to attribute no less weight to Spanish lack of planning and coordination, also to the division of opinion between those who wish to retain a special regime for this place and the advocates of its rapid absorption.   Among the former may be counted the local Spaniards, official and unofficial: protagonists of the latter course of action are said to be the exchange control people in Madrid.

WHITE

881.00/1799 : Telegram

The Diplomatic Agent and Consul General at Tangier (White) to the Secretary of State

TANGIER, December 13, 1940—4 p. m.
[Received December 13—3 p. m.]

85. My telegrams 82 [28] and 83.   Both submarines left port last night. This morning the non-Spanish departmental heads of the International Administration received definite notice to quit though some were requested to remain a few days more for the purpose of a less disorderly transfer to Spaniards.   As administrator Dr. Amieva has been replaced by his compatriot Colonel Gregori.   A number of police from the Spanish Zone have arrived to take the places of employees of this branch who are neither Moors nor Spaniards.

I am not informed as to when the Spanish Government realized that the harboring of the submarines was a greater annoyance to the British than its violations of the Statute of Tangier.   I should be surprised if it were not quite satisfied to be rid of this Italian incubus and it felt that this riddance had earned it enough merit with the British to warrant further annexationist measures.

WHITE

---

[28] Not printed.

881.00/1800 : Telegram

The Ambassador in Spain (Weddell) to the Secretary of State

MADRID, December 15, 1940—noon.
[Received 1 : 08 p. m.]

725. My 692, December 2, noon [*11 a. m.*]. Today's press published the following communiqué from the official news agency EFE:

By virtue of the law of November 23 which provides that the juridicial regime of Tangier shall be subject to the laws for the Spanish Protectorate in Morocco, the High Commissariat of Spain has assumed charge of the services of police, finance, health, public works and, in short, of all those services up to now dependent on the international administration of Tangier which has thus been replaced in the form foreseen.

Repeated to Tangier.

WEDDELL

852.48/817 : Telegram

The Ambassador in Spain (Weddell) to the Secretary of State

MADRID, December 16, 1940—noon.
[Received 4 : 55 p. m.]

726. My 723, December 13, 5 p. m.[29] Department's 346, December 14, 5 p. m.[30] The British Ambassador tells me this morning that the action by the Spanish Government concerning Tangier reported in my 725, December 15, noon, had come as a complete surprise to him and had produced a strong unfavorable reaction in London whose instructions he was now awaiting. He had seen the Minister for Foreign Affairs whose attitude was that this action flowed logically from the decree of November 23 reported in my 692, December 2, 11 a. m., and that the attitude of the British Government in protesting indicated a desire to dictate Spanish foreign policy. This latter, the Ambassador said he flatly countered, pointing out that precipitate action of this kind where interests of various friendly powers were involved was ill-considered. He further emphasized to the Minister the unpleasant impression produced in London, whose instructions he was awaiting, and added that he left the matter in the Minister's hands having the intention to see him today or tomorrow and learn if he was not prepared to suggest a solution.

The Ambassador who spoke in a more optimistic vein over the general outlook than I have yet observed is of opinion that in view of

[29] Not printed.
[30] Vol. II, p. 847.

British successes in Egypt and events in Albania announcement of relief measures for Spain by his and our Government would be particularly timely although recognizing the obstacle created by the action under reference. He said further that the Spanish shipping necessary for Canadian wheat shipments are now in North American ports and no physical delay need be anticipated.

WEDDELL

881.00/1801 : Telegram

The Diplomatic Agent and Consul General at Tangier (White) to the Secretary of State

TANGIER, December 16, 1940—7 p. m.
[Received December 16—6 : 17 p. m.]

86. Reference is made to Legation's telegram No. 83, December 13, 9 a. m. On the 11th, Serrano Suñer [31] gave verbal assurance in regard to Tangier to Sir Samuel Hoare. He said that he intended no hurried economic changes but proposed to maintain both currencies, provided that the French did not make a drive against the peseta; he agreed that lapse of Statute of Tangier would revive British capitulatory rights; that the Straits should not be fortified; perpetrators of the British Post Office incident should be punished, and in general that British rights be respected.

The good effect produced in London by these assurances did not survive the news of the events reported in my 85, December 13, 4 p. m., and my latest information is that if the British Cabinet agrees, the Foreign Secretary will cause credits and wheat shipments for Spain to be held up pending receipt of a statement in writing from the Spanish Minister for Foreign Affairs as to precisely how he will give effect to the above-mentioned verbal assurance.

The late administrator Amieva told me that while nothing had been decided, the tendency is towards a separate economic system for this city.

In the absence of orders from the Sultan or the use of force, the international customs officials and the Mendub [*Mendoub*] [32] are not relinquishing charge.

WHITE

[31] Spanish Minister for Foreign Affairs.
[32] Representative of the Sultan of Morocco in the Tangier Zone.

881.00/1803 : Telegram

The Diplomatic Agent and Consul General at Tangier (White) to the Secretary of State

TANGIER, December 18, 1940—11 a. m.
[Received December 18—9 : 05 a. m.]

88. Pending London Cabinet decision (see my telegram 86, December 16, 7 p. m.) as to whether or not to make the shipment of 1 million tons of wheat for Spain during the next 12 months dependent upon a written guarantee in regard to Tangier, the following may be of interest.

The night of the 13th Suñer took the position that although British rights in Tangier are to be guaranteed in so far as they do not run counter to his decrees, international government is no longer possible here and Spain cannot accept dictation even with the threat of famine. His claim that the post office disturbance showed the need for Spanish instead of international control suggests that said incident may have been a Spanish plant after all.

The British Ambassador has reported that Spanish public sentiment will support the Tangier policy of the Foreign Minister and that even pro-British army officers are solid for *Anschluss*. Hence my informant deduces that Suñer is using the annexation of Tangier to acquire popularity with the Spanish Army.

The Ambassador has also pointed out that the Spanish Government is not in a position to draw up on paper a program of confederacy such as that suggested by the Foreign Secretary; the British Foreign Office must draft it.

It appears that on December 9 Laval [33] telegraphed the French Consul General not to take the initiative in conversations with the Spaniards regarding Tangier but to leave the initiative to them; also to be conciliatory.

WHITE

881.00/1806 : Telegram

The Diplomatic Agent and Consul General at Tangier (White) to the Secretary of State

TANGIER, December 18, 1940—1 p. m.
[Received 2 : 05 p. m.]

90. My British colleague and my Dutch colleague have protested in writing to Colonel Yuste against ejection of international administrators.

---

[33] Pierre Laval, French Minister for Foreign Affairs.

The new Spanish administrator has written advising me and other colleagues of his assumption of office.

I understand that a Spanish Court of Justice will be instituted January 1 but that Mixed Court will remain some months longer for the purpose of finishing pending cases.

Yuste is reported to be disposed to restrict his activities to military affairs. He is stated to have said that all Moorish troops except 1,000 cavalry will leave Tangier, their place is being taken by peninsular Spaniards in numbers to constitute a total garrison of between 3 and 4 thousand. He denies arrival of additional artillery.

WHITE

881.00/1805 : Telegram

The Diplomatic Agent and Consul General at Tangier (White) to the Secretary of State

TANGIER, December 18, 1940—4 p. m.
[Received December 18—1 : 30 p. m.]

89. With reference to my telegrams 86, December 16, 7 p. m., and 88, December 18, 11 a. m., and with the same reservations as to secrecy, last night's instructions from London to Madrid were, to continue to press for concrete written assurance as regards British interests in Tangier. I understand that the Spanish Government's assurance should cover the points mentioned in my 83, December 13, 9 a. m. except that the demand for compensation of British officials dismissed from local government is to be insisted upon but not for their reinstatement.

Very significant was directive to the effect that events in Tangier are not of sufficient intrinsic importance to change Great Britain's Spanish policy but that they are of value as an indication of Spain's policy.

While the British Foreign Office authorized the Embassy at Madrid to draft a statement of assurances for the signature of the Spanish Minister for Foreign Affairs, it refused to do this work itself on the ground that it did not possess the necessary information.

WHITE

852.48/820 : Telegram

The Ambassador in Spain (Weddell) to the Secretary of State

MADRID, December 18, 1940—10 p. m.
[Received December 19—2 : 05 a. m.]

733. My 727, December 16, 7 p. m.[34] The British Ambassador told me tonight that he had not yet seen the Foreign Minister but ex-

[34] Not printed.

pected to call on him Friday morning and to then endeavor to secure from him formal promises to respect British rights in Tangier. The Ambassador has called his Consul General from the city named to post him fully in the matter.

The Ambassador said further that London continues to take a serious view of the whole subject because it seems tied in with the many cases of harsh treatment of British subjects and disregard of British interests in Spain. The Ambassador even feels the matter may grow into a white paper but in response to my question said he did not feel that this would necessarily further delay matters relating to relief to Spain.

The Ambassador admitted with some chagrin in reply to my further query that the morning following his conversation with the Foreign Minister reported in my telegram under reference the two Italian submarines in Tangier harbor had fled.

WEDDELL

881.00/1810 : Telegram

The Diplomatic Agent and Consul General at Tangier (White) to the Secretary of State

TANGIER, December 24, 1940—11 a. m.
[Received 11 : 45 a. m.]

93. My telegram to the Department 89, December 18, 4 p. m. My British colleague is proceeding to Madrid today to help draft a project of a *modus vivendi* with the Spanish Government for British interests in Tangier.

The Legation's telegram No. 92, December 21, 9 p. m.,[35] please disregard the final paragraph.

WHITE

852.48/825 : Telegram

The Ambassador in Spain (Weddell) to the Secretary of State

MADRID, December 26, 1940—3 p. m.
[Received December 27—3 a. m.]

744. My 733, December 18, 10 p. m., and 737, December 20, 8 p. m.[36] The British Ambassador told me today that he was endeavoring to arrange an early interview between representatives of his Embassy and the Spanish Foreign Office in order to submit to the latter the draft of an agreement relative to the protection of British interests in Tan-

---

[35] Not printed.
[36] For the latter, see vol. II, p. 850.

gier. He said that in the draft his Government was asking nothing unreasonable nor asking the Spanish Government to retrace its steps but only sought therein assurances concerning the interests named. These he added involved approximately 1700 British subjects some of them influential together with vested interests totaling £8,000,000.

(An Attaché of the Embassy had previously told me that essential demands would embrace: (1) adequate compensation to British employees in the Zone Government let out as a result of the recent Spanish action; (2) re-establishment of the British consular court; (3) arrangements under which British subjects could freely dispose of their Tangier properties; (4) a satisfactory adjustment of the new complicated currency; (5) Tangier not to be fortified).

The Ambassador then remarked that if suggested assurances were not given it would be necessary to negotiate further and that in this event it might be 3 weeks before his Government could make an announcement concerning credits for wheat to Spain. I expressed concern at this and pointed out that my own uneasiness over each day's delay arose from my [apprehension?] that under pressure of famine or otherwise this Government might embark on some unpredictable foolish adventure harmful to the general cause. The Ambassador's comment was that he was "equally nervous" and that if the anticipated meeting between his representatives and those of the Spanish Foreign Office did not indicate an early solution he meditated a telegram to his Government to urge on the Department of State immediate announcement of our intention to send shipments of wheat or flour to Spain,[37] not waiting on the announcement of British action.

WEDDELL

881.00/1792 : Telegram

The Secretary of State to the Chargé in France (Matthews)

WASHINGTON, December 27, 1940—7 p. m.

893. Your 1074, December 2, 5 p. m. The Department would be pleased to receive information concerning the present status of the territorial concessions Laval may have contemplated making in Morocco and Spain. The Department would also be interested in learning the views of the Foreign Office concerning the status of French interests in the Tangier Zone consequent upon the Spanish action in dissolving the international administration of that zone. Please keep the Department informed of all pertinent developments concerning the attitude of the French Government toward developments at Tangier.

HULL

---

[37] For correspondence on this subject, see vol. II, pp. 803 ff.

REPRESENTATIONS REGARDING JURISDICTION OVER AMERICAN NA-
TIONALS BY MILITARY AUTHORITIES IN THE FRENCH ZONE OF
MOROCCO AND BY SPANISH OCCUPATION FORCES IN THE TANGIER
ZONE

125.283H3/126 : Telegram

The Consul General at Casablanca (Goold) to the Secretary of State

CASABLANCA, July 10, 1940—3 p. m.
[Received July 10—1 : 58 p. m.]

67. In the event of war between Great Britain and France for which
preparations are being made, our two British clerks are apprehensive
of internment. I shall resist such a measure on the ground of our
extraterritoriality in accordance with the views of Mr. Blake.[38] But I
should appreciate instructions.

GOOLD

881.203/1

The Diplomatic Agent and Consul General at Tangier (Blake)
to the Secretary of State

No. 1547   TANGIER, July 12, 1940.
[Received July 22.]

SIR: I have the honor to inform the Department that the Spanish
Minister in Tangier has addressed a Note to me,[39] transmitting "for
my information" copy, in the French text, of an order issued by the
Colonel in Chief of the Spanish troops of occupation of Tangier. This
order proclaims that offenses committed against the members of the
forces, involving disrespect towards them, danger to their safety, or
obstruction to the performance of their duties, will be dealt with by
Spanish Courts Martial in Tangier, whosoever may be the person
charged with such offenses.

Mr. Goold, on the other hand, reports that in the Permanent
Court Martial at Fez, French Morocco, proceedings are now pending
against an American protégé, Rahamin Azoulay, charged with failure
to declare stocks, as required under the terms of a Dahir to which,
moreover, the American Government's assent has not been given.
In his representations in this connection to the Diplomatic Cabinet
at Rabat, Mr. Goold points out that the matter is further aggravated
by the fact that the civil courts in the French Zone continue to prose-
cute charges for similar offenses committed by non-American *ressortissants*, that is to say by persons other than those who, according to
the treaties are amenable to the jurisdiction of the American Consular Courts in Morocco.

---

[38] Maxwell Blake, Diplomatic Agent and Consul General at Tangier.
[39] Note of transmittal dated July 8, not printed.

In an instruction addressed to the American Ambassador in Paris, under date of January 3, 1921,[41] the latter, in connection with a similar violation of American extraterritorial jurisdiction in French Morocco, was directed to point out to the French Minister for Foreign Affairs that:

"The proclamation of Martial Law by the French Authorities of the Protectorate cannot, in the absence of an agreement to that effect with the Government of the United States, confer upon French military tribunals jurisdiction over American protegees, who, under the treaties in force and the existing usages, are liable to judicial proceedings only in the American Consular Courts, representing in Morocco not the dignity of His Shereefian Majesty but the sovereign authority of the United States."

(See last paragraph on page 7 of Enclosure to Instruction No. 191 of January 3, 1921, addressed to the American Agent and Consul General in Tangier. See also Instruction to American Ambassador, Paris, of November 19, 1921, Enclosure to Instruction to Tangier, No. 203 of November 19, 1921 [42]).

In view of the foregoing I respectfully request instructions, by cable should the Department deem it necessary, as to the action which it may be desired that I take in regard to each of the two cases above reported.

In so far as concerns the Spanish authorities, whether civil or military, it may be recalled that no formal recognition of their status in Morocco has yet been given by the Government of the United States.

Respectfully yours,   MAXWELL BLAKE

[Enclosure—Translation] [43]

Military Order by the Commander of the Spanish Occupation Troops in Tangier (*Yuste*)

Don Miguel Ponte y Manso de Zúñiga, Marqués de Bóveda de Limia, Lieutenant General, Chief of the Army Corps of Morocco, and in his name Don Antonio Yuste Segura, Colonel of Infantry, Chief of the Column of Occupation of the Tangier Zone.

I hereby give notice that:

The proper complement to the presence of the Forces of Occupation of my command in the Tangier Zone, as well as the guarantee of normal development of the complex functions entrusted to them, is the exercise and effectiveness of military jurisdiction which constitutes the fundamental power of a permanent character in the life of the accompanying army and provides the necessary arm for the execu-

---

[41] *Foreign Relations,* 1922, vol. II, p. 736.
[42] Not printed.
[43] File translation revised by the editors.

tion of the high commissions which have been entrusted to the army—a military jurisdiction which at all times follows the Forces of Occupation, wherever they may be, or whatever the reasons for the occupation, according to the basic principle of Public International Law.

In virtue of the foregoing, I ordain:

Article 1. The following matters shall be subjected to the Military Jurisdiction of the Forces of Occupation and tried by summary procedure whosoever may be the person charged:

(1) Espionage offences, mentioned and penalized under articles 228 and 230, both comprised in the Code of Spanish Military Justice, whenever the offence assumes the following military character:

(*a*) To penetrate clandestinely or in disguise without justified motive among the troops of occupation or into places where they are installed.

(*b*) To carry out, without proper authorization, reconnaissances, drawing of plans, or to obtain sketches of military posts or of places where the forces of occupation are permanently to be found.

(*c*) To protect, conceal or to favor in any other manner perpetrators of the above offences.

(*d*) Conspiracy or proposition to commit the above offences.

(2) Insulting offences to a sentinel, guard or the armed forces of the Troops of Occupation, and injuries or offences, open or disguised, against specified branches, classes, or corps of the service, or against the military authorities.

Article 2. The following shall be deemed guilty of the offence of rebellion, within the meaning of the Code of Military Justice, and shall be tried accordingly.

(1) Persons who disseminate false or tendentious news for the purpose of impairing the prestige of the Forces of Occupation.

(2) The authors, instigators, liaison agents, distributors or possessors of clandestine or subversive broadsheets or proclamations, the contents of which are prejudicial to discipline or security, or to the prestige of the elements composing the troops of occupation, or to the prestige of Spain.

(3) Persons who for the purpose of obstructing or preventing the action assigned to the forces of occupation, promote, or succeed in creating disturbance of public order such as to imperil the mission of the said forces.

(4) All persons who, whatever means they may employ, attempt to perform, or succeed in performing acts of sabotage or obstruction to roads, and means of communication, telephone or telegraph stations, highways or bridges, provided the ulterior object of such acts is to make difficult the functions entrusted to the troops of occupation, and are consequently directed against the latter.

(5) Persons engaged in the clandestine sale of fire arms for purposes which may prejudice the security of the forces of occupation or that of persons belonging to the same.

Article 3. No intimation or previous notice shall be required when armed force is used to repel attacks on sentinels, guards or on military forces.

Article 4. In respect of penal prosecutions the Military Jurisdiction in Morocco is extended to the Zone and town of Tangier, for the trial of specifically military offences.

In conclusion I hope to find the active co-operation of all those who desire public order, and who personify the traditional qualities of the Tangier population, in order to be assured of the greatest effectiveness, which is the essential factor in the execution of the important duties assigned today to the forces under my command.

TANGIER, July 3, 1940.

ANTONIO YUSTE

(Seal of the "Inspection of Shereefian Forces")

881.203/1 : Telegram

The Acting Secretary of State to the Diplomatic Agent and Consul General at Tangier (Blake)

WASHINGTON, July 25, 1940—5 p. m.

32. Your despatch no. 1547 of July 12, 1940 and Casablanca's telegram no. 67, July 10, 3 p. m. It would appear that the issue raised by Goold and that which has arisen in connection with the note addressed to you by your Spanish colleague have to do with a possible conflict of jurisdiction where the security of the forces of the Occupying Power may be affected. It will no doubt be apparent to you that a distinction may be made between the two cases in that the former is concerned with a possible menace to the security of the armed forces of a Power whose status in Morocco has been recognized by this Government, while in the latter no such recognition has ever been accorded. The Department would appreciate receiving by air mail an expression of your views concerning these two cases in order that appropriate consideration may be given them in connection with the examination now being made of this general subject.

With regard to Azoulay, in the event it appears to you that Mr. Goold's representations may be ineffectual or should you deem it desirable for other reasons, you are authorized to address a note to the French Protectorate authorities concerning the attempt of the French military tribunal to assume jurisdiction over this American protégé. In any note you may address to the French Protectorate authorities you should state that the proclamation of a state of siege in French Morocco cannot, in the absence of an agreement to that effect with this Government, confer upon French military tribunals jurisdiction over American nationals or American-protected persons who, under the treaties in force and in accordance with existing custom and usage, are liable to judicial proceedings only in American consular courts.

It should be added that this Government has no desire to interfere with the performance by the French Government of its proper undertakings in Morocco, but it cannot overlook contravention of American rights by the action of the French military authorities in Morocco in assuming jurisdiction over an American protégé charged with an offense that obviously does not threaten or in any way affect the security of the French military forces.

Appropriate reference may also be made in your discretion to the assurances which have been given the Protectorate authorities (see Department's instruction no. 1054 of December 4, 1939)[44] concerning the willingness of this Government to examine suggestions which those authorities might have to offer with a view to avoiding any special difficulties prejudicial to the interests of the Moroccan community which might result from the failure of this Government to give its approval to legislation enacted as a result of the exceptional circumstances in Morocco. It may be added that this Government's assent would not appear to have been requested to the application to American nationals and American-protected persons of the Dahir of which Azoulay is charged with non-observance.

Please inform Casablanca.

WELLES

881.203/2

The Diplomatic Agent and Consul General at Tangier (Blake) to the Secretary of State

No. 1551   TANGIER, July 30, 1940.
[Received August 8.]

SIR: I have the honor to acknowledge the receipt of cable Instruction No. 32 of July 25, 5 p. m., which replies to my despatch No. 1547 of July 12, 1940, and requests me to submit upon the two cases dealt with in that despatch, further comments which may be of assistance to the Department in its consideration of the action to be taken on the general subject of the interjection of military jurisdiction, whether French or Spanish, into the administration of justice in the French and Tangier Zones of Morocco.

---

[44] *Foreign Relations, 1939*, vol. IV, p. 692.

I note that the general principles cited in the Department's telegram are substantially those set forth in previous instructions to the American Embassy in Paris, to which reference was made in my No. 1547, namely:

That extraterritorial jurisdiction exercised in virtue of existing treaties, customs and usages, by American Consular Courts in Morocco, cannot be superseded by Military Courts of other powers, in the absence of express agreement with the Government of the United States.

The process for our vindication of the position in regard to French Morocco is a comparatively simple matter because of our recognition of the French Protectorate. Our reaction to the claims of Spanish Military Courts in Tangier (or indeed elsewhere in Morocco) is complicated by the fact, (pointed out in both in my despatch No. 1547 and in the Department's cable No. 32), that the American Government has given no formal recognition to the status of Spain, whether civil or military, in the Shereefian Empire.

The following background information may be helpful to the Department in the consideration of eventual action to be taken in the Spanish case:

(1) Whatever may have been the vicissitudes of the negotiations, the Spanish military occupation of Tangier [45] was the result of agreement, or at least connivance with France and Great Britain, two of the sponsors of the Tangier regime.

(2) The measures taken by French, British and Italian naval forces at Tangier for the preservation of order in the Zone during the Spanish civil war, is a precedent to which the Spaniards may point as justifying their occupation of Tangier, because of present international disturbances.

Moreover, under the Tangier regime which, from the point of view of the adherents to the "International" Statutes,[46] is an offspring of the Act of Algeciras,[47] the military police of the Zone, is under the supreme command of a Spanish officer, and the forces of occupation coming from the Spanish Zone are Moroccan troops officered by Spaniards.

(3) The promulgation of the notice by the Spanish Commander of the troops of occupation in Tangier, is claimed to have been necessitated by an incident of which I have just become apprised. Two persons were brought before the Tangier Mixed Tribunal on charges of affronting members of the Spanish military forces, but the Mixed Tribunal declared itself incompetent to deal with such charges. It

---

[45] For correspondence on this subject, see pp. 783 ff.
[46] Signed at Paris, December 18, 1923, League of Nations Treaty Series, vol. XXVIII, p. 541.
[47] *Foreign Relations*, 1906, pt. 2, p. 1495.

may be added that a Spaniard was the presiding magistrate of the section of the Mixed Court concerned, and the inference is that the incident was probably staged for the purpose in view.

Incidentally the creation of such motive to justify the introduction of Spanish Courts Martial into the Tangier Zone, would have seemed superfluous if, as Colonel Yuste implies in the preamble of his proclamation, (enclosure to my No. 1547) it is indeed "a recognized basic principle of public international law that military jurisdiction at all times follows the forces of occupation, whatever the reasons for the occupation."

At all events, our opposition to such pretensions stands upon our extraterritorial rights under the Moroccan treaties, while our Consular Courts, unlike the Tangier Mixed Court, are not prepared to acquiesce in any arbitrary abridgment of their competency to hear charges brought against American *ressortissants*.

While representations must necessarily be made for the safeguard of our treaty position in the Shereefian Empire, it is not easy, on account of the very complicated and confused political and diplomatic situation in Tangier, to determine what form these representations should take or to what Spanish authorities they might appropriately be addressed.

Here are some of the points which contribute to the complexity:

(1) Our exceptional position, among the other representatives of the powers in Tangier, because of the fact that we alone still retain the exercise of our capitulatory rights, in the "International" Zone.

(2) Our position of detachment from the Tangier organization, and consequently from the considerations which have induced other powers to assent to the Spanish military occupation of the Zone.

(3) The fact that we have not recognized Spain's position in Morocco,[43] whether in the Spanish or in the Tangier Zones, and that consequently official relations with the Spanish authorities in Morocco are debarred to the American representative in Tangier.

(4) Informal representations to the Administrative Authorities of the Spanish Zone have been effected by the American representative through his Spanish Colleague in Tangier. Should this same *modus vivendi* be extended to representations to the Spanish Military Authorities in Tangier?

The important question is whether our representations in the premises should be made at Tangier through my Spanish Colleague, or to the Spanish Government through the Spanish Ambassador in Washington, or through the American Ambassador in Madrid.

All things considered I believe address to the Government at Madrid to be the advisable one. It would simultaneously maintain our aloofness from the local political complications which present events

---

[43] For previous correspondence on this subject, see *Foreign Relations*, 1936, vol. III, pp. 422 ff.

have accentuated among the European powers in regard to Tangier, and be consistent with the absence of our formal recognition of Spanish Authority in Morocco.

At the same time the Department may consider it advisable that I should informally notify my Spanish Colleague of such "démarches" as may be taken by the Department vis-à-vis the Madrid Government.

In order to complete the Department's documentation on the subject, I enclose herewith copies of the French text together with English translations of:

(a) The Spanish Minister's Note to the individual representatives of the powers in Tangier, and (b) his circular as President of the Committee of Control to his fellow members of that Committee, concerning the establishment of Spanish Courts Martial in the Tangier Zone.[49]

Respectfully yours,   MAXWELL BLAKE

P. S. As regards the case of the American protégé under prosecution by the French Court Martial at Fez, I am in communication with the Consul General at Casablanca and according to his account of the actual situation, the matter will be dealt with in pursuance of the directions contained in the Department's cable instruction, hereby acknowledged, and a report of the action eventually taken, will follow by mail.

881.203/4

The Diplomatic Agent and Consul General at Tangier (White) to the Secretary of State

No. 5   TANGIER, August 6, 1940.
                                             [Received September 4.]

SIR: In reference to the Post Scriptum to Mr. Blake's despatch No. 1551 of July 30, 1940, I have the honor to transmit herewith to the Department copy of a Note dated August 1, 1940, addressed by my predecessor to the Resident General of France at Rabat, in regard to the recent unwarranted proceedings against an American *ressortissant* in the French Military Court at Fez.

It is believed that Mr. Blake's Note to General Noguès satisfactorily complies with the directions contained in the Department's cable instruction No. 32 of July 25, 5 p. m.

The Department will be kept informed of any further developments in the matter.

Respectfully yours,   J. C. WHITE

---

[49] Neither printed.

[Enclosure]

The American Diplomatic Agent and Consul General at Tangier (Blake) to the French Resident General in Morocco (Noguès)

TANGIER, August 1, 1940.

MR. RESIDENT GENERAL: I have the honor to inform Your Excellency that Mr. Herbert S. Goold, the American Consul General at Casablanca, has reported the prosecution of an American protégé, Rahamin Azoulay, by the Court Martial at Fez, apparently on a charge of concealment of stocks, in contravention of the provisions of a Dahir of September 13, 1938, concerning the general organization of the country in time of war.

On this subject, Mr. Goold addressed two Notes dated respectively June 10,[49a] and July 6, 1940,[50] to the Diplomatic Cabinet, pointing out that the American protégé concerned was under the exclusive jurisdiction of the American Consular Courts in Morocco. He consequently requested the good offices of the Diplomatic Cabinet to obtain desistance from the proceedings in the Military Court on the grounds of the lack of jurisdiction of that Court over the American protégé.

From a later report of Mr. Goold, it appears that this intervention on his part has proved ineffectual, since a judgment given by the Military Court on July 23, 1940, sentenced the American protégé to a suspended penalty of one month imprisonment, and to a fine of 1000 francs.

The matter has been brought to the attention of my Government, and the latter instructs me to point out to Your Excellency that the French Military Courts in Morocco cannot assume jurisdiction over American nationals or protégés by proclamation of state of siege, in the absence of an agreement to that effect with the Government of the United States, for the reason that, under the existing treaties, and by custom and usage, such persons are liable to judicial proceedings only in the Consular Courts of the United States of America in Morocco.

I am instructed to add that my Government has no desire to interfere with the French Government in the performance of its proper enterprises in Morocco but that it cannot admit violations of American rights by the French Military Authorities in Morocco in taking jurisdiction over an American protected person for an offense which obviously does not in any way threaten or affect the safety of the French forces.

Furthermore, I beg to recall that my Government's attitude towards emergency war time legislation in French Morocco was stated in two Notes which I had the honor to address to Your Excellency respec-

---

[49a] Not found in Department files.
[50] Not printed.

tively under dates of September 18, 1939 [51] and January 9, 1940.[52] In the latter Note, after indicating the reasons which prevented my Government from giving formal assent to such legislation, I informed Your Excellency that I was prepared to examine with the Protectorate Authorities, and report to the Department of State at Washington, suggestions designed to avoid special difficulties prejudicial to the interests of the Moroccan community, which might result from the failure of my Government to give its approval to legislation enacted as a result of the present exceptional circumstances.

In this connection the census of stocks held by American *ressortissants*—the basis of the case brought against the American protégé in the French Military Court at Fez—is a matter on which our mutual cooperation might well have fallen within the scope of such suggestions. It appears therefore to be deeply regrettable that instead of avail being taken of these friendly overtures, on my part, to deal with this question, resort should have been made to an unwarrantable action of the French Military Court at Fez in the premises.

In conclusion, while I have pleasure in reiterating to Your Excellency my readiness, in the future, to examine with the Protectorate Authorities, and to submit for the consideration of my Government the adoption of dispositions intended to overcome such special difficulties as may arise, I find myself obliged, in transmitting the observations of my Government upon the violation of American treaty rights involved in the action of the Court Martial at Fez against the American protégé, Rahamin Azoulay, to request that Your Excellency be good enough to cause the sentence of that Court to be quashed and the fine remitted.

Please accept [etc.]   MAXWELL BLAKE

881.203/2

The Secretary of State to the Diplomatic Agent and Consul General at Tangier (White)

No. 2   WASHINGTON, August 26, 1940.

SIR: The Department has received Mr. Blake's despatch no. 1551 of July 30, 1940 concerning cases involving a possible conflict between military and extraterritorial jurisdiction in Morocco.

You should address a note substantially as follows to your Spanish colleague in reply to his communication to Mr. Blake on July 8, 1940,[53] a copy of which was enclosed with the above-mentioned despatch:

---

[51] *Foreign Relations,* 1939, vol. IV, p. 692.
[52] *Ante,* p. 772.
[53] See despatch No. 1547, July 12, from the Diplomatic Agent and Consul General at Tangier, p. 805.

My predecessor did not fail to communicate to the Department of State at Washington a copy of your communication of July 8, 1940 enclosing a copy of an order purporting to indicate certain offenses which have been subjected to the military jurisdiction in the Tangier Zone.

I am now directed by my Government to inform you that, in view of the extraterritorial jurisdiction exercised by the United States of America, in Morocco, my Government cannot admit the validity of the assumption by the Spanish military forces of any jurisdiction over American nationals and American-protected persons in the Tangier Zone.

In forwarding to the Department a copy of the communication on the above subject which you have been directed to make to your Spanish colleague, you should submit at the same time your comments on Mr. Goold's telegram no. 67 of July 10, 1940, to the Department. The Department has noted that Mr. Blake inadvertently omitted from his despatch under reference the comments on that telegram which were requested in the Department's telegram no. 32 of July 25, 1940 to him.

Very truly yours,   For the Secretary of State:

A. A. BERLE, JR.

881.203/6

The Diplomatic Agent and Consul General at Tangier (White) to the Secretary of State

No. 17   TANGIER, August 30, 1940.
                                [Received September 30.]

SIR: I have the honor to refer to the Legation's despatches no. 1547 of July 12, 1940, 1551 of July 30, and 5 of August 6, 1940, and to telegram from the Department no. 32 of July 25, 5 p. m., all of which concern the prosecution of the American protégé, Rahamin Azoulay, by a French court martial at Fez, on the charge of concealing stocks.

It occurred to me that in as much as the American and French Governments appeared to have taken diametrically opposite views as to the competence of Military Tribunals in regard to American protégés, and as the attitude of the American Government has been formally and clearly set forth in writing in the note of August 1, 1940 addressed by my predecessor to the Resident General, a copy of which was enclosed with my despatch no. 5 above referred to, the best method of reaching a settlement would be to prevent any further action in this case prejudicial to American interests.

With this object, while I was in Fez, I interviewed Azoulay's attorney, Maitre Jacob, with a view to seeing whether, from the point of view of French jurisprudence, there was any flaw in the decision of the court which would afford the Resident General a convenient means of retreat from his position. The lawyer, however, said that the question of jurisdiction was the only point upon which the decision could be impugned.

In the meantime, Azoulay informed me that he had received a notice to pay the fine within ten days of August 15. I, therefore, telephoned the Cabinet Diplomatique asking them to postpone the execution of the sentence until I could talk the matter over.

When I reached Casablanca, I endeavored, with the assistance of Messrs. Goold and El Khazen,[56] to trace the decrees on the basis of which Azoulay had been brought before the court martial. The results of our investigation are to be found in enclosure 1).[57] I enclose the text, in original and translation, of the letter of May 1, 1940 [57] from the Chef du Service du Commerce et de l'Industrie, to which allusion is made in enclosure 1). The gentleman who wrote this letter appeared to be a relatively junior employee of the Service of Commerce and Industry. Exactly how this letter figured in the proceedings, I do not know. Azoulay's lawyer forwarded it to the Consulate at Casablanca without comment. Apparently the proceedings of French Military Tribunals are surrounded with a certain secrecy.

With this information, when I reached Rabat in the course of my return to Tangier, I approached M. Broustra, the Chief of the Diplomatic Cabinet. I began by reminding him that my Government definitely did not recognize the authority of the Military Tribunal; and then endeavored to demonstrate to him, on the basis of the enclosures 1) and 2), that even on the basis of the French-Moroccan legislation, the French did not have a particularly good case. In this connection I pointed out that a Frenchman or a Moor who had concealed stocks would be tried by their own civil courts and not by court martial. I also called attention to the inaccuracy of the statement in the letter of the Chief of the Service of Commerce and Industry, to the effect that the States which enjoyed extraterritoriality in Morocco, had never disputed the competence of the Military Tribunals in regard to their own "ressortissants".

In this connnection, I should state that there had just arrived and that I therefore had to hand the invaluable memorandum of July 24, 1940 [57] prepared by the Division of Near Eastern Affairs, entitled "Conflict between Extraterritorial and Military Jurisdiction", addressed to the Tangier and Casablanca offices as of date July 30, 1940. I was therefore able to make specific mention of the cases of Mohammad El Filaly in 1912,[58] and of El Mamoun in 1920,[59] pointing out that, in both instances, the action of the protégés was more likely to be a military menace than the non-reporting of stocks by Azoulay; yet

---

[56] Interpreter at the Consulate General at Casablanca.
[57] Not printed.
[58] See *Foreign Relations*, 1912, pp. 987 ff.
[59] See *ibid.*, 1922, vol. II, pp. 736 ff.

that, in the first case, the Military Tribunal appeared to have dropped the prosecution and, in the second case, the President of the French Republic had given a pardon.

I also pointed out, in connection with the last paragraph of the letter from the Chief of the Service of Commerce and Industry, that the decision of the Tribunal had been made after the armistice had been signed and, although I was aware that a state of war still existed, in law, yet this might be a circumstance to be considered. M. Broustra replied, in this connection, that the economic situation was more difficult now than ever.

M. Broustra then suggested that the decision of the court martial should be left in suspense indefinitely, without execution, and the fine not be collected.[60] He also requested me to inform Azoulay that he should not conceal stocks.

As this was the first case that I had taken up with the French authorities, as it seemed to me most unlikely that they would reverse their position so as to cover the principle involved, and as the non-collection of the fine should, if anything, strengthen the American contention in regard to the non-competence of courts martial to try American protégés, I replied that personally my aim was to avoid incidents and that, on that basis, this solution seemed satisfactory, though I also intimated that my Government would probably be better pleased were the sentence itself quashed.

As of possible interest, I might mention that in the course of my conversation with M. Broustra, he asked how it was possible to maintain the economic regime of the country if all American "ressortissants" could disregard the French regulations. I accordingly reminded him that in his letter of August 1 to the Residency, above mentioned, my predecessor had expressed his willingness to cooperate with the Residency, and that I and the Consulate at Casablanca were always at his disposal for that purpose.

I may mention that La Depêche Marocaine of August 30, 1940 quotes the following despatch from Vichy:

"Suppression of Military Tribunals"

"Vichy, August 30.—The permanent Military Tribunals of the Military Division of Fez, and the permanent Military Tribunal of Cassation at Rabat are suppressed.

"Algiers, the territories of the South, Tunisia, and the French Zone of Morocco, shall be within the jurisdiction of the permanent Military Tribunal of Cassation at Algiers."

Respectfully yours, J. C. WHITE

---

[60] In despatch No. 46, October 5, 1940, the Diplomatic Agent and Consul General at Tangier informed the Department that the French Resident General in a note of September 30 confirmed in writing that the execution of the judgment was suspended (881.203/8).

881.203/6

The Secretary of State to the Diplomatic Agent and Consul General at Tangier (White)

No. 8   WASHINGTON, October 16, 1940.

SIR: The Department has received your despatch no. 17 of August 30, 1940 concerning your representations to the French Protectorate authorities on behalf of Rahamin Azoulay, an American protected person, in a case involving his improper subjection to the jurisdiction of the military courts in French Morocco.

It appears that, as a result of your representations, the French Protectorate authorities have suggested that the decision of the Court Martial be left in suspense indefinitely, without execution, and that the fine should not be collected.

The Department approves the action taken by you in this case and, relying upon your recommendations, is disposed to accept the suggestion offered by the French Protectorate authorities for its settlement. The Department would prefer that the sentence imposed by the court martial on Mr. Azoulay be quashed but it is not disposed to insist on this action so long as the French Protectorate authorities refrain from any attempt to assert the validity of the judgment or any effort to enforce it. In view of the dissolution of the military court which imposed the sentence under reference, the Department assumes that the case may be regarded, for all practical purposes, as closed.

Very truly yours,   For the Secretary of State:
                                      R. WALTON MOORE

ASSOCIATION OF THE UNITED STATES WITH THE PROTEST BY THE DEAN OF THE CONSULAR CORPS AT CASABLANCA REGARDING THE EXPULSION OF BRITISH CONSULAR OFFICERS FROM THE FRENCH ZONE OF MOROCCO

702.4181/9

The Consul General at Casablanca (Goold) to the Secretary of State

No. 333   CASABLANCA, July 20, 1940.
                                      [Received August 5.]

SIR: I have the honor to enclose a copy of my letter of July 13th to the Honorable Maxwell Blake at Tangier together with its enclosures concerning the matter of a proposed protest to be made to the Protectorate Authorities with reference to the dismissal of British Consuls from the ports of the Protectorate, and Mr. Blake's reply. The proposed protest was to be based on the theory that the exequaturs of the Consuls were issued to them by the Sultan and counter-signed by the Resident General as the Sultan's Foreign Minister—all in accordance with the Protectorate treaty [61]—and that consequently the action of the French Government in dismissing the Consuls was illegal.

I do not know to what extent the Department is interested in the maintenance of the fiction of the Protectorate in Morocco, but if it is interested to any extent, here is undoubtedly an opportunity to make a point which the French may, when peace treaty making time comes, [have reason?] to be grateful for.

I have the honor to ask instructions.

Respectfully yours,   HERBERT S. GOOLD

[Enclosure 1]

The Consul General at Casablanca (Goold) to the Diplomatic Agent and Consul General at Tangier (Blake)

CASABLANCA, July 13, 1940.

SIR: As you know there was some question of our taking over British interests here, but you will note from Mr. Hurst's [62] letter to me of yesterday that the Consul at Marrakesh will continue to deal with the affairs of the posts at Rabat and Casablanca.

I am enclosing copies of Mr. Hurst's letter of the 12th together with its enclosures [63] for what it has to say of the manner in which he was asked to leave the country, and to point out to you that the action was taken without any reference to the Sultan. You will notice from Mr. Morize's [64] note of the 8th of July that it was the French Government which took the decision to invite British Consuls in Ports to leave for England.

Under the Protectorate régime, I take it that there is no doubt that this action was quite illegal and I send the papers to you to learn whether you would have any objection to my joining with my Belgian and other colleagues in bringing this matter to the attention of the Protectorate Government, and making a protest, or whether you would prefer to make the protest yourself, or whether you would prefer to make a protest in addition to the one which I make jointly with my colleagues.

Respectfully yours,   HERBERT S. GOOLD

---

[61] Signed at Fez, Morocco, March 30, 1912, *British and Foreign State Papers*, vol. CVI, p. 1023.
[62] British Consul General at Rabat.
[63] Enclosures not printed.
[64] Jean Morize of the French Residency General at Rabat.

[Subenclosure]

The British Consul General at Rabat (Hurst) to the American Consul General at Casablanca (Goold)

RABAT, 12 July, 1940.

SIR AND DEAR COLLEAGUE: I acknowledge with many thanks the receipt of your letter of yesterday confirming your readiness to place official seals on British Government property at Rabat, Casablanca, Mazagan and Saffi when requested to do so and to make a written declaration concerning the action taken in each place.

For your information I enclose a copy of the communication addressed to me by the Residency-General, No. 321 of the 8th July,[65] regarding the closure of British Consular posts at ports in the French Zone of Morocco and of my reply thereto, dated the 9th July. You will notice that the letter of the Residency-General speaks of the "French Government" only and makes no mention of His Majesty the Sultan of Morocco and is, in this respect and without prejudice to other irregularities, quite incorrect.

Mr. Parr, His Britannic Majesty's Consul at Marrakesh, whose functions (as those of Mr. F. H. Gamble, His Britannic Majesty's Consul at Fez) continue, will, as from the closure of the British Consular posts at Rabat and Casablanca deal with British communities and interests in those two Consular districts also.

Believe me, Sir and Dear Colleague,

Respectfully yours,   L. H. HURST

[Enclosure 2]

The Diplomatic Agent and Consul General at Tangier (Blake) to the Consul General at Casablanca (Goold)

TANGIER, July 17, 1940.

SIR: I have to acknowledge the receipt of your letter of July 13, 1940 (File No. 704/HSG/ib) and enclosures relating the circumstances of the expulsion of British Consular representatives from French Protectorate ports.

I hesitate to advise your joining in the protest contemplated by your Belgian colleague, although I deem this to be well founded. I suggest, however, that, by air mail, you should bring the matter to the attention of the Department, furnishing it with copies of the

---

[65] Not printed.

complete correspondence, and requesting instructions, by cable if the Department considers it advisable, as to what action, if any, you may be desired to take in the premises. Please send for our files a copy of the Department's reply.

Respectfully yours, MAXWELL BLAKE

702.4181/9 : Telegram

The Acting Secretary of State to the Consul General at Casablanca (Goold)

WASHINGTON, August 8, 1940—5 p. m.

55. Your despatch 333 of July 20. Please inform the Department by telegraph in Gray Code:

1. The precise terms of any protest which the Dean contemplates making to the French Protectorate authorities;

2. The countries represented by those of your colleagues who have signified their intention of associating themselves with such a protest; and

3. The character of any views, which may have been formulated by your colleagues, contrary to those entertained by the Dean, so far as they may be available.

WELLES

704.4181/18 : Telegram

The Consul General at Casablanca (Goold) to the Secretary of State

CASABLANCA, August 28, 1940—2 p. m.
[Received 10:25 p. m.]

102. Your telegram 55, August 8, 5 p. m. By mistake the Belgian Consul General filed the protest yesterday associating me with it. This morning I informed the Diplomatic Cabinet that the association was premature and to be disregarded. Mr. Barbanson [66] did the same.

The Swiss and the Japanese representatives joined in making the protest but the Greek received instructions not to do so under the present circumstances and the Spaniard held that the time had passed.

Under the circumstances and to save time may I telegraph the protest in the clear.

GOOLD

---

[66] Albert Barbanson, Belgian Consul General and Dean of the Consular Corps at Casablanca.

702.4181/11 : Telegram

The Consul General at Casablanca (Goold) to the Secretary of State

CASABLANCA, August 31, 1940.
[Received September 1—8 : 30 a. m.]

107. Your 68, August 30, noon [67]. Following is protest:

"Having recently learned of the unwonted language of the letter which your Residency General addressed to the Consul General of His Britannic Majesty inviting the Consuls of Great Britain in the ports together with their personnel to return to England, I took up the matter with my career colleagues.

In the first place it is not admissible that the notification should have been made in the name of the French Government, such a procedure being contrary to law. His Majesty, the Sultan, remains the sole sovereign of Morocco : the solemn declarations which you have often had occasion to make in the name of the French Government leave no place for doubt on this subject.

It is by virtue of his exequatur that Consuls perform their duties here. He only may withdraw this exequatur and it is thus in his name that notification should have been given. By the very terms of article 5 of the Protectorate Treaty the French Government has not the right to deal here with foreign representatives except as an intermediary through its representative, the Commissioner Resident General.

On the other hand, if a government undoubtedly has the right to consider a representative of a foreign power as *persona non grata* at a given moment or as a result of certain circumstances, it cannot be admitted that it should exercise this right by discourteous or violent proceedings. However, the manner in which the Consuls of His Britannic Majesty were asked to leave Morocco really constitutes an expulsion, and expulsion is a measure which in the unanimous opinion of the most authoritative writers cannot be justified even in an extreme case. If the Shereefian Government could have considered sending the Consuls away, it was none the less obligated to respect international law and custom in having recourse to the procedure of recall.

Consequently, in my capacity as Dean of the Consular Corps, it is my duty, Mr. Resident General, to raise the most formal protest against the illegal and discourteous procedure to which the Consuls of His Britannic Majesty in Morocco were submitted.

My colleagues of the United States, of Switzerland and of Japan associate themselves with this action. The Consul General of Spain in Rabat, the Consul of Portugal in Rabat, and the Vice Consul of Greece in Casablanca prefer to abstain."

GOOLD

---

[67] Not printed.

702.4181/14 : Telegram

The Consul General at Casablanca (Goold) to the Secretary of State

CASABLANCA, September 4, 1940—noon.
[Received September 4—11 : 42 a. m.]

111. My telegram 102, August 28. The Resident General has answered the Belgian Consul General saying that the matter does not concern the Dean of the Consular Corps of Casablanca but the French, Moroccan, and the British Governments exclusively.

GOOLD

702.4181/14 : Telegram

The Secretary of State to the Consul General at Casablanca (Goold)

WASHINGTON, September 6, 1940—7 p. m.

73. Your 107, August 31 and 111, September 4, noon. You should address the following communication to the appropriate French Protectorate authorities, a copy of which may be made available to the Belgian Consul General in his capacity as dean of the consular corps:

"I have been instructed by my Government to associate myself with the protest made by the dean of the consular corps at Casablanca concerning British consular officers in French Morocco, while observing that the status of American consular officers in Morocco is determined not only by the general principles of international law but also on the basis of extraterritorial rights."

Please furnish Department and Tangier by mail with copies of your communication.[68]

HULL

CONSENT BY THE UNITED STATES, WITH RESERVATIONS, TO THE APPLICATION OF CERTAIN DECREES IN THE FRENCH ZONE OF MOROCCO TO AMERICAN NATIONALS AND PROTÉGÉS

881.512/151

The Diplomatic Agent and Consul General at Tangier (Blake) to the Secretary of State

No. 1546   TANGIER, July 5, 1940.
[Received August 6.]

SIR: I have the honor to enclose herewith the French text and English translation of various taxation Dahirs of French Morocco. It

---

[68] In despatch No. 351, September 21, the Consul General at Casablanca reported the delivery of his letter of September 9 to the French Resident General and stated that on September 16 he had received a reply acknowledging the letter with thanks (702.4181/15).

was requested by the French Residency General that these measures be made applicable to American *ressortissants.*

The Dahirs in question concern the introduction of Income Tax (Enclosures Nos. 1 to 5); increases in or relief from the "Patente" Tax (Enclosure No. 6); the introduction of excess profits taxation (Enclosures 7 to 9); and modification of the City Buildings Tax (Enclosures Nos. 10 to 12).[69]

The request of the French Residency General was transmitted on February 12, 1940, but the translation of the legislation has of necessity been continuously interrupted because of exceptional pressure of other more urgent business on a short staffed office owing to the absence of myself and of Mr. Doolittle. It is only now therefore that it has been possible to despatch the matter.

Our position in regard to this legislation was briefly reviewed in my No. 1507 of November 23, 1939,[70] and is covered by the general reservation on all war time legislation, addressed to the French Residency General, in pursuance of the Department's Instruction No. 1054 of December 4, 1939 (File No. 681.006/67),[71] as reported in my No. 1521 of January 9, 1940.[72]

The Department's instructions are respectfully requested as to what, if any, further action should be taken in this connection.

Respectfully yours,   MAXWELL BLAKE

881.512/152

The Diplomatic Agent and Consul General at Tangier (White) to the Secretary of State

No. 27   TANGIER, September 12, 1940.
                                         [Received September 30.]

SIR: I have the honor to inform the Department that, by note dated August 21, 1940, the Resident General of France, as Minister for Foreign Affairs of the Shereefian Government, has requested that increased taxation on petroleum products decreed by a Dahir of August 8, 1940, be made applicable to American *ressortissants* in the French Zone of Morocco.

Copy of the French text and English translation of the Dahir in question are annexed hereto.[70]

Instruction No. 756 of August 3, 1933 (File No. 881.512/113),[70] indicates that the Department's assent to a similar taxation Dahir, dated February 27, 1933, was subjected to reservations of the following purport:

---

[69] Enclosures mentioned in this despatch not printed.
[70] Not printed.
[71] *Foreign Relations,* 1939, vol. IV, p. 692.
[72] *Ante,* p. 772.

1. The jurisdiction of the American Consular Courts over American nationals and *ressortissants* in the French Zone of Morocco is not abridged in any manner by reason of the Dahir in question.

2. The taxation referred to in the Dahir shall become applicable to American *ressortissants* as of the date of the notification of the Department's assent thereto.

3. The taxation measures in question shall be applied, without discrimination, to persons, concerns or groups of whatever nationality they may be.

4. Article 7 of the above Dahir refers to the search of private dwellings or business premises in the event of suspected concealment of stocks. As regards premises occupied by American *ressortissants*, such search may be carried out only with the previous consent of the American Consul and with the assistance of a delegate of the American Consulate at Casablanca.

If the object of the Dahir of August 8, 1940, now under consideration, is purely the creation of additional revenue, the Department's assent thereto might be given, subject to the above reservations.

I enclose herewith a copy of a letter dated September 9, 1940,[73] containing Mr. Goold's comments on this point, and also reporting the attitude of the Socony Vacuum Oil Company towards the question of this taxation.

It is not strictly correct to say that the Socony Vacuum Oil Company is the only American corporation doing business in Morocco under the extraterritorial regime. To speak only of oil companies, an American corporation, subsidiary of the Atlantic Refining Company, operates in Morocco on the same legal status as the Socony Company.

Nevertheless, in so far as their sales policy is concerned, it is true that the American Oil Companies, in order to conciliate the Moroccan authorities, usually submit to the Protectorate's taxation measures and to regulations concerning the local oil trade without reference to the treaty position.

Since therefore the American Oil Companies are in fact already paying the tax on their products, as decreed in the Dahir of August 8, 1940, the question of the Department's giving or withholding its assent thereto will have no practical influence upon the revenue purposes of the decree.

In so far as it is taxation upon a commodity of primary necessity, a consumption tax on gasoline at 1.45 francs per liter is rather a heavy tax. In actual circumstances, it is not gasoline taxation, whatever be the scale of increase, that will affect the Moroccan import trade in motor vehicles; however, this trade might be seriously impaired if taxation of this or perhaps greater severity were to be maintained with the return of normal facilities for the supply of motor fuels to Morocco.

---

[73] Not printed.

It is suggested, therefore, that the Dahir of August 8, 1940, herewith submitted, might be classed and treated as one of those exceptional war-time measures, in regard to which the Department's reservations, as indicated in Instruction No. 1054 of December 4, 1939 (File No. 681.006/67)[75] have already been made known to the French Residency General at Rabat.

Respectfully yours,   J. C. WHITE

881.512/153

The Diplomatic Agent and Consul General at Tangier (White) to the Secretary of State

No. 34   TANGIER, September 18, 1940.
                                          [Received October 21.]

SIR: I have the honor to enclose herewith the French text and English translation of a Dahir dated February 26, 1940,[76] modifying and completing the Dahir of October 9, 1920, which created a "Patente" Tax, or tax on professions and trades in French Morocco.

The Resident General at Rabat has requested that this modifying decree be made applicable to American nationals and *ressortissants* in the Zone of the French Protectorate.

As a matter of convenience I attach hereto a Memorandum [76] recapitulating the action taken by the Department in regard to the original "Patente" Tax decree of October 9, 1920, as well as to subsequent amending Dahirs previous to that of February 26, 1940, which is now submitted for the Department's consideration.

Subject to the usual reservations, there would appear to be no objection to the enforcement upon American nationals and *ressortissants* of this last mentioned decree.

An additional observation appears necessary however upon its final caption: "*Provisions Common to Tables A and B.*" This section of the Dahir of February 26, 1940, includes as an item of variable taxation, a charge of Francs 5.00 per horsepower unit on the maximum motor power of automobile vehicles employed in the pursuit of trades and professions.

In this connection it is recalled that the Department has raised objection to the principle of the use in Morocco of the H. P. unit as a basis of automobile taxation, on the grounds that this method of taxation involves discrimination against American made automobiles, (see Instruction No. 779 of February 15, 1934, File No. 881.512 Motor cars/28 [76]); moreover, the H. P. basis of taxation on motor vehicles in

---

[75] *Foreign Relations,* 1939, vol. IV, p. 692.
[76] Not printed.

French Morocco was abandoned and replaced by an increase of the consumption tax on gasoline. (Dahir of November 28, 1935, Articles 1 and 9).

In view of this indirect revival of the objectionable basis of taxation on motor cars by means of its introduction into a tax on trades and professions, the Department may consider it advisable to exclude the variable tax item on automobile Horse Power from its assent to the remainder of the provisions of the Dahir of February 26, 1940.

A similar situation was reported in my predecessor's despatch No. 1262 of February 27, 1937,[77] in connection with a request of the Residency General at Rabat for the American Government's assent to a Dahir dated September 21, 1936, also issued to complete the then existing decrees relative to the "Patente" Tax in French Morocco. No instruction has reached the Legation in reply to that despatch.

Respectfully yours,   J. C. WHITE

881.512/154

The Diplomatic Agent and Consul General at Tangier (White) to the Secretary of State

No. 55   TANGIER, October 14, 1940.
                [Received November 1.]

SIR: I have the honor to enclose herewith the French text and translation of a Vizirial Decree dated September 10, 1940,[77] which increases from 2000 to 3000 francs per hectoliter the internal consumption tax on alcohol in the French Zone of Morocco.

By Note dated October 9, 1940, the French Resident General at Rabat requests that this increased taxation on alcohol be made applicable to American nationals and protégés.

I am of the opinion that there would seem to be no objection to the Department's acquiescence in this request subject to the reservations which have been formulated by the Department in the past, with respect to the subjection of American *ressortissants* to the payment of the internal consumption tax on alcohol in French Morocco. (See cable Instruction No. 1 of January 7, 1925 and Instruction No. 459 of February 10, 1928, File 881.512/53 [78]).

Such reservations are the following:

1. That the tax shall be levied on all inhabitants of the French Zone alike;
2. That in so far as concerns American nationals and protected persons the increase in the taxation shall be effective as of the date of the notification to the Shereefian Government of the Department's assent to the legislation;

---

[77] Not printed.
[78] Neither printed.

303207—58——53

3. That the jurisdiction of the American Consular Court over American nationals and *ressortissants* in the French Zone of Morocco is not abridged in any manner by reason of the Vizirial Decree in question;

and 4. Since Article 3 of this Vizirial Decree invokes the application of Article 7 of the Dahir of June 30, 1930, providing for the search of private dwellings and offices suspected of harboring clandestine stocks, the stipulation that the search of premises of American *ressortissants* may take place only with the previous consent of the American Consul at Casablanca and with the assistance of his delegate.

Respectfully yours,   J. C. WHITE

881.512/152

The Secretary of State to the Diplomatic Agent and Consul General at Tangier (White) [79]

No. 11   WASHINGTON, November 1, 1940.

SIR: The Department has received your despatch no. 27 of September 12, 1940 transmitting a request of the French Resident General that the provisions of a dahir of August 8, 1940, providing for increased taxation on petroleum products, be made applicable to American nationals and American protected persons in the French Zone of Morocco.

You may inform the French Resident General that this Government consents to the application of this dahir to American nationals and American protected persons as of the date this Government's consent is conveyed to the French Resident General, provided that the dahir is applied also to all other nationals without discrimination and subject to the reservation of the jurisdiction of American Consular Courts over cases arising under this dahir, in which persons under American jurisdiction may be concerned. A specific reservation should be made to the effect that no search may be undertaken of private dwellings or business premises under the provisions of Article 7, except with the previous consent of the American Consul and with the assistance of a delegate of the American Consulate at Casablanca.

You should add in your communication to the French Resident General that your Government's consent to this tax has been given in view of the exceptional economic conditions in French Morocco and, accordingly, that such consent is temporary in character and subject to subsequent withdrawal.

Very truly yours,   For the Secretary of State:
                                                          R. WALTON MOORE

---

[79] Similar instructions as No. 12, November 1, and No. 18, November 25, in reply to despatches No. 1546, July 5, and No. 55, October 14, respectively, not printed.

881.512/153

The Secretary of State to the Diplomatic Agent and Consul General at Tangier (White)

No. 19   WASHINGTON, November 29, 1940.

SIR: The Department has received your despatch no. 34 of September 18, 1940, transmitting a request of the French Resident General that the provisions of a Dahir of February 26, 1940 modifying a Dahir of October 9, 1920, as amended by a Dahir of December 12, 1929, be made applicable to American nationals and American-protected persons in the French Zone of Morocco. Reference is made also to your predecessor's despatches no. 1250 of January 27 and no. 1262 of February 27, 1937,[80] concerning a similar request with respect to a Dahir of September 21, 1936 modifying the Dahir of October 9, 1920.

You may inform the French Resident General that this Government consents, with the exception noted below, to the application of the Dahirs of September 21, 1936 and February 26, 1940 to American nationals and American-protected persons as of the date this Government's consent is conveyed to the French Resident General, provided that the dahirs are applied also to all other nationals without discrimination and subject to the reservation of the jurisdiction of American Consular Courts over cases arising under these dahirs in which persons under American jurisdiction may be concerned. You should add that this Government's consent cannot be given to the application to American nationals and American-protected persons of the variable taxes included in the tables annexed to the dahirs, so far as these taxes involve an assessment on the basis of the horsepower unit of automotive vehicles, for the reason that such a basis of assessment is deemed to be discriminatory.

Very truly yours,   For the Secretary of State:
                                                      R. WALTON MOORE

---

[80] Neither printed.

PALESTINE

EFFECT OF THE EUROPEAN WAR UPON THE SITUATION IN PALESTINE; BRITISH POLICIES REGARDING JEWISH IMMIGRATION INTO PALESTINE [1]

867N.01/1685

The Consul General at Jerusalem (Wadsworth) to the Secretary of State

[Extracts]

No. 1187 JERUSALEM, January 8, 1940.
[Received February 5.]

SIR: I have the honor to submit herewith a brief résumé of the various major currents of thought in this country as I have found them during the month following my return from four months leave of absence. I shall take as my text a comment made by the High Commissioner: "You will find it a very different country to that you left last summer." He referred primarily to changes brought about by a world distraught by war.

Most notable of these changes, of course, is the ending of the three years of Arab insurrection. That, in fullest truth, there is today no Arab revolt is confirmed to me on every side, from British and Arab sources alike. The General Officer Commanding comments: "We have reestablished order and we shall maintain it." Able author George Antonius sees his people, as often throughout their history following a surge of effort, again carried backwards on an ebbing tide of almost fatalistic inaction. Their genius, he adds, unlike that of the Jews, does not include a capacity for long-sustained effort.

Among politically-minded Arabs I find an undercurrent of helplessness amounting almost to resignation. They are without effective leadership, largely impoverished. Their main support, the sympathy of the Arab and Moslem worlds, is largely inactive. They still mistrust British *bona fides* and fear Jewish influence in London and Washington.

In particular, these Arabs complain that the White Paper of last May [2] promised them restriction of Jewish immigration and land

---

[1] For previous correspondence, see *Foreign Relations*, 1939, vol. IV, pp. 694 ff.
[2] British Cmd. 6019: *Palestine, Statement of Policy.*

purchases. Instead, they have seen a legal immigration of 14,000 supplemented by some 20,000 illegal entrants. And they still await the long-promised land transfer regulations. Of late, Jewish purchasers are, if anything, on the increase; and current cables from the United States bring reports of a United Palestine Appeal for record contributions.

It follows, too, that among these Arabs I have found no enthusiasm for the Allied cause. That they are better off under the British than they would be under the Germans is readily admitted. But for them this means, as one put it, "but the less objectionable of two imperialisms." Definitely, they feel, it is not their war; and they see, in an allied victory, little hope of better things in Palestine. They speak often, with little veiled regret at their own impotency to act likewise, of the Indian Congress Party's stand.

Withal, however, I am assured, there is a general willingness among the Arabs to cooperate helpfully with the Administration in meeting the pressing problems of the moment. The Palestine Arab has always sensed the pro-Arab sympathies of the local British official. With the ending of the revolt, old friendships have been renewed. . . .

.   .   .   .

In Jewish circles I find less consideration given to the political aspects of the Palestine problem. There is readily voiced relief that the Arab revolt has ended and an evident underlying conviction that Zionism must ultimately triumph. But there is wanting that keenness—and bitterness—which has marked political discussion during the last four years. There is, in short, general acceptance of the proposition that, for the duration of the war, the question of the ultimate political status of the country is not to be raised. Meanwhile, it is their basic policy to consolidate and strengthen their position in the country and, by their support of the Allied cause, earn good will for the future.

In the latter field, as reported by Consul Steger,[3] there was, following the outbreak of the war, extensive organization of Jewish manpower for possible enlistment in the Allied forces. But, on the Jewish side, this reduced itself to a desire to form, under British and Jewish officers, strictly Jewish units for service only in Palestine or, in an emergency, in neighboring countries. The political implications of this attitude were patent. The comment is current in British circles that "what the Jews most wanted was that we should train a Jewish army to serve a post-war Jewish State."

.   .   .   .

Respectfully yours,   GEORGE WADSWORTH

---
[3] Christian T. Steger.

867N.55/200

*The Consul General at Jerusalem (Wadsworth) to the Secretary
of State*

No. 1207   JERUSALEM, January 24, 1940.
                                            [Received February 20.]

SIR: I have the honor to report that Jewish immigration into Palestine in 1939 showed remarkable increase in spite of having been governed by regulations especially designed to keep it under control on a quota basis.   The purpose of this despatch is to give a brief preliminary report on immigration during 1939—to be followed by the usual annual report when more detailed information is available—and to assess the significance of the figures given.   Advantage will also be taken of the opportunity to bring up to date the chronology of events in the field of illegal immigration left off with the Consulate General's despatch No. 1096 of September 21, 1939.[4]

Before giving the 1939 figures, it will be helpful to review, at the risk of too-frequent repetition, the regulations and conditions governing immigration in that year.   During the first three months, immigration was controlled by a schedule published on October 27, 1938, relating to the period October 1, 1938 to March 31, 1939.   Under this last of the schedules based on the temporary expedient of political high level, 7,788 Jews entered the country during the first quarter or registered as immigrants after arrival as visitors.   A new chapter in Palestine's ever-changing immigration problem was inaugurated with the publishing on June 15, 1939, of the first quota, which provided for the issuance of 10,350 immigration certificates to Jews for the period April 1st to September 30.   This quota, designed to replace the former schedules based on the traditional policy of economic absorptive capacity, gave effect to the immigration phase of the British White Paper of May 1939 which provided for the entry of 50,000 Jewish immigrants over a period of five years and for the admission of 25,000 Jewish refugees.   For a discussion of this new policy and of Jewish and Arab reaction thereto, the Department is referred to despatch No. 978 of June 26, 1939.[5]

Jewish immigration during the second quota period, October 1, 1939 to March 31, 1940, was completely suspended as a result of the widespread entry of Jews into the country illegally.   The determination of the British Government to suspend immigration for six months, or even longer if conditions warrant, was reported in despatch No. 1018 of July 21, 1939,[6] and the translation of this intention into legal act in a telegram of October 23, 1939.[7]   It should be emphasized

---

[4] *Foreign Relations,* 1939, vol. IV, p. 802.
[5] Not printed.
[6] *Foreign Relations,* 1939, vol. IV, p. 790.
[7] *Ibid.,* p. 809.

here that Palestine's immigration quotas represent immigration certificates to be issued and not persons to be admitted during the periods covered. Jewish immigrants presently arriving in considerable numbers thus bear certificates issued before September 30 and not, as many persons fall into the error of believing, during the present quota period.

Turning now to the main theme of this despatch, some 16,000 to 16,500 Jewish immigrants entered Palestine legally in 1939, which estimate includes, in addition to immigrant arrivals, temporary visitors given permission to remain permanently. (It may be observed here that this practice of registering visitors as immigrants has been discontinued). These figures are based on statistics of the Department of Migration showing the entry for the first 10 months of 14,161 Jews and on a semi-official estimate of immigration of about 2,000 for November and December. This compares with legal Jewish immigration of 12,868 in 1938 and 10,536 in 1937, the only years with which comparison is possible as arbitrary numerical restriction of immigration was not imposed until mid-1937. Figures for 1939 are much smaller, of course, than those of 29,727 for 1936 and 61,854 for 1935, when immigration, restricted only by the test of economic absorptive capacity, reached its peak.

This small increase in legal immigration as compared with 1937 and 1938 has, in itself, little political significance for an even greater increase was to be expected under the new policy based on the White Paper. In fact, had the quota for the present period not been suspended, more than 20,000 Jewish immigrants would probably have entered legally in 1939. The Government's intention, as indicated in the White Paper and as carried out in the first quota based on it, was—and apparently still is—to admit Jewish immigrants at the rate of 10,000 a year for five years, plus (during the early part of the five-year period) as many of the specially authorized 25,000 refugees as the country may be able to absorb. Obviously, however, the number of refugees to be admitted will depend on political and psychological as well as economic factors. It would appear, therefore, that, such factors permitting, the Government has contemplated the admission of some 20,000 Jews a year for the next two years; hence, the entry of 16,000 in 1939 seems to be in keeping with present policy.

The immigration picture is not, however, complete unless we look behind the figures on the legal entry of immigrants and see how they are affected by illegal immigration. It is in this field that we find much of political importance in 1939 and it is here that much of the battle of Zionism versus White Paper must be fought. It is estimated that some 14,000 to 15,000 Jews entered Palestine illegally in 1939.

Of this estimated number, some 10,200 are by actual count, having arrived on the 19 illegal immigrant ships listed in the Consulate General's despatches of May 3,[8] June 26, July 21, September 21 and in this despatch. A further four to five thousand may be estimated to have entered, as during the preceding year, singly and in smaller groups or to have stayed illegally after arrival as temporary visitors. Thus, during 1939, almost as many Jews entered the country illegally as legally, bringing the total of Jewish immigrants for the year to at least 30,000. This is double the entries for 1938 and 1937, even if we add to the figures for the two previous years the generally accepted estimate of illegal immigration at the rate of several thousand a year.

More important, however, than the mere figures is the fact that the Government appears to have been powerless to prevent the illegal flow, in spite of apparently sincere efforts to do so. Clearly, the problem is one of considerable magnitude, particularly since the Government is deprived, for obvious humanitarian reasons, of its most effective means of combatting the traffic—that of deportation.

There has been a lull in the arrival of illegal immigrant ships during the last few months, only two having discharged their human cargoes on the shores of Palestine since the Consulate General's despatch of September 21. These were the Bulgarian SS *Rudnitchan*, which landed its illegal immigrants, approximately 500 in number, in small boats near Tel Aviv on November 14 and an unnamed "auxiliary motor schooner" which landed 502 near Haifa on January 8, 1940. Excluding this latter vessel which arrived after January 1, our record shows that 19 ships landed some 10,200 illegal immigrants from the beginning of the first quota period on April 1 to the end of the year. The illegal immigrants were in all cases arrested but released shortly thereafter. The ships were, when it was possible to apprehend them, detained pending sequestration proceedings; most were confiscated by the Government but some were released on technical grounds. The crews were, also when they could be found, arrested; some were sentenced, others released for various reasons.

It is not to be supposed that the present lull in the arrival of shiploads of illegal immigrants indicates that the traffic has voluntarily ceased or that the Government has been successful in stopping it. It may, I believe, be attributed to three factors. First, the war has temporarily disrupted arrangements and made it difficult to obtain ships. Secondly, I am confidentially informed by an official of the Jewish Agency that that body is giving at present no active encouragement to the illegal traffic, as the arrival of thousands of penniless refugees has seriously hampered Jewish unemployment and relief work and has had disagreeable political consequences. Thirdly, the British

[8] *Foreign Relations,* 1939, vol. IV, p. 744.

Government is known to be putting pressure "behind the scenes" on the Governments of those European countries where illegal immigrants embark to obtain cooperation in preventing the departure of ships. That the British Government, however, does not believe the threat of further mass illegal immigration has passed is evident from the following statement reported by Reuters to have been made by the Foreign Office on January 8, 1940:

It is reported that certain shipping agencies are engaged in organizing the transport of emigrants from Danubian countries to Palestine. There is reason to believe that intending emigrants do not know that they will not be admitted into Palestine unless they possess immigration certificates issued by the Palestine Department of Immigration and that if they arrive in Palestine without these certificates they will be liable to serious penalties and deportation under Palestine laws.

Furthermore, it is alleged that the ships, on which the immigrants travel at great expense to themselves, are small and unsanitary and unseaworthy.

The captains and crews of these ships do not appear to know that if they carry passengers who are not legally entitled to land in Palestine they are themselves liable to arrest and heavy fine.

A high official of the Palestine Government has confidentially informed me that this statement was issued primarily as a warning to official and shipping circles in southeastern European countries rather than to prospective immigrants or Jewish organizations. Local officials, too, have recently received specific information that certain ships—apparently, I gathered, of Greek or Rumanian registry—are making arrangements to transport further illegal immigrants to this country.

In summary, the considerable increase in Jewish immigration in 1939 may be attributed almost entirely to the mass entry of illegal immigrants in especially chartered ships although a smaller increase was to have been expected as a result of the new policy based on the White Paper. Although ship-load traffic in illegal immigrants has fallen off greatly in the last few months, it is not unlikely that it will pick up again in 1940.

As to the immediate future of legal immigration, no prediction is possible. It would appear, however, that at least a small quota for the period beginning April 1 will be established, providing that illegal immigration does not increase in volume prior to that date. This belief is based on two considerations—one statistical and one political. The first is that Jewish immigration for the two semi-annual quota periods, April 1, 1939, to March 31, 1940, will probably amount to only some five to eight thousand more than the 20,000 or so the Government apparently intended to admit under the new policy. Thus, it would seem that further total suspension of the issuance of immigration certificates will not be justified in the light of the present policy and the decreased volume of illegal entries. The other, political, consideration is that the Government may wish to appease Jewish opinion which was hurt and outraged at the suspension of immigration at a time when the European refugee problem was so acute.

The Chief Secretary, in an after-dinner conversation last week, made a remark in discussing the possibility of a quota after April 1 which throws some light on this latter aspect of the matter and at the same time approaches the illegal immigration problem from a somewhat new and interesting angle. "There is a very good case," he said, "for a refugee quota after April 1, if only the Jewish Agency and leading Zionist organizations would come out into the open and declare that they disapprove of illegal immigration." By this he implied, in the light of preceding remarks, that although such organizations are in fact opposed to illegal immigration because disruptive of orderly development of the National Home, they hesitate openly to express themselves in that sense because of the unfavorable effect any such expression would have on world Jewry's support of the Zionist cause, faced as Jewry is with constant harrowing accounts of German persecution and as constant appeals for refugee relief contribution. A major element of strength in Zionism's current appeal is, of course, that Palestine still offers a place of asylum for many thousands of refugees from Central and Eastern Europe.

I venture to recall, in concluding, an observation made in my despatch No. 1018 of July 21, 1939, reviewing developments in this field following publication of the May 17 White Paper. It was to the effect that two contending forces, the Government and Zionism, were drawn up to do battle over Jewish immigration into Palestine. It would appear that the first round in this conflict has gone to the latter. Unless the Government can stem the flow of illegal immigrants, realization of the immigration phase, and indeed all, of the White Paper policy will be seriously prejudiced.

Respectfully yours,

GEORGE WADSWORTH

867N.01/1689

Memorandum of Conversation, by the Chief of the Division of Near Eastern Affairs (Murray)

[WASHINGTON,] February 6, 1940.

Participants: Dr. Chaim Weizmann;
Mr. Murray;
Mr. Alling;
Mr. Childs.

Dr. Weizmann, President of the World Zionist Organization and ex-officio President of the Jewish Agency, stated that he had come to this country, with Palestine as always uppermost in his mind, to raise $4,000,000 outside the United Palestine Appeal for strengthening the Jewish community in Palestine.

It was to be anticipated, Dr. Weizmann said, that at the end of the war there would be at least 2,500,000 Jews seeking refuge. Of these perhaps 1,000,000 would represent Jews with a future and the others Jews whose lives were behind them—"who were but little more than dust". He believed that it would be possible to settle in Palestine 1,000,000 of these refugees, so far as possible those with a future, one-fourth on the land, the remainder as an addition to the urban population. It was true that Palestine was not rich in the raw materials which were conducive to industrial development but Palestine did possess in its Jewish population the very quintessence of intellectual ability. It was not too much to expect, he thought, that Jewish brains might develop Palestine industrially in a way to make it fill the needs of the Near East in such items as pharmaceutical products for example. He had discussed this possibility in Turkey when he was there recently and had met with a favorable reaction to it.

Dr. Weizmann expressed the view that the most advantageous settlement of the Palestine question in his opinion would be the division of the country into Jewish and Arab cantons with wide powers of autonomy and the federation of Palestine and Trans-Jordan into one state under continued British supervision for some time to come. As Jewish cantons he would include Galilee (northern Palestine) and the coastal region of Palestine, and as Arab cantons the hill country and western Palestine, together with Trans-Jordan. The Negev or southern Palestine comprises 11,000,000 dunums of land inhabited by no more than 50,000 Bedouins. At least one-tenth of this region was cultivable and might serve as an eventual place of settlement of large numbers of people. He would leave this area, however, outside the cantonization plan for subsequent disposition.*

The hope was expressed by Dr. Weizmann that eventually such Jewish and Arab areas as might be set up in Palestine and Trans-Jordan could be merged in a larger federation of states, including

---

*According to the Palestine Partition Commission Report, the Negev comprises 12½ million dunums of which from 1,500,000 to 2,000,000 dunums are put under cultivation (one dunum equals 0.2217 acres or a little more than one-fifth of an acre). Well borings in this area, however, have not given promise of the possibility of irrigation from that source of water although Dr. Lowdermilk of the U. S. Department of Agriculture, who visited it recently, is of the opinion that greater utilization of the land might be possible through more scientific use of the rain water available. It may be said that, although the possibilities of the settlement of large numbers in the Negev remains to be demonstrated as feasible, the existence of so large an area comparatively unpopulated in Palestine makes it one of the most attractive potential possibilities for large-scale immigration in that country. [Footnote in the original.]

Syria and Iraq, but he was afraid that the French might be an obstacle to this.

The Jewish leader added that his proposed boundaries for cantonal settlement followed in general the lines of the partition proposals of the Royal Commission. He had succeeded in obtaining the approval of the partition proposals by the World Zionist Congress in 1937 as he felt that those proposals were something in hand which were worth accepting. Unfortunately, the partition scheme had had to be abandoned.

Dr. Weizmann stated that he would be one of the first to admit that the Jews had made many mistakes in Palestine. Twenty years had not been enough in which to reach a durable basis of settlement. It would take many more years than that.

Mr. Murray inquired what Dr. Weizmann's reaction had been to the statement in Parliament in 1938 of Viscount Samuel that the Arab nationalist movement in Palestine was as genuine as the Egyptian nationalist movement, the Irish nationalist movement, or the Indian nationalist movement.[9] Dr. Weizmann replied that he was in entire accord with Viscount Samuel as to this.

Mr. Murray observed that he did not think that Dr. Weizmann's views as to the advantages of the partition proposals of the Royal Commission or as to the significance of the Arab uprising of the past three years in Palestine were generally shared by American Zionists.

Dr. Weizmann replied that with all due respect to American Zionists he found them either too extreme in their views, on the one hand, or too lukewarm, on the other. By reason of their distance from the practical problems which the Jews had to face, American Zionists were insufficiently informed concerning the day-to-day development of those problems. As a result, American Zionists were either uncompromising in their outlook or completely disillusioned regarding the future.

Mr. Murray asked Dr. Weizmann whether he did not agree that the attainment of an Arab-Jewish understanding was of vital importance to the success of the Jewish National Home in Palestine; whether, in view of the, in general, higher intelligence, superior education and greater social consciousness of the Jews, the responsibility for effecting such an understanding rested to a far greater degree upon the Jews than upon the Arabs of Palestine; whether, in other words, it was not reasonable to expect that somewhere in World Jewry outstanding men of diplomatic skill and negotiating talent could be found to handle this all-important problem and to dispel the fear that had obsessed both Jews and Arabs in Palestine with such devastating

---

[9] Statement made by Viscount Samuel in the House of Lords, December 8, 1938. See United Kingdom, *Parliamentary Debates*, House of Lords, 5th ser., vol. 111, p. 425.

effect on the vital interests of both races. Dr. Weizmann replied that he heartily concurred in the views expressed by Mr. Murray and that he would be the first to admit that the Jews must share with the Arabs the blame for what had happened in Palestine. He made the interesting observation in this connection that, while some effort had been made for farseeing Jews to effect a reconciliation with the Arabs, they had been blocked in many quarters not only by Jews but also by certain British officials who seemed to have no interest in the success of such an endeavor. Mr. Murray expressed the view that if the Jews and Arabs could come to an understanding among themselves and could present the world with a plan mutually agreed upon by them it would be difficult, if not impossible, to raise effective objection in any quarter to the execution of such a plan. Dr. Weizmann confirmed this view, and stated that the great obstacle which the Jews had experienced hitherto in dealing with the Arabs was that they had at all times been obliged to deal through British officials instead of direct with the Arabs. He also observed that in order to gain the confidence of the Arabs and to dispel their very real fear of the Jews he felt it would be a wise and farseeing policy for the Jews to devote as much attention and care to the welfare and well-being of the Arabs in the country as had been expended upon the Jews. In other words, he would like to see the Jews set up model villages for the Arabs in the proposed Arab area equal in every respect to those provided for the Jews. In this way he would hope to bring about a lasting spirit of good will and confidence between the two races.

When Mr. Murray mentioned that there were reports of a new spirit animating the Arabs and Jews in Palestine, as evidenced by increasing friendly cooperation, the President of the World Zionist Organization observed that he himself had been heartened by these reports and he had hopes that they would continue. He did not believe that exaggerated importance should be attached to them but they were straws in the wind.

Dr. Weizmann remarked that Mr. Murray had asked him how it was the Jews, with their brains and ability, had not succeeded in coming to terms with the Arabs. The inquiry was a very pertinent one, the Jewish leader observed. He recalled that he himself had entered into negotiations with Feisal [10] in 1918 and that the two had signed an agreement with respect to Palestine [11] which had never been realized owing to subsequent developments. At that time Feisal was recognized as the spokesman of the Arabs and any agreement which he signed had the force of authority of the Arab world

---

[10] Emir Feisal, acting on behalf of his father, the King of Hedjaz.
[11] Signed at London, January 3, 1919; British Cmd. 5479: *Palestine Royal Commission Report*, July 1937, p. 26.

of the Near East behind it. Since that time, however, Feisal had died and the Arab world, at least so far as Palestine was concerned, had been without any single spokesman; consequently, it had been correspondingly difficult for the Jews to enter into negotiations with the Arabs with a view to reaching an understanding. That, of course, was what was most desired and he had hopes that it might still be possible to achieve it.

He added that while in London recently Mr. H. St. J. B. Philby, the great Near Eastern authority and friend of King Ibn Saud, had called on him and had stated that he would like to take back with him to Saudi Arabia some basis of settlement which the King might be willing to support. Dr. Weizmann said that he had remarked to Philby that the only thing the Jews had to offer was money. If an amount of a million pounds was wanted by the King of Saudi Arabia for enlisting his aid in achieving a settlement for Palestine he, Dr. Weizmann, would answer that the price was much too small; if the sum were fifteen or twenty million pounds he would answer that it was beyond hope of realization by the Jews but if the amount were three to four million pounds as the price of the King's support of a scheme whereby the Arabs of Palestine would be voluntarily transferred to Trans-Jordan and Iraq, Dr. Weizmann stated that he would prepare to undertake to raise the sum. Philby had promised to convey the offer to the King but Dr. Weizmann had no means of knowing whether anything would come of it. He did feel that King Ibn Saud would be an excellent spokesman for the Arabs and one with whom he could deal. Consequently, he was awaiting with interest information from Mr. Philby as to Ibn Saud's reactions to the discussions.

867N.01/1687 : Telegram

The Consul General at Jerusalem (Wadsworth) to the Secretary of State

JERUSALEM, March 3, 1940—noon.
[Received March 3—9 a. m.]

9. Local reaction to the publication last Wednesday of "land transfers regulations" [12] in substance prohibiting, except by special authorization and for limited special purposes, transfer of all Palestine Arab-owned land save to Palestine Arabs, other than in municipal areas, the Haifa industrial zone and a central coastal area of some one thousand square kilometres, may be summarized as follows.

---

[12] Announced in the House of Commons on February 28, 1940; for text, see British Cmd. 6180, Miscellaneous No. 2 (1940): *Palestine Land Transfers Regulations.*

Jewish opposition is as widespread and bitter as that following publication of the British White Paper of last May. General strike and synagogue services recall those of that month. Street demonstrations were probably prevented from deteriorating into serious rioting by prompt British police action and military imposition of curfew at Haifa and Tel Aviv. Placards carried by demonstrators demand repeal, calling "down with MacDonald [13] and his Nuremberg laws" and "Hitler smote us in front, the British in the back". The "free" coastal area is derisively termed a pale of settlement. The Jewish Agency has protested officially that the regulations "not only violate the terms of the mandate but completely nullify its primary purpose". Arab reaction is [not?] unfavorable but with undercurrent of continuing mistrust of British *bona fides* and apprehension that Jewish pressure will induce modification.

British officials welcome move as one showing intention to make White Paper policy with emphasis on the modifying clause of article 6 of the mandate. I sense that, as British Palestine policy last spring when war threatened was designed in large measure to re-establish good will in the Arab and Moslem worlds, it is today being implemented by immigration and land transfer restrictions not only because such action is believed to be just but also with that same larger political objective in view.

WADSWORTH

867N.01/1712

The Minister Resident in Iraq (Knabenshue) to the Secretary of State

No. 1541   BAGHDAD, April 8, 1940.
[Received May 16.]

SIR: I have the honor to give below a summary of recent comment in Iraq on the developments in Palestine.

Al-Istiqlal of March 26, 1940, gives the text of a letter sent by the Grand Mufti to the London *News Chronicle*, in response to its inquiry as to his attitude towards the recent land transfer regulations promulgated in Palestine. This article may be summarized by stating that the Grand Mufti expresses complete dissatisfaction. This letter has, in all probability, been reported by the Embassy in London, but a copy of it is enclosed,[14] as it may differ in some respects from the version published in London, which was subject to censorship.

An interesting sidelight on the attitude of political exiles from Palestine now residing in Baghdad is given by Abdul Razzak, leader of the

---

[13] Malcolm MacDonald, British Secretary of State for the Colonies.
[14] Not printed.

Palestine rebellion, who called at the Legation in connection with his desire to send his brother to the United States for graduate study. When it was remarked that conditions in Palestine seemed to be much more quiet in recent months, he replied succinctly, "That's because I'm here." His attitude regarding the land transfer regulations was essentially that of the Grand Mufti, namely that the Jews already possessed all of the good land, and that the regulation prohibiting further transfers would offer no solution for existing problems.

The then Prime Minister, and present Minister for Foreign Affairs, Nuri as-Said, made a statement regarding Palestine during the debate on the budget of the Foreign Office on March 29. While making no comment on the land transfers, he remarked, "I should like to point out once more, in the name of the Iraqi Government, the Iraqi Nation, and the whole of the Arab world, that the only way to settle the present difficulties in Palestine and Syria is to establish self government and independence in both countries." A translation of the complete statement is enclosed.[15]

The Iraqi Government has, through the Chamber of Deputies, made a further practical contribution to the Palestine Arabs in the form of a grant of I. D. 6,000 for the relief of distress in Palestine. This is in addition to an earlier contribution of I. D. 6,000.

The reaction of the Jews in Baghdad has not been particularly evident, and one gathers from conversations with local Jews that they regard the land transfer regulations as a logical outcome of the White Paper, and a matter which does not particularly concern them.

Respectfully yours,   P. KNABENSHUE

867N.55/204 : Telegram

The Consul General at Jerusalem (Wadsworth) to the Secretary of State

JERUSALEM, April 25, 1940—2 p. m.
[Received 4 : 48 p. m.]

25. By an order dated April 22 made under section 5A of the Immigration Ordinance the High Commissioner has authorized the issuance during the first 2 months of the semester begun April 1 of 2,050 immigration certificates to individual immigrants and of such additional certificates as are needed for wives and minor children of such immigrants and of immigrants previously admitted.

An appended explanatory note estimates at 3,000 the total number of certificates to be issued under this order and announcing as a matter of policy that there will be issued during each of the succeeding 2 bimonthly periods of the semester a similar total minus the number of

---

[15] Not printed.

illegal immigrants recorded during the immediately preceding bi-monthly period, thus providing for an estimated total immigration of 9,000 during the current semester. Of the 2,050 figure 1,950 certificates are reserved for Jews.

According to the note, total immigration during the year ended March 31 was approximately 26,000 of which 10,500 was legal, the remainder being made up of immigrants recorded as unlawfully arriving and/or remaining. Ten thousand of this total are therefore charged to last year's authorized immigration quota and 16,000 to the special 5 years' refugee quota, thus leaving 9,000 of the latter unfilled.

Of the current semester's estimated total immigration 5,000 is to be charged against the year's authorized immigration quota of 10,000 and 4,000 against the remainder of the refugee quota.

The significance of the new order lies in the fact that after 6 months' suspension, imposed to counterbalance illegal immigration, Palestine's immigration regime has [been] brought back in line with that announced in the British White Paper of last May.

An interesting modification provides that no certificates shall be issued to persons who have resided in enemy territory after the outbreak of war or in enemy occupied Poland after October 1st.

WADSWORTH

867N.55/210

The Consul General at Jerusalem (Wadsworth) to the Secretary of State

No. 1352   JERUSALEM, August 29, 1940.
                                              [Received September 25.]

SIR: Continuing the Consulate General's series of despatches on the subject of immigration in Palestine, I have the honor to report the issuance of a governmental order dated August 20, 1940, copy of which is transmitted herewith,[16] whereby the number of immigration certificates which may be issued during the months of August and September is fixed at about 3,500.

In despatch No. 1289 of May 6, 1940,[16] I enclosed and commented on an Order of the Palestine Government dated April 22, 1940, under which the country's immigration regime was, after six months' suspension, brought back in line with that announced in the British Government's White Paper on Palestine of May 17, 1939. The reason for the suspension, it will be recalled, had been the large illegal immigration (16,000 recorded) during 1939.

---

[16] Not printed.

This Order of April 22 laid down the policy to be followed during the current semester to end September 30 and authorized, for the first two months thereof, the issuance of an estimated total of 3,000 immigration certificates. The policy envisaged the issuance of a similar number of certificates during the succeeding second and third two-monthly periods of the semester and provided: 1) that, if the authorized number of certificates was not issued in any two-monthly period, the authorized number for the ensuing period might be increased accordingly; and 2) that deduction should be made from the resulting figure of the number of recorded illegal immigrants during the preceding two-monthly period.

The immigration schedule fixed by the Government for June and July was reported in my despatch No. 1309 of June 17 [12], 1940,[19] which mentioned that a total immigration of between 4,000 and 4,500 was authorized.

The schedule for August and September is the third, and last, of the three schedules covering the current semester to end September 30. The following table shows pertinent details of this latest schedule:

Jews: Basic schedule for the two months (i. e., the same figure as those authorized for the first two months and for the second two months of the semester) 1950

    Deduct recorded number of illegal immigrants during May, June and July (deductions for the month of April have been made from the provision for certificates in the months of June and July) 366

                                 Total Jews   1584

Others: Basic schedule for the two months (i. e., the same figure as those authorized for the first two months and for the second two months of the semester) 100

                                        Total   1684

Dependents: Estimated number of wives and minor children of the above and of immigrants previously admitted . . 1816

                            Grand total—about   3500

It will be recalled that in May 1939 His Majesty's Government declared its policy in regard to Jewish immigration into Palestine in the following terms:

"For each of the next five years a quota of 10,000 Jewish immigrants will be allowed, on the understanding that shortage in any one year may be added to the quotas for subsequent years, within the five years' period, if economic capacity permits.

In addition, as a contribution towards the solution of the Jewish refugee problem, 25,000 refugees will be admitted as soon as the High

[19] Not printed.

Commissioner is satisfied that adequate provision for their maintenance is ensured, special consideration being given to refugee children and dependents."

In the execution of that policy for the six months April–September 1940, the High Commissioner decided that approximately 9,000 Jewish immigrants would be admitted into Palestine on authorities granted during these six months, namely, 5,000 against the annual quota of 10,000, and about 4,000 against the remaining (unissued) 9,000 of the special refugee quota of 25,000.

For the second semester of the year (to begin October 1, 1940) it was envisaged, therefore, that there would be issued the remaining 5,000 certificates chargeable against the regular annual quota and an additional number of certificates (not to exceed the remaining unissued 5,000) chargeable against the special refugee quota.

Against this still remaining balance of the special refugee quota, however, 300 individual certificates have already been specially authorized (see despatch No. 1309 of June 12, 1940). For the current semester, therefore, total authorizations are as follows:

Period—1940	Individual Certificates	Estimated Dependents
April and May	2, 050	950
June and July	2, 557	1, 693
August and September	1, 684	1, 816
Totals	6, 291	4, 459

The foregoing table shows that a total immigration of 10,750 has been authorized for the current semester. While this shows an excess above the initially envisaged immigration of 9,000, actual immigration for the semester will in all probability be less than that figure because of the difficulty holders of certificates are having in securing passage to Palestine as a result of the war.

The above statement is borne out by official statistics published by the Government of Palestine which show that 3,840 legal immigrants entered the country during the first six months of 1940 as compared with 9,724 during the corresponding period of 1939, a decrease of approximately 60 per cent. Of the 1940 figure, 3,181 or 83 per cent were Jews, 241 Arabs (6 per cent) and 418 (11 per cent) were others. Of the 1939 figure, 8,509 or 88 per cent were Jews, 91 (1 per cent) were Arabs and 1,124 (about 12 per cent) were others.

On enclosure No. 2 to this despatch [20] there are given tables for the periods indicated above, showing immigrants by leading categories. Of special interest in the table covering the first six months of 1940

---

[20] Not printed.

may be mentioned the number of immigrants classified as capitalists, that is, persons with LP.1,000 and upwards. The total number under this category was 556 or approximately 14 per cent of the total, and the number of dependents on such persons was 790. The combined total of these two figures, viz. 1,346, represented 34 per cent of the total immigrants in this table. During the first six months of 1939 the number of capitalists and persons dependent upon them was 1,869 or 35 per cent of the total registered for that period.

There is given as enclosure No. 3 to this despatch [21] a table showing countries of origin of immigrants entering Palestine during the first six months' periods of 1939 and 1940. In both periods the greatest number of immigrants came from Germany (including Austria), the total 1940 figure being 728 or about 18 per cent of the total for that period, and 6,799 for the first six months of 1939, representing 57 per cent of the half year total. Poland in both periods furnished the second largest number of immigrants, the 1940 half-yearly figure being 556 or 14 per cent of the total, and 1,232 during the first half of 1939 or 10 per cent of the total.

Respectfully yours,   GEORGE WADSWORTH

867N.55/211 : Telegram

The Consul General at Jerusalem (Wadsworth) to the Secretary of State

JERUSALEM, October 17, 1940—2 p. m.
[Received October 18—2 : 05 a. m.]

140. Referring to standing instructions to keep the Department informed regarding Palestine immigration policy and quotas I have the honor to report that the Chief Secretary last evening gave me informally the following information.

1. Approximately one month ago the High Commissioner urged on the Colonial Office that no quota be authorized for the current semester beginning October 1, primarily for the reason that the country's economic situation precluded effective assimilation of further immigrants.

2. He has at the same time suggested postponement of such a decision pending receipt and study of the usual Jewish Agency recommendations in the matter.

3. In striking contrast to its past practice, however, the Agency submitted no recommendations, presumably because while recognizing the soundness of the Government's position it preferred for reasons of Zionist politics to refrain from admitting it openly.

---

[21] Not printed.

4. In the meantime reliable information was received that three ship-loads of intending illegal immigrants from Rumania totaling perhaps 3000 persons were nearing Palestine waters and that five other ships carrying an approximately equal number were known to be quitting Rumania, not improbably with the connivance of Germany which wishes thus further to embarrass the British position here.

5. This information not only constituted added reason for announcing the proposed decision but raised also the serious problem of what should be done with such illegal immigrants.

6. It is now proposed to reship them to Mauritius, an added reason for such action being the danger that among them are Nazi agents.

7. Simultaneously arrangements are being made for the evacuating to Australia of some 2000 interned non-Jewish Germans and Italians.

WADSWORTH

867N.55/212

The British Embassy to the Department of State

The Foreign Office state confidentially that they are thinking of granting the Jewish Agency's recent request that the ban on admission into Palestine of immigrants from enemy countries, or territories occupied by the enemy, might be relaxed in respect of children up to 15 years.

In present circumstances, of course the grant of this request naturally depends on the United States authorities in enemy territories being willing to undertake, in this connexion, the work formerly performed by British Passport Control Officers.

It is not thought that very much work would be involved, aside from the production of a certificate of health for the prospective immigrant and the establishment of his identity. Most of the applications for immigration certificates will no doubt be made by the children's relatives either in Palestine or in the United States and if they are approved the Government of Palestine will probably issue some form of immigration certificate which would be forwarded to the American Consulate concerned.

It is desired to know whether the State Department would be willing in principle that American Consular Officers concerned should assume these additional duties on behalf of His Majesty's Government. If so, the authorities in London will no doubt provide the necessary guidance for the Consular Officers concerned.

WASHINGTON, November 11, 1940.

840.48 Refugees/2305a : Telegram

The Acting Secretary of State to the Chargé in the United Kingdom (Johnson)

WASHINGTON, November 16, 1940—7 p. m.

3510. You may, at the request to us of interested Jewish groups in the United States, make a *pro forma* inquiry of the Foreign Office as to the veracity of reports which have been received by Jewish circles from Syria to the effect that the British authorities in Palestine will not permit 1700 refugees of German and Austrian origin to land from a Greek ship now off the Palestine coast and are suggesting that they proceed to Mauritius.

WELLES

840.48 Refugees/2306 : Telegram

The Chargé in the United Kingdom (Johnson) to the Secretary of State

LONDON, November 19, 1940—4 p. m.
[Received November 19—10 : 55 a. m.]

3783. Your 3510, November 16, 7 p. m. Foreign Office indicates informally that report is true and that the British Government contemplates attempting to send on to Mauritius any further shiploads of persons seeking illegal entry into Palestine. They consider this action necessary to discourage further traffic of this character.

Full information has been telegraphed confidentially to British Embassy in Washington. Foreign Office is consulting Colonial Office as to your inquiry and non-confidential reply to your 3510 will be transmitted shortly.

JOHNSON

840.48 Refugees/2307 : Telegram

The Chargé in the United Kingdom (Johnson) to the Secretary of State

LONDON, November 19, 1940—5 p. m.
[Received 12 : 10 p. m.]

3784. Your 3510, November 16, 7 p. m. Am advised by Foreign Office that British Government intends hereafter to refuse admission into Palestine to all illegal immigrants. Accommodation for such persons is to be arranged elsewhere. An announcement of the foregoing is to be made tomorrow in Palestine. British Embassy in Washington has been fully advised of details and instructed to advise you.

JOHNSON

867N.55/213 : Telegram

The Consul General at Jerusalem (Wadsworth) to the Secretary of State

JERUSALEM, November 20, 1940—noon.
[Received 7 p. m.]

165. Referring to my telegram No. 140 of October 17, 2 p. m.

1. On November 1 and 3, two small steamships flying the Panamanian flag, the *Pacific* and the *Mylos* with respectively Greek and mixed Turkish-Bulgarian crews, brought total of almost 1800 intending Jewish illegal immigrants to Haifa, where they are being held and well cared for aboard the detained French passenger liner *Patria*. Embarked last month at Rumanian Danubian ports and largely of Central European origin, many of them are known to have relatives or friends in this country, an advertisement carrying some 1100 of their names having been published in the three leading Hebrew afternoon papers of November 12 with the result that the papers have since been suspended.

2. While the British censorship authorities have prohibited any reference to the matter in the local press or in outgoing news agency cables it has become generally known, as have the facts that the High Commissioner has urged the British Government to authorize deportation aboard the *Patria* to Mauritius and that the Jewish Agency has lodged strong protest here and in London. This has resulted in growing bitterness in local Jewish circles where threats are current of widespread demonstrations similar to those of last March following publication of the land transfer regulations. A general strike has been called from noon to midnight today.

3. Yesterday I learned from reliable official sources that, while the British Colonial Secretary is expected to announce in Parliament this afternoon that the proposed deportation has been decided upon, no serious local disturbances are expected for the reason that the question has been fully thrashed out in London with competent Jewish leaders, in this latter connection I was told in strictest confidence that Dr. Weizmann had "played up very well".

4. Two other similar refugee steamers are known to be approaching Palestine waters, the Panamanian *Atlantic* and the Bulgarian *Pentcho*, carrying a total of almost 2400 persons.

WADSWORTH

840.48 Refugees/2358

Memorandum of Conversation, by Mr. J. Rives Childs of the Division of Near Eastern Affairs

[WASHINGTON,] November 22, 1940.

Mr. Malcolm [22] called and stated that he understood the Department had instructed the American Embassy in London to inquire of the Foreign Office concerning the reported decision that the British authorities in Palestine were refusing to permit illegal Jewish immigrants to land, but were suggesting that they should proceed to Mauritius. Mr. Malcolm stated that he wished to leave the attached memorandum, dated November 22, 1940,[23] which had been received from the Foreign Office on the subject. Mr. Malcolm added that he could leave with us also the attached printed confidential memorandum on Jewish illegal immigration into Palestine,[24] which he would ask us to return to him when we had an opportunity of reading it.

Mr. Malcolm stated that the Jewish [*sic*] were apparently finding it difficult to understand the British policy in this matter, but that it had to be emphasized that very vital issues were at stake, as was explained in the accompanying memorandum.

Mr. Malcolm stated that a copy of the memorandum of November 22, 1940 had been made available to the British Press Service in New York for use as background purposes in dealing with the Press on this subject.

840.48 Refugees/2358

The British Embassy to the Department of State

MEMORANDUM

The problem of illegal immigration into Palestine has given a great deal of trouble in the past especially since the publication of His Majesty's Government's statement of policy in May, 1939, which set a definite limit of 75,000 to further Jewish immigration except with Arab consent. The Zionists have never accepted this decision and ignoring the law of Palestine which regulates immigration by a system of half-yearly quotas, extreme Zionist organizations in Central Europe have organized the transport of considerable numbers of Jews of all ages and both sexes without immigration certificates to the shores of Palestine. These immigrants arrive in unseaworthy vessels generally chartered from Greek shipowners and, if not intercepted and brought into Haifa, hover off the coast at a distance of anything

---

[22] A. C. E. Malcolm, Second Secretary of the British Embassy.
[23] *Infra.*
[24] Not reprinted.

up to 50 miles and disembark their passengers at night in small boats which are left to make their way to the shore. The difficulty of detecting every small boat load by night has led the Palestine Government to pass legislation enabling it to seize any ships carrying prospective illegal immigrants whether they are inside Palestine territorial waters or not. Such ships have hitherto been brought into Haifa harbour, the captain and crew sentenced to long term imprisonment and ships confiscated. There has been no alternative but to release Jewish passengers after necessary period of quarantine and (so far as accommodation is available) of internment to become a burden on the Jewish community, deducting their numbers from the next six months quota.

This procedure, though unsatisfactory, served the purpose before the outbreak of war and in fact had a considerable deterrent effect. Lately, however, the problem has again become acute and under war conditions assumes a graver aspect. There are indications that the Axis powers are encouraging influx of Jews to Palestine (giving them choice of embarking on a ship for Palestine or remaining in a concentration camp) their object being not only to embarrass His Majesty's Government by inflaming Arab sentiment, but to introduce enemy agents into Palestine and the Middle East. To admit into Palestine any further shiploads of illegal immigrants and to allow the law of Palestine to be openly flouted would undoubtedly involve the risk of serious trouble with the Arabs and jeopardize our whole military position in the Middle East.

The Secretary of State for the Colonies has therefore approved strongly the recommendation of the High Commissioner for Palestine that the two shiploads (totalling one thousand seven hundred and seventy) who have already arrived at Haifa should be refused admission to Palestine and should be shipped at the earliest possible moment to Mauritius where it is hoped that provisions can be made for their detention during the period of the war. A further ship carrying Jewish "refugees" has since arrived off Cyprus, having run out of fuel, provisions and water, and unless (as is unlikely) she can be induced or compelled to proceed elsewhere it will be necessary to take her to Haifa and there to arrange for the deportation of the passengers. It is hoped that when it has been made widely known that illegal immigrants will no longer be admitted into Palestine but will be sent abroad for detention, the game will be found to be not worth the candle even with the Axis' encouragement, and traffic will cease; but we must allow for the possibility of having to accommodate anything up to three thousand Jews apart from those who are destined for Mauritius.

The Jews are already making a great grievance about the decision to refuse these people admission into Palestine. They enlarge upon the inhuman turning away of these "refugees from Nazi oppression"; they claim, without foundation, that every Jew has a right to enter Palestine as his homeland and they profess complete disregard to the immigration law of Palestine. They point out that the White Paper of 1939 itself provides for the admission into Palestine of twenty-five thousand refugees (included in the total of seventy-five thousand) but they ignore the proviso that these refugees are only to be admitted when the High Commissioner is satisfied that their maintenance can be assured.

[WASHINGTON,] November 22, 1940.

867N.55/212

The Department of State to the British Embassy

MEMORANDUM

The Department of State is in principle willing that its officers in charge of British interests serve, as indicated in the British Embassy's memorandum of November 11, 1940, as a medium of transmission for the delivery of immigration certificates to children up to fifteen years of age whose admission into Palestine is contemplated by the British authorities. It is understood that the Department's officers will not be called upon to act in a manner requiring interpretation or enforcement of the Palestine immigration law but will merely receive the certificates referred to for delivery to children specifically designated by the Palestine Government upon establishment of their identity and production of certificates of good health. The Department will, of course, instruct its officers to ascertain in advance that the appropriate local authorities entertain no objections before they proceed to act in the manner just outlined.

The Department assumes that it will in due course be informed if the British Government determines to put the contemplated arrangement into effect and that it will be given such general indications of the details of procedure which the British Government wishes observed as will enable the issuance to the Department's officers in charge of British interests of uniform instructions intended for their guidance.

WASHINGTON, November 23, 1940.

867N.55/215 : Telegram

The Consul General at Jerusalem (Wadsworth) to the Secretary of State

JERUSALEM, December 2, 1940—10 a. m.
[Received December 3—1 : 30 a. m.]

175. Supplementing my telegram No. 165 of November 20, noon.

(1) On that afternoon the expected official announcement was made here that the illegal immigrants in question numbering 1,771 and any similar parties which might reach Palestine in the future would be deported and detained in a British colony for the duration of the war. The Jewish protest strike was generally observed but without marked enthusiasm, largely because of dissension among Jewish leaders, many of whom had argued that overt action against British authority in wartime could but harm the Zionist cause.

(2) On November 22, when preparations for the sailing of the *Patria* on November 24 were all but complete, word was received that the 700-ton Panamanian steamship *Atlantic* carrying some 1900 more Jewish refugees from Rumania had been picked up by British naval patrol in Cyprus waters and held at Larnaca. I am informed confidentially that the Governor of Cyprus declined, because of unsanitary conditions on board, to permit its remaining there even temporarily. On the 24th it was brought into Haifa harbor, the sailing of the *Patria* being delayed to permit the transfer thereto of some 500 of its passengers.

(3) The following morning, after some 100 such transfers had been made, an explosion occurred aboard the *Patria* which caused it to sink in 15 minutes, port boats performed excellent rescue work. Of the approximately 1900 refugees on board, 30 are known to have drowned and 2 died in hospital, some 200 are missing, and the others, except for 13 reported to have escaped from Hadassah Hospital have been interned in detention camps. Of the missing the majority are also believed to have escaped. One British policeman and a ship's officer were also lost. The remaining *Atlantic* passengers who were to have been deported aboard a converted freighter have also been detained.

(4) I am assured by the Chief Secretary that the sinking has in no way caused the Government to modify its policy, but that some time must elapse before new arrangements for deportation can be made. Official circles are unanimous in condemning the act as a rank flouting of Government authority outstandingly serious in the light of conditions and increasing shortage of shipping. Responsible Jewish opinion recognizes the force of this view, and the Jewish Agency and other national institutions hotly deny any complicity.

(5) Although suggestions of fifth column sabotage are heard, there is general concurrence that some Jewish group is responsible. Several persons were seen to jump from the ship just before the explosion occurred. A revisionist or labor federation extremist youth group is naturally most suspect. A general staff political intelligence officer has commented categorically to me in this sense, adding that he believed the explosive was taken aboard as the vessel was coaling. However, the Government official in direct charge of frontier control tells me informally "there is not a shred of direct evidence". Both believe it improbable that the Navy will permit any vessel carrying these refugees to transit the Suez Canal.

WADSWORTH

867N.55/216 : Telegram

The Consul General at Jerusalem (Wadsworth) to the Secretary of State

JERUSALEM, December 10, 1940—6 p. m.
[Received December 12—6 : 20 a. m.]

183. Referring to my telegram No. 175 of December 2, 10 a. m.

1. On December 4 the Palestine Government issued an official statement exempting from deportation "as an exceptional act of mercy" the survivors of the steamship *Patria* but no others. The Chief Secretary has informed me in strict confidence that this was done under a decision of a special meeting of the British War Cabinet, that obviously the decision was the result of further representations of Jewish leaders in London and that it was so worded as to convince the High Commissioner and General Wavell [25] that no further discussion of the matter would be entertained.

2. Jewish reaction was one of high appreciation and hope that the Government could be induced on grounds of humanity and principle (that the Jew is in Palestine as of right and not on sufferance) similarly to exempt the 1800 other refugees who had arrived on the steamship *Atlantic*. Arab circles naturally argued that the decision was one more example of the power of Jewish influence on the British Government. British officials generally felt "let down" but the Chief Secretary assured me that no further exemptions would be made and that arrangements were being concluded with General Wavell for deporting the 1800 detainees.

3. Yesterday morning two Dutch ships arrived in Haifa harbor

---

[25] Gen. Sir Archibald P. Wavell, Commanding General of British forces in the Middle East.

which was closely cordoned. Into them the detainees were hurried under strong police escort and the vessels sailed at nightfall. Today, I have just been reliably informed, they safely transited the Suez Canal. I understand the Red Sea convoy by which the detainees will continue their journey to Mauritius should leave Suez tomorrow morning.

4. Reaction among Palestine Jews is one of bitter disappointment. As developments became known in Haifa yesterday afternoon a protest strike spontaneously developed. Last night their National Council published a strong condemnation of "this act which has outraged the national and humanitarian feelings of Palestine Jewry". Today there was a general Jewish strike throughout the country. There is, however, little fear that violent demonstrations will develop. Associated Press correspondent informs me all press cables are held by censor because ship movements are involved.

5. Meanwhile the number of recovered *Patria* victims has mounted to almost 60 and on December 7 a commission headed by a British puisne judge was appointed by the High Commissioner to inquire into and report regarding the circumstances of its sinking.

WADSWORTH

867N.55/218 : Telegram

The Chargé in the United Kingdom (Johnson) to the Secretary of State

LONDON, December 27, 1940—1 p. m.
[Received December 27—8 : 35 a. m.]

4216. Your 3567, November 23, 1 p. m.[26] Foreign Office note dated yesterday expresses appreciation for Department's offer of assistance [27] in transmitting Palestinian immigration certificates. It states that the Department's understanding of the procedure to be followed and the responsibilities involved is entirely correct. The High Commissioner in Palestine has been requested to furnish information concerning the procedure to be followed in connection with the issue of these certificates and a further communication on this subject is promised.

JOHNSON

---

[26] Not printed.
[27] See memorandum of November 23, p. 852.

867N.55/219 : Telegram

The Consul General at Jerusalem (Wadsworth) to the Secretary of State

JERUSALEM, December 30, 1940—noon.
[Received December 31—10 : 55 p. m.]

188. A notice issued December 26th under the Palestine Immigration Ordinance announces that no immigration quota will be prescribed for the current semester ending March 31st next. It then gives information regarding immigration under the preceding semester's quota and for the entire period from April 1, 1939, to September 30, 1940, during which the British White Paper policy of May 1939 has been enforced.

Against 9,400 authorities issued during the [apparent omission] semester only 1,300 persons were able to immigrate. The unused authorities have been extended to March 31 next, after which replacement certificates may be granted "in strictly limited number" only and where admission "will be to the clear advantage of the country".

Against the 75,000 certified to be issued over 5 years, 19,600 authorities were granted; but 28,800 arrivals were recorded. Of the latter some 12,300 were legal immigrants and 16,500 recorded illegal immigrants.

The last figure does not include the 1800 survivors from the steamship *Patria* referred to in recent telegrams nor to an unspecified smaller number of other illegal immigrants permitted to remain during the current semester, all of whom "will be deducted from the next quota".

If these latter be added to the 28,800 recorded arrivals and it be assumed that the approximately 8,000 outstanding authorities are all utilized, there will remain some 37,000 certificates to be issued during the balance of the White Paper 5-year period.

The controlling reasons for not prescribing a current quota are stated to be circumstances of international travel, difficulty of transferring new capital, restricted opportunities for investment and unemployment. December 31, 10 a. m.

WADSWORTH

REPRESENTATIONS REGARDING RESTRICTIVE TRADE MEASURES ADOPTED BY BRITISH AUTHORITIES IN PALESTINE IN VIOLATION OF AMERICAN TREATY RIGHTS [28]

667N.116/64

The Secretary of State to the Ambassador in the United Kingdom (Kennedy)

No. 1305   WASHINGTON, April 2, 1940.

SIR: In the Department's telegram no. 1638 of December 19, 1939,[29] you were requested to address a note to the Foreign Office and to inform the British Government that this Government confidently expected that that Government, in accordance with the obligations under its mandate conventions with the United States, would continue to recognize that American products must be admitted to Palestine and British mandated territories in Africa on a basis of full equality in all respects with British and all other products.

Subsequent to that telegram, the Department was informed by the American Consulate General in Jerusalem, in a despatch of January 23, 1940,[30] that the Palestine authorities were disclaiming "any intent to discriminate in favor of British trade" in the administration of the import licensing system in Palestine. However, Mr. Scott of the Consulate General was informed by Mr. Fletcher, the authority in Palestine administering the import licensing system, that:

"It had been decided to stop the importation of apples from the United States and Canada. When I pressed him for an answer as to whether, when the Australian apple export season begins, licenses would be granted for Australian apples, he replied that while the question had not yet definitely arisen he would have to admit that in all probability importers would be able to obtain licenses for Australian apples."

The Department decided that note should be taken of Mr. Fletcher's statements to Mr. Scott and, accordingly, in a letter dated February 29, 1940 [30] to Mr. Wadsworth, the American Consul General in Jerusalem, he was instructed to inform Mr. Fletcher "that the issuance by the authorities of licenses for the importation of any commodity such as apples from a source other than the United States, when permission for importation of the like commodity from the United States had been previously withheld, would be regarded as a breach of American treaty rights in Palestine".

The Department is now informed in a despatch No. 1225 of February 20, 1940 [30] from the American Consulate General in Jerusalem, a

---

[28] Continued from *Foreign Relations*, 1939, vol. IV, pp. 811–816.
[29] *Ibid.*, p. 815.
[30] Not printed.

copy of which was forwarded you by that office, that licenses have been refused an applicant desirous of importing apples from the United States although licenses to import into Palestine apples from Australia, Rumania and Turkey have been granted. The same despatch reports that a license applied for by an American firm to import Kolynos toothpaste from the United States has been refused, although the same firm was notified that an application to import the same toothpaste from the United Kingdom would be granted. The Consulate General reports at the same time that the Palestine agent of the R. J. Reynolds Tobacco Company has been refused permission to import Camel cigarettes.

You should address a note to the Foreign Office reciting the foregoing facts and stating that you have been instructed to make a formal protest against the action of the Palestine authorities in withholding licenses for the importation of commodities from the United States when permission is granted for the importation of similar commodities from sources other than the United States. You should add that such action is, of course, inconsistent with the terms of the American-British Mandate Convention of December 3, 1924,[31] assuring American trade with Palestine equality of treatment with that of the Mandatory Power or of any foreign state, and that this Government must hold the British Government responsible for any losses sustained by American interests in Palestine or in British mandated territories in Africa as a result of such violations of American treaty rights.

Please keep the Department informed of all developments in connection with this matter.

Very truly yours,   For the Secretary of State:
                                     R. WALTON MOORE

667N.116/68

The Ambassador in the United Kingdom (Kennedy) to the Secretary of State

No. 5043   LONDON, April 9, 1940.
                                     [Received April 23.]

SIR: Referring to my telegram No. 883 of April 9, 1940 [32] reporting the receipt of a note outlining the British Government's position with regard to the effect on American commercial rights of the exchange control and import licence system in Palestine, in other British mandated territories and in the British territories within the Congo Basin, I have the honor to enclose a copy of the note in question which is dated April 8, 1940 (File No. W 5104/280/49).

---

[31] *Foreign Relations*, 1924, vol. II, p. 212.
[32] *Ante*, p. 121.

There is also enclosed, in order to complete the Department's files, a copy of note No. 1716 of December 21, 1939, in which this Mission brought to the attention of the British Foreign Office the considerations embodied in the Department's telegram No. 1638 of December 19, 7: 00 p. m.,[33] regarding the effect on American commercial rights of the exchange control and import license system established in Palestine.

Previous correspondence referring to questions touched on in the enclosed note includes the Department's instruction No. 1134 of December 26, 1939 [34] (File No. 648T.006/), its telegram No. 38 of January 6, 4: 00 p. m.,[35] and this Mission's despatch No. 4392 of January 17, 1940.[35]

Respectfully yours,   For the Ambassador:

HERSCHEL V. JOHNSON

[Enclosure 1]

The British Secretary of State for Foreign Affairs (Halifax) to the American Ambassador (Kennedy)

No. W 5104/280/49   [LONDON,] 8 April, 1940.

YOUR EXCELLENCY: In Mr. Herschel Johnson's note No. 1716 of the 21st December, 1939,[36] he was good enough to draw my attention to the establishment by the Palestine Government of an import license system and to state that the United States Government were unable to recognize the necessity or justification for the administration of the exchange control and import license system in a manner to give preference to imports from British Empire sources, with a resultant discrimination against imports from the United States of America.

2. I would ask Your Excellency to assure the United States Government, first, that His Majesty's Government in the United Kingdom are determined to respect the rights of the United States of America in Palestine to the utmost of their ability and anxious to justify, or alternatively to rectify, any situation of fact or law which might seem inconsistent with those rights; and secondly, that whatever other motives may have led to the adoption of the measures to which Mr. Herschel Johnson's note refers, a desire to increase the export trade to Palestine of the United Kingdom or any other part of the British Empire at the expense of other countries was not among them.

---

[33] *Foreign Relations*, 1939, vol. IV, p. 815.
[34] Not printed.
[35] *Ante*, p. 118.
[36] Enclosure 2, *infra*.

3. I am confident that the United States Government will share the view of His Majesty's Government in the United Kingdom that the paramount obligation imposed upon the Mandatory Power by the Mandate for Palestine is to protect the interests of Palestine and its inhabitants, and that the rights conferred by the Mandate or by international instruments concluded within the framework of the Mandate upon third parties (whether these parties be the Mandatory Power itself, States Members of the League of Nations, countries like the United States of America with rights analogous to those of States Members or non-Members) must in case of conflict defer to this obligation.

4. The interests of Palestine and its inhabitants require first and foremost that Palestine territory should be protected from foreign aggression and it might well be argued that so long as the possibility of aggression continued this would in itself justify the Mandatory Power in taking any step, even if that step were at variance with the letter of its obligations under the Mandate to States Members or States with analogous rights, which might directly or indirectly increase its ability to protect this territory. His Majesty's Government, however, do not wish to rely unduly upon this general consideration in the present case, since the measures to which Mr. Herschel Johnson drew attention can, in their opinion, be justified by the more particular considerations arising out of the economic and financial interest of Palestine which are explained below, but they nevertheless regard it as lying at the basis of the Mandatory system.

5. It must be remembered that the export trade of Palestine has been seriously damaged by the war. As a result the purchasing power of the country has been greatly diminished and strict control of the import trade is necessary. In particular the very limited quantities of non-sterling currency which are now being received render the utmost economy in their use essential. The whole basis of the present system of control is that the best use should be made of the purchasing power available to Palestine and licenses are issued solely with that object in view. The legislation which has been introduced is non-discriminatory, the licenses being granted for imports both from the British Empire and from foreign sources, and although it is no doubt the case that the Palestine authorities are able to grant import licenses more freely for goods from most Empire sources than from foreign countries, since these goods are paid for in sterling, this does not apply to the whole British Empire as such, Canadian imports for example being treated on the same basis as United States imports in view of the similarity of the exchange position of Canada to that of the United States.

6. As regards United States goods in particular, the United States Government will no doubt realize that the balance of trade between the United States and Palestine has in the past been very favourable to the former, imports from the United States to Palestine in the three years 1936 to 1938 having averaged over £1,000,000 per annum, while the total exports to the United States from Palestine averaged under £100,000 per annum and has since fallen much below that figure. As Palestine currency is based on sterling, the large excess of imports from the United States during this and previous periods was in effect being paid for by the purchase of United States dollars with the proceeds of Palestine exports to other countries, that is (except to the extent that dollars were provided by an import of capital from the United States) mainly with the sterling proceeds of exports to the United Kingdom, the principal importer of Palestine products.

7. If, therefore, the emergency measures in force throughout the British Empire generally were not to be put into force in Palestine, the effect would be that the United Kingdom would have to provide Palestine importers with dollar exchange to finance Palestine imports from the United States in excess of those balanced by exports to the United States. The United States Government are aware that the United Kingdom is finding great difficulty in providing foreign exchange to meet her own essential imports, and she cannot continue to provide unrestricted exchange to meet Palestine imports of non-essential commodities from the United States or other countries from which Palestine cannot import without creating a drain on sterling.

8. It is not desired, nor would it be possible, to reduce United States exports to Palestine to the level of the Palestine exports to the United States and so to remove all exchange burdens on this account from the United Kingdom, but I trust that the United States Government will agree that it is inevitable that the Palestine authorities should not be able to grant import licenses for all applications whatsoever for imports from the United States, and reasonable in the circumstances that they should not be expected to try to do so.

9. I trust that these explanations will reassure the United States Government as to the manner in which His Majesty's Government and the Palestine administration intend to use the powers conferred upon them by the Palestine import and exchange control legislation, and I would ask Your Excellency to add, when transmitting them to the United States Government, that His Majesty's Government will gladly furnish any further explanations on points of detail which the United States Government may desire.

10. The same considerations apply *mutatis mutandis* to the position in other Mandated Territories administered by His Majesty's Government in the United Kingdom, and in the British territories within

the Congo Basin, regarding which an *Aide-Mémoire* was received from the United States Embassy on the 16th January.[38]

I have [etc.]   (For the Secretary of State)
                                                      N. B. Ronald

[Enclosure 2]

The American Chargé (Johnson) to the British Secretary of State for Foreign Affairs (Halifax)

No. 1716   London, December 21, 1939.

My Lord: Under instructions from my Government, based on information received from the American Consul General at Jerusalem, I have the honor to invite your Lordship's attention to the establishment by the Palestine Government of an import licence system, effective December 11, 1939, applicable to some 422 items of the total of 760 items of merchandise in the Palestine Customs classification list, including almost all articles imported from the United States.

The Department of State is also informed that in an interview on December 12, 1939 between a representative of the American Consulate General and the Economic Adviser of the Palestine Government, the latter stated that he was unable to give assurances that American trade will not be subject to restrictions placing it on a less favorable footing than British trade with Palestine.

The Economic Adviser is stated to have explained that the policy of the Palestine Government, in accordance with instructions from the British Government, is to accord preference to imports from British Empire sources, such a policy having been justified by the Economic Adviser on the ground that the British Government cannot cut Palestine adrift during the war but must afford its currency and economic interests the protection of emergency measures applied throughout the British Empire.

Any effort on the part of the Palestine authorities to discriminate against American imports into Palestine with a view to reducing the demand for foreign exchange or for exchange from countries outside the sterling exchange control area would, of course, be viewed by my Government as violation of American treaty rights in Palestine and particularly those embodied in Article 2 of the American British Mandate Convention of December 3, 1924, and the related Article 18 of the Mandate assuring American trade with Palestine equality of treatment with that of the mandatory power or of any foreign state.

While the United States Government is not disposed to raise any question regarding the adoption of measures in Palestine which may

---

[38] *Ante,* p. 119.

be reasonably necessary and consistent with the status of Palestine and the obligations of the British Government as mandatory for that territory, it cannot overlook illegal and unwarranted interferences with American treaty rights and it does not find itself able to recognize either the necessity or justification for the administration of the exchange control and import licence system in Palestine in a manner to give preference to imports from British Empire sources, with a resultant discrimination against imports from the United States.

The foregoing observations are deemed equally applicable, *mutatis mutandis*, to British mandated territories in Africa where a control import licence system is understood to have been introduced similar to that in Palestine.

I have the honor to add that the United States Government feels confident that, in accordance with the obligations under its mandate conventions with the United States, the British Government will continue to recognize that American products must be admitted to Palestine and British mandated territories in Africa on a basis of full equality in all respects with British and all other products.

I have [etc.]   HERSCHEL V. JOHNSON

667N.116/67 : Telegram

The Ambassador in the United Kingdom (*Kennedy*) *to the Secretary of State*

LONDON, April 20, 1940—4 p. m.
[Received April 20—10 : 48 a. m.]

1015. Your mail instruction 1305, April 2, and my 883 of April 9th [39] regarding discrimination against American products in Palestine. Since Embassy's despatch of April 9 enclosing Foreign Office note giving British position on this question crossed your instruction 1305, unless otherwise instructed, [apparent omission] pending opportunity for Department to consider British note.

KENNEDY

648T.116/18

Memorandum by Mr. Gordon P. Merriam of the Division of Near Eastern Affairs

[WASHINGTON,] December 19, 1940.

I asked Mr. Ward [40] for his views on the desirability of forwarding to the British Government a note such as the one drafted last summer,[41]

---

[39] *Ante*, pp. 857 and 121, respectively.
[40] Frank X. Ward, Assistant to the Legal Adviser.
[41] Not printed.

pressing the British on the question of trade restrictions which discriminate against imports of American goods into Palestine, British mandated territory in Africa, and British territory in the Congo Basin.

Mr. Ward considers that we have a clear case against the British of violation of treaty rights. This was made a matter of record by the Embassy's communications to the Foreign Office of December 21, 1939 and January 16, 1940.[42] After initialling the draft of a further communication, Mr. Ward came to the conclusion that, in view of the difficulties under which the British were operating, their position, while legally unjustifiable, was reasonable because the conservation and channelling of available dollar exchange to pay for armament manufactured in the United States was for them a matter of survival which outweighed the legal aspects of the matter and could even be considered as in our own basic self-interest. Moreover, since at that time there was no way to ship American goods to Palestine, the matter was in large part academic. Accordingly, Mr. Ward felt that it would be best to hold the instruction in abeyance.[43]

In the meantime the situation as regards Palestine has changed in two respects. The authorities there, from experience gained over the past few months, have decided that certain commodities, regarded as essential, can be secured from the United States and from no other source. They are allowing, or will allow, these to come in. Moreover, the question of transport from the United States, while far from satisfactory, is not quite as difficult as before. These are, however, minor factors.

Mr. Ward notes, however, that present developments point to the definite possibility or likelihood that in the near future, by one means or another, British war requirements from the United States will be financed by this country. If and when that occurs, it is to be presumed that the British need of dollar exchange will be greatly reduced. For that reason, and because of the important financial service which would be rendered by this country, Mr. Ward considers that when such an arrangement is in definite form and working order we could very properly approach the British again in regard to the discriminations against our trade, but he does not believe the time to do so has arrived quite yet.

We did, of course, press the French on the matter in August and apparently got no reply whatever.[44] The French were then no longer fighting or receiving war materials or much of anything else from the United States. Another justification for handling the British and

[42] Ante, pp. 862 and 119, respectively.
[43] The instruction was not sent.
[44] See pp. 926 ff.

the French differently in the matter, which seems to bulk rather largely in Mr. Ward's eyes, is that the French reply to our original representations was short, vague, and nasty, whereas the British reply gave every evidence of careful consideration on their part and of a desire to fulfil their legal obligations to the greatest possible extent, and they went to some pains to justify their departure therefrom by overwhelming necessity.

NON-RECOGNITION BY THE UNITED STATES OF THE RIGHT OF THE BRITISH GOVERNMENT TO ESTABLISH A NAVAL CONTRABAND CONTROL IN PALESTINE

740.00112 European War 1939/947a : Telegram

The Secretary of State to the Consul General at Jerusalem (Wadsworth)

WASHINGTON, January 15, 1940.

The Department assumes that, in view of the absence of reports from you on the subject, the British prize court and contraband control base reported to have been established in Palestine by the British Government have not attempted to function.

HULL

740.00112 European War 1939/956 : Telegram

The Consul General at Jerusalem (Wadsworth) to the Secretary of State

JERUSALEM, January 18, 1940—4 p. m.
[Received January 18—2 : 45 p. m.]

2. The following reply to the Department's telegram of January 15 is based on information informally given me yesterday by the Attorney General.

By Admiralty warrant issued in London September 3 Supreme Court of Palestine was authorized to proceed on all matters of Prize Court. British Prize Court rules are applicable and the Attorney General is designated to conduct proceedings on behalf of the Crown. On the same date a British naval contraband control base was established at Haifa.

Only 10 ships all west bound (8 Italian, 1 Dutch and 1 Swedish) have thus far been diverted to Haifa. All were boarded in the Red Sea and a British naval officer accompanied by two or three ratings put in charge.

The first six ships, handled prior to December 31, were released after unloading alleged contraband cargo. This cargo, seized by the naval control officer, was turned over to a civilian detaining officer representing the Attorney General, and the latter issued through the court registrar writs to all known interested persons. As yet, however, no case has come on for trial and the Attorney General expects that through sources out of court a considerable part of the detained goods will be released after study of pertinent documents.

The first week in January the "hold-back" guarantee system was introduced under orders from London. Under this system the next three ships (all Italian) and their cargoes were held only a few hours, the guarantee of the master and agent, countersigned by the Italian Consul, being taken that their alleged contraband cargo would not be delivered to the consignees except upon release of the British Ministry of Economic Warfare to be communicated through the British Embassy in Rome and if not so released would be returned to Haifa.

Under this system with which the Italian Government is cooperating the alleged contraband is detained in Government warehouse after unloading at Italian port.

Were an American ship to be similarly diverted to Haifa a similar guarantee would be accepted but my countersignature would not be taken unless believed by the Department helpful to American shipping interests.

The last ship handled was the *Conte Verdant* brought into Haifa yesterday morning with alleged contraband cargo for transshipment at Italian port to an American bound vessel. It was released after 3 hours detention on guarantee that the transshipment would be witnessed by a British Consul.

The Attorney General believes that under the new system only contraband cargo consigned to persons on the British blacklist will be detained at Haifa.

WADSWORTH

740.00112 European War 1939/956 : Telegram

The Secretary of State to the Consul General at Jerusalem
(Wadsworth)

WASHINGTON, January 23, 1940.

Your 2, January 18, 4 p. m. You should keep the Department fully and currently informed of all important action taken by the British Government tending to give Palestine a belligerent status. You should report in particular at once any effort on the part of the British authorities to extend any assumed jurisdiction of the British Prize Court in Palestine or the British contraband control base at Haifa over American vessels or goods.

The Department desires that you refrain from countersigning any guarantee under the arrangements referred to in your telegram or from taking any action that might possibly be construed as implying acquiescence by this Government or its representative in the application to Palestine of any belligerent measure.

HULL

740.00112 European War 1939/1082

The Secretary of State to the Consul General at Jerusalem
(Wadsworth)

WASHINGTON, March 22, 1940.

SIR: The Department has received your despatch no. 1201 of January 22, 1940,[45] quoting a telegram forwarded by you under date of January 18, 1940 regarding the British Contraband Control Base and Prize Court in Palestine and containing supplementary information furnished you by the Attorney General for facilitating the release of goods which may be detained by the Contraband Control at Haifa.

In consonance with the position indicated in the Department's telegram to you of January 23, 1940, and in order to avoid any possible implication that your transmission to the Department, at the suggestion of the Attorney General, of the information mentioned in the preceding paragraph constitutes acquiescence in the establishment of a British Contraband Control Base in Palestine, you are requested to inform the Attorney General that, in as much as this Government does not recognize the right of the British Government to establish a Naval Contraband Control in Palestine, it cannot, of course, give any recognition to any regulation or procedure adopted in connection with such control.

As you are no doubt aware, one of the practical consequences which would result from the recognition by this Government of the belligerent status of Palestine would be the application to that territory of the pertinent provisions of the Neutrality Act of 1939,[45a] including the prohibition of American vessels calling at Palestinian ports.

Very truly yours,   For the Secretary of State:
A. A. BERLE, JR.

---

[45] Not printed.
[45a] 54 Stat. 4.

OPPOSITION BY THE DEPARTMENT OF STATE TO THE GRANTING OF RED CROSS AID TO PALESTINE WITHOUT REFERENCE TO THE RELIEF NEEDS OF THE NEAR EAST AS A WHOLE

867N.48/53

Memorandum by the Chief of the Division of Near Eastern Affairs (Murray) to the Under Secretary of State (Welles)

[WASHINGTON,] September 23, 1940.

MR. WELLES: Mr. Ernest J. Swift, Vice Chairman in charge of Insular and Foreign Operations, of the American National Red Cross, called me by telephone this morning to state that, at the instance of Rabbi Silver,[46] a donation of $25,000 had been promised to the Jewish Agency in Palestine for the relief of sufferers from the recent Italian bombing raids in that country. Mr. Swift wished to know whether the above-mentioned amount could be transmitted by the Department to the American Consul General in Palestine for delivery to the Jewish Agency for relief purposes among the Jews.

I inquired of Mr. Swift whether it had not been the custom of the American Red Cross to ask the advice of the Department prior to the granting of donations of this kind and he said that it was but that the matter had been put through hurriedly last Saturday morning before the Department could be consulted.

I pointed out, in this connection, to Mr. Swift that, while there had as yet been only one bombing of the Jewish city of Tel Aviv, Palestine, Haifa had already been bombed three times with almost the same number of casualties among the Arabs and, in view of the fact that Haifa is one of the terminals of the Iraq Petroleum Company's pipeline to the Mediterranean and has large quantities of oil stored there in addition to the operation of its refinery, it appeared not unlikely that there would be further and more severe bombings at Haifa in the future with heavy loss of life among the overwhelmingly Arab population of the town.

I also inquired of Mr. Swift as to whether any thought had been given to transmitting funds for relief in Palestine to a relief organization administered by the British, who are the responsible authorities in the country, possibly to some British Red Cross organization there. I added that after all the Jewish Agency was exclusively a political organization designed to further the establishment of a national home in Palestine for the Jewish people and that it would appear highly improper for an American Consular Officer in that country to use exclusively for Jewish relief, funds raised in this country for general relief purposes at home or abroad. Such action would, I felt sure, create a deplorable impression not only among the non-Jewish two-thirds of the population of the country but also among British Gov-

---

[46] Rabbi Abba Hillel Silver, National Chairman of the United Palestine Appeal.

ernment officials and could scarcely fail to be compromising to Mr. Wadsworth [47] in his official capacity.

I added further that it seemed somewhat surprising that the American Red Cross should be donating $25,000 for the relief of the Jewish victims of the Italian bombings in Palestine where about one hundred had been killed when only $5,000 was originally donated to Turkey last winter after the earthquake in Anatolia when nearly 40,000 people were killed. While this sum was eventually increased to $10,000, our representatives in Turkey reported later that the assistance coming from this country during that appalling disaster compared unfavorably with the aid rendered by several other countries.

I have discussed this matter meanwhile with Mr. Berle [48] and he has talked with Mr. Norman Davis.[49] As a result of this discussion, it was agreed that the matter should be reopened with Rabbi Silver, informing him that it would not be feasible to donate the sum in question exclusively for Jewish relief in Palestine, and a means is being sought to generalize the use of funds for the relief of victims regardless of race or religion.

WALLACE MURRAY

867N.48/34a : Telegram

The Secretary of State to the Consul General at Jerusalem
(Wadsworth)

WASHINGTON, September 23, 1940—6 p. m.

The American Red Cross has received appeals that it make available funds for the relief of those stricken by air raid attacks in Palestine and it is considering the donation of $25,000 for such a purpose.

Please telegraph the Department whether the Palestine Red Cross mentioned in your despatch no. 1247 of March 21, 1940 [50] is adequately organized to ensure an efficient and impartial distribution of funds which might be made available by the American Red Cross, bearing in mind that the distribution would have to be made without distinction of religion and race. If in your opinion the Palestine Red Cross is not adequate, the Department desires your recommendation concerning other organizations through which such distribution might be made.

Please inform the Department also whether the British authorities have made plans for the relief of those affected by the air raid attacks and, if so, the extent of the financial aid envisaged.

HULL

---

[47] George Wadsworth, Consul General at Jerusalem.
[48] Adolf A. Berle, Jr., Assistant Secretary of State.
[49] Chairman, American Red Cross.
[50] Not printed.

867N.48/36 : Telegram

*The Consul General at Jerusalem (Wadsworth) to the Secretary
of State*

JERUSALEM, September 27, 1940—2 p. m.
[Received September 28—8 : 15 a. m.]

123. Referring to Department's telegram of September 23, 6 p. m.

1. In conversation yesterday with the Chief Secretary and confirmed today by informal personal note after discussion with the High Commissioner, he expressed keen appreciation of the provisional offer of American Red Cross funds and termed the suggested amount of $25,000 "very handsome indeed".

2. At the same time, he said, he felt it only fair to add that the Palestine Government did not view the situation resulting from the air raids to date on Haifa and that on Tel Aviv as being in the nature of an emergency such as would ordinarily warrant an appeal for Red Cross assistance from abroad.

3. The immediate needs of victims of the raids and their dependents, he explained, had thus far been cared for by local social welfare organizations, notably the Tel Aviv and Haifa municipalities, aided chiefly by Jewish organizations, the expense being borne from funds already at their disposal supplemented by a special Government grant of 2000 to the Tel Aviv municipality, by donations from local Red Cross funds of 500 each to Haifa and Tel Aviv municipalities, by a similar donation from Hadassah to the latter and by small gifts from many individuals wishing to show their sympathy for the victims.

4. Evacuation, and finally medical aid and direct relief to the air raid victims.

5. In the last mentioned field, he said, the Government is preparing a scheme based on current British practice and which will be retroactive for the payment of compensation to civilian victims, but this may be restricted to persons engaged in work contributing to the prosecution of the war or in vital industries and in transport in particular areas.

6. Thus far, we estimated roughly, there have been in the 8 raids on Haifa some 85 fatal casualties. In that on Tel Aviv there were 124. Of all these, however, but few would be considered victims in the sense of such a scheme. The same may be said of the somewhat lesser number who suffered serious injury.

7. There is no Palestine Red Cross but, in addition to the military service unit of the British Red Cross mentioned in my despatch under reference, there has been established a joint organization of the British Red Cross and Order of St. John of Jerusalem under the presidency of Lady MacMichael and the chairmanship of the Financial Secretary of the Government.

8. It was this organization which made from funds previously collected locally the two mentioned LP500 donations for expenditure by competent municipal agencies in Haifa and Tel Aviv. While it has not as yet seen the need for a centralized program of direct relief of air raid victims it could readily undertake and ensure through such agencies the impartial distribution of American Red Cross funds both for that specific purpose and, if desired, for general emergency needs of the Jewish and Arab communities such as those mentioned in paragraph 4 above.

WADSWORTH

867N.48/41

Memorandum of Conversation, by Mr. J. Rives Childs of the Division of Near Eastern Affairs

[WASHINGTON,] October 8, 1940.

Participants: Rabbi Breslau, of the Zionist Organization of America
Mr. Montor, Director of the United Palestine Appeal
(and also of the United Jewish Appeal)
Mr. Murray
Mr. Alling [51]
Mr. Childs

Rabbi Breslau and Mr. Montor stated they had been for some time in touch with the Red Cross with a view to Red Cross assistance for Palestine; that they had obtained what they regarded as a commitment from the Red Cross for the allocation of a sum of $25,000 for Palestine but that they had learned within the past few days some questions had been raised by the Department, first as to the distribution of such a sum among Arabs as well as Jews and, secondly, as to the advisability of extending the scope of the aid to include Egypt as well as Palestine.

Mr. Murray stated that he welcomed their visit as he thought it would afford an opportunity for a meeting of minds on the subject and would promote a clarification of our respective points of view. He added that when the question of Red Cross aid in Palestine had first come to the notice of the Department, Mr. Berle, as the executive officer having oversight over the Division of Near Eastern Affairs, had desired to consider the problem as a whole in relationship to the Near East. In such a survey a number of considerations had obtruded, including the fact that a neighboring country, Egypt, had suffered and was liable to suffer equally if not greater from the war than Palestine. It was pointed out in that connection that while

---

[51] Paul H. Alling, Assistant Chief of the Division of Near Eastern Affairs.

there had been only ten bombings of Palestine towns, Alexandria alone had suffered more than thirty bombings with a considerable loss of life, necessitating the evacuation of more than a third of the population of some 600,000 of that city.

Mr. Montor stated that he thought it would contribute to a clarification of the position of the United Palestine Appeal with reference to Red Cross aid for Palestine if he sketched briefly the background of that question. He observed that as early as April when the appropriation of a fifty million dollar grant by Congress to the Red Cross for war relief was under consideration the United Palestine Appeal had approached the President concerning the making available of a part of this for Jewish relief. The President had stated that the Red Cross would give consideration to Jewish needs as a part of the whole problem of war relief. Before the bombings in Palestine they had approached the Red Cross and had pointed out the pressing need of relief for those stricken by the war who had sought haven in Palestine. They had been concerned with that problem much before the bombings in Palestine and Egypt had taken place. The conversations with the Red Cross on the subject had been concerned with the alleviation of that general problem rather than with the special problem created by the bombings.

Mr. Murray observed that the problem as it had been presented to us by the Red Cross was one viewed in the light of the bombing of Tel Aviv, that we had understood that relief had been sought exclusively for the relief of the Jewish victims of that air raid and that it was felt that any restriction of Red Cross aid to only one element of the population in Palestine would have repercussions prejudicial to the British whose position was hanging in the balance, prejudicial to our own interests and prejudicial no less to Jewish interests. We had telegraphed to our Consul General in Jerusalem at the request of the Red Cross and he had consulted with the Jewish Agency and the Chief Secretary of the Palestine Government. The Chief Secretary had stated to the Consul General that the emergency was not such as would ordinarily warrant an appeal to the Red Cross and it would appear also from the statements made by the Chief Secretary to the Consul General that the Mandatory Power and local organizations were dealing adequately with the situation.

Mr. Montor replied that he thought that the British authorities might be deliberately minimizing the needs of Palestine out of a desire not to have to admit that the needs were greater than their own resources could meet. He added that he had understood from the Red Cross, in explanation of the difficulties that had developed incident to the extension of the promised Red Cross aid for Palestine, that a political angle had developed incident to the question. Mr.

Montor stated that he wished to make it quite plain that his organization was not seeking, and would not seek, to press the Red Cross to make an allocation of funds or of aid to Palestine which the American Government might consider contrary to the interests of the British cause or contrary to the interests of this Government.

Mr. Murray answered that the attitude expressed by Mr. Montor made it easier for us to see eye to eye. Mr. Murray continued by setting forth the larger aspects of the question, that the problem of relief for Palestine could not be isolated from the larger problem of relief for Egypt as well. There was stressed the importance of the world of Egypt, Iraq, Saudi Arabia and Yemen to Britain, the unfavorable repercussions which a grant to Palestine alone would have on that world. It was noted that in 1938 the King of Saudi Arabia had addressed himself to the President [52] expressing his concern over the attitude of this Government toward the Arabs. More recently there had been disquieting reports of a pro-German tendency of King Ibn Saud. It was pointed out that the Suez Canal was flanked by Egypt and that the Mosul oil fields and pipelines were in Arab territory; that Aden, important gateway to the Red Sea, was encompassed by Arabs. These considerations made it essential that nothing should be done to add to Britain's difficulties in the Near East, where the outcome of the battle in Egypt was only a little less vital to the British than the battle in Britain itself.

Mr. Montor stated he would like to interject the comment whether it was not more advisable for Britain to concern itself with the Jews in Palestine on whose loyalty it could count rather than to be concerned for the Arabs whose loyalty was uncertain. He also observed that Egypt was an independent country which had developed its own social services but Palestine was dependent for most of its social services on non-governmental organizations.

It was observed to Mr. Montor in that connection that the Egyptian Fellaheen who might be bombed would hardly be disposed to concern themselves with abstract considerations of governmental polity. It was observed also that our Consul General in Jerusalem had recently quoted the Palestine press as recognizing that Palestine's frontier was no longer at Sinai but on the Libyan frontier. It was further observed that if Egypt fell Palestine would inevitably fall with it and that therefore Palestine's fate was bound up with Egypt.

Rabbi Breslau inquired whether it might not be well to suggest to the Red Cross that they send an investigator to the Near East to study the problem of relief on the spot. Mr. Murray raised the question whether the needs in the Near East could be in any way comparable with those of Europe and particularly of London and else-

---

[52] *Foreign Relations*, 1938, vol. ΙΙ, p. 994.

where in England. He added further that established Jewish agencies in Palestine were excellently equipped to deal with the relief of those war refugees who might be finding their way to Palestine; that he could not imagine any war areas where refugees might find better equipped facilities for their aid than were to be found already in Palestine.

Mr. Montor stated that he felt Rabbi Breslau and himself had greatly profited from the extended discussion which had taken place. He had at first suggested the Jewish Agency as a suitable instrument through which Red Cross aid might be dispensed in Palestine, not with any thought of confining such aid to Jews alone but because the Government and the Arabs had no such organizations as Hadassah capable of dealing with the relief problem. He entirely shared the opinion that had been expressed that any aid given to Palestine should be extended to Arab and Jew alike. He added that he and Rabbi Breslau had come to the Department seeking enlightenment and instructions on how best to proceed and they were desirous of deferring in all respects to the opinions of the Government.

Mr. Murray expressed gratification at their attitude and said a telegram had gone out at the suggestion of the Red Cross to our Legation in Cairo [53] requesting a report on the situation in that country with reference to war relief. It was added that it was believed best to suspend consideration of Palestine relief until the report from Cairo had been received and we were in a position to consider the problem in its larger Near Eastern aspects.

Rabbi Breslau and Mr. Montor expressed themselves as in full agreement with this course.

883.48/7a : Telegram

The Secretary of State to the Minister in Egypt (Fish)

WASHINGTON, October 8, 1940—1 p. m.

113. For your confidential information, the American Red Cross is contemplating the donation of 25,000 dollars for war relief in Palestine, including in particular the relief of those stricken by air raid attacks in that country.

The Department is of the opinion that, for numerous reasons, it would be inadvisable for the Red Cross to attempt to isolate the relief problem in Palestine from the larger problem of war relief in the Near East, including in particular Egypt. The Department has in mind in that connection the reports which have been received from Egypt of the repeated bombing of Alexandria and of the evacua-

---

[53] *Infra.*

tion of a large proportion of the inhabitants of that city. It is believed, accordingly, that the war relief problem in Egypt is actually as well as potentially as serious, if not more serious than that of Palestine, and that contributions made by the Red Cross to Palestine alone would have most undesirable repercussions in Egypt as well as in other countries of the Near East.

In order to assist the Red Cross in reaching a decision you are requested to telegraph the Department as soon as possible (*a*) an estimate of the total number of civilian casualties resulting from Italian bombings in Egypt; (*b*) an estimate of the civilian property loss; (*c*) an estimate of the number of people who have evacuated their homes in consequence of the bombings of Egyptian towns and (*d*) the approximate amount of financial aid which the Egyptian Government and local organizations have provided for war relief.

The Department desires also your opinions and recommendations, based on all the considerations involved, regarding a possible allotment by the Red Cross for Egypt. In the event the Red Cross may find it possible to make a donation for Egypt in addition to that contemplated for Palestine the Department has in mind suggesting the Red Crescent as the agency through which the sum might most appropriately be administered. Your recommendations in this particular are also desired, bearing in mind that the Red Cross would expect an efficient and impartial administration of the funds.

HULL

883.48/9 : Telegram

The Minister in Egypt (Fish) to the Secretary of State

CAIRO, October 15, 1940—9 a. m.
[Received 8 : 10 p. m.]

243. Department's telegram No. 113, October 8, 1 p. m. Upon discreet discussion of the war relief problem in Egypt with several Egyptian officials and the Comptroller General of the Red Crescent the distinct impression was given that the existing relief question here is not regarded with serious concern and that there is no conscious need for further measures to meet the situation at this time.

As regards the four points on which information was requested the following observations were made by the officials consulted: (*a*) casualties resulting from bombings in Egypt have been small; (*b*) civilian property loss has been also small and a recent proposal made to the Prime Minister for Government compensation for such losses was shelved on the ground that the matter was not sufficiently consequential; (*c*) evacuees from Alexandria are estimated to have reached about 200,000 and from Cairo about 120,000 by August 1 but large numbers have since returned to both cities. It is to be noted that this evacuation movement was almost exclusively in anticipation of danger rather than in consequence of actual bombing. Casualties in Alexandria have usually been cared for by Government hospitals and dispensaries. The only assistance rendered by the Red Crescent has been donation of 500 Egyptian pounds to the Ministry of the Interior for relief of evacuees with an offer to provide additional funds if necessary but no such a request has been made.

In the light of the foregoing it is my considered opinion that there is no present need for outside assistance to meet the present relief situation in Egypt. However, the trend of present developments is such that an intensification of hostilities, with greatly increased loss of civilian life and property, is not improbable. In that event a very vital need for outside assistance might well result and it is respectfully suggested that the offer of aid by the American Red Cross be held in abeyance pending such an eventuality. At that time it is believed that the Red Crescent, which is a semi-official agency and whose head is Dr. Aly Ibrahim Pasha, Minister of Public Health, would be the appropriate agency through which to work.

The above recommendation is based entirely on the facts of the local situation and does not take into consideration the unhappy comparison which would very probably be drawn if relief were offered in Palestine and not here, in which respect I am in entire accord with the Department's views. At the risk of possibly seeming to express views not in my competence might I suggest that in Palestine as in Egypt the actual damage done thus far may be but a relatively mild foretaste of much more serious events to come, and that under these considerations it might seem advisable to leave relief in both areas to local agencies and reserve possible American assistance for the future.

FISH

867N.48/36 : Telegram

The Secretary of State to the Consul General at Jerusalem
(Wadsworth)

WASHINGTON, November 9, 1940—6 p. m.

Your 123, September 27, 2 p. m. In a letter which Rabbi Silver has addressed to the Chairman of the American Red Cross the statement is made that you have informed Kaplan [54] that on September 27 you had cabled the Department as follows:

"Palestine Jewry is faced with a real financial emergency in its efforts to meet various war-born problems, the absorption of indigent

---

[54] Elizer Kaplan, Financial Director of the Jewish Agency in Palestine.

refugees, and unemployment resulting from economic dislocation as well as those of air-raid precautions, possible urban evacuation, medical aid and direct relief for air-raid victims."

In as much as no such passage appears in your telegram under reference please telegraph the facts in order that the Department may be in a position to comment on the statement.

HULL

867N.4846 : Telegram

The Consul General at Jerusalem (Wadsworth) to the Secretary of State

JERUSALEM, November 11, 1940—5 p. m.
[Received November 12—4 : 35 p. m.]

155. Referring to Department's telegram of November 9, 6 p. m., I regret exceedingly that coded text of numbered paragraph 4 of my telegram No. 123 was either not given to typist or was omitted by her when copying.

It read as follows:

"4. He recognized, however, the force of the Jewish Agency's contention, stressed by its Financial Director in my conversation with him of the preceding day, that Palestine Jewry is faced with a very real financial emergency in its efforts to meet the various war-born problems of absorption of indigent refugees and unemployment resulting from economic dislocation as well as those of air raid precaution, possible urban evacuation, and, finally, medical aid and direct relief to air raid victims."

The Financial Director referred to in this paragraph is the Kaplan mentioned in the Department's telegram under reference. He concurred in the accuracy of my recapitulation of his statement. Doctor Magnes,[55] with whom I also discussed the matter, asks me to say that he "supports strongly the Kaplan statement and, while recognizing that no immediate emergency need exists for the relief of air raid victims, urges the desirability of an American Red Cross unit or representative because of developments in this part of the world".

As a matter of fact, Tel Aviv suffered its only air raid on September 9 and there has been no serious air raid at Haifa since that of September 21.

Lady MacMichael has discussed with me what might be done with the proposed American Red Cross gift if made, and we have suggested to Colonel Jardine of the British Red Cross, Middle East Headquarters, Cairo, that his organization consider duplicating in money or supplies the amount of any such American donation.

---

[55] Judah Leon Magnes, President of Hebrew University in Jerusalem.

Our common idea was that any such gifts should not be used for the care of past air raid victims but held as the nucleus of a special Red Cross fund to be used to supplement, in an emergency and where most needed, funds available to local social welfare agencies which are equipped, as her committee is not equipped, to render direct aid to future air raid victims in the Holy Land.

This idea is approved by the Chief Secretary as well as by Magnes, Kaplan and the Political Director of the Jewish Agency.

WADSWORTH

867N.48/46 : Telegram

The Secretary of State to the Consul General at Jerusalem
(Wadsworth)

WASHINGTON, November 27, 1940—9 p. m.

Your 155, November 11, 5 p. m. The American Red Cross, in consultation with the Department, has given careful consideration to the question of Red Cross relief in Palestine, and has reached the conclusion that the time has not yet arrived when the relief problem of Palestine and the whole problem of relief in the Near East can and should be dealt with.

The Red Cross understands that there are at present no immediate emergency needs for relief of air raid victims in Palestine. So far as concerns the problems of indigent refugees and unemployment, the Red Cross points out that these needs are matters for the consideration of the country as a whole and are hardly within the scope of the kind of emergency relief that the American Red Cross is usually prepared to extend. It is added "On the other hand, with developments in the Middle East threatening to involve Palestine in major difficulties, the Red Cross must stand ready to assist when the moment arrives."

In communicating these conclusions to Rabbi Silver of the United Palestine Appeal, the American Red Cross has assured him that "the way is being prepared to give this assistance when the time arrives in full cooperation and collaboration with your organization and the other agencies interested in relief in Palestine."

You may communicate the foregoing to the Palestine authorities and other interested individuals and groups with whom you have conferred on this subject.

HULL

PROBLEMS ARISING IN CONNECTION WITH EVACUATION AND REPATRIATION OF AMERICAN CITIZENS IN PALESTINE

340.1115A/651 : Telegram

The Consul General at Jerusalem (Wadsworth) to the Secretary of State

JERUSALEM, May 20, 1940—4 p. m.
[Received 5 : 15 p. m.]

30. Referring to Department's telegram No. 37 of May 16, 6 p. m. repeated from Ankara.[56] The Department of course is aware that the estimated 8,000-odd American citizens in Palestine present a very special problem.

Almost 90 percent are Jews, of whom at least two-thirds are naturalized citizens. They have been admitted to Palestine under immigration schedules on visas authorizing permanent residence. For the most part ardent Zionists, their dominant interest is Jewish settlement and realization of the National Home ideal. Their first and preeminent loyalty is to that ideal and its concomitant concept of Jewish statehood in their lifetime.

It follows that retention of American citizenship by these settlers is in many cases primarily a matter of not wanting to burn one's bridges. Few only among them, I believe, will want to leave Palestine even in the event of Italy entering the war and consequent hostilities in the Mediterranean. To these relatively few, of whom I anticipate most will apply to me for advice, I propose to communicate the pertinent substance of the telegram under reference and to extend all possible assistance in obtaining transportation.

Other American residents include several hundred naturalized citizens of Palestine, Arab origin, against at least a majority of whom presumption of expatriation due to protracted residence abroad has arisen. They are for the most part safely situated in scattered inland villages. If desirous of returning at this time, they may be counted on to consult my office. Its advice and assistance will be freely given.

There remain the Kellogg Company's 70-odd employees with 90-odd wives and children in Haifa and, including dependents, roughly 100 missionaries, consular staff, and others. The substance of the telegram under reference has been communicated privately, through heads of institutions to practically all of these.

In the circumstances set forth and because, in the light of Italy's threatening attitude, Mediterranean travel appears to involve serious risk, I should prefer not to issue any public notice inviting American

---

[56] Vol. II, p. 95.

citizens to leave Palestine. A further consideration, with respect to which I am consulting with the Legation in Cairo, is the difficulty of obtaining passage even on Mediterranean sailings.

At the same time, and after consulting Magnes, Totah and Miller (respectively heads of the Hebrew University, Ramallah Friends' Schools and the Y. M. C. A.), I have made tentative plans for the care of Americans, who, if Italy enters the war, may, from fear of bombing attacks, wish to leave Haifa or Tel Aviv. Kellogg Company families would be cared for at the Friends' Boys' School, Jews at the Hebrew University.

Also, and in line with the Department's telegram No. 42 of May 13, noon, to Bern [57] regarding which the Legation at Cairo consulted me, I have been assured of ample accommodation at the Y. M. C. A. and the School of Oriental Research for Legation and Consular families in Egypt who may wish to remove to the safety which no one doubts would be afforded by residence in the Holy City.

None of my American staff or members of their families desire to leave Jerusalem, although my wife hopes to depart on usual summer visit to the United States if and when safe means and route of travel are available.

WADSWORTH

340.1115A/683 : Telegram

The Consul General at Jerusalem (Wadsworth) to the
Secretary of State

JERUSALEM, May 23, 1940—9 p. m.
[Received May 24—7 : 48 a. m.]

33. Supplementing my telegram No. 30 of May 20, 4 p. m., as the following Reuters' message with today's Washington dateline is to appear in tomorrow morning's Palestine newspapers: "A general warning has been issued to all Americans in Iraq, Palestine, Tunis, Egypt and Tangier to leave while communications are still open." I have arranged with the Government Press Bureau that the following supplementary comment be concurrently published. "The American Consul General in Jerusalem explains in this connection that there is no insistence by the Government in Washington on the departure of American citizens from these countries and that each citizen must decide for himself whether to remain or to depart".

I believe and Magnes concurs that thus presented this warning will not occasion panic among resident American Jews. We have particularly wished to avoid this because according to Thomas Cook

---

[57] Vol. II, p. 87.

the only current sailings available for departures are on Italian steamer leaving for Venice May 30 which could accommodate some 200 persons and an east bound Japanese vessel leaving Port Said June 1st. American passenger vessel sailings are reported fully booked but the Legation at Cairo is endeavoring to arrange use of cargo ships if emergency arises. All current British sailings are reported diverted via the Cape.

WADSWORTH

340.1115A/651 : Telegram

The Secretary of State to the Consul General at Jerusalem (Wadsworth)

WASHINGTON, May 24, 1940—7 p. m.

Your 30, May 20, 4 p. m. Department deems it important that all American citizens alike receive the invitation to return to the United States while there still remains opportunity for them to do so. Department has noted your despatch No. 1003, July 12, 1939,[58] suggesting channels through which such invitation may be made.

HULL

340.1115A/700 : Telegram

The Consul General at Jerusalem (Wadsworth) to the Secretary of State

JERUSALEM, May 25, 1940—6 p. m.
[Received May 25—5 : 05 p. m.]

36. As the Department's telegram of May 24, 7 p. m., may have been sent without reference to my telegram No. 33 of May 23, 9 p. m., I desire to report that the Reuters' message and my supplementary comment, both quoted in my telegram under reference, were published prominently yesterday in all morning newspapers, namely the four Hebrew and three Arabic dailies and in the English language Palestine *Post.* The Department may rest assured that through such publication its warning to American citizens has become generally known throughout Palestine.

My telegram No. 33 reported that only two vessels are currently available for travel from Palestine. It now appears that departure by the former is not to be recommended because reliable reports received today have it that all Italian line sailings from Italy to New York have been canceled and that United States Line sailings are

---

[58] Not printed.

fully booked. This constitutes, I believe, a strong added reason for my taking no further steps at this time to invite American citizens here to return to the United States while, in the words of the Department's telegram, "There still remains opportunity for them to do so", such opportunity appears to exist in fact for at most a few hundreds of our more than 8,000 citizens in Palestine. I am therefore hesitant to add, by press release or other form of additional notification, further fuel to the smoldering fire of panic now reliably reported to be spreading in the Palestine Jewish community.

WADSWORTH

340.1115A/700 : Telegram

The Secretary of State to the Consul General at Jerusalem
(Wadsworth)

WASHINGTON, May 28, 1940.

Your 36, May 25, 6 p. m.   Your position approved.

HULL

340.1115A/1418

The Consul General at Jerusalem (Wadsworth) to the Secretary
of State

No. 1331   JERUSALEM, July 20, 1940.
[Received August 27.]

SIR: [Here follows information similar to that brought up to date in despatch No. 1411, November 15, printed *infra.*]

As to the general problem of evacuating American Jews from Haifa, and possibly Tel Aviv, I early suggested to Jewish-American leaders that these communities would do well to consider, through their local organizations, the question of how their position might be affected by a possible spread of hostilities to the Eastern Mediterranean, adding that the Consulate General would be glad to furnish advice and all possible assistance. This matter—the fourth and last subject to be treated in the present despatch—will be discussed in some detail below.

About the middle of May, also, I arranged for the formation of a small committee of three representative Americans with whom the Consulate General might consult informally regarding any emergency which might arise. Its members were:

Dr. J. L. Magnes, President of the Hebrew University
Dr. Totah, Director of the American Friends' Schools
Mr. A. L. Miller, Director of the Jerusalem Y. M. C. A.

Subsequently, and largely on Dr. Magnes' recommendation, we decided it would be advisable to form a special subcommittee of leading American Jews to consider the problems especially affecting resident citizens of that faith. Such a committee finally met with me on June 26. Its members were:

Dr. J. L. Magnes, as Chairman
Mr. J. Simon, President of the Palestine Economic Corporation
Dr. I. Kligler, of the Hadassah Medical Organization
Mr. H. Viteles, of the Central Bank of Cooperatives
Mr. H. Margalith, head of the Jerusalem branch of the American-Jewish Association of Palestine.

With members of this subcommittee and with representatives of the other two branches of the American-Jewish Association (at Tel Aviv and Haifa) the matter of organized arrangements for the assistance of American Jews has been discussed on several occasions. Tentative plans have already been made to receive and care for any needy refugees who may be forced by circumstances—such, for instance, as further bombing of Haifa—to leave dangerous areas.

The most notable contribution in this field is an offer made by Drs. Magnes and Kligler to house such refugees in buildings to be made available by the institutions they represent. And Mr. Simon has made a generous offer of financial assistance towards putting such buildings into "habitable" condition should need therefor arise.

Officials of the American-Jewish Association are also cooperating with the Consulate General in effecting a more complete registration of American Jewish residents of the country. In this latter connection the matter of the financial situation of these citizens will also be considered.

The ultimate aim of this move, which is the sub-committee's own proposal, is to perfect some arrangements for the collection of funds for the assistance of any who may find themselves evacuated and in real need. The investigation is at present proceeding.

In conclusion and to recapitulate the major points made in the present despatch and its enclosures:

1) Some 250 resident citizens have left Palestine since receipt of the Department's telegram of May 16 advising Americans to return to the United States; and an approximately equal number are known to wish to leave and to possess funds more or less sufficient for the purpose;

2) There remain in the country some 7,000 citizens (roughly 6,500 Jews, 400 Arabs and 100 others) against at least 3,000 of whom presumption of expatriation is believed to have arisen; and

3) Some 1,000 of these remaining citizens reside in Haifa, in which connection there exists a potential emergency evacuation—and possibly relief—problem of some magnitude.

Finally, and in explanation of the relative smallness of the numbers of citizens who have left or made known their desire to leave the country, I venture to quote the following paragraph from my telegram of May 20:

"About 90 per cent are Jews of whom at least two-thirds are naturalized citizens. They have been admitted to Palestine under immigration schedules on visas authorizing permanent residence. For the most part ardent Zionists their dominant interest is Jewish settlement and realization of the National Home ideal. Their first and preeminent loyalty is to that ideal and its concomitant concept of Jewish statehood in their lifetime."

Respectfully yours, G. WADSWORTH

340.1115A/1700

The Consul General at Jerusalem (Wadsworth) to the Secretary of State

No. 1411 JERUSALEM, November 15, 1940.
[Received December 23.]

Subject: War emergency problems affecting American citizens in Palestine.

SIR: In my despatch No. 1331 of July 20, 1940, there was submitted a detailed review of the above subject as presenting itself at the time. In the present despatch I shall have the honor to bring that review up to date. As to the number of American citizens involved, the situation was, briefly, as follows:

During the period from May 18 (date of the receipt of the Department's advice to American citizens to return to the United States) to July 15, some 250 resident citizens had left Palestine.

Approximately 7,000 citizens (then estimated at roughly 6,500 Jews, 400 Arabs and 100 "others") were believed to remain in the country.

Of these estimated 7,000, only some 250 were known to wish to leave and to possess more or less sufficient funds for the purpose.

Many more, it was believed, would wish to leave were the Middle East to become the scene of major hostilities and the country to be threatened by Axis invasion.

During the intervening four months, only some 150 citizens have left the country. This figure has been confirmed by enquiry made of local travel agencies. Fifty-odd departed in August on the Egyptian S. S. *El Nil* via the Red Sea and the Cape of Good Hope, the others via Iraq and India.

These departures included: all of the remaining American employees (23 in number) of the M. W. Kellogg Company, which had concluded its construction work of the new oil refinery at Haifa; one single missionary and one missionary family departing on furlough; and, the balance, 120-odd residents (for the most part Jews). In addition seven missionaries from Egypt who had spent the summer here returned to that country.

On the basis of these figures, there should remain in the country something over 6,000 American Jews, the originally estimated 400 naturalized citizens of local Arab origin and rather less than 100 "others". Further enquiries made during these intervening four months confirm the substantial accuracy of the latter two figures but suggest the desirability of reducing that of the number of American Jews.

As to "others" the following table is believed to be substantially correct as of the present date:

Institution	Adults	Dependents
Assembly of God	7	7
American Friends Mission	10	2
Franciscan Custody of the Holy Land	12	–
Southern Baptist Convention	4	7
Christian and Missionary Alliance	5	3
American Carmelite Fathers	5	–
Other "missionaries" (YMCA, American Colony Aid Association, etc.)	10	3
Total "missionaries"	53	23 [22]
Consulate General (including two F. S. O. families evacuated from Cairo)	10	10
Others registered at the Consulate	2	–
Total "others"	65	33 [32]

As to the estimated number of resident American Jews, it is to be noted that the survey—reported in my last despatch as having been undertaken by the American-Jewish Association of Palestine—has led the officials of that association to put the total at an outside figure of approximately 5,000. They suggest that the estimate prepared by the Consulate General erred in not allowing for a higher percentage of departures during recent years.

They argue, and I believe with considerable justification, that American Jews have adjusted themselves less readily than Europeans to conditions in Palestine and, therefore, especially during the "disturbances" of 1936–39, returned in considerably larger numbers than the Consulate's estimate showed for permanent residence in the United States. They suggest that this divergence was due in many instances to the fact that Jews so leaving Palestine were ashamed to admit that they were definitely "deserting the ship" and hence applied to the Consulate and to the Palestine Migration Department for passports or other services for seasonal travel only.

Be this as it may—and the Consulate's citizenship section is now engaged in a further study of the matter—the survey in question led the officers of the American-Jewish Association to the interesting conclusions set forth in my telegram No. 159 of November 13, 2 p. m.[59] A confirmation copy is transmitted herewith, together with a copy of the Association's letter of November 12 [59] which enclosed a draft text (which I did not modify) of the first and second numbered paragraphs of my telegram.

The most interesting point made in the Association's conclusions was that, of the 2,500 American Jews for whom it claimed to speak, only some 500 "wish to return to the United States at the present juncture or at an early date", the others "preferring to remain unless the country is threatened by Axis invasion."

Of these 500, the Association's survey showed, "barely 100 are financially able to pay present fares" and the remainder require assistance in the form either of cheaper fares or of full repatriation relief. The Association's officers believed that a somewhat similar situation would be found to exist among the other half of the Jewish American residents not directly represented by them.

If this be the case—and the Consulate's observations suggest its substantial accuracy—there are today in Palestine only some 800 American citizens (all Jews) who desire to return to the United States at this time and who do not possess sufficient funds for the purpose. And, of such 800, approximately one-half would be able to pay between $200 and $400 for steerage or tourist-class fares.

The numbers (of all categories) of those wishing to depart would, of course, as my telegram and earlier despatch suggested, multiply rapidly were the Eastern Mediterranean to become the scene of major hostilities and Palestine be threatened by Axis invasion.

In that latter event, the problem of the evacuation of American citizens from this country would indeed be one of serious magnitude and difficulty; and the Association's officers urge that the Department accord it full and sympathetic consideration. They present their case substantially as follows:

They came to and settled in this country primarily because inspired by the Zionist ideal. As Jews, they wished to make their contribution towards building the Jewish National Home. As Americans they wished that contribution—in the field of spiritual as well as material progress—to be representative of the best traditions of their former, American homeland.

They admit thus frankly to a dual loyalty; and they feel that that which they owe to Palestine precludes their deserting the Zionist ship now seriously endangered by but not as yet actually caught in

---

[59] Not printed.

the maelstrom of world war. They recognize, however, that in this stand they may be risking life itself, that as Jews (even though American citizens) they would receive short shrift at the hands of a Nazi invasion.

In the circumstances—which they feel may rightly be deemed to set them apart as unique among all Americans now resident abroad in war-threatened areas—they hold to the belief that, in dire emergency, their government should and will come to their aid with all the power (financial and otherwise) at its command.

In my many conversations with these and other leaders of the local Jewish-American community I have not encouraged them in this stand, and I have let no opportunity pass to impress on them— and through them on their community—the seriousness of the Department's advice that Americans should leave this and other Near Eastern countries.

I cannot but feel, however, that, even in the face of their failure to heed that advice, their Government could not "in dire emergency" wash its hands of all responsibility for their welfare and remain loyal to the humanitarian principles for which it has always stood. The vision is grim of what their lot would be in a Nazi-occupied Holy Land.

My hope is that, should such a tragedy come to pass, funds for their repatriation or relief would be made available by public American charity. It is a hope with which Dr. Judah Magnes, my chief counsellor in these matters, wishes very particularly to associate himself. Millions of dollars have been and, we gather, still are being contributed, notably by American Jewry, for the rendering of similar assistance to European Jews.

It might be well were the Department to consider drawing, through appropriate charitable institutions, the attention of these same American donors to this potential need of American Jews in Palestine.

Respectfully yours,   G. WADSWORTH

340.1115A/1700 : Telegram

The Secretary of State to the Consul General at Jerusalem
(Wadsworth)

WASHINGTON, January 25, 1941—2 p. m.

Your despatch 1411, November 15.

1. In accordance with the Department's instructions to its officers in the Near East, it was suggested by you to Americans in Palestine, in anticipation of the spread of hostilities to the Mediterranean, that they return to the United States while transportation facilities were available and opportunity remained for them to do so. Despite that

advice and the subsequent spread of hostilities to the Mediterranean and although there still exists means of transportation to the United States via the Persian Gulf and India, the large number of persons referred to in your despatch have remained and continue to remain in Palestine.

2. The persons in question admit a loyalty to Palestine impelling them to remain there and they do not propose to leave unless a dire emergency should occur when, they say, they will expect this Government to come to their aid with all the power at its command, financial and otherwise. The Government will, of course, at all times extend to bona fide citizens abroad every possible protection and assistance, but citizens choosing to remain in a dangerous situation must understand that the Government's efforts to protect and assist them may be vitiated by circumstances beyond its control. It is very possible that the Government would be unable in particular to arrange for the removal of Americans in Palestine, especially of such a large number as are remaining, should an emergency arise.

3. While the Department will continually endeavor to arrange, in so far as it can, for sufficient transportation facilities for Americans returning home from war areas, it is not the obligation of government to repatriate its citizens and the Congress has not appropriated funds for that purpose. The Department has on occasion since the outbreak of hostilities made allotments to its officers abroad for advances as loans against promissory notes to destitute Americans in hazardous areas for their transportation expenses to the United States. It has made these allotments from special funds which are limited by reason of other purposes for which they are used. When it is found necessary and possible to make such allotments, the loans therefrom may only be made to bona fide American citizens. In this regard the Department in its telegraphic instruction to its offices in France [60] covering the recent repatriation of Americans from that country defined bona fide American citizens for purposes of Government financial assistance for repatriation as:

"Persons resting under unrebutted presumption may not be afforded the benefit of the arrangements including the loan of government funds to qualify under Rule G. Bona fide citizens are those citizens who are in complete and unquestioned possession of their citizenship rights, including the right to passports and the full protection of this Government, who have ties in the United States and who have continually held themselves out while abroad as American citizens and are in every way identifiable as such. They are citizens temporarily abroad desiring to return home. They are not persons merely possessing some circumstantial claim to American citizenship which they have not validated by residence and maintenance of ties in the United States

---

[60] Telegram No. 857, December 18, 1940, to the Chargé in France, vol. II, p. 182.

and by truly identifying themselves abroad as bona fide citizens of the United States. The affording of transportation to the United States to the latter class of destitute persons, particularly with the aid of funds of this Government, would undoubtedly cause just public criticism of the action and is not the intent of the Department. Each and every officer concerned will take careful note of these instructions and be prepared to give the Department evidence as may be desired by it of his compliance therewith in any case which he should pass for repatriation."

While applications for loans when allotments are granted for that purpose are considered upon the merits of the individual case, it is hardly possible that persons, such as those referred to in your despatch, who have left the United States and settled in a foreign country to which they admit a loyalty at least equal to that which they may have for the United States, should be able to qualify as bona fide American citizens properly entitled to the use of the public funds of the United States.

4. You are authorized to use the foregoing in your discretion.

5. You are also authorized to state to the persons concerned, with reference to the possible need of those whom they may represent for repatriation or relief funds supplied by American charity, that the Department itself cannot properly undertake to solicit those funds.

HULL

SYRIA AND LEBANON

INTEREST OF THE UNITED STATES REGARDING THE IMPACT OF THE EUROPEAN WAR UPON SYRIA AND LEBANON

740.00111A Financial/90

The Secretary of State to the Consul General at Beirut (Palmer)

WASHINGTON, March 2, 1940.

SIR: The receipt is acknowledged of your despatch No. 464 of January 27, 1940,[1] in which a clarification is requested of the present status of Syria under the Neutrality Act of 1939.[2]

There are enclosed, for your information, a copy of the Neutrality Act of 1939, a copy of an analysis [2a] of the requirements of certain of the provisions of this Act, and copies of the President's Proclamations of November 4, 1939,[3] issued pursuant to certain provisions of the Act.

The term "France", as used in the President's Proclamation of November 4, 1939, making the provisions of the Neutrality Act applicable to that country, is considered to include all French colonies and protectorates and all territories mandated to France except the Class A mandate, Syria (including Lebanon). Accordingly, the provisions of the Neutrality Act do not in general apply at the present time to exports to Syria. Depending upon the manner in which shipment is made, however, there are certain provisions of the Neutrality Act which may, in one way or another, have some effect on shipments to Syria. For example, the provisions of Section 2 of the Act relating to transfer of title are applicable to shipments of goods consigned to Syria if shipment is routed via a belligerent port or territory not within an excepted area. This fact may account for the receipt by importers in Syria of the conflicting information referred to in the despatch under acknowledgment.

With reference to the extension of credit in connection with purchases made by or on behalf of the French Army stationed in the Levant, attention is invited to that provision of Section 7 of the Act which, as made applicable to France by the above-mentioned Proclamation, prohibits the extension of any credit (other than neces-

---

[1] Not printed.
[2] 54 Stat. 4.
[2a] Not attached to file copy of this document.
[3] Department of State *Bulletin*, November 4, 1939, p. 453, or 54 Stat. (pt. 2) 2671.

sary credits accruing in connection with the transmission of telegraph, cable, wireless, and telephone services) to the French Government, to any political subdivision thereof, or to any person acting for or on behalf of the French Government or any political subdivision thereof. Purchases made by private firms in Syria, on their own behalf, would not be affected by this credit provision of the Act.

There is enclosed, for your further information, a copy of a memorandum dated February 8, 1940,[3a] prepared by an officer of the Department on this general subject.

Very truly yours,   For the Secretary of State:
                                                    A. A. BERLE, JR.

740.0011 European War 1939/4128 : Telegram

The Consul General at Beirut (Palmer) to the Secretary of State

BEIRUT, June 23, 1940—2 p. m.
[Received June 23—1 : 02 p. m.]

38. Officers and men of the French forces here including colonial troops and naval and air force units are determined to carry on.[4] General Mittelhauser [5] informed me late yesterday afternoon that he was confident that the entire French Fleet and all other forces outside of France were united in such a determination. He says that with the pooled resources of the French and British Empires they will fight in the closest cooperation with, or even as a part of, the British forces; that they are firm in their resolve to effect a military and moral resurrection of France and to make any necessary sacrifice to this end.

He tells me that after conference here General Wavell [6] has proposed to the British Government the establishment of a commission in Cairo through which supplies for all British and French forces in Africa and the Near East will be obtained independently of supplies for British or French forces elsewhere. Pending British Government approval which he and General Wavell regard as certain he asks that this information be held in strictest confidence.

He states that French forces here are well equipped and have material sufficient for normal operations up to September or October but must be assured of replenishment before the exhaustion of this material and in the meantime have urgent need of aircraft. He emphasizes their dependency on the United States as a source of supply

---

[3a] Not attached to file copy of this document.
[4] The French-German armistice was signed on June 22. For text of the armistice treaty, see *Documents on German Foreign Policy, 1918–1945*, series D, vol. IX, p. 671.
[5] French Commander in Chief in the Eastern Mediterranean area.
[6] Gen. Sir Archibald P. Wavell, Commanding General of British forces in the Middle East.

for all material that can possibly be furnished and he hopes for encouraging assurances in this respect. The air force hopes for rapid expansion here and the organization of an important training center for pilots and is most anxious to have information as to the immediate or early availability of training and fighting planes.

Local rumors repeated abroad to the effect that there have been disturbances in Damascus and other centers are contradicted by American and other reliable residents, and the High Commissioner replies that such rumors are entirely unfounded.

PALMER

740.0011 European War 1939/4174d : Telegram

The Secretary of State to the Consul General at Beirut (Palmer)

WASHINGTON, June 24, 1940—1 p. m.

31. Please report regarding attitude of Allied army in Near East and of the French authorities in your area concerning present situation.

HULL

740.0011 European War 1939/4193 : Telegram

The Consul General at Beirut (Palmer) to the Secretary of State

BEIRUT, June 26, 1940—7 a. m.
[Received 10:48 a. m.]

39. With reference to the Department's telegram of June 24, 1 p. m. It is assumed that the Department now has my telegram of June 23, 2 p. m., which was despatched from Beirut at 5 p. m. via Imperial and Western Union. Confidence therein reported has been shaken by lack of confirmation of the unity that was then anticipated but determination and hopefulness still predominate. My telegram dated June 26, 8 a. m.,[7] with further information and comment is being despatched by cable.

PALMER

740.0011 European War 1939/4196 : Telegram

The Consul General at Beirut (Palmer) to the Secretary of State

BEIRUT, June 26, 1940—8 a. m.
[Received 12:20 p. m.]

40. Supplementing my telegram dated June 26, 7 a. m. High Commissioner [8] informs me in strictest confidence that he and General

---

[7] *Infra.*
[8] Gabriel Puaux.

Mittelhauser are now uncertain as to attitude of forces in North Africa and fleet and are profoundly disturbed. Their uncertainty and discouragement is causing great concern to the head of the British liaison mission with the French forces here. He tells me that he has discussed the situation frankly with the General and various officers and that while he is convinced of the former's courage and enheartened by the splendid morale of the great majority he shares their fear that if the French forces here find themselves without support from those in North Africa and the fleet some reservists will be tempted to accept the decision of the Bordeaux Government in the hope of being reunited with their families in France. He anticipates that in such an event many French officers and possibly entire units will join up with the British forces in Palestine or Egypt; and I know of a number of officers who are disposed to take such a step.

The High Commissioner assures me that the reaction to his declaration when the signing of the armistice was announced, to the effect that he and the General were in complete accord in their determination to carry on without any thought of capitulation, has been most gratifying not only in the enthusiastic and unanimous response of all French citizens here but also in manifestations of loyalty on the part of the native population and particularly in the case of Moslems. It is because of his responsibility toward [apparent omission] who have committed themselves in response to his appeal that he is now so bewildered.

If the Department prefers such telegrams in Brown code by direct wireless instead of in this cipher by round about cable route instructions would be appreciated.

PALMER

740.0011 European War 1939/4214 : Telegram

The Consul General at Beirut (Palmer) to the Secretary of State

BEIRUT, June 27, 1940—7 p. m.
[Received June 27—1 : 18 p. m.]

42. Referring to my telegram No. 41, June 27, 11 a. m.[9] Proclamation today by General Mittelhauser reads as follows:

"By virtue of the armistice conditions signed by the French Government, no change has taken place in the situation of the territory under mandate.

Consequently the general commander in chief of the theater of operations in the Eastern Mediterranean, in agreement with the High

---

[9] Not printed.

Commissioner, has ordered the cessation of hostilities. The French flag will continue to fly over this territory and France will pursue her mission in the Levant States."

Comment will follow by cable.

PALMER

740.0011 European War 1939/4259 : Telegram

The Consul General at Beirut (Palmer) to the Secretary of State

BEIRUT, June 28, 1940—9 a. m.
[Received 12: 30 p. m.]

43. Reference to my telegram No. 43 [*42*], June 27. The High Commissioner explained to me yesterday that his abandonment of previously declared determination to carry on is due to rejection by General Noguès [10] of General Mittelhauser's appeal to French forces in North Africa.

From authoritative British source I learned later that confidential telegram from Algeria indicates that many officers and troops in North Africa still hope to carry on and that their attitude may prevail; in which case British here feel that local French forces may resume resistance as many of officers and a considerable number of troops had hoped to do.

Meanwhile officers and men of air force and other units are understood to have made plans to leave for Palestine individually or in small groups but in considerable numbers. Planes have been flown there and other material is on the way.

High Commissioner assures me that notwithstanding demobilization in accordance with terms of armistice a sufficient force to maintain order will remain here; but native reaction to presence here of expected Italian commission to supervise armistice terms may render situation difficult.

PALMER

740.0011 European War 1939/4360 : Telegram

The Consul General at Beirut (Palmer) to the Secretary of State

BEIRUT, July 2, 1940—noon.
[Received 2: 46 p. m.]

45. Reference to my telegram No. 43, June 28. Except for a fully equipped Polish contingent of several thousand the number of officers

---

[10] Gen. Albert Noguès, French Resident General in French Morocco, and Commander in Chief of French forces in North Africa.

and soldiers and the quantities of supplies that have gone over to the British in Palestine have been much less than anticipated and are declared by higher French authorities here to be relatively unimportant.

The attitude of these authorities appears now to be primarily one of determination to support the Bordeaux Government unreservedly in carrying out the terms of the armistice in the hope of avoiding the presence here of an armistice commission with Italian and German members; secondarily, but increasingly one of distrust of the British.

General Massiet has taken over from General Le Petit command of the permanent local defense domain (*Armée du Levant*) and from General Mittelhauser command of the larger so-called expeditionary force pending its demobilization. The latter's chief of staff is under arrest for connivance with French officers in Damascus in plans for fully equipped units to join the British in Palestine.

British military mission here is leaving immediately in compliance with Bordeaux Government orders received yesterday morning in telegram from General Weygand.[11] Head of the mission told me yesterday noon that even as late as the day before French officers had been asking him to assure them that if they could get to Palestine they would be accepted by the British, and I am informed that all that have gone are being taken over without change of rank but with higher British pay. He maintains that at all times the French command here has been fully aware of his attitude and activities; but the High Commissioner later explained to me that the presence here of this British officer whose mission had actually terminated could no longer be tolerated since he had been directly involved in the Damascus plans which resulted in the arrest of General Mittelhauser's chief of staff.

In response to my inquiry as to the state of public security here and relations with neighboring countries, the High Commissioner told me yesterday afternoon that Noury [*Nuri*] Pasha[12] returning to Baghdad from Ankara had assured him of the good will of both Iraq and Turkey. As regards relations with Palestine the High Commissioner said that the Bordeaux Government were allowing him considerable freedom of action and that he would do his best to maintain these on a normal basis, but he added that he fears that certain British elements in Palestine might now again stir up trouble in the Djebel-druze. He emphasized that with such a possibility in mind it was essential that a well-disciplined French force be maintained here; also that he hopes that this and undeviating support of the Bordeaux

---

[11] Gen. Maxime Weygand became commander of the French forces in the Near East in September 1939, was called home and assumed command of the French Army in May 1940, and was appointed Minister for National Defense in the Pétain Cabinet on July 11, 1940.

[12] Iraqi Minister for Foreign Affairs.

Government will forestall the sending to Beirut of an armistice commission with Italian or German members whose presence here might lead to serious disturbances in this area.

PALMER

740.0011 European War 1939/4485a : Telegram

The Secretary of State to the Ambassador in the United Kingdom
(Kennedy)

WASHINGTON, July 3, 1940.

1578. Can you confirm press reports that the Foreign Office has issued a statement expressing the determination of Britain to prevent Syria and Lebanon from being occupied by any hostile power.

HULL

740.0011 European War 1939/4384 : Telegram

The Ambassador in the United Kingdom (Kennedy) to the Secretary
of State

LONDON, July 4, 1940.
[Received July 4—9 : 06 a. m.]

1971. Your 1578, July 3. Following statement published in morning papers July 2 is stated by Foreign Office to have been given out officially Monday evening:

"His Majesty's Government in the United Kingdom understand that General Mittelhauser, the Commander-in-Chief of the French forces in the Levant, has stated that hostilities have ceased in Syria. His Majesty's Government assume that this does not mean that if Germany or Italy sought to occupy Syria or the Lebanon and were to try to do so in the face of British command of the sea, no attempt would be made by the French forces to oppose them. In order, however, to set at rest doubts which may be felt in any quarter, His Majesty's Government declare that they could not allow Syria or the Lebanon to be occupied by any hostile power or to be used as a base for attacks upon those countries in the Middle East which they are pledged to defend or to become the scene of such disorder as to constitute a danger to those countries. They, therefore, hold themselves free to take whatever measures they may, in such circumstances, consider necessary in their own interests. Any action which they may hereafter be obliged to take in fulfilment of this declaration will be entirely without prejudice to the future status of the territories now under French Mandate."

KENNEDY

740.0011 European War 1939/4529a : Telegram

The Secretary of State to the Consul General at Beirut (Palmer)

WASHINGTON, July 8, 1940—6 p. m.

36. Please inform the Department regarding the French Fleet in your area, including particularly the units present and the attitude of the officers and men. Information is also desired regarding alleged fighting on the Syrian-Palestine border, regarding an announced determination of the French authorities to defend Syria "against any foreign encroachments", and regarding Weygand's present activities and influence in Syria.

Keep the Department advised by frequent short telegrams at least until the Franco-British situation is clarified.

HULL

740.0011 European War 1939/4551 : Telegram

The Consul General at Beirut (Palmer) to the Secretary of State

BEIRUT, July 10, 1940—9 a. m.
[Received July 10—8 : 50 a. m.]

50. In response to the Department's telegram No. 36, of the French naval vessels in this port at the time of the French request for an armistice 1 proceeded almost immediately to Alexandria; 2 submarines left subsequently undisclosed destination following news of British action against French at Oran; [13] 3 submarines and a mine layer are still here.

Prior to the armistice the attitude of the French naval authorities here was one of closest and most cordial cooperation with the local British Consulate General and with British naval authorities in Palestine and Egypt; up to the time of the Oran conflict reflected the pro-British sentiments of officers and men; since that time has been one of active support of the Pétain Government although the necessity for abandoning the British is generally regretted and it is understood that there is still some acceptance of British explanation regarding Oran.

PALMER

---

[13] British naval action against the French Fleet at Oran, July 3, 1940; see vol. II, pp. 469–473.

740.0011 European War 1939/4557 : Telegram

The Consul General at Beirut (Palmer) to the Secretary of State

BEIRUT, July 10, 1940—noon.
[Received 2:30 p. m.]

51. Reference Department's telegram No. 36, and my telegram No. 50. Strict compliance with orders of Pétain Government on the part of the naval authorities here is in complete accord with the attitude of General Massiet and High Commissioner Puaux, both of whom have expressed themselves as determined to maintain order within the country and to use all the means at their disposal to prevent disturbances of whatever nature or origin.

While they have not publicly voiced their apprehension as to foreign influences or aggression they have privately expressed satisfaction over the reassuring attitude of Turkey and Iraq toward Syria and are apparently hopeful of combating Italian and German propaganda and that the question of direct intervention here on the part of Germany or Italy will not arise.

They appear to be most concerned over the probability of subversive activities on the part of British agents in Syria and the possibility of British military action from Palestine with the excuse of alleged necessity for maintaining order in the adjoining territory. But the High Commissioner and the British Consul General have both categorically contradicted the rumor from abroad that there has been fighting on the Syrian-Palestine border and each has assured me that his Government not only desires to avoid open conflict here but also is prepared to cooperate in the maintenance of normal relations in this area; in which connection the British Consul General has let it be understood that British funds might be made available if necessary to meet local financial and economic requirements.

It is understood that Weygand whose influence here is still great, continues to manifest a particular interest in the Near East; but rumors of his presence here at various times since the armistice have been in informal conversation denied by the authorities and persons who have claimed to have seen him in Syria have been discredited.

PALMER

740.0011 European War 1939/4557 : Telegram

The Secretary of State to the Consul General at Beirut (Palmer)

WASHINGTON, July 11, 1940—6 p. m.

38. Your no. 51, July 10, noon, last paragraph. Please endeavor to obtain further information regarding Weygand's reported visit to Syria, several indications of which we have received. Lane reported

from Belgrade on July 1 [14] that the French Minister there had informed him that Weygand's recent trip to Syria was to persuade Mittelhauser to remain loyal to the Pétain Government. This would seem to verify a report from Cairo, dated July 3,[14] that Wavell's visit to Syria "several days ago" had coincided with that of Weygand. A German official broadcast from Athens is said to have reported that Weygand was in Athens on June 30 en route to Syria.

HULL

740.0011 European War 1939/4637 : Telegram

The Consul General at Beirut (Palmer) to the Secretary of State

BEIRUT, July 11, 1940—1 p. m.
[Received July 13—11 : 40 a. m.]

53. Department's No. 38, July 11, 6 p. m. The British Consul General assures me that Wavell's last visit was the one to which Mittelhauser referred in conversation with me on June 22 (see my telegram No. 38, June 23, 2 p. m.) and that he does not believe that Weygand had returned here up to that time or has since come here. He tells me that following the broadcast from Athens reporting Weygand there June 30 en route to Syria he cautioned the British authorities against accepting without verification reports from interested foreign sources regarding this area and later was informed officially that subsequent inquiry in Athens had failed to reveal anyone who had seen Weygand there and at various times since Weygand left here for France on March 29 I have inquired of High Commissioner Puaux as to the truth of successive reports that Weygand had returned. He has repeatedly told me that they were without foundation. Today he has authorized me to quote him as saying that at no time since that date has Weygand been in Syria or Lebanon; or in Greece, Turkey, Egypt or Palestine; or elsewhere outside of France as far as he is aware.

PALMER

740.0011 European War 1939/4610 : Telegram

The Consul General at Beirut (Palmer) to the Secretary of State

BEIRUT, July 12, 1940—6 p. m.
[Received 6 : 45 p. m.]

52. General Fourgère has arrived from France by airplane via Naples and Athens to relieve General Massiet who is to leave for France with General Mittelhauser.

---

[14] Not printed.

Admiral Gouton has arrived to relieve Admiral de Carpentier who has completed a normal 2-year tour of duty at this naval base.

French steamer from Egypt with officers and men of the French naval forces to be returned to France arrived here this morning.

PALMER

740.00115 European War 1939/499 : Telegram

The Consul General at Beirut (Palmer) to the Secretary of State

BEIRUT, August 8, 1940—9 a. m.
[Received 11 : 42 a. m.]

70. In response to an inquiry by the British Consul General, following a tip to the British Passport Officer by a personal friend in the Sûreté Général that British males under 50 would no longer be permitted to leave Lebanon and Syria, the Chief of the Political Bureau of the French High Commission yesterday confirmed the receipt of telegraphic instructions from Vichy, effective immediately, prohibiting the departure of all British, Dutch, Belgians, Czechs, Poles and Austrians of military age.

A request by the British Consul General for a 48-hour period of grace was neither granted nor refused but he was given to understand that if persons affected should apply this morning for exit permits these would be issued.

Notwithstanding British Consul General's representations two prominent members of the local British community traveling to Palestine and Egypt on business were turned back yesterday afternoon by the French authorities at the Palestine frontier although provided with the customary permits from the Sûreté Général for departure and return.

This action by the French Government, apparently a complete surprise to High Commissioner Puaux, is interpreted by many as preliminary to the arrival of a German and Italian commission, rumors of which he has consistently denied but the imminence of which is suggested by letters recently received here from the former Italian Consul General.

PALMER

740.00115 European War 1939/502 : Telegram

The Consul General at Beirut (Palmer) to the Secretary of State

BEIRUT, August 8, 1940—7 p. m.
[Received August 8—6 : 37 p. m.]

72. Reference my telegram No. 70, today's date. Order from Vichy prohibiting departure from Lebanon and Syria of certain aliens

strictly enforced from moment of receipt, provides for no exception. British Consul General's understanding that exit might be issued this morning to British and other nationals affected proved to be incorrect. Refusal of such permits to British women gave rise to rumors that all such nationals would be interned; but the High Commissioner tells me that such refusal was in error and assures me that the order affects only males between 18 and 48 years of age and does not envisage internment.

The High Commissioner explains that this order does not apply exclusively to this area but to all territory under French control. He admits the possibility of a German and Italian commission arriving in the near future and is increasingly concerned; but he states that he is still without official indications in this regard. Recurrent [rumors?] that a commission including Italian and German consular officers formerly at this post is about to arrive are traceable to letters which the Brazilian Consul General now in charge of Italian interests has from time to time received from the former Italian Consul General who has repeatedly referred to his prospective return with such a commission, but has not yet suggested any probable dates.

This latest move on the part of the French Government, within a few days of the internment here of the British merchant seamen whose arrest was reported in my telegram No. 63 of August 1,[16] leaves little hope in local French or Britannic circles for obtaining from London the necessary final approval of the clearing agreement with Palestine that is so anxiously awaited here.

PALMER

740.00115 European War 1939/507 : Telegram

The Consul General at Beirut (Palmer) to the Secretary of State

BEIRUT, August 12, 1940—11 a. m.
[Received August 12—10 : 20 a. m.]

75. Reference my telegram No. 72, August 8. Leading local British residents, including Canadians, have escaped to Palestine mostly by night, some disguised.

French authorities here are apparently not displeased at this evasion of an order that they privately regard as inspired by Berlin and that constitutes another obstacle to British approval of the clearing agreement with Palestine which had already been made contingent upon release of British seamen still interned here contrary to advice of High Commissioner Puaux.

PALMER

---

[16] Not printed.

740.0011 European War 1939/5178a : Telegram

The Acting Secretary of State to the Consul General at Beirut
(Palmer)

WASHINGTON, August 16, 1940—5 p. m.

51. The Department would appreciate receiving by telegraph any information which may be discreetly obtainable concerning: (1) the present number and status of the French Army in Syria and the Lebanon; (2) the number, if any, which have been demobilized but not repatriated; (3) the number which may have been repatriated; and (4) any reliable estimate available of the number which have passed into Palestine. In this connection the Department would be interested in learning whether plans have been formulated for the repatriation of any appreciable portion of the army in the near future and, if not, the reasons for the continued maintenance of such a force.

The Department should be promptly informed in the event of any significant changes at any time in the disposition of the French forces in your district.

WELLES

740.0011 European War 1939/5159 : Telegram

The Consul General at Beirut (Palmer) to the Secretary of State

BEIRUT, August 17, 1940—9 a. m.
[Received 1 p. m.]

79. With reference to my telegram No. 52, July 12. Eighteen hundred French naval officers and seamen who arrived at Beirut from Alexandria on July 12 aboard the French steamship *Providence* with the expectation of continuing to France a few days later left here for Marseille yesterday afternoon on the same ship.

Month's delay, due to withholding of Italian permission for this [apparent omission] that is understood to have been approved by the British prior to the departure from Alexandria, became a cause of serious concern to the French authorities here because of growing discontentment among the seamen. Rumors of insubordination which were persistent during the past fortnight were repeatedly denied but it is understood that the seamen's attitude finally forced the French authorities to make an insistent appeal for previously requested Italian permission which at last came through on August 12.

General Massiet who has been awaiting authorization to return to France by plane via Italy also sailed on the *Providence* but incognito. Six hundred tons of wheat which had not been covered by the British safe conduct but which they had learned might be shipped under a last minute authorization on the part of the competent French civil authorities at this port are understood to have been refused by the responsible French naval authorities.

Another ship is expected shortly with an additional contingent from the French naval vessels at Alexandria but with space also for the most discontented of the French Army reservists here whose repatriation at the earliest possible moment is locally recognized by French military and civil authorities alike as of primary importance. Any significant developments or indications as to the state of affairs in this regard will be promptly reported by telegraph.

PALMER

740.0011 European War 1939/5161 : Telegram

The Consul General at Beirut (Palmer) to the Secretary of State

BEIRUT, August 17, 1940—6 p. m.
[Received August 18—7 : 32 a. m.]

80. Consulate General has just received Department's telegram No. 51 dated August 15 [*16*], 5 p. m., but apparently despatched from Washington at 8 : 41 last evening.

Except for reservists from eastern Mediterranean countries French troops here have neither been repatriated nor demobilized; nor is demobilization and repatriation of any considerable number anticipated in the absence of transportation facilities and British and Italian authorization. The steamship *Athos* whose expected departure with naval reservists and more extreme malcontents among army reservists was mentioned in my telegram No. 79 of this morning is now in port and scheduled to leave shortly with these groups but no other ships are known to be on the way here.

Since my telegram No. 45 of July 2 reporting the number of French troops that had passed into Palestine as relatively unimportant, only a few small groups have gone over and the total is insignificant.

I hope to be able to telegraph within the next few days the figures and other information requested in the Department's telegram and will continue to keep Department informed of significant developments by telegraph as heretofore.

PALMER

740.0011 European War 1939/5206 : Telegram

The Consul General at Beirut (Palmer) to the Secretary of State

BEIRUT, August 20, 1940—9 a. m.
[Received 12: 38 p. m.]

82. Reference Department's 51, August 15 [*16*], and my 80, August 17. Present French Army in Syria and Lebanon not less than 80,000

nor more than 100,000 according to trustworthy sources of information. It will be recalled that last January in my despatch number 463 [17] following a visit to various military centers I reported my calculations giving these same figures and mentioned an estimated top figure of 140,000 as a high one. In the light of present information and assuming that these earlier calculations were essentially correct it would appear that arrivals during the spring which probably did not exceed 20,000 may have been later offset by secret departures on steamers arriving here with military supplies up to the end of May.

As reported in my telegram dated August 17, 6 p. m., reservists from Eastern Mediterranean countries were the first to be demobilized. Totaling less than 2000 altogether, many who are not residents of Syria and Lebanon have already been repatriated. To those should now be added 1200 men and 30 officers that left for France yesterday afternoon on the steamship *Athos* together with 150 naval reservists whose replacements from French regular naval forces at Alexandria brought here by this same steamer.

Further demobilization of reservists to a total of from 35,000 to 40,000 will take place as soon as ships for their repatriation are available. The Germans are insisting that the demobilization and the repatriation of these reservists and the retirement of regular officers in the French Army who have reached the recently lowered age limits should be completed by September 15. It is hoped that negotiations for safe conducts from the British and Italians that are now under way will be concluded shortly. As suggested in my telegram No. 79 of August 17, the importance of repatriating of reservists as rapidly as possible is locally recognized; and it is understood that the departure yesterday of the more troublesome elements and the prospect of early repatriation now anticipated by the remainder has gone a long way toward relieving the tension that had been causing anxiety here.

Subject to immediate retirement are a number of competent and energetic officers familiar with the Near East, most of whom are pro-British and some of whom would prefer to remain here rather than return to France under the present conditions. In general it may be said that reservists, including officers, are concerned primarily with rejoining their families after a long period of separation concluding with one of demoralizing inactivity; that many regular army officers while not now disposed to join the British are considering the possibility of carrying on with their former allies at some later date. Consequently the number of officers and men who originally passed into Palestine and have continued to go over in small groups that might have been larger if demobilization had taken place without any possibility of immediate repatriation, have now reached a total of but 400 or 500 according to both British consular and French military estimates.

---

[17] Not printed.

It will be observed that on the basis of the number of French troops now under arms here and of those supposed to be demobilized by September 15 the French military forces in Syria and Lebanon after that date should number between 40 and 60 thousand. It is understood that in local French military circles a force of 40 thousand is considered adequate to maintain order now that, according to military observers who have frequently and recently covered the entire area, native elements seem little inclined to trouble. The effect of German propaganda in Syria is still widely apparent but it is found in anti-British rather than in anti-French feeling and still has to overcome the handicap of association with Italy.

It is interesting to note that the determination of the French authorities here to use all the means at their disposal to prevent disturbances of whatever nature or origin, as reported in my telegram No. 51 of July 10, is frequently reiterated but no longer as at one time with apparent reference to a possible movement against Syria on the part of the British. While French troops are now stationed along the Palestine frontier in greater number and at more points than usual this is not believed to be intended as a warning to the British but rather as a manifestation of a determination to prevent clandestine crossing the border by French deserters or others. This may also have a relation to the prospective arrival of the commission mentioned in my telegram 77 dated August 16 [18] which the Consulate General has privately learned from an official source will consist of an Italian General and another Italian officer and is expected soon although probable date has not yet been announced. It is assumed that for the time being Italy and Germany are not averse to seeing a French force of from 40 to 60 thousand holding this area; and it is apparently the desire of the French authorities to satisfy these Italian officers that such a force should be maintained here and to avoid any action that might give rise to possible doubt in this regard.

PALMER

740.0011 European War 1939/5206

Memorandum by the Chief of the Division of Near Eastern Affairs
(Murray)

[WASHINGTON,] August 23, 1940.

The most important fact emerging from the attached telegram [19] from our Consul General in Beirut regarding the French Army in Syria and the Lebanon is the intention of the French authorities to maintain the strength of that army at from 40,000 to 60,000 men.

---

[18] Not printed.
[19] *Supra.*

As stated in the telegram, it is assumed that Italy and Germany would not be averse to the maintenance in Syria and the Lebanon of such a force. Although the reasons for this assumption are not given in the telegram they are, it is believed, fairly obvious.

The presence of such a number of French troops would immobilize an approximately equivalent number of British troops in Palestine and thus prevent the reinforcement by that number of British troops in Egypt in case of emergency.

Moreover, the presence of such troops constitutes a possible threat to Turkey's southwestern border and to that extent hampers Turkey's freedom of action.

It is not unlikely that, in the absence of any appreciable number of troops in Syria, the British would be tempted to endeavor to occupy the country to prevent its being used as a base against Palestine or Iraq. The Syrians and Lebanese, it is believed, would probably welcome such a British occupation as offering the possibility of the reunion of Palestine, Trans-Jordan and Syria, which the Arabs envisaged at the end of the first World War. As long as French troops are maintained in any considerable numbers in Syria the realization of that partial Arab unity is obstructed.

Moreover, the French troops relieve Italy of any present necessity of endeavoring to occupy the country with the consequent difficult problems of supply.

For all these reasons, accordingly, it appears reasonable to conclude that the continued maintenance of a French army of any appreciable strength in Syria is not contrary to Axis interests, but is even in the interests of Germany and Italy.

WALLACE MURRAY

740.00119 European War 1939/493 : Telegram

The Consul General at Beirut (Palmer) to the Secretary of State

BEIRUT, August 28, 1940—noon.
[Received August 30—8 : 45 a. m.]

84. Italian Armistice Commission delegation arrived Aleppo last night, expected in Beirut today, composed of General Giorgi, two colonels and major with eight non-commissioned officers as secretaries. Its mission is defined as (1) to take inventory of military material; (2) to verify liberation of Italians who had been interned. French delegation composed of General Arlabosse, Secretary of Embassy Conty (Chief of Political Bureau of High Commission), Colonel Keime (General Fougère's Chief of Staff), Colonel Alamichel and naval Captain Voisard with Captain Leridon as secretary.

PALMER

740.0011 European War 1939/5445 : Telegram

The Consul General at Beirut (Palmer) to the Secretary of State

BEIRUT, September 9, 1940—8 p. m.
[Received September 11—9 a. m.]

88. Reference to Department's telegram 51, August 15 [16] and my 82, August 20. Approximately 1,000 reservists originally due to leave for France yesterday on the steamship *Dessirada* are now scheduled to sail tomorrow. Departure of further equal contingent on steamship *Sidiabbas* likewise in port awaits British authorization. Remainder ready to leave on steamers expected shortly; but British Consul General recently communicated to High Commission warning of Admiral commanding British naval forces in the Mediterranean that, although British make no attempt to seize lentils and other foodstuffs unauthorizedly shipped on steamships *Providence* and *Athos* that left here on August 16 with reservists under safe conduct, no further such shipments will be allowed to pass. Consul General has referred to London request of French authorities here that one last shipment of 400 tons of lentils be authorized but he is not counting on the favorable reply that he has recommended as an easy step toward better official relations.

Persistent refusal of Vichy Government to agree to British proposal that French steamship *Patria* held at Haifa since armistice be exchanged for three British ships of approximately equivalent aggregate tonnage similarly held here until their formal seizure of July 31 when their crews were arrested, as reported in my telegrams 63 and 65 of August first,[20] continues to meet unyielding insistence of British naval authorities that British seamen concerned be allowed to leave on their ships.

These 40 British seamen, whose original internment in army barracks previously occupied by native troops and admitted by French Army officers to be unsanitary was the subject of energetic British protests, have recently been returned to these barracks from the former German and Italian internment camp near Sidon, to permit of the reinternment on September 7 of Germans unwilling to [return to?] Germany and therefore considered, the High Commissioner tells me, as entitled to "right of asylum" here.

The British Consul General informs me that the return of the seamen to the barracks was without the knowledge of the High Commissioner; that the latter promptly undertook to have them transferred to a mountain village; that because of the possibility that partial liberty might involve them in irritating incidents the Consulate General was instructed to request that they be quartered aboard their

---

[20] Neither printed.

ships; that this request has been refused by the French naval authorities who seem to be inclined to make concessions in respect to the seamen conditional upon receipt from Palestine of September quota of gasoline on which this month's rationing is based.

More disturbing than delays in settlement of immediate problem of fuel for motor transport are successive indications from London that British approval of Palestine clearing agreement will be withheld until both ships and seamen are released. Consequent necessity for control of gasoline and foodstuffs ordinarily obtained largely from abroad was explained by High Commissioner in recent radio broadcast as due to economic pressure on the part of the British in disregard of the well-being of the people of the Near East; but his address made little impression among the native population, either Moslem or Christian, and aroused no enthusiasm among the French here. He failed to discredit contrary statements in French and Arabic circular of undisclosed but suspected British origin that is understood to have been widely accepted in French military and native circles and to have given timely impetus to a growing sentiment in favor of the British which has been particularly noticeable since the arrival of military delegation of Italian armistice commission on August 28.

In general the relations of this delegation with local French delegation evolve no ground for dissatisfaction; but in respect to certain minor instances of Italian disregard for the French and with reference to indications that several Italian consular officers formerly stationed in Syria and Lebanon would soon be returning in a pseudo-military capacity as additional members of this delegation the High Commissioner has protested to Vichy.

Problem of repatriation of nearly 40,000 reservists still awaiting transportation is complicated by restlessness of colonial and other regular forces. Officers admit that this has increased considerably since arrival of Italian delegation and effective development of British propaganda, including daily French broadcasts from Jerusalem and Cairo. Troops have been cautioned against misrepresentative radio reports but individual departures for Palestine are not infrequent and even among officers there seems to be considerable satisfaction that some 30 planes reliably reported to have been flown to Palestine and Egypt since the armistice include several Curtiss bombers that have made their getaway since the Italian delegation's arrival.

High Commissioner has expressed himself to me with resentment in respect to British radio propaganda from Palestine and Egypt, but he assures me that he has no knowledge or [of] origin of obviously local interference that recently has practically obliterated these particular programs. His attitude reflects nervousness naturally resulting from strain of conscientiously endeavoring to safeguard this mandated area and protect French and native interests here while representing distant government in which many of his associates, a greater number of the military forces and a vast majority of the native population now lack confidence. Rumors allegedly current in Palestine that French Army in Near East will soon join forces with British are manifestly inspired and premature but in local military circles there is a definite trend of thought in that direction.

PALMER

890D.01/509 : Telegram

The Ambassador in Turkey (MacMurray) to the Secretary of State

ANKARA, September 18, 1940—4 p. m.
[Received 5 : 45 p. m.]

152. The French Chargé has made the following statement on the situation in Syria to one of the editors of the semi-official *Ulus:*

"Many unfounded rumors acrimoniously circulated recently on the situation in Syria. I should regret very much if these rumors should cause any doubt in Turkish opinion as to the firm intention of the French Government scrupulously to fulfill its mission in these countries under mandate. I am moreover in a position to point out to you : (1) that contrary to what has been insinuated, the Franco-Italian armistice convention²⁰ᵃ contains no secret clause concerning Syria; (2) that the French High Commission contemplates no abandonment of its military positions in the Levant which could jeopardize the internal or external security of the countries under mandate; (3) that no foreign influence is being exercised on the political activity of the French High Commission at Beirut. Since I have the pleasure of speaking to a Turkish journalist, permit me to add that France, deeply grateful for the sympathy which the Turkish nation has shown in its misfortunes, is firmly resolved to omit no effort in order that the friendly and confident character of Turco-Syrian relations may be maintained."

Repeated to Beirut.

MACMURRAY

740.0011 European War 1939/5609 : Telegram

The Consul General at Beirut (Palmer) to the Secretary of State

BEIRUT, September 20, 1940—11 a.m.
[Received September 21—8 : 40 a. m.]

93. With reference to telegram No. 152 of September 18 from Ankara. Statement of French Chargé d'Affaires at Ankara may be

²⁰ᵃ Signed June 24, 1940; for text, see *Documents on American Foreign Relations*, July 1939–June 1940, p. 436.

attributed to High Commissioner's annoyance over British propaganda and his growing concern over persistent reports from neighboring countries that resentment of Syrians and Lebanese has been aroused by presence of delegation of Italian Armistice Commission and that French authorities here are embarrassed by delegation's attitude and demands.

Monsieur Puaux's general nervousness and his particular annoyance over British propaganda, both of which were mentioned in my telegram 88, September 9, have unquestionably been aggravated by the continued presence of this delegation although he was relieved to find that there are no former Italian consular officers from Syria or Lebanon in the second group which arrived a week ago and which includes a naval officer and an air force officer.

Monsieur Puaux maintains that the entire delegation is military and assures me that it is correct in its attitude and is neither interfering in non-military matters nor making unreasonable demands; but the general public, native and French alike, and many officials and French military officers think otherwise.

Among the native population both Moslems and Christians freely express resentment of Italian authority, whatever its origin or scope, and disgust that the French should, in any respect, be obliged to conform to Italian wishes. Even in high places, normally pro-French, there is unconcealed admiration for the way the British are carrying on and confidentially expressed regret that at this time of stress this area is not under British control.

Well timed and well received by Syrian and Lebanese, Moslems in general and many Christians was the Emir Abdullah's [21] recent message broadcast through Jerusalem, Cairo and London in which he expressed the hope that the French authorities here, independently of the Vichy Government and in effective cooperation with the British, would prove worthy of the confidence of the Arab world by maintaining Syria and Lebanon free from Italian interference or other subjection to armistice terms unjustly applied to this mandated area.

Among the French there is a growing indignation that they should be humiliated by the presence here of those who are so widely held in contempt by Syrians and Lebanese but who come here with an official status as victors. Significant was a meeting of all French Army officers in Beirut who were called together by General Fougère last week on the eve of the arrival of the second group of Italian delegates.

At this meeting the General appealed to these officers to remain true to France and the Pétain [22] Government which he urged them to consider no longer as the Vichy Government but as the government of the French people. According to separate personal accounts on the

---

[21] Emir of Trans-Jordan.
[22] Henri Philippe Pétain, French Chief of State.

part of three of these officers, at the conclusion of the General's remarks which included a warning for those of pro-British sentiments, all but a few of those present maintained a reserved silence, to the apparent discomfiture of their commanding officer. In confidential conversation with me one of these officers who has an important command expressed the disappointment of the majority who had hoped that the meeting would prove to be the occasion for a declaration for leadership that would bring them back into the war beside the British.

Combined with the problem of leadership for the reputedly large number of officers and troops desirous of uniting with the British, is the increasingly acute one of reparation for an equal number of reservists whose sole desire is to return to their families and who are again becoming restless as the prospect of their homecoming seems more and more remote. The Consulate General has been reliably informed that the Italians are showing no disposition to facilitate arrangements for such repatriation requiring both their approval and that of the British; and with some 35,000 reservists still here out of a total of approximately 40,000 it seems likely that a large number will have to be reckoned with for some time to come and that optimistic predictions apparently current in Palestine, to the effect that the French here will join forces with the British within the next few weeks, are unwarranted.

PALMER

740.0011 European War 1939/5772 : Telegram

The Consul General at Beirut (Palmer) to the Secretary of State

BEIRUT, September 28, 1940—7 p. m.
[Received September 29—1 : 20 p. m.]

97. Reference my telegram No. 93, September 20. Developments of the past week have effectively broken up previously widespread and growing support here for de Gaulle [23] and have indefinitely set back the local movement to join forces with the British that gave some promise of action earlier in the month but lacked leadership.

These developments include not only those at Dakar [24] but also the unannounced arrival at Beirut of Colonel Bourget formerly General Weygand's chief of staff here; the arrest of several local de Gaulle supporters, both military and civilian, who in an ill-timed spirit of confidence that the moment for action was imminent expressed themselves too freely; a military ceremony at which decorations were conferred on numerous officers, including some frankly pro-British,

---

[23] Gen. Charles de Gaulle, leader of the Free French.
[24] Dakar, French West Africa, was unsuccessfully attacked by British and Free French forces, September 23–25, 1940.

and at the conclusion of which the High Commissioner in a private gathering appealed to these and other officers to maintain a spirit of unity in support of Marshal Pétain and of loyalty of France, to the exclusion of all other countries; and a radio broadcast in which the High Commissioner made a similar appeal to all French citizens here and urged the Syrians and Lebanese to unite with the French in the full confidence that French military forces will remain here and maintain order and security and that France will not forget Syrian and Lebanese aspirations.

Effect of Dakar incident has been to intensify anti-British feeling in certain French circles, principally naval, still resentful of British action at Oran; to revive anti-British feeling on the part of those who had made up their minds to forget Oran; to discredit de Gaulle among his former supporters; with a consequent lessening of the chances of any early movement here in favor of the British. But hope for the defeat of Germany by the British and that French forces here may eventually have an opportunity to contribute to such defeat is a predominant underlying sentiment, particularly among French Army officers.

Arrival of Bourget generally regarded as a personal messenger from Weygand [25] to his former officers in this [apparent omission], appears to have resulted in crystallizing this underlying sentiment but with emphasis on unity and discipline as essential to the maintenance of order and security here and to preparedness for eventual aggression on the part of Germany or Italy. Bourget's presence here where Weygand's prestige is still great undoubtedly paved the way for the favorable reception of the High Commissioner's appeal for unity on the part of the army officers; the reaction to his subsequent broadcast was largely one of indifference in French circles in general and of doubt in native circles as to whether France would ever again be in a position to bring about a realization of Syrian and Lebanese aspirations even if the High Commissioner's assurances in this regard should be recalled.

PALMER

740.0011 European War 1939/6117

Memorandum of Conversation, by the Chief of the Division of Near Eastern Affairs (Murray)

[WASHINGTON,] October 2, 1940.

During a call from M. Jacques Truelle, Counselor of the French Embassy, yesterday, he informed me that he had been instructed by

---

[25] General Weygand was appointed Delegate General of the Vichy Government in North Africa on September 6, 1940, but had not yet assumed his duties.

his Government to make a categorical denial of the reports published in the press in this country on September 26 to the effect that Premier Mussolini had demanded, in Italo-French armistice negotiations, that French naval bases, airdromes and military centers in Syria and the Lebanon should be turned over to Italian armed forces.

There is attached a clipping from the *New York Times* [25a] representing the United Press story emanating from Cairo and dated September 25. The story reports in detail eleven "demands" said to have been made by the Italians during the above-mentioned negotiations.

M. Truelle stated that it was obvious to him that this story emanating from Cairo as it did was entirely British propaganda and he expressed the view that it was deplorable beyond words that the British persist in spreading lies of this kind in times like these when France's fate is hanging in the balance. He added that, while he was not instructed by his Government to do so, he nevertheless earnestly hoped that officials of this Government would point out to British officials here and in London the folly of these methods and the disastrous consequences that might ensue for France if the British persist in spreading propaganda tales of this kind.

I told M. Truelle that I would bring his views to the attention of the appropriate authorities of the Department.

740.00119 European War 1939/516 : Telegram

The Secretary of State to the Consul General at Beirut (Palmer)

WASHINGTON, October 2, 1940—6 p. m.

71. A United Press despatch from Cairo dated September 25 reported that 11 demands had been made by the Italian armistice commission regarding Syria. These demands included demobilization of armed forces in Syria, repatriation of demobilized forces, delivery of all military, air and naval bases to Italy, administrative control by an Italian commission, ban against listening to radio broadcasts except from the Axis, Italian control of production and commerce, and the surrender of all army munitions, provisions, and gasoline to Italy.

On September 30 an Associated Press despatch from Cairo stated that "Authoritative reports" had reached there concerning further Italian demands regarding Syria, relating principally to permission for the return to Syria of German, Italian, and certain Arab propagandists. The United Press also carried this report on October 1 from Cairo, attributing the source to the News Agency Orient Arabe, Beirut.

[25a] Not reprinted.

On October 2 the United Press reported from Cairo that the Italian Commission had been unable to persuade French officials to turn over 800 aircraft and airdromes in Lebanon to Axis powers, that the Commissioners have been recalled and that a new commission will be appointed.

Please report by telegraph any basis which may exist for these reports, with your comments.

HULL

740.0011 European War 1939/5865 : Telegram

The Consul General at Beirut (Palmer) to the Secretary of State

BEIRUT, October 4, 1940—7 p. m.
[Received October 5—1 : 06 a. m.]

101. Department's No. 71, October 2, received today. The four press despatches mentioned are wholly incorrect according to the High Commissioner who qualifies as "false" each report and every item.

Prior inquiries on the part of the Consulate General with a view to determining the basis for similar reports previously current here confirmed none of them.

Comments including specific references to certain items will follow by telegram tomorrow morning.

PALMER

740.0011 European War 1939/5860 : Telegram

The Consul General at Beirut (Palmer) to the Secretary of State

BEIRUT, October 5, 1940—9 a. m.
[Received 6 : 25 p. m.]

102. Supplementing 101 of October 4th and referring to 82 of August 20 (final sentence), 93 of September 20 (third and last paragraphs) and 97 of September 28. High Commissioner reaffirms and attitude of French officers plainly indicates intention to maintain adequate armed forces in Syria and Lebanon.

He seems confident that Axis Powers are still satisfied to feel that there is a strong French force here and he denies that Italian Commission has demanded demobilization, delivery of any military air or naval base, or surrender of aircraft or any army munitions or provisions or gasoline (it is understood that all but 100 planes have been effectively unmobilized; that these 100 are allowed to fly over restricted courses on normal patrol incident to the maintenance of internal security; that if [one] of these planes leaves this mandated area the squadron to which it belongs will be permanently grounded with a consequent reduction in the total number available for such use.)

He emphasizes that military and other French authorities here are more interested than Italy and Germany in expediting repatriation of potentially troublesome reservists and he pointed out that whatever the wishes of the Axis Powers the repatriation cannot be expected without the consent of the British in the case of each ship.

He also points out that there is no prohibition here against listening to any radio broadcast and he insists that neither in this respect nor in respect to administrative matters or control of production and trade have there been any demands or interference on the part of the Italian Commission.

He declares that he has no knowledge of any proposal for the return here of Arab or other propagandists unless a former Italian Vice Consul in Beirut who recently returned with pseudo military status as a member of a third group of armistice commission delegates and personnel, notwithstanding the High Commissioner's objections previously expressed to Vichy, may be considered in this category.

False reports such as the press despatches mentioned in Department's telegram 71 of October 2 are generally based on rumors that circulate freely here and frequently appear in local Arab newspapers that are read also in Palestine. On more than one occasion the British Consul General has telegraphed the Foreign Office suggesting that radio broadcasting stations under British control be cautioned against the repetition of unconfirmed reports as to the situation here which discredit British sources of information that until recently were locally considered as generally reliable. It has been suggested that German and Italian agents may have found in the natives' weakness for rumors a means for spreading misleading reports that quickly reach neighboring countries, are almost certain to be included in British and American broadcasts and newspapers and are often the subject of official denials that offer Axis broadcasting stations and news services opportunities for undermining confidence in British broadcasts in general.

Latest reports of this nature based on false local rumors widely accepted in Palestine and repeated abroad picture bread lines in Syria and state that 2 or 3 Italian planes damaged by anti-aircraft fire in recent raid on Haifa came down in Lebanon or just off this coast and that 1 of these planes that made a forced landing near Beirut had a German observer on board. There are no bread lines here, nor any reason therefor. Only 1 such plane is known to have come down here, the one that made a forced landing near Beirut with no German but 5 Italians that have been interned.

PALMER

740.0011 European War 1939/5929 : Telegram

The Secretary of State to the Chargé in France (Matthews)

WASHINGTON, October 11, 1940—5 p. m.

589. Your 711, October 8, 4 p. m.[26] On October 7 the French Ambassador read to the Under Secretary a telegram from his Government[27] characterizing as totally false reports that Italy had made demands on France for the establishment of air bases in Syria, submarine bases in French North African possessions, or the complete demobilization of all French forces in Syria. The telegram authorized the Ambassador to inform this Government that no demands of any character with regard to Syria or other French African possessions had ever been formulated by Italy. On October 4 the French High Commissioner in Syria made similar denials to our Consul General at Beirut in regard to Italian activities in the mandated territories.

It is difficult to reconcile these denials with the statements made to you, as reported in the second paragraph of section 3 of your 711, October 8, 4 p. m., particularly the reference to Italian endeavors to stir up trouble in Syria.

We should appreciate your comments on the foregoing.

HULL

740.0011 European War 1939/6068 : Telegram

The Chargé in France (Matthews) to the Secretary of State

VICHY, October 14, 1940—9 p. m.
[Received October 15—7:25 a. m.]

747. Department's 589, October 11, 5 p. m. I have heard no confirmation here of any reports that Italy has made any formal demands on France for the establishment of air bases in Syria or for any submarine bases in French North Africa or that it has demanded the complete demobilization of all French forces in Syria. I learn from both French Foreign Office and several high French military sources that Italy has demanded the reduction of all French forces in North Africa to a total of 100,000. I have also been told by French War Department sources that Italy has required a reduction of French forces in Syria to the equivalent of the three divisions which were stationed there prior to September 1939: the French have agreed to this demand and would in any case have returned to North Africa the forces sent to Syria during the war.

[26] Not printed.
[27] See memorandum by the Under Secretary of State, October 7, vol. II, p. 384.

With the Department's telegram in mind I inquired of Charles Roux [28] this morning with regard to the Italian attitude in Syria and he replied literally as follows: "The Italians are causing us all possible trouble both in Syria and everywhere else. They are now behaving worse than the Germans." In spite of my questioning on Syria he would not be more specific other than to mention minor endeavors to stir up some trouble among the natives. He added "Through their armistice commission and other missions they are able to cause all sorts of annoyances and difficulties."

The above statements and those reported in my telegram 711, October 8, 4 p. m.[29] are of course at variance with the statements mentioned in the Department's telegram 589. There are several explanations. There is, as I have endeavored to stress, an important difference in views between the permanent personnel of the French Foreign Office who retain their ardent hopes for a British victory and who will talk sometimes with relative frankness in private conversation, and the other and more influential elements of the Government. It is more than possible that the telegram which the French Ambassador read to the Under Secretary was written by or transmitted under the instructions of Baudouin [30] himself or even under the orders of Laval.[31] This should be borne in mind, I feel, when the French Ambassador discusses with the Department various instructions received from Vichy.

It is my recollection that the "false reports" on Italian demands mentioned by the Ambassador emanated largely from the British radio in connection with appeals for support of the de Gaulle movement. As the Department is aware that movement is anathema to the entire French Government and any "false reports" mentioned by the B. B. C. in connection with the movement will be eagerly, promptly and publicly denied by Vichy. There is a further possibility that the Italians themselves may have brought sufficient pressure to compel the aforesaid denial. This is a point which French officialdom would be loath to discuss.

(The above mentioned comparison between the German and Italian attitudes today I have heard from military sources too.) Apparently the Germans are for the moment showing a greater willingness to comply with minor French requests. This may be due to one of two factors: As recent displeasure at growing applause for the British cause in movie theaters in occupied France has shown, the Germans are somewhat worried at increasing hostility toward them by the population of the occupied zone and may wish greater "cooperation"

---

[28] Secretary General of the French Ministry for Foreign Affairs.
[29] Not printed.
[30] Paul Baudouin, French Minister for Foreign Affairs.
[31] Pierre Laval, French Vice Premier.

from the French Government. In the second place the Germans may be relaxing their severity somewhat in the hope of French acquiescence in their demands for control of French Mediterranean ports. That such demands have actually been made I had confirmed today from another excellent source although they are still officially denied. The Germans may feel that by throwing a few sops the French Government may become more willing to accept their complete control and the loss of its remaining "independence".

MATTHEWS

740.0011 European War 1939/6068 : Telegram

The Secretary of State to the Consul General at Beirut (Palmer)

WASHINGTON, October 17, 1940—5 p. m.

80. Your 102, October 5, 9 a. m. Embassy at Vichy has been informed that through armistice commission and other missions the Italians are causing the French "all possible trouble" in Syria and elsewhere. In Syria Italians are said, among other things, to have endeavored to stir up trouble among the natives.

Please comment by telegraph. Avoid revealing source of your information in any discreet inquiries you may make. Sources other than the High Commission might be helpful, including your British colleague.

HULL

740.0011 European War 1939/6164 : Telegram

The Consul General at Beirut (Palmer) to the Secretary of State

BEIRUT, October 18, 1940—4 p. m.
[Received October 20—8 : 55 a. m.]

110. Referring to my telegram No. 109, today's date.[32] It is not certain but quite possible that the younger reservists are to be kept here for a time as a result of Colonel Bourget's visit, reported in my 97 of September 28. He left here by plane October 12, not for Africa as had been generally understood, but for France.

On the day before Colonel Bourget's departure he told me that he had come here to [survey?] the situation and that he had found it was rather confused, as he had expected. He stated that he had found officers and men, as well as officials of the High Commission and other French residents, divided as regards loyalty to government at Vichy and in many cases uncertain as to what stand to take. He admitted

[32] Not printed.

that this state of affairs was the natural consequence of lack of confidence and loss of discipline resulting from the wavering attitude of their leaders here immediately following the armistice. He said that he had been charged by Marshal Pétain with the mission of explaining to French officers and others in authority here the situation in France and the position of the French Government and of emphasizing the necessity for unity and discipline.

I had previously been informed on good authority that in his talks with French officers Colonel Bourget had not encouraged anti-British feelings but had been urging them to be neither pro-British nor anti-British and to devote their entire thought and time to achievement of French unity here as a part of Empire unity. In his talk with me he maintained a similar attitude although criticizing the British for dissatisfaction among the French troops here and, with considerable feeling, for paying bonuses to French aviators for planes in which the latter had gone over to the British. He admitted that it is quite natural that Frenchmen should desire a British victory as the only hope for the defeat of Germany but he suggested that those Frenchmen who wish to do their bit are not now in a position to contribute effectively to such a victory and that only by holding together could they prepare themselves for eventualities.

Subsequently the British Consul General told me that Colonel Bourget had severely criticized the British in addressing a gathering of French officials and heads of French institutions here; and the High Commissioner in response to inquiry on my part regarding Colonel Bourget's visit, expressed regret that the Government at Vichy apparently fails to appreciate the importance and recognize its possibility of facilitating more normal relations between this mandated area and adjacent territory under British control. But in reviewing Colonel Bourget's response to my request that he inform me as far as he might feel free to do so regarding the object and result of his unannounced return to Beirut, it is my impression that he wished to make it clear to me in my official capacity and as a friend of General Weygand that the mission which he had carried out here, involving disciplinary measures affecting both officers and civilians that have made for hard feeling against him, was not directed against the British but was considered necessary in relation to Empire unity now centering around General Weygand in North Africa [33] and offering a possibility of an eventual comeback on the part of the French.

From other sources also I have gained the impression that an increasing number of Frenchmen here and elsewhere now envisage the possibility of such a comeback.

---

[33] For correspondence on this subject, see vol. II, pp. 570 ff., especially pp. 597–631.

One of General Weygand's former officers, who is still on the General Staff here and who, immediately after the armistice, had told me that he and others were determined to carry on with the British, has assured me since Colonel Bourget's visit that their seeing the defeat of Germany and to have a part in it has not changed and that they hope that Empire unity centering around General Weygand in North Africa will offer them their opportunity.

The same idea of Empire unity as essential to an eventual French comeback against Germany was stressed in confidential conversation with me by Roger Garreau who arrived here from Vichy on October 14 en route to Batavia as Consul General. I had known Garreau as High Commissioner de Martel's delegate in the sanjak of Alexandretta up to the time of the Hatay settlement and he may be further identified by Childs [34] in the Division of Far Eastern Affairs who knew him in Cairo, and by our Embassy at Berlin concerning his arrest by the German authorities while he was Consul General at Hamburg. He informed me that apart from his consular functions he is charged with a special mission that will take him principally to French Indochina and the purpose of which is primarily the maintenance of Empire unity in anticipation of the time when anti-German sentiment in France, which he says is now rapidly being revived and is already widespread in occupied territory, will express itself in a movement there that will result in freedom of action for Frenchmen abroad even though it may not immediately free France from German domination.

PALMER

740.0011 European War 1939/6221 : Telegram

The Consul General at Beirut (Palmer) to the Secretary of State

BEIRUT, October 23, 1940—10 a. m.
[Received October 24—8 : 52 a. m.]

117. Department's No. 80, October 17. British Consul General, with whom I have been constantly in touch has again assured me that to the best of his knowledge and belief the Italian Commission here in its relations with the High Commission and the French military authorities has been careful to maintain a correct attitude and to avoid unjustifiable or unreasonable demands; that in his opinion Italian propaganda in Lebanon and Syria is of little consequence.

This opinion is shared by American consular dragomans here and in Damascus and by the British Consul General in the Syrian capital, with whom I dined there 2 days ago; also by other well-informed

[34] J. Rives Childs.

friends who have given me their views during the past few days and whose statements [merit?] full credence, including President Edde,[35] President Dodge of the American University and prominent Lebanese-born Palestine citizen George Antonius.

It is generally admitted that Italians are endeavoring, principally through schools and Maronite clergy, to raise Italy's prestige here at the cost of [apparent omission]; but their activities in this respect are merely cautious revival of activities that were no secret before Italy's entry into war and seem to cause little concern in local French official circles and to be discounted by British consular officers and others that might be disturbed if such activities were considered likely to be effective.

Considerable increase in number of Maronite students at American University this year, with corresponding decrease at French (Jesuit) University, it is believed to be due partly to Italian suggestions in Maronite circles that French may not count for much here in the future; but this in itself is obviously not likely to [disturb?] the French; and Maronite support is unquestionably prejudicial to such chances, if any, as the Italians may have had for success among Moslems.

Reports that Italian agents have been feeling out Kurds and certain Moslem Arab leaders, both tribal and political, including former Syrian Ministers Jamil Mardam and Saadalahjabri, come from well-informed sources; but such Kurdish support as may have been cannot be expected to be loyal or lasting and there is little encouragement to be found in receptiveness of political leaders who had already lost much influence before their recent flight from Syria (reported in my telegram 116 of yesterday [36]) following indictment for complicity in murder of principal political opponent.

Considering that Italians in general are heartily disliked by Moslems of Syria and Lebanon as well as by a majority of non-Moslem elements, it is difficult to understand how they could cause serious trouble for French if the Italian Commission were endeavoring to do so, which does not appear to be the case. It was reported soon after Commission's arrival that subordinate personnel had manifested an attitude of superiority in various public places that aroused unconcealed resentment on the part of Lebanese; but the head of the Commission and his fellow delegates appear to have avoided such incidents and to have taken steps to prevent further indiscretion on the part of their assistants.

Even as regards Maronite member of staff of this office tells me that Maronite Patriarch, generally regarded as past master in art of give

---

[35] Emile Edde, President of the Republic of Lebanon.
[36] Not printed.

and take, with emphasis on the latter, recently turned down suggestion of an influential member of his flock that his Beatitude invite Italian delegates to luncheon; the welcome conclusion among Maronites being that although Italy may now consider herself prospective successor of France in Lebanon, if not in Syria, Italian influence here falls far short of [apparent omission], and gives little promise of ever reaching a point where it would have to be reckoned with.

Further indication of lack of local French concern and apparent absence of grounds therefor in respect to Italian influence and activities is found in High Commissioner's reply 10 days ago to my inquiry whether Italian Commission was causing trouble in Lebanon or Syria. He assured me that it was not and told me that members of now discredited but potentially troublesome Parti Populaire Syrien had recently approached certain members of the Commission with a view to obtaining their support for pro-Axis activities here but had been turned down. Whether Italian stand was prompted by caution or by doubt as to usefulness of this group of malcontents, this incident suggests that French authorities here do not ignore possibility of trouble if Italians were disposed and able to make use of such opportunist elements but are satisfied that there is nothing to worry about as matters now stand.

Situation might change if German Commission were here, for there is considerable pro-German feeling among Moslems in Lebanon and even more in Syria and some such feeling in other circles. But only yesterday the High Commissioner emphasized that Germany has been showing surprisingly little direct interest in this mandated area, and he flatly contradicted persistent local rumors that Germans have recently arrived in this country to assist German delegate, Roser. Latter has now been here 3 weeks and the apparent correctness of his attitude, coupled with that of Italian Commission, may justify assumption that until Germans or Italians are in a position to establish themselves firmly here they will not risk playing into hands of British by irritating native population and antagonizing French authorities. The latter in fact find presence of the Italians here in itself and in so far as concerns their attitude and activities much less a cause for concern than successive disturbing incidents between French and British including British propaganda activities within and from outside Lebanon and Syria, and British repetition by broadcasts and otherwise of false misrepresentative reports that embarrass the French High Commission and irritate French military authorities.

PALMER

740.0011 European War 1939/6287 : Telegram

The Secretary of State to the Consul General at Beirut (Palmer)

WASHINGTON, October 31, 1940—3 p. m.

87. The Chargé d'Affaires at Vichy in reporting on French reaction to the Italian attack on Greece [37] states:

"It is privately admitted in certain official circles that if Turkey is drawn in, the allegiance of Syria to the Vichy regime will promptly be severed."

Please comment.

HULL

740.0011 European War 1939/557 : Telegram

The Consul General at Beirut (Palmer) to the Secretary of State

BEIRUT, October 31, 1940—5 p. m.
[Received November 1—8 : 30 a. m.]

123. Reference my telegram No. 121, October 28.[38] Local reaction to piecemeal reports regarding Pétain–Hitler understanding [39] is among the French continued distrust of Laval but desire to believe in Pétain. Resultant uncertainty in official circles is reflected throughout native population in growing disesteem for the French and increasing doubt as to their permanence in the Levant. Consequent widespread consideration of possible successors reveals, in contrast with general disdain for Italians, divided sentiment regarding British, Germans and Turks. British are strongly favored by most Christian communities, considerably by Druzes and to some extent by Moslems, latter principally in Lebanon. Germans are highly respected and hopefully awaited by most Moslems except where Turkish influence is still strong in North Syria and Tripoli.

With reference to persistent rumors as to nature and possible scope of eventual cooperation between France and Germany, local press on October 29 gave prominence to notice to the effect that the High Commission had been authorized to declare officially that there was no foundation for reports of peace preliminaries, or of cession of territory, or of the placing of strategic bases at the disposal of Germany or Italy, or of any attempt against French sovereignty in France or abroad. In response to query on my part as to whether this declaration could be made with assurance, the High Commissioner informed me that it was based on a telegram from Baudouin. The statement at

---

[37] Telegram No. 845, October 28, 9 p. m., not printed.
[38] Not printed.
[39] See telegram No. 3537, October 26, from the Chargé in the United Kingdom, and following documents, vol. II, pp. 395 ff.

first had a calming effect, but it has since been vitiated by the vagueness of successive announcements from Vichy which has caused disappointment among the French and disquietude in native circles.

PALMER

740.0011 European War 1939/6490 : Telegram

The Consul General at Beirut (Palmer) to the Secretary of State

BEIRUT, November 5, 1940—3 p. m.
[Received November 6—5 : 30 a. m.]

124. Reference Department's 87, October 31. Reports of Greek resistance against Italian aggression have been received here with general satisfaction, freely expressed by the native population but cautiously by the French; latter undoubtedly influenced by official attitude of Vichy as evidenced by prohibition of departure of locally resident Greeks of military age numbering approximately 350 according to the Greek Consul General.

Position of Turkey set in President Inonu's recent speech has likewise caused satisfaction here except among apprehensive Armenians and pro-German Moslems. Announcement regarding Turkish relations with Union of Soviet Socialist Republics and declaration of cooperation with Great Britain have enheartened pro-British elements both native and French and been welcomed in French military circles.

According to reliable information the French forces here have standing instructions to maintain order and French authority and resist aggression of whatever origin, and responsible officers insist that there would be no compromise if German or Italian military action were attempted here. The thought that any such action is unlikely now with the position of Turkey so clearly defined is not only a [apparent omission] to those who have lost interest in fighting since the armistice but also an encouragement to those who are anxiously but patiently awaiting an opportunity to fight against Germany.

The allegiance of these forces to the Vichy regime is primarily and essentially allegiance to Pétain based on their confidence in his integrity and their belief that he stands in the way of a complete manifestation of Laval's pro-Axis sympathies and will never agree to any concessions involving immediate or eventual military assistance to Germany or Italy.

There are no local indications that this allegiance has been weakened by President Inonu's definition of the attitude of Turkey or that it might be severed if Turkey were to come into the war or as a result of any initiative here. It appears on the contrary that allegiance to Pétain is stronger than ever and that only through some action on his part would severance of such allegiance be likely to take place. It is believed that if he were to cease to be the head of the French Government and particularly if he were to break with and be succeeded by Laval a majority of the French forces here might consider themselves as under no further obligation to support the Vichy regime, but it is admitted that among the elements now here there are none with personality or prestige adequate for the local leadership that would then be necessary and it has been suggested that such leadership would have to be provided from North Africa if not from France itself.

PALMER

740.0011 European War 1939/6577 : Telegram

The Consul General at Beirut (Palmer) to the Secretary of State

BEIRUT, November 8, 1940—6 p. m.
[Received November 9—5 : 15 a. m.]

127. Confidentially informed by unimpeachable source that Turkey has threatened to seize two stretches of Baghdad Railway in Syria unless it is allowed the right to transit war material from Basra to Turkey. Orders from Armistice Commission through Vichy have been received to forbid such use of railway. Turkey has right to transit war material under railway agreement which forms part of Treaty of Friendship and Good Neighborship recently concluded but which has not been put into effect as Turkey requested, delay in so doing on the ground that the situation was too unstable. Local authorities are searching for a practical solution satisfactory to Turks as they are convinced that if Turkey executes its threat Iraq will take portion of Jezireh, Druzes will rebel and English may move forward from Palestine. Same source states that British war material is reaching Alexandretta but that port facilities are too limited. Repeated to Vichy, Ankara, Baghdad and Jerusalem.

PALMER

740.0011 European War 1939/6807 : Telegram

The Consul General at Beirut (Palmer) to the Secretary of State

BEIRUT, November 21, 1940—noon.
[Received November 22—7 : 40 a. m.]

131. In a radio message on November 19, the High Commissioner referred to appeals from neighboring countries addressed to the French and explained that in order to avoid a misunderstanding that

might prove tragic and weigh heavily on the future he felt called upon to declare that the French in the Levant, whatever their beliefs, recognize Pétain as their only leader; that today as formerly they will not have recourse to arms except to defend themselves; that French civil and military leaders of all ranks in this mandated territory are ready to perform their duties in defending it; that these leaders know that they can count on the loyalty of the Syrians and Lebanese toward France which has been and will remain their faithful friend.

This suggests an appeal to the many Syrians and Lebanese who are outspokenly "through with the French" and to the considerable number of Frenchmen in Syria and Lebanon, largely in military and other official circles, who are earnestly pro-British in their desire for the defeat of Germany but are now mostly inactive and silent, even among themselves, since they have been persuaded that any manifestation of pro-British sentiments at present would serve no useful purpose and might result in their being denounced by non-sympathetic confidants, as reported in some instances.

It also reflects the High Commissioner's apprehension, following a recent series of local official incidents affecting the British Consulate General, as to possible developments in Anglo-French relations in the Eastern Mediterranean.

PALMER

RESERVATIONS BY THE UNITED STATES OF ITS TREATY RIGHTS WITH RESPECT TO EXPORT-IMPORT RESTRICTIONS IN FRENCH MANDATED TERRITORY

690D.006/1 : Telegram

The Consul General at Beirut (Palmer) to the Secretary of State

BEIRUT, December 4, 1939—4 p. m.
[Received December 4—1 : 20 p. m.]

28. Complete control over exchange and imports, exports instituted effective December 3. Merchandise already in transit or for which special permits previously issued may proceed but all other must obtain import authorization and exchange permits. Foreign currency proceeds of exports and all other transactions must be surrendered to Exchange Bureau. Banque de Syrie Liban acting as official exchange agents. Compagnie Algérienne and Crédit Foncier d'Algérie Tunisie also authorized. Products from France or territories exempted. Airmail report follows.[40]

PALMER

---

[40] Not printed.

600.90D9/12

The Consul General at Beirut (Palmer) to the Secretary of State

No. 448   BEIRUT, January 9, 1940.
                                          [Received January 31.]

SIR: I have the honor to confirm my cablegram No. 2 of today's date,[41] as follows:

"Wool export licenses no longer granted except for France. Authorizations before January 8 valid but destination may be changed to French Empire at the option of shipper."

It is of interest to note in this connection that during the last two years for which export statistics are available, of the total Syrian exports of wool, the United States accounted for 95 and 72 percent, respectively, while the whole French Empire took only 3 and 2 percent, respectively, during the same periods. A table of these exports follows:

SYRIAN EXPORTS OF WOOL

1938

Total	1, 722, 070 kg. (100%)	1, 430, 984 LS
U. S. A.	1, 236, 608 kg. (72%)	1, 016, 350 LS
French Empire .	40, 261 kg. (2%)	35, 310 LS

1937

Total	3, 911, 272 kg. (100%)	2, 968, 496 LS
U. S. A.	3, 698, 080 kg. (95%)	2, 831, 716 LS
French Empire .	107, 118 kg. (3%)	62, 752 LS

Since January 1, 1940, this office has received invoices covering wool shipments to the United States totalling over $478,000.

It is evident that this measure affects the United States in a far greater degree than any other country, and is much more in the nature of discrimination than the imposition of the exchange and general trade restrictions favoring France, inasmuch as the Syrian currency is attached to the franc.

Respectfully yours,   ELY E. PALMER

690D.116/1 : Telegram

The Consul General at Beirut (Palmer) to the Secretary of State

BEIRUT, January 18, 1940—11 a. m.
[Received 12 : 59 p. m.]

4. Following up several complaints made by local merchants I am informed orally by official of High Commission that acting on instructions just received from Paris local authorities are categorically

---

[41] Not printed.

refusing and will refuse for an indefinite period to sell dollar exchange in payment for merchandise ordered since December 3, 1939, except in those instances where import licenses have been obtained, and that these licenses will be given only in exceptional cases. Suggest that American exporters be immediately advised to refuse orders unless satisfied that Syrian client is in possession of import license.

PALMER

690D.116/2 : Telegram

The Consul General at Beirut (Palmer) to the Secretary of State

BEIRUT, January 22, 1940—4 p. m.
[Received 6 : 40 p. m.]

7. Following categorical orders from Paris on January 15 as reported in my telegram No. 4 dated January 18.

All requests for dollar exchange are being refused. Socony Vacuum Oil Company commitments for stocks already in country exceed $1,-500,000. Local Socony manager reports reasonably satisfactory but still unconfirmed assurances of favorable action by High Commission on these existing commitments but High Commission has warned him that future shipments of oil payable in dollars will not be permitted without authorization from Paris. He states that no sterling or franc oil is immediately available for this market.

Inasmuch as High Commission is without authority to take action in response to local representations this telegram is being sent also to the American Embassy at Paris but suggestions for the guidance of this office would be appreciated.

PALMER

690 D.116/5a

The Secretary of State to the Ambassador in France (Bullitt)

No. 1929   WASHINGTON, January 25, 1940.

SIR: The Department has noted that foreign exchange control was established in the French colonies and mandated territories in Africa by a decree of September 9, 1939, which was published in the *Journal Officiel* of September 10, providing for the application to those areas of the provisions of the French decree-law of the same date prohibiting or regulating in time of war the export of capital, exchange operations and trading in gold. A series of regulations issued simultaneously in implementation of the decree appear to be in all essentials identical, *mutatis mutandis*, with the exchange control measures applying to France itself.

A supplementary French decree of September 9, 1939, relating to the payment of imports and exports, also published in the *Journal Officiel* of September 10, made provision under Article 8 for its application to the French colonies and mandated territories in Africa. Among those provisions was the stipulation that all imports of foreign merchandise shall be subject to the prior obtainment of a certificate attesting either that the delivery of foreign exchange necessary to effect payment had been authorized, or that, according to the importer's declaration, no foreign exchange in payment was required. It appears, moreover, that an import license must accompany each such certificate; while in the case of exports, the foreign exchange received in full or partial payment must be sold to the Colonial Exchange Office within one month after receipt. If payment for exports is offered wholly or partially in French francs the exporters must undertake to accept in payment only foreign holdings in francs which the Colonial Exchange Office has authorized to be issued for the purchase of French products.

Article 9 of the same decree, however, specifically exempted from the control of the authorities all payments between France and the French colonies and mandates, in the following terms:

"Commercial settlements between the home country, Algeria, the colonies and African territories under mandate, as well as commercial settlements with Tunis and Morocco, will not be subject to the provisions of the present decree.

"The same will apply to commercial settlements with Syria and Lebanon as soon as provisions similar to those in the decree-law referred to above have been made applicable in Syria and Lebanon."

According to a telegram from the American Consulate General at Beirut dated December 4, 1939, complete control over foreign exchange and over imports and exports was instituted in the States of the Levant under French mandate on December 3, 1939, products from France and French territories being exempted under the regulations.

These exemptions from the exchange control regulations, in the case of transactions between France and the French mandated territories of Togoland and the Cameroons, are obviously inconsistent with the provisions of Article 6 of the respective mandates for those territories, to the benefits of which the United States and its nationals are entitled under the terms of the American-French convention signed at Paris on February 13, 1925 [*1923*].[42] Paragraph two of Article 6, it will be recalled, states in part that "the Mandatory shall ensure to all nationals of States Members of the League of Nations, on the same footing as his own nationals, freedom of transit and navigation, and complete economic, commercial and industrial equality".

---

[42] *Foreign Relations*, 1923, vol. II, p. 8.

The exemptions favoring French trade in the case of Syria and the Lebanon are clearly inconsistent with Article 11 of the Mandate, to the benefits of which the United States is entitled under the terms of the American-French Convention signed at Paris on April 4, 1924.[43]

Furthermore, the exchange restrictions and import regulations in general, in so far as they apply to those portions of French Equatorial Africa and the Cameroons lying within the specified region known as the Congo Basin, are clearly inconsistent with the provisions of the Convention signed at St. Germain-en-Laye on September 10, 1919,[44] to which the Governments of both France and the United States are parties. Article 2 of that Convention provides that merchandise belonging to the nationals of the signatory powers shall have free access to the interior of that specified region in Africa, and that no differential treatment shall be imposed on such merchandise on importation or exportation. The import permit requirements and exchange control regulations which have been applied to the region in question, apparently without the consent of the signatory powers to the St. Germain Convention, not only seem to overlook the right of free access but to involve discriminatory treatment of American goods.

While the Department is not disposed to question the adoption of measures in the French colonies and mandated areas referred to above which may reasonably be considered necessary and consistent with the status of those territories and the obligations of the French Government as mandatory or responsible for the government thereof, it cannot overlook illegal and unwarranted interference with American treaty rights and it is unable to recognize either the necessity or justification for the administration of the exchange control and import license system in those territories in a manner to give preference to imports from French Empire sources, with a resultant discrimination against their trade with the United States.

This Government confidently expects that the French Government will recognize the right of American merchandise to enter the French colonies and mandated territories freely and without discriminatory treatment under the terms of the pertinent mandate conventions and the Congo Basin Convention, and, in view of the adverse effect which the regulations may be expected to have on American trade, that appropriate steps will be promptly taken to this end. You should seek an early opportunity to discuss these matters with the French authorities, leaving with them an *aide-mémoire* in the sense of the

---

[43] *Foreign Relations*, 1924, vol. I, p. 741.
[44] Department of State Treaty Series No. 887, or 49 Stat. (pt. 2) 3027.

present instruction. You should make a general reservation with respect to American treaty rights covering trade relations with those French colonies and mandated areas to which the above-mentioned treaties apply. Please report by mail the results of your interview.

Very truly yours,　　　　　　　　　　For the Secretary of State:

R. WALTON MOORE

690D.116/2 : Telegram

The Secretary of State to the Consul General at Beirut (Palmer)

WASHINGTON, January 27, 1940—1 p. m.

3. Your No. 7, January 22, 4 p. m. The Embassy in Paris is being instructed by air mail to discuss with the French authorities the exchange and trade measures being taken in Syria and the Lebanon which favor trade with the French Empire and which are therefore contrary to the guarantee of non-discriminatory treatment contained in Article 11 of the Mandate for Syria. The Embassy is being requested to enter a general reservation of our treaty rights in this respect. A copy of the instruction to Paris is being sent to you by air mail.

HULL

600.90D9/12 : Telegram

The Secretary of State to the Ambassador in France (Bullitt)

WASHINGTON, February 3, 1940—noon.

89. Department's instruction No. 1929, January 25, 1940. With reference to despatch No. 448 from Beirut dated January 9, copy of which has been sent to the Embassy, the Department considers the refusal to grant licenses for the export of wool from Syria to any country except France to be a direct violation of Article 11 of the Syrian Mandate, providing for non-discriminatory treatment with respect to goods "destined for" any of the States members of the League of Nations. Guarantees given to members of the League in the Syrian Mandate were extended to the United States in the Convention signed at Paris April 4, 1924.

You should refer specifically to the wool embargo in Syria in your discussions with the French authorities consequent to the Department's instruction of January 25, and should protest against this discriminatory treatment.

HULL

690D.116/3 : Telegram

The Chargé in France (Murphy) to the Secretary of State

PARIS, February 9, 1940—noon.
[Received February 9—9 : 42 a. m.]

188. We left at the Foreign Office this morning an aide-mémoire along the lines of the Department's air mail instruction No. 1929 of January 25 and made as directed a general reservation with respect to American treaty rights covering trade relations with those French colonies and mandated areas to which the treaties under reference apply.

Rageot [45] read the aide-mémoire with evident perturbation. He said that all that the Department pointed out was unquestionably true but that the French Government's attitude was dictated by wartime necessity which were overwhelming.

Although Rageot promised that we would be provided at a later date, when an opportunity had been afforded for a careful study of our aide-mémoire, with a more comprehensive statement of the French position, which could be reported to the Department, he ventured the informal opinion that there could be no withdrawal from the policy which had been adopted and that the probability of protest such as ours had been discounted in advance of these various measures.

MURPHY

690D.006/2 : Telegram

The Consul General at Beirut (Palmer) to the Secretary of State

BEIRUT, February 17, 1940—noon.
[Received 2 : 40 p. m.]

15. Foreign Commerce Control Office of French High Commission has announced that from now on import permits from countries other than British Empire (except Canada, Newfoundland, and Hong Kong), Egypt, Sudan and Iraq will not be accepted unless requested in French francs and marked "payable by crediting to foreign account in francs." Local importers are therefore officially advised to come to an agreement with their suppliers in this matter.

American exporters should be urgently warned to make no shipments whatever to Syria unless they receive cash in advance or are willing to accept blocked francs. This applies immediately to all orders irrespective of date. The same announcement states that the provisions mentioned above will apply likewise to requests for authorization of importation of merchandise ordered before December 3,

---

[45] Maxime Rageot, Assistant Chief of the Division of Near East and African Affairs, French Ministry for Foreign Affairs.

1939, effective date of Syrian trade and exchange control. This is absolutely contrary to the assurances given to this office by the High Commission as previously reported.

PALMER

690D.116/3 : Telegram

The Secretary of State to the Chargé in France (Murphy)

WASHINGTON, February 27, 1940—11 a. m.

135. Your no. 188, February 9, noon. According to a telegram from the Consulate General in Beirut dated February 17, noon, the Department understands that the French High Commission there has announced that henceforth imports from countries other than British Empire, Egypt, Sudan and Iraq will not be permitted unless payment is accepted in French francs, that the restrictions will apply to all imports, including those ordered before December 3, 1939, the effective date of Syrian trade and exchange control, and that this action is absolutely contrary to assurances previously given to the Consulate General by the High Commission.

Please discuss the above with the appropriate French authorities, stating that without prejudice to the Department's general position with regard to the treatment of American trade in certain French colonies and mandated areas, the Department considers it particularly important that the French authorities adhere to the assurances given Mr. Palmer that orders for American goods placed prior to December 3, 1939 would be exempted from the exchange and import permit restrictions.

HULL

690D.116/6 : Telegram

The Chargé in France (Murphy) to the Secretary of State

PARIS, March 1, 1940—5 p. m.
[Received 5 : 38 p. m.]

279. Department's 135, February 27, 11 a. m. Lagarde [46] has promised to look without delay into the question of exemption from exchange and import restrictions of American goods ordered before December 3. He freely admits the force of the argument that the restrictions should not apply to goods on order before the effective date of the Syrian control and has given us to understand that he will do his utmost to obtain a satisfactory decision.

MURPHY

---

[46] Antoine Lagarde, Deputy Director of the Office of Near East and African Affairs, French Ministry for Foreign Affairs.

600.90D9/14

The Chargé in France (Murphy) to the Secretary of State

No. 6272   PARIS, March 20, 1940.
                                               [Received April 9.]

SIR: I have the honor to transmit copies and a translation of a note dated March 17, 1940, which has been received from the Sous-Direction d'Afrique-Levant of the Foreign Office in acknowledgment of protests filed by the Embassy, at the instance of the Department, on February 5 and 8, respectively, following the introduction into Syria and also in the French Colonies and Mandated Territories in Africa of measures of control and restriction considered to be in contravention of American treaty rights.

There are also enclosed, for the completion of the Department's files, copies of the Embassy's note to the Foreign Office of February 5,[47] based upon the Department's telegram No. 89 of February 3, and of the *aide-mémoire* left with the appropriate official in the Sous-Direction de l'Afrique-Levant on February 8,[48] following along the lines of the Department's airmail instruction No. 1929 of January 25, 1940.

Respectfully yours,   ROBERT D. MURPHY

[Enclosure—Translation]

The French Ministry for Foreign Affairs to the American Embassy

                                               PARIS, March 17, 1940.

Under dates of February 5 and 8 last, the Embassy of the United States of America was good enough to apprise the Ministry of Foreign Affairs of the views of the Department of State with respect to certain measures which have recently been adopted in Togo, the Cameroons, Syria and the Lebanon, as well as in the French possessions of Equatorial Africa, at least so far as the territory of these latter is situated within the Congo Basin as established by Convention.

The Ministry has the honor to inform the Embassy that these measures, including those by which the High Commissioner of the Republic at Beirut has regulated the export of wool, are inspired with a view to diminishing the consequences of the profound upheaval which the economic structure of the countries in question is undergoing.

Nevertheless it is the intention of the Government of the Republic to maintain this regime only so long as may be justified by circumstances. It will disappear with the conditions which called it into being.

---

[47] Not printed.
[48] *Aide-mémoire* not printed.

600.90D9/14

The Secretary of State to the Chargé in France (Murphy)

No. 2267   WASHINGTON, August 16, 1940.

SIR: The Department has received the Embassy's despatch No. 6272 of March 20, 1940, enclosing a copy of a note from the French Foreign Office in acknowledgment of protests filed by the Embassy on February 5 and 8, respectively, regarding the introduction into Syria and the Lebanon, the French mandated territories in Africa, and the French territories within the Congo Basin, of exchange control and other measures in contravention of American rights in those territories. In its reply the French Government makes no mention of its obligations under its mandate conventions with the United States and the Congo Basin Convention of September 10, 1919. Moreover, it is evidently the intention of the French Government to maintain the régime to which exception is taken as long "as may be justified by circumstances."

You are requested to take up this subject again with the French authorities and to leave with them a note along the following lines.

It will be recalled that in the communication which the Embassy made to the Foreign Office on February 8, 1940 the French Government was informed that this Government confidently expected that that Government, in accordance with the terms of the pertinent mandate conventions and the Congo Basin Convention, would continue to recognize that American trade with Syria and the Lebanon, the French mandated territories in Africa, and French territories within the Congo Basin be permitted on a basis of full equality in all respects with French and all other trade.

The Department was subsequently informed by the American Consulate General at Beirut that the French mandatory authorities for Syria and the Lebanon had officially announced that imports into the States under French mandate would as far as possible be made from the French Empire.

The Department has received a number of complaints in connection with the operation of the exchange control and import licensing system in the French African territories and mandates, where measures similar to those in effect in Syria and the Lebanon are operating to the disadvantage of American trade with the African areas.

As was pointed out in the Embassy's communication of February 8, 1940 to the French Government, the United States Government is not disposed to raise any question regarding the adoption of measures in Syria and the Lebanon and the French mandated territories in Africa which may be reasonably necessary and consistent with the status of those territories and the obligations of the French Government as mandatory for those territories. This Government, however, does not recognize the necessity for the administration of the controls of foreign exchange and imports and exports in the territories in question in a manner to give preference to imports from or exports to the French Empire or other sources, with a resultant discrimination against trade with the United States.

This Government considers that the action of the appropriate authorities in withholding licenses for the importation or exportation of commodities from or to the United States when permission is granted for the importation or exportation of similar commodities from or to sources other than the United States is inconsistent with the terms of the American-French Mandate Convention of April 4, 1924, concerning Syria and the Lebanon, and of the American-French Mandate Conventions of February 13, 1923, concerning the Cameroons and Togoland, assuring American trade with those territories equality of treatment with that of the mandatory power or of any foreign state. It also considers that the withholding of licenses in similar circumstances in French territories within the Congo Basin is in violation of the Congo Basin Convention of September 10, 1919. Accordingly, this Government must continue to make full reservations of all its rights in connection with the application of the controls of foreign exchange and imports and exports improperly affecting the rights of American nationals in the territories mentioned.

Please keep the Department informed of all developments with regard to this question. A copy of this instruction is being communicated to the American Consuls at Beirut, Lagos and Léopoldville.

Very truly yours,   For the Secretary of State:
HENRY F. GRADY

[No later correspondence regarding this question has been found in Department files.]

RESTRICTIONS ADOPTED BY FRENCH AUTHORITIES IN SYRIA AND LEBANON AGAINST TRANSFERS OF INHERITANCE PROCEEDS TO HEIRS DOMICILED IN THE UNITED STATES

890D.5151/15

The Consul at Beirut (Gwynn) to the Secretary of State

No. 504   BEIRUT, March 20, 1940.
[Received April 3.]

SIR: I have the honor to report that the Consulate General has recently received a number of requests for assistance in obtaining permission to transfer the proceeds from the liquidation of estates situated in the States of the Levant under French Mandate to persons domiciled in the United States, and that, as no provision for such transfer could be found in the decrees issued recently in Beirut concerning the control of foreign exchange operations,[49] a note was sent to the High Commission on February 24, 1940, a copy of which is enclosed, asking that the Consulate General be advised as to whether or not it is now possible for heirs of American nationality to withdraw

----

[49] For correspondence on this subject, see pp. 926 ff.

from Syria and Lebanon the proceeds from the sale of such inheritances. A note under date of March 13, 1940, has now been received, a copy and translation enclosed, stating that "the instructions at present followed concerning the control of foreign exchange do not permit assuring the transfer of the proceeds from the liquidation of successions opened in Syria and Lebanon."

After the receipt of the note I discussed the matter with M. François Conty, the Chief of the Political Bureau of the French High Commission, and asked him if it might not be possible to reconsider the matter. I told him that it was unlikely that the Department of State could accept without question such a ruling, and said that in all probability the amounts arising from the sale of inheritances transferred from the United States to the States of the Levant were greatly superior to the corresponding amounts transferred from Syria and Lebanon to America. I also told him that I recalled having seen within the last year references in the American press to correspondence between the American and German Governments, and that my impression was that Germany had finally assured the United States that no further difficulty would be put in the way of transferring the proceeds from the liquidation of inheritances in Germany to American citizens domiciled in the United States.[50] M. Conty promised to discuss the matter in a conference that the High Commissioner holds every day with his immediate advisers. He telephoned me yesterday to say that M. Ehrhardt, Financial Adviser at the High Commission, had said in one of these meetings that nothing could be done about the matter here in Beirut as the orders which are being followed came from Paris, and that any possible discussions should take place between the American and French Governments. M. Ehrhardt, it appears, stated that, whatever may have been the situation in the past, he did not believe that at the present time heirs in Syria or Lebanon would transfer dollar funds from the United States to the States of the Levant, and that if they did so they would doubtless buy their francs on the unofficial market at New York and that consequently there would be no immediate benefit to France in its efforts to acquire dollars.

Respectfully yours,   WILLIAM M. GWYNN

[Enclosure 1]

The American Consulate General at Beirut to the French High Commission in Syria and Lebanon

The Consulate General of the United States of America presents its compliments to the French High Commission and has the honor

---

[50] See memorandum by the Acting Secretary of State, December 20, 1938, *Foreign Relations*, 1938, vol. II, p. 479.

to request that it be advised whether or not, in view of the recently published Arrêtés concerning the control of foreign exchange, it is now possible for the heirs, of American citizenship, to estates of Syrian and Lebanese nationals, situated in the States of the Levant under French Mandate, to withdraw from these States to the United States the proceeds from the sale of these estates.

As the High Commission is doubtless aware, there are many American citizens interested as direct heirs in such estates, the majority of which are of small pecuniary value. Experience has shown that it is usual for the American heirs to liquidate their interests in these estates and to transfer the proceeds to the United States. Should it not be possible for them to do so at the present time, the Consulate General desires to be in a position so to inform them.

FEBRUARY 24, 1940.

[Enclosure 2—Translation]

The French High Commission in Syria and Lebanon to the American Consulate General at Beirut

BEIRUT, March 13, 1940.

The High Commission of the French Republic in Syria and Lebanon presents its compliments to the Consulate General of the United States of America at Beirut and, with reference to the note of the Consulate General No. 330/300 under date of February 24 last, has the honor to inform it that the instructions at present followed concerning the control of foreign exchange do not permit assuring the transfer of the proceeds from the liquidation of successions opened in Syria and Lebanon.

(SEAL)   HIGH COMMISSION OF THE FRENCH REPUBLIC
IN SYRIA AND LEBANON
Diplomatic Bureau

890D.5151/15

The Secretary of State to the Ambassador in France (Bullitt)

No. 2081   WASHINGTON, April 29, 1940.

SIR: There is enclosed herewith a copy of despatch no. 504, dated March 20, 1940, from the American Consulate General at Beirut,[51] reporting that regulations governing the control of exchange which have been placed into effect in the mandated territory affect the transfer of inheritances from that territory to the United States. The Consulate General reports that a number of requests for assistance

[51] *Supra.*

in obtaining permission to transfer the proceeds of such estates to persons domiciled in the United States have already been received. The Embassy is requested to report to the Department regarding the subject, including information concerning any regulations which may be in effect in continental France governing the transfer of estates to heirs domiciled in the United States. Since there are no Federal restrictions upon the transfer of inheritances from the United States, and considering that the few states of the United States which have enacted legislation controlling the transmission of funds from decedents' estates permit remittance to any foreign country on a basis of reciprocity, the restrictive measures placed into effect by the French authorities in Syria lack any basis of reciprocity when applied to residents of this country. The Embassy's comments with regard to possible representations on the subject will be of interest.

Very truly yours,   For the Secretary of State:

R. WALTON MOORE

890D.5151/15

The Secretary of State to the Consul General at Beirut (Palmer)

WASHINGTON, April 29, 1940.

The Secretary of State refers to the Consulate General's despatch no. 504, of March 20, 1940, regarding the transfer of inheritances from the mandated territory to heirs domiciled in the United States, and encloses herewith, for the Consulate General's information, a copy of an instruction on the subject which has been sent to the American Embassy in Paris.[52]

The Consulate General is requested to report to the Department any further information it may obtain concerning this subject, with particular regard to the question of discrimination against heirs domiciled in the United States as compared with heirs domiciled in France or Great Britain.

Copies of any despatches sent to the Department on the subject should be forwarded direct to the Embassy in Paris.

890D.5151/16

The Consul General at Beirut (Palmer) to the Secretary of State

No. 556   BEIRUT, June 11, 1940.

[Received July 12.]

SIR: I have the honor to refer to the Department's instruction of April 29, 1940 (file no. 890D.5151/15), regarding the transfer of

[52] *Supra.*

303207—58——60

inheritances from the mandated territory to heirs domiciled in the United States, and to enclose a memorandum of a further conversation on this subject that took place between an official of the French High Commission and an officer of the Consulate General.

The French official stated that the same restrictions that apply to heirs in the United States were applicable to heirs domiciled in other countries, including France and Great Britain. However, it is common knowledge that money can be transferred from the States of the Levant under French Mandate to France without difficulty, and that it is much easier to obtain foreign exchange in Sterling than in dollars.

It appears that for the present there is nothing that I can do beyond advising inquirers that the rules governing foreign exchange preclude the transfer to the United States of the proceeds from the sale of inheritances.

In view of the depreciation of the French franc, and of the Syro-Lebanese pound which is attached to it, and of the probability of further depreciation, it would appear advisable for American citizens who have interests in real estate in the mandated territory to retain those interests for the time being, and not to convert them into money until circumstances have changed. I have so advised a number of correspondents recently and shall continue to do so unless instructed otherwise.

In view of the present military situation, no copy of this despatch is being sent to Paris.

Respectfully yours, ELY E. PALMER

[Enclosure]

Memorandum of Conversation, by the Consul at Beirut (Gwynn)

[BEIRUT,] June 7, 1940.

The Department's instruction of April 29, 1940 (file no. 890D.5151/-15), having arrived, I called on M. Conty to discuss again the subject of the transfer of inheritances from the mandated territory to persons domiciled in the United States. I hoped to be able to convince him that it would be more politic to make some arrangement whereby the proceeds from the liquidation of estates, at least in certain cases where the amount involved is small, might be transferred than to adopt a hard and fast practice of refusing to consider such transfers. The Havas bulletins and the local press have carried a number of items recently concerning the very considerable sums that are now being raised in the United States for humanitarian uses in France. While the transfer of estates cannot be put into the same category, there is often a humanitarian side to the cases, particularly in those in which the amount to be transferred is small. This comes out clearly in correspondence which is currently received by the Consulate General, not only from the interested parties but also from relief workers and persons and organizations interested in assisting the destitute. These latter are certain to hear about cases where people in need in America are forced to ask for charity because they cannot obtain possession of money that is rightfully theirs and to resent the action that gives rise to such situations. However, M. Conty did not appear to see any merit in such an argument. He said that the matter had been discussed, a decision reached, and the question settled as far as Beirut is concerned. Should contrary instructions be received from Paris, they would, he said, be followed as a matter of course.

I was prepared to explain to him the detail of a number of cases. One of these is that of . . ., who has written several times: he and his family have about $150 due them, of which they appear to be in great need; the money, 306 Syrian pounds, is in the hands of Abraham Sabah, Khiam, Lebanon, who is anxious to send it, but cannot. However, in view of what had been said, I saw there was no use in going on.

I asked M. Conty if the same restrictions were applicable to countries other than the United States, particularly to Great Britain and France. He said that the restrictions were general and applied to all countries.

890D.5151/16

The Secretary of State to the Chargé in France (Barnes)

No. 2205 WASHINGTON, July 18, 1940.

The Secretary of State refers to his instruction No. 2081 of April 29, 1940, regarding the regulations in Syria governing the transfer of inheritances from that country to the United States, and encloses herewith a copy of a despatch from the American Consul General at Beirut, dated June 11, 1940,[53] furnishing further information in this regard.

The Department will be glad to receive any information the Embassy may be in a position to furnish with regard to the regulations in France and in French colonies and mandated areas regarding the transfer of inheritances to heirs in the United States.

---

[53] *Supra.*

890D.5151/17

*The First Secretary of Embassy in France (Barnes) to the
Secretary of State*

No. 6862   PARIS, September 4, 1940.
                                          [Received September 21.]

SIR: I have the honor to reply as follows to the Department's instructions Nos. 2081 and 2205 of April 29 and July 18, 1940, respectively, regarding the regulations in Syria governing the transfer of inheritances from that country to the United States.

In its instruction No. 2205 the Department requested information available with regard to the regulations in France and in French colonies and mandated territories with respect to the transfer of inheritances to heirs in the United States. The question was discussed with the Assistant Director of the Foreign Exchange Office in Paris and this official pointed out that no special ruling in this respect had been embodied in the exchange control law, but that, generally speaking, such transfers would come under article 9 of "prohibited and authorized operations" which provides that, under certain conditions: "permits may be granted for the transfer of means of payment in francs, properties in France, foreign stocks and bonds located in France, which belong to a person considered as foreign . . .".[54] In this connection please see pages 17 to 19 of Enclosure No. 7 to despatch No. 6577 of May 10, 1940.[55] One of the main conditions would be that the transfer related to an inheritance payable before September 10, 1939.

As concerns the question raised in the despatch from the American Consul General at Beirut, dated June 11, 1940, enclosed with the Department's instruction No. 2205, the official of the Foreign Exchange Office in Paris referred to above said that the Banque de Syrie et du Liban, the approved intermediary of the Foreign Exchange Office for the States of the Levant under French mandate, was alone competent to take decisions regarding such transfers, and that, while it was true that foreign exchange required for any transfers approved by the Banque de Syrie et du Liban must be obtained from the Foreign Exchange Office, the latter, generally speaking, did not concern itself with the reasons for the transfer. This official went on to say that there would appear to be no reason why the transfer of small inheritances may not be approved, but expressed the view that difficulties may be met with in securing the transfer of large sums.

---

[54] Omission indicated in the original despatch.
[55] Not printed.

In view of the information obtained from the Foreign Exchange Office at Paris, set forth above, and the attitude taken by the French authorities in Syria as indicated in the despatch from the American Consul at Beirut, the Paris Embassy is requesting the Embassy at Vichy to take the matter up with the French Foreign Office.[56]

Respectfully yours,   MAYNARD B. BARNES

[56] No record has been found in Department files of any further action on this subject.

TURKEY

REPURCHASE BY THE UNITED STATES OF TURKISH CHROME SOLD TO THE UNITED KINGDOM

811.20 Defense (Materials)/16 : Telegram

The Ambassador in the United Kingdom (Kennedy) to the Secretary of State

[Extract]

LONDON, June 22, 1940.
[Received June 22—11 : 13 a. m.]

1782. Embassy's 1781, June 22, 3 p. m.[1] The following strictly confidential information has been obtained in response to your request of June 15, 3 p. m.[1]

Chrome ore: As regards metallurgical grade British Government defined situation in Turkey as follows and made following informal proposal. Under Anglo-French-Turkish Agreement[2] British and French Governments have an option on total Turkish output which Turks agreed to limit to 250,000 tons, in proportion United Kingdom 11⁄15's, France 4⁄15's. Question of disposal of French portion now arises. British Government has no knowledge as to whether Turkey may put forward a claim to ship the French 4⁄15's to German controlled France or not. British are aware that Turkey using its option to hold up United States and have asked $23 per ton f. o. b. on an American Treasury purchase inquiry for 15,000 tons. Under Anglo-French-Turkish Agreement United Kingdom portion is to be at current London metal exchange price which in turn is based on price of Rhodesian ore which British Government state they are keeping at a reasonable figure as evidenced by a recent sale to the United States of 22,000 tons at 75 shillings per ton. British authorities state that they are fully prepared to facilitate supply of 100,000 to 150,000 tons of Turkish ore to United States if satisfactory settlement of French option can be made. They feel that a practical basis would be for them to offer to take the French 4⁄15's from Turkey for dollars if the United States in turn took it over. Although this would break the Turkish holdup price it would guarantee them a market and give them dollars and from British point of view would provide an other than German

---

[1] Not printed.
[2] For further information regarding this confidential agreement, see latter part of telegram No. 158, September 25, 6 p. m., from the Chargé in Turkey, p. 952.

outlet for the ore. British Government states that if satisfactory settlement of Turkish situation cannot be evolved British Empire might conceivably supply reasonable American requirements but situation would be extremely difficult and hazardous. Rhodesian output now at about 192,000 tons but apparently cannot be increased substantially. Present stocks Rhodesian ore roughly 100,000 tons.

. . . .

KENNEDY

811.20 Defense (Materials)/33 : Telegram

The Ambassador in the United Kingdom (Kennedy) to the Secretary of State

LONDON, June 27, 1940.
[Received June 27—12 : 37 p. m.]

1862. With reference to informal proposal regarding chrome ore reported in Embassy's 1781, June 22, 3 p. m.,[3] official of the Ministry of Economic Warfare has written indicating he has discussed the matter with his superiors and stating that "the general idea that we should be glad to cooperate with you in working out some solution to the Turkish problem has met with their approval and I am therefore at your disposal if you want to pursue the matter further".

KENNEDY

811.20 Defense (M)/33 : Telegram

The Secretary of State to the Ambassador in the United Kingdom (Kennedy)

WASHINGTON, July 9, 1940—6 p. m.

1680. Your 1862, June 27. The Government is distinctly interested in the possibility of acquiring chrome ore from Turkey and will welcome all further information and suggestions from the British Government as to what quantities may be available, on what terms, and in what form necessary purchase arrangements could be discussed. Procurement Division of Treasury, which arranges and carries through the actual buying, informs the Department that under present conditions it feels it necessary to contract such purchases on a c. i. f. New York basis, which we understand to be the usual basis. It has recently bought certain quantities of Turkish chrome ore through the intermediary of Mutual Chemical Company on this basis. Please discuss the matter with the British authorities and report.

---

[3] Not printed.

Because of our desire to build up these reserve stocks promptly and because of both the great expense and difficulty of making satisfactory shipping arrangements to carry the ore from Turkey, it would be distinctly helpful to us to get as much Rhodesian ore as the British authorities think they might spare.

Please report as promptly as possible.

HULL

811.20 Defense (M)/33 : Telegram

The Secretary of State to the Ambassador in the United Kingdom (Kennedy)

WASHINGTON, July 12, 1940—4 p. m.

1738. Your 1782, June 22, and Department's 1680, July 9. The Department has again discussed this question with the National Defense Commission and hopes that you will secure from the British Government promptly the information asked in Department's 1680.

The Procurement Division of the Treasury is authorized to buy large amounts of chromite and funds are now available for this purpose. It states that it knows of no basis on which it could carry through except c. i. f. American port. This would appear to make it necessary that shipping be arranged by the Turkish Government or its agents unless the British Government has a better arrangement to suggest.

Please advise Department whether it would expedite matter if it also took up this possibility with Embassy in Istanbul and if so along what lines.

This Government would also be definitely interested in acquiring stocks of Rhodesian ore if you can persuade the British Government to assist in supplying our reserve requirements by releasing additional amounts from that area.

HULL

811.20 Defense (M)/90 : Telegram

The Ambassador in the United Kingdom (Kennedy) to the Secretary of State

LONDON, July 16, 1940—7 a. m.
[Received 8 : 15 p. m.]

2212. Since the receipt of Department's 1680 July 9, 6 p. m. and 1738 July 12, 7 [4] p. m. detailed discussions have taken place with the Ministry of Supply and the Ministry of Economic Warfare as a result of which the following information has been obtained :

(1) As regards Rhodesian ore the metallurgical grade production is now running at the rate of 10,000 tons a month. The limiting factor

on Rhodesian production is said to be the number of technically competent white supervisors, a good many of whom have already been called up for military service. Of the 10,000 tons current production, 2,500 is going to Canada, 1,100 to the United Kingdom, and 7,000 to the United States. The 600 tons difference is at present being made up out of stocks. The Chrome Company has informed the Ministry of Supply that it could raise production by 2,000 tons per month, but to do so would have to change its specifications from 49 to 47–48 C. R. 203 and would be reluctant to take this step. As regards stocks, there are 35,000 tons in Rhodesia of metallurgical ore and this could be purchased by the Procurement Division of the Treasury for 90 shillings a ton f. o. b. Beira, payable at the official rate.

(2) As regards Turkey, the position is complicated and has changed from that set forth in my 1781, June 22, 3 p. m.[5] Due to the delay which ensued between my 1781, June 22, 3 p. m. and your reply No. 1680, July 9, 6 p. m., the British panicked and offered the Turks a guaranteed price of 100 shillings while acceding to Turkey's request to sell direct to the United States. The Turks then asked for 110 shillings and the current British counteroffer, which the Turks are now considering, is 105 shillings for the balance of 1940 which with stocks on hand will amount to approximately 180,000 tons of which roughly half is metallurgical grade.

However, the British have indicated that they are willing to do what they can to be of assistance to us and are going into the shipping question and will supply further information as soon as possible. They are of course desirous that we take up Turkish chrome rather than have it pile up there. They feel that Turkey does not have as strong a bargaining position as is apparent because it does not acquire free sterling for its sales of ore to the United Kingdom, much of the proceeds being credited against British loans and the rest being blocked. They believe that the Turks will hold us up if we turn ourselves into the eager buyer, but if we allow Turkey to become the ready seller we can make favorable terms.

They are prepared to pass a word to Russell, who is a British subject in charge of the Chrome Company which, as you know, is a British company owned by Union Carbide, suggesting that he urge the Turks to seek us out and also to instruct the British Embassy at Istanbul to discuss the position with our Embassy. We would of course have to deal direct with Turkey. If you wish such an instruction sent please notify me.

In any case I would appreciate an answer on the Rhodesian proposition and an indication of what you intend to do at Istanbul.

My own feeling is that if you think it really important to have Rhodesian production increased the British Government could do

---

[5] Not printed.

so by making an effort and perhaps calling back people who have been mobilized and the way to get that done is in connection with the helpful concessions which we for our part are making for the British which I gather is being done through Purvis.[6]

KENNEDY

811.20 Defense (M)/33 : Telegram

The Secretary of State to the Ambassador in the United Kingdom (Kennedy)

WASHINGTON, July 16, 1940—9 p. m.

1820. Department's 1680, July 9, 6 p. m. Mr. Marris of the Ministry of Economic Warfare, now in this country,[7] suggests that any approach to the Turkish Government by the British Government in connection with this Government's purchases of chromite would almost certainly become known and might endanger the safe passage of vessels through the Mediterranean carrying chromite to the United States. It may be desirable therefore for this Government to approach the Turkish Government directly but the Department will await a report on your conversations with British officials.

Marris also indicated that the British Government has been purchasing much more chromite from Turkey than it requires and probably would be willing to relinquish some of its present claim on Turkish chromite in favor of this Government so that the American proportion might be considerably higher than the former French allocation. Please explore this possibility since this Government will wish to secure reserve stocks as rapidly as possible. It is essential however that the Turkish Government should be able to arrange adequate shipping and should offer a reasonable price. The British Government might help on the price situation in order to rid itself of the necessity of purchasing unneeded supplies from Turkey.

HULL

811.20 Defense (M)/101 : Telegram

The Ambassador in the United Kingdom (Kennedy) to the Secretary of State

LONDON, July 17, 1940—5 p. m.
[Received July 17—1 p. m.]

2231. Department's 1820, July 16, 9 p. m. As indicated in the third from the last paragraph, my 2212, July 16, 7 p. m. [a. m.],

---

[6] Arthur B. Purvis, Director General of the British Purchasing Commission.
[7] A. D. Marris, First Secretary of the British Embassy.

Embassy concurs in Marris's view that American Government should approach Turkish Government directly.

As regards paragraph 2 of your 1820, July 16th, 9 p. m., according to Controller of Chrome Ministry of Supply, British Government has no need under present circumstances of obtaining any Turkish chromite and is quite prepared that the United States should acquire all the Turkish chrome it desires. But since it is guaranteeing Turkey a market for its total output its aid to the United States seems now to be limited to (1) facilitating the availability of shipping and (2) the suggestion contained in the third from the last paragraph of my 2212, July 16, 7 p. m. [*a. m.*]

Incidentally Marris was most helpful when in the Ministry of Economic Warfare. He is straightforward and exhibited a capacity for getting things done.

KENNEDY

811.20 Defense (M)/159a : Telegram

The Acting Secretary of State to the Ambassador in Turkey
(MacMurray)

WASHINGTON, July 26, 1940—6 p. m.

41. This Government has been given to understand that the British Government would be entirely willing for us to purchase from the Turkish Government as much chrome ore as can be arranged, the British Government relinquishing to us all or a part of the Turkish ore production now earmarked for Great Britain, it being understood that this Government would also take over that part of Turkish production formerly allocated to France.

This Government is definitely interested in securing a very substantial tonnage of Turkish chrome for reserve stocks in this country and is now prepared to make these purchases on contract if the Turkish Government can sell c. i. f. American ports, making satisfactory shipping arrangements itself or through its agents, and if it will offer an attractive price. It is believed that such bulk purchases, to be held in reserve stocks here entirely off the market, will justify a price offering by the Turkish Government quite considerably below the price paid by this Government on its recent small reserve stock purchase; the Procurement Division of the Treasury here paid what it considered to be an unreasonable price on the latter purchase merely because of the emergency shipping situation then existing.

This entire matter has been discussed with the British Government and they are prepared to assist in every way possible. It is considered wise, however, to avoid any indication whatever that they are taking this position since such indication might complicate the problem of successfully transporting Turkish chrome to this country. They are making an effort, however, to have the Turkish Government approach this Government with a proposal for sale of chrome and they are instructing the British Embassy at Istanbul to keep in touch with you regarding the matter.

All of the above is given you for background information only at the present time and the Department desires that you take no initiative on the matter until further instructions are received from the Department. You are of course free to discuss the matter with the British. Also you may indicate interest on the part of this Government, within the limitations indicated in the second paragraph of this telegram, if the Turkish Government approaches you regarding the subject.

Please report any new information or developments promptly to the Department.

WELLES

811.20 Defense (M)/281 : Telegram

The Secretary of State to the Ambassador in Turkey (MacMurray)

WASHINGTON, August 28, 1940—6 p. m.

66. Department's 41, July 26, 1940, 6 p. m. to Istanbul. High freight and insurance costs from Turkey to the United States and f. o. b. prices in Turkey based on the price of 105 shillings reached in negotiations between the British and Turkish Governments indicate a c. i. f. United States quotation for Turkish chrome between $43 and $45 per ton as compared with the current market price for Rhodesian chrome of approximately $29. The Procurement Division of the Treasury is unwilling to consider further purchases of Turkish chrome so long as such a price differential prevails.

Unless you see some likelihood that the Turkish Government could be persuaded to quote a price very considerably below the price guaranteed by the British, this Government will wish to drop, for the present, all attempts to purchase from the Turkish Government.

For your confidential information, this Government intends to explore the possibility of some arrangement with the British Government which would make Turkish chrome available to this Government at a price at or near the present market quotations here.

HULL

811.20 Defense (M)/281 : Telegram

The Secretary of State to the Ambassador in Turkey (MacMurray)

WASHINGTON, September 21, 1940—3 p. m.

71. Department's 66, August 28, 6 p. m. After exploring other possible sources of supply, the Defense Commission and Procurement Division are now convinced of the desirability of procuring Turkish chrome as soon as possible. The Department understands that there is approximately 100,000 tons of such chrome already mined in Turkey but that the British have taken title to it in accordance with the Anglo-Turkish financial agreement. The British authorities have indicated a willingness to sell this chrome to us (see Department's 41, July 26, 6 p. m.) but point out that their Financial Agreement with Turkey prevents resale without Turkey's permission.

You are instructed, therefore, to discuss with the Turkish Government urgently and vigorously arrangements whereby this Government could buy this chrome from Great Britain. The Turkish authorities will appreciate the fact that the purchase of this chrome by the United States is not intended to affect in any way the British-Turkish financial agreement or alter the continuing British undertaking to purchase chrome under that agreement.

The American Government desires to acquire the chrome now above ground in Turkey as a part of its defense program. You will therefore urge the Turkish authorities as a matter of the strongest interest of this Government that permission be granted for sale to us by the British as suggested above. You should, if necessary, remind the Turkish authorities that the United States, as a very exceptional measure, has recently permitted the exportation to Turkey of tetraethyl lead essential for aviation fuel. This permission was granted contrary to the firmly established policy of this Government and was made possible only as a result of the unusually friendly relations between the United States and Turkey. These considerations are well known to the Turkish Ambassador in Washington, who is now being informed of the present request of the American Government. It may also be pointed out that other Turkish requests of a similar nature, on which the Ambassador will be able to report, are now pending before this Government.

If, in spite of the above, the Turkish authorities refuse to permit our purchase of this chrome from Great Britain, you may suggest as an alternative, that the Turkish Government agree to the transfer to the Turkish Government of title to the chrome, and to the sale of this chrome by Turkey to the United States.

As regards the question of shipping, present indications are that a satisfactory solution to this problem may be found, possibly through the use of vessels of Panamanian registry.

HULL

811.20 Defense (M)/410

Memorandum of Conversation, by Mr. George V. Allen of the Division of Near Eastern Affairs

[WASHINGTON,] September 24, 1940.

Participants: Turkish Ambassador [8]
                 Mr. Murray [9]
                 Mr. Allen

The Turkish Ambassador, who had called at Mr. Murray's request, was informed of the desire of the American Government to purchase approximately 100,000 tons of Turkish chrome now understood to be above ground in Turkey. He was told of our understanding from the British Embassy that Great Britain had taken title to this chrome but that Britain could not sell it to us without the consent of the Turkish Government. The Ambassador's assistance was requested in connection with obtaining the consent of his Government to allow Great Britain to sell this chrome to the United States.

The Ambassador readily acquiesced to this request, saying that he would exercise his best endeavors with his Government in this respect. He said that our request appeared an entirely reasonable one to him considering the chrome matter alone, but that there were further strong considerations which made him particularly desirous of having his Government meet our wishes. He recalled his recent expression, following our exception in the tetraethyl lead case, of a desire to be able to reciprocate our friendly gesture and said that his Government's acquiescence in the chrome matter would improve his position in future instances of this kind.

811.20 Defense (M)/381 : Telegram

The Chargé in Turkey (Kelley) to the Secretary of State

ANKARA, September 25, 1940—6 p. m.
[Received September 26—2 : 13 p. m.]

158. Department's 71, September 21, 3 p. m.

1. I discussed this morning the question of the acquisition of Turkish chrome by the United States with the Secretary General of

---

[8] Mehmet Münir Ertegün.
[9] Wallace Murray, Chief of the Division of Near Eastern Affairs.

the Ministry of Foreign Affairs [10] (the most energetic official in the Foreign Office and the one who negotiated the chrome agreements with Great Britain). I explained the situation as set forth in the Department's telegram pointing out that the British Government was willing to sell to us the chrome to which they had taken title in Turkey but that under the chrome agreement of January 8, 1940, they could not resell Turkish chrome to a third country without Turkey's permission. I emphasized that the acquisition of this chrome was a matter of the greatest importance to my Government and urged most strongly that permission be granted for the sale of this chrome to us by Great Britain.

Numan inquired whether it was a question of the purchase of chrome in Turkey or chrome that had already been shipped to Great Britain. I replied that I understood that it was a question of chrome now above ground in Turkey. He said that in that case he would much prefer to work out an arrangement for the sale of this chrome directly to the United States by the Turkish Government.

Upon my inquiring whether this was possible under the Anglo-Turkish agreements he said that he was confident that it could be arranged and added that while the British Government was obliged to purchase chrome the Turkish Government was not obliged to sell it to Great Britain. (I gathered from his remarks that he contemplates working out an arrangement whereby the British Government will relinquish to us part of the ore now earmarked for Great Britain.) He said that one condition upon which he would insist was that the contemplated transaction would be recognized as a special one outside the scope of our trade agreement.[11] I said that offhand I did not think that there would be any difficulty on this score. He assured me that the Turkish Government was most eager to sell chrome to us since it had tremendous need of dollars to make purchases in the United States. He concluded by saying that he would personally take charge of this question, that he would take the matter up at once with the Director General of the E. T. I. Bank and the Minister of Finance and, as soon as he had all the facts in hand, with the Prime Minister. He promised to give me an answer within a few days. (During our conversation the Secretary General was handed a telegram which he said had just come in from the Turkish Ambassador in Washington relative to this matter.)

2. I also discussed today the chrome situation with the British Commercial Attaché [12] (who has negotiated the several chrome arrangements between Turkey and Great Britain) who gave me the

---

[10] Numan Menemencioglu.
[11] Signed at Ankara, April 1, 1939, Department of State Executive Agreement Series No. 163, or 54 Stat. 1870.
[12] S. R. Jordan.

following information which may be of interest to the Department. He said that under the confidential chrome agreement of January 8, 1940, the maximum annual output of Turkey was fixed at 250,000 tons and that Great Britain obligated itself to purchase this quantity (plus an amount of 50,000 tons then in stock) less the amount sold to the United States. It was also provided that Great Britain could not sell chrome purchased from Turkey to a third country.

Jordan stated that a supplementary agreement was concluded on July 1, 1940, which fixes at 130,000 tons the amount of chrome which Great Britain is obliged to purchase up to the end of 1940. The E. T. I. Bank reserves the right to deliver a supplementary quantity of 50,000 tons. Jordan explained that these two amounts represent the estimated total Turkish production in the period in question and that inasmuch as Great Britain has a lien on the 130,000 tons specified the 50,000 tons represents the total amount at the free disposal of Turkey. He said that the E. T. I. Bank has already shipped 19,000 tons to the United States and that consequently there now remains only 31,000 tons at the disposition of the Turkish Government.

Jordan states that according to information furished him by the E. T. I. Bank there were approximately 36,000 tons of chrome at ports on August 31, 1940. He does not know how much there is above ground at the mines but he is certain that the total mined is much less than 100,000 tons. He expressed the opinion that the chief difficulty in working out an arrangement for the resale of Turkish chrome by Great Britain to the United States would be the question of the disposal of the dollar proceeds.

Since the proceeds from the sale of the chrome to Great Britain are earmarked for the payment of interest on and principal of Turkish obligations held by Great Britain, the dollars received from the resale to the United States of Turkish chrome purchased by Great Britain would not be available to the Turkish authorities unless they made available for the payment of interest et cetera an equivalent amount of pounds (sterling) from other sources. He intimated that if the Turkish Government were willing to do this the British Government would probably not object to the dollar proceeds being placed at the disposition of the Turkish authorities. I gather that there is a good possibility of some satisfactory arrangement being worked out with regard to this point.

3. Jordan also informed me that during the past 6 weeks the representative of the British Chrome Association has been endeavoring to persuade the E. T. I. Bank to offer us the chrome at its disposal for $22.50 per ton f. o. b. which represents a dollar less than [apparent omission] price. Following the Department's telegram No. 66, August 28, 6 p. m., I pointed out in several conversations with inter-

ested British authorities that the principal difficulty confronting us in connection with the purchase of Turkish chrome was the high freight and insurance costs and that these high costs would not be offset by a reduction in the f. o. b. price of only one dollar per ton. I suggested to them, in view of the fact that the sale of Turkish chrome to the United States would be to the advantage of the British Government in that it would take off their hands chrome which Great Britain could not utilize, that the British Government provide ships to convey the chrome to the United States at operating cost. I pointed out that the ships would have a full cargo in proceeding from Great Britain to Turkey and in returning from the United States to Turkey and that the profits on these trips would offset the absence of a profit in transporting the chrome. It is understood that the British Commercial Attaché here has recommended a solution along these lines.

KELLEY

811.20 Defense (M)/391 : Telegram

The Chargé in Turkey (Kelley) to the Secretary of State

ISTANBUL, September 28, 1940—noon.
[Received 3 : 05 p. m.]

107. My 158, September 25, 6 p. m. The Secretary General of the Foreign Office informed me this morning that the Turkish Government is pleased to comply with our request and has already granted to the British Government the desired permission with regard to the sale of chrome to us. He said that the Government had decided that it was more feasible to arrange for our purchase of Turkish chrome through Great Britain than through a direct transaction between the Turkish Government and the United States. The Turkish Ambassador in Washington has been advised of the Turkish Government's action in this matter.

KELLEY

811.20 Defense (M)/391 : Telegram

The Secretary of State to the Ambassador in the United Kingdom (Kennedy)

WASHINGTON, September 30, 1940—2 p. m.

2951. Following cable just received from Ankara [*Istanbul*] (No. 107 of September 28) :
[Here follows text of telegram printed *supra.*]
Please consult at once with British authorities as to best means of executing this arrangement with the British Government.

Advise upon quantities and grades that will be available (the Defense Commission wants as much as it can get as soon as it can get it) and terms of payment. Also please discuss shipping arrangements.

HULL

811.20 Defense (M)/391 : Telegram

The Secretary of State to the Chargé in Turkey (Kelley)

WASHINGTON, September 30, 1940—2 p. m.

73. Your 107, September 28, noon. Department immediately asking Embassy in London to inaugurate discussions looking towards agreement with British Government. Please give as full as possible information regarding (a) amount of chrome by grades in stock in Turkey now, (b) prospective schedule of production under the agreement with Great Britain, (c) any other prospective production in Turkey.

HULL

811.20 Defense (M)/391 : Telegram

The Secretary of State to the Chargé in Turkey (Kelley)

WASHINGTON, October 4, 1940—6 p. m.

74. Department's 73 of September 30 and previous. American Embassy in London is, in response to Defense Commission's desire, in busy discussion with British Government regarding re-sale to us of Turkish chrome.

Apparently the British Government still lacks full independent confirmation of Turkish position reported in your 107 of September 28. Will you do your best, by whatever method is judged most effective, to have this confirmation passed on directly by the Turkish Government to the British representative.

In course of price discussions between ourselves and British, they have expressed uncertainty as to whether the Turkish Government will require them to turn over to it part of the dollars that may accrue from re-sale of Turkish chrome to us. We hope for speedy determination of this question, so that there may be no unnecessary delay.

HULL

811.20 Defense (M)/467 : Telegram

The Chargé in Turkey (Kelley) to the Secretary of State

ANKARA, October 9, 1940—5 p. m.
[Received 6 : 50 p. m.]

166. Department's 74, Oct. 4, 6 p. m. The Foreign Office having informed me that the Turkish Government was not disposed to take the initiative in formally advising the British Government of its position in the matter but that it would gladly and promptly give its formal consent to the resale to us of Turkish chrome if the British Government would make inquiry of it preferably through the British Embassy here, I took the matter up with the British Commercial Attaché, and he informed me today that the British Embassy would make formal inquiry immediately.

I shall continue to follow the matter closely with a view to expediting as much as possible the receipt by the British Government of the Turkish Government's formal consent.

KELLEY

811.20 Defense (M)/489 : Telegram

The Ambassador in Turkey (MacMurray) to the Secretary of State

ANKARA, October 15, 1940—5 p. m.
[Received 7 : 58 p. m.]

169. Embassy's 166, October 9, 5 p. m. The British Embassy received today the written consent of the Turkish Government to the resale of Turkish chrome to us by Great Britain.

MACMURRAY

INFORMAL SUGGESTION BY THE TURKISH AMBASSADOR THAT THE UNITED STATES GIVE SUPPORT TO THE CREATION OF A BLOC OF NATIONS (SOVIET UNION, TURKEY, GREECE, BULGARIA) TO RESIST AXIS AGGRESSION

740.0011 European War 1939/6126

Memorandum of Conversation, by the Assistant Secretary of State (Berle)

[WASHINGTON,] October 9, 1940.

The Turkish Ambassador [13] came in today, at his request. He said, first, that he wished to exchange views on the general situation, over which he was very much concerned.

---

[13] Mehmet Münir Ertegün.

Turkey, he observed, had sedulously maintained correct and friendly relations with Russia.[14]   On one occasion these had been gravely strained; but they had stood by their historic position, maintaining peaceful intentions, and maintaining their obligations and agreements with respect to the Straits.   In the long run this had worked out well; and he believed that there was respect between the two governments.

Now, the situation was shifting and the appearance of German troops in Roumania indicated that the tide was coming very close. Turkey, he said, was prepared for every eventuality, and proposed to resist any attempt at invasion.

But, he said, each of the European nations had been handling its affairs as though it were buying a ticket in the sweepstakes: if the number turned up, the nation might win, or preserve itself.   Actually, it had meant disaster.   He considered that there was still "the nick of time", as he put it, to work out a bloc between certain of the remaining countries, which might save the situation.   Specifically, he had thought of a bloc of Russia, Turkey, possibly Greece, and Bulgaria (in the latter country he said it would not be hard to separate the Russophile nation from its pro-German King) ; in which case they would like, of course, to count on the support of the United States.   In this case he considered there might be a reasonable chance to avoid the continuance of the disaster.

He said that Russia had always been an enigma, and probably would continue to be so; that no one was altogether sure of her real intentions; but that the Russians must know that the moment there was a sweeping Axis victory, she was completely helpless.   Even a threat, let alone an invasion, would cause the whole Russian edifice to crumble. He considered that Turkey had a unique position by reason of geography and her relationship with Russia.

I asked if this last suggestion were a suggestion inspired by instructions from his government.   He said no; but that he had been turning over in his mind the possibility of some measure which might lead to a healthier situation.   The Turkish position he thought was very like our own.   I said that I could, of course, only give him my personal analysis of the situation.   At the time of the Russo-German agreement in 1939,[15] we had reason to believe that the Germans had given the Russians to understand that they would not come to the Black Sea.   There had been a certain suspicion between the two governments, though it did not impede their staying by the agreement. But at the time of the Hungarian-Roumanian settlement a few weeks

---

[14] For correspondence concerning activities of the Soviet Union in the Balkans and Turkey, see vol. I, pp. 444 ff.

[15] Treaty of non-aggression, signed at Moscow on August 23, 1939; for text, see *Documents on German Foreign Policy, 1918–1945*, series D, vol. VII, p. 245.

ago, the Germans had guaranteed the Roumanian frontier,[16] which in practice meant going to the Black Sea, and taking into their orbit an area which Russia had marked out for her own. We had reason to believe that this had not been done after previous consultation with the Russians, and indeed Russia had felt that her rights in the Danube had not been adequately recognized. The appearance of German troops in Roumania reinforced this conclusion. I thought, therefore, that there had been a real breach of the spirit of the Russo-German agreement.

Further, I said, we had no reason to believe that the Germans had consulted Russia when they acquired transit rights across Finland. Finally, we had every reason to believe that though Russia was told about the Axis-Japanese agreement[17] before it was announced, the notification had been *pro forma*, and had not been a consultation in the sense envisaged by the Russo-German agreement.

Further, that the Axis-Japanese agreement had itself created certain tensions. The "greater Asiatic area" in the Japanese mind had always included certain areas which belonged to Russia now, such as the maritime provinces and eastern Siberia, and possibly part of Mongolia, and Sakhalin. Unless there had been discussions and some secret agreement by which Japan had limited her aspirations in these areas, which seemed unlikely, the alliance would appear to be a new threat to the Russian position. Grounds of national interest and expediency therefore would seem to lead the Russians towards some cooperation with powers not dominated by Germany.

But, I said, it was my view that the Russian policy would be more dominated by the proximity of a very large German army on her border, than by these obvious considerations. Her policy was not to risk war, if possible; she would therefore cooperate, at least in appearance, with the Germans until forced to do otherwise.[18] I said that it sounded plausible to believe that Russia had been promised some compensation in Persia; perhaps even to the extent of authorizing her to take over Persia and establish herself on the Persian gulf.

I said that I considered the invasion of Britain now improbable, and that the winter would presumably be spent in some sort of activity in the Mediterranean. This might be either by thrust towards Gibraltar; or by using the Italy–Sicily–Tunis route to strengthen the Italian attack on Egypt; or by a thrust through the Balkans, with a view

---

[16] For the Vienna Award of August 30, 1940, by which Rumania ceded large amounts of territory (in Transylvania) to Hungary, see telegram No. 3826, August 30, from the Chargé in Germany, vol. I, p. 501. For the simultaneous guarantee of the territorial integrity and inviolability of Rumania given by Germany and Italy, see telegram No. 3827, August 30, from the Chargé in Germany, vol. I, p. 502.

[17] Signed at Berlin, September 27, 1940, *Foreign Relations, Japan, 1931–1941,* vol. II, p. 165.

[18] For correspondence on wartime cooperation between Germany and the Soviet Union, see vol. I, pp. 539 ff.

ultimately to attacking Suez through Syria and Palestine. This last involved either making arrangements for transit through Russia— difficult, and probably impossible; or a thrust through Turkey, using the Turkish railway system. We had no information as to which of these alternatives Germany and Italy might choose; we had no information as to any decisions reached between Hitler and Mussolini; the Roumanian occupation seemed to indicate that demands might be made on Turkey, though this of course was a pure supposition.

Mr. Ertegün said that this was very much his own view; except that he leaned strongly to the idea that the eastern Mediterranean really was the key to the situation. By consequence, he regarded the situation as very serious. He felt that American public opinion had not given adequate attention to the eastern Mediterranean theatre; it was this, in part, which moved him to explore the possibility of the "bloc" which he had mentioned.

I said that I should be glad to think over the suggestion he made, and more particularly his indication of closer relations with Russia. As to that, I said that one point had to be kept in mind. We could not make arrangements of mere expediency. Our tangible difficulties with Russia were relatively small: questions of export rights, the handling of nationals, etc. These obviously were susceptible of ready adjustment.[19] But I thought firm relations with Russia would never be really established until two matters were cleared up. The first was the cessation of Russian revolutionary propaganda in the United States, directed against this government. The second was the Russian assertion of the right to take and seize territory by violence, as she had done in Latvia, Lithuania and Estonia[20] and had attempted to do, with some success, in Finland,[21] despite the fact that she herself had played a large part in setting these countries free. The United States had definitely set its face against that kind of thing; and we would find it difficult to establish really cordial relations with a country which pursued a policy of this kind. This was an objection of principle; but if we abandoned our principles in this matter, we had very little to stand on.

The Ambassador said that he conceded both points, at once. The fact that we did pursue policies based on principle made it possible, for instance, for him to talk to us thus frankly. But, he said, some of these questions could be minimized or left over for the time being, without prejudice to the position.

---

[19] For correspondence regarding attempts to find a solution to difficulties and to improve relations between the United States and the Soviet Union, see pp. 244 ff.

[20] See vol. I, pp. 357 ff.

[21] For correspondence on the Winter War and relations between Finland and the Soviet Union, see *ibid.*, pp. 269 ff.

I repeated that I would consider what he said; and after some friendly interchange about the chrome they had just sold us and the tetra-ethyl lead we had sold them ("It would never go to the Germans: the last drop would have been expended before they took over", said he), he departed.

A. A. BERLE, JR.

740.0011 European War 1939/6126

Memorandum by the Assistant Secretary of State (Berle) to the Chief of the Division of Near Eastern Affairs (Murray)

[WASHINGTON,] October 11, 1940.

MR. MURRAY: This conversation [22] is interesting, but it raised two or three solid questions in my mind:

(1) If no one does anything, will the Turks resist the Germans, or will they consider that they have no chance and let the Germans through? My feeling is that they will resist, but this is merely based on sentiment.

(2) If Turkey should resist, will Russia join her, or stab her in the back via Armenia and Persia? By hypothesis this would mean suicide for Russia; but the Russians have a habit of thinking things out and coming to conclusions opposite from anyone else.

(3) Are the Turks now in any shape to give some leadership to the Arab world—possibly operating through Baghdad and Iraq? This re-emergence of the Turkish Empire over a welter of hatred into co-operative form sounds impossible; but nothing is impossible these days.

A. A. B[ERLE], JR.

740.0011 European War 1939/6554

Memorandum of Conversation, by the Assistant Secretary of State (Berle)

[WASHINGTON,] October 15, 1940.

The Turkish Ambassador came in to see me, at my request. I said that we had been thinking over the suggestions which he had made on the occasion of his last conversation with me. The heart of them lay in the improvement of relations between the United States and Russia.

I said that I thought we should be glad to have any specific suggestions which he might care to make, for our consideration.

[22] See memorandum *supra*.

He said he would think it over. Further, his view was that matters were now so serious that little short of a definite agreement on our part to assist, by measures short of war, would be of any particular use. He felt that every day that went by now increased the danger; he held the personal view that something might happen within a week's time.

At the same time, he said, he was confident of ultimate victory, though there might be a very great deal of pain and suffering before that occurred.

A. A. BERLE, JR.

740.0011 European War 1939/6126

Memorandum by the Acting Chief of the Division of Near Eastern Affairs (Alling) to the Assistant Secretary of State (Berle)

[WASHINGTON,] October 16, 1940.

MR. BERLE: Replying to the queries in your attached memorandum: [23]

1. I think we can be reasonably certain that the Turks will fight if the Germans move against the Dardanelles. Military opinion seems to be that the Turks could not withstand for long the thrust of the German armies, but I think the Germans would not have an easy time getting through the Anatolian plateau and the Taurus Mountains or keeping up the long line of communications. In this connection, a further question arises, i. e., would the Germans head for the Suez Canal or the Iraq oil fields? Possibly they would try both. Even if the capture of the Mosul fields did not give Germany refined products (there is only one small refinery in Iraq and transportation of large quantities of oil to Europe would be difficult), it would at least be possible for them to cut off British supplies now going to Haifa via the pipeline.

2. Probably Eu [24] can estimate better than NE [25] what action Russia might take. We are inclined to believe that Russia would not move in a military way either for or against the Turks. The following factors have been considered in arriving at that conclusion: (*a*) the Russians are undoubtedly growing more and more suspicious of Axis aims, (*b*) they do not wish to become involved in hostilities either in Turkey or elsewhere because of the strategic situation (Japan and Germany) and because of internal weaknesses (*c*) they may hope to pick up important bits of territory either around the Dardanelles

---

[23] Memorandum of October 11, p. 961.
[24] Division of European Affairs.
[25] Division of Near Eastern Affairs.

(possibly joint-control with the Axis) or in Iran in the event of an Axis victory over Turkey, all without taking any military risks.

3. We are doubtful of the possibility of the Turks giving leadership to the Arab world as such. The Arabs respect the Turks but we are not sure that even now they fully trust them. The Arabs remember the comparatively recent cession of Alexandretta. Late in June the Iraqi Foreign Minister, Nuri Pasha, went to Ankara specifically to seek assurances, which were forthcoming, that Turkey would not encroach upon Syria or Iraq. The fact that the assurances were sought may indicate suspicion of the Turks on the part of the Iraqis.

The British exercise influence and control in Egypt and Iraq and actually administer Palestine, but they have been unable to stir up sufficient enthusiasm in any of those countries to bring them actively into the war. Probably the British could bring sufficient pressure on Egypt and Iraq to induce them to enter the war, but the Arabs would ask for certain engagements in return particularly in regard to Palestine and the Egyptians would want additional advantages. Apparently the British are loath to make any new promises to the Arabs or to the Egyptians or to raise any new Near Eastern questions at this time. The British have already explored the possibility of an Arab federation but that apparently is not practicable until all of the Arab states have obtained their independence. The Arab angle does not, therefore, appear promising at the moment.

There is, however, another group in which Turkey is influential and in which something might be done. It is with the members of the Saadabad Pact—Turkey, Iran, Afghanistan and Iraq.[26] Turkey might be able to stiffen the backbone of these people. It may be that the Turks have already looked into this possibility. If so, we have not heard of it. Of course, Iran and Afghanistan would be of no use in repelling a German invasion of Turkey and the Turks may feel that to approach them would be likely to stir up suspicions in Russia—something the Turks would probably want to avoid.

I do not believe we or the British are going to be able to induce Russians, Turks, Iraqis or anyone else to fight the Axis unless they can see what they are going to get out of it. In the case of the Turks, the motive would be protection of their hard-won independence. The question is, do we have anything to offer any of these people which might be a definite inducement? So far as Turkey is concerned, we have given her rather special facilities in obtaining certain military supplies and we should continue to do so.

We have apparently made some concessions recently in favor of Russia. I suppose the Russians may also be impressed by our firm

[26] The pact was signed at Teheran (in the Saadabad Palace) on July 8, 1937; for text, see League of Nations Treaty Series, vol. cxc, p. 21.

stand in the Far East. The sum of these various contributions on our part and our growing aid to the British unquestionably affect the Near Eastern countries, particularly the Arabs, who are always impressed by power. It seems to me that for the time being we are probably already taking about all the steps open to us, short of war, to encourage the Near Eastern countries to resist aggression. As our productive capacity increases, so can our aid to these countries.

PAUL H. ALLING

INSISTENCE BY THE UNITED STATES ON THE LIQUIDATION BY THE TURKISH GOVERNMENT OF THE EXCHANGE ARREARS FOR IMPORTS FROM THE UNITED STATES [27]

867.5151/169 : Telegram

The Ambassador in Turkey (MacMurray) to the Secretary of State

ISTANBUL, January 13, 1940—4 p. m.
[Received January 13—2 p. m.]

9. My telegram No. 76, December 29, 6 p. m.[28] Turkish authorities have issued instructions exempting from the exchange premium all American merchandise imported into Turkey prior to December 4, 1939. American merchandise imported between December 4, 1939, and January 2, 1940, will pay a premium of 37½ piasters per dollar and imports subsequent to January 2 a premium of 50 piasters.

Embassy has been informed that dollar transfers for the amounts covered by exchange permits, issued since December 15 but not utilized on account of the requirement to pay exchange premium (which totaled $2,271,000 on January 10) will start on January 15.

Applications on file on January 10 for which permits had not been issued totaled $4,356,000.

For the Ambassador:
KELLEY

867.5151/172 : Telegram

The Secretary of State to the Ambassador in Turkey (MacMurray)

WASHINGTON, February 2, 1940—6 p. m.

7. Department of Commerce reports that Turkish importers are advising American exporters that as a result of a recent financial agreement between the United States and Turkey, foreign exchange in Turkey is now available for immediate payment of new imports from the United States.

---

[27] For previous correspondence, see *Foreign Relations*, 1939, vol. IV, pp. 866 ff.
[28] *Ibid.*, p. 892.

You should take steps to correct any erroneous impression which may exist that the Turkish compensation premium system is a result of a bilateral agreement to which the United States is a party. Although our telegram no. 63 of December 22, 6 p. m.,[29] stated that the Department would not be disposed to object to an arrangement involving the temporary levy of premiums on new imports, we reserved the right to reconsider the matter in the light of actual practice and in accordance with the provisions of the trade agreement. We consider the recent Turkish regulations as entirely unilateral acts on the part of the Turkish Government.

You should continue to insist upon the chronological liquidation of arrears.

HULL

611.6151/666

The Ambassador in Turkey (MacMurray) to the Secretary of State

No. 1370   ANKARA, February 15, 1940.
                                            [Received April 2.]

SIR: Referring to my despatches No. 1314 [*1341*] of January 22, 1940, and No. 1316 of December 30, 1939,[30] with regard to developments in American-Turkish trade relations, I regret to have to report that a delay has occurred in the liquidation of the exchange arrears which appears to the Embassy entirely unwarranted.

The Department will recall that commencing December 15, 1939, exchange permits bore a notation which required the payment of an exchange premium of 37½ piasters per dollar. Such permits were not utilized since the holders were unwilling to pay the required exchange premium. The Exchange Control Office in Istanbul continued, however, to issue such permits up to January 2, 1940, when the issue of permits was discontinued in consequence of the decision made by the Inter-Ministerial Committee on that day that "no premium shall be applied to the countervalue of commercial imports made from America prior to December 4, 1939." As reported in my despatch No. 1341 of January 22, 1940, there was a delay of two weeks in the resumption of the issue of permits without a stamp requiring the payment of an exchange premium; such permits were to be issued in the first place, of course, in exchange for the permits with such a stamp given out between December 15 and January 2.

The Embassy had expected that the replacement of the permits issued between December 15 and January 2 would be accomplished with only

---

[29] *Foreign Relations*, 1939, vol. IV, p. 891.
[30] Neither printed.

a brief delay, and that the Exchange Office would then proceed to the issue of new permits. Weeks passed by, however, without any new permits being issued. In response to frequent inquiries made by a representative of the Embassy, the Director of the Exchange Office in Istanbul gave it as a reason for the delay in the issue of new permits that his office was busy with the issue of permits to replace those previously given out, and that no new permits would be issued until all the old ones had been replaced. While this reason appeared plausible at the beginning, it became less and less persuasive as time went on. The Director of the Exchange Office alleged also that the replacement of the old permits was delayed by the fact that a large number of local firms had failed to present their old permits for replacement by new ones. It is difficult to believe that there are any considerable number of such cases, inasmuch as the local importers have already deposited the countervalue of their invoices in local currency and would have no possible reason for refusing to exchange their permits.

After three weeks had elapsed without the issue of new permits being resumed, I decided to bring to the attention of the Minister for Foreign Affairs the situation obtaining in the matter of the liquidation of the exchange arrears. I took the matter up with him on February 9, 1940, and pointed out that no new exchange permits for the transfer of payments for commercial importations from the United States had been issued by the Exchange Control authorities in Istanbul since early in January, the only permits given out during the past month being those issued to replace permits previously issued. In view of the fact that the exchange arrears amounted to more than $4,000,000 and that the non-liquidation of these arrears was having a harmful effect on American-Turkish trade, I requested the Minister to look into the situation with a view to expediting the liquidation of the arrears. I also brought to his attention that, although the American-Turkish Trade Agreement [31] stipulated that the Turkish Government should make available exchange for commercial imports from the United States in the chronological order in which requests for exchange were made, and although there existed large arrears, the Embassy understood that considerable amounts of exchange had recently been allocated, through the opening of letters of credit, for new commercial imports from the United States; and I urgently requested the Minister to take steps to bring about the cessation of this practice and to have the money in question allocated to the liquidation of the arrears.

Respectfully yours,   J. V. A. MacMurray

---

[31] Signed at Ankara, April 1, 1939. Department of State Executive Agreement Series No. 163, or 54 Stat. (pt. 2) 1870.

611.6731/671

The Ambassador in Turkey (MacMurray) to the Secretary of State

No. 1381   ANKARA, February 29, 1940.
                                                       [Received April 2.]

SIR: Referring to my despatch No. 1370 of February 15, 1940, reporting the representations which I made to the Minister for Foreign Affairs on February 9 with regard to the cessation of the issue of exchange permits for the transfer of payments for commercial importations from United States, I have the honor to report that, after two weeks had elapsed without any reply being received from the Minister in response to my representations, I addressed a letter to him on February 24 pointing out the deplorable effect which the cessation of the issue of exchange permits was having upon the trade relations between Turkey and the United States, stating that we were at a loss to understand the cessation of the issue of exchange permits at the very time when large amounts of exchange were becoming available to the Turkish Government through the purchase of Turkish products by the United States,* and requesting the Minister to give the matter his urgent consideration with a view to bringing about the prompt resumption of the issue of exchange permits. A translation of my letter is enclosed for the Department's information.

I may add that the Exchange Control Officer in Istanbul continues to maintain that the delay in the issue of new exchange permits is due to the fact that the replacement of the permits issued between December 15, 1939, and January 2, 1940, has not been completed, and to state that he is unable to indicate when the issue of new permits will be resumed.

Respectfully yours,   J. V. A. MACMURRAY

[Enclosure—Translation]

The American Ambassador (MacMurray) to the Turkish Minister for Foreign Affairs (Saracoglu)

                                                       ANKARA, February 24, 1940.

DEAR MR. MINISTER: May I ask your indulgence to allow me to invite your attention again to the situation with regard to the cessation of the issue of exchange permits for the transfer of payments for commercial importations from the United States, which I discussed with you on February 9.

---

*It is estimated that the American tobacco companies have already sold about $4,400,000 in connection with their purchases of Turkish tobacco since December 1, 1939. Exchange permits issued since the beginning of December have totalled about $2,700,000. [Footnote in the original.]

I need not point out the deplorable effect of such delays upon the trade relations between Turkey and the United States. As time passes by without the settlement of past accounts and with uncertainty as to what may be expected in the future, American traders lose interest and confidence in the Turkish trade, and there is not only a dislocation of current business but also a disorganizing tendency to sever existing commercial connections. I cannot conceal the fact that we are profoundly disturbed by the continuation of this situation. As you know, my Government considers it essential that exchange be made available currently for American imports and we are at a loss to understand the cessation of the issue of exchange permits at the very time when large amounts of exchange are becoming available to the Turkish Government through the purchase of Turkish products by the United States.

In view of the long period which has already elapsed during which no permits have been issued, I hope that you will find it possible to give the matter your urgent consideration with a view to bringing about the prompt resumption of the issue of exchange permits in order that the exchange arrears may be liquidated as quickly as possible.

J. V. A. MacMurray

867.5151/176 : Telegram

The Ambassador in Turkey (MacMurray) to the Secretary of State

Ankara, March 5, 1940—4 p. m.
[Received 6 p. m.]

19. With reference to the Turkish exchange situation the Istanbul Exchange Office yesterday resumed the issuance of exchange transfer permits which has been interrupted for several weeks.

Unpaid arrears representing applications filed during the period June 20, 1939, to February 24, 1940, amount to $4,830,000.

Our best estimate is that the Turkish Government has available some $2,500,000 in exchange but the dilatoriness and secretiveness with which the interested authorities have handled this matter in recent months leads to some doubt as to the prospects of their dealing promptly and effectively with the question of arrears.

MacMurray

611.6731/666a : Telegram

The Secretary of State to the Ambassador in Turkey (MacMurray)

Washington, March 14, 1940—3 p. m.

19. Department's 22, April 7, 1939, 2 p. m.[32] You should at your earliest convenience obtain from the Turkish authorities the statistics

---

[32] *Foreign Relations*, 1939, vol. IV, p. 867.

necessary for giving effect to the exchange provisions of the trade agreement during 1939. For this purpose the following figures are desirable: (*a*) the total value of commercial imports from all countries into Turkey in the year 1939, (*b*) the amount to be deducted from this total as provided in paragraph 1 of the supplementary note to the trade agreement, (*c*) the total value of commercial imports of American origin in 1939, and (*d*) the exchange allotments actually made in 1939 for commercial imports of American origin taking place in 1939. The Department would also like to be informed of the amount of unpaid arrears representing applications filed in 1939 for American products imported in the same year.

HULL

867.5151/177 : Telegram

The Ambassador in Turkey (MacMurray) to the Secretary of State

ANKARA, March 16, 1940—1 a. m.
[Received 3 : 51 p. m.]

28. My telegram No. 19, March 5, 4 p. m., from Istanbul [*Ankara*]. Exchange Office there [Istanbul] advises that up to March 15 exchange permits issued since the resumption of exchange transfers on March 4 total $287,400. Transfers leave [*have?*] now been effected on all applications filed prior to July 1, 1939.

Total unpaid applications for exchange transfer permits on file as of March 14 amount to $4,680,000.

MACMURRAY

867.5151/174 : Telegram

The Secretary of State to the Ambassador in Turkey (MacMurray)

WASHINGTON, March 21, 1940—1 p. m.

20. Your despatches 1287 December 6 and 1316 December 30.[33]

1. Are all proceeds of Turkish exports to the United States now being liquidated at 1.625 Turkish pounds to the dollar?

2. Does the 1.625 rate now apply to all dollars offered for sale in Turkey from noncommercial and commercial transactions alike?

3. What kinds of transactions, if any, result in a higher or a lower rate than 1.625?

Please report by telegraph, elaborating in a despatch if necessary.

HULL

---

[33] Neither printed.

867.5151/178 : Telegram

The Ambassador in Turkey (MacMurray) to the Secretary of State

ANKARA, March 23, 1940—noon.
[Received 4:11 p. m.]

29. Department's 20, March 21, 1 p. m.

(1) All dollars sold in connection with Turkish exports to the United States are being purchased at the rate of 1.625 Turkish pounds to the dollar.

(2) This rate has not been made applicable to dollars sold for non-commercial purposes. It would appear from information obtained by the Embassy that the Turkish Government has decided to apply the uniturc rate (now approximately 1.95 to the dollar) to such dollars. This rate is being made available generally to dollars sold for noncommercial purposes provided that they have been brought into Turkey from abroad and provided that in the case of their being offered for sale by persons not connected with a foreign mission the transaction has in each case the approval of the Ministry of Finance. American newspapermen who have been recently in Ankara have been selling dollars at this rate and appear to have experienced no difficulty in obtaining the permission of that Ministry. Banks other than the Central Bank purchase dollars offered to them only at the official rate of approximately 1.30.

MACMURRAY

611.6731/673

The Ambassador in Turkey (MacMurray) to the Secretary of State

No. 1408
ISTANBUL, April 3, 1940.
[Received April 29.]

SIR: Supplementing my despatch No. 1381 of February 29, 1940, relative to the situation in respect to the liquidation of the exchange arrears, I have the honor to report that the Exchange Control Office in Istanbul resumed the issue of new exchange permits on March 4, presumably as the result of instructions received from Ankara in consequence of the Embassy's representations. The issue of exchange permits, however, proceeded at a very slow rate, less than $300,000 in permits being issued during the first ten days. In view of the interest manifested by the Minister of Commerce in improving the trade relations between the United States and Turkey, the Embassy considered that it would be helpful to bring to the Minister's personal attention the situation in respect to the issue of exchange permits for the transfer of payments for commercial importations from the United States. Arrangements were made for the Assistant Commercial Attaché to call upon the Minister with a view to pointing out to him the deplorable effect which the continued delay in the liquidation of the exchange arrears was having on American-Turkish trade. The Minister expressed surprise on learning that so little exchange had been transferred since the resumption of the issue of exchange permits, and said that he had supposed that at least a million dollars would have been transferred. He undertook to discuss the matter with the Minister of Finance; and on the following day, March 22, he stated that the Minister of Finance had promised to give at once the necessary instructions for the acceleration of the exchange transfers.

The Minister of Commerce was unable to obtain any definite information from the Minister of Finance as to the amount of dollar exchange which was available. (The latter did not know the details of the dollar exchange position and the officer in charge of the matter was ill.) The Minister of Commerce had made inquiries, however, at the Central Bank, and was informed that, since the beginning of December, the Bank had purchased approximately $5,900,000,* representing presumably the dollars sold by American companies to cover their tobacco purchases and the proceeds of other Turkish exports to the United States made during that period. He said that he felt that this figure was rather low and that he was inclined to believe that there had been some "flight" of dollars which should have been forthcoming from exports to the United States. The Minister declared that he would endeavor to obtain exact information with regard to the amount of dollar exchange now available and that he would insist upon full restitution if he discovered that dollar exchange which should have been utilized for the payment of commercial imports from the United States had been diverted to noncommercial purposes. He referred to shipments of gold made to New York last year, and intimated the possibility that a certain amount of the exchange received during recent months might have been used to repay the advances for which the gold shipments presumably were security. He indicated his readiness, in the event that there had been a diversion, to make available for the payment of the dollar arrears the exchange which he anticipated receiving in payment for wheat shipments to Mediterranean countries, which are payable in dollars. Apparently this exchange is the only dollar exchange over which the Minister of Commerce has direct control.

As reported in the Embassy's telegram No. 34 of March 30, 2 p. m.,[34] the Istanbul Exchange Office stated on that date that the amount of

---

*This figure checks approximately with the information obtained by the Embassy from the American tobacco companies to the effect that the sales of dollars effected by the three principal American purchasers since the opening of the tobacco market in early December total more than $5,300,000. [Footnote in the original.]

[34] Not printed.

exchange permits issued up to that time since March 4 totalled $927,400. This figure indicates that the issue of exchange permits during the last fifteen days of this period was considerably accelerated.

With respect to the question of the application of the rate established for the purchase of dollars sold in connection with the export of Turkish commodities to the United States, namely, the official rate plus an exchange premium of twenty-five per cent., it may be stated that, as reported in my telegram No. 29 of March 23, 12 noon, this rate has not been made applicable to dollars sold for non-commercial purposes, although the Minister of Commerce had stated that this rate would be applied to all transactions, involving the sale of dollars for Turkish currency, and although the Embassy had been given to understand by the Central Bank that regulations relating to this matter were being worked out. After a reasonable time had elapsed and no action had been taken to apply the exchange premium to the purchase of non-commercial dollars, the Embassy took the matter up with the Foreign Office which in turn consulted the Central Bank. The competent official in the Central Bank informed the Foreign Office that it had been decided to make available the Uniturc rate to dollars sold for non-commercial purposes. In the event that such dollars were offered for sale by persons not connected with a foreign mission, the transaction would have to have in each case the approval of the Ministry of Finance. It was stated that the approval of the Minister of Finance would be given promptly provided that the dollars in question had been brought into Turkey from abroad. The Foreign Office official indicated that in practice the official rate would be applied only to dollars presented by persons who were unable or did not desire to explain their origin, the assumption being that such dollars had been acquired illegally. After receiving this information, the Embassy sought to ascertain whether the Uniturc rate was actually being accorded to persons, not connected with a foreign mission, who offered dollars for sale. In view of the infrequency at the present time of the sale of dollars for non-commercial purposes by persons not connected with a foreign mission, some time elapsed before a sufficient number of cases had come to the Embassy's attention to justify the conclusion that the Uniturc rate was actually being made available generally to dollars sold for non-commercial purposes. The Embassy has now established that in half a dozen cases American newspaper men in Ankara have experienced no difficulty in obtaining the permission of the Ministry of Finance to dispose of their dollars at the Uniturc rate; and there has not come to the Embassy's attention any case in which this rate has been refused. The Embassy will follow developments in this matter, however, with a view to seeing whether the Uniturc rate continues to be made available to persons selling dollars for non-commercial purposes.

Respectfully yours,   J. V. A. MacMurray

867.5151/206

The Ambassador in Turkey (MacMurray) to the Secretary of State

No. 1480   ANKARA, June 12, 1940.
                                                  [Received July 19.]

SIR: I have the honor to refer to the Department's despatch No. 468 of May 15 [35] in which this Embassy is requested to furnish the Department any information it may be able to obtain regarding the suggestions made by the Goodyear Tire & Rubber Company to the effect that the Turkish authorities have been delaying the issuance of exchange permits in the expectation of a loan to be made to Turkey by the Export Import Bank.

It will be recalled that from January 5 to March 4, 1940, no new exchange transfer permits were issued by the exchange authorities, and no reasonable explanation of this delay was ever offered. The principal explanation given was that the Exchange Control Office was finding it more difficult than had been anticipated to recall and replace those permits issued between December 15, 1939, and January 5, 1940, which had not been utilized by holders by reason of the fact that they required the payment of an exchange premium. The Embassy did not at the time consider that the alleged difficulties were such as to occasion any such prolonged delay. On March 4, however, the issuance of new permits was resumed; and since that date, the Exchange Control Office has given out permits totalling approximately $2,400,000.

The Embassy did not attribute this prolonged delay primarily to the Turkish Government's hope of obtaining a loan from the Export Import Bank, although there was evidence that this hope was present in the minds of the Turkish authorities. On at least two occasions the Minister of Commerce, in discussing the exchange situation with the Assistant Commercial Attaché, stated that the arrears could all be cleared up promptly if the Turkish Government were granted a loan from the Export Import Bank. On both occasions the Minister was advised that the Turkish Government's request for a loan had been transmitted to the Department in December (my telegram No. 156 of December 12, 1939, 4 p. m.[36]), and that as no instructions had since been received there was nothing further that

---

[35] Not printed.
[36] *Foreign Relations*, 1939, vol. IV, p. 886.

the Embassy could say at that time. The Minister was told unofficially in December, at the time the loan was requested, and on subsequent occasions when he referred to the subject, that it would be unwise to count upon the loan being granted. However, it would appear from information which has recently become available that in spite of the fact that the Turkish authorities were discouraged from adopting too optimistic an attitude with regard to the loan, it was in the expectation of obtaining such a loan that the exchange transfers were held up during the period January 5 to March 4. The fact that the Turkish officials obviously could not admit to the Embassy that transfers were being held up for this reason would account for the very unsatisfactory excuses for the delay which were given at the time.

It was apparently the Turkish Government's intention to utilize any loan obtained from the Export Import Bank for the purpose of liquidating the outstanding arrears which, at the time the loan was first requested, totalled some $6,500,000, and to devote dollar exchange derived from the purchase of Turkish tobacco by American companies and other Turkish exports to the United States to making prompt dollar payment for new imports of American origin upon their arrival in Turkey and opening letter of credit in the United States to cover such new imports. This is borne out by several statements made by the Minister of Commerce in December and January to the effect that dollar exchange would be available to pay for new imports from the United States upon arrival here and that it would be possible to open letters of credit covering new purchases of American merchandise. When the Embassy pointed out to the competent Turkish authorities that such action would be in violation of the provisions of the Turkish-American Trade Agreement, the idea of effecting immediate dollar payment for new arrivals of merchandise of American origin was abandoned, and letters of credit for only some $400,000 were opened at that time.

It is probable that the resumption on March 4 of exchange transfers was due primarily to the Embassy's action in pressing for a more rapid liquidation of the arrears, rather than to the apparent failure to obtain the loan from the Export Import Bank, as during the latter part of April the Minister of Commerce while in Istanbul again referred hopefully to the loan in a conversation with a member of the Embassy staff.

Respectfully yours,   J. V. A. MacMurray

611.6731/683

The Ambassador in Turkey (MacMurray) to the Secretary of State

No. 1488   ANKARA, June 21, 1940.
                                         [Received July 19.]

SIR: In continuation of my despatch No. 1443 of May 6, 1940,[37] relative to the exchange situation, I have the honor to report that I took up again with the Minister for Foreign Affairs on May 8, 1940, the question of the allocation of exchange for the payment of arrears due on imports from the United States, with particular reference to the statement in the Ministry's note of April 24, 1940, that $1,755,071 were "in course of payment". There is enclosed, for the Department's records, a copy of the memorandum of my conversation with the Minister. I gained the impression that the Minister was genuinely surprised to learn that a large amount of the dollar exchange which had been allocated for the payment of imports from the United States had not been paid out.

In accordance with the Minister's suggestion, Mr. Kelley [38] called upon the Director General of the Department of Commercial and Economic Affairs on May 13, 1940, and explained the exchange situation fully to him. As of interest to the Department there is enclosed a copy of the memorandum which he left with Mr. Saman.

It would appear that following my representations, the Minister actively interested himself in the matter since, as will be seen from the table below, a very large amount of exchange has been made available since May 17 for the payment of imports from the United States.

Period	Amount of Exchange Permits Issued
April 12–18	$102, 000
April 19–25	40, 000
April 26–May 2	110, 000
May 3–9	99, 000
May 10–16	120, 000
May 17–23	221, 000
May 24–30	487, 000
May 31–June 6	625, 000
June 7–13	403, 000

It will be noted that whereas in the four weeks preceding May 17 the total amount of the exchange permits issued was $369,000, during the four weeks following that date exchange permits were issued to the amount of $1,736,000. Even though there be deducted from this latter amount the sum of $479,000, representing the value of the

---

[37] Not printed.
[38] Robert Kelley, First Secretary of Embassy.

exchange permits returned by the Ford Motor Company, as explained in my despatch No. 1475 of May 31, 1940,[39] the amount remaining exceeds the figure for the previous period by about $1,000,000. As a result of the large amount of exchange furnished since May 17, the arrears for imports from the United States effected prior to January 1, 1940, have been reduced to approximately $459,000 (as of June 14th). While the liquidation of the remaining arrears for pre-1940 imports may be delayed in consequence of recent international developments, the Embassy will continue to follow the matter closely with a view to expediting as much as possible the liquidation of these arrears.

I may add for the Department's information that the Embassy has not as yet received any reply to its note of March 19, 1940, requesting the information specified by the Department in its telegram No. 19 of March 14, 3 p. m. The Embassy has endeavored to expedite the procurement of this information through both oral and written representations to the Foreign Office, which maintains that it has been doing its best to obtain the data desired from the appropriate Departments of the Turkish Government.

Respectfully yours,   J. V. A. MACMURRAY

[Enclosure 1]

Memorandum of Conversation, by the Ambassador in Turkey
(MacMurray)

ANKARA, May 8, 1940.

I again brought this question up with the Minister,[40] pointing out that, although he had assured me a year ago that all exchange received from American purchases would be paid into a special account out of which 80 per cent. would be held available for the payment of American accounts, that had not in fact been done; apparently, during the period from January 5 to March 4 last, when the issuance of exchange permits was suspended, the very considerable sums received from the purchase of Turkish products by the United States had in large part been diverted to other uses. The consequence was that well over $2,000,000 of arrears for imports from the United States in 1939 remained unsettled; and although the Ministry's note of April 24th stated that the sum of $1,750,000 odd were in course of payment, the payments were in fact proceeding at a very slow and unsatisfactory rate.

Mr. Saracoglu expressed surprise, and said that he had been assured by the Minister of Finance that 80 per cent. of all dollars received

---

[39] Not printed.
[40] Turkish Minister for Foreign Affairs, Sükrü Saracoglu.

from American purchases had been made available for payments on American account. I pointed out that the Ministry's note itself indicated that something under $2,000,000 of the amount of exchange reserved for American account had not in fact been paid; and I handed him a copy of the note, so that he might refresh his memory. He read it with an air of surprise and of gravity. He then said that, since he himself did not have the details of the matter in mind, he would suggest that I have Mr. Kelley go into the matter fully in a conversation with Mr. Bedri Tahir Şaman, the Director General of the Department of Commercial and Economic Affairs, or, if I preferred, sum up the matter in an *Aide-Mémoire*. He promised that he would give the matter his personal attention, and do what he could to assist us in it.

For the first time in any of our conversations of recent months on this subject, he gave me the impression of taking this question seriously and recognizing a responsibility on the part of his Ministry in regard to it.

MACM[URRAY]

[Enclosure 2—Translation]

Memorandum by the First Secretary of Embassy in Turkey (Kelley) [41]

1. Exchange arrears for imports of American origin effected in 1939 amount to approximately $2,300,000.

2. The existence of these arrears is due to the fact that the Turkish Government has not made available currently for the payment of American imports 80 per cent. of the dollar exchange received from the purchase of Turkish products by the United States.

3. In May, 1939, following representations by the Embassy relative to the considerable amount of exchange arrears for American imports which had accumulated in the twelve months subsequent to May 11, 1938, as a result of the utilization by the Turkish Government for non-commercial purposes of the greater part of the dollar exchange received from Turkish exports to the United States in that period, the Turkish Government assured the Embassy that 80 per cent. of the exchange received from exports to the United States would be put into a special account and made available currently for the payment of American imports and that exchange transfer permits would be issued by the Exchange Control Officer in Istanbul in accordance with the exchange availabilities in this account.

[41] Handed by the First Secretary of Embassy to the Director General of the Turkish Department of Commercial and Economic Affairs.

4. This arrangement appears to have been adhered to up to January 5, 1940, when the issue of exchange permits was suspended. No new exchange permits were issued from that date until March 4, 1940, a period during which large amounts of exchange were becoming available to the Turkish Government from the purchase of Turkish products by the United States. Inasmuch as very small amounts of exchange have been made available since the resumption of the issue of exchange permits, it would appear that a large amount of exchange, approximately $2,000,000, which, under the above-mentioned arrangement, should have been made available for the payment of American imports, has been diverted to other purposes.

5. The American Government is quite disturbed by the fact that American trade with Turkey is seriously handicapped by the exchange arrears which have accumulated in consequence of the failure of the Turkish Government to allocate an adequate amount of exchange. As a result of the accumulation of exchange arrears in 1938–39 imports into Turkey of American origin have undergone a considerable decline and there is no question but that American imports in the present year will show a still further decrease in consequence of the existence of arrears for importations effected in 1939. According to Turkish statistics, American imports into Turkey declined from 17,294,000 Turkish pounds in 1937 to 15,680,000 in 1938, and to 11,686,000 in 1939, while Turkish exports to the United States have been maintained at a high level, amounting to 19,201,000 in 1937, 17,768,000 in 1938 and 18,212,000 in 1939.

Ankara, May 13, 1940.

867.5151/208

The Ambassador in Turkey (MacMurray) to the Secretary of State

No. 1513

Istanbul, August 6, 1940.
[Received August 22.]

Sir: I have the honor to refer to my despatch No. 1475 of May 31, 1940,[42] as well as to telegraphic despatches on the status of exchange transfers in payment of commercial imports of American origin.

On June 15, 1940 the Turkish Exchange Control Office temporarily ceased the issuance of permits for dollar exchange transfers. This suspension continued until around July 10 when the issuance of permits was resumed but on a limited scale. The Exchange Director gave varying reasons for the temporary suspension but it is believed probable that dollar exchange transfers were stopped by an order of the Ministry of Finance pending some clarification of the rather

---

[42] Not printed.

tense political situation in the Balkans which existed at that time. As a matter of fact, Namik Kemal Bey, the Director of the Istanbul Exchange Office, in a conversation with the Assistant Commercial Attaché on July 5th, made a definite statement to that effect. On July 10 the issuance of permits was again resumed but the amounts granted have not been large. From July 10 to August 1, inclusive, only $141,296 of permits have been issued. Since the Embassy's last telegraphic despatch on the exchange situation (June 29 [*30*], 1940) [43] until August 2nd new applications have been filed with the exchange authorities in the amount of $196,293.

On August 2nd the total unpaid applications on file covering commercial imports from the United States amounted to $3,283,017 of which $332,945 represented imports effected during 1939. It should be noted that the figure for the 1939 arrears is not, strictly speaking, an accurate one as the Embassy is obliged to make calculations based on data furnished by the Exchange Office and the Turkish authorities consider as 1939 arrears only those imports which were effected prior to December 4, 1939, the date on which the exchange premiums came into effect. The Department will recall that last December the Turkish Government finally agreed to continue to liquidate the old arrears without the collection of an exchange premium but that an exchange premium would be levied on new imports and the date fixed for the application of the exchange premiums was December 4. It is probable, therefore, that the figure given above as representing 1939 arrears is in error by a possible $200,000 almost all of which is believed to be due to the Socony Vacuum Oil Company.

With the entrance of Italy into the war the problem of effecting actual dollar transfers covered by permits issued became increasingly difficult. Although the Central Bank continued to issue dollar checks against exchange permits, local firms were extremely reluctant to make use of the ordinary post as the Turkish postal authorities, while accepting mail for the United States, were still undecided as to the means by which the mail would be forwarded (the Trans-Siberian route by way of Vladivostok and Japan was finally decided upon and is still being utilized). The Central Bank refused to sell dollars for cable transfer and the other banks were obliged to follow the lead of the Central Bank.

On June 13 the Embassy approached the Foreign Office with a request that the Central Bank be approached with a view to authorizing the sale of dollars for cable transfer. The Embassy pointed out that permits being issued by the exchange authorities covering commercial imports from the United States were of relatively little value if the local importer found it impossible to transfer to the United

---

[43] Not printed.

980 FOREIGN RELATIONS, 1940, VOLUME III

States the dollars granted him. As a result of the Embassy's efforts the Central Bank did effect cable transfers but by way of London, presumably through the sale in New York of Sterling from the Bank's London balances.

With the suspension in the issuance of permits the question of the actual transfer of the dollars lost its immediate importance but has again arisen with the resumption of the granting of permits. At the present time the only means of transfer of dollars is again by ordinary post. The Central Bank states that they are unable to make cable transfers as recent British regulations prevent transfer through London. Furthermore, the Central Bank will not permit the use of airmail for dollar remittances stating that the use of airmail for this purpose is against their regulations.

The Embassy believes that the attitude of the Central Bank is anything but a liberal one as it is the Embassy's understanding that practically all the dollar purchases of the Central Bank are by cable on New York. The tobacco companies have, since the early part of the year, been making their dollar sales for tobacco purchases and manipulation by cable in New York and it is consequently difficult to understand the refusal of the Central Bank to utilize their dollar balances in New York to sell dollars here for cable transfer. A specific example exists in the case of a permit for $74,000 granted the Socony Vacuum Oil Company more than three weeks ago. The American company has not to date been able to effect the transfer of this sum. It is believed that there are probably other instances although as most of the permits granted during the past few weeks have been for relatively small amounts it is possible that local holders have obtained the checks and mailed them by ordinary post.

The Embassy intends approaching the Central Bank directly with the request that they give serious consideration to the possibility of authorizing the sale of dollars for cable transfer at the same time calling attention to the Embassy's understanding that the dollar purchases of the bank are usually effected by cable on New York and citing as an example the case of the dollar sales of the tobacco companies. As an alternative measure, the use of airmail communications will be suggested.

Respectfully yours,

J. V. A. MacMurray

867.5151/207 : Telegram

The Ambassador in Turkey (MacMurray) to the Secretary of State

ISTANBUL, August 22, 1940—6 p. m.
[Received 8 : 15 p. m.]

94. The Minister of Commerce in an address delivered at the opening of the international fair at Izmir made the following remarks

relative to the liquidation of the existing exchange arrears for imports from the United States and Turkey's foreign exchange situation:

"On the other hand, we had a debt of $3,453,000 to the United States of America on August 1, 1940, and the overdrawn accounts with countries with the interchangeable regime amount to pounds Turkish 1,879,000.

However, we are now in a position already to settle these debts. These accounts could be liquidated in full by the shipment of 10,000 tons of cotton which could be exported before the commencement of the exportation of the 1940 crops, and it is, moreover, more than probable that we can obtain $10,000,000 from the export of wheat when the 1940 export season opens up, and another $10,000,000 from the export of 25,000 tons of cotton.

These new sources of free exchange are quite apart from our normal free exchange resources and may be regarded as an important asset contributed to the country's economy by the first year of war. Therefore towards the close of the year we shall have the means of paying from day to day the free exchange required by our imports. The functioning of our free exchange sources in the way I have mentioned will ensure the accumulation of a large reserve of free exchange in 1941 which will result in making our currency one of the soundest in Europe."

Subsequently, in summing up his remarks, he stated,

"Soon we shall have liquidated our debts in free exchange and we shall dispose of reserves for these sorts of independent payments."

The Embassy will endeavor to obtain from the Minister more definite information regarding the possibility mentioned by him of any early complete liquidation of our exchange arrears.

MACMURRAY

867.5151/209 : Telegram

The Ambassador in Turkey (MacMurray) to the Secretary of State

ISTANBUL, September 4, 1940—noon.
[Received September 4—11 : 40 a. m.]

97. My telegram No. 94 of August 22, 6 p. m. The Turkish Minister of Commerce has advised the Assistant Commercial Attaché that he is determined to clear up the exchange arrears for imports from the United States even though the immediate prospect for further imports from the United States is not bright. The Minister stated that he hoped to clear up by special arrangement the arrears due the Socony Vacuum and liquidate the remaining arrears from free exchange which he expected from cotton already sold to Yugoslavia and possible grain exports to Greece. Although the Minister was very definite as to the possibility of utilizing such exchange for

the liquidation of the American arrears, the Exchange Director when queried on this point took a less favorable view.

When asked for his opinion as to the possibilities of Basra–Baghdad–Istanbul route for Turkish-American trade, the Minister was optimistic, nor did he feel that much was to be expected from the Hellenic Lines New York to Istanbul regular ocean freight service much advertised here for some time past.

MacMurray

611.6731/689

The Ambassador in Turkey (MacMurray) to the Secretary of State

No. 1553   Istanbul, September 7, 1940.
[Received October 21.]

Sir: In continuation of my despatch No. 1488 of June 21, 1940, with regard to the liquidation of exchange arrears for imports from the United States, I have the honor to report the following developments relative to this matter which have occurred during the past two months:

As has been reported to the Department, the issuance of permits for the transfer of dollar exchange for the payment of imports from the United States was suspended on June 13, 1940. After two weeks had elapsed without the resumption of the issuance of permits, the Embassy took up again with the Foreign Office the question of the allocation of exchange for the liquidation of the outstanding exchange arrears. Mr. Kelley called upon the Director General of the Department of Commercial and Economic Affairs of the Foreign Office on July 1, 1940, and informed him that the Exchange Control Director at Istanbul had suspended on June 13, 1940, the issuance of exchange permits for the payment of imports from the United States and that the Embassy understood that this action had been taken as a result of instructions received from Ankara. He pointed out that the exchange arrears for imports from the United States amounted to approximately $3,228,000 and that of this sum approximately $460,000 represented arrears for imports effected in 1939, although six months had elapsed since the close of that year. He requested the Foreign Office to urge the competent authorities to allocate sufficient exchange to expedite the complete liquidation of the arrears.

The issuance of exchange permits was resumed on July 10, 1940, but from that date up to September 6, 1940, the total amount of the permits issued was only $350,600. The Turkish authorities in response to the Embassy's representations have maintained that the decrease in the amount of exchange permits issued was due, not to any intervention on the part of the Turkish authorities, but to the fact that the quantity of exchange becoming available to Turkey had diminished as a result of the termination of the export season and of the decrease in shipping facilities.

There is enclosed, for the Department's records, the text, together with a translation, of a note received from the Foreign Office dated July 4, 1940, commenting on certain statements contained in the Embassy's memorandum of May 13, 1940, a copy of which was enclosed with my despatch No. 1488 of June 21, 1940. The Foreign Office would have us believe that the accumulation of exchange arrears in 1938 was due to the circumstance that Turkey did not receive sufficient dollar exchange to pay for imports from the United States. Such a thesis is not supported by the facts. As the Embassy has reported to the Department (see my despatch No. 1153 of July 15, 1939 [44]), in the twelve month period following May 11, 1938, the Turkish Government made available for the payment of imports from the United States not much more than fifty per cent. of the dollar exchange received from the purchase of Turkish products by the United States. The Foreign Office also maintains that the recent decline in imports into Turkey from the United States was due, not to the reasons set forth in the Embassy's memorandum, but to the fact that "American firms since the outbreak of the war, have not stopped demanding payment in cash contrary to the chronological order provided for in the Turkish-American Agreement". As the Department is probably aware, the policy adopted early in 1939 by many American manufacturers of requiring payment by letter of credit for shipments to Turkey was dictated by the existence of large blocked arrears in Turkey and the delay experienced in the receipt of dollar remittances for previous shipments to Turkey. It will be observed that the Foreign Office declares that it has been the constant care of the Turkish Government to see that the engagements arising out of the American-Turkish Trade Agreement are carried out within the bounds of the material possibilities, and that "payments for American imports are proceeding at present in accordance with the foreign exchange availabilities".

The Embassy will continue to endeavor to expedite the liquidation of the outstanding exchange arrears which amounted to $3,216,000 on September 6, 1940. It would appear that the Minister of Commerce is determined to liquidate completely these arrears and that he is prepared to use for this purpose free exchange obtained from the export of cotton to Yugoslavia and of wheat to Greece. (My telegram No. 97 September 4, 12 noon). The Embassy understands that Turkey is to receive approximately $1,300,000 for cotton already sold to Yugoslavia. Inasmuch as an agreement in principle has been reached between the Turkish Government and the Socony-Vacuum Oil Company

---

[44] *Foreign Relations,* 1939, vol. IV, p. 869.

whereby that Company is to receive dollar obligations payable in two years for its outstanding exchange arrears which amount to approximately $1,000,000, the above mentioned amount of dollars would appear to be sufficient to settle all the remaining arrears. However, while the Minister of Commerce speaks very definitely of the possibility of utilizing such exchange for the liquidation of the American arrears, it is not at all clear at present that the Ministry of Finance shares his viewpoint.

Respectfully yours,   J. V. A. MacMurray

[Enclosure—Translation]

The Turkish Ministry for Foreign Affairs to the American Embassy

77387
28

The Ministry of Foreign Affairs duly transmitted to the competent Department Note No. 293 of March 19, 1940,[45] as well as the contents of the Memorandum dated May 13, 1940, which the Embassy of the United States of America was kind enough to forward to the Ministry on the subject of American imports into Turkey.

The competent Department cannot agree with the point of view of the Embassy of the United States as regards the reasons which brought about the existence of arrears arising out of these imports. It is, indeed, true that arrears accumulated during the year 1938 in consequence of an abnormal increase in American imports into Turkey and the exchange obtained from Turkish exports to the United States proved insufficient to cover them. However, since the conclusion of the Agreement of May 15, 1939, the competent Department has taken care to apply all the measures required for its sound application. As a matter of fact, an amount of $5,987,135, not including payments made by the State, was allotted up to May 31, 1940, for American imports.

The total of the payments made in the course of the last months alone amounts to $1,227,806. Payments for American imports are proceeding at present in accordance with the foreign exchange availabilities.

If the imports into Turkey have lately experienced a decrease, as pointed out in the Memorandum of the Honorable Embassy, this has nothing to do with the reasons set forth in this document but is due to the fact that American firms, since the outbreak of the war, have not stopped demanding payment in cash contrary to the chronological order provided for in the Turkish-American Agreement.

The Ministry of Foreign Affairs considers in view of the above

---

[45] See last paragraph of despatch No. 1488, June 21, p. 975.

facts that there does not appear to exist any indications susceptible of hampering—even in the slightest degree—the normal development of Turkish-American commercial relations, particularly as the Government of the Republic has constantly taken care to see to it that the engagements arising out of the abovementioned Agreement were carried out within the bounds of the material possibilities.

ANKARA, July 4, 1940.

867.5151/216 : Telegram

The Ambassador in Turkey (MacMurray) to the Secretary of State

ANKARA, October 24, 1940—noon.
[Received 5 : 44 p. m.]

175. The Socony Vacuum Oil Company has concluded an agreement with the Turkish Central Bank relative to the liquidation of the exchange arrears of itself, Shell and Steaua Romana for petroleum products imported from the United States whereby the oil companies turn over to the Turkish Government Turkish pounds deposited in the Central Bank for transfer and receive an exchange permit for $971,000 (representing the total arrears for imports from December 4, 1939, to date) which amount is to be paid in six equal installments: on January 1 and October 1, 1941, and on January 1, April 1, July 1 and October 1, 1942.

The bank informed the oil companies that the arrears for imports prior to December 4, 1939, amounting to $224,000 would be liquidated within 20 days. (Of this amount $102,000 was paid Tuesday.) The Embassy understands that the liquidation of these arrears will take place in accordance with the chronological order provided for by the trade agreement, the 20 days being the time which the Turkish Government estimates that it will require to liquidate all arrears for imports from the United States prior to December 4 (the oil companies' arrears for imports in 1939 comprise by far the greater part of the arrears outstanding for 1939 imports from the United States).

The Embassy has been informed by the General Manager, Levant Division, Socony Vacuum Oil Company, that the advantage gained by the oil companies from the agreement is protection against loss from possible decline in the value of the pound (Turkish) concerning which they have been greatly worried. The exchange permit issued Tuesday specifies the amount of dollars to be paid to them on the basis of the current exchange rate of 132.20. Consequently the liquidation of their arrears will not be affected by future exchange fluctuations and in return for this advantage they were willing to agree to a delay in the actual receipt of the dollars.

MACMURRAY

611.6731/691

The Ambassador in Turkey (MacMurray) to the Secretary of State

No. 1588   ANKARA, November 7, 1940.
                                            [Received December 11.]

SIR: I have the honor to refer to the Department's telegraphic instruction No. 19 of March 14, 3 p. m., requesting the information necessary for giving effect to the exchange provisions of the American-Turkish Trade Agreement in 1939, and to report that despite repeated requests, both written and oral, the desired information has not as yet been furnished by the Foreign Office.

The Embassy has reason to believe that in the case of the information concerning the amount of exchange allocated for the payment of commercial imports of American origin effected in 1939, the failure to furnish the data requested is due to the fact that, as pointed out in my despatch No. 1443 of May 6, 1940,[46] the relevant records of the Turkish Government have not been kept in such a way as to permit the compilation of this data. With regard to the information relative to the amount to be deducted from the total value of Turkey's commercial imports in accordance with Paragraph 1 of the Supplementary Note to the Trade Agreement, it is believed that the authorities simply do not desire to take the time and trouble to compile this information since they do not contemplate making any use of it. However, the Embassy will continue to press the Foreign Office with a view to expediting the procurement of the desired information.

Pending the receipt of official information from the Turkish Government, it is thought that the Department would desire to have at its disposal the most reliable data now available relative to the points in which the Department is interested:

(*a*) The total value of the commercial imports from all countries into Turkey in 1939:

According to the official publication of the Central Statistical Office, Turkey's total commercial imports in 1939 amounted to Ltqs. 118,248,934;

(*b*) Amount to be deducted from Turkey's total commercial imports as provided in Paragraph 1 of the Supplementary Note to the Trade Agreement:

There is no data available upon which to base an estimate of this amount;

(*c*) The total value of the commercial imports of American origin into Turkey in 1939:

According to the official publication of the Central Statistical Office, Turkey's commercial imports from the United States in 1939 amounted to Ltqs. 11,686,099, representing 9.89% of Turkey's total commercial imports;

---

[46] Not printed.

(*d*) Exchange allotments actually made for commercial imports of American origin effected in 1939:

The Embassy estimates that up to November 7, 1940, the Turkish authorities had allocated approximately $9,174,624 for the payment of imports from the United States effected in 1939. This figure is an approximate one because it includes (due to delay in filing applications for exchange permits) some exchange granted for the payment of imports actually effected prior to January 1, 1939. This estimate is based on the following figures:

Exchange allocated from the resumption of exchange payments in July, 1939, up to May 31, 1940	$5, 987, 135*
(From this figure should be deducted the estimated arrears for 1938 imports existing at the time of resumption of exchange payments)	$ 420, 000
	$5, 567, 135
Exchange permits issued May 31, 1940, to June 13, 1940	$1, 028, 000
Exchange permits issued July 10, 1940, to November 7, 1940	$1, 760, 489
Payments to oil companies under Special Permits January 1, 1939, to June 20, 1939† . .	$ 819, 000
	9, 174, 624

The Embassy estimates that the amount of unpaid arrears for American goods imported in 1939 amounted to approximately $300,000 on November 7, 1940.‡

Respectfully yours,   J. V. A. MacMurray

867.5151/221

The Ambassador in Turkey (MacMurray) to the Secretary of State

No. 1618   Ankara, December 10, 1940.
                                            [Received January 27, 1941.]

Sir: I have the honor to refer to my despatch No. 1548 of September 7,[47] and previous despatches on the Turkish exchange situation and to

---

*This figure was furnished by the Foreign Office in its note of July 4, 1940. It differs but slightly from the Embassy's estimates for the period in question. [Footnote in the original.]

†The total amount received by oil companies was $1,300,000. Of the amount received by the Socony-Vacuum Oil Company ($1,004,000), $619,000 covered payments for petroleum products imported in 1939 and $385,000 products imported in 1938. It is estimated that of the amount—$300,000—received by the other oil companies, $200,000 represented payments for 1939 imports. [Footnote in the original.]

‡Exchange Director at Istanbul stated on November 7, 1940, that he expected to liquidate "within a few days" the remaining arrears for 1939 imports. [Footnote in the original.]

[47] Not printed.

report that for the past six weeks exchange transfers have been proceeding at a very satisfactory rate. Since the first week in September exchange transfer permits had been issued for a total of $2,162,000 and during the past six weeks exchange transfers have averaged approximately $290,000 weekly. All applications for exchange filed during 1939 have now been covered by exchange transfer permits and the Istanbul Exchange Office advised the Embassy on December 6 that the permits then being issued covered applications up to March 26, 1940.

It is believed that little difficulty has been experienced in effecting the actual transfers, these having been done by cable remittance. The charge for cable transfers is, however, very high, in most instances 2 percent. Exceptions are apparently made for cable remittances covering imports of certain vital materials such as oil, iron and steel where the charge is at the regular rate of one half piaster.

Since the early part of the present year the Exchange Director in Istanbul has been supplying the Embassy weekly with figures covering exchange applications filed with and permits granted by his office. The Embassy was therefore able until fairly recently to figure currently the amount of the outstanding arrears, and occasionally to obtain some check on this figure. For example, in his speech at the opening of the Izmir Fair on August 20, 1940, the former Minister of Commerce referred to the total American arrears as of that date as $3,458,000. This figure, as reported in my despatch of September 7, was within $200,000 of the figure compiled by the Embassy based on data furnished by the Exchange Office, but it subsequently developed that that portion of the total representing 1939 arrears was much too small. The Embassy made repeated efforts during September and October to secure from the Exchange Office the exact figure for 1939 arrears but was put off with various excuses until on November 15th the Exchange Director advised the Embassy representative that the 1939 arrears had been completely liquidated. The Embassy assumes therefore that the permits issued between the early part of September and November 15, totalling approximately $1,000,000 were for the final liquidation of the 1939 arrears. According to the Exchange Director all permits issued since that date have covered applications filed during the current year. Since the statement of the Minister of Commerce regarding arrears, the new applications as furnished by the Istanbul Exchange Director total only some $245,000 and exchange permits granted since early September up to November 29 amount to $2,161,000. In addition to the regular exchange transfer permits issued, the outstanding arrears of the Socony Vacuum, the Shell, and Steaua Romana oil companies amounting to nearly $1,000,000 have been settled through a special arrangement. The outstanding arrears should, according to the Embassy's estimates, not be much in excess of $1,200,000.

However, on November 15 when the Assistant Commercial Attaché was discussing the question of exchange with the Director of the Istanbul Exchange Office, that official referred to the total arrears as between $4,000,000 and $5,000,000. When the Assistant Commercial Attaché expressed surprise that this figure was so much in excess of the Embassy estimate which was compiled from figures furnished weekly by the Exchange Office, and asked for an explanation of this very considerable difference, the Exchange Director stated that the difference undoubtedly arose from the fact that applications for large sums of exchange accepted some time ago by the exchange offices in other parts of Turkey had not been sent to him for inclusion in his records. The Embassy considers this explanation as most unsatisfactory as more than a year ago the Turkish Government, in order to simplify the handling of exchange applications and issuance of permits, centralized this work in the Istanbul Exchange Office. It seems incredible therefore that some $2,000,000 of exchange applications if regularly filed with other exchange offices would not have been reported promptly to the Central Exchange Office in Istanbul, particularly when it is borne in mind that for several months past there have been practically no imports from the United States. The Exchange Director was asked if he could furnish a total figure for the outstanding arrears and although he stated that he was engaged in compiling such a figure and would furnish it to the Embassy when available, he has not yet done so although the Embassy's desire to be furnished with this information has repeatedly been called to his attention. His reply invariably is that he has not yet completed his compilations.

The Embassy is at a loss to understand and can only surmise what has caused this enormous jump in the total arrears. In the normal course of events there would be every advantage in exchange offices outside of Istanbul forwarding any applications received to the Istanbul Office with as little delay as possible. It seems difficult to believe therefore that applications for large amounts were held in local exchange offices indefinitely for no apparent reason. For example, the Exchange Director spoke of applications for large amounts of dollar exchange being made in Samsun. This seems most unlikely as Samsun is not an importing center and in all probability any American merchandise brought into that port would have been already cleared through the customs in Istanbul and exchange applied for. As a possible explanation the Embassy ventures to suggest that exchange applications have been filed covering certain government purchases made in the United States and involving large sums. As these purchases were paid for through letters of credit it may be the intention of the Turkish Government to recover the foreign exchange originally provided for this purpose. The advantage to the Turkish Government in filing applications for the exchange made available to cover government purchases is obvious—the Turkish Government would in this manner have placed government purchases on the same basis as ordinary commercial imports from the United States and in consequence eventually recover the dollar exchange which had been utilized to open letters of credit in the United States to cover the government's imports of American merchandise.

The Embassy has no proof that such a course has been adopted by the Turkish Government and offers the above suggestion only as a possible explanation of the sudden jump in the amount of the outstanding arrears, and the coy behavior of and unsatisfactory explanation offered by the Exchange Director when pressed for details as to the origin of the exchange applications which would appear to have accounted for the sudden jump in the total arrears.

Respectfully yours,   J. V. A. MacMurray

CLOSING OF THE Y.M.C.A. AND ASSOCIATED SCHOOL AT ISTANBUL; GOOD OFFICES OF THE AMERICAN EMBASSY IN SECURING REOPENING OF SCHOOL

867.144/26

The Ambassador in Turkey (MacMurray) to the Secretary of State

No. 1329   ANKARA, January 15, 1940.
                                        [Received February 9.]

SIR: I have the honor to report that on December 27, 1939, the Y.M.C.A. at Istanbul and the affiliated American Language and Commercial School, fostered by the Y.M.C.A., but technically independent of it, together with the Student Hostel attached to the latter school, were closed by the police authorities, acting under the authority of the Governor of Istanbul. Although no notification has been made to either of these institutions by the authorities, a representative of the Y.M.C.A. was permitted to read the official order for the closing of the Y.M.C.A. held by the police officials, and a copy of this document made by him is enclosed.[48]

Of the three legal points apparently forming the basis for the closing of the Y.M.C.A. (and with it the School and Hostel housed in the same American-owned building) the most important is apparently that the Y.M.C.A. has been found to be an association having its headquarters in a foreign country, thus contravening Article 10 of the Turkish Law on Associations, which went into effect on July 14, 1938

---

[48] Enclosures to this despatch not printed.

(reported in the Embassy's despatch No. 828, September 15, 1938,[49] enclosing a translation of the law). The police had no authority for the closing of the Language and Commercial School, which, although occupying the major part of the premises of the building in question, holds a separate permit from the Ministry of Education (the Y.M.C.A. operated under a permit from the Ministry of the Interior). The Student Hostel was permitted to remain open temporarily as a result of protests made by the Turkish University students housed there, but the order for its closing is merely in suspense.

The Y.M.C.A., which has operated for 25 years in Istanbul, took cognizance of the new Law on Associations immediately upon its promulgation in 1938, and filed a petition with the appropriate authorities on June 13, 1939, for registration of its constitution under the new law. It hoped to obtain the permission of the Council of Ministers to continue its operations in Turkey in spite of the provisions of Article 10 of the law referred to above, by virtue of an exception contained in this Article, which reads as follows:

"Article 10. An association having its seat abroad may not open branches in Turkey. Associations pursuing international aims may not be founded.

"However, the Council of Ministers may authorize the foundation in Turkey of associations considered useful for the bringing about of understanding among nations, or the opening in Turkey of branches of already established associations of this kind . . .".[49a]

It appears that the petition of the Association was given consideration by the Department of Public Security at Ankara but that, so far as can be learned, it did not come to the attention of the Minister of the Interior. No reply has yet been received to this petition, nor has the Association received any communication concerning it.

While recognizing the legal basis for the closing of the Y.M.C.A., its local Directors immediately took steps to secure the reopening of the American Language and Commercial School, which maintains, in addition to its scholastic activities, the Student Hostel and a large gymnasium. The Director of the School, Bay Ilhami Polater, a Turkish citizen, called at the Vilayet on January 2 in company with Bay Hamid, the legal adviser of the Y.M.C.A., and Mr. Luther L. Fowle, one of the Directors (Treasurer of the American Board of Foreign Missions, headquarters at Istanbul), and presented a petition calling attention to the separate entity of the School and protesting against its illegal closing. A translation of the petition is enclosed herewith. The Governor immediately referred the petition to the Department of Education at Istanbul, and the latter on January 2

---

[49] Not printed.
[49a] Omission indicated in the original despatch.

returned to the Governor's office a recommendation which is believed to have been in favor of the reopening of the School.

At the request of the local directors of the Y.M.C.A. and with my approval, Mr. Latimer, the consular officer in charge at Istanbul, called on the Governor on January 8 to express the concern of the Consulate General over the closing of a respected American institution. He pointed out that the Y.M.C.A. had done its best to comply with the new law, that it had received no reply to its petition, and that it had been closed without warning. He also emphasized the separate entity of the American Language and Commercial School, which had been closed apparently without authority, and stated that the Directors of the Y.M.C.A., while recognizing the validity of its closing, desired to continue operating the Language and Commercial School, provided they could be assured of the support and approval of the Turkish authorities and public, which they believed themselves to have enjoyed up to the present. The Governor replied that the Language School had been closed only because it was in the same building with the Y.M.C.A., and the police had been unable to make a clear distinction between the two organizations. He assured Mr. Latimer that the closing of the Y.M.C.A. was due solely to the automatic application of the new Law on Associations which provided that an association having its headquarters in a foreign country could not operate in Turkey. He further stated that he had been on the point of ordering the reopening of the School when the legal question was raised as to whether an affiliate of an association which had been closed for non-conformity with the new law could be permitted to continue operating. This legal question, he said, had been referred to a special committee for decision. He agreed to expedite decision on this question, and gave evidence of his friendly and favorable attitude towards the matter. The Governor made it clear that there was not the slightest feeling against the American institutions involved, or against American institutions in general, and took pains to discredit an article published in the *Yeni Sabah* of December 28, referred to by Mr. Latimer, which attacked the Y.M.C.A. as an institution dangerous to Turkish youth and took upon the paper credit for its closing. Translations of the article in question, and of a matter-of-fact one from the more respectable newspaper *Tan*, are enclosed herewith. A memorandum prepared by Mr. Latimer concerning his interview is enclosed herewith.

In spite of the seemingly favorable attitude taken by the Department of Education and by the Governor, subsequent information obtained through private sources, particularly the Director of the School of Languages and Commerce, reveal that the trend of events did not augur well for a favorable decision. It was found that the question of the School's reopening had left the hands of the special committee appointed by the Governor (composed of the Assistant Governor, the Legal Advisor of the Vilayet and the Director of Education of Istanbul) without decision and had been privately referred to the Istanbul Committee of the People's Party, indicating that the issue had now become a local political matter. It had already been clear to the Directors that the "Halk Evi" (People's Homes), maintained by the People's Party, had evidenced a keen interest in obtaining the property of the Y.M.C.A., immediately upon its closing. In this connection it should be pointed out that the property of an association which is closed for non-conformity with the new Law on Associations automatically reverts to the Turkish Government.

On January 12th, the legal advisor of the Y.M.C.A. called on the Assistant Governor and on the Legal Advisor of the Vilayet to furnish complete details as to the organization and activities of the American institutions concerned, and both officials took the attitude that the whole affair was a closed issue and out of their hands, although the Y.M.C.A. representative was unable to learn from them what had been decided as regards the petition for the reopening of the Language and Commercial School or in whose hands the petition now rested.

At a meeting of the Board of Directors of the Y.M.C.A. on January 12, 1940, attended by Consul Latimer, who furnished a statement concerning his interview with the Governor, the members decided to abandon the branch of the Y.M.C.A. at Istanbul and to concentrate their efforts on the reopening of the American Language and Commercial School. The approval of the Head Office of the Y.M.C.A. for this move had already been obtained by cable. The Board further decided to make it clear to the local authorities that if the latter approved of the activities of the School, the Directors desired to continue it with its Turkish Director assisted by an American teacher whose salary would be provided through local American contributions and with an Advisory Board which would include Turkish citizens in its membership. A telegram was drafted advising the Y.M.C.A. Head Office at New York to postpone the sailing of the Secretary scheduled to leave for Turkey in February of this year (to replace Mr. Baker, present incumbent at Istanbul, who left Turkey on leave of absence several months ago). The Directors requested Mr. Fowle to draw up a memorandum (copy enclosed herewith) showing the background of the Y.M.C.A.'s operations in Turkey, the attitude of the Directors towards its present situation, and the future operations of the Language and Commercial School. The Directors requested that a copy of this memorandum be furnished Mr. Latimer for transmission to the Embassy, and it was urgently recommended that the Embassy be asked to intervene in the matter in order to assure a complete examination of the question by the highest Turkish authorities.

An examination of the several reports and memoranda which were sent to the Embassy by Mr. Latimer, and by Mr. Fowle on behalf of the Board of Directors of the Y.M.C.A., served to create a strong presumption that the municipal authorities had acted on their own responsibility, without the knowledge or approval of the central Government, and with their own ends in view. If this were true—and it was later found to be the case—the action of the municipal authorities might, when it was too late, be found to have been unwarranted, and, even if warranted, might, because it coincided with the awakening of a genuine sympathy in the United States for the victims of the Turkish earthquake, be seriously misunderstood and exert an unfortunately negative effect on American-Turkish relations. It was therefore deemed advisable to bring the matter to the attention of the Ministry of Foreign Affairs, but as a request for information and with a suggestion as to its possible effects, rather than as a formal complaint. A representative of the Embassy consequently called at the Ministry on January 13 and exposed the question in that light. A memorandum of the resulting conversation is enclosed for the Department's information. The Department will observe that the Foreign Office is not inclined to consider the action of the local authorities of Istanbul as being final.

Respectfully yours,   J. V. A. MacMurray

867.144/27

The Ambassador in Turkey (MacMurray) to the Secretary of State

No. 1360   Ankara, February 13, 1940.
                                 [Received March 19.]

Sir: I have the honor to refer to the Embassy's despatch No. 1329 of January 15, 1940, reporting the closing of the Y.M.C.A. at Istanbul and of two affiliated organizations, the American Language and Commercial School and the Student Hostel, and to report further developments in the matter, including the reopening on February 6, 1940, of the two affiliated institutions referred to.

As reported in my despatch under reference, the Embassy made inquiries at the Foreign Office on January 13 as to the status of the Y.M.C.A. and the two associated organizations, housed in the same building, which were closed simultaneously. Apparently as a direct result of the Embassy's inquiries, which were made in such a way as to point out the unfortunate result which the closing of these American organizations might have on public opinion in the United States, a distinct change of attitude toward the question became apparent almost immediately on the part of the officials in Istanbul through whose hands the closing had been effected, and although it was some time before this change of attitude was translated into effective action, assurances were given, within a few days after the Embassy's inquiries, that the American Language and Commercial School and the attached Student Hostel would be permitted to reopen.

On January 27, 1940, just a month after the Y.M.C.A. building had been closed and sealed, representatives of the Istanbul Police and Vilayet called again and removed seals from some of the rooms, also permitting the sign of the Language and Commercial School to be displayed again at the entrance. The officials showed some hesitancy as to just how liberal they should be in removing seals from rooms which might be considered as connected in some way with the work of the Y.M.C.A. proper. This hesitancy appears to have been at least partially justified, owing to the overlapping of the operations of the Association and the School. Altogether, five successive visits were made by the police and local administrative officials, at intervals of a few days, before the Language and Commercial School was actually in a position, on February 6, 1940, to resume operations.

To all intents and purposes the activities formerly conducted in the building can now be resumed, although work is still somewhat hampered by the fact that two office rooms pertaining chiefly to the School but also containing some Y.M.C.A. records are still sealed, as well as three safes used chiefly by the School. The office of the Y.M.C.A. Secretary, who is now absent, also remains closed. The Director of the Language and Commercial School has been encouraged by the officials who have recently called at the premises to believe that they may within a reasonable time remove the seals from the two closed office rooms pertaining to the School and possibly also from some of the safes, thus leaving an irreducible minimum of sealed premises (one office and one or more safes) to represent the Y.M.C.A., orders for the definite closing of which still remain in effect.

Although the main objective of the local Y.M.C.A. Directors and of the Embassy and the Consulate General has thus been substantially achieved, there remains the question of the final disposition to be made of the Y.M.C.A. property. If the matter is allowed to take its normal course, the liquidation of the Y.M.C.A. as an association which has been officially closed by the Turkish authorities for non-conformity with the Law on Associations will involve some difficulties. It will entail, for example, the opening and examining of the contents of the safes and the inventorying and appraisal of the property of the Association. It is possible, furthermore, that an attempt might be made to claim this property for the Government. In any case, a certain amount of unpleasantness before the affair can be finally disposed of would seem inevitable.

After discussion between the consular officer in charge at Istanbul and Directors of the Y.M.C.A., a suggestion has been formulated, with the approval of the Embassy, for presentation to the Vali of Istanbul with a view to obviating the development of possible further annoyance and difficulties in connection with this matter. The suggestion is, briefly, that the Vali should see to it that the petition presented by the Y.M.C.A. in June, 1939, receives a reply. To date, no reply has been received, excepting in the form of the abrupt closing of the Y.M.C.A. building by the police, which hardly seems appropriate treatment for a reputable institution which has operated in Istanbul for 25 years with the permission, successively, of the Ottoman Government and of the Turkish Republican Government. If the Government's reply to the petition proves unfavorable, then the Association should be given a reasonable period in which to wind up its affairs in a dignified manner and, as a friendly gesture, all seals should be removed from the premises and property of the Association. A representative of the Embassy made the foregoing suggestion to the Vali of Istanbul in a social conversation with him in Ankara during his recent visit to this city. The Vali replied that he was not sufficiently acquainted with the matter to give a decision on this suggestion, but requested that he be given time to acquaint himself more thoroughly with the problems involved and that the Consul at Istanbul be asked to call on him there to discuss the matter further.

The consular officer in charge at Istanbul has entered into contact with the Vali for this purpose and will, it is expected, call on him within a few days. The result of his interview will be promptly communicated to the Department.

Respectfully yours, J. V. A. MacMurray

867.144/28

The Ambassador in Turkey (MacMurray) to the Secretary of State

No. 1402 ANKARA, March 27, 1940.
[Received April 30.]

SIR: I have the honor to refer to the Embassy's despatch no. 1360 of February 13, 1940 reporting the reopening of the American Language and Commercial School and Student Hostel at Istanbul, which were closed together with their parent organization, the Y.M.C.A., last December, and to submit an account of recent developments concerning these institutions.

In pursuance of the plan mentioned in the closing paragraphs of the Embassy's recent despatch under reference, the consular officer in charge at Istanbul called on the Governor on February 16 to repeat the suggestion already made to him at Ankara by an official of this

Embassy that the Y.M.C.A. be permitted to liquidate its branch at Istanbul in a manner befitting the international standing of this respected American organization and that to this end all the remaining seals which had been placed by the Police on its property and that of its affiliated institutions should be removed. The Governor indicated his sympathetic attitude toward this suggestion but said that as no legal provision existed as to the manner of liquidation of an association which had been closed for non-conformity with the new Law on Associations, he had been obliged to refer the question to Ankara for decision. This seemed a favorable development, as the viewpoint of officials in Ankara relative to the Y.M.C.A. has consistently been broader and more friendly than that of the provincial and municipal authorities in Istanbul. A copy of Mr. Latimer's memorandum of his conversation with the Governor is enclosed.[50]

On March 3 the Consulate General at Istanbul was informed that the Y.M.C.A. had received an official reply from the Governor's Office to its petition of June 13, 1939 for approval of its constitution under the Law on Associations. This reply, a copy of which is enclosed, was noncommittal and consisted merely of a statement that the Y.M.C.A. had been closed because it had been found not to be in conformity with certain points of the Law on Associations. Reference to these points was made in the Embassy's despatch of January 15, 1940.

On March 8, Mr. Satterthwaite[51] of this Embassy called on Bay Faik Hozar, Director General of the Second Section of the Foreign Office, in order to call the Ministry's attention to the fact that the question of the final disposal of the Y.M.C.A. had been referred to Ankara by the Governor of Istanbul and to request that the Foreign Office follow up the matter with a view to reinforcing the suggestions already made to the Governor by the Consulate General. Bay Hozar evidenced a favorable attitude toward this request and agreed to take up the matter with the Ministry of the Interior. A copy of Mr. Satterthwaite's memorandum of his interview is enclosed.

Early in March Mr. Arnold E. Jenny, a Y.M.C.A. secretary sent out by the New York headquarters of the International Y.M.C.A., arrived at Istanbul. As stated in a letter of introduction to the Governor of Istanbul from Bay Munir Ertegün, Turkish Ambassador at Washington, which Mr. Jenny brought with him, he was sent here for the purpose of carrying out the liquidation of the Y.M.C.A. at Istanbul. Mr. Jenny has informed the Consulate General and the Governor of Istanbul that it is the further intention of his principals that he remain here for a period of about six months to act as advisor

---

[50] Enclosures to this despatch not printed.
[51] Joseph C. Satterthwaite, Second Secretary of Embassy.

to the American School of Language and Commerce during the transition period in which the School will take over the activities previously administered by the Y.M.C.A.

The Consulate General arranged an appointment for Mr. Jenny to present his letter of introduction to the Governor of Istanbul on March 13. He was introduced by Mr. Luther Fowle, Treasurer of the American Board of Foreign Missions headquarters at this city, who has voluntarily acted as the godfather of the Y.M.C.A. at Istanbul in the absence of an American secretary. The interview apparently took place in an informal and cordial atmosphere and when the request was made by Mr. Jenny that the seals be removed from the Y.M.C.A. premises so that the Association might carry out its liquidation and the School be relieved of the remaining restrictions on its activities, the Governor intimated that orders would be given along these lines. Although the Governor did not commit himself as to the exact action to be taken, Mr. Jenny and Mr. Fowle are hopeful that in due time approximately the results desired may be achieved, and the Embassy is inclined to agree with this viewpoint. Copies of Mr. Jenny's letter of introduction and of Mr. Fowle's memorandum on the interview with the Governor are enclosed.

It may be added that on February 16, 1940, an official permit was received by the Turkish Director of the American School of Language and Commerce and the Student Hostel from the Istanbul Department of Education confirming the previously granted verbal permission to reopen these two institutions. A copy of this permit is enclosed herewith.

Respectfully yours,   J. V. A. MacMurray

867.144/29

The Ambassador in Turkey (MacMurray) to the Secretary of State

No. 1505   Istanbul, July 10, 1940.
        [Received August 13.]

Sir: I have the honor to refer to the Embassy's despatch No. 1402 of March 27, 1940 regarding developments consequent upon the closing of the Y.M.C.A. at Istanbul, and to furnish herewith information bringing those developments up to date.

According to information received from the American Language and Commercial School, the provincial authorities at Istanbul on March 28, 1940 turned over the dossier covering the liquidation of the Y.M.C.A., closed in accordance with the new Law on Associations in December, 1939, to the Istanbul 5th Court of Justice of the Peace for final liquidation of the Y.M.C.A. property. Informal statements made at that time by local officials to the Turkish legal advisor of the Y.M.C.A. indicated that the property of this organization at Istanbul would probably be handed over, at the conclusion of the necessary legal formalities, to the duly empowered representatives of the International Committee of the Y.M.C.A.

On July 3, 1940 Mr. Eugene Jenny, who was sent to Istanbul this spring by the International Committee of the Y.M.C.A., informed the Consulate General that the requisite power of attorney naming him, and in addition Professor Scipio of the Engineering School of Robert College and Dr. Birge of the American Board Missions as its attorneys had finally been received from the International Committee of the Y.M.C.A. at New York and that a petition had been submitted to the local Court on June 17 requesting that the property of the Y.M.C.A. still remaining under police seal, consisting of three offices and two safes, be released and turned over to the duly empowered attorneys. No action has as yet been taken by the Court on this petition.

Although the work of the American Language and Commercial School was resumed on February 28, 1940 with a satisfactory enrolment and the usual summer school of the organization is now under way, the organization is handicapped by its inability to use the property still sealed by the police and by the fact that a permanent board of directors for the School has not yet been formed. Following the disbanding of the board of directors of the Y.M.C.A. after the closing of the latter organization in December, an unofficial and temporary board headed by Mr. Fowle of the American Board Missions, looked after the interests of the Y.M.C.A. until Mr. Jenny's arrival in March 1940. At present a provisional board appointed by Mr. Jenny is canvassing the possibilities for the successful continuation of the work of the School with the ultimate aim of enlisting the services of Turkish citizens as members of its board. This provisional board consists of Colonel Binns, a local British businessman, Mr. Goemans, a Dutch subject, Assistant Manager of the American Turkish Investment Corporation, and Professor Bliss of the School of Engineering at Robert College.

In a recent meeting of the former directors of the Y.M.C.A. and local residents interested in its work, the American Board Missions personnel formerly participating in the Y.M.C.A. board voluntarily withdrew from official participation in the direction of the School. This action, it has been learned, followed the declining of an invitation extended by Mr. Fowle to Dr. Wright, President of Robert College, to serve on the new board of directors. Dr. Wright stated, in declining, that as the head of a foreign educational institution which has only recently achieved a satisfactory standing with the Turkish public and officialdom after a long and critical struggle, he frankly could not afford to associate himself officially with an organization which (under the name of Y.M.C.A.) had acquired an unfavorable reputation in Turkish circles chiefly because of the suspicion attaching in their minds to all foreign institutions believed to have a missionary or religious purpose. Dr. Wright, in making his remarks, took pains to make clear his sincere respect for and friendly feelings toward the American Board Missions group in Turkey but stressed his belief that to have any chance of continuing successfully in Turkey the type of social and educational work which the Y.M.C.A. promotes, the directors of the American Language and Commercial School must be free, in the mind of the Turkish public, from associations with any missionary or religious enterprise. The Mission group (tacitly) as well as the business and professional men present at this meeting, agreed with Dr. Wright's viewpoint.

. . . .

The summer camp of the Y.M.C.A., which has been the most successful and popular branch of its activities, has not been operated since the status of the Y.M.C.A. came under examination under the new Law on Associations in 1939, and no attempt will be made to press the matter of its reopening until such time as the successor organization may have firmly established itself and regularized its legal status.

It is the Embassy's opinion that if the work of the successor organization to the Istanbul Y.M.C.A. is to continue at all, it must very shortly be furnished the guidance and energetic management of an American trained in social work and with a broad understanding of the Turkish viewpoint.

Respectfully yours,

J. V. A. MacMurray

867.144/30

The Ambassador in Turkey (MacMurray) to the Secretary of State

No. 1596   ISTANBUL, November 9, 1940.
[Received December 12.]

SIR: I have the honor to refer to the Embassy's despatch No. 1505, dated July 10, 1940, regarding developments in the liquidation of the Y.M.C.A. in Istanbul, and to report that according to a letter dated October 7, 1940 received from Mr. Luther Fowle, Treasurer of the American Board Missions at Istanbul, the remaining seals placed by the Istanbul police authorities on the safes and offices in the Y.M.C.A. building have now been removed by them and the entire property of the Association has been handed over by the Turkish courts to the duly empowered representatives appointed locally by the International Y.M.C.A., for disposal as they see fit. The only propery which has been kept by the Police is one rubber stamp bearing the seal of the Y.M.C.A., which has no value inasmuch as the Association no longer has the right to use this name in Turkey. The provisional board, composed of local American and British citizens, which has been supervising the operation of the successor organization to the Y.M.C.A., the American Language and Commercial School, continue to function and has chosen a permanent chairman, Dr. Kingsley Birge of the American Board Missions.

Respectfully yours, J. V. A. MacMurray

PROPOSED AGREEMENT BETWEEN THE UNITED STATES AND TURKEY REGARDING THE STATUS OF CERTAIN NATURALIZED AMERICAN CITIZENS NATIVES OF TERRITORY DETACHED FROM TURKEY BY THE TREATY OF LAUSANNE [52]

390D.11/186

The Secretary of State to the Ambassador in Turkey (MacMurray)

No. 445 WASHINGTON, January 19, 1940.

SIR: 1. Reference is made to your despatch No. 1277 of November 23, 1939,[53] and your telegram No. 75 of December 29, 2 p. m.,[54] regarding the proposed exchange of notes with Turkey intended to provide for the release from Turkish allegiance of certain natives of former parts of the Ottoman Empire. In response to the inquiry contained in your telegram under reference, the Department would prefer not to enter into a treaty covering merely the material intended to be included in the suggested exchange of notes. The Department does not consider that the proposed nationality agreement, dealing only with the release from Turkish allegiance of certain natives of former parts of the Ottoman Empire, would involve subject matter which would warrant the agreement being concluded in the form of a treaty, requiring ratification by the United States. Some type of executive agreement, whether in the form of an exchange of notes or otherwise, would be more appropriate from our point of view.

2. Should the Turkish authorities desire, for administrative reasons, to enter into an agreement to be ratified by the Grand National Assembly, we would interpose no objection, nor do we insist that the agreement take the form of an exchange of notes. The proposed nationality agreement might take the form of an executive agreement such as the Claims Agreement between the United States and Turkey

---

[52] Continued from *Foreign Relations,* 1939, vol. IV, pp. 849–861.
[53] *Ibid.,* p. 857.
[54] *Ibid.,* p. 860.

signed at Ankara on October 25, 1934,[55] a copy of which is enclosed. It will be observed that this agreement was ratified by the Turkish Assembly although our own procedure did not require its reference to the Senate. It is not unusual for agreements to be ratified by one of the parties, in accordance with its constitutional requirements, although not by the other.

3. It may be pointed out to the Turkish authorities, however, that the provisions of the proposed agreement appear similar in principle to the provisions included in the exchange of notes between France and Turkey on May 29, 1937,[56] and that the Department assumed in proposing our exchange of notes that the Turkish Government would be as readily disposed to enter into an exchange of notes with us. The delay in concluding the matter and the Turkish Government's late suggestion that the agreement take the form of a treaty are difficult to understand, unless there are differences in principle between the French situation and our own of which we are not aware.

4. As regards the Turkish Government's desire that we agree not to present claims on behalf of any of the persons to be covered, we are willing to include in the agreement a statement that none of the provisions thereof may be construed as obliging the government of either country to entertain a claim on behalf of a person who is a national of that country or who was a national of that country at the time the events out of which the claim arose took place.

5. As regards the Turkish Government's desire to include a statement that none of the persons covered will be permitted to return to Turkey, we are willing to state that nothing in the agreement shall be construed as affecting existing statutes or regulations of either country in relation to the immigration of aliens or the right of either country to enact such statutes.

6. With regard to the draft treaty proposed by the Turkish authorities and enclosed with your despatch of November 23, 1939, the Department is somewhat surprised that the Turkish authorities appear still to have in mind an agreement relating only to Syrians, in spite of the repeated emphasis which, so the Department assumes, the Embassy must have placed, in accordance with the Department's instruction, upon our desire to reach an agreement relating to natives of all parts of the Ottoman Empire detached by the Treaty of Lausanne.

7. If the Turkish Government is disposed to negotiate a general naturalization treaty with the United States, we would be glad to consider the question of including in such a treaty provisions covering the nationality of natives of former parts of the Ottoman Empire. The basis for the naturalization treaty might well be our Treaty of

---

[55] *Foreign Relations*, 1934, vol. II, p. 933.
[56] League of Nations, *Official Journal*, November 1937, p. 841.

Naturalization with Bulgaria signed at Sofia on November 23, 1923 [57] (Treaty Series 684. 43 Statutes at Large 1759). If the Turkish authorities are willing to negotiate a general naturalization treaty along these lines, you should inform the Department by telegraph, and a draft treaty will be forwarded to you by air mail for presentation to the Turkish Government. Should the Turkish Government accept a general provision similar to Article I of the Bulgarian treaty, recognizing the loss of Turkish citizenship by Turkish nationals naturalized in the United States, the necessity for any exchange of notes regarding natives of former parts of the Ottoman Empire would of course be obviated. If the Turkish Government is not willing to include provisions recognizing the loss of Turkish nationality by all Turkish citizens who are naturalized in the United States, other general provisions relating to nationality might possibly be agreed upon. However, although we should be very pleased to enter into a general naturalization treaty with Turkey, the negotiations of such a treaty would doubtless be difficult and prolonged, due to the divergence between the American and Turkish principles relating to nationality, and it would seem preferable to conclude the negotiations already undertaken before approaching the general treaty unless you are able to report that the prospects for the early conclusion of a general treaty are more favorable than the Department presumes.

Very truly yours,   For the Secretary of State:

                                           R. WALTON MOORE

390D.11/189 : Telegram

The Ambassador in Turkey (MacMurray) to the Secretary of State

ANKARA, February 29, 1940—11 a. m.
[Received 12 : 05 p. m.]

21. Department's instruction No. 445, January 19. The Ministry of Foreign Affairs is insisting that detailed lists as provided in their counterproposals be presented through the Department and while apparently willing that the lists be prepared by Syrian organizations, desires that the naturalization records of the persons appearing thereon be vouched for by our Government. Other points of divergence are being discussed by the Ministry of Foreign Affairs with the Ministry of the Interior. In the meantime it would be helpful to have the Department's views as to the lists as I am hopeful that all the other differences can be reconciled.

I have refrained from proposing the negotiation of a general naturalization treaty in the belief that even the suggestion might delay indefinitely the completion of the present negotiations.

                                         MACMURRAY

---

[57] *Foreign Relations*, 1923, vol. I, p. 464.

390D.11/189 : Telegram

The Secretary of State to the Ambassador in Turkey (MacMurray)

WASHINGTON, April 2, 1940—5 p. m.

23. Your 21, February 29, 11 a. m. and Department's 12, February 29, 11 a. m.[58] The Department is willing to transmit to Turkey requests of American citizens that they be released from Turkish allegiance, and will require satisfactory evidence that the persons whose requests are transmitted have acquired American citizenship.

HULL

390D.11/195 : Telegram

The Ambassador in Turkey (MacMurray) to the Secretary of State

ANKARA, April 17, 1940—5 p. m.
[Received April 17—4 : 30 p. m.]

41. Department's 23, April 2, 5 p. m. While considerable difficulty is being encountered chiefly on account of lack of interest in the conclusion of the nationality agreement on the part of the Ministry of the Interior which must be consulted with respect to every point I hope nevertheless to be able in the near future to forward a draft of the agreement acceptable to the Turks which the Department can approve.

While the Turks are insisting on the acceptance of article VI of their draft (forwarded in my despatch No. 1277, November 23, last [59]) we are endeavoring to persuade them to agree to the text suggested in the Department's instruction 455 [*445*], January 19, last, with the addition of a note from the Turkish Government stating that the persons in question will not be permitted to enter Turkey. In the event that they prove adamant on this point, however, I should like to know how far the Department is willing to go with respect to this article as we are told the Ministry of the Interior is insisting upon the Turkish draft as a *sine qua non* of concluding an agreement.

MACMURRAY

---

[58] Latter not printed.
[59] *Foreign Relations*, 1939, vol. IV, p. 857.

390D.11/195

*Memorandum of Conversation, by Mr. George V. Allen of the Division
of Near Eastern Affairs*

[WASHINGTON,] April 18, 1940.

Participants: Turkish Ambassador [60]

Mr. Murray [61]

Mr. Allen

During a call at the Division today, the Turkish Ambassador was informed of the receipt of a telegram from the American Embassy at Ankara (No. 41, April 17, 5 p. m.) reporting that the Turkish authorities were insisting that a provision be included in the nationality agreement stating specifically that the persons concerned would lose definitely the right to reenter Turkey.

Mr. Murray recalled that when the Turkish Government first made known to us, last year, its desire that a provision of this kind be included, we had suggested the insertion of an article similar to Article 1 of the Treaty of Establishment and Sojourn between the United States and Turkey,[62] providing that nothing in the agreement should be construed as affecting existing statutes or regulations of either country in relation to the immigration of aliens or the right of either country to enact such statutes. Mr. Murray suggested to the Ambassador the reasons for our being unable to accept the more categorical and definite wording desired by the Turkish Government. He pointed out that language similar to that we suggested was contained in several of our treaties, the ratification of which has been approved by the Senate. He thought it would be easy for us to conclude an agreement containing this wording, and probably difficult to obtain acceptance of any other. He pointed out that, furthermore, the Turkish wording, if adopted, would involve an agreement on the part of the American Government to a discrimination by Turkey against a group of naturalized American citizens as compared with native-born citizens as regards entry into Turkey. Mr. Murray said that it had long been a principle of American law, based on an Act of Congress enacted in 1868,[63] that no discrimination should be made by the American Government or its officials between native-born and naturalized citizens.

Mr. Murray expressed the opinion, moreover, that the Turkish Government's categorical language might not be in the best interests of Turkey itself, since a definite provision that all of the persons

---

[60] Mehmet Münir Ertegün.
[61] Wallace Murray, Chief of the Division of Near Eastern Affairs.
[62] Signed at Ankara, October 28, 1931, *Foreign Relations*, 1931, vol. II, p. 1042.
[63] An Act Concerning the Rights of American Citizens in Foreign States, Rev. Stat. 35.

affected would lose the right to reenter Turkey might unduly restrain the Turkish Government's freedom of action. Turkey might find it desirable, in some cases, to permit the individuals to reenter Turkey, and might find its own provision of some embarrassment.

Mr. Murray said that the purposes which the Turkish authorities have in mind would be entirely accomplished by our proposed language, which gives either party entire freedom of action with regard to the entry of aliens into its territory. He thought our wording would be more satisfactory for both Governments.

The Turkish Ambassador indicated that he himself was satisfied that our wording would accomplish the desired purpose of both parties, but that in an effort to discern the objections which might be in the minds of the Turkish negotiators, he presumed they were not entirely satisfied that our language would accomplish their purpose. He thought that our draft would have been more easily understood if worded more simply, or somewhat as follows:

Each nation reserves entire freedom of action with regard to the entry of aliens into its territory.

The Ambassador was informed that his wording expressed concisely and precisely our understanding of the meaning of the language of the American proposal. The Ambassador then said that he would write to his Government, attempting to persuade it to accept the language proposed by us, pointing out the reasons which caused us to prefer our wording and which prevented us from accepting the Turkish proposal. He said he would suggest that an interpretation of our language, as indicated above, be stated in a procès-verbal or subsidiary exchange of notes, if the Turkish authorities retained any doubts on the subject.

The Ambassador requested that a copy of the pertinent provisions of the Act of Congress of 1868, referred to by Mr. Murray, be furnished him.[64] He indicated that our reference to this law enabled him, for the first time, to understand clearly why we were unable to accept the language suggested by the Turkish Government.

390D.11/195 : Telegram

The Secretary of State to the Ambassador in Turkey (*MacMurray*)

WASHINGTON, April 26, 1940—4 p. m.

26. Your 41, April 17, 5 p. m. The Department would not be able to accept article 6 of the Turkish draft since we are prevented, by a

---

[64] On April 20, Mr. Murray sent to the Ambassador the pertinent provision of the Act of July 27, 1868, reading as follows:

"Section 2000. All naturalized citizens of the United States, while in foreign countries, are entitled to and shall receive from this Government the same protection of persons and property which is accorded to native-born citizens."

long-established principle of American law, from entering into an agreement specifically providing for a discrimination between naturalized and native-born American citizens as regards their rights abroad, which include their right of entry into a foreign country. This aspect has been discussed fully with the Turkish Ambassador here, who agrees that the language proposed in the Department's instruction of January 19 would assure to either Government entire freedom of action with regard to the entry of aliens into its territory and that it should be satisfactory to his Government.

Should the Turkish authorities entertain any doubts as to the meaning of our proposed language, you are authorized to include in a subsidiary exchange of notes or in a procès-verbal a statement to the effect that the American Government understands article — of the agreement to be a recognition of the fact that each Government enjoys entire freedom of action with regard to the entry of all aliens into its territory. This fact is recognized in the Treaty of Establishment and Sojourn now in effect between the United States and Turkey and is reasserted at the request of the Turkish Government.

HULL

390D.11/196 : Telegram

The Ambassador in Turkey (MacMurray) to the Secretary of State

ANKARA, May 9, 1940—6 p. m.
[Received May 9—4 : 14 p. m.]

50. Department's 26, April 26, 4 p. m. Being apprehensive of a deadlock in our negotiations I discussed the matter yesterday with the Foreign Minister.[65] He said that he himself was not yet fully convinced that our proposals were altogether satisfactory. He promised, however, to interest himself personally in trying to work out a satisfactory arrangement.

MACMURRAY

390D.11/199 : Telegram

The Ambassador in Turkey (MacMurray) to the Secretary of State

ANKARA, July 16, 1940—4 p. m.
[Received 8 : 50 p. m.]

124. My despatch No. 1466, May 23.[66] After repeated inquiries negotiations for the nationality agreement were finally renewed on July 1 when a new Turkish draft was presented and briefly discussed.

---

[65] Sükrü **Saracoglu**
[66] Not printed.

This draft was affirmed an improvement in some respects on the previous one but presented some new difficulties especially as regards claims. However, before we could obtain clarification of a number of points we were requested to ignore this latest draft inasmuch as the Minister for Foreign Affairs was giving the proclamation [sic] his personal consideration. I accordingly wrote him a personal letter again setting forth our position as regards claims and [apparent omission] and expressing the hope that his Government might find it possible to agree to the terminology of our assurances on these two points. He told me this morning that he had not yet read my letter but that he had all the papers at his house and hoped to be able to go over them soon.

MacMurray

390D.11/202 : Telegram

The Chargé in Turkey (Kelley) to the Secretary of State

ANKARA, October 7, 1940—6 p. m.
[Received 7:15 p. m.]

163. My 124, July 16, 4 p. m. The Embassy has been unable to continue the nationality agreement negotiations in spite of frequent inquiries because the dossier is still in the hands of the Minister of Foreign Affairs who informed the Ambassador on September 19 that he hoped to be able to study it in the near future. I took the matter up again today with the Assistant Secretary General who promised to do what he could to get the Minister to act on it.

KELLEY

390D.11/205 : Telegram

The Ambassador in Turkey (MacMurray) to the Secretary of State

ANKARA, November 23, 1940—noon.
[Received 12:33 p. m.]

210. Embassy's telegram number 163, October 7, 6 p. m., and despatch No. 1590, November 8.[67] I took up this matter yesterday with the Foreign Minister and expressed the hope that notwithstanding the urgent international problems now preoccupying him he would be able to look into this question soon. He said that he hoped that he would be able to do so in the near future.[68]

MacMurray

---

[67] Latter not printed.
[68] No further action, however, was taken by the Turkish authorities on this proposed agreement.

INDEX

INDEX[1]

[1] In indexing persons the intention has been to include all references to persons of significance for an understanding of the record, with the following exceptions: (1) The name of the Secretary of State or the Acting Secretary of State appearing as the signer of outgoing instructions unless there is a clear indication of the Secretary's or Acting Secretary's personal interest; (2) the name of an American Ambassador or Chargé appearing as the signer of reports to the Department of State, except for personal items and cross-references to subjects; (3) the names of persons to whom documents are addressed.

Persons are not identified by office in the index, but usually where a person is first mentioned in any section a footnote identification is given unless that person is identified in the text.

O